STRATEGIC MANAGEMENT PROCESS

SIMPLE AND STRAIGHTFORWARD
APPROACH TO
STRATEGIC PLANNING

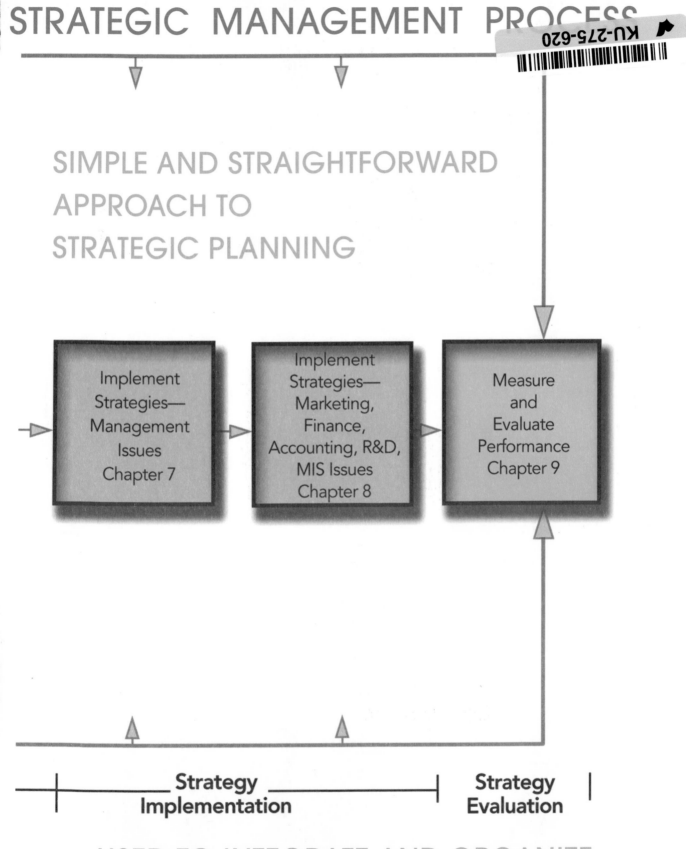

Implement Strategies— Management Issues Chapter 7

Implement Strategies— Marketing, Finance, Accounting, R&D, MIS Issues Chapter 8

Measure and Evaluate Performance Chapter 9

Strategy Implementation

Strategy Evaluation

USED TO INTEGRATE AND ORGANIZE
ALL CHAPTERS IN THIS TEXT

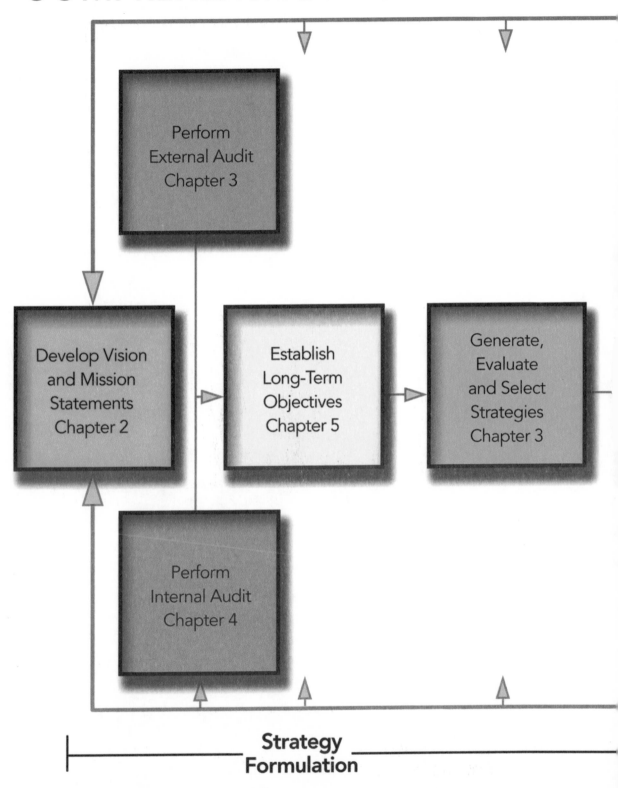

Perform
External Audit
Chapter 3

Develop Vision
and Mission
Statements
Chapter 2

Establish
Long-Term
Objectives
Chapter 5

Generate,
Evaluate
and Select
Strategies
Chapter 3

Perform
Internal Audit
Chapter 4

**Strategy
Formulation**

strategic management

concepts and cases

Tenth Edition

Fred R. David

Francis Marion University, Florence, South Carolina

PEARSON

Prentice
Hall

Pearson Education International

To Joy, Forest, Byron, and Meredith—my wife and children—
for their encouragement and love.

Editor-in-Chief: Jeff Shelstad
Acquisitions Editor: Michael Ablassmeir
Assistant Editor: Christine Genneken
Media Project Manager: Jessica Sabloff
Marketing Manager: Shannon Moore
Senior Managing Editor (Production): Judy Leale
Production Editor: Marcela Boos
Associate Director, Manufacturing: Vincent Scelta
Manufacturing Buyer: Diane Peirano
Design Manager: Maria Lange
Interior Design: Michael Fruhbeis
Cover Design: Michael Fruhbeis
Manager, Print Production: Christy Mahon
Project Management: Carlisle Communications
Printer/Binder: Courier Kendallville

Pearson Education LTD.
Pearson Education Singapore, Pte. Ltd
Pearson Education, Canada, Ltd
Pearson Education–Japan
Pearson Education Australia PTY, Limited

Pearson Education North Asia Ltd
Pearson Educación de Mexico, S.A. de C.V.
Pearson Education Malaysia, Pte. Ltd
Pearson Education Upper Saddle River, New Jersey

10 9 8 7 6 5 4 3 2 1
ISBN 0-13-127675-1

Brief Contents

Contents

SERVICE COMPANY CASES

TELECOMMUNICATIONS, INC.

AIRLINES

INTERNET COMPANIES

RETAILERS

ENTERTAINMENT

SMALL FOR-PROFIT BUSINESS

NONPROFIT ORGANIZATIONS

MANUFACTURING COMPANY CASES

TRANSPORTATION

Preface

The business world today is considerably different and more complex than it was just two years ago when the previous edition of this text was published. Today we experience improving economies, rising interest rates, extensive outsourcing, a migration of work to developing countries, more attention to business ethics, ballooning federal budget deficits, continued globalization, rising unemployment, a European Union of twenty-four countries instead of twelve, and intense rivalry in almost all industries. E-commerce too has changed the nature of business to its core. Thousands of strategic alliances and partnerships, even among competitors, have been formed in recent years. Hundreds of companies have declared bankruptcy and corporate scandals have highlighted the need for improved business ethics and corporate disclosure of financial transactions. Downsizing, rightsizing, reengineering, and countless divestitures, acquisitions, and liquidations have permanently altered the corporate landscape in the last two years. Thousands of firms have begun global operations and thousands more have merged. Thousands have prospered and yet thousands more have failed in the last two years. Many manufacturers have become e-commerce suppliers and long-held competitive advantages have eroded as new ones have formed. China has become the third country to send a person into space, and the war on terrorism threatens American economic stability. Both the challenges and opportunities facing organizations of all sizes today are greater than ever. There is less room than ever for error in the formulation and implementation of a strategic plan.

Changes made in this tenth edition are aimed squarely at illustrating the effect of this new world order on strategic-management theory and practice. Due to the magnitude of the changes in strategic-management theory, research, and practice as well as changes in companies, cultures, and countries, this edition has changed more substantially than any. The first edition was published in 1986. Thirteen reviewers of the ninth edition did outstanding work and their suggestions have dramatically improved this tenth edition. There are more brand-new cases in this edition than ever before and there is more coverage of strategic-management concepts, theory, research, and techniques in the chapters. Every sentence and paragraph has been scrutinized, modified, clarified, deleted, streamlined, updated, and improved to enhance the content and caliber of presentation. The structure of this edition parallels the last, with nine chapters and a Cohesion Case, but the improvements in readability and coverage are dramatic. Every chapter now features new strategic-management concepts and practices presented in a clear, focused, and relevant manner.

The skills-oriented, practitioner perspective that historically has been the foundation of this text is enhanced and strengthened in this edition. However, there is new and expanded coverage of strategic-management theories and research herein to reflect companies' use of concepts such as value chain analysis (VCA), Balanced Scorecard, resource-based view (RBV), and outsourcing. To survive and prosper in the new millennium, organizations must build and sustain competitive advantage. This text is now trusted around the world to provide future and present managers the latest skills and concepts needed to effectively formulate and efficiently implement a strategic plan—a game plan if you will—that can lead to sustainable competitive advantage for any type of business.

Our mission in preparing the tenth edition of *Strategic Management* was "to create the most current, well-written strategic management textbook on the market—a book that is exciting and valuable to both students and professors." To achieve this, every page has been revamped, updated, and improved. New strategic-management research and practice, such as the Industrial Organizational (I/O) Model and First Mover Advantages, are incorporated now and hundreds of new practical examples abound. There is a brand-new Cohesion Case on Krispy Kreme Doughnuts (KKD)—2004, an exciting company that is expanding aggressively around the world. Students will enjoy analyzing this case through exercises at the end of each chapter. Even if you have not previously utilized the Cohesion Case feature of this text, please give it a try, since this teaching tool is improved in this edition and anchored by KKD. There are also new Experiential Exercises on KKD provided at the end of each chapter.

A wonderful selection of brand-new cases in this edition include such companies as Verizon Communications, R.J. Reynolds Tobacco Co., Calloway Golf, the U.S. Postal Service, Gateway Computer, the American Red Cross, and others on well-known, student-exciting companies and organizations. The time basis for all cases included in this edition is 2004 since year-end 2003 financial statements are provided in most of the cases. This case lineup represents the most up-to-date compilation of cases ever assembled in a strategic-management text. There are more cases on technology companies this time, more nonprofit companies, more small business companies, and more global companies.

The reviewers and I believe you will find this tenth edition to be the best business policy textbook available for communicating both the excitement and value of strategic management. Concise and exceptionally well organized, this text is now published in nine different languages—English, Chinese, Spanish, German, Japanese, Pharsi, Indonesian, Indian, and Arabic. On five continents, this text is widely used in colleges and universities at both the graduate and undergraduate levels. In addition, thousands of companies, organizations, and governmental bodies use this text as a management guide, making it perhaps the most widely used strategic planning book in the world.

This textbook meets all AACSB guidelines for the business policy and strategic-management course at both the graduate and undergraduate levels, and previous editions have been used at more than 500 colleges and universities. It is now updated to reflect the twenty-first century in terms of appearance, topical coverage, and today's business environment.

Prentice Hall maintains a separate Web site for this text at **www.prenhall.com/ david**. The author maintains the Strategic Management Club Online at **www. strategyclub.com**, which offers many benefits for strategic-management and business policy students.

Tenth Edition Design Changes

There are some nice design changes in this edition as well. First, the comprehensive strategic-management model is displayed on the inside front cover of the text.

At the start of each chapter, the section of the comprehensive strategy model covered in that chapter is "highlighted and enlarged" so students can see the focus of each chapter in the basic running comprehensive model.

The "How to Analyze a Business Policy Case" section is moved from "before the chapters" to "before the cases." This introductory case analysis material is now expanded and divided into two parts: (1) "How to Prepare and Present a Strategic Management Case" and (2) "A Sample Case Analysis Outline." The sample case analysis part is brand new with this edition. Also in this introductory case material, the "Fifty Tips for Success in Case Analysis" are now organized into Content Tips and Process Tips for easier use.

This edition of the book is also more visually appealing. Reviewers told us that the picture of interlocking gears on the front cover and at the beginning of each chapter in the last edition represented a bygone era when manufacturing dominated. Thus, the outside cover has changed and for the first time pictures are provided in the chapter material.

A new case matrix is provided in the Preface to reveal topical areas emphasized in each case. This new case matrix lists the cases and suggestions on how the cases deal with the three themes and the nine chapters. For instance, details regarding which cases can be used to highlight mission/vision and which ones are best for strategy implementation are provided.

A new "About the Author" biography is also provided in the Preface.

Chapter Themes

Three themes still permeate all chapters in this edition and contribute significantly to making it timely, informative, exciting, and valuable. There are boxed insert "Perspectives" in each chapter that link concepts being presented to each theme.

However, the "Perspectives" in this edition are fewer in number and are tied more closely to chapter material. The three themes that permeate the nine chapters of this text are as follows:

1. Global Factors Affect Virtually All Strategic Decisions

The global theme is enhanced in this edition because doing business globally has become a necessity, rather than a luxury, in most industries. Nearly all strategic decisions today are affected by global issues and concerns. There is new global coverage in each chapter consistent with the growing interdependence among countries and companies worldwide. The dynamics of political, economic, and cultural differences across countries directly affect strategic-management decisions. Doing business globally is more risky and complex than ever. The global theme illustrates how organizations today can effectively do business in an interlocked and interdependent world community.

2. E-Commerce Is a Vital Strategic-Management Tool

The e-commerce theme is integrated throughout the chapters in response to immense e-commerce opportunities and threats facing organizations today. Almost all products can now be purchased on the Internet. Business-to-business e-commerce is ten times greater even than business-to-consumer e-commerce. Accelerating use of the Internet to gather, analyze, send, and receive information has changed the way strategic decisions are made. Since the last edition, literally millions of companies have established World Wide Web sites and are conducting e-commerce internationally. There has been a resurgence of technology firms and products in the last two years affecting all other firms.

3. Preserving the Natural Environment Is a Vital Strategic Issue

Unique to strategic-management texts, the natural environment theme is strengthened in this edition in order to promote and encourage firms to conduct operations in an environmentally sound manner. This theme now includes social responsibility and business ethics issues. Countries worldwide have enacted laws to curtail the pollution of streams, rivers, the air, land, and sea. Environmental concerns are a new point of contention in World Trade Organization (WTO) policies and practices. The strategic efforts of both companies and countries to preserve the natural environment are described herein, including new coverage of ISO 14001 and the BELL Program. Respect for the natural environment has become an important concern for consumers, companies, society, and the AACSB.

Time-Tested Features

This edition continues to offer many special time-tested features and content that have made this text so successful for nearly twenty years. Trademarks of this text that have been strengthened in this edition include:

Chapters: Time-Tested Features

- This text meets AACSB guidelines which support a practitioner orientation rather than a theory/research approach. It offers a skills-oriented approach to developing a vision and mission statement; performing an external audit; conducting an internal assessment; and formulating, implementing, and evaluating strategies.

- The global, natural environment, and e-commerce themes permeate all chapters and examine strategic-management concepts in these important perspectives.
- The author's writing style is concise, conversational, interesting, logical, lively, and supported by numerous current examples throughout.
- A simple, integrative strategic-management model appears in all chapters and on the inside front cover of the text. This model is widely utilized for strategic planning among consultants and companies worldwide. One reviewer said: "One thing I have admired about David's text is that he follows the fundamental sequence of strategy development, implementation, and evaluation. There is a basic flow from mission/purposes to internal/ external environmental scanning to strategy development, selection, implementation, and evaluation. This has been, and continues to be, a hallmark of the David text. Many other strategy texts are more disjointed in their presentation, and thus confusing to the student, especially at the undergraduate level."
- A Cohesion Case (Krispy Kreme Doughnuts—2004) follows Chapter 1 and is revisited at the end of each chapter. This exciting new Cohesion Case allows students to apply strategic-management concepts and techniques to a real organization as chapter material is covered. This integrative (cohesive) approach readies students for case analysis.
- End-of-chapter Experiential Exercises effectively apply concepts and techniques in a challenging, meaningful, and enjoyable manner. Eighteen exercises apply text material to the Cohesion Case; ten apply textual material to a college or university; another ten exercises send students into the business world to explore important strategy topics. The exercises are relevant, interesting, and contemporary.
- There is excellent pedagogy, including Notable Quotes and Objectives to open each chapter, and Key Terms, Current Readings, Discussion Questions, and Experiential Exercises to close each chapter.
- There is excellent coverage of strategy formulation issues such as business ethics, global versus domestic operations, vision/mission, matrix analysis, partnering, joint venturing, competitive analysis, governance, and guidelines for conducting an internal/external strategy assessment.
- There is excellent coverage of strategy implementation issues such as corporate culture, organizational structure, outsourcing, marketing concepts, financial analysis, and again, business ethics.
- A systematic, analytical approach is presented in Chapter 6, including matrices such as the SWOT (previously called TOWS), BCG, IE, GRAND, SPACE, and QSPM.
- The chapter material is again published in four-color.
- "Visit the Net" Internet exercises are available online at **www.prenhall. com/david** or at the **www.strategyclub.com** Web site and in the page margins of the text. This feature reveals the author's recommended Web sites for locating additional information on the concepts being presented, and greatly enhances classroom presentation in an Internet environment since the recommended sites have been screened closely to assure that each is well worth visiting in class. This feature also provides students with substantial additional material on chapter concepts.

- The Web site **www.prenhall.com/david** provides chapter and case updates and support materials.
- There are nine chapters organized in the same manner as the previous edition.
- A chapters-only paperback version of the text is available.
- Activebook, an Internet version of this text, is available.
- Custom-case publishing is available whereby an instructor can combine chapters from this text with cases from a variety of sources.
- For the chapter material, the outstanding ancillary package includes a comprehensive *Instructor's Manual,* and a computerized test bank.

Cases: Time-Tested Features

- This edition contains the most current set of cases in any strategic-management text on the market. All cases are based upon year-end 2003 financial data and information.
- The cases focus on well-known firms in the news making strategic changes. All cases are undisguised and most are exclusively written for this text to reflect current strategic-management problems and practices.
- Organized conveniently by industry (usually two competing firms per industry), the cases feature a great mix of small business, international, and not-for-profit firms.
- All cases have been class tested to ensure that they are interesting, challenging, and effective for illustrating strategic-management concepts.
- All cases provide complete financial information about the firm, an organizational chart, and a vision and mission statement for the organization if those were available.
- Customized inclusion of cases to comprise a tailored text is available to meet the special needs of some professors.
- A split paperback version including only cases is available.
- For the cases, the outstanding ancillary package includes an elaborate *Case Instructor's Manual,* PowerPoint, and other support on the **www. strategyclub.com** Web site.
- A special matrix provided in the Preface compares all cases in the text on important criteria such as size of firm, Web site of firm, address of firm, phone number of firm, and so on.

New Chapter Features/Changes/Content in This Edition

In addition to the special time-tested trademarks described above, this tenth edition includes some exciting new features, changes, and content designed to position this text as the clear leader and best choice for teaching business policy and strategic management.

First of all, the new Cohesion Case on Krispy Kreme Doughnuts (KKD) replaces the previous American Airlines Cohesion Case. Krispy Kreme is a rapidly growing, global company headquartered in Winston-Salem, North Carolina. (The previous American Airlines cohesion case is updated and included among the set of forty cases in the tenth edition.) Appearing after Chapter 1, the KKD case is considered the best Cohesion Case ever in a strategic-management text. Experiential Exercises at the end of each chapter apply concepts to KKD to ready students for case analysis when they complete the chapter material. Over the past twenty years, the Cohesion Case for this text has changed from Ponderosa Steakhouse in the first and second editions, to Hershey Foods in the third through seventh editions, to AOL in the eighth edition, to American Airlines in the ninth edition, and now to KKD, which is a fun company for students to focus upon throughout the semester. You or a team of students could on occasion bring donuts to class during the semester.

In this edition, new features, changes, and content common to all nine chapters include the following:

- New Global, E-commerce, and Natural Environment boxed inserts.
- New examples throughout.
- New Visit the Net (VTN) Web sites provided in the page margins.
- Improved coverage of global issues and concerns.
- Expanded coverage of business ethics.
- All new current readings at the end of each chapter reveal new, relevant strategic-management research.
- More international flavor than ever. American textbook authors should include substantial coverage of how business functions vary across countries, so there is excellent new coverage of cultural and conceptual strategic-management differences across countries.
- New research and theories of seminal thinkers in strategy development such as Ansoff, Chandler, Porter, Hamel, Prahalad, Mintzberg, and Barney are included. Scholars such as these made strategic management important and brought it to its present place in modern business. Practical aspects of strategic management, however, are still center-stage and the trademark of this text.
- New excellent Web sites that augment chapter concepts are provided in the text page margins throughout this edition because many universities now teach in Internet-ready classrooms and utilize Web sites during lectures. These sites are also hot-linked at **www.prenhall.com/david** and **www. strategyclub.com** Web sites.
- Substantial new material on business ethics throughout. Corporate fraud, scandals, and illegalities have become so numerous that we in academia must be certain to emphasize that "good ethics is good business." This notion is tied to the natural environment theme in this edition.
- On average, ten new review questions are provided at the end of each chapter.

In addition to the above new chapter features/changes/content, an overview of specific new chapter features/changes/content that characterize this tenth edition are given below:

Chapter 1

- New information is provided about gaining and sustaining competitive advantage. The Industrial/Organizational (I/O) and the Resource-Based View (RBV) theories of organizations are introduced for the first time as they are detailed in Chapters 3 and 4, respectively, of this edition.

- The new organizational chart position, Chief Strategy Officer (CSO), is introduced since it is becoming common in organizations.
- New coverage of ISO 14000 Certification is provided since more and more firms seek this natural environment stamp of approval.
- There is a new Strategies in Action Table featuring Nestlé, Legend, and Krispy Kreme Doughnuts.

Chapter 2

- The title was changed from "The Business Mission" to "The Business Vision and Mission" to reflect more coverage of vision and mission statements.
- New coverage on social responsibility is provided.
- New examples abound.
- New Business-to-Business (B2B) E-Commerce Perspective is provided.

Chapter 3

- New heading and coverage of the Industrial Organization (I/O) View of competitive advantage is provided.
- New coverage of Porter's Five-Forces Model is provided.
- New coverage of the business conditions in Russia, Mexico, China, and Europe is provided.
- New E-Commerce and Natural Environment Perspectives are provided.
- New EFE and CPM matrices are provided.

Chapter 4

- New heading and coverage of the Resource-Based View (RBV) of strategic management is provided.
- New discussion of inventory control being used as a competitive weapon is provided.
- New material on the use of dividends as a financial and investment tool is included.
- New heading and material on Value Chain Analysis (VCA) is provided.
- New IFE matrix is provided.
- New information on applying financial ratio analysis in not-for-profit settings is provided.

Chapter 5

- New discussion of objectives is provided, including a comparison of Financial versus Strategic objectives.
- New discussion of the Balanced Scorecard is provided.
- A new diagram and narrative on the "Levels of Strategies" is included to exemplify the corporate, divisional, functional, and operational levels in firms.
- New Tables on Divestitures, Mergers, and Joint Ventures are provided.
- New headings and discussions of "First Mover Advantages" and "Outsourcing" are provided.

- New coverage of joint ventures, cooperative arrangements, and partnerships is provided. Firms today more often form alliances than merge or acquire and this new trend is illustrated well.
- The value chain discussion is expanded and moved from this to the preceding chapter.

Chapter 6

- The section on "The Role of Boards of Directors" is renamed "Governance Issues" and expanded to include coverage of the Sarbanes-Oxley Act passed in July 2002.
- The TOWS acronym is replaced by SWOT throughout the chapter, to be consistent with strategic-planning practice.
- New Global and Natural Environment Perspectives are provided.
- New example SWOT and IE matrices are provided as well as new discussion of their limitations and implications.

Chapter 7

- The title was changed from "Implementing Strategies: Management Issues" to "Implementing Strategies: Management and Operations Issues" to reflect expanded coverage of production/operations issues related to strategic management.
- New discussion is provided that addresses whether companies consider natural environment training in business schools to be a factor in hiring decisions.
- Discussion of Mexican, Japanese, and Russian culture is improved. New discussion of other cultures (European, Chinese, South American) is now included. This emphasis accents the fact that the U.S. culture model is by no means the only model for doing business. Business students need exposure to business practices of other countries in order to appreciate differences among managers worldwide and thus be more effective practicing managers.
- A new organizational chart (for Sonoco Products Company) illustrates an SBU design.
- Increased coverage of issues related to women and minority managers is provided.

Chapter 8

- Expanded and improved coverage of financial statement analysis is provided to match current new thinking in regard to ethical and legal handling of financial reporting.
- New example EPS/EBIT and Value of the Company analyses, tables, and diagrams are provided.
- The word "proforma" is replaced with "projected" throughout the chapter as related to financial statements, to be more consistent with practice.
- New coverage of the Sarbanes-Oxley Act of 2002 dealing with CEO and CFO responsibilities regarding financial statements is provided.
- New coverage lists MBA programs that do especially well in providing coverage of natural environmental issues.

Chapter 9

- New coverage on "Twenty-first Century Challenges in Strategic Management" is provided, including:
    a. Whether the process should be more an art or a science.
    b. Whether strategies should be visible or hidden from stakeholders.
    c. Whether the process should be more top-down or bottom-up.
- New coverage of the Balanced Scorecard as a strategy evaluation tool is provided.

New Case Features/Changes/Content in This Edition

The following fifteen new cases by new authors are included in this tenth edition:

Two new telecommunications firms:

1. Verizon Communications
2. Nextel Communications

Four new small business strategy cases:

3. The Quarry, Inc.
4. First Reliance Bank
5. The Bridal Gallery
6. Champions Hydro-Lawn, Inc.

Three new nonprofit organization cases:

7. U.S. Postal Service
8. American Red Cross
9. Utah Valley State College

Two new computer company cases:

10. Apple Computer
11. Gateway

One new airline company case:

12. American Airlines (earlier version was the Cohesion Case)

Three other new exciting cases:

13. R.J. Reynolds
14. Anheuser-Busch
15. Calloway Golf

The following seventeen cases from the ninth edition were deleted, thus not included in this tenth edition:

1. U.S. Airways
2. Best Buy
3. Wachovia

4. First State Bank of Roans Prairie
5. Elkins Lake Baptist Church
6. Winn-Dixie
7. Strictly Roots Natural Hair Salon
8. Dell Computer
9. Hewlett-Packard
10. Heinz Foods
11. Playboy Enterprises
12. Reader's Digest
13. Coors
14. Hershey Foods
15. Harrah's
16. Carnival Cruise Lines
17. Riverbanks Zoo

The following seven cases from the ninth edition are fully updated by a new author and included in this tenth edition:

1. E*TRADE
2. eBay
3. Amazon
4. Royal Caribbean
5. Lockheed Martin
6. Reebok
7. Harley-Davidson

The following eighteen cases from the ninth edition are fully updated by the original author and included in this tenth edition:

1. Southwest Airlines
2. Limited Brands
3. Wal-Mart Stores
4. Target Corp.
5. Mandalay Resort Group
6. Audubon Nature Institute
7. Central United Methodist Church
8. Classic Car Club of America
9. Harley-Davidson
10. Winnebago Industries
11. Avon Products
12. Revlon
13. Pilgrim's Pride
14. Boeing
15. Stryker
16. Biomet
17. Nike
18. UST Inc.

Net Result: There are a total of forty cases in the tenth edition of this text.

Facts About the Tenth Edition Lineup of Cases

- The new mix of forty cases includes twenty-three service companies and seventeen manufacturing companies.
- The time setting of all the cases is year-end 2003, making them exceptionally up-to-date.
- Almost all the cases contain year-end 2003 financial statements, so students can project financial implications of their recommendations for 2004 and beyond.
- All of the cases are "comprehensive" in the sense that each focuses on multiple business functions, rather than addressing one particular business problem or issue. Students are generally asked to prepare a three-year strategic plan for each case company, rather than being asked to solve a particular business problem.
- The new mix of cases includes three purely e-commerce cases to support the new e-commerce theme; the cases are E*Trade, eBay, and Amazon.
- The new mix of cases includes four small business (for-profit) cases and six not-for-profit cases.
- The new mix of cases includes thirty-five "international" companies, which provides students with a better opportunity to evaluate and consider international aspects of doing business.
- All the cases are undisguised and feature real organizations in real industries, and use real names and real places.
- All the cases feature an organization "undergoing strategic change," thus offering students specific issues to evaluate and consider.
- All the cases feature organizations in familiar or interesting settings.
- All the cases provide excellent coverage of a firm's internal weaknesses and external threats, rather than focusing on the organization's strengths and opportunities.
- All the cases are written in a lively, concise writing style that captures the reader's interest and establishes a time setting, usually in the opening paragraph.
- The cases provide excellent quantitative information such as numbers, ratios, percentages, dollar values, graphs, statistics, and maps so students can prepare a more specific, rational, and defensible strategic plan for the organization.
- Each provides excellent information about the industry and competitors.
- Each case includes the organization's existing vision statement and mission statement, if available.
- Each case is supported by an excellent teacher's note.

Ancillary Materials

- A new running update of the Krispy Kreme Cohesion Case is provided at **www.prenhall.com/david**. The Krispy Kreme Cohesion Case is kept fully undated online for both professors and students. Scores of excellent hot links for the Krispy Kreme case are provided at **www.prenhall.com/david**.
- There is a dramatically improved **www.prenhall.com/david** Web site. This Web site, designed solely to support this textbook, has been revised with both professor and student content and information.

- The new PowerPoint Web site provided with this text offers professors easy lecture outlines for in-class presentations. Chapter headings and topics are highlighted on more than eighty PowerPoint slides per chapter in this edition.
- *Case Instructor's Manual.* Provides a comprehensive teacher's note for all forty cases. The teacher's notes feature detailed analyses, classroom discussion questions with answers, an external and internal assessment, specific recommendations, strategy implementation material, and an epilogue for each case.
- *Instructor's Manual.* Provides lecture notes, teaching tips, answers to all end-of-chapter Experiential Exercises and Review Questions, additional Experiential Exercises not in the text, a glossary with definitions of all end-of-chapter key terms and concepts, sample course syllabi, and a newly revamped test bank of nearly 1,500 mostly new questions with answers.
- *Fully Revised, Printed and Computerized Test Bank.* The test bank for this text includes 425 True/False questions, 450 multiple choice questions, 250 essay questions for the text chapters, and 250 discussion questions. Sample comprehensive tests for Chapters 1–5 and Chapters 6–9 are also given, and answers to all objective questions are provided. The test questions given in the *Instructor's Manual* are also available on computerized test software to facilitate preparing and grading tests.
- Ancillary Materials are provided to professors online, at **www.prenhall.com/ david**.

Special Note to Students

Welcome to business policy or strategic management, whichever title this course has at your university. This is a challenging and exciting course that will allow you to function as the owner or chief executive officer of different organizations. Your major task in this course will be to make strategic decisions and to justify those decisions through oral and written communication. Strategic decisions determine the future direction and competitive position of an enterprise for a long time. Decisions to expand geographically or to diversify are examples of strategic decisions.

Strategic decision making occurs in all types and sizes of organizations, from General Motors to a small hardware store. Many people's lives and jobs are affected by strategic decisions, so the stakes are very high. An organization's very survival is often at stake. The overall importance of strategic decisions makes this course especially exciting and challenging. You will be called upon in business policy to demonstrate how your strategic decisions could be successfully implemented.

In this course you can look forward to making strategic decisions both as an individual and as a member of a team. No matter how hard employees work, an organization is in real trouble if strategic decisions are not made effectively. Doing the right things (effectiveness) is more important than doing things right (efficiency). For example, companies such as Spiegel and WestPoint Stevens were very prosperous in the early 1990s, but ineffective strategies led to bankruptcy in 2003. Even firms such as Merck, Boeing, and Sun Microsystems have pursued ineffective strategies of late.

You will have the opportunity in this course to make actual strategic decisions, perhaps for the first time in your academic career. Do not hesitate to take a stand and defend specific strategies that you determine to be the best. The rationale for your strategic decisions will be more important than the actual decision, because no one knows for sure what the best strategy is for a particular organization at a given point in time. This fact accents the subjective, contingency nature of the strategic-management process.

Use the concepts and tools presented in this text, coupled with your own intuition, to recommend strategies that you can defend as being most appropriate for the organizations that you study. You will also need to integrate knowledge acquired in previous business courses. For this reason, business policy is often called a capstone course; you may want to keep this book for your personal library.

This text is practitioner-oriented and applications-oriented. It presents strategic-management concepts that will enable you to formulate, implement, and evaluate strategies in all kinds of profit and nonprofit organizations. The end-of-chapter Experiential Exercises allow you to apply what you've read in each chapter to the new Krispy Kreme Donut Cohesion Case and to your own university.

Definitely visit the Strategic Management Club Online at **www.strategyclub. com**. The templates and links there will save you time in performing analyses and will make your work look professional. Work hard in policy this term and have fun. Good luck!

Acknowledgments

Many persons have contributed time, energy, ideas, and suggestions for improving this text over ten editions. The strength of this text is largely attributed to the collective wisdom, work, and experiences of business policy professors, strategic-management researchers, students, and practitioners. Names of particular individuals whose published research is referenced in this edition of this text are listed alphabetically in the Name Index. To all individuals involved in making this text so popular and successful, I am indebted and thankful.

Many special persons and reviewers contributed valuable material and suggestions for this edition. I would like to thank my colleagues and friends at Auburn University, Mississippi State University, East Carolina University, and Francis Marion University. These are universities where I have served on the management faculty. Scores of students and professors at these schools helped shape the development of this text. Many thanks go to the thirteen outstanding reviewers of the tenth edition whose names are listed below:

1. Kunal Banerji, Florida Atlantic University
2. Drew L. Harris, Longwood University
3. Jo Ann M. Duffy, Sam Houston State University
4. Dave Flynn, Hofstra University
5. Debbie Gilliard, Metropolitan State College
6. Robert C. Losik, Southern New Hampshire University
7. Leslie C. Mueller, Northwestern State University of Louisiana
8. Kenneth R. Tillery, Middle Tennessee State University
9. John Cote, Baker College
10. Rodley C. Pineda, Tennessee Technological University
11. Michael G. Goldsby, Ball State University College of Business
12. Warren S. Stone, University of Arkansas at Little Rock
13. Lindle Hatton, California State University, Sacramento

Individuals who develop cases for the North American Case Research Association Meeting, the Midwest Society for Case Research Meeting, the Eastern Case Writers Association Meeting, the European Case Research Association Meeting, and Harvard Case Services are vitally important for continued progress in the field of strategic management. From a research perspective, writing business policy cases represents a valuable scholarly activity among faculty. Extensive research is required to structure business policy cases in a way that exposes strategic issues, decisions, and behavior. Pedagogically, business policy cases are essential for students in learning how to apply concepts, evaluate situations, formulate strategies, and resolve implementation problems. Without a continuous stream of updated business policy cases, the strategic-management course and discipline would lose much of its energy and excitement.

Professors who teach this course supplement lecture with simulations, guest speakers, experiential exercises, class projects, and/or outside readings. Case analysis, however, is typically the backbone of the learning process in most strategic-management courses across the country. This course is sometimes called business policy, but case analysis is almost always an integral part of the class.

Analyzing strategic-management cases gives students the opportunity to work in teams to evaluate the internal operations and external issues facing various organizations and to craft strategies that can lead these firms to success. Working in teams gives students practical experience solving problems as part of a group. In the business world, important decisions are generally made within groups; strategic-management students learn to deal with overly aggressive group members and also timid, noncontributing group members. This experience is valuable as strategic-management students near graduation and soon enter the working world on a full-time basis.

Students can improve their oral and written communication skills as well as their analytical and interpersonal skills by proposing and defending particular courses of action for the case companies. Analyzing cases allows students to view a company, its competitors, and its industry concurrently, thus simulating the complex business world. Through case analysis, students learn how to apply concepts, evaluate situations, formulate strategies, and resolve implementation problems. Instructors typically ask students to prepare a three-year strategic plan for the firm. Analyzing a strategic-management case entails students applying concepts learned across their entire business curriculum. Students gain experience dealing with a wide range of organizational problems that impact all the business functions.

The following individuals wrote cases that were selected for inclusion in this edition of this text. These persons helped develop the most current compilation of cases ever assembled in a strategic-management text:

Jill Austin, Middle Tennessee State University; Brian Barbour, Francis Marion University; Robert Barrett, Francis Marion University; Henry Beam, Western Michigan University; Melissa Birch, Francis Marion University; Eugene Bland, Texas A&M University at Corpus Christi; Mark Bube, Francis Marion University; Marilyn Butler, Sam Houston State University; Todd Butler, Francis Marion University; Jim Camerius, Northern Michigan University; Carol Cumber, South Dakota State University; Forest David, Campbell University; Marcelo de Mattos, Francis Marion University; Satish Deshpande, Western Michigan University; William Doulaveris, Francis Marion University; Caroline Fisher, Loyola University New Orleans; Michelle Ghoens, Francis Marion University; Lowell Glenn, Utah Valley State University; Andrew Graaff, Francis Marion University; James Harbin, East Texas State University; Suzanne Harrington, Francis Marion University; Marilyn Helms, Dalton State College;

David Johnson, Utah Valley State University; Joseph Kavanaugh, Sam Houston State University; Mike Keeffe, Southwest Texas State University; Harold Koch, Utah Valley State University; Benjamin Lanier, Francis Marion University; Lori Lyerly, Francis Marion University; Jim Meshaw, Francis Marion University; Bill Middlebrook, Southwest Texas State University; Bianca Ornclas, South Dakota State University; Misty Poissoit, Sam Houston State University; Paul Reed, Sam Houston State University; John Ross III, Southwest Texas State University; Corina San-Marina, Francis Marion University; Stephanie Schaller, Francis Marion University; Amit Shah, Frostburg State University; Matthew Sonfield, Hofstra University; Charles Sterrett, Frostburg State University; Robert Stevenson, Francis Marion University; Carolyn Stokes, Francis Marion University; Leslie Toombs, University of Texas at Tyler; Cleat Weaver, Francis Marion University; Brad Winn, Utah Valley State University; Ben Zhang, Francis Marion University

I especially appreciate the wonderful work completed by the tenth edition ancillary authors as follows:

Case Instructor's Manual—Forest R. David, Campbell University

Instructor's Manual—Tracy Ryan, Longwood College

Test Item File—Amit Shah, Frostburg State University

Scores of Prentice Hall employees and salespersons have worked diligently behind the scenes to make this text a leader in the business policy market. I appreciate the continued hard work of all those persons.

I also want to thank you, the reader, for investing the time and effort to read and study this text. It will help you formulate, implement, and evaluate strategies for any organization with which you become associated. I hope you come to share my enthusiasm for the rich subject area of strategic management and for the systematic learning approach taken in this text.

Finally, I want to welcome and invite your suggestions, ideas, thoughts, comments, and questions regarding any part of this text or the ancillary materials. Please call me at 843–661–1419, fax me at 843–661–1432, e-mail me at **Fdavid@Fmarion.edu**, or write me at the School of Business, Francis Marion University, Florence, South Carolina 29501. I sincerely appreciate and need your input to continually improve this text in future editions. Your efforts at drawing my attention to specific errors or deficiencies in coverage or exposition will especially be appreciated.

Thank you for using this text.

Fred R. David

About the Author

Dr. Fred R. David is the author of three mainstream strategic-management textbooks titled *Strategic Management, Concepts in Strategic Management,* and *Cases in Strategic Management.* These texts have been on a two-year revision cycle since 1986, when the first edition was published. They are among the best if not the best-selling strategic-management textbooks in the world and are used at more than 400 colleges and universities. Prestigious universities that have used Dr. David's textbook include Harvard University, Duke University, Carnegie-Mellon University, John Hopkins University, the University of Maryland, and Wake Forest University.

Dr. David's strategic-management textbook has been translated and published in Chinese, Japanese, Pharsi, Spanish, Indonesian, Indian, and Arabic, and is widely used across Asia and South America. It is the best-selling strategic-management textbook in Mexico, China, Peru, Chile, Japan, and number one or number two in the United States. Approximately 90,000 students read Dr. David's textbook annually as well as thousands of businesspersons. The book has led the field of strategic management for more than a decade in providing an applications/practitioner approach to the discipline.

A native of Whiteville, North Carolina, Fred R. David received a B.S. degree in Mathematics and an MBA from Wake Forest University before being employed as a bank manager with United Carolina Bank. He received a Ph.D. in Business Administration from the University of South Carolina where he majored in Management. Currently, the TranSouth Professor of Strategic Management at Francis Marion University (FMU) in Florence, South Carolina, Dr. David has also taught at Auburn University, Mississippi State University, East Carolina University, the University of South Carolina, and the University of North Carolina at Pembroke. He is the author of 145 referred publications, including 36 journal articles, 52 *Proceedings* publications, and 57 business policy cases. David has articles published in such journals as *Academy of Management Review, Academy of Management Executive, Journal of Applied Psychology, Long Range Planning*, and *Advanced Management Journal.*

In May 2003, Dr. David received a Lifetime Honorary Professorship Award from the Universidad Ricardo Palma in Lima, Peru. He delivered the keynote speech at the twenty-first Annual Latin American Congress on Strategy hosted by the Centrum School of Business in Peru. Dr. David recently delivered an eight-hour Strategic Planning Workshop to the faculty at Pontificia Universidad Catolica Del in Lima, Peru, and an eight-hour Case Writing/Analyzing Workshop to the faculty at Utah Valley State College in Orem, Utah. He has received numerous awards, including FMU's Board of Trustees Research Scholar Award, and the university's Award for Excellence in Research given annually to the best faculty researcher on campus. Dr. David has received the prestigious Phil Carroll Advancement of Management Award, given annually by the Society for the Advancement of Management (SAM) to a management scholar for outstanding recent contributions in management research.

David served for three years on the Southern Management Association's Board of Directors and currently serves on the Editorial Review Board of the *Advanced Management Journal*. Through his Web site, **www.checkmateplan.com**, Dr. David actively assists businesses across the country and around the world in doing strategic planning. He has developed and markets the *CheckMATE* Strategic Planning Software, which is an industry-leading business software package (**www.checkmateplan.com**).

CASE COMPANY INFORMATION MATRIX

	STOCK SYMBOL	STOCK EXCHANGE	TELEPHONE	HEADQUARTERS ADDRESS	WEB SITE ADDRESS
TENTH EDITION SERVICE COMPANY CASES					
TELECOMMUNICATIONS					
1. Verizon Communications	VZ	NY	212–395–2121	1095 Avenue of the Americas 36th Floor New York, NY 10036	**www.22.verizon.com**
2. Nextel Communications	NXTL	NASD	703–433–4000	2001 Edmund Halley Dr. Reston, VA 20191	**www.nextel.com**
AIRLINES					
3. Southwest Airlines	LUV	NY	214–792–4000	P.O. Box 36611 Dallas, TX 75235	**www.iflyswa.com** **www.southwest.com**
4. American Airlines	AMR	NY	817–963–1234	4333 Amon Carter Blvd. Fort Worth, TX 76155	**www.amrcorp.com**
E-COMMERCE COMPANIES					
5. E*TRADE	ET	NY	650–331–6000	4500 Bohannon Dr. Menlo Park, CA 94025	**www.etrade.com**
6. eBay	eBAY	NASD	408–376–7400	2145 Hamilton Ave. San Jose, CA 95125	**www.ebay.com**
7. Amazon	AMZN	NASD	206–266–1000	1200 12th Ave. Suite 1200 Seattle, WA 98144	**www.amazon.com**
RETAILERS					
8. Kroger Company	KR	NY	513–762–4000	1014 Vine St. Cincinnati, OH 45202	**www.kroger.com**
9. Limited Brands	LTD	NY	614–415–7000	3 Limited Pky. P.O. Box 16000 Columbus, OH 43216	**www.limited.com**
10. Wal-Mart Stores	WMT	NY	501–273–4000	702 SW Eighth St. Bentonville, AR 72716–8611	**www.wal-mart.com**
11. Target Corporation	TGT	NY	612–304–6073	1000 Nicollet Mall Minneapolis, MN 55403	**www.Target.com**
ENTERTAINMENT					
12. Mandalay Resort Group	MBG	NY	702–632–6700	3950 Las Vegas Blvd. Las Vegas, NV 89119	**www.mandalayresort group.com**
13. Royal Caribbean	RCL	NY	305–539–6000	1050 Caribbean Way Miami, FL 33132	**www.royalcaribbean.com**

(continued)

CASE COMPANY INFORMATION MATRIX (CONTINUED)

	STOCK SYMBOL	STOCK EXCHANGE	TELEPHONE	HEADQUARTERS ADDRESS	WEB SITE ADDRESS
SMALL BUSINESSES					
14. The Quarry, Inc.	NA		801–418–0266	2494 North University Pky. Provo, UT 84604	www.thequarry.net
15. First Reliance Bank	N/A		843–656–5000	F2145 Fernleaf Lane Florence, SC 29501	www.firstreliance.com
16. Bridal Gallery	N/A		936–295–8895	Vickie Cangelose 2400 Ave. I Huntsville, TX 77340	
17. Champions Hydro-Lawn	NA		281–445–2614	13226 Kaltenbrun Houston, TX 77086	www.championhydro lawn.com
NONPROFIT ORGANIZATIONS					
18. Audubon Nature Institute	N/A	N/A	504–581–4629	6500 Magazine St. New Orleans, LA 70118	www.auduboninstitute. org
19. Central United Methodist Church	NA	NA	843–662–3218	P.O. Box 87 Florence, SC 29501	www.centralumcsc. web.com
20. U.S. Postal Service	NA	NA		475 Lenfant Plaza SW Washington, DC 20260	www.usps.com
21. American Red Cross	NA	NA	202–303–4498	American Red Cross 431 18th St., NW Washington, DC 20006	www.redcross.org/
22. Classic Car Club of America	N/A	N/A	847–390–0443	1645 Des Plaines River Rd. Suite 7A Des Plaines, IL 60018	www.classiccarclub.org/
23. Utah Valley State College	N/A	N/A	801–863–INFO	800 West University Pky. Orem, Utah 84058	www.uvsc.edu/

TENTH EDITION MANUFACTURING COMPANY CASES

	STOCK SYMBOL	STOCK EXCHANGE	TELEPHONE	HEADQUARTERS ADDRESS	WEB SITE ADDRESS
TRANSPORTATION					
24. Harley-Davidson	HDI	NY	414–342–4680	3700 W. Juneau Ave. Milwaukee, WI 53208	www.harley-davidson.com
25. Winnebago Industries	WGO	NY	641–585–3535	P.O. Box 152 Forest City, IA 50436	www.winnebago ind.com
COSMETICS					
26. Avon Products	AVP	NY	212–282–5000	1345 Avenue of the Americas New York, NY 10105	www.avon.com
27. Revlon	REV	NY	212–527–4000	625 Madison Ave. New York, NY 10022	www.revlon.com

CASE COMPANY INFORMATION MATRIX (CONTINUED)

	STOCK SYMBOL	STOCK EXCHANGE	TELEPHONE	HEADQUARTERS ADDRESS	WEB SITE ADDRESS
FOOD AND BEVERAGE					
28. Pilgrim's Pride	CHX	NY	903–855–1000	110 South Texas St. Pittsburg, TX 75686	www.pilgrims pride.com
29. Anheuser-Busch	BUD	NY	314–577–2000	One Bush Place St. Louis, MO 63118	www.anheuserbusch. com
AEROSPACE					
30. Boeing	BA	NY	312–544–2000	100 N. Riverside Chicago, IL 60606	www.boeing.com
31. Lockheed Martin	LMT	NY	301–897–6000	6801 Rockledge Dr. Bethesda, MD 20817	www.lockheedmartin. com
COMPUTERS					
32. Apple Computer	AAPL	NASD	408–996–1010	1 Infinite Loop Cupertino, CA 95014	www.apple.com
33. Gateway	GTW	NY	858–848–3401	14303 Gateway Place Poway, CA 92064	www.gateway.com
MEDICAL					
34. Stryker	SYK	NY	616–385–2600	P.O. Box 4085 Kalamazoo, MI 49003	www.strykercorp.com
35. Biomet	BMET	NASD	574–267–6639	56 East Bell Dr. Warsaw, IN 46582	www.biomet.com
SPORTING GOODS					
36. Nike	NKE	NY	503–671–6453	1 Bowerman Dr. Beaverton, OR 97005	www.nike.com
37. Reebok	RBK	NY	781–401–5000	1895 J.W. Foster Blvd. Canton, MA 02021	www.reebok.com
38. Calloway Golf	ELY	NY	760–931–1771	2180 Rutherford Rd. Carlsbad, CA 92008–7328	www.callawaygolf.com
TOBACCO					
39. UST Inc.	UST	NY	203–661–1100	100 W. Putnam Ave. Greenwich, CT 06830	www.ustshareholder. com
40. R.J. Reynolds	RJR	NY	336–741–5500	401 North Main St. Winston-Salem, NC 27102	www.rjrt.com

CASE DESCRIPTION MATRIX

	TOPICAL CONTENT ISSUES													
	1	2	3	4	5	6	7	8	9	10	11	12	13	14
TENTH EDITION COHESION CASE														
Krispy Kreme Doughnuts, Inc.—2004	Y	N	Y	N	Y	Y	Y	Y	Y	N	Y	N	Y	Y
TENTH EDITION SERVICE COMPANY CASES														
TELECOMMUNICATIONS														
1. Verizon Communications, Inc.—2004	Y	N	Y	Y	Y	Y	N	Y	N	Y	N	Y	Y	Y
2. Nextel Communications, Inc.—2004	Y	N	Y	N	Y	Y	Y	Y	Y	N	Y	N	Y	Y
AIRLINES														
3. Southwest Airlines Co.—2004	Y	N	Y	N	N	Y	N	Y	Y	Y	N	N	N	Y
4. AMR Inc.—2004	Y	N	Y	N	Y	Y	Y	Y	N	Y	N	Y	Y	Y
INTERNET COMPANIES														
5. E*TRADE Financial, Corp.—2004	Y	N	Y	Y	Y	Y	N	Y	N	N	N	N	Y	N
6. eBay Inc.—2004	Y	Y	Y	Y	Y	Y	N	Y	N	Y	N	N	N	Y
7. Amazon.com, Inc.—2004	Y	Y	N	Y	Y	Y	N	Y	Y	Y	Y	N	N	Y
RETAILERS														
8. The Kroger Company—2003	N	Y	Y	N	Y	Y	Y	Y	Y	Y	Y	N	N	Y
9. Limited Brands—2004	N	Y	Y	Y	Y	Y	Y	Y	Y	Y	Y	Y	N	Y
10. Wal-Mart Stores, Inc.—2004	N	Y	Y	Y	N	Y	N	Y	Y	Y	N	N	N	Y
11. Target Corporation—2003	Y	N	Y	N	Y	Y	Y	Y	Y	N	Y	N	Y	Y
ENTERTAINMENT														
12. Mandalay Resort Group—2004	Y	N	Y	N	Y	Y	Y	Y	Y	N	Y	N	Y	Y
13. Royal Caribbean Cruises, Ltd.—2004	Y	N	Y	N	Y	Y	Y	Y	Y	N	Y	N	Y	Y
SMALL BUSINESSES														
14. The Quarry, Inc., Indoor Climbing Center—2004	Y	N	Y	N	Y	Y	Y	Y	Y	N	Y	N	Y	Y
15. First Reliance Bank—2003	Y	N	Y	N	Y	Y	Y	Y	Y	N	Y	N	Y	Y
16. Bridal Gallery—2003	Y	N	Y	N	Y	Y	Y	Y	Y	N	Y	N	Y	Y
17. Champions-Hydro Lawn, Inc.—2003	Y	N	Y	N	Y	Y	Y	Y	Y	N	Y	N	Y	Y
NONPROFIT ORGANIZATIONS														
18. The Audubon Nature Institute—2003	Y	N	Y	N	Y	Y	Y	Y	Y	N	Y	N	Y	Y
19. Central United Methodist Church—2004	Y	N	Y	N	Y	Y	Y	Y	Y	N	Y	N	Y	Y
20. The United States Postal Service—2004	Y	N	Y	N	Y	Y	Y	Y	Y	N	Y	N	Y	Y

CASE DESCRIPTION MATRIX (CONTINUED)

	TOPICAL CONTENT ISSUES													
	1	2	3	4	5	6	7	8	9	10	11	12	13	14
21. American Red Cross—2004	Y	N	Y	N	Y	Y	Y	Y	N	Y	N	Y	Y	Y
22. The Classic Car Club of America—2004	Y	N	Y	N	Y	Y	Y	Y	N	Y	N	Y	Y	Y
23. Utah Valley State College—2004	Y	N	Y	N	Y	Y	Y	Y	N	Y	N	Y	Y	Y

TENTH EDITION MANUFACTURING COMPANY CASES

TRANSPORTATION

	1	2	3	4	5	6	7	8	9	10	11	12	13	14
24. Harley-Davidson, Inc.—2004	Y	N	Y	N	Y	Y	Y	Y	N	Y	N	Y	Y	Y
25. Winnebago Industries—2004	Y	N	Y	N	Y	Y	Y	Y	N	Y	N	Y	Y	Y

COSMETICS

	1	2	3	4	5	6	7	8	9	10	11	12	13	14
26. Avon Products, Inc.—2004	Y	N	Y	N	Y	Y	Y	Y	N	Y	N	Y	Y	Y
27. Revlon, Inc.—2004	Y	N	Y	N	Y	Y	Y	Y	N	Y	N	Y	Y	Y

FOOD AND BEVERAGE

	1	2	3	4	5	6	7	8	9	10	11	12	13	14
28. Pilgrim's Pride Corporation—2004	Y	N	Y	N	Y	Y	Y	Y	N	Y	N	Y	Y	Y
29. Anheuser Busch Companies, Inc.—2004	Y	N	Y	N	Y	Y	Y	Y	N	Y	N	Y	Y	Y

AEROSPACE

	1	2	3	4	5	6	7	8	9	10	11	12	13	14
30. Boeing—2004	Y	N	Y	N	Y	Y	Y	Y	N	Y	N	Y	Y	Y
31. Lockheed Martin Corporation—2004	Y	N	Y	N	Y	Y	Y	Y	N	Y	N	Y	Y	Y

COMPUTERS

	1	2	3	4	5	6	7	8	9	10	11	12	13	14
32. Apple Computer, Inc.—2004	Y	N	Y	N	Y	Y	Y	Y	N	Y	N	Y	Y	Y
33. Gateway, Inc.—2004	Y	N	Y	N	Y	Y	Y	Y	N	Y	N	Y	Y	Y

MEDICAL

	1	2	3	4	5	6	7	8	9	10	11	12	13	14
34. Stryker Corporation—2004	Y	N	Y	N	Y	Y	Y	Y	N	Y	N	Y	Y	Y
35. Biomet, Inc.—2004	Y	N	Y	N	Y	Y	Y	Y	N	Y	N	Y	Y	Y

SPORTING GOODS

	1	2	3	4	5	6	7	8	9	10	11	12	13	14
36. Nike—2004	Y	N	Y	N	Y	Y	Y	Y	N	Y	N	Y	Y	Y
37. Reebok International, Ltd. (RBK)—2004	Y	N	Y	N	Y	Y	Y	Y	N	Y	N	Y	Y	Y
38. Calloway Golf Company—2004	Y	N	Y	N	Y	Y	Y	Y	N	Y	N	Y	Y	Y

TOBACCO

	1	2	3	4	5	6	7	8	9	10	11	12	13	14
39. UST Inc.—2004	Y	N	Y	N	Y	Y	Y	Y	N	Y	N	Y	Y	Y
40. R.J. Reynolds Tobacco Company—2004	Y	N	Y	N	Y	Y	Y	Y	N	Y	N	Y	Y	Y

(continued)

CASE DESCRIPTION MATRIX (CONTINUED)

Topical Content Areas (Y = Yes and N = No)

1. Year-end 2003 Financial Statements Included?

2. Year-end 2002 Financial Statements Included?

3. Is Organizational Chart Included?

4. Does Company Do Business Outside U.S.?

5. Is a Vision or Mission Statement Included?

6. E-Commerce Issues Included?

7. Natural Environment Issues Included?

8. Strategy Formulation Emphasis?

9. Strategy Implementation Included?

10. By-segment Financial Data Included?

11. Firm has Declining Revenues?

12. Firm has Declining Net Income?

13. Discussion of Competitors is Provided?

14. Case Appears in Text for the First Time Ever?

strategic management

concepts

The Nature of Strategic Management ①

chapter objectives

After studying this chapter, you should be able to do the following:

1. Describe the strategic-management process.

2. Explain the need for integrating analysis and intuition in strategic management.

3. Define and give examples of key terms in strategic management.

4. Discuss the nature of strategy formulation, implementation, and evaluation activities.

5. Describe the benefits of good strategic management.

6. Explain why good ethics is good business in strategic management.

7. Explain the advantages and disadvantages of entering global markets.

8. Discuss the relevance of Sun Tzu's The Art of War to strategic management.

9. Discuss how a firm may achieve sustained competitive advantage.

10. Explain ISO 9000, 14000, and 14001.

experiential exercises

"notable quotes"

If we know where we are and something about how we got there, we might see where we are trending—and if the outcomes which lie naturally in our course are unacceptable, to make timely change.
Abraham Lincoln

Without a strategy, an organization is like a ship without a rudder, going around in circles. It's like a tramp; it has no place to go.
Joel Ross and Michael Kami

Plans are less important than planning.
Dale McConkey

The formulation of strategy can develop competitive advantage only to the extent that the process can give meaning to workers in the trenches.
David Hurst

Most of us fear change. Even when our minds say change is normal, our stomachs quiver at the prospect. But for strategists and managers today, there is no choice but to change.
Robert Waterman, Jr.

If business is not based on ethical grounds, it is of no benefit to society and will, like all other unethical combinations, pass into oblivion.
C. Max Killan

If a man takes no thought about what is distant, he will find sorrow near at hand. He who will not worry about what is far off will soon find something worse than worry.
Confucius

This chapter provides an overview of strategic management. It introduces a practical, integrative model of the strategic-management process; it defines basic activities and terms in strategic management; and it discusses the importance of business ethics.

This chapter initiates several themes that permeate all the chapters of this text. First, *global considerations impact virtually all strategic decisions*! The boundaries of countries no longer can define the limits of our imaginations. To see and appreciate the world from the perspective of others has become a matter of survival for businesses. The underpinnings of strategic management hinge upon managers' gaining an understanding of competitors, markets, prices, suppliers, distributors, governments, creditors, shareholders, and customers worldwide. The price and quality of a firm's products and services must be competitive on a worldwide basis, not just on a local basis. A "Global Perspective" box is provided in all chapters of this text to emphasize the importance of global factors in strategic management.

A second theme is that *electronic commerce (e-commerce) has become a vital strategic-management tool.* An increasing number of companies are gaining a competitive advantage by using the Internet for direct selling and for communication with suppliers, customers, creditors, partners, shareholders, clients, and competitors who may be dispersed globally. E-commerce allows firms to sell products, advertise, purchase supplies, bypass intermediaries, track inventory, eliminate paperwork, and share information. In total, e-commerce is minimizing the expense and cumbersomeness of time, distance, and space in doing business, thus yielding better customer service, greater efficiency, improved products, and higher profitability.

The Internet and personal computers are changing the way we organize our lives; inhabit our homes; and relate to and interact with family, friends, neighbors, and even ourselves. The Internet promotes endless comparison shopping, which thus enables consumers worldwide to band together to demand discounts. The Internet has transferred power from businesses to individuals. Buyers used to face big obstacles when attempting to get the best price and service, such as limited time and data to compare, but now consumers can quickly scan hundreds of vendor offerings. Or they can go to Web sites, such as CompareNet.com, that offer detailed information on more than 100,000 consumer products.

The Internet has changed the very nature and core of buying and selling in nearly all industries. It has fundamentally changed the economics of business in every single industry worldwide. Broadband, e-trade, e-commerce, e-business, and e-mail have become an integral part of everyday life worldwide. Business-to-business e-commerce is five times greater than consumer e-commerce. Fully 74 percent of Americans think the Internet will change society more than the telephone and television combined.[1] An "E-commerce Perspective" box is included in each chapter to illustrate how electronic commerce impacts the strategic-management process.

A third theme is that *the natural environment has become an important strategic issue.* Global warming, bioterrorism, and increased pollution suggest that perhaps there is now no greater threat to business and society than the continuous exploitation and decimation of our natural environment. Mark Starik at George Washington University says, "Halting and reversing worldwide ecological destruction and deterioration . . . is a strategic issue that needs immediate and substantive attention by all businesses and managers." According to the International Standards Organization (ISO), and in this textbook, the word "environment" refers to the natural environment and is defined as "surroundings in which an organization operates, including air, water, land, natural resources, flora, fauna, humans, and their interrelation." A "Natural Environment Perspective" box is provided in all chapters to illustrate how firms are addressing natural environment concerns.

What Is Strategic Management?

VISIT THE NET

Designed by the publisher, Prentice Hall, especially for this textbook, this Web site provides sample tests and extra materials to supplement chapter concepts.

www.prenhall.com/david

Once there were two company presidents who competed in the same industry. These two presidents decided to go on a camping trip to discuss a possible merger. They hiked deep into the woods. Suddenly, they came upon a grizzly bear that rose up on its hind legs and snarled. Instantly, the first president took off his knapsack and got out a pair of jogging shoes. The second president said, "Hey, you can't outrun that bear." The first president responded, "Maybe I can't outrun that bear, but I surely can outrun you!" This story captures the notion of strategic management, which is to achieve and maintain competitive advantage.

Defining Strategic Management

Strategic management can be defined as the art and science of formulating, implementing, and evaluating cross-functional decisions that enable an organization to achieve its objectives. As this definition implies, strategic management focuses on integrating management, marketing, finance/accounting, production/operations, research and development, and computer information systems to achieve organizational success. The term *strategic management* in this text is used synonymously with the term *strategic planning.* The latter term is more often used in the business world, whereas the former is often used in academia. Sometimes the term *strategic management* is used to refer to strategy formulation, implementation, and evaluation, with *strategic planning* referring only to strategy formulation. The purpose of strategic management is to exploit and create new and different opportunities for tomorrow; *long-range planning,* in contrast, tries to optimize for tomorrow the trends of today.

The term *strategic planning* originated in the 1950s and was very popular between the mid-1960s and the mid-1970s. During these years, strategic planning was widely believed to be the answer for all problems. At the time, much of corporate America was "obsessed" with strategic planning. Following that "boom," however, strategic planning was cast aside during the 1980s as various planning models did not yield higher returns. The 1990s, however, brought the revival of strategic planning, and the process is widely practiced today in the business world.

A strategic plan is, in essence, a company's game plan. Just as a football team needs a good game plan to have a chance for success, a company must have a good strategic plan to be able to compete successfully. Profit margins among firms in most industries have been so reduced that there is little room for error in the overall strategic plan. A strategic plan results from tough managerial choices among numerous good alternatives, and signals commitment to specific markets, policies, procedures, and operations in lieu of other, "less desirable" courses of action.

The term *strategic management* is used at many colleges and universities as the subtitle for the capstone course in business administration, Business Policy, which integrates material from all business courses. The Strategic Management Club Online at **www.strategyclub.com** offers many benefits for business policy and strategic management students.

Stages of Strategic Management

The *strategic-management process* consists of three stages: strategy formulation, strategy implementation, and strategy evaluation. *Strategy formulation* includes developing a vision and mission, identifying an organization's external opportunities and threats, determining internal strengths and weaknesses, establishing long-term objectives, generating alternative strategies, and choosing particular strategies to pursue. Strategy-formulation issues include deciding what new businesses to enter, what businesses to abandon, how to allocate resources, whether to expand operations or diversify, whether to enter international markets, whether to merge or form a joint venture, and how to avoid a hostile takeover.

Because no organization has unlimited resources, strategists must decide which alternative strategies will benefit the firm most. Strategy-formulation decisions commit an organization to specific products, markets, resources, and technologies over an extended period of time. Strategies determine long-term competitive advantages. For better or worse, strategic decisions have major multifunctional consequences and enduring effects on an organization. Top managers have the best perspective to understand fully the ramifications of strategy-formulation decisions; they have the authority to commit the resources necessary for implementation.

Strategy implementation requires a firm to establish annual objectives, devise policies, motivate employees, and allocate resources so that formulated strategies can be executed. Strategy implementation includes developing a strategy-supportive culture, creating an effective organizational structure, redirecting marketing efforts, preparing budgets, developing and utilizing information systems, and linking employee compensation to organizational performance.

VISIT THE NET

Provides nice narrative regarding strategy formulation and implementation at Southern Polytechnic State University.
www.spsu.edu/planassess/
strategic.htm

Strategy implementation often is called the action stage of strategic management. Implementing strategy means mobilizing employees and managers to put formulated strategies into action. Often considered to be the most difficult stage in strategic management, strategy implementation requires personal discipline, commitment, and sacrifice. Successful strategy implementation hinges upon managers' ability to motivate employees, which is more an art than a science. Strategies formulated but not implemented serve no useful purpose.

Interpersonal skills are especially critical for successful strategy implementation. Strategy-implementation activities affect all employees and managers in an organization. Every division and department must decide on answers to questions, such as "What must we do to implement our part of the organization's strategy?" and "How best can we get the job done?" The challenge of implementation is to stimulate managers and employees throughout an organization to work with pride and enthusiasm toward achieving stated objectives.

Strategy evaluation is the final stage in strategic management. Managers desperately need to know when particular strategies are not working well; strategy evaluation is the primary means for obtaining this information. All strategies are subject to future modification because external and internal factors are constantly changing. Three fundamental strategy-evaluation activities are (1) reviewing external and internal factors that are the bases for current strategies, (2) measuring performance, and (3) taking corrective actions. Strategy evaluation is needed because success today is no guarantee of success tomorrow! Success always creates new and different problems; complacent organizations experience demise.

Strategy formulation, implementation, and evaluation activities occur at three hierarchical levels in a large organization: corporate, divisional or strategic business unit, and functional. By fostering communication and interaction among managers and employees across hierarchical levels, strategic management helps a firm function as a competitive team. Most small businesses and some large businesses do not have divisions or strategic business units; they have only the corporate and functional levels. Nevertheless, managers and employees at these two levels should be actively involved in strategic-management activities.

Peter Drucker says the prime task of strategic management is thinking through the overall mission of a business:

> . . . that is, of asking the question, "What is our Business?" This leads to the setting of objectives, the development of strategies, and the making of

today's decisions for tomorrow's results. This clearly must be done by a part of the organization that can see the entire business; that can balance objectives and the needs of today against the needs of tomorrow; and that can allocate resources of men and money to key results.[2]

Integrating Intuition and Analysis

The strategic-management process can be described as an objective, logical, systematic approach for making major decisions in an organization. It attempts to organize qualitative and quantitative information in a way that allows effective decisions to be made under conditions of uncertainty. Yet strategic management is not a pure science that lends itself to a nice, neat, one-two-three approach.

Based on past experiences, judgment, and feelings, most people recognize that *intuition* is essential to making good strategic decisions. Intuition is particularly useful for making decisions in situations of great uncertainty or little precedent. It is also helpful when highly interrelated variables exist or when it is necessary to choose from several plausible alternatives. Some managers and owners of businesses profess to have extraordinary abilities for using intuition alone in devising brilliant strategies. For example, Will Durant, who organized General Motors Corporation, was described by Alfred Sloan as "a man who would proceed on a course of action guided solely, as far as I could tell, by some intuitive flash of brilliance. He never felt obliged to make an engineering hunt for the facts. Yet at times, he was astoundingly correct in his judgment."[3] Albert Einstein acknowledged the importance of intuition when he said, "I believe in intuition and inspiration. At times I feel certain that I am right while not knowing the reason. Imagination is more important than knowledge, because knowledge is limited, whereas imagination embraces the entire world."[4]

Although some organizations today may survive and prosper because they have intuitive geniuses managing them, most are not so fortunate. Most organizations can benefit from strategic management, which is based upon integrating intuition and analysis in decision making. Choosing an intuitive or analytic approach to decision making is not an either-or proposition. Managers at all levels in an organization inject their intuition and judgment into strategic-management analyses. Analytical thinking and intuitive thinking complement each other.

Operating from the I've-already-made-up-my-mind-don't-bother-me-with-the-facts mode is not management by intuition; it is management by ignorance.[5] Drucker says, "I believe in intuition only if you discipline it. 'Hunch' artists, who make a diagnosis but don't check it out with the facts, are the ones in medicine who kill people, and in management kill businesses."[6] As Henderson notes:

> The accelerating rate of change today is producing a business world in which customary managerial habits in organizations are increasingly inadequate. Experience alone was an adequate guide when changes could be made in small increments. But intuitive and experience-based management philosophies are grossly inadequate when decisions are strategic and have major, irreversible consequences.[7]

In a sense, the strategic-management process is an attempt both to duplicate what goes on in the mind of a brilliant, intuitive person who knows the business and to couple it with analysis.

Adapting to Change

The strategic-management process is based on the belief that organizations should continually monitor internal and external events and trends so that timely changes

VISIT THE NET

Reveals that strategies may need to be constantly changed.
www.csuchico.edu/mgmt/strategy/module1/sld041.htm

can be made as needed. The rate and magnitude of changes that affect organizations are increasing dramatically. Consider, for example, e-commerce, laser surgery, the war on terrorism, economic recession, the aging population, the Enron scandal, and merger mania. To survive, all organizations must be capable of astutely identifying and adapting to change. The strategic-management process is aimed at allowing organizations to adapt effectively to change over the long run. As Waterman has noted:

> In today's business environment, more than in any preceding era, the only constant is change. Successful organizations effectively manage change, continuously adapting their bureaucracies, strategies, systems, products, and cultures to survive the shocks and prosper from the forces that decimate the competition.[8]

VISIT THE NET

Reveals that actual strategy results from planned strategy coupled with reactive changes.
www.csuchico.edu/mgmt/
strategy/module1/
sld032.htm

E-commerce and globalization are external changes that are transforming business and society today. On a political map, the boundaries between countries may be clear, but on a competitive map showing the real flow of financial and industrial activity, the boundaries have largely disappeared. The speedy flow of information has eaten away at national boundaries so that people worldwide readily see for themselves how other people live. People are traveling abroad more: 10 million Japanese travel abroad annually. People are emigrating more: Germans to England and Mexicans to the United States are examples. As the Global Perspective indicates, U.S. firms are challenged by competitors in many industries. We have become a borderless world with global citizens, global competitors, global customers, global suppliers, and global distributors!

The need to adapt to change leads organizations to key strategic-management questions, such as "What kind of business should we become?" "Are we in the right field(s)?" "Should we reshape our business?" "What new competitors are entering our industry?" "What strategies should we pursue?" "How are our customers changing?" "Are new technologies being developed that could put us out of business?"

Key Terms in Strategic Management

Before we further discuss strategic management, we should define nine key terms: competitive advantage, strategists, vision and mission statements, external opportunities and threats, internal strengths and weaknesses, long-term objectives, strategies, annual objectives, and policies.

Competitive Advantage

Strategic management is all about gaining and maintaining *competitive advantage*. This term can be defined as "anything that a firm does especially well compared to rival firms." When a firm can do something that rival firms cannot do, or owns something that rival firms desire, that can represent a competitive advantage. Getting and keeping competitive advantage is essential for long-term success in an organization. The Industrial/Organizational (I/O) and the Resource-Based View (RBV) theories of organization (as discussed in Chapters 3 and 4, respectively) present different perspectives on how best to capture and keep competitive advantage—that is, how best to manage strategically. Pursuit of competitive advantage leads to organizational success or failure. Strategic management researchers and practitioners alike desire to better understand the nature and role of competitive advantage in various industries.

Normally, a firm can sustain a competitive advantage for only a certain period due to rival firms imitating and undermining that advantage. Thus it is not adequate to simply obtain competitive advantage. A firm must strive to achieve *sustained competitive advantage* by (1) continually adapting to changes in external trends and events and internal capabilities, competencies, and resources; and by (2) effectively formulating, implementing, and evaluating strategies that capitalize upon those factors.

Strategists

Strategists are the individuals who are most responsible for the success or failure of an organization. Strategists have various job titles, such as chief executive officer, president, owner, chair of the board, executive director, chancellor, dean, or entrepreneur. Jay Conger, professor of organizational behavior at the London Business School and author of *Building Leaders*, says, "All strategists have to be chief learning officers. We are in an extended period of change. If our leaders aren't highly adaptive and great models during this period, then our companies won't adapt either, because ultimately leadership is about being a role model."

Strategists help an organization gather, analyze, and organize information. They track industry and competitive trends, develop forecasting models and scenario analyses, evaluate corporate and divisional performance, spot emerging market opportunities, identify business threats, and develop creative action plans. Strategic planners usually serve in a support or staff role. Usually found in higher levels of management, they typically have considerable authority for decision making in the firm. The CEO is the most visible and critical strategic manager. Any manager who has responsibility for a unit or division, responsibility for profit and loss outcomes, or direct authority over a major piece of the business is a strategic manager (strategist). In the last five years, the position of chief strategy officer (CSO) has emerged as a new addition to the top management ranks of many organizations, including Sun Microsystems, Network Associates, Clarus, Lante, Marimba, Sapient, Commerce One, BBDO, Cadbury Schweppes, General Motors, Ellie Mae, Cendant, Charles Schwab, Tyco, Campbell Soup, Morgan Stanley, and Reed-Elsevier. This new corporate officer title represents recognition of the growing importance of strategic planning in the business world.[9]

Strategists differ as much as organizations themselves, and these differences must be considered in the formulation, implementation, and evaluation of strategies. Some strategists will not consider some types of strategies because of their personal philosophies. Strategists differ in their attitudes, values, ethics, willingness to take risks, concern for social responsibility, concern for profitability, concern for short-run versus long-run aims, and management style. The founder of Hershey Foods, Milton Hershey, built the company to manage an orphanage. From corporate profits, Hershey Foods today cares for over one thousand boys and girls in its School for Orphans.

Vision and Mission Statements

Many organizations today develop a *vision statement* that answers the question, "What do we want to become?" Developing a vision statement is often considered the first step in strategic planning, preceding even development of a mission statement. Many vision statements are a single sentence. For example, the vision statement of Stokes Eye Clinic in Florence, South Carolina, is "Our vision is to take care of your vision." The vision of the Institute of Management Accountants is "Global leadership in education, certification, and practice of management accounting and financial management."

Mission statements are "enduring statements of purpose that distinguish one business from other similar firms. A mission statement identifies the scope of a firm's operations in product and market terms."[10] It addresses the basic question that faces

GLOBAL PERSPECTIVE

Do U.S. Firms Dominate All Industries?

The *Wall Street Journal's* annual ranking of the world's largest companies reveals that U.S. firms are being challenged in many industries. The world's largest oil-producing and public finance companies are listed below in rank order.

The top ten oil-producing companies in millions of barrels a day (2003):

Company Name (Country)	Production
Saudi Aramco (Saudi Arabia)	8.3
National Iranian Oil Co. (Iran)	3.8
Pomex (Mexico)	3.6
PDV (Venezuela)	3.2
ExxonMobil (U.S.)	2.5
Iraq National Oil Co. (Iraq)	2.4
Royal Dutch/Shell (Netherlands/UK)	2.2
PetroChina (China)	2.1
ChevronTexaco (U.S.)	2.0
BP (UK)	1.8

The top ten public finance companies in total assets (2003):

Mizuho Financial Group	Japan
Citigroup	U.S.
Allianz	Germany
Fannie Mae	U.S.
Sumitomo Mitsui Financial	Japan
UBS	Switzerland
Mitsubishi Tokyo Financial	Japan
Deutsche Bank	Germany
HSBC Holdings	UK
JP Morgan Chase	U.S.
ING Group	Netherlands
BNP Paribas	France
Bayerische Hypo Bank	Germany
Freddie Mac	U.S.
Credit Suisse	Switzerland

Source: Adapted from: Brian Callanan, "The Global Giants," *Wall Street Journal* (September 22, 2003): R10.

all strategists: "What is our business?" A clear mission statement describes the values and priorities of an organization. Developing a mission statement compels strategists to think about the nature and scope of present operations and to assess the potential attractiveness of future markets and activities. A mission statement broadly charts the future direction of an organization. An example of a mission statement is provided below for Microsoft.

> Microsoft's mission is to create software for the personal computer that empowers and enriches people in the workplace, at school and at home. Microsoft's early vision of a computer on every desk and in every home is coupled today with a strong commitment to Internet-related technologies that expand the power and reach of the PC and its users. As the world's leading software provider, Microsoft strives to produce innovative products that meet our customers' evolving needs. At the same time, we understand that long-term success is about more than just making great products. Find out what we mean when we talk about Living Our Values (www.microsoft.com/mscorp/).

External Opportunities and Threats

External opportunities and *external threats* refer to economic, social, cultural, demographic, environmental, political, legal, governmental, technological, and competitive trends and events that could significantly benefit or harm an organization in the future.

Opportunities and threats are largely beyond the control of a single organization—thus the word *external*. The wireless revolution, biotechnology, population shifts, changing work values and attitudes, space exploration, recyclable packages, and increased competition from foreign companies are examples of opportunities or threats for companies. These types of changes are creating a different type of consumer and consequently a need for different types of products, services, and strategies. Many companies in many industries face the severe external threat of online sales capturing increasing market share in their industry.

Other opportunities and threats may include the passage of a law, the introduction of a new product by a competitor, a national catastrophe, or the declining value of the dollar. A competitor's strength could be a threat. Unrest in the Middle East, rising energy costs, or the war against terrorism could represent an opportunity or a threat.

A basic tenet of strategic management is that firms need to formulate strategies to take advantage of external opportunities and to avoid or reduce the impact of external threats. For this reason, identifying, monitoring, and evaluating external opportunities and threats is essential for success. This process of conducting research and gathering and assimilating external information is sometimes called *environmental scanning* or industry analysis. Lobbying is one activity that some organizations utilize to influence external opportunities and threats.

Internal Strengths and Weaknesses

Internal strengths and *internal weaknesses* are an organization's controllable activities that are performed especially well or poorly. They arise in the management, marketing, finance/accounting, production/operations, research and development, and management information systems activities of a business. Identifying and evaluating organizational strengths and weaknesses in the functional areas of a business is an essential strategic-management activity. Organizations strive to pursue strategies that capitalize on internal strengths and eliminate internal weaknesses.

Strengths and weaknesses are determined relative to competitors. *Relative* deficiency or superiority is important information. Also, strengths and weaknesses can be determined by elements of being rather than performance. For example, a strength may involve ownership of natural resources or a historic reputation for quality. Strengths and weaknesses may be determined relative to a firm's own objectives. For example, high levels of inventory turnover may not be a strength to a firm that seeks never to stock-out.

Internal factors can be determined in a number of ways, including computing ratios, measuring performance, and comparing to past periods and industry averages. Various types of surveys also can be developed and administered to examine internal factors such as employee morale, production efficiency, advertising effectiveness, and customer loyalty.

Long-Term Objectives

Objectives can be defined as specific results that an organization seeks to achieve in pursuing its basic mission. *Long-term* means more than one year. Objectives are essential for organizational success because they state direction; aid in evaluation; create synergy; reveal priorities; focus coordination; and provide a basis for effective planning, organizing, motivating, and controlling activities. Objectives should be challenging, measurable, consistent, reasonable, and clear. In a multidimensional firm, objectives should be established for the overall company and for each division.

TABLE 1-1   Example Strategies in Action in 2004

NESTLÉ VERSUS UNILEVER

Nestlé SA recently acquired Dreyer's Grand Ice Cream Inc., to supplement its Häagen-Dazs and Drumstick brands. Swiss giant Nestlé is now waging an aggressive ice cream war against Unilever, the huge Anglo-Dutch firm that sells Good Humor, Ben & Jerry's, and Breyer's ice cream brands. Nestlé's Dreyer's acquisition pushes its ice cream market share to roughly equal Unilever's at 17 percent. Both firms are pursuing market penetration to make ice cream available everywhere. They aggressively compete for freezer space at convenience stores, gas stations, vending machines, and video shops around the world.

LEGEND GROUP LTD.

Legend Group Ltd., is the largest desktop personal-computer maker in China, but the company has little name recognition outside China. That is about to change as Legend has announced plans to expand worldwide. Legend also makes notebook computers, mobile phones, and MP3 music players. Sales of Legend's flagship product—desktop PCs—slipped 3 percent in fiscal 2003 to $2.6 billion and a 25 percent market share in China. However, Legend plans to boost its revenue outside of China from 7 percent in 2003 to 25 percent by 2007. Dell, H-P, and IBM should be aware of Legend on the horizon.

KRISPY KREME

Krispy Kreme's revenues have skyrocketed in the United States as its number of stores has grown from 144 in 2001 to 276 in 2003. Now the doughnut company is expanding into Great Britain with plans to open 25 shops there in the next five years. The first opened in mid-2003 in Harrod's in London. But Dunkin' Donuts, a major competitor, failed in the 1990s in its attempt to establish stores in Britain. Krispy Kreme believes it can tailor its doughnuts to British culture, as it has in South Korea where it offers fix, mango, and red-bean paste doughnuts.

Strategies

Strategies are the means by which long-term objectives will be achieved. Business strategies may include geographic expansion, diversification, acquisition, product development, market penetration, retrenchment, divestiture, liquidation, and joint ventures. Strategies currently being pursued by some companies are described in Table 1–1.

Strategies are potential actions that require top management decisions and large amounts of the firm's resources. In addition, strategies affect an organization's long-term prosperity, typically for at least five years, and thus are future-oriented. Strategies have multifunctional or multidivisional consequences and require consideration of both the external and internal factors facing the firm.

Annual Objectives

Annual objectives are short-term milestones that organizations must achieve to reach long-term objectives. Like long-term objectives, annual objectives should be measurable, quantitative, challenging, realistic, consistent, and prioritized. They should be established at the corporate, divisional, and functional levels in a large organization. Annual objectives should be stated in terms of management, marketing, finance/accounting, production/operations, research and development, and management information systems (MIS) accomplishments. A set of annual objectives is needed for each long-term objective. Annual objectives are especially important in strategy implementation, whereas long-term objectives are particularly important in strategy formulation. Annual objectives represent the basis for allocating resources.

Policies

Policies are the means by which annual objectives will be achieved. Policies include guidelines, rules, and procedures established to support efforts to achieve stated objectives. Policies are guides to decision making and address repetitive or recurring situations.

Policies are most often stated in terms of management, marketing, finance/accounting, production/operations, research and development, and computer information systems activities. Policies can be established at the corporate level and apply to an entire organization at the divisional level and apply to a single division, or at the functional level and apply to particular operational activities or departments. Policies, like annual objectives, are especially important in strategy implementation because they outline an organization's expectations of its employees and managers. Policies allow consistency and coordination within and between organizational departments.

Substantial research suggests that a healthier workforce can more effectively and efficiently implement strategies. The National Center for Health Promotion estimates that more than 80 percent of all American corporations have No Smoking policies. No Smoking policies are usually derived from annual objectives that seek to reduce corporate medical costs associated with absenteeism and to provide a healthy workplace. In 2004, Ireland banned smoking in all pubs and restaurants. Norway, Holland, and Greece are passing similar laws.

The Strategic-Management Model

The strategic-management process can best be studied and applied using a model. Every model represents some kind of process. The framework illustrated in Figure 1–1 is a widely accepted, comprehensive model of the strategic-management process.[11] This model does not guarantee success, but it does represent a clear and practical approach for formulating, implementing, and evaluating strategies. Relationships among major components of the strategic-management process are shown in the model, which appears in all subsequent chapters with appropriate areas shaped to show the particular focus of each chapter.

Identifying an organization's existing vision, mission, objectives, and strategies is the logical starting point for strategic management because a firm's present situation and condition may preclude certain strategies and may even dictate a particular course of action. Every organization has a vision, mission, objectives, and strategy, even if these elements are not consciously designed, written, or communicated. The answer to where an organization is going can be determined largely by where the organization has been!

The strategic-management process is dynamic and continuous. A change in any one of the major components in the model can necessitate a change in any or all of the other components. For instance, a shift in the economy could represent a major opportunity and require a change in long-term objectives and strategies; a failure to accomplish annual objectives could require a change in policy; or a major competitor's change in strategy could require a change in the firm's mission. Therefore, strategy formulation, implementation, and evaluation activities should be performed on a

FIGURE 1–1

A Comprehensive Strategic-Management Model

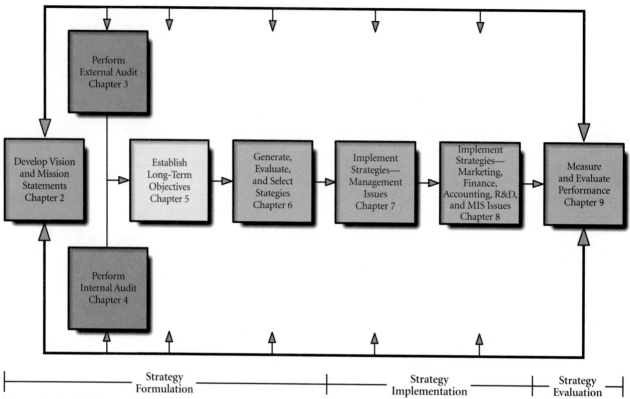

Source: Fred R. David, "How Companies Define Their Mission," *Long Range Planning* 22, no. 3 (June 1988): 40.

continual basis, not just at the end of the year or semi-annually. The strategic-management process never really ends.

The strategic-management process is not as cleanly divided and neatly performed in practice as the strategic-management model suggests. Strategists do not go through the process in lockstep fashion. Generally, there is give-and-take among hierarchical levels of an organization. Many organizations conduct formal meetings semiannually to discuss and update the firm's vision/mission, opportunities/threats, strengths/weaknesses, strategies, objectives, policies, and performance. These meetings are commonly held off-premises and are called *retreats.* The rationale for periodically conducting strategic-management meetings away from the work site is to encourage more creativity and candor from participants. Good communication and feedback are needed throughout the strategic-management process.

Application of the strategic-management process is typically more formal in larger and well-established organizations. Formality refers to the extent that participants, responsibilities, authority, duties, and approach are specified. Smaller businesses tend to be less formal. Firms that compete in complex, rapidly changing environments, such as technology companies, tend to be more formal in strategic planning. Firms that have many divisions, products, markets, and technologies also tend to be more formal in applying strategic-management concepts. Greater formality in applying the strategic-management process is usually positively associated with the cost, comprehensiveness, accuracy, and success of planning across all types and sizes of organizations.[12]

Benefits of Strategic Management

Strategic management allows an organization to be more proactive than reactive in shaping its own future; it allows an organization to initiate and influence (rather than just respond to) activities—and thus to exert control over its own destiny. Small bussiness owners, chief executive officers, presidents, and managers of many for-profit and non-profit organizations have recognized and realized the benefits of strategic management.

Historically, the principal benefit of strategic management has been to help organizations formulate better strategies through the use of a more systematic, logical, and rational approach to strategic choice. This certainly continues to be a major benefit of strategic management, but research studies now indicate that the process, rather than the decision or document, is the more important contribution of strategic management.[13] *Communication is a key to successful strategic management.* Through involvement in the process, managers and employees become committed to supporting the organization. Dialogue and participation are essential ingredients.

The manner in which strategic management is carried out is thus exceptionally important. A major aim of the process is to achieve the understanding of and commitment from all managers and employees. Understanding may be the most important benefit of strategic management, followed by commitment. When managers and employees understand what the organization is doing and why, they often feel that they are a part of the firm and become committed to assisting it. This is especially true when employees also understand linkages between their own compensation and organizational performance. Managers and employees become surprisingly creative and innovative when they understand and support the firm's mission, objectives, and strategies. A great benefit of strategic management, then, is the opportunity that the process provides to empower individuals. *Empowerment* is the act of strengthening employees' sense of effectiveness by encouraging them to participate in decision making and to exercise initiative and imagination, and rewarding them for doing so.

More and more organizations are decentralizing the strategic-management process, recognizing that planning must involve lower-level managers and employees. The notion of centralized staff planning is being replaced in organizations by decentralized line-manager planning. The process is a learning, helping, educating, and supporting activity, not merely a paper-shuffling activity among top executives. Strategic-management dialogue is more important than a nicely bound strategic-management document.[14] The worst thing strategists can do is develop strategic plans themselves and then present them to operating managers to execute. Through involvement in the process, line managers become "owners" of the strategy. Ownership of strategies by the people who have to execute them is a key to success!

Although making good strategic decisions is the major responsibility of an organization's owner or chief executive officer, both managers and employees must also be involved in strategy formulation, implementation, and evaluation activities. Participation is a key to gaining commitment for needed changes.

VISIT THE NET

Explains in detail how to develop a strategic plan and compares this document to a business plan.
www.planware.org/strategy.htm#1

An increasing number of corporations and institutions are using strategic management to make effective decisions. But strategic management is not a guarantee for success; it can be dysfunctional if conducted haphazardly.

VISIT THE NET

Provides excellent narrative on the "Benefits of Strategic Planning," "Pitfalls of Strategic Planning," and the "Steps in Doing Strategic Planning."
www.entarga.com/ stratplan/index.htm

Financial Benefits

Research indicates that organizations using strategic-management concepts are more profitable and successful than those that do not.[15] Businesses using strategic-management concepts show significant improvement in sales, profitability, and productivity compared to firms without systematic planning activities. High-performing firms tend to do systematic planning to prepare for future fluctuations in their external and internal environments. Firms with planning systems more closely resembling strategic-management theory generally exhibit superior long-term financial performance relative to their industry.

High-performing firms seem to make more informed decisions with good anticipation of both short- and long-term consequences. On the other hand, firms that perform poorly often engage in activities that are shortsighted and do not reflect good forecasting of future conditions. Strategists of low-performing organizations are often preoccupied with solving internal problems and meeting paperwork deadlines. They typically underestimate their competitors' strengths and overestimate their own firm's strengths. They often attribute weak performance to uncontrollable factors such as a poor economy, technological change, or foreign competition.

Dun & Bradstreet reports that more than 100,000 businesses in the United States fail annually. Business failures include bankruptcies, foreclosures, liquidations, and court-mandated receiverships. Although many factors besides a lack of effective strategic management can lead to business failure, the planning concepts and tools described in this text can yield substantial financial benefits for any organization. An excellent Web site for businesses engaged in strategic planning is **www.checkmateplan.com**.

Nonfinancial Benefits

Besides helping firms avoid financial demise, strategic management offers other tangible benefits, such as an enhanced awareness of external threats, an improved understanding of competitors' strategies, increased employee productivity, reduced resistance to change, and a clearer understanding of performance–reward relationships. Strategic management enhances the problem-prevention capabilities of organizations because it promotes interaction among managers at all divisional and functional levels. Firms that have nurtured their managers and employees, shared organizational objectives with them, empowered them to help improve the product or service, and recognized their contributions can turn to them for help in a pinch because of this interaction.

In addition to empowering managers and employees, strategic management often brings order and discipline to an otherwise floundering firm. It can be the beginning of an efficient and effective managerial system. Strategic management may renew confidence in the current business strategy or point to the need for corrective actions. The strategic-management process provides a basis for identifying and rationalizing the need for change to all managers and employees of a firm; it helps them view change as an opportunity rather than as a threat.

Greenley stated that strategic management offers the following benefits:

1. It allows for identification, prioritization, and exploitation of opportunities.
2. It provides an objective view of management problems.

3. It represents a framework for improved coordination and control of activities.
4. It minimizes the effects of adverse conditions and changes.
5. It allows major decisions to better support established objectives.
6. It allows more effective allocation of time and resources to identified opportunities.
7. It allows fewer resources and less time to be devoted to correcting erroneous or ad hoc decisions.
8. It creates a framework for internal communication among personnel.
9. It helps integrate the behavior of individuals into a total effort.
10. It provides a basis for clarifying individual responsibilities.
11. It encourages forward thinking.
12. It provides a cooperative, integrated, and enthusiastic approach to tackling problems and opportunities.
13. It encourages a favorable attitude toward change.
14. It gives a degree of discipline and formality to the management of a business.[16]

Why Some Firms Do No Strategic Planning

Some firms do not engage in strategic planning, and some firms do strategic planning but receive no support from managers and employees. Some reasons for poor or no strategic planning are as follows:

VISIT THE NET

Gives reasons why some organizations avoid strategic planning.
www.mindtools.com/ plfailpl.html

- *Poor Reward Structures*—When an organization assumes success, it often fails to reward success. When failure occurs, then the firm may punish. In this situation, it is better for an individual to do nothing (and not draw attention) than to risk trying to achieve something, fail, and be punished.
- *Fire-Fighting*—An organization can be so deeply embroiled in crisis management and fire-fighting that it does not have time to plan.
- *Waste of Time*—Some firms see planning as a waste of time since no marketable product is produced. Time spent on planning is an investment.
- *Too Expensive*—Some organizations are culturally opposed to spending resources.
- *Laziness*—People may not want to put forth the effort needed to formulate a plan.
- *Content with Success*—Particularly if a firm is successful, individuals may feel there is no need to plan because things are fine as they stand. But success today does not guarantee success tomorrow.
- *Fear of Failure*—By not taking action, there is little risk of failure unless a problem is urgent and pressing. Whenever something worthwhile is attempted, there is some risk of failure.
- *Overconfidence*—As individuals amass experience, they may rely less on formalized planning. Rarely, however, is this appropriate. Being overconfident or overestimating experience can bring demise. Forethought is rarely wasted and is often the mark of professionalism.
- *Prior Bad Experience*—People may have had a previous bad experience with planning, that is, cases in which plans have been long, cumbersome, impractical, or inflexible. Planning, like anything else, can be done badly.

- *Self-Interest*—When someone has achieved status, privilege, or self-esteem through effectively using an old system, he or she often sees a new plan as a threat.
- *Fear of the Unknown*—People may be uncertain of their abilities to learn new skills, of their aptitude with new systems, or of their ability to take on new roles.
- *Honest Difference of Opinion*—People may sincerely believe the plan is wrong. They may view the situation from a different viewpoint, or they may have aspirations for themselves or the organization that are different from the plan. Different people in different jobs have different perceptions of a situation.
- *Suspicion*—Employees may not trust management.[17]

Pitfalls in Strategic Planning

Strategic planning is an involved, intricate, and complex process that takes an organization into unchartered territory. It does not provide a ready-to-use prescription for success; instead, it takes the organization through a journey and offers a framework for addressing questions and solving problems. Being aware of potential pitfalls and being prepared to address them is essential to success.

Some pitfalls to watch for and avoid in strategic planning are provided below:

- Using strategic planning to gain control over decisions and resources
- Doing strategic planning only to satisfy accreditation or regulatory requirements
- Too hastily moving from mission development to strategy formulation
- Failing to communicate the plan to employees, who continue working in the dark
- Top managers making many intuitive decisions that conflict with the formal plan
- Top managers not actively supporting the strategic-planning process
- Failing to use plans as a standard for measuring performance
- Delegating planning to a "planner" rather than involving all managers
- Failing to involve key employees in all phases of planning
- Failing to create a collaborative climate supportive of change
- Viewing planning to be unnecessary or unimportant
- Becoming so engrossed in current problems that insufficient or no planning is done
- Being so formal in planning that flexibility and creativity are stifled[18]

VISIT THE NET

Provides nice discussion of the limitations of strategic planning process within an organization.
www.des.calstate.edu/ limitations.html

Guidelines for Effective Strategic Management

Failing to follow certain guidelines in conducting strategic management can foster criticisms of the process and create problems for the organization. An integral part of strategy evaluation must be to evaluate the quality of the strategic-management process. Issues such as "Is strategic management in our firm a people process or a paper process?" should be addressed.

Even the most technically perfect strategic plan will serve little purpose if it is not implemented. Many organizations tend to spend an inordinate amount of time, money, and effort on developing the strategic plan, treating the means and circumstances under which it will be implemented as afterthoughts! Change comes through implementation and evaluation, not through the plan.

A technically imperfect plan that is implemented well will achieve more than the perfect plan that never gets off the paper on which it is typed.[19]

Strategic management must not become a self-perpetuating bureaucratic mechanism. Rather, it must be a self-reflective learning process that familiarizes managers and employees in the organization with key strategic issues and feasible alternatives for resolving those issues. Strategic management must not become ritualistic, stilted, orchestrated, or too formal, predictable, and rigid. Words supported by numbers, rather than numbers supported by words, should represent the medium for explaining strategic issues and organizational responses. A key role of strategists is to facilitate continuous organizational learning and change.

R. T. Lenz offered some important guidelines for effective strategic management:

> Keep the strategic-management process as simple and nonroutine as possible. Eliminate jargon and arcane planning language. Remember, strategic management is a process for fostering learning and action, not merely a formal system for control. To avoid routinized behavior, vary assignments, team membership, meeting formats, and the planning calendar. The process should not be totally predictable, and settings must be changed to stimulate creativity. Emphasize word-oriented plans with numbers as back-up material. If managers cannot express their strategy in a paragraph or so, they either do not have one or do not understand it. Stimulate thinking and action that challenge the assumptions underlying current corporate strategy. Welcome bad news. If strategy is not working, managers desperately need to know it. Further, no pertinent information should be classified as inadmissible merely because it cannot be quantified. Build a corporate culture in which the role of strategic management and its essential purposes are understood. Do not permit "technicians" to co-opt the process. It is ultimately a process for learning and action. Speak of it in these terms. Attend to psychological, social, and political dimensions, as well as the information infrastructure and administrative procedures supporting it.[20]

An important guideline for effective strategic management is open-mindedness. A willingness and eagerness to consider new information, new viewpoints, new ideas, and new possibilities is essential; all organizational members must share a spirit of inquiry and learning. Strategists such as chief executive officers, presidents, owners of small businesses, and heads of government agencies must commit themselves to listen to and understand managers' positions well enough to be able to restate those positions to the managers' satisfaction. In addition, managers and employees throughout the firm should be able to describe the strategists' positions to the satisfaction of the strategists. This degree of discipline will promote understanding and learning.

No organization has unlimited resources. No firm can take on an unlimited amount of debt or issue an unlimited amount of stock to raise capital. Therefore, no organization can pursue all the strategies that potentially could benefit the firm. Strategic decisions thus always have to be made to eliminate some courses of action and to allocate organizational resources among others. Most organizations can afford to pursue only a few corporate-level strategies at any given time. It is a critical mistake for managers to pursue too many strategies at the same time, thereby spreading the firm's resources so thin that all strategies are jeopardized. Joseph Charyk, CEO of the Communication Satellite Corporation (Comsat), said, "We have to face the cold fact that Comsat may not be able to do all it wants. We must make hard choices on which ventures to keep and which to fold."

Strategic decisions require trade-offs such as long-range versus short-range considerations or maximizing profits versus increasing shareholders' wealth. There are ethics issues too. Strategy trade-offs require subjective judgments and preferences. In many cases, a lack of objectivity in formulating strategy results in a loss of competitive posture and profitability. Most organizations today recognize that strategic-management concepts and techniques can enhance the effectiveness of decisions. Subjective factors such as attitudes toward risk, concern for social responsibility, and organizational culture will always affect strategy-formulation decisions, but organizations need to be as objective as possible in considering qualitative factors.

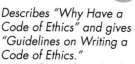

VISIT THE NET

Describes "Why Have a Code of Ethics" and gives "Guidelines on Writing a Code of Ethics."
www.ethicsweb.ca/codes

Business Ethics and Strategic Management

Business ethics can be defined as principles of conduct within organizations that guide decision making and behavior. Good business ethics is a prerequisite for good strategic management; good ethics is just good business!

A rising tide of consciousness about the importance of business ethics is sweeping America and the world. Strategists are the individuals primarily responsible for ensuring that high ethical principles are espoused and practiced in an organization. All strategy formulation, implementation, and evaluation decisions have ethical ramifications.

Newspapers and business magazines daily report legal and moral breaches of ethical conduct by both public and private organizations. For example, the Securities and Exchange Commission recently imposed on MCI (formerly WorldCom) a fine of $1.5 billion payable to shareholders for accounting fraud. MCI shareholders and bondholders in addition are now filing civil fraud claims against former CEO Bernard Ebbers, other MCI executives, and various banks involved in the scandal.

Managers and employees of firms must be careful not to become scapegoats blamed for company environmental wrongdoings. Harming the natural environment is unethical, illegal, and costly. When organizations today face criminal charges for polluting the environment, firms increasingly are turning on their managers and employees to win leniency for themselves. Employee firings and demotions are becoming common in pollution-related legal suits. Managers being fired at Darling International, Inc. and Niagara Mohawk Power Corporation for being indirectly responsible for their firms' polluting water exemplifies this corporate trend. Therefore, managers and employees today must be careful not to ignore, conceal, or disregard a pollution problem, or they may find themselves personally liable. In this regard, more and more companies are becoming ISO 14001 certified, as indicated in the "Natural Environment Perspective."

A new wave of ethics issues related to product safety, employee health, sexual harassment, AIDS in the workplace, smoking, acid rain, affirmative action, waste disposal, foreign business practices, cover-ups, takeover tactics, conflicts of interest, employee privacy, inappropriate gifts, security of company records, and layoffs has accented the need for strategists to develop a clear code of business ethics. United Technologies Corporation has issued a twenty-one-page Code of Ethics and named a new vice president of business ethics. Baxter Travenol Laboratories, IBM, Caterpillar Tractor, Chemical Bank, ExxonMobil, Dow Corning, and Celanese are firms that have formal codes of business ethics. A *code of business ethics* can provide a basis on which policies can be devised to guide daily behavior and decisions at the work site.

NATURAL ENVIRONMENT PERSPECTIVE

Using ISO 14000 Certification to Gain Strategic Advantage

Based in Geneva, Switzerland, the ISO (International Organization for Standardization) is a network of the national standards institutes of 147 countries, one member per country. ISO is the world's largest developer of standards. Widely accepted all over the world, ISO standards are voluntary since the organization has no legal authority to enforce their implementation. ISO itself does not regulate or legislate. Governmental agencies in various countries, such as the Environmental Protection Agency in the U.S. have adopted ISO standards as part of their regulatory framework, and the standards are the basis of much legislation. Adoptions are sovereign decisions by the regulatory authorities, governments, and/or companies concerned.

Two widely adopted ISO standards are ISO 9000, which focuses on quality control, and ISO 14000, which focuses on operating in an environmentally friendly manner. More than half a million organizations in more than 60 countries are implementing ISO 9000, which provides a framework for quality management throughout the production and distribution of products and services. ISO 9000 has become an international reference for quality requirements in most industries. Companies that are not ISO 9000–certified often cannot get work.

Almost 37,000 companies have adopted the ISO 14001 standard for Environmental Management Systems since it was published in 1995. However, just 17 percent of the companies adopting the ISO 14001 standard are in developing countries. ISO 14000–certified Ford Motor Company, as of July 2, 2003, required all of its suppliers and all of its manufacturing sites to be ISO 14001 certified. General Motors requires all of its suppliers to be certified to the ISO 14001 Standard. IBM Corporation strongly encourages its suppliers to be ISO 14001 certified. Skanska USA, Inc., was the first construction group in the United States to have all of its offices, jobsites, and operations ISO 14001 certified. Washtenaw County, Michigan, is implementing an EMS based on 14001 for its Sheriff's Department.

What Are ISO 14000 and ISO 14001?

ISO 14000 refers to a series of voluntary standards in the environmental field. The ISO 14000 family of standards concerns the extent to which a firm minimizes harmful effects on the environment caused by its activities and continually monitors and improves its own environmental performance. Included in the ISO 14000 series are the ISO 14001 standards in fields such as environmental auditing, environmental performance evaluation, environmental labeling, and life-cycle assessment. ISO 14001 is a set of standards adopted by thousands of firms worldwide to certify to their constituencies that they are conducting business in an environmentally friendly manner. ISO 14001 standards offer a universal technical standard for environmental compliance that more and more firms are requiring not only of themselves but also of their suppliers and distributors.

Requirements for ISO 14001 Certification

The ISO 14001 standard requires that a community or organization put in place and implement a series of practices and procedures that, when taken together, result in an environmental management system. ISO 14001 is not a technical standard and as such does not in any way replace technical requirements embodied in statutes or regulations. It also does not set prescribed standards of performance for organizations. The major requirements of an EMS under ISO 14001 include:

- Establish an EMS that includes commitments to prevention of pollution, continual improvement in overall environmental performance, and compliance with all applicable statutory and regulatory requirements.

- Identification of all aspects of the organization's activities, products, and services that could have a significant impact on the environment, including those that are not regulated.

- Setting performance objectives and targets for the management system which link back to three policies: (1) prevention of pollution, (2) continual improvement, and (3) compliance.

(continued)

- Implementing an EMS to meet environmental objectives that include training of employees, establishing work instructions and practices, and establishing the actual metrics by which the objectives and targets will be measured.
- Auditing the operation of the EMS.
- Taking corrective actions when deviations from the EMS occur.

Conclusion

ISO 14001 standards on air, water, and soil quality, and on emissions of gases and radiation, contribute to preserving the environment in which we all live and work. The U.S. Environmental Protection Agency (EPA) now offers a guide entitled "Environmental Management Systems (EMS): An Implementation Guide for Small and Medium Sized Organizations." The Guide offers a plain-English, commonsense guide to becoming ISO 14001 certified. Not being ISO 14001 certified can be a strategic disadvantage for towns, counties, and companies as people today expect organizations to minimize, or even better, eliminate environmental harm they cause.

Source: Adapted from the **www.iso.14000** Web site and the **www.epa.gov** Web site.

VISIT THE NET

An excellent Web site to obtain additional information regarding business ethics is www.ethicsweb.ca/codes; *it describes "Why Have a Code of Ethics" and gives "Guidelines on Writing a Code of Ethics."*

VISIT THE NET

Professor Hansen at Stetson University provides a strategic management slide show for this entire text. www.stetson.edu/ ~rhansen/strategy/

The explosion of the Internet into the workplace has raised many new ethical questions in organizations today.

The "E-Commerce Perspective" focuses on business ethics issues related to the Internet. Merely having a code of ethics, however, is not sufficient to ensure ethical business behavior. A code of ethics can be viewed as a public relations gimmick, a set of platitudes, or window dressing. To ensure that the code is read, understood, believed, and remembered, organizations need to conduct periodic ethics workshops to sensitize people to workplace circumstances in which ethics issues may arise.[21] If employees see examples of punishment for violating the code and rewards for upholding the code, this helps reinforce the importance of a firm's code of ethics.

An ethics "culture" needs to permeate organizations! To help create an ethics culture, Citicorp developed a business ethics board game that is played by forty thousand employees in forty-five countries. Called "The Word Ethic," this game asks players business ethics questions, such as, how do you deal with a customer who offers you football tickets in exchange for a new, backdated IRA? Diana Robertson at the Wharton School of business believes the game is effective because it is interactive. Many organizations, such as Prime Computer and Kmart, have developed a code-of-conduct manual outlining ethical expectations and giving examples of situations that commonly arise in their businesses. Harris Corporation's managers and employees are warned that failing to report an ethical violation by others could bring discharge.

One reason strategists' salaries are high compared to those of other individuals in an organization is that strategists must take the moral risks of the firm. Strategists are responsible for developing, communicating and enforcing the code of business ethics for their organizations. Although primary responsibility for ensuring ethical behavior rests with a firm's strategists, an integral part of the responsibility of all managers is to provide ethics leadership by constant example and demonstration. Managers hold positions that enable them to influence and educate many people. This makes managers responsible for developing and implementing ethical decision making. Gellerman and Drucker respectively, offer some good advice for managers:

> All managers risk giving too much because of what their companies demand from them. But the same superiors, who keep pressing you to do more, or to do it better, or faster, or less expensively, will turn on you

E-COMMERCE PERSPECTIVE

Business Ethics and the Internet

May employees use the Internet at work to conduct day trading of personal stocks? May employees send e-mail to personal friends and relatives from the workplace? Is it ethical for employees to shop online while at work? May employees hunt for a new job while online at work? May employees play games online while at work? Before answering these questions consider the following facts:

- Employee productivity can suffer immensely when many workers surf the Web at work.

- Unlike phone calls, e-mail can often be retrieved months or years later and can be used against the company in litigation.

- When employees surf the Web at work, they drag the company's name along with them everywhere. This could be harmful to the company if employees visit certain sites such as racist chat rooms or pornographic material.

- Software packages are now available to companies that report Web site visits by individual employees. Companies such as Telemate Net Software Inc. in Atlanta produce software that tells managers who went to what sites at what times and for how long.

- Some 27 percent of large U.S. firms have begun checking employee e-mail, up from 15 percent in 1997. BellSouth employees must regularly click OK to a message warning them against misuse of e-mail and the Internet and alerting them that their actions can be monitored.

- Many companies such as Boeing grant Internet usage to employees as a perk, but many of those firms are finding that this fringe benefit must be managed.

Lockheed Martin now directs its employees onto the Internet for extensive training sessions on topics that include business ethics, legal compliance sexual harassment, and day-trading. Lockheed even has an Internet ethics game, Ethics Challenge, which every single employee and manager must play once a year. During a recent six-month period, Lockheed discharged 25 employees for ethics violations, suspended 14 others, gave a written reprimand to 51 persons, and an oral reprimand to 146 employees.

Soon after installing the Telemate software, Wolverton & Associates learned that broadcast.com was the company's third-most visited site; people download music from that site. And E*TRADE was the company's eight-most visited site; people day-trade stocks at that site.

Recent research reveals that 38 percent of companies today choose to store and review employees e-mail messages; this represents a rise of 15 percent since 1997. In addition, 54 percent of companies also monitor employees' Internet connections, with 29 percent blocking access to unauthorized or inappropriate Web sites.

Source: Adapted from Michael McCarthy, "Virtual Morality. A New Workplace Quandary," *Wall Street Journal* (October 21, 1999): B1; Michael McCarthy, "Now the Boss Knows Where You're Clicking," *Wall Street Journal* (October 21, 1999); and Michael McCarthy, "How One Firm Tracks Ethics Electronically," *Wall Street Journal,* (October 21, 1999): B1.

should you cross that fuzzy line between right and wrong. They will blame you for exceeding instructions or for ignoring their warnings. The smartest managers already know that the best answer to the question "How far is too far?" is don't try to find out.[22]

A man (or woman) might know too little, perform poorly, lack judgment and ability, and yet not do too much damage as a manager. But if that person lacks character and integrity—no matter how knowledgeable, how brilliant, how successful—he destroys. He destroys people, the most valuable resource of the enterprise. He destroys spirit. And he destroys performance. This is particularly true of the people at the head of an enterprise. For the spirit of an organization is created from the top. If an organization is great in spirit, it is because the spirit of its top people is great. If it decays, it does so because the top rots. As the proverb has it, "Trees die from the top." No one should ever become a strategist unless he or she is willing to have his or her character serve as the model for subordinates.[23]

No society anywhere in the world can compete very long or successfully with people stealing from one another or not trusting one another, with every bit of information requiring notarized confirmation, with every disagreement ending up in litigation, or with government having to regulate businesses to keep them honest. Being unethical is a recipe for headaches, inefficiency, and waste. History has proven that the greater the trust and confidence of people in the ethics of an institution or society, the greater its economic strength. Business relationships are built mostly on mutual trust and reputation. Short-term decisions based on greed and questionable ethics will preclude the necessary self-respect to gain the trust of others. More and more firms believe that ethics training and an eithics culture create strategic advantage.

Some business actions considered to be unethical include misleading advertising or labeling, causing environmental harm, poor product or service safety, padding expense accounts, insider trading, dumping banned or flawed products in foreign markets, lack of equal opportunities for women and minorities, overpricing, hostile takeovers, moving jobs overseas, and using nonunion labor in a union shop.[24]

Internet fraud, including hacking into company computers and spreading viruses, has become a major unethical activity that plagues every sector of online commerce from banking to shopping sites. More than three hundred Web sites now show individuals how to hack into computers; this problem has become endemic nationwide and around the world.

Ethics training programs should include messages from the CEO emphasizing ethical business practices, the development and discussion of codes of ethics, and procedures for discussing and reporting unethical behavior. Firms can align ethical and strategic decision making by incorporating ethical considerations into long-term planning, by integrating ethical decision making into the performance appraisal process, by encouraging whistle-blowing or the reporting of unethical practices, and by monitoring departmental and corporate performance regarding ethical issues.

In a final analysis, ethical standards come out of history and heritage. Our fathers, mothers, brothers, and sisters of the past left us with an ethical foundation to build upon. Even the legendary football coach Vince Lombardi knew that some things were worth more than winning, and he required his players to have three kinds of loyalty: to God, to their families, and to the Green Bay Packers, "in that order."

Comparing Business and Military Strategy

A strong military heritage underlies the study of strategic management. Terms such as *objectives*, *mission*, *strengths*, and *weaknesses* first were formulated to address problems on the battlefield. According to *Webster's New World Dictionary*, strategy is "the science of planning and directing large-scale military operations, of maneuvering forces into the most advantageous position prior to actual engagement with the enemy." The word *strategy* comes from the Greek *strategos*, which refers to a military general and combines *stratos* (the army) and *ago* (to lead). The history of strategic planning began in the military. A key aim of both business and military strategy is "to gain competitive advantage." In many respects, business strategy is like military strategy, and military strategists have learned much over the centuries that can benefit business strategists today. Both business and military organizations try to use their own strengths to exploit competitor's weaknesses. If an organization's overall strategy is wrong (ineffective), then all the efficiency in the world may not be enough to allow success. Business or military success is generally not the happy result of accidental strategies. Rather, success is the product of both continuous attention to changing external and internal conditions and the formulation and implementation of insightful adaptations to those conditions. The element of surprise provides great competitive advantages in both military and business strategy; information systems that provide data on opponents' or competitors' strategies and resources are also vitally important.

Of course, a fundamental difference between military and business strategy is that business strategy is formulated, implemented, and evaluated with an assumption of *competition*, whereas military strategy is based on an assumption of *conflict*. Nonetheless, military conflict and business competition are so similar that many strategic-management techniques apply equally to both. Business strategists have access to valuable insights that military thinkers have refined over time. Superior strategy formulation and implementation can overcome an opponent's superiority in numbers and resources.

Both business and military organizations must adapt to change and constantly improve to be successful. Too often, firms do not change their strategies when their environment and competitive conditions dictate the need to change. Gluck offered a classic military example of this:

> When Napoleon won, it was because his opponents were committed to the strategy, tactics, and organization of earlier wars. When he lost—against Wellington, the Russians, and the Spaniards—it was because he, in turn, used tried-and-true strategies against enemies who thought afresh, who were developing the strategies not of the last war but of the next.[25]

Similarities can be construed from Sun Tzu writings to the practice of formulating and implementing strategies among businesses today. Table 1–2 provides narrative excerpts from *The Art of War*. As you read through Table 1–2, consider which of the principles of war apply to business strategy as companies today compete aggressively to survive and grow.

The Nature of Global Competition

For centuries before Columbus discovered America and surely for centuries to come, businesses have searched and will continue to search for new opportunities beyond their national boundaries. There has never been a more internationalized and economically competitive society than today's. Some American industries, such as textiles, steel, and consumer electronics, are in complete disarray as a result of the international challenge.

Organizations that conduct business operations across national borders are called *international firms* or *multinational corporations*. The term *parent company*

VISIT THE NET

Provides a nice account of strategic planning, tracing history back to the military.
www.des.calstate.edu/ history.html

TABLE 1-2   Excerpts from Sun Tzu's *The Art of War* Writings
(Note: Substitute the words *strategy* or *strategic planning* for *war* or *warfare*)

- War is a matter of vital importance to the state; a matter of life or death, the road either to survival or ruin. Hence, it is imperative that it be studied thoroughly.

- Warfare is based on deception. When near the enemy, make it seem that you are far away; when far away, make it seem that you are near. Hold out baits to lure the enemy. Strike the enemy when he is in disorder. Avoid the enemy when he is stronger. If your opponent is of choleric temper, try to irritate him. If he is arrogant, try to encourage his egotism. If enemy troops are well prepared after reorganization, try to wear them down. If they are united, try to sow dissension among them. Attack the enemy where he is unprepared, and appear where you are not expected. These are the keys to victory for a strategist. It is not possible to formulate them in detail beforehand.

- A speedy victory is the main object in war. If this is long in coming, weapons are blunted and morale depressed. When the army engages in protracted campaigns, the resources of the state will fall short. Thus, while we have heard of stupid haste in war, we have not yet seen a clever operation that was prolonged.

- Generally, in war the best policy is to take a state intact; to ruin it is inferior to this. To capture the enemy's entire army is better than to destroy it; to take intact a regiment, a company, or a squad is better than to destroy it. For to win one hundred victories in one hundred battles is not the acme of skill. To subdue the enemy without fighting is the supreme excellence. Those skilled in war subdue the enemy's army without battle.

- The art of using troops is this—When ten to the enemy's one, surround him. When five times his strength, attack him. If double his strength, divide him. If equally matched, you may engage him with some good plan. If weaker, be capable of withdrawing. And if in all respects unequal, be capable of eluding him.

- Know your enemy and know yourself, and in a hundred battles you will never be defeated. When you are ignorant of the enemy but know yourself, your chances of winning or losing are equal. If ignorant both of your enemy and of yourself, you are sure to be defeated in every battle.

- He who occupies the field of battle first and awaits his enemy is at ease, and he who comes later to the scene and rushes into the fight is weary. And therefore, those skilled in war bring the enemy to the field of battle and are not brought there by him. Thus, when the enemy is at ease, be able to tire him; when well fed, be able to starve him; when at rest, be able to make him move.

- Analyze the enemy's plans so that you will know his shortcomings as well as his strong points. Agitate him in order to ascertain the pattern of his movement. Lure him out to reveal his dispositions and to ascertain his position. Launch a probing attack in order to learn where his strength is abundant and where deficient. It is according to the situation that plans are laid for victory, but the multitude does not comprehend this.

- An army may be likened to water, for just as flowing water avoids the heights and hastens to the lowlands, so an army should avoid strength and strike weakness. And as water shapes its flow in accordance with the ground, so an army manages its victory in accordance with the situation of the enemy. And as water has no constant form, there are in warfare no constant conditions. Thus, one able to win the victory by modifying his tactics in accordance with the enemy situation may be said to be divine.

- If you decide to go into battle, do not announce your intentions or plans. Project "business as usual."

- Unskilled leaders work out their conflicts in courtrooms and battlefields. Brilliant strategists rarely go to battle or to court; they generally achieve their objectives through tactical positioning well in advance of any confrontation.

- When you do decide to challenge another company (or army), much calculating, estimating, analyzing, and positioning brings triumph. Little computation brings defeat.

- Skillful leaders do not let a strategy inhibit creative counter-movement. Not should commands from those at a distance interfere with spontaneous maneuvering in the immediate situation.

- When a decisive advantage is gained over a rival, skillful leaders do not press on. They hold their position and give their rivals the opportunity to surrender or merge. They do not allow their forces to be damaged by those who have nothing to lose.

- Brilliant strategists forge ahead with illusion, obscuring the area(s) of major confrontation, so that opponents divide their forces in an attempt to defend many areas. Create the appearance of confusion, fear, or vulnerability so the opponent is helplessly drawn toward this illusion of advantage.

Source: Adapted from *The Art of War* and from the Web site **www.ccs.neu.edu/home/thigpen/html/art_of_war.html**.

refers to a firm investing in international operations, while *host country* is the country where that business is conducted. The strategic-management process is conceptually the same for multi-national firms as for purely domestic firms; however, the process is more complex for international firms because of the presence of more variables and relationships. The social, cultural, demographic, environmental, political, govern-mental, legal, technological, and competitive opportunities and threats that face a multinational corporation are almost limitless, and the number and complexity of these factors increase dramatically with the number of products produced and the number of geographic areas served.

More time and effort are required to identify and evaluate external trends and events in multinational corporations, than in domestic corporations. Geographical distance, cultural and national differences, and variations in business practices often make communication between domestic headquarters and overseas operations diffi-cult. Strategy implementation can be more difficult because different cultures have different norms, values, and work ethics.

The global war on terrorism and advancements in telecommunications are drawing countries, cultures, and organizations worldwide closer together. Foreign revenue as a percent of total company revenues already exceeds 50 percent in hun-dreds of U.S. firms, including ExxonMobil, Gillette, Dow Chemical, Citicorp, Colgate-Palmolive, and Texaco. Joint ventures and partnerships between domestic and foreign firms are becoming the rule rather than the exception!

Fully 95 percent of the world's population lives outside the United States, and this group is growing 70 percent faster than the American population! The lineup of com-petitors in virtually all industries today is global. Global competition is more than a management fad. General Motors, Ford, and Chrysler compete with Toyota and Hyundai. General Electric and Westinghouse battle Siemens and Mitsubishi. Caterpillar and John Deere compete with Komatsu. Goodyear battles Michelin, Bridgestone/Firestone, and Pirelli. Boeing competes with Airbus. Only a few U.S. industries, such as furniture, printing, retailing, consumer packaged goods, and retail banking, are not yet greatly challenged by foreign competitors. But many products and components in these industries too are now manufactured in foreign countries. In the cellphone business in 2003, Nokia of Finland led the U.S. market with a 28 percent share while Motorola of Schamburg, Illinois, was number 2 with 27 percent. Fierce rivals, both firms are spending heavily on marketing as total U.S. cellphone sales increased 21 percent in the first half of 2003 alone.

International operations can be as simple as exporting a product to a single foreign country, or as complex as operating manufacturing, distribution, and marketing facilities in many countries. U.S. firms are acquiring foreign companies and forming joint ven-tures with foreign firms, and foreign firms are acquiring U.S. companies and forming joint ventures with U.S. firms. This trend is accelerating dramatically. International expansion is no guarantee of success, however, as Starbucks Corp. can attest. The highly successful domestic coffee company now has 1,532 coffee shops outside the U.S. and Canada. These overseas shops account for only 9 percent of company sales, yet they are 23 percent of the firm's stores. In its largest overseas market, Japan, Starbucks lost $3.9 million in 2002, and is losing market share in Europe and the Middle East too.

Advantages and Disadvantages of International Operations

Firms have numerous reasons for formulating and implementing strategies that initi-ate, continue, or expand involvement in business operations across national borders. Perhaps the greatest advantage is that firms can gain new customers for their products and services, thus increasing revenues. Growth in revenues and profits is a common organizational objective and often an expectation of shareholders because it is a measure of organizational success.

In addition to seeking growth, firms have the following potentially advantageous reasons to initiate, continue, and expand international operations:

1. Foreign operations can absorb excess capacity, reduce unit costs, and spread economic risks over a wider number of markets.
2. Foreign operations can allow firms to establish low-cost production facilities in locations close to raw materials and/or cheap labor.
3. Competitors in foreign markets may not exist, or competition may be less intense than in domestic markets.
4. Foreign operations may result in reduced tariffs, lower taxes, and favorable political treatment in other countries.
5. Joint ventures can enable firms to learn the technology, culture, and business practices of other people and to make contacts with potential customers, suppliers, creditors, and distributors in foreign countries.
6. Many foreign governments and countries offer varied incentives to encourage foreign investment in specific locations.
7. Economies of scale can be achieved from operation in global rather than solely domestic markets. Larger-scale production and better efficiencies allow higher sales volumes and lower price offerings.

A firm's power and prestige in domestic markets may be significantly enhanced with various stakeholder groups if the firm competes globally. Enhanced prestige can translate into improved negotiating power among creditors, suppliers, distributors, and other important groups.

There are also numerous potential disadvantages of initiating, continuing, or expanding business across national borders. One risk is that foreign operations could be seized by nationalistic factions. Other disadvantages include the following:

1. Firms confront different and often little-understood social, cultural, demographic, environmental, political, governmental, legal, technological, economic, and competitive forces when doing business internationally. These forces can make communication difficult between the parent firm and subsidiaries.
2. Weaknesses of competitors in foreign lands are often overestimated, and strengths are often underestimated. Keeping informed about the number and nature of competitors is more difficult when doing business internationally.
3. Language, culture, and value systems differ among countries, and this can create barriers to communication and problems managing people.
4. Gaining an understanding of regional organizations such as the European Economic Community, the Latin American Free Trade Area, the International Bank for Reconstruction and Development, and the International Finance Corporation is difficult but is often required in doing business internationally.
5. Dealing with two or more monetary systems can complicate international business operations.
6. The availability, depth, and reliability of economic and marketing information in different countries vary extensively, as do industrial structures, business practices, and the number and nature of regional organizations.

CONCLUSION

All firms have a strategy, even if it is informal, unstructured, and sporadic. All organizations are heading somewhere, but unfortunately some organizations do not know where they are going. The old saying "If you do not know where you are going, then any road will lead you there!" accents the need for organizations to use strategic-management concepts and techniques. The strategic-management process is becoming more widely used by small firms, large companies, nonprofit institutions, governmental organizations, and multinational conglomerates alike. The process of empowering managers and employees has almost limitless benefits.

Organizations should take a proactive rather than a reactive approach in their industry, and they should strive to influence, anticipate, and initiate rather than just respond to events. The strategic-management process embodies this approach to decision making. It represents a logical, systematic, and objective approach for determining an enterprise's future direction. The stakes are generally too high for strategists to use intuition alone in choosing among alternative courses of action. Successful strategists take the time to think about their businesses, where they are with the businesses, and what they want to be as organizations—and then to implement programs and policies to get from where they are to where they want to be in a reasonable period of time.

It is a known and accepted fact that people and organizations that plan ahead are much more likely to become what they want to become than those that do not plan at all. A good strategist plans and controls his or her plans, while a bad strategist never plans and then tries to control people! This textbook is devoted to providing you with the tools necessary to be a good strategist.

Success in business increasingly depends upon offering products and services that are competitive on a world basis, not just on a local basis. If the price and quality of a firm's products and services are not competitive with those available elsewhere in the world, the firm may soon face extinction. Global markets have become a reality in all but the most remote areas of the world. Certainly throughout the United States, even in small towns, firms feel the pressure of world competitors. Nearly half of all the automobiles sold in the United States, for example, are made in Japan and Germany.

We invite you to visit the David page on the Prentice Hall Companion Web site at *www.prenhall.com/david* for this chapter's World Wide Web exercises.

KEY TERMS AND CONCEPTS

Annual Objectives (p. 12)
Business Ethics (p. 20)
Code of Business Ethics (p. 20)
Competitive Advantage (p. 8)
Empowerment (p. 15)
Environmental Scanning (p. 11)
External Opportunities (p. 10)
External Threats (p. 10)
Host Country (p. 27)
Internal Strengths (p. 11)
Internal Weaknesses (p. 11)

International Firms (p. 25)
Intuition (p. 7)
ISO 9000 (p. 21)
ISO 14000 (p. 21)
ISO 14001 (p. 21)
Long-Range Planning (p. 5)
Long-Term Objectives (p. 11)
Mission Statements (p. 9)
Multinational Corporations (p. 25)
Parent Company (p. 25)
Policies (p. 13)

Strategic Management (p. 5)
Strategic-Management Model (p. 13)
Strategic-Management Process (p. 5)
Strategies (p. 12)
Strategists (p. 9)
Strategy Evaluation (p. 6)
Strategy Formulation (p. 5)
Strategy Implementation (p. 6)
Sustained Competitive
  Advantage (p. 9)
Vision Statement (p. 9)

ISSUES FOR REVIEW AND DISCUSSION

1. Explain why Strategic Management often is called a "capstone course."
2. What aspect of strategy formulation do you think requires the most time? Why?
3. Why is strategy implementation often considered the most difficult stage in the strategic-management process?
4. Why is it so important to integrate intuition and analysis in strategic management?
5. Explain the importance of a vision and mission statement.
6. Discuss relationships among objectives, strategies, and policies.
7. Why do you think some chief executive officers fail to use a strategic-management approach to decision making?
8. Discuss the importance of feedback in the strategic-management model.
9. How can strategists best ensure that strategies will be effectively implemented?
10. Give an example of a recent political development that changed the overall strategy of an organization.
11. Who are the major competitors of your college or university? What are their strengths and weaknesses? What are their strategies? How successful are these institutions compared to your college?
12. If you owned a small business, would you develop a code of business conduct? If yes, what variables would you include? If no, how would you ensure that ethical business standards were being followed by your employees?
13. Would strategic-management concepts and techniques benefit foreign businesses as much as domestic firms? Justify your answer.
14. What do you believe are some potential pitfalls or risks in using a strategic-management approach to decision making?
15. In your opinion, what is the single major benefit of using a strategic-management approach to decision making? Justify your answer.
16. Compare business strategy and military strategy.
17. What do you feel is the relationship between personal ethics and business ethics? Are they—or should they be—the same?
18. Why is it important for all business majors to study strategic management since most students will never become a chief executive officer nor even a top manager in a large company?
19. Explain why consumption patterns are becoming similar worldwide. What are the strategic implications of this trend?
20. What are the advantages and disadvantages of beginning export operations in a foreign country?
21. Describe the content available on the SMCO Web site at *www.strategyclub.com*.
22. List four financial and four nonfinancial benefits of a firm engaging in strategic planning.
23. Why is it that a firm can normally sustain a competitive advantage for only a limited period of time?
24. Why it is not adequate to simply obtain competitive advantage?
25. How can a firm best achieve sustained competitive advantage?
26. Compare and contrast ISO 9000, 14000, and 14001.

NOTES

1. Kevin Maney, "The Net Effect: Evolution or Revolution?" *USA Today* (August 9, 1999): B1.
2. Peter Drucker, *Management: Tasks, Responsibilities, and Practices* (New York: Harper & Row, 1974): 611.
3. Alfred Sloan, JR., *Adventures of the White Collar Man* (New York: Doubleday, 1941): 104.
4. Quoted in Eugene Raudsepp, "Can You Trust Your Hunches?" *Management Review* 49, no. 4 (April 1960): 7.
5. Stephen Harper, "Intuition: What Separates Executives from Managers," *Business Horizons* 31, no. 5 (September–October 1988): 16.
6. Ron Nelson, "How to Be a Manager," *Success* (July–August 1985): 69.
7. Bruce Henderson, *Henderson on Corporate Strategy* (Boston: Abt Books, 1979): 6.
8. Robert Waterman, Jr., *The Renewal Factor: How the Best Get and Keep the Competitive Edge* (New York: Bantam, 1987). See also *BusinessWeek* (September 14, 1987): 100. Also, see *Academy of Management Executive* 3, no. 2 (May 1989): 115.

9. Daniel Delmar, "The Rise of the CSO," *Organization Design* (March–April 2003): 8–10.

10. John Pearce II and Fred David, "The Bottom Line on Corporate Mission Statements," *Academy of Management Executive* 1, no. 2 (May 1987): 109.

11. Fred R. David, "How Companies Define Their Mission," *Long Range Planning* 22, no. 1 (February 1989): 91.

12. Jack Pearce and Richard Robinson, *Strategic Management,* 7th ed. (New York: McGraw-Hill, 2000): p. 8.

13. Ann Langley, "The Roles of Formal Strategic Planning," *Long Range Planning* 21, no. 3 (June 1988): 40.

14. Bernard Reimann, "Getting Value from Strategic Planning," *Planning Review* 16, no. 3 (May–June 1988): 42.

15. G. L. Schwenk and K. Schrader, "Effects of Formal Strategic Planning in Financial Performance in Small Firms: A Meta-Analysis," *Entrepreneurship and Practice* 3, no. 17 (1993): 53–64. Also, C. C. Miller and L. B. Cardinal, "Strategic Planning and Firm Performance: A Synthesis of More than Two Decades of Research," *Academy of Management Journal* 6, no. 27 (1994): 1649–1665; Michael Peel and John Bridge, "How Planning and Capital Budgeting Improve SME Performance," *Long Range Planning* 31, no. 6 (October 1998): 848–856;

Julia Smith, "Strategies for Start-Ups," *Long Range Planning* 31, no. 6 (October 1998): 857–872.

16. Gordon Greenley, "Does Strategic Planning Improve Company Performance?" *Long Range Planning* 19, no. 2 (April 1986): 106.

17. Adapted from: *www.mindtools.com/plreschn.html.*

18. Adapted from the Web sites: *www.des.calstate.edu/limitations.html* and *www.entarga.com/stratplan/purposes.html.*

19. Dale McConkey, "Planning in a Changing Environment," *Business Horizons* (September–October 1988): 66.

20. R. T. Lenz, "Managing the Evolution of the Strategic Planning Process," *Business Horizons* 30, no. 1 (January–February 1987): 39.

21. Joann Greco, "Privacy—Whose Right Is It Anyhow?" *Journal of Business Strategy* (January–February 2001): 32.

22. Saul Gellerman, "Why 'Good' Managers Make Bad Ethical Choices," *Harvard Business Review* 64, no. 4 (July–August 1986): 88.

23. Drucker, 462, 463.

24. Gene Laczniak, Marvin Berkowitz, Russell Brooker, and James Hale, "The Ethics of Business: Improving or Deteriorating?" *Business Horizons* 38, no. 1 (January–February 1995): 43.

25. Frederick Gluck, "Taking the Mystique Out of Planning," *Across the Board* (July–August 1985): 59.

CURRENT READINGS

Barney, Jay B. "Is the Resource-Based 'View' a Useful Perspective for Strategic Management Research? Yes." *Academy of Management Journal* 26, no. 1 (January 2001): 41.

Baruch, Y. "No Such Thing as a Global Manager." *Business Horizons* 45, no. 1 (January–February 2002): 36–42.

Clemons, Eric K., and Jason A. Santamaria. "Maneuver Warfare: Can Modern Military Strategy Lead You to Victory?" *Harvard Business Review* (April 2002): 56.

Drucker, Peter F. "They're Not Employees, They're People." *Harvard Business Review* (February 2002): 70.

Farjoun, M. "Towards an Organic Perspective on Strategy." *Strategic Management Journal* 23, no. 7 (July 2002): 561–594.

Hansen, F., and M. Smith. "Crisis in Corporate America: The Role of Strategy." *Business Horizons* 46, no. 1 (January–February 2003): 7–18.

Porter, Michael E. "Strategy and the Internet." *Harvard Business Review* (March 2001): 62.

Powell, T. C. "The Philosophy of Strategy." *Strategic Management Journal* 23, no. 9 (September 2002): 873–888.

Powell, T. C. "Strategy Without Ontology." *Strategic Management Journal* 24, no. 2 (March 2003): 285–291.

Priem, Richard L., and John E. Butler. "Is the Resource-Based 'View' a Useful Perspective for Strategic Management Research?" *Academy of Management Journal* 26, no. 1 (January 2001): 22.

Robertson, R. J., and R. Sarathy. "Executive Briefing/Digital Privacy." *Business Horizons* 45, no. 1 (January–February 2002): 2–5.

Rosen, Christine Meisner. "Environmental Strategy and Competitive Advantage: An Introduction." *California Management Review* 43, no. 3 (Spring 2001): 8.

KRISPY KREME DOUGHNUTS, INC.—2004

Cynthia Duff

Francis Marion University
Ticker Symbol: KKD
www.krispykreme.com

The neon sign "Hot Doughnuts Now," when illuminated, lures hungry customers into the local Krispy Kreme stores. The sign signals that Krispy Kreme's signature product, Hot Original Glazed doughnuts, are right now rolling under the glazing process and are ready to be devoured by anxiously waiting customers. There's nothing better than a hot, fresh, fluffy glazed doughnut that melts in your mouth to satisfy your sweet tooth.

Krispy Kreme Doughnuts went public on April 5, 2000, allowing its customers to have their doughnuts and eat them too. It opened a test doughnut-making store in a Wal-Mart Supercenter in October 2003.

HISTORY

Vernon Rudolph opened a doughnut company, Krispy Kreme, on July 13, 1937, in Winston-Salem, North Carolina. The company started out by selling doughnuts to local grocery stores. People walking in front of the bakery soon began stopping by to ask if they could purchase the doughnuts hot. Rudolph decided to cut a hole in the wall of the bakery so that his Hot Original Glazed doughnuts could be sold directly to the customer, marking the introduction of Krispy Kreme's retail service. During the 1950s, the doughnut-making process was mechanized with the new Krispy Kreme automatic doughnut cutter. Hand-cut doughnuts became a thing of the past. All processes in the bakery became entirely automatic. This was the initial version of Krispy Kreme's continuous yeast doughnut-making equipment.

The year 1962 saw new innovation for Krispy Kreme. Doughnuts were no longer cut; they were extruded by air pressure from a dough hopper directly to trays. On May 28, 1976, Krispy Kreme Doughnut Corporation became a wholly owned subsidiary of Beatrice Foods Company of Chicago, Illinois. The headquarters for Krispy Kreme remained in Winston-Salem, North Carolina. Krispy Kreme was then purchased back from Beatrice Foods Company on February 28, 1982, by a group of Krispy Kreme franchisees, led by Joseph A. McAleer Sr. Krispy Kreme made history when a contribution of Krispy Kreme artifacts was donated to the Smithsonian Institution's National Museum of American History in Washington, D.C., on July 17, 1997.

Krispy Kreme sought to enhance and broaden its beverage offerings to customers and therefore acquired Digital Java, Inc., in 2001. Digital Java was a small coffee roaster and brewing-equipment fabricator located in Chicago. Also in 2001, Krispy Kreme's common stock transferred to the New York Stock Exchange under the new ticker symbol KKD. On December 11, 2001, Krispy Kreme opened its first store outside the United States, in Canada. Then on June 19, 2003, it opened its first store outside of North America, in Australia.

PRESENT CONDITIONS

Krispy Kreme produces approximately 7.5 million doughnuts a day, serving customers in 302 stores operating in 41 states in the United States, and also in Canada and Australia. Exhibit 1 is a map of the locations of Krispy Kreme stores by state

EXHIBIT 1 Geographic Distributions of Stores by Ownership Category Map

Number of Stores ▲ Company ■ Area Developers ● Associates

AUSTRALIA

Source: Krispy Kreme Doughnuts, Inc., 2003 *Annual Report*, p. 73.

including the stores currently in Canada and Australia. Exhibit 2 provides locations listed by major metropolitan areas. Krispy Kreme doughnuts and snacks are also sold at thousands of supermarkets, convenience stores, and other retail outlets throughout the United States.

KKD acquired Montana Mills Bread Co., in early 2003. Under the terms of the merger agreement, the shares of Montana Mills common stock will be converted to Krispy Kreme stock. Krispy Kreme has plans to develop a bakery-café strategy with Montana Mills' product and brand as a basis for this new concept. Montana Mills offers more than eighty types of bread, muffins, rolls, scones, cookies, brownies, and cakes, which are sold through its twenty-two retail stores located primarily in suburban areas in New York, Ohio, Pennsylvania, and Connecticut. The stores cater to upscale customers, offering baked goods, ready-made sandwiches, specialty coffees, and gift items. Montana Mills went public in June 2002 and trades on the American Stock Exchange under the symbol MMX.

COMPANY PROFILE AND PHILOSOPHY

The principle business of KKD is high-volume sales and production of over twenty varieties of the finest quality doughnuts, including the signature Hot Original Glazed. Krispy Kreme's commitment to quality and consistency has created a long-standing devoted customer base. The doughnut-making stores, quality ingredients, and vertical integration are part of what makes Krispy Kreme capable of differentiating itself from competitors.

Krispy Kreme is dedicated to a strategic philosophy, which includes the following beliefs:

- All products will have a taste and quality that are second to none.
- Control product quality and freshness of the ingredients.
- Be thoroughly prepared to execute growth initiatives when they become needed.
- The keys to creating and maintaining a competitive advantage include observing that quality, service, and innovation are second to none.
- Instill the belief that the company is a set of capabilities, not just a product or brand.
- Have a passion that growth and success as a company is a natural result of the growth and success of our people.

BUSINESS STRUCTURE

Krispy Kreme is a vertically integrated company with three reportable segments: Company Store Operations, Franchise Operations, and Krispy Kreme Manufacturing and Distribution (KKM&D) unit. KKD company stores are owned by the KKD Company and are consolidated joint ventures; there are 114 units in this division. There are 188 franchise stores that are owned by either area developers or associates. These stores pay royalties to Krispy Kreme. Company stores and franchise stores both make and sell doughnuts and complementary products through on-premises and off-premises sales channels. The KKM&D division provides all supplies including foodstuffs, equipment, signage, and uniforms to all KKD locations.

KKD's company stores have both on- and off-premises sales. On-premises sales include direct in-store sales to customers visiting inside or at the drive-through window. Discounted sales for community organization fundraising purposes are also

EXHIBIT 2 Geographic Distributions of Stores by Ownership Category

Locations listed by major metropolitan areas

UNITED STATES

Alabama
Birmingham (3)
Dothan
Huntsville
Mobile (2)
Montgomery
Tuscaloosa
Arizona
Phoenix (4)
Tucson
California
Bakersfield
Fresno
Los Angeles (17)
Modesto
Oxnard
Sacramento (2)
San Diego (3)
San Francisco (7)
Santa Rosa
Stockton
Colorado
Colorado Springs
Denver (4)
Connecticut
Milford
Newington
Delaware
Wilmington
Florida
Clearwater
Daytona Beach
Fort Lauderdale (2)
Gainesville
Jacksonville (3)
Melbourne (2)
Miami
Orlando (2)
Panama City
Pensacola (2)
Tallahassee (2)
Tampa (3)
West Palm Beach
Georgia
Albany
Athens
Atlanta (8)

Augusta (3)
Macon
Savannah (2)
Hawaii
Maui
Idaho
Meridian
Illinois
Chicago (12)
Fairview Heights
Indiana
Fort Wayne
Indianapolis (3)
Schererville
Iowa
Cedar Rapids
Davenport
Des Moines
Kansas
Kansas City (2)
Wichita
Kentucky
Florence
Louisville (2)
Louisiana
Baton Rouge (2)
Lafayette
New Orleans (2)
Maryland
Baltimore (5)
Michigan
Detroit (4)
Grand Rapids
Minnesota
Minneapolis/St. Paul (4)
Mississippi
Gulfport
Jackson
Missouri
Kansas City
Springfield
St. Louis (5)
Nebraska
Omaha (2)
Nevada
Las Vegas (5)
Reno

New Mexico
Albuquerque
New York
Buffalo (2)
East Meadow
New York City (5)
Rochester (2)
North Carolina
Asheville
Charlotte (5)
Fayetteville
Goldsboro
Greensboro (2)
Greenville
Hickory
High Point
Raleigh
Rocky Mount
Wilmington
Winston-Salem
North Dakota
Fargo
Ohio
Akron (2)
Cincinnati (2)
Cleveland
Columbus (3)
Dayton
Toledo
Oklahoma
Oklahoma City (3)
Tulsa
Pennsylvania
Pittsburgh (4)
Philadelphia (3)
Scranton (2)
Rhode Island
Cranston
South Carolina
Charleston
Columbia
Florence (2)
Greenville
Myrtle Beach (3)
Spartanburg
Tennessee
Chattanooga

Kingsport
Knoxville (3)
Memphis (2)
Nashville (4)
Texas
Amarillo
Austin (3)
Beaumont
Dallas (5)
Ft. Worth
Houston (6)
San Antonio
Utah
Salt Lake City (4)
Virginia
Alexandria (2)
Ashland
Bristol
Charlottesville
Hampton
Richmond
Roanoke
Virginia Beach
Washington
Seattle (3)
Spokane
West Virginia
Charleston
Wisconsin
Milwaukee (3)
AUSTRALIA
Sydney
CANADA
Ontario
Toronto (4)
Windsor

Source: Krispy Kreme Doughnuts, Inc., 2003 *Annual Report*, p. 72.

included in on-premises sales. Off-premises sales include fresh-doughnut distributions of branded, unbranded, and/or private-label doughnuts to grocery and convenience stores. These doughnuts are sold packaged or unpackaged from a retailer's display case.

KKD Inc., offers franchise opportunities. Franchisees pay royalties to Krispy Kreme Doughnuts, Inc., in return, for the use of the Krispy Kreme name. Two franchise programs are offered. First, in the Associate Program, which is the original program, franchisees pay royalties of 3 percent of on-premises sales and 1 percent of all other sales with the exception of private labels. Second is the Area Developer Program developed in the mid-1990s, in which royalties of 4.5 percent of all sales are paid along with franchise fees ranging from $20,000 to $40,000 per store. Almost all area developers and associates contribute 1 percent of all sales to the national advertising and brand development fund. Krispy Kreme offers franchises in the U.S. market as well as the global market. Franchise stores and company stores are required to purchase all supplies from KKM&D.

The KKM&D unit buys and processes all ingredients used in the doughnut mixes and manufactures the doughnut-making equipment that all stores are required to purchase. KKM&D also includes the coffee roasting operations. KKM&D ships all food ingredients, juices, display cases, uniforms, and other items to Krispy Kreme locations on a weekly basis by common carrier.

Exhibit 3 provides a segmented account of revenues and expenses for Krispy Kreme. The largest segment of total revenue and total operating expenses is derived from Company Store Operations followed by KKM&D. Franchise Operations make

EXHIBIT 3   KKD Segmented Revenues and Expenses

Krispy Kreme Doughnuts, Inc.

SEGMENTED REVENUES AND EXPENSES (IN THOUSANDS)

YEAR ENDED	JAN. 28, 2001	FEB. 3, 2002	FEB. 2, 2003
REVENUES BY BUSINESS SEGMENT:			
Company Store Operations	$213,677	$266,209	$319,592
Franchise Operations	9,445	14,008	19,304
KKM&D	77,593	114,137	152,653
Total revenues	$300,715	$394,354	$491,549
OPERATING EXPENSES BY BUSINESS SEGMENT:			
Company Store Operations	$181,470	$217,419	$252,524
Franchise Operations	3,642	4,896	4,877
KKM&D	65,578	94,631	124,088
Total operating expenses	$250,690	$316,946	$381,489
Depreciation and Amortization Expenses:			
Company Store Operations	$ 4,838	$ 5,859	$ 8,854
Franchise Operations	72	72	108
KKM&D	303	507	1,723
Corporate administration	1,244	1,521	1,586
Total depreciation and amortization expenses	$ 6,457	$ 7,959	$ 12,271

Source: Krispy Kreme Doughnuts, Inc., 2003 *Annual Report*, p. 64.

EXHIBIT 4 Krispy Kreme Doughnuts, Inc. (KKD)—Income Statement

IN MILLIONS OF U.S. DOLLARS (EXCEPT FOR PER SHARE ITEMS) 52 WEEKS ENDING 02/02/03	2003	2002	2001
Revenue	$491.5	$394.4	$300.7
Other Revenue	—	—	—
Total Revenue	**491.5**	**394.4**	**300.7**
Cost of Revenue	381.5	316.9	250.7
Gross Profit	**110.1**	**77.4**	**50.0**
Selling/General/Administrative Expenses	28.9	27.6	20.1
Research and Development	—	—	—
Depreciation/Amortization	12.3	8.0	6.5
Interest Expense (Income), Net Operating	—	—	—
Unusual Expense (Income)	9.1	—	0.0
Other Operating Expenses	—	—	—
Total Operating Expense	**431.7**	**352.5**	**277.2**
Operating Income	**59.8**	**41.9**	**23.5**
Interest Expense, Net Non-Operating	(1.8)	(0.3)	(0.6)
Interest/Investment Income	(0.0)	2.4	1.6
Interest Income (Expense)	(1.8)	2.0	1.0
Gain (Loss) on Sale of Assets	(0.9)	(0.2)	(0.0)
Other, Net	(2.3)	(1.1)	(0.7)
Income Before Tax	54.8	42.5	23.8
Income Tax	21.3	16.2	9.1
Income After Tax	**33.5**	**26.4**	**14.7**
Minority Interest	—	—	—
Equity In Affiliates	—	—	—
Net Income Before Extra Items	**33.5**	**26.4**	**14.7**
Accounting Change	—	—	—
Discontinued Operations	—	—	—
Extraordinary Item	—	—	—
Net Income	**33.5**	**26.4**	**14.7**
Preferred Dividends	—	—	—
Income Available	**33.5**	**26.4**	**14.7**
Basic/Primary Weighted Average Shares	55.1	53.7	49.2

Source: www.investor.stockpoint.com

up only 3 to 4 percent of total revenue and 1 to 2 percent of total operating expenses. Exhibits 4 and 5 provide the company's consolidated Income Statement and Balance Sheet.

COMPETITION

The number-one competitor of Krispy Kreme is Dunkin' Donuts. Dunkin' Donuts is owned by Allied Domecq PLC, which is an international company whose core businesses are in spirits and wine, and quick-service restaurants. Dunkin' Donuts has

EXHIBIT 5 Krispy Kreme Doughnuts, Inc. (KKD)—Balance Sheet

IN MILLIONS OF U.S. DOLLARS (EXCEPT FOR PER SHARE ITEMS) AS OF 02/02/03

	2003	2002	2001
Cash and Equivalents	$ 32.2	$ 21.9	$ 7.0
Short Term Investments	23.0	15.3	18.1
Cash and Short Term Investments	55.2	37.2	25.1
Trade Accounts Receivable, Net	45.4	35.9	22.5
Other Receivables	0.9	2.8	2.3
Total Receivables, Net	46.3	38.7	24.7
Total Inventory	24.4	16.2	12.0
Prepaid Expenses	3.5	2.6	1.9
Other Current Assets	11.8	7.1	3.8
Total Current Assets	141.1	101.8	67.6
Property/Plant/Equipment—Gross	—	—	—
Accumulated Depreciation	(50.2)	(43.9)	(38.6)
Property/Plant/Equipment, Net	202.6	112.6	78.3
Goodwill, Net	—	—	—
Intangibles, Net	48.7	16.6	—
Long Term Investments	11.2	16.1	20.7
Other Long Term Assets	6.9	8.3	4.8
Total Assets	410.5	255.4	171.5
Accounts Payable	14.1	12.1	8.2
Accrued Expenses	21.0	26.7	21.2
Notes Payable/Short Term Debt	0.9	3.9	3.5
Current Port. LT Debt/Capital Leases	3.3	0.7	0.0
Other Current Liabilities	20.5	9.1	5.2
Total Current Liabilities	59.7	52.5	38.2
Long Term Debt	57.2	3.9	0.0
Capital Lease Obligations	—	—	—
Total Long Term Debt	57.2	3.9	0.0
Total Debt	61.4	8.5	3.5
Deferred Income Tax	9.8	3.9	0.6
Minority Interest	5.2	2.5	1.1
Other Liabilities	5.2	4.8	6.0
Total Liabilities	137.1	67.7	45.8
Redeemable Preferred Stock	—	—	—
Preferred Stock—Non Redeemable, Net	—	—	—
Common Stock	173.1	121.1	85.1
Additional Paid-In Capital	—	—	0.0
Retained Earnings (Accum. Deficit)	102.4	68.9	42.5
Treasury Stock—Common	—	—	—
Other Equity	(2.2)	(2.3)	(1.9)
Total Equity	273.4	187.7	125.7
Total Liability and Shareholders' Equity	410.5	255.4	171.5
Shares Outstanding—Common Stock	56.3	54.3	51.8
Total Common Shares Outstanding	56.3	54.3	51.8
Total Preferred Stock Shares Outstanding	—	—	—
Employees (actual figures)	3,913.0	3,371.0	3,200.0
Number of Common Shareholders	—	—	—

Source: www.investor.stockpoint.com

5,438 stores; 1,602 stores outside the United States and 3,836 located in the United States. Bill Rosenberg founded Dunkin' Donuts in Quincy, Massachusetts, and KKD has recently expanded into its home territory.

Sizing up the competition, one glazed doughnut from Dunkin' Donuts has 180 calories, while one Hot Original Glazed doughnut from Krispy Kreme has 200 calories. Dunkin' Donuts carries 25 varieties of doughnuts as well as beverages, bagels, and breakfast sandwiches. Krispy Kreme sells coffee espresso, forzen blends, plain or flavored milk, and has 25 varieties of doughnuts; in addition it has special flavors such as the Pumpkin Spice doughnut offered during the fall months. Dunkin' Donuts celebrated its fiftieth anniversary in 2000. In 2001, Dunkin' Donuts introduced a new beverage, Vanilla Chai, a creamy combination of tea, vanilla, honey, and spices. It also introduced a new logo the same year and then launched its new advertising tagline, JUST THE THING™ in 2002.

Since KKD sells drip coffee, espresso, frozen beverages, and plain or flavored milk, the company now considers Starbucks Corp. as a key competitor. Starbucks purchases and roasts high-quality whole bean coffees, which it sells, together with fresh, rich-brewed coffees, primarily through approximately 6,800 retail stores located in the United States, Asia-Pacific, Europe, the Middle East, Africa, and Latin America. Starbucks offers a wide selection of pastries and confections in addition to coffee and coffee-making equipment and accessories.

INDUSTRY OUTLOOK

The Standard & Poor's (S&P) Restaurants Index was up 22.08 percent year-to-date through August 22, 2003 versus a 13.6 percent rise in the S&P 1500. Shares in the Quick Service Restaurant (QSR) industry have begun to rebound from a recent drop caused by an aggressively competitive environment, including significant price discounts by industry leaders McDonald's and Burger King. Stable same-store sales growth and positive operating conditions may have contributed to the surge in casual-dining industry stocks.

The casual-dining sector continues to gain share from fast-food chains, as an older, wealthier population favors dining in full-service restaurants. This trend is estimated to continue. Food product price inflation remained modest through 2003, but began increasing in 2004. Major industry themes will likely incorporate an emphasis on lowering development costs of new restaurants and slowing expansion in the overstored U.S. fast-food market. Reducing the cost of new units should enhance companies' returns on investment and improve entry into smaller markets. Some fast-food companies are looking to international expansion for growth, while others are investigating new formulas to find ways to grow. There is a new trend toward providing "healthy" choices.

During the past two decades, an ever-increasing precentage of U.S. food dollars has gone to eating out. With a greater percentage of Americans working, there has been less time available for at-home food preparation. Krispy Kreme believes that this trend along with growth in two-income households will increase snack-food consumption and further growth of doughnut sales.

INTERNAL FACTORS
Marketing

On-premises KKD sales include counter sales and drive-through window sales. Krispy Kreme is involved in community organization fundraiser events in which it offers doughnuts at a discounted price for community fundraising projects. Off-premises sales include branded, unbranded, and private-label sales to grocery stores and convenience stores. Krispy Kreme entices customers with its doughnut-making "theaters," which are stores that have glass viewing areas that allow customers to watch the actual doughnut-making process. Generations of loyal customers have grown to love the one-of-a kind taste of Krispy Kreme doughnuts.

Production

Each Krispy Kreme Doughnut store is a doughnut factory which has the capacity to produce from 4,000 dozen to over 10,000 dozen doughnuts daily. KKM&D manufactures the doughnut-making equipment and produces the doughnut mixes that all stores are required to purchase. KKD relocated the Chicago-based Digital Java to its hometown—Winston-Salem, North Carolina. The full beverage program was implemented in approximately seventy KKD locations. It is anticipated that the remaining stores will receive the new beverage program, primarily espresso and frozen beverages, in the next twelve to eighteen months.

Management

KKD's upper management structure is comprised of eight officers, including the president and chief executive officer, and seven senior vice presidents. Exhibit 6 provides a graphic representation of the company's management structure.

EXHIBIT 6 Organizational Chart

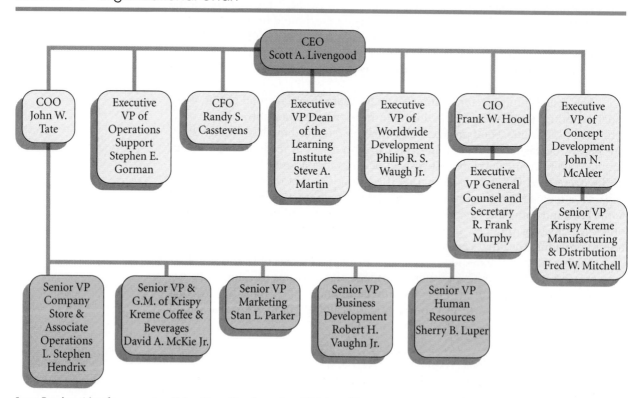

Source: Based on titles of top executives, Krispy Kreme Doughnuts, Inc., 2003 *Annual Report,* p. 75.

GLOBAL ISSUES

Krispy Kreme currently has international locations in Ontario, Canada, and British Columbia, Quebec, and Sydney, Australia, and has plans to open stores in Britain and Mexico in early 2004; over the next five years, it plans to open twenty-five stores outside the U.S. Krispy Kreme has teamed up with Harrod's department store as the place to debut doughnuts in Britain. The United States and Britain differ in eating habits and office etiquette. Brits are accustomed to their traditional English breakfast of eggs, bacon, and milk. KKD plans to convince the Brits to replace the biscuit, which is a cookie, with a doughnut for their snack food. Another concern for Krispy Kreme is persuading people to buy doughnuts by the dozen to take to the office. Most people in Britain do not have cars; therefore they cannot stop by the drive-through on their way to work. Office etiquette is more formal in Britain and a dozen Krispy Kreme Hot Glazed Original doughnuts would cost about five British pounds, which is about $8.00. Krispy Kreme will also offer the tea-drinking British its own custom brews of coffee.

KKD's largest competitor, Dunkin' Donuts, can be found throughout the world. Dunkin' Donuts currently has locations in Aruba, the Bahamas, Brazil, Brunei, Bulgaria, Canada, Chile, Colombia, the Dominican Republic, Ecuador, Germany, Greece, Guam, Guatemala, Indonesia, Korea, Lebanon, Malaysia, Mexico, New Zealand, Pakistan, Peru, the Philippines, Puerto Rico, Qatar, Saudi Arabia, Spain, Thailand, Turkey, the United States, and the UAE.

E-COMMERCE ISSUES

Krispy Kreme's Chief Information Officer, Frank Hood, has teamed up with Network Appliance to provide network storage solutions for KKD. Krispy Kreme's intranet, mykrispykreme.com, allows store operators and franchise owners access to real-time company information, including inventory updates, equipment maintenance, and store directories, dramatically improving communications between owners and the home office.

Krispy Kreme teamed up with Productivity Point International to provide the tools and knowledge necessary to help train employees to reach their top potential. Knowledge Publisher from Productivity Point allows employees to interact with trainers via real-time chat and e-mail. Training is conveyed visually, not just in words, creating an environment where specific techniques can be demonstrated.

Krispy Kreme Doughnuts can be found on the web at **www.krispykreme.com** and Dunkin' Donuts can be found at **www.dunkindonuts.com**. KKD's Web site is not as user friendly as Dunkin' Donuts.' Dunkin' Donuts offers online ordering of its coffee and gift baskets; KKD has no online ordering.

FUTURE OUTLOOK

Krispy Kreme plans to soon open stores in Japan, Mexico, South Korea, and Spain. But will other cultures love the same sweet, calorie-laden snacks that we Americans enjoy? One way for Krispy Kreme to balance its sweet bakery offerings is to consider developing healthier snack-food alternatives. According to the experts at the Centers for Disease Control and Prevention, based in Atlanta, one out of three adult Americans is overweight. Fast-food institutions, which are a major contributor to obesity, can be found anywhere in the United States, even in hospitals. Krispy Kreme has a doughnut

EXHIBIT 7 (All amounts in millions) Montana Mills Income Statement

INCOME STATEMENT	JAN. 02	JAN. 01
Revenue	10.8	7.6
Cost of Goods Sold	5.3	3.5
Gross Profit	5.5	4.1
Gross Profit Margin	—	54.1%
SG&A Expense	5.9	3.9
Depreciation & Amortization	0.6	—
Operating Income	(1.0)	0.2
Operating Margin	—	3.0%
Non-Operating Income	0.2	0.2
Non-Operating Expenses	0.8	0.4
Income Before Taxes	(1.6)	0.0
Income Taxes	(0.6)	0.0
Net Income After Taxes	(1.0)	0.0
Continuing Operations	(1.0)	0.0
Discontinued Operations	0.0	0.0
Total Operations	(1.0)	0.0
Total Net Income	(1.0)	0.0
Net Profit Margin	—	0.4%
Diluted EPS from Continuing Operations ($)	(0.25)	—
Diluted EPS from Discontinued Operations ($)	0.00	—
Diluted EPS from Total Operations ($)	(0.25)	—
Diluted EPS from Total Net Income ($)	(0.25)	—
Dividends per Share	0.00	—

Source: www.hoovers.com.

counter located inside Atlanta's St. Joseph's Hospital. Most fast-food restaurants are revising their menus to include "healthier" choices. Krispy Kreme continues to look for ways to integrate a complete range of products and services; perhaps it should develop a new "low-calorie" doughnut selection.

Exhibits 7 and 8 provide Montana Mills' Income Statement and Balance Sheet. Information for the fiscal year ending January 2003 was not a available. For the year ending January 2002, Montana Mills had a negative net income. Further integration into the bakery and café concept could lead KKD to consider acquiring companies such as Atlanta Bread Company. Montana Mills had a net loss of approximately $2.6 million for the 39-week period ending in October 2002; Krispy Kreme may have paid too much for it. The acquisition of Montana Mills has extended KKD's breadth of competitors,

EXHIBIT 8   (All amounts in millions) Montana Mills Balance Sheet

BALANCE SHEET	JAN. 02	JAN. 01
Assets		
Current Assets		
Cash	0.2	5.8
Net Receivables	0.3	0.0
Inventories	0.4	0.2
Other Current Assets	1.0	0.4
Total Current Assets	2.0	6.4
Net Fixed Assets	6.6	3.5
Other Noncurrent Assets	0.9	0.7
Total Assets	9.5	10.6
Liabilities and Shareholders' Equity		
Current Liabilities		
Accounts Payable	0.8	0.6
Short-Term Debt	0.0	0.0
Other Current Liabilities	0.3	0.2
Total Current Liabilities	1.2	0.9
Long-Term Debt	6.6	6.6
Other Noncurrent Liabilities	0.0	0.1
Total Liabilities	10.2	7.6
Shareholders' Equity		
Preferred Stock Equity	0.0	2.5
Common Stock Equity	(0.8)	0.4
Total Equity	(0.8)	2.9
Shares Outstanding (mil.)	5.0	—

Source: www.hoovers.com.

and Atlanta Bread Company is a bakery much like Montana Mills, except that it is a privately owned company.

Sales for Atlanta Bread Company in 2002 were $15 million; it has 150 stores in 24 states and covers some territory that is not covered by Montana Mills. Atlanta Bread Company is worth about $75 million, and acquiring it may be a good strategy for Krispy Kreme. Krispy Kreme also should accelerate its plans for the global market, which includes opening locations in the United Kingdom, Japan, Mexico, South Korea, and Spain.

Determine whether you think KKD paid too much for Montana Mills. Determine whether you think KKD should expand globally, and if so, where and how fast, or should the firm be expanding further domestically? Develop a three-year strategic plan for KKD, which is in a real fight with Dunkin' Donuts for market share.

experiential exercises

PURPOSE

The purpose of this exercise is to give you experience identifying an organization's opportunities, threats, strengths, and weaknesses. This information is vital to generating and selecting among alternative strategies.

INSTRUCTIONS

Step 1 Identify what you consider to be KKD's major opportunities, threats, strengths, and weaknesses. On a separate sheet of paper, list these key factors under separate headings. Describe each factor in specific terms.

Step 2 Through class discussion, compare your lists of external and internal factors to those developed by other students. From the discussion, add to your lists of factors. Keep this information for use in later exercises.

PURPOSE

This exercise can give you practice in developing a code of business ethics. Research was conducted to examine codes of business ethics from large manufacturing and service firms in the United States. The twenty-eight variables that follow were found to be included in a sample of more than eighty codes of business ethics. The variables are presented in order of how frequently they occurred. Thus, the first variable, "conduct business in compliance with all laws," was most often included in the sample documents; "firearms at work are prohibited" was least often included.

1. Conduct business in compliance with all laws.
2. Payments for unlawful purposes are prohibited.
3. Avoid outside activities that impair duties.
4. Comply with all antitrust and trade regulations.
5. Comply with accounting rules and controls.
6. Bribes are prohibited.
7. Maintain confidentiality of records.
8. Participate in community and political activities.
9. Provide products and services of the highest quality.
10. Exhibit standards of personal integrity and conduct.
11. Do not propagate false or misleading information.
12. Perform assigned duties to the best of your ability.
13. Conserve resources and protect the environment.
14. Comply with safety, health, and security regulations.
15. Racial, ethnic, religious, and sexual harassment at work is prohibited.
16. Report unethical and illegal activities to your manager.
17. Convey true claims in product advertisements.
18. Make decisions without regard for personal gain.
19. Do not use company property for personal benefit.
20. Demonstrate courtesy, respect, honesty, and fairness.
21. Illegal drugs and alcohol at work are prohibited.
22. Manage personal finances well.

23. Employees are personally accountable for company funds.
24. Exhibit good attendance and punctuality.
25. Follow directives of supervisors.
26. Do not use abusive language.
27. Dress in businesslike attire.
28. Firearms at work are prohibited.[1]

INSTRUCTIONS

Step 1   On a separate sheet of paper, write a code of business ethics for KKD. Include as many variables listed above as you believe appropriate to KKD's business. Limit your document to one hundred words or less.

Step 2   Read your code of ethics to the class. Comment on why you did or did not include certain variables.

Step 3   Explain why having a code of ethics is not sufficient for ensuring ethical behavior in an organization. What else does it take?

Notes

Donald Robin, Michael Giallourakis, Fred R. David, and Thomas E. Moritz, "A Different Look at Codes of Ethics," *Business Horizons* 32, no. 1 (January–February 1989): 66–73.

**Experiential
Exercise 1C**

*The Ethics of Spying on
Competitors*

PURPOSE

This exercise gives you an opportunity to discuss ethical and legal issues in class as related to methods being used by many companies to spy on competing firms. Gathering and using information about competitors is an area of strategic management that Japanese firms do more proficiently than American firms.

INSTRUCTIONS

On a separate sheet of paper, number from 1 to 18. For the 18 spying activities listed below, indicate whether or not you believe the activity is Ethical or Unethical and Legal or Illegal. Place either an *E* for ethical or *U* for unethical, and either an *L* for legal or an *I* for illegal for each activity. Compare your answers to your classmates', and discuss any differences.

1. Buying competitors' garbage.
2. Dissecting competitors' products.
3. Taking competitors' plant tours anonymously.
4. Counting tractor-trailer trucks leaving competitors' loading bays.
5. Studying aerial photographs of competitors' facilities.
6. Analyzing competitors' labor contracts.
7. Analyzing competitors' help-wanted ads.
8. Quizzing customers and buyers about the sales of competitors' products.
9. Infiltrating customers' and competitors' business operations.
10. Quizzing suppliers about competitors' level of manufacturing.
11. Using customers to buy out phony bids.

12. Encouraging key customers to reveal competitive information.
13. Quizzing competitors' former employees.
14. Interviewing consultants who may have worked with competitors.
15. Hiring key managers away from competitors.
16. Conducting phony job interviews to get competitors' employees to reveal information.
17. Sending engineers to trade meetings to quiz competitors' technical employees.
18. Quizzing potential employees who worked for or with competitors.

Experiential Exercise 1D

Strategic Planning for My University

PURPOSE

External and internal factors are the underlying bases of strategies formulated and implemented by organizations. Your college or university faces numerous external opportunities/threats and has many internal strengths/weaknesses. The purpose of this exercise is to illustrate the process of identifying critical external and internal factors.

External influences include trends in the following areas: economic, social, cultural, demographic, environmental, technological, political, legal, governmental, and competitive. External factors could include declining numbers of high school graduates; population shifts; community relations; increased competitiveness among colleges and universities; rising numbers of adults returning to college; decreased support from local, state, and federal agencies; increasing numbers of foreign students attending American colleges; and rising number of Internet courses.

Internal factors of a college or university include faculty, students, staff, alumni, athletic programs, the physical plant, grounds and maintenance, student housing, administration, fundraising, academic programs, food services, parking, placement, clubs, fraternities, sororities, and public relations.

INSTRUCTIONS

Step 1 On a separate sheet of paper, make four headings: External Opportunities, External Threats, Internal Strengths, and Internal Weaknesses.

Step 2 As related to your college or university, list five factors under each of the four headings.

Step 3 Discuss the factors as a class. Write the factors on the board.

Step 4 What new things did you learn about your university from the class discussion? How could this type of discussion benefit an organization?

Experiential Exercise 1E

Strategic Planning at a Local Company

PURPOSE

This activity is aimed at giving you practical knowledge about how organizations in your city or town are doing strategic planning. This exercise also will give you experience interacting on a professional basis with local business leaders.

INSTRUCTIONS

Step 1 Use the telephone to contact business owners or top managers. Find an organization that does strategic planning. Make an appointment to visit with the strategist (president, chief executive officer, or owner) of that business.

Step 2 Seek answers to the following questions during the interview:
- a. How does your firm formally conduct strategic planning? Who is involved in the process?
- b. Does your firm have a written mission statement? How was the statement developed? When was the statement last changed?
- c. What are the benefits of engaging in strategic planning?
- d. What are the major costs or problems in doing strategic planning in your business?
- e. Do you anticipate making any changes in the strategic planning process at your company? If yes, please explain.

Step 3 Report your findings to the class.

Experiential Exercise 1F

Does My University Recruit in Foreign Countries?

PURPOSE

A competitive climate is emerging among colleges and universities around the world. Colleges and universities in Europe and Japan are increasingly recruiting American students to offset declining enrollments. Foreign students already make up more than one-third of the student body at many American universities. The purpose of this exercise is to identify particular colleges and universities in foreign countries that represent a competitive threat to American institutions of higher learning.

INSTRUCTIONS

Step 1 Select a foreign country. Conduct research to determine the number and nature of colleges and universities in that country. What are the major educational institutions in that country? What programs are those institutions recognized for offering? What percentage of undergraduate and graduate students attending those institutions are American? Do these institutions actively recruit American students?

Step 2 Prepare a report for the class that summarizes your research findings. Present your report to the class.

Experiential Exercise 1G

Getting Familiar with SMCO

PURPOSE

This exercise is designed to get you familiar with the Strategic Management Club Online (SMCO), which offers many benefits for the strategy student. Note there is a student version of the popular CheckMATE Strategic Planning Software, which is described in more detail at the **www.checkmateplan.com** Web site. The corporate version of CheckMATE is the most popular strategic planning software in the world. The SMCO site also offers templates for doing case analyses in this course.

INSTRUCTIONS

Step 1 Go to the **www.strategyclub.com** Web site. Review the various sections of this site.

Step 2 Select a section of the SMCO site that you feel will be most useful to you in this class. Write a one-page summary of that section and why you feel it will benefit you most.

The Business Vision and Mission

After studying this chapter, you should be able to do the following:

1. Describe the nature and role of vision and mission statements in strategic management.

2. Discuss why the process of developing a mission statement is as important as the resulting document.

3. Identify the components of mission statements.

4. Discuss how clear vision and mission statements can benefit other strategic-management activities.

5. Evaluate mission statements of different organizations.

6. Write good vision and mission statements.

experiential exercises

"notable quotes"

A business is not defined by its name, statutes, or articles of incorporation. It is defined by the business mission. Only a clear definition of the mission and purpose of the organization makes possible clear and realistic business objectives.
Peter Drucker

A corporate vision can focus, direct, motivate, unify, and even excite a business into superior performance. The job of a strategist is to identify and project a clear vision.
John Keane

Where there is no vision, the people perish.
Proverbs 29:18

The last thing IBM needs right now is a vision. (July 1993)

What IBM needs most right now is a vision. (March 1996)
Louis V. Gerstner Jr., CEO, IBM Corporation

The best laid schemes of mice and men often go awry.
Robert Burns (paraphrased)

A strategist's job is to see the company not as it is . . . but as it can become.
John W. Teets, Chairman of Greyhound, Inc.

That business mission is so rarely given adequate thought is perhaps the most important single cause of business frustration.
Peter Drucker

The very essence of leadership is that you have to have vision. You can't blow an uncertain trumpet.
Theodore Hesburgh

This chapter focuses on the concepts and tools needed to evaluate and write business vision and mission statements. A practical framework for developing mission statements is provided. Actual mission statements from large and small organizations and for-profit and nonprofit enterprises are presented and critically examined. The process of creating a vision and mission statement is discussed.

We can perhaps best understand vision and mission by focusing on a business when it is first started. In the beginning, a new business is simply a collection of ideas. Starting a new business rests on a set of beliefs that the new organization can offer some product or service to some customers, in some geographic area, using some type of technology, at a profitable price. A new business owner typically believes that the management philosophy of the new enterprise will result in a favorable public image and that this concept of the business can be communicated to, and will be adopted by, important constituencies. When the set of beliefs about a business at its inception is put into writing, the resulting document mirrors the same basic ideas that underlie the vision and mission statements. As a business grows, owners or managers find it necessary to revise the founding set of beliefs, but those original ideas usually are reflected in the revised statements of vision and mission.

Vision and mission statements often can be found in the front of annual reports. They often are displayed throughout a firm's premises and are distributed with company information sent to constituencies. The statements are part of numerous internal reports, such as loan requests, supplier agreements, labor relations contracts, business plans, and customer service agreements. In a recent study, researchers concluded that 90 percent of all companies have used a mission statement sometime in the previous five years.[1]

What Do We Want to Become?

It is especially important for managers and executives in any organization to agree upon the basic vision that the firm strives to achieve in the long term. A vision statement should answer the basic question, "What do we want to become?" A clear vision provides the foundation for developing a comprehensive mission statement. Many organizations have both a vision and mission statement, but the vision statement should be established first and foremost. The vision statement should be short, preferably one sentence, and as many managers as possible should have input into developing the statement.

Several example vision statements are provided below and in Table 2–1.

VISIT THE NET

Gives an introduction to the vision concept.
www.csuchico.edu/mgmt/
strategy/module1/
sld007.htm

The Vision of the National Pawnbrokers Association is to have complete and vibrant membership that enjoys a positive public and political image and is the focal organization of all pawn associations.—National Pawnbrokers Association (**npa.ploygon.net**)

Our Vision as an independent community financial institution is to achieve superior long-term shareholder value, exercise exemplary corporate citizenship, and create an environment which promotes and rewards employee development and the consistent delivery of quality service to our customers.—First Reliance Bank of Florence, South Carolina

At CIGNA, we intend to be the best at helping our customers enhance and extend their lives and protect their financial security. Satisfying customers is the key to meeting employee needs and shareholder expectations, and will enable CIGNA to build on our reputation as a financially strong and highly respected company. (**www.cigna.com**)

TABLE 2-1   Vision and Mission Statement Examples

THE BELLEVUE HOSPITAL

Vision Statement

The Bellevue Hospital is the LEADER in providing resources necessary to realize the community's highest level of HEALTH throughout life.

Mission Statement

The Bellevue Hospital, with *respect*, *compassion*, *integrity*, and *courage*, honors the individuality and confidentiality of our patients, employees, and community, and is progressive in anticipating and providing future health care services.

U.S. POULTRY & EGG ASSOCIATION

Vision Statement

A national organization which represents its members in all aspects of poultry and eggs on both a national and an international level.

Mission Statement

1. We will partner with our affiliated state organizations to attack common problems.
2. We are committed to the advancement of all areas of research and education in poultry technology.
3. The International Poultry Exposition must continue to grow and be beneficial to both exhibitors and attendees.
4. We must always be responsive and effective to the changing needs of our industry.
5. Our imperatives must be such that we do not duplicate the efforts of our sister organizations.
6. We will strive to constantly improve the quality and safety of poultry products.

We will continue to increase the availability of poultry products.

JOHN DEERE, INC.

Vision Statement

John Deere is committed to providing Genuine Value to the company's stakeholders, including our customers, dealers, shareholders, employees, and communities. In support of that commitment, Deere aspires to:

- Grow and pursue leadership positions in each of our businesses.
- Extend our preeminent leadership position in the agricultural equipment market worldwide.
- Create new opportunities to leverage the John Deere brand globally.

Mission Statement

John Deere has grown and prospered through a long-standing partnership with the world's most productive farmers. Today, John Deere is a global company with several equipment operations and complementary service businesses. These businesses are closely interrelated, providing the company with significant growth opportunities and other synergistic benefits.

MANLEY BAPTIST CHURCH

The Vision of Manley Baptist Church is to be the people of God, on mission with God, motivated by a love for God, and a love for others.

The Mission of Manley Baptist Church is to help people in the Lakeway area become fully developed followers of Jesus Christ.

U.S. GEOLOGICAL SURVEY (USGS)

The Vision of USGS is to be a world leader in the natural sciences through our scientific excellence and responsiveness to society's needs.

The mission of USGS is to serve the Nation by providing reliable scientific information to

- describe and understand the Earth
- minimize loss of life and property from natural disasters
- manage water, biological, energy, and mineral resources; and enhance and protect our quality of life

(continued)

TABLE 2-1   Vision and Mission Statement Examples (*continued*)

MASSACHUSETTS DIVISION OF BANKS

Vision Statement

To protect the public interest, ensure competition, accessibility and fairness within the relevant financial services industries, respond innovatively to a rapidly changing environment, and foster a positive impact on the Commonwealth's economy.

Mission Statement

To maintain a safe and sound competitive banking and financial services environment throughout the Commonwealth and ensure compliance with community reinvestment and consumer protection laws by chartering, licensing, and supervising state regulated financial institutions in a professional and innovative manner.

OHIO DIVISION OF HAZARDOUS WASTE MANAGEMENT

Vision Statement

Ohio's Division of Hazardous Waste Management is recognized as a leader among state hazardous waste management programs through our expertise, effectiveness, application of sound science, and delivery of quality service to our stakeholders.

Mission Statement

The Division of Hazardous Waste Management protects and improves the environment and therefore the health of Ohio's citizens by promoting pollution prevention and the proper management and cleanup of hazardous waste. We provide quality service to our stakeholders by assisting them in understanding and complying with the hazardous waste management regulations, and by implementing our program effectively.

ATLANTA WEB PRINTERS, INC.

Vision Statement

To be the first choice in the printed communications business. The first choice is the best choice, and *being the best* is what Atlanta Web *pledges* to work hard at being—*every day!*

Mission Statement

- to make our clients feel welcome, appreciated, and worthy of our best efforts in everything we do . . . each and every day
- to be recognized as an exceptional leader in our industry and community
- to conduct all our relationships with an emphasis on long-term mutual success and satisfaction, rather than short-term gain
- to earn the trust and respect of all we work with as being a Company of honesty, integrity, and responsibility
- to provide an environment of positive attitude and action to accomplish our vision, by increasing positive feedback and recognition at all levels of the Company
- to train and motivate our employees and to develop cooperation and communication at all levels
- to use our resources, knowledge, and experience to create win/win relationships for our clients, employees, suppliers, and shareholders in terms of growing compensation, service, and value

CALIFORNIA ENERGY COMMISSION

Vision Statement

It is the vision of the California Energy Commission for Californians to have energy choices that are affordable, reliable, diverse, safe, and environmentally acceptable.

Mission Statement

It is the California Energy Commission's mission to assess, advocate, and act through public/private partnerships to improve energy systems that promote a strong economy and a healthy environment.

What Is Our Business?

Current thought on mission statements is based largely on guidelines set forth in the mid–1970s by Peter Drucker, who is often called "the father of modern management" for his pioneering studies at General Motors Corporation and for his twenty-two books and hundreds of articles. *Harvard Business Review* has called Drucker "the preeminent management thinker of our time."

Drucker says that asking the question "What is our business?" is synonymous with asking the question "What is our mission?" An enduring statement of purpose that distinguishes one organization from other similar enterprises, the *mission statement* is a declaration of an organization's "reason for being." It answers the pivotal question "What is our business?" A clear mission statement is essential for effectively establishing objectives and formulating strategies.

Sometimes called a *creed statement*, a statement of purpose, a statement of philosophy, a statement of beliefs, a statement of business principles, or a statement "defining our business," a mission statement reveals what an organization wants to be and whom it wants to serve. All organizations have a reason for being, even if strategists have not consciously transformed this reason into writing. As illustrated in Figure 2–1, carefully prepared statements of vision and mission are widely recognized by both practitioners and academicians as the first step in strategic management.

VISIT THE NET

Gives an introduction to the mission concept.
www.csuchico.edu/mgmt/ strategy/module1/sld008. htm

> A business mission is the foundation for priorities, strategies, plans, and work assignments. It is the starting point for the design of managerial jobs and, above all, for the design of managerial structures. Nothing may seem simpler or more obvious than to know what a company's business is. A steel mill makes steel, a railroad runs trains to carry freight and passengers, an insurance company underwrites fire risks, and a bank lends money. Actually, "What is our business?" is almost always a difficult question and the right answer is usually anything but obvious. The answer to this question is the first responsibility of strategists. Only strategists can make sure that this question receives the attention it deserves and that the answer makes sense and enables the business to plot its course and set its objectives.[2]

Some strategists spend almost every moment of every day on administrative and tactical concerns, and strategists who rush quickly to establish objectives and implement strategies often overlook the development of a vision and mission statement. This problem is widespread even among large organizations. Many corporations in America have not yet developed a formal vision or mission statement.[3] An increasing number of organizations are developing these statements.

Some companies develop mission statements simply because they feel it is fashionable, rather than out of any real commitment. However, as will be described in this chapter, firms that develop and systematically revisit their vision and mission statements, treat them as living documents, and consider them to be an integral part of the firm's culture realize great benefits. Johnson & Johnson (J&J) is an example firm. J&J managers meet regularly with employees to review, reword, and reaffirm the firm's vision and mission. The entire J&J workforce recognizes the value that top management places on this exercise, and these employees respond accordingly.

Vision versus Mission

Many organizations develop both a mission statement and a vision statement. Whereas the mission statement answers the question "What is our business," the *vision statement*

FIGURE 2-1

A Comprehensive Strategic-Management Model

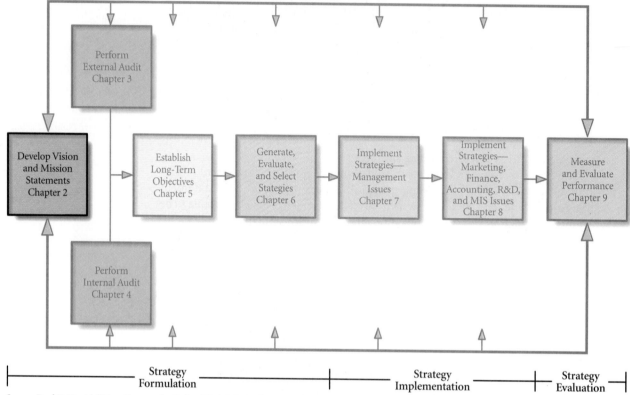

Source: Fred R. David, "How Companies Define Their Mission," *Long Range Planning* 22, no. 3 (June 1988): 40.

VISIT THE NET

Gives questions that help form an effective vision and mission statement.

www.csuchico.edu/mgmt/ strategy/module1/ sld009.htm

answers the question "What do we want to become?" Many organizations have both a mission and vision statement. Several examples are given in Table 2–1.

It can be argued that profit, not mission or vision, is the primary corporate motivator. But profit alone is not enough to motivate people.[4] Profit is perceived negatively by some employees in companies. Employees may see profit as something that they earn and management then uses and even gives away to shareholders. Although this perception is undesired and disturbing to management, it clearly indicates that both profit and vision are needed to effectively motivate a workforce.

When employees and managers together shape or fashion the vision and mission statements for a firm, the resultant documents can reflect the personal visions that managers and employees have in their hearts and minds about their own futures. Shared vision creates a commonality of interests that can lift workers out of the monotony of daily work and put them into a new world of opportunity and challenge.

The Process of Developing a Mission Statement

As indicated in the strategic-management model, a clear mission statement is needed before alternative strategies can be formulated and implemented. It is important to involve as many managers as possible in the process of developing a mission state-ment, because through involvement, people become committed to an organization.

A widely used approach to developing a mission statement is first to select sev-eral articles about mission statements and ask all managers to read these as back-ground information. Then ask managers themselves to prepare a mission statement for the organization. A facilitator, or committee of top managers, should then merge these statements into a single document and distribute this draft mission statement to all managers. A request for modifications, additions, and deletions is needed next, along with a meeting to revise the document. To the extent that all managers have input into and support the final mission statement document, organizations can more easily obtain managers' support for other strategy formulation, implementa-tion, and evaluation activities. Thus, the process of developing a mission statement represents a great opportunity for strategists to obtain needed support from all man-agers in the firm.

During the process of developing a mission statement, some organizations use discussion groups of managers to develop and modify the mission statement. Some organizations hire an outside consultant or facilitator to manage the process and help draft the language. Sometimes an outside person with expertise in developing mis-sion statements, who has unbiased views, can manage the process more effectively than an internal group or committee of managers. Decisions on how best to commu-nicate the mission to all managers, employees, and external constituencies of an orga-nization are needed when the document is in final form. Some organizations even develop a videotape to explain the mission statement and how it was developed.

An article by Campbell and Yeung emphasizes that the process of developing a mission statement should create an "emotional bond" and "sense of mission" between the organization and its employees.[5] Commitment to a company's strategy and intel-lectual agreement on the strategies to be pursued do not necessarily translate into an emotional bond; hence, strategies that have been formulated may not be imple-mented. These researchers stress that an emotional bond comes when an individual personally identifies with the underlying values and behavior of a firm, thus turning intellectual agreement and commitment to strategy into a sense of mission. Campbell and Yeung also differentiate between the terms *vision* and *mission*, saying that vision is "a possible and desirable future state of an organization" that includes specific goals, whereas mission is more associated with behavior and the present.

Importance of Vision and Mission Statements

The importance of vision and mission statements to effective strategic management is well documented in the literature, although research results are mixed. Rarick and Vitton found that firms with a formalized mission statement have twice the average return on shareholders' equity that those firms without a formalized mission state-ment have; Bart and Baetz found a positive relationship between mission statements and organizational performance; *BusinessWeek* reports that firms using mission state-ments have a 30 percent higher return on certain financial measures than those with-out such statements; however, some studies have found that having a mission state-ment does not directly contribute positively to financial performance.[6] The extent of manager and employee involvement in developing vision and mission statements can make a difference in business success. This chapter provides guidelines for developing these important documents. In actual practice, wide variations exist in the nature, composition, and use of both vision and mission statements. King and Cleland recommend that organizations carefully develop a written mission statement for the following reasons:

1. To ensure unanimity of purpose within the organization
2. To provide a basis, or standard, for allocating organizational resources
3. To establish a general tone or organizational climate
4. To serve as a focal point for individuals to identify with the organization's purpose and direction, and to deter those who cannot from participating further in the organization's activities
5. To facilitate the translation of objectives into a work structure involving the assignment of tasks to responsible elements within the organization
6. To specify organizational purposes and then to translate these purposes into objectives in such a way that cost, time, and performance parameters can be assessed and controlled[7]

Reuben Mark, former CEO of Colgate, maintains that a clear mission increasingly must make sense internationally. Mark's thoughts on vision are as follows:

> When it comes to rallying everyone to the corporate banner, it's essential to push one vision globally rather than trying to drive home different messages in different cultures. The trick is to keep the vision simple but elevated: "We make the world's fastest computers" or "Telephone service for everyone." You're never going to get anyone to charge the machine guns only for financial objectives. It's got to be something that makes people feel better, feel a part of something.[8]

A Resolution of Divergent Views

Developing a comprehensive mission statement is important because divergent views among managers can be revealed and resolved through the process. The question "What is our business?" can create controversy. Raising the question often reveals differences among strategists in the organization. Individuals who have worked together for a long time and who think they know each other suddenly may realize that they are in fundamental disagreement. For example, in a college or university, divergent views regarding the relative importance of teaching, research, and service often are expressed during the mission statement development process. Negotiation, compromise, and eventual agreement on important issues are needed before people can focus on more specific strategy formulation activities.

> "What is our mission?" is a genuine decision; and a genuine decision must be based on divergent views to have a chance to be a right and effective decision. Developing a business mission is always a choice between alternatives, each of which rests on different assumptions regarding the reality of the business and its environment. It is always a high-risk decision. A change in mission always leads to changes in objectives, strategies, organization, and behavior. The mission decision is far too important to be made by acclamation. Developing a business mission is a big step toward management effectiveness. Hidden or half-understood disagreements on the definition of a business mission underlie many of the personality problems, communication problems, and irritations that tend to divide a top-management group. Establishing a mission should never be made on plausibility alone, should never be made fast, and should never be made painlessly.[9]

Considerable disagreement among an organization's strategists over vision and mission statements can cause trouble if not resolved. For example, unresolved disagreement over the business mission was one of the reasons for W. T. Grant's bankruptcy and eventual liquidation. As one executive reported:

> There was a lot of dissension within the company whether we should go the Kmart route or go after the Montgomery Ward and JCPenney position. Ed Staley and Lou Lustenberger (two top executives) were at loggerheads over the issue, with the upshot being we took a position between the two and that consequently stood for nothing.[10]

Too often, strategists develop vision and business mission statements only when the organization is in trouble. Of course, it is needed then. Developing and communicating a clear mission during troubled times indeed may have spectacular results and even may reverse decline. However, to wait until an organization is in trouble to develop a vision and mission statement is a gamble that characterizes irresponsible management. According to Drucker, the most important time to ask seriously, "What do we want to become?" and "What is our business?" is when a company has been successful:

> Success always obsoletes the very behavior that achieved it, always creates new realities, and always creates new and different problems. Only the fairy tale story ends, "They lived happily ever after." It is never popular to argue with success or to rock the boat. The ancient Greeks knew that the penalty of success can be severe. The management that does not ask, "What is our mission?," when the company is successful is, in effect, smug, lazy, and arrogant. It will not be long before success will turn into failure. Sooner or later, even the most successful answer to the question, "What is our business?," becomes obsolete.[11]

In multidivisional organizations, strategists should ensure that divisional units perform strategic-management tasks, including the development of a statement of vision and mission. Each division should involve its own managers and employees in developing a vision and mission statement that is consistent with and supportive of the corporate mission.

An organization that fails to develop a vision statement as well as a comprehensive and inspiring mission statement loses the opportunity to present itself favorably to existing and potential stakeholders. All organizations need customers, employees, and managers, and most firms need creditors, suppliers, and distributors. The vision and mission statements are effective vehicles for communicating with important internal and external stakeholders. The principal value of these statements as tools of strategic management is derived from their specification of the ultimate aims of a firm:

> They provide managers with a unity of direction that transcends individual, parochial, and transitory needs. They promote a sense of shared expectations among all levels and generations of employees. They consolidate values over time and across individuals and interest groups. They project a sense of worth and intent that can be identified and assimilated by company outsiders. Finally, they affirm the company's

An effective mission statement should not be too lengthy; recommended length is less than 200 words. An effective mission statement also arouses positive feelings and emotions about an organization; it is inspiring in the sense that it motivates readers to action. An effective mission statement generates the impression that a firm is successful, has direction, and is worthy of time, support, and investment—from all socioeconomic groups of people.

It reflects judgments about future growth directions and strategies that are based upon forward-looking external and internal analyses. A business mission should provide useful criteria for selecting among alternative strategies. A clear mission statement provides a basis for generating and screening strategic options. The statement of mission should be dynamic in orientation, allowing judgments about the most promising growth directions and those considered less promising.

A Customer Orientation

A good mission statement describes an organization's purpose, customers, products or services, markets, philosophy, and basic technology. According to Vern McGinnis, a mission statement should (1) define what the organization is and what the organization aspires to be, (2) be limited enough to exclude some ventures and broad enough to allow for creative growth, (3) distinguish a given organization from all others, (4) serve as a framework for evaluating both current and prospective activities, and (5) be stated in terms sufficiently clear to be widely understood throughout the organization.[14]

A good mission statement reflects the anticipations of customers. Rather than developing a product and then trying to find a market, the operating philosophy of organizations should be to identify customers' needs and then provide a product or service to fulfill those needs. Since more and more customers are using the Internet, all firms should post their vision and mission statements at the company's home page—as indicated in the "E-Commerce Perspective."

Good mission statements identify the utility of a firm's products to its customers. This is why AT&T's mission statement focuses on communication rather than on telephones; it is why ExxonMobil's mission statement focuses on energy rather than on oil and gas; it is why Union Pacific's mission statement focuses on transportation rather than on railroads; it is why Universal Studio's mission statement focuses on entertainment rather than on movies. The following utility statements are relevant in developing a mission statement:

Do not offer me things.
Do not offer me clothes. Offer me attractive looks.
Do not offer me shoes. Offer me comfort for my feet and the pleasure of walking.
Do not offer me a house. Offer me security, comfort, and a place that is clean and happy.
Do not offer me books. Offer me hours of pleasure and the benefit of knowledge.
Do not offer me records. Offer me leisure and the sound of music.
Do not offer me tools. Offer me the benefits and the pleasure that come from making beautiful things.
Do not offer me furniture. Offer me comfort and the quietness of a cozy place.
Do not offer me things. Offer me ideas, emotions, ambience, feelings, and benefits.
Please, do not offer me *things*.

A major reason for developing a business mission statement is to attract customers who give meaning to an organization. Hotel customers today want to use the

E-COMMERCE PERSPECTIVE

Business over the Internet Skyrocketing

BusinessWeek reported in mid-2003 that business-to-business (B2B) e-commerce now exceeds $2.4 trillion annually and consumer e-commerce exceeds $100 billion. The Internet has truly connected people and businesses around the world, enabled companies to slash costs, and increased productivity. Businesses everywhere now communicate with their customers, suppliers, distributors, shareholders, and creditors instantaneously and inexpensively and are passing these cost savings on to consumers. Thousands of new consumers and businesses are coming online around the world every day. U.S. household subscriptions to broadband are growing at 57 percent annually and had surpassed 29 million households at year-end 2003; they are expected to surpass 40 million by the end of 2004. The annual growth rate of broadband is even higher in Canada, Japan, Korea, and a few other countries. More than one-quarter of all U.S. households now have high-speed Internet access, which is crucial to Web entertainment, banking, and shopping.

Internet-based companies now dominate business in many industries, as evidenced below:

- **Automobiles**—eBay has become the largest U.S. used-car dealer.

- **Travel**—Expedia has become the largest travel agency. Thirteen percent of traditional travel agencies closed in 2002, partly due to Expedia and other Internet-based travel service firms.
- **Computers**—Dell dominates and competitors try to imitate its Internet operations.
- **Financial Services**—LendingTree is growing 70 percent annually and already dominating.
- **Health Care**—WebMD and similar firms are gaining rapidly in popularity.
- **Retailing**—Amazon joined the top 40 U.S. retailers in 2003 and eBay joined the top 15. Even Wal-Mart's online tactics are crushing traditional retailers such as Kmart.
- **Education**—Phoenix and other universities are growing dramatically. Cisco Systems saved $133 million in 2002 by moving training sessions to the Internet.
- **Music**—Apple Computer sells music downloads. Consumers now download more than 35 billion songs annually, mostly at no cost.

Source: Adapted from Timothy Mullaney and Heather Green, "The E-Biz Surprise," *BusinessWeek* (May 12, 2003): 60–68.

Internet, so more and more hotels are providing Internet service. A classic description of the purpose of a business reveals the relative importance of customers in a statement of mission:

> It is the customer who determines what a business is. It is the customer alone whose willingness to pay for a good or service converts economic resources into wealth and things into goods. What a business thinks it produces is not of first importance, especially not to the future of the business and to its success. What the customer thinks he/she is buying, what he/she considers value, is decisive—it determines what a business is, what it produces, and whether it will prosper. And what the customer buys and considers value is never a product. It is always utility, meaning what a product or service does for him or her. The customer is the foundation of a business and keeps it in existence.[15]

A Declaration of Social Policy

The term *social policy* embraces managerial philosophy and thinking at the highest levels of an organization. For this reason, social policy affects the development of a business mission statement. Social issues mandate that strategists consider not only what the organization owes its various stakeholders but also what responsibilities the firm has to consumers, environmentalists, minorities, communities, and other groups. After decades of debate on the topic of social responsibility, many firms still struggle to determine appropriate social policies.

The issue of social responsibility arises when a company establishes its business mission. The impact of society on business and vice versa is becoming more pronounced each year. Social policies directly affect a firm's customers, products and services, markets, technology, profitability, self-concept, and public image. An organization's social policy should be integrated into all strategic-management activities, including the development of a mission statement. Corporate social policy should be designed and articulated during strategy formulation, set and administered during strategy implementation, and reaffirmed or changed during strategy evaluation.[16] The emerging view of social responsibility holds that social issues should be attended to both directly and indirectly in determining strategies. In 2003, the *Wall Street Journal* rated the top companies for social responsibility to be as follows:[17]

1. Alexander & Baldwin
2. Johnson & Johnson
3. American Express
4. Altria Group
5. United Parcel Service
6. BP America
7. Procter & Gamble
8. Administaff
9. Medtronic
10. Merck

VISIT THE NET

Provides example mission and vision statements that can be critiqued.
www.csuchico.edu/mgmt/
strategy/module1/
sld015.htm; www.csuchico.
edu/mgmt/strategy/
module1/sld014.htm;
www.csuchico.edu/mgmt/
strategy/module1/
sld017.htm

Firms should strive to engage in social activities that have economic benefits. For example, Merck & Co. recently developed the drug ivermectin for treating river blindness, a disease caused by a fly-borne parasitic worm endemic in poor, tropical areas of Africa, the Middle East, and Latin America. In an unprecedented gesture that reflected its corporate commitment to social responsibility, Merck then made ivermectin available at no cost to medical personnel throughout the world. Merck's action highlights the dilemma of orphan drugs, which offer pharmaceutical companies no economic incentive for development and distribution.

Despite differences in approaches, most American companies try to assure outsiders that they conduct their businesses in socially responsible ways. The mission statement is an effective instrument for conveying this message.

Some strategists agree with Ralph Nader, who proclaims that organizations have tremendous social obligations. Others agree with Milton Friedman, the economist, who maintains that organizations have no obligation to do any more for society than is legally required. Most strategists agree that the first social responsibility of any business must be to make enough profit to cover the costs of the future, because if this is not achieved, no other social responsibility can be met. Strategists should examine social problems in terms of potential costs and benefits to the firm, and they should address social issues that could benefit the firm most.

Components of a Mission Statement

Mission statements can and do vary in length, content, format, and specificity. Most practitioners and academicians of strategic management feel that an effective statement exhibits nine characteristics or components. Because a mission statement is often the most visible and public part of the strategic-management process, it is important that it includes all of these essential components:

1. *Customers*—Who are the firm's customers?
2. *Products or services*—What are the firm's major products or services?
3. *Markets*—Geographically, where does the firm compete?
4. *Technology*—Is the firm technologically current?
5. *Concern for survival, growth, and profitability*—Is the firm committed to growth and financial soundness?
6. *Philosophy*—What are the basic beliefs, values, aspirations, and ethical priorities of the firm?
7. *Self-concept*—What is the firm's distinctive competence or major competitive advantage?
8. *Concern for public image*—Is the firm responsive to social, community, and environmental concerns?
9. *Concern for employees*—Are employees a valuable asset of the firm?

Excerpts from the mission statements of different organizations are provided in Table 2–2 to exemplify the nine essential mission statement components.

Writing and Evaluating Mission Statements

Perhaps the best way to develop a skill for writing and evaluating mission statements is to study actual company missions. Therefore, six mission statements are presented in Table 2–3. These statements are then evaluated in Table 2–4 based on the nine criteria presented above.

There is no one best mission statement for a particular organization, so good judgment is required in evaluating mission statements. In Table 2–4, a *Yes* indicates that the given mission statement answers satisfactorily the question posed in Table 2–2 for the respective evaluative criteria. Some individuals are more demanding than others in rating mission statements in this manner. For example, if a statement includes the word *employees* or *customer*, is that alone sufficient for the respective component? Some companies answer this question in the affirmative and some in the negative. You may ask yourself this question: "If I worked for this company, would I have done better with regard to including a particular component in its mission statement?" Perhaps the important issue here is that mission statements include each of the nine components in some manner.

As indicated in Table 2–4, the Dell Computer mission statement was rated to be the best among the six statements evaluated. Note, however, that the Dell Computer statement lacks inclusion of the "Philosophy" and the "Concern for Employees" components. The PepsiCo mission statement was evaluated as the worst because it included only three of the nine components. Note that only one of these six statements included the "Technology" component in its document.

VISIT THE NET

Provides the NIH Clinical Center's vision and mission statements and its overall strategic plan.
www.cc.nih.gov/od/ strategic/index.html

TABLE 2-2   Examples of the Nine Essential Components of a Mission Statement

1. CUSTOMERS
We believe our first responsibility is to the doctors, nurses, patients, mothers, and all others who use our products and services. (Johnson & Johnson)
To earn our customers' loyalty, we listen to them, anticipate their needs, and act to create value in their eyes. (Lexmark International)

2. PRODUCTS OR SERVICES
AMAX's principal products are molybdenum, coal, iron ore, copper, lead, zinc, petroleum and natural gas, potash, phosphates, nickel, tungsten, silver, gold, and magnesium. (AMAX Engineering Company)
Standard Oil Company (Indiana) is in business to find and produce crude oil, natural gas, and natural gas liquids; to manufacture high-quality products useful to society from these raw materials; and to distribute and market those products and to provide dependable related services to the consuming public at reasonable prices. (Standard Oil Company)

3. MARKETS
We are dedicated to the total success of Corning Glass Works as a worldwide competitor. (Corning Glass Works)
Our emphasis is on North American markets, although global opportunities will be explored. (Blockway)

4. TECHNOLOGY
Control Data is in the business of applying micro-electronics and computer technology in two general areas: computer-related hardware; and computing-enhancing services, which include computation, information, education, and finance. (Control Data)
We will continually strive to meet the preferences of adult smokers by developing technologies that have the potential to reduce the health risks associated with smoking. (RJ Reynolds)

5. CONCERN FOR SURVIVAL, GROWTH, AND PROFITABILITY
In this respect, the company will conduct its operations prudently and will provide the profits and growth which will assure Hoover's ultimate success. (Hoover Universal)
To serve the worldwide need for knowledge at a fair profit by adhering, evaluating, producing, and distributing valuable information in a way that benefits our customers, employees, other investors, and our society. (McGraw-Hill)

6. PHILOSOPHY
Our world-class leadership is dedicated to a management philosophy that holds people above profits. (Kellogg)
It's all part of the Mary Kay philosophy—a philosophy based on the golden rule. A spirit of sharing and caring where people give cheerfully of their time, knowledge, and experience. (Mary Kay Cosmetics)

7. SELF-CONCEPT
Crown Zellerbach is committed to leapfrogging ongoing competition within 1,000 days by unleashing the constructive and creative abilities and energies of each of its employees. (Crown Zellerbach)

8. CONCERN FOR PUBLIC IMAGE
To share the world's obligation for the protection of the environment. (Dow Chemical)
To contribute to the economic strength of society and function as a good corporate citizen on a local, state, and national basis in all countries in which we do business. (Pfizer)

TABLE 2-2   Examples of the Nine Essential Components of a Mission Statement (*continued*)

9. CONCERN FOR EMPLOYEES

To recruit, develop, motivate, reward, and retain personnel of exceptional ability, character, and dedication by providing good working conditions, superior leadership, compensation on the basis of performance, an attractive benefit program, opportunity for growth, and a high degree of employment security. (The Wachovia Corporation)

To compensate its employees with remuneration and fringe benefits competitive with other employment opportunities in its geographical area and commensurate with their contributions toward efficient corporate operations. (Public Service Electric & Gas Company)

TABLE 2-3   Mission Statements of Six Organizations

PepsiCo's mission is to increase the value of our shareholders' investment. We do this through sales growth, cost controls, and wise investment resources. We believe our commercial success depends upon offering quality and value to our consumers and customers; providing products that are safe, wholesome, economically efficient, and environmentally sound; and providing a fair return to our investors while adhering to the highest standards of integrity.

Ben & Jerry's mission is to make, distribute, and sell the finest quality all-natural ice cream and related products in a wide variety of innovative flavors made from Vermont dairy products. To operate the Company on a sound financial basis of profitable growth, increasing value for our shareholders, and creating career opportunities and financial rewards for our employees. To operate the Company in a way that actively recognizes the central role that business plays in the structure of society by initiating innovative ways to improve the quality of life of a broad community— local, national, and international.

The Mission of the Institute of Management Accountants (IMA) is to provide to members personal and professional development opportunities through education, association with business professionals, and certification in management accounting and financial management skills. The IMA is globally recognized by the financial community as a respected institution influencing the concepts and ethical practices of management accounting and financial management.

The Mission of Genentech, Inc., is to be the leading biotechnology company, using human genetic information to develop, manufacture, and market pharmaceuticals that address significant unmet medical needs. We commit ourselves to high standards of integrity in contributing to the best interests of patients, the medical profession, and our employees, and to seek significant returns to our stockholders based on the continued pursuit of excellent science.

The Mission of Barrett Memorial Hospital is to operate a high-quality health care facility, providing an appropriate mix of services to the residents of Beaverhead County and surrounding areas. Service is given with ultimate concern for patients, medical staff, hospital staff, and the community. Barrett Memorial Hospital assumes a strong leadership role in the coordination and development of health-related resources within the community.

Dell Computer's mission is to be the most successful computer company in the world at delivering the best customer experience in markets we serve. In doing so, Dell will meet customer expectations of highest quality; leading technology; competitive pricing; individual and company accountability; best-in-class service and support; flexible customization capability; superior corporate citizenship; financial stability.

TABLE 2-4   An Evaluation Matrix of Mission Statements

COMPONENTS

Organization	Customers	Products/ Services	Markets	Technology	Concern for Survival, Growth, Profitability
PepsiCo	Yes	No	No	No	Yes
Ben & Jerry's	No	Yes	Yes	No	Yes
Institute of Management Accountants	Yes	Yes	Yes	No	No
Genentech, Inc.	Yes	Yes	No	No	Yes
Barrett Memorial Hospital	Yes	Yes	Yes	No	No
Dell Computer	Yes	Yes	Yes	Yes	Yes

Organization	Philosophy	Self-Concept	Concern for Public Image	Concern for Employees
PepsiCo	Yes	No	No	No
Ben & Jerry's	No	Yes	Yes	Yes
Institute of Management Accountants	Yes	Yes	Yes	No
Genentech, Inc.	Yes	Yes	Yes	Yes
Barrett Memorial Hospital	No	Yes	Yes	Yes
Dell Computer	No	Yes	Yes	No

CONCLUSION

Every organization has a unique purpose and reason for being. This uniqueness should be reflected in vision and mission statements. The nature of a business vision and mission can represent either a competitive advantage or disadvantage for the firm. An organization achieves a heightened sense of purpose when strategists, managers, and employees develop and communicate a clear business vision and mission. Drucker says that developing a clear business vision and mission is the "first responsibility of strategists."

A good mission statement reveals an organization's customers; products or services; markets; technology; concern for survival, growth, and profitability; philosophy; self-concept; concern for public image; and concern for employees. These nine basic components serve as a practical framework for evaluating and writing mission statements. As the first step in strategic management, the vision and mission statements provide direction for all planning activities.

Well-designed vision and mission statements are essential for formulating, implementing, and evaluating strategy. Developing and communicating a clear business vision and mission is one of the most commonly overlooked tasks in strategic management. Without clear statements of vision and mission, a firm's short-term actions can be counterproductive to long-term interests. Vision and mission statements always should be subject to revision, but, if carefully prepared, they will require infrequent major changes. Organizations usually reexamine their vision and mission statements annually. Effective mission statements stand the test of time.

Vision and mission statements are essential tools for strategists, a fact illustrated in a short story told by Porsche former CEO Peter Schultz:

Three people were at work on a construction site. All were doing the same job, but when each was asked what his job was, the answers varied: "Breaking rocks," the first replied; "Earning a living," responded the second; "Helping to build a cathedral," said the third. Few of us can build cathedrals. But to the extent we can see the cathedral in whatever cause we are following, the job seems more worthwhile. Good strategists and a clear mission help us find those cathedrals in what otherwise could be dismal issues and empty causes.[18]

We invite you to visit the David page on the Prentice Hall Companion Web site at *www.prenhall.com/david* for this chapter's World Wide Web exercises.

KEY TERMS AND CONCEPTS

Concern for Employees (p. 63)

Concern for Public Image (p. 63)

Concern for Survival, Growth, and Profitability (p. 63)

Creed Statement (p. 53)

Customers (p. 63)

Markets (p. 63)

Mission Statement (p. 53)

Mission Statement Components (p. 63)

Philosophy (p. 63)

Products or Services (p. 63)

Self-Concept (p. 63)

Social Policy (p. 62)

Stakeholders (p. 58)

Technology (p. 63)

Vision Statement (p. 53)

ISSUES FOR REVIEW AND DISCUSSION

1. Compare and contrast vision statements with mission statements in terms of composition and importance.
2. Do local service stations need to have written vision and mission statements? Why or why not?
3. Why do you think organizations that have a comprehensive mission tend to be high performers? Does having a comprehensive mission cause high performance?
4. Explain why a mission statement should not include strategies and objectives.
5. What is your college or university's self-concept? How would you state that in a mission statement?
6. Explain the principal value of a vision and a mission statement.
7. Why is it important for a mission statement to be reconciliatory?
8. In your opinion, what are the three most important components that should be included when writing a mission statement? Why?
9. How would the mission statements of a for-profit and a nonprofit organization differ?
10. Write a vision and mission statement for an organization of your choice.
11. Go to *www.altavista.com* and conduct a search with the keywords *vision statement* and *mission statement*. Find various company vision and mission statements and evaluate the documents.
12. Who are the major stakeholders of the bank that you do business with locally? What are the major claims of those stakeholders?
13. How could a strategist's attitude toward social responsibility affect a firm's strategy? What is your attitude toward social responsibility?
14. List the characteristics of a mission statement.
15. List the benefits of a having a clear mission statement.
16. How often do you think a firm's vision and mission statements should be changed?

NOTES

1. Barbara Bartkus, Myron Glassman, and Bruce McAfee, "Mission Statements: Are They Smoke and Mirrors?" *Business Horizons* (November–December 2000): 23.
2. Peter Drucker, *Management: Tasks, Responsibilities, and Practices* (New York: Harper & Row, 1974): 61.
3. Fred David, "How Companies Define Their Mission," *Long Range Planning* 22, no. 1 (February 1989): 90–92; John Pearce II and Fred David, "Corporate Mission Statements: The Bottom Line," *Academy of Management Executive* 1, no. 2 (May 1987): 110.
4. Joseph Quigley, "Vision: How Leaders Develop It, Share It and Sustain It," *Business Horizons* (September–October 1994): 39.

5. Andrew Campbell and Sally Yeung, "Creating a Sense of Mission," *Long Range Planning* 24, no. 4 (August 1991): 17.
6. Charles Rarick and John Vitton, "Mission Statements Make Cents," *Journal of Business Strategy* 16 (1995): 11. Also, Christopher Bart and Mark Baetz, "The Relationship Between Mission Statements and Firm Performance: An Exploratory Study," *Journal of Management Studies* 35 (1998): 823; "Mission Possible," *Business Week* (August 1999): F12.
7. W. R. King and D. I. Cleland, *Strategic Planning and Policy* (New York: Van Nostrand Reinhold, 1979): 124.
8. Brian Dumaine, "What the Leaders of Tomorrow See," *Fortune* (July 3, 1989): 50.
9. Drucker: 78, 79.
10. "How W. T. Grant Lost $175 Million Last Year," *BusinessWeek* (February 25, 1975): 75.
11. Drucker, 88.
12. John Pearce II, "The Company Mission as a Strategic Tool," *Sloan Management Review* 23, no. 3 (Spring 1982): 74.
13. George Steiner, *Strategic Planning: What Every Manager Must Know* (New York: The Free Press, 1979): 160.
14. Vern McGinnis, "The Mission Statement: A Key Step in Strategic Planning," *Business* 31, no. 6 (November–December 1981): 41.
15. Drucker, 61.
16. Archie Carroll and Frank Hoy, "Integrating Corporate Social Policy into Strategic Management," *Journal of Business Strategy* 4, no. 3 (Winter 1984): 57.
17. *www.fortune.com*
18. Robert Waterman, Jr., *The Renewal Factor: How the Best Get and Keep the Competitive Edge* (New York: Bantam, 1987); *BusinessWeek* (September 14, 1987): 120.

CURRENT READINGS

Baetz, Mark C., and Christopher K. Bart, "Developing Mission Statements Which Work." *Long Range Planning* 29, no. 4 (August 1996): 526–533.

Bartkus, Barbara, Myron Glassman, and R. Bruce McAfee. "Mission Statements: Are They Smoke and Mirrors?" *Business Horizons* 43, no. 6 (November–December 2000): 23.

Brabet, Julienne, and Mary Klemm. "Sharing the Vision: Company Mission Statements in Britain and France." *Long Range Planning* (February 1994): 84–94.

Buysse, K., and A. Verbeke. "Proactive Environmental Strategies: A Stakeholder Management Perspective." *Strategic Management Journal* 24, no. 5 (May 2003): 453–470.

Collins, James C., and Jerry I. Porras. "Building a Visionary Company." *California Management Review* 37, no. 2 (Winter 1995): 80–100.

Collins, James C., and Jerry I. Porras. "Building Your Company's Vision." *Harvard Business Review* (September–October 1996): 65–78.

Cummings, Stephen, and John Davies. "Brief Case—Mission, Vision, Fusion." *Long Range Planning* 27, no. 6 (December 1994): 147–150.

Davies, Stuart W., and Keith W. Glaister. "Business School Mission Statements—The Bland Leading the Bland?" *Long Range Planning* 30, no. 4 (August 1997): 594–604.

Gratton, Lynda. "Implementing a Strategic Vision—Key Factors for Success." *Long Range Planning* 29, no. 3 (June 1996): 290–303.

Hemphill, T. "Executive Briefing/Online Privacy and E-commerce." *Business Horizons* 46, no. 1 (January–February 2003): 3–6.

Hough, J. R., and M. A. White. "Environmental Dynamism and Strategic Decision-Making Rationality: An Examination at the Decision-Level." *Strategic Management Journal* 24, no. 5 (May 2003): 481.

Larwood, Laurie, Cecilia M. Falbe, Mark P. Kriger, and Paul Miesing. "Structure and Meaning of Organizational Vision." *Academy of Management Journal* 38, no. 3 (June 1995): 740–769.

Lissak, Michael, and Johan Roos. "Be Coherent, Not Visionary." *Long Range Planning* 34, no. 1 (February 2001): 53.

McTavish, Ron. "One More Time: What Business Are You In?" *Long Range Planning* 28, no. 2 (April 1995): 49–60.

Oswald, S. L., K. W. Mossholder, and S. G. Harris. "Vision Salience and Strategic Involvement: Implications for Psychological Attachment to Organization and Job." *Strategic Management Journal* 15, no. 6 (July 1994): 477–490.

Starkey, K., and A. Crane. "Toward Green Narrative: Management and the Evolutionary Epic." *Academy of Management Review* 28, no. 2 (April 2003): 220–237.

experiential exercises

PURPOSE

A business mission statement is an integral part of strategic management. It provides direction for formulating, implementing, and evaluating strategic activities. This exercise will give you practice evaluating mission statements, a skill that is prerequisite to writing a good mission statement.

INSTRUCTIONS

Step 1   Your instructor will select some or all of the following mission statements to evaluate. On a separate sheet of paper, construct an evaluation matrix like the one presented in Table 2–4. Evaluate the mission statements based on the nine criteria presented in this chapter.

Step 2   Record a *yes* in appropriate cells of the evaluation matrix when the respective mission statement satisfactorily meets the desired criteria. Record a *no* in appropriate cells when the respective mission statement does not meet the stated criteria.

MISSION STATEMENTS

Criterion Productions, Inc.

The mission statement of Criterion Productions, Inc., is to increase the success of all who avail themselves of our products and services by providing image enhancement and a medium that communicates our customer's corporate identity and unique message to a targeted audience. In this, our tenth year of business, Criterion Productions, Inc., pledges to offer a distinct advantage and a superior value in all of your video production needs. We will assist our customers in their endeavors to grow and prosper through celebrity associations that are "effectively appropriate" to their industry, and/or who possess the qualities and characteristics most respected by our customers.

Mid-America Plastics, Inc.

"Continuous Improvement Every Day, In Everything We Do."

   In order for us to accomplish our mission, every employee must be "Committed to Excellence" in everything he or she does by performing his or her job right the first time.

Hatboro Area YMCA

To translate the principles of the YMCA's Christian heritage into programs that nurture children, strengthen families, build strong communities, and develop healthy minds, bodies, and spirits for all.

Integrated Communications, Inc.

Our mission is to be perceived by our customers as providing the highest quality of customer service and salesmanship, delivered with a sense of ownership, friendliness, individual pride, and team spirit. We will accomplish this with the quality of our Wireless Products that supply complete solutions to our customers' needs. And, through unyielding loyalty to our customers and suppliers, ICI will provide opportunities and security to our employees as well as [maximize] our long-term financial growth.

American Counseling Association (ACA)
The Mission of ACA is to promote public confidence and trust in the counseling profession.

Idaho Hospital Association
The mission of the Idaho Hospital Association is to provide representation, advocacy and assistance for member hospitals, healthcare systems and the healthcare services they provide. The Association, through leadership and collaboration among healthcare providers and others, promotes quality healthcare that is adequately financed and accessible to all Idahoans.

Experiential Exercise 2B

Writing a Vision and Mission Statement for Krispy Kreme Doughnuts (KKD)

PURPOSE

There is no one best vision or mission statement for a given organization. Analysts feel that KKD needs a clear vision and mission statement to prosper. Writing a mission statement that includes desired components—and at the same time is inspiring and reconciliatory—requires careful thought. Mission statements should not be too lengthy; statements under two hundred words are desirable.

INSTRUCTIONS

Step 1   Take 15 minutes to write vision and mission statements for KKD. Scan the case for needed details as you prepare your statements.

Step 2   Join with three other classmates to form a group of four people. Read each others' statements silently. As a group, select the best vision statement and best mission statement from your group.

Step 3   Read those "best" statements to the class.

Experiential Exercise 2C

Writing a Vision and Mission Statement for My University

PURPOSE

Most universities have a vision and mission statement. The purpose of this exercise is to give you practice writing a vision and mission statement for a nonprofit organization such as your own university.

INSTRUCTIONS

Step 1   Take 15 minutes to write a vision statement and a mission statement for your university. Your mission statement should not exceed two hundred words.

Step 2   Read your vision and mission statements to the class.

Step 3   Determine whether your institution has a vision and/or mission statement. Look in the front of the college handbook. If your institution has a written statement, contact an appropriate administrator of the institution to inquire as to how and when the statement was prepared. Share this information with the class. Analyze your college's mission statement in light of concepts presented in this chapter.

Experiential Exercise 2D

Conducting Mission Statement Research

PURPOSE

This exercise gives you the opportunity to study the nature and role of vision and mission statements in strategic management.

INSTRUCTIONS

Step 1 Call various organizations in your city or county to identify firms that have developed a formal vision and/or mission statement. Contact nonprofit organizations and government agencies in addition to small and large businesses. Ask to speak with the director, owner, or chief executive officer of each organization. Explain that you are studying vision and mission statements in class and are conducting research as part of a class activity.

Step 2 Ask several executives the following four questions, and record their answers.
   1. When did your organization first develop its vision and/or mission statement? Who was primarily responsible for its development?
   2. How long have your current statements existed? When were they last modified? Why were they modified at that point in time?
   3. By what process are your firm's vision and mission statements altered?
   4. How are your vision and mission statements used in the firm?

Step 3 Provide an overview of your findings to the class.

The External Assessment

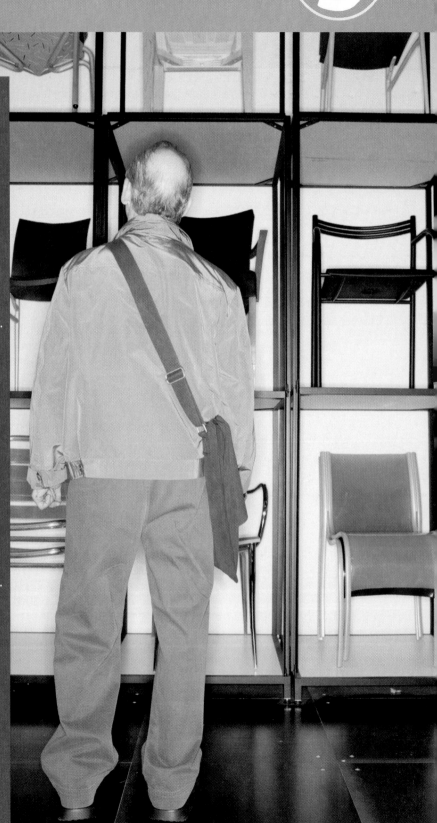

After studying this chapter, you should be able to do the following:

1. Describe how to conduct an external strategic-management audit.

2. Discuss ten major external forces that affect organizations: economic, social, cultural, demographic, environmental, political, governmental, legal, technological, and competitive.

3. Identify key sources of external information, including the Internet.

4. Discuss important forecasting tools used in strategic management.

5. Discuss the importance of monitoring external trends and events.

6. Explain how to develop an EFE Matrix.

7. Explain how to develop a Competitive Profile Matrix.

8. Discuss the importance of gathering competitive intelligence.

9. Describe the trend toward cooperation among competitors.

10. Discuss the economic environment in Russia.

11. Discuss the global challenge facing American firms.

experiential exercises

"notable quotes"

If you're not faster than your competitor, you're in a tenuous position, and if you're only half as fast, you're terminal.
George Salk

The opportunities and threats existing in any situation always exceed the resources needed to exploit the opportunities or avoid the threats. Thus, strategy is essentially a problem of allocating resources. If strategy is to be successful, it must allocate superior resources against a decisive opportunity.
William Cohen

Organizations pursue strategies that will disrupt the normal course of industry events and forge new industry conditions to the disadvantage of competitors.
Ian C. Macmillan

The idea is to concentrate our strength against our competitor's relative weakness.
Bruce Henderson

If everyone is thinking alike, then somebody isn't thinking.
George Patton

It is not the strongest of the species that survive, nor the most intelligent, but the one most responsive to change.
Charles Darwin

Nothing focuses the mind better than the constant sight of a competitor who wants to wipe you off the map.
Wayne Calloway

This chapter examines the tools and concepts needed to conduct an external strategic management audit (sometimes called *environmental scanning* or *industry analysis*). An *external audit* focuses on identifying and evaluating trends and events beyond the control of a single firm, such as increased foreign competition, population shifts to the Sunbelt, an aging society, consumer fear of traveling, and stock market volatility. An external audit reveals key opportunities and threats confronting an organization so that managers can formulate strategies to take advantage of the opportunities and avoid or reduce the impact of threats. This chapter presents a practical framework for gathering, assimilating, and analyzing external information. The Industrial Organization (I/O) view of strategic management is introduced.

The Nature of an External Audit

VISIT THE NET

Reveals how strategic planning evolved from long-range planning and environmental scanning (external audit or assessment).
horizon.unc.edu/projects/ seminars/futuresresearch/ strategic.asp#planning

The purpose of an *external audit* is to develop a finite list of opportunities that could benefit a firm and threats that should be avoided. As the term *finite* suggests, the external audit is not aimed at developing an exhaustive list of every possible factor that could influence the business; rather, it is aimed at identifying key variables that offer actionable responses. Firms should be able to respond either offensively or defensively to the factors by formulating strategies that take advantage of external opportunities or that minimize the impact of potential threats. Figure 3–1 illustrates how the external audit fits into the strategic-management process.

FIGURE 3–1

A Comprehensive Strategic-Management Model

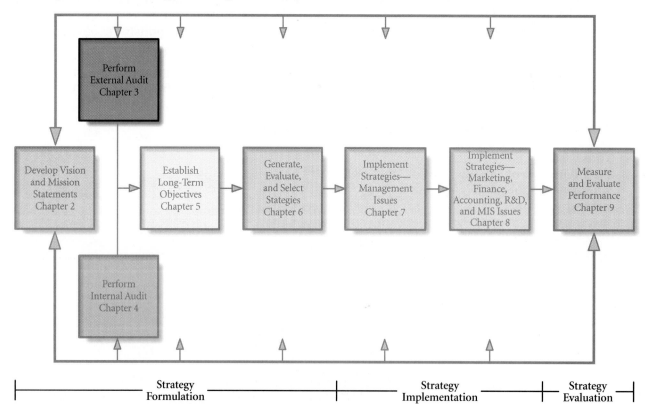

Key External Forces

External forces can be divided into five broad categories: (1) economic forces; (2) social, cultural, demographic, and environmental forces; (3) political, governmental, and legal forces; (4) technological forces; and (5) competitive forces. Relationships among these forces and an organization are depicted in Figure 3–2. External trends and events significantly affect all products, services, markets, and organizations in the world.

Changes in external forces translate into changes in consumer demand for both industrial and consumer products and services. External forces affect the types of products developed, the nature of positioning and market segmentation strategies, the type of services offered, and the choice of businesses to acquire or sell. External forces directly affect both suppliers and distributors. Identifying and evaluating external opportunities and threats enables organizations to develop a clear mission, to design strategies to achieve long-term objectives, and to develop policies to achieve annual objectives.

The increasing complexity of business today is evidenced by more countries developing the capacity and will to compete aggressively in world markets. Foreign businesses and countries are willing to learn, adapt, innovate, and invent to compete successfully in the marketplace. There are more competitive new technologies in Europe and the Far East today than ever before. American businesses can no longer beat foreign competitors with ease.

The Process of Performing an External Audit

The process of performing an external audit must involve as many managers and employees as possible. As emphasized in earlier chapters, involvement in the strategic management process can lead to understanding and commitment from organizational members. Individuals appreciate having the opportunity to contribute ideas and to gain a better understanding of their firm's industry, competitors, and markets.

To perform an external audit, a company first must gather competitive intelligence and information about economic, social, cultural, demographic, environmental, political, governmental, legal, and technological trends. Individuals can be asked to monitor various sources of information, such as key magazines, trade journals, and newspapers. These persons can submit periodic scanning reports to a committee of

FIGURE 3–2

Relationships Between Key External Forces and an Organization

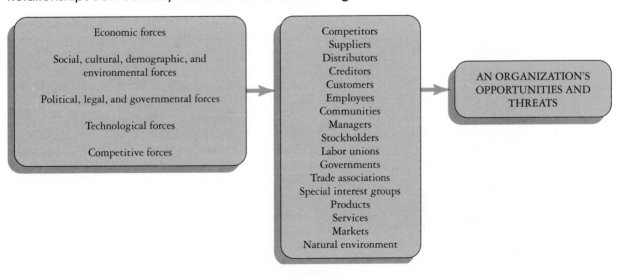

managers charged with performing the external audit. This approach provides a continuous stream of timely strategic information and involves many individuals in the external-audit process. The Internet provides another source for gathering strategic information, as do corporate, university, and public libraries. Suppliers, distributors, salespersons, customers, and competitors represent other sources of vital information.

VISIT THE NET

Describes the external audit process in a university setting.
horizon.unc.edu/projects/ seminars/futuresresearch/ stages.asp

Once information is gathered, it should be assimilated and evaluated. A meeting or series of meetings of managers is needed to collectively identify the most important opportunities and threats facing the firm. These key external factors should be listed on flip charts or a blackboard. A prioritized list of these factors could be obtained by requesting that all managers rank the factors identified, from 1 for the most important opportunity/threat to 20 for the least important opportunity/threat. These key external factors can vary over time and by industry. Relationships with suppliers or distributors are often a critical success factor. Other variables commonly used include market share, breadth of competing products, world economies, foreign affiliates, proprietary and key account advantages, price competitiveness, technological advancements, population shifts, interest rates, and pollution abatement.

Freund emphasized that these key external factors should be (1) important to achieving long-term and annual objectives, (2) measurable, (3) applicable to all competing firms, and (4) hierarchical in the sense that some will pertain to the overall company and others will be more narrowly focused on functional or divisional areas.[1] A final list of the most important key external factors should be communicated and distributed widely in the organization. Both opportunities and threats can be key external factors.

The Industrial Organization (I/O) View

The *Industrial Organization (I/O)* approach to competitive advantage advocates that external (industry) factors are more important than internal factors in a firm achieving competitive advantage. Proponents of the I/O view, such as Michael Porter, contend that organizational performance will be primarily determined by industry forces. Porter's Five-Forces Model, presented later in this chapter, is an example of the I/O perspective, which focuses upon analyzing external forces and industry variables as a basis for getting and keeping competitive advantage. Competitive advantage is determined largely by competitive positioning within an industry, according to I/O advocates. Managing strategically from the I/O perspective entails firms striving to compete in attractive industries, avoiding weak or faltering industries, and gaining a full understanding of key external factor relationships within that attractive industry. I/O research was mainly conducted from the 1960s to the 1980s and provided important contributions to our understanding of how to gain competitive advantage.

I/O theorists contend that the industry in which a firm chooses to compete has a stronger influence on the firm's performance than do the internal functional decisions managers make in marketing, finance, and the like. Firm performance, they contend, is primarily based more on industry properties, such as economies of scale, barriers to market entry, product differentiation, and level of competitiveness than on internal resources, capabilities, structure, and operations. Research findings suggest that approximately 20 percent of a firm's profitability can be explained by the industry, whereas 36 percent of the variance in profitability is attributed to the firm's internal factors (see the RBV discussion in the next chapter).[2]

The I/O view has enhanced our understanding of strategic management. However, it is not a question of whether external or internal factors are more important in gaining and maintaining competitive advantage. Effective integration and understanding of *both* external and internal factors is the key to securing and keeping a competitive advantage. In fact, as will be discussed in Chapter 6, matching key external opportunities/threats with key internal strengths/weaknesses provides the basis for successful strategy formulation.

Economic Forces

As domestic and global economies slowly recover from recession, consumer confidence and disposable income are the lowest in a decade, whereas unemployment and consumer debt are the highest in a decade. Stock prices, interest rates, corporate profits, exports, and imports are all very low in the United States and abroad.

Increasing numbers of two-income households is an economic trend in America. As affluence increases, individuals place a premium on time. Improved customer service, immediate availability, trouble-free operation of products, and dependable maintenance and repair services are becoming more important. Americans today are more willing than ever to pay for good service if it limits inconvenience.

Economic factors have a direct impact on the potential attractiveness of various strategies. For example, when interest rates rise, funds needed for capital expansion become more costly or unavailable. Also, when interest rates rise, discretionary income declines, and the demand for discretionary goods falls. When stock prices increase, the desirability of equity as a source of capital for market development increases. Also, when the market rises, consumer and business wealth expands. A summary of economic variables that often represent opportunities and threats for organizations is provided in Table 3–1.

Trends in the dollar's value have significant and unequal effects on companies in different industries and in different locations. For example, the pharmaceutical, tourism, entertainment, motor vehicle, aerospace, and forest products industries benefit greatly when the dollar falls against the yen and euro. Agricultural and

VISIT THE NET

Provides excellent narrative on NASA's strategic-management process, especially its external assessment activities. Provides NASA's entire strategic plan with outstanding narrative and illustrations about how to do strategic planning.
www.hq.nasa.gov/office/ nsp/toc.htm

TABLE 3–1   Key Economic Variables to Be Monitored

Shift to a service economy in the United States	Import/export factors
Availability of credit	Demand shifts for different categories of goods and services
Level of disposable income	Income differences by region and consumer groups
Propensity of people to spend	
Interest rates	Price fluctuations
Inflation rates	Export of labor and capital from the United States
Money market rates	
Federal government budget deficits	Monetary policies
Gross domestic product trend	Fiscal policies
Consumption patterns	Tax rates
Unemployment trends	European Economic Community (EEC) policies
Worker productivity levels	
Value of the dollar in world markets	Organization of Petroleum Exporting Countries (OPEC) policies
Stock market trends	Coalitions of Lesser Developed Countries (LDC) policies
Foreign countries' economic conditions	

petroleum industries are hurt by the dollar's rise against the currencies of Mexico, Brazil, Venezuela, and Australia. Generally, a strong or high dollar makes American goods more expensive in overseas markets. This worsens America's trade deficit. When the value of the dollar falls, tourism-oriented firms benefit because Americans do not travel abroad as much when the value of the dollar is low; rather, foreigners visit and vacation more in the United States.

A low value of the dollar means lower imports and higher exports; it helps U.S. companies' competitiveness in world markets. In 2004, the dollar fell to four-year lows against the euro and yen, which makes U.S. goods cheaper to foreign consumers and combats deflation by pushing up prices of imports. However, European firms such as Volkswagen AG, Nokia Corp., and Michelin complain that the strong euro hurts their financial performance. The low value of the dollar benefits the U.S. economy in many ways. First, it helps to stave off the risks of deflation in the U.S. and also reduces the U.S. trade deficit. In addition, the low value of the dollar raises the foreign sales and profits of domestic firms, thanks to dollar-induced gains, and encourages foreign countries to lower interest rates and loosen fiscal policy, which stimulates worldwide economic expansion. Some sectors, such as consumer staples, energy, materials, technology, and health care, especially benefit from a low value of the dollar. Manufacturers in many domestic industries in fact benefit because of a weak dollar, which forces foreign rivals to raise prices and extinguish discounts. Domestic firms with big overseas sales, such as McDonald's, greatly benefit from a weak dollar.

In Europe, there are ten countries from Eastern Europe, the Baltics, and the Mediterranean scheduled to join the twelve-country European Union (EU) in May 2004. These countries are excited about adopting the euro as their currency. However, Sweden, in late 2003, rejected the euro as its currency although it has been an EU member since 1994. Denmark and Britain have delayed a vote until 2006 on whether to adopt the euro. Some European countries are having trouble meeting the euro requirement that a member country keep its federal budget deficits below 3 percent of gross domestic product (GDP). Germany and France have conspicuously and brazenly violated this rule since 2001, although they strongly demanded budget discipline as a condition for EU membership in 1997. Both countries' deficit is about 4 percent of GDP.

In the United States, inflation is as low as the Federal Reserve (Fed) wants, even so low that the economy could move into deflation. Yet the Fed's main weapon to guard against deflation is the federal funds rate (the interest rate at which banks can borrow money) which is at a forty-five-year low of 1 percent. With unemployment rates over 6 percent, the Fed is holding interest rates constant, but many analysts forecast rising interest rates as the economy improves.

Every business day, thousands of American workers learn that they will lose their jobs. More than 500,000 annual employee layoffs by U.S. firms in the 1990s led to terms such as *downsizing, rightsizing*, and *decruiting* becoming common. European firms, too, are downsizing. The U.S. and world economies face a sustained period of slow, low-inflationary expansion, global overcapacity, high unemployment, price wars, and increased competitiveness. Thousands of laid-off workers are being forced to become entrepreneurs to make a living. The United States is becoming more entrepreneurial every day.

In Europe, an economic rebound still eluded most countries as 2003 came to an end. Rising joblessness and nervousness about the euro coupled with rising unemployment still curtails consumer spending. In Japan, the economy is in its healthiest state in three years despite lower corporate profits due to a soaring yen. The Japanese government expects GDP to rise 2.1 percent in 2004 with slow but steady economic improvement. Interest rates are low but are expected to rise as economies improve.

Russia's Economy

As the year 2004 begins, Russia's economy has never been healthier. Gross domestic product is growing 6 percent annually, investment is growing 14 percent annually, inflation is falling, foreign debt is low, foreign exchange reserves are mushrooming, and government finances are in surplus.[3] Higher prices for Russian oil are building trade surpluses by $30 billion annually, which is increasing the country's money supply by 40 percent each year. Real incomes of the Russian people are increasing 10 percent annually and the Russian stock market advanced over 30 percent in 2003. Real estate in Moscow increased 25 percent in 2003. However, the question is whether President Putin will make needed reforms before or after the March 2004 election. He should be cutting bureaucracy, overhauling tax and legal procedures, reducing organized crime, toughening up regulations on banks, and making sure Russia's economy does not grow too fast for its own good. In addition, many Russians are struggling to make ends meet. However, President Putin easily won re-election. One-fourth of Russia's population still lives below the poverty line, and this group of people is the main source of support for the Communist Party.[4]

Although Russia is still not a member of the World Trade Organization (WTO), President Putin has made joining the global group of trading partners one of his main economic goals. Moody's Investors Service granted Russia an investment-grade credit rating in October 2003 for the first time ever. One sticking point is that Russia continues to fight hard to limit foreign access to its banking, insurance, and telecommunications markets and also highly regulates prices of its natural gas and fuel exports. In the Fall of 2004, General Motors will begin producing the Opel Astra at its plant in the Southern Russian town of Togliatti. GM has a joint venture with the Russian firm Avtovaz.

Social, Cultural, Demographic, and Environmental Forces

Social, cultural, demographic, and environmental changes have a major impact upon virtually all products, services, markets, and customers. Small, large, for-profit and non-profit organizations in all industries are being staggered and challenged by the opportunities and threats arising from changes in social, cultural, demographic, and environmental variables. In every way, the United States is much different today than it was yesterday, and tomorrow promises even greater changes.

The United States is getting older and less Caucasian. The oldest members of America's 76 million baby boomers plan to retire in 2011, and this has lawmakers and younger taxpayers deeply concerned about who will pay their social security, Medicare, and Medicaid. Individuals age 65 and older in the United States as a percent of the population will rise to 18.5 percent by 2025.

By the year 2075, the United States will have no racial or ethnic majority. This forecast is aggravating tensions over issues such as immigration and affirmative action. Hawaii, California, and New Mexico already have no majority race or ethnic group.

Population of the world passed 6 billion on October 12, 1999; the United States has less than 300 million people. That leaves billions of people outside the United States who may be interested in the products and services produced through domestic firms. Remaining solely domestic is an increasingly risky strategy, especially as the world population continues to grow to estimated numbers of 7 billion in 2013, 8 billion in 2028, and 9 billion in 2054.

Social, cultural, demographic, and environmental trends are shaping the way Americans live, work, produce, and consume. New trends are creating a different type of consumer and, consequently, a need for different products, different services, and different strategies. There are now more American households with people living alone or with unrelated people than there are households consisting of married couples with children. American households are making more and more purchases online, but still are not that comfortable purchasing clothes online—as indicated in the "E-Commerce Perspective." Federated Stores is one of many brick-and-mortar firms pulling back from Internet operations. Federated is substantially reducing its macys.com and its bloomingdales.com Internet catalog operations. Federated has found that customers shopping online are more comfortable buying hard goods, such as jewelry and gifts, than apparel. These two Federated Web sites have never been profitable, but they still remain in operation, primarily as marketing sites. Other traditional retailers are scaling back their Internet operations, including, Kmart with bluelight.com and Wal-Mart with walmart.com, as well as Toys "R" Us and Saks Fifth Avenue.

The United States Census Bureau projects that the number of Hispanics will increase to 15 percent of the population by 2021, when they will become a larger minority group than African Americans in America. Revenues of Hispanic-owned companies in the U.S. are growing faster than other firms.[5] The five largest domestic firms owned by Hispanics are Burt Automotive in Englewood, Colorado, Goya Foods in Secaucus, New Jersey, and three firms in Miami: Brightstar, MasTec, and Related Group of Florida.

During the 1990s, the number of individuals age fifty and over increased 18.5 percent—to 76 million. In contrast, the number of Americans under age fifty grew by just 3.5 percent. The trend toward an older America is good news for restaurants, hotels, airlines, cruise lines, tours, resorts, theme parks, luxury products and services, recreational vehicles, home builders, furniture producers, computer manufacturers, travel services, pharmaceutical firms, automakers, and funeral homes. Older Americans are especially interested in healthcare, financial services, travel, crime prevention, and leisure. The world's longest-living people are the Japanese, with Japanese women living to 86.3 years and men living to 80.1 years on average. By 2050, the Census Bureau projects that the number of Americans age 100 and older will increase to over 834,000 from just under 100,000 centenarians in the United States in 2000. Senior citizens are also senior executives at hundreds of American companies. Examples include 87-year-old William Dillard at Dillard's Department Stores; 79-year-old Sumner Redstone, CEO of Viacom; 71-year-old Ellen Gordon, president of Tootsie Roll Industries; 77-year-old Richard Jacobs, CEO of the Cleveland Indians; 76-year-old Leslie Quick, CEO of Quick & Reilly; 83-year-old Ralph Roberts, chairman of Comcast; and 76-year-old Alan Greenspan, chairman of the Federal Reserve. Americans age 65 and over will increase from 12.6 percent of the U.S. population in 2000 to 20.0 percent by the year 2050.

The aging American population affects the strategic orientation of nearly all organizations. Apartment complexes for the elderly, with one meal a day, transportation, and utilities included in the rent, have increased nationwide. Called *lifecare facilities*, these complexes now exceed 2 million. Some well-known companies building these facilities include Avon, Marriott, and Hyatt. By the year 2005, individuals age 65 and older in the United States will rise to 13 percent of the total population; Japan's elderly population ratio will rise to 17 percent, and Germany's to 19 percent.

Americans are on the move in a population shift to the South and West (Sunbelt) and away from the Northeast and Midwest (Frost Belt). The Internal Revenue Service provides the Census Bureau with massive computer files of demographic data. By comparing individual address changes from year to year, the Census

E-COMMERCE PERSPECTIVE

Do You Purchase Clothes Online?

Although Wal-Mart and other retailers have abandoned the idea of selling apparel online, Sears recently acquired Lands' End, which is successful selling apparel online, and also acquired Structure from Limited Brands. Sears has announced plans to sell clothing online by the end of 2004. It began selling tools online in 1997 and appliances online in 1999. Its new strategy to add clothing to its online sales offerings follows up on Jupiter Research, which estimates that online sales of apparel and accessories increased 42 percent in 2002 to $4.7 billion or 2.7 percent of total sales of such merchandise.

Amazon.com added an apparel department to its Web site in 2002. Wal-Mart and other retailers found that customer returns of clothing items was logically too cumbersome to make the business profitable, but Sears has plans to somehow minimize that problem.

Source: Adapted from Amy Merrick, "Sears to Sell Clothing on Its Web Site," *Wall Street Journal* (September 26, 2003): B2.

Bureau publishes extensive information about population shifts across the country. For example, Nevada is the fastest-growing state. Arizona, Colorado, and Florida are close behind. States incurring the greatest loss of people are North Dakota, West Virginia, Iowa, Louisiana, and Pennsylvania. This type of information can be essential for successful strategy formulation, including where to locate new plants and distribution centers and where to focus marketing efforts.

Americans are becoming less interested in fitness and exercise. Fitness participants declined in the United States by 3.5 percent annually in the 1990s. Makers of fitness products, such as Nike, Reebok International, and CML Group—which makes NordicTrack—are experiencing declines in sales growth. *American Sports Data* in Hartsdale, New York, reports that "the one American in five who exercises regularly is now outnumbered by three couch potatoes."

Except for terrorism, no greater threat to business and society exists than the voracious, continuous decimation and degradation of our natural environment. The U.S. Clean Air Act went into effect in 1994. The U.S. Clean Water Act went into effect in 1984. A summary of important social, cultural, demographic, and environmental variables that represent opportunities or threats for virtually all organizations is given in Table 3–2.

The U.S.-Mexican Border

Stretching 2,100 miles from the Pacific Ocean to the Gulf of Mexico, this 180-mile-wide strip of land is North America's fastest-growing region. The two nations meet along this border, where there are shantytowns just down the street from luxury residential neighborhoods.

There are now over 1,500 *maquiladoras* (assembly plants) on the Mexican side of the border. However, the *maquiladoras* have been under slow, steady assault from China despite the SARS epidemic there. China replaced Mexico in 2003 as the largest exporter to the U.S. For the first time in 2002 and again in 2003, China replaced the U.S. as the world's hottest destination for foreign direct investment. Because of China, Asia overtook Europe for the first time in 2003 as the continent receiving the most *foreign direct investment.* China has cheaper labor than Mexico and China gives companies more site location incentives than Mexico. An assembly-line worker in

TABLE 3-2   Key Social, Cultural, Demographic, and Environmental Variables

Childbearing rates	Attitudes toward retirement
Number of special interest groups	Attitudes toward leisure time
Number of marriages	Attitudes toward product quality
Number of divorces	Attitudes toward customer service
Number of births	Pollution control
Number of deaths	Attitudes toward foreign peoples
Immigration and emigration rates	Energy conservation
Social security programs	Social programs
Life expectancy rates	Number of churches
Per capita income	Number of church members
Location of retailing, manufacturing, and service businesses	Social responsibility
Attitudes toward business	Attitudes toward careers
Lifestyles	Population changes by race, age, sex, and level of affluence
Traffic congestion	Attitudes toward authority
Inner-city environments	Population changes by city, county, state, region, and country
Average disposable income	
Trust in government	Value placed on leisure time
Attitudes toward government	Regional changes in tastes and preferences
Attitudes toward work	
Buying habits	Number of women and minority workers
Ethical concerns	Number of high school and college graduates by geographic area
Attitudes toward saving	
Sex roles	Recycling
Attitudes toward investing	Waste management
Racial equality	Air pollution
Use of birth control	Water pollution
Average level of education	Ozone depletion
Government regulation	Endangered species

Guadalajara, Mexico, earns $2.50 to $3.50 an hour, whereas his counterpart in Guangdong, China, makes 50 cents to 80 cents. China joined the World Trade Organization (WTO) in 2001 and now has thousands of seasoned supplier companies available to firms locating there. Mexico's exports to the U.S. grew 1.2 percent in 2002 while China's exports to the U.S. surged 19 percent.[6] China is a ferocious technological competitor, whereas Mexico recently ranked number forty-seven by the World Economic Forum behind Botswana in technological development. Mexico's corporate income tax rate is 34 percent, double China's rate. Mexico's electricity rates are 40 percent higher than China's. Not all companies are relocating from Mexico to China, but hundreds are, and thousands more are choosing China over Mexico for new operations. The impact of this trend on the economic well-being of both Mexico and the U.S. is profound.

Political, Governmental, and Legal Forces

Federal, state, local, and foreign governments are major regulators, deregulators, subsidizers, employers, and customers of organizations. Political, governmental, and legal factors, therefore, can represent key opportunities or threats for both small and large organizations.

For industries and firms that depend heavily on government contracts or subsidies, political forecasts can be the most important part of an external audit. Changes in patent laws, antitrust legislation, tax rates, and lobbying activities can affect firms significantly. The U.S. Justice Department offers excellent information at its Web site (**www.usdoj.gov**) on such topics.

In the world of biopolitics, Americans are still deeply divided over issues such as assisted suicide, genetic testing, genetic engineering, cloning, stem-cell research, and abortion. Americans are also divided regarding feelings toward the natural environment policies and practices of the Bush administration—as indicated in the "Natural Environment Perspective." Political issues have great ramifications for companies in many industries, ranging from pharmaceuticals to computers.

The increasing global interdependence among economies, markets, governments, and organizations makes it imperative that firms consider the possible impact of political variables on the formulation and implementation of competitive strategies.

For example, the United States, Japan, and Europe are critical of the Chinese government for its fixed exchange rate, which analysts contend takes jobs from other countries and artificially cuts the cost of China's exports by significantly undervaluing its currency. A rise in the value of China's currency would make Chinese-made goods more expensive abroad. China's currency is called the yuan, which is fixed at 8.30 yuan to $1.00.

In Europe, many large multinational firms such as John Deere, Polo Ralph Lauren, Gillette, Cargill, and General Mills are moving their headquarters from France, Netherlands, and Germany to Switzerland and Ireland in order to avoid costs associated with *tax harmonization*—a term that refers to the EU's effort to end competitive tax breaks among member countries. In the World Economic Forum's most recent annual report on global competitiveness, ratings for the Netherlands, Belgium, France, and Germany plunged while the ratings for Switzerland, a non-EU member, surged. Although the EU strives to standardize tax breaks, member countries vigorously defend their right to politically and legally set their own tax rates. Behind Switzerland as the most attractive European location for corporations, Ireland keeps its corporate tax rates low which is why Ingersoll-Rand recently moved much of its operations there. About 650 American companies already have operations in Switzerland.

Political forecasting can be especially critical and complex for multinational firms that depend on foreign countries for natural resources, facilities, the distribution of products, special assistance, or customers. Strategists today must possess skills that enable them to deal more legalistically and politically than previous strategists, whose attention was directed more toward economic and technical affairs of the firm. Strategists today are spending more time anticipating and influencing public policy actions. They spend more time meeting with government officials, attending hearings and government-sponsored conferences, giving public speeches, and meeting with trade groups, industry associations, and government agency directors. Before entering or expanding international operations, strategists need a good understanding of the political and decision-making processes in countries where their firms may conduct business. For example, republics that made up the former Soviet Union differ greatly in wealth, resources, language, and lifestyle.

NATURAL ENVIRONMENT PERSPECTIVE

Environmentalists Are Concerned About Bush Administration Policies

Politicians and government policies can and do have tremendous impact on business, society and, yes, the natural environment. The George Bush administration has come under increasing criticism from environmentalists who contend that U.S. government policies are too severely easing environmental standards regarding clean air, water, and land. For example, in 2003, the Environmental Protection Agency (EPA) created loopholes in the Clean Air Act that allow factories to upgrade facilities without installing improved pollution control devices. New rules also restrict jurisdiction of the Clean Water Act. Similarly, the U.S. Interior Department is pushing proposed lease sales that would allow offshore oil and gas development in the Beaufort Sea off Alaska's northern coast and the Arctic National Wildlife Refuge. Also, the Forest Service has refused to grant wilderness protection to 3 million acres of Alaska's Tongass National Forest, which is the largest roadless area in the U.S. Logging and clearcutting can now begin there. The Bush administration also has ended the 25-year-old ban on the sale of land polluted with polychlorinated biphenyls (PCBs). This ban was preventing hundreds of polluted sites from being redeveloped in ways that could spread the toxins and raise public health risks. More than 1,000 pieces of land nationwide are contaminated. The Department of Interior differs sharply with the Yellowstone National Park staff in its assessments of the threats facing that natural treasure. President Bush was the only major head of state who refused to attend 2003's most important environmental meeting—the World Summit on Sustainable Development held in South Africa. The list of such environmentalists' concerns is very extensive and should be a concern to all of us.

Increasingly in our world, what is good for the environment is good for business because a healthy environment is good for business and society. We should strive to protect rather than further harm our air, water, land, and oceans. Our belief that no one owns the ocean, for example, has allowed us seemingly to tolerate no one caring about the ocean's health. Scientists have documented that soot, which is too small to see in the air and arises from factories, power plants, cars, buses, and trucks, causes heart, lung, and other diseases. Cities in the U.S. with the most soot include Atlanta, Birmingham, Chicago, Cincinnati, Cleveland, Detroit, Indianapolis, Knoxville, Los Angeles, Louisville, Pittsburgh, and St. Louis. Soot levels exceed EPA limits in all these cities.

Facts such as those that follow exemplify our need to do as much as we can to preserve rather than harm the environment, and more than the Bush administration mandates.

1. Oil running off U.S. streets and driveways and ultimately flowing into the oceans is equal to an *Exxon Valdez* oil spill (10.9 million gallons) every eight months.
2. More than 13,000 U.S. beaches are closed or under pollution advisory this year, and this number increased 20 percent from last year.
3. U.S. coastal marshes, which filter pollutants and serve as nurseries for wildlife, are disappearing at a rate of 20,000 acres per year.
4. Global air temperature is expected to warm by 2.5 degrees to 10.4 degrees in the twenty first century, raising the global sea level by 4 to 35 inches.

Sources: Adapted from Christopher Tulou (Executive Director), *Pew Oceans Commission Summary Report* (May 2003): 1–37. Peter Eisler, "EPA Lifts Ban on Selling PCB Sites," *USA Today* (September 2, 2003): 1A. Also, Traci Watson, "EPA Urges Look at Lower Soot Limits," *USA Today* (September 3, 2002): 3A; John Carey, "How Green is the White House," *BusinessWeek* (November 3, 2003): 96–98.

Increasing global competition accents the need for accurate political, governmental, and legal forecasts. Many strategists will have to become familiar with political systems in Europe, Africa, and Asia and with trading currency futures. East Asian countries already have become world leaders in labor-intensive industries. A world market has emerged from what previously was a multitude of distinct national markets, and the climate for international business today is much more favorable than yesterday. Mass communication and high technology are creating similar patterns of consumption in diverse cultures worldwide. This means that many companies may find it difficult to survive by relying solely on domestic markets.

It is no exaggeration that in an industry that is, or is rapidly becoming, global, the riskiest possible posture is to remain a domestic competitor. The domestic competitor will watch as more aggressive companies use this growth to capture economies of scale and learning. The domestic competitor will then be faced with an attack on domestic markets using different (and possibly superior) technology, product design, manufacturing, marketing approaches, and economies of scale. A few examples suggest how extensive the phenomenon of world markets has already become. Hewlett-Packard's manufacturing chain reaches halfway around the globe, from well-paid, skilled engineers in California to low-wage assembly workers in Malaysia. General Electric has survived as a manufacturer of inexpensive audio products by centralizing its world production in Singapore.[7]

Local, state, and federal laws, regulatory agencies, and special interest groups can have a major impact on the strategies of small, large, for-profit, and nonprofit organizations. Many companies have altered or abandoned strategies in the past because of political or governmental actions. A summary of political, governmental, and legal variables that can represent key opportunities or threats to organizations is provided in Table 3–3.

TABLE 3-3   Some Political, Governmental, and Legal Variables

Government regulations or deregulations	Sino-American relationships
Changes in tax laws	Russian-American relationships
Special tariffs	European-American relationships
Political action committees	African-American relationships
Voter participation rates	Import-export regulations
Number, severity, and location of government protests	Government fiscal and monetary policy changes
Number of patents	Political conditions in foreign countries
Changes in patent laws	Special local, state, and federal laws
Environmental protection laws	Lobbying activities
Level of defense expenditures	Size of government budgets
Legislation on equal employment	World oil, currency, and labor markets
Level of government subsidies	Location and severity of terrorist activities
Antitrust legislation	Local, state, and national elections

Technological Forces

Revolutionary technological changes and discoveries are having a dramatic impact on organizations. Superconductivity advancements alone, which increase the power of electrical products by lowering resistance to current, are revolutionizing business operations, especially in the transportation, utility, healthcare, electrical, and computer industries.

The *Internet* is acting as a national and even global economic engine that is spurring productivity, a critical factor in a country's ability to improve living standards; and it is saving companies billions of dollars in distribution and transaction costs from direct sales to self-service systems.

The Internet is changing the very nature of opportunities and threats by altering the life cycles of products, increasing the speed of distribution, creating new products and services, erasing limitations of traditional geographic markets, and changing the historical trade-off between production standardization and flexibility. The Internet is altering economies of scale, changing entry barriers, and redefining the relationship between industries and various suppliers, creditors, customers, and competitors.

To effectively capitalize on e-commerce, a number of organizations are establishing two new positions in their firms: *chief information officer (CIO)* and *chief technology officer (CTO)*. This trend reflects the growing importance of *information technology (IT)* in strategic management. A CIO and CTO work together to ensure that information needed to formulate, implement, and evaluate strategies is available where and when it is needed. These individuals are responsible for developing, maintaining, and updating a company's information database. The CIO is more a manager, managing the overall external-audit process; the CTO is more a technician, focusing on technical issues such as data acquisition, data processing, decision-support systems, and software and hardware acquisition.

Technological forces represent major opportunities and threats that must be considered in formulating strategies. Technological advancements can dramatically affect organizations' products, services, markets, suppliers, distributors, competitors, customers, manufacturing processes, marketing practices, and competitive position. Technological advancements can create new markets, result in a proliferation of new and improved products, change the relative competitive cost positions in an industry, and render existing products and services obsolete. Technological changes can reduce or eliminate cost barriers between businesses, create shorter production runs, create shortages in technical skills, and result in changing values and expectations of employees, managers, and customers. Technological advancements can create new competitive advantages that are more powerful than existing advantages. No company or industry today is insulated against emerging technological developments. In high-tech industries, identification and evaluation of key technological opportunities and threats can be the most important part of the external strategic-management audit.

Organizations that traditionally have limited technology expenditures to what they can fund after meeting marketing and financial requirements urgently need a reversal in thinking. The pace of technological change is increasing and literally wiping out businesses every day. An emerging consensus holds that technology management is one of the key responsibilities of strategists. Firms should pursue strategies that take advantage of technological opportunities to achieve sustainable, competitive advantages in the marketplace.

Technology-based issues will underlie nearly every important decision that strategists make. Crucial to those decisions will be the ability to approach technology planning analytically and strategically. . . . technology can be planned and managed using formal techniques similar to those used in business and capital investment planning. An effective technology strategy is built on a penetrating analysis of technology opportunities and threats, and an assessment of the relative importance of these factors to overall corporate strategy.[8]

In practice, critical decisions about technology too often are delegated to lower organizational levels or are made without an understanding of their strategic implications. Many strategists spend countless hours determining market share, positioning products in terms of features and price, forecasting sales and market size, and monitoring distributors; yet too often, technology does not receive the same respect.

Not all sectors of the economy are affected equally by technological developments. The communications, electronics, aeronautics, and pharmaceutical industries are much more volatile than the textile, forestry, and metals industries. For strategists in industries affected by rapid technological change, identifying and evaluating technological opportunities and threats can represent the most important part of an external audit.

For example, in the office supply industry, business customers find that purchasing supplies over the Internet is more convenient than shopping in a store. Office Depot was the first office supply company to establish a Web site for this purpose and remains the largest Internet office supply retailer, with close to $1 billion in sales. Staples, Inc., has recently also entered the Internet office supply business with its **staples.com** Web site, but it has yet to make a profit on these operations, although revenue from the site is growing dramatically.

Competitive Forces

The top five U.S. competitors in four different industries are identified in Table 3–4. An important part of an external audit is identifying rival firms and determining their strengths, weaknesses, capabilities, opportunities, threats, objectives, and strategies.

Collecting and evaluating information on competitors is essential for successful strategy formulation. Identifying major competitors is not always easy because many firms have divisions that compete in different industries. Most multidivisional firms generally do not provide sales and profit information on a divisional basis for competitive reasons. Also, privately held firms do not publish any financial or marketing information.

However, many businesses use the Internet to obtain most of their information on competitors. The Internet is fast, thorough, accurate, and increasingly indispensable in this regard. Addressing questions about competitors such as those presented in Table 3–5 is important in performing an external audit.

Competition in virtually all industries can be described as intense—and sometimes as cutthroat. For example, when Italian car maker Fiat Auto had financial troubles in 2003, Ford Motor boosted advertising and marketing spending 10 to 20 percent in Italy, even though Ford was slashing expenses elsewhere. Renault SA

VISIT THE NET

Provides information regarding the importance of gathering information about competitors. This Web site offers audio answers to key questions about intelligence systems.
www.fuld.com

TABLE 3-4   The Top Five U.S. Competitors in Four Different Industries in 2003

	2003 SALES (IN MILLIONS)	% CHANGE FROM 2002	2003 PROFITS (IN MILLIONS)	% CHANGE FROM 2002
BEVERAGES				
PepsiCo	26,971	+ 7	3,568	+ 19
Coca-Cola Enterprises	17,330	+ 8	676	+ 37
Anheuser-Busch	14,146	+ 4	2,075	+ 7
Pepsi Bottling Group	10,265	+11	422	− 1
Coors (Adolph)	4,000	+ 6	174	+ 8
PHARMACEUTICALS				
Pfizer	45,188	+40	1,639	− 82
Johnson & Johnson	41,862	+15	7,197	+ 9
Merck	22,485	+ 5	6,589	− 3
Bristol-Myers Squibb	20,671	+14	2,952	+ 45
Abbott Laboratories	19,680	+11	2,753	− 1
MACHINERY				
Caterpillar	22,763	+13	1,099	+ 38
Deere	15,534	+11	643	+101
Illinois Tool Works	10,035	+ 6	1,040	+ 12
Ingersoll-Rand	9,876	+11	593	+ 62
Paccar	8,194	+14	526	+ 42
COMPUTERS				
IBM	89,131	+10	7,613	+ 43
Hewlett-Packard	73,061	+29	2,539	None
Dell	39,667	+18	2,499	+ 27
Sun Microsystems	11,196	− 8	−1,446	None
Apple Computer	6,741	+15	137	+552

Source: Adapted from *BusinessWeek,* February 23, 2004, pp. 60–84.

and Peugeot SA, other rivals to Fiat, also boosted consumer incentives in the Italian market. Fiat's market share in Italy has recently dropped from 40 percent to 27 percent. If a firm detects weakness in a competitor, no mercy at all is shown in capitalizing on its problems.

Seven characteristics describe the most competitive companies in America: (1) Market share matters; the 90th share point isn't as important as the 91st, and nothing is more dangerous than falling to 89; (2) Understand and remember precisely what business you are in; (3) Whether it's broke or not, fix it—make it better; not just products, but the whole company, if necessary; (4) Innovate or evaporate; particularly in technology-driven businesses, nothing quite recedes like success; (5) Acquisition is essential to growth; the most successful purchases are in niches that add a technology or a related market; (6) People make a difference; tired of hearing it? Too bad; (7) There is no substitute for quality and no greater

TABLE 3-5   Key Questions About Competitors

1. What are the major competitors' strengths?
2. What are the major competitors' weaknesses?
3. What are the major competitors' objectives and strategies?
4. How will the major competitors most likely respond to current economic, social, cultural, demographic, environmental, political, governmental, legal, technological, and competitive trends affecting our industry?
5. How vulnerable are the major competitors to our alternative company strategies?
6. How vulnerable are our alternative strategies to successful counterattack by our major competitors?
7. How are our products or services positioned relative to major competitors?
8. To what extent are new firms entering and old firms leaving this industry?
9. What key factors have resulted in our present competitive position in this industry?
10. How have the sales and profit rankings of major competitors in the industry changed over recent years? Why have these rankings changed that way?
11. What is the nature of supplier and distributor relationships in this industry?
12. To what extent could substitute products or services be a threat to competitors in this industry?

threat than failing to be cost-competitive on a global basis; these are complementary concepts, not mutually exclusive ones.[9]

Competitive Intelligence Programs

What is competitive intelligence? *Competitive intelligence (CI)*, as formally defined by the Society of Competitive Intelligence Professionals (SCIP), is a systematic and ethical process for gathering and analyzing information about the competition's activities and general business trends to further a business's own goals (SCIP Web site).

Good competitive intelligence in business, as in the military, is one of the keys to success. The more information and knowledge a firm can obtain about its competitors, the more likely it is that it can formulate and implement effective strategies. Major competitors' weaknesses can represent external opportunities; major competitors' strengths may represent key threats.

According to *BusinessWeek*, there are more than 5,000 corporate spies now actively engaged in intelligence activities, and nine out of ten large companies have employees dedicated solely to gathering competitive intelligence.[10] The article contends that many large U.S. companies spend more than $1 million annually tracking their competitors. Evidence suggests that the benefits of corporate spying include increased revenues, lower costs, and better decision making.

Unfortunately, the majority of U.S. executives grew up in times when American firms dominated foreign competitors so much that gathering competitive intelligence seemed not worth the effort. Too many of these executives still cling to these attitudes—to the detriment of their organizations today. Even most MBA programs do not offer a course in competitive and business intelligence, thus reinforcing this attitude. As a consequence, three strong misperceptions about business intelligence prevail among American executives today:

1. Running an intelligence program requires lots of people, computers, and other resources.
2. Collecting intelligence about competitors violates antitrust laws; business intelligence equals espionage.
3. Intelligence gathering is an unethical business practice.[11]

VISIT THE NET

Describes the nature and role of strategic planning in a firm.
www.nonprofits.org/ npofaq/03/22.html

All three of these perceptions are totally misguided. Any discussions with a competitor about price, market, or geography intentions could violate antitrust statutes, but this fact must not lure a firm into underestimating the need for and benefits of systematically collecting information about competitors for the purpose of enhancing a firm's effectiveness. The Internet has become an excellent medium for gathering competitive intelligence. Information gathering from employees, managers, suppliers, distributors, customers, creditors, and consultants also can make the difference between having superior or just average intelligence and overall competitiveness.

Firms need an effective competitive intelligence (CI) program. The three basic missions of a CI program are (1) to provide a general understanding of an industry and its competitors, (2) to identify areas in which competitors are vulnerable and to assess the impact strategic actions would have on competitors, and (3) to identify potential moves that a competitor might make that would endanger a firm's position in the market.[12] Competitive information is equally applicable for strategy formulation, implementation, and evaluation decisions. An effective CI program allows all areas of a firm to access consistent and verifiable information in making decisions. All members of an organization—from the chief executive officer to custodians—are valuable intelligence agents and should feel themselves to be a part of the CI process. Special characteristics of a successful CI program include flexibility, usefulness, timeliness, and cross-functional cooperation.

The increasing emphasis on *competitive analysis* in the United States is evidenced by corporations putting this function on their organizational charts under job titles such as Director of Competitive Analysis, Competitive Strategy Manager, Director of Information Services, or Associate Director of Competitive Assessment. The responsibilities of a *director of competitive analysis* include planning, collecting data, analyzing data, facilitating the process of gathering and analyzing data, disseminating intelligence on a timely basis, researching special issues, and recognizing what information is important and who needs to know. Competitive intelligence is not corporate espionage because 95 percent of the information a company needs in order to make strategic decisions is available and accessible to the public. Sources of competitive information include trade journals, want ads, newspaper articles, and government filings, as well as customers, suppliers, distributors, competitors themselves, and the Internet.

Unethical tactics such as bribery, wiretapping, and computer break-ins should never be used to obtain information. Marriott and Motorola—two American companies that do a particularly good job of gathering competitive intelligence—agree that all the information you could wish for can be collected without resorting to unethical tactics. They keep their intelligence staffs small, usually under five people, and spend less than $200,000 per year on gathering competitive intelligence.

Unilever recently sued Procter & Gamble (P&G) over that company's corporate-espionage activities to obtain the secrets of its Unilever hair-care business.

After spending $3 million to establish a team to find out about competitors in the domestic hair-care industry, P&G allegedly took roughly eighty documents from garbage bins outside Unilever's Chicago offices. P&G produces Pantene and Head & Shoulders shampoos, while Unilver has hair-care brands such as ThermaSilk, Suave, Salon Selectives, and Finesse. Similarly, Oracle Corp. recently admitted that detectives it hired paid janitors to go through Microsoft Corp.'s garbage, looking for evidence to use in court.

An interesting aspect of any competitive analysis discussion is whether strategies themselves should be secret or open within firms. The Chinese warrior Sun Tzu and military leaders today strive to keep strategies secret, as war is based on deception. However, for a business organization, secrecy may not be best. Keeping strategies secret from employees and stakeholders at large could severely inhibit employee and stakeholder communication, understanding, and commitment and also forgo valuable input that these persons could have regarding formulation and/or implementation of that strategy. Thus strategists in a particular firm must decide for themselves whether the risk of rival firms easily knowing and exploiting a firm's strategies is worth the benefit of improved employee and stakeholder motivation and input. Most executives agree that some strategic information should remain confidential to top managers, and that steps should be taken to ensure that such information is not disseminated beyond the inner circle. For a firm that you may own or manage, would you advocate openness or secrecy in regard to strategies being formulated and implemented?

Cooperation Among Competitors

Strategies that stress cooperation among competitors are being used more. For example, Lockheed teamed up with British Aerospace PLC to compete against Boeing Company to develop the next-generation U.S. fighter jet. Lockheed's cooperative strategy with a profitable partner in the Airbus Industrie consortium encourages broader Lockheed–European collaboration as Europe's defense industry consolidates. The British firm offers Lockheed special expertise in the areas of short takeoff and vertical landing technologies, systems integration, and low-cost design and manufacturing.

Cooperative agreements between competitors are even becoming popular. For example, Boeing and Lockheed are working together to modernize the United States' overburdened air-traffic-control system. Northrop Grumman, also a competitor in the defense industry, may join the cooperative agreement too. For collaboration between competitors to succeed, both firms must contribute something distinctive, such as technology, distribution, basic research, or manufacturing capacity. But a major risk is that unintended transfers of important skills or technology may occur at organizational levels below where the deal was signed.[13] Information not covered in the formal agreement often gets traded in the day-to-day interactions and dealings of engineers, marketers, and product developers. Firms often give away too much information to rival firms when operating under cooperative agreements! Tighter formal agreements are needed.

Fierce competitors America Online, Microsoft, and Yahoo! for the first time joined forces in 2003 to form a united front against spam. Spam costs U.S. companies nearly $10 billion annually and now accounts for one-half of all e-mail sent. "The Internet quality of life has deteriorated due to out-of-control spammers," says Nicholas Graham at AOL. Spammers, like hackers, change tactics frequently and are growing in numbers because it is a cheap way to reach millions of consumers. Worldwide spam messages sent

VISIT THE NET

Gives 30+ pages of excellent detail on "Developing a Business Strategy."
www.planware.org/strategy.htm

daily grew from 4.0 to 8.8 billion from 2001 to 2004.[14] The three large competing ISP firms are jointly developing software and guidelines to combat spam, which bogs down Internet traffic worldwide and steals time from almost all Internet users.

Perhaps the best example of rival firms in an industry forming alliances to compete against each other is the airline industry. There were three major alliances that encompassed 40 airlines in late 2003. The Star Alliance has 16 airlines such as Air Canada, Mixicana, Spanair, United, and Varig, while the OneWorld Alliance has 8 airlines such as American, British Air, and LanChile, and finally, SkyTeam Alliance has 6 airlines such as Air France, Delta, and Korean Air. KLM is set to join SkyTeam soon, Swiss International is scheduled to join OneWorld, and USAirways is scheduled to join Star Alliance. Firms are moving to compete as groups within alliances more and more as it becomes increasingly difficult to survive alone in some industries.

The idea of joining forces with a competitor is not easily accepted by Americans, who often view cooperation and partnerships with skepticism and suspicion. Indeed, joint ventures and cooperative arrangements among competitors demand a certain amount of trust if companies are to combat paranoia about whether one firm will injure the other. However, multinational firms are becoming more globally cooperative, and increasing numbers of domestic firms are joining forces with competitive foreign firms to reap mutual benefits. Kathryn Harrigan at Columbia University says, "Within a decade, most companies will be members of teams that compete against each other."

American companies often enter alliances primarily to avoid investments, being more interested in reducing the costs and risks of entering new businesses or markets than in acquiring new skills. In contrast, *learning from the partner* is a major reason why Asian and European firms enter into cooperative agreements. American firms, too, should place learning high on the list of reasons to be cooperative with competitors. American companies often form alliances with Asian firms to gain an understanding of their manufacturing excellence, but Asian competence in this area is not easily transferable. Manufacturing excellence is a complex system that includes employee training and involvement, integration with suppliers, statistical process controls, value engineering, and design. In contrast, American know-how in technology and related areas more easily can be imitated. American firms thus need to be careful not to give away more intelligence than they receive in cooperative agreements with rival Asian firms.

Competitive Analysis: Porter's Five-Forces Model

As illustrated in Figure 3–3, *Porter's Five-Forces Model* of competitive analysis is a widely used approach for developing strategies in many industries. The intensity of competition among firms varies widely across industries. Table 3–6 reveals the average return on equity for firms in twenty-four different industries in 2003. Intensity of competition is highest in lower-return industries. For example, in the electrical and electronics industry, collective impact of competitive forces is so brutal that the industry is clearly "unattractive" from a profit-making standpoint. Rivalry among existing firms is severe, new rivals can enter the industry with relative ease, and both suppliers and customers can exercise considerable bargaining leverage. Note in Table 3–6 that the average 2003 return on equity among firms in this industry was

FIGURE 3–3

The Five-Forces Model of Competition

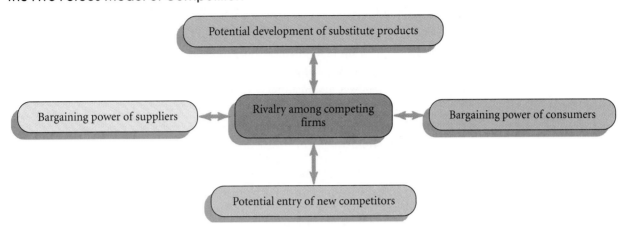

TABLE 3–6   Intensity of Competition Among Firms in Different Industries—2003 Results Provided

RANK	INDUSTRY	2003 AVERAGE RETURN ON EQUITY
1.	Materials	5.1
2.	Semiconductors and Equipment	5.3
3.	Real Estate	6.8
4.	Technology Hardware	7.6
5.	Transportation	8.8
6.	Automobiles and Components	9.0
7.	Media	9.0
8.	Utilities	9.1
9.	Telecommunication Services	10.0
10.	Hotels/Restaurants/Leisure	10.5
11.	Insurance	11.5
12.	Software and Services	12.6
13.	Capital Goods	14.5
14.	Retailing	14.6
15.	Pharmaceuticals and Biotechnology	15.4
16.	Diversified Financials	16.6
17.	Commercial Services and Supplies	16.7
18.	Food and Staples Retailing	17.9
19.	Energy	18.3
20.	Banks	18.3
21.	Consumer Durables and Apparel	18.3
22.	Health Care Equipment/Services	19.0
23.	Food/Beverage/Tobacco	20.3
24.	Household and Personal Products	36.6

Source: Adapted from *BusinessWeek*, February 23, 2004, p. 60–84.

negative 44.6 percent. According to Porter, the nature of competitiveness in a given industry can be viewed as a composite of five forces:

1. Rivalry among competing firms
2. Potential entry of new competitors
3. Potential development of substitute products
4. Bargaining power of suppliers
5. Bargaining power of consumers

Rivalry Among Competing Firms

Rivalry among competing firms is usually the most powerful of the five competitive forces. The strategies pursued by one firm can be successful only to the extent that they provide competitive advantage over the strategies pursued by rival firms. Changes in strategy by one firm may be met with retaliatory countermoves, such as lowering prices, enhancing quality, adding features, providing services, extending warranties, and increasing advertising.

In the Internet world, competitiveness is fierce. Amazon.com watches in dismay as customers use its site's easy-to-use format, in-depth reviews, expert recommendations—and then bypass the cash register as they click their way over to deep-discounted sites such as Buy.com to make their purchases. Buy.com's CEO says, "The Internet is going to shrink retailers' margins to the point where they will not survive." Price-comparison Web sites allow consumers to efficiently find the lowest-priced seller on the Internet. Kate Delhagen of Forrester Research says, "If you're a consumer and you're thinking about any kind of researched purchase, you're leaving thousands of dollars on the table if you don't at least look online."[15] The costs of setting up a great e-commerce site are nothing compared to the cost of acquiring real estate for building retail stores—or even printing and mailing catalogs.

Free-flowing information on the Internet is driving down prices and inflation worldwide. The Internet, coupled with the common currency in Europe, enables consumers to easily make price comparisons across countries. Just for a moment, consider the implications for car dealers who used to know everything about a new car's pricing, while you, the consumer, knew very little. You could bargain, but being in the dark, you rarely could win. Now you can go to Web sites such as CarPoint or Edmunds.com and know more about new car prices than the car salesperson, and you can even shop online in a few hours at every dealership within five hundred miles to find the best price and terms. So you, the consumer, can win. This is true in many, if not most, business-to-consumer and business-to-business sales transactions today.

The intensity of rivalry among competing firms tends to increase as the number of competitors increases, as competitors become more equal in size and capability, as demand for the industry's products declines, and as price cutting becomes common. Rivalry also increases when consumers can switch brands easily; when barriers to leaving the market are high; when fixed costs are high; when the product is perishable; when rival firms are diverse in strategies, origins, and culture; and when mergers and acquisitions are common in the industry. As rivalry among competing firms intensifies, industry profits decline, in some cases to the point where an industry becomes inherently unattractive.

Potential Entry of New Competitors

Whenever new firms can easily enter a particular industry, the intensity of competitiveness among firms increases. Barriers to entry, however, can include the need to gain economies of scale quickly, the need to gain technology and specialized know-how, the lack of experience, strong customer loyalty, strong brand preferences, large capital requirements, lack of adequate distribution channels, government regulatory policies, tariffs, lack of access to raw materials, possession of patents, undesirable locations, counterattack by entrenched firms, and potential saturation of the market.

Despite numerous barriers to entry, new firms sometimes enter industries with higher-quality products, lower prices, and substantial marketing resources. The strategist's job, therefore, is to identify potential new firms entering the market, to monitor the new rival firms' strategies, to counterattack as needed, and to capitalize on existing strengths and opportunities.

Potential Development of Substitute Products

In many industries, firms are in close competition with producers of substitute products in other industries. Examples are plastic container producers competing with glass, paperboard, and aluminum can producers, and acetaminophen manufacturers competing with other manufacturers of pain and headache remedies. The presence of substitute products puts a ceiling on the price that can be charged before consumers will switch to the substitute product.

Competitive pressures arising from substitute products increase as the relative price of substitute products declines and as consumers' switching costs decrease. The competitive strength of substitute products is best measured by the inroads into the marketshare those products obtain, as well as those firms' plans for increased capacity and market penetration.

Bargaining Power of Suppliers

The bargaining power of suppliers affects the intensity of competition in an industry, especially when there is a large number of suppliers, when there are only a few good substitute raw materials, or when the cost of switching raw materials is especially costly. It is often in the best interest of both suppliers and producers to assist each other with reasonable prices, improved quality, development of new services, just-in-time deliveries, and reduced inventory costs, thus enhancing long-term profitability for all concerned.

Firms may pursue a backward integration strategy to gain control or ownership of suppliers. This strategy is especially effective when suppliers are unreliable, too costly, or not capable of meeting a firm's needs on a consistent basis. Firms generally can negotiate more favorable terms with suppliers when backward integration is a commonly used strategy among rival firms in an industry.

Bargaining Power of Consumers

When customers are concentrated or large, or buy in volume, their bargaining power represents a major force affecting the intensity of competition in an industry. Rival firms may offer extended warranties or special services to gain customer loyalty whenever the bargaining power of consumers is substantial. Bargaining power of consumers also is higher when the products being purchased are standard or undifferentiated. When this is the case, consumers often can negotiate selling price, warranty coverage, and accessory packages to a greater extent. Even for a huge company such as Wal-Mart, the drastic increase in bargaining power of consumers caused by Internet usage is a major external threat.

Sources of External Information

A wealth of strategic information is available to organizations from both published and unpublished sources. Unpublished sources include customer surveys, market research, speeches at professional and shareholders' meetings, television programs, interviews, and conversations with stakeholders. Published sources of strategic information include periodicals, journals, reports, government documents, abstracts, books, directories, newspapers, and manuals. The Internet has made it easier for firms to gather, assimilate, and evaluate information.

The Internet offers consumers and businesses a widening range of services and information resources from all over the world. Interactive services offer users not only access to information worldwide but also the ability to communicate with the person or company that created the information. Historical barriers to personal and business success—time zones and diverse cultures—are being eliminated. The Internet has become as important to our society as television and newspapers.

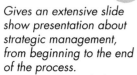

VISIT THE NET

Gives an extensive slide show presentation about strategic management, from beginning to the end of the process.
www.csuchico.edu/mgmt/strategy/

Forecasting Tools and Techniques

Forecasts are educated assumptions about future trends and events. Forecasting is a complex activity because of factors such as technological innovation, cultural changes, new products, improved services, stronger competitors, shifts in government priorities, changing social values, unstable economic conditions, and unforeseen events. Managers often must rely upon published forecasts to identify key external opportunities and threats effectively.

A sense of the future permeates all action and underlies every decision a person makes. People eat expecting to be satisfied and nourished—in the future. People sleep assuming that in the future they will feel rested. They invest energy, money, and time because they believe their efforts will be rewarded in the future. They build highways assuming that automobiles and trucks will need them in the future. Parents educate children on the basis of forecasts that they will need certain skills, attitudes, and knowledge when they grow up. The truth is we all make implicit forecasts throughout our daily lives. The question, therefore, is not whether we should forecast but rather how we can best forecast to enable us to move beyond our ordinarily unarticulated assumptions about the future. Can we obtain information and then make educated assumptions (forecasts) to better guide our current decisions to achieve a more desirable future state of affairs. We should go into the future with our eyes and our minds open, rather than stumble into the future with our eyes closed.[16]

Many publications and sources on the Internet forecast external variables. Several published examples include *Industry Week's* "Trends and Forecasts," *BusinessWeek's* "Investment Outlook," and Standard & Poor's *Industry Survey*. The reputation and continued success of these publications depend partly on accurate forecasts, so published sources of information can offer excellent projections.

Sometimes organizations must develop their own projections. Most organizations forecast (project) their own revenues and profits annually. Organizations sometimes forecast market share or customer loyalty in local areas. Because forecasting is so important in strategic management and because the ability to forecast (in contrast to the ability to use a forecast) is essential, selected forecasting tools are examined further here.

Forecasting tools can be broadly categorized into two groups: quantitative techniques and qualitative techniques. Quantitative forecasts are most appropriate when historical data are available and when the relationships among key variables are expected to remain the same in the future. *Linear regression*, for example, is based on the assumption that the future will be just like the past—which, of course, it never is. As historical relationships become less stable, quantitative forecasts become less accurate.

No forecast is perfect, and some forecasts are even wildly inaccurate. This fact accents the need for strategists to devote sufficient time and effort to study the underlying bases for published forecasts and to develop internal forecasts of their own. Key external opportunities and threats can be effectively identified only through good forecasts. Accurate forecasts can provide major competitive advantages for organizations. Forecasts are vital to the strategic-management process and to the success of organizations.

Making Assumptions

Planning would be impossible without assumptions. McConkey defines assumptions as the "best present estimates of the impact of major external factors, over which the manager has little if any control, but which may exert a significant impact on performance or the ability to achieve desired results."[17] Strategists are faced with countless variables and imponderables that can be neither controlled nor predicted with 100 percent accuracy.

By identifying future occurrences that could have a major effect on the firm and by making reasonable assumptions about those factors, strategists can carry the strategic-management process forward. Assumptions are needed only for future trends and events that are most likely to have a significant effect on the company's business. Based on the best information at the time, assumptions serve as checkpoints on the validity of strategies. If future occurrences deviate significantly from assumptions, strategists know that corrective actions may be needed. Without reasonable assumptions, the strategy-formulation process could not proceed effectively. Firms that have the best information generally make the most accurate assumptions, which can lead to major competitive advantages.

The Global Challenge

Foreign competitors are battering U.S. firms in many industries. In its simplest sense, the international challenge faced by U.S. business is twofold: (1) how to gain and maintain exports to other nations and (2) how to defend domestic markets against imported goods. Few companies can afford to ignore the presence of international competition. Firms that seem insulated and comfortable today may be vulnerable tomorrow; for example, foreign banks do not yet compete or operate in most of the United States.

America's economy is becoming much less American. A world economy and monetary system is emerging. Corporations in every corner of the globe are taking advantage of the opportunity to share in the benefits of worldwide economic development. Markets are shifting rapidly and in many cases converging in tastes, trends, and prices. Innovative transport systems are accelerating the transfer of technology, and shifts in the nature and location of production systems are reducing the response time to changing market conditions.

More and more countries around the world are welcoming foreign investment and capital. As a result, labor markets have steadily become more international. East Asian countries have become market leaders in labor-intensive industries, Brazil offers abundant natural resources and rapidly developing markets, and Germany offers skilled labor and technology. The drive to improve the efficiency of global business operations is leading to greater functional specialization. This is not limited to a search for the familiar low-cost labor in Latin America or Asia. Other considerations include the cost of energy, availability of resources, inflation rates, existing tax rates, and the nature of trade regulations.

Multinational Corporations

Multinational corporations (MNCs) face unique and diverse risks, such as expropriation of assets, currency losses through exchange rate fluctuations, unfavorable foreign court interpretations of contracts and agreements, social/political disturbances, import/export restrictions, tariffs, and trade barriers. Strategists in MNCs are often confronted with the need to be globally competitive and nationally responsive at the same time. With the rise in world commerce, government and regulatory bodies are more closely monitoring foreign business practices. The United States Foreign Corrupt Practices Act, for example, defines corrupt practices in many areas of business. A sensitive issue is that some MNCs sometimes violate legal and ethical standards of the home country, but not of the host country.

Before entering international markets, firms should scan relevant journals and patent reports, seek the advice of academic and research organizations, participate in international trade fairs, form partnerships, and conduct extensive research to broaden their contacts and diminish the risk of doing business in new markets. Firms can also reduce the risks of doing business internationally by obtaining insurance from the U.S. government's Overseas Private Investment Corporation (OPIC). Note in the "Global Perspective" that U.S. firms are doing more extensive research today before entering particular global markets.

Globalization

Globalization is a process of worldwide integration of strategy formulation, implementation, and evaluation activities. Strategic decisions are made based on their impact upon global profitability of the firm, rather than on just domestic or other individual country considerations. A global strategy seeks to meet the needs of customers worldwide, with the highest value at the lowest cost. This may mean locating production in countries with the lowest labor costs or abundant natural resources, locating research and complex engineering centers where skilled scientists and engineers can be found, and locating marketing activities close to the markets to be served. A global strategy includes designing, producing, and marketing products with global needs in mind, instead of considering individual countries alone. A global strategy integrates actions against competitors into a worldwide plan.

Globalization of industries is occurring for many reasons, including a worldwide trend toward similar consumption patterns, the emergence of global buyers and sellers, and e-commerce and the instant transmission of money and information across continents. The European Economic Community (EEC), religions, the Olympics, the World Bank, world trade centers, the Red Cross, the Internet, environmental conferences, telecommunications, and economic summits all contribute to global interdependencies and the emerging global marketplace.

It is clear that different industries become global for different reasons. The need to amortize massive R&D investments over many markets is a major reason why the aircraft manufacturing industry became global. Monitoring globalization in one's industry is an important strategic-management activity. Knowing how to use that

GLOBAL PERSPECTIVE

The Old Way versus the New Way to Take a Company Global

The old way to take a company global was to get in fast, do minimal research, strike deals with top officials, make quick acquisitions, focus on upscale consumers, and watch local customers begin buying up the company's products. That approach, however, failed more often that it succeeded.

The new, more effective approach to taking a company global is to do extensive homework regarding culture, distributors, suppliers, and customers before placing operations in a foreign land. Successful globalization today requires investing time and energy to understand the nature of business in those countries and to methodically build a presence from the ground up. Companies successfully going global today work closely with bureaucrats, entrepreneurs, social groups, and other potential customers at the grassroots level. These companies are also targeting individuals in countries where the average income is low yet whose numbers far exceed those of the richest 10 percent of countries and customers. These companies have come to realize that developing nations are growing much faster than the industrial nations. Fully four billion people who earn the equivalent of $1,500 or less annually live in developing nations, and this group is growing more rapidly than well-to-do citizens and countries.

A number of companies are using this new approach to be successful globally. Hewlett-Packard is presently marketing its products heavily in Central America and Africa. Citibank also is following this new approach by persuading its corporate customers in developing countries to set up retail bank accounts for their entire staffs—from janitors to top managers. Kodak also is following this new approach for being successful globally. Kodak has struggled in the United States recently, but the company's sales in Asia are up nicely. The company has increased its number of Kodak Express photo supply shops in China from 6,000 in early 2001 to 10,000 in 2002. A final example of a company using this new approach to be successful globally is Whirlpool, which invested fourteen months of research in the effort before rolling out what has become the leading brand of washing machines in India.

Source: Adapted from "Smart Globalization," *BusinessWeek* (August 27, 2001): 132–137.

information for one's competitive advantage is even more important. For example, firms may look around the world for the best technology and select one that has the most promise for the largest number of markets. When firms design a product, they design it to be marketable in as many countries as possible. When firms manufacture a product, they select the lowest-cost source, which may be Japan for semiconductors, Sri Lanka for textiles, Malaysia for simple electronics, and Europe for precision machinery. MNCs design manufacturing systems to accommodate world markets. One of the riskiest strategies for a domestic firm is to remain solely a domestic firm in an industry that is rapidly becoming global.

China: Opportunities and Threats

U.S. firms increasingly are doing business in China as market reforms create a more businesslike arena daily. Foreign direct investment in China is about $50 billion annually.

Risks that still deter firms from initiating business with China include the following:

- Poor infrastructure
- Disregard for the natural environment
- Absence of a legal system
- Rampant corruption

- Lack of freedom of press, speech, and religion
- Severe human rights violations
- Little respect for patents, copyrights, brands, and logos
- Counterfeiting, fraud, and pirating of products
- Little respect for legal contracts
- No generally accepted accounting principles

The minimum wage in China is twelve cents per hour, but many firms pay even less. Chinese workers usually have no healthcare and no compensation for injury. Few factories have fire extinguishers. Bribes are often paid to officials to avoid fines and shutdowns. Labor unions are illegal and nonexistent in China. Child labor is commonplace. Political and religious oppression and imprisonment occur. Levi Strauss has pulled all its business operations out of China to protest its human rights violations.

China's leaders are determined these days to minimize foreign policy problems so they can focus on domestic economic development, which is booming. China's new President Hu Jintao, who replaced Jiang Zemin, has put China's economic goals at the forefront of policy and practice. China is expected to surpass India by 2006 as the country of choice for information technology (IT) outsourcing. China's economy is booming and thousands of foreign companies have set up manufacturing bases on the Chinese mainland. In Shanghai, an engineer is paid on average $500 a month compared to $700 in India and $4,000 in the U.S. As margins shrink in many industries due to increased competitiveness, more and more firms see China as more attractive even than Mexico or India for conducting business, especially IT operations.

For the first time ever, China attracted more foreign direct investment (FDI) than the U.S. in the year 2002. FDI in the U.S. fell from $144 billion in 2001 to just $30 billion in 2002, while fast-growing China attracted $53 billion FDI in 2002, up 12 percent from 2001 levels.[18] China was one of the only countries worldwide in 2002 with increasing FDI as worldwide FDI fell 21 percent that year due to weak global economies. Less FDI in the U.S. cuts value from the dollar which helps exporters but hurts importers and also can lead to higher interest rates. The U.S. dollar lost 14 percent of its value against major currencies from January 2003 to January 2004. But the low value of the dollar boosts the profits of U.S. based multinational companies and is considered a positive for the U.S. economy.

The Dutch company Philips Electronics NV plans to double its revenue from China by 2007 from $6.7 billion in 2002. Philips is transferring much of its manufacturing to take advantage of China's deep pool of low-cost labor and well-trained engineers. Philips currently has $2.5 billion worth of investment in China spread out over 30 wholly owned enterprises and joint ventures that employ 18,000 people and produce everything from semiconductors and lighting to medical diagnostic imaging equipment.

German chipmaker Infineon Technologies AG plans to invest $1.2 billion in China between 2003 and 2006 to gain a share of this market that is expected to reach $80 billion by 2007. The company has a joint venture with China-Singapore Suzhou Industrial Park Venture to produce dynamic random-access memory, or DRAM, chip assembly-and-test facilities.

Hong Kong is the centerpiece of China's efforts to reform, privatize, and expand imports and exports worldwide. The map in Figure 3–4 illustrates Hong Kong's strategic location for China. With its 6.3 million people, magnificent harbor, financial wealth, 500 banks from 43 countries, the world's eighth-largest stock market, and

FIGURE 3–4
Hong Kong's Strategic Location

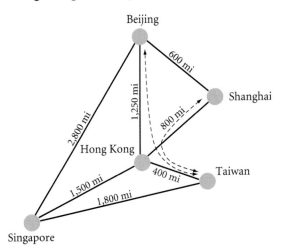

minimum taxation, Hong Kong serves as the gateway to a fast-growing China. U.S. companies alone have 178 regional headquarters in Hong Kong and $10.5 billion in direct investment.

Industry Analysis: The External Factor Evaluation (EFE) Matrix

An *External Factor Evaluation (EFE) Matrix* allows strategists to summarize and evaluate economic, social, cultural, demographic, environmental, political, governmental, legal, technological, and competitive information. Illustrated in Table 3–7, the EFE Matrix can be developed in five steps:

1. List key external factors as identified in the external-audit process. Include a total of from ten to twenty factors, including both opportunities and threats, that affect the firm and its industry. List the opportunities first and then the threats. Be as specific as possible, using percentages, ratios, and comparative numbers whenever possible.

2. Assign to each factor a weight that ranges from 0.0 (not important) to 1.0 (very important). The weight indicates the relative importance of that factor to being successful in the firm's industry. Opportunities often receive higher weights than threats, but threats too can receive high weights if they are especially severe or threatening. Appropriate weights can be determined by comparing successful with unsuccessful competitors or by discussing the factor and reaching a group consensus. The sum of all weights assigned to the factors must equal 1.0.

3. Assign a 1-to-4 rating to each key external factor to indicate how effectively the firm's current strategies respond to the factor, where 4 = *the response is superior*, 3 = *the response is above average*, 2 = *the response is average*, and 1 = *the response is poor*. Ratings are based on effectiveness of the firm's strategies.

TABLE 3-7   An Example External Factor Evaluation Matrix
for UST, Inc.

KEY EXTERNAL FACTORS	WEIGHT	RATING	WEIGHTED SCORE
Opportunities			
1. Global markets are practically untapped by smokeless tobacco market	.15	1	.15
2. Increased demand caused by public banning of smoking	.05	3	.15
3. Astronomical Internet advertising growth	.05	1	.05
4. Pinkerton is leader in discount tobacco market	.15	4	.60
5. More social pressure to quit smoking, thus leading users to switch to alternatives	.10	3	.30
Threats			
1. Legislation against the tobacco industry	.10	2	.20
2. Production limits on tobacco increases competition for production	.05	3	.15
3. Smokeless tobacco market is concentrated in southeast region of United States	.05	2	.10
4. Bad media exposure from the FDA	.10	2	.20
5. Clinton administration	.20	1	.20
TOTAL	1.00		2.10

Ratings are thus company-based, whereas the weights in Step 2 are industry-based. It is important to note that both threats and opportunities can receive a 1, 2, 3, or 4.

4. Multiply each factor's weight by its rating to determine a weighted score.
5. Sum the weighted scores for each variable to determine the total weighted score for the organization.

Regardless of the number of key opportunities and threats included in an EFE Matrix, the highest possible total weighted score for an organization is 4.0 and the lowest possible total weighted score is 1.0. The average total weighted score is 2.5. A total weighted score of 4.0 indicates that an organization is responding in an outstanding way to existing opportunities and threats in its industry. In other words, the firm's strategies effectively take advantage of existing opportunities and minimize the potential adverse effects of external threats. A total score of 1.0 indicates that the firm's strategies are not capitalizing on opportunities or avoiding external threats.

An example of an EFE Matrix is provided in Table 3–7 for UST, Inc., the manufacturer of Skoal and Copenhagen smokeless tobacco. Note that the Clinton administration was considered to be the most important factor affecting this industry, as indicated by the weight of 0.20. UST was not pursuing strategies that effectively capitalized on this opportunity, as indicated by the rating of 1.0. The total weighted score of 2.10 indicates that UST is below average in its effort to pursue strategies that capitalize on external opportunities and avoid threats. It is important to note here that a thorough understanding of the factors being used in the EFE Matrix is more important than the actual weights and ratings assigned.

Another example EFE Matrix is provided in Table 3–8, for Gateway Computer Company in late 2003. Note that Gateway China is viewed as an outstanding opportunity yet Gateway is not capitalizing on this factor as indicated by the low (1) ratings.

TABLE 3-8   EFE Matrix for Gateway Computer (2003)

KEY EXTERNAL FACTORS	WEIGHT	RATING	WEIGHTED SCORE
Opportunities			
1. Global PC market expected to grow 20% in 2004, compared to 12% in 2003	0.10	3	0.30
2. Cost of PC component parts expected to decrease 10% in 2004	0.10	3	0.30
3. Internet use growing rapidly	0.05	2	0.10
4. China entered WTO which lowered taxes for importing PCs	0.10	1	0.10
5. The average income for PC worker has declined from $40,000/year to $30,000/year	0.05	3	0.15
6. Modernization of business firms and government agencies	0.05	2	0.10
7. U.S. (and world) economies recovering	0.05	3	0.15
8. 30% of Chinese population can afford a PC; only 10% of Chinese homes have a PC	0.05	1	0.05
Threats			
1. Intense rivalry in industry	0.10	2	0.20
2. Severe price cutting in PC industry	0.05	3	0.15
3. Different countries have different regulations and infrastructure for PCs	0.05	1	0.05
4. Palm and PDA becoming substitute for PC	0.05	3	0.15
5. Demand exceeds supply of experienced PC workers	0.05	4	0.20
6. Birth rate in U.S. is declining annually	0.05	3	0.15
7. U.S. consumers and businesses delaying purchase of PCs	0.05	2	0.10
8. PC firms diversifying into consumer electronics	0.05	3	0.15
TOTAL	1.00		2.40

The Competitive Profile Matrix (CPM)

The *Competitive Profile Matrix (CPM)* identifies a firm's major competitors and its particular strengths and weaknesses in relation to a sample firm's strategic position. The weights and total weighted scores in both a CPM and EFE have the same meaning. However, *critical success* factors in a CPM include both internal and external issues; therefore, the ratings refer to strengths and weaknesses, where 4 = major strength, 3 = minor strength, 2 = minor weakness, and 1 = major weakness. There are some important differences between the EFE and CPM. First of all, the critical success factors in a CPM are broader, they do not include specific or factual data and even may focus on internal issues. The critical success factors in a CPM also are not grouped into opportunities and threats as they are in an EFE. In a CPM, the ratings and total weighted scores for rival firms can be compared to the sample firm. This comparative analysis provides important internal strategic information.

A sample Competitive Profile Matrix is provided in Table 3–9. In this example, advertising and global expansion are the most important critical success factors, as indicated by a weight of 0.20. Avon's and L'Oreal's product quality is superior, as evidenced by a rating of 4; L'Oreal's "financial position" is good, as indicated by a rating of 3; Procter & Gamble is the weakest firm overall, as indicated by a total weighted score of 2.80.

Other than the critical success factors listed in the example CPM, factors often included in this analysis include breadth of product line, effectiveness of sales distribution, proprietary or patent advantages, location of facilities, production capacity and efficiency, experience, union relations, technological advantages, and e-commerce expertise.

A word on interpretation: Just because one firm receives a 3.2 rating and another receives a 2.8 rating in a Competitive Profile Matrix, it does not follow that the first firm is 20 percent better than the second. Numbers reveal the relative strengths of firms, but their implied precision is an illusion. Numbers are not magic. The aim is not to arrive at a single number, but rather to assimilate and evaluate information in a meaningful way that aids in decision making.

Another Competitive Profile Matrix is provided in Table 3–10 for Gateway Computer Company. Note that Apple has the best product quality and management

TABLE 3-9   An Example Competitive Profile Matrix

Critical Success Factors	Weight	AVON Rating	Score	L'OREAL Rating	Score	PROCTER & GAMBLE Rating	Score
Advertising	0.20	1	0.20	4	0.80	3	0.60
Product Quality	0.10	4	0.40	4	0.40	3	0.30
Price Competitiveness	0.10	3	0.30	3	0.30	4	0.40
Management	0.10	4	0.40	3	0.30	3	0.30
Financial Position	0.15	4	0.60	3	0.45	3	0.45
Customer Loyalty	0.10	4	0.40	4	0.40	2	0.20
Global Expansion	0.20	4	0.80	2	0.40	2	0.40
Market Share	0.05	1	0.05	4	0.20	3	0.15
TOTAL	1.00		3.15		3.25		2.80

Note: (1) The ratings values are as follows: 1 = major weakness, 2 = minor weakness, 3 = minor strength, 4 = major strength. (2) As indicated by the total weighted score of 2.8, Competitor 3 is weakest. (3) Only eight critical success factors are included for simplicity; this is too few in actuality.

TABLE 3-10   Competitive Profile Matrix for Gateway Computer (2003)

Critical Success Factors	Weight	GATEWAY Rating	GATEWAY Weighted Score	APPLE Rating	APPLE Weighted Score	DELL Rating	DELL Weighted Score
Market share	0.15	3	0.45	2	0.30	4	0.60
Inventory system	0.08	2	0.16	2	0.16	4	0.32
Financial position	0.10	2	0.20	3	0.30	3	0.30
Product quality	0.08	3	0.24	4	0.32	3	0.24
Consumer loyalty	0.02	3	0.06	3	0.06	4	0.08
Sales distribution	0.10	3	0.30	2	0.20	3	0.30
Global expansion	0.15	3	0.45	2	0.30	4	0.60
Organization structure	0.05	3	0.15	3	0.15	3	0.15
Production capacity	0.04	3	0.12	3	0.12	3	0.12
E-commerce	0.10	3	0.30	3	0.30	3	0.30
Customer service	0.10	3	0.30	2	0.20	4	0.40
Price competitive	0.02	4	0.08	1	0.02	3	0.06
Management experience	0.01	2	0.02	4	0.04	2	0.02
TOTAL	1.00		2.83		2.47		3.49

experience; Dell has the best market share and inventory system; and Gateway has the best price as indicated by the four ratings.

CONCLUSION

Increasing turbulence in markets and industries around the world means the external audit has become an explicit and vital part of the strategic-management process. This chapter provides a framework for collecting and evaluating economic, social, cultural, demographic, environmental, political, governmental, legal, technological, and competitive information. Firms that do not mobilize and empower their managers and employees to identify, monitor, forecast, and evaluate key external forces may fail to anticipate emerging opportunities and threats and, consequently, may pursue ineffective strategies, miss opportunities, and invite organizational demise. Firms not taking advantage of the Internet are falling behind technologically.

A major responsibility of strategists is to ensure development of an effective external-audit system. This includes using information technology to devise a competitive intelligence system that works. The external-audit approach described in this chapter can be used effectively by any size or type of organization. Typically, the external-audit process is more informal in small firms, but the need to understand key trends and events is no less important for these firms. The EFE Matrix and Porter's Five-Forces Model can help strategists evaluate the market and industry, but these tools must be accompanied by good intuitive judgment. Multinational firms especially need a systematic and effective external-audit system because external forces among foreign countries vary so greatly.

We invite you to visit the David page on the Prentice Hall Companion Web site at *www.prenhall.com/david* for this chapter's World Wide Web exercises.

KEY TERMS AND CONCEPTS

Chief Information Officer
(CIO) (p. 86)
Chief Technology Officer
(CTO) (p. 86)
Competitive Analysis (p. 90)
Competitive Intelligence
(CI) (p. 89)
Competitive Profile Matrix
(CPM) (p. 104)
Decruiting (p. 78)
Director of Competitive
Analysis (p. 90)

Downsizing (p. 78)
Environmental Scanning (p. 74)
External Audit (p. 74)
External Factor Evaluation (EFE)
Matrix (p. 101)
External Forces (p. 75)
Foreign Direct Investment
(FDI) (p. 81)
Industrial/Organization
(I/O) (p. 74)
Industry Analysis (p. 74)

Information Technology
(IT) (p. 86)
Internet (p. 86)
Learning from the Partner (p. 92)
Linear Regression (p. 97)
Lifecare Facilities (p. 80)
Porter's Five-Forces Model (p. 92)
Rightsizing (p. 78)
Tax Harmonization (p. 83)

ISSUES FOR REVIEW AND DISCUSSION

1. Explain how to conduct an external strategic-management audit.
2. Identify a recent economic, social, political, or technological trend that significantly affects financial institutions.
3. Discuss the following statement: Major opportunities and threats usually result from an interaction among key environmental trends rather than from a single external event or factor.
4. Identify two industries experiencing rapid technological changes and three industries that are experiencing little technological change. How does the need for technological forecasting differ in these industries? Why?
5. Use Porter's Five-Forces Model to evaluate competitiveness within the U.S. banking industry.
6. What major forecasting techniques would you use to identify (1) economic opportunities and threats and (2) demographic opportunities and threats? Why are these techniques most appropriate?
7. How does the external audit affect other components of the strategic-management process?
8. As the owner of a small business, explain how you would organize a strategic-information scanning system. How would you organize such a system in a large organization?

9. Construct an EFE Matrix for an organization of your choice.
10. Make an appointment with a librarian at your university to learn how to use online databases. Report your findings in class.
11. Give some advantages and disadvantages of cooperative versus competitive strategies.
12. As strategist for a local bank, explain when you would use qualitative versus quantitative forecasts.
13. What is your forecast for interest rates and the stock market in the next several months? As the stock market moves up, do interest rates always move down? Why? What are the strategic implications of these trends?
14. Explain how information technology affects strategies of the organization where you worked most recently.
15. Let's say your boss develops an EFE Matrix that includes sixty-two factors. How would you suggest reducing the number of factors to twenty?
16. Discuss the ethics of gathering competitive intelligence.
17. Discuss the ethics of cooperating with rival firms.
18. Visit the SEC Web site at *www.sec.gov*, and discuss the benefits of using information provided there.

19. What are the major differences between U.S. and multinational operations that affect strategic management?
20. Why is globalization of industries a common factor today?
21. Discuss the opportunities and threats a firm faces in doing business in China.
22. Do you agree with I/O theorists that external factors are more important than internal factors to a firm's achieving competitive advantage? Explain both your and their position.
23. Define, compare, and contrast the Weights versus Ratings in an EFEM versus IFEM.
24. Develop a Competitive Profile Matrix for your university. Include six factors.
25. List the ten external areas that give rise to opportunities and threats.
26. Discuss recent trends in Russia's economic condition.
27. True or False: China replaced Mexico in 2003 as the largest exporter to the United States. Discuss this statement.
28. Define and discuss implications of "tax harmonization" in Europe.
29. Do you believe strategies themselves should be secret or open within firms? Explain.
30. True or False: For the first time in 100 years, China attracted more foreign direct investment (FDI) than the United States in the year 2002.

NOTES

1. York Freund, "Critical Success Factors," *Planning Review* 16, no. 4 (July–August 1988): 20.
2. A. M. McGahan, "Competition, Strategy and Business Performance," *California Management Review* 41, no. 3 (1999): 74–101; A. McGahan and M. Porter, "How Much Does Industry Matter Really?," *Strategic Management Journal* 18, no. 8 (1997): 15–30.
3. Jason Bush, "Sizzling Growth Could Singe Russia's Economy," *BusinessWeek* (July 23, 2003): 52
4. Gregory White, "Pro-Putin Forces Struggle to Hold Political Ground," *Wall Street Journal* (September 17, 2003): A12.
5. Jim Hopkins, "Hispanic-owned Companies See Strong Growth Spurt," *USA Today* (July 2, 2003): B1.
6. Geri Smith, "Despite SARS, Mexico is Still Losing Export Ground to China," *BusinessWeek* (June 2, 2003): 44.
7. Frederick Gluck, "Global Competition in the 1990s," *Journal of Business Strategy* (Spring 1983): 22–24.
8. John Harris, Robert Shaw, Jr., and William Sommers, "The Strategic Management of Technology," *Planning Review* 11, no. 11 (January–February 1983): 28, 35.
9. Bill Saporito, "Companies That Compete Best," *Fortune* (May 22, 1989): 36.
10. Louis Lavelle, "The Case of the Corporate Spy," *BusinessWeek* (November 26, 2001): 56–57.
11. Kenneth Sawka, "Demystifying Business Intelligence," *Management Review* (October 1996): 49.
12. John Prescott and Daniel Smith, "The Largest Survey of 'Leading-Edge' Competitor Intelligence Managers," *Planning Review* 17, no. 3 (May–June 1989): 6–13.
13. Gary Hamel, Yves Doz, and C. K. Prahalad, "Collaborate with Your Competitors—and Win," *Harvard Business Review* 67, no. 1 (January–February 1989): 133.
14. Jon Swartz, "Rivals Form United Front Against Spam," *USA Today* (April 29, 2003): 2B.
15. David Bank, "A Site-Eat-Site World," *Wall Street Journal* (July 12, 1999): R8.
16. *horizon.unc.edu/projects/seminars/futuresresearch/rationale.asp*
17. Dale McConkey, "Planning in a Changing Environment," *Business Horizons* 31, no. 5 (September–October 1988): 67.
18. Barbara Hagenbaugh, "China Draws More Foreign Money Than USA," *USA Today* (September 5, 2003): 3B.

CURRENT READINGS

Adner, R. "When Are Technologies Disruptive: A Demand-Based View of the Emergence of Competition." *Strategic Management Journal* 23, no. 8 (August 2002): 667–688.

Arend, R. J. "Revisiting the Logical and Research Considerations of Competitive Advantage." *Strategic Management Journal* 24, no. 3 (March 2003): 279–284.

Durand, R. "Competitive Advantages Exist: A Critique of Powell." *Strategic Management Journal* 23, no. 9 (September 2002): 867–872.

Garg, V. K., B. A. Walters, and R. L. Priem. "Chief Executive Scanning Emphasis, Environmental Dynamism and Manufacturing Firm Performance." *Strategic Management Journal* 24, no. 8 (August 2003): 725–744.

Hawawini, G., V. Subramanian, and P. Verdin. "Is Performance Driven by Industry—or Firm-specific Factors? A New Look at the Evidence." *Strategic Management Journal* 24, no. 1 (January 2003): 1–17.

Shankar, V., and B. L. Bayus. "Network Effects and Competition: An Empirical Analysis of the Home Video Game Industry." *Strategic Management Journal* 24, no. 4 (April 2003): 375–384.

Stanley, S. F., and E. M. Olson. "A Fresh Look at Industry and Market Analysis." *Business Horizons* 45, no. 1 (January–February 2002): 15–22.

experiential exercises

Experiential Exercise 3A

Developing an EFE Matrix for Krispy Kreme Doughnuts (KKD)

PURPOSE

This exercise will give you practice developing an EFE Matrix. An EFE Matrix summarizes the results of an external audit. This is an important tool widely used by strategists.

INSTRUCTIONS

Step 1 Join with two other students in class, and jointly prepare an EFE Matrix for KKD. Refer back to the Cohesion Case and to Experiential Exercise 1A, if necessary, to identify external opportunities and threats.

Step 2 All three-person teams participating in this exercise should record their EFE total weighted scores on the board. Put your initials after your score to identify it as your team's.

Step 3 Compare the total weighted scores. Which team's score came closest to the instructor's answer? Discuss reasons for variation in the scores reported on the board.

Experiential Exercise 3B

The External Assessment

PURPOSE

This exercise will help you become familiar with important sources of external information available in your college library. A key part of preparing an external audit is searching the Internet and examining published sources of information for relevant economic, social, cultural, demographic, environmental, political, governmental, legal, technological, and competitive trends and events. External opportunities and threats must be identified and evaluated before strategies can be formulated effectively.

INSTRUCTIONS

Step 1 Select a company or business where you currently or previously have worked. Conduct an external audit for this company. Find opportunities and threats in recent issues of newspapers and magazines. Search for information using the Internet.

Step 2 On a separate sheet of paper, list ten opportunities and ten threats that face this company. Be specific in stating each factor.

Step 3 Include a bibliography to reveal where you found the information.

Step 4 Write a three-page summary of your findings, and submit it to your instructor.

Experiential Exercise 3C

Developing an EFE Matrix for My University

PURPOSE

More colleges and universities are embarking upon the strategic-management process. Institutions are consciously and systematically identifying and evaluating external opportunities and threats higher education in your state, the nation, and the world.

INSTRUCTIONS

Step 1 Join with two other individuals in class, and jointly prepare an EFE Matrix for your institution.

Step 2 Go to the board and record your total weighted score in a column that includes the scores of all three-person teams participating. Put your initials after your score to identify it as your team's.

Step 3 Which team viewed your college's strategies most positively? Which team viewed your college's strategies most negatively? Discuss the nature of the differences.

Experiential Exercise 3D

Developing a Competitive Profile Matrix for Krispy Kreme Doughnuts (KKD)

PURPOSE

Monitoring competitors' performance and strategies is a key aspect of an external audit. This exercise is designed to give you practice evaluating the competitive position of organizations in a given industry and assimilating that information in the form of a Competitive Profile Matrix.

INSTRUCTIONS

Step 1 Turn back to the Cohesion Case and review the section on competitors.

Step 2 On a separate sheet of paper, prepare a Competitive Profile Matrix that includes Krispy Kreme Doughnuts (KKD) and Dunkin' Donuts.

Step 3 Turn in your Competitive Profile Matrix for a classwork grade.

Experiential Exercise 3E

Developing a Competitive Profile Matrix for My University

PURPOSE

Your college or university competes with all other educational institutions in the world, especially those in your own state. State funds, students, faculty, staff, endowments, gifts, and federal funds are areas of competitiveness. The purpose of this exercise is to give you practice thinking competitively about the business of education in your state.

INSTRUCTIONS

Step 1 Identify two colleges or universities in your state that compete directly with your institution for students. Interview several persons who are aware of particular strengths and weaknesses of those universities. Record information about the two competing universities.

Step 2 Prepare a Competitive Profile Matrix that includes your institution and the two competing institutions. Include the following factors in your analysis:
   1. Tuition costs
   2. Quality of faculty
   3. Academic reputation
   4. Average class size

  5. Campus landscaping
  6. Athletic programs
  7. Quality of students
  8. Graduate programs
  9. Location of campus
 10. Campus culture

Step 3   Submit your Competitive Profile Matrix to your instructor for evaluation.

The Internal Assessment

After studying this chapter, you should be able to do the following:

1. Describe how to perform an internal strategic-management audit.

2. Discuss the Resource-Based View (RBV) in strategic management.

3. Discuss key interrelationships among the functional areas of business.

4. Compare and contrast culture in America with other countries.

5. Identify the basic functions or activities that make up management, marketing, finance/accounting, production/operations, research and development, and management information systems.

6. Explain how to determine and prioritize a firm's internal strengths and weaknesses.

7. Explain the importance of financial ratio analysis.

8. Discuss the nature and role of management information systems in strategic management.

9. Develop an Internal Factor Evaluation (IFE) Matrix.

experiential exercises

Experiential Exercise 4A
Performing a Financial Ratio Analysis for Krispy Kreme Doughnuts (KKD)

Experiential Exercise 4B
Constructing an IFE Matrix for Krispy Kreme Doughnuts (KKD)

Experiential Exercise 4C
Constructing an IFE Matrix for My University

"notable quotes"

Like a product or service, the planning process itself must be managed and shaped, if it is to serve executives as a vehicle for strategic decision-making.
Robert Lenz

The difference between now and five years ago is that information systems had limited function. You weren't betting your company on it. Now you are.
William Gruber

Weak leadership can wreck the soundest strategy.
Sun Zi

A firm that continues to employ a previously successful strategy eventually and inevitably falls victim to a competitor.
William Cohen

Sad but true, U.S. businesspeople have the lowest foreign language proficiency of any major trading nation. U.S. business schools do not emphasize foreign languages, and students traditionally avoid them.
Ronald Dulek

Great spirits have always encountered violent opposition from mediocre minds.
Albert Einstein

This chapter focuses on identifying and evaluating a firm's strengths and weaknesses in the functional areas of business, including management, marketing, finance/accounting, production/operations, research and development, and management information systems. Relationships among these areas of business are examined. Strategic implications of important functional area concepts are examined. The process of performing an internal audit is described. The Resource-Based View (RBV) of strategic management is introduced as well as the Value Chain Analysis (VCA) concept.

The Nature of an Internal Audit

VISIT THE NET

Excellent strategic planning quotes.
www.planware.org/quotes.htm#3

All organizations have strengths and weaknesses in the functional areas of business. No enterprise is equally strong or weak in all areas. Maytag, for example, is known for excellent production and product design, whereas Procter & Gamble is known for superb marketing. Internal strengths/weaknesses, coupled with external opportunities/threats and a clear statement of mission, provide the basis for establishing objectives and strategies. Objectives and strategies are established with the intention of capitalizing upon internal strengths and overcoming weaknesses. The internal-audit part of the strategic-management process is illustrated in Figure 4–1.

Key Internal Forces

It is not possible in a business policy text to review in depth all the material presented in courses such as marketing, finance, accounting, management, management infor-

FIGURE 4–1

A Comprehensive Strategic-Management Model

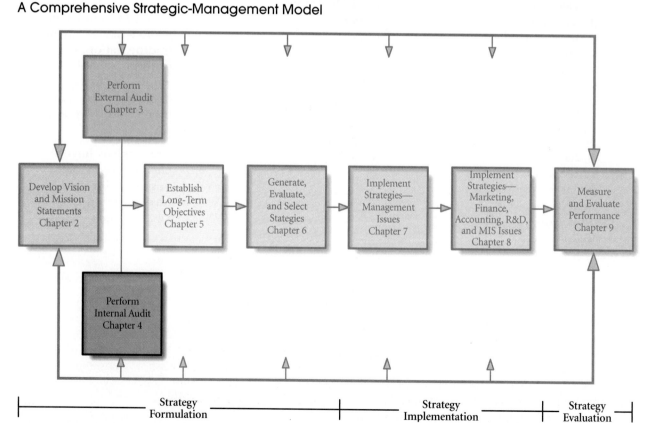

mation systems, and production/operations; there are many subareas within these functions, such as customer service, warranties, advertising, packaging, and pricing under marketing.

For different types of organizations, such as hospitals, universities, and government agencies, the functional business areas, of course, differ. In a hospital, for example, functional areas may include cardiology, hematology, nursing, maintenance, physician support, and receivables. Functional areas of a university can include athletic programs, placement services, housing, fundraising, academic research, counseling, and intramural programs. Within large organizations, each division has certain strengths and weaknesses.

A firm's strengths that cannot be easily matched or imitated by competitors are called *distinctive competencies*. Building competitive advantages involves taking advantage of distinctive competencies. For example, 3M exploits its distinctive competence in research and development by producing a wide range of innovative products. Strategies are designed in part to improve on a firm's weaknesses, turning them into strengths—and maybe even into distinctive competencies.

Some researchers emphasize the importance of the internal audit part of the strategic-management process by comparing it to the external audit. Robert Grant concluded that the internal audit is more important, saying:

> In a world where customer preferences are volatile, the identity of customers is changing, and the technologies for serving customer requirements are continually evolving; an externally focused orientation does not provide a secure foundation for formulating long-term strategy. When the external environment is in a state of flux, the firm's own resources and capabilities may be a much more stable basis on which to define its identity. Hence, a definition of a business in terms of what it is capable of doing may offer a more durable basis for strategy than a definition based upon the needs which the business seeks to satisfy.[1]

The Process of Performing an Internal Audit

The process of performing an *internal audit* closely parallels the process of performing an external audit. Representative managers and employees from throughout the firm need to be involved in determining a firm's strengths and weaknesses. The internal audit requires gathering and assimilating information about the firm's management, marketing, finance/accounting, production/operations, research and development (R&D), and management information systems operations. Key factors should be prioritized as described in Chapter 3 so that the firm's most important strengths and weaknesses can be determined collectively.

Compared to the external audit, the process of performing an internal audit provides more opportunity for participants to understand how their jobs, departments, and divisions fit into the whole organization. This is a great benefit because managers and employees perform better when they understand how their work affects other areas and activities of the firm. For example, when marketing and manufacturing managers jointly discuss issues related to internal strengths and weaknesses, they gain a better appreciation of the issues, problems, concerns, and needs of all the functional areas. In organizations that do not use strategic management, marketing, finance, and manufacturing managers often do not interact with each other in significant ways. Performing an internal audit thus is an excellent vehicle or forum for improving the process of communication in the organization. Communication may be the most important word in management.

VISIT THE NET

Gives excellent information about the need for planning.
www.mindtools.com/plintro.html

Performing an internal audit requires gathering, assimilating, and evaluating information about the firm's operations. Critical success factors, consisting of both strengths and weaknesses, can be identified and prioritized in the manner discussed in Chapter 3. According to William King, a task force of managers from different units of the organization, supported by staff, should be charged with determining the ten to twenty most important strengths and weaknesses that should influence the future of the organization. He says:

> The development of conclusions on the 10 to 20 most important organizational strengths and weaknesses can be, as any experienced manager knows, a difficult task, when it involves managers representing various organizational interests and points of view. Developing a 20-page list of strengths and weaknesses could be accomplished relatively easily, but a list of the 10 to 15 most important ones involves significant analysis and negotiation. This is true because of the judgments that are required and the impact which such a list will inevitably have as it is used in the formulation, implementation, and evaluation of strategies.[2]

VISIT THE NET

Provides the complete strategic plan for the Wyoming Insurance Department Agency, including its list of strengths and weaknesses.
www.state.wy.us/ state/strategy/ insurance.html

Strategic management is a highly interactive process that requires effective coordination among management, marketing, finance/accounting, production/ operations, R&D, and management information systems managers. Although the strategic-management process is overseen by strategists, success requires that managers and employees from all functional areas work together to provide ideas and information. Financial managers, for example, may need to restrict the number of feasible options available to operations managers, or R&D managers may develop products that marketing managers need to set higher objectives. A key to organizational success is effective coordination and understanding among managers from all functional business areas. Through involvement in performing an internal strategic-management audit, managers from different departments and divisions of the firm come to understand the nature and effect of decisions in other functional business areas in their firm. Knowledge of these relationships is critical for effectively establishing objectives and strategies.

A failure to recognize and understand relationships among the functional areas of business can be detrimental to strategic management, and the number of those relationships that must be managed increases dramatically with a firm's size, diversity, geographic dispersion, and the number of products or services offered. Governmental and nonprofit enterprises traditionally have not placed sufficient emphasis on relationships among the business functions. Some firms place too great an emphasis on one function at the expense of others. Ansoff explained:

> During the first fifty years, successful firms focused their energies on optimizing the performance of one of the principal functions: production/operations, R&D, or marketing. Today, due to the growing complexity and dynamism of the environment, success increasingly depends on a judicious combination of several functional influences. This transition from a single function focus to a multifunction focus is essential for successful strategic management.[3]

Financial ratio analysis exemplifies the complexity of relationships among the functional areas of business. A declining return on investment or profit margin ratio could be the result of ineffective marketing, poor management policies, research and development errors, or a weak management information system. The effectiveness of strategy formulation, implementation, and evaluation activities hinges upon a clear understanding of how major business functions affect one another. For strategies to succeed, a coordinated effort among all the functional areas of business is needed. In the case of planning, George wrote:

> We may conceptually separate planning for the purpose of theoretical discussion and analysis, but in practice, neither is it a distinct entity nor is it capable of being separated. The planning function is mixed with all other business functions and, like ink once mixed with water, it cannot be set apart. It is spread throughout and is a part of the whole of managing an organization.[4]

The Resource-Based View (RBV)

Gaining in popularity in the 1990s and continuing today, the RBV approach to competitive advantage contends that internal resources are more important for a firm than external factors in achieving and sustaining competitive advantage. In contrast to the I/O theory presented in the previous chapter, proponents of the RBV view, led by Jay Barney, contend that organizational performance will primarily be determined by internal resources which can be grouped into three all encompassing categories: physical resources, human resources, and organizational resources.[5] Physical resources include all plant and equipment, location, technology, raw materials, machines; human resources include all employees, training, experience, intelligence, knowledge, skills, abilities; and organizational resources include firm structure, planning processes, information systems, patents, trademarks, copyrights, databases, and so on. RBV theory asserts that resources are actually what helps a firm exploit opportunities and neutralize threats.

The basic premise of the RBV is that the mix, type, amount, and nature of a firm's internal resources should be considered first and foremost in devising strategies that can lead to sustainable competitive advantage. Managing strategically according to the RBV involves developing and exploiting a firm's unique resources and capabilities, and continually maintaining and strengthening those resources. The theory asserts that it is advantageous for a firm to pursue a strategy that is not currently being implemented by any competing firm. When other firms are unable to duplicate a particular strategy, then the focal firm has a sustainable competitive advantage, according to RBV theorists. In order for a resource to be valuable, however, it must be either (1) rare, (2) hard to imitate, or (3) not easily substitutable. Often called "empirical indicators," these three characteristics of resources enable a firm to implement strategies that improve its efficiency and effectiveness and lead to a sustainable competitive advantage. The more a resource(s) is rare, nonimitable, and nonsubstitutable, the stronger a firm's competitive advantage will be and the longer it will last.

Rare resources are resources that other competing firms do not possess. If many firms have the same resource, then those firms will likely implement similar strategies, thus giving no one firm a sustainable competitive advantage. This is not to say that resources that are common are not valuable; they do indeed aid the firm in its chance for economic prosperity. However, to sustain a competitive advantage, it is more advantageous if the resource(s) is also rare.

It is also important that these same resources be difficult to imitate. If firms cannot easily gain the resources, say RBV theorists, then those resources will lead to a competitive advantage more so than resources easily imitable. Even if a firm employs resources that are rare, a sustainable competitive advantage may be achieved only if other firms cannot easily obtain these resources.

The third empirical indicator that can make resources a source of competitive advantage is substitutability. Borrowing from Porter's Five-Forces Model, to the degree that there are no viable substitutes, a firm will be able to sustain its competitive advantage. However, even if a competing firm cannot imitate a firm's resource perfectly, it can still obtain a sustainable competitive advantage of its own by obtaining resource substitutes.

The RBV has continued to grow in popularity and continues to seek a better understanding of the relationship between resources and sustained competitive advantage in strategic management. However, as eluded to in Chapter 3, one cannot say with any degree of certainty that either external or internal factors will always or even consistently be more important in seeking competitive advantage. Understanding both external and internal factors, and more importantly, understanding the relationships among them, will be the key to effective strategy formulation (discussed in Chapter 6). Since both external and internal factors continually change, strategists seek to identify and take advantage of positive changes and buffer against negative changes in a continuing effort to gain and sustain a firm's competitive advantage. This is the essence and challenge of strategic management and oftentimes survival of the firm hinges on this work.

Integrating Strategy and Culture

Relationships among a firm's functional business activities perhaps can be exemplified best by focusing on organizational culture, an internal phenomenon that permeates all departments and divisions of an organization. *Organizational culture* can be defined as "a pattern of behavior [that has been] developed by an organization as it learns to cope with its problem of external adaptation and internal integration, [and] that has worked well enough to be considered valid and to be taught to new members as the correct way to perceive, think, and feel."[6] This definition emphasizes the importance of matching external with internal factors in making strategic decisions.

Organizational culture captures the subtle, elusive, and largely unconscious forces that shape a workplace. Remarkably resistant to change, culture can represent a major strength or weakness for the firm. It can be an underlying reason for strengths or weaknesses in any of the major business functions.

Defined in Table 4–1, *cultural products* include values, beliefs, rites, rituals, ceremonies, myths, stories, legends, sagas, language, metaphors, symbols, heroes, and heroines. These products or dimensions are levers that strategists can use to influence and direct strategy formulation, implementation, and evaluation activities. An organization's culture compares to an individual's personality in the sense that no two organizations have the same culture and no two individuals have the same personality. Both culture and personality are fairly enduring and can be warm, aggressive, friendly, open, innovative, conservative, liberal, harsh, or likable.

Dimensions of organizational culture permeate all the functional areas of business. It is something of an art to uncover the basic values and beliefs that are deeply buried in an organization's rich collection of stories, language, heroes, and rituals, but cultural products can represent both important strengths and weaknesses. Culture is an aspect of an organization that can no longer be taken for granted in performing an internal strategic-management audit because culture and strategy must work together.

VISIT THE NET

Provides an excellent "Business and Strategic Planning Bibliography." home.att.net/~nichols/ strategy.htm

TABLE 4-1   Cultural Products and Associated Definitions

Rites	Relatively elaborate, dramatic, planned sets of activities that consolidate various forms of cultural expressions into one event, carried out through social interactions, usually for the benefit of an audience
Ceremonial	A system of several rites connected with a single occasion or event
Ritual	A standardized, detailed set of techniques and behaviors that manage anxieties, but seldom produce intended, technical consequences of practical importance
Myth	A dramatic narrative of imagined events, usually used to explain origins or transformations of something. Also, an unquestioned belief about the practical benefits of certain techniques and behaviors that is not supported by facts
Saga	A historical narrative describing the unique accomplishments of a group and its leaders, usually in heroic terms
Legend	A handed-down narrative of some wonderful event that is based on history but has been embellished with fictional details
Story	A narrative based on true events, sometimes a combination of truth and fiction
Folktale	A completely fictional narrative
Symbol	Any object, act, event, quality, or relation that serves as a vehicle for conveying meaning, usually by representing another thing
Language	A particular form or manner in which members of a group use sounds and written signs to convey meanings to each other
Metaphors	Shorthand words used to capture a vision or to reinforce old or new values
Values	Life-directing attitudes that serve as behavioral guidelines
Belief	An understanding of a particular phenomenon
Heroes/Heroines	Individuals whom the organization has legitimized to model behavior for others

Source: Adapted from H. M. Trice and J. M. Beyer, "Studying Organizational Cultures through Rites and Ceremonials," *Academy of Management Review* 9, no. 4 (October 1984): 655.

The strategic-management process takes place largely within a particular organization's culture. Lorsch found that executives in successful companies are emotionally committed to the firm's culture, but he concluded that culture can inhibit strategic management in two basic ways. First, managers frequently miss the significance of changing external conditions because they are blinded by strongly held beliefs. Second, when a particular culture has been effective in the past, the natural response is to stick with it in the future, even during times of major strategic change.[7] An organization's culture must support the collective commitment of its people to a common purpose. It must foster competence and enthusiasm among managers and employees.

Organizational culture significantly affects business decisions and thus must be evaluated during an internal strategic-management audit. If strategies can capitalize on cultural strengths, such as a strong work ethic or highly ethical beliefs, then management often can implement changes swiftly and easily. However, if the firm's culture is not supportive, strategic changes may be ineffective or even counterproductive. A firm's culture can become antagonistic to new strategies, with the result being confusion and disorientation. An organization's culture should infuse individuals with enthusiasm for implementing strategies. Allarie and Firsirotu emphasized the need to understand culture:

> Culture provides an explanation for the insuperable difficulties a firm encounters when it attempts to shift its strategic direction. Not only has the "right" culture become the essence and foundation of corporate excellence, it is also claimed that success or failure of reforms hinges on management's sagacity and ability to change the firm's driving culture in time and in time with required changes in strategies.[8]

The potential value of organizational culture has not been realized fully in the study of strategic management. Ignoring the effect that culture can have on relationships among the functional areas of business can result in barriers to communication, lack of coordination, and an inability to adapt to changing conditions. Some tension between culture and a firm's strategy is inevitable, but the tension should be monitored so that it does not reach a point at which relationships are severed and the culture becomes antagonistic. The resulting disarray among members of the organization would disrupt strategy formulation, implementation, and evaluation. On the other hand, a supportive organizational culture can make managing much easier.

Internal strengths and weaknesses associated with a firm's culture sometimes are overlooked because of the interfunctional nature of this phenomenon. It is important, therefore, for strategists to understand their firm as a sociocultural system. Success is often determined by linkages between a firm's culture and strategies. The challenge of strategic management today is to bring about the changes in organizational culture and individual mind-sets that are needed to support the formulation, implementation, and evaluation of strategies.

American versus Foreign Cultures

To successfully compete in world markets, U.S. managers must obtain a better knowledge of historical, cultural, and religious forces that motivate and drive people in other countries. In Japan, for example, business relations operate within the context of *Wa*, which stresses group harmony and social cohesion. In China, business behavior revolves around *guanxi*, or personal relations. In Korea, activities involve concern for *inhwa*, or harmony based on respect of hierarchical relationships, including obedience to authority.[9] Note in the Global Perspective box that it is important to be sensitive to foreign business cultures.

In Europe, it is generally true that the farther north on the continent, the more participatory the management style. Most European workers are unionized and enjoy more frequent vacations and holidays than U.S. workers. A ninety-minute lunch break plus twenty-minute morning and afternoon breaks are common in European firms. Guaranteed permanent employment is commonly a part of employment contracts in Europe. In socialist countries such as France, Belgium, and the United Kingdom, the only ground for immediate dismissal from work is a criminal offense. A six-month trial period at the beginning of employment is usually part of the contract with a European firm. Many Europeans resent pay-for-performance, commission salaries, and objective measurement and reward systems. This is true especially of workers in southern Europe. Many Europeans also find the notion of team spirit difficult to grasp because the unionized environment has dichotomized worker–management relations throughout Europe.

A weakness that U.S. firms have in competing with Pacific Rim firms is a lack of understanding of Far Eastern cultures, including how Asians think and behave. Spoken Chinese, for example, has more in common with spoken English than with spoken Japanese or Korean. Managers around the world face the responsibility of having to exert authority while at the same time trying to be liked by subordinates. U.S. managers consistently put more weight on being friendly and liked, whereas Asian and European managers exercise authority often without this concern. Americans tend to use first names instantly in business dealings with foreigners, but foreigners find this presumptuous. In Japan, for example, first names are used only among family members and intimate friends; even longtime business associates and co-workers shy away from the use of first names. Other cultural differences or pitfalls that U.S. managers need to know about are given in Table 4–2.

U.S. managers have a low tolerance for silence, whereas Asian managers view extended periods of silence as important for organizing and evaluating one's thoughts. U.S. managers are much more action-oriented than their counterparts around the world; they rush to appointments, conferences, and meetings—and then feel the day has been productive. But for foreign managers, resting, listening, meditating, and thinking is considered productive. Sitting through a conference without talking is unproductive in the United States, but it is viewed as positive in Japan if one's silence helps preserve unity.

TABLE 4-2   Cultural Pitfalls That You Need to Know

- Waving is a serious insult in Greece and Nigeria, particularly if the hand is near someone's face.
- Making a "good-bye" wave in Europe can mean "no," but it means "come here" in Peru.
- In China, last names are written first.
- A man named Carlos Lopez-Garcia should be addressed as Mr. Lopez in Latin America, but as Mr. Garcia in Brazil.
- Breakfast meetings are considered uncivilized in most foreign countries.
- Latin Americans are on average twenty minutes late to business appointments.
- Direct eye contact is impolite in Japan.
- Don't cross your legs in Arab or many Asian countries—it's rude to show the sole of your shoe.
- In Brazil, touching your thumb and first finger—an American "OK" sign—is the equivalent of raising your middle finger.
- Nodding or tossing your head back in southern Italy, Malta, Greece, and Tunisia means "no." In India, this body motion means "yes."
- Snapping your fingers is vulgar in France and Belgium.
- Folding your arms across your chest is a sign of annoyance in Finland.
- In China, leave some food on your plate to show that your host was so generous that you couldn't finish.
- Do not eat with your left hand when dining with clients from Malaysia or India.
- One form of communication works the same worldwide. It's the smile—so take that along wherever you go.

U.S. managers also put greater emphasis on short-term results than foreign managers do. In marketing, for example, Japanese managers strive to achieve "everlasting customers," whereas many Americans strive to make a one-time sale. Marketing managers in Japan see making a sale as the beginning, not the end, of the selling process. This is an important distinction. Japanese managers often criticize U.S. managers for worrying more about shareholders, whom they do not know, than employees, whom they do know. Americans refer to "hourly employees," whereas many Japanese companies still refer to "lifetime employees."

Rose Knotts recently summarized some important cultural differences between U.S. and foreign managers:[10]

1. Americans place an exceptionally high priority on time, viewing time as an asset. Many foreigners place more worth on relationships. This difference results in foreign managers often viewing U.S. managers as "more interested in business than people."

2. Personal touching and distance norms differ around the world. Americans generally stand about three feet from each other when carrying on business conversations, but Arabs and Africans stand about one foot apart. Touching another person with the left hand in business dealings is taboo in some countries. American managers need to learn the personal space rules of foreign managers with whom they interact in business.

3. People in some cultures do not place the same significance on material wealth as American managers often do. Lists of the "largest corporations" and "highest-paid" executives abound in the United States. "More is better" and "bigger is better" in the United States, but not everywhere. This can be a consideration in trying to motivate individuals in other countries.

4. Family roles and relationships vary in different countries. For example, males are valued more than females in some cultures, and peer pressure, work situations, and business interactions reinforce this phenomenon.

5. Language differs dramatically across countries, even in countries where people speak the same language. Words and expressions commonly used in one country may be disrespectful in another.

6. Business and daily life in some societies is governed by religious factors. Prayer times, holidays, daily events, and dietary restrictions, for example, need to be respected by American managers not familiar with these practices in some countries.

7. Time spent with the family and the quality of relationships are more important in some cultures than the personal achievement and accomplishments espoused by the traditional American manager. For example, where a person stands in the hierarchy of a firm's organizational structure, how large the firm is, and where the firm is located are much more important factors to American managers than to many foreign managers.

8. Many cultures around the world value modesty, team spirit, collectivity, and patience much more than the competitiveness and individualism that are so important in America.

9. Punctuality is a valued personal trait when conducting business in America, but it is not revered in many of the world's societies. Eating habits also differ dramatically across cultures. For example, belching is acceptable in many countries as evidence of satisfaction with the food that has been prepared. Chinese culture considers it good manners to sample a portion of each food served.

10. To prevent social blunders when meeting with managers from other lands, one must learn and respect the rules of etiquette of others. Sitting on a toilet seat is viewed as unsanitary in most countries, but not in the United States. Leaving food or drink after dining is considered impolite in some countries, but not in China. Bowing instead of shaking hands is customary in many countries. Many cultures view Americans as unsanitary for locating toilet and bathing facilities in the same area, whereas Americans view people of some cultures as unsanitary for not taking a bath or shower every day.

11. Americans often do business with individuals they do not know, but this practice is not accepted in many other cultures. In Mexico and Japan, for example, an amicable relationship is often mandatory before conducting business.

In many countries, effective managers are those who are best at negotiating with government bureaucrats rather than those who inspire workers. Many U.S. managers are uncomfortable with nepotism and bribery, which are common in many countries. In almost every country except the United States, bribery is tax deductible.

The United States has gained a reputation for defending women from sexual harassment and minorities from discrimination, but not all countries embrace the same values. For example, in the Czech Republic, it is considered a compliment when the boss openly flirts with his female secretary and invites her to dinner. U.S. managers in the Czech Republic who do not flirt seem cold and uncaring to some employees.

American managers in China have to be careful about how they arrange office furniture because Chinese workers believe in *feng shui*, the practice of harnessing natural forces. American managers in Japan have to be careful about *nemaswashio*, whereby Japanese workers expect supervisors to alert them privately of changes rather than informing them in a meeting. Japanese managers have little appreciation for versatility, expecting all managers to be the same. In Japan, "If a nail sticks out, you hit it into the wall," says Brad Lashbrook, an international consultant for Wilson Learning.

Probably the biggest obstacle to the effectiveness of U.S. managers—or managers from any country working in another—is the fact that it is almost impossible to change the attitude of a foreign workforce. "The system drives you; you cannot fight the system or culture," says Bill Parker, president of Phillips Petroleum in Norway.

Management

The *functions of management* consist of five basic activities: planning, organizing, motivating, staffing, and controlling. An overview of these activities is provided in Table 4–3.

Planning

The only thing certain about the future of any organization is change, and *planning* is the essential bridge between the present and the future that increases the likelihood of achieving desired results. Planning is the process by which one determines whether to attempt a task, works out the most effective way of reaching desired objectives, and prepares to overcome unexpected difficulties with adequate resources. Planning is the start of the process by which an individual or business may turn empty dreams into achievements. Planning enables one to avoid the trap of working extremely hard but achieving little.

Planning is an up-front investment in success. Planning helps a firm achieve maximum effect from a given effort. Planning enables a firm to take into account relevant

TABLE 4-3   The Basic Functions of Management

FUNCTION	DESCRIPTION	STAGE OF STRATEGIC-MANAGEMENT PROCESS WHEN MOST IMPORTANT
Planning	Planning consists of all those managerial activities related to preparing for the future. Specific tasks include forecasting, establishing objectives, devising strategies, developing policies, and setting goals.	Strategy Formulation
Organizing	Organizing includes all those managerial activities that result in a structure of task and authority relationships. Specific areas include organizational design, job specialization, job descriptions, job specifications, span of the control, unity of command, coordination, job design, and job analysis.	Strategy Implementation
Motivating	Motivating involves efforts directed toward shaping human behavior. Specific topics include leadership, communication, work groups, behavior modification, delegation of authority, job enrichment, job satisfaction, needs fulfillment, organizational change, employee morale, and managerial morale.	Strategy Implementation
Staffing	Staffing activities are centered on personnel or human resource management. Included are wage and salary administration, employee benefits, interviewing, hiring, firing, training, management development, employee safety, affirmative action, equal employment opportunity, union relations, career development, personnel research, discipline policies, grievance procedures, and public relations.	Strategy Implementation
Controlling	Controlling refers to all those managerial activities directed toward ensuring that actual results are consistent with planned results. Key areas of concern include quality control, financial control, sales control, inventory control, expense control, analysis of variances, rewards, and sanctions.	Strategy Evaluation

factors and focus on the critical ones. Planning helps ensure that the firm can be prepared for all reasonable eventualities and for all changes that will be needed. Planning enables a firm to gather the resources needed and carry out tasks in the most efficient way possible. Planning enables a firm to conserve its own resources, avoid wasting ecological resources, make a fair profit, and be seen as an effective, useful firm. Planning enables a firm to identify precisely what is to be achieved and to detail precisely the who, what, when, where, why, and how needed to achieve desired objectives. Planning enables a firm to assess whether the effort, costs, and implications associated with achieving desired objectives are warranted.[11] Planning is the cornerstone of effective strategy formulation. But even though it is considered the foundation of management, it is commonly the task that managers neglect most. Planning is essential for successful strategy implementation and strategy evaluation, largely because organizing, motivating, staffing, and controlling activities depend upon good planning.

The process of planning must involve managers and employees throughout an organization. The time horizon for planning decreases from two to five years for top-level to less than six months for lower-level managers. The important point is that all managers do planning and should involve subordinates in the process to facilitate employee understanding and commitment.

Planning can have a positive impact on organizational and individual performance. Planning allows an organization to identify and take advantage of external opportunities as well as minimize the impact of external threats. Planning is more than extrapolating from the past and present into the future. It also includes developing a mission, forecasting future events and trends, establishing objectives, and choosing strategies to pursue.

An organization can develop synergy through planning. *Synergy* exists when everyone pulls together as a team that knows what it wants to achieve; synergy is the 2 + 2 = 5 effect. By establishing and communicating clear objectives, employees and managers can work together toward desired results. Synergy can result in powerful competitive advantages. The strategic-management process itself is aimed at creating synergy in an organization.

Planning allows a firm to adapt to changing markets and thus to shape its own destiny. Strategic management can be viewed as a formal planning process that allows an organization to pursue proactive rather than reactive strategies. Successful organizations strive to control their own futures rather than merely react to external forces and events as they occur. Historically, organisms and organizations that have not adapted to changing conditions have become extinct. Swift adaptation is needed today more than ever before because changes in markets, economies, and competitors worldwide are accelerating.

Organizing

The purpose of *organizing* is to achieve coordinated effort by defining task and authority relationships. Organizing means determining who does what and who reports to whom. There are countless examples in history of well-organized enterprises successfully competing against—and in some cases defeating—much stronger but less-organized firms. A well-organized firm generally has motivated managers and employees who are committed to seeing the organization succeed. Resources are allocated more effectively and used more efficiently in a well-organized firm than in a disorganized firm.

The organizing function of management can be viewed as consisting of three sequential activities: breaking tasks down into jobs (work specialization), combining jobs to form departments (departmentalization), and delegating authority. Breaking tasks down into jobs requires the development of job descriptions and job specifications. These tools clarify for both managers and employees what particular jobs entail. In *Wealth of Nations*, published in 1776, Adam Smith cited the advantages of work specialization in the manufacture of pins:

> One man draws the wire, another straightens it, a third cuts it, a fourth points it, a fifth grinds it at the top for receiving the head. Ten men working in this manner can produce 48,000 pins in a single day, but if they had all wrought separately and independently, each might at best produce twenty pins in a day.[12]

Combining jobs to form departments results in an organizational structure, span of control, and a chain of command. Changes in strategy often require changes in structure because positions may be created, deleted, or merged. Organizational structure dictates how resources are allocated and how objectives are established in a firm. Allocating resources and establishing objectives geographically, for example, is much different from doing so by product or customer.

The most common forms of departmentalization are functional, divisional, strategic business unit, and matrix. These types of structure are discussed further in Chapter 7.

Delegating authority is an important organizing activity, as evidenced in the old saying "You can tell how good a manager is by observing how his or her department functions when he or she isn't there." Employees today are more educated and more capable of participating in organizational decision making than ever before. In most cases, they expect to be delegated authority and responsibility, and to be held accountable for results. Delegation of authority is embedded in the strategic-management process.

Motivating

Motivating can be defined as the process of influencing people to accomplish specific objectives.[13] Motivation explains why some people work hard and others do not. Objectives, strategies, and policies have little chance of succeeding if employees and managers are not motivated to implement strategies once they are formulated. The motivating function of management includes at least four major components: leadership, group dynamics, communication, and organizational change.

When managers and employees of a firm strive to achieve high levels of productivity, this indicates that the firm's strategists are good leaders. Good leaders establish rapport with subordinates, empathize with their needs and concerns, set a good example, and are trustworthy and fair. Leadership includes developing a vision of the firm's future and inspiring people to work hard to achieve that vision. Kirkpatrick and Locke reported that certain traits also characterize effective leaders: knowledge of the business, cognitive ability, self-confidence, honesty, integrity, and drive.[14]

Research suggests that democratic behavior on the part of leaders results in more positive attitudes toward change and higher productivity than does autocratic behavior. Drucker said:

> Leadership is not a magnetic personality. That can just as well be demagoguery. It is not "making friends and influencing people." That is flattery. Leadership is the lifting of a person's vision to higher sights, the raising of a person's performance to a higher standard, the building of a person's personality beyond its normal limitations.[15]

Group dynamics play a major role in employee morale and satisfaction. Informal groups or coalitions form in every organization. The norms of coalitions can range from being very positive to very negative toward management. It is important, therefore, that strategists identify the composition and nature of informal groups in an organization to facilitate strategy formulation, implementation, and evaluation. Leaders of informal groups are especially important in formulating and implementing strategy changes.

Communication, perhaps the most important word in management, is a major component in motivation. An organization's system of communication determines whether strategies can be implemented successfully. Good two-way communication is vital for gaining support for departmental and divisional objectives and policies. Top-down communication can encourage bottom-up communication. The strategic-management process becomes a lot easier when subordinates are encouraged to discuss their concerns, reveal their problems, provide recommendations, and give suggestions. A primary reason for instituting strategic management is to build and support effective communication networks throughout the firm.

> The manager of tomorrow must be able to get his people to commit themselves to the business, whether they are machine operators or junior vice-presidents. Ah, you say, participative management. Have a cigar. But just because most

managers tug a forelock at the P word doesn't mean they know how to make it work. Today, throwing together a few quality circles won't suffice. The key issue will be empowerment, a term whose strength suggests the need to get beyond merely sharing a little information and a bit of decision making.[16]

Staffing

The management function of *staffing*, also called *personnel management* or *human resource management*, includes activities such as recruiting, interviewing, testing, selecting, orienting, training, developing, caring for, evaluating, rewarding, disciplining, promoting, transferring, demoting, and dismissing employees, as well as managing union relations.

Staffing activities play a major role in strategy-implementation efforts, and for this reason, human resource managers are becoming more actively involved in the strategic-management process. It is important to identify strengths and weaknesses in the staffing area.

The complexity and importance of human resource activities have increased to such a degree that all but the smallest organizations now need a full-time human resource manager. Numerous court cases that directly affect staffing activities are decided each day. Organizations and individuals can be penalized severely for not following federal, state, and local laws and guidelines related to staffing. Line managers simply cannot stay abreast of all the legal developments and requirements regarding staffing. The human resources department coordinates staffing decisions in the firm so that an organization as a whole meets legal requirements. This department also provides needed consistency in administering company rules, wages, and policies.

Human resource management is particularly challenging for international companies. For example, the inability of spouses and children to adapt to new surroundings has become a major staffing problem in overseas transfers. The problems include premature returns, job performance slumps, resignations, discharges, low morale, marital discord, and general discontent. Firms such as Ford Motor and ExxonMobil have begun screening and interviewing spouses and children before assigning persons to overseas positions. 3M Corporation introduces children to peers in the target country and offers spouses educational benefits.

Strategists are becoming increasingly aware of how important human resources are to effective strategic management. Human resource managers are becoming more involved and more proactive in formulating and implementing strategies. They provide leadership for organizations that are restructuring, or they allow employees to work at home.

Controlling

The *controlling* function of management includes all of those activities undertaken to ensure that actual operations conform to planned operations. All managers in an organization have controlling responsibilities, such as conducting performance evaluations and taking necessary action to minimize inefficiencies. The controlling function of management is particularly important for effective strategy evaluation. Controlling consists of four basic steps:

1. Establishing performance standards
2. Measuring individual and organizational performance
3. Comparing actual performance to planned performance standards
4. Taking corrective actions

Measuring individual performance is often conducted ineffectively or not at all in organizations. Some reasons for this shortcoming are that evaluations can create confrontations that most managers prefer to avoid, can take more time than most managers are willing to give, and can require skills that many managers lack. No single approach to measuring individual performance is without limitations. For this reason, an organization should examine various methods, such as the graphic rating scale, the behaviorally anchored rating scale, and the critical incident method, and then develop or select a performance appraisal approach that best suits the firm's needs. Increasingly, firms are striving to link organizational performance with managers' and employees' pay. This topic is discussed further in Chapter 7.

Management Audit Checklist of Questions

The checklist of questions provided below can help determine specific strengths and weaknesses in the functional area of business. An answer of *no* to any question could indicate a potential weakness, although the strategic significance and implications of negative answers, of course, will vary by organization, industry, and severity of the weakness. Positive or *yes* answers to the checklist questions suggest potential areas of strength.

1. Does the firm use strategic-management concepts?
2. Are company objectives and goals measurable and well communicated?
3. Do managers at all hierarchical levels plan effectively?
4. Do managers delegate authority well?
5. Is the organization's structure appropriate?
6. Are job descriptions and job specifications clear?
7. Is employee morale high?
8. Are employee turnover and absenteeism low?
9. Are organizational reward and control mechanisms effective?

Marketing

Marketing can be described as the process of defining, anticipating, creating, and fulfilling customers' needs and wants for products and services. There are seven basic *functions of marketing*: (1) customer analysis, (2) selling products/services, (3) product and service planning, (4) pricing, (5) distribution, (6) marketing research, and (7) opportunity analysis.[17] Understanding these functions helps strategists identify and evaluate marketing strengths and weaknesses.

Customer Analysis

Customer analysis—the examination and evaluation of consumer needs, desires, and wants—involves administering customer surveys, analyzing consumer information, evaluating market positioning strategies, developing customer profiles, and determining optimal market segmentation strategies. The information generated by customer analysis can be essential in developing an effective mission statement. Customer profiles can reveal the demographic characteristics of an organization's customers. Buyers, sellers, distributors, salespeople, managers, wholesalers, retailers, suppliers, and creditors can all participate in gathering information to identify customers' needs and wants successfully. Successful organizations continually monitor present and potential customers' buying patterns.

Selling Products/Services

Successful strategy implementation generally rests upon the ability of an organization to sell some product or service. *Selling* includes many marketing activities, such as advertising, sales promotion, publicity, personal selling, sales force management, customer relations, and dealer relations. These activities are especially critical when a firm pursues a market penetration strategy. The effectiveness of various selling tools for consumer and industrial products varies. Personal selling is most important for industrial goods companies, and advertising is most important for consumer goods companies. During the CBS telecast of Super Bowl XXXVIII on February 1, 2004, a 30-second advertisement cost $2.3 million, up 9 percent from 2003. There were 62 ad slots sold by CBS for this Super Bowl. Determining organizational strengths and weaknesses in the selling function of marketing is an important part of performing an internal strategic-management audit.

With regard to advertising products and services on the Internet, a new trend is to base advertising rates exclusively on sales rates. This new accountability contrasts sharply with traditional broadcast and print advertising, which bases rates on the number of persons expected to see a given advertisement. The new cost-per-sale online advertising rates are possible because any Web site can monitor which user clicks on which advertisement and then can record whether that consumer actually buys the product. If there are no sales, then the advertisement is free.

Product and Service Planning

Product and service planning includes activities such as test marketing; product and brand positioning; devising warranties; packaging; determining product options, product features, product style, and product quality; deleting old products; and providing for customer service. Product and service planning is particularly important when a company is pursuing product development or diversification.

One of the most effective product and service planning techniques is *test marketing*. Test markets allow an organization to test alternative marketing plans and to forecast future sales of new products. In conducting a test market project, an organization must decide how many cities to include, which cities to include, how long to run the test, what information to collect during the test, and what action to take after the test has been completed. Test marketing is used more frequently by consumer goods companies than by industrial goods companies. Test marketing can allow an organization to avoid substantial losses by revealing weak products and ineffective marketing approaches before large-scale production begins.

Pricing

Five major stakeholders affect *pricing* decisions: consumers, governments, suppliers, distributors, and competitors. Sometimes an organization will pursue a forward integration strategy primarily to gain better control over prices charged to consumers. Governments can impose constraints on price fixing, price discrimination, minimum prices, unit pricing, price advertising, and price controls. For example, the Robinson-Patman Act prohibits manufacturers and wholesalers from discriminating in price among channel member purchasers (suppliers and distributors) if competition is injured.

Competing organizations must be careful not to coordinate discounts, credit terms, or condition of sale; not to discuss prices, markups, and costs at trade association meetings; and not to arrange to issue new price lists on the same date, to rotate low bids on contracts, or to uniformly restrict production to maintain high prices. Strategists should view price from both a short-run and a long-run perspective, because competitors can copy price changes with relative ease. Often a dominant firm will aggressively match all price cuts by competitors.

With regard to pricing, as the value of the dollar increases, U.S. multinational companies have a choice. They can raise prices in the local currency of a foreign country or risk losing sales and market share. Alternatively, multinational firms can keep prices steady and face reduced profit when their export revenue is reported in the United States in dollars.

In late 2003, Wrigley's raised the price of its chewing gum by five cents, to thirty cents, the first such price hike in sixteen years. The price of plasma televisions has dropped to below $2,000 in 2004 from above $8,000 several years ago. Intense price competition coupled with Internet price-comparative shopping in most industries has reduced profit margins to bare minimum levels for most companies. For example, airline tickets, rental car prices, and even computer prices are lower today than they have been in many years.

Prices on handheld computers are falling dramatically because distributors have excess inventory due to slowing consumer demand. Analysts contend that handheld computers will soon become as inexpensive as cellphones—and eventually may be given away when a consumer purchases the company's wireless Internet service. Palm is the largest handheld-computer maker, but other competitors include Casio, Handspring, and Hewlett-Packard. While the current economic downturn has wreaked havoc for companies on Wall Street, it has benefited consumers on Main Street, who have seen lower prices almost everywhere they shop.

Distribution

Distribution includes warehousing, distribution channels, distribution coverage, retail site locations, sales territories, inventory levels and location, transportation carriers, wholesaling, and retailing. Most producers today do not sell their goods directly to consumers. Various marketing entities act as intermediaries; they bear a variety of names such as wholesalers, retailers, brokers, facilitators, agents, vendors—or simply distributors.

Distribution becomes especially important when a firm is striving to implement a market development or forward integration strategy. Some of the most complex and challenging decisions facing a firm concern product distribution. Intermediaries flourish in our economy because many producers lack the financial resources and expertise to carry out direct marketing. Manufacturers who could afford to sell directly to the public often can gain greater returns by expanding and improving their manufacturing operations. Even General Motors would find it very difficult to buy out its more than eighteen thousand independent dealers.

Successful organizations identify and evaluate alternative ways to reach their ultimate market. Possible approaches vary from direct selling to using just one or many wholesalers and retailers. Strengths and weaknesses of each channel alternative should be determined according to economic, control, and adaptive criteria. Organizations should consider the costs and benefits of various wholesaling and retailing options. They must consider the need to motivate and control channel members and the need to adapt to changes in the future. Once a marketing channel is chosen, an organization usually must adhere to it for an extended period of time.

Marketing Research

Marketing research is the systematic gathering, recording, and analyzing of data about problems relating to the marketing of goods and services. Marketing research can uncover critical strengths and weaknesses, and marketing researchers employ numerous scales, instruments, procedures, concepts, and techniques to gather information. Marketing research activities support all of the major business functions of an organization. Organizations that possess excellent marketing research skills have a definite strength in pursuing generic strategies.

> The President of PepsiCo [said], "Looking at the competition is the company's best form of market research. The majority of our strategic successes are ideas that we borrow from the marketplace, usually from a small regional or local competitor. In each case, we spot a promising new idea, improve on it, and then out-execute our competitor."[18]

As indicated in the "E-Commerce Perspective," market researchers should be careful not to use spam as a marketing tool because consumers intensely reject this method of gathering information. Spam slows down business for millions of firms.

E-COMMERCE PERSPECTIVE

Spam Is Choking E-Commerce

Spam, unwanted, unsolicited, undesirable e-mail messages, is choking e-commerce globally. Spam now accounts for over 50 percent of all Internet traffic and annually delivers more than 1,000 mailings to every person who uses the Internet. This traffic jams individual and business servers and computers around the globe and clogs and slows down transactions. Companies are being forced to buy more and more hardware and software to handle the avalanche of spam while their workers waste precious time every day combing through it. Current estimates are that spam is costing companies $874 a year per worker. Spammers are as bad for e-commerce as vandals who create worms and viruses or thieves who steal credit card numbers and extort. The FBI now lists cybercrime as its third-ranking priority, behind only the war against terror and counterespionage.

California has the nation's toughest anti-spam law because it requires e-mail marketers either to have an existing business relationship with each recipient, or to receive permission from the recipient to send a commercial e-mail. Also, California law allows lawyers to sue the senders of unwanted e-mail; the law carries penalties of $1,000 for each unsolicited message sent and a $1 million fine for each "campaign." Since there is as yet no U.S. federal law against spamming, e-mail marketers still fre-

quently change their e-mail address, route their e-mails through multiple computers to disguise their identity, and send e-mails from outside the United States. Thirty-five states have laws regulating spam in some form, but California's and Delaware's are more stringent.

In an attempt to halt the spread of disruptive computer viruses and spam, more and more companies are eliminating employee use of AOL, Yahoo!, and other outside e-mail services to protect their own networks. Companies are also eliminating Web surfing by employees. Phone4U, a mobile-phone retailer in England, for example, now prohibits its 2,500 employees from e-mailing one another, although customers can still e-mail the company. Analysts estimate that in 2003 roughly half of all external corporate e-mail, or more than two trillion messages, was spam. Maret researcher Cipher-Trust Research says that up to 80 percent of all U.S. businesses will have policies in place in 2004 to combat spam and viruses.

Sources: Adapted from Heather Green, Ira Sager, Steve Rosenbush, and Andrew Park, "Where Danger Lurks," *BusinessWeek* (August 25, 2003): 114–118; Mylene Mangalindan, "California Gets Serious About Spam," *Wall Street Journal* (September 24, 2003): A4; Jon Swartz, "More Workers Get Shut Out of E-mail," *USA Today* (September 29, 2003): B1.

Opportunity Analysis

The seventh function of marketing *is opportunity analysis*, which involves assessing the costs, benefits, and risks associated with marketing decisions. Three steps are required to perform a *cost/benefit analysis*: (1) compute the total costs associated with a decision, (2) estimate the total benefits from the decision, and (3) compare the total costs with the total benefits. When expected benefits exceed total costs, an opportunity becomes more attractive. Sometimes the variables included in a cost/benefit analysis cannot be quantified or even measured, but usually reasonable estimates can be made to allow the analysis to be performed. One key factor to be considered is risk. Cost/benefit analyses should also be performed when a company is evaluating alternative ways to be socially responsible.

Marketing Audit Checklist of Questions

The following questions about marketing, much like the earlier questions for management, are pertinent:

1. Are markets segmented effectively?
2. Is the organization positioned well among competitors?
3. Has the firm's market share been increasing?
4. Are present channels of distribution reliable and cost-effective?
5. Does the firm have an effective sales organization?
6. Does the firm conduct market research?
7. Are product quality and customer service good?
8. Are the firm's products and services priced appropriately?
9. Does the firm have an effective promotion, advertising, and publicity strategy?
10. Are marketing, planning, and budgeting effective?
11. Do the firm's marketing managers have adequate experience and training?

Finance/Accounting

Financial condition is often considered the single best measure of a firm's competitive position and overall attractiveness to investors. Determining an organization's financial strengths and weaknesses is essential to formulating strategies effectively. A firm's liquidity, leverage, working capital, profitability, asset utilization, cash flow, and equity can eliminate some strategies as being feasible alternatives. Financial factors often alter existing strategies and change implementation plans.

An especially good Web site to obtain financial information about a company is **finance.yahoo.com** or **www.quicken.com**, which provide excellent financial ratio, stock, and valuation information on all publicly-held companies. Simply insert the company's stock symbol when the screen first loads and a wealth of information follows. Another nice site for obtaining financial information is **www.forbes.com**. Be sure to access the Manufacturing and Service section of **www.strategyclub.com** for excellent financial-related Web sites.

Finance/Accounting Functions

According to James Van Horne, the *functions of finance/accounting* comprise three decisions: the investment decision, the financing decision, and the dividend decision.[19] Financial ratio analysis is the most widely used method for determining an organization's strengths and weaknesses in the investment, financing, and dividend areas. Because the functional areas of business are so closely related, financial ratios can signal strengths or weaknesses in management, marketing, production, research and development, and management information systems activities. It is important to note here that financial ratios are equally applicable in for-profit and nonprofit organizations. Even though nonprofit organizations obviously would not have return-on-investment or earnings-per-share type ratios, they would routinely monitor many other special ratios. For example, a church would monitor the ratio of dollar contributions to number of members, while a zoo would monitor dollar food sales to number of visitors. A university would monitor number of students divided by number of professors. Therefore, be creative when performing ratio analysis for nonprofit organizations because they strive to be financially sound just as for-profit firms do.

The *investment decision*, also called *capital budgeting*, is the allocation and reallocation of capital and resources to projects, products, assets, and divisions of an organization. Once strategies are formulated, capital budgeting decisions are required to implement strategies successfully. The *financing decision* determines the best capital structure for the firm and includes examining various methods by which the firm can raise capital (for example, by issuing stock, increasing debt, selling assets, or using a combination of these approaches). The financing decision must consider both short-term and long-term needs for working capital. Two key financial ratios that indicate whether a firm's financing decisions have been effective are the debt-to-equity ratio and the debt-to-total-assets ratio.

Dividend decisions concern issues such as the percentage of earnings paid to stockholders, the stability of dividends paid over time, and the repurchase or issuance of stock. Dividend decisions determine the amount of funds that are retained in a firm compared to the amount paid out to stockholders. Three financial ratios that are helpful in evaluating a firm's dividend decisions are the earnings-per-share ratio, the dividends-per-share ratio, and the price-earnings ratio. The benefits of paying dividends to investors must be balanced against the benefits of retaining funds internally, and there is no set formula on how to balance this trade-off. For the reasons listed here, dividends are sometimes paid out even when funds could be better reinvested in the business or when the firm has to obtain outside sources of capital:

1. Paying cash dividends is customary. Failure to do so could be thought of as a stigma. A dividend change is considered a signal about the future.
2. Dividends represent a sales point for investment bankers. Some institutional investors can buy only dividend-paying stocks.
3. Shareholders often demand dividends, even in companies with great opportunities for reinvesting all available funds.
4. A myth exists that paying dividends will result in a higher stock price.

Many companies, such as Goodyear Tire & Rubber, have recently suspended paying dividends due to consistently falling revenues and earnings. Goodyear's stock price fell 17 percent to $4.22 on news of the board's decision to eliminate the firm's 12-cents-a-share quarterly dividend in early 2003. In contrast, Microsoft in 2003 began paying dividends for the first time in seventeen years, spurred by both its huge cash reserves and President Bush's plan to eliminate federal taxes on dividends. Citigroup and Wells Fargo raised their dividend payouts by 75 percent and 50 percent, respectively, in mid-2003. In the bear stock market of 2002, dividend-paying stocks held their value much better than non-dividend-paying stocks, losing only 13 percent of their value compared to 30 percent. Only 365 companies in the

S&P 500 stock index pay dividends today, up from 351 at year-end 2002, but still fewer than the 438 companies in 1990. However, nearly 250 of the S&P 500 companies increased their dividend payout in 2003, up from 113 firms in 2002. McDonald's raised its dividend payout by 70 percent in 2003, the largest increase for the firm in 25 years. In contrast, Kodak cut its dividend by 70 percent in late 2003, the first such cut by the company in 101 years. Instead of paying out $3 billion in dividends, Kodak is investing that money in digital photography, away from camera film. From January through October of 2003, 194 S&P 500 companies introduced or raised dividends while only 16 lowered or suspended them.[20]

Basic Types of Financial Ratios

Financial ratios are computed from an organization's income statement and balance sheet. Computing financial ratios is like taking a picture because the results reflect a situation at just one point in time. Comparing ratios over time and to industry averages is more likely to result in meaningful statistics that can be used to identify and evaluate strengths and weaknesses. Trend analysis, illustrated in Figure 4–2, is a useful technique that incorporates both the time and industry average dimensions of financial ratios. Note that the dotted lines reveal projected ratios. Some Web sites, such as **finance.yahoo.com**, calculate financial ratios and provide data with charts. Four major sources of industry-average financial ratios follow:

VISIT THE NET

Enter your stock symbol and then access the up-to-date financial news about the company.
finance.yahoo.com

1. Dun & Bradstreet's *Industry Norms and Key Business Ratios*—Fourteen different ratios are calculated in an industry-average format for eight hundred different types of businesses. The ratios are presented by Standard Industrial Classification (SIC) number and are grouped by annual sales into three size categories.

FIGURE 4–2

A Financial Ratio Trend Analysis

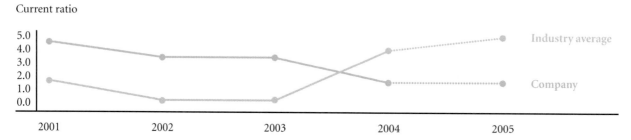

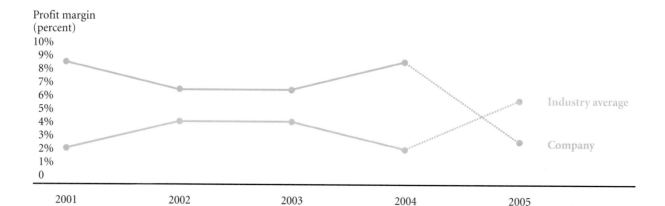

2. Robert Morris Associates' *Annual Statement Studies*—Sixteen different ratios are calculated in an industry-average format. Industries are referenced by SIC numbers published by the Bureau of the Census. The ratios are presented in four size categories by annual sales for all firms in the industry.
3. *Almanac of Business & Industrial Financial Ratios*—Twenty-two financial ratios and percentages are provided in an industry-average format for all major industries. The ratios and percentages are given for twelve different company-size categories for all firms in a given industry.
4. *Federal Trade Commission Reports*—The FTC publishes quarterly financial data, including ratios on manufacturing companies. FTC reports include analyses by industry group and asset size.

Table 4–4 provides a summary of key financial ratios showing how each ratio is calculated and what each ratio measures. However, all the ratios are not significant for all industries and companies. For example, accounts receivable turnover and average collection period are not very meaningful to a company that primarily does a cash receipts business. Key financial ratios can be classified into the following five types:

1. **Liquidity ratios** measure a firm's ability to meet maturing short-term obligations.
   Current ratio
   Quick (or acid-test) ratio
2. **Leverage ratios** measure the extent to which a firm has been financed by debt.
   Debt-to-total-assets ratio
   Debt-to-equity ratio
   Long-term debt-to-equity ratio
   Times-interest-earned (or coverage) ratio
3. **Activity ratios** measure how effectively a firm is using its resources.
   Inventory-turnover
   Fixed assets turnover
   Total assets turnover
   Accounts receivable turnover
   Average collection period
4. **Profitability ratios** measure management's overall effectiveness as shown by the returns generated on sales and investment.
   Gross profit margin
   Operating profit margin
   Net profit margin
   Return on total assets (ROA)
   Return on stockholders' equity (ROE)
   Earnings per share (EPS)
   Price-earnings ratio
5. **Growth ratios** measure the firm's ability to maintain its economic position in the growth of the economy and industry.
   Sales
   Net income
   Earnings per share
   Dividends per share

TABLE 4–4   A Summary of Key Financial Ratios

RATIO	HOW CALCULATED	WHAT IT MEASURES
Liquidity Ratios		
Current Ratio	$\dfrac{\text{Current assets}}{\text{Current liabilities}}$	The extent to which a firm can meet its short-term obligations
Quick Ratio	$\dfrac{\text{Current assets minus inventory}}{\text{Current liabilities}}$	The extent to which a firm can meet its short-term obligations without relying upon the sale of its inventories
Leverage Ratios		
Debt-to-Total-Assets Ratio	$\dfrac{\text{Total debt}}{\text{Total assets}}$	The percentage of total funds that are provided by creditors
Debt-to-Equity Ratio	$\dfrac{\text{Total debt}}{\text{Total stockholders' equity}}$	The percentage of total funds provided by creditors versus by owners
Long-Term Debt-to-Equity Ratio	$\dfrac{\text{Long-term debt}}{\text{Total stockholders' equity}}$	The balance between debt and equity in a firm's long-term capital structure
Times-Interest-Earned Ratio	$\dfrac{\text{Profits before interest and taxes}}{\text{Total interest charges}}$	The extent to which earnings can decline without the firm becoming unable to meet its annual interest costs
Activity Ratios		
Inventory Turnover	$\dfrac{\text{Sales}}{\text{Inventory of finished goods}}$	Whether a firm holds excessive stocks of inventories and whether a firm is selling its inventories slowly compared to the industry average
Fixed Assets Turnover	$\dfrac{\text{Sales}}{\text{Fixed assets}}$	Sales productivity and plant and equipment utilization
Total Assets Turnover	$\dfrac{\text{Sales}}{\text{Total assets}}$	Whether a firm is generating a sufficient volume of business for the size of its asset investment
Accounts Receivable Turnover	$\dfrac{\text{Annual credit sales}}{\text{Accounts receivable}}$	The average length of time it takes a firm to collect credit sales (in percentage terms)
Average Collection Period	$\dfrac{\text{Accounts receivable}}{\text{Total credit sales/365 days}}$	The average length of time it takes a firm to collect on credit sales (in days)
Profitability Ratios		
Gross Profit Margin	$\dfrac{\text{Sales minus cost of goods sold}}{\text{Sales}}$	The total margin available to cover operating expenses and yield a profit
Operating Profit Margin	$\dfrac{\text{Earnings before interest and taxes (EBIT)}}{\text{Sales}}$	Profitability without concern for taxes and interest
Net Profit Margin	$\dfrac{\text{Net income}}{\text{Sales}}$	After-tax profits per dollar of sales

TABLE 4-4   A Summary of Key Financial Ratios (*continued*)

RATIO	HOW CALCULATED	WHAT IT MEASURES
Profitability Ratios (continued)		
Return on Total Assets (ROA)	$\dfrac{\text{Net income}}{\text{Total assets}}$	After-tax profits per dollar of assets; this ratio is also called return on investment (ROI)
Return on Stockholders' Equity (ROE)	$\dfrac{\text{Net income}}{\text{Total stockholders' equity}}$	After-tax profits per dollar of stockholders' investment in the firm
Earnings Per Share (EPS)	$\dfrac{\text{Net income}}{\text{Number of shares of common stock outstanding}}$	Earnings available to the owners of common stock
Price-earnings Ratio	$\dfrac{\text{Market price per share}}{\text{Earnings per share}}$	Attractiveness of firm on equity markets
Growth Ratios		
Sales	Annual percentage growth in total sales	Firm's growth rate in sales
Net Income	Annual percentage growth in profits	Firm's growth rate in profits
Earnings Per Share	Annual percentage growth in EPS	Firm's growth rate in EPS
Dividends Per Share	Annual percentage growth in dividends per share	Firm's growth rate in dividends per share

Financial ratio analysis is not without some limitations. First of all, financial ratios are based on accounting data, and firms differ in their treatment of such items as depreciation, inventory valuation, research and development expenditures, pension plan costs, mergers, and taxes. Also, seasonal factors can influence comparative ratios. Therefore, conformity to industry composite ratios does not establish with certainty that a firm is performing normally or that it is well managed. Likewise, departures from industry averages do not always indicate that a firm is doing especially well or badly. For example, a high inventory turnover ratio could indicate efficient inventory management and a strong working capital position, but it also could indicate a serious inventory shortage and a weak working capital position.

It is important to recognize that a firm's financial condition depends not only on the functions of finance, but also on many other factors that include (1) management, marketing, management production/operations, research and development, and management information systems decisions; (2) actions by competitors, suppliers, distributors, creditors, customers, and shareholders; and (3) economic, social, cultural, demographic, environmental, political, governmental, legal, and technological trends. Even natural environment liabilities can affect financial ratios, as indicated in the "Natural Environment Perspective." So financial ratio analysis, like all other analytical tools, should be used wisely.

Finance/Accounting Audit Checklist of Questions

The following finance/accounting questions, like the similar questions about marketing and management earlier, should be examined:

1. Where is the firm financially strong and weak as indicated by financial ratio analyses?
2. Can the firm raise needed short-term capital?

3. Can the firm raise needed long-term capital through debt and/or equity?
4. Does the firm have sufficient working capital?
5. Are capital budgeting procedures effective?
6. Are dividend payout policies reasonable?
7. Does the firm have good relations with its investors and stockholders?
8. Are the firm's financial managers experienced and well trained?

NATURAL ENVIRONMENT PERSPECTIVE

Is Your Business Polluting the Air or Water?

Air

More than 1.5 billion people around the world live in urban areas with dangerous levels of air pollution. Alarmingly, cities are growing too rapidly to reverse this trend. Seven of the ten worst cities for sulfur dioxide and carbon monoxide are in developing countries. These and other pollutants cause acute and chronic lung disease, heart disease, lung cancer, and lead-induced neurological damage in children. Lung cancer alone kills over one million people annually, and more than a million new cases of lung cancer are diagnosed annually. In the European Union countries, a 33 percent increase in female lung cancer cases is predicted by 2005. There is no effective treatment for lung cancer—only 10 percent of patients are alive five years after diagnosis. Polluted air knows no city, state, country, or continent boundaries.

Water

Is your business polluting the water? Contaminated water is blamed for as much as 80 percent of all disease in developing countries. Well over one billion people in the world still are without safe water to drink, bathe, cook, and clean. Less than 2 percent of the domestic and industrial wastewater generated in developing countries receives any kind of treatment; it just runs into rivers and groundwater resources, thus poisoning populations, the environment, and the planet. Unsafe drinking water is a prime cause of diarrhea, malaria, cancer, infant deformities, and infant mortality. A few statistics reveal the severity, harshness, and effect of water pollution.

- More than five million babies born in developing countries die annually in the first month of life, mainly because of polluted water.
- About four million babies are born with deformities annually.
- Diarrhea and dysentery kill 2.5 million people annually.
- Malaria kills 2.1 million people annually.

Industrial discharge, a major water problem even in the United States, contributes significantly to the dramatic rise in cancer both here and abroad. More than 10 million new cases of cancer are diagnosed annually, and about 6.5 million people die of cancer annually. More than 1.2 billion of these deaths are caused by stomach and colon cancer, two types often associated with poor water and eating habits. Besides deaths, the anguish, sickness, suffering, and expense inflicted upon people directly or indirectly because of contaminated water is immeasurably high even in the United States. Dangerous industrial chemicals are used here as fertilizers, pesticides, solvents, food additives, fuels, medicines, cosmetics, and in a wide range of manufacturing processes.

Source: Adapted from William Miller, "Clean-Air Contention," *Industry Week* (May 5, 1997): 14. Also, *World Health Organization Report* (1997).

Production/Operations

The *production/operations function* of a business consists of all those activities that transform inputs into goods and services. Production/operations management deals with inputs, transformations, and outputs that vary across industries and markets. A manufacturing operation transforms or converts inputs such as raw materials, labor, capital, machines, and facilities into finished goods and services. As indicated in Table 4–5, Roger Schroeder suggested that production/operations management comprises five functions or decision areas: process, capacity, inventory, workforce, and quality.

Most automakers require a thirty-day notice to build vehicles, but Toyota Motor fills a buyer's new car order in just five days. Honda Motor was considered the industry's fastest producer, filling orders in fifteen days. Automakers have for years operated under just-in-time inventory systems, but Toyota's 360 suppliers are linked to the company via computers on a virtual assembly line. The new Toyota production system was developed in the company's Cambridge, Ontario, plant and now applies to its Solara, Camry, Corolla, and Tacoma vehicles.

Capacity utilization for light trucks in the automobile industry has dropped from 107 percent in 2000 to an expected 75 percent in 2005, due to oversupply and falling demand. Light trucks, which include SUVs, minivans, and pickups, account for much of the profits for Ford, DaimlerChrysler, and General Motors. American automobile producers have been slow to upgrade their car models, and consequently, foreign makes of cars now comprise more than half of the market share for all cars sold in the United States.

TABLE 4-5   The Basic Functions of Production Management

FUNCTION	DESCRIPTION
1. Process	Process decisions concern the design of the physical production system. Specific decisions include choice of technology, facility layout, process flow analysis, facility location, line balancing, process control, and transportation analysis.
2. Capacity	Capacity decisions concern determination of optimal output levels for the organization—not too much and not too little. Specific decisions include forecasting, facilities planning, aggregate planning, scheduling, capacity planning, and queuing analysis.
3. Inventory	Inventory decisions involve managing the level of raw materials, work-in-process, and finished goods. Specific decisions include what to order, when to order, how much to order, and materials handling.
4. Workforce	Workforce decisions are concerned with managing the skilled, unskilled, clerical, and managerial employees. Specific decisions include job design, work measurement, job enrichment, work standards, and motivation techniques.
5. Quality	Quality decisions are aimed at ensuring that high-quality goods and services are produced. Specific decisions include quality control, sampling, testing, quality assurance, and cost control.

Source: Adapted from R. Schroeder, *Operations Management* (New York: McGraw-Hill Book Co., 1981): 12.

Production/operations activities often represent the largest part of an organization's human and capital assets. In most industries, the major costs of producing a product or service are incurred within operations, so production/operations can have great value as a competitive weapon in a company's overall strategy. Strengths and weaknesses in the five functions of production can mean the success or failure of an enterprise. For example, a major production strength for the JCPenney company is its inventory control system, as explained in the "Global Perspective."

Many production/operations managers are finding that cross-training of employees can help their firms respond to changing markets faster. Cross-training of workers can increase efficiency, quality, productivity, and job satisfaction. For example, at General Motors' Detroit gear and axle plant, costs related to product defects were reduced 400 percent in two years as a result of cross-training workers. A shortage of qualified labor in America is another reason cross-training is becoming a common management practice.

Singapore rivals Hong Kong as an attractive site for locating production facilities in Southeast Asia. Singapore is a city-state near Malaysia. An island nation of

GLOBAL PERSPECTIVE

JCPenney's Global Inventory Control System Best in the Industry

JCPenney is widely considered to have the best inventory control system in the mass merchandising industry and its system is global in all respects. When a Penney's store in Atlanta sells a dress shirt, a record of that sale goes to a Hong Kong computer company, TAL Apparel Ltd., which instructs a factory worker in Taiwan that same day to ship another identical shirt to that Atlanta store. Penney stores today keep almost no extra inventory of dress shirts, whereas a decade ago, Penney would have had warehouses across the United States keeping thousands of dress shirts in inventory, tying up capital as the shirts slowly went out of style. Formerly, Penney stores would each keep three months of inventory on hand and the warehouses would keep six months of inventory on hand. This was very expensive. Now, the Taiwanese manufacturer ships shirts directly to Penney stores, bypassing warehouses and corporate decision makers.

As mass retailers today cut costs to bare minimum and respond swiftly to changing consumer needs, they are relying on suppliers more and more to manage their own inventory. And these suppliers are increasingly located in the Far East, rather than in Mexico or South America. TAL in Hong Kong supplies apparel name brands J. Crew, Calvin Klein, Banana Republic, Tommy Hilfiger, Liz Claiborne,

Ralph Lauren, and Brooks Brothers to U.S. retailers and does so on a minute's notice. TAL is also actively involved in sales forecasting and inventory management as suppliers today become active production/operations consultants. TAL has manufacturing operations for apparel in Guangdong, Thailand, Malaysia, Taiwan, and Hong Kong.

For other companies such as Lands' End, TAL stitches made-to-measure pants in Malaysia and flies them straight to U.S. consumers with a Lands' End invoice included. Wal-Mart Stores actually pioneered this type of inventory control system years ago when it opened its computer systems to suppliers worldwide, who track sales and replenish inventory on a just-in-time basis. Penney has turned over immense power to TAL. Wai Chan Chan, a principal at McKinsey & Co. in Hong Kong says, "You are giving away a pretty important function when you outsource your inventory management. That's something most retailers do not want to part with." JCPenney is considering allowing TAL to do for its underwear what it does for its shirts. In fact, TAL and Penney are discussing a joint venture to allow TAL to control all of Penney's inventory.

Source: Adapted from Gabriel Kahn, "Invisible Supplier Has Penney's Shirts All Buttoned Up," *Wall Street Journal* (September 11, 2003): A1.

about 4 million, Singapore is changing from an economy built on trade and services to one built on information technology. A large-scale program in computer education for older (over age 26) residents is very popular. Singapore children receive outstanding computer training in schools. All government services are computerized nicely. Singapore lures multinational businesses with great tax breaks, world-class infrastructure, excellent courts that handle business disputes efficiently, exceptionally low tariffs, large land giveaways, impressive industrial parks, excellent port facilities, and a government very receptive to and cooperative with foreign businesses. Foreign firms now account for 70 percent of manufacturing output in Singapore.

There is much reason for concern that many organizations have not taken sufficient account of the capabilities and limitations of the production/operations function in formulating strategies. Scholars contend that this neglect has had unfavorable consequences on corporate performance in America. As shown in Table 4–6, James Dilworth outlined several types of strategic decisions that a company might make with production/operations implications of those decisions. Production capabilities and policies can also greatly affect strategies.

Production/Operations Audit Checklist of Questions

Questions such as the following should be examined:

1. Are supplies of raw materials, parts, and subassemblies reliable and reasonable?
2. Are facilities, equipment, machinery, and offices in good condition?
3. Are inventory-control policies and procedures effective?
4. Are quality-control policies and procedures effective?
5. Are facilities, resources, and markets strategically located?
6. Does the firm have technological competencies?

Research and Development

The fifth major area of internal operations that should be examined for specific strengths and weaknesses is *research and development* (R&D). Many firms today conduct no R&D, and yet many other companies depend on successful R&D activities for survival. Firms pursuing a product development strategy especially need to have a strong R&D orientation.

Organizations invest in R&D because they believe that such an investment will lead to a superior product or service and will give them competitive advantages. Research and development expenditures are directed at developing new products before competitors do at improving product quality, or at improving manufacturing processes to reduce costs.

Effective management of the R&D function requires a strategic and operational partnership between R&D and the other vital business functions. A spirit of partnership and mutual trust between general and R&D managers is evident in the best-managed firms today. Managers in these firms jointly explore; assess; and decide the what, when, where, why, and how much of R&D. Priorities, costs, benefits, risks, and rewards associated with R&D activities are discussed openly and shared. The overall mission of R&D thus has become broad-based, including supporting existing

TABLE 4-6   Impact of Strategy Elements on Production Management

POSSIBLE ELEMENTS OF STRATEGY	CONCOMITANT CONDITIONS THAT MAY AFFECT THE OPERATIONS FUNCTION AND ADVANTAGES AND DISADVANTAGES
1. Compete as low-cost provider of goods or services	Discourages competition Broadens market Requires longer production runs and fewer product changes Requires special-purpose equipment and facilities
2. Compete as high-quality provider	Often possible to obtain more total profit from a smaller volume of sales Requires more quality-assurance effort and higher operating cost Requires more precise equipment, which is more expensive Requires highly skilled workers, necessitating higher wages and greater training efforts
3. Stress customer service	Requires broader development of servicepeople and service parts and equipment Requires rapid response to customer needs or changes in customer tastes, rapid and accurate information system, careful coordination Requires a higher inventory investment
4. Provide rapid and frequent introduction of new products	Requires versatile equipment and people Has higher research and development costs Has high retraining costs and high tooling and changeover in manufacturing Provides lower volumes for each product and fewer opportunities for improvements due to the learning curve
5. Strive for absolute growth	Requires accepting some projects or products with lower marginal value, which reduces ROI Diverts talents to areas of weakness instead of concentrating on strengths
6. Seek vertical integration	Enables company to control more of the process May not have economies of scale at some stages of process May require high capital investment as well as technology and skills beyond those currently available within the organization
7. Maintain reserve capacity for flexibility	Provides ability to meet peak demands and quickly implement some contingency plans if forecasts are too low Requires capital investment in idle capacity Provides capability to grow during the lead time normally required for expansion
8. Consolidate processing (Centralize)	Can result in economies of scale Can locate near one major customer or supplier Vulnerability: one strike, fire, or flood can halt the entire operation
9. Disperse processing of service (Decentralize)	Can be near several market territories Requires more complex coordination network: perhaps expensive data transmission and duplication of some personnel and equipment at each location If each location produces one product in the line, then other products still must be transported to be available at all locations If each location specializes in a type of component for all products, the company is vulnerable to strike, fire, flood, etc. If each location provides total product line, then economies of scale may not be realized
10. Stress the use of mechanization, automation, robots	Requires high capital investment Reduces flexibility May affect labor relations Makes maintenance more crucial
11. Stress stability of employment	Serves the security needs of employees and may develop employee loyalty Helps to attract and retain highly skilled employees May require revisions of make-or-buy decisions, use of idle time, inventory, and subcontractors as demand fluctuates

Source: J. Dilworth, *Production and Operations Management: Manufacturing and Nonmanufacturing,* 2nd ed. Copyright © 1983 by Random House, Inc. Reprinted by permission of Random House, Inc.

businesses, helping launch new businesses, developing new products, improving product quality, improving manufacturing efficiency, and deepening or broadening the company's technological capabilities.[21]

The best-managed firms today seek to organize R&D activities in a way that breaks the isolation of R&D from the rest of the company and promotes a spirit of partnership between R&D managers and other managers in the firm. R&D decisions and plans must be integrated and coordinated across departments and divisions by having the departments share experiences and information. The strategic-management process facilitates this cross-functional approach to managing the R&D function.

Internal and External R&D

Cost distributions among R&D activities vary by company and industry, but total R&D costs generally do not exceed manufacturing and marketing startup costs. Four approaches to determining R&D budget allocations commonly are used: (1) financing as many project proposals as possible, (2) using a percentage-of-sales method, (3) budgeting about the same amount that competitors spend for R&D, or (4) deciding how many successful new products are needed and working backward to estimate the required R&D investment.

R&D in organizations can take two basic forms: (1) internal R&D, in which an organization operates its own R&D department, and/or (2) contract R&D, in which a firm hires independent researchers or independent agencies to develop specific products. Many companies use both approaches to develop new products. A widely used approach for obtaining outside R&D assistance is to pursue a joint venture with another firm. R&D strengths (capabilities) and weaknesses (limitations) play a major role in strategy formulation and strategy implementation.

Most firms have no choice but to continually develop new and improved products because of changing consumer needs and tastes, new technologies, shortened product life cycles, and increased domestic and foreign competition. A shortage of ideas for new products, increased global competition, increased market segmentation, strong special-interest groups, and increased government regulations are several factors making the successful development of new products more and more difficult, costly, and risky. In the pharmaceutical industry, for example, only one out of every few thousand drugs created in the laboratory ends up on pharmacists' shelves. Scarpello, Boulton, and Hofer emphasized that different strategies require different R&D capabilities:

> The focus of R&D efforts can vary greatly depending on a firm's competitive strategy. Some corporations attempt to be market leaders and innovators of new products, while others are satisfied to be market followers and developers of currently available products. The basic skills required to support these strategies will vary, depending on whether R&D becomes the driving force behind competitive strategy. In cases where new product introduction is the driving force for strategy, R&D activities must be extensive. The R&D unit must then be able to advance scientific and technological knowledge, exploit that knowledge, and manage the risks associated with ideas, products, services, and production requirements.[22]

U.S. companies increased R&D spending 0.1 percent in 2003, following a 0.3 percent rise in 2002 and a 5.0 percent rise back in 2001.[23] In other words, R&D

expenditures are flat. Some companies spend a large percentage of their revenues on R&D; for example, Microsoft spends about 16 percent ($4.3 billion) of its annual revenues on R&D and Medtronic spends about 10 percent ($650 million). In contrast to flat corporate increases in R&D spending, U.S. government R&D expenditures increased 11 percent in 2002 and were expected to increase another 10.5 percent in 2003 to about $90 billion. Technology companies cut their R&D expenses by an average of 9.0 percent in 2002 although a few tech companies such as Intel increased the R&D expenditures.[24] Analysts expect the cuts to slow innovation and new-product development.

Research and Development Audit Checklist of Questions

Questions such as the following should be asked in performing an R&D audit:

1. Does the firm have R&D facilities? Are they adequate?
2. If outside R&D firms are used, are they cost-effective?
3. Are the organization's R&D personnel well qualified?
4. Are R&D resources allocated effectively?
5. Are management information and computer systems adequate?
6. Is communication between R&D and other organizational units effective?
7. Are present products technologically competitive?

Management Information Systems

Information ties all business functions together and provides the basis for all managerial decisions. It is the cornerstone of all organizations. Information represents a major source of competitive management advantage or disadvantage. Assessing a firm's internal strengths and weaknesses in information systems is a critical dimension of performing an internal audit. The company motto of Mitsui, a large Japanese trading company, is "Information is the lifeblood of the company." A satellite network connects Mitsui's two-hundred worldwide offices.

A management information system's purpose is to improve the performance of an enterprise by improving the quality of managerial decisions. An effective information system thus collects, codes, stores, synthesizes, and presents information in such a manner that it answers important operating and strategic questions. The heart of an information system is a database containing the kinds of records and data important to managers.

A *management information system* receives raw material from both the external and internal evaluation of an organization. It gathers data about marketing, finance, production, and personnel matters internally, and social, cultural, demographic, environmental, economic, political, governmental legal, technological, and competitive factors externally. Data are integrated in ways needed to support managerial decision making.

There is a logical flow of material in a computer information system, whereby data are input to the system and transformed into output. Outputs include computer printouts, written reports, tables, charts, graphs, checks, purchase orders, invoices, inventory records, payroll accounts, and a variety of other documents. Payoffs from alternative strategies can be calculated and estimated. *Data* become *information* only when they are evaluated, filtered, condensed, analyzed, and organized for a specific purpose, problem, individual, or time.

An effective management information system utilizes computer hardware, software, models for analysis, and a database. Some people equate information systems with the advent of the computer, but historians have traced recordkeeping and non-computer data processing to Babylonian merchants living in 3500 B.C. Benefits of an effective information system include an improved understanding of business functions, improved communications, more informed decision making, a better analysis of problems, and improved control.

Because organizations are becoming more complex, decentralized, and globally dispersed, the function of information systems is growing in importance. Spurring this advance is the falling cost and increasing power of computers. There are costs and benefits associated with obtaining and evaluating information, just as with equipment and land. Like equipment, information can become obsolete and may need to be purged from the system. An effective information system is like a library, collecting, categorizing, and filing data for use by managers throughout the organization. Information systems are a major strategic resource, monitoring internal and external issues and trends, identifying competitive threats, and assisting in the implementation, evaluation, and control of strategy.

We are truly in an information age. Firms whose information-system skills are weak are at a competitive disadvantage. On the other hand, strengths in information systems allow firms to establish distinctive competencies in other areas. Low-cost manufacturing and good customer service, for example, can depend on a good information system.

Strategic-Planning Software

Some strategic decision support systems, however, are too sophisticated, expensive, or restrictive to be used easily by managers in a firm. This is unfortunate because the strategic-management process must be a people process to be successful. People make the difference! Strategic-planning software should thus be simple and unsophisticated. Simplicity allows wide participation among managers in a firm and participation is essential for effective strategy implementation.

One strategic-planning software product that parallels this text and offers managers and executives a simple yet effective approach for developing organizational strategies is *CheckMATE*. This personal computer software performs planning analyses and generates strategies a firm could pursue. *CheckMATE* incorporates the most modern strategic-planning techniques. No previous experience with computers or knowledge of strategic planning is required of the user. *CheckMATE* thus promotes communication, understanding, creativity, and forward thinking among users.

CheckMATE is not a spreadsheet program or database; it is an expert system that carries a firm through strategy formulation and implementation. A major strength of the new 2002 version of *CheckMATE* strategic-planning software is its simplicity and participative approach. The user is asked appropriate questions, responses are recorded, information is assimilated, and results are printed. Individuals can work through the software independently and then the program will develop joint recommendations for the firm.

Specific analytical procedures included in the *CheckMATE* program are Strategic Position and Action Evaluation (SPACE) analysis, Strengths-Weaknesses-Opportunities-Threats (SWOT) analysis, Internal-External (IE) analysis, and

Grand Strategy Matrix analysis. These widely used strategic-planning analyses are described in Chapter 6.

An individual license for *CheckMATE* costs $495. More information about *CheckMATE* can be obtained at **www.checkmateplan.com** or 910-579-5744 (phone).

Management Information Systems Audit Checklist of Questions

Questions such as the following should be asked when conducting this audit:

1. Do all managers in the firm use the information system to make decisions?
2. Is there a chief information officer or director of information systems position in the firm?
3. Are data in the information system updated regularly?
4. Do managers from all functional areas of the firm contribute input to the information system?
5. Are there effective passwords for entry into the firm's information system?
6. Are strategists of the firm familiar with the information systems of rival firms?
7. Is the information system user-friendly?
8. Do all users of the information system understand the competitive advantages that information can provide firms?
9. Are computer training workshops provided for users of the information system?
10. Is the firm's information system continually being improved in content and user-friendliness?

The Value Chain

According to Porter, the business of a firm can best be described as a *value chain*, in which total revenues minus total costs of all activities undertaken to develop and market a product or service yields value. All firms in a given industry have a similar value chain, which includes activities such as obtaining raw materials, designing products, building manufacturing facilities, developing cooperative agreements, and providing customer service. A firm will be profitable as long as total revenues exceed the total costs incurred in creating and delivering the product or service. Firms should strive to understand not only their own value chain operations, but also their competitors', suppliers', and distributors' value chains.

Value Chain Analysis (VCA) refers to the process whereby a firm determines the costs associated with organizational activities from purchasing raw materials to manufacturing product(s) to marketing those products. VCA aims to identify where low-cost advantages or disadvantages exist anywhere along the value chain from raw material to customer service activities. VCA can enable a firm to better identify its own strengths and weaknesses, especially as compared to competitors' value chain analyses and their own data examined over time.

Substantial judgment may be required in performing a VCA because different items along the value chain may impact other items positively or negatively, so there exist complex interrelationships. For example, exceptional customer service may be especially expensive yet may reduce the costs of returns and increase revenues. Despite the complexity of VCA, the initial step in implementing this procedure is to divide a firm's operations into specific activities or business processes. Then the analyst attempts to attach a cost to each discrete activity and the costs could be in terms of both time and money. Finally, the analyst converts the cost data into information by looking for competitive cost strengths and weaknesses that may yield competitive advantage or disadvantage. Conducting a VCA is supportive of the RBV's examination of a firm's assets and capabilities as sources of distinctive competence.

More and more companies are using VCA to gain and sustain competitive advantage by being especially efficient and effective along various parts of the value chain. For example, Wal-Mart has built powerful value advantages by focusing on exceptionally tight inventory control, volume purchasing of products, and offering exemplary customer service. Computer companies in contrast compete aggressively along the distribution end of the value chain. Of course, price competitiveness is a key component of effectiveness among both mass retailers and computer firms.

The Internal Factor Evaluation (IFE) Matrix

A summary step in conducting an internal strategic-management audit is to construct an *Internal Factor Evaluation (IFE) Matrix*. This strategy-formulation tool summarizes and evaluates the major strengths and weaknesses in the functional areas of a business, and it also provides a basis for identifying and evaluating relationships among those areas. Intuitive judgments are required in developing an IFE Matrix, so the appearance of a scientific approach should not be interpreted to mean this is an all-powerful technique. A thorough understanding of the factors included is more important than the actual numbers. Similar to the EFE Matrix and Competitive Profile Matrix described in Chapter 3, an IFE Matrix can be developed in five steps:

1. List key internal factors as identified in the internal-audit process. Use a total of from ten to twenty internal factors, including both strengths and weaknesses. List strengths first and then weaknesses. Be as specific as possible, using percentages, ratios, and comparative numbers.
2. Assign a weight that ranges from 0.0 (not important) to 1.0 (all-important) to each factor. The weight assigned to a given factor indicates the relative importance of the factor to being successful in the firm's industry. Regardless of whether a key factor is an internal strength or weakness, factors considered to have the greatest effect on organizational performance should be assigned the highest weights. The sum of all weights must equal 1.0.
3. Assign a 1-to-4 rating to each factor to indicate whether that factor represents a major weakness (rating = 1), a minor weakness (rating = 2), a minor strength (rating = 3), or a major strength (rating = 4). Note that strengths must receive a 4 or 3 rating and weaknesses must receive a 1 or 2 rating. Ratings are thus company-based, whereas the weights in Step 2 are industry-based.
4. Multiply each factor's weight by its rating to determine a weighted score for each variable.
5. Sum the weighted scores for each variable to determine the total weighted score for the organization.

Regardless of how many factors are included in an IFE Matrix, the total weighted score can range from a low of 1.0 to a high of 4.0, with the average score being 2.5. Total weighted scores well below 2.5 characterize organizations that are weak internally, whereas scores significantly above 2.5 indicate a strong internal position. Like the EFE Matrix, an IFE Matrix should include from 10 to 20 key factors. The number of factors has no effect upon the range of total weighted scores because the weights always sum to 1.0.

When a key internal factor is both a strength and a weakness, the factor should be included twice in the IFE Matrix, and a weight and rating should be assigned to each statement. For example, the Playboy logo both helps and hurts Playboy Enterprises; the logo attracts customers to *Playboy* magazine, but it keeps the Playboy cable channel out of many markets.

An example of an IFE Matrix for Mandalay Bay is provided in Table 4–7. Note that the firm's major strengths are its size, occupancy rates, property, and long-range planning as indicated by the rating of 4. The major weaknesses are locations and recent joint ventures. The total weighted score of 2.75 indicates that this large gaming corporation is above average in its overall internal strength.

In multidivisional firms, each autonomous division or strategic business unit should construct an IFE Matrix. Divisional matrices then can be integrated to develop an overall corporate IFE Matrix.

An example IFE Matrix for Gateway Computer in late 2003 is provided in Table 4–8. Note that Gateway was recently *Consumer Reports'* number-one rated computer. Gateway's total weighted score of 2.85 is above the average value of 2.50.

TABLE 4–7   A Sample Internal Factor Evaluation Matrix for Mandalay Bay

KEY INTERNAL FACTORS	WEIGHT	RATING	WEIGHTED SCORE
Internal Strengths			
1. Largest casino company in the United States	.05	4	.20
2. Room occupancy rates over 95% in Las Vegas	.10	4	.40
3. Increasing free cash flows	.05	3	.15
4. Owns one mile on Las Vegas Strip	.15	4	.60
5. Strong management team	.05	3	.15
6. Buffets at most facilities	.05	3	.15
7. Minimal comps provided	.05	3	.15
8. Long-range planning	.05	4	.20
9. Reputation as family-friendly	.05	3	.15
10. Financial ratios	.05	3	.15
Internal Weaknesses			
1. Most properties are located in Las Vegas	.05	1	.05
2. Little diversification	.05	2	.10
3. Family reputation, not high rollers	.05	2	.10
4. Laughlin properties	.10	1	.10
5. Recent loss of joint ventures	.10	1	.10
TOTAL	1.00		2.75

TABLE 4-8   IFE Matrix for Gateway Computer

KEY INTERNAL FACTORS	WEIGHT	RATING	WEIGHTED SCORE
Strengths			
1. Several new senior executives with world-class skills and leadership experience	0.05	4	0.40
2. Continuous decline in operating costs and cost of goods sold	0.05	3	0.15
3. Well-known brand name	0.05	3	0.15
4. *Consumer Reports* (September 2002) recommended Gateway 500X as #1	0.10	4	0.40
5. As a direct seller, Gateway holds high brand recognition	0.05	3	0.15
6. Gateway is diversifying into non-PC products	0.10	3	0.30
7. Good relationship with its suppliers	0.05	4	0.20
8. Economies of scale, the 6th largest PC maker in the world	0.05	4	0.20
9. Gateway retail stores excellent	0.05	3	0.15
Weaknesses			
1. High operating expense (22% of revenue vs. 10% for Dell)	0.05	1	0.05
2. Almost no budget for R&D vs. Dell's 18% of revenue	0.10	1	0.10
3. Low return-on-assets ratio	0.025	2	0.05
4. No niche market	0.025	2	0.05
5. Shortage of cash due to successive losses	0.10	2	0.20
6. Limited number Gateway stores	0.05	2	0.10
7. Weak performance in overseas market	0.10	2	0.20
TOTAL	1.00		2.85

CONCLUSION

Management, marketing, finance/accounting, production/operations, research and development, and management information systems represent the core operations of most businesses. A strategic-management audit of a firm's internal operations is vital to organizational health. Many companies still prefer to be judged solely on their bottom-line performance. However, an increasing number of successful organizations are using the internal audit to gain competitive advantages over rival firms.

Systematic methodologies for performing strength-weakness assessments are not well developed in the strategic-management literature, but it is clear that strategists must identify and evaluate internal strengths and weaknesses in order to formulate and choose among alternative strategies effectively. The EFE Matrix, Competitive Profile Matrix, IFE Matrix, and clear statements of vision and mission provide the basic information needed to formulate competitive strategies successfully. The process of performing an internal audit represents an opportunity for managers and employees throughout the organization to participate in determining the future of the firm. Involvement in the process can energize and mobilize managers and employees.

We invite you to visit the David page on the Prentice Hall Companion Web site at *www.prenhall.com/david* for this chapter's World Wide Web exercises.

KEY TERMS AND CONCEPTS

Activity Ratios (p. 135)
Capital Budgeting (p. 133)
Communication (p. 126)
Controlling (p. 127)
Cost/Benefit Analysis (p. 132)
Cultural Products (p. 118)
Customer Analysis (p. 128)
Distinctive Competencies (p. 115)
Distribution (p. 130)
Dividend Decisions (p. 133)
Empirical Indicators (p. 117)
Financial Ratio Analysis (p. 116)
Financing Decision (p. 133)
Functions of Finance/
    Accounting (p. 132)
Functions of Management (p. 123)
Functions of Marketing (p. 128)
Functions of Production/
    Operations (p. 140)

Growth Ratios (p. 135)
Human Resource Management
    (p. 127)
Internal Audit (p. 115)
Internal Factor Evaluation (IFE)
    Matrix (p. 147)
Investment Decision (p. 133)
Leverage Ratios (p. 135)
Liquidity Ratios (p. 135)
Management Information
    System (p. 144)
Marketing Research (p. 130)
Motivating (p. 126)
Opportunity Analysis (p. 132)
Organizational Culture (p. 118)
Organizing (p. 125)
Personnel Management (p. 127)
Planning (p. 123)

Pricing (p. 129)
Product and Service
    Planning (p. 129)
Production/Operations
    Function (p. 139)
Profitability Ratios (p. 135)
Research and Development
    (R&D) (p. 141)
Resource-Based View
    (RBV) (p. 114)
Selling (p. 129)
Staffing (p. 127)
Synergy (p. 125)
Test Marketing (p. 129)
Value Chain Analysis
    (VCA) (p. 146)

ISSUES FOR REVIEW AND DISCUSSION

1. Explain why prioritizing the relative importance of strengths and weaknesses in an IFE Matrix is an important strategic-management activity.
2. How can delegation of authority contribute to effective strategic management?
3. Diagram a formal organizational chart that reflects the following positions: a president, two executive officers, four middle managers, and eighteen lower-level managers. Now, diagram three overlapping and hypothetical informal group structures. How can this information be helpful to a strategist in formulating and implementing strategy?
4. Which of the three basic functions of finance/accounting do you feel is most important

in a small electronics manufacturing concern? Justify your position.
5. Do you think aggregate R&D expenditures for American firms will increase or decrease next year? Why?
6. Explain how you would motivate managers and employees to implement a major new strategy.
7. Why do you think production/operations managers often are not directly involved in strategy-formulation activities? Why can this be a major organizational weakness?
8. Give two examples of staffing strengths and two examples of staffing weaknesses of an organization with which you are familiar.

9. Would you ever pay out dividends when your firm's annual net profit is negative? Why? What effect could this have on a firm's strategies?

10. If a firm has zero debt in its capital structure, is that always an organizational strength? Why or why not?

11. Describe the production/operations system in a police department.

12. After conducting an internal audit, a firm discovers a total of 100 strengths and 100 weaknesses. What procedures then could be used to determine the most important of these? Why is it important to reduce the total number of key factors?

13. Why do you believe cultural products affect all the functions of business?

14. Do you think cultural products affect strategy formulation, implementation, or evaluation the most? Why?

15. Identify cultural products at your college or university. Do these products, viewed collectively or separately, represent a strength or weakness for the organization?

16. Describe the management information system at your college or university.

17. Explain the difference between data and information in terms of each being useful to strategists.

18. What are the most important characteristics of an effective management information system?

19. Compare and contrast American versus foreign cultures in terms of doing business.

20. Do you agree or disagree with the RBV theorists that internal resources are more important for a firm than external factors in achieving and sustaining competitive advantage? Explain your and their position.

21. Define and discuss "empirical indicators."

22. Define and discuss the "spam" problem in the U.S.

23. Discuss JCPenney's inventory control system. Why is that a competitive advantage for the firm?

24. Define and explain value chain analysis (VCA).

25. List five financial ratios that may be used by your university to monitor operations.

NOTES

1. Robert Grant, "The Resource-Based Theory of Competitive Advantage: Implications for Strategy Formulation," *California Management Review* (Spring 1991): 116.

2. Reprinted by permission of the publisher from "Integrating Strength-Weakness Analysis into Strategic Planning," by William King, *Journal of Business Research* 2, no. 4: p. 481. Copyright 1983 by Elsevier Science Publishing Co., Inc.

3. Igor Ansoff, "Strategic Management of Technology" *Journal of Business Strategy* 7, no. 3 (Winter 1987): 38.

4. Claude George, Jr., *The History of Management Thought*, 2nd ed. (Englewood Cliffs, N.J.: Prentice-Hall, 1972): 174.

5. J. B. Barney, "Firm Resources and Sustained Competitive Advantage," *Journal of Management* 17 (1991): 99–120; J. B. Barney, "The Resource-Based Theory of the Firm," *Organizational Science* 7 (1996): 469; J. B. Barney, "Is the Resource-Based 'View' a Useful Perspective for Strategic Management Research? Yes." *Academy of Management Review* 26, no. 1 (2001): 41–56.

6. Edgar Schein, *Organizational Culture and Leadership* (San Francisco: Jossey-Bass, 1985): 9.

7. John Lorsch, "Managing Culture: The Invisible Barrier to Strategic Change," *California Management Review* 28, no. 2 (1986): 95–109.

8. Y. Allarie and M. Firsirotu, "How to Implement Radical Strategies in Large Organizations," *Sloan Management Review* (Spring 1985): 19.

9. Jon Alston, "Wa, Guanxi, and Inhwa: Managerial Principles in Japan, China and Korea," *Business Horizons* 32, no. 2 (March–April 1989): 26.

10. Rose Knotts, "Cross-Cultural Management: Transformations and Adaptations," *Business Horizons* (January–February 1989): 29–33.

11. *www.mindtools.com/plfailpl.html*

12. Adam Smith, *Wealth of Nations* (New York: Modern Library, 1937): 3–4.

13. Richard Daft, *Management*, 3rd ed. (Orlando, FL: Dryden Press, 1993): 512.

14. Shelley Kirkpatrick and Edwin Locke, "Leadership: Do Traits Matter?" *Academy of Management Executive* 5, no. 2 (May 1991): 48.

15. Peter Drucker, *Management Tasks, Responsibilities, and Practice* (New York: Harper & Row, 1973): 463.

16. Brian Dumaine, "What the Leaders of Tomorrow See," *Fortune* (July 3, 1989): 51.

17. J. Evans and B. Bergman, *Marketing* (New York: Macmillan, 1982): 17.

18. Quoted in Robert Waterman, Jr., "The Renewal Factor," *BusinessWeek* (September 14, 1987): 108.

19. J. Van Horne, *Financial Management and Policy* (Englewood Cliffs, N.J.: Prentice-Hall, 1974): 10.

20. Michelle Kessler, "Kodak Cuts Dividend 70%, Plans Big Move into Digital," *USA Today* (September 26, 2003): 3B.

21. Philip Rousebl, Kamal Saad, and Tamara Erickson, "The Evolution of Third Generation R&D," *Planning Review* 19, no. 2 (March–April 1991): 18–26.

22. Vida Scarpello, William Boulton, and Charles Hofer, "Reintegrating R&D into Business Strategy," *Journal of Business Strategy* 6, no. 4 (Spring 1986): 50–51.

23. Amy Frank, "Businesses Keep Tight Budget on R&D Amid Weak Stocks," *Wall Street Journal* (January 2, 2002): A4.

24. Michelle Kessler, "Many Companies Cut Research Budgets," *USA Today* (February 24, 2003): 1B.

CURRENT READINGS

Akhter, S. "Strategic Planning, Hypercompetition, and Knowledge Management." *Business Horizons* 46, no. 1 (January–February 2003): 19–24.

Arend, R. J. "Revisiting the Logical and Research Considerations of Competitive Advantage." *Strategic Management Journal* 24, no. 3 (March 2003): 279–284.

Barney, J. B. "Firm Resources and Sustained Competitive Advantage." *Journal of Management*, no. 17 (1991): 99–120.

Barney, J. B. "The Resource-Based Theory of the Firm." *Organizational Science*, no. 7 (1996): 469.

Barney, J. B. "Is the Resource-Based View a Useful Perspective for Strategic Management Research? Yes." *Academy of Management Review* 27 (2002): 41–56.

Bates, K. A., and J. E. Flynn. "Innovation History and Competitive Advantage: A Resource-Based View Analysis of Manufacturing Technology Innovations." *Academy of Management Best Papers Proceedings* (1995): 235–239.

Castrogiovanni, G. J. "Organization Task Environments: Have They Changed Fundamentally Over Time?" *Journal of Management* 28, no. 2 (2002): 129–150.

Coff, R. W. "Human Assets and Management Dilemmas: Coping with Hazards on the Road to Resource-Based Theory." *Academy of Management Review*, no. 22 (1997): 374–402.

Conner, K. R., and C. K. Prahalad. "A Resource-Based Theory of the Firm: Knowledge Versus Opportunism." *Organizational Science*, no. 7 (1996): 477–501.

Dutta, S., J. M. Zbaracki, and M. Bergen. "Pricing Process as a Capability: A Resource-Based Perspective." *Strategic Management Journal* 24, no. 7 (July 2003): 615–630.

Jassawalla, A. R., and H. C. Sashittal. "Cultures That Support Product-Innovation Processes." *Academy of Management Executive* 16, no. 16 (August 2002): 42–54.

Makhija, M. "Comparing the Resource-Based and Market-Based Views of the Firm: Empirical Evidence from Czech Privatization." *Strategic Management Journal* 24, no. 5 (May 2003): 433–452.

McGahan, A. M., and M. E. Porter. "How Much Does Industry Matter, Really?" *Strategic Management Journal* 17 (1997): 15–30.

Oliver, C. "Sustainable Competitive Advantage: Combining Institutional and Resource-Based Views." *Strategic Management Journal*, no. 18 (1997): 697–713.

Priem, R. L., and J. E. Butler. "Is the Resource-Based 'View' a Useful Perspective for Strategic Management?" *Academy of Management Review* 26, no. 1 (2001): 22–40.

Priem, R. L., and J. E. Butler. "Tautology in the Resource-Based View and the Implications of Externally Determined Resource Value: Further Comments." *Academy of Management Review* 26, no. 1 (2001): 57–66.

Rouse, M. J., and U. S. Daellenbach. "Rethinking Research Methods for the Resource-Based Perspective." *Strategic Management Journal* 20 (1999): 487–494.

Ruefli, T. W., and R. R. Wiggins. "Industry, Corporate and Segment Effects and Business Performance: A Non-Parametric Approach." *Strategic Management Journal* 24, no. 9 (September 2003): 861–880.

Rugman, A., and A. Verbeke. "Edith Penrose's Contribution to the Resource-Based View of Strategic Management." *Strategic Management Journal* 23, no. 5 (August 2002): 769–780.

Wernerfelt, B. "A Resource-Based View of the Firm." *Strategic Management Journal*, no. 5 (May 1984): 171–180.

Wernerfelt, B. "The Resource-Based View of the Firm: Ten Years After." *Strategic Management Journal* 16 (1995): 171–174.

experiential exercises

Experiential Exercise 4A

Performing a Financial Ratio Analysis for Krispy Kreme Doughnuts (KKD)

PURPOSE

Financial ratio analysis is one of the best techniques for identifying and evaluating internal strengths and weaknesses. Potential investors and current shareholders look closely at firms' financial ratios, making detailed comparisons to industry averages and to previous periods of time. Financial ratio analyses provide vital input information for developing an IFE Matrix.

INSTRUCTIONS

Step 1 On a separate sheet of paper, number from 1 to 20. Referring to KKD's income statement and balance sheet (pp. 37–38), calculate twenty financial ratios for 2003 for the company. Use Table 4–4 as a reference.

Step 2 Go to *finance.yahoo.com* and find financial ratio information for Starbucks (stock symbol = SBUX). Starbucks is a KKD competitor. Record the SBUX values in the second column on your paper. Calculate by hand any SBUX ratios that you cannot find on the Internet.

Step 3 In a third column, indicate whether you consider each ratio to be a strength, a weakness, or a neutral factor for KKD.

Experiential Exercise 4B

Constructing an IFE Matrix for Krispy Kreme Doughnuts (KKD)

PURPOSE

This exercise will give you experience in developing an IFE Matrix. Identifying and prioritizing factors to include in an IFE Matrix fosters communication among functional and divisional managers. Preparing an IFE Matrix allows human resource, marketing, production/operations, finance/accounting, R&D, and management information systems managers to articulate their concerns and thoughts regarding the business condition of the firm. This results in an improved collective understanding of the business.

INSTRUCTIONS

Step 1 Join with two other individuals to form a three-person team. Develop a team IFE Matrix for KKD.

Step 2 Compare your team's IFE Matrix to other teams' IFE Matrices. Discuss any major differences.

Step 3 What strategies do you think would allow KKD to capitalize on its major strengths? What strategies would allow KKD to improve upon its major weaknesses?

Experiential Exercise 4C

Constructing an IFE Matrix for My University

PURPOSE

This exercise gives you the opportunity to evaluate your university's major strengths and weaknesses. As will become clearer in the next chapter, an organization's strategies are largely based upon striving to take advantage of strengths and improving upon weaknesses.

INSTRUCTIONS

Step 1 Join with two other individuals to form a three-person team. Develop a team IFE Matrix for your university. You may use the strengths/weaknesses determined in Experimental Exercise 1D.

Step 2 Go to the board and diagram your team's IFE Matrix.

Step 3 Compare your team's IFE Matrix to other teams' IFE Matrices. Discuss any major differences.

Step 4 What strategies do you think would allow your university to capitalize on its major strengths? What strategies would allow your university to improve upon its major weaknesses?

Strategies in Action

experiential exercises

"notable quotes"

Alice said, "Would you please tell me which way to go from here?" The cat said, "That depends on where you want to get to."
Lewis Carroll

Tomorrow always arrives. It is always different. And even the mightiest company is in trouble if it has not worked on the future. Being surprised by what happens is a risk that even the largest and richest company cannot afford, and even the smallest business need not run.
Peter Drucker

Planning. Doing things today to make us better tomorrow. Because the future belongs to those who make the hard decisions today.
Eaton Corporation

One big problem with American business is that when it gets into trouble, it redoubles its effort. It's like digging for gold. If you dig down twenty feet and haven't found it, one of the strategies you could use is to dig twice as deep. But if the gold is twenty feet to the side, you could dig a long time and not find it.
Edward De Bono

Even if you're on the right track, you'll get run over if you just sit there.
Will Rogers

Strategies for taking the hill won't necessarily hold it.
Amar Bhide

The early bird may get the worm, but the second mouse gets the cheese.
Unknown

Hundreds of companies today, including Sears, IBM, Searle, and Hewlett-Packard, have embraced strategic planning fully in their quest for higher revenues and profits. Kent Nelson, former chair of UPS, explains why his company has created a new strategic-planning department: "Because we're making bigger bets on investments in technology, we can't afford to spend a whole lot of money in one direction and then find out five years later it was the wrong direction."[1]

This chapter brings strategic management to life with many contemporary examples. Sixteen types of strategies are defined and exemplified, including Michael Porter's generic strategies: cost leadership, differentiation, and focus. Guidelines are presented for determining when it is most appropriate to pursue different types of strategies. An overview of strategic management in nonprofit organizations, governmental agencies, and small firms is provided.

Long-Term Objectives

Long-term objectives represent the results expected from pursuing certain strategies. Strategies represent the actions to be taken to accomplish long-term objectives. The time frame for objectives and strategies should be consistent, usually from two to five years.

The Nature of Long-Term Objectives

VISIT THE NET

Gives the basic principles of strategic planning.
www.eaglepointconsulting.com/sp_principles.html

Objectives should be quantitative, measurable, realistic, understandable, challenging, hierarchical, obtainable, and congruent among organizational units. Each objective should also be associated with a time line. Objectives are commonly stated in terms such as growth in assets, growth in sales, profitability, market share, degree and nature of diversification, degree and nature of vertical integration, earnings per share, and social responsibility. Clearly established objectives offer many benefits. They provide direction, allow synergy, aid in evaluation, establish priorities, reduce uncertainty, minimize conflicts, stimulate exertion, and aid in both the allocation of resources and the design of jobs.

Long-term objectives are needed at the corporate, divisional, and functional levels of an organization. They are an important measure of managerial performance. Many practitioners and academicians attribute a significant part of U.S. industry's competitive decline to the short-term, rather than long-term, strategy orientation of managers in the United States. Arthur D. Little argues that bonuses or merit pay for managers today must be based to a greater extent on long-term objectives and strategies. A general framework for relating objectives to performance evaluation is provided in Table 5–1. A particular organization could tailor these guidelines to meet its own needs, but incentives should be attached to both long-term and annual objectives.

Clearly stated and communicated objectives are vital to success for many reasons. First, objectives help stakeholders understand their role in an organization's future. They also provide a basis for consistent decision making by managers whose values and attitudes differ. By reaching a consensus on objectives during strategy-formulation activities, an organization can minimize potential conflicts later during implementation. Objectives set forth organizational priorities and stimulate exertion and accomplishment. They serve as standards by which individuals, groups, departments, divisions, and entire organizations can be evaluated. Objectives provide the basis for designing jobs and organizing activities to be performed in an organization. They also provide direction and allow for organizational synergy.

TABLE 5-1   Varying Performance Measures
             by Organizational Level

ORGANIZATIONAL LEVEL	BASIS FOR ANNUAL BONUS OR MERIT PAY
Corporate	75% based on long-term objectives 25% based on annual objectives
Division	50% based on long-term objectives 50% based on annual objectives
Function	25% based on long-term objectives 75% based on annual objectives

Without long-term objectives, an organization would drift aimlessly toward some unknown end. It is hard to imagine an organization or individual being successful without clear objectives. Success only rarely occurs by accident; rather, it is the result of hard work directed toward achieving certain objectives.

Financial versus Strategic Objectives

Two types of objectives are especially common in organizations—financial and strategic objectives. Financial objectives include those associated with growth in revenues, growth in earnings, higher dividends, larger profit margins, greater return on investment, higher earnings per share, a rising stock price, improved cash flow, and so on; while strategic objectives include things such as a larger market share, quicker on-time delivery than rivals, shorter design-to-market times than rivals, lower costs than rivals, higher product quality than rivals, wider geographic coverage than rivals, achieving ISO 14001 certification, and so on.

Although financial objectives are especially important in firms, oftentimes there is a trade-off between financial and strategic objectives such that crucial decisions have to be made. For example, there are things a firm can do to maximize short-term financial objectives which would harm long-term strategic objectives. To improve financial position in the short run through higher prices may, for example, jeopardize long-term market share. The dangers associated with trading off long-term strategic objectives with near-term bottom-line performance are especially severe if competitors relentlessly pursue increased market share at the expense of short-term profitability. And there are other trade-offs between financial and strategic objectives, related to riskiness of actions, concern for business ethics, need to preserve the natural environment, and social responsibility issues.

Dell Computer, in late 2003, announced its corporate objective to grow revenues by 15 percent annually through 2006 and to reach $60 billion in total revenues by that year. To achieve this goal, Dell established specific annual objectives on a per-segment basis. These are shown in Table 5–2.

Not Managing by Objectives

An unknown educator once said, "If you think education is expensive, try ignorance." The idea behind this saying also applies to establishing objectives. Strategists should avoid the following alternative ways to "not managing by objectives."

- *Managing by Extrapolation*—adheres to the principle "If it ain't broke, don't fix it." The idea is to keep on doing about the same things in the same ways because things are going well.

VISIT THE NET

Provides a short essay about the resurgence of strategic planning in companies.
www.businessweek.com/ 1996/35/b34901.htm

TABLE 5-2   Dell Computer's Revenue Objectives
Through 2006 (in $Billions)

DIVISION	2002	2003	2004	2005	2006
PC's	$23	$26	$27	$29	$30
Servers/Storage	5	7	8	9	10
Services	4	4	5	7	9
Software/Peripherals	4	4	7	10	13
TOTAL	$36	$41	$47	$54	$62

Source: Adapted from Andrew Park and Peter Burrows, "What You Don't Know About Dell," *BusinessWeek*
(November 3, 2003): 81.

- *Managing by Crisis*—based on the belief that the true measure of a really good strategist is the ability to solve problems. Because there are plenty of crises and problems to go around for every person and every organization, strategists ought to bring their time and creative energy to bear on solving the most pressing problems of the day. Managing by crisis is actually a form of reacting rather than acting and of letting events dictate the whats and when of management decisions.

- *Managing by Subjectives*—built on the idea that there is no general plan for which way to go and what to do; just do the best you can to accomplish what you think should be done. In short, "Do your own thing, the best way you know how" (sometimes referred to as *the mystery approach to decision making* because subordinates are left to figure out what is happening and why).

- *Managing by Hope*—based on the fact that the future is laden with great uncertainty, and that if we try and do not succeed, then we hope our second (or third) attempt will succeed. Decisions are predicted on the hope that they will work and the good times are just around the corner, especially if luck and good fortune are on our side![2]

Levels of Strategies

Strategy making is not just a task for top executives. As discussed in Chapter 1, middle and lower-level managers too must be involved in the strategic-planning process to the extent possible. In large firms, there are actually four levels of strategies: corporate, divisional, functional, and operational—as illustrated in Figure 5–1. However, in small firms, there are actually three levels of strategies: company, functional, and operational.

In large firms, the persons primarily responsible for having effective strategies at the various levels include the CEO at the corporate level; the president or executive vice president at the divisional level; the respective Chief Finance Officer (CFO), Chief Information Officer (CIO), Human Resource Manager (HRM), Chief Marketing Officer (CMO), and so on, at the functional level; and the plant manager, regional sales manager, and so on, at the operational level. In small firms, the persons primarily responsible for having effective strategies at the various levels include the business owner or president at the company level and then the same range of persons at the lower two levels as with a large firm.

It is important to note that all persons responsible for strategic planning at the various levels ideally participate and understand the strategies at the other organizational levels to help assure coordination, facilitation, and commitment while avoid-

FIGURE 5-1

Levels of Strategies with Persons Most Responsible

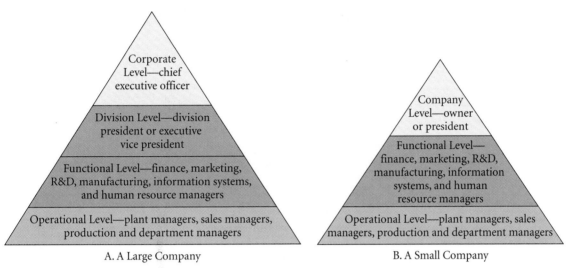

A. A Large Company   B. A Small Company

ing inconsistency, inefficiency, and miscommunication. Plant managers, for example, need to understand and be supportive of the overall corporate strategic plan (game plan) while the president and the CEO need to be knowledgeable of strategies being employed in various sales territories and manufacturing plants.

Types of Strategies

The model illustrated in Figure 5–2 provides a conceptual basis for applying strategic management. Defined and exemplified in Table 5–3, alternative strategies that an enterprise could pursue can be categorized into twelve actions—forward integration, backward integration, horizontal integration, market penetration, market development, product development, concentric diversification, conglomerate diversification, horizontal diversification, retrenchment, divestiture, and liquidation. Each alternative strategy has countless variations. For example, market penetration can include adding salespersons, increasing advertising expenditures, couponing, and using similar actions to increase market share in a given geographic area.

Many, if not most, organizations pursue a combination of two or more strategies simultaneously, but a *combination strategy* can be exceptionally risky if carried too far. No organization can afford to pursue all the strategies that might benefit the firm. Difficult decisions must be made. Priority must be established. Organizations, like individuals, have limited resources. Both organizations and individuals must choose among alternative strategies and avoid excessive indebtedness.

Hansen and Smith recently explained that strategic planning involves "choices that risk resources" and "trade-offs that sacrifice opportunity." In other words, if you have a strategy to go north, then you must buy snowshoes and warm jackets (spend resources) and forgo the opportunity of population increases you would have by going south. You cannot have a strategy to go north and then take a step east, south, or west "just to be on the safe side." Firms spend resources and focus on a finite number of opportunities in pursuing strategies to achieve an uncertain outcome in the

FIGURE 5-2
A Comprehensive Strategic-Management Model

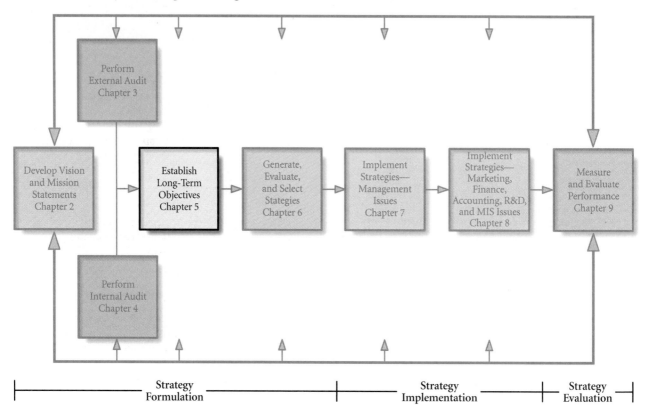

future. Strategic planning is much more than a roll of the dice; it is a wager based on predictions and hypotheses that are continually tested and refined by knowledge, research, experience, and learning. Survival of the firm itself may hinge on your strategic plan.[3]

Organizations cannot do too many things well because resources and talents get spread thin and competitors gain advantage. In large diversified companies, a combination strategy is commonly employed when different divisions pursue different strategies. Also, organizations struggling to survive may employ a combination of several defensive strategies, such as divestiture, liquidation, and retrenchment, simultaneously.

The Balanced Scorecard

Developed in 1993 by Harvard Business School professors Robert Kaplan and David Norton, and refined continually through today, the Balanced Scorecard is a strategy evaluation and control technique.[4] Balanced Scorecard derives its name from the perceived need of firms to "balance" financial measures which are oftentimes used exclusively in strategy evaluation and control with nonfinancial measures such as product quality and customer service. The overall aim of the Balanced Scorecard is to "balance" shareholder objectives with customer and operational objectives. Obviously, these sets of objectives interrelate and many even conflict. For example, customers want low price and high service which may conflict with shareholders' desire for a high return on their investment. The Balanced Scorecard concept is consistent with the notions of continuous improvement in management (CIM) and total quality management (TQM).

TABLE 5-3   Alternative Strategies Defined and Exemplified

STRATEGY	DEFINITION	2003 EXAMPLES
Forward Integration	Gaining ownership or increased control over distributors or retailers	Doll maker and mail order firm, Pleasant Co., just opened a retail store in Manhattan.
Backward Integration	Seeking ownership or increased control of a firm's suppliers	McDonald's recently acquired a paper cup producer.
Horizontal Integration	Seeking ownership or increased control over competitors	Callaway Golf recently acquired Top-Flite Golf Company.
Market Penetration	Seeking increased market share for present products or services in present markets through greater marketing efforts	SABMiller Plc spent $500 million in 2003 on marketing its Miller brands of beer.
Market Development	Introducing present products or services into new geographic area	JetBlue is adding dozens of new routes.
Product Development	Seeking increased sales by improving present products or services or developing new ones	GM developing hydrogen-powered automobiles or Pfizer developing a new antismoking pill.
Concentric Diversification	Adding new but related products or services	Microsoft launched its first personal computers that double as entertainment centers.
Conglomerate Diversification	Adding new, unrelated products or services	The video-rental firm Blockbuster may acquire the DVD and music direct-marketing firm Columbia House.
Horizontal Diversification	Adding new, unrelated products or services for present customers	Viacom acquired Comedy Central, an all-humor cable channel known for The Man Show and The Daily Show, from AOL.
Retrenchment	Regrouping through cost and asset reduction to reverse declining sales and profit	America West Airlines closing its hub at Columbus, Ohio, and laying off 390 employees.
Divestiture	Selling a division or part of an organization	ConocoPhillips recently sold its Circle K convenience store chain to Alimentation Couche-Tard, a Canadian firm.
Liquidation	Selling all of a company's assets, in parts, for their tangible worth	Sprint liquidated its Web-hosting division.

Although the Balanced Scorecard concept will be covered in more detail in Chapter 9 as it relates to evaluating strategies, it should be noted here that clearly firms should establish objectives and evaluate strategies on items other than financial measures. This is the basic tenet of the Balanced Scorecard. Financial measures and ratios are vitally important. However, of equal importance are factors such as customer service, employee morale, product quality, pollution abatement, business ethics, social responsibility, community involvement, and other such items. In conjunction with financial measures, these "softer" factors comprise an integral part of both the objective-setting process and the strategy-evaluation process. These factors can vary by organization, but such items, along with financial measures, comprise the essence of a Balanced Scorecard. A Balanced Scorecard for a firm is simply a listing of all key objectives to work toward, along with an associated time dimension of when each objective is to be accomplished, as well as a primary responsibility or contact person, department, or division for each objective.

Integration Strategies

Forward integration, backward integration, and horizontal integration are sometimes collectively referred to as *vertical integration* strategies. Vertical integration strategies allow a firm to gain control over distributors, suppliers, and/or competitors.

Forward Integration

Forward integration involves gaining ownership or increased control over distributors or retailers. Increasing numbers of manufacturers (suppliers) today are pursuing a forward integration strategy by establishing Web sites to sell products directly to consumers. This strategy is causing turmoil in some industries. For example, Dell Computer began pursuing forward integration in 2003 by establishing its own stores-within-a-store in Sears, Roebuck. This strategy supplements Dell's mall-based kiosks, which enable customers to see and try Dell computers before they purchase one. Neither the Dell kiosks nor the Dell stores-within-a-store will stock computers. Customers still will order Dells exclusively by phone or over the Internet which historically differentiated Dell from other computer firms.

Another company betting heavily on forward integration today is Staples, which is adding "delivery of office products to businesses" as a service at more and more of its 1,400 stores nationwide and in Europe. Staples, however, is playing catch-up to Office Depot which in June 2003 acquired a French delivery business that doubled its European sales.

An effective means of implementing forward integration is *franchising*. Approximately 2,000 companies in about fifty different industries in the United States use franchising to distribute their products or services. Businesses can expand rapidly by franchising because costs and opportunities are spread across many individuals. Total sales by franchises in the United States are about $1 trillion annually.

However, a growing trend is for franchisees, who for example may operate ten franchised restaurants, stores, or whatever, to buy out their part of the business from their franchiser (corporate owner). There is a growing rift between franchisees and franchisers as the segment often outperforms the parent. For example, often to increase growth, a franchiser will allow new owners to locate near existing franchisee operations, or will cut back on services and training to reduce costs.[5]

The huge forest products firm Boise Cascade, which owns 2.3 million acres of timberlands and more than two dozen paper and building-products mills, continues to pursue forward integration as evidenced by its recent acquisition of OfficeMax, the third-largest retail-office-products company after Staples and Office Depot. OfficeMax has more than 1,000 superstores and has lately focused on boosting domestic sales and remodeling stores, rather than expanding internationally. A risk to Boise Cascade in making this acquisition is that Staples and Office Depot could drop the Boise Cascade line of products viewing them now to be more a competitor than a supplier.

Six guidelines for when forward integration may be an especially effective strategy are:[6]

- When an organization's present distributors are especially expensive, or unreliable, or incapable of meeting the firm's distribution needs.
- When the availability of quality distributors is so limited as to offer a competitive advantage to those firms that integrate forward.
- When an organization competes in an industry that is growing and is expected to continue to grow markedly; this is a factor because forward integration reduces an organization's ability to diversify if its basic industry falters.
- When an organization has both the capital and human resources needed to manage the new business of distributing its own products.
- When the advantages of stable production are particularly high; this is a consideration because an organization can increase the predictability of the demand for its output through forward integration.
- When present distributors or retailers have high profit margins; this situation suggests that a company profitably could distribute its own products and price them more competitively by integrating forward.

Backward Integration

Both manufacturers and retailers purchase needed materials from suppliers. *Backward integration* is a strategy of seeking ownership or increased control of a firm's suppliers. This strategy can be especially appropriate when a firm's current suppliers are unreliable, too costly, or cannot meet the firm's needs.

When you buy a box of Pampers diapers at Wal-Mart, a scanner at the store's checkout counter instantly zaps an order to Procter & Gamble Company. In contrast, in most hospitals, reordering supplies is a logistical nightmare. Inefficiency caused by lack of control of suppliers in the healthcare industry is, however, rapidly changing as many giant healthcare purchasers, such as the U.S. Defense Department and Columbia/HCA Healthcare Corporation, move to require electronic bar codes on every supply item purchased. This allows instant tracking and recording without invoices and paperwork. Of the estimated $83 billion spent annually on hospital supplies, industry reports indicate that $11 billion can be eliminated through more effective backward integration.

Some industries in the United States (such as the automotive and aluminum industries) are reducing their historical pursuit of backward integration. Instead of owning their suppliers, companies negotiate with several outside suppliers. Ford and Daimler-Chrysler buy over half of their component parts from outside suppliers such as TRW, Eaton, General Electric, and Johnson Controls. Deintegration makes sense in industries that have global sources of supply. Companies today shop around, play one seller against another, and go with the best deal. Small steel manufacturers such as Arrowhead Steel Company and Worthington Steel Company are pursuing backward integration today through the use of the Internet. Owners of most small steel firms now click on Web sites such as MetalSite LP, based in Pittsburgh, or e-Steel Corporation, based in New York, to find the lowest-priced supplier of scrap steel that they need. These two sites give buyers and sellers of steel the opportunity to trade, buy, and sell metal from a variety of companies. Many steel companies now have Web sites to capitalize on backward integration opportunities in the industry.

Global competition is also spurring firms to reduce their number of suppliers and to demand higher levels of service and quality from those they keep. Although traditionally relying on many suppliers to ensure uninterrupted supplies and low prices, American firms now are following the lead of Japanese firms, which have far fewer suppliers and closer, long-term relationships with those few. "Keeping track of so many suppliers is onerous," says Mark Shimelonis, formerly of Xerox.

Seven guidelines for when backward integration may be an especially effective strategy are:[7]

- When an organization's present suppliers are especially expensive, or unreliable, or incapable of meeting the firm's needs for parts, components, assemblies, or raw materials.
- When the number of suppliers is small and the number of competitors is large.
- When an organization competes in an industry that is growing rapidly; this is a factor because integrative-type strategies (forward, backward, and horizontal) reduce an organization's ability to diversify in a declining industry.
- When an organization has both capital and human resources to manage the new business of supplying its own raw materials.
- When the advantages of stable prices are particularly important; this is a factor because an organization can stabilize the cost of its raw materials and the associated price of its product(s) through backward integration.
- When present supplies have high profit margins, which suggests that the business of supplying products or services in the given industry is a worthwhile venture.
- When an organization needs to acquire a needed resource quickly.

Horizontal Integration

Horizontal integration refers to a strategy of seeking ownership of or increased control over a firm's competitors. One of the most significant trends in strategic management today is the increased use of horizontal integration as a growth strategy. Mergers, acquisitions, and takeovers among competitors allow for increased economies of scale and enhanced transfer of resources and competencies. Kenneth Davidson makes the following observation about horizontal integration:

> The trend towards horizontal integration seems to reflect strategists' misgivings about their ability to operate many unrelated businesses. Mergers between direct competitors are more likely to create efficiencies than mergers between unrelated businesses, both because there is a greater potential for eliminating duplicate facilities and because the management of the acquiring firm is more likely to understand the business of the target.[8]

In 2003, Krispy Kreme bought Montana Mills, a thirty-store bakery chain, to extend its penetration into the bakery-café business nationwide. By acquiring National Steel for just over $1 billion, U.S. Steel recently surpassed International Steel as the largest domestic producer, even though International Steel had itself acquired Bethlehem Steel earlier in 2003. U.S. Steel also recently acquired bankrupt Serbian Steel as part of the firm's overall horizontal integration strategy.

Five guidelines for when horizontal integration may be an especially effective strategy are:[9]

- When an organization can gain monopolistic characteristics in a particular area or region without being challenged by the federal government for "tending substantially" to reduce competition.
- When an organization competes in a growing industry.
- When increased economies of scale provide major competitive advantages.

VISIT THE NET

Provides Dr. Hansen's course syllabus which includes excellent hot links.
www.stetson.edu/
~rhansen/stratsyl.html

- When an organization has both the capital and human talent needed to successfully manage an expanded organization.
- When competitors are faltering due to a lack of managerial expertise or a need for particular resources that an organization possesses; note that horizontal integration would not be appropriate if competitors are doing poorly, because in that case overall industry sales are declining.

Intensive Strategies

Market penetration, market development, and product development are sometimes referred to as *intensive strategies* because they require intensive efforts if a firm's competitive position with existing products is to improve.

Market Penetration

A *market-penetration* strategy seeks to increase market share for present products or services in present markets through greater marketing efforts. This strategy is widely used alone and in combination with other strategies. Market penetration includes increasing the number of salespersons, increasing advertising expenditures, offering extensive sales promotion items, or increasing publicity efforts. For example, Toyota is rapidly increasing its market share in North America, where the firm now makes 75 percent of its worldwide profit and has increased its market share from 7 percent in 2002 to 9 percent in 2003. Jeff Schuster, of J. D. Power and Associates, says, "Toyota functions and behaves very much like a domestic brand and American company." Toyota's new pickup plant in San Antonio will produce 150,000 trucks when it opens in 2006, and the company's Lexus division is the top luxury car in the United States.[10]

Five guidelines for when market penetration may be an especially effective strategy are:[11]

- When current markets are not saturated with a particular product or service.
- When the usage rate of present customers could be increased significantly.
- When the market shares of major competitors have been declining while total industry sales have been increasing.
- When the correlation between dollar sales and dollar marketing expenditures historically has been high.
- When increased economies of scale provide major competitive advantages.

Market Development

Market development involves introducing present products or services into new geographic areas. Krispy Kreme opened 77 new stores in 2003, as the Winston-Salem-based company pursues market development throughout North America, and for the first time also is opening stores in Australia, New Zealand, Mexico, and the United Kingdom. Doughnuts are the fastest-growing segment of the restaurant business in the United States, according to Technomic, a restaurant consulting firm. More than ten times the size of Krispy Kreme, Dunkin' Donuts, with over 3,600 stores, also was pursuing market development by adding 300 new domestic restaurants in 2003. Dunkin' Donuts is also in negotiation with Home Depot to place restaurants in these stores. Even Tim Horton's, a donut chain of 160 restaurants, enjoyed a 20 percent increase in revenues in 2003. Dennis Lombardi at Technomic says, "Americans now often drive to the health club while eating a doughnut."

Discount airlines such as AirTran, JetBlue, and Southwest are pursuing market development by expanding routes nationwide, just as the large airlines are cutting back on routes and employees. Both JetBlue and AirTran purchased 100 new planes in 2003 to fly to new cities in the Americas. However, JetBlue recently stopped flying into Atlanta due to heavy competition in that market.

McDonald's plans to open 100 new stores in China in 2004 and another 100 in China in 2005. By mid-2003, McDonald's had 566 restaurants in 94 cities in China, representing the company's seventh-largest market. McDonald's serves about 2 million customers in China every day and plans to aggressively boost that number. Kentucky Fried Chicken (KFC) has more outlets than McDonald's in many of China's cities, such as the inland city of Xian where KFC has 24 outlets and McDonald's has but 3.

Six guidelines for when market development may be an especially effective strategy are:[12]

- When new channels of distribution are available that are reliable, inexpensive, and of good quality.
- When an organization is very successful at what it does.
- When new untapped or unsaturated markets exist.
- When an organization has the needed capital and human resources to manage expanded operations.
- When an organization has excess production capacity.
- When an organization's basic industry is becoming rapidly global in scope.

Product Development

Product development is a strategy that seeks increased sales by improving or modifying present products or services. Product development usually entails large research and development expenditures.

Fast-food chains from Arby's to McDonald's are pursuing product development, testing gourmet-like sandwiches—because customers increasingly are willing to pay more for fast food crafted with quality ingredients. People more and more want food that not only tastes good but that they can feel good about eating. McDonald's now has design-your-own deli sandwiches and Arby's sells chi-chi sandwiches, which is a chicken salad blended with pecans, apples, and grapes. Subway is testing a healthy Kids Pak and Wendy's is testing fruit cups and milk as options in its Kids Meals.

Verizon Communications, the largest local phone company in the United States, recently began installing wireless Internet service at its pay phones, including 1,000 pay phones in New York City alone. A similar product-development strategy is being pursued by rival SBC Communications, another large phone company, and by rival Comcast, a large cable company. Phone companies currently have 35 percent of the high speed Internet market in the United States compared to 62 percent for cable. Phone and cable companies aggressively compete against each other in the Internet service business.

Banks are expanding geographically by adding branches aggressively. Washington Mutual, the seventh-largest domestic bank, opened 250 new branches in 2003, a 17 percent increase. Similarly, the largest U.S. bank, Bank of America, is adding 500 branches between 2003 and 2005, a 13 percent increase.

Five guidelines for when product development may be an especially effective strategy to pursue are:[13]

- When an organization has successful products that are in the maturity stage of the product life cycle; the idea here is to attract satisfied customers to try new (improved) products as a result of their positive experience with the organization's present products or services.

- When an organization competes in an industry that is characterized by rapid technological developments.
- When major competitors offer better-quality products at comparable prices.
- When an organization competes in a high-growth industry.
- When an organization has especially strong research and development capabilities.

Diversification Strategies

There are three general types of *diversification strategies:* concentric, horizontal, and conglomerate. Overall, diversification strategies are becoming less popular as organizations are finding it more difficult to manage diverse business activities. In the 1960s and 1970s, the trend was to diversify so as not to be dependent on any single industry, but the 1980s saw a general reversal of that thinking. Diversification is now on the retreat. Michael Porter, of the Harvard Business School, says, "Management found [it] couldn't manage the beast." Hence, businesses are selling, or closing, less profitable divisions in order to focus on core businesses.

There are, however, a few companies today that pride themselves on being conglomerates, from small firms such as Pentair Inc., and Blount International to huge companies such as Textron, Allied Signal, Emerson Electric, General Electric, Viacom, and Samsung. Samsung, for example, now has global market share leadership in many diverse areas, including cell-phones (10%), big-screen televisions (32%), MP3 players (13%), DVD players (11%), and microwave ovens (25%).[14] Similarly, Textron, through numerous diverse acquisitions, now produces and sells Cessna airplanes, Bell helicopters, Jacobsen lawn mowers, golf products, transmissions, consumer loans, and telescopic machinery. Conglomerates prove that focus and diversity are not always mutually exclusive.

Peters and Waterman's advice to firms is to "stick to the knitting" and not to stray too far from the firm's basic areas of competence. However, diversification is still an appropriate strategy sometimes, especially when the company is competing in an unattractive industry. For example, United Technologies is diversifying away from its core aviation business due to the slumping airline industry. Most recently, United Technologies acquired British electronic-security company Chubb PLC, which follows up its acquisition of Otis Elevator Company and Carrier air conditioning to reduce its dependence on the volatile airline industry. Hamish Maxwell, Philip Morris's former CEO, says, "We want to become a consumer-products company." Diversification makes sense for Philip Morris because cigarette consumption is declining, product liability suits are a risk, and some investors reject tobacco stocks on principle.

Concentric Diversification

Adding new, but related, products or services is widely called *concentric diversification*. An example of this strategy is Amazon.com Inc.'s recent move to sell personal computers through its online store. Rather than keeping the computers in its warehouses, however, Amazon will simply transmit orders for computers to wholesaler Ingram Micro, based in Santa Ana, California. Ingram will package and send the computers to customers, so Amazon is minimizing its own risk in this diversification initiative.

Dell Computer is pursuing concentric diversification by manufacturing and marketing consumer electronics products such as flat-panel televisions and MP3 players. Also, Dell has recently opened an online music-downloading store. These are examples of concentric diversification strategies for Dell, as the company sees the

NATURAL ENVIRONMENT PERSPECTIVE

Songbirds and Coral Reefs in Trouble

Songbirds

Bluebirds are one of seventy-six songbird species in the United States that have dramatically declined in numbers in the last two decades. Not all birds are considered songbirds, and why birds sing is not clear. Some scientists say they sing when calling for mates or warning of danger, but many scientists now contend that birds sing for sheer pleasure. Songbirds include chickadees, orioles, swallows, mockingbirds, warblers, sparrows, vireos, and the wood thrush. "These birds are telling us there's problem, something's out of balance in our environment," says Jeff Wells, bird conservation director for the National Audubon Society. Songbirds may be telling us that their air or water is too dirty or that we are destroying too much of their habitat. People collect Picasso paintings and save historic buildings. "Songbirds are part of our natural heritage. Why should we be willing to watch songbirds destroyed anymore than allowing a great work of art be destroyed?" asks Wells. Whatever message songbirds are singing to us today about their natural environment, the message is becoming less and less heard nationwide. Listen when you go outside today. Each of us as individuals, companies, states, and countries should do what we reasonably can to help improve the natural environment for songbirds.

Coral Reefs

The ocean covers more than 71 percent of the Earth. The destructive effect of commercial fishing on ocean habitats coupled with increasing pollution runoff into the ocean and global warming of the ocean have decimated fisheries, marine life, and coral reefs around the world. The unfortunate consequence of fishing over the last century has been *overfishing*—with the principal reasons being politics and greed. Trawl fishing with nets destroys coral reefs and has been compared to catching squirrels by cutting down forests, since bottom nets scour and destroy vast areas of the ocean. The great proportion of marine life caught in a trawl is "by-catch" juvenile fish and other life that are killed and discarded. Warming of the ocean due to CO_2 emissions also kills thousands of acres of coral reefs annually. The total area of fully protected marine habitats in the United States is only about 50 square miles, compared to some 93 million acres of national wildlife refuges and national parks on the nation's land. Ocean ecosystems and a healthy ocean is vital to the economic and social future of the nation—and, indeed, all countries of the world. Everything we do on land ends up in the ocean, so we all must become better stewards of this last frontier on Earth in order to sustain human survival and the quality of life.

Sources: Adapted from Tom Brook, "Declining Numbers Mute Many Birds' Songs," *USA Today* (September 11, 2001): 4A. Also adapted from John Ogden, "Maintaining Diversity in the Oceans," *Environment* (April 2001): 29–36.

personal computer business becoming more aligned with the entertainment business because both are becoming more and more digital. Simply put, computing and consumer electronics are converging into one industry. Dell as well as Hewlett-Packard and Gateway are among the computer firms that now compete with Sony, Matsushita, and Samsung in consumer electronics.

Motorola exited the television-producing business in 1974 in order to focus on semiconductors and wireless products. However, Motorola reentered the television-making business in late 2003 by hiring a Chinese company, Proview International Holdings of Hong Kong, to produce flat-panel screens, televisions, and other products under the Motorola name. Motorola's concentric diversification strategy also involves the firm trying to divest its semiconductor division so it can focus more on wireless and electronic household products.

Six guidelines for when concentric diversification may be an effective strategy are provided below.[15]

- When an organization competes in a no-growth or a slow-growth industry.
- When adding new, but related, products would significantly enhance the sales of current products.
- When new, but related, products could be offered at highly competitive prices.
- When new, but related, products have seasonal sales levels that counterbalance an organization's existing peaks and valleys.
- When an organization's products are currently in the declining stage of the product's life cycle.
- When an organization has a strong management team.

Horizontal Diversification

Adding new, unrelated products or services for present customers is called *horizontal diversification*. This strategy is not as risky as conglomerate diversification because a firm already should be familiar with its present customers. For example, consider the increasing number of hospitals that are creating miniature malls by offering banks, bookstores, coffee shops, restaurants, drugstores, and other retail stores within their buildings. Many hospitals previously had only cafeterias, gift shops, and maybe a pharmacy, but the movement into malls and retail stores is aimed at improving the ambiance for patients and their visitors. The new University Pointe Hospital in West Chester, Ohio, has 75,000 square feet of retail space. The CEO says, "Unless we diversify our revenue, we won't be able to fulfill our mission of providing healthcare. We want our hospital to be a place that people want to go to."[16] An example of horizontal diversification strategy would be the recent General Electric (GE) acquisition of Vivendi Universal Entertainment (VUE). VUE is a television and theme park empire while GE is a highly diversified conglomerate. VUE owns and operates Universal Studios theme parks. GE owns the National Broadcasting Corporation (NBC) and also produces home appliances and scores of other products. The new NBC Universal segment of GE will generate over $14 billion in revenue in 2004. GE will own 80 percent of NBC Universal while Vivendi will own 20 percent.

Four guidelines for when horizontal diversification may be an especially effective strategy are:[17]

- When revenues derived from an organization's current products or services would increase significantly by adding the new, unrelated products.
- When an organization competes in a highly competitive and/or a no-growth industry, as indicated by low industry profit margins and returns.
- When an organization's present channels of distribution can be used to market the new products to current customers.
- When the new products have countercyclical sales patterns compared to an organization's present products.

Conglomerate Diversification

Adding new, unrelated products or services is called *conglomerate diversification*. For example, in 2003, the huge battery company Energizer Holdings, acquired the Schick-Wilkinson Sword razor business from Pfizer for $930 million. Schick was the nation's second-largest shaving products company, with 18 percent global market share in the wet-shaving business. This conglomerate diversification strategy puts Energizer in direct competition with industry leader Gillette, which, interestingly, owns the Duracell battery brand and has 70 percent global market share in the wet-shaving business. So Gillette and Energizer are examples of highly diversified firms competing aggressively against each other in both batteries and razors.

The coffee shop company Starbucks entered the prepaid card and credit card business in late 2003 by developing its Duetto card. This card competes with Visa, MasterCard, and American Express, which also want increased market share in the growing prepaid card market. Starbucks' Duetto card is one of the first dual prepaid/credit cards. This conglomerate diversification strategy of creating the Duetto card will act as a lure, Starbucks expects, to keep consumers coming back into its shops.

Six guidelines for when conglomerate diversification may be an especially effective strategy to pursue are listed below.[18]

- When an organization's basic industry is experiencing declining annual sales and profits.
- When an organization has the capital and managerial talent needed to compete successfully in a new industry.
- When an organization has the opportunity to purchase an unrelated business that is an attractive investment opportunity.
- When there exists financial synergy between the acquired and acquiring firm (note that a key difference between concentric and conglomerate diversification is that the former should be based on some commonality in markets, products, or technology, whereas the latter should be based more on profit considerations).
- When existing markets for an organization's present products are saturated.
- When antitrust action could be charged against an organization that historically has concentrated on a single industry.

General Electric is a classic firm that is highly diversified. GE makes locomotives, lightbulbs, power plants, and refrigerators; GE manages more credit cards than American Express; GE owns more commercial aircraft than American Airlines.

Defensive Strategies

In addition to integrative, intensive, and diversification strategies, organizations also could pursue retrenchment, divestiture, or liquidation.

Retrenchment

Retrenchment occurs when an organization regroups through cost and asset reduction to reverse declining sales and profits. Sometimes called a turnaround or reorganizational strategy, retrenchment is designed to fortify an organization's basic distinctive competence. During retrenchment, strategists work with limited resources and face pressure from shareholders, employees, and the media. Retrenchment can entail selling off land and buildings to raise needed cash, pruning product lines, closing marginal businesses, closing obsolete factories, automating processes, reducing the number of employees, and instituting expense control systems.

Lord & Taylor, a division of May Department Stores, closed 32 of its 86 stores in 2003 and laid off 3,700 employees as part of a retrenchment strategy. The store closures represented 19 percent of the division's sales and 3 percent of corporate sales. Gateway Computer Company is using a retrenchment strategy as it closed 2 manufacturing plants and 80 stores in 2003 while struggling to fend off rival Dell Computer.

In 2003, Levi Strauss closed its remaining plants in the United States and Canada, eliminating nearly 2,000 jobs. From 1996 to 2002, sales of Levi clothing plummeted by $3 billion. Cone Mills, which makes fabric for Levi's jeans, filed Chapter 11 bankruptcy in 2003 and actively is pursuing a retrenchment strategy in an effort to survive a hostile buyout attempt by financier Wilbur Ross. Both companies are in severe financial trouble.

In some cases, *bankruptcy* can be an effective type of retrenchment strategy. Bankruptcy can allow a firm to avoid major debt obligations and to void union contracts. There are five major types of bankruptcy: Chapter 7, Chapter 9, Chapter 11, Chapter 12, and Chapter 13.

Chapter 7 bankruptcy is a liquidation procedure used only when a corporation sees no hope of being able to operate successfully or to obtain the necessary creditor agreement. All the organization's assets are sold in parts for their tangible worth.

Chapter 9 bankruptcy applies to municipalities. A municipality that successfully declared bankruptcy is Camden, New Jersey, the state's poorest city and the fifth-poorest city in the United States. A crime-ridden city of 87,000, Camden received $62.5 million in state aid and has withdrawn its bankruptcy petition. Between 1980 and 2000, only eighteen U.S. cities declared bankruptcy. Some states do not allow municipalities to declare bankruptcy.

Chapter 11 bankruptcy allows organizations to reorganize and come back after filing a petition for protection. Among all bankruptcy filings in 2002, personal bankruptcies comprised 97.6 percent of the total, while consumer (business) bankruptcies comprised 2.4 percent. Consumer bankruptcies increased 6 percent in 2002 to 1.54 million, an all-time record. However, corporate bankruptcy filings in 2002 declined 4 percent to about 40,000 cases.[19] For the twelve-month period that ended June 30, 2003, bankruptcy filings in federal court rose 9.6 percent to a new annual record of 1.65 million cases. Among these, nonbusiness filings increased 10 percent while business filings actually declined 5.15 percent to 37,182. Still, that is a lot of U.S. business bankruptcies for a twelve-month period.

Based in Lewisville, Texas, Fleming Companies, one of the largest distributors of supermarkets and convenience stores in the U.S., filed for Chapter 11 bankruptcy in 2003. Weeks earlier the company fired its CEO Mark Hansen. Fleming once received more than 20 percent of its revenues from Kmart, which also is operating under Chapter 11 bankruptcy.

Spiegel, parent of Eddie Bauer, Newport News, and the Spiegel Catalog, filed for Chapter 11 bankruptcy protection in mid-2003. The retailer plans, however, to keep all of its stores and catalog operations running. WestPoint Stevens, based in West Point, Georgia, also recently filed for bankruptcy protection from its creditors, joining other textile makers such as Guilford Mills and Burlington Industries, all of whom have been forced to restructure under bankruptcy because of overseas competition, cheap imports, and excessive debt. WestPoint makes bath products under brand names such as Ralph Lauren, Martha Stewart, and Joe Boxer.

Chapter 12 bankruptcy was created by the Family Farmer Bankruptcy Act of 1986. This law became effective in 1987 and provides special relief to family farmers with debt equal to or less than $1.5 million.

Chapter 13 bankruptcy is a reorganization plan similar to Chapter 11, but it is available only to small businesses owned by individuals with unsecured debts of less than $100,000 and secured debts of less than $350,000. The Chapter 13 debtor is allowed to operate the business while a plan is being developed to provide for the successful operation of the business in the future.

Five guidelines for when retrenchment may be an especially effective strategy to pursue are as follows.[20]

- When an organization has a clearly distinctive competence but has failed to meet its objectives and goals consistently over time.
- When an organization is one of the weaker competitors in a given industry.
- When an organization is plagued by inefficiency, low profitability, poor employee morale, and pressure from stockholders to improve performance.
- When an organization has failed to capitalize on external opportunities, minimize external threats, take advantage of internal strengths, and overcome internal weaknesses over time; that is, when the organization's strategic managers have failed (and possibly will be replaced by more competent individuals).
- When an organization has grown so large so quickly that major internal reorganization is needed.

Divestiture

Selling a division or part of an organization is called *divestiture*. Divestiture often is used to raise capital for further strategic acquisitions or investments. Divestiture can be part of an overall retrenchment strategy to rid an organization of businesses that are unprofitable, that require too much capital, or that do not fit well with the firm's other activities. For example, Walt Disney Company recently divested its Anaheim Angels baseball team, which ended Disney's financially disappointing ownership of the team that won the World Series in 2002. Disney is also trying to divest its only other sports team, the Mighty Ducks of Anaheim of the National Hockey League, which is unprofitable. Disney has had trouble merging professional sports teams into its entertainment empire.

Best Buy, based in Eden Prairie, Minnesota, recently divested its 1,200-store Musicland retail business to Sun Capital Partners based in Boca Raton, Florida. The Musicland division had been operating at a loss with Best Buy since its acquisition in 2001, due largely to declining sales of compact discs, increased online music-swapping, and growing competition from large discounters.

Bombardier recently divested its recreational products business to Bain Capital. This division of Bombardier makes snowmobiles and watercraft under such brand names as Ski-Doo snowmobiles and Sea-Doo jet skis. Based in Montreal, Canada, Bombardier had made snowmobiles for more than sixty years, but "need for cash" was a major reason for the divestiture. Abbott recently divested its hospital products business in order to focus more on the firm's pharmaceutical and vascular medicine products. Abbott's hospital products division historically had not performed well. More examples of divestitures in 2003–2004 are listed in Table 5–4.

Six guidelines for when divestiture may be an especially effective strategy to pursue are listed below.[21]

- When an organization has pursued a retrenchment strategy and failed to accomplish needed improvements.
- When a division needs more resources to be competitive than the company can provide.

TABLE 5-4   Recent Divestitures

PARENT COMPANY	PART BEING DIVESTED	ACQUIRING COMPANY
Abbey National PLC	Consumer-finance business	General Electric Co.
U.S. Bancorp	Piper Jaffray	Shareholders
AFC Enterprises	Seattle Coffee	Starbucks
Cablevision	Clearview Cinemas	Shareholders
Cablevision	Rainbow DBS	Shareholders
National Assoc. of Securities Dealers	American Stock Exchange	GTCR Golder Rauner LLC
ConAgra Foods	Chicken Processing	Pilgrim's Pride
Credit Suisse Group	Churchill Insurance PLC	Royal Bank of Scotland Group
Odyssey Investment	TransDigm	Warburg Pincus
ANC Rental Corp.	Alamo Car Rental	Cerberus Capital Mgt.
ANC Rental Corp.	National Car Rental	Cerberus Capital Mgt.
Magna	Real estate operations	
Magna	Horse racing operations	
General Electric	GE Edison Life Insurance	American International
Lincolnshire Mgt.	Riddell Sports Group	Fenway Partners, Inc.
Sears, Roebuck	Credit Card Business	Citigroup
Loral	NA Telecommunications	Intelsat
KirchMedia	ProSiebenSat.1AG	Haim Saban
General Electric	Financial Guaranty Insurance	
Aegon NV	TransAmerica	General Electric
W. L. Gore	Glide	Procter & Gamble
Sears, Roebuck	National Tire & Battery	TBC Corp.
Walter Industries	Applied Industrial Materials	Oxbow Group
Motorola	Semiconductor operations	
Women's Capital	Plan B	Barr Laboratories

- When a division is responsible for an organization's overall poor performance.
- When a division is a misfit with the rest of an organization; this can result from radically different markets, customers, managers, employees, values, or needs.
- When a large amount of cash is needed quickly and cannot be obtained reasonably from other sources.
- When government antitrust action threatens an organization.

Liquidation

Selling all of a company's assets, in parts, for their tangible worth is called *liquidation*. Liquidation is a recognition of defeat and consequently can be an emotionally difficult strategy. However, it may be better to cease operating than to continue losing large sums of money. For example, National Century Financial Enterprises, Inc., based in Dublin, Ohio, liquidated in 2003 after operating under Chapter 11 bankruptcy for less than a year. National Century specialized in providing financing for healthcare companies, several of which declared bankruptcy themselves soon after National Century ceased operations. Another example is the recent liquidation of Consolidated Freightways Corp., based in Vancouver, Washington, which ceased operations in the trucking industry.

Based in Kannapolis, North Carolina, Pillowtex is a large textile maker that declared bankruptcy and then liquidated in 2003 as the firm closed all sixteen of its plants and sold off all its assets. Pillowtex made Cannon and Fieldcrest towels and sheets for more than 100 years, but cheap imports and heavy debt obligations sealed the firm's demise.

Based in Waltham, Massachusetts, StorageNetworks liquidated in 2003 after its stock price fell to $1 from a high in 2000 of over $90. The firm had marketed off-site computer data storage "farms" but companies never really trusted their sensitive computer data being outsourced.

Thousands of small businesses in the United States liquidate annually without ever making the news. It is tough to start and successfully operate a small business. In China and Russia, thousands of government-owned businesses liquidate annually as those countries try to privatize and consolidate industries.

Three guidelines for when liquidation may be an especially effective strategy to pursue are:[22]

- When an organization has pursued both a retrenchment strategy and a divestiture strategy, and neither has been successful.
- When an organization's only alternative is bankruptcy; liquidation represents an orderly and planned means of obtaining the greatest possible cash for an organization's assets. A company can legally declare bankruptcy first and then liquidate various divisions to raise needed capital.
- When the stockholders of a firm can minimize their losses by selling the organization's assets.

Michael Porter's Generic Strategies

Probably the three most widely read books on competitive analysis in the 1980s were Michael Porter's (**www.hbs.edu/bios/mporter**) *Competitive Strategy* (Free Press, 1980), *Competitive Advantage* (Free Press, 1985), and *Competitive Advantage of Nations* (Free Press, 1989). According to Porter, strategies allow organizations to gain competitive advantage from three different bases: cost leadership, differentiation, and focus. Porter calls these bases *generic strategies*. *Cost leadership* emphasizes producing standardized products at a very low per-unit cost for consumers who are price-sensitive. *Differentiation* is a strategy aimed at producing products and services considered unique industrywide and directed at consumers who are relatively price-insensitive. *Focus* means producing products and services that fulfill the needs of small groups of consumers.

Porter's strategies imply different organizational arrangements, control procedures, and incentive systems. Larger firms with greater access to resources typically compete on a cost leadership and/or differentiation basis, whereas smaller firms often compete on a focus basis.

Porter stresses the need for strategists to perform cost-benefit analyses to evaluate "sharing opportunities" among a firm's existing and potential business units. Sharing activities and resources enhances competitive advantage by lowering costs or raising differentiation. In addition to prompting sharing, Porter stresses the need for firms to "transfer" skills and expertise among autonomous business units effectively in order to gain competitive advantage. Depending upon factors such as type of industry, size of firm, and nature of competition, various strategies could yield advantages in cost leadership, differentiation, and focus.

Cost Leadership Strategies

A primary reason for pursuing forward, backward, and horizontal integration strategies is to gain cost leadership benefits. But cost leadership generally must be pursued in conjunction with differentiation. A number of cost elements affect the relative attractiveness of generic strategies, including economies or diseconomies of scale achieved, learning and experience curve effects, the percentage of capacity utilization achieved, and linkages with suppliers and distributors. Other cost elements to consider in choosing among alternative strategies include the potential for sharing costs and knowledge within the organization, R&D costs associated with new product development or modification of existing products, labor costs, tax rates, energy costs, and shipping costs.

Striving to be the low-cost producer in an industry can be especially effective when the market is composed of many price-sensitive buyers, when there are few ways to achieve product differentiation, when buyers do not care much about differences from brand to brand, or when there are a large number of buyers with significant bargaining power. The basic idea is to underprice competitors and thereby gain market share and sales, driving some competitors out of the market entirely.

A successful cost leadership strategy usually permeates the entire firm, as evidenced by high efficiency, low overhead, limited perks, intolerance of waste, intensive screening of budget requests, wide spans of control, rewards linked to cost containment, and broad employee participation in cost control efforts. Some risks of pursuing cost leadership are that competitors may imitate the strategy, thus driving overall industry profits down; that technological breakthroughs in the industry may make the strategy ineffective; or that buyer interest may swing to other differentiating features besides price. Several example firms that are well known for their low-cost leadership strategies are Wal-Mart, BIC, McDonald's, Black and Decker, Lincoln Electric, and Briggs and Stratton.

Differentiation Strategies

Different strategies offer different degrees of differentiation. Differentiation does not guarantee competitive advantage, especially if standard products sufficiently meet customer needs or if rapid imitation by competitors is possible. Durable products protected by barriers to quick copying by competitors are best. Successful differentiation can mean greater product flexibility, greater compatibility, lower costs, improved service, less maintenance, greater convenience, or more features. Product development is an example of a strategy that offers the advantages of differentiation.

A differentiation strategy should be pursued only after a careful study of buyers' needs and preferences to determine the feasibility of incorporating one or more differentiating features into a unique product that features the desired attributes. A successful differentiation strategy allows a firm to charge a higher price for its product and to gain customer loyalty because consumers may become strongly attached to the differentiation features. Special features that differentiate one's product can include superior service, spare parts availability, engineering design, product performance, useful life, gas mileage, or ease of use.

A risk of pursuing a differentiation strategy is that the unique product may not be valued highly enough by customers to justify the higher price. When this happens, a cost leadership strategy easily will defeat a differentiation strategy. Another risk of pursuing a differentiation strategy is that competitors may develop ways to copy the differentiating features quickly. Firms thus must find durable sources of uniqueness that cannot be imitated quickly or cheaply by rival firms.

Common organizational requirements for a successful differentiation strategy include strong coordination among the R&D and marketing functions and substantial amenities to attract scientists and creative people. Firms pursuing a differentiation strategy include Dr. Pepper, Jenn-Air, The Limited, BMW, Grady-White, Ralph Lauren, Maytag, and Cross.

Focus Strategies

A successful focus strategy depends on an industry segment that is of sufficient size, has good growth potential, and is not crucial to the success of other major competitors. Strategies such as market penetration and market development offer substantial focusing advantages. Midsize and large firms can effectively pursue focus-based strategies only in conjunction with differentiation or cost leadership-based strategies. All firms in essence follow a differentiated strategy. Because only one firm can differentiate itself with the lowest cost, the remaining firms in the industry must find other ways to differentiate their products.

Focus strategies are most effective when consumers have distinctive preferences or requirements and when rival firms are not attempting to specialize in the same target segment. Starbucks, the largest U.S. coffeehouse chain, is pursuing a focus strategy as it recently acquired Seattle Coffee's U.S. and Canadian operations for $72 million. Based in Seattle, Starbucks now owns Seattle's 150 coffee shops as well as Seattle's wholesale contracts with about 12,000 grocery stores and food service stores that distribute Seattle coffee beans.

In the insurance industry, Safeco recently divested its life insurance and investment management divisions to focus exclusively on property casualty insurance operations. The Seattle-based company's strategy is just one of many examples of consolidation in the insurance industry where firms strive to focus on one type of insurance rather than many types.

Risks of pursuing a focus strategy include the possibility that numerous competitors will recognize the successful focus strategy and copy it, or that consumer preferences will drift toward the product attributes desired by the market as a whole. An organization using a focus strategy may concentrate on a particular group of customers, geographic markets, or on particular product-line segments in order to serve a well-defined but narrow market better than competitors who serve a broader market.

Means for Achieving Strategies

Joint Venture/Partnering

Joint venture is a popular strategy that occurs when two or more companies form a temporary partnership or consortium for the purpose of capitalizing on some opportunity. Often, the two or more sponsoring firms form a separate organization and have shared equity ownership in the new entity. Other types of *cooperative arrangements* include research and development partnerships, cross-distribution agreements, cross-licensing agreements, cross-manufacturing agreements, and joint-bidding consortia. Burger King recently formed a "conceptual agreement" with its fierce rival, Hungry Jacks, in Australia, whereby the two firms will join forces against market leader McDonald's. All Burger Kings in Australia are being renamed Hungry Jacks, but Burger King retains ownership under the unusual agreement. With this agreement, Australia becomes Burger King's fourth-largest country market, tied with Spain.

Nestlé SA and Colgate-Palmolive recently formed a joint venture to develop and sell candy and chewing gum that can reduce plaque and clean teeth. This intensely competitive industry is dominated by Cadbury Schweppes PLC's Adams and Chicago-based Wm. Wrigley Jr. Co. Called the "functional confectionary segment," gum and candy sales that have health or aesthetic benefits are growing almost 6 percent annually, twice the growth rate of standard gum and candy. Nestlé had no functional confectionary products prior to the joint venture. Adams is the world leader in functional confectionery, with a 26 percent share and products such as tooth-whitening Trident White and Recaldent. Wrigley has 21 percent of the market with products such as Orbit White and Airwaves.

Joint ventures and cooperative arrangements are being used increasingly because they allow companies to improve communications and networking, to globalize operations, and to minimize risk. Kathryn Rudie Harrigan, professor of strategic management at Columbia University, summarizes the trend toward increased joint venturing:

> In today's global business environment of scarce resources, rapid rates of technological change, and rising capital requirements, the important question is no longer "Shall we form a joint venture?" Now the question is "Which joint ventures and cooperative arrangements are most appropriate for our needs and expectations?" followed by "How do we manage these ventures most effectively?"[23]

In a global market tied together by the Internet, joint ventures, partnerships, and alliances are proving to be a more effective way to enhance corporate growth than mergers and acquisitions.[24] Strategic partnering takes many forms, including outsourcing, information sharing, joint marketing, and joint research and development. Many companies such as Eli Lilly even now host partnership training classes for their managers and partners. There are today more than 10,000 joint ventures formed annually, more than all mergers and acquisitions. There are countless examples of successful strategic alliances, such as Starbucks' recent joint venture with China's President Coffee to open hundreds of new Starbuck coffee shops in China. For 4,500 years, China has been a country of tea drinkers, but Seattle-based Starbucks is having success building Chinese taste for coffee.

A major reason why firms are using partnering as a means to achieve strategies is globalization. Wal-Mart's successful joint venture with Mexico's Cifra is indicative of how a domestic firm can benefit immensely by partnering with a foreign company to gain substantial presence in that new country. Technology also is a major reason behind the need to form strategic alliances, with the Internet linking widely dispersed partners. The Internet paved the way and legitimized the need for alliances to serve as the primary means for corporate growth.

Evidence is mounting that firms should use partnering as a means for achieving strategies. However, the sad fact is that most American firms in many industries, such as financial services, forest products, and metals and retailing, still operate in a merger or acquire mode to obtain growth. Partnering is not yet taught at most business schools and is often viewed within companies as a financial issue rather than a strategic issue. However, partnering has become a core competency, a strategic issue of such importance that top management involvement initially and throughout the life of an alliance is vital.[25]

Air France's recent linkup with KLM Royal Dutch Airlines falls short of a merger but links Europe's largest and fourth-largest airlines by establishing a jointly owned Franco-Dutch holding company. With a market value of $3.71 billion, Air France is about six times larger than KLM, which has been especially hard hit by the downturn in air travel and is pursuing retrenchment. Joint ventures among once rival firms are commonly being used to pursue strategies ranging from retrenchment to market development.

Although ventures and partnerships are preferred over mergers as a means for achieving strategies, certainly they are not all successful. The good news is that joint ventures and partnerships are less risky for companies than mergers, but the bad news is that many alliances fail. *Forbes* recently reported that about 30 percent of all joint ventures and partnership alliances are outright failures, while another 17 percent have limited success and then dissipate due to problems.[26] There are countless examples of failed joint ventures. A few common problems that cause joint ventures to fail are as follows:

1. Managers who must collaborate daily in operating the venture are not involved in forming or shaping the venture.
2. The venture may benefit the partnering companies but may not benefit customers who then complain about poorer service or criticize the companies in other ways.
3. The venture may not be supported equally by both partners. If supported unequally, problems arise.
4. The venture may begin to compete more with one of the partners than the other.[27]

Six guidelines for when a joint venture may be an especially effective strategy to pursue are:[28]

- When a privately owned organization is forming a joint venture with a publicly owned organization; there are some advantages to being privately held, such as closed ownership; there are some advantages of being publicly held, such as access to stock issuances as a source of capital. Sometimes, the unique advantages of being privately and publicly held can be synergistically combined in a joint venture.
- When a domestic organization is forming a joint venture with a foreign company; a joint venture can provide a domestic company with the opportunity for obtaining local management in a foreign country, thereby reducing risks such as expropriation and harassment by host country officials.
- When the distinct competencies of two or more firms complement each other especially well.
- When some project is potentially very profitable but requires overwhelming resources and risks; the Alaskan pipeline is an example.
- When two or more smaller firms have trouble competing with a large firm.
- When there exists a need to introduce a new technology quickly.

Some recent joint ventures include Wachovia Brokerage uniting with Prudential Brokerage to form Wachovia Securities. Also, Nestlé and Colgate-Palmolive just formed a joint venture, as mentioned previously. Orange SA just entered into two joint ventures, one with Alcatel SA and the other with Nokia Corp.

Joint Ventures in Russia

A joint venture strategy offers a possible way to enter the Russian market. Joint ventures create a mechanism to generate hard currency, which is important because of problems valuing the ruble. Russia's joint venture law has been revised to allow foreigners to own up to 99 percent of the venture and to allow a foreigner to serve as chief executive officer.

The following guidelines are appropriate when considering a joint venture in Russia. First, avoid regions with ethnic conflicts and violence. Also, make sure the potential partner has a proper charter that has been amended to permit joint venture participation. Be aware that businesspeople in these lands have little knowledge of marketing, contract law, corporate law, fax machines, voice mail, and other business practices that Westerners take for granted.

Business contracts with Russian firms should address natural-environment issues because Westerners often get the blame for air and water pollution problems and habitat destruction. Work out a clear means of converting rubles to dollars before entering a proposed joint venture, because neither Russian banks nor authorities can be counted on to facilitate foreign firms' getting dollar profits out of a business. Recognize that chronic shortages of raw materials hamper business in Russia, so make sure an adequate supply of competitively priced, good-quality raw materials is reliably available. Finally, make sure the business contract limits the circumstances in which expropriation would be legal. Specify a lump sum in dollars if expropriation should occur unexpectedly, and obtain expropriation insurance before signing the agreement.

BP PLC is an example of a company that is betting its future on a $6.75 billion joint venture in Russia to drill for oil. Formed in 2003, the new joint venture aims to produce 1.2 million barrels of oil per day and is the largest ever foreign-equity investment in Russia. BP has a 50 percent stake in the new venture that becomes Russia's third-largest oil producer.

Merger/Acquisition

Merger and acquisition are two commonly used ways to pursue strategies. A *merger* occurs when two organizations of about equal size unite to form one enterprise. An *acquisition* occurs when a large organization purchases (acquires) a smaller firm, or vice versa. When a merger or acquisition is not desired by both parties, it can be called a *takeover* or *hostile takeover*. For example, Canadian aluminum maker Alcan Inc., in mid-2003, launched a $3.9 billion unsolicited takeover bid for French rival Pechiney SA, aimed at creating the world's largest aluminum company. This was the first hostile takeover of a French firm since Nestlé SA bought Perrier in the early 1990s; France jealously guards national firms against unsolicited foreign incursions, although such protectionism is waning. Also in mid-2003, Oracle launched a hostile takeover of PeopleSoft, and Zimmer Holdings made an unsolicited bid for Swiss orthopedics firm Centerpulse AG. In addition, ArvinMeritor launched a $2.2 billion hostile bid for rival autoparts maker Dana in a bid to create the number-three domestic auto supplier behind number-one Delphi Corp., and number-two Visteon Corp. Hostile takeovers are often difficult to pull off.

In contrast, if the acquisition is desired by both firms, it is termed a *friendly merger*. For example, the Nike acquisition of Converse in mid-2003 was a friendly merger. Nike executive Thomas Clarke said, "we intend to leave Converse's current management, headed by Jack Boys in place. He's really established a great brand that has a lot of elasticity. We like Converse's business plan and we don't plan on making any changes." Maker of the world's lowest-tech sneakers, Converse is the antithesis of Nike, maker of the world's highest-tech sneakers. There are numerous and powerful forces driving once-fierce rivals to merge around the world. Some of these forces are deregulation, technological change, excess capacity, inability to boost profits through price increases, a depressed stock market, and the need to gain economies of scale.

There are bargains available as companies struggle and while stock prices are low. Among domestic media companies, for example, numerous mergers are expected since the Federal Communications Commission, in June 2003, lifted the decades-old restrictions on the size of media firms. That ruling allows newspapers to now own television and radio stations in the markets where they publish. Also, network television companies can now own stations reaching up to 45 percent of the nation's viewers, up from 35 percent. Companies such as Tribune, Media General, Sinclair Broadcast Group, LIN TV, NewsCorp, Fox, NBC, ABC, CBS, and others are expected to be merging in the 2004–2006 time period.

Not all mergers are effective and successful. Pricewaterhouse Coopers LLP recently researched mergers and found that the average acquirer's stock was 3.7 percent lower than its industry peer group a year later. *BusinessWeek* and the *Wall Street Journal* studied mergers and concluded that about half produced negative returns to shareholders. Warren Buffett once said in a speech that "too-high purchase price for the stock of an excellent company can undo the effects of a subsequent decade of favorable business developments." So a merger between two firms can yield great benefits, but the price and reasoning must be right.

Among mergers, acquisitions, and takeovers in recent years, same-industry combinations have predominated. A general market consolidation is occurring in many industries, especially banking, insurance, defense, and healthcare, but also in pharmaceuticals, food, airlines, accounting, publishing, computers, retailing, financial services, and biotechnology.

The total value of U.S. merger deals in 2002 fell 41 percent to $447.8 billion, its lowest level since 1994, and down 74 percent from the peak year in 2000.[29] Globally, the number of mergers in 2002 fell to 24,786 or 28 percent from 29,786 in 2001. In addition to the weak economy hurting the merger business, accounting scandals, poor earnings, low stock prices, and global uncertainty also reduced interest in merging. This sharp decline enabled the number and dollar volume of mergers and acquisitions in Europe to surpass those in the United States in 2002 for the first time since 1991. European deals in 2002 totaled about $477.8 billion, a 9.8 percent decline from 2001 but still 7.0 percent more than in the United States. However, in 2003, merger activity really picked up again, both domestically and globally, as economies improved, investor confidence improved, and stock prices remained relatively cheap.

In Mexico, the number of mergers and acquisitions increased 300 percent in 2002 to more than $12 billion. A reason for the increase in activity in Mexico is that the peso is strong compared to the weaker currencies of Argentina, Brazil, and Colombia, even though the Mexican peso depreciated 10 percent against the U.S. dollar in 2002.[30]

The world's largest drug company, Pfizer, recently acquired Pharmacia for $53 billion, to become nearly 50 percent larger than the number-two drug company in the world, GlaxoSmithKline. The acquisition gives Pfizer 11 percent of the global market share for prescription drugs. Also in mid-2003, trucking company Yellow Corp. paid a 49 percent premium to acquire its major competitor, Roadway, to become the largest single company in the less-than-truckload shipment industry. The new company is called Yellow-Roadway Corp.

Table 5–5 shows some mergers and acquisitions completed in 2003–2004. There are many reasons for mergers and acquisitions, including the following:

- To provide improved capacity utilization
- To make better use of the existing sales force

TABLE 5-5   Some Recent Example Mergers

ACQUIRING FIRM	ACQUIRED FIRM
IBM	Rational Software Corporation
Yahoo!	Inktomi Corp.
HSBC Holdings PLC	Household International
Credit Agricole SA	Credit Lyonnais SA
U.S. Steel	National Steel Corp.
Johnson & Johnson	Scios
Moore Corp.	Wallace Computer Services
Berkshire Hathaway Inc.	Burlington Industries, Inc.
Constellation Brands Inc.	BRL Hardy
Canada Life Financial	Great-West Lifeco
Devon Energy Corp.	Ocean Energy Inc.
Pfizer	Pharmacia
Krispy Kreme Doughnuts	Montana Mills
PeopleSoft	J. D. Edwards
Oracle	PeopleSoft
Palm	Handspring
WellPoint Health Networks	Cobalt Corp.
General Dynamics	Veridian
Community Bank Systems	Grange National Bank
Mercury Interactive	Kitana
Biogen	Idec
Nike	Converse
Yellow Corp.	Roadway Corp.
EMC Corp.	Legato Systems Inc.
VF Corp.	Nautica Enterprises
Sun Microsystems	Pixo
Yahoo!	Overture Services
Business Objects SA	Crystal Decisions
American Express	Rosenbluth
Kodak	Practice Works
Lockheed Martin	Titan
Avio Holding	FlatAvio
Investor Group	Transdigm
Eurazeo	Eutelsat
DRS Technologies	Integrated Defense Tech
L-3 Communications Hldg.	Goodrich Avionics Systems
Alcan	Pechiney
Manulife Financial	John Hancock Financial

- To reduce managerial staff
- To gain economies of scale
- To smooth out seasonal trends in sales
- To gain access to new suppliers, distributors, customers, products, and creditors
- To gain new technology
- To reduce tax obligations

The volume of mergers completed annually worldwide is growing dramatically and exceeds $1 trillion. There are more than 10,000 mergers annually in the United States that total more than $700 billion.

The proliferation of mergers is fueled by companies' drive for market share, efficiency, and pricing power as well as by globalization, the need for greater economies of scale, reduced regulation and antitrust concerns, the Internet, and e-commerce.

A *leveraged buyout* (LBO) occurs when a corporation's shareholders are bought (hence *buyout*) by the company's management and other private investors using borrowed funds (hence *leverage*).[31] Besides trying to avoid a hostile takeover, other reasons for initiating an LBO are senior management decisions that particular divisions do not fit into an overall corporate strategy or must be sold to raise cash, or receipt of an attractive offering price. An LBO takes a corporation private.

First Mover Advantages

First mover advantages refers to the benefits a firm may achieve by entering a new market or developing a new product or service prior to rival firms.[32] Some advantages of being a first mover include securing access to rare resources, gaining new knowledge of key factors and issues, and carving out market share and a position that is easy to defend and costly for rival firms to overtake. First mover advantages are analogous to taking the high ground first which puts one in an excellent strategic position to launch aggressive campaigns and to defend territory. There would, however, be risks associated with being the first mover, such as unexpected and unanticipated problems and costs that occur from being the first firm doing business in the new market.

Strategic-management research indicates that first mover advantages tend to be greatest when competitors are roughly the same size and possess similar resources. If competitors are not similar in size, then larger competitors can wait while others make initial investments and mistakes, and then respond with greater effectiveness and resources.

Outsourcing

Business-process outsourcing (BPO) is a rapidly growing new business that involves companies taking over the functional operations, such as human resources, information systems, payroll, accounting, customer service, and even marketing of other firms. Companies are choosing to outsource their functional operations more and more for several reasons: (1) it is less expensive, (2) it allows the firm to focus on its core businesses, and (3) it enables the firm to provide better services. In other words, BPO is a means for achieving strategies that are similar to partnering and joint venturing. According to the *Wall Street Journal*, the worldwide BPO market rose 10.5 percent in 2003 to $122 billion and is expected to exceed $173 billion by 2007.[33]

Two of many firms selling BPO services today are IBM and Affiliated Computer Services (ACS). IBM has a $400 million, ten-year contract to handle Procter & Gamble's human resources tasks. ACS generated nearly 70 percent of its $3.8 billion in 2003 revenues from BPO services, up 63 percent from 2002. ACS handles all of Motorola's human resources but also does extensive BPO work for government agencies and even academic institutions.

Many firms such as Dearborn, Michigan-based Visteon Corp., and J. P. Morgan Chase & Co. outsource their computer operations to IBM, who competes with firms such as Electronic Data Systems and Computer Sciences Corp., in the computer outsourcing business. 3M Corp., in 2004, is outsourcing all of its manufacturing operations to Flextronics International Ltd. of Singapore or Jabil Circuit in Florida. 3M is also outsourcing all design and manufacturing of low-end standardized volume products by building a new design center in Taiwan.

Strategic Management in Nonprofit and Governmental Organizations

The strategic-management process is being used effectively by countless nonprofit and governmental organizations, such as the Girl Scouts and Boy Scouts, the Red Cross, chambers of commerce, educational institutions, medical institutions, public utilities, libraries, government agencies, and churches. The nonprofit sector, surprisingly, is by far America's largest employer. Many nonprofit and governmental organizations outperform private firms and corporations on innovativeness, motivation, productivity, and strategic management. For many nonprofit examples of strategic planning in practice, click on Strategic Planning Links found at the **www. strategyclub.com** Web site.

Compared to for-profit firms, nonprofit and governmental organizations may be totally dependent on outside financing. Especially for these organizations, strategic management provides an excellent vehicle for developing and justifying requests for needed financial support.

Educational Institutions

Educational institutions are using strategic-management techniques and concepts more frequently. Richard Cyert, president of Carnegie-Mellon University, says, "I believe we do a far better job of strategic management than any company I know." Population shifts nationally from the Northeast and Midwest to the Southeast and West are but one factor causing trauma for educational institutions that have not planned for changing enrollments. Ivy League schools in the Northeast are recruiting more heavily in the Southeast and West. This trend represents a significant change in the competitive climate for attracting the best high school graduates each year.

The first all-Internet law school, Concord University School of Law, boasts nearly two hundred students who can access lectures anytime and chat at fixed times with professors. Online college degrees are becoming common and represent a threat to traditional colleges and universities. "You can put the kids to bed and go to law school," says Andrew Rosen, chief operating officer of Kaplan

Education Centers, a subsidiary of the Washington Post Company, that owns Concord. Concord is not accredited by the American Bar Association, which prohibits study by correspondence and requires more than one thousand hours of classroom time.

For a list of college strategic plans, click on Strategic Planning Links found at the **www.strategyclub.com** Web site, and scroll down through the academic sites.

Medical Organizations

The $200 billion American hospital industry is experiencing declining margins, excess capacity, bureaucratic overburdening, poorly planned and executed diversification strategies, soaring healthcare costs, reduced federal support, and high administrator turnover. The seriousness of this problem is accented by a 20 percent annual decline in inpatient use nationwide. Declining occupancy rates, deregulation, and accelerating growth of health maintenance organizations, preferred provider organizations, urgent care centers, outpatient surgery centers, diagnostic centers, specialized clinics, and group practices are other major threats facing hospitals today. Many private and state-supported medical institutions are in financial trouble as a result of traditionally taking a reactive rather than a proactive approach in dealing with their industry.

Hospitals—originally intended to be warehouses for people dying of tuberculosis, smallpox, cancer, pneumonia, and infectious diseases—are creating new strategies today as advances in the diagnosis and treatment of chronic diseases are undercutting that earlier mission. Hospitals are beginning to bring services to the patient as much as bringing the patient to the hospital; healthcare is more and more being concentrated in the home and in the residential community, not on the hospital campus. Chronic care will require day-treatment facilities, electronic monitoring at home, user-friendly ambulatory services, decentralized service networks, and laboratory testing. A successful hospital strategy for the future will require renewed and deepened collaboration with physicians, who are central to hospitals' well-being, and a reallocation of resources from acute to chronic care in home and community settings.

Current strategies being pursued by many hospitals include creating home health services, establishing nursing homes, and forming rehabilitation centers. Backward integration strategies that some hospitals are pursuing include acquiring ambulance services, waste disposal services, and diagnostic services. Millions of persons annually research medical ailments online, which is causing a dramatic shift in the balance of power between doctor, patient, and hospitals.[34] The number of persons using the Internet to obtain medical information is skyrocketing. A motivated patient using the Internet can gain knowledge on a particular subject far beyond his or her doctor's knowledge, because no person can keep up with the results and implications of billions of dollars' worth of medical research reported weekly. Patients today often walk into the doctor's office with a file folder of the latest articles detailing research and treatment options for their ailments. On Web sites such as America's Doctor (**www.americasdoctor.com**), consumers can consult with a physician in an online chat room twenty-four hours a day. Excellent consumer health Web sites are proliferating, boosted by investments from such firms as Microsoft, AOL, Reader's Digest, and CBS. Drug companies such as Glaxo Wellcome are getting involved, as are hospitals. The whole strategic landscape of healthcare is changing because of the Internet. Intel recently began offering a new secure medical service whereby doctors and patients can conduct sensitive business on the Internet, such as sharing results of medical tests and prescribing medicine. The ten most successful hospital strategies today are providing free-standing outpatient surgery centers, outpatient surgery and

diagnostic centers, physical rehabilitation centers, home health services, cardiac rehabilitation centers, preferred provider services, industrial medicine services, women's
medicine services, skilled nursing units, and psychiatric services.[35]

Governmental Agencies and Departments

Federal, state, county, and municipal agencies and departments, such as police
departments, chambers of commerce, forestry associations, and health departments,
are responsible for formulating, implementing, and evaluating strategies that use taxpayers' dollars in the most cost-effective way to provide services and programs.
Strategic-management concepts are generally required and thus widely used to
enable governmental organizations to be more effective and efficient. For a list of
government agency strategic plans, click on Strategic Planning Links found at the
www.strategyclub.com Web site, and scroll down through the government sites.

But strategists in governmental organizations operate with less strategic
autonomy than their counterparts in private firms. Public enterprises generally cannot diversify into unrelated businesses or merge with other firms. Governmental
strategists usually enjoy little freedom in altering the organizations' missions or
redirecting objectives. Legislators and politicians often have direct or indirect control over major decisions and resources. Strategic issues get discussed and debated in
the media and legislatures. Issues become politicized, resulting in fewer strategic
choice alternatives. There is now more predictability in the management of public
sector enterprises.

Government agencies and departments are finding that their employees get
excited about the opportunity to participate in the strategic-management process
and thereby have an effect on the organization's mission, objectives, strategies, and
policies. In addition, government agencies are using a strategic-management
approach to develop and substantiate formal requests for additional funding.

Strategic Management in Small Firms

Strategic management is vital for large firms' success, but what about small firms?
The strategic-management process is just as vital for small companies. From their
inception, all organizations have a strategy, even if the strategy just evolves from day-
to-day operations. Even if conducted informally or by a single owner/entrepreneur,
the strategic-management process can significantly enhance small firms' growth and
prosperity. Recent data clearly show that an ever-increasing number of men and
women in the United States are starting their own businesses. This means that more
individuals are becoming strategists. Widespread corporate layoffs have contributed
to an explosion in small businesses and new ideas.

Numerous magazine and journal articles have focused on applying strategic-
management concepts to small businesses.[36] A major conclusion of these articles is
that a lack of strategic-management knowledge is a serious obstacle for many small
business owners. Other problems often encountered in applying strategic-
management concepts to small businesses are a lack of both sufficient capital to
exploit external opportunities and a day-to-day cognitive frame of reference.
Research also indicates that strategic management in small firms is more informal
than in large firms, but small firms that engage in strategic management outperform
those that do not.

VISIT THE NET

Site provides sixty sample business plans for small businesses.
www.bplans.com/sp/ index.cfm?a=bc

GLOBAL PERSPECTIVE

Mexico's Lure Starting to Wane

As consumer demand falls and global economies falter, the lure of locating or even keeping business operations in Mexico has faded. Scores of companies such as General Electric, SCI Systems, Goodyear, Michelin, and Flextronics are moving their operations from the U.S.–Mexico border to China and Malaysia. What do China and Malaysia have to offer companies over Mexico? The answer: Wages as low as sixty cents an hour, tax incentives, center tariffs, and close proximity to markets that are growing instead of contracting.

Mexico has long suffered from poor schools, rampant corruption, and outmoded infrastructure, but its close proximity to the United States, its low wages, and the passage of NAFTA were appealing to companies. Mexican President Vicente Fox has promised to boost education spending from 5 percent of Gross Domestic Product (GDP) to 8 percent, but many companies feel this is too little, too late. Telephone penetration in Mexico is among the lowest in Latin America, and Mexico's judicial system is prone to corruption. Mexicans average fewer

than seven years of education, compared with about ten years for Koreans and Poles. Malaysia and Singapore charge no corporate taxes on electronics assembly, while China and Ireland tax rates are about 10 percent. In contrast, Mexico's tax rate is 34 percent. The level of spending on research and development as a percentage of GDP in Mexico is 0.25 percent, compared to 0.75 percent, 0.85 percent and 2.6 percent in China, India, and the United States, respectively.

Mexico indeed is at a crossroads. To compete more effectively with other low-wage-rate countries such as China, Singapore, Malaysia, and Brazil, Mexico must improve its education system and infrastructure, and it must fight against drug trafficking to attract companies in the twenty-first century. Low wages and hard-working employees are no longer sufficient attractors.

Source: Adapted from Geri Smith, "Is the Magic Starting to Fade?" *BusinessWeek* (August 6, 2001): 42–43.

CONCLUSION

The main appeal of any managerial approach is the expectation that it will enhance organizational performance. This is especially true of strategic management. Through involvement in strategic-management activities, managers and employees achieve a better understanding of an organization's priorities and operations. Strategic management allows organizations to be efficient, but more important, it allows them to be effective. Although strategic management does not guarantee organizational success, the process allows proactive rather than reactive decision making. Strategic management may represent a radical change in philosophy for some organizations, so strategists must be trained to anticipate and constructively respond to questions and issues as they arise. The sixteen strategies discussed in this chapter can represent a new beginning for many firms, especially if managers and employees in the organization understand and support the plan for action.

We invite you to visit the David page on the Prentice Hall Companion Web site at *www.prenhall.com/david* for this chapter's World Wide Web exercises.

KEY TERMS AND CONCEPTS

Acquisition (p. 181)

Backward Integration (p. 165)

Bankruptcy (p. 173)

Business Processing Outsourcing (BPO) (p. 184)

Combination Strategy (p. 161)

Concentric Diversification (p. 169)

Conglomerate Diversification (p. 171)

Cooperative Arrangements (p. 178)

Cost Leadership (p. 176)

Differentiation (p. 176)

Diversification Strategies (p. 169)

Divestiture (p. 174)

First Mover Advantages (p. 184)

Focus (p. 176)

Forward Integration (p. 164)

Franchising (p. 164)

Friendly Merger (p. 181)

Generic Strategies (p. 176)

Horizontal Diversification (p. 171)

Horizontal Integration (p. 166)

Hostile Takeover (p. 181)

Integration Strategies (p. 164)

Intensive Strategies (p. 167)

Joint Venture (p. 178)

Leveraged Buyout (p. 184)

Liquidation (p. 175)

Long-Term Objectives (p. 158)

Market Development (p. 167)

Market Penetration (p. 167)

Merger (p. 181)

Product Development (p. 168)

Retrenchment (p. 172)

Takeover (p. 181)

Vertical Integration (p. 164)

ISSUES FOR REVIEW AND DISCUSSION

1. How does strategy formulation differ for a small versus a large organization? How does it differ for a for-profit versus a nonprofit organization?
2. Give recent examples of market penetration, market development, and product development.
3. Give recent examples of forward integration, backward integration, and horizontal integration.
4. Give recent examples of concentric diversification, horizontal diversification, and conglomerate diversification.
5. Give recent examples of joint venture, retrenchment, divestiture, and liquidation.
6. Do you think hostile takeovers are unethical? Why or why not?
7. What are the major advantages and disadvantages of diversification?
8. What are the major advantages and disadvantages of an integrative strategy?
9. How does strategic management differ in profit and nonprofit organizations?
10. Why is it not advisable to pursue too many strategies at once?
11. Consumers can purchase tennis shoes, food, cars, boats, and insurance on the Internet. Are there any products today than cannot be purchased online? What is the implication for traditional retailers?
12. What are the pros and cons of a firm merging with a rival firm?
13. Does the United States lead in small business start ups globally?
14. Visit the *CheckMATE* strategic-planning software Web site at *www.checkmateplan.com*, and discuss the benefits offered.
15. Compare and contrast financial objectives with strategic objectives. Which type is more important in your opinion? Why?
16. Diagram a two-division organizational chart that includes a CEO, COO, CIO, CSO, CFO, CMO, HRM, R&D, and two division presidents. Hint: Division presidents report to the COO.
17. How do the levels of strategy differ in a large firm versus a small firm?
18. List ten types of strategies. Give a hypothetical example of each strategy listed.
19. Discuss the nature of as well as the pros and cons of a "friendly merger" versus "hostile takeover" in acquiring another firm. Give an example of each.
20. Define and explain "first mover advantages."
21. Define and explain "outsourcing."
22. Discuss the business of offering a BBA or MBA degree online.

NOTES

1. John Byrne, "Strategic Planning—It's Back," *BusinessWeek* (August 26, 1996): 46.
2. Steven C. Brandt, *Strategic Planning in Emerging Companies* (Reading, MA: Addison-Wesley, 1981). Reprinted with permission of the publisher.
3. F. Hansen and M. Smith, "Crisis in Corporate America: The Role of Strategy," *Business Horizons* (January–February 2003): 9.
4. R. Kaplan and D. Norton, "Putting the Balanced Scorecard to Work," *Harvard Business Review* (September–October, 1993): 147.
5. Jeff Bailey, "Franchisees Group to Take Control," *Wall Street Journal* (December 24, 2002): B2.
6. Adapted from F. R. David, "How Do We Choose Among Alternative Growth Strategies?" *Managerial Planning* 33, no. 4 (January–February 1985): 14–17, 22.
7. Ibid.
8. Kenneth Davidson, "Do Megamergers Make Sense?" *Journal of Business Strategy* 7, no. 3 (Winter 1987): 45.
9. op. cit., David.
10. David Kiley and Earle Eldridge, "San Antonio Plant Is Part of Strategy," *USA Today* (February 6, 2003): 3B.
11. Ibid.
12. op. cit., David.
13. Ibid.
14. "The Samsung Way," *BusinessWeek* (June 16, 2003): 56–60.
15. Sheila Muto, "Seeing a Boost, Hospitals Turn to Retail Stores," *Wall Street Journal* (November 7, 2001): B1, B8.
16. op. cit., David.
17. op. cit., David.
18. Ibid.
19. Christine Dugas, "Bankruptcy Filings Set Record in 2002," *USA Today* (February 17, 2003): 6B.
20. op. cit., David.
21. Ibid.
22. Ibid.
23. Kathryn Rudie Harrigan, "Joint Ventures: Linking for a Leap Forward," *Planning Review* 14, no. 4 (July–August 1986): 10.
24. Matthew Schifrin, "Partner or Perish," *Forbes* (May 21, 2001): 26.
25. Ibid., p. 28.
26. Nikhil Hutheesing, "Marital Blisters," *Forbes* (May 21, 2001): 32.
27. Ibid., p. 32.
28. Steven Rattner, "Mergers: Windfalls or Pitfalls?" *Wall Street Journal* (October 11, 1999): A22; Nikhil Deogun, "Merger Wave Spurs More Stock Wipeouts," *Wall Street Journal* (November 29, 1999): C1.
29. Robert Frank, "Merger Market Gets Year-End Jump-Start," *Wall Street Journal* (January 2, 2003): R6.
30. Joel Millman, "Mexican Mergers/Acquisitions Triple from 2001," *Wall Street Journal* (December 27, 2002): A2.
31. Robert Davis, "Net Empowering Patients," *USA Today* (July 14, 1999): 1A.
32. M. J. Gannon, K. G. Smith, and C. Grimm, "An Organizational Information-processing Profile of First Movers," *Journal of Business Research* 25 (1992): 231–241; M. B. Lieberman and D. B. Montgomery, "First Mover Advantages," *Strategic Management Journal* 9 (Summer 1988): 41–58.
33. Peter Loftus, "Outsourcing Gets Expanded Uses by Businesses," *Wall Street Journal* (September 24, 2003): B13B.
34. *Hospital* (May 5, 1991): 16.
35. Some articles are Keith D. Brouthers, Floris Andriessen, and Igor Nicolaes, "Driving Blind: Strategic Decision-Making in Small Companies," *Long Range Planning* 31 (1998): 130–138; Javad Kargar, "Strategic Planning System Characteristics and Planning Effectiveness in Small Mature Firms," *Mid-Atlantic Journal of Business* 32, no. 1 (1996): 19–35; Michael J. Peel and John Bridge, "How Planning and Capital Budgeting Improve SME Performance," *Long Range Planning* 31, no. 6 (1998): 848–856; Larry R. Smeltzer, Gail L. Fann, and V. Neal Nikolaisen, "Environmental Scanning Practices in Small Business," *Journal of Small Business Management* 26, no. 3 (1988): 55–63; and Michael P. Steiner and Olaf Solem, "Factors for Success in Small Manufacturing Firms," *Journal of Small Business Management* 26, no. 1 (1988): 51–57.
36. Anne Carey and Grant Jerding, "Internet's Reach on Campus," *USA Today* (August 26, 1999): A1; Bill Meyers, "It's a Small-Business World," *USA Today* (July 30, 1999): B1–2.

CURRENT READINGS

Akhter, S. H. "Strategic Planning, Hypercompetition, and Knowledge Management." *Business Horizons* 46, no. 1 (January–February 2003): 19–24.

Anderson, U., M. Forsgren, and U. Holm. "The Strategic Impact of External Networks: Subsidiary Performance and Competence Development in the Multinational Corporation." *Strategic Management Journal* 23, no. 11 (November 2002): 979–998.

Busco, C. "Growing Global by Acquisitions: The Role of Measurement as GE in Italy." *Business Horizons* 46, no. 1 (January–February 2003): 37.

Combs, J. G., and D. J. Ketchen. "Why Do Firms Use Franchising as an Entrepreneurial Strategy? A Meta-Analysis." *Journal of Management* 29, no. 3 (2003): 443.

Danneels, E. "The Dynamics of Product Innovation and Firm Competencies." *Strategic Management Journal* 23, no. 12 (December 2002): 1095–1122.

Draulans, J., A. P. deMan, and H. W. Volberda. "Building Alliance Capability: Management Techniques for Superior Alliance Performance." *Long Range Planning* 36, no. 2 (April 2003): 151–166.

Gates, S., and P. Very. "Measuring Performance During M&A Integration." *Long Range Planning* 36, no. 2 (April 2003): 167–186.

Ireland, R. D., M. A. Hitt, and D. Vaidyanath. "Alliance Management as a Source of Competitive Advantage." *Journal of Management* 28, no. 3 (2002): 413–446.

Johnson, J. P., M. A. Korsgaard, and H. J. Sapienze. "Perceived Fairness, Decision Control, and Commitment in International Joint Venture." *Strategic Management Journal* 23, no. 12 (December 2002): 1141–1160.

Kale, P., J. H. Dyer, and H. Singh. "Alliance Capability, Stock Market Response, and Long Term Alliance Success: The Role of the Alliance Function." *Strategic Management Journal* 23, no. 8 (August 2002): 747–768.

Kerns, C. D. "An Entrepreneurial Approach to Strategic Direction Setting." *Business Horizons* 45, no. 4 (July–August 2002): 2–6.

Koka, B. R., and J. E. Prescott. "Strategic Alliances as Social Capital: A Multidimensional View." *Strategic Management Journal* 23, no. 9 (September 2002): 795–816.

Luo, Y. "Contract, Cooperation and Performance in International Joint Ventures." *Strategic Management Journal* 23, no. 10 (October 2002): 903–920.

Osegowitsch, T., and A. Madhok. "Vertical Integration Is Dead, Or Is It?" *Business Horizons* 46, no. 2 (March–April 2003): 25–34.

Park, C. "Prior Performance Characteristics of Related and Unrelated Acquirers." *Strategic Management Journal* 24, no. 5 (May 2003): 471–480.

Reuer, J. J., and A. Arino. "Contractual Renegotiations in Strategic Alliances." *Journal of Management* 28, no. 1 (2002): 47–68.

Robins, J. A., S. Tallman, and K. Fladmoe-Lindquist. "Autonomy and Dependence of International Cooperative Ventures: An Exploration of the Strategic Performance of U.S. Ventures in Mexico." *Strategic Management Journal* 23, no. 10 (October 2002): 881–902.

Robinson, W. T., and J. Chiang. "Product Development Strategies for Established Market Pioneers, Early Followers and Late Entrants." *Strategic Management Journal* 23, no. 9 (September 2002): 855–866.

Rugman, A. M., and A. Verbeke. "Edith Penrose's Contribution to the Resource-Based View of Strategic Management." *Strategic Management Journal* 23, no. 8 (August 2002): 769–781.

Shepherd, D. A. "Learning from Business Failure: Propositions of Grief Recovery for the Self-Employed." *Academy of Management Review* 28, no. 2 (April 2003): 318.

Tsang, E. W. "Acquiring Knowledge by Foreign Partners from International Joint Ventures in a Transition Economy: Learning-by-Doing and Learning Myopia." *Strategic Management Journal* 23, no. 9 (September 2002): 835–854.

Wagner, S. M., and R. Boutellier. "Capabilities for Managing a Portfolio of Supplier Relationships." *Business Horizons* 45, no. 6 (November–December 2002): 79–88.

experiential exercises

Experiential
Exercise 5A

*What Strategies Should
Krispy Kreme Doughnuts
(KKD) Pursue in
2004–2005?*

PURPOSE

In performing business policy case analysis, you can find information about the respective company's actual and planned strategies. Comparing what is planned versus *what you recommend* is an important part of case analysis. Do not recommend what the firm actually plans, unless in-depth analysis of the situation reveals those strategies to be best among all feasible alternatives. This exercise gives you experience conducting library and Internet research to determine what KKD should do in 2004–2005.

INSTRUCTIONS

Step 1   Look up KKD and Dunkin' Donuts on the Internet. Find some recent articles about firms in this industry. Scan Moody's, Dun & Bradstreet, and Standard & Poor's publications for information. Check the *finance.yahoo.com* Web site and the *www.strategyclub.com* Web site.

Step 2   Summarize your findings in a three-page report entitled "Strategies for KKD in 2004–2005."

PURPOSE

Strategy articles can be found weekly in journals, magazines, and newspapers. By reading and studying strategy articles, you can gain a better understanding of the strategic-management process. Several of the best journals in which to find corporate strategy articles are *Advanced Management Journal, Business Horizons, Long Range Planning, Journal of Business Strategy,* and *Strategic Management Journal.* These journals are devoted to reporting the results of empirical research in management. They apply strategic-management concepts to specific organizations and industries. They introduce new strategic-management techniques and provide short case studies on selected firms.

Other good journals in which to find strategic-management articles are *Harvard Business Review, Sloan Management Review, California Management Review, Academy of Management Review, Academy of Management Journal, Academy of Management Executive, Journal of Management,* and *Journal of Small Business Management.*

In addition to journals, many magazines regularly publish articles that focus on business strategies. Several of the best magazines in which to find applied strategy articles are *Dun's Business Month, Fortune, Forbes, BusinessWeek, Inc.,* and *Industry Week.* Newspapers such as *USA Today, Wall Street Journal, New York Times,* and *Barrons* cover strategy events when they occur—for example, a joint venture announcement, a bankruptcy declaration, a new advertising campaign start, acquisition of a company, divestiture of a division, a chief executive officer's hiring or firing, or a hostile takeover attempt.

In combination, journal, magazine, and newspaper articles can make the strategic-management course more exciting. They allow current strategies of profit and nonprofit organizations to be identified and studied.

INSTRUCTIONS

Step 1 Go to your college library and find a recent journal article that focuses on a strategic-management topic. Select your article from one of the journals listed earlier, not from a magazine. Copy the article and bring it to class.

Step 2 Give a three-minute oral report summarizing the most important information in your article. Include comments giving your personal reaction to the article. Pass your article around in class.

Experiential Exercise 5C
Classifying Some Year 2004 Strategies

PURPOSE

This exercise can improve your understanding of various strategies by giving you experience classifying strategies. This skill will help you use the strategy-formulation tools presented later. Consider the following ten (actual or possible) year-2004 strategies by various firms:

1. J. P. Morgan Chase acquired Bank One for $60 billion.
2. KB Toys filed for bankruptcy and announced plans to close half of its 1,217 stores in the USA. Toys R Us is the #1 specialty toy retailer. KB is #2.
3. Viacom sold its 82 percent stake in Blockbuster.
4. RJR and Brown & Williamson, two large tobacco firms, merged.
5. FedEx acquired Kinko's for $2.5 billion in order to gain thousands of retail shipping locations.
6. Fishing Charters, Inc. acquired a local radio station.
7. Marriott acquired a furniture manufacturer.
8. Lonestar Steakhouse expanded into Europe.
9. IBM began opening its own chain of retail stores to exclusively sell its own products.
10. Avon doubled its advertising efforts worldwide.

INSTRUCTIONS

Step 1 On a separate sheet of paper, number from 1 to 10. These numbers correspond to the strategies described above.

Step 2 What type of strategy best describes the ten actions cited above? Indicate your answers.

Step 3 Exchange papers with a classmate, and grade each other's paper as your instructor gives the right answers.

Experiential Exercise 5D
How Risky Are Various Alternative Strategies?

PURPOSE

This exercise focuses on how risky various alternative strategies are for organizations to pursue. Different degrees of risk are based largely on varying degrees of *externality*, defined as movement away from present business into new markets and products. In general, the greater the degree of externality, the greater the probability of loss resulting from unexpected events. High-risk strategies generally are less attractive than low-risk strategies.

INSTRUCTIONS

Step 1   On a separate sheet of paper, number vertically from 1 to 10. Think of 1 as "most risky," 2 as "next most risky," and so forth to 10, "least risky."

Step 2   Write the following strategies beside the appropriate number to indicate how risky you believe the strategy is to pursue: horizontal integration, horizontal diversification, liquidation, forward integration, backward integration, product development, market development, market penetration, joint venture/partnering, and conglomerate diversification.

Step 3   Grade your paper as your teacher gives you the right answers and supporting rationale. Each correct answer is worth 10 points.

Experiential Exercise 5E

Developing Alternative Strategies for My University

PURPOSE

It is important for representatives from all areas of a college or university to identify and discuss alternative strategies that could benefit faculty, students, alumni, staff, and other constituencies. As you complete this exercise, notice the learning and understanding that occurs as people express differences of opinion. Recall that *the process of planning is more important than the document.*

INSTRUCTIONS

Step 1   Recall or locate the external opportunity/threat and internal strength/weakness factors that you identified as part of Experiential Exercise 1D. If you did not do that exercise, discuss now as a class important external and internal factors facing your college or university.

Step 2   Identify and put on the chalkboard alternative strategies that you feel could benefit your college or university. Your proposed actions should allow the institution to capitalize on particular strengths, improve upon certain weaknesses, avoid external threats, and/or take advantage of particular external opportunities. List at least twenty possible strategies on the board. Number the strategies as they are written on the board.

Step 3   On a separate sheet of paper, number from 1 to the total number of strategies listed on the board. Everyone in class individually should rate the strategies identified, using a 1 to 3 scale, where 1 = *I do not support implementation*, 2 = *I am neutral about implementation*, and 3 = *I strongly support implementation*. In rating the strategies, recognize that your institution cannot do everything desired or potentially beneficial.

Step 4   Go to the board and record your ratings in a row beside the respective strategies. Everyone in class should do this, going to the board perhaps by rows in the class.

Step 5   Sum the ratings for each strategy so that a prioritized list of recommended strategies is obtained. This prioritized list reflects the collective wisdom of your class. Strategies with the highest score are deemed best.

Step 6 Discuss how this process could enable organizations to achieve understanding and commitment from individuals.

Step 7 Share your class results with a university administrator, and ask for comments regarding the process and top strategies recommended.

Experiential Exercise 5F

Lessons in Doing Business Globally

PURPOSE

The purpose of this exercise is to discover some important lessons learned by local businesses that do businesses internationally.

INSTRUCTIONS

Contact several local business leaders by phone. Find at least three firms that engage in international or export operations. Visit the owner or manager of each business in person. Ask the businessperson to give you several important lessons that his or her firm has learned in doing business globally. Record the lessons on paper, and report your findings to the class.

Strategy Analysis and Choice

chapter objectives

After studying this chapter, you should be able to do the following:

1. Describe a three-stage framework for choosing among alternative strategies.

2. Explain how to develop a SWOT Matrix, SPACE Matrix, BCG Matrix, IE Matrix, and QSPM.

3. Identify important behavioral, political, ethical, and social responsibility considerations in strategy analysis and choice.

4. Discuss the role of intuition in strategic analysis and choice.

5. Discuss the role of organizational culture in strategic analysis and choice.

6. Discuss the role of a board of directors in choosing among alternative strategies.

experiential exercises

"notable quotes"

Strategic management is not a box of tricks or a bundle of techniques. It is analytical thinking and commitment of resources to action. But quantification alone is not planning. Some of the most important issues in strategic management cannot be quantified at all.
Peter Drucker

Objectives are not commands; they are commitments. They do not determine the future; they are the means to mobilize resources and energies of an organization for the making of the future.
Peter Drucker

Life is full of lousy options.
General P. X. Kelley

When a crisis forces choosing among alternatives, most people will choose the worst possible one.
Rudin's Law

Strategy isn't something you can nail together in slapdash fashion by sitting around a conference table.
Terry Haller

Planning is often doomed before it ever starts, either because too much is expected of it or because not enough is put into it.
T. J. Cartwright

Whether it's broke or not, fix it—make it better. Not just products, but the whole company if necessary.
Bill Saporito

Strategy analysis and choice largely involve making subjective decisions based on objective information. This chapter introduces important concepts that can help strategists generate feasible alternatives, evaluate those alternatives, and choose a specific course of action. Behavioral aspects of strategy formulation are described, including politics, culture, ethics, and social responsibility considerations. Modern tools for formulating strategies are described, and the appropriate role of a board of directors is discussed.

The Nature of Strategy Analysis and Choice

As indicated by Figure 6–1, this chapter focuses on generating and evaluating alternative strategies, as well as selecting strategies to pursue. Strategy analysis and choice seeks to determine alternative courses of action that could best enable the firm to achieve its mission and objectives. The firm's present strategies, objectives, and mission, coupled with the external and internal audit information, provide a basis for generating and evaluating feasible alternative strategies.

Unless a desperate situation confronts the firm, alternative strategies will likely represent incremental steps that move the firm from its present position to a desired future position. Alternative strategies do not come out of the wild blue yonder, they are derived from the firm's vision, mission, objectives, external audit, and internal audit; they are consistent with, or build on, past strategies that have worked well. Note from the "Natural Environment Perspective" box that the strategies of both

FIGURE 6–1

A Comprehensive Strategic-Management Model

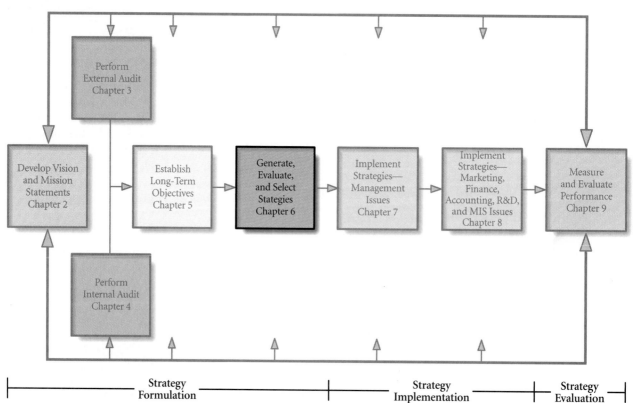

What Is a Pollution Register?

No business wants a reputation as being a big polluter; that could hurt it in the marketplace, jeopardize its standing in the community, and invite scrutiny by regulators, investors, and environmentalists. Accordingly, governments increasingly encourage businesses to behave responsibly. Various governments mandate that businesses publicly report the pollutants and wastes their facilities produce.

Perhaps the best-known pollution register is the Toxics Release Inventory (TRI) administered by the EPA in the United States. The TRI is a plant-by-plant accounting of industrial pollution that the government makes publicly accessible via the Internet and published reports. The TRI has been instrumental in cutting industrial pollutant releases of tracked chemicals by 48 percent from 1988 to 2000, pressuring some firms not only to comply with government regulations, but to reduce pollution beyond their legal obligation.

The United States, Canada, the Netherlands, Norway, and the United Kingdom all have at least a decade of experience operating comprehensive pollution registers like the TRI. In response to the success of these registers, other countries have instituted or are in the process of creating their own national pollution registers, which are generically termed "Pollutant Release and Transfer Registers" or "PRTRs." Today, about sixty countries have developed or are in the process of developing such registers. The attractiveness of a country to foreign direct investment, to some extent, hinges on that country's environmental policies and practices.

Pollution registers clearly provide information that interests and empowers citizens, investors, and reporters. Since the first release of TRI data in 1989, these pollution listings have become the subject of media reports. Journalists were particularly likely to report on a company with pollution concentrated at a few facilities, or on chemical releases from companies that were not traditionally considered big polluters. The TRI data have affected the decisions of stock market investors as well. On the day that TRI data first became available in 1989, the companies included in the inventory suffered statistically significant declines in the market value of their stock. For companies whose emissions were the subject of a media story, the loss in stock value was greater—an average of $6.2 million, according to one analysis. In other words, investors were surprised by the quantity of pollution their companies produced, and worried about negative publicity and potential cleanup costs.

The TRI can provide useful data for communities to pressure companies to reduce emissions from local factories. Citizens in any community in the United States can use the Internet to print a tailored emission report from the TRI database for their county, and can even send a message or question about their findings to the government. Similarly, in Canada, the Canadian National Pollutant Release Inventory (NPRI) provides communities and consumers with information that they have used to pressure Canadian companies to reduce their emissions. Within two days of its rollout, some 3 million Internet users visited the Pollution Watch Web site created by Canadian NGOs to give easy access to NPRI data, and sent roughly 1,200 faxes to polluting companies listed there.

Countries operating a pollution register in 2004 are: Australia, Ireland, Korea, Norway, United Kingdom, Canada, Japan, Netherlands, Slovak Republic, United States, and Mexico. Countries that do not have a pollution register in 2004, but as members of the EU are required to participate in the European Polluting Emissions Register are: Austria, Estonia, Hungary, Luxembourg, Slovenia, Belgium, Finland, Italy, Malta, Spain, Cyprus, France, Latvia, Poland, Sweden, Czech Republic, Germany, Lithuania, Portugal, Switzerland, Denmark, and Greece. Countries that do not have a pollution register, but have indicated some interest in designing one, or that participate in the Aarhus Protocol on Pollutant Release and Transfer Registers are: Albania, Brazil, Ecuador, Kazakhstan, South Africa, Argentina, Bulgaria, Egypt, Romania, Ukraine, Armenia, Chile, Georgia, Russia, Uzbekistan, Azerbaijan, Costa Rica, Macedonia, Serbia, Montenegro, Taiwan, Belarus, Croatia, Moldova, Tajikistan, Turkey, Bosnia, Herzegovina, Cuba, and Monaco. All other countries, including Russia and China, indicate no interest in pollution registers.

Sources: Adapted from World Resources Institute 2002–2004, *Decisions for the Earth: Balance, Voice, and Power;* United Nations Development Programme, United Nations Environment Programme, World Bank; USEPA 2002:12.

companies and countries are increasingly scrutinized and evaluated from a natural environment perspective, as indicated by the presence of pollution registers. Even the *Wall Street Journal* is advocating and reporting that a growing number of business schools offer separate courses and even a concentration in environmental management or *sustainability*, the idea that a business can meet its financial goals without hurting the environment.[1] Note that China and Russia are two of many countries that shun the idea of companies having to publicly report the pollutants and wastes their facilities produce.

The Process of Generating and Selecting Strategies

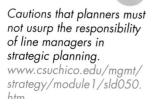

VISIT THE NET

Cautions that planners must not usurp the responsibility of line managers in strategic planning.
www.csuchico.edu/mgmt/strategy/module1/sld050.htm

Strategists never consider all feasible alternatives that could benefit the firm, because there are an infinite number of possible actions and an infinite number of ways to implement those actions. Therefore, a manageable set of the most attractive alternative strategies must be developed. The advantages, disadvantages, trade-offs, costs, and benefits of these strategies should be determined. This section discusses the process that many firms use to determine an appropriate set of alternative strategies.

Identifying and evaluating alternative strategies should involve many of the managers and employees who earlier assembled the organizational vision and mission statements, performed the external audit, and conducted the internal audit. Representatives from each department and division of the firm should be included in this process, as was the case in previous strategy-formulation activities. Recall that involvement provides the best opportunity for managers and employees to gain an understanding of what the firm is doing and why, and to become committed to helping the firm accomplish its objectives.

All participants in the strategy analysis and choice activity should have the firm's external and internal audit information by their sides. This information, coupled with the firm's mission statement, will help participants crystallize in their own minds particular strategies that they believe could benefit the firm most. Creativity should be encouraged in this thought process.

Alternative strategies proposed by participants should be considered and discussed in a meeting or series of meetings. Proposed strategies should be listed in writing. When all feasible strategies identified by participants are given and understood, the strategies should be ranked in order of attractiveness by all participants, with 1 = should not be implemented, 2 = possibly should be implemented, 3 = probably should be implemented, and 4 = definitely should be implemented. This process will result in a prioritized list of best strategies that reflects the collective wisdom of the group.

A Comprehensive Strategy-Formulation Framework

Important strategy-formulation techniques can be integrated into a three-stage decision-making framework, as shown in Figure 6–2. The tools presented in this framework are applicable to all sizes and types of organizations and can help strategists identify, evaluate, and select strategies.

Stage 1 of the formulation framework consists of the EFE Matrix, the IFE Matrix, and the Competitive Profile Matrix (CPM). Called the Input Stage, Stage 1 summarizes the basic input information needed to formulate strategies. Stage 2, called the Matching Stage, focuses upon generating feasible alternative strategies by aligning key external and internal factors. Stage 2 techniques include the Strengths-Weaknesses-Opportunities-Threats (SWOT) Matrix, the Strategic Position and

FIGURE 6–2

The Strategy-Formulation Analytical Framework

STAGE 1: THE INPUT STAGE		
External Factor Evaluation (EFE) Matrix	Competitive Profile Matrix (CPM)	Internal Factor Evaluation (IFE) Matrix

STAGE 2: THE MATCHING STAGE				
Strengths-Weaknesses-Opportunities-Threats (SWOT) Matrix	Strategic Position and Action Evaluation (SPACE) Matrix	Boston Consulting Group (BCG) Matrix	Internal-External (IE) Matrix	Grand Strategy Matrix

STAGE 3: THE DECISION STAGE
Quantitative Strategic Planning Matrix (QSPM)

Action Evaluation (SPACE) Matrix, the Boston Consulting Group (BCG) Matrix, the Internal-External (IE) Matrix, and the Grand Strategy Matrix. Stage 3, called the Decision Stage, involves a single technique, the Quantitative Strategic Planning Matrix (QSPM). A QSPM uses input information from Stage 1 to objectively evaluate feasible alternative strategies identified in Stage 2. A QSPM reveals the relative attractiveness of alternative strategies and thus provides objective basis for selecting specific strategies.

All nine techniques included in the *strategy-formulation framework* require the integration of intuition and analysis. Autonomous divisions in an organization commonly use strategy-formulation techniques to develop strategies and objectives. Divisional analyses provide a basis for identifying, evaluating, and selecting among alternative corporate-level strategies.

Strategists themselves, not analytic tools, are always responsible and accountable for strategic decisions. Lenz emphasized that the shift from a words-oriented to a numbers-oriented planning process can give rise to a false sense of certainty; it can reduce dialogue, discussion, and argument as a means for exploring understandings, testing assumptions, and fostering organizational learning.[2] Strategists therefore must be wary of this possibility and use analytical tools to facilitate, rather than to diminish, communication. Without objective information and analysis, personal biases, politics, emotions, personalities, and *halo error* (the tendency to put too much weight on a single factor) unfortunately may play a dominant role in the strategy-formulation process.

VISIT THE NET

Gives purpose and characteristics of objectives.
www.csuchico.edu/mgmt/strategy/module1/sld022.htm

The Input Stage

Procedures for developing an EFE Matrix, an IFE Matrix, and a CPM were presented in the previous two chapters. The information derived from these three matrices provides basic input information for the matching and decision stage matrices described later in this chapter.

The input tools require strategists to quantify subjectivity during early stages of the strategy-formulation process. Making small decisions in the input matrices regarding the relative importance of external and internal factors allows strategists to generate and evaluate alternative strategies more effectively. Good intuitive judgment is always needed in determining appropriate weights and ratings.

The Matching Stage

VISIT THE NET

Gives example objectives.
www.csuchico.edu/mgmt/
strategy/module1/sld024.
htm

Strategy is sometimes defined as the match an organization makes between its internal resources and skills and the opportunities and risks created by its external factors.[3] The matching stage of the strategy-formulation framework consists of five techniques that can be used in any sequence: the SWOT Matrix, the SPACE Matrix, the BCG Matrix, the IE Matrix, and the Grand Strategy Matrix. These tools rely upon information derived from the input stage to match external opportunities and threats with internal strengths and weaknesses. *Matching* external and internal critical success factors is the key to effectively generating feasible alternative strategies. For example, a firm with excess working capital (an internal strength) could take advantage of the cell phone industry's 20 percent annual growth rate (an external opportunity) by acquiring Cellfone, Inc., a firm in the cell phone industry. This example portrays simple one-to-one matching. In most situations, external and internal relationships are more complex, and the matching requires multiple alignments for each strategy generated. The basic concept of matching is illustrated in Table 6–1.

Any organization, whether military, product-oriented, service-oriented, governmental, or even athletic, must develop and execute good strategies to win. A good offense without a good defense, or vice versa, usually leads to defeat. Developing strategies that use strengths to capitalize on opportunities could be considered an offense, whereas strategies designed to improve upon weaknesses while avoiding threats could be termed defensive. Every organization has some external opportunities and threats and internal strengths and weaknesses that can be aligned to formulate feasible alternative strategies.

The Strengths-Weaknesses-Opportunities-Threats (SWOT) Matrix

The *Strengths-Weaknesses-Opportunities-Threats (SWOT) Matrix* is an important matching tool that helps managers develop four types of strategies: SO (strengths-opportunities) Strategies, WO (weaknesses-opportunities) Strategies, ST (strengths-threats) Strategies, and WT (weaknesses-threats) Strategies.[4] Matching key external

TABLE 6–1 Matching Key External and Internal Factors to Formulate Alternative Strategies

KEY INTERNAL FACTOR		KEY EXTERNAL FACTOR		RESULTANT STRATEGY
Excess working capacity (an internal strength)	+	20% annual growth in the cell phone industry (an external opportunity)	=	Acquire Cellfone, Inc.
Insufficient capacity (an internal weakness)	+	Exit of two major foreign competitors from the industry (an external opportunity)	=	Pursue horizontal integration by buying competitors' facilities
Strong R&D expertise (an internal strength)	+	Decreasing numbers of younger adults (an external threat)	=	Develop new products for older adults
Poor employee morale (an internal weakness)	+	Strong union activity (an external threat)	=	Develop a new employee benefits package

and internal factors is the most difficult part of developing a SWOT Matrix and requires good judgment—and there is no one best set of matches. Note in Table 6–1 that the first, second, third, and fourth strategies are SO, WO, ST, and WT strategies, respectively.

SO Strategies use a firm's internal strengths to take advantage of external opportunities. All managers would like their organizations to be in a position in which internal strengths can be used to take advantage of external trends and events. Organizations generally will pursue WO, ST, or WT strategies in order to get into a situation in which they can apply SO Strategies. When a firm has major weaknesses, it will strive to overcome them and make them strengths. When an organization faces major threats, it will seek to avoid them in order to concentrate on opportunities.

WO Strategies aim at improving internal weaknesses by taking advantage of external opportunities. Sometimes key external opportunities exist, but a firm has internal weaknesses that prevent it from exploiting those opportunities. For example, there may be a high demand for electronic devices to control the amount and timing of fuel injection in automobile engines (opportunity), but a certain auto parts manufacturer may lack the technology required for producing these devices (weakness). One possible WO Strategy would be to acquire this technology by forming a joint venture with a firm having competency in this area. An alternative WO Strategy would be to hire and train people with the required technical capabilities.

ST Strategies use a firm's strengths to avoid or reduce the impact of external threats. This does not mean that a strong organization should always meet threats in the external environment head-on. An example of ST Strategy occurred when Texas Instruments used an excellent legal department (a strength) to collect nearly $700 million in damages and royalties from nine Japanese and Korean firms that infringed on patents for semiconductor memory chips (threat). Rival firms that copy ideas, innovations, and patented products are a major threat in many industries. This is still a major problem for U.S. firms selling products in China.

WT Strategies are defensive tactics directed at reducing internal weakness and avoiding external threats. An organization faced with numerous external threats and internal weaknesses may indeed be in a precarious position. In fact, such a firm may have to fight for its survival, merge, retrench, declare bankruptcy, or choose liquidation.

A schematic representation of the SWOT Matrix is provided in Figure 6–3. Note that a SWOT Matrix is composed of nine cells. As shown, there are four key factor cells, four strategy cells, and one cell that is always left blank (the upper-left cell). The four strategy cells, labeled *SO, WO, ST,* and *WT,* are developed after completing four key factor cells, labeled *S, W, O,* and *T.* There are eight steps involved in constructing a SWOT Matrix:

1. List the firm's key external opportunities.
2. List the firm's key external threats.
3. List the firm's key internal strengths.
4. List the firm's key internal weaknesses.
5. Match internal strengths with external opportunities, and record the resultant SO Strategies in the appropriate cell.
6. Match internal weaknesses with external opportunities, and record the resultant WO Strategies.
7. Match internal strengths with external threats, and record the resultant ST Strategies.
8. Match internal weaknesses with external threats, and record the resultant WT Strategies.

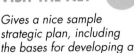

VISIT THE NET

Gives a nice sample strategic plan, including the bases for developing a SWOT Matrix.
www.planware.org/ strategicsample.htm

FIGURE 6–3
The SWOT Matrix

Always leave blank	STRENGTHS—S 1. 2. 3. 4. 5. 6. 7. 8. 9. 10. List strengths	WEAKNESSES—W 1. 2. 3. 4. 5. 6. 7. 8. 9. 10. List weaknesses
OPPORTUNITIES—O 1. 2. 3. 4. 5. 6. 7. 8. 9. 10. List opportunities	SO STRATEGIES 1. 2. 3. 4. 5. 6. 7. 8. 9. 10. Use strengths to take advantage of opportunities	WO STRATEGIES 1. 2. 3. 4. 5. 6. 7. 8. 9. 10. Overcome weaknesses by taking advantage of opportunities
THREATS—T 1. 2. 3. 4. 5. 6. 7. 8. 9. 10. List threats	ST STRATEGIES 1. 2. 3. 4. 5. 6. 7. 8. 9. 10. Use strengths to avoid threats	WT STRATEGIES 1. 2. 3. 4. 5. 6. 7. 8. 9. 10. Minimize weaknesses and avoid threats

The purpose of each Stage 2 matching tool is to generate feasible alternative strategies, not to select or determine which strategies are best. Not all of the strategies developed in the SWOT Matrix, therefore, will be selected for implementation. A sample SWOT Matrix for Carnival Cruise Lines, is provided in Figure 6–4.

Another example of a SWOT Matrix is provided in Figure 6–5, for the Riverbanks Zoo in Columbia, South Carolina. Note that the zoo is considering eight possible strategies for the future.

The strategy-formulation guidelines provided in Chapter 5 can enhance the process of matching key external and internal factors. For example, when an organization has both the capital and human resources needed to distribute its own products (internal strength) and distributors are unreliable, costly, or incapable of meeting the firm's needs (external threat), then forward integration can be an attractive ST

FIGURE 6–4

SWOT Matrix for Carnival Cruise Lines

	STRENGTHS—S	WEAKNESSES—W
	1. Holds 34% market share 2. Largest fleet of ships 3. Six different cruise lines 4. Innovator in cruise travel industry 5. Largest variety of ships 6. Building largest cruise ship 7. High brand recognition 8. Headquartered in Miami 9. Internet friendly with online booking	1. Major loss in affiliated operations 2. Increased debt from building new ships 3. Not serving Asian market
OPPORTUNITIES—O 1. Air travel has decreased (9/11) 2. Asian market not being served 3. Possible acquisition of Princess Cruise Lines 4. New weather forecasting systems available 5. Rising demand for all-inclusive vacation packages 6. Families have increased disposable incomes 7. Marriage rates are up—more honeymoons	**SO STRATEGIES** 1. Increase capacity of ships to obtain travelers from air industry (S6, O1, O3) 2. Display the weather of vacation locations on Web site (S9, O4) 3. Offer Trans-Atlantic cruises (S6, O4) 4. Acquire P & O Princess (S1, O3)	**WO STRATEGIES** 1. Begin serving Japan and Pacific Islands (W3, O2, O3, O4) 2. Use weather forecasting to alert customers of potential storm during their vacation (W1, O4)
THREATS—T 1. Decrease in travel since 9/11 2. Terrorism 3. Competition within industry 4. Competition among other types of vacations 5. Economic recession 6. Chance of natural disasters 7. Increasing fuel prices 8. Changing government regulations	**ST STRATEGIES** 1. Advertise Carnival's ship variety, brand recognition, and safety policies (S3, S7, T1, T2, T5) 2. Advertise alternate vacations that are not affected by hurricane season (S3, T5, T7) 3. Offer discounts on Carnival Web site (S9, T6)	**WT STRATEGIES** 1. Lower prices of cruises during hurricane season (W1, T6) 2. Research viability of entering other foreign markets (W2, W3, T8, S9)

Strategy. When a firm has excess production capacity (internal weakness) and its basic industry is experiencing declining annual sales and profits (external threat), then concentric diversification can be an effective WT Strategy. It is important to use specific, rather than general, strategy terms when developing a SWOT Matrix. In addition, it is important to include the "S1, O2"-type notation after each strategy in the SWOT Matrix. This notation reveals the rationale for each alternative strategy.

FIGURE 6–5

SWOT Matrix for Riverbanks (2003)

	STRENGTHS—S	WEAKNESSES—W
	1. The Riverbanks Zoo and Garden are ranked among the top zoos in North America.	1. Weak advertising effort.
	2. Winner of the 2002 Governor's cup for most outstanding tourist attraction in South Carolina.	2. Few foul-weather retreats at the zoo.
	3. Riverbank Zoo and Garden is the premium choice for education and recreation, including school programs, educational classes, and overnight and day camps.	3. Not actively soliciting businesses.
	4. Riverbanks Zoo is home to some of the Earth's most popular and spectacular creatures, like African lions and tigers.	
	5. Education and conservation efforts increase the number of visitors.	
	6. The zoo has been treating endangered species for over twenty-five years.	
	7. Riverbanks Zoo is home to more than 2,000 magnificent, fascinating, and exotic animals.	
	8. Guests are able to feed lots of the animals, including the giraffes.	
	9. Riverbanks Zoo and Garden supports conservation and science by being an active member of American Zoo and Aquarium (AZA).	
	10. Excellent financial condition.	
OPPORTUNITIES—O	**SO STRATEGIES**	**WO STRATEGIES**
1. Increase in revenue annually.	1. A program that offers credit to high school seniors by helping care for and feed the animals. (S3, S5, S7, S8, S9, O2, O4, O5)	1. Interactive Web site that allows customers to vote on a feature animal or plant of the month. (W1, O3, O6)
2. Governmental support increased to 26.8% for the year 2001.	2. A program that offers credit to college students by helping care for and feed the animals. (S3, S5, S7, O3)	2. Seek more business/corporate sponsorships of animals. (W1, W3, O3, O4)
3. Columbia, S.C. is a growing area.		
4. Active memberships increased from 27,000 in 2001 to about 32,000 in 2002.		
5. Attendance increased from around 800,000 in 2001 to over 1,000,000 visitors in 2002, including 25% who came from outside the state.		
6. The Internet enables visitors to access information about the zoo and garden before attending.		
7. Families spending more time on entertainment.		

FIGURE 6-5
Continued

THREATS—T	ST STRATEGIES	WT STRATEGIES
1. Weak economy.	1. Conduct a monthly scavenger hunt for youth and adults with prizes given. (S3, S5, S10, T2)	1. Add a prehistoric/extinct animal museum in the zoo area. (W1, T3)
2. Local attractions remain a big part of the zoo's competition.	2. Develop partnerships with local Columbia events such as USC ballgames and coliseum concerts. (S1, T2)	2. Add a covered walkway trail in and about the zoo. (W2, T5)
3. Animal extinctions; less than 1.5 million elephants survive in all of Africa. There are only about 400 African elephants in zoos in North America.		
4. The black rhino is highly endangered. There are only about 2,500 rhinos left in the wild.		
5. Admission revenues are affected by weather conditions because most of the attractions are outdoors.		
6. Animal movement can be costly and risky (from overseas to the zoos). It cost $49,000 to import, e.g., Warthogs from Africa or Asia to U.S. for each pair.		
7. Animal diet can be costly. For example, elephants alone feed up to sixteen hours per day (ten pounds of mixed vegetables and fruits, one to two bales of coastal grass hay per day, and sixty gallons of water per day).		

The Strategic Position and Action Evaluation (SPACE) Matrix

The *Strategic Position and Action Evaluation (SPACE) Matrix*, another important Stage 2 matching tool, is illustrated in Figure 6–6. Its four-quadrant framework indicates whether aggressive, conservative, defensive, or competitive strategies are most appropriate for a given organization. The axes of the SPACE Matrix represent two internal dimensions (*financial strength [FS]* and *competitive advantage [CA]*) and two external dimensions (*environmental stability [ES]* and *industry strength [IS]*). These four factors are the most important determinants of an organization's overall strategic position.[5]

Depending upon the type of organization, numerous variables could make up each of the dimensions represented on the axes of the SPACE Matrix. Factors that were included earlier in the firm's EFE and IFE matrices should be considered in developing a SPACE Matrix. Other variables commonly included are given in Table 6–2. For example, return on investment, leverage, liquidity, working capital, and cash flow are commonly considered to be determining factors of an organization's financial strength. Like the SWOT Matrix, the SPACE Matrix should be both tailored to the particular organization being studied and based on factual information as much as possible.

FIGURE 6-6
The SPACE Matrix

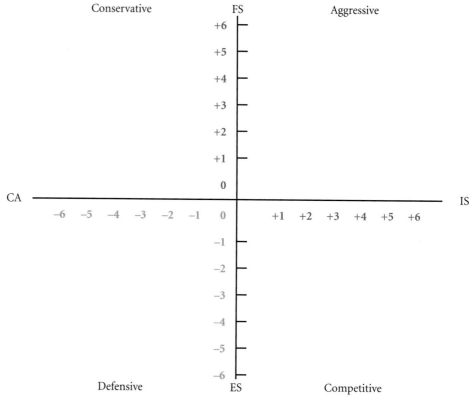

Source: H. Rowe, R. Mason, and K. Dickel, *Strategic Management and Business Policy: A Methodological Approach* (Reading, MA: Addison-Wesley Publishing Co. Inc., © 1982): 155. Reprinted with permission of the publisher.

The steps required to develop a SPACE Matrix are as follows:

1. Select a set of variables to define financial strength (FS), competitive advantage (CA), environmental stability (ES), and industry strength (IS).

2. Assign a numerical value ranging from +1 (worst) to +6 (best) to each of the variables that make up the FS and IS dimensions. Assign a numerical value ranging from −1 (best) to −6 (worst) to each of the variables that make up the ES and CA dimensions. On the FS and CA axes, make comparison to competitors. On the IS and ES axes, make comparison to other industries.

3. Compute an average score for FS, CA, IS, and ES by summing the values given to the variables of each dimension and then by dividing by the number of variables included in the respective dimension.

4. Plot the average scores for FS, IS, ES, and CA on the appropriate axis in the SPACE Matrix.

5. Add the two scores on the *x*-axis and plot the resultant point on *X*. Add the two scores on the *y*-axis and plot the resultant point on *Y*. Plot the intersection of the new *xy* point.

6. Draw a *directional vector* from the origin of the SPACE Matrix through the new intersection point. This vector reveals the type of strategies recommended for the organization: aggressive, competitive, defensive, or conservative.

TABLE 6-2   Example Factors that Make Up the SPACE
Matrix Axes

INTERNAL STRATEGIC POSITION	EXTERNAL STRATEGIC POSITION
Financial Strength (FS)	*Environmental Stability (ES)*
Return on investment	Technological changes
Leverage	Rate of inflation
Liquidity	Demand variability
Working capital	Price range of competing products
Cash flow	Barriers to entry into market
	Competitive pressure
	Ease of exit from market
	Price elasticity of demand
	Risk involved in business
Competitive Advantage (CA)	*Industry Strength (IS)*
Market share	Growth potential
Product quality	Profit potential
Product life cycle	Financial stability
Customer loyalty	Technological know-how
Competition's capacity utilization	Resource utilization
Technological know-how	Ease of entry into market
Control over suppliers and distributors	Productivity, capacity utilization

Source: H. Rowe, R. Mason, and K. Dickel, *Strategic Management and Business Policy: A Methodological Approach* (Reading, MA: Addison-Wesley Publishing Co. Inc., © 1982): 155–156. Reprinted with permission of the publisher.

Some examples of strategy profiles that can emerge from a SPACE analysis are shown in Figure 6–7. The directional vector associated with each profile suggests the type of strategies to pursue: aggressive, conservative, defensive, or competitive. When a firm's directional vector is located in the *aggressive quadrant* (upper-right quadrant) of the SPACE Matrix, an organization is in an excellent position to use its internal strengths to (1) take advantage of external opportunities, (2) overcome internal weaknesses, and (3) avoid external threats. Therefore, market penetration, market development, product development, backward integration, forward integration, horizontal integration, conglomerate diversification, concentric diversification, horizontal diversification, or a combination strategy all can be feasible, depending on the specific circumstances that face the firm.

The directional vector may appear in the *conservative quadrant* (upper-left quadrant) of the SPACE Matrix, which implies staying close to the firm's basic competencies and not taking excessive risks. Conservative strategies most often include market penetration, market development, product development, and concentric diversification. The directional vector may be located in the lower-left or *defensive quadrant* of the SPACE Matrix, which suggests that the firm should focus on rectifying internal weaknesses and avoiding external threats. Defensive strategies include retrenchment, divestiture, liquidation, and concentric diversification. Finally, the

FIGURE 6–7
Example Strategy Profiles

Aggressive Profiles

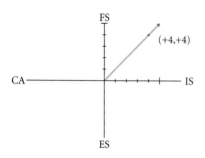

A financially strong firm that has achieved major competitive advantages in a growing and stable industry

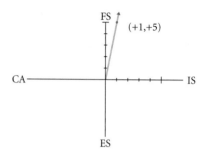

A firm whose financial strength is a dominating factor in the industry

Conservative Profiles

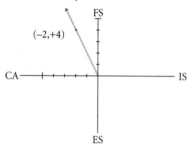

A firm that has achieved financial strength in a stable industry that is not growing; the firm has no major competitive advantages

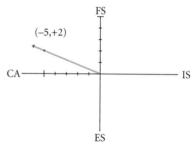

A firm that suffers from major competitive disadvantages in an industry that is technologically stable but declining in sales

Competitive Profiles

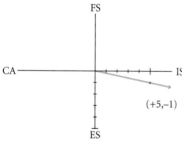

A firm with major competitive advantages in a high–growth industry

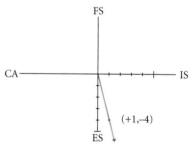

An organization that is competing fairly well in an unstable industry

Defensive Profiles

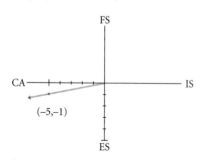

A firm that has a very weak competitive position in a negative growth, stable industry

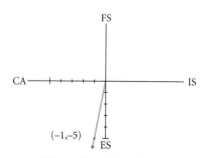

A financially troubled firm in a very unstable industry

Source: H. Rowe, R. Mason, and K. Dickel, *Strategic Management and Business Policy: A Methodological Approach* (Reading, MA: Addison-Wesley Publishing Co. Inc., © 1982): 155. Reprinted with permission of the publisher.

directional vector may be located in the lower-right or *competitive quadrant* of the SPACE Matrix, indicating competitive strategies. Competitive strategies include backward, forward, and horizontal integration; market penetration; market development; product development; and joint ventures.

A SPACE Matrix analysis for a bank is provided in Table 6–3. Note that the competitive strategies are recommended.

TABLE 6-3   A SPACE Matrix for a Bank

FINANCIAL STRENGTH	RATINGS
The bank's primary capital ratio is 7.23 percent, which is 1.23 percentage points over the generally required ratio of 6 percent.	1.0
The bank's return on assets is negative 0.77, compared to a bank industry average ratio of positive 0.70.	1.0
The bank's net income was $183 million, down 9 percent from a year earlier.	3.0
The bank's revenues increased 7 percent to $3.46 billion.	4.0
	9.0

INDUSTRY STRENGTH	
Deregulation provides geographic and product freedom.	4.0
Deregulation increases competition in the banking industry.	2.0
Pennsylvania's interstate banking law allows the bank to acquire other banks in New Jersey, Ohio, Kentucky, the District of Columbia, and West Virginia.	4.0
	10.0

ENVIRONMENTAL STABILITY	
Less-developed countries are experiencing high inflation and political instability.	−4.0
Headquartered in Pittsburgh, the bank historically has been heavily dependent on the steel, oil, and gas industries. These industries are depressed.	−5.0
Banking deregulation has created instability throughout the industry.	−4.0
	−13.0

COMPETITIVE ADVANTAGE	
The bank provides data processing services for more than 450 institutions in 38 states.	−2.0
Superregional banks, international banks, and nonbanks are becoming increasingly competitive.	−5.0
The bank has a large customer base.	−2.0
	−9.0

CONCLUSION

ES Average is −13.0 ÷ 3 = −4.33 IS Average is + 10.0 ÷ 3 = 3.33

CA Average is −9.0 ÷ 3 = −3.00 FS Average is + 9.0 ÷ 4 = 2.25

Directional Vector Coordinates: x-axis: −3.00 + (+3.33) = +0.33
y-axis: −4.33 + (+2.25) = −2.08

The bank should pursue Competitive Strategies.

The Boston Consulting Group (BCG) Matrix

Autonomous divisions (or profit centers) of an organization make up what is called a *business portfolio*. When a firm's divisions compete in different industries, a separate strategy often must be developed for each business. The *Boston Consulting Group (BCG) Matrix* and the *Internal-External (IE) Matrix* are designed specifically to enhance a multidivisional firm's efforts to formulate strategies. (BCG is a private management consulting firm based in Boston. BCG employs about 1,400 consultants worldwide but is cutting its workforce by 12 percent in 2002.)

The BCG Matrix graphically portrays differences among divisions in terms of relative market share position and industry growth rate. The BCG Matrix allows a multidivisional organization to manage its portfolio of businesses by examining the relative market share position and the industry growth rate of each division relative to all other divisions in the organization. *Relative market share position* is defined as the ratio of a division's own market share in a particular industry to the market share held by the largest rival firm in that industry.

Relative market share position is given on the *x*-axis of the BCG Matrix. The midpoint on the *x*-axis usually is set at .50, corresponding to a division that has half the market share of the leading firm in the industry. The *y*-axis represents the industry growth rate in sales, measured in percentage terms. The growth rate percentages on the *y*-axis could range from −20 to +20 percent, with 0.0 being the midpoint. These numerical ranges on the *x*- and *y*-axes are often used, but other numerical values could be established as deemed appropriate for particular organizations.

An example of a BCG Matrix appears in Figure 6–8. Each circle represents a separate division. The size of the circle corresponds to the proportion of corporate revenue generated by that business unit, and the pie slice indicates the proportion of corporate profits generated by that division. Divisions located in Quadrant I of the BCG Matrix are called Question Marks, those located in Quadrant II are called Stars, those located in Quadrant III are called Cash Cows, and those divisions located in Quadrant IV are called Dogs.

- *Question Marks*—Divisions in Quadrant I have a low relative market share position, yet they compete in a high-growth industry. Generally these firms' cash needs are high and their cash generation is low. These businesses are called *Question Marks* because the organization must decide whether to strengthen them by pursuing an intensive strategy (market penetration, market development, or product development) or to sell them.

- *Stars*—Quadrant II businesses (often called *Stars*) represent the organization's best long-run opportunities for growth and profitability. Divisions with a high relative market share and a high industry growth rate should receive substantial investment to maintain or strengthen their dominant positions. Forward, backward, and horizontal integration; market penetration; market development; product development; and joint ventures are appropriate strategies for these divisions to consider.

- *Cash Cows*—Divisions positioned in Quadrant III have a high relative market share position but compete in a low-growth industry. Called *Cash Cows* because they generate cash in excess of their needs, they are often milked. Many of today's Cash Cows were yesterday's Stars. Cash Cow divisions should be managed to maintain their strong position for as long as possible. Product development or concentric diversification may be attractive strategies for strong Cash Cows. However, as a Cash Cow division becomes weak, retrenchment or divestiture can become more appropriate.

FIGURE 6–8

The BCG Matrix

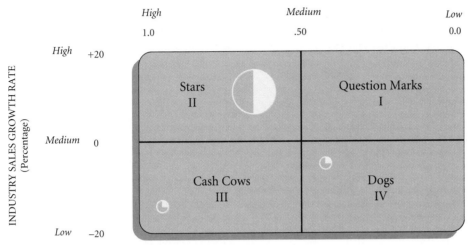

Source: Adapted from Boston Consulting Group, *Perspectives on Experience* (Boston: The Boston Consulting Group, 1974).

- **Dogs**—Quadrant IV divisions of the organization have a low relative market share position and compete in a slow- or no-market-growth industry; they are *Dogs* in the firm's portfolio. Because of their weak internal and external position, these businesses are often liquidated, divested, or trimmed down through retrenchment. When a division first becomes a Dog, retrenchment can be the best strategy to pursue because many Dogs have bounced back, after strenuous asset and cost reduction, to become viable, profitable divisions.

The major benefit of the BCG Matrix is that it draws attention to the cash flow, investment characteristics, and needs of an organization's various divisions. The divisions of many firms evolve over time: Dogs become Question Marks, Question Marks become Stars, Stars become Cash Cows, and Cash Cows become Dogs in an ongoing counter-clockwise motion. Less frequently, Stars become Question Marks, Question Marks become Dogs, Dogs become Cash Cows, and Cash Cows become Stars (in a clockwise motion). In some organizations, no cyclical motion is apparent. Over time, organizations should strive to achieve a portfolio of divisions that are Stars.

One example of a BCG Matrix is provided in Figure 6–9, which illustrates an organization composed of five divisions with annual sales ranging from $5,000 to $60,000. Division 1 has the greatest sales volume, so the circle representing that division is the largest one in the matrix. The circle corresponding to Division 5 is the smallest because its sales volume ($5,000) is least among all the divisions. The pie slices within the circles reveal the percent of corporate profits contributed by each division. As shown, Division 1 contributes the highest profit percentage, 39 percent. Notice in the diagram that Division 1 is considered a Star, Division 2 is a Question Mark, Division 3 is also a Question Mark, Division 4 is a Cash Cow, and Division 5 is a Dog.

The BCG Matrix, like all analytical techniques, has some limitations. For example, viewing every business as either a Star, Cash Cow, Dog, or Question Mark is an oversimplification; many businesses fall right in the middle of the BCG Matrix and thus are not easily classified. Furthermore, the BCG Matrix does not

FIGURE 6-9

An Example BCG Matrix

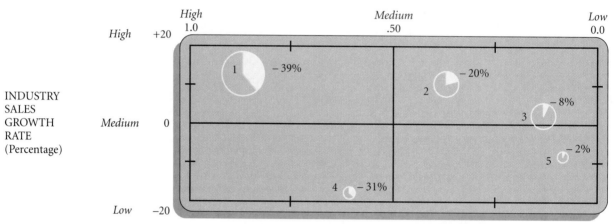

Division	Revenues	Percent Revenues	Profits	Percent Profits	Percent Market Share	Percent Growth Rate
1	$60,000	37	$10,000	39	80	+15
2	40,000	24	5,000	20	40	+10
3	40,000	24	2,000	8	10	+1
4	20,000	12	8,000	31	60	−20
5	5,000	3	500	2	5	−10
Total	$165,000	100	$25,500	100		

reflect whether or not various divisions or their industries are growing over time; that is, the matrix has no temporal qualities, but rather it is a snapshot of an organization at a given point in time. Finally, other variables besides relative market share position and industry growth rate in sales, such as size of the market and competitive advantages, are important in making strategic decisions about various divisions.

The Internal-External (IE) Matrix

The *Internal-External (IE) Matrix* positions an organization's various divisions in a nine-cell display, illustrated in Figure 6–10. The IE Matrix is similar to the BCG Matrix in that both tools involve plotting organization divisions in a schematic diagram; this is why they are both called portfolio matrices. Also, the size of each circle represents the percentage sales contribution of each division, and pie slices reveal the percentage profit contribution of each division in both the BCG and IE Matrix.

But there are some important differences between the BCG Matrix and the IE Matrix. First, the axes are different. Also, the IE Matrix requires more information about the divisions than the BCG Matrix. Furthermore, the strategic implications of each matrix are different. For these reasons, strategists in multidivisional firms often develop both the BCG Matrix and the IE Matrix in formulating alternative strategies. A common practice is to develop a BCG Matrix and an IE Matrix for the present and then develop projected matrices to reflect expectations of the future. This before-and-after analysis forecasts the expected effect of strategic decisions on an organization's portfolio of divisions.

FIGURE 6–10
The Internal-External (IE) Matrix

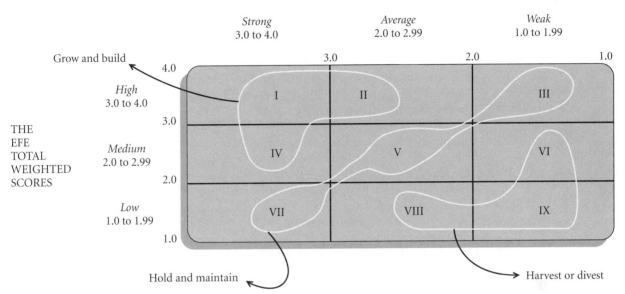

Source: The IE Matrix was developed from the General Electric (GE) Business Screen Matrix. For a description of the GE Matrix see Michael Allen, "Diagramming GE's Planning for What's WATT," in R. Allio and M. Pennington, eds., *Corporate Planning: Techniques and Applications* (New York: AMACOM, 1979).

GLOBAL PERSPECTIVE

Use the U.S. Department of Commerce Global Web Site

BuyUSA.com is an e-marketplace sponsored by the U.S. Department of Commerce. This sophisticated combination of online and offline services pairs the vast global resources of the U.S. Department of Commerce with the power of the Internet. BuyUSA.com brings together suppliers of U.S. products and services and international companies outside the United States, and gives both groups the advocacy and services they need to conduct successful business worldwide.

U.S. Commercial Service offers valuable assistance to help your business export goods and services to markets worldwide. From this site you can access a global listing of trade events, international market research, and practical tools to help with every step of the export process.

Export.gov is the U.S. government's online entry point for U.S. exporters. The site organizes export-related programs, services, and market research information from across nineteen federal agencies and provides a sophisticated cross-agency search capability.

Trade Development offers a well-coordinated, economical, and accessible array of services to help small businesses increase their export potential.

Export America Magazine is the federal source for Global Business Needs.

Central and Eastern Europe Business Information Center is a business facilitation program for U.S. firms interested in expanding into the Central and Eastern Europe and markets.

Business Information Services for the Newly Independent States is the U.S. government's primary market information center for U.S. companies exploring business opportunities in Russia and other Newly Independent States.

Platinum Key Service allows U.S. companies to take advantage of longer-term, sustained, and customized U.S. Commercial Service assistance on a range of issues.

Source: **www.commerce.gov/trade_opportunities.html**.

The IE Matrix is based on two key dimensions: the IFE total weighted scores on the *x*-axis and the EFE total weighted scores on the *y*-axis. Recall that each division of an organization should construct an IFE Matrix and an EFE Matrix for its part of the organization. The total weighted scores derived from the divisions allow construction of the corporate-level IE Matrix. On the *x*-axis of the IE Matrix, an IFE total weighted score of 1.0 to 1.99 represents a weak internal position; a score of 2.0 to 2.99 is considered average; and a score of 3.0 to 4.0 is strong. Similarly, on the *y*-axis, an EFE total weighted score of 1.0 to 1.99 is considered low; a score of 2.0 to 2.99 is medium; and a score of 3.0 to 4.0 is high.

The IE Matrix can be divided into three major regions that have different strategy implications. First, the prescription for divisions that fall into cells I, II, or IV can be described as *grow and build.* Intensive (market penetration, market development, and product development) or integrative (backward integration, forward integration, and horizontal integration) strategies can be most appropriate for these divisions. Second, divisions that fall into cells III, V, or VII can be managed best with *hold and maintain* strategies; market penetration and product development are two commonly employed strategies for these types of divisions. Third, a common prescription for divisions that fall into cells VI, VIII, or IX is *harvest or divest.* Successful organizations are able to achieve a portfolio of businesses positioned in or around cell I in the IE Matrix.

An example of a completed IE Matrix is given in Figure 6–11, which depicts an organization composed of four divisions. As indicated by the positioning of the

FIGURE 6–11

An Example IE Matrix

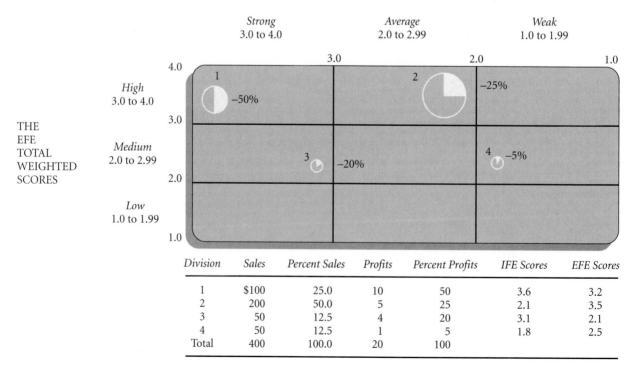

THE IFE TOTAL WEIGHTED SCORES

Division	Sales	Percent Sales	Profits	Percent Profits	IFE Scores	EFE Scores
1	$100	25.0	10	50	3.6	3.2
2	200	50.0	5	25	2.1	3.5
3	50	12.5	4	20	3.1	2.1
4	50	12.5	1	5	1.8	2.5
Total	400	100.0	20	100		

circles, *grow and build* strategies are appropriate for Division 1, Division 2, and Division 3. Division 4 is a candidate for *harvest or divest*. Division 2 contributes the greatest percentage of company sales and thus is represented by the largest circle. Division 1 contributes the greatest proportion of total profits; it has the largest-percentage pie slice.

As indicated in Figure 6–12 and Figure 6–13, Harrah's recently constructed two IE Matrices, one for its four geographic segments and one for its five product segments. Note that its Central Region and its Casino Division have the largest revenues (as indicated by the largest circles) and the largest profits (as indicated by the largest pie slices) in the matrices, respectively. Harrah's could also develop a Land-Based versus Riverboat versus Indian Gaming IE Matrix with three circles. It is common for organizations to develop both geographic and product-based IE Matrices in order to more effectively formulate strategies and allocate resources among divisions. In addition, firms often prepare an IE (or BCG) Matrix for its competitors. Furthermore, firms will often prepare "before and after" IE (or BCG) Matrices to reveal the situation at present versus the expected situation after one year. This latter idea minimizes the limitation of these matrices being a "snapshot in time." In performing case analysis, feel free to estimate the IFE and EFE scores for the various divisions based upon your research into the company and industry—rather than preparing a separate IE Matrix for each division.

FIGURE 6–12

The Internal-External (IE) Matrix for Harrah's (2003) (Based on Region)

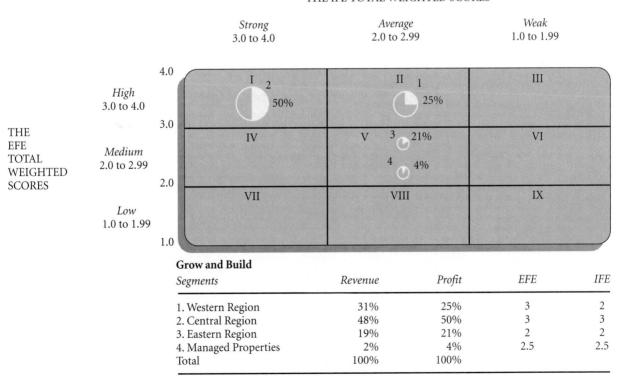

Grow and Build				
Segments	Revenue	Profit	EFE	IFE
1. Western Region	31%	25%	3	2
2. Central Region	48%	50%	3	3
3. Eastern Region	19%	21%	2	2
4. Managed Properties	2%	4%	2.5	2.5
Total	100%	100%		

FIGURE 6–13

The Internal-External (IE) for Harrah's (2003) (Based on Product)

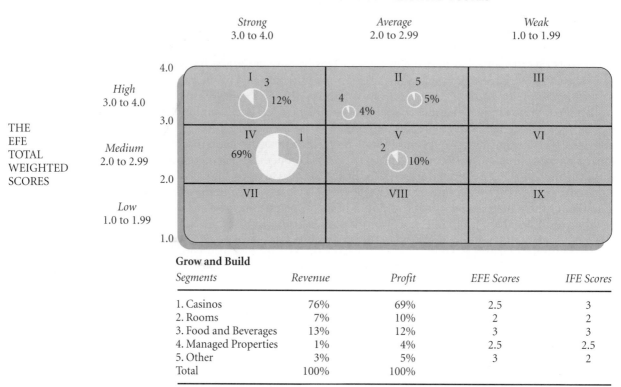

Grow and Build

Segments	Revenue	Profit	EFE Scores	IFE Scores
1. Casinos	76%	69%	2.5	3
2. Rooms	7%	10%	2	2
3. Food and Beverages	13%	12%	3	3
4. Managed Properties	1%	4%	2.5	2.5
5. Other	3%	5%	3	2
Total	100%	100%		

The Grand Strategy Matrix

In addition to the SWOT Matrix, SPACE Matrix, BCG Matrix, and IE Matrix, the *Grand Strategy Matrix* has become a popular tool for formulating alternative strategies. All organizations can be positioned in one of the Grand Strategy Matrix's four strategy quadrants. A firm's divisions likewise could be positioned. As illustrated in Figure 6–14, the Grand Strategy Matrix is based on two evaluative dimensions: competitive position and market growth. Appropriate strategies for an organization to consider are listed in sequential order of attractiveness in each quadrant of the matrix.

Firms located in Quadrant I of the Grand Strategy Matrix are in an excellent strategic position. For these firms, continued concentration on current markets (market penetration and market development) and products (product development) is an appropriate strategy. It is unwise for a Quadrant I firm to shift notably from its established competitive advantages. When a Quadrant I organization has excessive resources, then backward, forward, or horizontal integration may be effective strategies. When a Quadrant I firm is too heavily committed to a single product, then concentric diversification may reduce the risks associated with a narrow product line. Quadrant I firms can afford to take advantage of external opportunities in several areas: They can take risks aggressively when necessary.

FIGURE 6–14
The Grand Strategy Matrix

RAPID MARKET GROWTH

Quadrant II
1. Market development
2. Market penetration
3. Product development
4. Horizontal integration
5. Divestiture
6. Liquidation

Quadrant I
1. Market development
2. Market penetration
3. Product development
4. Forward integration
5. Backward integration
6. Horizontal integration
7. Concentric diversification

WEAK COMPETITIVE POSITION

STRONG COMPETITIVE POSITION

Quadrant III
1. Retrenchment
2. Concentric diversification
3. Horizontal diversification
4. Conglomerate diversification
5. Divestiture
6. Liquidation

Quadrant IV
1. Concentric diversification
2. Horizontal diversification
3. Conglomerate diversification
4. Joint ventures

SLOW MARKET GROWTH

Source: Adapted from Roland Christensen, Norman Berg, and Malcolm Salter, *Policy Formulation and Administration* (Homewood, IL: Richard D. Irwin, 1976): 16–18.

Firms positioned in Quadrant II need to evaluate their present approach to the marketplace seriously. Although their industry is growing, they are unable to compete effectively, and they need to determine why the firm's current approach is ineffective and how the company can best change to improve its competitiveness. Because Quadrant II firms are in a rapid-market-growth industry, an intensive strategy (as opposed to integrative or diversification) is usually the first option that should be considered. However, if the firm is lacking a distinctive competence or competitive advantage, then horizontal integration is often a desirable alternative. As a last resort, divestiture or liquidation should be considered. Divestiture can provide funds needed to acquire other businesses or buy back shares of stock.

Quadrant III organizations compete in slow-growth industries and have weak competitive positions. These firms must make some drastic changes quickly to avoid further decline and possible liquidation. Extensive cost and asset reduction (retrenchment) should be pursued first. An alternative strategy is to shift resources away from the current business into different areas (diversify). If all else fails, the final options for Quadrant III businesses are divestiture or liquidation.

Finally, Quadrant IV businesses have a strong competitive position but are in a slow-growth industry. These firms have the strength to launch diversified programs into more promising growth areas: Quadrant IV firms have characteristically high cash-flow levels and limited internal growth needs and often can pursue concentric, horizontal, or conglomerate diversification successfully. Quadrant IV firms also may pursue joint ventures.

The Decision Stage

Analysis and intuition provide a basis for making strategy-formulation decisions. The matching techniques just discussed reveal feasible alternative strategies. Many of these strategies will likely have been proposed by managers and employees participating in the strategy analysis and choice activity. Any additional strategies resulting from the matching analyses could be discussed and added to the list of feasible alternative options. As indicated earlier in this chapter, participants could rate these strategies on a 1 to 4 scale so that a prioritized list of the best strategies could be achieved.

The Quantitative Strategic Planning Matrix (QSPM)

Other than ranking strategies to achieve the prioritized list, there is only one analytical technique in the literature designed to determine the relative attractiveness of feasible alternative actions. This technique is the *Quantitative Strategic Planning Matrix (QSPM)*, which comprises Stage 3 of the strategy-formulation analytical framework.[6] This technique objectively indicates which alternative strategies are best. The QSPM uses input from Stage 1 analyses and matching results from Stage 2 analyses to decide objectively among alternative strategies. That is, the EFE Matrix SWOT, IFE Matrix, and Competitive Profile Matrix that make up Stage 1, coupled with the SWOT Matrix, SPACE Matrix, BCG Matrix, IE Matrix, and Grand Strategy Matrix that make up Stage 2, provide the needed information for setting up the QSPM (Stage 3). The QSPM is a tool that allows strategists to evaluate alternative strategies objectively, based on previously identified external and internal critical success factors. Like other strategy-formulation analytical tools, the QSPM requires good intuitive judgment.

The basic format of the QSPM is illustrated in Table 6–4. Note that the left column of a QSPM consists of key external and internal factors (from Stage 1), and the top row consists of feasible alternative strategies (from Stage 2). Specifically, the left column of a QSPM consists of information obtained directly from the EFE Matrix and IFE Matrix. In a column adjacent to the critical success factors, the respective weights received by each factor in the EFE Matrix and the IFE Matrix are recorded.

The top row of a QSPM consists of alternative strategies derived from the SWOT Matrix, SPACE Matrix, BCG Matrix, IE Matrix, and Grand Strategy Matrix. These matching tools usually generate similar feasible alternatives. However, not every strategy suggested by the matching techniques has to be evaluated in a QSPM. Strategists should use good intuitive judgment in selecting strategies to include in a QSPM.

Conceptually, the QSPM determines the relative attractiveness of various strategies based on the extent to which key external and internal critical success factors are capitalized upon or improved. The relative attractiveness of each strategy within a set of alternatives is computed by determining the cumulative impact of each external and internal critical success factor. Any number of sets of alternative strategies can be included in the QSPM, and any number of strategies can make up a given set, but only strategies within a given set are evaluated relative to each other. For example, one set of strategies may include concentric, horizontal, and conglomerate diversification, whereas another set may include issuing stock and selling a division to raise needed capital. These two sets of strategies are totally different, and

TABLE 6–4   The Quantitative Strategic Planning Matrix—QSPM

		STRATEGIC ALTERNATIVES		
Key Factors	*Weight*	*Strategy 1*	*Strategy 2*	*Strategy 3*
Key External Factors				
Economy				
Political/Legal/Governmental				
Social/Cultural/Demographic/Environmental				
Technological				
Competitive				
Key Internal Factors				
Management				
Marketing				
Finance/Accounting				
Production/Operations				
Research and Development				
Management Information Systems				

the QSPM evaluates strategies only within sets. Note in Table 6–4 that three strategies are included, and they make up just one set.

A QSPM for a food company is provided in Table 6–5. This example illustrates all the components of the QSPM: Strategic Alternatives, Key Factors, Weights, Attractiveness Scores (AS), Total Attractiveness Scores (TAS), and the Sum Total Attractiveness Score. The three new terms just introduced—(1) Attractiveness Scores, (2) Total Attractiveness Scores, and (3) the Sum Total Attractiveness Score—are defined and explained below as the six steps required to develop a QSPM are discussed.

Step 1 *Make a list of the firm's key external opportunities/threats and internal strengths/weaknesses in the left column of the QSPM.* This information should be taken directly from the EFE Matrix and IFE Matrix. A minimum of ten external critical success factors and ten internal critical success factors should be included in the QSPM.

Step 2 *Assign weights to each key external and internal factor.* These weights are identical to those in the EFE Matrix and the IFE Matrix. The weights are presented in a straight column just to the right of the external and internal critical success factors.

Step 3 *Examine the Stage 2 (matching) matrices, and identify alternative strategies that the organization should consider implementing.* Record these strategies in the top row of the QSPM. Group the strategies into mutually exclusive sets if possible.

Step 4 *Determine the Attractiveness Scores (AS)* defined as numerical values that indicate the relative attractiveness of each strategy in a

TABLE 6-5   A QSPM for Campbell Soup Company

		STRATEGIC ALTERNATIVES			
		Joint Venture in Europe		Joint Venture in Asia	
Key Factors	Weight	AS	TAS	AS	TAS
Opportunities					
1. One European currency—euro	.10	4	.40	2	.20
2. Rising health consciousness in selecting foods	.15	4	.60	3	.45
3. Free market economies arising in Asia	.10	2	.20	4	.40
4. Demand for soups increasing 10% annually	.15	3	.45	4	.60
5. NAFTA	.05	–	–	–	–
Threats					
1. Food revenues increasing only 1% annually	.10	3	.30	4	.40
2. ConAgra's Banquet TV Dinners lead market with 27.4 percent share	.05	–	–	–	–
3. Unstable economies in Asia	.10	4	.40	1	.10
4. Tin cans are not biodegradable	.05	–	–	–	–
5. Low value of the dollar	.15	4	.60	2	.30
	1.0				
Strengths					
1. Profits rose 30%	.10	4	.40	2	.20
2. New North American division	.10	–	–	–	–
3. New health-conscious soups are successful	.10	4	.40	2	.20
4. Swanson TV dinners' market share has increased to 25.1%	.05	4	.20	3	.15
5. One-fifth of all managers' bonuses is based on overall corporate performance	.05	–	–	–	–
6. Capacity utilization increased from 60% to 80%	.15	3	.45	4	.60
Weaknesses					
1. Pepperidge Farm sales have declined 7%	.05	–	–	–	–
2. Restructuring cost $302 million	.05	–	–	–	–
3. The company's European operation is losing money	.15	2	.30	4	.60
4. The company is slow in globalizing	.15	4	.60	3	.45
5. Pretax profit margin of 8.4% is only one-half industry average	.05	–	–	–	–
Sum Total Attractiveness Score	1.0		5.30		4.65

AS = Attractiveness Score; TAS = Total Attractiveness Score
Attractiveness Score: 1 = not attractive; 2 = somewhat attractive; 3 = reasonably attractive; 4 = highly attractive.

given set of alternatives. *Attractiveness Scores (AS)* are determined by examining each key external or internal factor, one at a time, and asking the question, "Does this factor affect the choice of strategies being made?" If the answer to this question is *yes,* then the strategies should be compared relative to that key factor. Specifically, Attractiveness Scores should be assigned to each strategy to indicate the relative attractiveness of one strategy over others, considering the particular factor. The range for Attractiveness Scores is 1 = not attractive, 2 = somewhat attractive, 3 = reasonably attractive, and 4 = highly attractive. If the answer to the above question is no, indicating that the respective key factor has not effect upon the specific choice being made, then do not assign Attractiveness Scores to the strategies in that set. Use a dash to indicate that the key factor does not affect the choice being made. Note: If you assign an AS score to one strategy, then assign AS score(s) to the other. In other words, if one strategy receives a dash, then all others must receive a dash in a given row.

Step 5   ***Compute the Total Attractiveness Scores.*** *Total Attractiveness Scores (TAS)* are defined as the product of multiplying the weights (Step 2) by the Attractiveness Scores (Step 4) in each row. The Total Attractiveness Scores indicate the relative attractiveness of each alternative strategy, considering only the impact of the adjacent external or internal critical success factor. The higher the Total Attractiveness Score, the more attractive the strategic alternative (considering only the adjacent critical success factor).

Step 6   ***Compute the Sum Total Attractiveness Score.*** Add Total Attractiveness Scores in each strategy column of the QSPM. The *Sum Total Attractiveness Scores (STAS)* reveal which strategy is most attractive in each set of alternatives. Higher scores indicate more attractive strategies, considering all the relevant external and internal factors that could affect the strategic decisions. The magnitude of the difference between the Sum Total Attractiveness Scores in a given set of strategic alternatives indicates the relative desirability of one strategy over another.

In Table 6–5, two alternative strategies—establishing a joint venture in Europe and establishing a joint venture in Asia—are being considered by Campbell Soup.

Note that NAFTA has no impact on the choice being made between the two strategies, so a dash (–) appears several times across that row. Several other factors also have no effect on the choice being made, so dashes are recorded in those rows as well. If a particular factor affects one strategy but not the other, it affects the choice being made, so attractiveness scores should be recorded. The sum total attractiveness score of 5.30 in Table 6–5 indicates that the joint venture in Europe is a more attractive strategy when compared to the joint venture in Asia.

You should have a rationale for each AS score assigned. In Table 6–5, the rationale for the AS scores in the first row is that the unification of Western Europe creates more stable business conditions in Europe than in Asia. The AS score of 4 for the joint venture in Europe and 2 for the joint venture in Asia indicates that the European venture is highly attractive and the Asian venture is somewhat attractive, considering only the first critical success factor. AS scores, therefore, are not mere guesses; they should be rational, defensible, and reasonable. Avoid giving each strategy the same AS score. Note in Table 6–5 that dashes are inserted all the way across the row when used. Also note that double 4s, or double 3s, or double 2s, or double 1s, are never in a given row. These are important guidelines to follow in constructing a QSPM.

Positive Features and Limitations of the QSPM

A positive feature of the QSPM is that sets of strategies can be examined sequentially or simultaneously. For example, corporate-level strategies could be evaluated first, followed by division-level strategies, and then function-level strategies. There is no limit to the number of strategies that can be evaluated or the number of sets strategies that can be examined at once using the QSPM.

Another positive feature of the QSPM is that it requires strategists to integrate pertinent external and internal factors into the decision process. Developing a QSPM makes it less likely that key factors will be overlooked or weighted inappropriately. A QSPM draws attention to important relationships that affect strategy decisions. Although developing a QSPM requires a number of subjective decisions, making small decisions along the way enhances the probability that the final strategic decisions will be best for the organization. A QSPM can be adapted for use by small and large for-profit and nonprofit organizations and can be applied to virtually any type of organization. A QSPM can especially enhance strategic choice in multinational firms because many key factors and strategies can be considered at once. It also has been applied successfully by a number of small businesses.[7]

The QSPM is not without some limitations. First, it always requires intuitive judgments and educated assumptions. The ratings and attractiveness scores require judgmental decisions, even though they should be based on objective information. Discussion among strategists, managers, and employees throughout the strategy-formulation process, including development of a QSPM, is constructive and improves strategic decisions. Constructive discussion during strategy analysis and choice may arise because of genuine differences of interpretation of information and varying opinions. Another limitation of the QSPM is that it can be only as good as the prerequisite information and matching analyses upon which it is based.

Cultural Aspects of Strategy Choice

All organizations have a culture. *Culture* includes the set of shared values, beliefs, attitudes, customs, norms, personalities, heroes, and heroines that describe a firm. Culture is the unique way an organization does business. It is the human dimension that creates solidarity and meaning, and it inspires commitment and productivity in an organization when strategy changes are made. All human beings have a basic need to make sense of the world, to feel in control, and to make meaning. When events threaten meaning, individuals react defensively. Managers and employees may even sabotage new strategies in an effort to recapture the status quo.

It is beneficial to view strategic management from a cultural perspective because success often rests upon the degree of support that strategies receive from a firm's culture. If a firm's strategies are supported by cultural products such as values, beliefs, rites, rituals, ceremonies, stories, symbols, language, heroes, and heroines, then managers often can implement changes swiftly and easily. However, if a supportive culture does not exist and is not cultivated, then strategy changes may be ineffective or even counter-productive. A firm's culture can become antagonistic to new strategies, and the result of that antagonism may be confusion and disarray.

Strategies that require fewer cultural changes may be more attractive because extensive changes can take considerable time and effort. Whenever two firms merge, it becomes especially important to evaluate and consider culture-strategy linkages. For example, Hewlett-Packard (HP) and Compaq completed their merger in 2002, but their company cultures are quite different. Compaq's culture is top-down-oriented, whereas the H-P culture, called the H-P Way, is based on "management by walking around." Compaq was a marketer that spent only 3.5 percent of revenues on R&D, whereas H-P is an inventor that spends 6 percent of its revenues annually on R&D. Compaq focused on a few major products, whereas H-P boasts a wide array of products in many categories. Compaq's management style was described as outgoing, whereas H-P's is introspective and analytical.[8] Compaq's workforce is highly competitive, aggressive, and takes risks, whereas the H-P Way is to base decisions more on experience, professionalism, and careful analysis.

Culture provides an explanation for the difficulties a firm encounters when it attempts to shift its strategic direction, as the following statement explains:

> Not only has the "right" corporate culture become the essence and
> foundation of corporate excellence, but success or failure of needed corporate
> reforms hinges on management's sagacity and ability to change the firm's
> driving culture in time and in tune with required changes in strategies.[9]

The Politics of Strategy Choice

All organizations are political. Unless managed, political maneuvering consumes valuable time, subverts organizational objectives, diverts human energy, and results in the loss of some valuable employees. Sometimes political biases and personal preferences get unduly embedded in strategy choice decisions. Internal politics affect the choice of strategies in all organizations. The hierarchy of command in an organization, combined with the career aspirations of different people and the need to allocate scarce resources, guarantees the formation of coalitions of individuals who strive to take care of themselves first and the organization second, third, or fourth. Coalitions of individuals often form around key strategy issues that face an enterprise. A major responsibility of strategists is to guide the development of coalitions, to nurture an overall team concept, and to gain the support of key individuals and groups of individuals.

In the absence of objective analyses, strategy decisions too often are based on the politics of the moment. With development of improved strategy-formation tools, political factors become less important in making strategic decisions. In the absence of objectivity, political factors sometimes dictate strategies, and this is unfortunate. Managing political relationships is an integral part of building enthusiasm and esprit de corps in an organization.

A classic study of strategic management in nine large corporations examined the political tactics of successful and unsuccessful strategists.[10] Successful strategists were found to let weakly supported ideas and proposals die through inaction and to establish additional hurdles or tests for strongly supported ideas considered unacceptable but not openly opposed. Successful strategists kept a low political profile on unacceptable proposals and strived to let most negative decisions come from subordinates or a group consensus, thereby reserving their personal vetoes for big issues and crucial moments. Successful strategists did a lot of chatting and informal questioning to stay abreast of how things were progressing and to know when to intervene. They led strategy but did not dictate it. They gave few orders, announced few decisions, depended heavily on informal questioning, and sought to probe and clarify until a consensus emerged.

Successful strategists generously and visibly rewarded key thrusts that succeeded. They assigned responsibility for major new thrusts to *champions,* the individuals most strongly identified with the idea or product and whose futures were linked to its success. They stayed alert to the symbolic impact of their own actions and statements so as not to send false signals that could stimulate movements in unwanted directions.

Successful strategists ensured that all major power bases within an organization were represented in, or had access to, top management. They interjected new faces and new views into considerations of major changes. (This is important because new employees and managers generally have more enthusiasm and drive than employees who have been with the firm a long time. New employees do not see the world the same old way; nor do they act as screens against changes.) Successful strategists minimized their own political exposure on highly controversial issues and in circumstances in which major opposition from key power centers was likely. In combination, these findings provide a basis for managing political relationships in an organization.

Because strategies must be effective in the marketplace and capable of gaining internal commitment, the following tactics used by politicians for centuries can aid strategists:

- *Equifinality*—It is often possible to achieve similar results using different means or paths. Strategists should recognize that achieving a successful outcome is more important than imposing the method of achieving it. It may be possible to generate new alternatives that give equal results but with far greater potential for gaining commitment.
- *Satisfying*—Achieving satisfactory results with an acceptable strategy is far better than failing to achieve optimal results with an unpopular strategy.
- *Generalization*—Shifting focus from specific issues to more general ones may increase strategists' options for gaining organizational commitment.
- *Focus on Higher-Order Issues*—By raising an issue to a higher level, many short-term interests can be postponed in favor of long-term interests. For instance, by focusing on issues of survival, the auto and steel industries were able to persuade unions to make concessions on wage increases.
- *Provide Political Access on Important Issues*—Strategy and policy decisions with significant negative consequences for middle managers will motivate intervention behavior from them. If middle managers do not have an opportunity to take a position on such decisions in appropriate political forums, they are capable of successfully resisting the decisions after they are made. Providing such political access provides strategists with information that otherwise might not be available and that could be useful in managing intervention behavior.[11]

Governance Issues

A "director," according to *Webster's Dictionary,* is "one of a group of persons entrusted with the overall direction of a corporate enterprise." A *board of directors* is a group of individuals who are elected by the ownership of a corporation to have oversight and guidance over management and who look out for shareholders' interests. The act of oversight and direction is referred to as *governance*. The National Association of Corporate Directors defines governance as "the characteristic of ensuring that long-term strategic objectives and plans are established and that the proper management structure is in place to achieve those objectives, while at the same time making sure that the structure functions to maintain the corporation's integrity, reputation, and responsibility to its various constituencies." This broad scope of responsibility for the board shows how boards are being held accountable for the entire performance of the firm. In the Worldcom, Tyco, and Enron bankruptcies and scandals, the firms' boards of directors were sued by shareholders for mismanaging their interests. New accounting rules in the United States and Europe are being passed to enhance coporate-governance codes and to require much more extensive financial disclosure among publicly held firms. The roles and duties of a board of directors can be divided into four broad categories, as indicated in Table 6–6.

Until recently, boards of directors did most of their work sitting around polished wooden tables. However, Hewlett-Packard's board of directors, among many others, now log onto their own special board Web site twice a week and conduct business based on extensive confidential briefing information posted there by the firm's top management team. Then the board members meet face-to-face and fully informed every two months to discuss the biggest issues facing the firm. The "E-Commerce Perspective" focuses on "doing governance online."

Today, boards of directors are composed mostly of outsiders who are becoming more involved in organizations' strategic management. The trend in America is toward much greater board member accountability with smaller boards, now averaging twelve members rather than eighteen as they did a few years ago. *BusinessWeek* recently evaluated the boards of most large American companies and provided the following "principles of good governance":

1. No more than two directors are current or former company executives.
2. No directors do business with the company or accept consulting or legal fees from the firm.
3. The audit, compensation, and nominating committees are made up solely of outside directors.
4. Each director owns a large equity stake in the company, excluding stock options.
5. At least one outside director has extensive experience in the company's core business and at least one has been CEO of an equivalent-size company.
6. Fully employed directors sit on no more than four boards and retirees sit on no more than seven.
7. Each director attends at least 75 percent of all meetings.
8. The board meets regularly without management present and evaluates its own performance annually.
9. The audit committee meets at least four times a year.
10. The board is frugal on executive pay, diligent in CEO succession oversight responsibilities, and prompt to act when trouble arises.
11. The CEO is not also the Chairperson of the Board.
12. Shareholders have considerable power and information to choose and replace directors.
13. Stock options are considered a corporate expense.
14. There are no interlocking directorships (where a director or CEO sits on another director's board).[12]

VISIT THE NET

Elaborates on role of a board of directors.

www.csuchico.edu/mgmt/
strategy/module1/
sld054.htm

TABLE 6–6   Board of Director Duties and Responsibilities

1. CONTROL AND OVERSIGHT OVER MANAGEMENT
   a. Select the Chief Executive Officer
   b. Sanction the CEO's team
   c. Provide the CEO with a forum
   d. Assure managerial competency
   e. Evaluate management's performance
   f. Set management's salary levels, including fringe benefits
   g. Guarantee managerial integrity through continuous auditing
   h. Chart the corporate course
   i. Devise and revise policies to be implemented by management

2. ADHERENCE TO LEGAL PRESCRIPTIONS
   a. Keep abreast of new laws
   b. Ensure the entire organization fulfills legal prescriptions
   c. Pass bylaws and related resolutions
   d. Select new directors
   e. Approve capital budgets
   f. Authorize borrowing, new stock issues, bonds, and so on

3. CONSIDERATION OF STAKEHOLDERS' INTERESTS
   a. Monitor product quality
   b. Facilitate upward progression in employee quality of work life
   c. Review labor policies and practices
   d. Improve the customer climate
   e. Keep community relations at the highest level
   f. Use influence to better governmental, professional association, and educational contacts
   g. Maintain good public image

4. ADVANCEMENT OF STOCKHOLDERS' RIGHTS
   a. Preserve stockholders' equity
   b. Stimulate corporate growth so that the firm will survive and flourish
   c. Guard against equity dilution
   d. Assure equitable stockholder representation
   e. Inform stockholders through letters, reports, and meetings
   f. Declare proper dividends
   g. Guarantee corporate survival

BusinessWeek identified some of the "worst" boards as those at Apple, Conseco, Gap, Kmart, Qwest, Tyson Foods, and Xerox and the "best" boards as those at 3M, Apria Healthcare, Colgate-Palmolive, General Electric, Home Depot, Intel, Johnson & Johnson, Medtronic, Pfizer, and Texas Instruments. Being a member of a board of directors today requires much more time, is much more difficult, and requires much more technical knowledge and financial commitment than in the past. Jeff

E-COMMERCE PERSPECTIVE

Board of Directors Doing Their Work Online

Directors today must have a better understanding of their firms' operations and doing business online on their own private, secure sites is now the practice of 23 percent of corporations in the U.S. In addition to H-P, other firms that have boards doing most of their business online include Cinergy, Albertson's, Intel, Motorola, and Tyco International. Some of these firms say they feel safer sending out confidential information electronically than relying on couriers to hand-deliver briefing packets.

The Sarbanes-Oxley Act of 2002 includes governance reforms that require audit committees of boards to meet far more frequently than in the past, so online meetings are especially well received by these members of boards. This Act establishes "best practices" of boards of directors of public firms; even private firms are rapidly moving to adopt these new standards and procedures.

Several lessons that pioneering firms offer to others in bringing boards of directors online are:

1. Establish strong security, password protected log-in, and firewalls on the special board of directors Web site.

2. Keep bulky graphics to a minimum since many directors at home or in hotels do not have fast Internet access.

3. Establish a telephone hotline to provide directors with technical support as needed.

4. Design the site in an easy manner where directors can easily access historical speeches, and so on.

5. Establish instant messaging, e-mail, and Web conferencing so directors can interact vigorously even though they may be thousands of miles apart.

An advantage of online board meetings is that the most talkative, strong-willed directors are less able to dominate discussions. E-mail allows more private contact between directors and this is an advantage. However, some CEOs feel threatened by directors who can scheme and plan together on their own through the special board Web site.

Source: Adapted from George Anders, "Run a Board Meeting," *Wall Street Journal* (September 15, 2003): R6.

Sonnerfeld, associate dean of the Yale School of Management, says: "Boards of directors are now rolling up their sleeves and becoming much more closely involved with management decision-making." Since the Enron and Worldcom scandals, company CEOs and boards are required to personally certify financial statements; company loans to company executives and directors are illegal, and there is faster reporting of insider stock transactions.

Just as directors are beginning to place more emphasis on staying informed about an organization's health and operations, they are also taking a more active role in ensuring that publicly issued documents are accurate representations of a firm's status. It is becoming widely recognized that a board of directors has legal responsibilities to stockholders and society for all company activities, for corporate performance, and for ensuring that a firm has an effective strategy. Failure to accept responsibility for auditing or evaluating a firm's strategy is considered a serious breach of a director's duties. Stockholders, government agencies, and customers are filing legal suits against directors for fraud, omissions, inaccurate disclosures, lack of due diligence, and culpable ignorance about a firm's operations with increasing frequency. Liability insurance for directors has become exceptionally expensive and has caused numerous directors to resign.

The Sarbanes-Oxley Act passed in July 2002 resulted in scores of boardroom overhauls among publicly traded companies. The jobs of chief executive and chairman are now held by separate persons and board audit committees must now have at least one financial expert as a member. Board audit committees now meet ten or more times per year, rather than three or four times as they did prior to the Act. The Act put an end to the "country club" atmosphere of most boards and has shifted power from CEOs to directors. Although aimed at public companies, the Act has also had a similar impact on privately owned companies.[13]

In Sweden, a new law has recently been passed requiring 25 percent female representation in boardrooms. The Norwegian government has passed a similar law that requires 40 percent of corporate director seats to go to women. In the United States, women currently hold about 13 percent of board seats at S&P 500 firms and 10 percent at S&P 1500 firms. The Investor Responsibility Research Center in Washington, D.C., reports that minorities hold just 8.8 percent of board seats of S&P 1500 companies. Progressive firms realize that women and minorities ask different questions and make different suggestions in boardrooms than white men, which is helpful because women and minorities comprise much of the consumer base everywhere.

A direct response of increased pressure on directors to stay informed and execute their responsibilities is that audit committees are becoming commonplace. A board of directors should conduct an annual strategy audit in much the same fashion that it reviews the annual financial audit. In performing such an audit, a board could work jointly with operating management and/or seek outside counsel. Boards should play a role beyond that of performing a strategic audit. They should provide greater input and advice in the strategy-formulation process to ensure that strategists are providing for the long-term needs of the firm. This is being done through the formation of three particular board committees: nominating committees to propose candidates for the board and senior officers of the firm; compensation committees to evaluate the performance of top executives and determine the terms and conditions of their employment; and audit committees to give board-level attention to company accounting and financial policies and performance.

CONCLUSION

VISIT THE NET

Provides answers to "Frequently Asked Questions About Strategic Planning."
www.allianceonline.org/
faqs.html

The essence of strategy formulation is an assessment of whether an organization is doing the right things and how it can be more effective in what it does. Every organization should be wary of becoming a prisoner of its own strategy, because even the best strategies become obsolete sooner or later. Regular reappraisal of strategy helps management avoid complacency. Objectives and strategies should be consciously developed and coordinated and should not merely evolve out of day-to-day operating decisions.

An organization with no sense of direction and no coherent strategy precipitates its own demise. When an organization does not know where it wants to go, it usually ends up some place it does not want to be. Every organization needs to consciously establish and communicate clear objectives and strategies.

Modern strategy-formulation tools and concepts are described in this chapter and integrated into a practical three-stage framework. Tools such as the SWOT Matrix, SPACE Matrix, BCG Matrix, IE Matrix, and QSPM can significantly enhance the quality of strategic decisions, but they should never be used to dictate the choice of strategies. Behavioral, cultural, and political aspects of strategy generation and selection are always important to consider and manage. Because of increased legal pressure from outside groups, boards of directors are assuming a more active role in strategy analysis and choice. This is a positive trend for organizations.

We invite you to visit the David page on the Prentice Hall Companion Web site at *www.prenhall.com/david* for this chapter's World Wide Web exercises.

KEY TERMS AND CONCEPTS

Aggressive Quadrant (p. 209)

Attractiveness Scores (AS) (p. 222)

Board of Directors (p. 226)

Boston Consulting Group (BCG) Matrix (p. 212)

Business Portfolio (p. 212)

Cash Cows (p. 212)

Champions (p. 226)

Competitive Advantage (CA) (p. 207)

Competitive Quadrant (p. 211)

Conservative Quadrant (p. 209)

Culture (p. 224)

Decision Stage (p. 201)

Defensive Quadrant (p. 209)

Directional Vector (p. 208)

Dogs (p. 213)

Environmental Stability (ES) (p. 207)

Financial Strength (FS) (p. 207)

Governance (p. 227)

Grand Strategy Matrix (p. 218)

Halo Error (p. 201)

Industry Strength (IS) (p. 207)

Input Stage (p. 200)

Internal-External (IE) Matrix (p. 214)

Matching (p. 202)

Matching Stage (p. 200)

Quantitative Strategic Planning Matrix (QSPM) (p. 220)

Question Marks (p. 212)

Relative Market Share Position (p. 212)

SO Strategies (p. 203)

ST Strategies (p. 203)

Stars (p. 212)

Strategic Position and Action Evaluation (SPACE) Matrix (p. 207)

Strategy-Formulation Framework (p. 201)

Sum Total Attractiveness Scores (STAS) (p. 223)

Strengths-Weaknesses-Opportunities-Threats (SWOT) Matrix (p. 202)

Sustainability (p. 200)

Total Attractiveness Scores (TAS) (p. 223)

WO Strategies (p. 203)

WT Strategies (p. 203)

ISSUES FOR REVIEW AND DISCUSSION

1. How would application of the strategy-formulation framework differ from a small to a large organization?
2. What types of strategies would you recommend for an organization that achieves total weighted scores of 3.6 on the IFE and 1.2 on the EFE Matrix?
3. Given the following information, develop a SPACE Matrix for the XYZ Corporation: FS = +2; ES = −6; CA = −2; IS = +4.
4. Given the information in the table below, develop a BCG Matrix and an IE Matrix:

Divisions	1	2	3
Profits	$10	$15	$25
Sales	$100	$50	$100
Relative Market Share	0.2	0.5	0.8
Industry Growth Rate	+.20	+.10	−.10
IFE Total Weighted Scores	1.6	3.1	2.2
EFE Total Weighted Scores	2.5	1.8	3.3

5. Explain the steps involved in developing a QSPM.

6. How would you develop a set of objectives for your school or business?
7. What do you think is the appropriate role of a board of directors in strategic management? Why?
8. Discuss the limitations of various strategy-formulation analytical techniques.
9. Explain why cultural factors should be an important consideration in analyzing and choosing among alternative strategies.
10. How are the SWOT Matrix, SPACE Matrix, BCG Matrix, IE Matrix, and Grand Strategy Matrix similar? How are they different?
11. How would for-profit and nonprofit organizations differ in their applications of the strategy-formulation framework?
12. Calculate the Relative Market Share Position of Nextel based on section C of Table 6–4 data.
13. Develop a SPACE Matrix for a company that is weak financially and is a weak competitor. The

industry for this company is pretty stable but the industry's projected growth in revenues and profits is not good. Label all axes and quadrants.

14. List four limitations of a BCG Matrix.

15. Make up an example to show clearly and completely that you can develop an IE Matrix for a three-division company, where each division has $10, $20, and $40 in revenues and $2, $4, and $1 in profits. State other assumptions needed. Label axes and quadrants.

16. What procedures could be necessary if the SPACE vector falls right on the axis between the Competitive and Defensive quadrants?

17. In a BCG Matrix or the Grand Strategy Matrix, what would you consider to be a rapid market (or industry) growth rate.

18. What are the pros and cons of a company (and country) participating in a Pollution Register?

19. How does the Sarbanes-Oxley Act of 2002 impact boards of directors?

20. Rank *BusinessWeek*'s "principles of good governance" from 1 to 14 (1 being most important and 14 least important), to reveal your assessment of these new rules.

21. Why is it important to work row-by-row instead of column-by-column in preparing a QSPM?

22. Why should one avoid putting double 4's in a row in preparing a QSPM?

23. Envision a QSPM with no weight column. Would that still be a useful analysis? Why or why not? What do you lose by deleting the weight column?

24. Prepare a BCG Matrix for a two-division firm with sales of $5 and $8 versus profits of $3 and $1, respectively? State assumptions for the RMSP and IGR axes to enable you to construct the diagram.

25. Consider developing a before-and-after BCG or IE Matrix to reveal the expected results of your proposed strategies. What limitation of the analysis would this procedure somewhat overcome?

26. If a firm has the leading market share in its industry, where on the BCG Matrix would the circle lie?

27. If a firm competes in a very unstable industry such as telecommunications, where on the ES axis of the SPACE Matrix would you plot the appropriate point?

28. Why do you think the SWOT Matrix is the most widely used of all strategy matrices?

29. The strategy templates described at the *www.strategyclub.com* Web site have templates for all of the Chapter 6 matrices. How could those templates be useful in preparing an example BCG or IE Matrix?

NOTES

1. Jane Kim, "Business Schools Take a Page from Kinder, Gentler Textbook," *Wall Street Journal* (October 22, 2003): B2C.

2. R. T. Lenz, "Managing the Evolution of the Strategic Planning Process," *Business Horizons* 30, no. 1 (January–February 1987): 37.

3. Robert Grant, "The Resource-Based Theory of Competitive Advantage: Implications for Strategy Formulation," *California Management Review* (Spring 1991): 114.

4. Heinz Weihrich, "The TOWS Matrix: A Tool for Situational Analysis," *Long Range Planning* 15, no. 2 (April 1982): 61. Note: Although Dr. Weihrich first modified SWOT analysis to form the TOWS matrix, the acronym SWOT is much more widely used than TOWS in practice, so this tenth edition reflects a change to SWOT from the use of TOWS in earlier editions.

5. H. Rowe, R. Mason, and K. Dickel, *Strategic Management and Business Policy: A Methodological Approach* (Reading, MA: Addison-Wesley Publishing Co. Inc., 1982): 155–156. Reprinted with permission of the publisher.

6. Fred David, "The Strategic Planning Matrix—A Quantitative Approach," *Long Range Planning* 19, no. 5 (October 1986): 102; Andre Gib and Robert Margulies, "Making Competitive Intelligence Relevant to the User," *Planning Review* 19, no. 3 (May–June 1991): 21.

7. Fred David, "Computer-Assisted Strategic Planning in Small Businesses," *Journal of Systems Management* 36, no. 7 (July 1985): 24–34.

8. Jon Swartz, "How Will Compaq, H-P Fit Together?" *USA Today* (September 6, 2001): 3B.

9. Y. Allarie and M. Firsirotu, "How to Implement Radical Strategies in Large Organizations," *Sloan Management Review* 26, no. 3 (Spring 1985): 19. Another excellent article is P. Shrivastava, "Integrating Strategy Formulation

with Organizational Culture," *Journal of Business Strategy* 5, no. 3 (Winter 1985): 103–111.

10. James Brian Quinn, *Strategies for Changes: Logical Incrementalism* (Homewood, IL: Richard D. Irwin, 1980): 128–145. These political tactics are listed in A. Thompson and A. Strickland, *Strategic Management: Concepts and Cases* (Plano, TX: Business Publications, 1984): 261.

11. William Guth and Ian MacMillan, "Strategy Implementation Versus Middle Management Self-Interest," *Strategic Management Journal* 7, no. 4 (July–August 1986): 321.

12. Louis Lavelle, "The Best and Worst Boards," *BusinessWeek* (October 7, 2002): 104–110.

13. Matt Murray, "Private Companies Also Feel Pressure to Clean Up Acts," *Wall Street Journal* (July 22, 2003): B1.

CURRENT READINGS

Aguilera, R. V., and G. Jackson. "The Cross-National Diversity of Corporate Governance: Dimensions and Determinants." *Academy of Management Review* 28, no. 3 (July 2003): 447–465.

Certo, S. T. "Influencing Initial Public Offering Investors with Prestige: Signaling with Board Structures." *Academy of Management Review* 28, no. 3 (July 2003): 432–446.

Daily, C. M., and D. R. Dalton. "Executive Briefing/Corporate Governance Digest." *Business Horizons* 46, no. 3 (May–June 2003): 2–5.

Daily, C. M., D. R. Dalton, and N. Rajagopalan. "Governance Through Ownership: Centuries of Practice, Decades of Research." *Academy of Management Journal* 46, no. 2 (April 2003): 151–159.

Daily, C. M., P. P. McDougall, J. G. Covin, and D. R. Dalton. "Governance and Strategic Leadership in Enterpreneurial Firms." *Journal of Management* 28, no. 3 (2002): 387–412.

Englehardt, C., and M. Nastanski. "Polling: An Element of Effective Corporate Governance." *Business Horizons* 45, no. 5 (September–October 2002): 19–26.

Filatotchev, I., and K. Bishop. "Board Composition: Share Ownership and 'Underpricing' of U.K. IPO Firms." *Strategic Management Journal* 23, no. 10 (October 2002): 941–956.

Hansen, F., and M. Smith. "Crisis in Corporate America: The Role of Strategy." *Business Horizons* 46, no. 1 (January–February 2003): 7–18.

Harrison, J. S., and D. D. Bergh. "Failed Takeover Attempts, Corporate Governance and Refocusing." *Strategic Management Journal* 24, no. 1 (January 2003): 87–95.

Henderson, J., and K. Cool. "Corporate Governance, Investment Bandwagons and Overcapacity: An Analysis of the Worldwide Petrochemical Industry, 1975–95." *Strategic Management Journal* 24, no. 4 (April 2003): 349–374.

Hillman, A. J., and T. Dalziel. "Boards of Directors and Firm Performance: Integrating Agency and Resource Dependence Perspectives." *Academy of Management Review* 28, no. 3 (July 2003): 383–396.

Lynall, M. D., B. R. Golden, and A. J. Hillman. "Board Composition from Adolescence to Maturity: A Multitheoretic View." *Academy of Management Review* 28, no. 3 (July 2003): 416–431.

Robins, J. A, and M. F. Wiersema. "The Measurement of Corporate Portfolio Strategy: Analysis of the Content Validity of Related Diversification Indexes." *Strategic Management Journal* 24, no. 1 (January 2003): 39–60.

Song, M., R. J. Calantone, and C. A. Di Benedetto. "Competitive Forces and Strategic Choice Decisions: An Experimental Investigation in the United States and Japan." *Strategic Management Journal* 23, no. 10 (October 2002): 969–980.

Sundaramurthy, C., and M. Lewis. "Control and Collaboration: Paradoxes of Governance." *Academy of Management Review* 28, no. 3 (July 2003): 397–415.

Tihanyi, L., R. A. Johnson, R. E. Hoskisson, and M. A. Hitt. "Institutional Ownership Differences and International Diversification: The Effects of Boards of Directors and Technological Opportunity." *Academy of Management Journal* 46, no. 2 (April 2003): 195–211.

Tuschke, A., and W. G. Sanders. "Antecedents and Consequences of Corporate Governance Reform: The Case of Germany." *Strategic Management Journal* 24, no. 7 (July 2003): 631–650.

Implementing Strategies: Management and Operations Issues

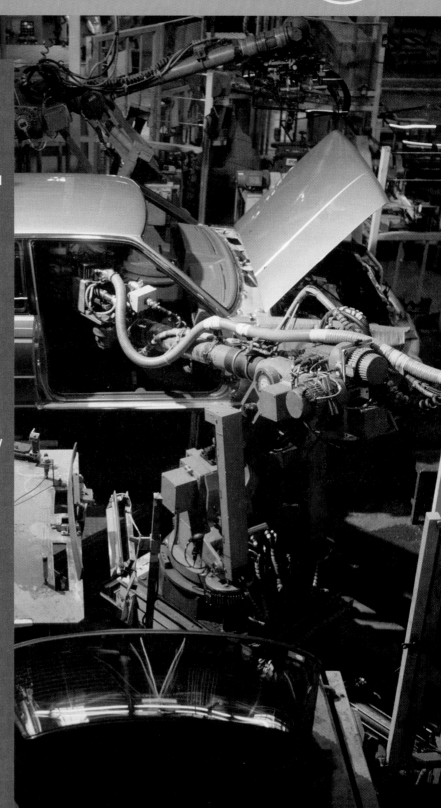

chapter objectives

After studying this chapter, you should be able to do the following:

1. Explain why strategy implementation is more difficult than strategy formulation.

2. Discuss the importance of annual objectives and policies in achieving organizational commitment for strategies to be implemented.

3. Explain why organizational structure is so important in strategy implementation.

4. Compare and contrast restructuring and reengineering.

5. Describe the relationships between production/operations and strategy implementation.

6. Explain how a firm can effectively link performance and pay to strategies.

7. Discuss employee stock ownership plans (ESOPs) as a strategic-management concept.

8. Describe how to modify an organizational culture to support new strategies.

9. Discuss the culture in Mexico, Russia, and Japan.

10. Describe the glass ceiling in the United States.

experiential exercises

Experiential Exercise 7A
Revising Krispy Kreme Doughnuts' (KKD's) Organizational Chart

Experiential Exercise 7B
Do Organizations Really Establish Objectives?

Experiential Exercise 7C
Understanding My University's Culture

"notable quotes"

You want your people to run the business as if it were their own.
William Fulmer

Poor Ike; when he was a general, he gave an order and it was carried out. Now, he's going to sit in that office and give an order and not a damn thing is going to happen.
Harry Truman

Changing your pay plan is a big risk, but not changing it could be a bigger one.
Nancy Perry

Objectives can be compared to a compass bearing by which a ship navigates. A compass bearing is firm, but in actual navigation, a ship may veer off its course for many miles. Without a compass bearing, a ship would neither find its port nor be able to estimate the time required to get there.
Peter Drucker

The best game plan in the world never blocked or tackled anybody.
Vince Lombardi

Pretend that every single person you meet has a sign around his or her neck that says, "Make me feel important."
Mary Kay Ash

The strategic-management process does not end when the firm decides what strategy or strategies to pursue. There must be a translation of strategic thought into strategic action. This translation is much easier if managers and employees of the firm understand the business, feel a part of the company, and through involvement in strategy-formulation activities have become committed to helping the organization succeed. Without understanding and commitment, strategy-implementation efforts face major problems.

Implementing strategy affects an organization from top to bottom; it affects all the functional and divisional areas of a business. It is beyond the purpose and scope of this text to examine all of the business administration concepts and tools important in strategy implementation. This chapter focuses on management issues most central to implementing strategies in the year 2003, and Chapter 8 focuses on marketing, finance/accounting, R&D, and management information systems issues.

VISIT THE NET

Gives a good definition of strategy implementation.
www.csuchico.edu/mgmt/
strategy/module/
sld044.htm

Even the most technically perfect strategic plan will serve little purpose if it is not implemented. Many organizations tend to spend an inordinate amount of time, money, and effort on developing the strategic plan, treating the means and circumstances under which it will be implemented as afterthoughts! Change comes through implementation and evaluation, not through the plan. A technically imperfect plan that is implemented well will achieve more than the perfect plan that never gets off the paper on which it is typed.[1]

The Nature of Strategy Implementation

The strategy-implementation stage of strategic management is revealed in Figure 7–1. Successful strategy formulation does not guarantee successful strategy implementation. It is always more difficult to do something (strategy implementation) than to say you are going to do it (strategy formulation)! Although inextricably linked, strategy implementation is fundamentally different from strategy formulation. Strategy formulation and implementation can be contrasted in the following ways:

- Strategy formulation is positioning forces before the action.
- Strategy implementation is managing forces during the action.
- Strategy formulation focuses on effectiveness.
- Strategy implementation focuses on efficiency.
- Strategy formulation is primarily an intellectual process.
- Strategy implementation is primarily an operational process.
- Strategy formulation requires good intuitive and analytical skills.
- Strategy implementation requires special motivation and leadership skills.
- Strategy formulation requires coordination among a few individuals.
- Strategy implementation requires coordination among many individuals.

Strategy-formulation concepts and tools do not differ greatly for small, large, forprofit, or nonprofit organizations. However, strategy implementation varies substantially among different types and sizes of organizations. Implementing strategies requires such actions as altering sales territories, adding new departments, closing facilities, hiring new employees, changing an organization's pricing strategy, devel-

FIGURE 7–1

Comprehensive Strategic-Management Model

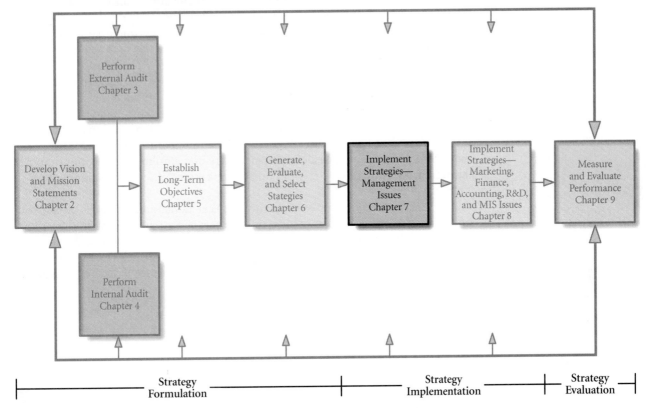

oping financial budgets, developing new employee benefits, establishing cost-control procedures, changing advertising strategies, building new facilities, training new employees, transferring managers among divisions, and building a better management information system. These types of activities obviously differ greatly between manufacturing, service, and governmental organizations.

Management Perspectives

In all but the smallest organizations, the transition from strategy formulation to strategy implementation requires a shift in responsibility from strategists to divisional and functional managers. Implementation problems can arise because of this shift in responsibility, especially if strategy-formulation decisions come as a surprise to middle- and lower-level managers. Managers and employees are motivated more by perceived self-interests than by organizational interests, unless the two coincide. Therefore, it is essential that divisional and functional managers be involved as much as possible in strategy-formulation activities. Of equal importance, strategists should be involved as much as possible in strategy-implementation activities.

Management issues central to strategy implementation include establishing annual objectives, devising policies, allocating resources, altering an existing organizational structure, restructuring and reengineering, revising reward and incentive plans, minimizing resistance to change, matching managers with strategy, developing a strategy-supportive culture, adapting production/operations processes, developing an effective human resource function and, if necessary, downsizing.

Management changes are necessarily more extensive when strategies to be implemented move a firm in a major new direction.

Managers and employees throughout an organization should participate early and directly in strategy-implementation decisions. Their role in strategy implementation should build upon prior involvement in strategy-formulation activities. Strategists' genuine personal commitment to implementation is a necessary and powerful motivational force for managers and employees. Too often, strategists are too busy to actively support strategy-implementation efforts, and their lack of interest can be detrimental to organizational success. The rationale for objectives and strategies should be understood and clearly communicated throughout an organization. Major competitors' accomplishments, products, plans, actions, and performance should be apparent to all organizational members. Major external opportunities and threats should be clear, and managers' and employees' questions should be answered. Top-down flow of communication is essential for developing bottom-up support.

Firms need to develop a competitor focus at all hierarchical levels by gathering and widely distributing competitive intelligence; every employee should be able to benchmark her or his efforts against best-in-class competitors so that the challenge becomes personal. This is a challenge for strategists of the firm. Firms should provide training for both managers and employees to ensure that they have and maintain the skills necessary to be world-class performers.

Annual Objectives

Establishing annual objectives is a decentralized activity that directly involves all managers in an organization. Active participation in establishing annual objectives can lead to acceptance and commitment. *Annual objectives* are essential for strategy implementation because they (1) represent the basis for allocating resources; (2) are a primary mechanism for evaluating managers; (3) are the major instrument for monitoring progress toward achieving long-term objectives; and (4) establish organizational, divisional, and departmental priorities. Considerable time and effort should be devoted to ensuring that annual objectives are well conceived, consistent with long-term objectives, and supportive of strategies to be implemented. Approving, revising, or rejecting annual objectives is much more than a rubber-stamp activity. The purpose of annual objectives can be summarized as follows:

> Annual objectives serve as guidelines for action, directing and channeling efforts and activities of organization members. They provide a source of legitimacy in an enterprise by justifying activities to stakeholders. They serve as standards of performance. They serve as an important source of employee motivation and identification. They give incentives for managers and employees to perform. They provide a basis for organizational design.[2]

Clearly stated and communicated objectives are critical to success in all types and sizes of firms. Annual objectives, stated in terms of profitability, growth, and market share by business segment, geographic area, customer groups, and product are common in organizations. Figure 7–2 illustrates how the Stamus Company could establish annual objectives based on long-term objectives. Table 7–1 reveals associ-

FIGURE 7–2

The Stamus Company's Hierarchy of Aims

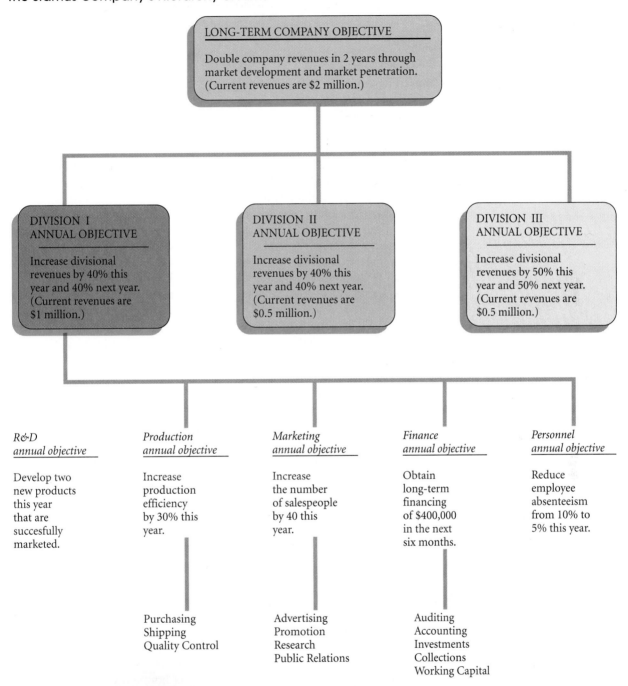

ated revenue figures that correspond to the objectives outlined in Figure 7–2. Note that, according to plan, the Stamus Company will slightly exceed its long-term objective of doubling company revenues between 2004 and the year 2006.

Figure 7–2 also reflects how a hierarchy of annual objectives can be established based on an organization's structure. Objectives should be consistent across hierarchical levels and form a network of supportive aims. *Horizontal consistency of objectives* is

TABLE 7–1   The Stamus Company's Revenue Expectations (in millions of dollars)

	2004	2005	2006
Division I Revenues	1.0	1.400	1.960
Division II Revenues	0.5	0.700	0.980
Division III Revenues	0.5	0.750	1.125
Total Company Revenues	2.0	2.850	4.065

as important as *vertical consistency of objectives.* For instance, it would not be effective for manufacturing to achieve more than its annual objective of units produced if marketing could not sell the additional units.

Annual objectives should be measurable, consistent, reasonable, challenging, clear, communicated throughout the organization, characterized by an appropriate time dimension, and accompanied by commensurate rewards and sanctions. Too often, objectives are stated in generalities, with little operational usefulness. Annual objectives such as "to improve communication" or "to improve performance" are not clear, specific, or measurable. Objectives should state quantity, quality, cost, and time—and also be verifiable. Terms and phrases such as *maximize, minimize, as soon as possible,* and *adequate* should be avoided.

Annual objectives should be compatible with employees' and managers' values and should be supported by clearly stated policies. More of something is not always better! Improved quality or reduced cost may, for example, be more important than quantity. It is important to tie rewards and sanctions to annual objectives so that employees and managers understand that achieving objectives is critical to successful strategy implementation. Clear annual objectives do not guarantee successful strategy implementation, but they do increase the likelihood that personal and organizational aims can be accomplished. Overemphasis on achieving objectives can result in undesirable conduct, such as faking the numbers, distorting the records, and letting objectives become ends in themselves. Managers must be alert to these potential problems.

Policies

Changes in a firm's strategic direction do not occur automatically. On a day-to-day basis, policies are needed to make a strategy work. Policies facilitate solving recurring problems and guide the implementation of strategy. Broadly defined, *policy* refers to specific guidelines, methods, procedures, rules, forms, and administrative practices established to support and encourage work toward stated goals. Policies are instruments for strategy implementation. Policies set boundaries, constraints, and limits on the kinds of administrative actions that can be taken to reward and sanction behavior; they clarify what can and cannot be done in pursuit of an organization's objectives. For example, Carnival's *Paradise* ship has a no-smoking policy anywhere, anytime aboard ship. It is the first cruise ship to comprehensively ban smoking. Another example of corporate policy relates to surfing the Web while at work. About 40 percent of companies today do not have a formal policy preventing employees from surfing the Internet, but software is being marketed now that allows firms to monitor how, when, where, and how long various employees use the Internet at work.

Policies let both employees and managers know what is expected of them, thereby increasing the likelihood that strategies will be implemented successfully. They provide a basis for management control, allow coordination across organizational units, and reduce the amount of time managers spend making decisions. Policies also clarify what work is to be done and by whom. They promote delegation of decision making to appropriate managerial levels where various problems usually arise. Many organizations have a policy manual that serves to guide and direct behavior. Wal-Mart has a policy that it calls the "10 Foot" Rule, whereby customers can find assistance within ten feet of anywhere in the store. This is a welcomed policy in Japan where Wal-Mart is trying to gain a foothold; 58 percent of all retailers in Japan are mom-and-pop stores and consumers historically have had to pay "top yen" rather than "discounted prices" for merchandise.

Policies can apply to all divisions and departments (for example, "We are an equal opportunity employer"). Some policies apply to a single department ("Employees in this department must take at least one training and development course each year"). Whatever their scope and form, policies serve as a mechanism for implementing strategies and obtaining objectives. Policies should be stated in writing whenever possible. They represent the means for carrying out strategic decisions. Examples of policies that support a company strategy, a divisional objective, and a departmental objective are given in Table 7–2.

Some example issues that may require a management policy are as follows:

- To offer extensive or limited management development workshops and seminars
- To centralize or decentralize employee-training activities
- To recruit through employment agencies, college campuses, and/or newspapers
- To promote from within or to hire from the outside
- To promote on the basis of merit or on the basis of seniority
- To tie executive compensation to long-term and/or annual objectives
- To offer numerous or few employee benefits
- To negotiate directly or indirectly with labor unions
- To delegate authority for large expenditures or to retain this authority centrally
- To allow much, some, or no overtime work
- To establish a high- or low-safety stock of inventory
- To use one or more suppliers
- To buy, lease, or rent new production equipment
- To stress quality control greatly or not
- To establish many or only a few production standards
- To operate one, two, or three shifts
- To discourage using insider information for personal gain
- To discourage sexual harassment
- To discourage smoking at work
- To discourage insider trading
- To discourage moonlighting

TABLE 7-2   A Hierarchy of Policies

Company Strategy
Acquire a chain of retail stores to meet our sales growth and profitability objectives.

Supporting Policies
1. "All stores will be open from 8 A.M. to 8 P.M. Monday through Saturday." (This policy could increase retail sales if stores currently are open only 40 hours a week.)
2. "All stores must submit a Monthly Control Data Report." (This policy could reduce expense-to-sales ratios.)
3. "All stores must support company advertising by contributing 5 percent of their total monthly revenues for this purpose." (This policy could allow the company to establish a national reputation.)
4. "All stores must adhere to the uniform pricing guidelines set forth in the Company Handbook." (This policy could help assure customers that the company offers a consistent product in terms of price and quality in all its stores.)

Divisional Objective
Increase the division's revenues from $10 million in 2004 to $15 million in 2005.

Supporting Policies
1. "Beginning in January 2004, each one of this division's salespersons must file a weekly activity report that includes the number of calls made, the number of miles traveled, the number of units sold, the dollar volume sold, and the number of new accounts opened." (This policy could ensure that salespersons do not place too great an emphasis in certain areas.)
2. "Beginning in January 2004, this division will return to its employees 5 percent of its gross revenues in the form of a Christmas bonus." (This policy could increase employee productivity.)
3. "Beginning in January 2004, inventory levels carried in warehouses will be decreased by 30 percent in accordance with a Just-in-Time (JIT) manufacturing approach." (This policy could reduce production expenses and thus free funds for increased marketing efforts.)

Production Department Objective
Increase production from 20,000 units in 2004 to 30,000 units in 2005.

Supporting Policies
1. "Beginning in January 2004, employees will have the option of working up to 20 hours of overtime per week." (This policy could minimize the need to hire additional employees.)
2. "Beginning in January 2004, perfect attendance awards in the amount of $100 will be given to all employees who do not miss a workday in a given year." (This policy could decrease absenteeism and increase productivity.)
3. "Beginning in January 2004, new equipment must be leased rather than purchased." (This policy could reduce tax liabilities and thus allow more funds to be invested in modernizing production processes.)

Resource Allocation

Resource allocation is a central management activity that allows for strategy execution. In organizations that do not use a strategic-management approach to decision making, resource allocation is often based on political or personal factors. Strategic management enables resources to be allocated according to priorities established by annual objectives.

Nothing could be more detrimental to strategic management and to organizational success than for resources to be allocated in ways not consistent with priorities indicated by approved annual objectives.

All organizations have at least four types of resources that can be used to achieve desired objectives: financial resources, physical resources, human resources, and technological resources. Allocating resources to particular divisions and departments does not mean that strategies will be successfully implemented. A number of factors commonly prohibit effective resource allocation, including an overprotection of resources, too great an emphasis on short-run financial criteria, organizational politics, vague strategy targets, a reluctance to take risks, and a lack of sufficient knowledge.

Below the corporate level, there often exists an absence of systematic thinking about resources allocated and strategies of the firm. Yavitz and Newman explain why:

> Managers normally have many more tasks than they can do. Managers must allocate time and resources among these tasks. Pressure builds up. Expenses are too high. The CEO wants a good financial report for the third quarter. Strategy formulation and implementation activities often get deferred. Today's problems soak up available energies and resources. Scrambled accounts and budgets fail to reveal the shift in allocation away from strategic needs to currently squeaking wheels.[3]

The real value of any resource allocation program lies in the resulting accomplishment of an organization's objectives. Effective resource allocation does not guarantee successful strategy implementation because programs, personnel, controls, and commitment must breathe life into the resources provided. Strategic management itself is sometimes referred to as a "resource allocation process."

Managing Conflict

Interdependency of objectives and competition for limited resources often leads to conflict. *Conflict* can be defined as a disagreement between two or more parties on one or more issues. Establishing annual objectives can lead to conflict because individuals have different expectations and perceptions, schedules create pressure, personalities are incompatible, and misunderstandings between line managers (such as production supervisors) and staff managers (such as human resource specialists) occur. For example, a collection manager's objective of reducing bad debts by 50 percent in a given year may conflict with a divisional objective to increase sales by 20 percent.

Establishing objectives can lead to conflict because managers and strategists must make trade-offs, such as whether to emphasize short-term profits or long-term growth, profit margin or market share, market penetration or market development, growth or stability, high risk or low risk, and social responsiveness or profit maximization. Conflict is unavoidable in organizations, so it is important that conflict be managed and resolved before dysfunctional consequences affect organizational performance. Conflict is not always bad. An absence of conflict can signal indifference and apathy. Conflict can serve to energize opposing groups into action and may help managers identify problems.

Various approaches for managing and resolving conflict can be classified into three categories: avoidance, defusion, and confrontation. *Avoidance* includes such actions as ignoring the problem in hopes that the conflict will resolve itself or physically separating the conflicting individuals (or groups). *Defusion* can include playing down differences between conflicting parties while accentuating similarities and common interests, compromising so that there is neither a clear winner nor loser, resorting to majority rule, appealing to a higher authority, or redesigning present positions. *Confrontation* is exemplified by exchanging members of conflicting parties so that each can gain an appreciation of the other's point of view, or holding a meeting at which conflicting parties present their views and work through their differences.

Matching Structure with Strategy

VISIT THE NET

Provides software to draw organizational charts easily.
www.smartdraw.com
You may download the SmartDraw software and use it free for thirty days.

Changes in strategy often require changes in the way an organization is structured for two major reasons. First, structure largely dictates how objectives and policies will be established. For example, objectives and policies established under a geographic organizational structure are couched in geographic terms. Objectives and policies are stated largely in terms of products in an organization whose structure is based on product groups. The structural format for developing objectives and policies can significantly impact all other strategy-implementation activities.

The second major reason why changes in strategy often require changes in structure is that structure dictates how resources will be allocated. If an organization's structure is based on customer groups, then resources will be allocated in that manner. Similarly, if an organization's structure is set up along functional business lines, then resources are allocated by functional areas. Unless new or revised strategies place emphasis in the same areas as old strategies, structural reorientation commonly becomes a part of strategy implementation.

Changes in strategy lead to changes in organizational structure. Structure should be designed to facilitate the strategic pursuit of a firm and, therefore, follows strategy. Without a strategy or reasons for being (mission), companies find it difficult to design an effective structure. Chandler found a particular structure sequence to be often repeated as organizations grow and change strategy over time; this sequence is depicted in Figure 7–3.

There is no one optimal organizational design or structure for a given strategy or type of organization. What is appropriate for one organization may not be appropriate for a similar firm, although successful firms in a given industry do tend to

FIGURE 7–3
Chandler's Strategy-Structure Relationship

Source: Adapted from Alfred Chandler, *Strategy and Structure* (Cambridge, MA: MIT Press, 1962).

organize themselves in a similar way. For example, consumer goods companies tend to emulate the divisional structure-by-product form of organization. Small firms tend to be functionally structured (centralized). Medium-sized firms tend to be divisionally structured (decentralized). Large firms tend to use a SBU (strategic business unit) or matrix structure. As organizations grow, their structures generally change from simple to complex as a result of concatenation, or the linking together of several basic strategies.

Numerous external and internal forces affect an organization; no firm could change its structure in response to every one of these forces, because to do so would lead to chaos. However, when a firm changes its strategy, the existing organizational structure may become ineffective. Symptoms of an ineffective organizational structure include too many levels of management, too many meetings attended by too many people, too much attention being directed toward solving interdepartmental conflicts, too large a span of control, and too many unachieved objectives. Changes in structure can facilitate strategy-implementation efforts, but changes in structure should not be expected to make a bad strategy good, to make bad managers good, or to make bad products sell.

Structure undeniably can and does influence strategy. Strategies formulated must be workable, so if a certain new strategy required massive structural changes it would not be an attractive choice. In this way, structure can shape the choice of strategies. But a more important concern is determining what types of structural changes are needed to implement new strategies and how these changes can best be accomplished. We examine this issue by focusing on seven basic types of organizational structure: functional, divisional by geographic area, divisional by product, divisional by customer, divisional process, strategic business unit (SBU), and matrix.

VISIT THE NET

Lists some items that strategy implementation must include.
www.csuchico.edu/mgmt/ strategy/module1/ sld045.htm

The Functional Structure

The most widely used structure is the functional or centralized type because this structure is the simplest and least expensive of the seven alternatives. A *functional structure* groups tasks and activities by business function, such as production/operations, marketing, finance/accounting, research and development, and management information systems. A university may structure its activities by major functions that include academic affairs, student services, alumni relations, athletics, maintenance, and accounting. Besides being simple and inexpensive, a functional structure also promotes specialization of labor, encourages efficiency, minimizes the need for an elaborate control system, and allows rapid decision making. Some disadvantages of a functional structure are that it forces accountability to the top, minimizes career development opportunities, and is sometimes characterized by low employee morale, line/staff conflicts, poor delegation of authority, and inadequate planning for products and markets. Most large companies abandoned the functional structure in favor of decentralization and improved accountability.

The Divisional Structure

The *divisional* or *decentralized structure* is the second-most common type used by American businesses. As a small organization grows, it has more difficulty managing different products and services in different markets. Some form of divisional structure generally becomes necessary to motivate employees, control operations, and compete successfully in diverse locations. The divisional structure can be organized in one of four ways: by geographic area, by product or service, by customer, or by process. With a divisional structure, functional activities are performed both centrally and in each separate division.

Cisco Systems recently discarded its divisional structure by customer and reorganized into a functional structure. CEO John Chambers replaced the three-customer structure based on big businesses, small businesses, and telecoms, and now the company has centralized its engineering and marketing units so that they focus on technologies such as wireless networks. Chambers says the goal was to eliminate duplication, but the change should not be viewed as a shift in strategy. Chambers' span of control in the new structure is reduced from fifteen to twelve managers reporting directly to him. He continues to operate Cisco without a chief operating officer or a number-two executive.

Kodak recently reduced its number of business units from seven by-customer divisions to five by-product divisions. As consumption patterns become increasingly similar worldwide, a by-product structure is becoming more effective than a by-customer or a by-geographic type divisional structure. In the restructuring, Kodak eliminated its global operations division and distributed those responsibilities across the new by-product divisions.

A divisional structure has some clear advantages. First and perhaps foremost, accountability is clear. That is, divisional managers can be held responsible for sales and profit levels. Because a divisional structure is based on extensive delegation of authority, managers and employees can easily see the results of their good or bad performances. As a result, employee morale is generally higher in a divisional structure than it is in a centralized structure. Other advantages of the divisional design are that it creates career development opportunities for managers, allows local control of situations, leads to a competitive climate within an organization, and allows new businesses and products to be added easily.

The divisional design is not without some limitations, however. Perhaps the most important limitation is that a divisional structure is costly, for a number of reasons. First, each division requires functional specialists who must be paid. Second, there exists some duplication of staff services, facilities, and personnel; for instance, functional specialists are also needed centrally (at headquarters) to coordinate divisional activities. Third, managers must be well qualified because the divisional design forces delegation of authority; better-qualified individuals require higher salaries. A divisional structure can also be costly because it requires an elaborate, headquarters-driven control system. Finally, certain regions, products, or customers may sometimes receive special treatment, and it may be difficult to maintain consistent, companywide practices. Nonetheless, for most large organizations and many small firms, the advantages of a divisional structure more than offset the potential limitations.

A *divisional structure by geographic area* is appropriate for organizations whose strategies need to be tailored to fit the particular needs and characteristics of customers in different geographic areas. This type of structure can be most appropriate for organizations that have similar branch facilities located in widely dispersed areas. A divisional structure by geographic area allows local participation in decision making and improved coordination within a region.

The *divisional structure by product (or services)* is most effective for implementing strategies when specific products or services need special emphasis. Also, this type of structure is widely used when an organization offers only a few products or services, or when an organization's products or services differ substantially. The divisional structure allows strict control over and attention to product lines, but it may also require a more skilled management force and reduced top management control. General Motors, DuPont, and Procter & Gamble use a divisional structure by product to implement strategies. Huffy, the largest bicycle company in the world, is another firm that is highly decentralized based on a divisional-by-product structure. Based in Ohio, Huffy's divisions are the Bicycle division, the Gerry Baby Products division, the

Huffy Sports division, YLC Enterprises, and Washington Inventory Service. Harry Shaw, Huffy's chairman, believes decentralization is one of the keys to Huffy's success.

Eastman Chemical established a new by-product divisional organizational structure. The company's two new divisions, Eastman Company and Voridian Company, focus on chemicals and polymers, respectively. The Eastman division focuses on coatings, adhesives, inks, and plastics, whereas the Voridian division focuses on fibers, polyethylene, and other polymers.

When a few major customers are of paramount importance and many different services are provided to these customers, then a *divisional structure by customer* can be the most effective way to implement strategies. This structure allows an organization to cater effectively to the requirements of clearly defined customer groups. For example, book publishing companies often organize their activities around customer groups such as colleges, secondary schools, and private commercial schools. Some airline companies have two major customer divisions: passengers and freight or cargo services. Merrill Lynch is organized into separate divisions that cater to different groups of customers, including wealthy individuals, institutional investors, and small corporations. Motorola's semiconductor chip division is also organized divisionally by customer, having three separate segments that sell to (1) the automotive and industrial market, (2) the mobile phone market, and (3) the data-networking market. The automotive and industrial segment is doing well but the other two segments are faltering, which is a reason why Motorola is trying to divest its semiconductor operations.

A *divisional structure by process* is similar to a functional structure, because activities are organized according to the way work is actually performed. However, a key difference between these two designs is that functional departments are not accountable for profits or revenues, whereas divisional process departments are evaluated on these criteria. An example of a divisional structure by process is a manufacturing business organized into six divisions: electrical work, glass cutting, welding, grinding, painting, and foundry work. In this case, all operations related to these specific processes would be grouped under the separate divisions. Each process (division) would be responsible for generating revenues and profits. The divisional structure by process can be particularly effective in achieving objectives when distinct production processes represent the thrust of competitiveness in an industry.

The Strategic Business Unit (SBU) Structure

As the number, size, and diversity of divisions in an organization increase, controlling and evaluating divisional operations become increasingly difficult for strategists. Increases in sales often are not accompanied by similar increases in profitability. The span of control becomes too large at top levels of the firm. For example, in a large conglomerate organization composed of ninety divisions, the chief executive officer could have difficulty even remembering the first names of divisional presidents. In multidivisional organizations, an SBU structure can greatly facilitate strategy-implementation efforts.

The SBU *structure* groups similar divisions into strategic business units and delegates authority and responsibility for each unit to a senior executive who reports directly to the chief executive officer. This change in structure can facilitate strategy implementation by improving coordination between similar divisions and channeling accountability to distinct business units. In the ninety-division conglomerate just mentioned, the ninety divisions could perhaps be regrouped into ten SBUs according

FIGURE 7–4

Sonoco Products' SBU Organizational Chart

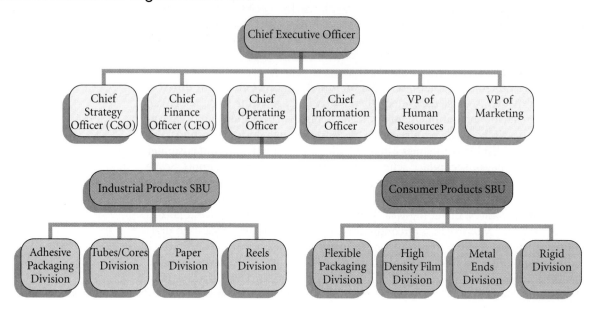

to certain common characteristics, such as competing in the same industry, being located in the same area, or having the same customers.

Two disadvantages of an SBU structure are that it requires an additional layer of management, which increases salary expenses, and the role of the group vice president is often ambiguous. However, these limitations often do not outweigh the advantages of improved coordination and accountability. Atlantic Richfield and Fairchild Industries are examples of firms that successfully use an SBU-type structure.

As illustrated in Figure 7–4, Sonoco Products Corporation, based in Hartsville, South Carolina, utilizes an SBU organizational structure. Note that Sonoco's SBU's, Industrial Products and Consumer Products, each have four autonomous divisions that have their own sales, manufacturing, R&D, finance, HRM, and MIS functions.

The Matrix Structure

A *matrix structure* is the most complex of all designs because it depends upon both vertical and horizontal flows of authority and communication (hence the term *matrix*). In contrast, functional and divisional structures depend primarily on vertical flows of authority and communication. A matrix structure can result in higher overhead because it creates more management positions. Other characteristics of a matrix structure that contribute to overall complexity include dual lines of budget authority (a violation of the unity-of-command principle), dual sources of reward and punishment, shared authority, dual reporting channels, and a need for an extensive and effective communication system.

Despite its complexity, the matrix structure is widely used in many industries, including construction, healthcare, research, and defense. Some advantages of a matrix structure are that project objectives are clear, there are many channels of communication, workers can see the visible results of their work, and shutting down a project can be accomplished relatively easily.

In order for a matrix structure to be effective, organizations need participative planning, training, clear mutual understanding of roles and responsibilities, excellent internal communication, and mutual trust and confidence. The matrix structure is being used more frequently by American businesses because firms are pursuing strategies that add new products, customer groups, and technology to their range of activities. Out of these changes are coming product managers, functional managers, and geographic-area managers, all of whom have important strategic responsibilities. When several variables, such as product, customer, technology, geography, functional area, and line of business, have roughly equal strategic priorities, a matrix organization can be an effective structural form.

Restructuring, Reengineering and E-Engineering

Restructuring and reengineering are becoming commonplace on the corporate landscape across the United States and Europe. *Restructuring*—also called downsizing, rightsizing, or *delayering*—involves reducing the size of the firm in terms of number of employees, number of divisions or units, and number of hierarchical levels in the firm's organizational structure. This reduction in size is intended to imporve both efficiency and effectiveness. Restructuring is concerned primarily with shareholder well-being rather than employee well-being.

VISIT THE NET

Provides a PowerPoint presentation on downsizing (restructuring).
www.cl.uh.edu/bpa/hadm/
HADM_5731/ppt_
presentations/7down/
index.htm

Recessionary economic conditions have forced many European companies to downsize, laying off managers and employees. This was almost unheard of prior to the mid-1990s because European labor unions and laws required lengthy negotiations or huge severance checks before workers could be terminated. In contrast to the United States, labor union executives sit on most boards of directors of large European firms.

Job security in European companies is slowly moving toward a U.S. scenario, in which firms lay off almost at will. From banks in Milan to factories in Mannheim, European employers are starting to show people the door in an effort to streamline operations, increase efficiency, and compete against already slim and trim U.S. firms. Massive U.S.-style layoffs are still rare in Europe, but unemployment rates throughout the continent are rising quite rapidly. European firms still prefer to downsize by attrition and retirement rather than by blanket layoffs because of culture, laws, and unions.

VISIT THE NET

Provides a PowerPoint presentation on reengineering.
www.cl.uh.edu/bpa/hadm/
HADM_5731/ppt_
presentations/6reengin/
index.htm

In contrast, *reengineering* is concerned more with employee and customer well-being than shareholder well-being. Reengineering—also called process management, process innovation, or process redesign—involves reconfiguring or redesigning work, jobs, and processes for the purpose of improving cost, quality, service, and speed. Reengineering does not usually affect the organizational structure or chart, nor does it imply job loss or employee layoffs. Whereas restructuring is concerned with eliminating or establishing, shrinking or enlarging, and moving organizational departments and divisions, the focus of reengineering is changing the way work is actually carried out.

Reengineering is characterized by many tactical (short-term, business-function–specific) decisions, whereas restructuring is characterized by strategic (long-term, affecting all business functions) decisions.

The Internet is ushering in a new wave of business transformation. No longer is it enough for companies to put up simple Web sites for customers and employees. To take full advantage of the Internet, companies need to change the way they distribute goods, deal with suppliers, attract customers, and serve customers. The Internet eliminates the geographic protection/monopoly of local businesses. Basically, companies need to reinvent the way they do business to take full advantage of the Internet. This whole process is being called e-engineering.[4] Dow Corning Corporation and many others have recently appointed an e-commerce top executive.

Restructuring

Firms often employ restructuring when various ratios appear out of line with competitors as determined through benchmarking exercises. *Benchmarking* simply involves comparing a firm against the best firms in the industry on a wide variety of performance-related criteria. Some benchmarking ratios commonly used in rationalizing the need for restructuring are headcount-to-sales-volume, or corporate-staff-to-operating-employees, or span-of-control figures.

The primary benefit sought from restructuring is cost reduction. For some highly bureaucratic firms, restructuring can actually rescue the firm from global competition and demise. But the downside of restructuring can be reduced employee commitment, creativity, and innovation that accompanies the uncertainty and trauma associated with pending and actual employee layoffs.

Another downside of restructuring is that many people today do not aspire to become managers, and many present-day managers are trying to get off the management track.[5] Sentiment against joining management ranks is higher today than ever. About 80 percent of employees say they want nothing to do with management, a major shift from just a decade ago when 60 to 70 percent hoped to become managers. Managing others historically led to enhanced career mobility, financial rewards, and executive perks; but in today's global, more competitive, restructured arena, managerial jobs demand more hours and headaches with fewer financial rewards. Managers today manage more people spread over different locations, travel more, manage diverse functions, and are change agents even when they have nothing to do with the creation of the plan or even disagree with its approach. Employers today are looking for people who can do things, not for people who make other people do things. Restructuring in many firms has made a manager's job an invisible, thankless role. More workers today are self-managed, entrepreneurs, interpreneurs, or team-managed. Managers today need to be counselors, motivators, financial advisors, and psychologists. They also run the risk of becoming technologically behind in their areas of expertise. "Dilbert" cartoons commonly portray managers as enemies or as morons.

Massive restructuring among companies during the economic downturn of 2002–2003 resulted in huge layoffs. An upside to restructuring, however, is that when there are layoffs, those left behind have more opportunity to advance upwards in the firm. Layoff survivors also have more opportunity to gain experience in varied areas of the firm and may be given more responsibilities.[6]

America's oldest department store retailer, Sears, Roebuck & Company is restructuring. The company is abandoning its position as a moderate-priced department store and becoming much more like a mass-discount retailer with central checkouts similar to Target and Kohl's. Sears is restructuring to become neither a department store nor a discounter; it is setting itself up to be positioned exactly between the two. The Sears restructuring includes layoffs of 36,000 salaried employees and 1,300 additional employees at its Hoffman Estates, Illinois, headquarters. Apparel, the most troubled part of Sears' business, will become more classic, casual, and moderately priced. More national brands will be on the shelves, and footwear will become self-service. Sears will strive to develop a prominent Sears line of apparel similar to its Craftsman tools and Kenmore appliances.

It is interesting to note that in France, laying off employees is almost impossible due to labor laws that require lengthy negotiations and expensive severance packages for any individuals who are laid off. French CEOs feel that the strict layoff policies are crippling France's economy and companies. This is true because other European countries such as Germany have recently made it much easier for companies to lay off employees in order to stay competitive—and indeed to survive. Moulinex is an example of a French company that recently tried to lay off 670 employees but was denied this option, so the firm fell into bankruptcy and possible liquidation.

Reengineering

The argument for a firm engaging in reengineering usually goes as follows: Many companies historically have been organized vertically by business function. This arrangement has led over time to managers' and employees' mind-sets being defined by their particular functions rather than by overall customer service, product quality, or corporate performance. The logic is that all firms tend to bureaucratize over time. As routines become entrenched, turf becomes delineated and defended, and politics takes precedence over performance. Walls that exist in the physical workplace can be reflections of "mental" walls.

In reengineering, a firm uses information technology to break down functional barriers and create a work system based on business processes, products, or outputs rather than on functions or inputs. Cornerstones of reengineering are decentralization, reciprocal interdependence, and information sharing. A firm that exemplifies complete information sharing is Springfield Remanufacturing Corporation, which provides to all employees a weekly income statement of the firm, as well as extensive information on other companies' performances.

The *Wall Street Journal* recently noted that reengineering today must go beyond knocking down internal walls that keep parts of a company from cooperating effectively; it must also knock down the external walls that prohibit or discourage cooperation with other firms—even rival firms.[7] A maker of disposable diapers echoes this need differently when it says that to be successful "cooperation at the firm must stretch from stump to rump."

Hewlett-Packard is a good example of a company that has knocked down the external barriers to cooperation and practices modern reengineering. The H-P of today shares its forecasts with all of its supply-chain partners and shares other critical information with its distributors and other stakeholders. H-P does all the buying of resin for its many manufacturers, giving it a volume discount of up to 5 percent. H-P has established many alliances and cooperative agreements of the kind discussed in Chapter 5.

A benefit of reengineering is that it offers employees the opportunity to see more clearly how their particular jobs affect the final product or service being marketed by the firm. However, reengineering can also raise manager and employee anxiety, which, unless calmed, can lead to corporate trauma.

Linking Performance and Pay to Strategies

Most companies today are practicing some form of pay-for-performance for employees and managers other than top executives. The average employee performance bonus is 6.8 percent of pay for individual performance, 5.5 percent of pay for group productivity, and 6.4 percent of pay for companywide profitability.

Staff control of pay systems often prevents line managers from using financial compensation as a strategic tool. Flexibility regarding managerial and employee compensation is needed to allow short-term shifts in compensation that can stimulate efforts to achieve long-term objectives.

How can an organization's reward system be more closely linked to strategic performance? How can decisions on salary increases, promotions, merit pay, and bonuses be more closely aligned to support the long-term strategic objectives of the organization? There are no widely accepted answers to these questions, but a dual bonus system based on both annual objectives and long-term objectives is becoming common. The percentage of a manager's annual bonus attributable to short-term versus long-term results should vary by hierarchical level in the organization. A chief executive officer's annual bonus could, for example, be determined on a 75 percent short-term and 25 percent long-term basis. It is important that bonuses not be based solely on short-term results because such a system ignores long-term company strategies and objectives.

DuPont Canada has a 16 percent return-on-equity objective. If this objective is met, the company's 4,000 employees receive a "performance sharing cash award" equal to 4 percent of pay. If return-on-equity falls below 11 percent, employees get nothing. If return-on-equity exceeds 28 percent, workers receive a 10 percent bonus.

In an effort to cut costs and increase productivity, more and more Japanese companies are switching from seniority-based pay to performance-based approaches. Toyota has switched to a full merit system for 20,000 of its 70,000 white-collar workers. Fujitsu, Sony, Matsushita Electric Industrial, and Kao also have switched to merit pay systems. Nearly 30 percent of all Japanese companies have switched to merit pay from seniority pay.[8] This switching is hurting morale at some Japanese companies, which have trained workers for decades to cooperate rather than to compete and to work in groups rather than individually.

Richard Brown, CEO of Electronic Data Systems (EDS), recently removed the bottom 20 percent of EDS's sales force and said,

> You have to start with an appraisal system that gives genuine feedback and differentiates performance. Some call it ranking people. That seems a little harsh. But you can't have a manager checking a box that says you're either stupendous, magnificent, very, good, or average. Concise, constructive feedback is the fuel workers use to get better. A company that doesn't differentiate performance risks losing its best people.[9]

Profit sharing is another widely used form of incentive compensation. More than 30 percent of American companies have profit sharing plans, but critics emphasize that too many factors affect profits for this to be a good criterion. Taxes, pricing, or an acquisition would wipe out profits, for example. Also, firms try to minimize profits in a sense to reduce taxes.

Still another criterion widely used to link performance and pay to strategies is gain sharing. *Gain sharing* requires employees or departments to establish performance targets; if actual results exceed objectives, all members get bonuses. More than 26 percent of American companies use some form of gain sharing; about 75 percent of gain sharing plans have been adopted since 1980. Carrier, a subsidiary of United Technologies, has had excellent success with gain sharing in its six plants in Syracuse, New York; Firestone's tire plant in Wilson, North Carolina, has experienced similar success with gain sharing.

Criteria such as sales, profit, production efficiency, quality, and safety could also serve as bases for an effective *bonus system.* If an organization meets certain understood, agreed-upon profit objectives, every member of the enterprise should share in the harvest. A bonus system can be an effective tool for motivating individuals to support strategy-implementation efforts. BankAmerica, for example, recently overhauled its incentive system to link pay to sales of the bank's most profitable products and services. Branch managers receive a base salary plus a bonus based both on the number of new customers and on sales of bank products. Every employee in each branch is also eligible for a bonus if the branch exceeds its goals. Thomas Peterson, a top BankAmerica executive, says, "We want to make people responsible for meeting their goals, so we pay incentives on sales, not on controlling costs or on being sure the parking lot is swept."

Five tests are often used to determine whether a performance-pay plan will benefit an organization:

1. ***Does the plan capture attention?*** Are people talking more about their activities and taking pride in early successes under the plan?
2. ***Do employees understand the plan?*** Can participants explain how it works and what they need to do to earn the incentive?
3. ***Is the plan improving communication?*** Do employees know more than they used to about the company's mission, plans, and objectives?
4. ***Does the plan pay out when it should?*** Are incentives being paid for desired results—and being withheld when objectives are not met?
5. ***Is the company or unit performing better?*** Are profits up? Has market share grown? Have gains resulted in part from the incentives?[10]

In addition to a dual bonus system, a combination of reward strategy incentives such as salary raises, stock options, fringe benefits, promotions, praise, recognition, criticism, fear, increased job autonomy, and awards can be used to encourage managers and employees to push hard for successful strategic implementation. The range of options for getting people, departments, and divisions to actively support strategy-implementation activities in a particular organization is almost limitless. Merck, for example, recently gave each of its 37,000 employees a ten-year option to buy one hundred shares of Merck stock at a set price of $127. Steven Darien, Merck's vice president of human resources, says, "We needed to find ways to get everyone in the workforce on board in terms of our goals and objectives. Company executives will begin meeting with all Merck workers to explore ways in which employees can contribute more."

Increasing criticism aimed at chief executive officers for their high pay has resulted in executive compensation being linked to performance of their firms more closely than ever before. Although the linkage between CEO pay and corporate performance is getting closer, CEO pay in the United States still can be astronomical. Salaries and bonuses of CEOs in the U.S. increased 10 percent in 2002, compared to a 3.5 percent improvement among all other white-collar nonunion salaried employees.[11] Total average compensation to CEOs in the U.S. increased 15 percent to $3.02 million in 2002. However, as a result of accounting scandals, bankruptcies, and investor outrage over stock options abuse, boards of directors are increasingly rethinking and reducing CEO compensation and tightening the correlation between compensation and firm performance. In fact, Booz Allen Hamilton reported that the number of U.S. CEOs fired for poor performance increased 70 percent in 2002 over 2001. Richard Brown's 2002 compensation at EDS, for example, declined 82.4 percent to $1.5 million as the firm's net income fell to negative $18.1 million. Mr. Brown owns over $17 million worth of EDS stock, which is typical in the sense that CEOs of large firms generally own very large amounts of their firm's stock.

Managing Resistance to Change

No organization or individual can escape change. But the thought of change raises anxieties because people fear economic loss, inconvenience, uncertainty, and a break in normal social patterns. Almost any change in structure, technology, people, or strategies has the potential to disrupt comfortable interaction patterns. For this reason, people resist change. The strategic-management process itself can impose major changes on individuals and processes. Reorienting an organization to get people to think and act strategically is not an easy task.

Resistance to change can be considered the single greatest threat to successful strategy implementation. Resistance in the form of sabotaging production machines, absenteeism, filing unfounded grievances, and an unwillingness to cooperate regularly occurs in organizations. People often resist strategy implementation because they do not understand what is happening or why changes are taking place. In that case, employees may simply need accurate information. Successful strategy implementation hinges upon managers' ability to develop an organizational climate conducive to change. Change must be viewed as an opportunity rather than as a threat by managers and employees.

Resistance to change can emerge at any stage or level of the strategy-implementation process. Although there are various approaches for implementing changes, three commonly used strategies are a force change strategy, an educative change strategy, and a rational or self-interest change strategy. A *force change strategy* involves giving orders and enforcing those orders; this strategy has the advantage of being fast, but it is plagued by low commitment and high resistance. The *educative change strategy* is one that presents information to convince people of the need for change; the disadvantage of an educative change strategy is that implementation becomes slow and difficult. However, this type of strategy evokes greater commitment and less resistance than does the force change strategy. Finally, a *rational* or *self-interest change strategy* is one that attempts to convince individuals that the change is to their personal advantage. When this appeal is successful, strategy implementation can be relatively easy. However, implementation changes are seldom to everyone's advantage.

The rational change strategy is the most desirable, so this approach is examined a bit further. Managers can improve the likelihood of successfully implementing change by carefully designing change efforts. Jack Duncan described a rational or self-interest change strategy as consisting of four steps. First, employees are invited to participate in the process of change and in the details of transition; participation allows everyone to give opinions, to feel a part of the change process, and to identify their own self-interests regarding the recommended change. Second, some motivation or incentive to change is required; self-interest can be the most important motivator. Third, communication is needed so that people can understand the purpose for the changes. Giving and receiving feedback is the fourth step: everyone enjoys knowing how things are going and how much progress is being made.[12]

Igor Ansoff summarized the need for strategists to manage resistance to change as follows:

> Observation of the historical transitions from one orientation to another shows that, if left unmanaged, the process becomes conflict-laden, prolonged, and costly in both human and financial terms. Management of resistance involves anticipating the focus of resistance and its intensity. Second, it involves eliminating unnecessary resistance caused by misperceptions and insecurities. Third, it involves mustering the power base necessary to assure support for the change. Fourth, it involves planning the process of change. Finally, it involves monitoring and controlling resistance during the process of change.[13]

Because of diverse external and internal forces, change is a fact of life in organizations. The rate, speed, magnitude, and direction of changes vary over time by industry and organization. Strategists should strive to create a work environment in which change is recognized as necessary and beneficial so that individuals can adapt

VISIT THE NET

Provides a PowerPoint presentation on organizational change and managing resistance to change.
www.cl.uh.edu/bpa/
hadm/HADM_5731/
ppt_presentations/
5orgchg/index.htm

to change more easily. Adopting a strategic-management approach to decision making can itself require major changes in the philosophy and operations of a firm.

Strategists can take a number of positive actions to minimize managers' and employees' resistance to change. For example, individuals who will be affected by a change should be involved in the decision to make the change and in decisions about how to implement the change. Strategists should anticipate changes and develop and offer training and development workshops so that managers and employees can adapt to those changes. They also need to communicate the need for changes effectively. The strategic-management process can be described as a process of managing change. Robert Waterman describes how successful organizations involve individuals to facilitate change:

> Implementation starts with, not after, the decision. When Ford Motor Company embarked on the program to build the highly successful Taurus, management gave up the usual, sequential design process. Instead [it] showed the tentative design to the workforce and asked [its] help in devising a car that would be easy to build. Team Taurus came up with no less than 1,401 items suggested by Ford employees. What a contrast from the secrecy that characterized the industry before. When people are treated as the main engine rather than interchangeable parts, motivation, creativity, quality, and commitment to implementation go up.[14]

Organizational change should be viewed today as a continuous process rather than as a project or event. The most successful organizations today continuously adapt to changes in the competitive environment, which themselves continue to change at an accelerating rate. It is not sufficient today to simply react to change. Managers need to anticipate change and ideally be the creator of change. Viewing change as a continuous process is in stark contrast to an old management doctrine regarding change, which was to unfreeze behavior, change the behavior, and then refreeze the new behavior. The new "continuous organizational change" philosophy should mirror the popular "continuous quality improvement philosophy."

VISIT THE NET

Gives good information about why employees may resist change.
www.mindtools.com/plreschn.html

Managing the Natural Environment

All business functions are affected by natural environment considerations or by striving to make a profit. However, both employees and consumers are especially resentful of firms that take from more than give to the natural environment; likewise, people today are especially appreciative of firms that conduct operations in a way that mends rather than harms the environment.

The U.S. Justice Department recently issued new guidelines for companies to uncover environmental wrongdoing among their managers and employees without exposing themselves to potential criminal liability. The new guidelines give nine hypothetical examples to illustrate the new legal requirements. The examples include Company A, which regularly conducts a comprehensive environmental audit, goes straight to the government as soon as something wrong is turned up, disciplines the responsible people in the company, and gives their names as well as all relevant documentation to the government. The Justice Department will prosecute but be lenient in this case. The extreme example is Company K, which tries to cover up an environmental violation and does not cooperate with the government or provide names. Its audit is narrow, and its compliance program is "no more than a collection of paper." No leniency is likely for this firm.

Creating a Strategy-Supportive Culture

Strategists should strive to preserve, emphasize, and build upon aspects of an existing *culture* that support proposed new strategies. Aspects of an existing culture that are antagonistic to a proposed strategy should be identified and changed. Substantial research indicates that new strategies are often market-driven and dictated by competitive forces. For this reason, changing a firm's culture to fit a new strategy is usually more effective than changing a strategy to fit an existing culture. Numerous techniques are available to alter an organization's culture, including recruitment, training, transfer, promotion, restructure of an organization's design, role modeling, and positive reinforcement.

Jack Duncan described *triangulation* as an effective, multimethod technique for studying and altering a firm's culture.[15] Triangulation includes the combined use of obtrusive observation, self-administered questionnaires, and personal interviews to determine the nature of a firm's culture. The process of triangulation reveals changes that need to be made to a firm's culture in order to benefit strategy.

Schein indicated that the following elements are most useful in linking culture to strategy:

1. Formal statements of organizational philosophy, charters, creeds, materials used for recruitment and selection, and socialization.
2. Designing of physical spaces, facades, buildings.
3. Deliberate role modeling, teaching, and coaching by leaders.
4. Explicit reward and status system, promotion criteria.
5. Stories, legends, myths, and parables about key people and events.
6. What leaders pay attention to, measure, and control.
7. Leader reactions to critical incidents and organizational crises.
8. How the organization is designed and structured.
9. Organizational systems and procedures.
10. Criteria used for recruitment, selection, promotion, leveling off, retirement, and "excommunication" of people.[16]

In the personal and religious side of life, the impact of loss and change is easy to see.[17] Memories of loss and change often haunt individuals and organizations for years. Ibsen wrote, "Rob the average man of his life illusion and you rob him of his happiness at the same stroke."[18] When attachments to a culture are severed in an organization's attempt to change direction, employees and managers often experience deep feelings of grief. This phenomenon commonly occurs when external conditions dictate the need for a new strategy. Managers and employees often struggle to find meaning in a situation that changed many years before. Some people find comfort in memories; others find solace in the present. Weak linkages between strategic management and organizational culture can jeopardize performance and success. Deal and Kennedy emphasized that making strategic changes in an organization always threatens a culture:

> people form strong attachments to heroes, legends, the rituals of daily life, the hoopla of extravaganza and ceremonies, and all the symbols of the workplace. Change strips relationships and leaves employees confused, insecure, and often angry. Unless something can be done to provide support for transitions from old to new, the force of a culture can neutralize and emasculate strategy changes.[19]

The Mexican Culture

Mexico always has been and still is an authoritarian society in terms of schools, churches, businesses, and families. Employers seek workers who are agreeable, respectful, and obedient, rather than innovative, creative, and independent. Mexican workers tend to be activity-oriented rather than problem solvers. When visitors walk into a Mexican business, they are impressed by the cordial, friendly atmosphere. This is almost always true because Mexicans desire harmony rather than conflict; desire for harmony is part of the social fabric in worker–manager relations. There is a much lower tolerance for adversarial relations or friction at work in Mexico as compared to the United States.

VISIT THE NET

Provides nice information on "What is Culture" and also provides additional excellent hot links to other culture sites.

www.mapnp.org/library/ org_thry/culture/culture.htm

Mexican employers are paternalistic, providing workers with more than a paycheck, but in return they expect allegiance. Weekly food baskets, free meals, free bus service, and free day care are often a part of compensation. The ideal working conditions for a Mexican worker is the family model, with people all working together, doing their share, according to their designated roles. Mexican workers do not expect or desire a work environment in which self-expression and initiative are encouraged. Whereas U.S. business embodies individualism, achievement, competition, curiosity, pragmatism, informality, spontaneity, and doing more than expected on the job, Mexican businesses stress collectivism, continuity, cooperation, belongingness, formality, and doing exactly what you're told.

In Mexico, business associates rarely entertain each other at their homes, which are places reserved exclusively for close friends and family. Business meetings and entertaining are nearly always done at a restaurant. Preserving one's honor, saving face, and looking important is also exceptionally important in Mexico. This is why Mexicans do not accept criticism and change easily; many find it humiliating to acknowledge having made a mistake. A meeting among employees and managers in a business located in Mexico is a forum for giving orders and directions rather than for discussing problems or participating in decision making. Mexican workers want to be closely supervised, cared for, and corrected in a civil manner. Opinions expressed by employees are often regarded as back talk in Mexico. Mexican supervisors are viewed as weak if they explain the rationale for their orders to workers.

Mexicans do not feel compelled to follow rules that are not associated with a particular person in authority they know well or work for. Thus, signs to wear earplugs or safety glasses, or attendance or seniority policies, and even one-way street signs are often ignored. Whereas Americans follow the rules, Mexicans often do not.

Life is slower in Mexico than in the United States. People do not wear watches. The first priority is often assigned to the last request, rather than to the first. Telephone systems break down. Banks may suddenly not have pesos. Phone repair can take months. Electricity for an entire plant or town can be down for hours or even days. Business and government offices open and close at different hours. Buses and taxis may be hours off schedule. Meeting times for appointments are not rigid. Tardiness is common everywhere. Doing business effectively in Mexico requires knowledge of the Mexican way of life, culture, beliefs, and customs.

The Russian Culture

In America, unsuccessful business entrepreneurs are viewed negatively as failures, whereas successful small-business owners enjoy high esteem and respect. In Russia, however, there is substantial social pressure against becoming a successful entrepreneur. Being a winner in Russia makes you the object of envy and resentment, a member of the elite rather than of the masses. Although this is slowly changing, personal

ambition and success in Russia are often met with vindictiveness and derision. Initiative is met with indifference at best and punishment at worst. In the face of public ridicule and organized crime, however, thousands of Russians, particularly young persons, are opening all kinds of businesses. Public scorn and their own guilt from violating the values they were raised with do not deter many. Because Russian society scorns success, publicizing achievements, material possessions, awards, or privileges earned by Russian workers is not an effective motivational tool for those workers.

The Russian people are best known for their drive, boundless energy, tenacity, hard work, and perseverance in spite of immense obstacles. This is as true today as ever. The notion that the average Russian is stupid or lazy is nonsense; Russians on average are more educated than their American counterparts and bounce up more readily from failure.

In the United States, business ethics and personal ethics are essentially the same. Deception is deception and a lie is a lie whether in business or personal affairs in America. However, in Russia, business and personal ethics are separate. To deceive someone, bribe someone, or lie to someone to promote a business transaction is ethical in Russia, but to deceive a friend or trusted colleague is unethical. There are countless examples of foreign firms being cheated by Russian business partners. The implication of this fact for American businesses is to forge strong personal relationships with their Russian business partners whenever possible; spend time with the Russians, eating, relaxing, and exercising; and in the absence of a personal relationship, be exceptionally cautious with agreements, partnerships, payments, and when granting credit.

The Russian people have great faith and confidence in as well as respect for American products and services. Russians generally have low self-confidence. American ideas, technology, and production practices are viewed by Russians as a panacea that can save them from a gloomy existence. For example, their squeaky telephone system and lack of fax machines make them feel deprived. This mind-set presents great opportunity in Russia for American products of all kinds.

Russia has historically been an autocratic state. This cultural factor is evident in business; Russian managers generally exercise power without ever being challenged by subordinates. Delegation of authority and responsibility is difficult and often nonexistent in Russian businesses. The American participative management style is not well received in Russia.

The Russian republic of Ingushetia recently passed a decree legalizing the practice of polygamy that allows men to have multiple wives, even a harem. The new law is a direct challenge to the Russian government, which has jurisdiction over eighty-nine republics. The Russian Constitution prohibits polygamy, but the criminal code does not provide for any penalty. Ingushetian men take more than one wife, especially when the first wife does not have a son, despite the scientific discovery in 1959 that the father's contribution alone in procreation determines a child's sex.

The Japanese Culture

The Japanese place great importance upon group loyalty and consensus, a concept called *Wa*. Nearly all corporate activities in Japan encourage *Wa* among managers and employees. *Wa* requires that all members of a group agree and cooperate; this results in constant discussion and compromise. Japanese managers evaluate the potential attractiveness of alternative business decisions in terms of the long-term effect on the group's *Wa*. This is why silence, used for pondering alternatives, can be plus in a formal Japanese meeting. Discussions potentially disruptive to *Wa* are generally conducted in very informal settings, such as at a bar, so as to minimize harm to the group's *Wa*. Entertaining is an important business activity in Japan because it strengthens *Wa*. Formal meetings are

GLOBAL PERSPECTIVE

American versus Foreign Communication Differences

As Americans increasingly interact with managers in other countries, it is important to be sensitive to foreign business cultures. Americans too often come across as intrusive, manipulative, and garrulous, and this impression reduces their effectiveness in communication. *Forbes* recently provided the following cultural hints from Charis Intercultural Training:

1. Italians, Germans, and French generally do not soften up executives with praise before they criticize. Americans do soften up folks, and this practice seems manipulative to Europeans.
2. Israelis are accustomed to fast-paced meetings and have little patience for American informality and small talk.
3. British executives often complain that American executives chatter too much. Informality, egalitarianism, and spontaneity from Americans in business settings jolt many foreigners.

4. Europeans feel they are being treated like children when asked to wear name tags by Americans.
5. Executives in India are used to interrupting one another. Thus, when American executives listen without asking for clarification or posing questions, they are viewed by Indians as not paying attention.
6. When negotiating orally with Malaysian or Japanese executives, periodically allow for a time of silence. However, do not pause when negotiating in Israel.

Refrain from asking foreign managers questions such as "How was your weekend?" That is intrusive to foreigners, who tend to regard their business and private lives as totally separate.

Source: Adapted from Lalita Khosla, "You Say Tomato," *Forbes* (May 21, 2001): 36.

often conducted in informal settings. When confronted with disturbing questions or opinions, Japanese managers tend to remain silent, whereas Americans tend to respond directly, defending themselves through explanation and argument.

Note in the "Global Perspective" that when negotiating orally with Japanese executives, one must periodically allow for a time of silence and must not ask, "How was your weekend?" which could be viewed as intrusive.

Most Japanese managers are reserved, quiet, distant, introspective, and other-oriented, whereas most U.S. managers are talkative, insensitive, impulsive, direct, and individual-oriented. Americans often perceive Japanese managers as wasting time and carrying on pointless conversations, whereas U.S. managers often use blunt criticism, ask prying questions, and make quick decisions. These kinds of cultural differences have disrupted many potentially productive Japanese–American business endeavors. Viewing the Japanese communication style as a prototype for all Asian cultures is a stereotype that must be avoided.

Americans have more freedom to control their own fates than do the Japanese. Life in the United States and life in Japan are very different; the United States offers more upward mobility to its people. This is a great strength of the United States. Sherman explained:

America is not like Japan and can never be. America's strength is the opposite: It opens its doors and brings the world's disorder in. It tolerates social change that would tear most other societies apart. This openness encourages Americans to adapt as individuals rather than as a group.

Americans go west to California to get a new start; they move east to Manhattan to try to make the big time; they move to Vermont or to a farm to get close to the soil. They break away from their parents' religions or values or class; they rediscover their ethnicity. They go to night school; they change their names.[20]

Production/Operations Concerns When Implementing Strategies

Production/operations capabilities, limitations, and policies can significantly enhance or inhibit the attainment of objectives. Production processes typically constitute more than 70 percent of a firm's total assets. A major part of the strategy-implementation process takes place at the production site. Production-related decisions on plant size, plant location, product design, choice of equipment, kind of tooling, size of inventory, inventory control, quality control, cost control, use of standards, job specialization, employee training, equipment and resource utilization, shipping and packaging, and technological innovation can have a dramatic impact on the success or failure of strategy-implementation efforts.

Examples of adjustments in production systems that could be required to implement various strategies are provided in Table 7–3 for both for-profit and nonprofit organizations. For instance, note that when a bank formulates and selects a strategy to add ten new branches, a production-related implementation concern is site location. The largest bicycle company in the United States, Huffy, recently ended its own production of bikes and now contracts out those services to Asian and Mexican manufacturers. Huffy focuses instead on the design, marketing, and distribution of bikes, but it no longer produces bikes itself. The Dayton, Ohio, company closed its plants in Ohio, Missouri, and Mississippi.

Just-in-Time (JIT) production approaches have withstood the test of time. JIT significantly reduces the costs of implementing strategies. With JIT, parts and materials are delivered to a production site just as they are needed, rather than being stockpiled as a hedge against later deliveries. Harley-Davidson reports that at one plant alone, JIT freed $22 million previously tied up in inventory and greatly reduced reorder lead time.

TABLE 7-3   Production Management and Strategy Implementation

TYPE OF ORGANIZATION	STRATEGY BEING IMPLEMENTED	PRODUCTION SYSTEM ADJUSTMENTS
Hospital	Adding a cancer center (Product Development)	Purchase specialized equipment and add specialized people.
Bank	Adding ten new branches (Market Development)	Perform site location analysis.
Beer brewery	Purchasing a barley farm operation (Backward Integration)	Revise the inventory control system.
Steel manufacturer	Acquiring a fast-food chain (Conglomerate Diversification)	Improve the quality control system.
Computer company	Purchasing a retail distribution chain (Forward Integration)	Alter the shipping, packaging, and transportation systems.

Factors that should be studied before locating production facilities include the availability of major resources, the prevailing wage rates in the area, transportation costs related to shipping and receiving, the location of major markets, political risks in the area or country, and the availability of trainable employees.

For high-technology companies, production costs may not be as important as production flexibility because major product changes can be needed often. Industries such as biogenetics and plastics rely on production systems that must be flexible enough to allow frequent changes and the rapid introduction of new products. An article in *Harvard Business Review* explained why some organizations get into trouble:

> They too slowly realize that a change in product strategy alters the tasks of a production system. These tasks, which can be stated in terms of requirements for cost, product flexibility, volume flexibility, product performance, and product consistency, determine which manufacturing policies are appropriate. As strategies shift over time, so must production policies covering the location and scale of manufacturing facilities, the choice of manufacturing process, the degree of vertical integration of each manufacturing facility, the use of R&D units, the control of the production system, and the licensing of technology.[21]

A common management practice, cross-training of employees, can facilitate strategy implementation and can yield many benefits. Employees gain a better understanding of the whole business and can contribute better ideas in planning sessions. Production/operations managers need to realize, however, that cross-training employees can create problems related to the following issues:

1. It can thrust managers into roles that emphasize counseling and coaching over directing and enforcing.
2. It can necessitate substantial investments in training and incentives.
3. It can be very time-consuming.
4. Skilled workers may resent unskilled workers who learn their jobs.
5. Older employees may not want to learn new skills.

Human Resource Concerns When Implementing Strategies

The job of human resource manager is changing rapidly as companies continue to downsize and reorganize. Strategic responsibilities of the human resource manager include assessing the staffing needs and costs for alternative strategies proposed during strategy formulation and developing a staffing plan for effectively implementing strategies. This plan must consider how best to manage spiraling healthcare insurance costs. Employers' health coverage expenses consume an average 26 percent of firms' net profits, even though most companies now require employees to pay part of their health insurance premiums. The plan must also include how to motivate employees and managers during a time when layoffs are common and workloads are high.

The human resource department must develop performance incentives that clearly link performance and pay to strategies. The process of empowering managers and employees through their involvement in strategic-management activities yields the greatest benefits when all organizational members understand clearly how they will benefit personally if the firm does well. Linking company and personal benefits is a major new strategic responsibility of human resource managers. Other new responsibilities for human resource managers may include establishing and administering an *employee stock ownership plan (ESOP)*, instituting an effective child-care policy, and providing leadership for managers and employees in a way that allows them to balance work and family.

A well-designed strategic-management system can fail if insufficient attention is given to the human resource dimension. Human resource problems that arise when businesses implement strategies can usually be traced to one of three causes: (1) disruption of social and political structures, (2) failure to match individuals' aptitudes with implementation tasks, and (3) inadequate top management support for implementation activities. [22]

Strategy implementation poses a threat to many managers and employees in an organization. New power and status relationships are anticipated and realized. New formal and informal groups' values, beliefs, and priorities may be largely unknown. Managers and employees may become engaged in resistance behavior as their roles, prerogatives, and power in the firm change. Disruption of social and political structures that accompany strategy execution must be anticipated and considered during strategy formulation and managed during strategy implementation.

A concern in matching managers with strategy is that jobs have specific and relatively static responsibilities, although people are dynamic in their personal development. Commonly used methods that match managers with strategies to be implemented include transferring managers, developing leadership workshops, offering career development activities, promotions, job enlargement, and job enrichment.

A number of other guidelines can help ensure that human relationships facilitate rather than disrupt strategy-implementation efforts. Specifically, managers should do a lot of chatting and informal questioning to stay abreast of how things are progressing and to know when to intervene. Managers can build support for strategy-implementation efforts by giving few orders, announcing few decisions, depending heavily on informal questioning, and seeking to probe and clarify until a consensus emerges. Key thrusts that succeed should be rewarded generously and visibly.

It is surprising that so often during strategy formulation, individual values, skills, and abilities needed for successful strategy implementation are not considered. It is rare that a firm selecting new strategies or significantly altering existing strategies possesses the right line and staff personnel in the right positions for successful strategy implementation. The need to match individual aptitudes with strategy-implementation tasks should be considered in strategy choice.

Inadequate support from strategists for implementation activities often undermines organizational success. Chief executive officers, small business owners, and government agency heads must be personally committed to strategy implementation and express this commitment in highly visible ways. Strategists' formal statements about the importance of strategic management must be consistent with actual support and rewards given for activities completed and objectives reached. Otherwise, stress created by inconsistency can cause uncertainty among managers and employees at all levels.

Perhaps the best method for preventing and overcoming human resource problems in strategic management is to actively involve as many managers and employees as possible in the process. Although time-consuming, this approach builds understanding, trust, commitment, and ownership and reduces resentment and hostility. The true potential of strategy formulation and implementation resides in people.

Employee Stock Ownership Plans (ESOPs)

An *ESOP* is a tax-qualified, defined-contribution, employee-benefit plan whereby employees purchase stock of the company through borrowed money or cash contributions. ESOPs empower employees to work as owners; this is a primary reason why the number of ESOPs grew dramatically throughout the 1980s and 1990s to more than 10,000 plans covering more than 15 million employees. ESOPs now control more than $80 billion in corporate stock in the United States.

Besides reducing worker alienation and stimulating productivity, ESOPs allow firms other benefits, such as substantial tax savings. Principal, interest, and dividend payments on ESOP-funded debt are tax deductible. Banks lend money to ESOPs at interest rates below prime. This money can be repaid in pretax dollars, lowering the debt service as much as 30 percent in some cases.

If an ESOP owns more than 50 percent of the firm, those who lend money to the ESOP are taxed on only 50 percent of the income received on the loans. ESOPs are not for every firm, however, because the initial legal, accounting, actuarial, and appraisal fees to set up an ESOP are about $50,000 for a small or midsized firm, with annual administration expenses of about $15,000. Analysts say ESOPs also do not work well in firms that have fluctuating payrolls and profits. Human resource managers in many firms conduct preliminary research to determine the desirability of an ESOP, and then they facilitate its establishment and administration if benefits outweigh the costs.

Many companies are following the lead of Polaroid, which established an ESOP as a tactic for preventing a hostile takeover. Polaroid's CEO MacAllister Booth says, "Twenty years from now we'll find that employees have a sizable stake in every major American corporation." (It is interesting to note here that Polaroid is chartered in the state of Delaware, which requires corporate suitors to acquire 85 percent of a target company's shares to complete a merger; over 50 percent of all American corporations are incorporated in Delaware for this reason.) Wyatt Cafeterias, a southwestern U.S. operator of 120 cafeterias, also adopted the ESOP concept to prevent a hostile takeover. Employee productivity at Wyatt has greatly increased since the ESOP began, as illustrated in the following quote:

> The key employee in our entire organization is the person serving the customer on the cafeteria line. In the past, because of high employee turnover and entry-level wages for many line jobs, these employees received far less attention and recognition than managers. We now tell the tea cart server, "You own the place. Don't wait for the manager to tell you how to do your job better or how to provide better service. You take care of it." Sure, we're looking for productivity increases, but since we began pushing decisions down to the level of people who deal directly with customers, we've discovered an awesome side effect—suddenly the work crews have this "happy to be here" attitude that the customers really love.[23]

Balancing Work Life and Home Life

Work/family strategies have become so popular among companies today that the strategies now represent a competitive advantage for those firms that offer such benefits as elder care assistance, flexible scheduling, job sharing, adoption benefits, an on-site summer camp, employee help lines, pet care, and even lawn service referrals. New corporate titles such as Work/Life Coordinator and Director of Diversity are becoming common.

Working Mother magazine, in late 2001, published its listing of "The 100 Best Companies for Working Mothers" (**workingmother.com/100BestList.shtml**). Three especially important variables used in the ranking were availability of flextime, advancement opportunities, and equitable distribution of benefits among companies. *Working Mother*'s top ten best companies for working women in 2003 are listed here:

1. Abbott Laboratories
2. Booz Allen Hamilton
3. Bristol-Meyers Squibb
4. Eli Lilly Company
5. Fannie Mae
6. General Mills
7. IBM Corporation
8. Prudential Financial Group
9. S. C. Johnson & Son
10. Wachovia Corporation

VISIT THE NET

Provides a great overview of the strategic planning process.
www.mapnp.org/library/plan_dec/str_plan.html

Human resource managers need to foster a more effective balancing of professional and private lives because nearly 60 million people in the United States are now part of two-career families. A corporate objective to become more lean and mean must today include consideration for the fact that a good home life contributes immensely to a good work life.

The work/family issue is no longer just a women's issue. Some specific measures that firms are taking to address this issue are providing spouse relocation assistance as an employee benefit, providing company resources for family recreational and educational use, establishing employee country clubs such as those at IBM and Bethlehem Steel, and creating family/work interaction opportunities. A study by Joseph Pleck of Wheaton College found that in companies that do not offer paternity leave for fathers as a benefit, most men take short, informal paternity leaves anyway by combining vacation time and sick days.

Some organizations have developed family days, when family members are invited into the workplace, taken on plant or office tours, dined by management, and given a chance to see exactly what other family members do each day. Family days are inexpensive and increase the employee's pride in working for the organization. Flexible working hours during the week are another human resource response to the need for individuals to balance work life and home life. The work/family topic is being made part of the agenda at meetings and thus is being discussed in many organizations.

According to Catalyst, a New York–based women's advocacy group, women in mid-2003 made up 15.7 percent of the top-ranking executives at America's largest companies. This is up from less than 9 percent in 1995. This is good news for women because more than 2,000 out of 14,000 corporate officers among the *Fortune* 500 companies now are women. However, only six of the *Fortune* 500 firms have a woman CEO and 71 of the *Fortune* 500 firms have no women corporate officers at all. Thus there is great room for improvement in removing the glass ceiling domestically, especially considering that women make up 47 percent of the U.S. labor force. As listed in Table 7–4, female CEOs (strategists) among large U.S. firms include Carly Fiorina at Hewlett-Packard, Patricia Russo at Lucent, Anne Mulcahy at Xerox, Andrea Jung at Avon, and Besty Holden at Kraft Foods. There still is great room for improvement in the United States in terms of women being promoted into executive positions, but progress is being made; the United States leads the world in promoting women and minorities into mid- and top-level managerial positions in business. Wal-Mart is an

TABLE 7–4   Some Women CEOs in the United States in 2004

CEO	COMPANY	CEO'S AGE
1. Carly Fiorina	Hewlett-Packard	49
2. Meg Whitman	eBay	47
3. Andrea Jung	Avon Products	45
4. Anne Mulcahy	Xerox	50
5. Majorie Magner	Citigroup	54
6. Betsy Holden	Kraft Foods	47
7. Ann Moore	AOL Time Warner	53
8. Sallie Krawcheck	Smith Barney	38
9. Shelly Lazarus	Ogilvy & Mather Worldwide	56
10. Pat Russo	Lucent Technologies	51
11. Mary Sammons	Rite Aid	57
12. Maria Lagomasino	J. P. Morgan Chase	45

example of a company in some legal trouble, since about 15 percent of its managers are female, yet women make up about 70 percent of the Wal-Mart workforce.

USA Today reports that among all *Fortune* 500 companies, 393 have no women among their top five executives.[24] Even three of the six female *Fortune* 500 CEOs, Marce Fuller at Mirant, Pat Russo at Lucent Technologies, and Marion Sandler at Golden West Financial, have no women reporting to them among the next four highest-paid executives. The other three—Carly Fiorina at Hewlett-Packard, Andrea Jung at Avon, and Anne Mulcahy at Xerox—each have but one woman in the next four spots.

The U.S. military has been a leader in women's rights. For example, in the U.S. Air Force, women make up 19.4 percent of its personnel, followed by the Army with 15.4 percent, the Navy with 14.4 percent, and finally the Marines with 6.0 percent.

Benefits of a Diverse Workforce

When Toyota was threatened with a boycott by African Americans in late 2001, the company committed almost $8 billion over ten years to diversify its workforce and to use more minority suppliers. Hundreds of other firms, such as Ford Motor Company and Coca-Cola, are also striving to become more diversified in their workforces. TJX Companies, the parent of 1,500 T. J. Maxx and Marshall's stores, has reaped great benefits and is an exemplary company in terms of diversity. A recent *Wall Street Journal* article listed, in order of importance, the following major benefits of having a diverse workforce:[25]

1. Improves corporate culture
2. Improves employee morale
3. Leads to a higher retention of employees
4. Leads to an easier recruitment of new employees
5. Decreases complaints and litigation
6. Increases creativity
7. Decreases interpersonal conflict between employees
8. Enables the organization to move into emerging markets
9. Improves client relations

10. Increases productivity
11. Improves the bottom line
12. Maximizes brand identity
13. Reduces training costs

An organization can perhaps be most effective when its workforce mirrors the diversity of its customers. For global companies, this goal can be optimistic, but it is a worthwhile goal. It is interesting that online shopping by Hispanics is growing at more than three times overall online shopping.[26] Consequently, many retailers are launching Spanish language Web sites. JetBlue Airways, Nissan North America, Office Depot, and Honda Motors are among dozens of companies that now offer Spanish-language Web sites. In the 2001 U.S. Census, Hispanics numbered 31 million, almost outnumbering blacks as the largest minority group.

CONCLUSION

Successful strategy formulation does not at all guarantee successful strategy implementation. Although inextricably interdependent, strategy formulation and strategy implementation are characteristically different. In a single word, strategy implementation means *change*. It is widely agreed that "the real work begins after strategies are formulated." Successful strategy implementation requires the support of as well as discipline and hard work from motivated managers and employees. It is sometimes frightening to think that a single individual can sabotage strategy-implementation efforts irreparably.

Formulating the right strategies is not enough, because managers and employees must be motivated to implement those strategies. Management issues considered central to strategy implementation include matching organizational structure with strategy, linking performance and pay to strategies, creating an organizational climate conducive to change, managing political relationships, creating a strategy-supportive culture, adapting production/operations processes, and managing human resources. Establishing annual objectives, devising policies, and allocating resources are central strategy-implementation activities common to all organizations. Depending on the size and type of the organization, other management issues could be equally important to successful strategy implementation.

We invite you to visit the David page on the Prentice Hall Companion Web site at *www.prenhall.com/david* for this chapter's World Wide Web exercises.

KEY TERMS AND CONCEPTS

Annual Objectives (p. 244)

Avoidance (p. 249)

Benchmarking (p. 256)

Bonus System (p. 258)

Conflict (p. 249)

Confrontation (p. 250)

Culture (p. 264)

Defusion (p. 249)

Delayering (p. 255)

Decentralized Structure (p. 251)

Divisional Structure by Geographic Area, Product, Customer, or Process (pp. 251–253)

Downsizing (p. 255)

Educative Change Strategy (p. 260)

Employee Stock Ownership Plans (ESOP) (p. 270)

Establishing Annual Objectives (p. 244)

Force Change Strategy (p. 260)

Functional Structure (p. 251)

ISSUES FOR REVIEW AND DISCUSSION

1. Allocating resources can be a political and an ad hoc activity in firms that do not use strategic management. Why is this true? Does adopting strategic management ensure easy resource allocation? Why?

2. Compare strategy formulation with strategy implementation in terms of each being an art or a science.

3. Describe the relationship between annual objectives and policies.

4. Identify a long-term objective and two supporting annual objectives for a familiar organization.

5. Identify and discuss three policies that apply to your present business policy class.

6. Explain the following statement: Horizontal consistency of goals is as important as vertical consistency.

7. Describe several reasons why conflict may occur during objective-setting activities.

8. In your opinion, what approaches to conflict resolution would be best for resolving a disagreement between a personnel manager and a sales manager over the firing of a particular salesperson? Why?

9. Describe the organizational culture of your college or university.

10. Explain why organizational structure is so important in strategy implementation.

11. In your opinion, how many separate divisions could an organization reasonably have without using an SBU-type organizational structure? Why?

12. Would you recommend a divisional structure by geographic area, product, customer, or process for a medium-sized bank in your local area? Why?

13. What are the advantages and disadvantages of decentralizing the wage and salary functions of an organization? How could this be accomplished?

14. Consider a college organization with which you are familiar. How did management issues affect strategy implementation in that organization?

15. As production manager of a local newspaper, what problems would you anticipate in implementing a strategy to increase the average number of pages in the paper by 40 percent?

16. Do you believe expenditures for child care or fitness facilities are warranted from a cost-benefit perspective? Why or why not?

17. Explain why successful strategy implementation often hinges on whether the strategy-formulation process empowers managers and employees.

18. Compare and contrast the cultures in Mexico, Russia, and Japan.

19. Discuss the glass ceiling in the United States, giving your ideas and suggestions.

20. Discuss three ways discussed in this book for linking performance and pay to strategies.

21. List the different types of organizational structure. Diagram what you think is the most complex of these structures and label your chart clearly.

22. List the advantages and disadvantages of a functional versus a divisional organizational structure.

23. Compare and contrast the U.S. business culture with the Mexican business culture.

24. Discuss recent trends in women and minorities becoming top executives in the United States.

25. Discuss recent trends in firms downsizing family-friendly programs.

26. Research the latest developments in the class-action lawsuit involving women managers versus Wal-Mart Stores and report your findings to the class.

NOTES

1. Dale McConkey, "Planning in a Changing Environment," *Business Horizons* (September–October 1988): 66.
2. A. G. Bedeian and W. F. Glueck, *Management,* 3rd ed. (Chicago: The Dryden Press, 1983): 212.
3. Boris Yavitz and William Newman, *Strategy in Action: The Execution, Politics, and Payoff of Business Planning* (New York: The Free Press, 1982): 195.
4. Steve Hamm and Marcia Stepanek, "From Reengineering to E-engineering," *BusinessWeek* (March 22, 1999): EB15.
5. "Want to Be a Manager? Many People Say No, Calling Job Miserable," *Wall Street Journal* (April 4, 1997): 1; Also, Stephanie Armour, "Management Loses Its Allure," *USA Today* (October 10, 1997): 1B.
6. Stephanie Armour, "Layoff Survivors Climb Ladder Faster," *USA Today* (September 10, 2001), B1.
7. Paul Carroll, "No More Business as Usual, Please. Time to Try Something Different," *Wall Street Journal* (October 23, 2001): A24.
8. Julie Schmit, "Japan Shifts to Merit Pay," *USA Today* (July 23, 1999): 5B.
9. Richard Brown, "Outsider CEO: Inspiring Change With Force and Grace," *USA Today* (July 19, 1999): 3B.
10. Yavitz and Newman, 58.
11. JoAnn Lub, "Why the Get-Rich-Quick Days May Be Over," *Wall Street Journal* (April 14, 2003): R1.
12. Jack Duncan, *Management* (New York: Random House, 1983): 381–390.
13. H. Igor Ansoff, "Strategic Management of Technology," *Journal of Business Strategy* 7, no. 3 (Winter 1987): 38.
14. Robert Waterman, Jr., "How the Best Get Better," *BusinessWeek* (September 14, 1987): 104.
15. Jack Duncan, "Organizational Culture: Getting a Fix on an Elusive Concept," *Academy of Management Executive* 3, no. 3 (August 1989): 229.
16. E. H. Schein, "The Role of the Founder in Creating Organizational Culture," *Organizational Dynamics* (Summer 1983): 13–28.
17. T. Deal and A. Kennedy, "Culture: A New Look Through Old Lenses," *Journal of Applied Behavioral Science* 19, no. 4 (1983): 498–504.
18. H. Ibsen, "The Wild Duck," in O. G. Brochett and L. Brochett (eds.), *Plays for the Theater* (New York: Holt, Rinehart & Winston, 1967); R. Pascale, "The Paradox of 'Corporate Culture': Reconciling Ourselves to Socialization," *California Management Review* 28, no. 2 (1985): 26, 37–40.
19. T. Deal and A. Kennedy, *Corporate Cultures: The Rites and Rituals of Corporate Life* (Reading, MA: Addison-Wesley, 1982): 256.
20. Stratford Sherman, "How to Beat the Japanese," *Fortune* (April 10, 1989): 145.
21. Robert Stobaugh and Piero Telesio, "Match Manufacturing Policies and Product Strategy," *Harvard Business Review* 61, no. 2 (March–April 1983): 113.
22. R. T. Lenz and Marjorie Lyles, "Managing Human Resource Problems in Strategy Planning Systems," *Journal of Business Strategy* 60, no. 4 (Spring 1986): 58.
23. J. Warren Henry, "ESOPs with Productivity Payoffs," *Journal of Business Strategy* (July–August 1989): 33.
24. Stephanie Armour, "More Women Cruise to the Top," *USA Today* (June 25, 2003): 3B; Del Jones, "Few Women Hold Top Executive Jobs, Even When CEOs Are Female," *USA Today* (January 27, 2003): B1.
25. Julie Bennett, "Corporate Downsizing Doesn't Deter Search for Diversity," *Wall Street Journal* (October 23, 2001): B18.
26. Jon Swartz, "Retailers Offer Web Sites in Spanish," *USA Today* (May 29, 2003): B1.

CURRENT READINGS

Cascio, W. F. "Strategies for Responsible Restructuring." *Academy of Management Executive* 16, no. 3 (August 2002): 80–91.

Dobni, B. "Creating a Strategy Implementation Environment." *Business Horizons* 46, no. 2 (March–April 2003): 43–46.

Foley, S., D. L. Kidder, and G. N. Powell. "The Perceived Glass Ceiling and Justice Perceptions: An Investigation of Hispanic Law Associates." *Journal of Management* 28, no. 4 (2002): 471–496.

Gomex-Mejia, L. R., M. Larraza-Kintana, and M. Makri. "The Determinants of Executive Compensation in Family-Controlled Public Corporations." *Academy of Management Journal* 46, no. 2 (April 2003): 226–237.

Love, L. G., R. L. Priem, and G. T. Lumpkin. "Explicitly Articulated Strategy and Firm Performance under Alternative Levels of Centralization." *Journal of Management* 28, no. 5 (2002): 611–628.

Porter, T. W., and S. C. Harper. "Tactical Implementation: The Devil Is in the Details." *Business Horizons* 46, no. 1 (January–February 2003): 53–60.

Richardson, H. A., R. J. Vandeberg, T. C. Blum, and P. M. Roman. "Does Decentralization Make a Difference for the Organization? An Examination of the Boundary Conditions Circumscribing Decentralized Decision-Making and Organizational Financial Performance." *Journal of Management* 28, no. 2 (2002): 217.

Rynes, S. L., K. G. Brown, and A. E. Colbert. "Seven Common Misconceptions about Human Resource Practices: Research Findings versus Practitioner Beliefs." *Academy of Management Executive* 16, no. 3 (August 2002): 92.

Shen, W., and A. A. Cannella. "Will Succession Planning Increase Shareholder Wealth? Evidence from Investor Reactions to Relay CEO Successions." *Strategic Management Journal* 24, no. 2 (February 2003): 191.

Siciliano, J. I. "Governance and Strategy Implementation: Expanding the Board's Involvement." *Business Horizons* 45, no. 6 (November–December 2002): 53–60.

Strategies have no chance of being implemented successfully in organizations that do not market goods and services well, in firms that cannot raise needed working capital, in firms that produce technologically inferior products, or in firms that have a weak information system. This chapter examines marketing, finance/accounting, R&D, and management information systems (MIS) issues that are central to effective strategy implementation. Special topics include market segmentation, market positioning, evaluating the worth of a business, determining to what extent debt and/or stock should be used as a source of capital, developing pro forma financial statements, contracting R&D outside the firm, and creating an information support system. Manager and employee involvement and participation are essential for success in marketing, finance/accounting, R&D, and MIS activities.

The Nature of Strategy Implementation

The quarterback can call the best play possible in the huddle, but that does not mean the play will go for a touchdown. The team may even lose yardage unless the play is executed (implemented) well. Less than 10 percent of strategies formulated are successfully implemented! There are many reasons for this low success rate, including failing to segment markets appropriately, paying too much for a new acquisition, and falling behind competitors in R&D.

Strategy implementation directly affects the lives of plant managers, division managers, department managers, sales managers, product managers, project managers, personnel managers, staff managers, supervisors, and all employees. In some situations, individuals may not have participated in the strategy-formulation process at all and may not appreciate, understand, or even accept the work and thought that went into strategy formulation. There may even be foot dragging or resistance on their part. Managers and employees who do not understand the business and are not committed to the business may attempt to sabotage strategy-implementation efforts in hopes that the organization will return to its old ways. The strategy-implementation stage of the strategic-management process is emphasized in Figure 8–1.

Marketing Issues

VISIT THE NET

An excellent PowerPoint presentation on marketing issues related to strategic management.
www.cl.uh.edu/bpa/ hadm/HADM_5731/ ppt_presentations/ 3mktpln/index.htm

Countless marketing variables affect the success or failure of strategy implementation, and the scope of this text does not allow us to address all those issues. Some examples of marketing decisions that may require policies are as follows:

1. To use exclusive dealerships or multiple channels of distribution.
2. To use heavy, light, or no TV advertising.
3. To limit (or not) the share of business done with a single customer.
4. To be a price leader or a price follower.
5. To offer a complete or limited warranty.
6. To reward salespeople based on straight salary, straight commission, or a combination salary/commission.
7. To advertise online or not.

A marketing issue of increasing concern to consumers today is the extent to which companies can track individuals' movements on the Internet—and even be able to identify an individual by name and e-mail address. Individuals' wanderings on the

FIGURE 8–1

A Comprehensive Strategic-Management Model

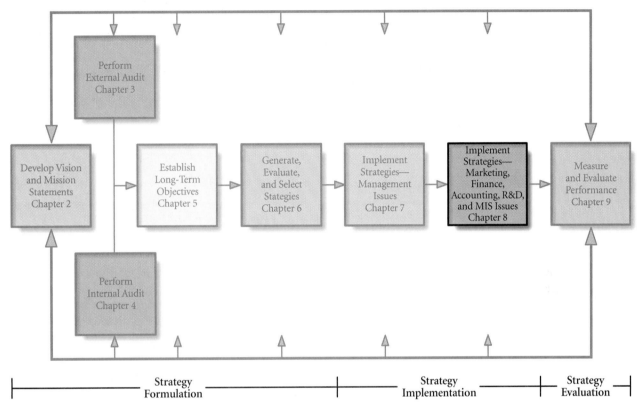

Internet are no longer anonymous, as many persons believe. Marketing companies such as Doubleclick, Flycast, AdKnowledge, AdForce, and Real Media have sophisticated methods to identify who you are and your particular interests.[1] If you are especially concerned about being tracked, visit the **www.networkadvertising.org** Web site that gives details about how marketers today are identifying you and your buying habits.

Two variables are of central importance to strategy implementation: *market segmentation* and *product positioning.* Market segmentation and product positioning rank as marketing's most important contributions to strategic management.

Market Segmentation

Market segmentation is widely used in implementing strategies, especially for small and specialized firms. Market segmentation can be defined as the subdividing of a market into distinct subsets of customers according to needs and buying habits.

Market segmentation is an important variable in strategy implementation for at least three major reasons. First, strategies such as market development, product development, market penetration, and diversification require increased sales through new markets and products. To implement these strategies successfully, new or improved market-segmentation approaches are required. Second, market segmentation allows a firm to operate with limited resources because mass production, mass distribution, and mass advertising are not required. Market segmentation enables a small firm to compete successfully with a large firm by maximizing per-unit profits and per-segment sales. Finally, market segmentation decisions directly affect *marketing mix variables*: product, place, promotion, and price, as indicated in Table 8–1. For example,

VISIT THE NET

Provides CheckMATE, the industry leader in strategic planning software worldwide. This is easy-to-use software that is Windows-based. Twenty-three different industry versions are available.
www.checkmateplan.com

TABLE 8-1   The Marketing Mix Component Variables

PRODUCT	PLACE	PROMOTION	PRICE
Quality	Distribution channels	Advertising	Level
Features and options	Distribution coverage	Personal selling	Discounts and allowances
Style	Outlet location	Sales promotion	Payment terms
Brand name	Sales territories	Publicity	
Packaging	Inventory levels and locations		
Product line	Transportation carriers		
Warranty			
Service level			
Other services			

Source: E. Jerome McCarthy, *Basic Marketing: A Managerial Approach*, 9th ed. (Homewood, IL: Richard D. Irwin, Inc., 1987): 37–44.

SnackWells, a pioneer in reduced-fat snacks, has shifted its advertising emphasis from low-fat to great taste as part of its new market-segmentation strategy.

Perhaps the most dramatic new market-segmentation strategy is the targeting of regional tastes. Firms from McDonald's to General Motors are increasingly modifying their products to meet different regional preferences within the United States. Campbell's has a spicier version of its nacho cheese soup for the Southwest, and Burger King offers breakfast burritos in New Mexico but not in South Carolina. Geographic and demographic bases for segmenting markets are the most commonly employed, as illustrated in Table 8–2. Note that gender is a popular demographic segmentation variable; it is discussed further in the "E-Commerce Perspective" box.

Evaluating potential market segments requires strategists to determine the characteristics and needs of consumers, to analyze consumer similarities and differences, and to develop consumer group profiles. Segmenting consumer markets is generally much simpler and easier than segmenting industrial markets, because industrial products, such as electronic circuits and forklifts, have multiple applications and appeal to diverse customer groups. Note in Figure 8–2 that customer age is used to segment automobile car purchases. Note that some older buyers especially like Cadillacs and Buicks.

Segmentation is a key to matching supply and demand, which is one of the thorniest problems in customer service. Segmentation often reveals that large, random fluctuations in demand actually consist of several small, predictable, and manageable patterns. Matching supply and demand allows factories to produce desirable levels without extra shifts, overtime, and subcontracting. Matching supply and demand also minimizes the number and severity of stock-outs. The demand for hotel rooms, for example, can be dependent on foreign tourists, businesspersons, and vacationers. Focusing on these three market segments separately, however, can allow hotel firms to predict overall supply and demand more effectively.

Banks now are segmenting markets to increase effectiveness. "You're dead in the water if you aren't segmenting the market," says Anne Moore, president of a bank consulting firm in Atlanta. As indicated in the "E-Commerce Perspective" box, the Internet makes market segmentation easier today because consumers naturally form "communities" on the Web.

VISIT THE NET

Gives the strategic plan for the Medical University of South Carolina, including a section on strategy implementation.
www.musc.edu/plan

TABLE 8-2   Alternative Bases for Market Segmentation

VARIABLE	TYPICAL BREAKDOWNS
GEOGRAPHIC	
Region	Pacific, Mountain, West North Central, West South Central, East North Cental, East South Central, South Atlantic, Middle Atlantic, New England
County Size	A,B,C,D
City Size	Under 5,000; 5,000–20,000; 20,000–50,000; 50,000–100,000; 100,000–250,000; 250,000–500,000; 500,000–1,000,000; 1,000,000–4,000,000; 4,000,000 or over
Density	Urban, suburban, rural
Climate	Northern, southern
DEMOGRAPHIC	
Age	Under 6, 6–11, 12–19, 20–34, 35–49, 50–64, 65+
Gender	Male, female
Family Size	1–2, 3–4, 5+
Family Life Cycle	Young, single; young, married, no children; young, married, youngest child under 6; young, married, youngest child 6 or over; older, married, with children; older, married, no children under 18; older, single; other
Income	Under $10,000; $10,001–$15,000; $15,001–$20,000; $20,001–$30,000; $30,001–$50,000; $50,001–$70,000; $70,001–$100,000; over $100,000
Occupation	Professional and technical; managers, officials, and proprietors; clerical, sales; craftsmen, foremen; operatives; farmers; retired; students; housewives; unemployed
Education	Grade school or less; some high school; high school graduate; some college; college graduate
Religion	Catholic, Protestant, Jewish, Islamic, other
Race	White, Asian, Hispanic, African American
Nationality	American, British, French, German, Scandinavian, Italian, Latin American, Middle Eastern, Japanese
PSYCHOGRAPHIC	
Social Class	Lower lowers, upper lowers, lower middles, upper middles, lower uppers, upper uppers
Personality	Compulsive, gregarious, authoritarian, ambitious
BEHAVIORAL	
Use Occasion	Regular occasion, special occasion
Benefits Sought	Quality, service, economy
User Status	Nonuser, ex-user, potential user, first-time user, regular user
Usage Rate	Light user, medium user, heavy user
Loyalty Status	None, medium, strong, absolute
Readiness Stage	Unaware, aware, informed, interested, desirous, intending to buy
Attitude Toward Product	Enthusiastic, positive, indifferent, negative, hostile

Source: Adapted from Philip Kotler, *Marketing Management: Analysis, Planning and Control*, © 1984: 256. Adapted by permission of Prentice-Hall, Inc., Englewood Cliffs, New Jersey.

FIGURE 8-2

Average Age of Automobile Buyers, by Brand

Plymouth	38	Pontiac	42	Infiniti	45
Mitsubishi	38	Acura	42	Subaru	45
Volkswagen	38	Hyundai	42	Oldsmobile	46
Honda	41	Suzuki	42	Saturn	46
Isuzu	41	Audi	42	Chrysler	47
Kia	41	Daewoo	43	Lexus	47
Land Rover	41	Chevrolet	43	Jaguar	49
Mazda	41	Porsche	43	Mercury	50
Nissan	41	Saab	43	Lincoln	51
BMW	42	GMC	44	Cadillac	53
Dodge	42	Toyota	44	Buick	57
Jeep	42	Volvo	44		
Ford	42	Mercedes-Benz	45		

Source: Adapted from Norihiko Shirouzu, "This Is Not Your Father's Toyota," *Wall Street Journal* (March 26, 2002): B1.

E-COMMERCE PERSPECTIVE

Male versus Female Internet Usage Globally

Note from the table below that the United States and Canada are the only countries in the world where female Internet usage is higher than male usage. Note that in many countries, including Germany, Italy, and India, male usage exceeds female usage by more than 20 percent.

COUNTRY	FEMALE	MALE
Argentina	45.4%	54.6%
Australia	46.9	53.1
Austria	42.8	57.2
Belgium	40.5	59.5
Brazil	43.1	56.9
Canada	51.9	48.1
Denmark	44.8	55.2
Finland	47.0	53.0
France	39.8	60.2
Germany	39.0	61.0
Hong Kong	43.9	56.1
India	33.9	66.1
Ireland	45.2	64.8
Israel	42.6%	57.4%
Italy	36.4	63.6
Japan	42.3	57.7
Mexico	40.6	59.4
Netherlands	43.1	57.0
New Zealand	49.6	50.4
Norway	43.4	56.6
Singapore	45.0	55.0
South Africa	43.1	56.9
South Korea	45.9	54.1
Spain	41.1	58.9
Sweden	44.9	55.1
Switzerland	41.4	58.6
Taiwan	45.0	55.0
United Kingdom	44.5	55.5
United States	51.4	48.6

Source: Adapted from Brad Reagan, "The Great Divide," *Wall Street Journal* (April 15, 2002): R4.

E-COMMERCE PERSPECTIVE

Hotels Adding Wi-Fi Wireless Internet Service

By the end of 2003, 9,000 hotels in the United States and Canada were offering wireless Internet service in their lobbies. That number is up from 4,000 in 2002 and 1,000 in 2001. Hotel companies consider this to be the next must-have amenity because so many customers today bring their laptops with them to hotels. Wi-Fi availability means customers do not need to hook into the hotel's phone system to get online. Adding Wi-Fi in hotel lobbies could be classified as "product development," since it is adding another feature to the lodging product/service. Some hotels are even adding Wi-Fi in all their hotel rooms. This strategy, like many strategies, is very expensive and cost-benefit analyses may or may not justify the expenditure, depending on the particular company and the location of its units relative to rival hotels.

Source: Dan Reed, "Hotels Plan to Hook Guests with Wi-Fi," *USA Today* (September 17, 2003): 1E.

Does the Internet Make Market Segmentation Easier?

Yes. The segments of people that marketers want to reach online are much more precisely defined than the segments of people reached through traditional forms of media, such as television, radio, and magazines. For example, **Quepasa.com** is widely visited by Hispanics. Marketers aiming to reach college students, who are notoriously difficult to reach via traditional media, focus on sites such as **collegeclub.com** and **studentadvantage.com**. The gay and lesbian population, which is estimated to comprise about 5 percent of the U. S. population, has always been difficult to reach via traditional media but now can be focused on sites such as **gay.com**. Marketers can reach persons interested in specific topics, such as travel or fishing, by placing banners on related Web sites.

People all over the world are congregating into virtual communities on the Web by becoming members/customers/visitors of Web sites that focus on an endless range of topics. People in essence segment themselves by nature of the Web sites that comprise their "favorite places," and many of these Web sites sell information regarding their "visitors." Businesses and groups of individuals all over the world pool their purchasing power in Web sites to get volume discounts.

Product Positioning

After markets have been segmented so that the firm can target particular customer groups, the next step is to find out what customers want and expect. This takes analysis and research. A severe mistake is to assume the firm knows what customers want and expect. Countless research studies reveal large differences between how customers define service and rank the importance of different service activities and how producers view services. Many firms have become successful by filling the gap between what customers and producers see as good service. What the customer believes is good service is paramount, not what the producer believes service should be.

Identifying target customers upon whom to focus marketing efforts sets the stage for deciding how to meet the needs and wants of particular consumer groups. Product positioning is widely used for this purpose. Positioning entails developing schematic representations that reflect how your products or services compare to competitors' on dimensions most important to success in the industry. The following steps are required in product positioning:

1. Select key criteria that effectively differentiate products or services in the industry.
2. Diagram a two-dimensional product-positioning map with specified criteria on each axis.
3. Plot major competitors' products or services in the resultant four-quadrant matrix.
4. Identify areas in the positioning map where the company's products or services could be most competitive in the given target market. Look for vacant areas (niches).
5. Develop a marketing plan to position the company's products or services appropriately.

Because just two criteria can be examined on a single product-positioning map, multiple maps are often developed to assess various approaches to strategy implementation. Multidimensional scaling could be used to examine three or more criteria simultaneously, but this technique requires computer assistance and is beyond the scope of this text. Some examples of product-positioning maps are illustrated in Figure 8–3.

Some rules for using product positioning as a strategy-implementation tool are the following:

1. Look for the hole or *vacant niche.* The best strategic opportunity might be an unserved segment.
2. Don't squat between segments. Any advantage from squatting (such as a larger target market) is offset by a failure to satisfy one segment. In decision-theory terms, the intent here is to avoid suboptimization by trying to serve more than one objective function.
3. Don't serve two segments with the same strategy. Usually, a strategy successful with one segment cannot be directly transferred to another segment.
4. Don't position yourself in the middle of the map. The middle usually means a strategy that is not clearly perceived to have any distinguishing characteristics. This rule can vary with the number of competitors. For example, when there are only two competitors, as in U. S. presidential elections, the middle becomes the preferred strategic position.[2]

An effective product-positioning strategy meets two criteria: (1) it uniquely distinguishes a company from the competition, and (2) it leads customers to expect slightly less service than a company can deliver. Firms should not create expectations that exceed the service the firm can or will deliver. Network Equipment Technology is an example of a company that keeps customer expectations slightly below perceived performance. This is a constant challenge for marketers. Firms need to inform customers about what to expect and then exceed the promise. Underpromise and then overdeliver!

VISIT THE NET

Provides the 2000 Strategic Plan of the National Archives and Records Administration, including "What Must We Do to Get There?" (implementation) issues.
www.archives.gov/about_us/strategic_planning_and_reporting/2003_strategic_plan.html

Finance/Accounting Issues

In this section, we examine several finance/accounting concepts considered to be central to strategy implementation: acquiring needed capital, developing pro forma financial statements, preparing financial budgets, and evaluating the worth of a business. Some examples of decisions that may require finance/accounting policies are:

FIGURE 8-3

Examples of Product-Positioning Maps

A. A PRODUCT-POSITIONING MAP
   FOR BANKS

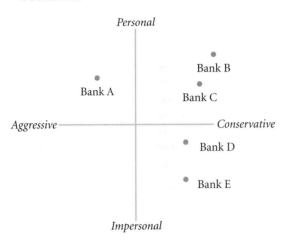

B. A PRODUCT-POSITIONING MAP
   FOR PERSONAL COMPUTERS

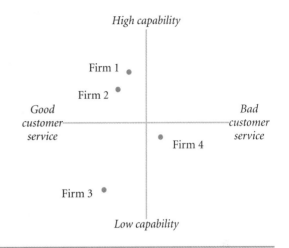

C. A PRODUCT-POSITIONING MAP FOR
   MENSWEAR RETAIL STORES

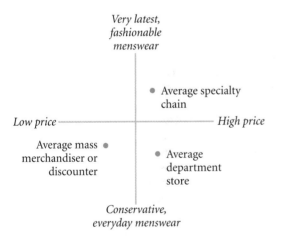

D. A PRODUCT-POSITIONING MAP
   FOR THE RENTAL CAR MARKET

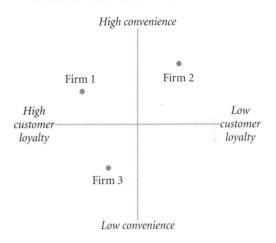

1. To raise capital with short-term debt, long-term debt, preferred stock, or common stock.

2. To lease or buy fixed assets.

3. To determine an appropriate dividend payout ratio.

4. To use LIFO (Last-in, First-out), FIFO (First-in, First-out), or a market-value accounting approach.

5. To extend the time of accounts receivable.

6. To establish a certain percentage discount on accounts within a specified period of time.

7. To determine the amount of cash that should be kept on hand.

Acquiring Capital
to Implement Strategies

Successful strategy implementation often requires additional capital. Besides net profit from operations and the sale of assets, two basic sources of capital for an organization are debt and equity. Determining an appropriate mix of debt and equity in a firm's capital structure can be vital to successful strategy implementation. An *Earnings Per Share/Earnings Before Interest and Taxes (EPS/EBIT) analysis* is the most widely used technique for determining whether debt, stock, or a combination of debt and stock is the best alternative for raising capital to implement strategies. This technique involves an examination of the impact that debt versus stock financing has on earnings per share under various assumptions as to EBIT.

Theoretically, an enterprise should have enough debt in its capital structure to boost its return on investment by applying debt to products and projects earning more than the cost of the debt. In low earning periods, too much debt in the capital structure of an organization can endanger stockholders' returns and jeopardize company survival. Fixed debt obligations generally must be met, regardless of circumstances. This does not mean that stock issuances are always better than debt for raising capital. Some special concerns with stock issuances are dilution of ownership, effect on stock price, and the need to share future earnings with all new shareholders.

Without going into detail on other institutional and legal issues related to the debt versus stock decision, EPS/EBIT may be best explained by working through an example. Let's say the Brown Company needs to raise $1 million to finance implementation of a market-development strategy. The company's common stock currently sells for $50 per share, and 100,000 shares are outstanding. The prime interest rate is 10 percent, and the company's tax rate is 50 percent. The company's earnings before interest and taxes next year are expected to be $2 million if a recession occurs, $4 million if the economy stays as is, and $8 million if the economy significantly improves. EPS/EBIT analysis can be used to determine if all stock, all debt, or some combination of stock and debt is the best capital financing alternative. The EPS/EBIT analysis for this example is provided in Table 8–3.

As indicated by the EPS values of 9.5, 19.50, and 39.50 in Table 8–3, debt is the best financing alternative for the Brown Company if a recession, boom, or normal year is expected. An EPS/EBIT chart can be constructed to determine the breakeven point, where one financing alternative becomes more attractive than

TABLE 8–3   EPS/EBIT Analysis for the Brown Company (in millions)

	COMMON STOCK FINANCING			DEBT FINANCING			COMBINATION FINANCING		
	Recession	*Normal*	*Boom*	*Recession*	*Normal*	*Boom*	*Recession*	*Normal*	*Boom*
EBIT	$2.0	$ 4.0	$ 8.0	$2.0	$ 4.0	$ 8.0	$2.0	$ 4.0	$ 8.0
Interest[a]	0	0	0	.10	.10	.10	.05	.05	.05
EBT	2.0	4.0	8.0	1.9	3.9	7.9	1.95	3.95	7.95
Taxes	1.0	2.0	4.0	.95	1.95	3.95	.975	1.975	3.975
EAT	1.0	2.0	4.0	.95	1.95	3.95	.975	1.975	3.975
#Shares[b]	.12	.12	.12	.10	.10	.10	.11	.11	.11
EPS[c]	8.33	16.66	33.33	9.5	19.50	39.50	8.86	17.95	36.14

[a]The annual interest charge on $1 million at 10% is $100,000 and on $0.5 million is $50,000. This row is in $, not %.
[b]To raise all of the needed $1 million with stock, 20,000 new shares must be issued, raising the total to 120,000 shares outstanding. To raise one-half of the needed $1 million with stock, 10,000 new shares must be issued, raising the total to 110,000 shares outstanding.
[c]EPS = Earnings After Taxes (EAT) divided by shares (number of shares outstanding).

another. Figure 8–4 indicates that issuing common stock is the least attractive financing alternative for the Brown Company.

EPS/EBIT analysis is a valuable tool for making the capital financing decisions needed to implement strategies, but several considerations should be made whenever using this technique. First, profit levels may be higher for stock or debt alternatives when EPS levels are lower. For example, looking only at the earnings after taxes (EAT) values in Table 8–3, you can see that the common stock option is the best alternative, regardless of economic conditions. If the Brown Company's mission includes strict profit maximization, as opposed to the maximization of stockholders' wealth or some other criterion, then stock rather than debt is the best choice of financing.

Another consideration when using EPS/EBIT analysis is flexibility. As an organization's capital structure changes, so does its flexibility for considering future capital needs. Using all debt or all stock to raise capital in the present may impose fixed obligations, restrictive covenants, or other constraints that could severely reduce a firm's ability to raise additional capital in the future. Control is also a concern. When additional stock is issued to finance strategy implementation, ownership and control of the enterprise are diluted. This can be a serious concern in today's business environment of hostile takeovers, mergers, and acquisitions.

Dilution of ownership can be an overriding concern in closely held corporations in which stock issuances affect the decision-making power of majority stockholders. For example, the Smucker family owns 30 percent of the stock in Smucker's, a well-known jam and jelly company. When Smucker's acquired Dickson Family, Inc., the company used mostly debt rather than stock in order not to dilute the family ownership.

When using EPS/EBIT analysis, timing in relation to movements of stock prices, interest rates, and bond prices becomes important. In times of depressed stock prices, debt may prove to be the most suitable alternative from both a cost and a demand standpoint. However, when cost of capital (interest rates) is high, stock issuances become more attractive.

Table 8–4 provides an EPS/EBIT for two companies—Best Buy and Heinz. Notice in those analyses that the combination stock/debt options vary from 50/50 to 80/20 and 60/40. Any number of combinations could be explored. Also notice that the graphs again reflect parallel lines. However, sometimes in preparing the EPS/EBIT graphs, the lines will intersect thus revealing breakeven points at which one financing

FIGURE 8–4

An EPS/EBIT Chart for the Brown Company

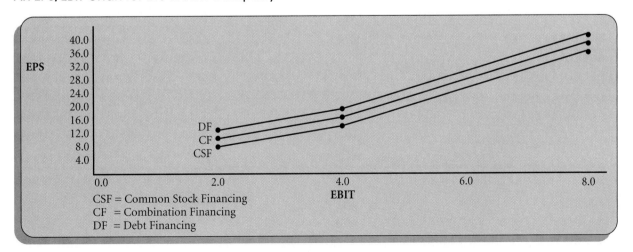

CSF = Common Stock Financing
CF   = Combination Financing
DF   = Debt Financing

TABLE 8-4   EPS/EBIT Analysis for Best Buy and Heinz

EPS/EBIT Analysis (in $millions for Best Buy at year-end 2001)
$Amount Needed: $500
Stock Price $30
EBIT Range $1000 to $2000
Tax Rate 366/936 = .4 = 40%
Interest Rate 5%
# of Shares Outstanding 321

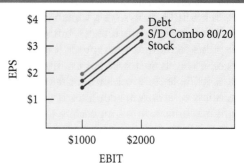

	(S) STOCK FINANCING		(D) FINANCING		80/20 S/D FINANCING	
	High	*Low*	*High*	*Low*	*High*	*Low*
EBIT ($937 in 2001)	$2000	$1000	$2000	$1000	$2000	$1000
Interest (5%)	0	0	25	25	5	5
EBT	2000	1000	1975	975	1995	995
Taxes 40%	800	400	790	390	797	398
EAT	1200	600	1185	585	1198	597
# of Shares Outstanding	337	337	321	321	334	334
EPS	3.56	1.78	3.69	1.82	3.59	1.79

Conclusion: Best Buy should use debt to raise the $500 million.

EPS/EBIT Analysis (in $millions for Heinz at year-end 2001)
$Amount Needed: $500
Stock Price $40
EBIT Range $1000 to $2000
Tax Rate 175/673 = .26 = 26%
Interest Rate 5%
# of Shares Outstanding 350

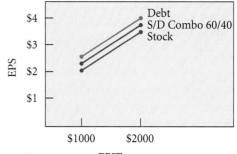

	(S) STOCK FINANCING		(D) FINANCING		60/40 S/D FINANCING	
	High	*Low*	*High*	*Low*	*High*	*Low*
EBIT ($982.4 in 2001)	$2000	$1000	$2000	$1000	$2000	$1000
Interest (5%)	0	0	25	25	10	10
EBT	2000	1000	1975	975	1990	990
Taxes 26%	520	260	514	254	517	257
EAT	1480	740	1461	721	1473	733
# of Shares Outstanding	362.5	362.5	350	350	357.5	357.5
EPS	4.08	2.04	4.17	2.06	4.12	2.05

Conclusion: Heinz should use debt to raise the $500 million.

alternative becomes more or less attractive than another. The slope of these lines will be determined by a combination of factors including stock price, interest rate, number of shares, and amount of capital needed. Also, it should be noted here that even though Debt financing is recommended in the two examples, Stock or the Combo approaches oftentimes will be best, as indicated by the highest EPS values. Finally in Table 8–4, note that the tax rates for companies vary considerably and should be computed from the respective income statements by dividing taxes paid by income before taxes.

Projected Financial Statements

Projected financial statement analysis is a central strategy-implementation technique because it allows an organization to examine the expected results of various actions and approaches. This type of analysis can be used to forecast the impact of various implementation decisions (for example, to increase promotion expenditures by 50 percent to support a market-development strategy, to increase salaries by 25 percent to support a market-penetration strategy, to increase research and development expenditures by 70 percent to support product development, or to sell $1 million of common stock to raise capital for diversification). Nearly all financial institutions require at least three years of projected financial statements whenever a business seeks capital. A projected income statement and balance sheet allow an organization to compute projected financial ratios under various strategy-implementation scenarios. When compared to prior years and to industry averages, financial ratios provide valuable insights into the feasibility of various strategy-implementation approaches.

Primarily as a result of the Enron collapse and accounting scandal, and the ensuring Sarbanes-Oxley Act, companies today are being much more diligent in preparing projected financial statements to "reasonably rather than too optimistically" project future expenses and earnings. There is much more care not to mislead shareholders and other constituencies.[3]

A 2005 projected income statement and balance sheet for the Litten Company are provided in Table 8–5. The projected statements for Litten are based on five assumptions: (1) The company needs to raise $45 million to finance expansion into foreign markets; (2) $30 million of this total will be raised through increased debt and $15 million through common stock; (3) sales are expected to increase 50 percent; (4) three new facilities, costing a total of $30 million, will be constructed in foreign markets; and (5) land for the new facilities is already owned by the company. Note in Table 8–5 that Litten's strategies and their implementation are expected to result in a sales increase from $100 million to $150 million and in a net increase in income from $6 million to $9.75 million in the forecasted year.

There are six steps in performing projected financial analysis:

1. Prepare the projected income statement before the balance sheet. Start by forecasting sales as accurately as possible. Be careful not to blindly push historical percentages into the future with regard to revenue (sales) increases. Be mindful of what the firm did to achieve those past sales increases, which may not be appropriate for the future unless the firm takes similar or analogous actions (such as opening a similar number of stores, for example). If dealing with a manufacturing firm, also be mindful that if the firm is operating at 100 percent capacity running three eight-hour shifts per day, then probably new manufacturing facilities (land, plant, and equipment) will be needed to increase sales further.

2. Use the percentage-of-sales method to project cost of goods sold (CGS) and the expense items in the income statement. For example, if CGS is 70 percent

TABLE 8-5   A Projected Income Statement and Balance Sheet
               for the Litten Company (in millions)

	PRIOR YEAR 2004	PROJECTED YEAR 2005	REMARKS
PROJECTED INCOME STATEMENT			
Sales	100	150.00	50% increase
Cost of Goods Sold	70	105.00	70% of sales
Gross Margin	30	45.00	
Selling Expense	10	15.00	10% of sales
Administrative Expense	5	7.50	5% of sales
Earnings Before Interest and Taxes	15	22.50	
Interest	3	3.00	
Earnings Before Taxes	12	19.50	
Taxes	6	9.75	50% rate
Net Income	6	9.75	
Dividends	2	5.00	
Retained Earnings	4	4.75	
PROJECTED BALANCE SHEET			
Assets			
Cash	5	7.75	Plug figure
Accounts Receivable	2	4.00	100% increase
Inventory	20	45.00	
Total Current Assets	27	56.75	
Land	15	15.00	
Plant and Equipment	50	80.00	Add 3 new plants at $10 million each
Less Depreciation	10	20.00	
Net Plant and Equipment	40	60.00	
Total Fixed Assets	55	75.00	
Total Assets	82	131.75	
Liabilities			
Accounts Payable	10	10.00	
Notes Payable	10	10.00	
Total Current Liabilities	20	20.00	
Long-term Debt	40	70.00	Borrowed $30 million
Additional Paid-in-Capital	20	35.00	Issued 100,000 shares at $150 each
Retained Earnings	2	6.75	2 + 4.75
Total Liabilities and Net Worth	82	131.75	

of sales in the prior year (as it is in Table 8–4), then use that same percentage to calculate CGS in the future year—unless there is a reason to use a different percentage. Items such as interest, dividends, and taxes must be treated independently and cannot be forecasted using the percentage-of-sales method.

3. Calculate the projected net income.

4. Subtract from the net income any dividends to be paid for that year. This remaining net income is Retained Earnings. Bring this retained earnings amount for that year (NI − DIV = RE) over to the balance sheet by adding it to the prior year's RE shown on the balance sheet. In other words, every year a firm adds its RE for that particular year (from the income statement) to its historical RE total on the balance sheet. Therefore the RE amount on the balance sheet is a cumulative number rather than money available for strategy implementation! Note that RE is the first projected balance sheet item to be entered. Due to this accounting procedure in developing projected financial statements, the RE amount on the balance sheet is usually a large number. However, it also can be a low or even negative number if the firm has been incurring losses. The only way for RE to decrease from one year to the next on the balance sheet is: (1) if the firm incurred an earnings loss that year, or (2) the firm had positive net income for the year but paid out dividends more than the net income. Be mindful that RE is the key link between a projected income statement and balance sheet, so be careful to make this calculation correctly.

5. Project the balance sheet items, beginning with retained earnings and then forecasting stockholders' equity, long-term liabilities, current liabilities, total liabilities, total assets, fixed assets, and current assets (in that order). Use the cash account as the plug figure—that is, use the cash account to make the assets total the liabilities and net worth. Then make appropriate adjustments. For example, if the cash needed to balance the statements is too small (or too large), make appropriate changes to borrow more (or less) money than planned.

6. List comments (remarks) on the projected statements. Any time a significant change is made in an item from a prior year to the projected year, an explanation (remark) should be provided. Remarks are essential because otherwise pro formas are meaningless.

The U. S. Securities and Exchange Commission (SEC) conducts fraud investigations if projected numbers are misleading or if they omit information that's important to investors. Projected statements must conform with generally accepted accounting principles (GAAP) and must not be designed to hide poor expected results. The Sarbanes-Oxley Act passed in 2002 requires CEOs and CFOs of corporations to personally sign their firms' financial statements attesting to their accuracy. These executives could thus be held personally liable for misleading or inaccurate statements. The collapse of the Arthur Andersen accounting firm in 2002, along with its client Enron has fostered a "zero tolerance" policy among auditors and shareholders with regard to a firm's financial statements. But, plenty of firms still "inflate" their financial projections and call them "pro formas," so investors, shareholders, and other stakeholders must still be wary of different companies' financial projections.[4]

Financial Budgets

A *financial budget* is a document that details how funds will be obtained and spent for a specified period of time. Annual budgets are most common, although the period of time for a budget can range from one day to more than ten years.

Fundamentally, financial budgeting is a method for specifying what must be done to complete strategy implementation successfully. Financial budgeting should not be thought of as a tool for limiting expenditures but rather as a method for obtaining the most productive and profitable use of an organization's resources. Financial budgets can be viewed as the planned allocation of a firm's resources based on forecasts of the future.

There are almost as many different types of financial budgets as there are types of organizations. Some common types of budgets include cash budgets, operating budgets, sales budgets, profit budgets, factory budgets, capital budgets, expense budgets, divisional budgets, variable budgets, flexible budgets, and fixed budgets. When an organization is experiencing financial difficulties, budgets are especially important in guiding strategy implementation.

Perhaps the most common type of financial budget is the *cash budget*. The Financial Accounting Standards Board (FASB) has mandated that every publicly held company in the United States must issue an annual cash-flow statement in addition to the usual financial reports. The statement includes all receipts and disbursements of cash in operations, investments, and financing. It supplements the Statement on Changes in Financial Position formerly included in the annual reports of all publicly held companies. A cash budget for the year 2005 for the Toddler Toy Company is provided in Table 8–6. Note that Toddler is not expecting to have surplus cash until November 2005.

Financial budgets have some limitations. First, budgetary programs can become so detailed that they are cumbersome and overly expensive. Overbudgeting

TABLE 8–6   A Six-Month Cash Budget for the Toddler Toy Company in 2005

CASH BUDGET (IN THOUSANDS)	JULY	AUG.	SEPT.	OCT.	NOV.	DEC.	JAN.
Receipts							
Collections	$12,000	$21,000	$31,000	$35,000	$22,000	$18,000	$11,000
Payments							
Purchases	14,000	21,000	28,000	14,000	14,000	7,000	
Wages and Salaries	1,500	2,000	2,500	1,500	1,500	1,000	
Rent	500	500	500	500	500	500	
Other Expenses	200	300	400	200	—	100	
Taxes	—	8,000	—	—	—	—	
Payment on Machine	—	—	10,000	—	—	—	
Total Payments	$16,200	$31,800	$41,400	$16,200	$16,000	$8,600	
Net Cash Gain (Loss) During Month	−4,200	−10,800	−10,400	18,800	6,000	9,400	
Cash at Start of Month if No Borrowing Is Done	6,000	1,800	−9,000	−19,400	−600	5,400	
Cumulative Cash (Cash at start plus gains or minus losses)	1,800	−9,000	−19,400	−600	5,400	14,800	
Less Desired Level of Cash	−5,000	−5,000	−5,000	−5,000	−5,000	−5,000	
Total Loans Outstanding to Maintain $5,000 Cash Balance	$3,200	$14,000	$24,400	$5,600	—	—	
Surplus Cash	—	—	—	—	400	9,800	

or underbudgeting can cause problems. Second, financial budgets can become a substitute for objectives. A budget is a tool and not an end in itself. Third, budgets can hide inefficiencies if based solely on precedent rather than on periodic evaluation of circumstances and standards. Finally, budgets are sometimes used as instruments of tyranny that result in frustration, resentment, absenteeism, and high turnover. To minimize the effect of this last concern, managers should increase the participation of subordinates in preparing budgets.

Evaluating the Worth of a Business

Evaluating the worth of a business is central to strategy implementation because integrative, intensive, and diversification strategies are often implemented by acquiring other firms. Other strategies, such as retrenchment and divestiture, may result in the sale of a division of an organization or of the firm itself. Thousands of transactions occur each year in which businesses are bought or sold in the United States. In all these cases, it is necessary to establish the financial worth or cash value of a business to successfully implement strategies.

All the various methods for determining a business's worth can be grouped into three main approaches: what a firm owns, what a firm earns, or what a firm will bring in the market. But it is important to realize that valuation is not an exact science. The valuation of a firm's worth is based on financial facts, but common sense and intuitive judgment must enter into the process. It is difficult to assign a monetary value to some factors—such as a loyal customer base, a history of growth, legal suits pending, dedicated employees, a favorable lease, a bad credit rating, or good patents—that may not be reflected in a firm's financial statements. Also, different valuation methods will yield different totals for a firm's worth, and no prescribed approach is best for a certain situation. Evaluating the worth of a business truly requires both qualitative and quantitative skills.

The first approach in evaluating the worth of a business is determining its net worth or stockholders' equity. Net worth represents the sum of common stock, additional paid-in capital, and retained earnings. After calculating net worth, add or subtract an appropriate amount for goodwill and overvalued or undervalued assets. This total provides a reasonable estimate of a firm's monetary value. If a firm has goodwill, it will be listed on the balance sheet, perhaps as "intangibles." It should be noted that Financial Accounting Standard Board (FASB) Rule 142 requires companies to admit once a year if the premiums they paid for acquisitions, called goodwill, were a waste of money. Goodwill is not a good thing to have on a balance sheet. Companies with the "too much" goodwill in 2003 include AOL Time Warner ($81.7 billion, 51% of total assets), Viacom ($57.5 billion, 64% of total assets), and Kraft Foods ($36.4 billion, 64% of total assets). AOL converted $54 billion of its goodwill into an earnings loss in 2002 and another $45.5 billion "write down" in 2003, as the firm struggles to avoid bankruptcy.[5] As noted in the "Global Perspective" box, accounting standards worldwide are converging.

The second approach to measuring the value of a firm grows out of the belief that the worth of any business should be based largely on the future benefits its owners may derive through net profits. A conservative rule of thumb is to establish a business's worth as five times the firm's current annual profit. A five-year average profit level could also be used. When using the approach, remember that firms normally suppress earnings in their financial statements to minimize taxes.

The third approach, letting the market determine a business's worth, involves three methods. First, base the firm's worth on the selling price of a similar company. A potential problem, however, is that sometimes comparable figures are not easy to locate, even though substantial information on firms that buy or sell to other firms is available in major libraries. The second approach is called the *price-earnings ratio method*. To use

GLOBAL PERSPECTIVE

Standardizing Accounting Standards Globally

The Financial Accounting Standards Board (FASB) in the U.S. and its counterpart, the International Accounting Standards Board (IASB), are each modifying its "rules" in an effort to converge accounting standards globally. It is unusual for the FASB to change simply to meet the IASB, but there is more and more movement from both sides towards convergence. And yes, the FASB is changing too. Standard setters in both the U. S. and other countries mutually desire the financial statements of a company—say in France—one day be comparable to those in the U. S. Accounting standards convergence would greatly simplify cross-border investment, interaction, and trade.

The FASB and the IASB began meeting twice yearly in 2002 which is good. The European Union of countries has agreed to adopt the IASB's standards by 2005. Actually about 91 countries worldwide will require their companies to comply with IASB standards by 2005. However, there still exist many differences though between FASB and IASB

standards. For example, the FASB does not allow for upward re-evaluation of property, plant, and equipment, whereas the IASB permits periodic re-evaluation up or down of assets. Thus, property, plant, and equipment on the statements of U. S. firms is often worth a lot more than reflected on the books. For another example, the IASB wants to remove net income from the income statement, but the FASB has not reached a decision on this issue. There are also differences between FASB and IASB in accounting for acquisitions as well as differences between when revenue should be booked.

One day decades in the future, there may be one currency worldwide. Certainly, convergence between accounting systems among countries worldwide would be step in that direction. Establishment of the Euro was a big step too in that direction. Convergence of accounting systems simply makes doing business much easier among businesses worldwide.

Source: Adapted from: Cassell Bryan-Low, "Accounting's Global Rule Book," *Wall Street Journal* (November 28, 2003): C1.

this method, divide the market price of the firm's common stock by the annual earnings per share and multiply this number by the firm's average net income for the past five years. The third approach can be called the *outstanding shares method*. To use this method, simply multiply the number of shares outstanding by the market price per share and add a premium. The premium is simply a per-share dollar amount that a person or firm is willing to pay to control (acquire) the other company. As indicated in the "Global Perspective," European firms aggressively are acquiring American firms, using these and perhaps other methods for evaluating the worth of their target companies.

Business evaluations are becoming routine in many situations. Businesses have many strategy-implementation reasons for determining their worth in addition to preparing to be sold or to buy other companies. Employee plans, taxes, retirement packages, mergers, acquisitions, expansion plans, banking relationships, death of a principal, divorce, partnership agreements, and IRS audits are other reasons for a periodic valuation. It is just good business to have a reasonable understanding of what your firm is worth. This knowledge protects the interests of all parties involved.

Table 8–7 provides the cash value analyses for three companies—Wachovia, Best Buy, and Heinz—for year-end 2001. Notice that there is significant variation among the four methods used to determine cash value. For example, Wachovia's cash value ranged from $249 billion to $33 billion. Obviously, if you were selling your company, you would seek the larger values while if purchasing a company, you would seek the lower values. In practice, substantial negotiation takes place in reaching a final compromise (or averaged) amount. Also recognize that if a firm's net income is negative,

TABLE 8-7   Cash Value Analyses for Wachovia, Best Buy, and Heinz

A. Cash Value of Wachovia in $millions at year-end 2001	
1. Stockholders' Equity + Goodwill = 28,455 + 12,772	$ 41,227
2. Net Income × 5 = $6,671 × 5	$ 33,355
3. Share price = $56 /EPS = $1.55 × Net Income $6,671	$ 241,016
4. Number of Shares Outstanding × Share Price = 4,450 × $56	$ 249,200
Method Average	**$ 141,199**
B. Cash Value of Best Buy in $millions at year-end 2001	
1. Stockholders' Equity + Goodwill = $2,521 + 773	$ 3,294
2. Net Income × 5 = $570 × 5	$ 2,850
3. Share price = $30 /EPS = $2.65 × Net Income $570	$ 2,049
4. Number of Shares Outstanding × Share Price = 321 × $30	$ 6,450
Method Average	**$ 3,660**
C. Cash Value of Heinz in $millions at year-end 2001	
1. Stockholders' Equity + Goodwill = $1,374 + 2,700	$ 4,074
2. Net Income × 5 = $478 × 5	$ 2,390
3. Share price = $40 /EPS = $1.41 × Net Income $478	$ 13,560
4. Number of Shares Outstanding × Share Price = 350 × $40	$ 14,000
Method Average	**$ 8,506**

theoretically the approaches involving that figure would result in a negative number, implying that the firm would pay you to acquire them. Of course, you obtain all of the firm's debt and liabilities in an acquisition, so theoretically this would be possible.

Deciding Whether to Go Public

Going public means selling off a percentage of your company to others in order to raise capital; consequently, it dilutes the owners' control of the firm. Going public is not recommended for companies with less than $10 million in sales because the initial costs can be too high for the firm to generate sufficient cash flow to make going public worthwhile. One dollar in four is the average total cost paid to lawyers, accountants, and underwriters when an initial stock issuance is under $1 million; one dollar in twenty will go to cover these costs for issuances over $20 million.

In addition to initial costs involved with a stock offering, there are costs and obligations associated with reporting and management in a publicly held firm. For firms with more than $10 million in sales, going public can provide major advantages: It can allow the firm to raise capital to develop new products, build plants, expand, grow, and market products and services more effectively.

Research and Development (R&D) Issues

Research and development (R&D) personnel can play an integral part in strategy implementation. These individuals are generally charged with developing new products and improving old products in a way that will allow effective strategy implementation. R&D

employees and managers perform tasks that include transferring complex technology, adjusting processes to local raw materials, adapting processes to local markets, and altering products to particular tastes and specifications. Strategies such as product development, market penetration, and concentric diversification require that new products be successfully developed and that old products be significantly improved. But the level of management support for R&D is often constrained by resource availability.

Technological improvements that affect consumer and industrial products and services shorten product life cycles. Companies in virtually every industry are relying on the development of new products and services to fuel profitability and growth.[6] Surveys suggest that the most successful organizations use an R&D strategy that ties external opportunities to internal strengths and is linked with objectives. Well-formulated R&D policies match market opportunities with internal capabilities. R&D policies can enhance strategy implementation efforts to:

1. Emphasize product or process improvements.
2. Stress basic or applied research.
3. Be leaders or followers in R&D.
4. Develop robotics or manual-type processes.
5. Spend a high, average, or low amount of money on R&D.
6. Perform R&D within the firm or to contract R&D to outside firms.
7. Use university researchers or private sector researchers.

There must be effective interactions between R&D departments and other functional departments in implementing different types of generic business strategies. Conflicts between marketing, finance/accounting, R&D, and information systems departments can be minimized with clear policies and objectives. Table 8–8 gives some examples of R&D activities that could be required for successful implementation of various strategies. Many American utility, energy, and automotive companies are employing their research and development departments to determine how the firm can effectively reduce its gas emissions.

Many firms wrestle with the decision to acquire R&D expertise from external firms or to develop R&D expertise internally. The following guidelines can be used to help make this decision:

1. If the rate of technical progress is slow, the rate of market growth is moderate, and there are significant barriers to possible new entrants, then in-house R&D is the preferred solution. The reason is that R&D, if successful, will result in a temporary product or process monopoly that the company can exploit.

TABLE 8-8 Research and Development Involvement in Selected Strategy-Implementation Situations

TYPE OF ORGANIZATION	STRATEGY BEING IMPLEMENTED	R&D ACTIVITY
Pharmaceutical company	Product development	Test the effects of a new drug on different subgroups.
Boat manufacturer	Concentric diversification	Test the performance of various keel designs under various conditions.
Plastic container manufacturer	Market penetration	Develop a biodegradable container.
Electronics company	Market development	Develop a telecommunications system in a foreign country.

The best-formulated and best-implemented strategies become obsolete as a firm's external and internal environments change. It is essential, therefore, that strategists systematically review, evaluate, and control the execution of strategies. This chapter presents a framework that can guide managers' efforts to evaluate strategic-management activities, to make sure they are working, and to make timely changes. Management information systems being used to evaluate strategies are discussed. Guidelines are presented for formulating, implementing, and evaluating strategies.

The Nature of Strategy Evaluation

VISIT THE NET

Gives excellent additional information about evaluating strategies, including some analytical tools.
www.mindtools.com/
plevplan.html

The strategic-management process results in decisions that can have significant, long-lasting consequences. Erroneous strategic decisions can inflict severe penalties and can be exceedingly difficult, if not impossible, to reverse. Most strategists agree, therefore, that strategy evaluation is vital to an organization's well-being; timely evaluations can alert management to problems or potential problems before a situation becomes critical. Strategy evaluation includes three basic activities: (1) examining the underlying bases of a firm's strategy, (2) comparing expected results with actual results, and (3) taking corrective actions to ensure that performance conforms to plans. The strategy-evaluation stage of the strategic-management process is illustrated in Figure 9–1.

FIGURE 9-1 A Comprehensive Strategic-Management Model

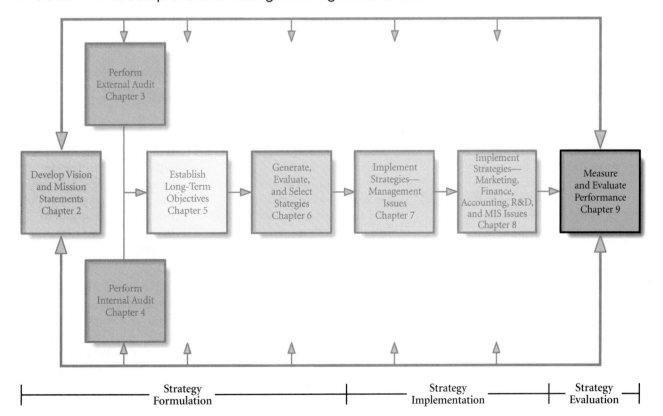

experiential exercises

"notable quotes"

Complicated controls do not work. They confuse. They misdirect attention from what is to be controlled to the mechanics and methodology of the control.
Seymour Tilles

Although Plan A may be selected as the most realistic . . . the other major alternatives should not be forgotten. They may well serve as contingency plans.
Dale McConkey

Organizations are most vulnerable when they are at the peak of their success.
R. T. Lenz

Strategy evaluation must make it as easy as possible for managers to revise their plans and reach quick agreement on the changes.
Dale McConkey

While strategy is a word that is usually associated with the future, its link to the past is no less central. Life is lived forward but understood backward. Managers may live strategy in the future, but they understand it through the past.
Henry Mintzberg

Unless strategy evaluation is performed seriously and systematically, and unless strategists are willing to act on the results, energy will be used up defending yesterday. No one will have the time, resources, or will to work on exploiting today, let alone to work on making tomorrow.
Peter Drucker

Executives, consultants, and B-school professors all agree that strategic planning is now the single most important management issue and will remain so for the next five years. Strategy has become a part of the main agenda at lots of organizations today. Strategic planning is back with a vengeance.
John Byrne

Planners should not plan, but serve as facilitators, catalysts, inquirers, educators, and synthesizers to guide the planning process effectively.
A. Hax and N. Majluf

Strategy Review, Evaluation, and Control

chapter objectives

After studying this chapter, you should be able to do the following:

1. Describe a practical framework for evaluating strategies.

2. Explain why strategy evaluation is complex, sensitive, and yet essential for organizational success.

3. Discuss the importance of contingency planning in strategy evaluation.

4. Discuss the role of auditing in strategy evaluation.

5. Explain how computers can aid in evaluating strategies.

6. Discuss the Balanced Scorecard.

7. Discuss three twenty-first century challenges in strategic management.

Step 4   Compare your projected statements to the statements of other students. What major differences exist between your analysis and the work of other students?

Experiential Exercise 8D

Determining the Cash Value of Krispy Kreme Doughnuts (KKD)

PURPOSE

It is simply good business practice to periodically determine the financial worth or cash value of your company. This exercise gives you practice determining the total worth of a company using several methods. Use 2003 as the sample year.

INSTRUCTIONS

Step 1   Calculate the financial worth of KKD based on four methods: (1) the net worth or stockholders' equity, (2) the future value of KKD earnings, (3) the price-earnings ratio, and (4) the outstanding shares method.

Step 2   In a dollar amount, how much is KKD worth?

Step 3   Compare your analyses and conclusions with those of other students.

Experiential Exercise 8E

Developing a Product-Positioning Map for My University

PURPOSE

The purpose of this exercise is to give you practice developing product-positioning maps. Nonprofit organizations, such as universities, are increasingly using product-positioning maps to determine effective ways to implement strategies.

INSTRUCTIONS

Step 1   Join with two other people in class to form a group of three.

Step 2   Jointly prepare a product-positioning map that includes your institution and four other colleges or universities in your state.

Step 3   Go to the blackboard and diagram your product-positioning map.

Step 4   Discuss differences among the maps diagrammed on the board.

Experiential Exercise 8F

Do Banks Require Projected Financial Statements?

PURPOSE

The purpose of this exercise is to explore the practical importance and use of projected financial statements in the banking business.

INSTRUCTIONS

Contact two local bankers by phone and seek answers to the questions listed below. Record the answers you receive, and report your findings to the class.

1. Does your bank require projected financial statements as part of a business loan application?
2. How does your bank use projected financial statements when they are part of a business loan application?
3. What special advice do you give potential business borrowers in preparing projected financial statements?

experiential exercises

**Experiential
Exercise 8A**
*Developing a Product-
Positioning Map for
Krispy Kreme Doughnuts
(KKD)*

PURPOSE

Organizations continually monitor how their products and services are positioned relative to competitors. This information is especially useful for marketing managers, but is also used by other managers and strategists.

INSTRUCTIONS

Step 1   On a separate sheet of paper, develop a product-positioning map for KKD.

Step 2   Go to the blackboard and diagram your product-positioning map.

Step 3   Compare your product-positioning map with those diagrammed by other students. Discuss any major differences.

PURPOSE

An EPS/EBIT analysis is one of the most widely used techniques for determining the extent that debt and/or stock should be used to finance strategies to be implemented. This exercise can give you practice performing EPS/EBIT analysis.

INSTRUCTIONS

Let's say KKD needs to raise $1 billion to expand around the world in 2004. Determine whether KKD should have used all debt, all stock, or a 50-50 combination of debt and stock to finance this market-development strategy. Assume a 38 percent tax rate, 5 percent interest rate, KKD stock price of $25 per share, and an annual dividend of $2.00 per share of common stock. The EBIT range for 2004 is between $1 billion and $100 million. A total of 60 million shares of common stock are outstanding. Develop an EPS/EBIT chart to reflect your analysis.

**Experiential
Exercise 8C**
*Preparing Projected
Financial Statements for
Krispy Kreme Doughnuts
(KKD)*

PURPOSE

This exercise is designed to give you experience preparing pro forma financial statements. Pro forma analysis is a central strategy-implementation technique because it allows managers to anticipate and evaluate the expected results of various strategy-implementation approaches.

INSTRUCTIONS

Step 1   Work with a classmate. Develop a 2004 projected income statement and balance sheet for KKD. Assume that KKD plans to raise $900 million in 2004 to begin serving new countries and plans to obtain 50 percent financing from a bank and 50 percent financing from a stock issuance. Make other assumptions as needed, and state them clearly in written form.

Step 2   Compute KKD's current ratio, debt-to-equity ratio, and return-on-investment ratio for 2001, 2002, and 2003. How do your 2004 projected ratios compare to the 2002 and 2003 ratios? Why is it important to make this comparison?

Step 3   Bring your projected statements to class, and discuss any problems or questions you encountered.

100% COMMON STOCK	100% DEBT FINANCING	20%DEBT–80%STOCK
EBIT		
Interest		
EBT		
Taxes		
EAT		
# Shares		
EPS		

NOTES

1. Leslie Miller and Elizabeth Weise, "E-Privacy—FTC Studies 'Profiling' by Web Sites," *USA Today* (November 8, 1999): 1A, 2A.

2. Ralph Biggadike, "The Contributions of Marketing to Strategic Management," *Academy of Management Review* 6, no. 4 (October 1981): 627.

3. Phyllis Plitch, "Companies in Many Sectors Give Earnings a Pro Forma Makeover, Survey Finds," *Wall Street Journal* (January 22, 2002): A4.

4. Michael Rapoport, "Pro Forma Is a Hard Habit to Break," *Wall Street Journal* (September 18, 2003): B3A.

5. Matt Krantz, "Accounting Rule Targets Goodwill," *USA Today* (February 6, 2003): 3B.

6. Amy Merrick, "U. S. Research Spending to Rise Only 3.2 Percent," *Wall Street Journal* (December 28, 2001): A2.

7. Pier Abetti, "Technology: A Key Strategic Resource," *Management Review* 78, no. 2 (February 1989): 38.

8. Adapted from Edward Baig, "Welcome to the Officeless Office," *BusinessWeek* (June 26, 1995).

CURRENT READINGS

Dobni, C. B., and G. Luffman. "Determining the Scope and Impact of Market Orientation Profiles on Strategy Implementation and Performance." *Strategic Management Journal* 24, no. 6 (June 2003): 577.

Kuperman, J. C. "Communicating Strategy to Financial Analysts." *Business Horizons* 45, no. 5 (September–October 2002): 11–18.

Lee, P. M., and H. M. O'Neill, "Ownership Structures and R&D Investments of U. S. and Japanese Firms: Agency and Stewardship Perspectives." *Academy of Management Journal* 46, no. 2 (April 2003): 212–225.

Lowry, J. R. "Marketing in Metamorphosis: Breaking Boundaries." *Business Horizons* 46, no. 3 (May–June 2003): 41.

Lubatkin, M., and B. Schulze. "Risk, Strategy, and Finance: Unifying Two World Views." *Long Range Planning* 36, no. 1 (February 2003): 7–8.

O'Brien, J. P. "The Capital Structure Implications of Pursuing a Strategy of Innovation." *Strategic Management Journal* 24, no. 5 (May 2003): 415–422.

Pollock, T. G., H. M. Fischer, and J. B. Wade. "The Role of Power and Politics in the Repricing of Executive Options." *Academy of Management Journal* 45, no. 6 (December 2002): 1172–1182.

Sakakibara, M. "Formation of R&D Consortia: Industry and Company Effects." *Strategic Management Journal* 23, no. 11 (November 2002): 1033–1050.

Schnatterly, K. "Increasing Firm Value Through Detection and Prevention of White-Collar Crime." *Strategic Management Journal* 24, no. 7 (July 2003): 587–614.

ISSUES FOR REVIEW AND DISCUSSION

1. Suppose your company has just acquired a firm that produces battery-operated lawn mowers, and strategists want to implement a market-penetration strategy. How would you segment the market for this product? Justify your answer.

2. Explain how you would estimate the total worth of a business.

3. Diagram and label clearly a product-positioning map that includes six fast-food restaurant chains.

4. Explain why EPS/EBIT analysis is a central strategy-implementation technique.

5. How would the R&D role in strategy implementation differ in small versus large organizations?

6. Discuss the limitations of EPS/EBIT analysis.

7. Explain how marketing, finance/accounting, R&D, and management information systems managers' involvement in strategy formulation can enhance strategy implementation.

8. Consider the following statement: "Retained earnings on the balance sheet are not monies available to finance strategy implementation." Is it true or false? Explain.

9. Explain why projected financial statement analysis is considered both a strategy-formulation and a strategy-implementation tool.

10. Describe some marketing, finance/accounting, R&D, and management information systems activities that a small restaurant chain might undertake to expand into a neighboring state.

11. Discuss the management information system at your college or university.

12. What effect is e-commerce having on firms' efforts to segment markets?

13. How has the Sarbanes-Oxley Act of 2002 changed CEOs' and CFOs' handling of financial statements?

14. To what extent have you been exposed to natural environment issues in your business courses? Which course has provided the most coverage? What percentage of your business courses provided no coverage? Comment.

15. Complete the following EPS/EBIT analysis for a company whose stock price is $20, interest rate on funds is 5%, tax rate is 20%, number of shares outstanding is 500 million, and EBIT range is $500 million to $1 billion. The firm needs to raise $200 million in capital. Use table on the next page to complete the work

16. Under what conditions would Retained Earnings on the Balance Sheet decrease from one year to the next?

17. In your own words, list all the steps in developing projected financial statements.

18. Based on the financial statements provided for Krispy Kreme Doughnuts (KKD Cohesion Case), how much dividends in dollars did KKD pay in 2002?

19. Based on the financial statements provided in this chapter for the Litten Company, calculate the value of this company if you know that its stock price is $20 and it has 1 million shares outstanding. Calculate four different ways and average.

20. Why should you be careful not to use historical percentages blindly in developing projected financial statements?

21. In developing projected financial statements, what should you do if the $ amount you must put in the Cash account (to make the statement balance) is far more (or less) than desired?

22. Why is it both important and necessary to segment markets and target groups of customers, rather than market to all possible consumers?

23. In full detail, explain the following EPS/EBIT chart.

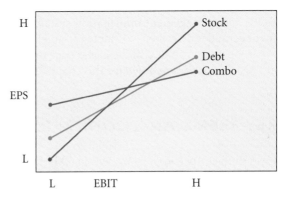

PeopleSoft, and Twentieth Century Fox average over thirty computer intrusion attempts daily. Thousands of companies today are plagued by computer hackers who include disgruntled employees, competitors, bored teens, sociopaths, thieves, spies, and hired agents. Computer vulnerability is a giant, expensive headache.

Dun & Bradstreet is an example of a company that has an excellent information system. Every D&B customer and client in the world has a separate nine-digit number. The database of information associated with each number has become so widely used that it is like a business social security number. D&B reaps great competitive advantages from its information system.

In many firms, information technology is doing away with the workplace and allowing employees to work at home or anywhere, anytime. The mobile concept of work allows employees to work the traditional 9-to-5 workday across any of the twenty-four time zones around the globe. Affordable desktop videoconferencing software developed by AT&T, Lotus, or Vivo Software allows employees to "beam in" whenever needed. Any manager or employee who travels a lot away from the office is a good candidate for working at home rather than in an office provided by the firm. Salespersons or consultants are good examples, but any person whose job largely involves talking to others or handling information could easily operate at home with the proper computer system and software. The accounting firm Ernst & Young has reduced its office space requirements by 2 million square feet over the past three years by allowing employees to work at home.

Many people see the officeless office trend as leading to a resurgence of family togetherness in American society. Even the design of homes may change from having large open areas to having more private small areas conducive to getting work done.[8]

CONCLUSION

Successful strategy implementation depends on cooperation among all functional and divisional managers in an organization. Marketing departments are commonly charged with implementing strategies that require significant increases in sales revenues in new areas and with new or improved products. Finance and accounting managers must devise effective strategy-implementation approaches at low cost and minimum risk to that firm. R&D managers have to transfer complex technologies or develop new technologies to successfully implement strategies. Information systems managers are being called upon more and more to provide leadership and training for all individuals in the firm. The nature and role of marketing, finance/accounting, R&D, and management information systems activities, coupled with the management activities described in Chapter 7, largely determine organizational success.

We invite you to visit the David page on the Prentice Hall Companion Web site at *www.prenhall.com/david* for this chapter's World Wide Web exercises.

KEY TERMS AND CONCEPTS

Cash Budget (p. 296)

EPS/EBIT Analysis (p. 290)

Financial Budget (p. 295)

Management Information
  Systems (MIS) (p. 301)

Market Segmentation (p. 283)

Marketing Mix Variables (p. 283)

Outstanding Shares
  Method (p. 298)

Price-Earnings Ratio
  Method (p. 297)

Product Positioning (p. 283)

Projected Financial Statement
  Analysis (p. 293)

Research and Development
  (R&D) (p. 299)

Vacant Niche (p. 288)

NATURAL ENVIRONMENT PERSPECTIVE

MBA Programs That Cover Natural Environment Issues Especially Well

Extensive research by the Business-Environment-Learning-Leadership (BELL) organization identifies the following universities that offer Master of Business Administration (MBA) programs that provide especially good coverage of natural environment issues in their curricula. The BELL program is a one-of-a-kind effort that focuses on greening management courses through curriculum resources, MBA benchmarking, and field experience. Annual BELL conferences act as a platform for exposing professors to new tools and methods and the sharing of green curricula. BELL's biennial report, *Beyond Grey Pinstripes* (2003), co-produced with the Aspen Institute, evaluates how well MBA programs train their students to manage for sustainability.

    Case Western Reserve University
    George Washington University
    Harvard University
    Hong Kong Polytechnic University
    Illinois Institute of Technology
    Loyola Marymount University
    Rensselaer Polytechnic Institute
    Stanford University

    University of California, Berkeley
    University of California, Los Angeles
    University of Jyvaeskylae
    University of Michigan-Ann Arbor
    University of New Mexico
    University of North Carolina at Chapel Hill
    University of Pennsylvania, The Wharton School
    University of Pittsburgh
    Vanderbilt University
    Wake Forest University
    Yale University
    York University, Schulich

Roughly 20 percent of students who attend UNC's Kenan-Flagler Business School do so because of its concentration in sustainable enterprise. Net Impact, an organization of MBA graduates with an interest in environmental business issues, had grown to 8,000 members by late 2003, from 1,350 in 1998. The number of Net Impact chapters has increased to 85 now from 45 in 1998.

Sources: Adapted from **www.worldresourcesinstitute.com**; **bell.wri.org**; Jane Kim, "Business Schools Take a Page from Kinder, Gentler Textbook," *Wall Street Journal* (October 22, 2003): B2C.

establishing a new approach to information systems, one that blends the technical knowledge of the computer experts with the vision of senior management.

Information collection, retrieval, and storage can be used to create competitive advantages in ways such as cross-selling to customers, monitoring suppliers, keeping managers and employees informed, coordinating activities among divisions, and managing funds. Like inventory and human resources, information is now recognized as a valuable organizational asset that can be controlled and managed. Firms that implement strategies using the best information will reap competitive advantages in the twenty-first century.

A good information system can allow a firm to reduce costs. For example, online orders from salespersons to production facilities can shorten materials ordering time and reduce inventory costs. Direct communications between suppliers, manufacturers, marketers, and customers can link elements of the value chain together as though they were one organization. Improved quality and service often result from an improved information system.

Firms must increasingly be concerned about computer hackers and take specific measures to secure and safeguard corporate communications, files, orders, and business conducted over the Internet. Gap, Playboy Enterprises, Hitachi America,

2. If technology is changing rapidly and the market is growing slowly, then a major effort in R&D may be very risky, because it may lead to the development of an ultimately obsolete technology or one for which there is no market.

3. If technology is changing slowly but the market is growing quickly, there generally is not enough time for in-house development. The prescribed approach is to obtain R&D expertise on an exclusive or nonexclusive basis from an outside firm.

4. If both technical progress and market growth are fast, R&D expertise should be obtained through acquisition of a well-established firm in the industry.[7]

There are at least three major R&D approaches for implementing strategies. The first strategy is to be the first firm to market new technological products. This is a glamorous and exciting strategy but also a dangerous one. Firms such as 3M and General Electric have been successful with this approach, but many other pioneering firms have fallen, with rival firms seizing the initiative.

A second R&D approach is to be an innovative imitator of successful products, thus minimizing the risks and costs of start-up. This approach entails allowing a pioneer firm to develop the first version of the new product and to demonstrate that a market exists. Then, laggard firms develop a similar product. This strategy requires excellent R&D personnel and an excellent marketing department.

A third R&D strategy is to be a low-cost producer by mass-producing products similar to but less expensive than products recently introduced. As a new product is accepted by customers, price becomes increasingly important in the buying decision. Also, mass marketing replaces personal selling as the dominant selling strategy. This R&D strategy, requires substantial investment in plant and equipment, but fewer expenditures in R&D than the two approaches described earlier.

R&D activities among American firms need to be more closely aligned to business objectives. There needs to be expanded communication between R&D managers and strategists. Corporations are experimenting with various methods to achieve this improved communication climate, including different roles and reporting arrangements for managers and new methods to reduce the time it takes research ideas to become reality.

Perhaps the most current trend in R&D management has been lifting the veil of secrecy whereby firms, even major competitors, are joining forces to develop new products. Collaboration is on the rise due to new competitive pressures, rising research costs, increasing regulatory issues, and accelerated product development schedules. Companies not only are working more closely with each other on R&D, but they are also turning to consortia at universities for their R&D needs. More than 600 research consortia are now in operation in the United States. Lifting of R&D secrecy among many firms through collaboration has allowed the marketing of new technologies and products even before they are available for sale.

Management Information Systems (MIS) Issues

Firms that gather, assimilate, and evaluate external and internal information most effectively are gaining competitive advantages over other firms. Recognizing the importance of having an effective *management information system (MIS)* will not be an option in the future; it will be a requirement. Information is the basis for understanding in a firm. In many industries, information is becoming the most important factor in differentiating successful from unsuccessful firms. The process of strategic management is facilitated immensely in firms that have an effective information system. Many companies are

Adequate and timely feedback is the cornerstone of effective strategy evaluation. Strategy evaluation can be no better than the information on which it operates. Too much pressure from top managers may result in lower managers contriving numbers they think will be satisfactory.

Strategy evaluation can be a complex and sensitive undertaking. Too much emphasis on evaluating strategies may be expensive and counterproductive. No one likes to be evaluated too closely! The more managers attempt to evaluate the behavior of others, the less control they have. Yet too little or no evaluation can create even worse problems. Strategy evaluation is essential to ensure that stated objectives are being achieved.

In many organizations, strategy evaluation is simply an appraisal of how well an organization has performed. Have the firm's assets increased? Has there been an increase in profitability? Have sales increased? Have productivity levels increased? Have profit margin, return on investment, and earnings-per-share ratios increased? Some firms argue that their strategy must have been correct if the answers to these types of questions are affirmative. Well, the strategy or strategies may have been correct, but this type of reasoning can be misleading, because strategy evaluation must have both a long-run and short-run focus. Strategies often do not affect short-term operating results until it is too late to make needed changes.

It is impossible to demonstrate conclusively that a particular strategy is optimal or even to guarantee that it will work. One can, however, evaluate it for critical flaws. Richard Rumelt offered four criteria that could be used to evaluate a strategy: consistency, consonance, feasibility, and advantage. Described in Table 9–1, *consonance* and *advantage* are mostly based on a firm's external assessment, whereas *consistency* and *feasibility* are largely based on an internal assessment.

Strategy evaluation is important because organizations face dynamic environments in which key external and internal factors often change quickly and dramatically. Success today is no guarantee of success tomorrow! An organization should never be lulled into complacency with success. Countless firms have thrived one year only to struggle for survival the following year. Organizational trouble can come swiftly, as further evidenced by the examples described in Table 9–2.

Strategy evaluation is becoming increasingly difficult with the passage of time, for many reasons. Domestic and world economies were more stable in years past, product life cycles were longer, product development cycles were longer, technological advancement was slower, change occurred less frequently, there were fewer competitors, foreign companies were weak, and there were more regulated industries. Other reasons why strategy evaluation is more difficult today include the following trends:

VISIT THE NET

Describes the how and why of strategy evaluation.
www.csuchico.edu/mgmt/
strategy/module1/
sld046.htm

1. A dramatic increase in the environment's complexity
2. The increasing difficulty of predicting the future with accuracy
3. The increasing number of variables
4. The rapid rate of obsolescence of even the best plans
5. The increase in the number of both domestic and world events affecting organizations
6. The decreasing time span for which planning can be done with any degree of certainty[1]

A fundamental problem facing managers today is how to effectively control employees in light of modern organizational demands for greater flexibility, innovation, creativity, and initiative from employees.[2] How can managers today ensure that empowered employees acting in an entrepreneurial manner do not put the well-being of the business at risk? Recall that Kidder, Peabody & Company lost $350 million when

TABLE 9-1   Rumelt's Criteria for Evaluating Strategies

CONSISTENCY

A strategy should not present inconsistent goals and policies. Organizational conflict and interdepartmental bickering are often symptoms of managerial disorder, but these problems may also be a sign of strategic inconsistency. There are three guidelines to help determine if organizational problems are due to inconsistencies in strategy:

- If managerial problems continue despite changes in personnel and if they tend to be issue-based rather than people-based, then strategies may be inconsistent.
- If success for one organizational department means, or is interpreted to mean, failure for another department, then strategies may be inconsistent.
- If policy problems and issues continue to be brought to the top for resolution, then strategies may be inconsistent.

CONSONANCE

Consonance refers to the need for strategists to examine *sets of trends* as well as individual trends in evaluating strategies. A strategy must represent an adaptive response to the external environment and to the critical changes occurring within it. One difficulty in matching a firm's key internal and external factors in the formulation of strategy is that most trends are the result of interactions among other trends. For example, the daycare explosion came about as a combined result of many trends that included a rise in the average level of education, increased inflation, and an increase in women in the workforce. Although single economic or demographic trends might appear steady for many years, there are waves of change going on at the interaction level.

FEASIBILITY

A strategy must neither overtax available resources nor create unsolvable subproblems. The final broad test of strategy is its feasibility; that is, can the strategy be attempted within the physical, human, and financial resources of the enterprise? The financial resources of a business are the easiest to quantify and are normally the first limitation against which strategy is evaluated. It is sometimes forgotten, however, that innovative approaches to financing are often possible. Devices such as captive subsidiaries, sale-leaseback arrangements, and tying plant mortgages to long-term contracts have all been used effectively to help win key positions in suddenly expanding industries. A less quantifiable, but actually more rigid, limitation on strategic choice is that imposed by individual and organizational capabilities. In evaluating a strategy, it is important to examine whether an organization has demonstrated in the past that it possesses the abilities, competencies, skills, and talents needed to carry out a given strategy.

ADVANTAGE

A strategy must provide for the creation and/or maintenance of a competitive advantage in a selected area of activity. Competitive advantages normally are the result of superiority in one of three areas: (1) resources, (2) skills, or (3) position. The idea that the positioning of one's resources can enhance their combined effectiveness is familiar to military theorists, chess players, and diplomats. Position can also play a crucial role in an organization's strategy. Once gained, a good position is defensible—meaning that it is so costly to capture that rivals are deterred from full-scale attacks. Positional advantage tends to be self-sustaining as long as the key internal and environmental factors that underlie it remain stable. This is why entrenched firms can be almost impossible to unseat, even if their raw skill levels are only average. Although not all positional advantages are associated with size, it is true that larger organizations tend to operate in markets and use procedures that turn their size into advantage, while smaller firms seek product/marker positions that exploit other types of advantage. The principal characteristic of good position is that it permits the firm to obtain advantage from policies that would not similarly benefit rivals without the same position. Therefore, in evaluating strategy, organizations should examine the nature of positional advantages associated with a given strategy.

Source: Adapted from Richard Rumelt, "The Evaluation of Business Strategy," in W. F. Glueck (ed.), *Business Policy and Strategic Management* (New York: McGraw-Hill, 1980): 359–367.

TABLE 9-2   Examples of Organizational Demise

A. SOME LARGE COMPANIES THAT EXPERIENCED A LARGE DROP (%) IN REVENUES IN 2003		B. SOME LARGE COMPANIES THAT EXPERIENCED A LARGE DROP (%) IN PROFITS IN 2003	
ConAgra Foods	−30%	Monaco Coach	−50%
RJ Reynolds Tobacco	−15%	Eastman Kodak	−70%
Astoria Financial	−14%	Caesars Entertainment	−66%
Fluor	−12%	Starwood Hotels	−58%
Shaw Group	−20%	Reader's Digest Association	−62%
VeriSign	−14%	Dillards	−81%
Cadence Design Systems	−13%	Hollywood Entertainment	−66%
Siebel Systems	−17%	Payless ShoeSource	−67%
Applied Materials	−12%	Winn-Dixie Stores	−85%
KLA-Tencor	−12%	Ralcorp	−89%
Lucent Technologies	−20%	AmeriCredit	−57%
Tellabs	−26%	Pfizer	−82%
Gateway	−18%	Boeing	−70%
Silicon Graphics	−17%	Goodrich	−70%
Georgia-Pacific	−13%	CSX	−60%
		PeopleSoft	−53%
		Nucor	−61%

Source: Adapted from *BusinessWeek,* February 23, 2004, pp. 60–84.

one of its traders allegedly booked fictitious profits; Sears, Roebuck and Company took a $60 million charge against earnings after admitting that its automobile service businesses were performing unnecessary repairs. The costs to companies such as these in terms of damaged reputations, fines, missed opportunities, and diversion of management's attention are enormous.

When empowered employees are held accountable for and pressured to achieve specific goals and are given wide latitude in their actions to achieve them, there can be dysfunctional behavior. For example, Nordstrom, the upscale fashion retailer known for outstanding customer service, was subjected to lawsuits and fines when employees underreported hours worked in order to increase their sales per hour—the company's primary performance criterion. Nordstrom's customer service and earnings were enhanced until the misconduct was reported, at which time severe penalties were levied against the firm.

The Process of Evaluating Strategies

Strategy evaluation is necessary for all sizes and kinds of organizations. Strategy evaluation should initiate managerial questioning of expectations and assumptions, should trigger a review of objectives and values, and should stimulate creativity in generating alternatives and formulating criteria of evaluation.[3] Regardless of the size of the organization, a certain amount of *management by wandering around* at all levels is essential to effective strategy evaluation. Strategy-evaluation activities should be performed on a continuing basis, rather than at the end of specified periods of time or just after problems occur. Waiting until the end of the year, for example, could result in a firm closing the barn door after the horses have already escaped.

VISIT THE NET

Elaborates on the "taking corrective actions" phase of strategy evaluation.
www.csuchico.edu/mgmt/
strategy/module 1/
sld047.htm

Evaluating strategies on a continuous rather than on a periodic basis allows benchmarks of progress to be established and more effectively monitored. Some strategies take years to implement; consequently, associated results may not become apparent for years. Successful strategies combine patience with a willingness to take corrective actions promptly when necessary. There always comes a time when corrective actions are needed in an organization! Centuries ago, a writer (perhaps Solomon) made the following observations about change:

> There is a time for everything,
>
> A time to be born and a time to die,
>
> A time to plant and a time to uproot,
>
> A time to kill and a time to heal,
>
> A time to tear down and a time to build,
>
> A time to weep and a time to laugh,
>
> A time to mourn and a time to dance,
>
> A time to scatter stones and a time to gather them,
>
> A time to embrace and a time to refrain,
>
> A time to search and a time to give up,
>
> A time to keep and a time to throw away,
>
> A time to tear and a time to mend,
>
> A time to be silent and a time to speak,
>
> A time to love and a time to hate,
>
> A time for war and a time for peace.[4]

Managers and employees of the firm should be continually aware of progress being made toward achieving the firm's objectives. As critical success factors change, organizational members should be involved in determining appropriate corrective actions. If assumptions and expectations deviate significantly from forecasts, then the firm should renew strategy-formulation activities, perhaps sooner than planned. In strategy evaluation, like strategy formulation and strategy implementation, people make the difference. Through involvement in the process of evaluating strategies, managers and employees become committed to keeping the firm moving steadily toward achieving objectives.

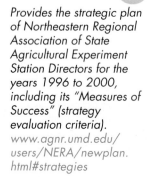

VISIT THE NET

Provides the strategic plan of Northeastern Regional Association of State Agricultural Experiment Station Directors for the years 1996 to 2000, including its "Measures of Success" (strategy evaluation criteria).
www.agnr.umd.edu/ users/NERA/newplan. html#strategies

A Strategy-Evaluation Framework

Table 9–3 summarizes strategy-evaluation activities in terms of key questions that should be addressed, alternative answers to those questions, and appropriate actions for an organization to take. Notice that corrective actions are almost always needed except when (1) external and internal factors have not significantly changed and (2) the firm is progressing satisfactorily toward achieving stated objectives. Relationships among strategy-evaluation activities are illustrated in Figure 9–2.

TABLE 9-3 A Strategy-Evaluation Assessment Matrix

HAVE MAJOR CHANGES OCCURRED IN THE FIRM'S INTERNAL STRATEGIC POSITION?	HAVE MAJOR CHANGES OCCURRED IN THE FIRM'S EXTERNAL STRATEGIC POSITION?	HAS THE FIRM PROGRESSED SATISFACTORILY TOWARD ACHIEVING ITS STATED OBJECTIVES?	RESULT
No	No	No	Take corrective actions
Yes	Yes	Yes	Take corrective actions
Yes	Yes	No	Take corrective actions
Yes	No	Yes	Take corrective actions
Yes	No	No	Take corrective actions
No	Yes	Yes	Take corrective actions
No	Yes	No	Take corrective actions
No	No	Yes	Continue present strategic course

Reviewing Bases of Strategy

As shown in Figure 9–2, *reviewing the underlying bases of an organization's strategy* could be approached by developing a revised EFE Matrix and IFE Matrix. A *revised IFE Matrix* should focus on changes in the organization's management, marketing, finance/accounting, production/operations, R&D, and management information systems strengths and weaknesses. A *revised EFE Matrix* should indicate how effective a firm's strategies have been in response to key opportunities and threats. This analysis could also address such questions as the following:

1. How have competitors reacted to our strategies?
2. How have competitors' strategies changed?
3. Have major competitors' strengths and weaknesses changed?
4. Why are competitors making certain strategic changes?
5. Why are some competitors' strategies more successful than others?
6. How satisfied are our competitors with their present market positions and profitability?
7. How far can our major competitors be pushed before retaliating?
8. How could we more effectively cooperate with our competitors?

Numerous external and internal factors can prohibit firms from achieving long-term and annual objectives. Externally, actions by competitors, changes in demand, changes in technology, economic changes, demographic shifts, and governmental actions may prohibit objectives from being accomplished. Internally, ineffective strategies may have been chosen or implementation activities may have been poor. Objectives may have been too optimistic. Thus, failure to achieve objectives may not be the result of unsatisfactory work by managers and employees. All organizational members need to know this to encourage their support for strategy-evaluation activities. Organizations desperately need to know as soon as possible when their strategies are not effective. Sometimes managers and employees on the front lines discover this well before strategists.

External opportunities and threats and internal strengths and weaknesses that represent the bases of current strategies should continually be monitored for

VISIT THE NET

The Small Business Administration Web site provides a forty-page Business Plan Outline.
www.sba.gov/starting/businessplan.html

FIGURE 9-2 A Strategy-Evaluation Framework

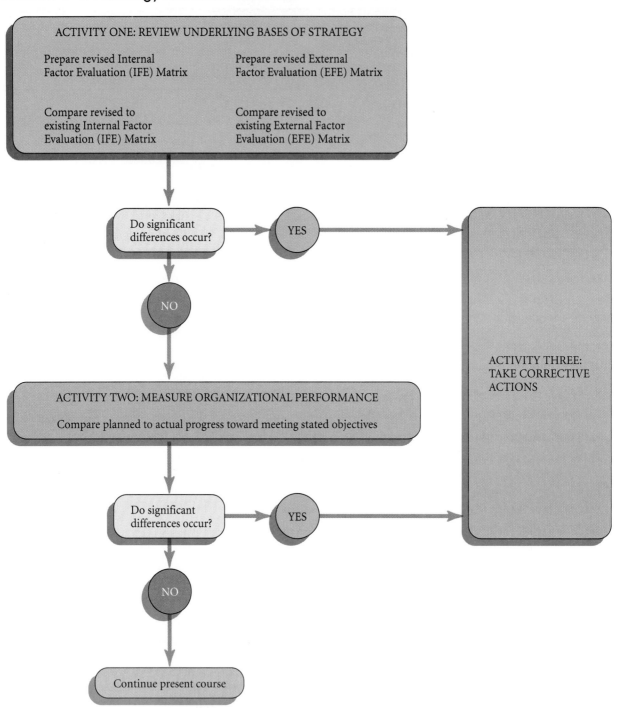

change. It is not really a question of whether these factors will change, but rather when they will change and in what ways. Some key questions to address in evaluating strategies are given here.

1. Are our internal strengths still strengths?
2. Have we added other internal strengths? If so, what are they?

3. Are our internal weaknesses still weaknesses?

4. Do we now have other internal weaknesses? If so, what are they?

5. Are our external opportunities still opportunities?

6. Are there now other external opportunities? If so, what are they?

7. Are our external threats still threats?

8. Are there now other external threats? If so, what are they?

9. Are we vulnerable to a hostile takeover?

Measuring Organizational Performance

Another important strategy-evaluation activity is *measuring organizational performance*. This activity includes comparing expected results to actual results, investigating deviations from plans, evaluating individual performance, and examining progress being made toward meeting stated objectives. Both long-term and annual objectives are commonly used in this process. Criteria for evaluating strategies should be measurable and easily verifiable. Criteria that predict results may be more important than those that reveal what already has happened. For example, rather than simply being informed that sales in the last quarter were 20 percent under what was expected, strategists need to know that sales in the next quarter may be 20 percent below standard unless some action is taken to counter the trend. Really effective control requires accurate forecasting.

Failure to make satisfactory progress toward accomplishing long-term or annual objectives signals a need for corrective actions. Many factors, such as unreasonable policies, unexpected turns in the economy, unreliable suppliers or distributors, or ineffective strategies, can result in unsatisfactory progress toward meeting objectives. Problems can result from ineffectiveness (not doing the right things) or inefficiency (doing the right things poorly).

Determining which objectives are most important in the evaluation of strategies can be difficult. Strategy evaluation is based on both quantitative and qualitative criteria. Selecting the exact set of criteria for evaluating strategies depends on a particular organization's size, industry, strategies, and management philosophy. An organization pursuing a retrenchment strategy, for example, could have an entirely different set of evaluative criteria from an organization pursuing a market-development strategy. Quantitative criteria commonly used to evaluate strategies are financial ratios, which strategists use to make three critical comparisons: (1) comparing the firm's performance over different time periods, (2) comparing the firm's performance to competitors', and (3) comparing the firm's performance to industry averages. Some key financial ratios that are particularly useful as criteria for strategy evaluation are as follows:

1. Return on investment (ROI)
2. Return on equity (ROE)
3. Profit margin
4. Market share
5. Debt to equity
6. Earnings per share
7. Sales growth
8. Asset growth

VISIT THE NET

Provides strategic management handbooks with detailed instructions for planning in certain U.S. states.

www.opm.state.ct.us/ mgmt/busguide/50states/ guides.htm

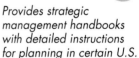

But there are some potential problems associated with using quantitative criteria for evaluating strategies. First, most quantitative criteria are geared to annual objectives rather than long-term objectives. Also, different accounting methods can provide different results on many quantitative criteria. Third, intuitive judgments are almost always involved in deriving quantitative criteria. For these and other reasons, qualitative criteria are also important in evaluating strategies. Human factors such as high absenteeism and turnover rates, poor production quality and quantity rates, or low employee satisfaction can be underlying causes of declining performance. Marketing, finance/accounting, R&D, or management information systems factors can also cause financial problems. Seymour Tilles identified six qualitative questions that are useful in evaluating strategies:

1. Is the strategy internally consistent?
2. Is the strategy consistent with the environment?
3. Is the strategy appropriate in view of available resources?
4. Does the strategy involve an acceptable degree of risk?
5. Does the strategy have an appropriate time framework?
6. Is the strategy workable?[5]

Some additional key questions that reveal the need for qualitative or intuitive judgments in strategy evaluation are as follows:

1. How good is the firm's balance of investments between high-risk and low-risk projects?
2. How good is the firm's balance of investments between long-term and short-term projects?
3. How good is the firm's balance of investments between slow-growing markets and fast-growing markets?
4. How good is the firm's balance of investments among different divisions?
5. To what extent are the firm's alternative strategies socially responsible?
6. What are the relationships among the firm's key internal and external strategic factors?
7. How are major competitors likely to respond to particular strategies?

Taking Corrective Actions

The final strategy-evaluation activity, *taking corrective actions*, requires making changes to reposition a firm competitively for the future. Examples of changes that may be needed are altering an organization's structure, replacing one or more key individuals, selling a division, or revising a business mission. Other changes could include establishing or revising objectives, devising new policies, issuing stock to raise capital, adding additional salespersons, allocating resources differently, or developing new performance incentives. Taking corrective actions does not necessarily mean that existing strategies will be abandoned or even that new strategies must be formulated.

> The probabilities and possibilities for incorrect or inappropriate actions increase geometrically with an arithmetic increase in personnel. Any person directing an overall undertaking must check on the actions of the participants as well as the results that they have achieved. If either the actions or results do not comply with preconceived or planned achievements, then corrective actions are needed.[6]

No organization can survive as an island; no organization can escape change. Taking corrective actions is necessary to keep an organization on track toward achieving stated objectives. In his thought-provoking books, *Future Shock* and *The Third Wave*, Alvin Toffler argued that business environments are becoming so dynamic and complex that they threaten people and organizations with *future shock*, which occurs when the nature, types, and speed of changes overpower an individual's or organization's ability and capacity to adapt. Strategy evaluation enhances an organization's ability to adapt successfully to changing circumstances. Brown and Agnew referred to this notion as *corporate agility*.[7]

Taking corrective actions raises employees' and managers' anxieties. Research suggests that participation in strategy-evaluation activities is one of the best ways to overcome individuals' resistance to change. According to Erez and Kanfer, individuals accept change best when they have a cognitive understanding of the changes, a sense of control over the situation, and an awareness that necessary actions are going to be taken to implement the changes.[8]

Strategy evaluation can lead to strategy-formulation changes, strategy-implementation changes, both formulation and implementation changes, or no changes at all. Strategists cannot escape having to revise strategies and implementation approaches sooner or later. Hussey and Langham offered the following insight on taking corrective actions:

> Resistance to change is often emotionally based and not easily overcome by rational argument. Resistance may be based on such feelings as loss of status, implied criticism of present competence, fear of failure in the new situation, annoyance at not being consulted, lack of understanding of the need for change, or insecurity in changing from well-known and fixed methods. It is necessary, therefore, to overcome such resistance by creating situations of participation and [a] full explanation when changes are envisaged.[9]

Corrective actions should place an organization in a better position to capitalize upon internal strengths; to take advantage of key external opportunities; to avoid, reduce, or mitigate external threats; and to improve internal weaknesses. Corrective actions should have a proper time horizon and an appropriate amount of risk. They should be internally consistent and socially responsible. Perhaps most important, corrective actions strengthen an organization's competitive position in its basic industry. Continuous strategy evaluation keeps strategists close to the pulse of an organization and provides information needed for an effective strategic-management system. Carter Bayles described the benefits of strategy evaluation as follows:

> Evaluation activities may renew confidence in the current business strategy or point to the need for actions to correct some weaknesses, such as erosion of product superiority or technological edge. In many cases, the benefits of strategy evaluation are much more far-reaching, for the outcome of the process may be a fundamentally new strategy that will lead, even in a business that is already turning a respectable profit, to substantially increased earnings. It is this possibility that justifies strategy evaluation, for the payoff can be very large.[10]

An example company that today is taking major corrective actions is Sun Microsystems. For nearly two decades, Sun Microsystems dismissed the standard chips and software that ran most computers in favor of its own souped-up custom designs.[11] Although more powerful than Intel and Microsoft chips and servers, Sun products were also more expensive. However, today Intel and Microsoft and similar firms produce generic chips and software that are less expensive than Sun's and just as powerful, so Sun increasingly is unable to compete on price, quality, or power. Sun's revenues and profits are declining rapidly, and the firm is actively engaged in the strategy-evaluation process. This is an example of a company that basically began with step two in the process illustrated; today firms must begin with step one due to intense competition in virtually all industries.

The Balanced Scorecard

Introduced earlier in the Chapter 5 discussion of Objectives, the Balanced Scorecard also is an important strategy-evaluation topic. It is a process that allows firms to evaluate strategies from four perspectives: financial performance, customer knowledge, internal business processes, and learning and growth. The Balanced Scorecard analysis requires that firms seek answers to the following questions and utilize that information, in conjunction with financial measures, to adequately and more effectively evaluate strategies being implemented:

1. How well is the firm continually improving and creating value along measures such as innovation, technological leadership, product quality, operational process efficiencies, and so on?
2. How well is the firm sustaining and even improving upon its core competencies and competitive advantages?
3. How satisfied are the firm's customers?

A sample Balanced Scorecard is provided in Table 9–4. Notice that the firm examines six key issues in evaluating its strategies: (1) Customers, (2) Managers/Employees, (3) Operations/Processes, (4) Community/Social Responsibility, (5) Business Ethics/Natural Environment, and (6) Financial. The basic form of a Balanced Scorecard may differ for different organizations. The Balanced Scorecard approach to strategy evaluation aims to balance long-term with short-term concerns, to balance financial with nonfinancial concerns, and to balance internal with external concerns. It can be an excellent management tool and it is used successfully today by Chemical Bank, Exxon/Mobil Corporation, CIGNA Property and Casualty Insurance, and numerous other firms. The Scorecard would be constructed differently, that is, adapted, to particular firms in various industries with the underlying theme or thrust being the same, which is to evaluate the firm's strategies based upon both key quantitative and qualitative measures.

Published Sources of Strategy-Evaluation Information

A number of publications are helpful in evaluating a firm's strategies. For example, *Fortune* annually identifies and evaluates the *Fortune* 1,000 (the largest manufacturers) and the *Fortune* 50 (the largest retailers, transportation companies, utilities, banks, insurance companies, and diversified financial corporations in the United States). *Fortune* ranks the best and worst performers on various factors such as return on investment, sales volume, and profitability. In its March issue each year, *Fortune* publishes its strategy-evaluation research in an article entitled "America's Most Admired Companies." Nine key attributes serve as evaluative criteria: quality of management; innovativeness; quality of products or services; long-term investment value; financial soundness; community and environmental responsibility; ability to attract, develop, and keep talented people; use of corporate assets; and

TABLE 9-4   An Example Balanced Scorecard

AREA OF OBJECTIVES	MEASURE OR TARGET	TIME EXPECTATION	PRIMARY RESPONSIBILITY
Customers			
1.			
2.			
3.			
4.			
Managers/Employees			
1.			
2.			
3.			
4.			
Operations/Processes			
1.			
2.			
3.			
4.			
Community/Social Responsibility			
1.			
2.			
3.			
4.			
Business Ethics/Natural Environment			
1.			
2.			
3.			
4.			
Financial			
1.			
2.			
3.			
4.			

international acumen. In October of each year, *Fortune* publishes additional strategy-evaluation research in an article entitled "The World's Most Admired Companies." Note from the "Natural Environment Perspective" that countries themselves are evaluated according to their responsiveness to environmental issues. The Kyoto treaty is an important measure of a country's commitment to environmental issues. *Fortune's* 2003 evaluation in Table 9–5 reveals the firms ranked as the top ten most admired (best managed).

Another excellent evaluation of corporations in America, "The Annual Report on American Industry," is published annually in the January issue of *Forbes*. It provides a detailed and comprehensive evaluation of hundreds of American

NATURAL ENVIRONMENT PERSPECTIVE

European Countries' Compliance with the Kyoto Agreement

The fifteen countries in the European Union (EU) adopted the Kyoto Protocol on global warming and the release of harmful carbon dioxide emissions. Some countries are ahead of schedule in meeting gas emission requirements and some are behind. The following list reveals in rank order the countries that are doing the best (#1) to the worst (#15) in complying with Kyoto Agreement provisions regarding air pollution:

1. Luxembourg
2. Germany
3. Sweden
4. United Kingdom
5. France
6. Finland
7. Netherlands
8. Greece
9. Belgium
10. Italy
11. Denmark
12. Austria
13. Portugal
14. Spain
15. Ireland

Although the U.S. did not ratify the Kyoto treaty, many American firms have factories in the EU and all these must comply with the treaty. It is unclear whether Russia will ratify the Kyoto treaty, and it must for the treaty itself to go into effect. Russia is not a member of the World Trade Organization (WTO), although President Putin is determined to gain entry. Many countries and companies already are taking steps to comply with the Kyoto treaty in anticipation of its provisions becoming standard worldwide sooner rather than later.

Source: Adapted from Jeffrey Ball, "In Europe, Clues to Kyoto's Impact," *Wall Street Journal* (October 10, 2003): A12.

companies in many different industries. *BusinessWeek, Industry Week,* and *Dun's Business Month* also periodically publish detailed evaluations of American businesses and industries. Although published sources of strategy-evaluation information focus primarily on large, publicly held businesses, the comparative ratios and related information are widely used to evaluate small businesses and privately owned firms as well.

TABLE 9–5   Most Admired Companies

RANK	COMPANY
1	Wal-Mart
2	Southwest Airlines
3	Berkshire Hathaway
4	Dell Computer
5	General Electric
6	Johnson & Johnson
7	Microsoft
8	FedEx
9	Starbucks
10	Procter & Gamble

Source: www.fortune.com/fortune/mostadmired

Characteristics of an Effective Evaluation System

Strategy evaluation must meet several basic requirements to be effective. First, strategy-evaluation activities must be economical; too much information can be just as bad as too little information; and too many controls can do more harm than good. Strategy-evaluation activities also should be meaningful; they should specifically relate to a firm's objectives. They should provide managers with useful information about tasks over which they have control and influence. Strategy-evaluation activities should provide timely information; on occasion and in some areas, managers may need information daily. For example, when a firm has diversified by acquiring another firm, evaluative information may be needed frequently. However, in an R&D department, daily or even weekly evaluative information could be dysfunctional. Approximate information that is timely is generally more desirable as a basis for strategy evaluation than accurate information that does not depict the present. Frequent measurement and rapid reporting may frustrate control rather than give better control. The time dimension of control must coincide with the time span of the event being measured.

Strategy evaluation should be designed to provide a true picture of what is happening. For example, in a severe economic downturn, productivity and profitability ratios may drop alarmingly, although employees and managers are actually working harder. Strategy evaluations should portray this type of situation fairly. Information derived from the strategy-evaluation process should facilitate action and should be directed to those individuals in the organization who need to take action based on it. Managers commonly ignore evaluative reports that are provided for informational purposes only; not all managers need to receive all reports. Controls need to be action-oriented rather than information-oriented.

The strategy-evaluation process should not dominate decisions; it should foster mutual understanding, trust, and common sense. No department should fail to cooperate with another in evaluating strategies. Strategy evaluations should be simple, not too cumbersome, and not too restrictive. Complex strategy-evaluation systems often confuse people and accomplish little. The test of an effective evaluation system is its usefulness, not its complexity.

Large organizations require a more elaborate and detailed strategy-evaluation system because it is more difficult to coordinate efforts among different divisions and functional areas. Managers in small companies often communicate with each other and their employees daily and do not need extensive evaluative reporting systems. Familiarity with local environments usually makes gathering and evaluating information much easier for small organizations than for large businesses. But the key to an effective strategy-evaluation system may be the ability to convince participants that failure to accomplish certain objectives within a prescribed time is not necessarily a reflection of their performance.

There is no one ideal strategy-evaluation system. The unique characteristics of an organization, including its size, management style, purpose, problems, and strengths, can determine a strategy-evaluation and control system's final design. Robert Waterman offered the following observation about successful organizations' strategy-evaluation and control systems:

> Successful companies treat facts as friends and controls as liberating. Morgan Guaranty and Wells Fargo not only survive but thrive in the troubled waters of bank deregulation, because their strategy evaluation and control systems are sound, their risk is contained, and they know themselves and the competitive situation so well. Successful companies have a voracious

hunger for facts. They see information where others see only data. They love comparisons, rankings, anything that removes decision making from the realm of mere opinion. Successful companies maintain tight, accurate financial controls. Their people don't regard controls as an imposition of autocracy but as the benign checks and balances that allow them to be creative and free.[12]

Contingency Planning

A basic premise of good strategic management is that firms plan ways to deal with unfavorable and favorable events before they occur. Too many organizations prepare contingency plans just for unfavorable events; this is a mistake, because both minimizing threats and capitalizing on opportunities can improve a firm's competitive position.

Regardless of how carefully strategies are formulated, implemented, and evaluated, unforeseen events such as strikes, boycotts, natural disasters, arrival of foreign competitors, and government actions can make a strategy obsolete. To minimize the impact of potential threats, organizations should develop contingency plans as part of their strategy-evaluation process. *Contingency plans* can be defined as alternative plans that can be put into effect if certain key events do not occur as expected. Only high-priority areas require the insurance of contingency plans. Strategists cannot and should not try to cover all bases by planning for all possible contingencies. But in any case, contingency plans should be as simple as possible.

Some contingency plans commonly established by firms include the following:

1. If a major competitor withdraws from particular markets as intelligence reports indicate, what actions should our firm take?
2. If our sales objectives are not reached, what actions should our firm take to avoid profit losses?
3. If demand for our new product exceeds plans, what actions should our firm take to meet the higher demand?
4. If certain disasters occur—such as loss of computer capabilities; a hostile takeover attempt; loss of patent protection; or destruction of manufacturing facilities because of earthquakes, tornados, or hurricanes—what actions should our firm take?
5. If a new technological advancement makes our new product obsolete sooner than expected, what actions should our firm take?

Too many organizations discard alternative strategies not selected for implementation although the work devoted to analyzing these options would render valuable information. Alternative strategies not selected for implementation can serve as contingency plans in case the strategy or strategies selected do not work.

When strategy-evaluation activities reveal the need for a major change quickly, an appropriate contingency plan can be executed in a timely way. Contingency plans can promote a strategist's ability to respond quickly to key changes in the internal and external bases of an organization's current strategy. For example, if underlying assumptions about the economy turn out to be wrong and contingency plans are ready, then managers can make appropriate changes promptly.

In some cases, external or internal conditions present unexpected opportunities. When such opportunities occur, contingency plans could allow an organization to capitalize on them quickly. Linneman and Chandran reported that contingency planning gave users such as DuPont, Dow Chemical, Consolidated Foods, and Emerson Electric three major benefits: (1) It permitted quick response to change, (2) it prevented panic in crisis situations, and (3) it made managers more adaptable by encouraging them to appreciate just how variable the future can be. They suggested that effective contingency planning involves a seven-step process:

1. Identify both beneficial and unfavorable events that could possibly derail the strategy or strategies.
2. Specify trigger points. Calculate about when contingent events are likely to occur.
3. Assess the impact of each contingent event. Estimate the potential benefit or harm of each contingent event.
4. Develop contingency plans. Be sure that contingency plans are compatible with current strategy and are economically feasible.
5. Assess the counter impact of each contingency plan. That is, estimate how much each contingency plan will capitalize on or cancel out its associated contingent event. Doing this will quantify the potential value of each contingency plan.
6. Determine early warning signals for key contingent events. Monitor the early warning signals.
7. For contingent events with reliable early warning signals, develop advance action plans to take advantage of the available lead time.[13]

Auditing

A frequently used tool in strategy evaluation is the audit. *Auditing* is defined by the American Accounting Association (AAA) as "a systematic process of objectively obtaining and evaluating evidence regarding assertions about economic actions and events to ascertain the degree of correspondence between these assertions and established criteria, and communicating the results to interested users."[14] Since the Enron, Worldcom, and Johnson & Johnson scandals in 2002, auditing has taken on greater emphasis and care in companies. Independent auditors basically are certified public accountants (CPAs) who provide their services to organizations for a fee; they examine the financial statements of an organization to determine whether they have been prepared according to generally accepted accounting principles (GAAP) and whether they fairly represent the activities of the firm. Independent auditors use a set of standards called generally accepted auditing standards (GAAS). Public accounting firms often have a consulting arm that provides strategy-evaluation services.

Two government agencies—the General Accounting Office (GAO) and the Internal Revenue Service (IRS)—employ government auditors responsible for making sure that organizations comply with federal laws, statutes, and policies. GAO and IRS auditors can audit any public or private organization. The third group of auditors consists of employees within an organization who are responsible for safeguarding company assets, for assessing the efficiency of company operations, and for ensuring that generally accepted business procedures are practiced.

The Environmental Audit

For an increasing number of firms, overseeing environmental affairs is no longer a technical function performed by specialists; rather, it has become an important strategic-management concern. Product design, manufacturing, transportation, customer use, packaging, product disposal, and corporate rewards and sanctions should reflect environmental considerations. Firms that effectively manage environmental affairs are benefiting from constructive relations with employees, consumers, suppliers, and distributors.

Shimell emphasized the need for organizations to conduct environmental audits of their operations and to develop a Corporate Environmental Policy (CEP).[15] Shimell contended that an environmental audit should be as rigorous as a financial audit and should include training workshops in which staff can help design and implement the policy. The CEP should be budgeted, and requisite funds should be allocated to ensure that it is not a public relations facade. A Statement of Environmental Policy should be published periodically to inform shareholders and the public of environmental actions taken by the firm.

Instituting an environmental audit can include moving environmental affairs from the staff side of the organization to the line side. Some firms are also introducing environmental criteria and objectives in their performance appraisal instruments and systems. Conoco, for example, ties compensation of all its top managers to environmental action plans. Occidental Chemical includes environmental responsibilities in all its job descriptions for positions.

Twenty-First-Century Challenges in Strategic Management

Three particular challenges or decisions that face all strategists today are (1) deciding whether the process should be more an art or a science, (2) deciding whether strategies should be visible or hidden from stakeholders, and (3) deciding whether the process should be more top-down or bottom-up in their firm.[16]

The Art or Science Issue

This textbook is consistent with most of the strategy literature in advocating that strategic management be viewed more as a science than an art. This perspective contends that firms need to systematically assess their external and internal environments, conduct research, carefully evaluate the pros and cons of various alternatives, perform analyses, and then decide upon a particular course of action. In contrast, Mintzberg's notion of "crafting" strategies embodies the artistic model which suggests that strategic decision making be based primarily on holistic thinking, intuition, creativity, and imagination.[17] Mintzberg and his followers reject strategies that result from objective analysis, preferring instead subjective imagination. "Strategy scientists" reject strategies that emerge from emotion, hunch, creativity, and politics. Proponents of the artistic view often consider strategic planning exercises to be time poorly spent. The Mintzberg philosophy insists on informality whereas strategy scientists (and this text) insist on more formality. Mintzberg refers to strategic planning as an "emergent" process whereas strategy scientists use the term "deliberate" process.[18]

The answer to the art versus science question is one that strategists must decide for themselves, and certainly the two approaches are not necessarily mutually exclusive. In deciding which approach is more effective, however, consider that the business world today has become increasingly complex and more intensely competitive. There is less room for error in strategic planning. Recall that Chapter 1 discussed the importance of intuition and experience and subjectivity in strategic planning, and even the weights and ratings discussed in Chapters 3, 4, and 6 certainly require good judgment. But the idea of deciding upon strategies for any firm without thorough research and analysis, at least in the mind of this writer, is unwise. Certainly, in smaller firms there can be more informality in the process compared to larger firms, but even for smaller firms, a wealth of competitive information is available on the Internet and elsewhere, and should be collected, assimilated, and evaluated before deciding on a course of action upon which survival of the firm may hinge. The livelihood of countless employees and shareholders may hinge on the effectiveness of strategies selected. Too much is at stake to be less than thorough in formulating strategies. It may not behoove a strategist to rely too heavily on gut feeling and opinion instead of research data, competitive intelligence, and analysis in formulating strategies.

The Visible or Hidden Issue

There are certainly good reasons to keep the strategy process and strategies themselves visible and open rather than hidden and secret. There are also good reasons to keep strategies hidden from all but top-level executives. Strategists must decide for themselves what is best for their firm. This text comes down largely on the side of being visible and open but certainly this may not be best for all strategists and all firms. As pointed out in Chapter 1, Zun Tzu argued that all war is based on deception and that the best maneuvers are those not easily predicted by rivals. Business is analogous to war.

Some reasons to be completely open with the strategy process and resultant decisions are:

1. Managers, employees, and other stakeholders can readily contribute to the process. They often have excellent ideas. Secrecy would forgo many excellent ideas.
2. Investors, creditors, and other stakeholders have greater basis for supporting a firm when they know what the firm is doing and where the firm is going.
3. Visibility promotes democracy whereas secrecy promotes autocracy. Domestic firms and most foreign firms prefer democracy over autocracy as a management style.
4. Participation and openness enhances understanding, commitment, and communication within the firm.

Reasons why some firms prefer to conduct strategic planning in secret and keep strategies hidden from all but the highest-level executives are as follows:

1. Free dissemination of a firm's strategies may easily translate into competitive intelligence for rival firms who could exploit the firm given that information.
2. Secrecy limits criticism, second guessing, and hindsight.
3. Participants in a visible strategy process become more attractive to rival firms who may lure them away.
4. Secrecy limits rival firms from imitating or duplicating the firm's strategies and undermining the firm.

The obvious benefits of the visible versus hidden extremes suggest that a working balance must be sought between the apparent contradictions. Parnell says that in a perfect world all key individuals both inside and outside the firm should be involved in strategic planning, but in practice particularly sensitive and confidential information should always remain strictly confidential to top managers.[19] This balancing act is difficult but essential for survival of the firm.

The Top-Down or Bottom-Up Approach

Proponents of the top-down approach contend that top executives are the only persons in the firm with the collective experience, acumen, and fiduciary responsibility to make key strategy decisions. In contrast, bottom-up advocates argue that lower- and middle-level managers and employees who will be implementing the strategies need to be actively involved in the process of formulating the strategies to assure their support and commitment. Recent strategy research and this textbook emphasize the bottom-up approach, but earlier work by Schendel and Hofer stressed the need for firms to rely on perceptions of their top managers in strategic planning.[20] Strategists must reach a working balance of the two approaches in a manner deemed best for their firm at a particular time, while cognizant of the fact that current research supports the bottom-up approach, at least among American firms. Increased education and diversity of the work-force at all levels are reasons why middle- and lower-level managers—and even nonmanagers—should be invited to participate in the firm's strategic planning process, at least to the extent that they are willing and able to contribute.

CONCLUSION

This chapter presents a strategy-evaluation framework that can facilitate accomplishment of annual and long-term objectives. Effective strategy evaluation allows an organization to capitalize on internal strengths as they develop, to exploit external opportunities as they emerge, to recognize and defend against threats, and to mitigate internal weaknesses before they become detrimental.

Strategists in successful organizations take the time to formulate, implement, and then evaluate strategies deliberately and systematically. Good strategists move their organization forward with purpose and direction, continually evaluating and improving the firm's external and internal strategic position. Strategy evaluation allows an organization to shape its own future rather than allowing it to be constantly shaped by remote forces that have little or no vested interest in the well-being of the enterprise.

Although not a guarantee for success, strategic management allows organizations to make effective long-term decisions, to execute those decisions efficiently, and to take corrective actions as needed to ensure success. Computer networks and the Internet help to coordinate strategic-management activities and to ensure that decisions are based on good information. The *Checkmate* Strategic Planning Software is especially good in this regard (*www.checkmateplan.com*). A key to effective strategy evaluation and to successful strategic management is an integration of intuition and analysis:

> A potentially fatal problem is the tendency for analytical and intuitive issues to polarize. This polarization leads to strategy evaluation that is dominated

by either analysis or intuition, or to strategy evaluation that is discontinuous, with a lack of coordination among analytical and intuitive issues.[21]

Strategists in successful organizations realize that strategic management is first and foremost a people process. It is an excellent vehicle for fostering organizational communication. People are what make the difference in organizations.

The real key to effective strategic management is to accept the premise that the planning process is more important than the written plan, that the manager is continuously planning and does not stop planning when the written plan is finished. The written plan is only a snapshot as of the moment it is approved. If the manager is not planning on a continuous basis—planning, measuring, and revising—the written plan can become obsolete the day it is finished. This obsolescence becomes more of a certainty as the increasingly rapid rate of change makes the business environment more uncertain.[22]

We invite you to visit the David page on the Prentice Hall Companion Web site at *www.prenhall.com/david* for this chapter's World Wide Web exercises.

KEY TERMS AND CONCEPTS

Advantage (p. 311)
Auditing (p. 325)
Balanced Scorecard (p. 320)
Consistency (p. 311)
Consonance (p. 311)
Contingency Plans (p. 324)
Corporate Agility (p. 319)
Feasibility (p. 311)

Future Shock (p. 318)
Management by Wandering
    Around (p. 313)
Measuring Organizational
    Performance (p. 317)
Reviewing the Underlying Bases
    of an Organization's
    Strategy (p. 315)

Revised EFE Matrix (p. 315)
Revised IFE Matrix (p. 315)
Taking Corrective Actions (p. 318)

ISSUES FOR REVIEW AND DISCUSSION

1. Why has strategy evaluation become so important in business today?
2. BellSouth Services is considering putting divisional EFE and IFE matrices online for continual updating. How would this affect strategy evaluation?
3. What types of quantitative and qualitative criteria do you think David Glass, CEO of Wal-Mart, uses to evaluate the company's strategy?
4. As owner of a local, independent supermarket, explain how you would evaluate the firm's strategy.

5. Under what conditions are corrective actions not required in the strategy-evaluation process?
6. Identify types of organizations that may need to evaluate strategy more frequently than others. Justify your choices.
7. As executive director of the state forestry commission, in what way and how frequently would you evaluate the organization's strategies?
8. Identify some key financial ratios that would be important in evaluating a bank's strategy.
9. As owner of a chain of hardware stores, describe how you would approach contingency planning.

10. Strategy evaluation allows an organization to take a proactive stance toward shaping its own future. Discuss the meaning of this statement.
11. Explain and discuss the Balanced Scorecard.
12. Why is the Balanced Scorecard an important topic both in devising objectives and in evaluating strategies?
13. Develop a Balanced Scorecard for a local fast-food restaurant.
14. Do you believe strategic management should be more visible or hidden as a process in a firm? Explain.
15. Do you feel strategic management should be more a top-down or bottom-up process in a firm? Explain.
16. Do you believe strategic management is more an art or a science? Explain.

NOTES

1. Dale McConkey, "Planning in a Changing Environment," *Business Horizons* (September–October 1988): 64.
2. Robert Simons, "Control in an Age of Empowerment," *Harvard Business Review* (March–April 1995): 80.
3. Dale Zand, "Reviewing the Policy Process," *California Management Review* 21, no. 1 (Fall 1978): 37.
4. Eccles. 3: 1–8.
5. Seymour Tilles, "How to Evaluate Corporate Strategy," *Harvard Business Review* 41 (July–August 1963): 111–121.
6. Claude George, Jr., *The History of Management Thought* (Englewood Cliffs, New Jersey: Prentice-Hall, 1968): 165–166.
7. John Brown and Neil Agnew, "Corporate Agility," *Business Horizons* 25, no. 2 (March–April 1982): 29.
8. M. Erez and F. Kanfer, "The Role of Goal Acceptance in Goal Setting and Task Performance," *Academy of Management Review* 8, no. 3 (July 1983): 457.
9. D. Hussey and M. Langham, *Corporate Planning: The Human Factor* (Oxford, England: Pergamon Press, 1979): 138.
10. Carter Bayles, "Strategic Control: The President's Paradox," *Business Horizons* 20, no. 4 (August 1977): 18.
11. Pui-Wing Tam, "Cloud Over Sun Microsystems: Plummeting Computer Prices," *Wall Street Journal* (October 16, 2003): A1.
12. Robert Waterman, Jr., "How the Best Get Better," *BusinessWeek* (September 14, 1987): 105.
13. Robert Linneman and Rajan Chandran, "Contingency Planning: A Key to Swift Managerial Action in the Uncertain Tomorrow," *Managerial Planning* 29, no. 4 (January–February 1981): 23–27.
14. American Accounting Association, *Report of Committee on Basic Auditing Concepts* (1971): 15–74.
15. Pamela Shimell, "Corporate Environmental Policy in Practice," *Long Range Planning* 24, no. 3 (June 1991): 10.
16. John Parnell, "Five Critical Challenges in Strategy Making," *SAM Advanced Management Journal* 68, no. 2 (Spring 2003): 15–22.
17. Henry Mintzberg, "Crafting Strategy," *Harvard Business Review* (July–August, 1987): 66–75.
18. Henry Mintzberg and J. Waters, "Of Strategies, Deliberate and Emergent," *Strategic Management Journal* 6, no. 2: 257–272.
19. Parnell, 15–22.
20. D. E. Schendel and C. W. Hofer (Eds.), *Strategic Management* (Boston: Little, Brown, 1979).
21. Michael McGinnis, "The Key to Strategic Planning: Integrating Analysis and Intuition," *Sloan Management Review* 26, no. 1 (Fall 1984): 49.
22. McConkey, 72.

CURRENT READINGS

Marginson, D. E. "Management Control Systems and Their Effects on Strategy Formation at Middle-Management Levels: Evidence from a U.K. Organization. "*Strategic Management Journal* 23, no. 11 (November 2002): 1019–1032.

Peng, M. W. "Institutional Transitions and Strategic Choices." *Academy of Management Review* 28, no. 2 (April 2003): 275–296.

Roney, C. W. "Planning for Strategic Contingencies." *Business Horizons* 46, no. 2 (March–April 2003): 35–42.

experiential exercises

<table>
<tr><td>

Experiential Exercise 9A

Preparing a Strategy-Evaluation Report for Krispy Kreme Doughnuts (KKD)

</td><td>

PURPOSE

This exercise can give you experience locating strategy-evaluation information. Use of the Internet coupled with published sources of information can significantly enhance the strategy-evaluation process. Performance information on competitors, for example, can help put into perspective a firm's own performance.

INSTRUCTIONS

Step 1 Visit **www.forbes.com** to locate strategy-evaluation information on competitors. Read five to ten articles written in the last six months that discuss the fast-food industry.

Step 2 Summarize your research findings by preparing a strategy-evaluation report for your instructor. Include in your report a summary of KKD's strategies and performance in 2003 and a summary of your conclusions regarding the effectiveness of KKD's strategies.

Step 3 Based on your analysis, do you feel that KKD is pursuing effective strategies? What recommendations would you offer to KKD's chief executive officer?

</td></tr>
<tr><td>

Experiential Exercise 9B

Evaluating My University's Strategies

</td><td>

PURPOSE

An important part of evaluating strategies is determining the nature and extent of changes in an organization's external opportunities/threats and internal strengths/weaknesses. Changes in these underlying critical success factors can indicate a need to change or modify the firm's strategies.

INSTRUCTIONS

As a class, discuss positive and negative changes in your university's external and internal factors during your college career. Begin by listing on the board new or emerging opportunities and threats. Then identify strengths and weaknesses that have changed significantly during your college career. In light of the external and internal changes that were identified, discuss whether your university's strategies need modifying. Are there any new strategies that you would recommend? Make a list to recommend to your department chair, dean, or chancellor.

</td></tr>
<tr><td>

Experiential Exercise 9C

Who Prepares an Environmental Audit?

</td><td>

PURPOSE

The purpose of this activity is to determine the nature and prevalence of environmental audits among companies in your state.

</td></tr>
</table>

INSTRUCTIONS

Contact by phone at least five different plant managers or owners of large businesses in your area. Seek answers to the questions listed below. Present your findings in a written report to your instructor.

1. Does your company conduct an environmental audit? If yes, please describe the nature and scope of the audit.
2. Are environmental criteria included in the performance evaluation of managers? If yes, please specify the criteria.
3. Are environmental affairs more a technical function or a management function in your company?
4. Does your firm offer any environmental workshops for employees? If yes, please describe them.

How to Prepare and Present a Case Analysis

objectives

After studying this chapter, you should be able to do the following:

1. Describe the case method for learning strategic-management concepts.

2. Identify the steps in preparing a comprehensive written case analysis.

3. Describe how to give an effective oral case analysis presentation.

4. Discuss special tips for doing case analysis.

sample case analysis outline

"notable quotes"

Two heads are better than one.
Unknown Author

One reaction frequently heard is, "I don't have enough information." In reality strategists never have enough information because some information is not available and some is too costly.
William Glueck

I keep six honest serving men. They taught me all I know. Their names are What, Why, When, How, Where, and Who.
Rudyard Kipling

Don't recommend anything you would not be prepared to do yourself if you were in the decision maker's shoes.
A. J. Strickland III

A picture is worth a thousand words.
Unknown Author

The purpose of this section is to help you analyze strategic-management cases. Guidelines for preparing written and oral case analyses are given, and suggestions for preparing cases for class discussion are presented. Steps to follow in preparing case analyses are provided. Guidelines for making an oral presentation are described.

What Is a Strategic-Management Case?

A *strategic-management (or business policy) case* describes an organization's external and internal condition and raises issues concerning the firm's mission, strategies, objectives, and policies. Most of the information in a business policy case is established fact, but some information may be opinions, judgments, and beliefs. Strategic-management cases are more comprehensive than those you may have studied in other courses. They generally include a description of related management, marketing, finance/accounting, production/operations, R&D, computer information systems, and natural environment issues. A strategic-management case puts the reader on the scene of the action by describing a firm's situation at some point in time. Strategic-management cases are written to give you practice applying strategic-management concepts. The case method for studying strategic management is often called *learning by doing*.

Guidelines for Preparing Case Analyses

The Need for Practicality

There is no such thing as a complete case, and no case ever gives you all the information you need to conduct analyses and make recommendations. Likewise, in the business world, strategists never have all the information they need to make decisions: information may be unavailable or too costly to obtain, or it may take too much time to obtain. So in preparing strategic-management cases, do what strategists do every day—make reasonable assumptions about unknowns, state assumptions clearly, perform appropriate analyses, and make decisions. *Be practical*. For example, in performing a projected financial analysis, make reasonable assumptions, state them appropriately, and proceed to show what impact your recommendations are expected to have on the organization's financial position. Avoid saying, "I don't have enough information." You can always supplement the information provided in a case with Internet and library research.

The Need for Justification

The most important part of analyzing cases is not what strategies you recommend, but rather how you support your decisions and how you propose that they be implemented. There is no single best solution or one right answer to a case, so give ample justification for your recommendations. This is important. In the business world, strategists usually do not know if their decisions are right until resources have been allocated and consumed. Then it is often too late to reverse a decision. This cold fact accents the need for careful integration of intuition and analysis in preparing business policy case analyses.

The Need for Realism

Avoid recommending a course of action beyond an organization's means. *Be realistic*. No organization can possibly pursue all the strategies that could potentially benefit the firm. Estimate how much capital will be required to implement what you recommended. Determine whether debt, stock, or a combination of debt and stock could be used to obtain the capital. Make sure your recommendations are feasible. Do not prepare a case analysis that omits all arguments and information not supportive of your recommendations. Rather, present the major advantages and disadvantages of several feasible alternatives. Try not to exaggerate, stereotype, prejudge, or overdramatize. Strive to demonstrate that your interpretation of the evidence is reasonable and objective.

The Need for Specificity

Do not make broad generalizations such as "The company should pursue a market penetration strategy." *Be specific* by telling *what*, *why*, *when*, *how*, *where*, and *who*. Failure to use specifics is the single major shortcoming of most oral and written case analyses. For example, in an internal audit say, "The firm's current ratio fell from 2.2 in 2003 to 1.3 in 2004, and this is considered to be a major weakness," instead of, "The firm's financial condition is bad." Rather than concluding from a Strategic Position and Action Evaluation (SPACE) Matrix that a firm should be defensive, be more specific, saying, "The firm should consider closing three plants, laying off 280 employees, and divesting itself of its chemical division, for a net savings of $20.2 million in 2005." Use ratios, percentages, numbers, and dollar estimates. Businesspeople dislike generalities and vagueness.

The Need for Originality

Do not necessarily recommend the course of action that the firm plans to take or actually undertook, even if those actions resulted in improved revenues and earnings. The aim of case analysis is for you to consider all the facts and information relevant to the organization at the time, to generate feasible alternative strategies, to choose among those alternatives, and to defend your recommendations. Put yourself back in time to the point when strategic decisions were being made by the firm's strategists. Based on the information available then, what would you have done? Support your position with charts, graphs, ratios, analyses, and the like—not a revelation from the library. You can become a good strategist by thinking through situations, making management assessments, and proposing plans yourself. *Be original.* Compare and contrast what you recommend versus what the company plans to do or did.

The Need to Contribute

Strategy formulation, implementation, and evaluation decisions are commonly made by a group of individuals rather than by a single person. Therefore, your professor may divide the class into three- or four-person teams and ask you to prepare written or oral case analyses. Members of a strategic-management team, in class or in the business world, differ on their aversion to risk, their concern for short-run versus long-run benefits, their attitudes toward social responsibility, and their views concerning globalization. There are no perfect people, so there are no perfect strategies. Be open-minded to others' views. *Be a good listener and a good contributor.*

Preparing a Case for Class Discussion

Your professor may ask you to prepare a case for class discussion. Preparing a case for class discussion means that you need to read the case before class, make notes regarding the organization's external opportunities/threats and internal strengths/

weaknesses, perform appropriate analyses, and come to class prepared to offer and defend some specific recommendations.

The Case Method versus Lecture Approach

The case method of teaching is radically different from the traditional lecture approach, in which little or no preparation is needed by students before class. The *case method* involves a classroom situation in which students do most of the talking; your professor facilitates discussion by asking questions and encouraging student interaction regarding ideas, analyses, and recommendations. Be prepared for a discussion along the lines of "What would you do, why would you do it, when would you do it, and how would you do it?" Prepare answers to the following types of questions:

- What are the firm's most important external opportunities and threats?
- What are the organization's major strengths and weaknesses?
- How would you describe the organization's financial condition?
- What are the firm's existing strategies and objectives?
- Who are the firm's competitors, and what are their strategies?
- What objectives and strategies do you recommend for this organization? Explain your reasoning. How does what you recommend compare to what the company plans?
- How could the organization best implement what you recommend? What implementation problems do you envision? How could the firm avoid or solve those problems?

The Cross-Examination

Do not hesitate to take a stand on the issues and to support your position with objective analyses and outside research. Strive to apply strategic-management concepts and tools in preparing your case for class discussion. Seek defensible arguments and positions. Support opinions and judgments with facts, reasons, and evidence. Crunch the numbers before class! Be willing to describe your recommendations to the class without fear of disapproval. Respect the ideas of others, but be willing to go against the majority opinion when you can justify a better position.

Business policy case analysis gives you the opportunity to learn more about yourself, your colleagues, strategic management, and the decision-making process in organizations. The rewards of this experience will depend on the effort you put forth, so do a good job. Discussing business policy cases in class is exciting and challenging. Expect views counter to those you present. Different students will place emphasis on different aspects of an organization's situation and submit different recommendations for scrutiny and rebuttal. Cross-examination discussions commonly arise, just as they occur in a real business organization. Avoid being a silent observer.

Preparing a Written Case Analysis

In addition to asking you to prepare a case for class discussion, your professor may ask you to prepare a written case analysis. Preparing a written case analysis is similar to preparing a case for class discussion, except written reports are generally more structured and more detailed. There is no ironclad procedure for preparing a written case analysis because cases differ in focus; the type, size, and complexity of the organizations being analyzed also vary.

When writing a strategic-management report or case analysis, avoid using jargon, vague or redundant words, acronyms, abbreviations, sexist language, and ethnic or racial slurs. And watch your spelling! Use short sentences and paragraphs and simple words and phrases. Use quite a few subheadings. Arrange issues and ideas from the most important to the least important. Arrange recommendations from the least controversial to the most controversial. Use the active voice rather than the passive voice for all verbs; for example, say, "Our team recommends that the company diversify," rather than, "It is recommended by our team to diversify." Use many examples to add specificity and clarity. Tables, figures, pie charts, bar charts, time lines, and other kinds of exhibits help communicate important points and ideas. Sometimes a picture *is* worth a thousand words.

The Executive Summary

Your professor may ask you to focus the written case analysis on a particular aspect of the strategic-management process, such as (1) to identify and evaluate the organization's existing mission, objectives, and strategies; or (2) to propose and defend specific recommendations for the company; or (3) to develop an industry analysis by describing the competitors, products, selling techniques, and market conditions in a given industry. These types of written reports are sometimes called *executive summaries*. An executive summary usually ranges from three to five pages of text in length, plus exhibits.

The Comprehensive Written Analysis

Your professor may ask you to prepare a *comprehensive written analysis*. This assignment requires you to apply the entire strategic-management process to the particular organization. When preparing a comprehensive written analysis, picture yourself as a consultant who has been asked by a company to conduct a study of its external and internal environment and to make specific recommendations for its future. Prepare exhibits to support your recommendations. Highlight exhibits with some discussion in the paper. Comprehensive written analyses are usually about ten pages in length, plus exhibits.

Steps in Preparing a Comprehensive Written Analysis

In preparing a comprehensive written analysis, you could follow the steps outlined here, which correlate to the stages in the strategic-management process and the chapters in this text.

Step 1	Identify the firm's existing vision, mission, objectives, and strategies.
Step 2	Develop vision and mission statements for the organization.
Step 3	Identify the organization's external opportunities and threats.
Step 4	Construct a Competitive Profile Matrix (CPM).
Step 5	Construct an External Factor Evaluation (EFE) Matrix.
Step 6	Identify the organization's internal strengths and weaknesses.
Step 7	Construct an Internal Factor Evaluation (IFE) Matrix.
Step 8	Prepare a Strengths-Weaknesses-Opportunities-Threats (SWOT) Matrix, Strategic Position and Action Evaluation (SPACE) Matrix,

Boston Consulting Group (BCG) Matrix, Internal-External (IE) Matrix, Grand Strategy Matrix, and Quantitative Strategic Planning Matrix (QSPM) as appropriate. Give advantages and disadvantages of alternative strategies.

Step 9 Recommend specific strategies and long-term objectives. Show how much your recommendations will cost. Itemize these costs clearly for each projected year. Compare your recommendations to actual strategies planned by the company.

Step 10 Specify how your recommendations can be implemented and what results you can expect. Prepare forecasted ratios and projected financial statements. Present a timetable or agenda for action.

Step 11 Recommend specific annual objectives and policies.

Step 12 Recommend procedures for strategy review and evaluation.

Making an Oral Presentation

Your professor may ask you to prepare a strategic-management case analysis, individually or as a group, and present your analysis to the class. Oral presentations are usually graded on two parts: content and delivery. *Content* refers to the quality, quantity, correctness, and appropriateness of analyses presented, including such dimensions as logical flow through the presentation, coverage of major issues, use of specifics, avoidance of generalities, absence of mistakes, and feasibility of recommendations. *Delivery* includes such dimensions as audience attentiveness, clarity of visual aids, appropriate dress, persuasiveness of arguments, tone of voice, eye contact, and posture. Great ideas are of no value unless others can be convinced of their merit through clear communication. The guidelines presented here can help you make an effective oral presentation.

Organizing the Presentation

Begin your presentation by introducing yourself and giving a clear outline of topics to be covered. If a team is presenting, specify the sequence of speakers and the areas each person will address. At the beginning of an oral presentation, try to capture your audience's interest and attention. You could do this by displaying some products made by the company, telling an interesting short story about the company, or sharing an experience you had that is related to the company, its products, or its services. You could develop or obtain a video to show at the beginning of class; you could visit a local distributor of the firm's products and tape a personal interview with the business owner or manager. A light or humorous introduction can be effective at the beginning of a presentation.

Be sure the setting of your presentation is well organized, with chairs, flip charts, a transparency projector, and whatever else you plan to use. Arrive at least fifteen minutes early at the classroom to organize the setting, and be sure your materials are ready to go. Make sure everyone can see your visual aids well.

Controlling Your Voice

An effective rate of speaking ranges from 100 to 125 words per minute. Practice your presentation a loud to determine if you are going too fast. Individuals commonly speak too fast when nervous. Breathe deeply before and during the presentation to help yourself slow down. Have a cup of water available; pausing to take a drink will wet your throat, give you time to collect your thoughts, control your nervousness, slow you down, and signal to the audience a change in topic.

Avoid a monotone by placing emphasis on different words or sentences. Speak loudly and clearly, but don't shout. Silence can be used effectively to break a monotone voice. Stop at the end of each sentence, rather than running sentences together with *and* or *uh*.

Managing Body Language
Be sure not to fold your arms, lean on the podium, put your hands in your pockets, or put your hands behind you. Keep a straight posture, with one foot slightly in front of the other. Do not turn your back to the audience; doing so is not only rude, but it also prevents your voice from projecting well. Avoid using too many hand gestures. On occasion, leave the podium or table and walk toward your audience, but do not walk around too much. Never block the audience's view of your visual aids.

Maintain good eye contact throughout the presentation. This is the best way to persuade your audience. There is nothing more reassuring to a speaker than to see members of the audience nod in agreement or smile. Try to look everyone in the eye at least once during your presentation, but focus more on individuals who look interested than on those who seem bored. Use humor and smiles as appropriate throughout your presentation to stay in touch with your audience. A presentation should never be dull!

Speaking from Notes
Be sure not to read to your audience, because reading puts people to sleep. Perhaps worse than reading is memorizing. Do not try to memorize anything. Rather, practice using notes unobtrusively. Make sure your notes are written clearly so you will not flounder when trying to read your own writing. Include only main ideas on your note cards. Keep note cards on a podium or table if possible so that you won't drop them or get them out of order; walking with note cards tends to be distracting.

Constructing Visual Aids
Make sure your visual aids are legible to individuals in the back of the room. Use color to highlight special items. Avoid putting complete sentences on visual aids; rather, use short phrases and then elaborate on issues orally as you make your presentation. Generally, there should be no more than four to six lines of text on each visual aid. Use clear headings and subheadings. Be careful about spelling and grammar; use a consistent style of lettering. Use masking tape or an easel for posters—do not hold posters in your hand. Transparencies and handouts are excellent aids; however, be careful not to use too many handouts or your audience may concentrate on them instead of you during the presentation.

Answering Questions
It is best to field questions at the end of your presentation, rather than during the presentation itself. Encourage questions, and take your time to respond to each one. Answering questions can be persuasive because it involves you with the audience. If a team is giving the presentation, the audience should direct questions to a specific person. During the question-and-answer period, be polite, confident, and courteous. Avoid verbose responses. Do not get defensive with your answers, even if a hostile or

confrontational question is asked. Staying calm during potentially disruptive situations, such as a cross-examination, reflects self-confidence, maturity, poise, and command of the particular company and its industry. Stand up throughout the question-and-answer period.

Tips for Success in Case Analysis

Strategic-management students who have used this text over nine editions offer you the following tips for success in doing case analysis. The tips are grouped into two basic sections: (1) Content Tips and (2) Process Tips. Content tips relate especially to the content of your case analysis, whereas the Process tips relate mostly to the process that you and your group mates undergo in preparing and delivering your case analysis/presentation.

Content Tips

1. Use the **www.strategyclub.com** Web site resources. The software described there is especially useful.
2. In preparing your external assessment, use the S&P Industry Survey material in your college library.
3. Go to the Web site and put your company's stock symbol in the lower right corner. Then use the information there.
4. View your case analysis and presentation as a product that must have some competitive factor to differentiate it favorably from the case analyses of other students.
5. Develop a mind-set of *why*, continually questioning your own and others' assumptions and assertions.
6. Since business policy is a capstone course, seek the help of professors in other specialty areas when necessary.
7. Read your case frequently as work progresses so you don't overlook details.
8. At the end of each group session, assign each member of the group a task to be completed for the next meeting.
9. Become friends with the library.
10. Be creative and innovative throughout the case analysis process.
11. A goal of case analysis is to improve your ability to think clearly in ambiguous and confusing situations; do not get frustrated that there is no single best answer.
12. Do not confuse symptoms with causes; do not develop conclusions and solutions prematurely; recognize that information may be misleading, conflicting, or wrong.
13. Work hard to develop the ability to formulate reasonable, consistent, and creative plans; put yourself in the strategist's position.
14. Develop confidence in using quantitative tools for analysis. They are not inherently difficult, it is just practice and familiarity you need.
15. Strive for excellence in writing and in the technical preparation of your case. Prepare nice charts, tables, diagrams, and graphs. Use color and unique pictures. No messy exhibits! Use PowerPoint.
16. Do not forget that the objective is to learn; explore areas with which you are not familiar.
17. Pay attention to detail.

18. Think through alternative implications fully and realistically. The consequences of decisions are not always apparent. They often affect many different aspects of a firm's operations.

19. Provide answers to such fundamental questions as *what*, *when*, *where*, *why*, *who*, and *how*.

20. Do not merely recite ratios or present figures. Rather, develop ideas and conclusions concerning the possible trends. Show the importance of these figures to the corporation.

21. Support reasoning and judgment with factual data whenever possible.

22. Your analysis should be as detailed and specific as possible.

23. A picture speaks a thousand words, and a creative picture gets you an A in many classes.

24. Emphasize the Recommendations and Strategy Implementation sections. A common mistake is to spend too much time on the external or internal analysis parts of your paper. Always remember that the meat of the paper or presentation is the recommendations and implementation sections.

Process Tips

1. In working within a team, encourage most of the work to be done individually. Use team meetings mostly to assimilate work. This approach is most efficient.

2. If allowed to do so, invite questions throughout your presentation.

3. During the presentation, keep good posture, eye contact, voice tone, and project confidence. Do not get defensive under any conditions or with any questions.

4. Prepare your case analysis far enough in advance of the due date to allow time for reflection and practice. Do not procrastinate.

5. Maintain a positive attitude about the class, working *with* problems rather than against them.

6. Keep in tune with your professor, and understand his or her values and expectations.

7. Other students will have strengths in functional areas that will complement your weaknesses, so develop a cooperative spirit that moderates competitiveness in group work.

8. When preparing a case analysis as a group, divide into separate teams to work on the external analysis and internal analysis.

9. Have a good sense of humor.

10. Capitalize on the strengths of each member of the group; volunteer your services in your areas of strength.

11. Set goals for yourself and your team; budget your time to attain them.

12. Foster attitudes that encourage group participation and interaction. Do not be hasty to judge group members.

13. Be prepared to work. There will be times when you will have to do more than your share. Accept it, and do what you have to do to move the team forward.

14. Think of your case analysis as if it were really happening; do not reduce case analysis to a mechanical process.

15. To uncover flaws in your analysis and to prepare the group for questions during an oral presentation, assign one person in the group to actively play the devil's advocate.

16. Do not schedule excessively long group meetings; two-hour sessions are about right.

17. Push your ideas hard enough to get them listened to, but then let up; listen to others and try to follow their lines of thinking; follow the flow of group discussion, recognizing when you need to get back on track; do not repeat yourself or others unless clarity or progress demands repetition.

18. Develop a case-presentation style that is direct, assertive, and convincing; be concise, precise, fluent, and correct.

19. Have fun when at all possible. It is frustrating at times, but enjoy it while you can; it may be several years before you are playing CEO again.

20. In group cases, do not allow personality differences to interfere. When they occur, they must be understood for what they are—and then put aside.

21. Get things written down (drafts) as soon as possible.

22. Read everything that other group members write, and comment on it in writing. This allows group input into all aspects of case preparation.

23. Adaptation and flexibility are keys to success; be creative and innovative.

24. Neatness is a real plus; your case analysis should look professional.

25. Let someone else read and critique your presentation several days before you present it.

26. Make special efforts to get to know your group members. This leads to more openness in the group and allows for more interchange of ideas. Put in the time and effort necessary to develop these relationships.

27. Be constructively critical of your group members' work. Do not dominate group discussions. Be a good listener and contributor.

28. Learn from past mistakes and deficiencies. Improve upon weak aspects of other case presentations.

29. Learn from the positive approaches and accomplishments of classmates.

Sample Case Analysis Outline

There are musicians who play wonderfully without notes and there are chefs who cook wonderfully without recipes, but most of us prefer a more orderly cookbook approach, at least in the first attempt at doing something new. Therefore the eight steps discussed below may serve as a basic outline for you in presenting a strategic plan for your firm's future. This outline is not the only approach used in business and industry for communicating a strategic plan, but this approach is time-tested, it does work, and it does cover all of the basics. You may amend the content, tools, and concepts given below to suit your own company, audience, assignment, and circumstances, but it helps to know and understand the rules before you start breaking them.

Depending upon whether your class is 50 minutes or 75 minutes and how much time your professor allows for your case presentation, the following outline details what generally needs to be covered. A recommended time (in minutes) as part of the presentation is given for an overall 50-minute event. Of course all cases are different, some being profit and some not-for-profit organizations for example, so the scope and content of your analysis may vary. Even if you do not have time to cover all areas given below in your oral presentation, you may be asked to prepare these areas and give them to your professor as a "written case analysis." Be sure in an oral presentation to manage time knowing that your recommendations and associated costs are the most important part. You should go to **www.strategyclub.com** and utilize that information and software in preparing your case analysis. Good luck.

sample case analysis outline

Experiential Exercise 9AA

1. Introduction
(2 minutes)

a. Introduce yourselves by name and major. Establish time setting of your case and analysis. Prepare your strategic plan for the three years 2004–2006 (or 2005–2007 if you have the 2004 year-end financials).

b. Introduce your company and its products/services; capture interest.

c. Show outline of presentation and tell who is doing what parts.

Experiential Exercise 9AB

2. Mission/Vision
(4 minutes)

a. Show existing mission and vision statements if available from firm's Web site, or annual report, or elsewhere.

b. Show your "improved" mission and vision and tell why it is improved.

c. Compare your mission and vision to a leading competitor's statements.

d. Comment on your vision and mission in terms of how they support the strategies you envision for your firm.

Experiential Exercise 9AC

3. Internal Assessment
(8 minutes)

a. Give your financial ratio analysis. Highlight especially good and bad ratios. Do not give definitions of the ratios and do not highlight all the ratios.

b. Show the firm's organizational chart found or "created based on executive titles." Identify type of chart as well as good and bad aspects. Unless all white males comprise the chart, peoples' names are generally not important because positions reveal structure as people come and go.

c. Give your improved/recommended organizational chart. Tell why you feel it is improved over the existing chart.

d. Show a market positioning map with firm and competitors. Discuss the map in light of strategies you envision for firm versus competitors' strategies.

e. Identify the marketing strategy of the firm in terms of good and bad points versus competitors and in light of strategies you envision for the firm.

f. Show a map locating the firm's operations. Discuss in light of strategies you envision.

g. Discuss (and perhaps show) the firm's Web site and e-commerce efforts/abilities in terms of good and bad points.

h. Show your "value of the firm" analysis.

i. List up to twenty of the firm's strengths and weaknesses. Go over each one listed without "reading" them verbatim.

j. Show and explain your Internal Factor Evaluation (IFE) Matrix.

Experiential Exercise 9AD

4. External Assessment
(8 minutes)

a. Identify and discuss major competitors. Use pie charts, maps, tables, and/or figures to show intensity of competition in the industry.

b. Show your Competitive Profile Matrix. Include at least twelve factors and two competitors.

c. Summarize key industry trends citing Standard & Poor's *Industry Survey* or Chamber of Commerce statistics, etc. Highlight key external trends as they impact the firm, in areas such as the economic, social, cultural, demographic, geographic, technological, political, legal, governmental, and natural environment.

d. List up to twenty of the firm's opportunities and threats. Make sure your opportunities are not stated as strategies. Go over each one listed without "reading" them verbatim.

e. Show and explain your External Factor Evaluation (EFE) Matrix.

Experiential Exercise 9AE

5. Strategy Formulation (14 minutes)

a. Show and explain your SWOT Matrix, highlighting each of your strategies listed.

b. Show and explain your SPACE Matrix, using half of your "space time" on calculations and the other half on implications of those numbers. Strategy implications need to be specific rather than generic. In other words, use of a term such as "market penetration" is not satisfactory alone as a strategy implication.

c. Show your Boston Consulting Group (BCG) Matrix. Again focus on both the numbers and the strategy implications. Do multiple BCG Matrices if possible, including domestic versus global, or another geographic breakdown. Develop a product BCG if at all possible. Comment on changes to this matrix as per strategies you envision. Develop this matrix even if you do not know the profits per division and even if you have to estimate the axes information. However, make no wild guesses on axes or revenue/profit information.

d. Show your Internal-External (IE) Matrix. Since this analysis is similar to the BCG, see the above comments.

e. Show your Grand Strategy Matrix. Again focus on implications after giving quadrant selection. Reminder: Use of a term such as "market penetration" is not satisfactory alone as a strategy implication. Be more specific. Elaborate.

f. Show your Quantitative Strategic Planning Matrix (QSPM). Be sure to explain your strategies to start with here. Do not go back over the internal and external factors. Avoid having more than one 4, 3, 2, or 1 in a row. If you rate one strategy, you need to rate the other because that particular factor is affecting the choice. Work row by row rather than column by column on preparing the QSPM.

g. Give your Recommendations Page. This is the most important page in your presentation. Be specific in terms of both strategies and estimated costs of those strategies. *Total up your estimated costs.* You should have six or more strategies. Divide your strategies into two groups: (1) Existing Strategies to Be Continued, and (2) New Strategies to Be Started.

Experiential Exercise 9AF

6. Strategy Implementation (8 minutes)

a. Show and explain your EPS/EBIT analysis to reveal whether stock, debt, or a combination is best to finance your recommendations. Graph the analysis. Decide which approach to use if there are any given limitations of the analysis.

b. Show your projected income statement. Relate changes in the items to your recommendations rather than blindly going with historical percentage changes.

c. Show your projected balance sheet. Relate changes in your items to your recommendations. Be sure to show the retained earnings calculation and the results of your EPS/EBIT decision.

d. Show your projected financial ratios and highlight several key ones to show benefits of your strategic plan.

Experiential Exercise 9AG

7. Strategy Evaluation

(2 minutes)

a. Prepare a Balanced Scorecard to show your expected financial and non-financial objectives recommended for the firm.

Experiential Exercise 9AH

8. Conclusion (4 minutes)

a. Compare and contrast your strategic plan versus the company's own plans for the future.

b. Thank the audience for their attention. Seek and answer questions.

Name Index

Subject Index

Company Index

strategic
management
cases

1

Verizon Communications, Inc.— 2004

Melissa Birch and Fred R. David
Francis Marion University

VZ

www22.verizon.com

In October 2003, Verizon Communications reduced its profit outlook for 2004 and communicated a $49 billion dollar debt load. Verizon's stock price plummeted on the news. Verizon also made the news recently when it settled with 78,000 Communications Workers of America and the International Brotherhood of Electrical Workers unions by giving all their employees a raise and job security. Verizon is the largest provider of local and wireless telecommunications in the United States. It is also the largest telephone directory publisher in the world.

History

Verizon Communications, Inc. was formed on June 30, 2000, by the merger of Bell Atlantic Corp. and GTE Corp. These companies have a history that goes back to the late nineteenth century in the telephone business. GTE was one of the world's largest telecommunications companies. It served approximately 35 million telephone access lines through subsidiaries in the United States, Canada, and the Dominican Republic, and through affiliates in Canada, Puerto Rico, and Venezuela. GTE was a leading wireless operator in the United States with more than 7.1 million wireless customers. Internationally, GTE served approximately 6.7 million customers for wireless networks through subsidiaries in Argentina, Canada, and the Dominican Republic, and affiliates in Canada, Puerto Rico, Venezuela, and Taiwan. GTE also provided Internetworking services, ranging from dial-up services for residential and small business consumers to Web-based applications for *Fortune* 500 companies. It was the leader in directories and telecommunication-based information services and systems.

Bell Atlantic was also one of the largest telecommunications providers. Domestic Telecom unit served 43 million Bell Atlantic mobile customers in the United States and international wireless in Latin America, Europe, and the Pacific Rim. Bell Atlantic was the world's largest provider of directory information, with operations in the United States, China, the Czech Republic, Gibraltar, Greece, Poland, and Slovakia. Valued at more than $52 billion, the merger was to create a combined company with the scale and scope to compete as one of the telecommunications industry's top-tier companies. It would provide long-distance and data services nationwide as a part of a full package of other communications services.

Verizon has been based in New York since it was incorporated in Delaware. Trading began on the New York Stock Exchange under the symbol "VZ" on July 3, 2003. "The symbol was selected because it uses the two letters of the Verizon logo that graphically portray speed, while also echo the geneses of the company name: *veritas,* the Latin word connoting certainty and reliability and horizon, signifying forward-looking and visionary."[1]

Internal Issues

Verizon serves 49 of the top 50 markets in the United States and has 32.5 million customers. Revenues rose to $67.7 billion in 2003 but net income declined to $3.1 billion. Verizon is the largest provider of local, long-distance, data, and broadband services to customers in two-thirds of the top 100 markets in the U.S. It has more than 30 million residential customers and 10.4 million long-distance customers. There are 1.8 million Digital Subscriber Lines, otherwise known as DSL lines. Verizon is the leading print and online directory publisher with 2,100 directories in the United States and 13 other countries. Its directories circulate to 156 million people worldwide. There are 57 million monthly searches on Verizon's SuperPages.com.

Business Structure

Verizon operates as four separate business units: (1) Information Services, (2) International, (3) Domestic Telecom, and (4) Domestic Wireless. The Information Services division consists of the domestic and international publishing businesses,

EXHIBIT 1
Verizon's Organizational Chart

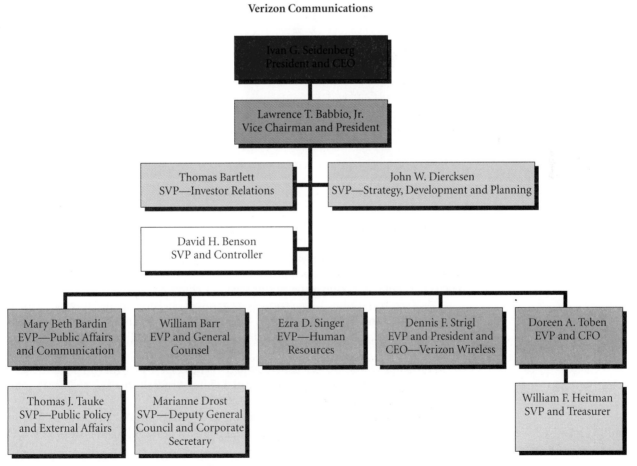

Source: investor.verizon.com/corp_gov/corp_officers.html.

EXHIBIT 2

Verizon's Information Services Division

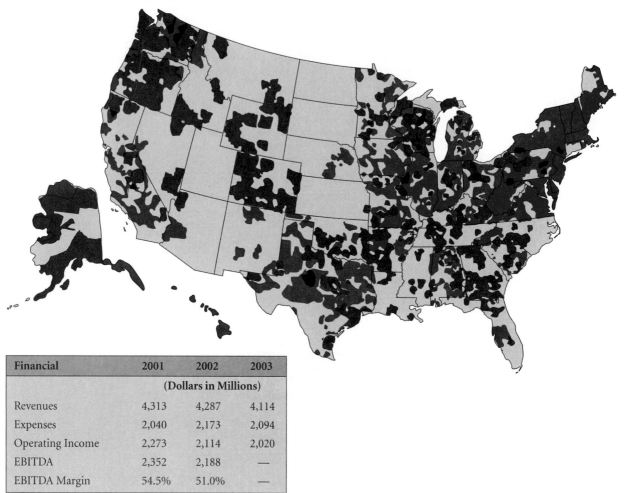

Financial	2001	2002	2003
	(Dollars in Millions)		
Revenues	4,313	4,287	4,114
Expenses	2,040	2,173	2,094
Operating Income	2,273	2,114	2,020
EBITDA	2,352	2,188	—
EBITDA Margin	54.5%	51.0%	—

Source: investor.verizon.com/business/infoserv.html.

including print SuperPages® and electronic SuperPages.com® directories. In 2002, Information Services made up approximately 6 percent of Verizon's total revenues and 4 percent of total operating expenses, as seen in Exhibit 2.

As seen in Exhibit 3, Verizon's International division made up 4 percent of total revenues and 4 percent of total operating expenses in 2002; and its global presence extends to over 30 countries in the Americas, Europe, Asia, and the Pacific.

Verizon's Domestic Telecom segment is the largest provider of wireline and voice communications in the United States. Exhibit 4 reveals that this segment's total revenues increased to over $42 billion in 2002.

Verizon's Domestic Wireless segment, with total revenues over $19 billion in 2002, is the second-largest division of the company. Exhibit 5 provides details on this division.

EXHIBIT 3
Verizon's International Division

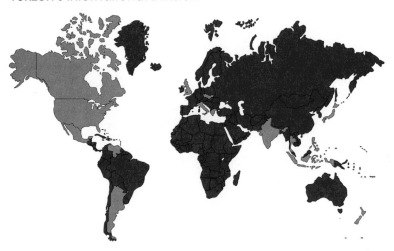

Americas
Argentina
Canada
Brazil
Dominican Republic
Mexico
Puerto Rico
United States

Europe
Czech Republic
Gibraltar
Italy
Slovakia
United Kingdom

Asia
India
Indonesia
Japan
Micronesia
New Zealand
Philippines
Singapore

Financial	2001	2002	2003
	(Dollars in Millions)		
Revenues	3,172	2,962	1,949
Expenses	2,584	2,355	1,611
Operating Income	624	607	338
EBITDA	1,159	1,139	—
EBITDA Margin	36.5%	38.5%	17.3%
Income from Unconsolidated Businesses	754	861	—

Source: investor.verizon.com/business/international.html.

Goals and Values
The mission and vision statements are not clearly identified by Verizon Communications. It has stated its goals and values for the organization in the 2002 *Annual Report* to its shareholders.

> At Verizon, our goal is to be the market leader in delivering innovative, integrated communications solutions to customers at home, at work and on the go. The more people connected to a network, the more valuable it is to those who use it. That's the idea that underlies our business. It's also the philosophy behind our commitment to our communities. Our aim is to mobilize and empower the millions of individuals and organizations— employees, retirees, customers, and nonprofits—that comprise the Verizon community, putting the tools for progress into the hands of people who can make a difference on the local level. We promote employee volunteerism through matching gift programs that recognize contributions of money and time. And we are helping build a strong and lasting infrastructure for progress by making sure people have the fundamental skills—like literacy and access to technology—to succeed in the digital era.[2]

EXHIBIT 4
Verizon's Domestic Telecom Division

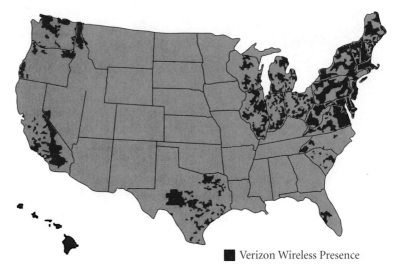

Verizon Wireless Presence

Financial	2001	2002	2003
	(Dollars in Millions)		
Revenues	42,081	40,712	39,602
Expenses	32,847	31,730	32,442
Operating Income	9,234	8,982	7,160
Operating Income Margin	21.9%	22.1%	18.1%
EBITDA	18,482	18,415	—
EBITDA Margin	43.9%	45.2%	—

Source: investor.verizon.com/business/wireline.html.

Financial Issues

Verizon had more than $67 billion in annual revenues and 229,500 employees in 2002, but it also has $49 billion in long-term debt. Verizon's net income for year-end 2002 was $4 billion, which was $3.7 billion higher than 2001, as seen in Exhibits 6 and 7. The Verizon International Foundation donated $25,000 in 2003 to the American Red Cross, to assist with relief efforts in the Dominican Republic in connection with the recent earthquake. The company invested $12 billion in wireless and telecom networks in 2002 by adding 400,000 miles of fiber-optic cable, extending DSL to 60 percent of their lines.

External Factors

Current and potential competitors in telecommunications services include long-distance companies, other local telephone companies, cable companies, wireless service providers, foreign telecommunications providers, electric utilities, Internet service providers, and other companies that offer network services. Many of these companies have a strong market presence, brand recognition, and existing customer relationships, all of which contribute to intensifying competition in the industry.

EXHIBIT 5

Verizon's Domestic Wireless Division

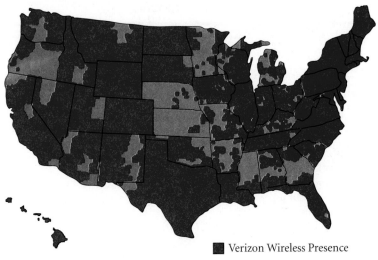

■ Verizon Wireless Presence

Financial	2001	2002	2003
	(Dollars in Millions)		
Revenues	17,393	19,260	22,489
Expenses	15,088	15,620	18,405
Operating Income	2,305	3,640	4,084
EBITDA	6,014	6,933	—
EBITDA Margin	37.6%	39.1%	—

Source: investor.verizon.com/business/wireless.html.

As indicated in Exhibit 8, competitors to Verizon are Alltel Corp., BellSouth Corp., SBC Communications, Vodafone Group, Sprint FON Group, and AT&T Wireless Services. Verizon competes against five national wireless service providers: AT&T Wireless, Cingular Wireless, Nextel Communications, Sprint PCS, and T-Mobile (formerly VoiceStream). In addition, the company competes against several regional wireless companies in markets where it provides service.

AT&T Wireless Services, Inc., is a provider of wireless voice and data services using time division multiple access (TDMA), analog, and cellular digital packet data (CDPD) technologies. In the first two quarters of 2003, AT&T's revenues rose 8 percent to $8.11 billion and net income totaled $357 million. These results reflect growth in new subscribers and a higher operating margin.

Alltel provides wireline and wireless communications and information services, including local, long-distance, network access, and Internet services, and information processing services. Alltel's revenues rose 18 percent to $3.92 billion in the first two quarters of 2003. Its net income from continued operations rose 17 percent to $451.7 million. These results reflect growth in new customers but it is partially offset by expenses related to its branding campaign.

Sprint FON Group is comprised of Sprint's wireline telecommunications operations, including long distance, local phone, product distribution, and directory publishing. Sprint's revenues fell 8 percent to $7.11 billion in the first two quarters of

EXHIBIT 6

Verizon Communications, Inc. (VZ)—Income Statement
(dollars in millions, except per share amounts)

YEAR ENDED DEC. 31,	2003	2002	2001
Revenue	$67,752.0	67,304.0	67,190.0
Other Revenue	—	—	—
Total Revenue	**67,752.0**	**67,304.0**	**67,190.0**
Cost of Revenue	21,783.0	19,911.0	41,651.0
Gross Profit	**45,969.0**	**47,393.0**	**25,539.0**
Selling/General/Adm Exp.	24,999.0	21,846.0	—
Research & Development	—	—	—
Depreciation/Amortization	13,617.0	13,290.0	13,657.0
Interest Expense (Income)	—	—	—
Unusual Expense (Income)	—	—	—
Other Operating Expenses	(141.0)	(2,747.0)	350.0
Total Operating Expense	**60,258.0**	**52,300.0**	**55,658.0**
Operating Income	**7,494.0**	**15,004.0**	**11,532.0**
Interest Expense, Net	(2,797.0)	(3,130.0)	(3,369.0)
Interest/Investment Income	1,278.0	(1,547.0)	—
Interest Income (Expense)	(1,519.0)	(4,677.0)	(3,369.0)
Gain (Loss) on Sale of Assets	—	—	—
Other, Net	(1,214.0)	(4,069.0)	(5,397.0)
Income Before Tax	**4,761.0**	**6,258.0**	**2,766.0**
Income Tax	1,252.0	1,597.0	2,176.0
Income After Tax	**3,509.0**	**4,661.0**	**590.0**
Minority Interest	—	—	—
Equity In Affiliates	—	—	—
Net Income Before Extra	**3,509.0**	**4,661.0**	**590.0**
Accounting Change	503.0	(496.0)	(182.0)
Discontinued Operations	(935.0)	(86.0)	—
Extraordinary Item	—	—	(19.0)
Net Income	**$ 3,077.0**	**4,079.0**	**389.0**

Source: www.investor.stockpoint.com

2003. Its net income from continued operations rose 19 percent to $373 million. These revenues reflect a decline in sales in its Global Markets Division. The earnings were from improved gross margins and lower debt levels. Sprint is offering bundled services on a nationwide basis.

BellSouth serves more than 45 million customers in 14 countries providing wireline network access services for voice, digital and data, cable and digital TV and advertising services, Web design, and hosting and Internet access. BellSouth's revenues fell 1 percent to $11.17 billion in 2003. Its net income rose 34 percent to $1.87 billion. BellSouth has entered into a partnership with SBC Communications, otherwise known as Cingular, to offer a more profitable service line.

Vodafone Group is a leading international mobile telecommunications provider with operations in 28 countries across 5 continents, and servicing over 119 million customers. Vodafone's fiscal year ended with its revenues rising 33 percent to

EXHIBIT 7

Verizon Communications, Inc. (VZ)—Balance Sheet
(dollars in millions, except per share amounts)

YEAR ENDED DEC. 31,	2003	2002	2001
Cash & Equivalents	$ 699.0	1,422.0	979.0
Short Term Investments	2,172.0	2,042.0	1,991.0
Cash and Short Term Investments	2,871.0	3,464.0	2,970.0
Trade Accounts Receivable, Net	9,905.0	12,496.0	14,254.0
Other Receivables	—	—	—
Total Receivables, Net	9,905.0	12,496.0	14,254.0
Total Inventory	1,283.0	1,497.0	1,968.0
Prepaid Expenses	4,234.0	3,331.0	2,796.0
Other Current Assets	0.0	1,305.0	1,199.0
Total Current Assets	**18,293.0**	**22,093.0**	**23,187.0**
Property/Plant/Equipment—Gross	—	—	—
Accumulated Depreciation	(105,659.0)	(103,080.0)	(95,167.0)
Property/Plant/Equipment, Net	75,316.0	73,758.0	74,419.0
Goodwill, Net	1,389.0	1,339.0	—
Intangibles, Net	45,640.0	45,000.0	44,262.0
Long Term Investments	5,789.0	4,986.0	10,202.0
Other Long Term Assets	19,541.0	20,292.0	18,725.0
Total Assets	**$165,968.0**	**167,468.0**	**170,795.0**
Accounts Payable	—	—	—
Accrued Expenses	—	—	—
Notes Payable/Short Term Debt	5,967.0	9,267.0	18,669.0
Current Port. LT Debt/Capital Leases	—	—	—
Other Current Liabilities	5,904.0	6,020.0	5,404.0
Total Current Liabilities	**26,570.0**	**27,929.0**	**38,020.0**
Long Term Debt	39,413.0	44,003.0	45,657.0
Capital Lease Obligations	—	—	—
Total Long Term Debt	**39,413.0**	**44,003.0**	**45,657.0**
Total Debt	**45,380.0**	**53,270.0**	**64,326.0**
Deferred Income Tax	21,708.0	19,467.0	16,543.0
Minority Interest	24,348.0	24,057.0	22,149.0
Other Liabilities	20,463.0	19,396.0	15,887.0
Total Liabilities	**$132,502.0**	**134,852.0**	**138,256.0**
Redeemable Preferred Stock	—	—	—
Preferred Stock—Non Redeemable, Net	—	—	—
Common Stock	277.0	275.0	275.0
Additional Paid-In Capital	25,363.0	24,685.0	24,676.0
Retained Earnings (Accum. Deficit)	9,409.0	10,536.0	10,704.0
Treasury Stock—Common	(115.0)	(218.0)	(1,182.0)
Other Equity	(1,250.0)	(2,110.0)	(1,187.0)
Total Equity	**33,466.0**	**32,616.0**	**32,539.0**
Total Liability & Shareholders' Equity	**$165,968.0**	**167,468.0**	**170,795.0**
Shares Outs.—Common Stock	2,765.0	2,745.8	2,717.2
Total Common Shares Outstanding	**2,765.0**	**2,745.8**	**2,717.2**
Total Preferred Stock Shares Outs.	—	—	—
Employees (actual figures)	229,500.0	247,309.0	263,552.0
Number of Common Shareholders	1,121,000.0	1,197,000.0	1,335,000.0

Source: www.investor.stockpoint.com

EXHIBIT 8
Cellphone Carrier Data

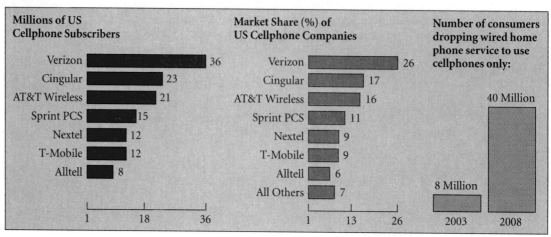

Source: Adapted from *USA Today*, November 24, 2003, p. 2B.

$30.38 billion. [However, the company's net loss increased to $9.06 billion.] The revenues reflect increased sales activity from the European and Asia Pacific markets. Vodafone has entered into a venture with Verizon Wireless to help deliver service on a low-cost basis.

SBC Communications

SBC Communications (SBC), otherwise known as Cingular, has just entered into a partnership with BellSouth to provide wireless services to BellSouth's local customers. SBC has also entered into an agreement with EchoStar to offer satellite video in the bundles. SBC is a holding company whose subsidiaries provide wireline and wireless telecommunications services and equipment, directory advertising, electronic security services, and cable television services. In the first two quarters of 2003, total revenues fell 4 percent to $20.54 billion; its net income rose 13 percent to $3.84 billion.

Industry Outlook

Homeowners are replacing landlines with mobile communications. In 2003, long distance and local calling decreased by 32 and 30 percent, respectively. During the same time, Internet and wireless expenditures increased by 44 and 41 percent, respectively. Customers with cell phones in the United States, as of November 2003, are able to take their phone numbers with them when they switch wireless service providers. Although the economy in the United States is slowly rebounding, the costs of phone services and sales are steadily rising.

Future Outlook

Standard and Poor's anticipates that access lines will decline at least 4 percent as wireless and cable offerings continue to increase. It also predicts that pricing pressures will continue and telecommunications companies will continue to invade each others' territories. Growth will come from traditional voice services and text messaging. All industries face the possibility of new competitors entering their markets. Wireless carriers may have to merge to compete. Which firms in the industry do you think Verizon should consider acquiring?

Verizon's $800 million sale of its Telecommunications Services division will allow the company to reduce its long-term debt and expand its operations in the data and wireless services. Verizon is now ranked as the third-largest long-distance carrier in the United States but it is awash in $49 billion in long-term debt. Like BellSouth, Verizon has also won approval to offer long-distance phone service in local territories, and is embarking on an aggressive plan to extend fiber-optic lines to homes and businesses to compete against cable companies.

Develop a three-year strategic plan for Verizon.

Notes

1. investor.verizon.com/profile/index.html.
2. Verizon Communications *Annual Report 2002*.

2 Nextel Communications, Inc.—2004

J. Brian Barbour
Francis Marion University

NXTL

www.nextel.com

Let the Battle Begin. Nextel Communications, Inc., has recently been embroiled in a controversy with Verizon over its walkie-talkie service. Walkie-talkie is a service that allows phones to send voice messages to each other instantaneously. Nextel and Verizon have been in court trying to settle a dispute over Verizon's recent announcement of "Push to Talk." Nextel has used its Direct Connect walkie-talkie service as its major competitive advantage, and has accused Verizon of false advertising and stealing the slogan "Push to Talk." Nextel has known about competitors' intentions to use walkie-talkie service offerings for some time. If Verizon succeeds, it could potentially take some of the walkie-talkie service market share from Nextel. How effectively Nextel reacts to this penetration of its market will determine how long it can remain the market leader in this type of service.

For 2003, Nextel's revenues rose 24 percent to $10.82 billion and earnings fell 11 percent to $1.47 billion. As of February 2004, Nextel had 15,200 employees.

History

Nextel became the large corporation it is today by a series of mergers and acquisitions that have lasted over a decade. Nextel was founded as Fleet Call in April of 1987. It issued an IPO in 1992 (NASDAQ:CALL). Fleet Call was originally founded as a two-way radio service, which eventually became the backbone technology of Nextel's present business. After a series of mergers and acquisitions, the company eventually became Nextel Communications in March of 1993. In 2003, Nextel and Nextel Partners service became available in 197 of the top 200 U.S. metropolitan areas, which is where 242 million Americans live or work.

Nextel has been dealing with negative profit reports since its inception, until 2002 when the business turned its first profit. The telecommunications market is saturated with competition, so Nextel is trying to differentiate itself with marketing strategies, technological advances, and infrastructure improvements. The business is aggressively increasing its distribution channels and network capability. Nextel has also done test marketing for Boost Mobile in California and Nevada, which is targeting the youth market.

Current Situation

Nextel has 8.2 percent market share among the top six national wireless carriers as of year-end 2002, as evidenced in Exhibit 1. As noted in Exhibit 2, Nextel has also garnered 14.1 percent of new wireless subscribers, which is helping to build market share growth. In 2002, the company posted significant growth in revenue and subscribers and had its first full year of net income.

EXHIBIT 1

Market Share of the Largest Cell Phone Firms in the United States in 2003

Verizon	24.3%
Cingular	15.9
AT&T Wireless	15.1
Sprint PCS	10.7
Nextel	8.2
T-Mobile	8.0

Source: Ken Brown and Jesse Drucker, "Take a Number: Portability Clouds Cellphone Firms' Future," *Wall Street Journal,* October 8, 2003, p. C1.

Nextel's major competitive advantage is Nextel Direct Connect, which is a two-way walkie-talkie service. Customers can instantly have private or group conferences within their local calling area. In 2002, this system was upgraded to allow customers to interact with Direct Connect nationally on the Nextel network. Direct Connect is continually updated and is now allowing customers to interact with other Direct

EXHIBIT 2

Annual Revenue Trends

	FOR THE YEARS ENDED DECEMBER 31		
	2002	*2001*	*2000*
Average monthly revenue per handset in service (1)	$ 70	71	74
Handsets in service, end of period (in thousands) (2) (3)	10,612	8,667	6,678
Net handset additions (in thousands) (2)	1,956	1,988	2,163
Transmitter and receiver sites in service end of period	16,300	15,500	12,700
Net transmitter and receiver sites placed in service	800	2,800	3,900
Switches in service, end of period	84	81	75
System minutes of use (in billions)	73.5	52.5	31.9
Average monthly billable minutes of use per handset	630	565	470

(1) Average monthly revenue per handset/unit in service, or ARPU, is an industry term that measures service revenues per month from our customers divided by the weighted average number of handsets in commercial services during that month, excluding the impact of test markets such as the Boost Mobile program. ARPU is not a measurement under accounting principles generally accepted in the United States and may not be similar to ARPU measures of other companies.

(2) Amount excludes the impact of test markets such as the Boost Mobile program.

(3) In the fourth quarter 2002, Nextel completed the analysis of our subscriber records after the conversion of our billing system, and Nextel identified nonrevenue generating units that were incorrectly introduced into the subscriber base prior to 2002. Therefore, in 2002, Nextel reduced our subscriber base by about 10,500 subscribers, including about 7,000 as of the beginning of the fourth quarter of 2002.

Source: 2002 Nextel *Form 10-K,* p. 44.

EXHIBIT 3
Wireless Industry Market Trends 2002

CARRIER	SERVICE REV. (MIL. $)	ARPU ($)	CHURN (%)	CAPITAL EXPENDITURES (MIL. $)
Verizon	4,713.0	49.23	2.10	1,373.0
Cingular	3,413.0	51.13	2.70	1,313.0
AT&T Wireless	3,738.0	60.00	2.40	2,146.0
Sprint PCS	2,773.0	62.00	3.50	590.0
Nextel	2,184.0	70.00	2.10	545.0
T-Mobile	1,408.0	50.00	2.45	1,749.0
Alltel	1,066.0	46.98	2.76	171.6
Total	19,295.0	—	—	7,887.6

Source: Standard & Poor's Industry Survey, *Telecommunications: Wireless Industry Survey,* May 29, 2003, p. 10.

Connect users traveling with them outside of the local market. This feature is key among competitors' initiatives to copy and improve upon. Verizon is first on the list of competitors to introduce walkie-talkie service. Features like this help Nextel to attract high-value customers. As seen in Exhibit 3, Nextel is the leader in Average Revenue per User (ARPU) at $70.00.

Affiliations

Nextel owns 32 percent of Nextel Partners, which provides digital wireless communications services under the Nextel brand name in small to midsized markets. Nextel Partners possesses the right to operate in 57 of the top 200 metropolitan areas of the United States ranked by population. Nextel Partners allows Nextel Communications, Inc., to focus on other aspects of the business. **www.nextelpartners.com**.

Bells and whistles attract consumers in today's culture. Handset technology is an important factor in the telecommunications market. All of the company's handsets are manufactured by Motorola except for the Blackberry 6510, which is made by Research in Motion, Ltd. All handsets incorporate iDEN technology and offer digital wireless service, Nextel Direct Connect, wireless Internet, and two-way messaging capabilities. Often, consumers will choose wireless services based on the types of phones provided. Having Motorola make considerable technological advancements will help Nextel secure customers in the future. **www.motorola.com**.

As of December 31, 2002, Nextel owned 36 percent of the outstanding common stock of NII Holdings, previously known as Nextel International, which sells wireless communications service to Latin America. NII Holdings filed for Chapter 11 bankruptcy in 2001 but emerged from bankruptcy in November 2002. Prior to its reorganization, NII Holdings was Nextel's wholly owned subsidiary. **www.niiholdings.com**.

Mission/Vision

Mission and vision statements were not found on either the Nextel Web site or in the *Nextel 2002 Annual Report.* However, Nextel Partners, the company partially owned by Nextel that markets its services, has a mission statement on its Web site, but no vision statement.

EXHIBIT 4
Nextel Organization Chart

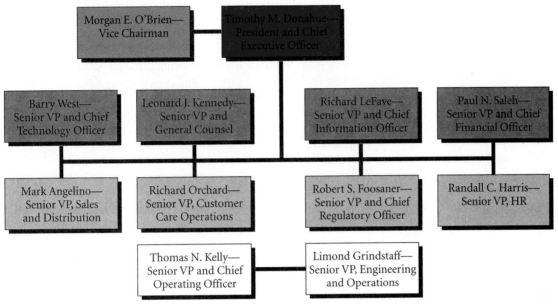

Source: Adapted from *2002 Nextel Annual Report* Officers' Titles.

Mission Statement and Guiding Principles—Nextel Partners

Our mission is to provide high-quality, integrated wireless service that maximizes customer and investor value.

Guiding principles:

- Strive for 100 percent partner satisfaction
- Strive for 100 percent customer satisfaction
- Achieve targeted revenue growth with a low cost structure
- Achieve win–win results through the power of teamwork
- Work smart while remaining humble

www.nextelpartners.com/mission.htm.

Organizational Chart

The organizational chart illustrated in Exhibit 4 was devised using the titles of executives in the *2002 Annual Report*. Nextel has a functional structure since most of its VPs have functional leadership titles. CEO Tim Donahue has been at the helm since August 1999. He joined the company as COO in 1996. Mr. Donahue was previously Northeast Regional President at AT&T and is a graduate of John Carroll University with a B.A. in English Literature.

Wireless Environment

The U.S. wireless market has entered a transition phase on the path from start-up to maturity. A number of large carriers have emerged as market leaders, offering nationwide service, bundled minutes, and one-rate pricing plans. The improved service and greater affordability has boosted market penetration—more than half of the U.S. population has now signed up for wireless service. Major carriers have invested heavily in upgrades to their networks to 2.5G technology, so that they can support Internet and other data-related offerings.

For carriers to grow their revenues, firms must look for largely untapped markets. This is no easy task since analysts consider wireless communications a mature product. Upper- and middle-class consumers are already hooked, therefore those demographic sets are difficult to penetrate. Most of the carriers are currently targeting the youth market with prepaid wireless plans. Another trend appearing is the all-you-can-talk plans. Carriers are now competing by offering more minutes at lower prices, which in turn has caused the ARPU (average revenue per user) to rise only 2 percent in 2002.

Wireless is beginning to replace landline communication services. With an onslaught of plans offering more minutes at an affordable price, many consumers, primarily young adults, have switched to wireless only. For example, college students sometimes live at dorms and at home during the same year.

Consolidation among major players in the communications industry seems likely with subscriber growth slowing, heavy capital requirements, and stiff competition. Some carriers like Cingular have 15.9 percent U.S. market share and need radio frequency rights, while T-Mobile has high fixed cost and needs more customers. Sprint PCS and Verizon have common technology platforms; however, as with any merger, there are obstacles, such as Department of Justice approval and management.

In the wireless business, customer churn is an important measurement of business performance. Customer churn is a measurement of customer retention and is defined as the monthly percentage of the customer base that disconnects. Churn measures both voluntary and involuntary disconnects. Involuntary disconnection usually refers to nonpayment situations. Voluntary churn is when the customer decides to disconnect the service. To calculate customer churn, divide the number of handsets disconnected from service by the average number of handsets in use during the period. It's important to have a low churn rate because it is much more costly to acquire new customers than to retain the existing ones. In Exhibit 3, churn rates are given for the major U.S. wireless industry competitors.

Legal and Governmental Issues

Access to radio frequencies for transmission, or spectrum, is the basic regulatory barrier to entering the wireless industry. The portion of the spectrum that's useable is from below AM frequencies to infrared. As technology improves, wireless providers are moving up the spectrum to higher frequencies. The Federal Communications Commission (FCC) assigns the range of spectrum associated with different types of technologies. Cellular wireless is between 824–849 MHz and 869–894 MHz. PCS provides between 1850 and 1990 Mhz. Spectrum is a very valuable asset in the wireless communications industry.

On September 23, 2003, Nextel announced its intentions to sue Verizon for false advertising of its walkie-talkie service "Push to Talk." The feud between Nextel and Verizon has been going on for some time with Verizon suing Nextel in June 2003, for testing unreleased handsets in what Verizon described as "corporate espionage." With competition so intense for unique product offerings, legal battles could continue in the wireless industry.

Economic Issues

The U.S. economy is rebounding. The wireless industry and Nextel's market share grew significantly even during the economic recession. Apparently, economic uncertainty, high unemployment rates, and war have not affected the demand for wireless communications services. Even though consumers are demanding wireless service, they are also demanding lower prices, which has and will likely continue to shrink ARPU. Inherently, this will force lower margins if considerable cost reduction is not implemented.

Cultural, Social, Demographic Issues

Our society is on the move and people are busy. Wireless communications allows people on the move to communicate freely without slowing down. Even lower-income people are warming up to wireless services. This market has been predominantly untapped. The lower-income market may not increase ARPU but it will definitely generate more revenue. As noted in Exhibit 5, there is a positive trend in the use of wireless communications. From 1998 to 2002, wireless communications use increased by over 500 billion minutes in the United States.

Internal Forces

Marketing

Effective marketing strategies are important for success in the wireless industry. Establishing a strong, loyal customer base is key to being successful. A company's advertising program is a key component of the marketing plan, particularly in the mass market. The effectiveness of marketing in this industry can be gauged in terms of penetration growth and net subscriber additions relative to expenditures. Education is also important in achieving growth. Companies must convince potential customers to pay for innovation. As the wireless market reaches saturation, companies are focusing on retaining customers more than attracting new ones.

In 2003, Nextel won the naming rights to NASCAR's (National Association for Stock Car Auto Racing) premier racing series. Previously known as Winston Cup, it will now be known as Nextel Cup. This will cost Nextel $700 million over 10 years. Many of the top American companies were bidding on the package once it was reported that RJR-Nabisco would no longer pick up the naming rights. NASCAR is an attractive marketing tool and has experienced phenomenal growth throughout the entire country. Nextel is hoping to benefit by offering unique, sports-related products and creating greater brand awareness. With NASCAR's market development, Nextel will try to follow suit with more market growth.

Retaining customers in the wireless business is of the utmost importance and arguably more important than attracting new ones. Average monthly churn rate was 2.1 percent in 2002, down from 2.3 percent in 2001, as noted in Exhibit 3. Strategies

EXHIBIT 5
U.S. Wireless Service Use

TOTAL U.S. MARKET WIRELESS MINUTES OF USE	
Year	Minutes Used (Billions)
1998	100
1999	125
2000	210
2001	470
2002	605

Source: Cellular Telecommunications and Internet Association.

have been implemented to reduce disconnections that include customer-focused programs and efforts to migrate customers to more preferable pricing plans. Also represented by the churn rate is the effort of Nextel to acquire higher-quality subscribers that are less likely to switch around.

Information Systems

Nextel has been awarded the best B2B Web site award among telecommunications carriers in BtoB's 2003 NetMarketing top 100 list. It was recognized for its account management systems, online demonstrations, customer support, and interactive features. Nextel has shown a strong focus on meeting its customers' needs through Web technology; the information systems initiatives are part of its strategy to lower churn rate. Quality information systems will help Nextel to be more responsive to its current customer-base needs. Quickly identifying key market drivers will help it stay ahead of the competition.

Finance

Nextel's Annual Income Statement and Balance Sheet are included in Exhibits 6 and 7. Note that Nextel has recently reduced debt on its balance sheet by reducing its interest payments and increasing equity. Fitch has upgraded Nextel's rating on senior unsecured notes from "B+" to "BB−". However, significant long-term debt still exists which could cause problems in the future if Nextel experiences low margins and/or high customer churn.

Revenue per customer, or ARPU, is down over the past few years, as seen in Exhibit 2. Nextel has traditionally been the leader in attracting the high-revenue-generating customers with its unique product offerings. If the ARPU continues to fall there could be a significant impact on profitability and there could be difficulties in covering overhead costs. However, if Nextel can gain new customers while keeping ARPU high, it could be tremendously profitable in the future. If the customer base remains the same size and ARPU rises, then profit margin will increase simultaneously.

Competition

Verizon

"Can you hear me now?" Yeah, we've heard that a million times. Verizon is the leader in wireless communications for year-end 2002; it is number one nationally in market share with 32.5 million customers, and revenues of $135.8 million. It operates in 29 states and has 10.4 million long-distance subscribers ranking it third in that particular market; it is also a directory publisher and has a global presence in 32 countries. Verizon is divided up into four segments: Domestic Telecom, Domestic Wireless, International Services, and Information Services. Other services provided include wireless voice, data services, and equipment sales in the Unites States and internationally. In 2003, Verizon marketed its "Push to Talk" feature versus Nextel's DirectConnect. **www.verizon.com**.

Cingular

Cingular tries to emphasize freedom of expression in its marketing strategy. Cingular is a joint venture of BellSouth and SBC. It is currently the second-largest provider of wireless communications services in the United States. Its name was chosen to symbolize unity and individuality. SBC owns 60 percent of Cingular and 40 percent of BellSouth. Its customer base is around 22 million. Eleven old brand names were replaced by the Cingular brand. Cingular has been in touch with

EXHIBIT 6
Nextel Income Statement

ANNUAL INCOME STATEMENT

In Millions of U.S. Dollars (except for per share items)	12 Months Ending 12/31/02	12 Months Ending 12/31/01 Restated 12/31/02
Revenue	$8,721.0	7,689.0
Other Revenue	—	—
Total Revenue	**8,721.0**	**7,689.0**
Cost of Revenue	2,516.0	2,869.0
Gross Profit	**6,205.0**	**4,820.0**
Selling/General/Administrative Expenses	3,039.0	3,020.0
Research & Development	—	—
Depreciation/Amortization	1,595.0	1,746.0
Interest Expense (Income), Net Operating	—	—
Unusual Expense (Income)	35.0	1,769.0
Other Operating Expenses	—	—
Total Operating Expense	**7,185.0**	**9,404.0**
Operating Income	**1,536.0**	**(1,715.0)**
Interest Expense, Net Non-Operating	(1,048.0)	(1,403.0)
Interest/Investment Income, Non-Operating	(244.0)	112.0
Interest Income (Expense), Net Non-Operating	(1,292.0)	(1,291.0)
Gain (Loss) on Sale of Assets	0.0	47.0
Other, Net	1,533.0	199.0
Income Before Tax	**1,777.0**	**(2,760.0)**
Income Tax	391.0	(135.0)
Income After Tax	**1,386.0**	**(2,625.0)**
Minority Interest	—	—
Equity In Affiliates	—	—
Net Income Before Extra. Items	**1,386.0**	**(2,625.0)**
Accounting Change	—	—
Discontinued Operations	—	—
Extraordinary Item	—	—
Net Income	**$1,386.0**	**(2,625.0)**

Source: investor.stockpoint.com/quote.asp?Mode=INCOME&Symbol=NXTL&Exchange=US.

T-Mobile USA about a potential merger. Recently, the company has cut 2,500 jobs (7 percent of its workforce). **www.cingular.com**.

AT&T Wireless
AT&T Wireless Services, Inc., operates as a wireless communications service provider in the United States. AT&T sometimes markets itself with regional brand names, such as SunCom in the southeastern United States. The company provides

EXHIBIT 7

ANNUAL BALANCE SHEET

In Millions of U.S. Dollars (except for per share items)	As of 12/31/02	As of 12/31/01 Restated 12/31/02
Cash & Equivalents	$ 1,846.0	2,481.0
Short Term Investments	840.0	1,236.0
Cash and Short-Term Investments	2,686.0	3,717.0
Trade Accounts Receivable, Net	1,077.0	1,111.0
Other Receivables	—	—
Total Receivables, Net	1,077.0	1,111.0
Total Inventory	245.0	260.0
Prepaid Expenses	609.0	533.0
Other Current Assets	33.0	102.0
Total Current Assets	**4,650.0**	**5,723.0**
Property/Plant/Equipment—Gross	—	—
Accumulated Depreciation	(5,007.0)	(3,667.0)
Property/Plant/Equipment, Net	8,918.0	9,274.0
Goodwill, Net	—	—
Intangibles, Net	6,607.0	6,067.0
Long-Term Investments	145.0	188.0
Other Long-Term Assets	1,164.0	812.0
Total Assets	**$21,484.0**	**22,064.0**
Accounts Payable	515.0	756.0
Accrued Expenses	1,749.0	1,470.0
Notes Payable/Short-Term Debt	0.0	1,865.0
Current Port. LT Debt/Capital Leases	251.0	145.0
Other Current Liabilities	241.0	341.0
Total Current Liabilities	**2,756.0**	**4,577.0**
Long-Term Debt	12,299.0	14,720.0
Capital Lease Obligations	—	—
Total Long-Term Debt	**12,299.0**	**14,720.0**
Total Debt	**12,550.0**	**16,730.0**
Deferred Income Tax	1,619.0	669.0
Minority Interest	—	—
Other Liabilities	949.0	566.0
Total Liabilities	**$17,623.0**	**20,532.0**
Redeemable Preferred Stock	1,015.0	2,114.0
Preferred Stock—Non-Redeemable, Net	136.0	283.0
Common Stock	1.0	1.0
Additional Paid-In Capital	10,530.0	8,581.0
Retained Earnings (Accum. Deficit)	(7,793.0)	(9,179.0)
Treasury Stock—Common	—	0.0
Other Equity	(28.0)	(268.0)
Total Equity	**3,861.0**	**1,532.0**
Total Liability & Shareholders' Equity	**$21,484.0**	**22,064.0**
Shares Outs.—Common Stock	968.0	763.0
Total Common Shares Outstanding	**1,004.0**	**799.0**
Total Preferred Stock Shares Outs.	**4.0**	**8.0**
Employees (actual figures)	15,200.0	13,400.0
Number of Common Shareholders (actual figures)	3,900.0	3,700.0

Source: investor.stockpoint.com/quote.asp?Mode5BALANCE&Symbol5NXTL&Exchange=US.

wireless voice and data services over two separate, overlapping networks. One network uses time division multiple access (TDMA) as its signal transmission technology. As of December 31, 2002, the company's TDMA network covered an aggregate population (POPS) of approximately 203 million, or 70 percent, of the U.S. population. It also provides voice and enhanced data services over a separate network that uses the signal transmission technology known as global system for mobile (GSM) communications and general packet radio service (GPRS). As of December 31, 2002, this network covered approximately 63 percent of the U.S. population, or 181 million POPS. As of December 31, 2002, AT&T Wireless's two networks covered an aggregate of approximately 213 million POPS, or 74 percent of the U.S. population, and operated in 83 U.S. metropolitan areas. **www.att.com**; **www.suncom.com**

Sprint PCS

Sprint PCS (personal communications system) Group, together with its third-party affiliates, offers services in over 300 metropolitan markets. Sprint PCS has licenses to operate in all of the United States. Sprint PCS Group has affiliations with other companies that use the same network system. These companies offer wireless services with the Sprint brand name and bear the expense of the network. In August 2003, Horizon PCS Inc., an affiliate of the PCS Group, filed for Chapter 11 bankruptcy protection along with two of its subsidiaries. **www.sprintpcs.com**.

Deutsche Telecom/T-Mobile

T-Mobile was formerly known by the name Voicestream and is a subsidiary of Deutsch Telecom. It is one of Europe's top wireless communications companies. T-Mobile has major operations in Germany, United Kingdom, and Austria. In 2001, it acquired Voicestream Wireless and Powertel in the United States. T-Mobile currently owns 60 percent of the U.K. company T-Motion, and focuses on prepaid wireless services, which causes them to have a small ARPU. It is also the fastest-growing wireless provider in the United States, as seen in Exhibit 8. **www.t-mobile.com**.

EXHIBIT 8

New Subscribers of Major Wireless Companies

NEW SUBSCRIBERS OF MAJOR WIRELESS COMPANIES			
Carrier	3rd Qtr 2002 Net Adds	Carrier	4th Qtr 2002 Net Adds
T-Mobile	869,000	T-Mobile	1,017,000
Verizon	803,000	Verizon	970,000
Nextel	480,000	AT&T Wireless	705,000
AT&T Wireless	201,000	Nextel	496,000
US Cellular	76,000	Sprint PCS	250,000
Alltel	67,648	US Cellular	160,000
Sprint PCS	(78,000)	Alltel	51,608
Cingular	(107,000)	Cingular	(121,000)
Total	2,311,648	Total	3,528,608

Source: Standard & Poor's Industry Survey, *Telecommunications: Wireless Industry Survey,* May 29, 2003, p. 1.

EXHIBIT 9
Europe Wireless Market Forecast

YEAR	SERVICE REVENUES (BILLIONS)
2002	$ 97
2003	$105
2004	$114
2005	$121
2006	$126
2007	$131

Source: RCR Wireless News, November 25, 2002, p. 18(1)

Global Perspective

Only 20 percent of the world has access to wireless communications services, according to Jorma Ollila, CEO of Nokia. The global wireless market is expected to reach over 1.75 billion customers by 2007. Since traditional wireless communications markets are saturated, companies will likely look at new markets to grow their business.

There are more cellular phones in China than there are in the United States. According to the Chinese Ministry of Information, there are 250 million of them in use. China is a highly populated nation with inferior landline infrastructure. Some companies are looking at developing nations such as China to increase revenues.

There are many risks involved with entering markets such as the Middle East. Physical risks such as terrorism and political instability are legitimate threats to doing business. However, wireless communications companies have to look at these areas to grow revenue.

Europe is predicted to have substantial wireless communications market growth, which is expected to reach $131 billion in service revenues by 2007, as noted in Exhibit 9. However, most of this market growth will be in areas other than voice. Europe's global market share will decrease from 30 percent to 20 percent because of high growth rates in Asia and the Americas.

Nextel is being marketed to Latin America by NII Holdings (Nextel International Incorporated), which used to be wholly owned by Nextel Communications, Inc. This market has considerably less competition and is more politically stable than the Middle East and Asia. This could be a potential growth area for Nextel in the future as the U.S. market becomes more and more saturated with competition.

Future Outlook

Nextel will continue to push its walkie-talkie service as its chief competitive advantage; it will have to increase its coverage area and make pricing competitive. It also expects to leverage its relationship with NASCAR auto racing to boost its market share and brand awareness. For Nextel to become the dominant player in the wireless communications industry, it will have to focus on retaining customers while encouraging people to switch over. The threat of mergers is very real and something could occur in the next few years. Competition over unique services such as walkie-talkie will continue to increase. Nextel is also looking to expand to rural areas of the United States where there is less competition. It is repurchasing debt to reduce interest expense and risk, and distribution channels are also being expanded so more people can easily sign onto Nextel service. Customer-centered operations will continue to be a focus so that high-value customers can be retained and customer churn rate will be lowered. Develop a clear three-year strategic plan for Nextel.

3

Southwest Airlines Co.—2004

Amit J. Shah, Charles R. Sterrett, and William L. Anderson
Frostburg State University

LUV

www.iflyswa.com

Despite terrorist attacks, new security measures, dramatic increases in aviation insurance costs, industry downsizing, rising energy costs, and a severe reduction in consumer air travel, Southwest Airlines is still poised for success. For twelve consecutive years (1991 through 2002), the Department of Transportation (DOT) Air Travel Consumer Report listed Southwest Airlines (tel. 214-792-4000 or 1-800-I-FLY-SWA) as among the top five of all major carriers for on-time performance, best baggage handling, and fewest customer complaints. In a highly competitive industry, all carriers continually strive to place first in any of these categories of the DOT report; Southwest is the only airline to ever hold the Triple Crown (first in all of the categories) for its annual performance. In addition to this honor, Southwest is consistently among *Fortune* magazine's most admired companies (second in 2002), and it is also on the magazine's list of the 100 best companies to work for.

In 2002, Southwest ranked first among airlines for customer service satisfaction, as reported in the *Wall Street Journal*. In addition, Southwest ranked first in *Money Magazine*'s feature for "The 30 Best Stocks" since 1972. Southwest continues to operate profitably despite geopolitical tensions: In 2003, it had $442.0 million in net income on $5.8 billion in revenues (Southwest *Annual Report,* 2003).

In an industry that historically has been awash in red ink, where airlines continually go in and out of bankruptcy or fail, Southwest has an enviable record of over thirty consecutive years of operating at a profit. But, considering the tremendous strain in current economical and political environments, can this record of success continue?

In their best-selling book *Nuts,* Kevin and Jackie Freiburg point to a company with people who are committed to working hard and having fun and who avoid following industry trends. The Freiburgs note that Southwest, based in Dallas, Texas, is a company that likes to keep prices at rock bottom; believes the customer comes second; runs recruiting ads that say, "Work at a place where wearing pants is optional"; paints its $30 million assets to look like killer whales and state flags; avoids trendy management programs; avoids formal, documented strategic planning; spends more time at planning parties than writing policies; and once settled a legal dispute by arm wrestling. This strategy has always worked, but will it continue to work?

History and Growth of Southwest Airlines

Rollin King and Herb Kelleher completed the necessary paperwork to create Air Southwest Co. (later renamed Southwest Airlines). Then the two filed for approval with the FAA; and on February 20, 1968, the Texas Aeronautical Commission approved their plans to fly between the three cities.

In the 1980s and 1990s, Southwest continued to expand, and by 1993, it was serving 34 cities in 15 states. Southwest slowly, but methodically, moved across the Southwestern states into California, the Midwest, and the Northwest. It added new destinations in Florida and on the East Coast. With its low prices and no-frills approach, it quickly dominated the markets it entered. In some markets, after Southwest entered, competitors soon withdrew, allowing the airline to expand even faster than projected. For example, when Southwest entered the California market in 1990, it quickly became the second-largest player, with over 20 percent of the intrastate market. Several competitors soon abandoned the Los Angeles–San Francisco route because they were unable to match Southwest's $59 one-way fare. Before Southwest entered this market, fares had been as high as $186 one way.

California offers a good example of the real dilemma facing competing carriers, which often referred to Southwest as a "500-pound cockroach that was too big to stamp out." While airfares were dropping, passenger traffic increased dramatically. But competitors, such as American and US Airways, were losing money on several key route segments, even though they cut service drastically. In late 1994, United began to fight back by launching a low-cost, high-frequency shuttle service on the West Coast. But it found that even a shuttle could not win against Southwest in a head-to-head battle. So United repositioned its shuttle away from Southwest's routes and even abandoned some routes altogether. According to the DOT, eight airlines surrendered West Coast routes to Southwest; at the same time, one-way fares fell by over 30 percent to an average of $60, and traffic increased by almost 60 percent. The major problem for the larger airlines was the fact that many of these West Coast routes were critical for feeding traffic into their highly profitable transcontinental and transpacific routes, and Southwest was cutting into that market.

Southwest is currently the fourth-largest domestic carrier in terms of customers boarded. The airline has transformed itself from a regional carrier operating out of Dallas into a truly national carrier. At year-end 2002, the airline served 58 cities in 30 states and operated more than 2,800 flights a day with its fleet of 375 Boeing 737s. In 2002, Southwest flew 45.4 billion revenue passenger miles (RPMs) compared with 44.5 billion RPMs in 2001. But most remarkable is its thirtieth year in a row of profitable operations, with total operating revenue in 2002 of $5.52 billion—a decrease of 0.6 percent over 2001. Operating income in 2002 fell by 33.9 percent in 2001. Net income fell by 52.9 percent from $511.1 million in 2001 to $241.0 million in 2002 (Southwest *Annual Report*, 2003). Nonetheless, Southwest was the only profitable major U.S. airline in 2002. Financial statements are shown in Exhibits 1 and 2.

Management

Lamar Muse led Southwest in its climb to profitability; but, in a dispute with the board, he was ousted in 1978. With Muse out, Kelleher moved into the top position, and ran the airline until June 19, 2001. On that date, Kelleher was succeeded as CEO by Southwest's vice president and general counsel, James F. Parker, 54. Colleen C. Barrett, 56, who started her collaboration with Mr. Kelleher thirty-four years earlier as his legal secretary, would be president and chief operating officer. Mr. Kelleher is slated to remain as chairman for three years. Exhibit 3 shows the organizational chart of the company.

Mr. Parker has been the airline's top labor negotiator, making him well known to the company's employees, and, according to Mr. Kelleher, he has had a say in every important decision for a "long, long time." Ms. Barrett, the unsung hero of Southwest, has been the keeper and crusader of Southwest's culture, and she has successfully indoctrinated thousands of new workers into Southwest's ways. Parker's plan as CEO is to stay with the blueprint—keep Southwest the low-cost, low-fare, no-frills airline it

EXHIBIT 1

Operating Statistics for Southwest Airlines

CONSOLIDATED HIGHLIGHTS			
(in thousands except per-share amounts)	*2002*	*2001*	*Change*
Operating revenues	$5,521,771	$5,555,174	(0.6)%
Operating expenses	$5,104,433	$4,924,052	3.7%
Operating income	$417,338	$631,122	(33.9)%
Operating margin	7.6%	11.4%	(3.8)pts.
Net income	$240,969	$511,147	(52.9)%
Net margin	4.4%	9.2%	(4.8)pts.
Net income per share—basic	$0.31	$0.67	(53.7)%
Net income per share—diluted	$0.30	$0.63	(52.4)%
Stockholders' equity	$4,421,617	$4,014,053	10.2%
Return on average stockholders' equity	5.7%	13.7%	(8.0)pts.
Stockholders' equity per common share outstanding	$5.69	$5.24	8.6%
Revenue passengers carried	63,045,988	64,446,773	(2.2)%
Revenue passenger miles (RPMs) (000s)	45,391,903	44,493,916	2.0%
Available seat miles (ASMs) (000s)	68,886,546	65,295,290	5.5%
Passenger load factor	65.9%	68.1%	(2.2)pts.
Passenger revenue yield per RPM	11.77¢	12.09¢	(2.6)%
Operating revenue yield per ASM	8.02¢	8.51¢	(5.8)%
Operating expenses per ASM	7.41¢	7.54¢	(1.7)%
Employees at year-end	33,705	31,580	6.7%

has always been. "There will be no change in our core philosophy and our basic business model," he says. It's a model he helped shape as general counsel for fifteen years.

Southwest's management team drives home the feeling that all of its people are part of one big family. Southwest's Culture Committee, formerly headed by Colleen Barrett, has unique ways to preserve the company's underdog background and can-do spirit. She constantly reinforces the message that employees should be treated like customers, and continually celebrates workers who go above and beyond the call of duty. Barrett also regularly visits each of the company's stations to reiterate the airline's history and to motivate employees. As keeper of the company's culture, Barrett commemorates all employee birthdays and special events with cards signed, "Herb and Colleen." Employees know the culture and expect others to live up to it. Donna Conover, another longtime Southwest employee who also understands and supports the company's culture, will succeed Barrett as president and COO.

Strategy

Southwest's operation under Herb Kelleher has a number of characteristics that seem to contribute to its success. It has always been able to quickly seize a strategic opportunity whenever one arises. Other key factors are its conservative growth pattern, its cost-containment policy, and the commitment of its employees.

Kelleher always resisted attempts to expand too rapidly. His philosophy was to expand only when there were resources available to go into a new location with ten to twelve flights per day—not just one or two. For years, he also resisted the temptation to begin transcontinental operations or to get into a head-to-head battle with the

EXHIBIT 2
Southwest Airlines Co.—Income Statement

YEAR ENDED DEC. 31,	2003	2002	2001
Revenue	$5,835.0	5,426.0	5,470.0
Other Revenue	102.0	95.7	85.2
Total Revenue	**5,937.0**	**5,521.8**	**5,555.2**
Cost of Revenue	4,087.0	3,731.1	3,630.4
Gross Profit	**1,748.0**	**1,694.9**	**1,839.5**
Selling/General/Administrative Expenses	—	—	—
Research & Development	—	—	—
Depreciation/Amortization	384.0	356.3	317.8
Interest Expense (Income), Net Operating	—	—	—
Unusual Expense (Income)	—	—	—
Other Operating Expenses	983.0	1,017.0	975.8
Total Operating Expense	**5,454.0**	**5,104.4**	**4,924.1**
Operating Income	**483.0**	**417.3**	**631.1**
Interest Expense, Net Non-Operating	(58.0)	(89.3)	(49.3)
Interest/Investment Income	24.0	37.0	42.6
Interest Income (Expense), Net	(34.0)	(52.3)	(6.7)
Gain (Loss) on Sale of Assets	—	—	—
Other, Net	259.0	27.7	203.2
Income Before Tax	**708.0**	**392.7**	**827.7**
Income Tax	266.0	151.7	316.5
Income After Tax	**442.0**	**241.0**	**511.1**
Minority Interest	—	—	—
Equity In Affiliates	—	—	—
Net Income Before Extra. Items	**$442.0**	**241.0**	**511.1**
Accounting Change	0.0	0.0	(22.1)
Discontinued Operations	—	—	—
Extraordinary Item	—	—	—
Net Income	**442.0**	**241.0**	**511.1**
Preferred Dividends	—	—	—
Income Available to Common	**442.0**	**241.0**	**511.1**
Income Available to Common Inc.	**442.0**	**241.0**	**511.1**
Basic/Primary Weighted Avg. shares	783.0	772.6	763.0
Basic/Primary EPS Excl. Extra.	**0.565**	**0.312**	**0.670**
Basic/Primary EPS Incl. Extra.	**0.565**	**0.312**	**0.670**
Dilution Adjustment	0.0	0.0	0.0
Diluted Weighted Average Shares	822.0	809.4	807.1

Source: www.investor.stockpoint.com (in thousands, except for per share amounts).

major carriers on long-distance routes. But even with a conservative approach, Southwest expanded at a vigorous pace. Its debt has remained the lowest among U.S. carriers, and, with an A-rating, Southwest has the highest Standard & Poor's credit rating in the industry.

Southwest has made its mark by concentrating on flying large numbers of passengers on high-frequency, short hops (usually one hour or less) at bargain fares. It

EXHIBIT 3
Southwest Organizational Chart

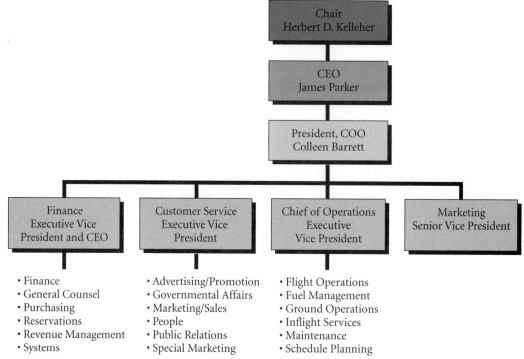

Source: Southwest Airlines Co. (February 1998).

has avoided the hub-and-spoke operations of its larger rivals, taking its passengers directly from city to city. Southwest also tends to avoid the more congested major airports in favor of smaller satellite fields. Kelleher revealed the niche strategy of Southwest when he noted that whereas other airlines set up hub-and-spoke systems in which passengers are shuttled to a few major hubs from which they are transferred to other planes going to their destinations, "we wound up with a unique market niche: We are the world's only short-haul, high-frequency, low-fare, point-to-point carrier. . . . We wound up with a market segment that is peculiarly ours, and everything about the airline has been adapted to serving that market segment in the most efficient and economical way possible." (See Exhibit 4.)

However, this strategy may be changing. Southwest has begun to introduce longer, nonstop trips on such routes as Baltimore, Maryland, to Las Vegas, Nevada (2,099 miles), and Austin, Texas, to Los Angeles, California (1,234 miles). Even one-stop trips are being added through central cities such as Nashville and Kansas City for coast-to-coast travel. The prospect of Southwest going long-haul on a grand scale is what "the genie [rivals] always hoped would not come out of the bottle," says analyst Kevin C. Murphy of Morgan Stanley Dean Witter. He believes that Southwest will continue its expansion and that it "will really rewrite the economics of the airline industry." This shifting strategy is downplayed by the fact that Southwest still flies about 80 percent of its flights on routes that are shorter than 750 miles. In 2002, the average flight was 548 miles and had duration of 1.5 hours. "We're built for the short-haul markets, and we know that," says Chief Financial Officer Gary C. Kelly. Kelleher explains the jump into routes that are 1,000-plus miles as a way to deal with the changes in the 1997 federal ticket tax, which was pushed by the bigger carriers. The incorporation of the new tax system replaced a percentage tax with a tax that included a flat, per-segment fee, which hits low-fare carriers harder.

EXHIBIT 4
Southwest Airlines Co. Balance Sheet

	2003	2002	2001
Cash & Equivalents	$1,865.0	1,815.4	2,279.9
Short Term Investments	—	—	—
Cash and Short Term Investments	1,865.0	1,815.4	2,279.9
Trade Accounts Receivable, Net	132.0	174.4	71.3
Other Receivables	—	—	—
Total Receivables, Net	132.0	174.4	71.3
Total Inventory	93.0	86.0	70.6
Prepaid Expenses	59.0	43.4	52.1
Other Current Assets	164.0	112.8	46.3
Total Current Assets	**2,313.0**	**2,232.0**	**2,520.2**
Property/Plant/Equipment—Gross	—	—	—
Accumulated Depreciation	(3,107.0)	(2,810.2)	(2,456.2)
Property/Plant/Equipment, Net	7,443.0	6,645.5	6,445.5
Goodwill, Net	—	—	—
Intangibles, Net	—	—	—
Long Term Investments	—	—	—
Other Long Term Assets	122.0	76.3	31.4
Total Assets	**$9,878.0**	**8,953.8**	**8,997.1**
Accounts Payable	405.0	362.0	504.8
Accrued Expenses	650.0	529.1	547.5
Notes Payable/Short Term Debt	—	0.0	475.0
Current Port. LT Debt/Capital Leases	206.0	130.5	39.6
Other Current Liabilities	462.0	412.2	672.2
Total Current Liabilities	**1,723.0**	**1,433.8**	**2,239.2**
Long Term Debt	1,332.0	1,552.8	1,327.2
Capital Lease Obligations	—	—	—
Total Long Term Debt	**1,332.0**	**1,552.8**	**1,327.2**
Total Debt	**1,538.0**	**1,683.2**	**1,841.7**
Deferred Income Tax	1,420.0	1,227.5	1,058.1
Minority Interest	—	—	—
Other Liabilities	351.0	318.0	358.6
Total Liabilities	**$4,826.0**	**4,532.1**	**4,983.1**
Redeemable Preferred Stock	—	—	—
Preferred Stock—Non Redeemable	—	—	—
Common Stock	789.0	776.7	766.8
Additional Paid-In Capital	258.0	135.8	50.4
Retained Earnings (Accum. Deficit)	3,883.0	3,455.4	3,228.4
Treasury Stock—Common	—	—	0.0
Other Equity	122.0	53.7	(31.5)
Total Equity	**5,052.0**	**4,421.6**	**4,014.1**
Total Liability & Share's Equity	**$9,878.0**	**8,953.8**	**8,997.1**
Shares Outs.—Common Stock	789.4	776.7	766.8
Total Common Shares Outs.	**789.4**	**776.7**	**766.8**
Total Preferred Stock Shares Outs.	—	—	—
Employees (actual figures)	32,847.0	33,705.0	31,580.0
Number of Common Shareholders	12,114.0	11,858.0	11,324.0

Source: www.investor.stockpoint.com

Competitors believe that Southwest would have moved strongly into the long-haul flights market despite the altered tax requirements. "They've dug all the shallow holes," says Rona J. Dutta, senior vice president for planning at United Airlines, Inc. He also replies that other low-fare units are increasing the competition in Southwest's core markets. As all other major airlines have performed poorly since the 2001 terrorist attacks, many are expanding or developing low-fare flight programs in an effort to increase profits. Short-haul lines such as JetBlue, Spirit, ATA, AirTran, SkyWest, and Frontier Airlines, as well as Delta's Song and Continental's JetExpress, may be affecting Southwest's profitability, but with its lower costs and impressive balance sheet, Southwest still prevails. Nonetheless, some low-fare lines have ended operations because they were unsuccessful in competing with existing low-fare lines. These include US Airways' MetroJet, Shuttle by United, Vanguard, and National airlines.

Southwest continues to be the lowest-cost airline in its markets. Even when trying to match Southwest's cut-rate fares, the larger carriers could not do so without incurring substantial losses. Southwest continues to operate with the lowest cost-per-available-seat mile (the number of seats multiplied by the distance flown) among all major airlines, with an average of 15 to 25 percent below its rivals. One of the major factors in this enviable record is that all of its planes used to be of a single type—Boeing 737s—which dramatically lowered the company's cost of training, maintenance, and inventory. Because all Southwest crews know the 737 inside and out, they could substitute personnel rapidly from one flight to another in an emergency. In addition, Southwest recognized that planes only earn you money while they are in the air, so the company worked hard to achieve a faster turnaround time on the ground. Most airlines take up to one hour to unload passengers, clean and service the plane, and board new passengers. Southwest has a turnaround time for most flights of twenty minutes or less. Thorough knowledge of the 737 has helped in this achievement.

Southwest has also cut costs in the customer service area as well. Because its flights are usually one hour or less, it does not offer meals—only peanuts and drinks. Boarding passes are reusable plastic cards, and boarding time is saved since the airline has no assigned seating. The airline does not subscribe to any centralized reservation service. It will not even transfer baggage to other carriers: That is the passenger's responsibility. Even with this frugality, passengers do not seem to object, since the price is right.

This ability to turn planes around rapidly, surprisingly, has not been jeopardized by the events after September 11, but this did not happen without incurring added expenses. Initially, new government-mandated security procedures did cause delays and longer check-in times. Since then, Southwest has added new automated systems and technologies that have streamlined the check-in process. This includes computer-generated baggage tags and boarding passes and self-service Rapid Check-in kiosks. Because of these additions, Southwest reports that check-in times are almost back to normal.

Southwest has achieved a team spirit that others can only envy. One of the reasons for this team spirit is that the company truly believes that employees come first, not the customers. Southwest is known for providing its employees with tremendous amounts of information that will enable them to better understand the company, its mission, its customers, and its competition. Southwest believes that information is power. It is the resource that enables employees to do their jobs better. Armed with this knowledge, they are able to serve the customer better, and customers who deal with Southwest rarely get the runaround.

Even though unionized, Southwest has been able to negotiate flexible work rules that enabled it to meet the rapid turnaround schedules. It's not unusual for pilots to help flight attendants clean the airplanes or to help the ground crew load baggage. Consequently, employee productivity is very high, and the airline is able to maintain a lean staff. In good times, Kelleher resisted the temptation to overhire, and so avoided layoffs during lean times. Southwest has only laid off three people in twenty-five years—and it immediately hired them back. The airline industry as a whole has furloughed approximately 100,000 employees as a result of the 2001 attacks. Not only did Southwest lay off no one, it also hired employees in 2002 and increased overall salaries, wages, and benefits. This was made possible by reductions in other areas: New plane deliveries were delayed, renovations to the company head-quarters were scrapped—but layoffs were not considered. Said CEO Parker, "We are willing to suffer some damage, even to our stock price, to protect the jobs of our peo-ple." This employee retention policy has contributed to employees' feelings of secu-rity and a fierce sense of loyalty. The people of Southwest see themselves as crusaders whose mission is to give ordinary people the opportunity to fly.

Maximizing profitability is a major goal at Southwest. This leads to a drive to keep costs low and quality high. The airline's ideal service consists of safe, frequent, low-cost flights that get passengers to their destinations on time—and often closer to their destination than the major airlines do, because its competitors use larger air-ports farther from the cities. Southwest uses Dallas's Love Field, Houston's Hobby Airport, and Chicago's Midway, which are closer to their respective downtown areas, are less congested, and are, therefore, more convenient for the business traveler. This also helps Southwest's on-time performance.

In its marketing approach, Southwest always tries to set itself apart from the rest of the industry. It also plays up its fun-loving, rebel reputation. In the early years, when the big airlines were trying to run Southwest out of business by undercutting its low fares, Southwest made its customers an unprecedented offer. In response to a Braniff ad offering a $13 fare to fly between Houston and Dallas, Southwest placed an ad that read, "Nobody's going to shoot Southwest Airlines out of the sky for a lousy $13." It then offered passengers the opportunity to purchase a ticket from Southwest for the same price, which was half the normal fare, or to buy a full-fare ticket for $26 and receive a bottle of premium whiskey along with it. The response was unprece-dented. Southwest's planes were full and, for a short time, Southwest was one of the top liquor distributors in the state of Texas.

Southwest's ads always try to convince the customer that what the airline offers them is of real value to them. It also believes it is in the business of making flying fun. With its ads, the company wants customers to know that when they fly Southwest, they'll have an experience unlike any other. It promises safe, reliable, frequent, low-cost air transportation that is topped off with outstanding service. By keeping its promises, Southwest has earned extremely high credibility in every market it serves.

e-Business

Southwest has been aggressively marketing its services on the Internet, and it was the first airline to establish a home page on the Web. When *Fortune* magazine asked the experts which businesses have Web sites that work, the answer they got was "not many." However, Southwest was one of ten cited as a business doing it right. In the Internet travel race, many observers think Southwest has lost the battle to a subsidiary of American Airlines, Travelocity. Yet while American has been getting most of the atten-tion, Southwest has been getting the business. According to a Nielsen/NetRatings' sur-vey, 13.8 percent of the people who visited Southwest's site booked a flight. The com-pany's "look-to-book" ratio is twice that of Travelocity and higher than that of any traditional retailer on the Web. Southwest, it seems, has been a success in turning browsers into buyers. In March 2002, *InternetWeek* reported that Southwest experienced an Internet traffic gain of 16 percent. Southwest reports that approximately 50 percent of its passenger revenue is generated by online bookings. Its cost-per-booking via the Internet is about $1; in comparison, the cost-per-booking via a travel agent is about $10.

Southwest's Web site has also been named the top-ranking Web site for customer satisfaction among major travel sites, according to research conducted by Harris Interactive. The Southwest site scored a rating of 8.62 out of 10, with its Web site attracting 4 million unique visitors during March 2001. In the June 11, 2001, issue of *InternetWeek,* Southwest's Web site was named as one of the top 100 e-businesses in the United States, as determined by the publication's survey.

Competitors

Since September 11, 2001, competition for Southwest Airlines has shifted from major airlines to low-fare airlines. This happened mainly because major airlines incurred losses in 2002. Before September 11, 2001, United, the second-largest airline with over 100,000 employees, was one of Southwest's most formidable competitors. Since then, the company has downsized to approximately 85,000 employees. Because of financial losses, United filed for bankruptcy in December 2002. Since United Shuttle service ceased operations shortly after September 11, 2001, direct competition with Southwest Airlines has diminished.

Following September 11, 2001, Delta, the third-largest U.S. carrier, cut 21 percent of its workforce and in 2003 was operating with approximately 75,000 employees. Delta flies to about 225 U.S. and foreign locations, and remains particularly strong throughout much of the southern tier of the United States, where two of its major hubs—Atlanta and Dallas/Fort Worth—are located. In the summer of 2003, Delta replaced its low-fare regional carrier service Delta Express with Song, in an effort to better compete with low-fare airlines like Southwest. Delta has also acquired a minority stake in three regional airlines which can feed passengers into its several hubs, and has established an alliance with Continental and Northwest Airlines.

A third past competitor, America West, is faring better than both Delta and United. In July 2002, America West recalled virtually all employees furloughed after the September 11, 2001, attacks. Despite net income losses of $388 million in 2002, American West expects to restructure its finances with the help of federal loan guarantees totaling $380 million. It has about 11,000 employees and serves 144 cities in the United States with foreign locations in Mexico and Canada. America West has strong positions in its hubs, Phoenix and Las Vegas. These locations put it into direct competition with Southwest. With Continental and Mesa Airlines, which have small stakes in America West, America West has formed alliances which give it access to another thirty-five destinations.

The low-fare carriers are doing better because they don't rely on high business fares and don't offer the frills the major carriers offer. They tend to gravitate toward secondary airports where less congestion and lower fees keep costs down. Many also fly point-to-point without stops, and in general have relied on highly efficient e-business. Most importantly, low-fare airlines have succeeded in appealing to the customer in ways that major airlines never could by using creative market strategies and promoting individualism. As a result, customers are intrigued by this new mode of transport and after trying it, are convinced that it is the new way to travel. In 1994, revenues earned by low-fare carriers represented 5 percent of the $76 billion U.S. air travel market. By 2003, their share was over 20 percent, according to *CFO* magazine, up from just 10 percent in 2000. Experts predict that low-fare airlines will have 25 to 35 percent of the market share by the end of 2004, an increase that may restructure the airline industry forever.

JetBlue is one of Southwest's newest and possibly most noteworthy competitors. In 2002, JetBlue was the only other airline to report profits, with $55 million on revenues of $635 million. In 2003, despite geopolitical tensions, JetBlue was hiring an average of six new employees a day to accommodate growth. JetBlue's founder and CEO is David Neeleman, who was employed in the inner circle of Southwest for over a year. Thus it is no surprise that JetBlue is structured similarly to Southwest: a low-cost, low-fare airline with high employee productivity, a laid-back attitude, and a single aircraft model. Perhaps these are the reasons that JetBlue continues to grow and earn profits. It may also explain why Southwest's CFO Gary Kelly stated, "We've got to be prepared for intense competition." In fact, Southwest gave model JetBlue planes to its executives with a note: "Know your enemy." Currently, the two airlines don't compete in many of the same markets, but being the only two airlines experiencing significant growth, they are certainly affecting each other's potential growth.

All of the competitors have come into head-to-head competition with Southwest on several occasions. Southwest always welcomed competition and firmly believes it can come out ahead in any of those situations. Kelleher, when asked about his thoughts on facing a competitor such as the United Shuttle head-on, stated, "I think its good to have some real competitive activity that gets your people stirred up and renews their vigor and their energy and their desire to win."

Long-haul success for Southwest will put pressure on the profits realized by its bigger competitors. The cost advantage for Southwest includes the rapid twenty-minute gate turnarounds; an efficient all-Boeing 737 fleet, including new 737-700s that can fly cross-country nonstop; and a more productive workforce. Even if longer flights increase the costs, Southwest still realizes a significant competitive advantage. Roberts, Roach & Associates Inc., an airline consultant in Hayward, California, says that Southwest has at least a 59 percent cost advantage over bigger rivals at flights of 500 miles, as well as a 35 percent lead for flights at 1,500 miles. "It's a huge threat," says a rival airline executive. Already, according to an estimate by analyst Samuel C. Buttrick from Paine Webber, Inc., nonstop flights longer than 1,000 miles account for more than 16 percent of Southwest's capacity. Southwest is not the only low-fare airline that has expanded long-haul services in recent years. According to a report from the Department of Transportation, AirTran Airways, ATA Airways, Frontier Airlines, JetBlue Airways, and Spirit Airlines, along with Southwest, have expanded long-haul services by 26 percent between 2000 and 2002. Will longer flights for these airlines also mean a loss in profits due to increased costs, or could low-fare airlines win an even larger portion of the market to reign in the American skies?

For now, considerations for serious expansion have been put on hold as many airlines are still trying to recover from losses over the past two years. Southwest will continue its strategy to capitalize conservatively and increase growth steadily. It is capitalizing on the schedule cutbacks other airlines have made, but as a result, the door is also open for other low-fare carriers to profit.

The Future

Today, Southwest provides service to only fifty-eight cities, so there are tremendous opportunities for expansion. The problem: Competitors have learned from Southwest and its unique management strategies, and they are using these tactics as well as unique ones to win over consumers. Southwest has always utilized conservative growth tactics, but this may hurt it if new competitors opt for faster growth strategies. Over 100 cities have asked Southwest to begin service in their communities because of the positive impact the company has had when it began operations in a new location. But if Southwest doesn't do it, another low-fare airline will.

Develop a clear three-year strategic plan for Southwest.

4   AMR Inc.—2004

Andrew Graaff
Francis Marion University

AMR

www.amrcorp.com

AMR Inc., the parent company of American Airlines (American) and American Eagle, is seemingly turning the corner. Despite losses of $3.51 billion and $1.76 billion in 2001 and 2002, respectively, enormous challenges to its business model from low-cost carriers, and aggressive price cutting by rivals, AMR is working hard to change and become profitable.

After winning important concessions from the employees' labor union, American Airlines, the largest airline in the United States, is improving revenues and narrowing losses. AMR's share price was as low as $1.41 per share on March 12, 2003 but it improved to trade at $12.24 on September 24, 2003 and then to $15.70 on February 27, 2004. AMR has achieved these results by negotiating reductions in labor costs with unions, cutting unprofitable routes, laying off thousands of employees, developing and expanding partnerships, and improving load rates. In addition, AMR is developing global partnerships, refining routes, improving automation, and leveraging its position as the largest company in the global airline industry. Analysts expect AMR to be profitable in 2004 but the air carrier posted 2003 revenues of $17.4 billion but incurred an annual loss of $ 1.2 billion.

History

American Airlines was formed in New York City under the name Aviation Corporation (AVCO) in 1929. The founder, Sherman Fairchild, combined 85 small airlines in 1930 to create American Airways. In 1934, when American Airways was having difficulty due to the suspension of airmail, Mr. E. L. Cord, successor to CEO C. R. Smith, gave it the name American Airlines. Smith had been responsible for commissioning the building of the first plane capable of paying for itself without the need for postal revenue, the Douglas DC-3.

In 1964, American Airlines revolutionized the airline industry with the introduction of SABRE, the first computerized airline ticket reservation system. In 1978, the airline industry was deregulated and the following year AMR moved its headquarters to Dallas/Fort Worth. In 1980, American hired a new CEO, former Chief Financial Officer (CFO) Bob Crandall. Crandall's first major accomplishment was to introduce another first for the industry, the frequent flier program. Crandall brilliantly leveraged the information that was available in the SABRE system to track traveler mileage.

In 1982, American created a new holding company, AMR. AMR purchased the domestic airline Nashville Eagle in 1987 and turned it into American Eagle. After successfully preventing Donald Trump from purchasing American in 1989, the company bought routes to Japan, Latin America, and London from competitors.

In 1996, 20 percent of SABRE was sold and a code-sharing agreement was reached with British Airways (BA). This began a series of similar agreements which led to the formation of Oneworld, an alliance of major airlines around the world, in 1999. Donald Carty replaced Crandall as CEO in 1998 just as American Eagle unveiled new jets to replace the old turbo-prop-powered planes. AMR decided to focus on airlines and sold off other businesses such as aviation services, call centers, and ground services. In 2000, AMR sold its share of Canadian Airlines and the balance of what it owned of SABRE.

In 2001, AMR bought the assets of the failed TWA for $743 million and pursued regulatory clearance to continue the code-sharing deal with British Airways. Two American Airlines planes were hijacked in the attacks of September 11, 2001. Later that year, AMR laid off 20,000 employees and reduced flights by 20 percent in anticipation of reduced demand for flights. More bad news followed when another American jet crashed in New York killing 260 passengers. No sooner had the U.S. Department of Transportation (DOT) approved (2002) the code-sharing agreement with BA than it decided to end the agreement, thus requiring BA and AMR to give up 224 slots at London's Heathrow airport.

Industry Overview

The worldwide airline industry amassed losses of $7.6 billion and $11.3 billion in 2001 and 2002, respectively, and Standard & Poor's forecast a loss of $6.5 billion in 2003. Industry capacity declined by 4.4 percent in 2002 and the average airfare for a 1,000 mile flight declined by 9.3 percent. The overall market capacity remains too high for an industry rebound, yet some carriers increased their capacity in 2003. There is continued downward pressure on both domestic and international airfares.

Low-fare carriers are proving to be in the best position to thrive in an industry that Standard & Poor's believes has excess capacity. Low-fare carriers have lower labor costs, lower fixed costs, and use a point-to-point method of transporting passengers to their destination. Larger airlines that use the hub-and-spoke method to transport passengers to their destinations have significantly higher costs associated with maintaining a hub and generally unfavorable wage rates as a result of labor agreements.

Reducing costs is seen as the best survival solution in an environment where air travel is not expected to increase and overcapacity in the industry is expected to remain. Passengers now empowered by the Internet have almost complete airfare price information from anywhere 24 hours a day. This has made airfare prices even more price-sensitive and it has become virtually impossible to sell airline tickets at premium prices. US Airways, United, and American Airlines are examples of large U.S. airlines that are undergoing the painful process of changing the way business is done as a result of not being able to receive premium prices for airfares. These airlines are no longer able to dominate routes and charge high rates as a result of competition and easy access to airfares. Even business passengers are mostly flying coach due to cost cutting by businesses and the increase of alternate methods of business communication. In contrast, low-fare airlines often do not offer first-class fares and have never been reliant on business travelers.

Competitors

American Airlines' competitors fall into two primary categories: those that use the traditional hub-and-spoke method and those that use the point-to-point method. Primary hub-and-spoke competitors are UAL, owner of United Airlines, the second-largest carrier; Northwest Airlines; and Delta. Point-to-point competitors include SouthWest Airlines, JetBlue, and AirTran.

UAL is the world's second-largest carrier and flies 565 jets to more than 130 local destinations and 27 to other countries. UAL is part of the Star Alliance, which includes Lufthansa and others; it is currently in Chapter 11 bankruptcy and laid off 1,500 management and salaried positions in 2003. The company is planning the creation of a low-cost, low-fare airline utilizing regional jets, and expects to be profitable in 2004.

Delta is the world's third-largest airline and is expanding regional operations and building strong global alliances. Delta flies to nearly 220 U.S. cities and about 45 foreign destinations. Code-sharing agreements allow Delta to serve an additional 220 U.S. cities and nearly 120 destinations abroad. In the United States, Delta owns regional carriers Delta Express, Atlantic Southeast Airlines, and Comair, and has a fleet of 830 aircraft. Delta has also faced financial difficulties and has reduced its workforce by 21,000 employees. The company launched a budget carrier called Song in 2003, to compete with other low-fare carriers like Southwest and JetBlue.

Northwest Airlines is the fourth-largest airline in the United States and flies to more than 175 cities worldwide from hubs in Detroit, Memphis, Minneapolis/St. Paul, Osaka, and Tokyo. It also owns Memphis regional carrier Express Airlines. Code-sharing agreements allow Northwest to reach 750 destinations in 120 countries. Northwest has about 575 aircraft, including more than 50 regional jets. The company cut its flight schedule in 2003 and decreased demand and has reduced its workforce by 10,000.

Hubs have high fixed costs and variable costs. The alternative to hubs, point-to-point is used by smaller and start-up airlines. Southwest Airlines is the most successful airline to use a point-to-point method. AirTran and JetBlue are imitating Southwest and are becoming increasingly successful. American Airlines operates five hubs: Dallas/Fort Worth, Chicago O'Hare, Miami, St. Louis, and San Juan, Puerto Rico. AMR's two largest competitors, Delta Air Lines and United, have hub operations at Dallas/Fort Worth and Chicago O'Hare, respectively. American Eagle serves smaller markets in the United States and feeds customers to American's hubs. American has contracts with other regional airlines called American Connection to provide connecting service through its St. Louis hub. Exhibit 1 provides a view of the magnitude of hub operations and provides details on each of American's hubs.

Global Alliances and Code-Sharing

Code sharing is an agreement between two airlines on specific routes and destinations. American has been moving actively to increase code-sharing agreements and open up new markets. Currently, American has code-sharing programs with Aer Lingus, Air Pacific, Alaska Airlines, Asiana Airlines, Swiss Air, China Eastern Airlines, EVA Air, Finnair, Gulf Air, Hawaiian Airlines, Iberia, Japan Airlines, LanChile, LOT Polish Airlines, Qantas Airways, SNCF, TACA Group, the TAM Group, TAP Air Portugal, Thalys, and Turkish Airlines. American Eagle also has code-sharing programs with Continental, Delta, Midwest Express, and Northwest. AMR is working to add code sharing with Cathay Pacific Airways and Vietnam Airlines. The most recent extension of code-sharing agreements was on September 16, 2003, between American and British Airways (BA). The agreement increases the destinations available to passengers on each airline. American now offers flights to Amsterdam and Abu Dhabi through a code sharing agreement.

Currently, there are three major global alliances, Oneworld, SkyTeam, and Star Alliance. American and BA are the major airlines that form Oneworld, but it also includes eleven other airlines as members. The Star Alliance is probably strongest and includes United Airlines and Lufthansa as major members. The SkyTeam alliance includes Delta, Air France, Continental, KLM, and Northwest Airlines.

Restructuring

The CEO of AMR is also the CEO of American Airlines. Likewise, the Vice President of Marketing and Chief Financial Officer (CFO) for AMR have the same position for American Airlines. An organizational chart shown in Exhibit 2.

In an effort to reach profitability, AMR is doing major restructuring. Labor cost consume a significant portion of revenues. Standard & Poor's estimates that labor

EXHIBIT 1
AMR Corp. Hubs

HUB	DALLAS/ FORT WORTH	CHICAGO O'HARE	MIAMI	LUIS MUÑOZ MARIN	LAMBERT– ST. LOUIS
AA Hub Established	1981	1982	1989	1986	2001
Eagle Hub Established	1984	1985	1989	1986	2001
Number of Gates	75	69	47	19	51
Daily AA Jet Departures	471	286	192	54	226
Daily American Eagle/American Connection Departures	229	183	37	90	196
AA Nonstop Cities Served	107	57	73	20	95
Eagle Nonstop Cities Served	37	24	7	23	—
International Routes	25	11	47	21	5
Total Airport Employees	15,493	11,916	10,081	2,659	7,375
AA Employees	13,241	10,394	9,231	1,268	7,375
American Eagle/American Connection Employees	2,252	1,522	850	1,391	700
2002 Total Passengers Boarded	17,917,311	12,838,098	8,757,634	4,048,868	10,501,409
2002 AA Passengers Boarded	15,697,311	9,390,550	7,363,129	2,351,004	8,765,896
2002 Eagle/Connection Passengers Boarded	2,220,000	3,447,548	1,394,505	1,697,864	1,735,513
Average Bags Handled Per Day	58,600	34,195	33,210	—	45,000
Number of Admirals Clubs	4	2	2	1	1
Ticket Counter Check-In Positions	137	78	190	52	52
Cargo Warehouse Size (sq. feet)	190,355	95,000	166,000	100,000	55,529

Source: Adapted from www.amrcorp.com/corpinfo.htm.

EXHIBIT 2
AMR Corporation's Organizational Structure

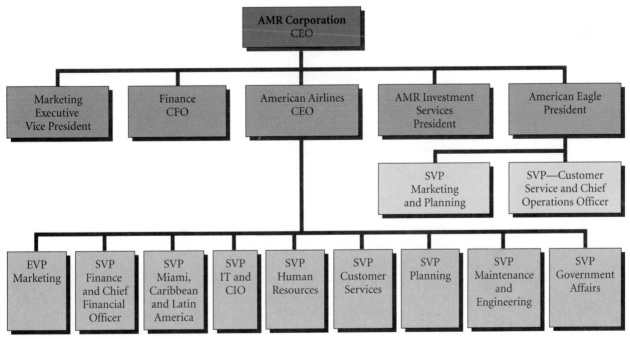

Source: Adapted from amrcorp.com/corpinfo.htm.

costs consumed as much as 43.9 percent of all airline industry revenues in 2002. AMR reached an agreement with union officials to reduce labor costs by $1.4 billion initially and $2 billion by the end of 2004. It's not just the regular employees who are getting less; the Board of Directors and the CEO volunteered to work without pay while AMR worked to become profitable.

American has reduced the number of flights to some destinations from its Dallas/Fort Worth and O'Hare hubs. Passengers will have a longer wait as a result of less-frequent flights. These steps were taken to gain efficiencies in operations. In total American reduced its flights by 20 percent in 2002 and early 2003 and reduced its workforce by 27,000 employees. More layoffs may be needed for the company to survive.

American is accelerating the retirement of its older aircraft that are more expensive to run. Fokker jets in particular are being replaced. The company has closed 105 travel centers, six Admiral's Clubs, and five Platinum Centers. Passengers can expect less food and beverages in-flight and American is looking at initiatives to sell food and beverages to passengers.

AMR Fleet

AMR has a vast fleet of aircraft as described in Exhibit 3. American Eagle has 286 aircraft and is looking to purchase newer, larger regional aircraft that that have better fuel consumption. Traditionally, these smaller aircraft have seated approximately 50 passengers, but airlines are moving to aircraft that seat between 75 and 100 passengers for regional flights. American had 819 aircraft at the end of 2002, but is reducing the number.

Fuel and Security

Fuel comprises approximately 12 percent of all airline costs, but varies depending on efficiency of the aircraft and length of flight, as take-offs and landings use significant volumes of fuel. Jet fuel prices averaged 76.8 cents in 2002. During the second quarter of 2003, American's average fuel cost was 83 cents per gallon.

The federal government has mandated certain security measures which have led to an increase in security costs. These costs have been subsidized by the federal government but not at a level that would absorb all the additional expenses. Airlines now pay a fee of $5 per passenger to help with the government's additional security expenses. Cockpit doors are now reinforced, all bags are screened for explosives, and each passenger's baggage is matched to a passenger seated on a flight. Longer waiting lines have reduced the convenience of flying, potentially lowering the demand for air travel.

EXHIBIT 3
AMR Fleet

AMERICAN AIRLINES 2002		AMERICAN EAGLE FLEET	
Aircraft	*No.*	*Aircraft*	*No.*
McDonnell Douglas MD-80	362	ATR-42	26
Boeing 757-200	151	Bombardier CRJ-700	8
Boeing 737-800	77	Embraer 135	40
Fokker 100	74	Embraer 140	43
Boeing 767-300	49	Embraer 145	50
Boeing 777-200	43	Super ATR	42
Airbus A300-600R	34	Saab 340B	52
Boeing 767-200	29	Saab 340B Plus	25

Source: www.aa.com.

Operating Statistics

Revenue passenger-miles (RPMs) is an indicator that measures the total number of passengers carried by the industry's airlines, multiplied by the number of miles flown. The RPM numbers are available on a monthly basis from the Air Transport Association (ATA), an industry trade group. RPMs continued to decline by 2.2 percent in 2002, following a 7.7 percent decline in 2001. This is in contrast to the industry's ten-year growth rate of about 4 percent.

Calculated on a monthly basis, available seats per mile (ASM) is an indicator that measures the total number of seats in the active fleet, multiplied by the number of miles flown, for either an individual airline or the entire industry. The ATA compiles an industrywide figure on a monthly basis. Changes in ASMs are an indication of changes in the industry's fleet, seating mix of aircraft, and how quickly the industry turns around its aircraft between flights. ASMs for the U.S. airline industry declined 5.2 percent in 2002 to $829.8 billion.

Load factor is an indicator, compiled monthly by the ATA, that measures the percentage of available seating capacity that is filled with passengers. It may be calculated as a percentage of a single airline's seats, or of all seats in the industry. Fortunately for AMR, once its load factor moves past the breakeven point, it can expect profit margins to expand quickly. Both American Eagle and American achieved record load factors in 2003. This helped in the second quarter of 2003 as AMR achieved an operating profit before other expenses. Load factor can also be calculated by dividing a carrier's RPMs by its total ASMs. AMR's revenue per available seat mile increased in the second quarter of 2003 by 2.6 percent to 8.74 cents. Exhibit 4 provides complete statistics for 2003, 2002, and 2001.

AAdvantage Travel Awards Program

American Airlines' AAdvantage is the largest travel awards program in the world. Starting in 1981 with 283,000 members, the program has grown to 45 million members worldwide. Members earn mileage credits when they fly American Airlines, American Eagle, AmericanConnection, and Oneworld carriers, as well as other airline participants. Members also earn mileage credits by purchasing products/services from nonairline AAdvantage participant businesses now numbering in excess of 1,500 companies, including 35 hotel chains, 75 brands, 2 airlines, 8 car rental companies, and 25 major retail/financial companies. Members can also earn miles by using any of 60 affinity cards available in 30 countries.

E-Commerce

When it comes to the proportion of airline tickets purchased online, American is behind competitors such as Southwest airlines, which sells more than 50 percent of its tickets over the Internet. Selling tickets via the Internet is lucrative because it lowers costs and reduces the portion paid to agencies. AMR is taking steps to improve its performance by adding services to its Web site, making it easier to use the Web site, and also adding features such as a My Reservations area, Flight check-in, view flight schedules, a flight status notification area, the ability to purchase upgrades, and e-mail subscriptions.

American will also launch an online cargo shipments tool on its Web site in early 2004. It will be possible to go to **www.aacargo.com** and book a shipment. American Cargo now ships more than 100 million pounds of cargo each week.

E-tickets are used by 89 percent of all AMR passengers. AMR is promoting e-tickets by working with alliance and code-sharing partners to make e-tickets available on code-sharing flights. E-tickets eliminate some of the hassle passengers experience as a result of tighter security by allowing tickets to be transferred without the need to print out a new ticket. American is working with Interline e-ticketing and partner airlines to make it possible to check in all the way to a final destination, even when traveling on multiple airlines.

EXHIBIT 4

AMR Corp.—Annual Income Statement

IN MILLIONS OF U.S. DOLLARS (EXCEPT FOR PER SHARE ITEMS) YEAR ENDING 12/31	2003	2002	2001
Revenue	$17,440.0	17,420.0	18,969.0
Other Revenue	—	—	—
Total Revenue	**17,440.0**	**17,420.0**	**18,969.0**
Cost of Revenue	14,430.0	15,961.0	16,429.0
Gross Profit	**3,010.0**	**1,459.0**	**2,540.0**
Selling/General/Adm. Exp.	—	—	—
Research & Development	—	—	—
Depreciation/Amortization	1,377.0	1,366.0	1,404.0
Interest Expense (Income)	—	—	—
Unusual Expense (Income)	49.0	708.0	610.0
Other Operating Expenses	2,428.0	2,715.0	2,996.0
Total Operating Expense	**18,284.0**	**20,750.0**	**21,439.0**
Operating Income	**(844.0)**	**(3,330.0)**	**(2,470.0)**
Interest Expense	(632.0)	(599.0)	(394.0)
Interest/Investment Income	55.0	71.0	110.0
Interest Income (Expense)	(577.0)	(528.0)	(284.0)
Gain (Loss) on Sale of Assets	—	—	—
Other, Net	113.0	(2.0)	(2.0)
Income Before Tax	**(1,308.0)**	**(3,860.0)**	**(2,756.0)**
Income Tax	(80.0)	(1,337.0)	(994.0)
Income After Tax	**(1,228.0)**	**(2,523.0)**	**(1,762.0)**
Accounting Change	0.0	(988.0)	0.0
Discontinued Operations	—	—	—
Extraordinary Item	—	0.0	0.0
Net Income	**$(1,228.0)**	**(3,511.0)**	**(1,762.0)**
Preferred Dividends	—	—	—
Income Available	**(1,226.0)**	**(2,530.0)**	**(1,760.0)**
Inc Avail Incl. Extras	**(1,226.0)**	**(3,518.0)**	**(1,760.0)**
Weighted Average Shares	158.0	156.0	154.0
EPS	**(7.759)**	**(16.218)**	**(11.429)**
EPS Incl. Extras	**(7.759)**	**(22.551)**	**(11.429)**

Source: www.investor.stockpoint.com.

Conclusion

AMR appears to be on the path to recovery and could be profitable in 2004; it needs to continue efforts to reduce costs and to delete routes that are unprofitable. AMR should consider selling off subsidiaries that are not part of the core business of providing air travel. Cash from the sale of these subsidiaries could be used to pay down debt. The company must continue accelerating the retirement of high-cost aircraft and consider upgrading regional jets, and it needs to focus on improving e-sales in order to better compete for the growing market segment that purchases tickets online.

Prepare a three-year strategic plan for AMR.

EXHIBIT 5

AMR Corp.—Balance Sheet

IN MILLIONS OF U.S. DOLLARS (EXCEPT FOR PER SHARE ITEMS) AS OF 12/31/03	2003	2002	2001
Cash & Equivalents	—	—	—
Short Term Investments	$ 2,486.0	1,846.0	2,386.0
Cash and Short Term Investments	2,606.0	1,950.0	2,488.0
Trade Accounts Receivable, Net	796.0	909.0	1,162.0
Other Receivables	0.0	572.0	252.0
Total Receivables, Net	796.0	1,481.0	1,414.0
Total Inventory	516.0	627.0	822.0
Prepaid Expenses	—	—	—
Other Current Assets	764.0	879.0	1,847.0
Total Current Assets	**4,682.0**	**4,937.0**	**6,571.0**
Property/Plant/Equipment—Gross	—	—	—
Accumulated Depreciation	(9,543.0)	(9,379.0)	(10,004.0)
Property/Plant/Equipment, Net	19,101.0	18,927.0	18,726.0
Goodwill, Net	—	0.0	1,392.0
Intangibles, Net	1,253.0	1,292.0	1,325.0
Long Term Investments	—	—	—
Other Long Term Assets	4,294.0	5,111.0	4,827.0
Total Assets	**$29,330.0**	**30,267.0**	**32,841.0**
Accounts Payable	967.0	1,198.0	1,785.0
Accrued Expenses	1,989.0	2,560.0	2,192.0
Notes Payable/Short Term Debt	—	—	—
Current Port. LT Capital Leases	804.0	868.0	772.0
Other Current Liabilities	2,799.0	2,614.0	2,763.0
Total Current Liabilities	**6,559.0**	**7,240.0**	**7,512.0**
Long Term Debt	11,901.0	10,888.0	8,310.0
Capital Lease Obligations	1,225.0	1,422.0	1,524.0
Total Long Term Debt	**13,126.0**	**12,310.0**	**9,834.0**
Total Debt	**13,930.0**	**13,178.0**	**10,606.0**
Deferred Income Tax	—	0.0	1,627.0
Minority Interest	—	—	—
Other Liabilities	9,599.0	9,760.0	8,495.0
Total Liabilities	**$29,284.0**	**29,310.0**	**27,468.0**
Redeemable Preferred Stock	—	—	—
Preferred Stock—Non Redeemable, Net	—	0.0	0.0
Common Stock	182.0	182.0	182.0
Additional Paid-In Capital	2,605.0	2,795.0	2,865.0
Retained Earnings (Accum. Deficit)	(551.0)	677.0	4,188.0
Treasury Stock—Common	(1,405.0)	(1,621.0)	(1,716.0)
Other Equity	(785.0)	(1,076.0)	(146.0)
Total Equity	**46.0**	**957.0**	**5,373.0**
Total Liability & Shareholder's Equity	**$29,330.0**	**30,267.0**	**32,841.0**
Shares Outs.—Common Stock	159.6	156.1	154.6
Total Common Shares Outs.	**159.6**	**156.1**	**154.6**
Total Preferred Stock Shares Outs.	**—**	**—**	**—**
Employees (actual figures)	96,400.0	109,600.0	122,820.0
Number of Common Shareholders	16,739.0	13,000.0	13,700.0

Source: www.investor.stockpoint.com.

5

E*TRADE Financial, Corp.—2004

William Doulaveris
Francis Marion University

NYSE: ET

www.etrade.com

Twenty years ago, did you ever think that you would be doing so much on a computer? Probably not. But today the reality is that almost everything is or can be done on a personal computer. From banking to investing, E*TRADE is capitalizing on the computer and Internet revolution.

E*TRADE FINANCIAL, Corp., known as E*TRADE Group, Inc. until October 2003, is an online brokerage firm that allows you to trade equities, keep your portfolio updated, and obtain market information around the clock. E*TRADE receives a commission from each trade and receives interest on the short positions of its clients. Its more than 4 million account holders trade stock using the Internet and phone. E*TRADE is also active in Germany, Australia, Canada, New Zealand, Denmark, Hong Kong, Japan, Korea, Sweden, and the United Kingdom. It offers over 15,200 automated teller machines (ATMs), and is positioning itself to be much more than simply a brokerage firm. Slowly but surely, E*TRADE is becoming a complete financial support and execution portal for individuals, offering every service you need in your financial life.

History

Founded as a service bureau in 1982 by Bill Porter, a physicist and inventor, the early E*TRADE provided online quote and trading services to Fidelity, Charles Schwab, and Quick & Reilly. Seeing the opportunity to capitalize on a potentially huge discount brokerage, Porter came up with an idea that would allow individuals to use their personal computers to invest, paying far less than the traditional brokerage fees. It would take several years for the world to catch up with his vision. In 1992, E*TRADE Securities, Inc., was born and began to offer online investing services through America Online and CompuServe. With the launch of **www.etrade.com** in 1996, the demand for E*TRADE's services exploded.

The company went public in August 1996 and completed another stock offering one year later when Porter handed over the reins to Christos Cotsakos, who came to E*TRADE with over twenty years of senior management experience at Federal Express and A. C. Neilsen. Under Cotsakos' guidance, E*TRADE became a global leader in online personal financial services with branded Web sites around the world. The company introduced E*TRADE Bank in 2000 with the purchase of Telebanc Financial (now E*TRADE Financial), an online bank with more than 100,000 depositors. It also bought Card Capture Services (now E*TRADE Access), an operator of more than 9,000 ATMs across the United States. Continuing to expand its global reach, E*TRADE acquired Canadian firm VERSUS Technologies, a provider of electronic trading services, and teamed up with UBS Warburg to allow non-U.S. investors to buy U.S. securities without needing to trade in dollars. Later, its E*TRADE International Capital announced plans to offer an initial public offering (IPO) to European investors.

In 2001, E*TRADE entered the consumer-lending business when it acquired online mortgage originator LoansDirect (now E*TRADE Mortgage). Headquartered in Menlo Park, California, it had 3,500 employees at year-end 2003 down just five employees from 2002. In 2003, E*TRADE's revenues rose to $2008 million and net income rose to $203 million.

External Factors

Despite the best effort of companies in the investment services industry to reduce cyclicality, their business is still closely tied to the economy, corporate earnings, and the stock market. The U.S. economy slipped into a recession in 2001, causing the stock market to experience one of its biggest slides in history, with the S&P 500 Index falling about 13 percent and the Nasdaq Index falling about 21 percent. What followed in 2002 was worse when the S&P 500 and Nasdaq dropped 23 percent and 34 percent, respectively. The year 2003 witnessed a mild rebound.

Although U.S. real gross domestic product (GDP) grew 2.4 percent in 2002, the recovery has remained tentative. Concerns that the U. S. economy may fall back into recession prompted the Federal Reserve to lower interest rates in November 2002. Amid the threat of another global slowdown, geopolitical fears, and numerous corporate scandals, stock markets have remained turbulent. Year-to-date through April 11, 2003, the S&P 500 Composite Stock Index was down 1.3 percent, while the Nasdaq Composite rose 1.7 percent. Overseas markets have been slightly better.

A flood of corporate accounting and other scandals have weighed on stock prices and led to a crisis of confidence among investors. Industry regulators are working to promote increased integrity and transparency among corporations and investment business, but it may take some time to restore investors' confidence. Until investor confidence is restored, conditions in the brokerage industry will remain challenging.

In 2002, the aggregate pretax profits of the 240 or so firms registered with the New York Stock Exchange (NYSE) fell 33 percent to $7.0 bilion, after having been cut in half in 2001 to $10.4 billion. Although pretax profits improved in 2003, the increases were driven largely by lower operating costs. Net revenue growth was on average to be weak.

Investment Services annual industry revenues fell 24 percent in 2002, year-to-year, to $148.7 billion. Commission revenues for the Investment Services industry firms totaled $27.6 billion in 2002, up 2.7 percent, year-to-year, as declining and volatile stock prices led to increased trading activity. Average daily volume on the NYSE rose to 1.4 billion shares, while Nasdaq volume slowed 11 percent to 1.825 billion shares a day.

Since 2001, online brokers have slashed costs in order to increase productivity and shore up profitability. That year, E*TRADE incurred more than $227 million in charges to restructure its operations. The company consolidated several centers, reduced headcount, and exited several foreign markets. At the same time, E*TRADE expanded into new businesses, such as market-making and mortgage lending, that would complement its core businesses.

Competitors

The market for electronic financial services over the Internet and other alternative channels continues to quickly grow and is extremely competitive. As E*TRADE continues to diversify and expand its services beyond online domestic retail brokerage offerings to inlcude banking, global cross-border trading, mutual fund offerings, market-making, consumer lending, institutional investing, financial advice, and insurance, the number of competitors in these varied market places is also increasing. E*TRADE faces direct competition from full-commission brokerage firms, discount brokerage firms, online brokerage firms, pure-play Internet banks, traditional "brick and mortar" commercial banks, and savings banks. These competitors provide touch-tone telephone, voice response, online banking services, electronic bill payment services, and a host of other financial products. In addition, E*TRADE competes with mutual fund companies, which provide money market funds and cash management accounts.

Some mutual fund firms, such as Putnam, have recently been accused of ethical wrongdoing. Putnam was the first investment management company charged with fraud amid a widening probe into illegal trading practices in the mutual fund industry by state and federal regulators. Recently, there has been a far-reaching probe into the mutual fund industry, causing widespread wrongdoing and market manipulation. Firms in the mutual fund industry have been accused of using two illegal practices: (1) late-day trading and (2) market timing. In late-day trading, a firm illegally buys shares after the market closes in order to take advantage of early evening news that will pump up the stock price by morning, allowing it to sell the next day at a profit. In market timing, firms quickly trade large blocks of shares, hoping to reap big profits by small fluctuations in share price. While the practice is not illegal, mutual funds were allowing powerful investors to make the risky trades at the expense of small-time, long-term investors, who are barred from the practice. As a result of these wrongdoings, more and more customers are moving away from mutual fund firms, such as Putnam, and turning toward investing companies such as E*TRADE.

E*TRADE's main competitors are Schwab (Charles) (SCH), Ameritrade Holding Corp.-CI (AMTD), Financial Institutions (FISI), A. B. Watley Group (ABWG), and JB Oxford Holdings (JBOH). Schwab is the largest broker in the industry, with 35 percent of the market share and revenues totaling almost $4.23 billion at year-end 2002. E*TRADE's market share was 30 percent based upon $2 billion in revenues. For the second-quarter 2003, Charles Schwab reported revenues of $1,082 million, up from $689 million in the first quarter. Ameritrade has market share of 15 percent and $650 million in revenues. The Warsaw, New York–based firm, Financial Institutions, has a market share of 5 percent and $140 million in revenues. JB Oxford Holdings and A. B. Watley Group collectively claim about 5 percent market share, and all other online brokerage firms represent the remaining 10 percent.

Based in Omaha, Nebraska, Ameritrade provides online brokerage services, an Internet-based personal financial management service, touch-tone telephone and market data, and research tools. Ameritrade's services are very similar to those of E*TRADE, with the major exception being the lack of ATMs. Ameritrade is an up-and-coming company that has potential. For the second-quarter 2003, Ameritrade reported revenues of $152.3 million, which was up from $89 million in the first quarter.

Internal Factors

E*TRADE's Vision Statement

E*TRADE's vision is "to empower self-directed investors to make informed investment decisions and take control of their financial future with anytime, anywhere access to the world's major investment markets."

E*TRADE's Mission Statement

Using technology to set the standard for innovation, service, and value for investors seeking more control over their investments. E*TRADE's rich suite of products and services can be customized to reflect a customer's unique needs and interests, including portfolio tracking, free real-time quotes, market news, and research available 24 hours a day, seven days a week. Customers can access their E*TRADE accounts virtually any time anywhere around the world.

Organizational Structure

In attempts to cut costs and streamline the organization as a whole, E*TRADE has reduced the amount of people needed to maintain the firm. The organization structure is shown in Exhibit 1, and was adapted based on titles of top executives. Note that E*TRADE uses a divisional structure with two segments: Brokerage and Banking.

The brokerage segment comprises E*TRADE Securities, which offers Internet domestic retail brokerage services. The banking segment includes E*TRADE Bank,

EXHIBIT 1
E*TRADE's Organizational Chart

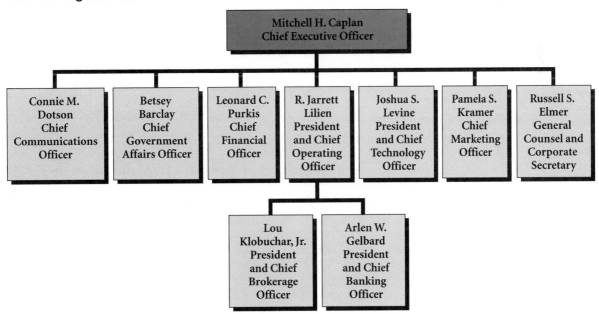

Source: Adapted based on titles of top executives.

E*TRADE Access, a network of 15,200 ATMs, E*TRADE Mortgage, and E*TRADE Zone. VERSUS Technologies, Inc., which provides services to international investors, and also TIR Holdings Limited, a service center for institutional investors, comprises the Global and Institutional segment of E*TRADE.

E*TRADE banking revenues increased 26 percent in 2002, while its brokerage revenues fell 5 percent; it reported net losses of $186.4 million in fiscal 2002, which includes an accounting change of $293.7 million. Consolidated financial statements for E*TRADE are listed in Exhibit 2 and Exhibit 3.

E*TRADE is trying to regain investor confidence after former CEO Christos Cotsakos received a 2001 pay package valued at $80 million, even as the company's share price plummeted. Although Cotsakos repaid $20 million, the company was still in desperate need of new leadership. Mitchell Caplan replaced Cotsakos in January 2003 and is in the process of restructuring the organization further and cutting more unnecessary expenditures, like the $14,000 a month concierge service for 200 or so employees in Rancho Cordova, California. E*TRADE TV was liquidated and the name E*TRADE Group replaced to distinguish it from other media companies or dot-com companies.

Marketing

E*TRADE is in the process of searching for a new advertising agency to replace the current Goodby, Silverstein & Partners. E*TRADE discontinued advertising in the Super Bowl in 2001, and uses co-branding to market its services at a discounted price. E*TRADE and Hilton HHonors Worldwide have a marketing relationship that provides Hilton HHonors members with HHonors bonus points when they open an account with E*TRADE. The agreement offers HHonors members the opportunity to earn 5,000 HHonors points when they open a new E*TRADE account, and enables E*TRADE to reach a large and highly attractive group of consumers with an expressed allegiance to one of the world's leading frequent-traveler programs.

In August 2003, E*TRADE and Genmar Holdings, Inc., a builder of recreational boats, announced the launch of Genmar Retail Financial Services (GRFS), a private-label retail marine finance program. Under the program, the companies will begin rolling out a variety of private-label retail financial services designed to meet the needs of Genmar dealers.

Conclusion

Under the leadership of CEO Mitchell Caplan, E*TRADE may want to acquire 8,000 new ATMs in the United Kingdom, Germany, Denmark, New Zealand, and Sweden to increase its ATM and global business. It could also open brick and mortar banks or brokerage offices in the United Kingdom, Germany, Denmark, New Zealand, and Sweden in order to further diversify its offerings. E*TRADE could try to acquire Ameritrade or another online brokerage firm to gain economies of scale and market share.

Develop a three-year strategic plan for E*TRADE.

EXHIBIT 2
E-TRADE—Balance Sheet

IN MILLIONS OF U.S. DOLLARS (EXCEPT FOR PER SHARE ITEMS) AS OF DECEMBER 31	2003	2002	2001
Cash & Equivalents	$ 2,566.0	2,222.7	1,600.9
Short Term Investments	—	—	—
Cash and Short Term Investments	2,566.0	2,222.7	1,600.9
Trade Accounts Receivable, Net	17,586.2	13,907.1	12,090.1
Other Receivables	—	—	—
Total Receivables, Net	17,586.2	13,907.1	12,090.1
Total Inventory	—	—	—
Prepaid Expenses	—	—	—
Other Current Assets	—	—	—
Total Current Assets	—	—	—
Property/Plant/Equipment—Gross	—	—	—
Accumulated Depreciation	—	(340.2)	(247.5)
Property/Plant/Equipment, Net	301.3	370.9	331.7
Goodwill, Net	402.3	385.1	557.3
Intangibles, Net	144.0	157.9	132.9
Long Term Investments	3,551.7	1,851.2	1,225.1
Other Long Term Assets	—	—	—
Total Assets	**$26,036.8**	**21,455.9**	**18,172.4**
Accounts Payable	3,691.2	2,713.7	2,700.0
Accrued Expenses	—	—	—
Notes Payable/Short Term Debt	—	—	—
Current LT Debt/Capital Leases	695.3	695.3	760.3
Other Current Liabilities	—	—	—
Total Current Liabilities	—	—	—
Long Term Debt	0.0	143.4	69.5
Capital Lease Obligations	—	—	—
Total Long Term Debt	**0.0**	**143.4**	**69.5**
Total Debt	**695.3**	**838.7**	**829.8**
Deferred Income Tax	—	—	—
Minority Interest	—	—	—
Other Liabilities	19,001.6	15,779.5	12,506.6
Total Liabilities	**$24,118.5**	**19,950.1**	**16,601.5**
Redeemable Preferred Stock	—	—	—
Preferred Stock—Non Redeemable	—	—	—
Common Stock	3.7	3.6	3.5
Additional Paid-In Capital	2,247.9	2,190.2	2,072.7
Retained Earnings (Accum. Deficit)	(230.5)	(433.5)	(247.1)
Treasury Stock—Common	—	—	—
Other Equity	(102.9)	(254.5)	(258.2)
Total Equity	**1,918.3**	**1,505.8**	**1,570.9**
Total Liability & Shareholders' Equity	**$26,036.8**	**21,455.9**	**18,172.4**
Shares Outs.—Common Stock	366.6	358.0	347.6
Total Common Shares Outs.	**366.6**	**358.0**	**347.6**
Total Preferred Stock Shares Outs.	—	—	—
Employees (actual figures)	—	3,500.0	3,495.0
Number of Common Shareholders	—	2,591.0	2,507.0

Source: www.investor.stockpoint.com

EXHIBIT 3
E*TRADE—Income Statement

IN MILLIONS OF U.S. DOLLARS (EXCEPT FOR PER SHARE ITEMS) AS OF DECEMBER 31	2003	2002	2001
Revenue	$2,008.4	1,901.7	2,062.1
Other Revenue	—	—	—
Total Revenue	**2,008.4**	**1,901.7**	**2,062.1**
Cost of Revenue	1,143.0	1,143.1	1,382.3
Gross Profit	**865.3**	**758.6**	**679.8**
Selling/General/Adm. Expenses	428.8	414.3	489.8
Research & Development	60.7	55.7	88.7
Depreciation/Amortization	33.0	28.3	43.1
Interest Expense (Income)	—	—	—
Unusual Expense (Income)	136.4	28.0	213.9
Other Operating Expenses	—	(23.5)	30.2
Total Operating Expense	**1,802.0**	**1,645.8**	**2,248.1**
Operating Income	**206.4**	**255.9**	**(186.0)**
Interest Expense	(45.6)	(47.7)	(52.9)
Interest/Investment Income	21.4	21.7	16.0
Interest Income (Expense)	(24.2)	(26.0)	(36.9)
Gain (Loss) on Sale of Assets	147.5	(18.5)	(49.8)
Other, Net	(19.3)	(17.4)	11.7
Income Before Tax	310.4	193.9	(260.9)
Income Tax	112.4	85.1	(19.9)
Income After Tax	**198.0**	**108.8**	**(241.1)**
Minority Interest	5.1	(1.6)	(0.5)
Equity in Affiliates	—	—	—
Net Inc. Before Extras	**203.0**	**107.3**	**(241.5)**
Accounting Change	—	(293.7)	—
Discontinued Operations	—	—	—
Extraordinary Items	—	—	—
Net Income	**$ 203.0**	**(186.4)**	**(241.5)**
Preferred Dividends	—	—	—
Inc. Available to Common	**203.0**	**107.3**	**(241.5)**
Inc. Available to Common	**203.0**	**(186.4)**	**(241.5)**
Weighted Average Shares	358.3	355.1	332.4
Basic/Primary EPS	**0.567**	**0.302**	**(0.727)**
Basic/Primary EPS	**(0.525)**	**(0.727)**	**0.004**
Dilution Adjustment	—	0.0	0.0
Diluted Weight Avg. Shares	367.4	361.1	332.4
Diluted EPS	**0.553**	**0.297**	**(0.727)**
Diluted EPS	**0.553**	**(0.516)**	**(0.727)**
Dividends per Share	0.000	0.000	0.000
Gross Dividends	0.0	0.0	0.0
Stock Based Compensation	—	14.2	38.5

Source: www.investor.stockpoint.com

References

A. B. Watley Group Inc. *Annual Report & Form 10K* (2002). www.freeedgar.com.

Ameritrade Inc. *Annual Report & Form 10K* (2002). www.freeedgar.com.

Charles Schwab, Inc. *Annual Report & Form 10K* (2002). www.freeedgar.com.

E*TRADE Group, Inc. *Annual Report & Form 10K* (2002). www.freeedgar.com.

JB Oxford Holdings. *Annual Report & Form 10K* (2002). www.freeedgar.com.

Wall Street Journal (August 2003). www.hoovers.com; www.investorstockpoint.com.

6   eBay Inc.—2004

Marcelo Brandao de Mattos
Francis Marion University

eBay

www.ebay.com

Going once. Going twice. Cybergone! Forget all the inventory and warehouses. Instead, imagine an online marketplace where people can find and list their own products to buy and sell. This is eBay, the world's largest and most popular marketplace on the Web.

Since eBay Inc., an Internet-based company located in San Jose, California, was founded, it has increased in all aspects exponentially. The number of users from 1995 to 2002 increased 150,488 percent to 61.7 million and revenues grew to $2.165 billion in 2003. The new goal is to reach $3 billion in sales in 2005. The company has performed very well since it was founded and today is worth more than such companies as McDonald's and Boeing.

The eBay formula is simple: Provide a worldwide market and collect revenue as transactions occur. eBay has established a Web community of buyers and sellers who get together in an auction format to buy and sell items ranging from electronics and collectibles to cars and real estate.

History

eBay was started in September 1995 by Pierre Omidyar, in his apartment. Born in France and raised in the United States, Omidyar moved to the West Coast after graduating from college as a computer programmer.

The Pez candy dispenser (a novelty item) story has been told and retold in countless popular accounts of eBay's history (the story says the business was started for his then-girlfriend, an avid Pez candy dispenser collector, to contact others who shared her interest in Pez dispensers). Omidyar revealed that this is just a romantic vision of eBay's founding. The truth is, in the summer of 1995, Omidyar was obsessed with finding ways to profit from the Internet. His solution was an online auction. He listed a broken laser pointer for sale on his Web site, and it was then that he realized its true potential. In the first week, he got no bids, then someone bid $3, then $4, and eventually the bidding reached $14 for an item he thought was worth almost nothing.

The original site, called Auction Web, made no promises or guarantees. Individuals logged on and bid for items, and made transactions. At that time, there were no fees, no registrations, no security, few items, seven categories, and little business. Omidyar then made one very positive marketing decision: He listed his trading site on the National Center for Supercomputing Applications' "What's Cool List," and the rest is history. After the listing was posted, business started to pick up. In February

1996, Omidyar had to institute a fee to cover his rising Internet service-provider cost. By the end of March 1996, the business turned a profit and by 1997, the company was doubling every three months. The business continued to grow, and in 1998 the company, now renamed eBay, went public.

The eBay community has become more diverse than ever, featuring homemakers, major corporations, and everyone in between. Those users listed more than a billion items on the site in 2003. Sales continue to grow, and today eBay is the largest Internet auction site; gross merchandise sales (value of all items sold on eBay) increased to $25 billion in 2003. At the end of the first year after eBay started, it had 41,000 users. By the end of 2003 this number had increased to 100 million. As a truly global marketplace, eBay has presence in 150 countries around the world. In total, users can find more than 30,000 categories in the Web site on any given day.

Vision and Mission Statements

eBay does not have a formal vision statement. The company mission statement is as follows: "Our mission is to build the world's most efficient and abundant marketplace in which anyone, anywhere, can buy or sell practically anything. We pioneered online trading by developing a Web-based marketplace in which a community of buyers and sellers are brought together in an entertaining, intuitive, easy-to-use environment to browse, buy, and sell an enormous variety of items. Through our PayPal service, we enable any business or consumer with e-mail to send and receive online payments securely, conveniently, and cost-effectively."

eBay Trade Experience

Anyone who has access to the Internet can visit the eBay homepage at **www.ebay.com** or any of eBay's international sites. Users can search for items to browse and buy, go to a specific item category, go to a specialty site such as eBay Stores or eBay Motors, and begin listing an item for sale. If you wish to bid on items listed or list items for sale, you must register.

The registration process is simple and quick. It takes less than five minutes and once registered, you can immediately bid on or list items for sale. All buyers and sellers must be eighteen or older to bid on or list items.

Once a user has found an item and registered, the user may enter a bid for the maximum amount he or she is willing to pay at that time. Alternatively, those listings that offer the Buy-It-Now feature can be purchased immediately by accepting the price established by the seller. In the event of competitive bids, the eBay service automatically increases bidding in increments based upon the current high bid, up to the bidder's maximum price. Potential buyers wishing additional information about a listed item can contact the seller through e-mail. During the course of the transaction, eBay notifies bidders immediately via indirect e-mail if they are outbid. Buyers are not charged for making bids or purchases through eBay.

When the bidding on a particular auction has ended, eBay will determine if a bid exceeds the reserve and opening price. eBay will then notify both buyer and seller via e-mail, and the buyer and seller complete the transaction independently of eBay. The buyer and seller agree upon and arrange for shipment and payment. eBay has no power to force the buyer and seller to complete the transaction, but it can ban either or both offending parties from trading on eBay in the future.

As noted in Exhibit 1, for as little as 30 cents a person can list an item and market it to millions of potential buyers. Users can sell items on eBay by registering and selling items on their own, or with the help of a Trade Assistant, who can assist in the sale of items for a fee. After a seller selects the opening and reserve price for opening bids, he or she has to say if the sale will last three, five, seven, or ten days. If a seller receives one or more bids above the stated minimum or reserve price, whichever is higher, the seller is obligated to complete a transaction.

After a transaction is completed, eBay buyers and sellers can exchange money by the payment method of their choice. Options include: credit card, cash, barter, check, money order, or eBay's recent acquisition, PayPal global payments platform. Through PayPal, eBay can accelerate the velocity of transactions and eliminate numerous obstacles presented by traditional payment methods. Businesses and consumers from 38 countries, including the United States, can receive online payments in a secure, convenient, and cost-effective way.

The eBay platform supports all the services that the organization offers, from selling and buying processes to bulletin board and chat areas. The total expenses in the operations platform in 2002 totaled $120.1 million, an increase of 48 percent over 2001. With the exception of once-a-week maintenance that takes a few hours, the system operates seven days a week, twenty-four hours a day.

eBay Customer Support consists of employees in five major, and multiple smaller worldwide centers who help eBay members make the most of their experience. Buyers and sellers can contact eBay through e-mail, text, chat, and phone twenty-four hours a day, seven days a week. eBay announced in April 2003 that Burnaby, British Columbia, part of the greater Vancouver metropolitan area, has been chosen as the site for its new international customer support center. This center will provide customer support to eBay members from its American, Canadian, and Australian Web sites. The Burnaby office will join existing operations in Salt Lake City, Omaha, and Dreilinden (Germany) to be eBay's fourth customer center worldwide.

EXHIBIT 1
Listing Fees

MINIMUM BID, OPENING VALUE OR RESERVE PRICE	LISTING FEE		SPECIAL CATEGORIES	LISTING FEE
$0.01–$9.99	$0.30		Passenger Vehicles or Other Vehicles	$40.00
$10.00–$24.99	$0.55			
$25.00–$49.99	$1.10		Motorcycles	$25.00
$50.00–$199.99	$2.20		Real Estate	$50.00–$300.00
$200.00 and up	$3.30			

RESERVE PRICE	RESERVE PRICE FEE*
$0.01–$24.99	$0.50
$25.00–$99.99	$1.00
$100.00 and up	1% of reserve price (up to a maximum fee of $100.00)

*Reserve price fee is fully refundable if item sells.

Source: eBay *Annual Report,* 2002.

The eBay Community

In providing a place for the trading of various items, eBay attempts to foster a sense of community among its users. CEO and President Meg Whitman has stated that eBay began with commerce but quickly grew into a very large community. eBay users believe that this sense of community is what separates it from other Internet auction and retail sites, and it invests heavily in the programs that make users feel that their transactions and information are safe from Internet thieves and fraudulent users.

One method used to establish the reputation of users is eBay's Feedback Forum, which encourages users to record comments, both favorable and unfavorable, about the trading partners. All this feedback information is recorded and creates a feedback rating for a specific person. Naturally, too many negative comments will likely cause users to avoid transactions with the individual in question.

eBay users' reputations are described with a percentage figure and star icons. The star is color-coded and indicates the amount of positive feedback that the user has received. A percentage value is also listed comparing the amount of positive to total feedback. Users may review a person's feedback profile prior to doing business with that person.

The Feedback Forum is a self-regulating system: Users police themselves. However, some users may be tempted to manipulate the system in order to discredit other users or to enhance their own reputations. eBay has several policies in place to prevent this, and the system has several automated features in place to detect and to prevent various forms of abuse.

Dealing with unknown individuals over the Internet can be a cause for concern for some and may cause many others to not use eBay. In order to ease users' fears, eBay has instituted what is called its SafeHarbor™ program, which provides trading guidelines and rules; provides information to help resolve disputes among users; provides addresses; and responds to misuse of the eBay system. The SafeHarbor™ group is organized into three areas: investigation, fraud prevention, and community watch. These groups investigate possible misuse of the system and will take appropriate action, which may include suspension from buying or selling on the site. SafeHarbor™ provides users with information to assist with disputes over the quality of goods and with possible fraudulent activities. If fraudulent activities occur, eBay will usually suspend the offending party or parties from further eBay activity. According to eBay, fewer than thirty auctions per million generate a possible fraud complaint. The company wants to lower the number of complaints and eliminate the potential for an unhappy experience. In response to fraud concerns, the company has established new rules preventing sellers from bidding on their own items; tougher ID checks; penalties if bidders do not complete transactions; and free buyer's insurance.

Because community plays such an important part in the eBay experience, the company has focused resources on its efforts to establish a community experience. The company believes that the eBay community is one of the strongest on the Internet. eBay offers a wide array of features that support the community, and these features solidify the eBay community and ensure its continued growth and loyalty. The company uses e-mail to provide users with category-specific chatrooms, the eBay café (a chatroom for the entire community), a bulletin board for feedback on new features, and announcements that cover new features and eBay news. Customer-support bulletin boards and an "items wanted" listing where users can post their requests for specific items are also provided.

My eBay gives users a report on recent activity, watch list, and favorite searches. Users who have their own Web pages can post links to their homepage, and those without a Web site can use About Me to create a homepage free of charge.

Revenue

There is no charge for buyers to shop on eBay. Bidding is free also. Revenue is derived from fees that sellers are charged for listing and selling items, as noted in Exhibit 1.

Additional revenue from listings can come in a variety of ways, as shown in Exhibit 2. eBay offers sellers many ways to enhance their listed items to attract bidders. Sellers can feature their auctions by paying additional incremental fees for various highlights.

If the seller is successful in selling his/her item, he/she must pay eBay a commission. At the time of notification of a winning bid, eBay charges the seller a final value fee based on the selling price. Final value fees are shown in Exhibit 3.

In the event that the buyer and seller cannot complete the transaction, the seller can notify eBay to credit the amount of the final fee. All invoices for placement fees, highlight fees, and successful selling fees are sent to sellers via e-mail on a monthly basis. Many sellers maintain credit accounts with eBay. At no time does eBay take possession of the merchandise or hold the receivable for the item.

eBay third-party advertising revenues come principally from the sale of online banner and sponsorship advertisements for cash and through barter

EXHIBIT 2
Feature Fees

SELLER FEATURE	DESCRIPTION	FEATURE FEE
Home Page Featured	Item is listed in a Special Featured section and is also rotated on the eBay home page.	$99.95
Featured Plus!	Item appears in the category's Featured Item section and in bidder's search results.	$19.95
Highlight	Item listing is emphasized with a colored band.	$5.00
Bold	Item title is listed in bold.	$1.00
Buy-It-Now	Allows the seller to close an auction instantly for a specified price.	$0.05

Source: eBay *Annual Report*, 2002.

EXHIBIT 3
Final Value Fees

SALE PRICE	FINAL VALUE FEE
Up to $25	5.25% of sale price
$25.01 to $1,000	Above plus 2.75% of amount over $25
Over $1,000	Above plus 1.5% of the amount over $1,000

SPECIAL CATEGORIES	FINAL VALUE FEE
Passenger Vehicles or Other Vehicles	$40.00
Motorcycles	$25.00

Source: eBay *Annual Report*, 2002.

arrangements. Third-party advertising net revenues are about 5 percent. These revenues were primarily from the U.S. segment.

Global Expansion and Acquisitions

eBay has become a truly global company. The corporation is establishing a strong presence in countries whose populations generate the majority of the world's e-commerce revenue like Germany, the United States, and England, and by the end of 2002, increased its presence in 27 countries. Today, eBay is present in 150 countries through wholly owned and majority owned subsidiaries and affiliates.

In 2002, eBay acquired NeoCom Technology Corporation, which is an online Chinese-language marketplace for the trading of goods and services in Taiwan. Also in 2002, eBay acquired the remaining 50 percent of the eBay Australia and New Zealand joint venture held by Ecorp Limited. For this transaction, eBay paid approximately $65.5 million. In October 2002, eBay acquired 100 percent of PayPal Inc., a company that provides a global payments platform.

In 2003, eBay paid $150 million to acquire the remaining outstanding stock of EachNet Inc., which, in cooperation with local subsidiaries, operates the leading e-commerce company in China. eBay's international net revenue increased 177 percent in 2002 due to strong performance in Germany, the United Kingdom, Canada, and South Korea. eBay's acquisitions in 2001 and 2002 are listed in Exhibit 4. In March 2002, eBay closed its subsidiary in Japan after two years of operation.

Growth

Since eBay was founded, growth has increased exponentially as measured by several factors. In all articles that list the sites that are visited the most, number of items listed, merchandise sales, registered users, number of log-ons, or number of minutes on the site per user, eBay is always one of the most popular sites on the Web. By all measures, eBay is one of the most active and widely visited Internet sites. For the month of August 2003, it was the fifth most-visited Web site in the United States, with a total audience of 33.15 million people.

EXHIBIT 4
Acquisitions

Company Name	Acquisition Date	Post Acquisition Ownership	Net Tangible Assets	Identifiable Intangible Assets	Deferred Tax Liabilities	Unearned Compensation	Goodwill	Minority Interest	Aggregate Purchase Price
Internet Auction	February 2001	50.1%	$ 67,670	$ 9,000	$ (3,600)	$ —	$ 82,691	$(33,834)	$ 121,927
iBazar	May 2001	100%	4,696	2,140	(856)	—	119,606	—	125,586
Billpoint	January 2002	100%	6,643	1,750	(700)	—	35,848	—	43,541
EachNet	March 2002	38%	9,379	2,280	(912)	—	19,253	—	30,000
NeoCom	April 2002	100%	1,446	165	(66)	—	9,760	—	11,305
PayPal	October 2002	100%	104,965	277,000	(34,958)	9,943	1,135,554	—	1,492,504
eBay Australia and New Zealand	October 2002	100%	444	4,650	(1,860)	—	62,266	—	65,500
Total			$195,243	$296,985	$(42,952)	$9,943	$1,464,978	$(33,834)	$1,890,363

Source: eBay *Annual Report,* 2002.

EXHIBIT 5
eBay Growth

YEAR ENDED DECEMBER 31 (IN MILLIONS)	2000	2001	2002
Supplemental Operating Data:			
Number of registered users at end of period	22.5	42.4	61.7
Number of items listed	264.7	423.1	638.3
Gross merchandise sales	$5,422	$9,319	$14,868
PayPal accounts at end of period	—	—	23.3
PayPal number of payments(1)	—	—	39.2
PayPal total payment volume(1)	—	—	$ 2,138

(1) Amounts shown are for the post-acquisition period from October 4, 2002 through December 21, 2002.
Source: eBay *Annual Report,* 2002.

Net income grew from $249 million at the end of 2002 to $447 million in 2003, as shown in Exhibit 7.

Marketing

Traditionally, eBay relied on word of mouth to promote its Web site and has occasionally used links and sponsorship with other Web sites. Today, it uses strategic purchase of online advertising in areas in which it can reach its target audience. It also has marketing activities in traditional media, such as TV, radio, trade shows,

EXHIBIT 6
eBay's Organizational Chart

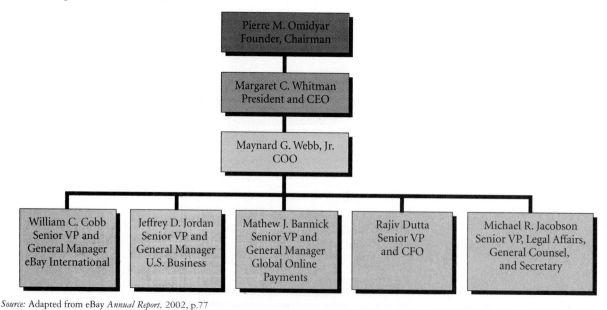

Source: Adapted from eBay *Annual Report,* 2002, p.77

and other events. eBay extended a contract it has with AOL until March 2004 and will pay AOL up to $15 million for its advertising services on a new user-performance basis.

eBay also has an agreement with The Walt Disney Company to provide advertisements and promotions, and develop a co-branded version of eBay's online service. By the end of 2002, eBay incurred $16.9 million in sales and marketing expenses associated with the Disney agreement. The company has agreements with Microsoft that obligate it to purchase software and related services through September 2003. Similarly, Microsoft agreed to buy online advertising and other services from eBay totaling $7 million through 2004.

Competition

The Internet has enabled millions of people worldwide to share information, communicate, and conduct electronic commerce transactions. According to Nielsen Net Ratings, 580 million people have Internet access. The United States accounts for 29 percent of the global Internet access universe, followed by Europe with 23 percent, Asia-Pacific with 13 percent, and Latin America with 2 percent.

Currently, eBay is the number-one online auction business and had one of the best performances in e-commerce and technology in 2003. eBay competes with several companies, serving particular categories of goods as well as those serving broader ranges of goods. Its competitors include traditional department and general merchandise stores such as Wal-Mart, Target, Sears, Sam's Club, and other online auction Web sites such as Yahoo! Auctions, Amazon, and uBid. At the present time, eBay dominates the online auction business and represents 2 percent of all of U.S. e-commerce transactions. eBay, Amazon, and Yahoo! Auctions lead the list of Web retailers.

Yahoo! Auctions is present in 25 international sites and generates most of its revenue from banner advertising sales and sponsorship ads. Yahoo! annual sales for 2002 were $953.1 million and the revenues for the six-month period ended 06/03 were $604.4 million. Four years ago Yahoo! executives were considering eBay as a possible acquisition. They opted, instead, to develop their own online auction business.

The biggest long-term threat to eBay's dominance in the Internet auction commerce is Amazon.com. The organization has customers in all 50 American states and more than 150 countries. Books, videos, and music are the core of the business. For the first quarter of 2003, Amazon's revenue was $2.2 billion. Amazon was the online department store most visited in August 2003, with 42.79 percent of market share.

The ACSI (American Customer Satisfaction Index), a study of customer satisfaction scored eBay an 82, Amazon an 88, and Yahoo! a 78. The highest score is 100. This score considers customer expectations, perceived quality, perceived value, customer complaints, and customer loyalty. In August 2003, eBay was the fifth most-visited Web site in the United States. Yahoo! was the third most-visited Web site, with an audience of 69.5 million people and with an average time spent per person of 116 minutes. The tenth most-visited Web site was Amazon, where 19.1 million people spent 16 minutes on average on the site.

The principal competitive factors for eBay include: brand recognition, ability to attract buyers, selection of goods, and customer service. With respect to eBay's online competition, additional competitive factors are community interaction, system reliability, the reliability of delivery and payment, Web site convenience and accessibility, level of service fees, and the quality of search tools. Some of eBay's competitors have great financial, marketing, and technical resources. As a result, eBay constantly monitors the activities of all competitors and adjusts its services to counter competitive activity. While eBay's rivals have been retrenching, the company has been expanding its own operations and maintaining its dominant status in auctions.

Government Regulations and Legal Proceedings

Because eBay does not take possession of any of the items that are sold on its site or hold any receivables for merchandise sold, the company does not collect sales taxes associated with the transactions. The individual seller must conduct any tax requirements resulting from transactions. Today, very few laws govern Internet sales. As Internet commerce becomes more popular, it is likely that laws will be enacted to address user contracts, privacy, price structures, freedom of expression, security, and other areas. Additional costs may result.

Third parties have claimed that eBay is infringing on intellectual property rights. eBay expects that it will increasingly be subject to infringement claims as the number of services and direct competitors grows. These claims could be time-consuming, result in costly litigation, cause service upgrade delays, require expensive changes in its methods of doing business, and may require eBay to enter into costly royalty or licensing agreements, if available. As a result, these claims could harm the business.

Financial Statements

eBay's income statement and balance sheet for 2001, 2002, and 2003 are provided in Exhibits 7 and 8. Note in these Exhibits that eBay has experienced remarkable growth and is financially in a great position. The company is one of few online Internet corporations to enjoy positive net income for the past four years.

eBay has two primary reporting segments: online and offline trading service. The online trading services segment consists of the operation of eBay, half.com, PayPal, and all other international online trading platforms. The offline segment consists of seller commissions, buyer premiums, and auction-related services. eBay reported in 2002 net revenues of $1.19 billion for online and $21.8 million for offline.

Conclusion

Early in 2004, virtually every Internet company is suffering with the poor economy and failing, but eBay has a very profitable Internet business and has become the number-one online auctioneer.

eBay has a great opportunity to grow as a global company. The organization may keep acquiring and making joint ventures with companies overseas and going after new markets; it may also improve its position as a business-to-business (B2B) trading platform. According to a quarterly review from the Institute for Supply Management and Forrester Research, 84 percent of large companies now use the Web to purchase materials and services. Hoping to extend its popularity into the small and midsized business markets, eBay launched a new section called eBay Business in February 2003.

EXHIBIT 7

eBay Inc.—Income Statement

IN MILLIONS OF U.S. DOLLARS (EXCEPT FOR PER SHARE ITEMS) AS OF DECEMBER 31	2003	2002	2001
Revenue	$2,165.1	1,214.1	748.8
Other Revenue	—	—	—
Total Revenue	**2,165.1**	**1,214.1**	**748.8**
Cost of Revenue	416.1	213.9	134.8
Gross Profit	**1,749.0**	**1,000.2**	**614.0**
Selling/General/Adm. Exp.	879.9	525.5	361.7
Research & Development	159.3	104.6	75.3
Depreciation/Amortization	50.7	15.9	36.6
Interest Expense (Income)	—	—	—
Unusual Expense (Income)	31.2	3.8	16.2
Other Operating Expenses	—	—	—
Total Operating Expense	**1,537.1**	**863.7**	**624.6**
Operating Income	**628.0**	**350.4**	**124.2**
Interest Expense	(4.3)	(1.5)	(2.9)
Interest/Investment Inc.	—	—	—
Interest Income (Expense)	(4.3)	(1.5)	(2.9)
Gain (Loss) on Sale of Assets	—	—	—
Other, Net	37.8	49.2	41.6
Income Before Tax	**661.5**	**398.1**	**162.9**
Income Tax	206.7	145.9	80.0
Income After Tax	**454.8**	**252.2**	**82.9**
Minority Interest	(7.6)	(2.3)	7.5
Equity In Affiliates	—	—	—
Net Inc. Before Extras	**447.2**	**249.9**	**90.4**
Accounting Change	(5.4)	0.0	—
Discontinued Operations	—	—	—
Extraordinary Item	—	—	—
Net Income	**$ 441.8**	**249.9**	**90.4**
Preferred Dividends	—	—	—
Income Available to Common	**447.2**	**249.9**	**90.4**
Inc. Avail. to Common Incl.	**441.8**	**249.9**	**90.4**
Wtd Avg. # Shares	638.3	575.0	537.9
Basic/Primary EPS	**0.701**	**0.435**	**0.168**
Basic/Primary EPS	**0.692**	**0.435**	**0.168**
Dilution Adjustment	0.0	0.0	0.0
Weighted Avg. Shares	656.7	585.6	561.2
Diluted EPS	**0.681**	**0.427**	**0.161**
Diluted EPS	**0.673**	**0.427**	**0.161**
Dividends per Share	0.000	0.000	0.000
Gross Dividends	0.0	0.0	0.0
Stock Based Compensation	—	186.9	208.4

Source: www.investor.stockpoint.com

EXHIBIT 8

eBay Inc.—Balance Sheet

IN MILLIONS OF U.S. DOLLARS (EXCEPT FOR PER SHARE ITEMS) AS OF DECEMBER 31	2003	2002	2001
Cash & Equivalents	$1,381.5	1,109.3	524.0
Short Term Investments	340.6	89.7	199.5
Cash and Short Term Investments	1,722.1	1,199.0	723.4
Trade Accounts Receivable	305.8	172.5	101.7
Other Receivables	—	—	—
Total Receivables, Net	305.8	172.5	101.7
Total Inventory	—	—	—
Prepaid Expenses	—	—	—
Other Current Assets	118.0	97.0	58.7
Total Current Assets	**2,145.9**	**1,468.5**	**883.8**
Property/Plant/Equipment	—	—	—
Accumulated Depreciation	—	(161.8)	(121.7)
Property/Plant/Equipment	601.8	218.0	142.3
Goodwill, Net	1,719.3	1,456.0	187.8
Intangibles, Net	274.1	279.5	10.8
Long Term Investments	934.2	470.2	287.0
Other Long Term Assets	144.9	148.0	166.7
Total Assets	**$5,820.1**	**4,040.2**	**1,678.5**
Accounts Payable	171.2	97.8	33.2
Accrued Expenses	356.5	199.3	94.6
Notes Payable/STerm Debt	2.8	3.0	16.1
Current Port. LT Debt	—	—	—
Other Current Liabilities	116.7	86.1	36.2
Total Current Liabilities	**647.3**	**386.2**	**180.1**
Long Term Debt	124.5	13.8	12.0
Capital Lease Obligations	—	—	—
Total Long Term Debt	**124.5**	**13.8**	**12.0**
Total Debt	**127.3**	**16.8**	**28.1**
Deferred Income Tax	79.2	27.6	3.6
Minority Interest	39.4	33.2	37.8
Other Liabilities	33.5	22.9	15.9
Total Liabilities	**$ 923.9**	**483.8**	**249.4**
Redeemable Preferred Stock	—	—	—
Preferred Stock	—	—	—
Common Stock	—	0.3	0.3
Additional Paid-In Capital	—	3,108.4	1,275.2
Retained Earnings	—	414.5	164.6
Treasury Stock—Common	—	—	—
Other Equity	4,896.2	33.2	(11.0)
Total Equity	**4,896.2**	**3,556.5**	**1,429.1**
Total Liability & Shareholder's Equity	**$5,820.1**	**4,040.2**	**1,678.5**
Shares Outs.—Common Stock	646.8	622.6	554.5
Total Com. Shares Outstanding	**646.8**	**622.6**	**554.5**
Total Preferred Stock Shares Outs.	—	—	—
Employees (actual figures)	—	4,000.0	2,560.0
Number of Shareholders	—	2,000.0	1,500.0

Source: www.investor.stockpoint.com

References

ebay Inc. *Annual Report*. December 2002.
"Hot links":

a. www.investor.stockpoint.com
b. www.strategyclub.com
c. www.marketguide.com
d. www.nielsen-netratings.com
e. www.hoovers.com
f. www.fortune.com
g. www.forbes.com
h. www.hoovers.com
i. www.ecommercetimes.com
j. www.nytimes.com
k. www.shareholder.com

7 Amazon.com, Inc.—2004

Corina San-Marina
Francis Marion University

Amzn

www.amazon.com

"So, this is the Amazon. Very cool. I've heard so much about it. Look, there is a parrot. Listen to the birds. The insects. The monkeys. Smell the tropical flowers. The Amazon sure is cool. It's nothing like their Web site." (Sherman's Lagoon)

"Our vision is the world's most customer-centric company. The place where people come to find and discover anything that they might want to buy online. The company's six core values: customer obsession, ownership, bias for action, frugality, high hiring bar, and innovation. The company motto: 'Work Hard, Have Fun, and Make History.'"

This is founder and CEO Jeff Bezos's view of Amazon.com. In less than seven years, Amazon.com went from zero to $3.2 billion-plus in sales. The company went from four people in a renovated garage to a 160,000 square-foot renovated former medical center and more than 7,500 employees in the United States and Europe. At year-end 2003, Amazon's sales were $5.26 billion, up from $3.93 billion in 2002.

History

Jeff Bezos is the eldest son of Miguel Bezos, an Exxon Corp. executive, and Jacklyn Gise Bezos. After graduating summa cum laude from Princeton University in 1986, Bezos joined FITEL, a high-tech start-up company in New York. Two years later, Bezos began working for Bankers Trust Company in New York, and in 1990 became the company's youngest vice president. From 1990 to 1994, Bezos worked for D. E. Shaw & Co., and in 1992 became its youngest senior vice president.

While working for Shaw & Co., Bezos was given the assignment to investigate Internet business opportunities and found that Web usage was growing 2,300 percent a year. Looking for the best product to be sold on the Web, Bezos compiled a list of possibilities. Music was eliminated because of the way the industry was set up, with six major record companies dominating the business and controlling the distribution. Selling computer software or office supplies was complicated because product description and comparison would have to be provided so the customer could make an informed decision. Bookselling was large and fragmented, with no dominant 800-pound gorillas. His final recommendation to David Shaw was selling books. To Bezos's surprise, the idea was rejected.

Bezos decided to resign and follow his idea. The next step was choosing a location. The criteria were: to be in an area with a large pool of technical talent; to be in a state with a relatively small population because only the residents of that state would be charged state sales tax; and finally, to be near a major book wholesaler. The choice was Seattle, Washington. The new company was incorporated in the state of Washington on July 5, 1994, as Cadabra, Inc, but was soon renamed Amazon.com and reregistered as a Delaware corporation. In November 1994, Jeff Bezos and two associates set up shop in a converted garage and began the task of creating Amazon.com. During the late spring of 1995, the company began beta-testing the Web site and in July 1995, began selling to the public.

Expansion 1996–2003

In 1996, "Get Big Fast" became the mantra at Amazon.com. The momentum began to pick up when Amazon.com secured $8 million in cash based on a $60 million valuation. The capital raised was used for heavy advertising, to build brand recognition, and to hire the best middle managers and executives. On May 15, 1997, the company went public with an opening price of $18 a share. Amazon.com began doing more of its own distribution. Bezos also wanted to extend Amazon.com's presence beyond the borders of the United States. In April 1998, the company acquired Bookpages, a British electronic bookstore, and Telebuch (Telebook) Inc., a major online bookstore in Germany. They were renamed Amazon.co.uk. and Amazon.co.de., and relaunched in October.

The mantra for 1999 and 2000 was "Get Bigger Faster." In 1999, the company bought 46 percent of drugstore.com and launched its own auction site to challenge eBay, the market leader in person-to-person auctions. Also, the company bought 50 percent of Pets.com. The next move was acquiring 1.7 percent stake in Sotheby's Holdings. The two companies formed a joint online auction site, sothebys.amazon.com. In 1999, Amazon.com paid $200 million to acquire e-Niche, Inc., and MusicFind, and then bought Accept.com and Alexa Internet Co. Also in 1999, Amazon.com bought 35 percent of HomeGrocer.com, 49 percent of Gear.com, and introduced zShops, which was Amazon.com's online mall. It also added tools, video games, software, gifts, and a co-branded credit card with Nextcard Inc.

In 2000, Amazon.com launched amazon.co.jp with a comprehensive book catalog as well as amazon.fr in France. In 2001, it opened the Amazon.com Travel store and announced plans to open a Target store at **www.amazon.com**, which expanded product offerings available at Amazon.com. Other partnerships for 2001 were with BabiesRUS, ToysRUS, and Borders Group.

In 2002, Virgin Entertainment Group and Amazon.com relaunched **www.virginmega.com** as a co-branded Web site. Office Depot, the world's largest seller of office products, and Amazon.com announced an e-commerce strategic alliance with the launch of the Office Products store at Amazon.com. Also in 2002, Amazon.com launched Amazon.ca, bringing Canadians the selection, convenience, and value of the Amazon shopping experience.

In January 2003, Amazon.com announced that the Free Super Saver Shipping on orders over $25 is going to be available year-round. The company also offers free shipping options at its U.K., German, French, Japanese, and Canadian sites. In April 2003, amazon.de and amazon.co.uk opened new shops for kitchen and housewares. In June 2003, Amazon.ca launched two new stores—Software and Computer and Video Games. These new stores mark the first expansion of Amazon.ca's product offering beyond books, music, videos, and DVDs.

In July 2003, Amazon.co.jp announced the launch of its new Electronics store. The launch marks the fourth Electronics store for Amazon.com, which also offers electronics items on Amazon.com, Amazon.co.uk, and Amazon.de. In August 2003, Amazon.com announced an extension of its e-commerce agreement with Target Corporation. This amended contract extends the original five-year agreement to August 2008. In September 2003, Amazon.com launched its new Sporting Goods store—offering more than 3,000 popular brands covering more than 50 sports. The company also announced it has teamed up with Los Angeles Clipper Elton Brand and sporting goods merchants to support Boys' and Girls' Clubs of America.

EXHIBIT 1
Organizational Chart

JEFFREY BEZOS
PRESIDENT, CEO & CHAIRMAN OF THE BOARD

Richard Dalzell	Mark Peek	Diego Piacentini	Thomas Szkutak	Jeff Wilke	Michelle Wilson
Senior VP, CIO	VP, Chief Accounting Officer	Senior VP, Worldwide Retail & Marketing	Senior VP, CFO	Senior VP, Worldwide Operations & Customer Service	Senior VP, HR, General Counsel & Secretary

Source: Adapted from Amazon.com *Annual Report,* 2002, p. 17.

Internal Assessment

One of the reasons Amazon.com is successful is the corporate culture that Bezos has tried to create since the company's inception. For Bezos, corporate culture is "a blend of 30 percent what you set out for it to be, 30 percent who your early employees happen to be, and 40 percent random chance." Ever since its inception, Bezos has been involved in hiring the best professionals he could find. He lured executives from Wal-Mart, Microsoft, Barnes & Noble, and Symantec, covering areas such as marketing, software development, financing, and distribution. Exhibit 1 shows the organizational chart for Amazon.com.

Building a strong brand name was another of Jeff Bezos's objectives. The Amazon.com brand name is mainly derived from two areas: a large product selection complemented by additional information about these products; and pricing policy which offers considerable discounts for many of its products. Amazon.com is the fifty-seventh most-valuable brand worldwide, according to a report from a British marketing firm. The brand is recognized by over 52 percent of adults in the United States and Europe. Marketing expenses, net of cooperative marketing reimbursements, were $125 million, $138 million, and $180 million for 2002, 2001, and 2000, representing 3, 4, and 7 percent of net sales, respectively. In January 2003, advertisement expenses were reduced compared with previous years in an effort to provide customers with everyday low prices and free shipping for qualified orders.

Amazon.com has built a strong customer service support. The company offers comprehensive help files on its Web sites, and in addition to positive feedback, it seeks to maximize customized services by providing fast acknowledgement of orders, and fast responses on customer queries. There is also a round-the-clock telephone service. Exhibit 2 presents the Customer Service Center locations.

Amazon.com has developed a proprietary technology called "1-Click," which automatically invokes all the relevant customer details by one click of the mouse on repeat orders. Amazon.com also launched Amazon Friends & Favorites, an area that gives customers the opportunity to help each other discover products and services. In a 2002 American Customer Satisfaction Index, Amazon.com scored 88, the highest score ever recorded in any service industry.

The Associates Program, started in 1996, allows the company to establish exclusive contracts with owners of cyberspace real estate. The program enables associated Web sites to make their products available to their respective audiences, with order fulfillment by Amazon.com. Amazon.com has currently enrolled 530,000 Web sites in the Associates Program.

Amazon.com has invested heavily in automated distribution centers across the United States and overseas, and has the infrastructure to fill customer orders faster than the competition, especially in peak periods like the holidays. Analysts agree that

EXHIBIT 2
Customer Service Centers

1. Tacoma, Washington
2. Huntington, West Virginia
3. Grand Forks, North Dakota
4. Slough, United Kingdom
5. Regensburg, Germany
6. Sapporo, Japan
7. India (has outsourcing agreement with Daksh.com)

Source: Amazon.com *Annual Report,* 2002, p. 4.

EXHIBIT 3
Distribution Centers

1. Fernley, Nevada
2. Coffeyville, Kansas
3. Campbellsville, Kentucky
4. Lexington, Kentucky
5. New Castle, Delaware
6. Grand Forks, North Dakota
7. Marston Gate, United Kingdom
8. Orléans, France
9. Bad Hersfeld, Germany
10. Japan (joint management with Nippon Express)
11. Canada (joint management with Assured Logistics)

Source: Amazon.com *Annual Report,* 2002, p. 4.

this infrastructure gives Amazon.com tremendous competitive advantage over other online competitors. Plus, operating a handful of automated warehouses is still far cheaper and easier than operating a thousand retail stores. Exhibit 3 presents Amazon.com's Distribution Center locations.

Software and technology are the real assets of Amazon.com. It has a continuous program to add additional software and hardware and further develop and upgrade its existing technology, transaction-processing systems, and network infrastructure. This need is particularly acute given the increasing traffic on its Web site and expanding sales volume through its transaction-processing systems. Technology and content expenses were $216 million, $241 million, and $269 million for 2002, 2001, and 2000, representing 5, 8, and 10 percent of net sales, respectively.

Financial Results—2003
Exhibits 4 and 5 present the Income Statement and Balance Sheet for 2001–2003.

Business Structure
Amazon.com has organized operations into four principal segments:

- The Books, Music, and Video/DVD (BMVD) Segment includes retail sales from **www.amazon.com** and **www.amazon.ca**, commissions from sales through Amazon Marketplace, Merchants@ program, and Syndicated Stores program. Net sales were $1.87 billion, $1.69 billion, and $1.70 billion in 2002, 2001, and 2000, respectively.
- The Electronics, Tools, and Kitchen (ETK) Segment includes retail sales from amazon.com and mail-order catalog sales, commissions from sales through Amazon Marketplace, Merchants@ program, and Syndicated Stores program. Net sales were $645 million, $547 million, and $484 million in 2002, 2001, and 2000, respectively.
- The International Segment includes all retail sales from the international sites **www.amazon.co.uk**, **www.amazon.de**, **www.amazon.fr**, **www.amazon.co.jp**. Net sales were $1.17 billion, $661 million, and $381 million in 2002, 2001, and 2000, respectively.
- The Services Segment consists of commissions, fees, and other amounts earned from the services business, Auctions, zShops, Amazon Payments, and miscellaneous marketing and promotional agreements. Net sales were $246 million, $225 million, and $198 million in 2002, 2001, and 2000, respectively.

EXHIBIT 4

Amazon.com Inc.—Income Statement

IN MILLIONS OF U.S. DOLLARS (EXCEPT FOR PER SHARE ITEMS) AS OF DECEMBER 31	2003	2002	2001
Revenue	$5,263.7	3,932.9	3,122.4
Other Revenue	—	—	—
Total Revenue	**5,263.7**	**3,932.9**	**3,122.4**
Cost of Revenue	4,006.5	2,940.3	2,323.9
Gross Profit	**1,257.2**	**992.6**	**798.6**
Selling/General/Adm. Exp.	775.9	665.8	607.0
Research & Development	207.8	215.6	241.2
Depreciation/Amortization	2.8	5.5	181.0
Interest Expense (Income)	—	—	—
Unusual Expense (Income)	0.1	41.6	181.6
Other Operating Expenses	—	—	—
Total Operating Expense	**4,993.1**	**3,868.8**	**3,534.7**
Operating Income	**270.6**	**64.1**	**(412.3)**
Interest Expense	(130.0)	(142.9)	(139.2)
Interest/Investment Inc.	22.0	23.7	29.1
Interest Income (Expense)	(108.0)	(119.2)	(110.1)
Gain (Loss) on Sale of Assets	(129.7)	(96.3)	(2.1)
Other, Net	2.8	5.6	(1.9)
Income Before Tax	**35.7**	**(145.8)**	**(526.4)**
Income Tax	0.0	0.0	0.0
Income After Tax	**35.7**	**(145.8)**	**(526.4)**
Minority Interest	—	—	—
Equity in Affiliates	(0.4)	(4.2)	(30.3)
Net Income Before Extra.	**35.3**	**(149.9)**	**(556.8)**
Accounting Change	0.0	0.8	(10.5)
Discontinued Operations	—	—	—
Extraordinary Item	—	—	—
Net Income	$ **35.3**	**(149.1)**	**(567.3)**
Preferred Dividends	—	—	—
Income Available to Com.	35.3	(149.9)	(556.8)
Income Available to Com.	**35.3**	**(149.1)**	**(567.3)**
Weighted Avg. Shares	395.5	378.4	364.2
Basic/Primary EPS	**0.089**	**(0.396)**	**(1.529)**
Basic/Primary EPS	**0.089**	**(0.394)**	**(1.558)**

Source: www.investor.stockpoint.com

Starting with the first quarter of 2003, Amazon.com reports its operating results along two lines: North America and International. The North America segment consists of amounts earned from retail sales through **www.amazon.com** and **www.amazon.ca**, Syndicated Stores and mail-order catalogs, Merchant.com, marketing, and promotional agreements. The International segment consists of amounts earned from retail sales through **www.amazon.co.uk**, **www.amazon.de**,

EXHIBIT 5

Amazon.com Inc.—Balance Sheet

IN MILLIONS OF U.S. DOLLARS (EXCEPT FOR PER SHARE ITEMS) AS OF DECEMBER 31	2003	2002	2001
Cash & Equivalents	$1,102.3	738.3	540.3
Short Term Investments	292.6	562.7	456.3
Cash and Short Term Investments	1,394.8	1,301.0	996.6
Trade Accounts Receivable, Net	—	—	—
Other Receivables	—	—	—
Total Receivables, Net	—	—	—
Total Inventory	293.9	202.4	143.7
Prepaid Expenses	132.1	112.3	67.6
Other Current Assets	—	—	—
Total Current Assets	**1,820.8**	**1,615.7**	**1,207.9**
Property/Plant/Equipment	—	—	
Accumulated Depreciation	—	(243.3)	(166.4)
Property/Plant/Equipment, Net	224.3	239.4	271.8
Goodwill, Net	69.1	70.8	45.4
Intangibles, Net	0.5	3.5	34.4
Long Term Investments	14.8	15.4	28.4
Other Long Term Assets	32.5	45.7	49.8
Total Assets	**$2,162.0**	**1,990.4**	**1,637.5**
Accounts Payable	819.8	618.1	444.7
Accrued Expenses	317.7	314.9	305.1
Notes Payable/Short Term Debt	—	—	—
Current Port. LT Debt/Capital Leases	4.2	13.3	15.0
Other Current Liabilities	110.9	119.6	156.6
Total Current Liabilities	**1,252.7**	**1,066.0**	**921.4**
Long Term Debt	1,945.4	2,277.3	2,156.1
Capital Lease Obligations	—	—	—
Total Long Term Debt	**1,945.4**	**2,277.3**	**2,156.1**
Total Debt	**1,949.7**	**2,290.6**	**2,171.1**
Deferred Income Tax	—	—	—
Minority Interest	—	—	—
Other Liabilities	—	—	—
Total Liabilities	**$3,198.1**	**3,343.3**	**3,077.5**
Redeemable Preferred Stock	—	—	—
Preferred Stock—Non Redeemable, Net	—	—	—
Common Stock	4.0	3.9	3.7
Additional Paid-In Capital	1,899.4	1,649.9	1,462.0
Retained Earnings (Accum. Deficit)	(2,974.4)	(3,009.7)	(2,860.6)
Treasury Stock—Common	—	—	—
Other Equity	34.9	3.1	(45.9)
Total Equity	**(1,036.1)**	**(1,352.8)**	**(1,440.0)**
Total Liability & Shareholders' Equity	**$2,162.0**	**1,990.4**	**1,637.5**
Shares Outs.—Common Stock	403.4	387.9	373.2
Total Common Shares Outstanding	**403.4**	**387.9**	**373.2**
Total Preferred Stock Shares Outs.	—	—	—
Employees (actual figures)	7,800.0	7,500.0	7,800.0
Number of Common Shareholders	—	4,229.0	4,013.0

Source: www.investor.stockpoint.com

EXHIBIT 6

Historical Segment Information for 2001–2002 (in thousands)

HISTORICAL SEGMENT INFORMATION	YEARS ENDED DECEMBER 31,	
	2002	2001
North America		
Net sales	$2,761,457	$2,460,336
Cost of sales	2,020,472	1,803,107
Gross profit	740,985	657,229
Direct segment operating expenses	561,318	599,728
Segment operating income (loss)	179,667	57,501
International		
Net sales	1,171,479	662,097
Cost of sales	919,846	520,768
Gross profit	251,633	141,329
Direct segment operating expenses	251,198	243,832
Segment operating income (loss)	435	(102,503)
Consolidated		
Net sales	3,932,936	3,122,433
Cost of sales	2,940,318	2,323,875
Gross profit	992,618	798,558
Direct segment operating expenses	812,516	843,560
Segment operating income (loss)	180,102	(45,002)
Stock-based compensation	68,927	4,637
Amortization of other intangibles	5,478	181,033
Restructuring-related and other	41,573	181,585
Income from operations	64,124	(412,257)
Total nonoperating expenses, net	(209,888)	(114,170)
Equity in losses of equity-method, net	(4,169)	(30,327)
Cumulative effect of change in accounting principle	801	(10,523)
Net income (loss)	$ (149,132)	$ (567,277)

Source: www.amazon.com/investorrelations/financialanalysis.

www.amazon.fr, and **www.amazon.co.jp**, Syndicated Stores, and international focused marketing and promotional agreements. The financial results for these two segments are presented in Exhibit 6. Note that in the year 2002, the International segment for the first time had a positive operating income of $435,000. In 2002, the North America segment had an operating income of $179.6 million compared with the 2001 operating income of $57.5 million.

Business Model

Amazon.com has pioneered a new business model for electronic commerce. It has transformed the book trade from a commodity-based, supplier-driven industry into a service-based, book-buying community. It has built up an extensive community of buyers through positive feedback, and in addition, has accumulated a substantial database of customers' preferences and buying patterns, tied to their e-mail and postal addresses. Such information has enabled Amazon.com to build up a large community of loyal customers, generating an impressive "repeat orders" rate of over

70 percent. Amazon.com has pioneered syndicate selling on the Web—Web sites passing clients on to each other by implementing links and taking a commission on sales.

Second, the business model has broken the principle of critical mass for the book market. For the first time, small and independent publishers as well as authors could place their products directly in an online store with global reach and without investments. Amazon.com has created two segments: business-to-consumers (B2C) e-commerce and business-to-business (B2B) e-commerce. The two groups that specialize in B2B e-commerce are Amazon Advantage, which offers services for publishers, and Amazon Associates, which deals with book resellers.

Online retailing is a low-margin affair and the ease with which comparison-shopping can be done on the Internet will always keep prices low. In a low-margin business, the companies that ultimately succeed are those that can keep operating costs low. Amazon.com, being the largest, is in the process of building efficiencies of scale. This means not only cost savings in terms of its massive bulk buying power with suppliers, but also in terms of the fast and efficient distribution system Amazon.com has set up. Cost savings that Amazon.com can pass on to its consumers and which ultimately should lead the company to a profit.

External Assessment

The Internet Tax Freedom Act, enacted in 1998, prohibits taxes on Internet access; taxation by multiple states on products purchased over the Internet; and discriminatory taxes that treat Internet purchases differently from other types of sales. The law expired in October 2001, but President Bush extended the ban on Internet taxes until November 1, 2003. At the beginning of 2003, Representative Cox and Senator Wyden introduced legislation to extend indefinitely the ban on new and discriminatory taxes on the Internet, arguing that "Given the continued softness in the tech economy, this is hardly the time for new taxes on the Internet. Rather, providing long-term certainty about tax policy is one of the necessary ingredients for a tech rebound." Also, President Bush promised that he will sustain any moratorium on Internet taxes.

In July 2003, Internet companies AOL Time Warner Inc., eBay Inc., and Amazon.com started levying hefty new taxes on products downloaded by customers in Europe over the Internet, including software, music, and videos. Until then, these sales, including eBay's auction services, had escaped value-added tax (VAT). Physical products such as books and cameras purchased on the Internet and shipped to customers in Europe were already subject to VAT.

The number of Internet users will continue to grow strongly in the next five years. Most of the growth is coming from Asia, Latin America, and parts of Europe. By year-end 2005, the number of worldwide Internet users will double to 1.12 billion. The number of Internet users in the United States will be 193 million in 2004 and 236 million in 2007; in Western Europe it will be 208 million in 2004 and 290 million in 2007; in Asia-Pacific it will be 357 million in 2004 and 612 million in 2007. The average American Internet user is young, white, employed, well educated, affluent, and suburban. Gender is balanced equally among Internet users. Only 8 percent of Internet users are black and 9 percent Hispanic, compared to 77 percent whites. Forty-seven percent of users are between 30 and 49 years old, 29 percent between 18 and 29 years old, 18 percent between 50 and 64 years old, and 4 percent older than 65. The level of education also is an important factor: 37 percent of users have college and/or graduate school degrees; 34 percent have some college education, compared to 5 percent who are not high school graduates. Fifty-two percent of users live in a suburban location, 26 percent in an urban location, and 21 percent in a rural community.

Improved technology such as broadband access helps Internet retailers. According to an ACNielsen survey, consumers with high-speed Internet connections express the most confidence in what the Internet can offer, beating out dial-up users by 21 percent. ACNielsen says the difference between the two groups can be attributed to broadband users' increased comfort levels with online credit-card use, plus the convenience of faster Internet access. A Nielsen//Netratings study showed that 33.6 million U.S. residents accessed the Internet via a broadband connection in December 2002—a 59 percent increase from a year earlier. Besides the convenience of an always-on Internet connection, broadband users also have access to more multi-media shopping experiences, including use of 3D virtual models, 360-degree virtual-reality tours, and audio and video tools that let them view and evaluate products more thoroughly before making a purchase.

Global Issues

Latino and Hispanic Americans represent the fastest-growing online ethnic group, according to new data from Nielsen//NetRatings. Based on the research group's find-ings, the number of Latinos online in the United States grew to 7.6 million in 2003—a 13 percent jump from 2001, marking the greatest increase of any ethnic group. The rate of Hispanic and Latino Americans coming online also far outpaced the national average, which expanded at 3 percent during the same period, to about to 105 mil-lion. Minority groups respond well to advertising specifically targeted to them. A recent study from Knowledge Networks/SRI and The Home Technology Monitor indicates that Latinos are more likely to own devices like PDAs, DVD players, and home theaters than other ethnic groups.

Currency fluctuation also plays an important role for Amazon.com. Recently, the dollar slumped to a 33-month low against the yen. There are concerns over the effects the rising yen will have on exports. According to Briefing.com, the dollar's weaker position compared to the yen and the euro is in no way a negative for U.S. stocks or business—as the profits of multinational companies are boosted by a lower dollar. A weaker dollar means that imports cost more in the United States, which improves the competitive position of U.S. companies both here and abroad. Furthermore, a weaker dollar increases the dollar value of profits achieved in yen, or other currencies. A weaker dollar has a broad, positive impact on the U.S. economy.

The Euro area is expected to recover modestly during 2004. Economic senti-ment and consumer confidence continued to decline in both January and February of 2003. In the International Monetary Fund's 2003 World Economic Outlook, the projected 1.1 percent gross domestic product (GDP) growth for the Euro region is slightly higher than its 2002 GDP growth. This pickup in growth is expected to come primarily from declining energy prices. A reduction in oil prices would boost real disposable incomes, increase consumption, and correspondingly decrease inventory stockpiles. All of these factors should expand business investments and boost business and consumer sentiment, as well as be positive for the Euro. Of par-ticular concern is the economic performance of the European Union's largest coun-tries, Germany and France. There is a lack of evidence that Germany could rebound from its current state of stagnation. [However, the country] continues to be weak, with the jobless rate at three-year highs, retail sales declining, and business confi-dence weakening. France's outlook is also negative, marked by weak consumer con-fidence and a soft labor market. The economies of France and Germany are funda-mentally weak and unless they find measures to turn their economies around, they will pose severe risks for further Euro appreciation when the U.S. economy begins to recover.

E-Commerce

Electronic commerce is growing and thriving in many parts of the world. Asia and the Pacific lead the developing world in the deployment of broadband, government support for the new technologies, and workforce computer skills. Fifty million new Internet users are going online in the region each year. Latin America is also progressing, though the greatest Internet advances are being made by only a handful of countries in the region. As many as 70 percent of Latin American enterprises have Internet access and are expanding in B2B. Africa is the farthest behind of the developing regions. There was a 30 percent increase in data traffic from the continent last year, but rate of use among the population remains low—only 1 in 118.

Elsewhere in the world, the transition economies are seeing a rapid rise in both B2B and B2C, but very modest volumes overall, and it is unlikely that e-commerce there will reach 1 percent of global e-commerce before 2005. B2C volumes remain considerably lower in Europe, however, and although the arrival of the "physical" euro has probably encouraged more intra-European e-commerce, in some sectors the market remains fragmented due to cultural and linguistic barriers and differing consumer preferences.

According to the United Nations Conference on Trade and Development report, *E-Commerce and Development Report 2002,* developing countries accounted for almost one-third of new Internet users worldwide in 2001. Worldwide e-commerce estimates range from $1.5 billion to $3.8 billion in 2003. In one of the most optimistic forecasts, e-commerce would represent about 18 percent of worldwide business-to-business and retail transactions in 2006.

Competitors

According to The State of Retailing Online 6.0, a Shop.org annual study conducted by Forrester Research of more than 130 retailers, online retail sales soared to $76 billion in 2002, up 48 percent over the prior year. Online sales reached 4.5 percent of total retail sales in 2003, up from 3.6 percent in 2002 and 2.4 percent in 2001. Online retail sales grew 26 percent in 2003 to $96 billion. According to the study, several product categories have reached double-digit penetration of total retail sales: 32 percent of computer hardware and software are sold online; 17 percent of event tickets are sold online; and 12 percent of books are sold online. In 2003, nine categories exceeded 5 percent penetration compared with seven categories in 2002.

Due to the low barriers to entry, Amazon.com will always have meaningful competition, certainly as more and more offline companies are coming online. Until recently, bricks-and-mortar retailers had rarely shown a coherent online strategy, but this is changing fast. Some of the biggest competitors that the company is facing are Wal-Mart, Barnes & Noble, and eBay.

Wal-Mart

Wal-Mart Stores, Inc., is the world's largest retailer. As of July 2003, there were 1,508 Wal-Mart stores, 1,356 Supercenters, 528 Sam's Clubs, and 53 Neighborhood Markets in the United States. Internationally, Wal-Mart operates units in Argentina (11), Brazil (24), Canada (213), Germany (92), Mexico (610), Puerto Rico (52), South Korea (15), and the United Kingdom (260) and under joint venture agreements, in China (28). The company employs more than 1.3 million associates worldwide.

Founded in January 2000, Wal-mart.com is a subsidiary of Wal-Mart Stores, Inc., with headquarters in the San Francisco Bay area. Wal-Mart, along with VC firm Accel Partners, made a $100 million investment in Walmart.com, spinning off the company into an independent entity, with Accel controlling 20 percent of

Walmart.com. Walmart.com offers 600,000 products including: music (80,000 titles), books (500,000), movies (10,000), sporting goods, home and garden items, jewelry, toys, video games, photography items, electronics, and computers. In 2003 it introduced DVD rental online for $15.54 per month. Both companies are similar in the items they sell on the Internet; the differences lie in the prices and services the Web sites offer. Talks about a possible merger between Amazon.com and Walmart.com, with Amazon.com running the Wal-Mart site have not materialized. At the present moment, Amazon.com is the Wal-Mart of the online retailing.

Barnes & Noble

Barnes & Noble is the largest U.S. bookseller, with 868 bookstores as of September 15, 2003. Through its 75 percent interest in Barnes&Noble.com, Inc., the company is also one of the largest online booksellers. In addition, through its 63 percent interest in GameStop Corp., Barnes & Noble operates 1,393 video game and entertainment software stores. Barnes & Noble operates 886 bookstores, 628 stores operate under the Barnes & Noble Booksellers, Bookstop, and Bookstar trade names and 258 stores operate under the B. Dalton Bookseller, Doubleday Book Shops, and Scribner's Bookstore trade names.

Since opening its online store in March 1997, Barnes&Noble.com has attracted more than 14.4 million customers in 230 countries. Barnes&Noble.com offers its customers fast delivery, easy and secure ordering, and rich editorial content. According to Jupiter Media Metrix, in December 2002, Barnes & Noble's Web site was the ninth most-trafficked shopping site and was among the top 50 largest Web properties on the Internet. For the fourth quarter of 2002, Barnes&Noble.com received one of the top three scores in customer satisfaction of the 190 companies contained in the latest American Customer Satisfaction Index (ACSI), a quarterly survey of consumer attitudes by the University of Michigan. In addition, Barnes&Noble.com scored 87 out of 100, an increase of 6.1 percent over the prior year's rating and 13.0 percent over the past three years.

In September 2003, the company acquired Bertelsmann's 36.8 percent interest in Barnes & Noble, for $164 million. As a result of its acquisitions of Babbage's Etc. and Funco in October 1999 and June 2000, respectively, Barnes & Noble is the largest U.S. video game and PC entertainment software specialty retailer. The company publishes books under the Barnes & Noble Books imprint, for exclusive sale through its retail stores and mail-order catalogs. In January 2003, Barnes & Noble acquired Sterling Publishing Co., Inc., a leading publisher of how-to books, for $126 million.

In 2002 sales increased 4.5 percent to $422.8 million from $404.6 million in the previous year. The company expects net sales to range between $430 million and $470 million for the year ended December 31, 2003. In 2002 gross profit increased to $95.6 million from $91.2 million as a result of the company's 4.5 percent increase in net sales.

eBay

eBay is The World's Online Marketplace™ for the sale of goods and services by a diverse community of individuals and businesses. Today, the eBay community includes tens of millions of registered members from around the world. People spend more time on eBay than any other online site, making it the most popular shopping destination on the Internet. On any given day, there are more than 16 million items listed on eBay across 27,000 categories. In 2002, eBay members transacted $14.87 billion in annualized gross merchandise sales.

People come to the eBay marketplace to buy and sell items across multiple categories, including antiques and art, books, business and industrial, cars and other vehicles, clothing and accessories, coins, collectibles, crafts, dolls and bears, electronics and computers, home furnishings, jewelry and watches, movies and DVDs, music, musical instruments, pottery and glass, real estate, sporting goods and memorabilia, stamps, tickets, toys and hobbies, and travel.

eBay has local sites that serve Australia, Austria, Belgium, Canada, France, Germany, Ireland, Italy, Korea, the Netherlands, New Zealand, Singapore, Spain, Sweden, Switzerland, Taiwan, and the United Kingdom. In addition, eBay has a presence in Latin America and China through its investments in MercadoLibre.com and EachNet, respectively. eBay offers a wide variety of features and services that enable members to buy and sell on the site quickly and conveniently. Buyers have the option to purchase items in auction-style format or items can be purchased at fixed price through a feature called Buy-It-Now. In addition, items at a fixed price are also available at **half.com**, an eBay company.

Conclusion

According to Value Line Investment Survey, the outlook for the Internet industry continues to improve, fueled by the improving domestic economy and robust online revenues. E-retail sales exceeded $100 billion in 2003, more than a 25 percent increase over 2002. Internet advertising rose steadily in 2003, following two years of steep declines. Develop a three-year strategic plan for Amazon.com.

References

Amazon.com, Inc. *Annual Report,* 10-K.

Berry, John. "Fed Holds Rates Steady, Citing Risks." Retrieved from **www.washingtonpost. com/wp-dyn/articles/A21711–2003Sep16.html**.

Computer Almanac Industry. "Internet Users Will Top 1 Billion in 2005." Retrieved from **www.c-i-a.com/pr032102.htm**.

cox.house.gov/.

Gongloff, Mark. "Will the Job Market Ever Get Better?" Retrieved from **money.cnn.com/ 2003/07/02/news/economy/jobs_walkup/**.

Greenspan, Robyn (June 2003). "Internet Not for Everyone." *The Big Picture Demographics.* Retrieved from **cyberatlas.internet.com/big_picture/demographics/article/0,,5901_ 2192251,00.html**.

retailindustry.about.com/library/weekly/01/aa010327a.htm.

Saunders, Christopher. "Latinos Outpace Other Groups' Online Growth." *The Big Picture Demographics.* Retrieved from **cyberatlas.internet.com/big_picture/demographics/ article/0,1323,5901_1428231,00**.

Standard & Poor's 500 *Industry Survey.* August 2003.

The Value Line Investment Survey (Part 3—Ratings & Reports) 58 (52) (August), p. 222.

www.amazon.com.

www.census.gov/mrts/www/current.html.

www.ecommercetimes.com/perl/story/20512.html.

www.dailyfx.com/currency_euro_forecast.html.

www.multexinvestor.com/KeyDevelopments.

www.theacsi.org/fourth_quarter.htm#ret.

www.ug.it.usyd.edu.au/isys1003/assignments/amazoncase.doc.

www.usabilitynews.com/news/article637.asp.

www.usatoday.com/tech/news/techpolicy/2003–07–31-tax-ban-advances_x.htm.

www.usembassy.it/pdf/other/RL31293.pdf.

www.usembassy.it/file2002_11/alia/a2112012.htm.

8

The Kroger Company—2003

Alen Badal
The Union Institute

KR

www.kroger.com

The Kroger Company, with its headquarters in Cincinnati, Ohio (513–762–4000), achieved annual sales of $ 51.8 billion in 2003, compared to $ 50.1 billion in 2002, and a net income of over $1.5 billion in 2003.[1] The company has been in existence for over 100 years and is the number-one grocery chain in the United States with over 2,400 grocery stores represented in 32 states.[2] Kroger and its subsidiary operations market food/drug, food processing, and jewelry commodities, and have approximately 290,000 employees.[3] Note that Kroger's fiscal year ends in February.

While the majority of the company's operations are in food/drug, The Kroger Company totals about 3,600 businesses under many banners, such as Barclay, Fred Meyer, and Littman jewelry stores; and Food4Less, to mention a few.[4] The company continues to expand its food businesses, and in 1999 acquired the Fred Meyer operations of about 800 stores in the West, for about $13 billion. It also purchased 20 former Hannaford locations in Virginia (in 2000) and 17 food-store locations from Fleming.[5] The purpose of continuous expansion is to reduce the company's debt.[6] Additional expansion into the West included purchases of 18 Raley's stores in Las Vegas, Nevada, each averaging 46,000 square feet.[7]

History

Experience in the industry dating back more than a century has yielded a number-one position for Kroger within the supermarket chain. This company is best described as driven by charitable contributions to the community, delivering a diverse product line, and expanding store locations within the United States. In 1883, The Kroger Company, pioneered by Barney Kroger, emerged and began its business in the supermarket chain industry.[8] The financial milestones of Kroger which began over a century ago, are shown in Exhibit 1.

Many recent unfortunate and negative events in the United States have affected the supermarket chain industry and Kroger. Unforeseen events, such as the September 11 attacks, have had a direct impact on our economy. More specifically, Kroger has been impacted by industry competition/consolidation and a generally slow economy.[9] Bankruptcies and unemployment rates have also caused the economy to decline.

The national retailer Wal-Mart has had an influence on all grocers as its presence is felt not only in the United States but abroad as well. Wal-Mart's Supercenters have emerged as the leading sellers of groceries.[10] However, Kroger is the number-one pure grocery chain in the United States.[11]

EXHIBIT 1
The Kroger Company Financial Developments Timeline

- 1883 First store opened in Cincinnati, Ohio
- 1901 Kroger is the first grocery company to operate its own bakeries
- 1925 Kroger opens a new warehouse to serve Cincinnati stores
- 1929 Kroger operating 5,529 stores
- 1952 Kroger sales top $1 billion
- 1963 Kroger achieved $2 billion in sales
- 1968 Kroger sales achieved $3 billion
- 1975 Sales exceeded $5 billion
- 1979 Kroger became the nation's second-largest food retailing company
- 1980 Company sales reach $10 billion
- 1986 Kroger stock splits
- 2001 Sales top $50 billion
- 2003 Net income tops $1.5 billion

Source: **www.kroger.com**.

Mission

The mission statement of Kroger is clear and detailed, outlining divisional objectives for the company. Exhibit 2 outlines the respective focuses of the company, including social statements to the community at large. The statements indicate a sensitivity to diversity, and to the well-being among associates and the customer base.

Divisions

The Kroger Company, as of February of 2003, operated 2,488 supermarkets that consisted of mostly leased buildings, representing the following types of stores:[12]

1. Combination food and drug stores (combo stores)
2. Superstores
3. Conventional stores
4. Multidepartment stores
5. Price impact warehouse stores
6. Jewelry stores[13]

Kroger and its subsidiaries are dispersed across the United States, consisting of 17 divisions under the Kroger umbrella. Exhibit 3 shows the divisions, headquarters, and the number of store locations. A greater description of the business follows.

Combination Grocery Store and Superstores

The combination stores are Kroger's conventional grocery stores, which potentially can achieve a return above the cost of capital by way of capturing a customer base from a radius of 2–2.5 miles. Distinguishing features of such stores include large layouts enabling a housing of departments such as health, pharmacy, general merchandise, seafood, and organic products. The combo stores operate under different banners, such as Ralphs, Hilander, and Kroger. Additionally, the combo locations average

EXHIBIT 2
Kroger's Mission Statement

OUR MISSION is to be a leader in the distribution and merchandising of food, health, personal care, and related consumable products and services. By achieving this objective, we will satisfy our responsibilities to shareowners, associates, customers, suppliers, and the communities we serve.

We will conduct our business to produce financial returns that reward investment by shareowners and allow the Company to grow. Investments in retailing, distribution and food processing will be continually evaluated for their contribution to our corporate return objectives.

We will constantly strive to satisfy the needs of customers as well as, or better than, the best of our competitors. Operating procedures will increasingly reflect our belief that the organization levels closest to the customer are best positioned to serve changing consumer needs.

We will provide all associates and customers with a safe, friendly work and shopping environment and will treat each of them with respect, openness, honesty, and fairness. We will solicit and respond to the ideas of our associates and reward their meaningful contributions to our success.

We value America's diversity and will strive to reflect that diversity in our work force, the companies with which we do business, and the customers we serve. As a Company, we will convey respect and dignity to all individuals.

We will encourage our associates to be active and responsible citizens and will allocate resources for activities that enhance the quality of life for our customers, our associates and the communities we serve.

David B. Dillon
Chief Executive Officer

Source: www.kroger.com.

55,000 square feet each at a mean cost of $9.4 million including real estate. Furthermore, certain sites also include petroleum centers.

The Superstores resemble combination locations, but differ in that they do not house pharmacies and have limited specialty departments as compared to the combo store locations.[14] Kroger is the world's largest florist with 2,163 floral shops and employs approximately 290,000 associates on either a full- or part-time basis.[15]

Convenience Stores

The conventional locations represent grocery products housed in stores of typically less than 25,000 square feet which means that because of limited space, perishable foods are not carried.[16] The convenience store locations operate under six different banners, representing 784 locations in 16 states in 2002, which comprised 2.7 percent of The Kroger Company, and 1.7 percent of Kroger's cash flow. One advantage of such stores is lower operating costs, because they are all served by Kroger distribution centers. Represented in five states, these stores resemble Supercenters, carrying anything from groceries to clothing lines. There are currently over 137 locations.[17]

Convenience stores are located in areas with typically less than 75,000 residents and are placed strategically near highways and traffic-corners; of the

EXHIBIT 3

The Kroger Company, Major Markets in the United States

DIVISION	HEADQUARTERS	# OF STORES
Ralphs	Los Angeles, CA	345
Kroger Great Lakes	Columbus, OH	229
Kroger Atlanta	Atlanta, GA	215
Kroger Southwest	Houston, TX	213
Kroger Mid-South	Louisville, KY	151
Kroger Central	Indianapolis, IN	144
Kroger Mid-Atlantic	Roanoke, VA	136
Fred Meyer Stores	Portland, OR	132
Food4Less	Los Angeles, CA	130
King Soopers/City Market	Denver, CO	126
Smith's	Salt Lake City, UT	125
Kroger Delta	Memphis, TN	113
Dillon Stores	Hutchinson, KS	110
Fry's	Phoenix, AZ	105
Kroger Cincinnati	Cincinnati, OH	100
Quality Food Centers (QFC)	Seattle, WA	86
Jay C	Seymour, IN	28

Source: www.kroger.com.

784 locations, 689 have petroleum centers.[18] These locations average 2,761 square feet and capture a mean of 6,700 customers, weekly; they carry approximately 3,000 products, and about 70 percent of sales derive from beer/soft drinks, candy, and tobacco items. However, in 2002, gasoline sales comprised 57 percent of convenience store sales.[19] Exhibit 4 shows the convenience store divisions and states in which they are represented.

EXHIBIT 4

Convenience Store Divisions of Kroger Company

C-STORE DIVISION	STATES	# STORES		
		2000	2001	2002
Tom Thumb Food Stores	FL, AL	116	117	120
Kwik Shop, Inc.	KS, IA, NE, IL	165	165	153
Quick Stop Markets, Inc.	CA, NV	108	105	106
Loaf 'N Jug/Mini Mart	CO, NM, NE, MT ND, OK, SD, WY	176	177	177
Turkey Hill Minit Markets	PA	224	225	228
Total		**789**	**789**	**784**

Source: www.kroger.com.

Multidepartment Stores

The multidepartment stores function under the names Fred Meyer and Fry's, and offer one-stop shopping. Fred Meyer operations include 132 locations in Oregon, Washington, Alaska, Idaho, and Utah by year-end 2002; they typically are housed in store formats ranging from 130,000 to 160,000 square feet and feature general home and food/apparel items (over 225,000 items).[20] Additionally, these locations carry brand-name products.

According to the company, the following distinguishing features set this facet of Kroger's division apart from its competition: fine food items (quality beef, organic produce, natural food center, etc.); in apparel, national brand-name men's, women's, and children's sportswear; in home products, brand-name and décor merchandise, including a garden center; in home electronics, audio/visual, phones, cameras, and so on.[21]

Price-Impact Warehouse Operations

The price-impact warehouse stores operate under Food4Less and Foods Company banners, averaging 54,661 square feet and offering budgetary shoppers' amenities, such as meat and dairy products, in a warehouse-style format. Strategic initiatives include the opening of three additional Food4Less locations in the Chicago area; currently, Food4Less locations have been launched in several California and Nevada markets (see Exhibit 3).[22]

Jewelry Stores

The Kroger Company jewelry division was operating 441 fine jewelry stores in 34 states by fiscal year-end 2002, thereby ranking the company as the fourth-largest fine jewelry retailer in America. Of the 441 locations, 117 were housed in Fred Meyer locations; 324 in shopping malls, operating under the names of Littman and Barclay jewelers. The company offers shareholders an additional 10 percent discount on fine jewelry ("offer not valid on unmounted diamonds or with any other promotional offer or discount").[23]

Exhibit 5 shows jewelry store locations throughout the United States.

EXHIBIT 5
The Kroger Company Jewelry Operations

STATE	# STORES	STATE	# STORES	STATE	# STORES
Alaska	10	Iowa	6	North Carolina	1
Arizona	10	Kansas	2	Ohio	11
California	45	Maryland	17	Oklahoma	1
Colorado	2	Massachusetts	5	Oregon	52
Connecticut	5	Michigan	24	Pennsylvania	37
Delaware	3	Minnesota	4	Tennessee	7
Florida	16	Missouri	3	Utah	12
Georgia	2	Nebraska	1	Virginia	6
Idaho	12	Nevada	4	Washington	60
Illinois	8	New Jersey	23	West Virginia	3
Indiana	9	New Mexico	1	Wisconsin	11
		New York	28		

Source: www.kroger.com.

Technological/Logistical Advances

The Kroger Company, is ranked number eighteen on the *Fortune* 500 list, as one of the nation's largest retail grocery chains.[24] The company has made capital investments in the following systems, which have produced returns above expectations:

- New point-of-sale systems
- Self-Checkout technology
- Time and attendance systems
- Labor scheduling technology
- Computer-assisted ordering
- Pharmacy systems
- Store cash optimization system
- "Voice-pick" technology for our distribution centers
- A new real-time warehouse management system
- Internet-based inbound freight management

The above systems will significantly improve efficiency and effectiveness, such as improved refrigeration temperature controls, monitoring of distributions, and additional square footage for storage of seasonal and promotional items.[25]

Kroger stands alone in the industry with the inception of a nationwide, three-tier distribution system, where the first tier consists of dry grocery, perishables, and freezer buildings that deliver to stores within a 200-mile radius, handling quick-turn and perishable items.[26]

The second tier services retail stores within a 350-mile radius with such products as pharmaceuticals and dry grocery items; the Peyton consolidation centers allow for greater buying power due to larger quantities, with either piece, sleeve, or case packages delivered on a frequency of two to three times weekly.

The third tier, a part of the Peyton network, distributes seasonal and promotional products to stores in a larger geographic area than the consolidation centers; Kroger operates five Peyton centers currently.[27]

Branding and Manufacturing

Kroger carries private-label products, which are produced and marketed in a three-tier quality fashion:

1. *Private selections*—These selections represent premium brands, geared toward the "gourmet" or "upscale" clientele. At fiscal year-end 2002, 600 different private selection items were offered.

2. *Banner brands*—Kroger, Ralphs, and King Soopers are among the outlets carrying such brands, labeled with "Try it, Like it, or Get the National Brand Free," as such brands are considered by Kroger as the same, if not better than national brands, at a lower cost to the consumer. Kroger, in order to stand by its statement, puts each private label product to the following test:
   a. Quality must be equal to or better than the national brand
   b. Must be able to sell at a retail price lower than the national brand equivalent
   c. Must be able to make more pennies-per-item profit

3. *For Maximum Value (FMV)*—Is the brand designated to deliver good quality at an affordable price?[28]

The Kroger product lines continue to increase as additional private-label lines fill more shelf spaces in stores, such as school supplies, Bath & Body Therapies, Mototech, and so on. In April of 2003, Kroger launched its Naturally Preferred brand, which is its own line of premium quality natural and organic products consisting of about 140 items, to include baby food, cereal, snacks, pastas, and so on. Such product lines include natural/organic ingredients that are certified.[29]

Kroger Manufacturing Plants and Pharmacies

Kroger produces bread, dairy products, meat, and many other grocery products, as this helps reduce costs. Currently, Kroger operates fifteen dairies and three ice cream plants; seven bakeries, two frozen dough plants, and two deli plants. Kroger also operates two cheese plants and three meat plants, and five grocery and three beverage plants. The plants exist in seventeen different states.[30]

Kroger is one of the top-ten pharmacy operators in the United States, with nearly 1,800 locations within food stores. Such technology as "EasyFill" enables customers to request prescriptions online; this process has helped to double the volume of prescriptions filled. Kroger also offers mail-order service through its Postal Prescription Service (PPS) facility.[31] The aforementioned Kroger operations have yielded impressive financial results for the company (see Exhibits 6 and 7).

Competition

The Kroger Company, like other national retailers, is continuing to keep one eye on Wal-Mart. This is not surprising when one understands Wal-Mart's market share and global presence. Kroger competes in not only the grocery chain arena, but also indirectly with the drugstore chain and foodmakers.

Currently, Kroger does not rank among the top ten foodmakers; Nestlé ranks number one followed by Kraft Foods. However, Kroger ranks number four among the global food retailers, behind number-one-ranked Wal-Mart, Carrefour, and Royal Ahold; also Kroger is not ranked among the top-five drugstore chains.[32] Exhibit 8 shows the direct competitor comparisons among four retailers in the grocery division and the industry. As you will note in the exhibit, Kroger's net income is much greater than industry rivals Albertson's and Safeway.

Albertson's, Inc.(**www.albertsons.com**), operates 2,287 locations represented in 31 states; of these locations, 1,313 are combo food/drug locations, 708 drugstores, and 266 conventional and warehouse locations. Additionally, the retailer is bannered under the following names: Albertson's, Albertsons-Osco, Albertsons-Sav-on, Jewel-Osco, Acme, Sav-on Drugs, Osco Drug, Max Foods, and Super Saver Foods; it also operates 17 major distribution centers.[33] The company evolved in 1939 and currently has no international presence.[34]

Safeway Inc. (**www.safeway.com**), operates 1,695 stores in the United States and Canada. A news flash announced Safeway is exiting the Chicago market by selling its Dominick's locations. The company also has its own product lines and operates divisions under the banners of Pak n' Save Foods, Vons, Pavilions, Carrs, Randalls, Tom Thumb, and Genuardi's Family Markets.[35] In many of the locations a shopper can expect to find Starbucks and petroleum stations, coupled with an array of departments ranging from deli to pharmacy.[36]

Wal-Mart Stores, Inc. (**www.walmartstores.com**), is a retail giant whose slogan is "Our People Make the Difference"; it consists of two divisions: retail and specialty. The retail division consists of Sam's Clubs, Wal-Mart Stores, Neighborhood Market, International, and walmart.com; the specialty divisions include Tire & Lube Express, Wal-Mart Optical, Wal-Mart Pharmacy, Wal-Mart

EXHIBIT 6
Kroger Company—Income Statement

IN MILLIONS OF U.S. DOLLARS (EXCEPT FOR PER SHARE ITEMS) AS OF FEBRUARY 1	2003	2002	2001
Revenue	$51,760.0	50,098.0	49,000.0
Other Revenue	—	—	—
Total Revenue	**51,760.0**	**50,098.0**	**49,000.0**
Cost of Revenue	37,810.0	36,398.0	35,804.0
Gross Profit	**13,950.0**	**13,700.0**	**13,196.0**
Selling/General/Administrative Expenses	10,274.0	10,133.0	9,799.0
Research & Development	—	—	—
Depreciation/Amortization	1,087.0	1,076.0	1,008.0
Interest Expense (Income), Net Operating	—	—	—
Unusual Expense (Income)	16.0	132.0	206.0
Other Operating Expenses	—	—	—
Total Operating Expense	**49,187.0**	**47,739.0**	**46,817.0**
Operating Income	**2,573.0**	**2,359.0**	**2,183.0**
Interest Expense, Net Non-Operating	(600.0)	(648.0)	(675.0)
Interest/Investment Income, Non-Operating	—	—	—
Interest Income (Expense), Net Non-Operating	(600.0)	(648.0)	(675.0)
Gain (Loss) on Sale of Assets	—	—	—
Other, Net	—	—	—
Income Before Tax	**1,973.0**	**1,711.0**	**1,508.0**
Income Tax	740.0	668.0	628.0
Income After Tax	**1,233.0**	**1,043.0**	**880.0**
Minority Interest	—	—	—
Equity In Affiliates	—	—	—
Net Income Before Extra. Items	**1,233.0**	**1,043.0**	**880.0**
Accounting Change	(16.0)	0.0	—
Discontinued Operations	—	—	—
Extraordinary Item	(12.0)	0.0	(3.0)
Net Income	**$ 1,205.0**	**1,043.0**	**877.0**
Preferred Dividends	—	—	—
Income Available	**1,233.0**	**1,043.0**	**880.0**
Income Available to Common	**1,205.0**	**1,043.0**	**877.0**
Basic/Primary Weighted Average Shares	778.8	804.5	823.0
Basic/Primary EPS Excl. Extra. Items	**1.583**	**1.296**	**1.069**
Basic/Primary EPS Incl. Extra. Items	**1.547**	**1.296**	**1.066**

Source: www.investor.stockpoint.com

Vacations, and Wal-Mart's Used Fixture Auctions.[37] Wal-Mart's international division is impressive, with over 1,000 store locations represented in 9 countries (Argentina, Brazil, Canada, China, Germany, Korea, Mexico, Puerto Rico, and the United Kingdom).[38] Wal-Mart currently is the second-largest grocer in the United Kingdom with its ASDA Group Limited stores (ranking second behind Tesco) operating 250 locations.[39]

EXHIBIT 7

Kroger Company—Balance Sheets

IN MILLIONS OF U. S. DOLLARS (EXCEPT FOR PER SHARE ITEMS) AS OF FEBRUARY 1	2003	2002	2001
Cash & Equivalents	—	—	—
Short Term Investments	—	—	—
Cash and Short Term Investments	$ 171.0	161.0	161.0
Trade Accounts Receivable, Net	677.0	679.0	687.0
Other Receivables	—	—	—
Total Receivables, Net	677.0	679.0	687.0
Total Inventory	4,175.0	4,178.0	4,063.0
Prepaid Expenses	543.0	494.0	501.0
Other Current Assets	—	—	—
Total Current Assets	**5,566.0**	**5,512.0**	**5,412.0**
Property/Plant/Equipment—Gross	—	—	—
Accumulated Depreciation	(6,881.0)	(6,020.0)	(5,421.0)
Property/Plant/Equipment, Net	10,548.0	9,657.0	8,813.0
Goodwill, Net	3,575.0	3,594.0	3,639.0
Intangibles, Net	—	—	—
Long Term Investments	—	—	—
Other Long Term Assets	413.0	306.0	315.0
Total Assets	**$20,102.0**	**19,069.0**	**18,179.0**
Accounts Payable	3,278.0	3,005.0	3,009.0
Accrued Expenses	571.0	584.0	603.0
Notes Payable/Short Term Debt	—	—	—
Current Port. LT Debt/Capital Leases	352.0	436.0	336.0
Other Current Liabilities	1,407.0	1,460.0	1,434.0
Total Current Liabilities	**5,608.0**	**5,485.0**	**5,382.0**
Long Term Debt	8,222.0	8,394.0	8,210.0
Capital Lease Obligations	—	—	—
Total Long Term Debt	**8,222.0**	**8,394.0**	**8,210.0**
Total Debt	**8,574.0**	**8,830.0**	**8,546.0**
Deferred Income Tax	—	—	—
Minority Interest	—	—	—
Other Liabilities	2,422.0	1,688.0	1,498.0
Total Liabilities	**$16,252.0**	**15,567.0**	**15,090.0**
Redeemable Preferred Stock	—	—	—
Preferred Stock—Non Redeemable, Net	—	—	—
Common Stock	908.0	901.0	891.0
Additional Paid-In Capital	2,317.0	2,217.0	2,092.0
Retained Earnings (Accum. Deficit)	3,352.0	2,147.0	1,104.0
Treasury Stock—Common	(2,521.0)	(1,730.0)	(998.0)
Other Equity	(206.0)	(33.0)	0.0
Total Equity	**3,850.0**	**3,502.0**	**3,089.0**
Total Liability & Shareholders' Equity	**$20,102.0**	**19,069.0**	**18,179.0**
Shares Outs.—Common Stock	758.0	795.0	815.0
Total Common Shares Outstanding	**758.0**	**795.0**	**815.0**
Total Preferred Stock Shares Outs.	**—**	**—**	**—**
Employees (actual figures)	290,000	288,000	312,000
Number of Common Shareholders	52,920	54,506	54,673

Source: www.investor.stockpoint.com

EXHIBIT 8
Direct Competitor Comparison

	KR	ABS	SWY	WMT	INDUSTRY
Market Cap	14.04B	7.66B	10.25B	251.14B	843.86M
Employees	290,000	202,000	172,000	1,400,000	8.60K
Rev. Growth	3.30%	−6.10%	−5.50%	12.20%	6.70%
Revenue	51.76B	35.63B	32.40B	246.52B	2.02B
Gross Margin	26.92%	28.92%	30.45%	22.02%	28.44%
EBITDA	3.63B	2.51B	2.18B	18.07B	124.50M
Oper. Margins	4.71%	4.36%	4.08%	5.31%	3.19%
Net Income	1.19B	724.00M	334.30M	8.46B	39.58M
EPS	1.46	1.91	0.8	1.94	0.89
PE	12.52	10.68	28.89	29.41	21.54
PEG	1.40	1.45	1.11	1.74	1.51
PS	0.26	0.21	0.31	0.99	0.31

KR: The Kroger Company
ABS: Albertson's, Inc.
SWY: Safeway Inc.
WMT: Wal-Mart Stores, Inc.
Industry: Supermarkets, Drugstores, and Mass Merchandisers
Source: finance.yahoo.com/q/co?s=KR.

The discussions thus far represent direct competitors of Kroger; however, the mass-merchandising arena, foodmakers, coupled with the drugstores and other supermarkets (industry) result in further competition to The Kroger Company.

The Retail Grocery Industry
The industry can best be summarized as fierce, as competitor giant Wal-Mart has forced the competition to reduce profit margins (approximately 3% of sales), and some chains have considered acquisitions to remedy the lack of margins. To this end, some competitors have attempted to delve into other aspects of retailing, such as convenience stores, as Kroger has done, while others have invested in food service distribution.

The fierce competition has also led to better customer service and product lines; traditionally, as companies compete, the consumer generally reaps the benefits. Companies such as Wal-Mart (operating in 9 different countries) and Carrefour (the second-largest global retailer behind Wal-Mart) are looking to continue global expansion into Asian, Eastern European, and South American markets, where competition, including Wal-Mart, is absent.[40] The international grocery arena is continuing to focus on such strategies as the inclusion of petroleum stations, online sales, and "dressing-up" store format.[41]

The grocery industry is experiencing a rise in organic food sales, currently offered at 7-Eleven convenience stores (some snacks), and soy-based vegetarian hot dogs, sold at some football stadiums.[42] According to the Organic Trade Association, annual growth rate for organic types of foods is about 20 percent, among educated, affluent, and safe-eating consumers; perhaps this is the reason Kroger has been expanding its organic product lines.

In sum, the industry remains lean as competition is continuously looking to capture more market share. Meanwhile, consumers are finding more grocery purchasing options at discounted prices, as a result of the fierce competition among grocery retailers.

Operational Strategies

The results of Kroger's Strategic Growth Plan after one year of implementation were the following:

1. Elimination of approximately 1,500 management and clerical positions.
2. Consolidation of the Nashville division office and distribution center into the Mid-South and Atlanta divisions.
3. Centralization of additional merchandising categories to drive down product costs.
4. Reduction of selected product categories and markets with intent to strengthen competitive position.
5. Achieved cost savings of $306 million.[43]

Additional strategies include further operational consolidation of the Columbus and Michigan divisions into one, and continuous price reductions and expansion of product lines.

In sum, the growth plan of Kroger led to some drastic outcomes, but further stress and expenses in the Nashville and Mid-South divisions may still remain as a result of consolidation. Moreover, the organizational impact regarding job cuts may or may not affect things such as associates' morale and commitment to the company.

Company Web site

A visit to the company's Web site (**www.kroger.com**) will yield a homepage that is informative, containing links to such information as the company profile and financial information, links to gifts, and pharmacy offerings. Additionally, the site offers Internet coupons, which eliminates coupon-clipping.

A distinct feature of the site is the ads that are available, which are categorized by city and state. The site contains traditional information, such as company profile and careers available. On a final note, links to the different subsidiary banners are also available.

The international retail grocery landscape differs somewhat from that of the United States; purchasing behaviors are different, depending on the country. Additionally, frequencies differ, too, such as amount of grocery buying. It is very common for consumers in England to purchase dinner on their way home from work, merely stopping by the grocery store to pick up a few items that can be carried in a shopping basket; unlike in the United States, where going into a grocery store may necessitate the use of a shopping cart instead of a basket. Finally, departmental grocery items may differ, too. If a majority of foods purchased are ready-to-eat items, such as packaged sandwiches, this particular department may be located at or near the entrance/check-out stands.

Strategic-Management Considerations

1. Considering Kroger's current position in the industry, would you advise an international expansion strategy? If so, in what international market(s)? How would you suggest entrance with respect to location selections and number of units?

EXHIBIT 9
Kroger's Organizational Structure

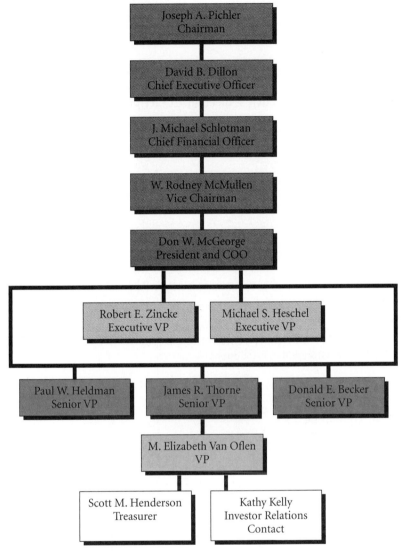

Source: Standard & Poor's Corporate Descriptions Plus News.

2. If international expansion is one recommended strategy, please discuss the pros and cons of hiring expatriate leadership/management teams.

3. Discuss cultural diversity/sensitivity management, as it applies to The Kroger Company. How might it differ and what should Kroger consider/incorporate if international expansion efforts are proposed?

4. Discuss how Kroger can take advantage of the concept of synergy.

5. How can Kroger, if at all, keep competitors at a distance? In your response please discuss expansion in the United States, product line(s), and portfolio management.

6. How effective is the "Strategic Growth Plan?" Would you change and/or recommend any additions?

7. Is there any evidence of knowledge management in practice within the company? If not, how would you advise corporate officials to incorporate the practice of knowledge management?

8. What influence, if any, may consumption purchasing behavior have on an organization's (grocery retail) considerations to transition abroad? Please discuss:

   • Specialty outlets, such as butcher/meat shops, outdoor produce and flower markets, etc.

   • Sociological factors, such as diet and grocery purchasing frequencies, etc.

Notes

1. LexisNexis™. Standard & Poor's Corporate Descriptions Plus News, September 13, 2003. Retrieved: September 21, 2003.
2. *Hoover's Handbook of American Business*, 2003, pp. 834–835.
3. LexisNexis™. Standard & Poor's Corporate Description Plus News, September 13, 2003. Retrieved: September 21, 2003.
4. *Hoover's Handbook of American Business*, 2003, pp. 834–835.
5. Ibid.
6. LexisNexis™. Standard & Poor's Daily News, June 27, 2003. Retrieved: September 21, 2003.
7. InfoTrac Web: Expanded Academic ASAP. Kroger (Flash! Frozen) (18 Raley's stores acquired in Las Vegas). *Frozen Food Age* 51(3) (October 2002): 5(1). Retrieved: September 21, 2003.
8. www.kroger.com.
9. InfoTrac Web: Expanded Academic ASAP. Kroger (Flash! Frozen) (18 Raley's stores acquired in Las Vegas). *Frozen Food Age* 51(3) (October 2002): 5(1). Retrieved: September 21, 2003.
10. Hoover's Online. Grocery Retail-Industry Overview. Retrieved: September 22, 2003.
11. *Hoover's Handbook*, 2003.
12. LexisNexis™. Standard & Poor's Corporate Descriptions Plus News, September 13, 2002. Retrieved: September 21, 2003.
13. www.kroger.com.
14. Ibid.
15. Ibid.
16. Ibid.
17. Ibid.
18. Ibid.
19. Ibid.
20. Ibid.
21. Ibid.
22. Ibid.
23. Ibid.
24. Ibid.
25. Ibid.
26. Ibid.
27. Ibid.
28. Ibid.
29. Ibid.
30. Ibid.
31. Ibid.
32. Hoover's Online. Grocery Retail-Industry Overview. Retrieved: September 22, 2003.
33. finance.yahoo.com/q?s=abs.
34. www.albertsons.com/abs_aboutalbertsons/ourhistory/default.asp.
35. finance.yahoo.com/q/pr?s=swy.
36. www.safeway.com/ourcompany.asp.
37. www.walmartstores.com/wmstore/wmstores/HomePage.jsp.

38. finance.yahoo.com/q/pr?s=wmt.
39. Hoover's Online. ASDA Group Limited-Fact Sheet. Retrieved: September 22, 2003.
40. Hoover's Online. Grocery Retail-Industry Overview. Retrieved: September 22, 2003.
41. Hoover's Online. Tesco PLC-Fact Sheet. Retrieved: September 22, 2003.
42. bix.yahoo.com/rc/031005/bizfeature_food_organic_1.html.
43. www.kroger.com.

9   Limited Brands—2004

M. Jill Austin
Middle Tennessee State University

Ltd

www.Limited.Brands.com

> Our brands are about innovation—about next. . . . We embrace change.
> Frankly, we like it. It's challenging, stimulating, and it's embedded in
> our culture.

This is chairman and CEO Leslie Wexner's view of Limited Brands in 2003. For almost forty years, Wexner's Limited stores have achieved success by "breaking the rules" in the specialty retailing industry. Instead of offering a wide variety of types of clothing, the stores offer a limited assortment of sportswear in large quantities and a variety of colors. In the mid–1990s, The Limited, Inc., made a strategic decision to develop strong "brand" associations for its stores. Today the company has a number of store brand leaders, including Victoria's Secret and Bath & Body Works. Net sales from 2001 to 2002 increased 7 percent to $8.445 billion. Operating income was $837 million in 2002, down from $882 million in 2001. Stores now number 4,036.

Present Conditions

In 2002, Limited Brands acquired a minority interest (14 percent) in Intimate Brands, Inc. (IBI), for $1.6 billion so that the brands of IBI (Victoria's Secret, Bath & Body Works, and White Barn Candle Company) could become a wholly owned subsidiary of Limited Brands. Lerner New York was sold in February 2003 for $79 million and a new beauty company called aura science was introduced in 2002. The company was officially renamed Limited Brands in 2002. According to Wexner, Limited Brands continues "to simplify our business structure dramatically through spin-offs, split-offs, and sales of businesses." The growth of Limited Brands is shown in Exhibit 1.

Limited Brands continues to be successful, in spite of significant changes in its business structure and major organizational changes in some of its store brands. Net sales increased for Victoria's Secret, Bath & Body Works, Limited Stores, and Express from 2001 to 2002. All brands except Bath & Body Works and Other Retail Businesses had increases in operating income. Bath & Body Works' operating income decreased by 14 percent from $347 million in 2001 to $300 million in 2002. The greatest increase in net sales from 2001 to 2002 was at Victoria's Secret ($3.27 billion to $3.586 billion) while the greatest increase in operating income during this time was at the apparel division's Express and Limited Stores ($55 million to $115 million). The vision and mission for Limited Brands continues to include growth and dominance in specialty retailing, as indicated in Exhibit 2.

EXHIBIT 1

Limited Brands' Stores and Selling Square Feet
(a summary of stores and selling square feet by business)

		END OF YEAR			CHANGE FROM	
		PLAN 2003	**2002**	**2001**	**2003–2002**	**2002–2001**
Victoria's Secret Stores	Stores	1,014	1,014	1,002	—	12
	Selling square feet	4,771,000	4,636,000	4,458,000	108,000	205,000
Bath & Body Works	Stores	1,622	1,639	1,615	(17)	24
	Selling square feet	3,575,000	3,568,000	3,463,000	7,000	105,000
Express Women's	Stores	559	624	667	(65)	(43)
	Selling square feet	3,483,000	3,927,000	4,280,000	(444,000)	(353,000)
Express Men's	Stores	321	358	439	(37)	(81)
	Selling square feet	1,298,000	1,458,000	1,774,000	(160,000)	(316,000)
Express Dual Gender	Stores	112	49	—	63	49
	Selling square feet	1,030,000	467,000	—	563,000	467,000
Total Express	Stores	992	1,031	1,106	(39)	(75)
	Selling square feet	5,811,000	5,852,000	6,054,000	(41,000)	(202,000)
Limited Stores	Stores	346	351	368	(5)	(17)
	Selling square feet	2,108,000	2,179,000	2,313,000	(71,000)	(134,000)
Total apparel businesses	Stores	1,338	1,382	1,474	(44)	(92)
	Selling square feet	7,919,000	8,031,000	8,367,000	(112,000)	(336,000)
Henri Bendel	Stores	1	1	—	—	—
	Selling square feet	35,000	35,000	35,000	—	—
Lerner New York	Stores	—	—	522	—	(522)
	Selling square feet	—	—	3,823,000	—	(3,823,000)
Total retail businesses	Stores	3,975	4,036	4,614	(61)	(578)
	Selling square feet	16,300,000	16,297,000	20,146,000	3,000	(3,849,000)

Source: Limited Brands *2002 Annual Report*, p. 28.

EXHIBIT 2

Vision and Mission for Limited Brands, Inc.

VISION—Build a "family of the world's best fashion brands."

MISSION—"Create sustained growth of shareholder value by focusing its time, talent, and capital on the highest return opportunities."

Source: www.LimitedBrands.com.

Business Structure

Limited Brands operates as five separate business groups: Victoria's Secret, Bath & Body Works, Apparel, Other Retail Brands, and Support Businesses. Stores/ operations included in each business group and net sales for each are shown in Exhibit 3.

EXHIBIT 3

Sales and Income Data (in millions)

NET SALES (Millions)	2002	2001	★2000	% CHANGE 2002–2001	% CHANGE 2001–2000
Victoria's Secret Stores	$2,647	$2,403	$2,339	10%	3%
Victoria's Secret Direct	939	869	962	8%	(10%)
Total Victoria's Secret	$3,586	$3,272	$3,301	10%	(1%)
Bath & Body Works	$1,781	$1,747	$1,785	2%	(2%)
Express	$2,073	$2,044	$2,163	1%	(6%)
Limited Stores	638	618	673	3%	(8%)
Total apparel businesses	$2,711	$2,662	$2,836	2%	(6%)
Other♦	$367	$742	$1,158	nm	nm
Total net sales	$8,445	$8,423	$9,080	0%	(7%)
OPERATING INCOME (Millions)					
Victoria's Secret	$614	$454	$468	35%	(3%)
Bath & Body Works	300	347	418	(14%)	(17%)
Apparel	115	55	75	109%	(27%)
Other♦	(157)	(130)	(119)	nm	nm
Subtotal	872	726	842	20%	(14%)
Special and nonrecurring items▲	(34)	170	(10)	nm	nm
Total operating income	$838	$896	$832	(6%)	8%

★ Fifty-three-week fiscal year.

♦ Other includes Corporate, Mast, Henri Bendel, and Lane Bryant through its sale on August 16, 2001.

▲ Special and nonrecurring items include the following: 2002—a $35 million non-cash charge related to the Intimate Brands, Inc. recombination, 2001—a $170 million gain resulting from the sale of Lane Bryant, and 2000—a $10 million charge to close Bath & Body Works' nine stores in the United Kingdom.

nm not meaningful

The above summarized financial data compares reported 2002 sales and operating income results to the comparable periods for 2001 and 2000.

COMPARABLE STORE SALES	2002	2001	2000
Victoria's Secret	6%	0%	5%
Bath & Body Works	(3%)	(11%)	1%
Express	2%	(3%)	10%
Limited Stores	7%	(2%)	5%
Total apparel businesses	3%	(3%)	9%
Lane Bryant (through August 16, 2001)	—	3%	2%
Henri Bendel	7%	(6%)	(1%)
Total comparable store sales	3%	(3%)	5%

The above summarized financial data compares reported 2002 results to the comparable periods of 2001 and 2000.

Source: Limited Brands *2002 Annual Report,* p. 21.

Victoria's Secret
Victoria's Secret Stores
Victoria's Secret is the largest intimate apparel chain in the world. The stores sell fashion-inspired collections with a modern look and bath and fragrance products. In 2003, a 25,000-square-foot store was opened in New York City; it has a contemporary look with cream and black colors, silver fixtures, and marble floors. Some variation of this color scheme will be incorporated into other Victoria's Secret stores as they are remodeled in the next few years. There are 1,014 Victoria's Secret stores in the United States.

Victoria's Secret Direct (Catalogue/E-commerce)
Since its purchase by Limited in 1982, the catalogue has steadily increased its operations. Victoria's Secret Catalogue is the dominant lingerie catalogue in the world. In 1996, a Victoria's Secret phone center was established in Japan so that market could be established for mail-order sales. At the end of 1998, the company launched a Web site (**www.VictoriasSecret.com**) so consumers worldwide could shop online. Sales of Victoria's Secret Direct in 2002 reached $939 million.

Victoria's Secret Beauty
This division sells high-quality beauty products in stand-alone stores or within Victoria's Secret lingerie stores, and had net sales of $640 million in 2002.

Bath & Body Works
In response to demand by consumers for natural personal care products, Limited opened six Bath & Body Works stores in 1990. Remodeling of these stores began in 2002 with wood shelving and the red-checked fabric and country atmosphere being replaced by white walls, pale-green armoire-style shelving, and hardwood floors. The company launched it Web site, **www.BathandBodyWorks.com**, in 2002. Bath & Body Works wants to be seen as a "twentyfirst-century apothecary of well-being" and began selling two new brands, "Aromatherapy" and "True Blue Spa," in 2003. There are 1,639 Bath & Body Works stores.

White Barn Candle Company
This division offers an assortment of fragrance products including high-quality candles, home fragrances, and home accessories. In 1999, 50 Bath & Body Works stores were converted to White Barn Candle Company stores. There are 123 White Barn Candle Company stores, most of them located adjacent to other Limited store operations. The company's Web site is **www.whitebarncandlecompany.com**.

Apparel Division
Limited Stores
This is the flagship division of the organization. Originally, merchandise in these stores was targeted to women between the ages of 16 and 25, but Limited stores now focus on fashion-conscious women who want a "sexy, sophisticated style." These stores sell medium-priced clothing and accessories. Most of the 351 Limited stores are located in regional shopping centers or malls across the United States. The number of Limited stores has been reduced significantly in recent years; there were 778 locations in 1990.

Express
The company describes its Express as being a "modern fashion leader for women and men" that offers cutting-edge styles. Express added a lingerie department in 1999, and beginning in 2001, it began to merge the men's Structure stores into Express. This brand is still making the transition to a dual-gender brand through remodeling of the stores. Sixty-three more stores should be remodeled in 2003 with a new store

design that reflects both sophistication and the casual style of urban professionals. The 1,031 Express stores in operation are located primarily in shopping malls.

Other Retail Businesses

Henri Bendel

Limited purchased this upscale fashion store in 1985. The store offers the best in clothing and accessories from international designers. Products are designed for "higher income 30-something women." This is the only upscale store owned by Limited Brands. The division was expanded to six stores in 1996, but the company closed five Henri Bendel stores in 1998.

aura science

Limited Brands owns 51 percent of aura science with Japanese cosmetics company Shiseido. The product line is foundations, concealers, powders, and colors for lips, nails, eyes, and cheeks, with options for women in four phases of skin aging. The first store opened in 2002, and by the end of the year there were nine aura science stores.

Support Businesses

Limited Logistics Services

Limited Brands' distribution center is located in Columbus, Ohio. The center now has seven distribution facilities and two shipping facilities with about 5 million square feet of space.

Limited Real Estate

This division handles store leases for the retail divisions. By the end of 1996, the total selling space of Limited operations was 28.4 million square feet. Selling space decreased to 16.3 million square feet by the end of 2002.

Limited Design Services

This division manages the design of apparel and merchandise for the retail stores.

Limited Brand and Creative Services

This division works with the individual businesses and Wexner to create brands that have a distinctive character.

Limited Technology Services

This division handles the telecommunications and computing needs for the company.

Mast Industries

The business of this division is to arrange for the manufacture and importation of apparel and other products from around the world, and to wholesale this merchandise to Limited Brands' stores and to other companies. This division delivers more than 200 million garments to Limited Brands each year.

Competition

The retailing of women's clothing is a very competitive business. Competitors of Limited Brands include nationally, regionally, and locally owned department stores; specialty stores; and mail-order catalogue businesses. Some of Limited Brands' major competitors are: Gap, American Eagle, Federated Department Stores, Dayton-Hudson, Dillard's, May Department Stores, Abercrombie & Fitch, Talbots, Spiegel/Eddie Bauer, Nordstrom, Sears, and JC Penney. In addition to these large chains, smaller chains such as Chico's FAS, J. Jill, and The Wet Seal are serious competitors for the teen market.

EXHIBIT 4
Top Fifteen Apparel Chains

| COMPANY | SALES (in thousands) | | % CHANGE |
	2002	2001	
Gap	$14,454,709	13,847,873	+4.4
TJX	11,981,207	10,708,998	+11.9
Limited Brands	8,444,654	8,422,724	+0.3
Ross Stores	3,531,349	2,986,596	+18.2
Charming Shoppes	2,412,409	1,993,843	+21.0
Abercrombie & Fitch	1,595,757	1,364,853	+16.9
Talbots	1,595,325	1,612,513	−1.1
American Eagle Outfitters	1,463,141	1,371,899	+6.7
Retail Brand Alliance	1,450,000	1,500,000	−3.3
Stein Mart	1,408,648	1,320,190	+6.7
Ann Taylor	1,380,966	1,299,573	+6.3
Men's Warehouse	1,295,049	1,273,154	+1.7
Goody's Family Clothing	1,193,405	1,192,546	+0.1
L.L. Bean	1,150,000	1,110,000	+3.6
Stage Stores	875,557	855,575	+2.3

Source: "Top 100 Retailers (2003)," **www.stores.com.**

According to *Stores,* Limited Brands was the number-three apparel chain in the United States during both 2001 and 2002. (The top fifteen apparel chains are shown in Exhibit 4.) Other apparel retailers who were among the top fifteen chains for sales volume in 2001 and 2002 include Gap, Charming Shoppes, and Talbots.

Two of Limited Brands' major competitors are discussed below.

Gap Inc.

At the end of August 2003, Gap Inc. had 4,252 apparel stores in operation. Gap has several divisions that compete directly with Limited Brands stores. Gap sells casual sportswear items for both men and women. Casual and active wear for children are sold under the GapKids brand. There are currently 2,309 U.S. Gap and GapKids stores. Banana Republic (441 stores) sells upscale casual wear. Old Navy Clothing Company, the company's fastest-growing division (842 stores), sells budget-priced casual clothing. Gap Inc. also operates 660 GapKids, Gap, and Banana Republic stores in Canada, Japan, Germany, the United Kingdom, and France. Gap, Banana Republic, and Old Navy have Internet sites. Financial information for Gap Inc. is shown in Exhibit 5.

TJX Companies

TJX Companies is the largest off-price apparel chain in the United States. Target customers for TJX include middle-income women between the ages of 25 and 50. Most TJX stores are located in strip shopping centers. At the end of January 2003, TJX Companies had 1,862 apparel stores in operation. The apparel division includes: T. J. Maxx (715 stores), Marshalls (633 stores), Winners Apparel Ltd. (151 stores), Home Goods (144 stores), A. J. Wright (77 stores), HomeSense (19 stores), and T. K. Maxx

EXHIBIT 5
Financial Information for Gap Inc.
($ in millions except per share amount)

	2001	2002
Gross Revenue	$13,847	14,454
Net Income	128.9	477.5
Long-Term Debt	1961.4	2895.8
Net Worth	3009.6	3658.2
Earnings Per Share	.15	.54

Source: Value Line.

EXHIBIT 6
Financial Information for TJX Companies
($ in millions except per share amount)

	2001	2002
Gross Revenue	$10,709	11,981
Net Income	540.4	578.4
Long-Term Debt	702.4	693.8
Net Worth	1340.7	1409.1
Earnings Per Share	.97	1.08

Source: Value Line.

(123 stores). T. K. Maxx is an off-price apparel store located in the United Kingdom, A. J. Wright is a Canadian off-price retailer, and HomeSense is a Canadian home fashions store. Plans call for an additional 60 HomeSense stores in Canada. The company launched the TJX Visa card in 2002, which provides customers with low interest rates and purchase rewards. Financial information for TJX Companies is shown in Exhibit 6.

Demographic and Societal Trends

Generation Y (ages 10–24) is an increasingly important group for apparel retailers. There are currently 31 million people ages 12–19, and this number is expected to increase to the largest teen population in U.S. history: 34 million by 2010. Another new target for retailers is the current "tween" age group of 7- to 12-year-olds who will be a part of the teenage population in 2010. Teens ages 12–19 spent approximately $200 billion in 2002 with one-third of this spending in fashion. Gaining brand and store loyalty among these younger shoppers is essential for apparel retailers.

Female baby boomers have begun to reach their fifties, but retailers and manufacturers of women's apparel have not provided for this group's needs. This large market group for women's apparel has found only youthful fashions and fads available for purchase. As a result, large numbers of customers began staying away from the stores entirely or purchasing fewer clothing items. In addition, many baby boomers have placed retirement savings, college tuition, and mortgages at a higher priority than spending for apparel. As more companies sell their items through the Internet, retail stores will have to learn how to contend with these competitors.

General e-commerce sales were up 25 percent in 2002 with spending at $35.9 billion, indicating that shoppers are willing to make purchases online. While this Internet spending represents only 3 percent of total U.S. retail sales and only a small portion of these sales are for fashion items, this selling approach has been adopted by many retailers. Because of busy lifestyles, many consumers have become "precision shoppers." They shop only for what they need and purchase it quickly, limiting their time in stores. Internet sites are an important channel for these shoppers because they can purchase online and/or browse for clothing online before going into the stores. Another trend related to time-conscious consumers is their willingness to drive greater distances to shop at superstores. These trends provide some challenges for specialty retail stores.

Another trend impacting the apparel industry is the increasing acceptance of the casual workplace. Over half of white-collar workers wear casual clothes to work each day. Fewer dress work clothes are being sold and those retailers who sell casual apparel have an easier time generating sales, especially in a slow economy. Adults are busy with work and family, so shopping is not the recreational activity it once was. More and more consumers see shopping as a chore and retailers who make shopping easy on their customers are likely to have an advantage in the marketplace.

Economic Conditions

The U.S. economy saw slow growth in 2003 since consumer confidence began to decline in fall 2000. After the terrorist attacks in September 2001, consumer confidence continued to falter. Analysts hope that the federal tax cuts will encourage more consumer spending. In fall 2003, 25 million U.S. households (with children) received tax rebates totaling $13 billion. There are some signs that the economy may be improving, but consumer confidence continued to decrease in fall 2003 and rising interest rates may lead to lower consumer spending, even with the dollars introduced into the economy by the tax rebates.

Household debt has continued to increase since 1994, and U.S. consumer debt reached $9 billion by fall 2003. Consumers are likely to change their purchasing habits for items such as clothing so they can pay off credit card debt. The gap between rich and poor also continues to grow; the number of "downscale" shoppers is increasing. Because many adults owe significant debt for cars and homes and are unable to spend much money for apparel, they often purchase clothing at outlet malls or discount stores. Occasionally, however, "downscale" shoppers may want to indulge themselves by purchasing fashion items from specialty stores. Also, many of the women in the baby-boom group spend their disposable income on items for their children and not clothing for themselves.

Apparel retailers also have economic concerns. Several major retail chains have filed for reorganization under Chapter 11 bankruptcy and many others have not been profitable in years. It is difficult for retail chains to predict consumer spending patterns. In the past 50 years, apparel retailers have seen about 17 different economic cycles. The longest cycle was six years while the shortest was about a year. Since these cycles corresponded with the business cycle 60 percent of the time; it appears that apparel sales are likely to stay strong when the economy is good and will be significantly reduced when the economy is not growing.

Specialty retailers may have to take more gambles to gain a competitive advantage in this volatile industry. They have gained a competitive advantage in the past by predicting a fashion trend early and purchasing inventory to provide that trend to customers. If a specialty retailer purchases inventory for a fashion trend but cannot turn it over, the store loses profit and cannot afford to take more risks. However, if they do not gamble by trying to keep up with fashion trends, it is impossible to make a profit when the economy turns around because the merchandise will be out-of-date.

Internal Factors for Limited Brands

Marketing

Wexner believes that his company is "reinventing the specialty store business." Since Limited Brands' retail store divisions sell clothing and related goods of different price ranges and styles, he has created the impact of a department store in many malls by locating the stores in close proximity. Wexner considers his stores as a collection of "brands" rather than a group of stores. He says,

> When you think of yourself as a brand, you think more broadly. You think of the efficacy of the brand, the reputation, the integrity, the channels of distribution, whether that be in a store, a catalogue, on television, or overseas.

Brand building includes defining each store's image, fashion, advertising, price, and market position. In the past, Limited divisions copied each others' designs so that the only difference in some divisions was prices charged for the items sold. Design teams are now assigned to each business and the fashions are designed around narrowly defined brand positions for each division. Wexner believes this is "good for now. Even better for the long-run."

The Limited spent very little money on advertising campaigns in its first twenty years. Instead, the company relied on walk-in traffic in malls to sell its products. The company launched its first national advertising campaign in November 1989. The $10 million campaign included advertisements in Vogue, Vanity Fair, and other women's magazines and was an attempt to increase brand recognition for the company's private labels. Wexner's approach to advertising has changed dramatically in recent years. In 1999, the company created Limited Brand and Creative Services, a department that serves as an in-house advertising agency for Limited Brands' brands. Its television commercials during the Super Bowl in January 1999 announcing a live online fashion show generated 1 million hits to the Victoria's Secret Web site. The 2003 televised fashion show had a Broadway theme and included models Tyra Banks, Gisele Bundchen, and Heidi Klum. Approximately $411 million was spent on advertising and catalogues in 2002.

Limited's distribution center is located in Columbus, Ohio. Over 60 percent of the U.S. population is located within a 500-mile radius of Columbus, so Wexner feels this is an ideal location for a distribution center. Another advantage of the Columbus location is its nearness to New York City, the port where incoming merchandise produced in foreign countries is received by Mast Industries. All merchandise arriving in New York is shipped directly to the distribution center for allocation among Limited Brands' stores. A computerized system aids distributors in their selections for each store's inventory. This system allows Limited Brands to monitor inventory levels, the merchandise mix, and the sales pattern at each store so that appropriate adjustments can be made as needed. Approximately 40 percent of the inventory enters the United States by air and can be delivered from Columbus, Ohio, to any Limited Brands store within 72 hours.

Production

Limited Brands does not produce its own clothing, but it has a division that contracts for the manufacture of clothing. Mast Industries specializes in contracting for production of high-quality, low-cost products. Leslie Wexner believes that having private-label brands allows Limited Brands to keep merchandise inventory current and unique. Limited Brands can also maintain control over its clothing and other products supply through Mast Industries. Company managers try to maintain a 1,000-hour turnaround time between recognizing a new style and delivering the merchandise to stores. Mast can send high-resolution computer images of clothing designs by satellite to Far Eastern manufacturers. In addition, computer information that is collected from all individual stores is used to determine what needs to be produced in the Far East the next day. In a few days, the newly produced items arrive at the Columbus distribution center and are sent to the stores.

In 2002, Mast purchased merchandise from approximately 2,500 different suppliers, but no more than 10 percent of Limited Brands' inventory was purchased from any single manufacturer. The coordination of work with so many factories makes it difficult to ensure consistent quality. However, the company builds alliances with suppliers so that innovative ideas are executed.

Management

Wexner has been a guiding force for the company since its beginning. His risk-taking style has concerned some investors, but his ability to create new marketing concepts has made Limited Brands the envy of other specialty retailers. The company uses a centralized process for planning, with Wexner leading the process. This approach to leadership allows him to remain involved in each store brand, without being involved in every detail of brand operations. The organization chart in Exhibit 7 shows major divisions of the company.

In March 2003, Limited Brands was named the most admired specialty retailer in the world by *Fortune* magazine. Wexner said, "I believe companies should be a source for good. For us. For our communities. For the world." The

EXHIBIT 7
Major Organizational Divisions of Limited Brands, Inc.

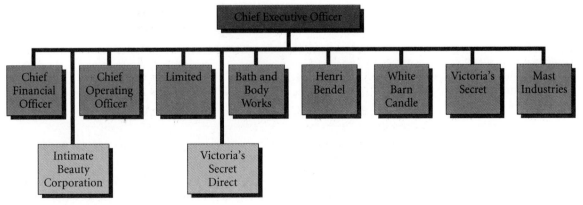

Source: Limited Brands *2002 Annual Report*, p. 44.

company focuses on charitable giving in the areas of empowering women, improving educational opportunities, and mentoring children. In the last five years, Limited Brands has contributed $60 million to community organizations. The company has allowed employees to volunteer on company time to tutor inner-city children, for a total of more than 100,000 hours. Some charities the company is involved with include: United Way, Susan G. Koman Breast Cancer Race for the Cure, and Make a Wish Foundation. In addition to charitable activities, Wexner believes that employees should have a "moral compass" and should be ethical in all their daily activities.

Financial Condition

Note in Exhibit 8 that while Limited Brands' net sales increased slightly from 2001 to 2002, the company's net income was reduced. The balance sheet (Exhibit 9) shows the company's current assets and total assets were more for 2003 than for 2002. [The company's long-term debt and current liabilities were reduced in 2003.] At the end of 2002, Wexner said, "We have resources to do almost anything we can imagine."

EXHIBIT 8

Consolidated Statements of Income (in millions except per-share amount)

	2002	2001	2000
Net sales	$8,445	$8,423	$9,080
Costs of goods sold, buying and occupancy	(5,351)	(5,407)	(5,895)
Gross income	3,094	3,016	3,185
General, administrative and store operating expenses	(2,222)	(2,290)	(2,343)
Special and nonrecurring items	(34)	170	(10)
Operating income	838	896	832
Interest expense	(30)	(34)	(58)
Interest income	29	24	42
Other income (loss)	—	(2)	(22)
Minority interest	(6)	(64)	(69)
Gains on investees' stock	6	62	—
Income from continuing operations before income taxes	837	882	725
Income tax expense	341	376	318
Net income from continuing operations	496	506	407
Income from discontinued operations (including loss on disposal of $4 in 2002), net of tax	6	13	21
Net income	$502	$519	$428
Income per basic share:			
Continuing operations	$0.97	$1.18	$0.95
Discontinued operations	0.01	0.03	0.05
Net income per basic share	$0.98	$1.21	$1.00
Income per diluted share:			
Continuing operations	$0.95	$1.16	$0.91
Discontinued operations	0.01	0.03	0.05
Net income per diluted share	$0.96	$1.19	$0.96

Source: Limited Brands *2002 Annual Report*, p. 31.

EXHIBIT 9

Consolidated Balance Sheets (in millions except per-share amount)

ASSETS	FEBRUARY 1, 2003	FEBRUARY 2, 2002
Current assets		
Cash and equivalents	$2,262	$1,495
Accounts receivable	151	80
Inventories	966	966
Other	227	243
Total current assets	3,606	2,784
Property and equipment, net	1,492	1,599
Deferred income taxes	—	67
Goodwill	1,311	121
Trade names and other intangible assets	447	31
Other assets	390	492
Total assets	$7,246	$5,094
LIABILITIES AND SHAREHOLDERS' EQUITY		
Current liabilities		
Accounts payable	$ 456	$ 365
Current portion of long-term debt	—	150
Accrued expenses and other	607	663
Income taxes	196	276
Total current liabilities	1,259	1,454
Deferred income taxes	125	—
Long-term debt	547	250
Other long-term liabilities	455	469
Commitments and contingencies		
Minority interest	—	177
SHAREHOLDERS' EQUITY		
Preferred stock—$1.00 par value; 10 shares authorized; none issued	—	—
Common stock—$0.50 par value; 1,000 shares authorized;		
523 and 432 shares issued in 2002 and 2001	261	216
Paid-in capital	1,693	46
Retained earnings	2,906	2,552
Less: treasury stock, at average cost; 3 shares in 2001	—	(70)
Total shareholders' equity	4,860	2,744
Total liabilities and shareholders' equity	$7,246	$5,094

Source: Limited Brands *2002 Annual Report*, p. 31.

Future Outlook

Wexner says he is "determined to build a Company of powerful, differentiated retail brands that maintain and strengthen our position as the world's dominant specialty retailer." He wants to maintain the company's financial strength and use the company's capital on the highest financial-return opportunities. He says, "Invent the concept. Prove it. Move forward fast." Some critics suggest that Wexner has the talent to identify unserved markets and create a marketing concept around them, but that he has not yet demonstrated skill at reinventing mature businesses. Wexner responds,

"My view is that whether you are turning around a business—that is reconceptualizing it—or whether you are starting from scratch, your vision of what you are driving toward is the same."

The company's plans for the future include the following:

1. Almost all stores in the top 160 malls in the country will be remodeled by 2007.
2. Approximately $400 million in capital expenditures will be made in 2003, with $300 million spent for new stores and remodeling of existing stores.
3. During 2003 the company expects to close as many as 90 underperforming stores and open 30 new stores. Selling space will remain relatively stable at 16.3 million square feet.
4. The company leaders will continue to refocus the company through brand building.
5. Wexner will focus on keeping the talented managers (and hiring new ones) so the company can continue the strategy of innovation in brand development.

Additional strategies include improving the merchandise mix and quality of products in the stores, continuing to take advantage of company name recognition and the supplier opportunities provided by Mast Industries, and building new retailing concepts. Wexner hopes these plans will allow Limited Brands to maintain its position in the specialty retailing industry.

However, the potential for serious problems exists for Wexner. Some of these include: (1) the possibility of downturns in the growth-oriented lingerie and personal care brands, (2) a continued downturn or recession in the U.S. economy, (3) a saturation of Limited Brands stores in U.S. malls, (4) difficulty finding reliable foreign suppliers, and (5) increased competition from Internet sales and other retail stores.

The following list presents some of the concerns that Wexner—and you— might consider:

1. Will the "branding" concept help Limited Brands to improve its market segmentation strategies?
2. Is locating stores in close proximity in malls a good idea for Limited Brands? Should the company locate some of its stores in strip shopping centers?
3. Is Limited Brands' strategy of spending more money on print and television advertising a good one?
4. What is the likelihood of a continued downturn in the U.S. economy that could negatively impact the women's apparel industry?
5. Will Wexner be able to "turn around" the Structure/Express Men's and Limited brands? What approach should he take in addition to concentrating on "branding"?
6. How serious are the potential problems Limited Brands could face in the future?
7. Should the company continue its strategy of developing a company and splitting it off as a separate company?
8. Should Limited Brands reorganize the company so the personal care brands are in a separate division?

References

Berner, Robert, and Christopher Palmeri. "Just How Deep Are Those Teen Pockets?" *BusinessWeek* (July 30, 2001).
Gill, Penny. "Les Wexner: Unlimited Success Story." *Stores* (January 1993).

Limited Brands. *Annual Reports* (1996, 1998, 2000, 2002).

Machan, Dyan. "Knowing Your Limits." *Forbes* (June 5, 1995).

"More Than Just a Bad Patch at the Gap." *BusinessWeek* (February 11, 2002).

"New Prestige Beauty Brand Unveiled by The Limited, Inc. and Shiseido Co., Ltd." *PR Newswire Association* (April 12, 2002).

"Retailing: Specialty." *Industry Surveys* (March 6, 2003).

Shein, Ester. "Intranet Logistics Goes High Fashion." *PC Week* (September 8, 1997).

Wilson, Marianne. "Limitless Possibilities." *Chain Store Age* (January 2003).

www.BathandBodyWorks.com.

www.limited.com.

www.tjx.com.

www.VictoriasSecret.com.

10 Wal-Mart Stores, Inc.—2004

Amit Shah, Evan Offstein, and Tyra Phipps
Frostburg State University

WMT

www.walmart.com

On February 18, 2003, *Fortune* announced that Wal-Mart was number one on the magazine's annual survey of Most Admired Companies. This marked the first time in the survey's 21-year history that the nation's largest company was also the most admired. This recognition represents the end result of Wal-Mart's efforts to overcome the recent economic downturn while still maintaining the level of reputation that the company is noted for.

Headquartered in Bentonville, Arkansas, Wal-Mart's sales rose from $217.8 billion in fiscal year 2002 to $244.5 billion in 2003. Net income rose from $6.7 billion to $8.0 billion during that period. For more than a decade, Wal-Mart has been growing by leaps and bounds and rolling over large competitors such as Kmart and thousands of small businesses. Financial statements are shown in Exhibit 1 and Exhibit 2. (Note: Wal-Mart's fiscal year ends January 31.)

In 1995, Wal-Mart ended a five-year battle with local leaders in Bennington, Vermont, and opened its first store in that state, thereby laying claim to having stores in all 50 states (see Exhibit 3). The Bennington store brought Wal-Mart's total number to 2,158. To get approval for this store, Wal-Mart abandoned its usual 200,000 square-foot store near a major highway exit and instead located in a downtown building containing just 50,000 square feet. Environmentalists in Vermont say the rural character of the state is endangered by "sprawl-mart development." As of the end of fiscal year 2003, there are still only four Wal-Mart stores in Vermont.

Wal-Mart does not have a formal mission statement. When asked about Wal-Mart's lack of a mission, Public Relations Coordinator Kim Ellis recently replied, "We believe that our customers are most interested in other aspects of our business, and we are focused on meeting their basic consumer needs." If, in fact, we did have a formal mission statement, it would be something like this: "To provide quality products at an everyday low price and with extended customer service . . . always." The Wal-Mart culture is based on three basic beliefs of Sam Walton: (1) respect for the individual, (2) service to our customers, and (3) strive for excellence.

History

No word better describes Wal-Mart than growth. In 1945, Sam Walton opened his first Ben Franklin franchise in Newport, Arkansas. Living in rural Bentonville, Arkansas, at the time, Walton, his wife Helen, and his brother Bud operated the nation's most successful Ben Franklin franchises. "We were a small chain," said Walton of his 16 store operation. "Things were running so smoothly [that] we even had time for our families." What more could a man want? A great deal, as it turned out.

EXHIBIT 1

Wal-Mart Stores—Income Statement

IN MILLIONS OF U.S. DOLLARS (EXCEPT FOR PER SHARE ITEMS) FISCAL YEAR ENDED JANUARY 31,	2003	2002	2001
Revenue	$244,524.0	217,799.0	191,329.0
Other Revenue	2,001.0	1,872.0	1,787.0
Total Revenue	**246,525.0**	**219,671.0**	**193,116.0**
Cost of Revenue	191,838.0	171,562.0	150,255.0
Gross Profit	**52,686.0**	**46,237.0**	**41,074.0**
Selling/General/Adm. Exp.	41,043.0	36,172.0	31,550.0
Research & Development	—	—	—
Depreciation/Amortization	—	—	—
Interest Expense (Income)	1,063.0	1,357.0	1,383.0
Unusual Expense (Income)	—	—	—
Other Operating Expenses	—		
Total Operating Expense	**233,806.0**	**208,920.0**	**183,000.0**
Operating Income	**12,719.0**	**10,751.0**	**10,116.0**
Interest Expense	—	—	—
Interest/Investment Income	—	—	—
Interest Income (Expense)	—	—	—
Gain (Loss) on Sale of Assets	—	—	—
Other, Net	—	—	—
Income Before Tax	**12,719.0**	**10,751.0**	**10,116.0**
Income Tax	4,487.0	3,897.0	3,692.0
Income After Tax	**8,232.0**	**6,854.0**	**6,424.0**
Minority Interest	(193.0)	(183.0)	(129.0)
Equity in Affiliates	—	—	—
Net Income	**8,039.0**	**6,671.0**	**6,295.0**
Accounting Change	0.0	0.0	0.0
Discontinued Operations	—	—	—
Extraordinary Item	—	—	—
Net Income	**8,039.0**	**6,671.0**	**6,295.0**
Preferred Dividends	—	—	—
Basic/Primary Wtd. Avg. Shares	4,430.0	4,465.0	4,465.0
Basic/Primary EPS	**1.815**	**1.494**	**1.410**
Basic/Primary EPS	**$ 1.815**	**1.494**	**1.410**

Source: www.investor.stockpoint.com

The company opened its first discount department store (Wal-Mart) in November 1962. The early stores had bare tile floors and pipe racks. Wal-Mart did not begin to revamp its image significantly until the mid–1970s, and growth in the early years was slow. However, once the company went public in 1970, sales began to increase rapidly. When it initially went public, 100 shares of Wal-Mart stock would have cost $1,650. Now, those 100 shares are worth over $6 million. Wal-Mart's stock was up 106 percent in 1999 and was named the number-one stock on the Dow.

Such retailers as Target, Venture, and Kmart provided the examples that Wal-Mart sought to emulate in its growth. The old Wal-Mart store colors, dark blue and

EXHIBIT 2
Consolidated Balance Sheet

	(AMOUNTS IN MILLIONS)	
JANUARY 31,	2003	2002
Assets		
Current Assets		
Cash and cash equivalents	$ 2,758	$ 2,161
Receivables	2,108	2,000
Inventories:		
At replacement cost	25,056	22,746
Less LIFO reserve	165	135
Inventories at LIFO cost	24,891	22,614
Prepaid expenses and other	726	1,103
Total Current Assets	30,483	27,878
Property, Plant and Equipment, at Cost		
Land	11,228	10,241
Building and improvements	33,750	28,527
Fixtures and equipment	15,946	14,135
Transportation equipment	1,313	1,089
	62,237	53,992
Less accumulated depreciation	13,537	11,436
Net property, plant and equipment	48,700	42,556
Property Under Capital Lease		
Property under capital lease	4,814	4,626
Less accumulated amortization	1,610	1,432
Net property under capital leases	3,204	3,194
Other Assets and Deferred Charges		
Net goodwill and other acquired intangible assets	9,521	8,566
Other assets and deferred charges	2,777	1,333
Total Assets	$94,685	$83,527
Liabilities and Shareholders' Equity		
Current Liabilities		
Commercial paper	$ 1,079	$ 743
Accounts payable	17,140	15,617
Accrued liabilities	8,945	7,174
Accrued income taxes	739	1,343
Long-term debt due within one year	4,538	2,257
Obligations under capital leases due within one year	176	148
Total Current Liabilities	32,617	27,282
Long-Term Debt	16,607	15,687
Long-Term Obligations Under Capital Leases	3,001	3,045
Deferred Income Taxes and Other	1,761	1,204
Minority Interest	1,362	1,207
Shareholders' Equity		
Preferred stock ($0.10 par value; 100 shares authorized, none issued)		
Common stock ($0.10 par value; 11,000 shares authorized, 4,395 and 4,453 issued and outstanding in 2003 and 2002, respectively)	440	445
Capital in excess of par value	1,482	1,484
Retained earnings	37,924	34,441
Other accumulated comprehensive income	(509)	(1,268)
Total Shareholders' Equity	39,337	35,102
Total Liabilities and Shareholders' Equity	$94,685	$83,527

Source: Wal-Mart *Annual Report, 2003.*

EXHIBIT 3
Fiscal 2003 End-of-Year Store Count

STATE	DISCOUNT STORES	SUPERCENTERS	SAM'S CLUBS	NEIGHBORHOOD MARKETS
Alabama	34	49	9	2
Alaska	6	0	3	0
Arizona	24	17	10	0
Arkansas	35	43	4	6
California	133	0	30	0
Colorado	17	29	14	0
Connecticut	27	2	3	0
Delaware	3	3	1	0
Florida	66	87	37	1
Georgia	42	61	20	0
Hawaii	6	0	1	0
Idaho	5	11	1	0
Illinois	81	33	27	0
Indiana	42	42	14	0
Iowa	27	24	7	0
Kansas	29	23	6	0
Kentucky	34	41	5	0
Louisiana	35	47	12	0
Maine	12	9	3	0
Maryland	32	5	13	0
Massachusetts	41	1	3	0
Michigan	48	14	22	0
Minnesota	34	9	12	0
Mississippi	21	41	5	1
Missouri	56	58	14	0
Montana	5	6	1	0
Nebraska	10	11	3	0
Nevada	11	7	5	0
New Hampshire	19	6	4	0
New Jersey	30	0	8	0
New Mexico	6	18	5	0
New York	52	22	18	0
North Carolina	47	52	17	0
North Dakota	8	0	2	0
Ohio	70	28	26	0
Oklahoma	41	40	7	12
Oregon	24	3	0	0
Pennsylvania	50	43	20	0
Rhode Island	8	0	1	0
South Carolina	22	37	9	0
South Dakota	6	4	2	0
Tennessee	33	57	15	2
Texas	117	155	68	24
Utah	6	15	7	1
Vermont	4	0	0	0
Virginia	21	52	13	0
Washington	29	6	2	0
West Virginia	8	20	3	0
Wisconsin	49	20	11	0
Wyoming	2	7	2	0
U.S. Totals	**1,568**	**1,258**	**525**	**49**

(continued)

EXHIBIT 3 *(continued)*

STATE	DISCOUNT STORES	SUPERCENTERS	SAM'S CLUBS	NEIGHBORHOOD MARKETS
INTERNATIONAL/WORLDWIDE				
Argentina	0	11	0	0
Brazil	0	12	8	2*
Canada	213	0	0	0
China	0	20	4	2
Germany	0	94	0	0
Korea	0	15	0	0
Mexico	472†	75	50	0
Puerto Rico	9	1	9	33**
United Kingdom	248‡	10	0	0
International Totals	**942**	**238**	**71**	**37**
Grand Totals	**2,510**	**1,496**	**596**	**86**

*Brazil includes Todo Dias

†Mexico includes 118 Bodegas, 50 Suburbias, 44 Superamas, 260 Vips

**Puerto Rico includes 33 Amigos

‡United Kingdom includes 248 ASDA Stores

Source: Wal-Mart *Annual Report, 2003*

white (too harsh), were dumped in favor of a three-tone combination of light beige, soft blue, and burnt orange. Carpeting, which had long been discarded on apparel sales floors, was put back. New racks were put into use that displayed the entire garment instead of only an outer edge.

In 1987, Wal-Mart implemented two new concepts: (1) Hypermarkets, which are 200,000 square-foot stores that sell everything, including food; and (2) Supercenters, which are scaled-down supermarkets. Also in 1987, Walton named David Glass as the new chief executive officer (CEO), while he remained chairman of the board. In 2000, H. Lee Scott was named president and CEO of Wal-Mart Stores, Inc. Exhibit 4 specifies the current organizational structure of Wal-Mart and identifies the individuals holding top management positions within the organization.

Sam Walton died in 1992. Bud Walton died in 1995. Wal-Mart's *1995 Annual Report* was dedicated to Bud. Sam Walton once said about Bud, "Of course, my number-one retail partner has been my brother, Bud. Bud's wise counsel and guidance kept us from many a mistake. Often, Bud would advise taking a different direction or maybe changing the timing. I soon learned to listen to him because he has exceptional judgment and a great deal of common sense."

Wal-Mart's current president and CEO, H. Lee Scott, commends the past leadership and management standards set by Sam Walton. He states, "While our history is rich with success, there's no question that our best years are yet to come."

Divisions

Wal-Mart Stores

Most Wal-Mart stores are located in towns of 5,000 to 25,000. On occasion, smaller stores are built in communities of less than 5,000. As indicated in Exhibit 3 for fiscal 2003, Wal-Mart, Inc., currently operates domestically 1,568 Wal-Mart discount stores, 1,258 Supercenters, 525 SAM's Clubs, and 49 Neighborhood Markets. Most of Wal-Mart's $244.5 billion in fiscal 2003 sales came from Wal-Mart stores and Supercenters. Exhibit 5 provides a breakdown of net sales per division, while Exhibit 6 provides other pertinent financial data per division.

EXHIBIT 4
Wal-Mart's Organizational Chart

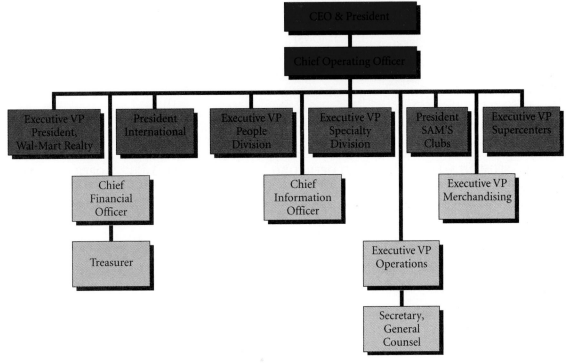

Source: www.freeedgar.com.

EXHIBIT 5
Net Sales by Operating Segment

The company and each of its operating segments had net sales (in millions) for the three fiscal years ended January 31, 2003 as follows:

FISCAL YEAR	WAL-MART STORES	SAM'S CLUB	INTERNATIONAL	OTHER	TOTAL COMPANY	TOTAL COMPANY INCREASE FROM PRIOR FISCAL YEAR
2003	**$157,121**	**$31,702**	**$40,794**	**$14,907**	**$244,524**	**12%**
2002	139,131	29,395	35,485	13,788	217,799	14%
2001	121,889	26,798	32,100	10,542	191,329	16%

Net sales grew by 12% in fiscal 2003 when compared with fiscal 2002. That increase resulted from our domestic and international expansion programs, and a domestic comparative store sales increase of 5% when compared with fiscal 2002. The sales increase of 14% in fiscal 2002, when compared with fiscal 2001, resulted from our domestic and international expansion programs, and a domestic comparative store sales increase of 6%. We consider comparative stores sales to be sales at stores that were open as of February 1st of the prior fiscal year and have not been expanded or relocated since February 1st of the prior fiscal year. Stores that were expanded or relocated during that period are not included in the calculation of comparative store sales. Comparative store sales are also referred to as same-store sales within the retail industry. The Wal-Mart stores and SAM'S CLUB segments include domestic units only. Wal-Mart stores and SAM'S CLUBS located outside the United States are included in the International segment.

Source: Wal-Mart *Annual Report, 2003.*

EXHIBIT 6
Wal-Mart Segment Data

A. WAL-MART STORES SEGMENT

FISCAL YEAR	SEGMENT SALES INCREASE FROM PRIOR FISCAL YEAR	SEGMENT OPERATING INCOME (IN BILLIONS)	SEGMENT OPERATING INCOME INCREASE FROM PRIOR YEAR	OPERATING INCOME AS A PERCENTAGE OF SEGMENT SALES
2003	12.9%	$11.9	16.2%	7.6%
2002	14.1%	10.2	6.3%	7.3%
2001	12.1%	9.6	10.5%	7.9%

The Wal-Mart Stores segment sales amounted to 64.3% of total company sales in fiscal 2003, which compares to 63.9% and 63.7% in fiscal 2002 and 2001, respectively.

B. SAM'S CLUB SEGMENT

FISCAL YEAR	SEGMENT SALES INCREASE FROM PRIOR FISCAL YEAR	SEGMENT OPERATING INCOME (IN BILLIONS)	SEGMENT OPERATING INCOME INCREASE FROM PRIOR YEAR	OPERATING INCOME AS A PERCENTAGE OF SEGMENT SALES
2003	7.8%	$1,028	0.00%	3.2%
2002	9.7%	1,028	9.1%	3.5%
2001	8.1%	0.942	10.8%	3.5%

The SAM'S Club segment net sales amounted to 13.0% of total company net sales in fiscal 2003, which compares to 13.5% and 14.0% in fiscal 2002 and 2001, respectively.

C. INTERNATIONAL SEGMENT

FISCAL YEAR	SEGMENT SALES INCREASE FROM PRIOR FISCAL YEAR	SEGMENT OPERATING INCOME (IN BILLIONS)	SEGMENT OPERATING INCOME INCREASE FROM PRIOR YEAR	OPERATING INCOME AS A PERCENTAGE OF SEGMENT SALES
2003	15.0%	$2,033	55.8%	5.0%
2002	10.5%	1,305	37.5%	3.7%
2001	41.2%	0.949	41.6%	3.0%

Wal-Mart's International segment is comprised of wholly owned operations in Argentina, Canada, Germany, South Korea, Puerto Rico, and the United Kingdom; operations through joint ventures in China; and operations through majority-owned subsidiaries in Brazil and Mexico and through a minority investment in Japan. International sales accounted for approximately 16.7% of total company sales in fiscal 2003 compared with 16.3% in fiscal 2002 and 16.8% in fiscal 2001.

D. OTHER

FISCAL YEAR	SEGMENT SALES INCREASE FROM PRIOR FISCAL YEAR	SEGMENT OPERATING LOSS (IN BILLIONS)	SEGMENT OPERATING LOSS INCREASE FROM PRIOR YEAR	OPERATING LOSS AS A FISCAL YEAR PERCENTAGE OF SEGMENT SALES
2003	8.1%	($1,290)	(109.1%)	(8.7%)
2002	30.8%	(0.617)	(214.8%)	(4.5%)
2001	20.3%	(0.196)	34.0%	(1.9%)

McLane net sales to unaffiliated purchasers accounted for approximately 6.1% of total company sales in fiscal 2003 compared with 6.3% in fiscal 2002 and 5.5% in fiscal 2001.

Operating losses for the segment in each of the fiscal years presented primarily resulted from corporate overhead expenses including insurance costs, corporate bonuses, various other expenses and in fiscal 2003, the unfavorable impact of a $30 million LIFO adjustment. These corporate overhead expenses are partially offset by McLane operating income and the favorable impact of LIFO adjustments of $67 million and $176 million in fiscal 2002 and 2001, respectively.

Source: Wal-Mart Annual Report, 2003 p. 6.

International sales accounted for approximately 16.7 percent of total company sales in fiscal 2003. This is up from 16.3 percent in fiscal 2002. For fiscal 2003, Wal-Mart operated internationally in 9 countries, with 942 discount stores, 238 Supercenters, 71 SAM's Clubs and 37 Neighborhood Markets.

Wal-Mart grouped its smaller discount stores, such as the one in Bennington, Vermont, into a new Hometown USA program. This strategy allows the company to give special attention to customers in smaller markets in rural America. Hometown USA consists of the stores that are less than 50,000 square feet and that are under one regional manager. The idea is to enable these stores to develop locally and with a different mix from the large prototypes. Although these stores represent Wal-Mart's heritage, they had become lost in the shuffle as the company opened 120,000 to 150,000 square-foot stores.

Wal-Mart stores generally have 36 departments and offer a wide variety of merchandise, including apparel for women, girls, men, boys, and infants. Each store also carries curtains, fabrics and notions, shoes, housewares, hardware, electronics, home supplies, sporting goods, toys, cameras and supplies, health and beauty aids, pharmaceuticals, and jewelry. Nationally advertised merchandise accounts for a majority of sales of the stores. Wal-Mart has begun marketing limited lines of merchandise under the brand name SAM's American Choice. The merchandise is carefully selected to ensure quality and must be made in the United States. Wal-Mart has also developed new apparel lines, such as the Kathie Lee career sportswear and dress collection, Basic Equipment sportswear, and McKids children's clothing.

McLane's

McLane's is the nation's largest distributor of food and merchandise to convenience stores. McLane's offers a wide variety of grocery and nongrocery products, including perishable and nonperishable items. The nongrocery products consist primarily of tobacco products, merchandise, health and beauty aids, toys, and stationery. McLane's is a wholesale distributor that sells merchandise to a variety of retailers, including Wal-Mart stores, SAM's Clubs, and Supercenters.

On May 2, 2003, Wal-Mart announced that it had entered into an agreement with Berkshire Hathaway, Inc., for the sale of McLane Company, Inc. Lee Scott, Wal-Mart's president and CEO, was quoted as saying, "This transaction is positive for both Wal-Mart and McLane." The sale will allow Wal-Mart to focus exclusively on core retail business. Following the acquisition, McLane will be a wholly owned subsidiary of Berkshire Hathaway, Inc.

SAM's Clubs

SAM's Clubs are membership-only, cash-and-carry operations. A financial service credit card program (Discover Card) is available in all clubs. In fiscal 2003, business members paid an annual membership fee of $30 for the primary membership card, with a spouse card available at no additional cost. The annual membership fee for an individual member is $35 for the primary membership card, with a spouse card available at no additional cost. The Elite Membership Program offers additional benefits and services such as automotive extended service contracts, roadside assistance, home improvement, auto brokering, and pharmacy discounts. The annual membership fee for an Elite Member is $100.

SAM's offers bulk displays of name-brand merchandise, some soft goods, and institutional-size grocery items. SAM's Clubs usually offer over 3,500 items, which are used most often by the consumers they serve, and each store also carries jewelry, sporting goods, toys, tires, stationery, and books. Most clubs have fresh-food departments, such as bakery, meat, and produce sections.

need to work smarter every day. With this technology, Wal-Mart is getting better, quicker, and more accurate information to manage and control every aspect of its business.

wal-mart.com

Wal-Mart is in the retail business, which now includes Internet e-tailing. The Internet has interesting aspects and will definitely serve a growing market throughout the twenty-first century. Profits are not easily made over the Internet, and issues of cost of delivery, merchandise returns, and data security are top concerns prior to building business over the Internet. Wal-Mart moved into the Internet in 1996 with the introduction of Wal-Mart On-line, and then it relaunched the site on January 1, 2000, as Wal-Mart.com. Wal-Mart looks at Internet retailing as another store with possibility, but without walls.

Wal-Mart.com, with its headquarters located in the San Francisco Bay area, is a wholly owned subsidiary of Wal-Mart Stores, Inc. This location choice affords Wal-Mart.com access to the best pool of Internet executive and technical talent. The company was able to attract a top retail management talent in Jeanne Jackson as the CEO of Wal-Mart.com. This venture combines the better of two worlds, technology and retailing, in order to provide customers easy access to more things at Wal-Mart 24 hours a day, 7 days a week. Its distinct purpose is to provide consumers with a convenient and rewarding online shopping experience. Wal-Mart.com has a separate management team and board of directors. Ultimately, it might choose to go public; however, Wal-Mart Stores will retain a majority ownership of the venture.

Operations

Wal-Mart's expense structure, measured as a percentage of sales, continues to be among the lowest in the industry. Although Walton watched expenses, he rewarded sales managers handsomely. Sales figures are available to every employee at Wal-Mart. Monthly figures for each department are ranked and made available throughout the organization. Employees who do better than average get rewarded with raises, bonuses, and a pat on the back. Poor performers are only rarely fired, although demotions are possible.

All employees (called "associates") have a stake in the financial performance of the company. Store managers earn as much as $100,000 to $150,000 per year. Even part-time clerks qualify for profit sharing and stock-purchase plans. Millionaires among Wal-Mart's middle managers are not uncommon. Executives frequently solicit ideas for improving the organization from employees and often put them to use. Due to Wal-Mart's stock selling at 35 to 40 times earnings, an almost incredible price, Walton presided over a sizable fortune before his death.

The Walton family owns 39 percent of Wal-Mart stock. Family holdings are worth nearly $16 billion. Continuing a Walton tradition, Wal-Mart invites over 100 analysts and institutional investors to the field house at the University of Arkansas for its annual meeting in mid-June. During the day-and-a-half session, investors meet top executives as well as Wal-Mart district managers, buyers, and 200,000 hourly salespeople. Investors see a give-and-take meeting between buyers and district managers.

Employee Benefits

Wal-Mart management takes pride in the ongoing development of its people. Training is seen as critical to outstanding performance, and new programs are often implemented in all areas of the company. The combination of grassroots meetings, the open-door policy, videos, printed material, classroom and home study, year-end management meetings, and on-the-job training has enabled employees to prepare themselves for advancement and added responsibilities.

Wal-Mart managers stay current with new developments and needed changes. Executives spend one week each year in hourly jobs in various stores. Walton himself once traveled at least three days per week, visiting competitors' stores and attending the openings of new stores, leading the Wal-Mart cheer, "Give me a W, give me an A. . . ."

Wal-Mart encourages employee stock purchases. Under the Stock Purchase Plan, Wal-Mart will contribute 15 percent each year toward an associate's stock purchases, up to $1,800 per year. Wal-Mart has a 401(k) plan, to which it contributes on an associate's behalf, whether the associate participates or not. The contribution is annual and is based on the company's performance. Associates may contribute up to 15 percent of pre-tax income toward retirement and they also have choices as to how their money is invested. Wal-Mart also has a corporate profit-sharing plan. The purposes of the profit-sharing plan are to furnish an incentive for increased efficiency, to provide progressive recognition of service, and to encourage careers with the company by Wal-Mart associates. This is a trustee-administered plan, which means that the company's contributions are made only out of net profits and are held by a trustee. The company from time to time contributes 10 percent of net profits to the trust.

Company contributions can be withdrawn only on termination. If employment is terminated because of retirement, death, or permanent disability, the company contribution is fully vested (meaning the entire amount is nonforfeitable). If termination of employment occurs for any other reason, the amount that is nonforfeitable depends on the number of years of service with the company. After completion of the third year of service with the company, 20 percent of each participant's account is nonforfeitable for each subsequent year of service. After seven years of service, a participant's account is 100-percent vested.

Policies and Legal Problems

Sam Walton was admittedly old-fashioned in many respects. Wal-Mart store policies reflect many of his values. For example, store policies forbid employees to date other employees without the prior approval of the executive committee. Also, women are rarely found in management positions. However, promotions have recently been made where there are now women in senior officer positions. Walton also resisted placing women on the board of directors; however, there are two women on the board at this time. Wal-Mart is an EEO/AA employer, but until 2003 managed to get away with certain past discriminatory policies. However, women now have a class action lawsuit against Wal-Mart based on so few women being among its managers, given that a majority of its workforce is female. Also in 2003, Wal-Mart had problems relating to hiring illegal Hispanic workers to clean its stores.

Wal-Mart has instituted several initiatives to increase the recruitment and promotion of women and minorities, including:

- A mentoring program encompassing more than 750 women and minority managers.
- A women's leadership group, in partnership with Herman Miller and ServiceMaster, to develop opportunities for high-potential female managers.
- Store internships during the summer for college students between their junior and senior years, with 70 percent being women or minorities.

Philanthropy and Community Involvement

Wal-Mart's community involvement year after year is phenomenal. Education is a primary beneficiary of Wal-Mart charitable giving. Some examples of its largesse follow.

- Each store awards a $1,000 college scholarship to a qualifying high school senior. More than $11 million in scholarships has been awarded since the program's inception.
- The company has made a major commitment to the United Negro College Fund. Wal-Mart pledged $1 million to UNCF over a four-year period.
- The company sponsors the Competitive Edge Scholarship Fund, which makes four-year scholarships—each worth $20,000—available to students pursuing technology-related college degrees.

During 2002, Wal-Mart provided $1 million in community disaster-relief funds to local Salvation Army and American Red Cross chapters. These efforts were recognized in May 2002 when President Bush honored Wal-Mart with the prestigious Ron Brown Corporate Leadership Award. This award is presented to the best corporate citizens in America. It recognizes companies that have demonstrated a deep level of commitment to empower employees and communites, while also advancing in business interests. Wal-Mart's corporate citizenship extends well beyond U. S. borders and into every country in which it operates.

Marketing

The discount retailing business is seasonal to a certain extent. Generally, the highest volume of sales and net income occurs in the fourth fiscal quarter, and the lowest volume occurs during the first fiscal quarter. Wal-Mart draws customers into the store by radio and television advertising, monthly circulars, and weekly newspaper ads. Television advertising is used to convey an image of everyday low prices and quality merchandise. Radio is used to a lesser degree to promote specific products that are usually in high demand. Newspaper advertisements and monthly circulars are major contributors to the program, emphasizing deeply discounted items, and they are effective at luring customers into the stores.

Efforts are also made to discount corporate overhead. Visitors often mistake corporate headquarters for a warehouse because of its limited decor and lack of "show." Wal-Mart executives share hotel rooms when traveling, to reduce expenses. The company avoids spending money on consultants and marketing experts. Instead, decisions are made based on the intuitive judgments of managers and employees and on the assessment of strategies of other retail chains.

Wal-Mart censors some products. The company has banned recordings and removed magazines based on certain types of lyrics and graphics; it has also stopped marketing teen rock magazines. Wal-Mart advertises a "Buy American" policy in an effort to keep production at home. Consequently, Wal-Mart buyers are constantly seeking vendors in grassroots America. In Tulsa, Oklahoma, Zebco, the fishing equipment company, responded to Wal-Mart's challenge by bucking the trend toward overseas fishing tackle manufacturing. Zebco created more than 200 U.S. jobs to assemble rods and to manufacture bait-and-cast reels. The company's bait-and-cast reels are the first to be manufactured in the United States in 30 years.

Competitors

Kmart is one of Wal-Mart's key competitors. However, compared to Wal-Mart, the scope of Kmart's problem becomes evident. Kmart's sales were around $31 billion in fiscal year 2002. This dollar figure is drastically lower than that of Wal-Mart's sales figure. Should Wal-Mart, the price leader in discounting, choose to sacrifice $0.10 to $0.15 of its estimated earnings per share, it virtually could ensure that Kmart would not operate above the breakeven point. During 2002, Kmart closed some 600 stores in the United States, Guam, Puerto Rico, and the U.S. Virgin Islands. Following a damaging move into specialty retailing and numerous failed turnaround attempts, Kmart began offering groceries in it stores. However, in January 2002 Kmart filed for Chapter 11 bankruptcy protection.

Supercenters are revolutionizing the discount store battlefield, just as tanks redefined trench warfare. Wal-Mart started 1995 with 68 Supercenters but increased this number to 1,496 in fiscal 2003. The goal of each new store is to shatter the profit potential of at least one older Kmart discount store. This is the dusk of the discount store era, and improvements in the merchandising and systems of Kmart's discount stores might do little to forestall its decline.

Target has now become a fierce competitor of Wal-Mart. Target operates about 1,500 stores in three formats: Target, a discount chain with more than 1,100 stores; Mervyn's midrange department stores; and Marshall Field's upscale department stores. Target, including SuperTarget and Target Greatland, account for more than 80 percent of Target Corporation's sales. Target has created a niche for itself by offering more upscale, fashionable merchandise than that of Wal-Mart.

Costco Wholesale Corporation has also become a competitor of Wal-Mart. Costco competes with the SAM's Club segment. It is the largest wholesale club operator in the United States, just ahead of SAM's.

Future Strategies

What strategies would you recommend to current CEO H. Lee Scott? How can Wal-Mart benefit from Internet retailing? How aggressively should Wal-Mart expand internationally and where? Should Wal-Mart get a foothold in Europe before competitors seize the initiative? Should Wal-Mart expand further in Mexico, the United States, or Canada? Should Wal-Mart make further acquisitions, like its Woolco acquisition in Canada? Is Wal-Mart's rate of growth of Supercenters too fast? What private-label products should Wal-Mart consider developing? What can Wal-Mart do to improve its SAM's Clubs operations? Develop a three-year strategic plan for CEO H. Lee Scott.

11 Target Corporation—2003

Henry Beam
Western Michigan University

TGT

www.target.com

Target Corporation is the country's third-largest general merchandise retailer, behind Wal-Mart and Sears Roebuck but Target does no business outside the United States. Company revenues were $43.9 billion in 2002, a 10.2 percent increase over 2001. Earnings were $1.6 billion, an increase of 20.9 percent over 2001. Headquartered in Minneapolis, Minnesota, the company caters to all income groups through three operating divisions: Mervyn's, Marshall Field's, and Target. Marshall Field's department stores are strong in the upper Midwest, controlling significant shares of the market in Detroit, Chicago, and Minneapolis. Target's upscale general merchandise discount stores are spread across the country and account for over 80 percent of the company's sales and pre-tax profits. Mervyn's, with stores primarily in California, caters to lower- to middle-income shoppers.

The Target division has been so successful that the company, formerly called Dayton Hudson, changed its name to Target Corporation in 2000. In addition, all Hudson's or Dayton's department stores were renamed Marshall Field's. Reflecting the corporate emphasis on service, all divisions refer to their customers as guests.

Sometimes, a Target store will be located near a Mervyn's and a Marshall Field's department store, or both. A mall in Kalamazoo, Michigan, has a Marshall Field's and a Mervyn's, while less than a mile away there is a Target store in a shopping center. Despite such proximity of locations, Target Corporation has made little attempt to associate the divisions with each other in the eyes of consumers, many of whom aren't aware that the three divisions are part of the same company.

History

Joseph Hudson opened a men's clothing store in Detroit in 1873. Among his merchandising innovations were return privileges and price-marking in place of bargaining, and by 1891, Hudson's was the largest retailer of men's clothing in America. When Hudson died in 1928, his four nephews took over and expanded the business. In 1928, Hudson's built a new building in downtown Detroit, and eventually grew to 25 stories, each with 49 acres of floor space that exuded quality throughout. The Detroit store was closed in 1982 and demolished in 1998 to make room for a downtown Detroit redevelopment project. In 1903, George Dayton, a former banker, opened his Dayton Dry Goods store in Minneapolis, where there was high foot traffic. Like Hudson, Dayton offered return privileges and liberal credit, and his store expanded to a full-line department store that was 12 stories tall.

After World War II, both companies saw that the future of retailing lay in the suburbs. In 1954, Hudson's built Northland at the northwest edge of Detroit, then the largest shopping center in the United States. Dayton's built the world's first fully enclosed shopping mall, Southdale, in Minneapolis in 1956. In an attempt to diversify, Dayton's opened its first Target discount store in 1962, and after going public in 1966, grew through numerous acquisitions. In 1969, it acquired the family-owned Hudson's for stock, forming Dayton Hudson Corporation, and in 1978, the company added the California-based Mervyn's retail chain of 47 stores. Its last major acquisition came in 1990, when it purchased Marshall Field's upscale department stores, assuming $1 billion of debt in the process. Marshall Field's grew out of a dry-goods business that predated the Civil War. Marshall Field bought the store in 1865, named the company after himself, and built it into one of Chicago's biggest retailers. His motto, "Give the lady what she wants," was a precursor of customer-oriented retailing. The company's original and largest store is located in downtown Chicago and is a major tourist attraction. Marshall Field's 111 STATE line of fashion apparel was named after the street address of this store.

Target Corporation's executive office provides leadership for all divisions and establishes the values under which those divisions operate. Each of the divisions has its own CEO and president and is run like an independent business, even though they are encouraged to share advances in technology and coordinate purchasing and financial management. An organization chart for the company and its operating divisions is given in Exhibit 1.

Divisions

Target

At the end of 2003, the Target division consisted of 1,225 stores located in all 48 continental states. Target is an upscale discount retailer that provides good-quality, family-oriented merchandise at attractive prices in a clean, spacious, and customer-friendly environment. Its motto is, "Expect more, pay less." A 1999 *Fortune* article on Target noted, "Going to Target is a cool experience, and everybody now considers it cool to save money. On the other hand, is it cool to save at Kmart, at Wal-Mart? I don't think so." Target offers innovative, well-designed merchandise at reasonable prices, such as Philips Kitchen Appliances, Calphalon cookware, Michael Graves–designed small appliances, and Eddie Bauer camping gear. Target stores, which average 125,000 square feet in size, are typically located in small, freestanding malls. Regional distribution centers process 90 percent of all freight for the stores. The objective of the distribution centers is to provide next-day service to all locations. Target invites evaluation from its customers on evaluation forms entitled "Be Our Guest Commentator," which are available at checkout counters. Target's micromarketing program has helped improve its merchandise assortments on a store-by-store basis. Micromarketing is Target's system for tailoring merchandise assortments to

EXHIBIT 1

Organization Chart for Target Corporation

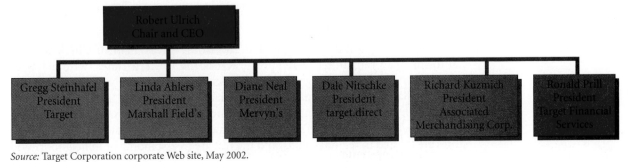

Source: Target Corporation corporate Web site, May 2002.

customers' needs in individual stores or markets, based on regional, climatic, demographic, and ethnic factors. This permits stores as close as fifteen miles apart to offer different merchandise mixes. The typical Target customer is a married woman with children, who is part of a two-wage-earner family with an average household income of $50,000, considerably higher than that of the typical Kmart or Wal-Mart customer. The average household income in the United States is $39,000.

Target advertises through multipage inserts placed in local newspapers, and television advertisements, featuring the familiar red circular bull's eye symbol. Target plans to continue opening stores in less-penetrated markets, such as Boston, New York, and Philadelphia, but increasingly, it is building new stores in more mature markets such as Atlanta, Denver, Indianapolis, and Phoenix. Although the cost of a store site in these more densely populated regions is generally higher, so is the sales potential. Over the past five years, Target's square footage has grown at a compound annual rate of 10 percent and is expected to continue to grow at that rate for the next few years. In 1995, Target opened its first two supercenter-type stores (SuperTargets) in the Plains states. The stores are about 180,000 square feet in size, with a fourth of the space devoted to grocery items, including its own line of grocery products marketed under the Archer Farms label. Certain categories, such as health and beauty aids and paper products, link the grocery and general merchandise areas and facilitate crossover shopping. The stores also feature a Starbucks Coffee Shop. The company anticipates that it will operate more than 200 SuperTarget stores by 2010. According to CEO Robert Ulrich, SuperTargets bring "fashion to food" and offer "a store that is attractive to our guests and as differentiated from our competition as are our discount stores."

Marshall Field's (www.fields.com)

At the end of 2003, Marshall Field's operated 62 department stores in eight Midwestern states. About half of the department stores are located in the major markets of Chicago, Detroit, and Minneapolis/St. Paul. Historically, they have emphasized fashion leadership, quality merchandise, and superior customer service, and today, the stores offer strong national brands with competitive prices in men's and women's apparel, accessories, and home furnishings. The typical customer for the department stores is a married woman in her early forties with a median family income of $50,000; over half have earned a college degree, and two-thirds hold white-collar positions. In addition to building new stores in selected locations, such as the new 200,000 square-foot store in the Rivertown Crossing Mall in Grand Rapids, Michigan, the division is also renovating some of its older stores.

In 2003, Marshall Field's and Yahoo!, a leading global Internet company, announced that Yahoo! would lease space in Marshall Field's flagship State Street store. A senior Yahoo! executive commented, "This initiative gives us the opportunity to put Yahoo! into the hands of the consumers in a retail environment. Both Yahoo! and Marshall Field's offer a broad array of products to a diverse customer base, making this partnership an ideal brand-building opportunity." Marshall Field's also sells Yahoo!-branded products that include digital cameras, webcams, keyboards, and speakers.

Mervyn's (www.mervyns.com)

At the end of 2003, Mervyn's operated 266 stores, nearly half of which were in California. The remainder were spread across the western states, with a few in Michigan and Minnesota. Mervyn's is a moderately priced family department store chain emphasizing brand-name and private-label casual apparel and home fashions that complement the offerings of Target and Marshall Field's. Its motto is "Big brands, small prices." Mervyn's typical customer is similar to that of Target. Half its stores are located in regional malls, and the rest are free-standing or in neighborhood shopping centers. While Mervyn's showed improved sales and profitability in 2003, performance in recent years has been disappointing. Like Target, Mervyn's advertises through weekly multipage inserts in local newspapers.

Direct Marketing and target.direct

The direct merchandising and electronic retailing division of Target Corporation is called target.direct. It was formed in 2000 by combining Target's e-commerce operation with its Rivertown Trading Company direct merchandising unit to create a single organization. This division produces six retail catalogs, four of which also have their own Web sites. The two largest catalogs are *Wireless,* and *Signals,* each of which offer a broad selection of gifts, including videos, art prints, distinctive jewelry, and creative toys. All catalogs and online shopping services can be accessed through Target Corporation's corporate Web site, **www.target.com**. All merchandise purchased through target.com may be returned to any Target store location.

Competition

Since its three main divisions, taken together, compete across all major merchandising categories except large appliances, Target Corporation faces a wide range of competitors. The largest division, Target, competes directly with "the marts": Kmart and Wal-Mart.

Kmart traces its roots to the S. S. Kresge Company dime store chain which was incorporated in 1912. By the 1950s, Kresge had become one of the largest general retailers in the nation, with stores primarily in urban locations. The first Kmart was opened in 1962 in a suburb of Detroit after an extensive study of retailing trends made in 1958 by its future CEO, Harry B. Cunningham. Designed to appeal to low- and middle-income shoppers, the Kmart large-store format was so successful that the company concentrated on it, rapidly opening Kmarts from coast to coast and closing dime stores as they became unprofitable. In 1977, the company officially changed its name to Kmart Corporation. Although Kmart features the popular Martha Stewart line of home furnishings and garden equipment, its stores are generally perceived as older, smaller, and less attractive than those of Wal-Mart or Target. In January 2002, Kmart became the largest retailing firm to seek bankruptcy protection. It emerged in May 2003. Realizing it has fallen far behind both Target and Wal-Mart in the discount store business, Kmart's post-bankruptcy strategy has been to operate "stores of the neighborhood" which cater to urban ethnic communities.

Wal-Mart Stores is one of the best-known success stories in America. Sam Walton opened his first Wal-Mart store in Rogers, Arkansas, in 1962. Growth, slow at first, accelerated during the 1970s. Wal-Mart established highly automated distribution centers to reduce shipping time and implemented an advanced computer system to track inventory and to speed up checkout and reordering. Its motto is displayed on each of its stores: "We sell for less, satisfaction guaranteed." Wal-Mart is the world's largest company. It operates nearly 5,000 stores worldwide, and about one-third of those are Supercenters which also carry groceries. At an average size of about 180,000 square feet, these stores are more than twice the size of the company's traditional discount stores and significantly more profitable. By the end of 2003, Wal-Mart's Supercenters outnumbered its traditional discount stores for the first time. It has overtaken Kroger to become the nation's largest seller of groceries and plans to open about 200 new Supercenters in the United States every year for the foreseeable future.

Target, Marshall Field's, and Mervyn's also compete with large national retailers such as JC Penney and Sears, as well as with regional discount department store chains such as Kohl's in the Midwest, Dillard's Department Stores in the South, and

May Department Stores in the East. Target's recent balance sheet gives sales and net income figures for the five largest general merchandise firms.

Financial Aspects

Balance sheet and income statement data on Target Corporation are given in Exhibits 2 and 3.

Financial Services

Financial services, including the credit card operation, are an increasingly important component of Target's profitability. Over the past five years, pretax profits from financing grew at a compound annual rate of 17 percent. Each division has its own credit card. The transactions are handled through Target Corporation's wholly owned Retailer's National Bank, chartered in 1994. The divisions will also take other credit cards, such as VISA and MasterCard. The recently introduced Target VISA card has been issued to 9 million customers. In an attempt to provide one-stop-shopping convenience, many Target stores now provide access to integrated banking and to brokerage and investment planning services through its alliance with E*TRADE, a leading online discount brokerage service.

Corporate Social Responsibility

Target Corporation is considered a model corporate citizen by consumer groups. It has contributed 5 percent of its pretax profits to philanthropic purposes every year since 1946. (By contrast, most large corporations in the United States, including Wal-Mart, contribute about 1 percent.) In 2003, the three operating divisions and the Target Corporation Foundation (funded by the corporation) gave over $50 million to local nonprofit programs that make their communities safer and more attractive places to live. Target will also donate 1 percent of purchases made on the Target Guest Card to the school of the guest's choice.

Robert Ulrich, Chairman and CEO

Robert Ulrich, Chairman and CEO of Target Corporation since 1994, is a graduate of the University of Michigan and the Executive Program at the Stanford University Graduate School of Business. His whole career has been with Target and its predecessor companies; he started as a merchandise trainee at Marshall Field's in 1967. Ulrich is a devotee of the arts and serves on the board of the Minneapolis Institute of Arts. The company does not have a formal mission statement, but Mr. Ulrich's first letter to shareholders after becoming chairman set forth his vision and growth goals for Target that still apply:

> We are committed to serving our guests better than the competition with trend-right, high-quality merchandise at very competitive prices. We are committed to being a low-cost, high-quality distributor of merchandise through "boundaryless" functioning—through leverage resources, expertise, and economies across divisions. Our primary objective is to maximize shareholder value over time. We believe we will achieve a compound annual fully diluted earnings per share growth of 15 percent over time, while maintaining a prudent and flexible capital structure.

Target Corporation has adhered closely to this management philosophy during Ulrich's tenure as CEO. Wall Street liked what it saw, since the price of Target

EXHIBIT 2

Target Corp (TGT)—Income Statement

IN MILLIONS OF U.S. DOLLARS (EXCEPT FOR PER SHARE ITEMS)	52 WEEKS 2/1/03	52 WEEKS 2/2/02	53 WEEKS 2/3/01
Revenue	$43,917.00	39,826.00	36,851.00
Other Revenue	—	—	—
Total Revenue	**43,917.00**	**39,826.00**	**36,851.00**
Cost of Revenue	30,025.00	27,606.00	25,504.00
Gross Profit	**13,892.00**	**12,220.00**	**11,347.00**
Selling/General/Administrative Expenses	9,416.00	8,461.00	7,928.00
Research & Development	—	—	—
Depreciation/Amortization	1,212.00	1,079.00	940
Interest Expense (Income), Net Operating	588	473	426
Unusual Expense (Income)	—	—	—
Other Operating Expenses	—	—	—
Total Operating Expense	**41,241.00**	**37,619.00**	**34,798.00**
Operating Income	**2,676.00**	**2,207.00**	**2,053.00**
Interest Expense, Net Non-Operating	—	—	—
Interest/Investment Income, Non-Operating	—	—	—
Interest Income (Expense), Net Non-Operating	—	—	—
Gain (Loss) on Sale of Assets	—	—	—
Other, Net	—	—	—
Income Before Tax	**2,676.00**	**2,207.00**	**2,053.00**
Income Tax	1,022.00	839	789
Income After Tax	**1,654.00**	**1,368.00**	**1,264.00**
Minority Interest	—	—	—
Equity in Affiliates	—	—	—
Net Income Before Extra. Items	**1,654.00**	**1,368.00**	**1,264.00**
Accounting Change	—	—	—
Discontinued Operations	—	—	—
Extraordinary Item	—	—	—
Net Income	**$ 1,654.00**	**1,368.00**	**1,264.00**
Preferred Dividends	—	—	0
Income Available to Common Excl. Extra. Items	**1,654.00**	**1,368.00**	**1,264.00**
Income Available to Common Incl. Extra. Items	**1,654.00**	**1,368.00**	**1,264.00**
Basic/Primary Weighted Average Shares	908	901.5	903.5
Basic/Primary EPS Excl. Extra. Items	**1.822**	**1.517**	**1.399**
Basic/Primary EPS Incl. Extra. Items	**1.822**	**1.517**	**1.399**
Dilution Adjustment	0	0	0
Diluted Weighted Average Shares	914	909.8	913
Diluted EPS Excl. Extra. Items	**1.81**	**1.504**	**1.384**
Diluted EPS Incl. Extra. Items	**1.81**	**1.504**	**1.384**
Dividends per Share—Common Stock	0.24	0.225	0.215
Gross Dividends—Common Stock	218	203	194
Stock Based Compensation	31	28	17

Source: www.investor.stockpoint.com

EXHIBIT 3

Target Corp (TGT)—Balance Sheet

IN MILLIONS OF U.S. DOLLARS (EXCEPT FOR PER SHARE ITEMS)	AS OF 2/1/03	AS OF 2/2/02	AS OF 2/3/01
Cash & Equivalents	$ 758	499	356
Short Term Investments	—	—	—
Cash and Short Term Investments	758	499	356
Trade Accounts Receivable, Net	5,565.00	3,831.00	1,941.00
Other Receivables	—	—	—
Total Receivables, Net	5,565.00	3,831.00	1,941.00
Total Inventory	4,760.00	4,449.00	4,248.00
Prepaid Expenses	—	—	—
Other Current Assets	852	869	759
Total Current Assets	**11,935.00**	**9,648.00**	**7,304.00**
Property/Plant/Equipment—Gross	—	—	—
Accumulated Depreciation			
Property/Plant/Equipment, Net	15,307.00	13,533.00	11,418.00
Goodwill, Net	—	—	—
Intangibles, Net	—	—	—
Long Term Investments	—	—	—
Other Long Term Assets	1,361.00	973	768
Total Assets	**$28,603.00**	**24,154.00**	**19,490.00**
Accounts Payable	4,684.00	4,160.00	3,576.00
Accrued Expenses	1,545.00	1,566.00	1,507.00
Note Payable/Short Term Debt	—	—	—
Current Port. LT Debt/Capital Leases	975	905	857
Other Current Liabilities	319	423	361
Total Current Liabilities	**7,523.00**	**7,054.00**	**6,301.00**
Long Term Debt	10,186.00	8,088.00	5,634.00
Capital Lease Obligations	—	—	—
Total Long Term Debt	**10,186.00**	**8,088.00**	**5,634.00**
Total Debt	**11,161.00**	**8,993.00**	**6,491.00**
Deferred Income Tax	1,451.00	1,152.00	1,036.00
Minority Interest	—	—	—
Other Liabilities	—	—	—
Total Liabilities	**19,160.00**	**16,294.00**	**12,971.00**
Redeemable Preferred Stock	—	—	—
Preferred Stock—Non Redeemable, Net	—	—	—
Common Stock	76	75	75
Additional Paid-In Capital	1,256.00	1,098.00	902
Retained Earnings (Accum. Deficit)	8,107.00	6,687.00	5,542.00
Treasury Stock—Common	—	—	—
Other Equity	4	0	—
Total Equity	**9,443.00**	**7,860.00**	**6,519.00**
Total Liability & Shareholders' Equity	**28,603.00**	**24,154.00**	**19,490.00**
Shares Outs.—Common Stock	909.8	905.2	897.8
Total Common Shares Outstanding	**909.8**	**905.2**	**897.8**
Total Preferred Stock Shares Outstanding	—	—	—
Employees (actual figures)	306,000.00	280,000.00	254,000.00
Number of Common Shareholders (actual figures)	17,108.00	15,773.0	13,883.00

Source: www.investor.stockpoint.com

Corporation's stock, adjusted for splits, has doubled in the past five years, largely due to increased sales and earnings at the Target division. Some financial analysts think Target Corporation's performance would be even better if it divested itself of its underperforming Marshall Field's and Mervyn's units whose sales and pretax profits were higher in 1998 than in 2003. Thus far, CEO Ulrich has been steadfast in his periodic reaffirmation to keep Mervyn's and Marshall Field's, even though they represent less than 20 percent of the corporation's sales and pretax profits.

References

Branch, Shelly. "How Target Got Hot." *Fortune* (May 24, 1999): 168–174.

Odell, Patricia. "Yahoo! Brings Products to Retail at Marshall Field's." *PROMO Xtra* (September 9, 2003). **www.promomagazine.com/ar/marketing_yahoo_brings_products/**.

Zutierman, Gregory and Ann Zimmerman. "Investors Aim Their Displeasure at Target." *Wall Street Journal* (February 4, 2004).

12 Mandalay Resort Group—2004

John K. Ross III, Mike Keeffe, and Bill Middlebrook
Southwest Texas State University

MBG

www.mandalayresortgroup.com

At year-end 2003, Las Vegas, the kingdom of glitz and glamour, seems to have recovered completely from the terrorist attacks of September 11, 2001 and the falling economy. Where two years before only crickets could be heard on the strip, there are now the sounds of laughter and the clink of coins falling from slot machines. Flights to Las Vegas (although fewer) are full, the colossal hotels/casinos are back in action (thanks to steep discounting), the bright lights are on, and the large crowds are back.

Mandalay describes itself as being in the business of entertainment, and it has been one of the innovators in the theme resort concept that is popular in casino gaming. Its areas of operation are the extravagant vacation and convention centers of Las Vegas, Reno, and Laughlin, Nevada, as well as other locations in the United States and abroad. Historically, Mandalay's marketing of its products had been called "right out of the bargain basement" and had catered to "low rollers." However, beginning with the opening of the Excalibur in 1990, Mandalay broadened its market to target the middle-income gambler and family-oriented vacationer. The Luxor further broadened the target market and the addition of Mandalay Bay helps bring in the prestigious and profitable "high roller."

Mandalay began as Circus Circus in 1974, when partners William G. Bennett, an aggressive cost-cutter who ran furniture stores before entering the gaming industry in 1965, and William N. Pennington bought a small and unprofitable casino operation for $50,000. The partners were able to rejuvenate Circus Circus with fresh marketing; they went public with a stock offering in October 1983, and experienced rapid growth and high profitability. Within the five-year period between 1993 and 1997, the average return on invested capital was 16.5 percent, and Mandalay generated over $1 billion in free cash flow. Today, Mandalay is one of the major players in the Las Vegas, Laughlin, and Reno markets in terms of both the square footage of casino space and the number of hotel rooms. It has achieved this success despite the incredible competitive growth in all gaming markets. For Mandalay, casino gaming operations provide slightly less than one-half of total revenues, and that trend continued into 2003 (see Exhibit 1). In 2003, Mandalay reported a net income of $115.6 million on revenues of $2.35 billion.

Mission

Mandalay currently does not seem to have a formally stated mission. No publicly stated vision statement is available; however, the development of the Mandalay Mile continues to be the core of Mandalay's future. The Mandalay Mile consists of three interconnected gaming resorts in Las Vegas on 230 acres.

EXHIBIT 1

Mandalay's Revenues by Segment

	2003	2002	2001	2000	1999	1998
Casinos	51.2%	51.1%	51.3%	46.3%	48.0%	46.7%
Food & Beverage	17.6	17.5	17.5	16.9	16.7	15.9
Rooms	24.2	24.8	25.7	26.0	24.0	24.4
Other	14.2	14.1	12.6	12.2	11.5	10.5
Unconsolidated	na	na	na	4.8	5.7	7.3
Less: Complementary Allowances	7.2	7.5	7.1	6.3	5.9	4.8

Note: 2002 column is for fiscal year ending 1-31-03.

Source: Mandalay Resort Group, *Form 10K* (January 31, 1996–2003), John K. Ross III, Mike Keeffe, and Bill Middlebrook.

Operations

Mandalay defines entertainment as pure play and fun, and it goes out of its way to see that customers have plenty of opportunities for both. Each Mandalay location has a distinctive personality, and the Mandalay corporate structure seems to allow each site to exploit that difference to its best advantage. Although Mandalay does not publish its organization chart, it appears that Mandalay Resort Group provides overall direction and strategic leadership as well as functional coordination in the areas of finance, accounting, human resources, legal issues, and marketing. Each resort, in turn, has its own functional structure that enables it to handle the specific activities required to successfully operate a large, combined hotel, casino, and entertainment resort.

The largest hotel/casino—and the crown jewel of the Mandalay group—is Mandalay Bay, which was completed in the first quarter of 1999 and opened on March 2 of that year at an estimated cost of $950 million (excluding land). This is the third addition to the Mandalay Mile, a contiguous mile at the southern end of the Las Vegas strip that currently contains the Mandalay Bay, Excalibur, and Luxor resorts (see Exhibit 2 for a map of the Las Vegas "Strip" and the locations of the major hotel/casinos). All three themed hotels/casinos are connected by an elevated monorail system. Located next to the Luxor, Mandalay Bay aims for the upscale traveler and player and is styled as a South Seas adventure.

The Mandalay Bay hotel/casino contains a 43-story hotel/casino with over 3,700 rooms and an 11-acre aquatic environment. The aquatic environment contains a surfing beach, a swim-up shark tank, and a snorkeling reef. A Four Seasons Hotel with some 424 rooms complements the remainder of Mandalay Bay and strives for the high-roller gamblers. Mandalay anticipates that the remainder of the "Masterplan Mile" will eventually consist of at least one additional casino resort, a convention center, and a number of stand-alone hotels and amusement centers. A planned convention center was placed on hold after the September 11 terrorist attacks but was completed by January 1, 2003. The convention center contains nearly 1 million square feet of exhibit space on two levels and the largest ballroom in the nation. In November of 2003 a new 1,122-suite tower opened and a new retail concourse located between Mandalay Bay and Luxor opened. Additionally, the resort acts as the background casino for the current TV show "Las Vegas" on NBC and helps showcase both the interior and exterior amenities of Mandalay Bay.

Circus Circus-Las Vegas is the world of the Big Top, where live circus acts perform free every 30 minutes. Kids may cluster around video games while the adults migrate to nickel slot machines and dollar game tables. Located at the north end of the Vegas strip, Circus Circus-Las Vegas sits on 69 acres of land with 3,744 hotel rooms, shopping areas,

EXHIBIT 2
The Las Vegas Strip

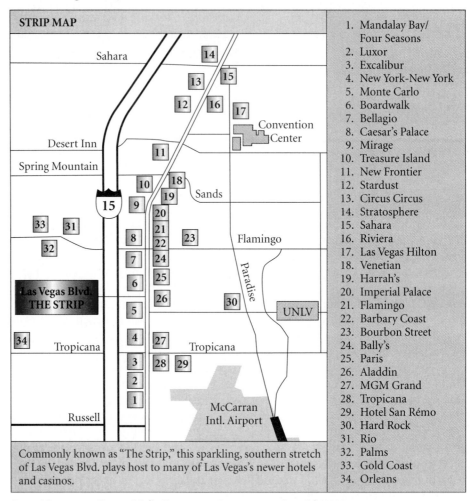

Source: Map courtesy Donrey Media Group, www.lasvegas.com, Copyright 2001.

two specialty restaurants, a buffet with seating for 1,200, fast-food shops, cocktail lounges, video arcades, and 109,000 square feet of casino space, and it includes the Grand Slam Canyon, a five-acre glass enclosed theme park, including a four-loop roller coaster.

Luxor, an Egyptian-themed hotel and casino complex, opened on October 15, 1993, and 10,000 people entered to play the 2,245 slot and video poker games and 110 table games in the 120,000 square-foot casino in the hotel atrium (reported to be the world's largest). By the end of the opening weekend, 40,000 people per day were visiting the 30-story bronze pyramid that encases the hotel and entertainment facilities.

Luxor features a 30-story pyramid and two new 22-story hotel towers, including 492 suites. It is connected to Excalibur by a climate-controlled skyway with moving walkways. Situated at the south end of the Las Vegas strip on a 64-acre site adjacent to Excalibur, Luxor features a food and entertainment area on three different levels beneath the hotel atrium. The pyramid's hotel rooms can be reached from the four corners of the building by state-of-the-art "inclinators" that travel at a 39-degree angle. Parking is available for nearly 3,200 vehicles, including a covered garage that contains approximately 1,800 spaces.

The Luxor underwent major renovations costing $323.3 million during fiscal 1997 and another $116.5 million in fiscal 1998. The resulting complex contains 4,425 hotel rooms, extensively renovated casino space, an additional 20,000 square feet of convention area, an 800-seat buffet, a series of IMAX attractions, 5 theme restaurants, 7 cocktail lounges, and a variety of specialty shops. Mandalay expects to draw significant walk-in traffic to the newly refurbished Luxor, which is one of the principal components of the Masterplan Mile.

Located next to the Luxor, Excalibur is one of the first sights travelers see as they exit Interstate 15 (management was confident that the sight of a giant, colorful medieval castle would make a lasting impression on mainstream tourists and vacationing families arriving in Las Vegas). Guests cross a drawbridge that is over a moat and proceed onto a cobblestone walkway where multicolored spires, turrets, and battlements loom above. The castle walls are four 28-story hotel towers containing a total of 4,008 rooms. Inside is a medieval world complete with a Fantasy Faire inhabited by strolling jugglers, fire-eaters and acrobats, as well as a Royal Village complete with peasants, serfs, and ladies-in-waiting who wander around medieval theme shops. The 110,000 square-foot casino encompasses 2,442 slot machines, more than 89 game tables, a sports book, and a poker and keno area. There are 12 restaurants that are capable of feeding more than 20,000 people daily, and a 1000-seat amphitheater. Excalibur, which opened in June 1990, was built for $294 million and was primarily financed with internally generated funds. In fiscal year-end January 31, 2002 and January 31, 2001, Excalibur contributed 12 percent of the organization's revenues.

Situated between the two anchors on the Las Vegas strip are two smaller casinos owned and operated by Mandalay. The Silver City Casino and Slots-A-Fun primarily depend on the foot traffic along the strip for their gambling patrons. Combined, they offer more than 1,202 slot machines and 46 gaming tables on 34,900 square feet of casino floor.

All of Mandalay's operations do well in the city of Las Vegas with a combined hotel room occupancy rate that has (until recently) remained above 90 percent. This has been due, in part, to low room rates (from $39 at Circus Circus-Las Vegas) and popular buffets. Each of the major properties contains large, inexpensive buffets that management believes make staying with Mandalay more attractive. As can be seen in Exhibit 3, the total earnings from each property continue to increase as the entire market for gaming continues to increase. Room occupancy rates vary between 76 and 95 percent due to the building boom in Las Vegas, the higher room rates at some locations ($99 to $399 for special occasions at Mandalay Bay), and the consuming public's attraction to newer properties. Also note the continued rise in room rates reflecting the general trend in Las Vegas of generating more revenue from sources other than gaming (i.e., rooms, restaurants, shows, and other attractions).

The company's other big-top facility is Circus Circus-Reno. With the addition of Skyway Tower in 1985, this big top now offers a total of 1,605 hotel rooms, 60,600 square feet of casino, a buffet which can seat 700 people, shops, video arcades, cocktail lounges, midway games, and circus acts. Circus Circus-Reno had several marginal years, but it has become one of the leaders in the Reno market. Mandalay anticipates that recent remodeling, at a cost of $25.6 million, will increase this property's revenue-generating potential.

Three properties purchased in 1995 and located in Jean and Henderson, Nevada, represent continuing investments by Mandalay in outlying markets. The Gold Strike and Nevada Landing service the highway I-15 market between Las Vegas and southern California. These properties have over 73,000 square feet of casino space, 2,140 slot machines, and 42 gaming tables combined. Each has limited hotel space (1,116 rooms total) and depends heavily on I-15 traffic. The Railroad Pass is

EXHIBIT 3

Mandalay's Income by Property

(IN MILLIONS)	2002			2001		
	OPERATING INCOME	DEPRECIATION	EBITDA	OPERATING INCOME	DEPRECIATION	EBITDA
Mandalay Bay	$ 41.6	$ 43.4	$ 85.0	$ 38.4	$ 40.8	$ 79.2
Luxor	74.9	33.8	108.7	85.9	37.3	123.2
Excalibur	67.6	17.9	85.5	79.0	16.9	95.9
Circus Circus-Las Vegas	39.8	23.0	62.8	47.7	23.6	71.3
Gold Strike-Tunica	11.0	12.8	23.8	19.4	12.8	32.2
Colorado Belle/Edgewater	10.5	11.5	22.0	13.6	11.3	24.9
Circus Circus-Reno	14.4	9.2	23.6	18.9	9.8	28.7
Gold Strike properties	(55.6)	10.2	(45.4)	7.7	10.4	18.1
MotorCity Casino	72.2	39.1	111.3	49.3	37.5	86.8
Unconsolidated joint ventures	107.1	6.5	113.6	108.5	6.5	115.0
Other	(3.7)	0.9	(2.8)	(4.9)	0.3	(4.6)
Subtotal	379.8	208.3	588.1	463.5	207.2	670.7
Corporate expense	(28.7)	7.7	(21.0)	(32.0)	10.8	(21.2)
Total	$351.1	$216.0	$567.1	$431.5	$218.0	$649.5

Source: Mandalay Group *2002 Annual Report*, p. 51.

considered a local casino and is dependent on Henderson residents as its market. This smaller casino contains only 395 slot machines and 11 gaming tables.

Gold Strike-Tunica (formally Circus Circus-Tunica) is a dockside casino located in Tunica, Mississippi. Opened in 1994 on 24 acres of land located along the Mississippi River, it lies approximately 20 miles south of Memphis.

Joint Ventures

In Las Vegas, Mandalay joined with Mirage Resorts to build and operate the Monte Carlo, a hotel-casino with 3,002 rooms designed along the lines of the grand casinos of the Mediterranean. It is located on 46 acres (with 600 feet on the Las Vegas strip) between the New York-New York casino and the Bellagio; all three casinos are connected by monorail. The Monte Carlo features a 90,000 square-foot casino containing 2,221 slot machines and 95 gaming tables, along with a 550-seat bingo parlor, high-tech arcade rides, restaurants and buffets, a microbrewery, approximately 15,000 square feet of meeting and convention space, and a 1,200-seat theater. Opened on June 21, 1996, the Monte Carlo generated $14.6 million as Mandalay's share in operating income for the first seven months of operation.

In Elgin, Illinois, Mandalay is in a 50 percent partnership with Hyatt Development Corporation in The Grand Victoria. Styled to resemble a Victorian riverboat, this floating casino and land-based entertainment complex includes some 36,000 square feet of casino space, containing 977 slot machines and 56 gaming tables. The adjacent land-based complex contains 2 movie theaters, a 240-seat buffet, restaurants, and parking for approximately 2,000 vehicles. Built for a total of $112 million, The Grand Victoria returned all of Mandalay's initial investment.

The third joint venture is a 50 percent partnership with Eldorado Limited in the Silver Legacy. Opened in 1995, this casino is located between Circus Circus-Reno and the Eldorado Hotel and Casino on two city blocks in downtown Reno, Nevada. The Silver Legacy has 1,711 hotel rooms, 85,000 square feet of casino, 2,275 slot machines, and 89 gaming tables. Management seems to believe that the Silver Legacy holds

EXHIBIT 4
Mandalay Resort GRP (MBG)—Balance Sheet

IN MILLIONS OF U.S. DOLLARS (EXCEPT FOR PER SHARE ITEMS) AS OF JANUARY 31,	2003	2002	2001
Cash & Equivalents	$ 148.4	105.9	105.9
Short Term Investments	—	—	—
Cash and Short Term Investments	148.4	105.9	105.9
Trade Accounts Receivable, Net	55.3	58.4	78.4
Other Receivables	13.1	13.5	0.0
Total Receivables, Net	68.4	71.9	78.4
Total Inventory	30.6	30.6	31.2
Prepaid Expenses	47.4	40.8	41.0
Other Current Assets	16.5	13.2	30.2
Total Current Assets	**311.4**	**262.4**	**286.6**
Property/Plant/Equipment—Gross	—	—	—
Accumulated Depreciation	(1,266.5)	(1,162.2)	(1,077.3)
Property/Plant/Equipment, Net	3,201.6	3,049.8	3,236.8
Goodwill, Net	38.3	45.4	65.8
Intangibles, Net	115.2	23.0	—
Long Term Investments	617.0	589.8	588.0
Other Long Term Assets	71.1	62.0	71.0
Total Assets	**$4,354.7**	**4,032.5**	**4,248.3**
Accounts Payable	37.0	33.5	37.3
Accrued Expenses	235.7	215.0	199.1
Notes Payable/Short Term Debt	—	—	—
Current Port. LT Debt/Capital Leases	20.3	39.3	42.3
Other Current Liabilities	24.4	21.5	18.0
Total Current Liabilities	**317.4**	**309.2**	**296.7**
Long Term Debt	2,763.6	2,482.1	2,623.6
Capital Lease Obligations	—	—	—
Total Long Term Debt	**2,763.6**	**2,482.1**	**2,623.6**
Total Debt	**2,783.9**	**2,521.3**	**2,665.9**
Deferred Income Tax	227.7	194.9	235.8
Minority Interest	18.6	(3.6)	(18.7)
Other Liabilities	144.5	109.3	42.0
Total Liabilities	**3,471.7**	**3,091.9**	**3,179.3**
Redeemable Preferred Stock	—	—	—
Preferred Stock—Non Redeemable, Net	—	—	—
Common Stock	1.9	1.9	1.9
Additional Paid-In Capital	581.2	573.0	569.8
Retained Earnings (Accum. Deficit)	1,490.0	1,374.4	1,321.3
Treasury Stock—Common	(1,173.2)	(986.8)	(817.3)
Other Equity	(16.9)	(21.9)	(6.8)
Total Equity	**882.9**	**940.6**	**1,068.9**
Total Liability & Shareholders' Equity	**$4,354.7**	**4,032.5**	**4,248.3**
Shares Outs.—Common Stock	62.6	68.4	76.3
Total Common Shares Outstanding	**62.6**	**68.4**	**76.3**
Total Preferred Stock Shares Outs.	**—**	**—**	**—**
Employees (actual figures)	26,800.0	33,300.0	35,000.0
Number of Common Shareholders	2,775.0	2,966.0	3,200.0

Source: www.investor.stockpoint.com

EXHIBIT 5

Mandalay Resort—Income Statement

IN MILLIONS OF U.S. DOLLARS (EXCEPT FOR PER SHARE ITEMS) 12 MONTHS ENDING JANUARY 31,	2003	2002	2001
Revenue	$2,020.1	2,016.3	2,081.4
Other Revenue	334.0	332.3	299.8
Total Revenue	**2,354.1**	**2,348.5**	**2,381.1**
Cost of Revenue	1,346.1	1,370.2	1,373.6
Gross Profit	**674.1**	**646.0**	**707.8**
Selling/General/Administrative Expenses	436.6	438.1	430.8
Research & Development	—	—	—
Depreciation/Amortization	145.0	216.0	218.0
Interest Expense (Income), Net Operating	—	—	—
Unusual Expense (Income)	18.4	52.0	0.0
Other Operating Expenses	53.7	34.3	42.0
Total Operating Expense	**1,901.8**	**1,997.5**	**1,949.6**
Operating Income	**452.3**	**351.1**	**431.5**
Interest Expense, Net Non-Operating	(214.3)	(228.9)	(229.8)
Interest/Investment Income, Non-Operating	—	—	—
Interest Income (Expense), Net Non-Operating	(214.3)	(228.9)	(229.8)
Gain (Loss) on Sale of Assets	—	—	—
Other, Net	(42.7)	(29.2)	(7.3)
Income Before Tax	**195.3**	**93.0**	**194.4**
Income Tax	77.9	40.0	74.7
Income After Tax	**117.5**	**53.0**	**119.7**
Minority Interest	—	—	—
Equity In Affiliates	—	—	—
Net Income Before Extra. Items	**117.5**	**53.0**	**119.7**
Accounting Change	(1.9)	0.0	0.0
Discontinued Operations	—	—	—
Extraordinary Item	—	—	—
Net Income	**$ 115.6**	**53.0**	**119.7**
Preferred Dividends	—	—	—
Income Available	**117.5**	**53.0**	**119.7**
Income Available to Common	**115.6**	**53.0**	**119.7**
Basic/Primary Weighted Average Shares	67.6	72.8	78.3
Basic/Primary EPS Excl. Extra. Items	**1.739**	**0.729**	**1.528**
Basic/Primary EPS Incl. Extra. Items	**1.711**	**0.729**	**1.528**

Source: www.investor.stockpoint.com

promise; however, the Reno market is suffering, and the opening of the Silver Legacy has cannibalized the Circus Circus-Reno market.

A final current joint venture is with the Atwater Casino Group to build and operate a hotel/casino in Detroit, Michigan. A temporary 75,000 square-foot casino was built under a plan agreed to by the city of Detroit. Future plans call for the construction of an approximately 800-room hotel, expansion of the gaming areas, the addition of new restaurants, more retail space, more convention space, and other amenities. Total costs are estimated at some $600 million, with Mandalay contributing 20 percent and the remainder being funded by debt with the joint venture. On August 2, 2002, the Detroit City Council approved a revised development agreement allowing for the expansion of MotorCity Casino facility by December 31, 2005.

Mandalay has achieved success through an aggressive growth strategy and a renovated corporate structure designed to enhance that growth. A strong cash position, innovative ideas, and attention to cost control have allowed Mandalay to satisfy the bottom line during a period when competitors were typically taking on large debt obligations to finance new projects. Yet the market is changing. Gambling of all kinds has spread across the country; no longer does the average individual need to go to Las Vegas or Atlantic City. Instead, gambling can be found as close as the local quick market (lottery), bingo hall, many Indian reservations, the Mississippi River, and of course on the Internet. There are now almost 300 casinos in Las Vegas alone, 60 in Colorado, and 160 in California. In order to maintain a competitive edge, Mandalay has continued to invest heavily in the renovation of existing properties (a strategy common to the entertainment/amusement industry); it continues to develop new projects, and it has shifted from a strategy dependent on gaming to one focusing as well on income from hotels, food, and entertainment.

The Gaming Industry

The gaming industry has captured a large portion of the vacation/leisure-time dollars spent in the United States. Casino gambling accounts for 40.6 percent of all legal gambling expenditures, still ahead of spending on second-place lotteries at 32.2 percent and third-place Indian reservations at 15.4 percent. The popularity of casino gambling may be credited to more frequent and somewhat higher pay-outs as compared to lotteries and racetracks; however, as winnings are recycled, the multiplier effect restores a high return to casino operators.

Geographic expansion has slowed considerably since no additional states have approved casino-type gambling since 1993. Growth has occurred in developed locations, with Las Vegas, Nevada, and Atlantic City, New Jersey, leading the way. Although the Internet as a gaming venue has exploded, Las Vegas remains the largest U.S. gaming market and one of the largest convention markets. Las Vegas hotel and casino capacity has continued to expand with some 12,300 rooms opened in 1999, another 4,219 in 2000, 3,099 in 2001, and 3,070 in 2002. However, the rapid expansion of rooms during the 1990s is not expected to continue. According to the Las Vegas Convention and Visitor Authority, Las Vegas is a destination market, with most visitors planning their trips more than a week in advance (81 percent), arriving by car (43 percent) or airplane (46 percent), and staying in a hotel (72 percent). Gamblers are typically return visitors (79 percent), averaging 2.2 trips per year because they like playing the slots (65 percent).

For Atlantic City, besides the geographical separation, the primary differences in the two markets reflect the different types of consumers frequenting these markets. While Las Vegas attracts overnight resort-seeking vacationers, Atlantic City's clientele is predominantly day-trippers traveling by automobile or bus. Gaming revenues are split between 12 casinos/hotels currently operating. Growth in the Atlantic City area will be concentrated in the Marina section of town, where Mirage Resorts has entered into an agreement with the city to develop 150 acres of the Marina as a destination resort. This development will include a resort wholly owned by Mirage, a casino/hotel developed by Mandalay, and a complex developed by a joint venture with Mirage and Boyd Corp. Currently in Atlantic City, Donald Trump's gaming empire holds the largest market share with Trump Marina, Trump Plaza, and the Trump Taj Mahal (total market share is 29 percent). The next closest in market share is Bally's (12.1 percent), Caesar's (11.2 percent), Tropicana (9.9 percent), and Harrah's (9.5 percent).

There remain a number of smaller markets located around the United States, primarily in Mississippi, Louisiana, Illinois, Missouri, and Indiana. Each state has imposed various restrictions on the development of casino operations within the state. In Illinois, for example, where there are only ten gaming licenses available, growth opportunities and revenues have been severely restricted. In other states, such as Mississippi and Louisiana, revenues are up 7 percent and 6 percent, respectively, in riverboat operations.

Native American casinos continue to be developed on federally controlled Indian land. These casinos are not publicly held but do tend to be managed by publicly held corporations. Overall, these other locations present a mix of opportunities and generally constitute only a small portion of overall gaming revenues. However, in 2000, California began allowing "Nevada-Style" gaming on Native American reservations. This has significantly impacted some of Mandalay's properties, particularly those in Reno, Laughlin, and Jean, Nevada.

Major Industry Players

Over the past several years, there have been numerous changes as mergers and acquisitions have reshaped the gaming industry. As of year-end 2003, the industry was a combination of corporations ranging from those engaged solely in gaming to multinational conglomerates. The largest competitors, in terms of revenues, combined multiple industries to generate both large revenues and substantial profits. However, those engaged primarily in gaming could also be extremely profitable.

Park Place was founded from the separation of the lodging and gaming operations of Hilton Hotels in December 1998. Park Place merged with the Mississippi gaming operations of Grand Casinos, and then it bought Caesar's from Starwood. Now it consists of a total of 29 casinos, 20 of which are located in the United States. Its latest venture is the Paris Las Vegas Casino & Resort located next to Bally's in Las Vegas. The Paris features a 50-story replica of the Eiffel Tower, 85,000 square feet of casino space, 13 restaurants, and 130,000 square feet of convention space. Park Place is the largest casino operator in the world, with approximately 2 million square feet of gaming space, 28,000 rooms, and a net loss of $282.4 million on revenues of $4.6 billion in 2002.

Harrah's Entertainment, Inc., is primarily engaged in the gaming industry, with casinos/hotels in Reno, Lake Tahoe, Las Vegas, and Laughlin, Nevada, as well as in Atlantic City, New Jersey. It has riverboats in Joliet, Illinois; Vicksburg and Tunica, Mississippi; Shreveport, Louisiana; and Kansas City, Kansas; two Indian casinos; and one casino in Auckland, New Zealand. In June 1998, Harrah's purchased the assets of Showboat and its operations in Atlantic City and Las Vegas, and in January 1999 it merged with Rio Hotel and Casino, Inc. In 2000, it sold the Showboat and purchased Players International and in 2002 acquired the common shares of JCC Holding Company (Harrah's-New Orleans). As of December 2002, the company had a total of over 1,547,645 square feet of casino space; 42,585 slot machines; 1,167 table games; 14,431 hotel rooms or suites; approximately 365,422 square feet of convention space; and 108 restaurants. Harrah's attempts to target the experienced gambler who likes to play in multiple markets by establishing strong brand names of consistent high quality.

MGM Mirage (formally known as the MGM Grand) owns and operates 16 hotel/casinos worldwide. These properties include the MGM Grand Hotel; MGM Grand Australia; MGM Grand Detroit; the Bellagio in Las Vegas; the Beau Rivage in Biloxi, Mississippi; the Golden Nugget-Downtown in Las Vegas; the Mirage on the strip in Las Vegas; Treasure Island; Holiday Inn-Boardwalk; and the Golden Nugget-Laughlin. Additionally, it is a 50 percent owner of the Monte Carlo with Mandalay. The MGM Las Vegas is located on approximately 116 acres at the northeast corner of Las Vegas Boulevard across the street from New York-New York Hotel and Casino. The casino is approximately 171,500 square feet in size, and it is one of the largest casinos in the world, with 3,669 slot machines and 157 table games. Through a wholly owned subsidiary, MGM owns and operates the MGM Grand Diamond Beach Hotel and a hotel/casino resort in Darwin, Australia. The company intends to expand the Bellagio with an additional 928 rooms in the Spa Tower by 2004.

Future Considerations

Mandalay was one of the innovators of the gaming resort concept and has continued to be a leader in that field. However, the mega-entertainment resort industry and the traditional casino gaming industry operate differently. In the past, consumers would visit a casino to experience the thrill of gambling. Now they not only gamble but also expect to be dazzled by enormous entertainment complexes that cost billions of dollars to build. The competition has continued to increase at the same time growth rates have been slowing. Intense price competition among the gaming companies and casinos has driven profit margins down.

Develop a three-year strategic plan for Mandalay Bay.

Bibliography

"AGA Fact Sheets," American Gaming Association, retrieved October 17, 2001 from www.americangaming.org/casino_entertainment/aga_facts/.

Aztar Corp., 1997, 1998, 1999, and 2000 10K, retrieved from EDGAR Data Base, www.sec.gov/Archives/edgar/data/.

"Economic Impacts of Casino Gaming in the United States," by Arthur Andersen, for the American Gaming Association (May 1997).

Harrah's Entertainment, Inc., 1997, 1998, 1999, and 2000 10K, retrieved from EDGAR Data Base, www.sec.gov/Archives/edgar/data/.

"Harrah's Survey of Casino Entertainment," Harrah's Entertainment, Inc. (1996).

Industry Surveys—Lodging and Gaming, Standard & Poor's Industry Surveys (June 19, 1997).

"ITT Board Rejects Hilton's Offer as Inadequate, Reaffirms Belief That ITT's Comprehensive Plan Is in the Best Interest of ITT Shareholders," press release (August 14, 1997).

ITT Corp., 1997 10K, retrieved from EDGAR Data Base, www.sec.gov/Archives/edgar/data/.

Mandalay Resort Group (formally Circus Circus), *Annual Report to Shareholders* (January 31, 1989; January 31, 1990; January 31, 1993; January 31, 1994; January 31, 1995; January 31, 1996; January 31, 1997; January 31, 1998; January 31, 1999; January 31, 2000; January 31, 2001).

MGM Mirage 1997, 1998, 1999, and 2000 10K, retrieved from EDGAR Database, www.sec.gov/Archives/edgar/data/.

Strow, David. "LV Casinos Look at Layoffs." *Las Vegas Sun* (September 17, 2001).

13

Royal Caribbean Cruises Ltd.—2004

Robert L. Stevenson
Francis Marion University

RCL

www.royalcaribbean.com
www.celebrity.com
www.rclinvestor.com

Royal Caribbean Cruises LTD's. newest (RCCL) ship in its Voyager class, *Mariner of the Seas*, made its maiden voyage on November 16, 2003. Despite a challenging U.S. economy and serious risks to passenger safety, from the threat of terrorism to viral outbreaks, RCCL continues to expand capacity and grow revenues. RCCL chairman and CEO Richard D. Fain said, commenting on 2002 results, "While 2002 has been a very trying year for everyone in the tourism business, we are pleased to have held our own so well during these challenging times. Who would have ever imagined after September 11 that we would be able to achieve net revenue yields close to last year's levels with a 15 percent capacity increase."

History

RCCL was founded in 1968 with one ship. Today its ships operate worldwide with a selection of itineraries that call on approximately 200 destinations in the Caribbean, North America, South America, and Europe. RCCL is the world's second-largest cruise company, behind Carnival Cruise Lines, and operates a total of 26 ships under two brands, Royal Caribbean International and Celebrity Cruises.

Only 10 percent of the vacationing public in the United States has tried the cruise experience, leaving great opportunities for further market growth, toward which RCCL is moving to capitalize on through an aggressive expansion program. In 1997, RCCL acquired Celebrity Cruises. In 2001, it attempted to purchase United Kingdom–based P&O Princess, but the deal was terminated prior to its consummation, and P&O Princess was ultimately purchased by Carnival. During the same period, RCCL introduced its Voyager-class ships, the largest in the world, beginning with *Voyager of the Seas* in November 1999; and since then three additional Voyager-class ships, each costing approximately $700 million, have been put into operation, with the latest, *Mariner of the Seas*. Today the company has a total capacity of 53,042 berths.

Internal Issues

Vision and Mission Statements

Vision Statement

Royal Caribbean Cruises LTD. will build on its reputation of an unwavering commitment to service and a desire to deliver the best cruise vacation possible. Our

27,300 employees are singularly focused on one goal: providing the highest level of service and the best vacation experience on land or sea.

Mission Statement

Royal Carribbean Cruises LTD. strives to:

- Compete principally on the basis of quality of ships, quality of service, variety of itineraries, and price.
- Improve our competitive position with respect to the quality and innovation of our on-board product and state-of-the-art cruise ships.
- Serve markets and provide itineraries worldwide.
- Value its employees as the company's most valuable asset. They are counted on to represent the company professionally and do the utmost to serve the company's customers.
- Value the environment and remain committed to protecting and preserving environmental resources and preventing pollution.
- Maintain strong relationships with travel agencies, the principal industry distribution system.
- Participate in and make grants to numerous community charity organizations with priority to those helping children and families and education and the environment.

Source: Vision and Mission Statements adapted from information provided in www.rclinvestor.com and www.celebrity.com.

Organizational Structure

EXHIBIT 1

Royal Caribbean Cruises LTD. Organizational Chart

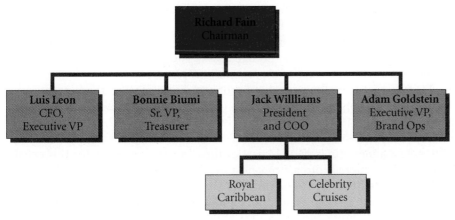

Source: Adapted from RCCL *Annual Report*, 2002, p. 12.

Global Issues

RCCL operates 26 ships on a selection of worldwide itineraries ranging from 3 to 17 nights that call on approximately 200 destinations. Referring to Exhibit 2, RCCL's fleet was deployed in over 31 locations in the United States and internationally during 2003. RCCL uses a flexible basing strategy, moving a portion of its

EXHIBIT 2
Fleet Deployment in 2003

DOMESTIC		INTERNATIONAL	
Baltimore, MD	New Orleans, LA	Barcelona, Spain	Rome, Italy
Boston, MA	New York, NY	Buenos Aires, Argentina	San Juan, Puerto Rico
Charleston, SC	Philadelphia, PA	Dover, England	S. Hampton, England
Fort Lauderdale, FL	Port Canaveral, FL	Ensinada, Mexico	Stockholm, Sweden
Galveston, TX	San Diego, CA	Hamburg, Germany	Valparaiso, Chile
Honolulu, HA	San Francisco, CA	Harwich, England	Vancouver, B. C.
Jacksonville, FL	Seward, AK	Oslo, Norway	Venice, Italy
Los Angeles, CA	Tampa, FL		
Miami, FL			

Source: www.royalcaribbean.com, and www.celebrity.com.

fleet throughout the year to meet seasonal demand. Continuing expansion of its fleet has allowed RCCL to expand into new destinations, itineraries, and markets. The American Automobile Association projects that the number of Americans driving to their vacation destinations will increase to 84 percent because of higher airline ticket prices and avoidance of air travel. To meet this demand in 2003, RCCL added new itineraries departing from major U.S. drive-to markets, including Tampa, New Orleans, Galveston, Port Canaveral, San Francisco, San Diego, Baltimore, and Charleston. Also in 2003, RCCL expanded its mix of itineraries in Alaska and Europe in order to provide vacationers with a wider range of options over and above those currently offered in the eastern, western, and southern Caribbean, Mexican Riviera, Bermuda, New England, Canada, Hawaii, and South America.

In 2001, RCCL began offering land-tour packages through Royal Celebrity Tours. This tour company offers land-tour programs in Alaska in combination with RCCL's Alaska cruise packages. The land-tour package includes a tour by motorcoach or rail with glass-domed railcars through Alaska and the Canadian Rockies. RCCL also launched a European land-tour program in 2003.

Despite recent weakness in the European cruise market, the percentage of international passengers on RCCL ships grew from approximately 7 percent of total passengers in 1991 to approximately 16 percent in 2002. RCCL is actively working to expand the number of international passengers through fleet deployment and expanded itineraries. As part of the company's strategy for this expansion, in 2000 it entered into a strategic alliance with First Choice Holidays PLC, one of the United Kingdom's largest tour operators. RCCL now holds approximately a 17 percent stake in First Choice Holidays PLC. In a separate joint venture, RCCL and First Choice Holidays PLC will launch a new cruise brand, Island Cruises (**www.islandcruises.com**). *Viking Serenade,* a 1,512-passenger ship which operated under the Royal Caribbean International brand until February 14, 2002, is the first ship to be operated by Island Cruises and will offer itineraries in the Mediterranean. In a separate attempt to expand further into the European market, RCCL made a failed bid in 2001 to acquire P&O Princess Cruises, which is based in the United Kingdom. This expansion comes at a time when the European cruise market is generally weak, especially in the Mediterranean region, due to the reluctance of Americans to travel too far from home.

Capital Expansion Issues

Currently, RCCL's combined fleet has an average age of approximately five years, which is one of the youngest of any major cruise company. Based on the ships currently on order, by December 31, 2004, RCCL's year-end capacity is expected to increase to 60,308 berths. This represents a capacity increase of 65 percent since the beginning of 2001.

RCCL is currently engaged in a capital expansion program, by driving revenue growth through the purchase of new and larger ships, as shown by the recent and planned fleet expansion in Exhibit 3. Since 2001, RCCL has placed two additional Voyager-class ships, *Adventure of the Seas* and *Navigator of the Seas*, in service in its Royal Caribbean Line; it has one additional Voyager-class ship on order. These are the largest cruise ships currently in service. Each one has a variety of innovative design features including the cruise industry's first horizontal atrium (which is four decks tall, longer than a football field, and provides entertainment, shopping, and dining experiences); recreational activities such as ice skating, rock climbing, miniature golf, and full-court basketball; enhanced staterooms; expanded dining options; and a variety of intimate spaces. Also, as part of the capital expansion program, RCCL introduced three Radiance-class ships: *Radiance of the Seas*, *Brilliance of the Seas*, and *Serenade of the Seas* in 2001, 2002, and 2003, respectively, to its Royal Caribbean Line. By increasing its average ship size, RCCL is able to achieve economies of scale in the operation of the ships. The increase in fleet size also provides a larger revenue base to absorb marketing, selling, and administrative expenses.

RCCL has also been expanding its Celebrity Cruise Line. Celebrity Cruises recently completed a capital expansion program by adding *Infinity*, *Summit*, and *Constellation*, the new Millennium-class series, from 2001 through 2002.

Continuing with its program to expand passenger capacity, the company announced in September of 2003 that a deal was signed with Finland's Kvaerner-Masa Yards to build a new class of Ultra Voyager ships with a capacity of

EXHIBIT 3
Recent and Future Fleet Expansion

	YEAR IN SERVICE	CAPACITY	GROSS TONS
Royal Caribbean			
Serenade of the Seas	2003	2,100	90,000
Navigator of the Seas	2002	3,100	142,000
Brilliance of the Seas	2002	2,100	90,000
Adventure of the Seas	2001	3,100	142,000
Radiance of the Seas	2001	2,100	90,000
Celebrity Cruises			
Constellation	2002	2,000	91,000
Summit	2001	2,000	91,000
Infinity	2001	2,000	91,000
Future			
Mariner of the Seas	4Q 2003	3,100	142,000
Jewel of the Seas	2Q 2004	2,100	90,000
Ultra Voyager Class	2Q 2006	3,600	—

Source: Adapted from data provided at Web site www.rclinvestor.com.

3,600 passengers, 500 greater than the current Voyager class. The first Ultra Voyager class ship will be delivered in May 2006, with an option to purchase a second ship for delivery in 2007. Fleet expansion is expected to decline to about 5 percent per year in the years 2004 to 2007 from an average of about 17 percent per year in the prior three years.

Passenger Safety Issues

Travelers vacationing on cruise ships are exposed to certain safety, health, and security risks including accidents, illnesses, and other incidents at sea. Recently, terrorist attacks, war, and other hostilities, and the resulting political instability and concerns over safety and security aspects of traveling have had an adverse impact on demand and pricing in the vacation industry. In response, heightened security has been put into place on RCCL ships including 100 percent screening of luggage and carry-ons as well as 100 percent photo identification of passengers and crew. Electronic photo identification of RCCL passengers is made at the time of initial boarding and is checked upon reboarding at each port of call. Passengers are being prescreened before cruise time to verify identity. Also, access areas to sensitive vessel operations, such as the bridge and engine room has been restricted. These increased measures are a response to the increased risk of terrorism targeted at cruise ships.

Illness aboard cruise ships has also been in the news recently. In November 2002, about 100 people aboard the *Magic*, a Disney cruise ship, became ill with stomach symptoms associated with the Norwalk virus, a gastrointestinal ailment with symptoms similar to the stomach flu. The *Magic* was the second ship to experience a viral outbreak. Passengers also contracted a Norwalk-like virus on Holland America's *Amsterdam*. During 2002, about 450 passengers on four cruises of the *Amsterdam* suffered from a similar virus before the ship was eventually sanitized by the Center for Disease Control.

Physical attacks involving passengers have also been reported on cruise ships. In 2002, a Miami-Dade County resident claims that she was assaulted by a crew member during a cruise on RCCL's *Voyager of the Seas*. A suit filed in Miami-Dade Circuit Court seeks unspecified damages. RCCL "maintains a zero-tolerance policy regarding sexual harassment" aboard its ships.

Finance Issues

During 2002 and 2003, RCCL experienced weaker margins due to pricing pressure caused by a weak U.S. economy, traveler safety concerns, and increasing capacity. RCCL cruise prices include a wide variety of activities and amenities, such as meals and entertainment. Prices vary depending on the destination, cruise length, cabin style, and the time of year the voyage takes place. The base price of a typical seven-day cruise in 2002 was about $100 per day. While many shipboard activities are included in the base price of the cruise, additional revenues are generated from airline tickets, shipboard gaming, the sale of alcoholic beverages, gift shop sales, photography, spa services, and shore excursions. Referring to Exhibit 4, total revenue per passenger cruise day was $190, $205, and $220 in 2002, 2001, and 2000, respectively.

For the six months ending June 30, 2003, RCCL's revenues increased 10 percent to $1.79 billion over the same period in 2002. Net income fell 9 percent to $108.8 million. Results reflect a 13.5 percent increase in capacity due to the additions of *Constellation*, *Brilliance of the Seas*, and *Navigator of the Seas* in 2002. The capacity increases were partially offset by lower operating margins due to lower yields and

EXHIBIT 4

Key Operating and Financial Statistics

	ROYAL CARIBBEAN	CELEBRITY	RCCL
Number of Ships (2003)	17	9	26
Number of Berths (2003)	38,800	16,354	55,154
	2002	**2001**	**2000**
Total Guests (includes Celebrity)	2,768,475	2,438,849	2,049,902
Company Share of North American Guests	36.2%	35.3%	29.8%
Occupancy	104.5%	101.8%	104.4%
Passenger Cruise Days (in thousands)	18,113	15,342	13,020
Revenues (in thousands)	$3,434,347	$3,145,250	$2,865,846
Revenue per Passenger Cruise Day	$190	$205	$220
Net Income	351,284	254,457	445,363
Earnings per Share	1.79	1.32	2.31
	2003	**2002**	**2001**
Estimated Capacity Growth	13%	15%	22%

Source: Adapted from RCCL *Annual Report*, 2002, pp. 13 and 14, and data provided on Web site **www.rclinvestor.com**.

ticket prices, and higher marketing costs related to reduced demand due to a weak U.S. economy and ongoing conflict in the Middle East.

Refering to Exhibit 4, net income increased 38.1 percent to $351.3 million or $1.79 per share on a diluted basis in 2002 compared to $254.5 million or $1.32 per share in 2001. The increase in net income was primarily the result of an increase in capacity associated with the addition of *Infinity*, *Radiance of the Seas*, *Summit*, and *Adventure of the Seas* in 2001, and Constellation, *Brilliance of the Seas*, and *Navigator of the Seas* in 2002.

The company took delivery of two ships in 2003 and one ship in 2004. Capital expenditures for 2003, 2004, and 2005 are estimated to be $1.1 billion, $0.5 billion, and $0.1 billion, respectively, not accounting for the planned acquisition of an Ultra-Voyager class ship in 2006. RCCL has financed recent ship acquisitions by issuing debt. The company is highly leveraged with a LT debt-to-equity ratio of 1.31, which is much higher than the industry average of 0.69. Assuming no significant changes in interest rates, net interest expense is expected to be in the range of $290 to $310 million in 2003. RCCL's preference for debt financing may be attributed to the high percentage of concentrated ownership. The company is 49 percent owned by the Wilhelmsen family of Norway and Pritzker family of Chicago, Illinois. Both families may be concerned about dilution of ownership that would accompany any stock issuance.

Marketing Issues

RCCL operates in the volume cruise vacation market, which is categorized into contemporary and premium segments. The contemporary segment consists of cruises that are typically seven days or shorter and feature a casual ambience, while the premium segment consists of cruises that are typically 7 to 14 days and appeal to the more seasoned, affluent cruiser. Celebrity Cruises primarily serves the premium segment, and has a higher proportion of its fleet deployed in seasonal markets (i.e, Alaska, Bermuda, Europe, and South America) than the Royal Caribbean International brand. Royal Caribbean International's marketing focuses on active adults and families who are vacation enthusiasts interested in exploring new destinations and seeking new experiences. The Alaska "Get Out There" campaign, created by Arnold Worldwide, is an extension of the original "Get Out There" initiative launched in 2000 to reposition the brand, dispel consumer misperceptions of cruising, and generate increased demand for Royal Caribbean. The advertising campaign is designed to appeal to consumers who are classified as "Explorers"—active and adventurous travelers who want to do, learn, and experience more while on vacation. The advertising campaign brings together a variety of media, including print, television, the Internet, and has resulted in increased name recognition for the Royal Caribbean brand. Expenses for media advertising were $97.9 million, $103.4 million, and $98.9 million in 2002, 2001, and 2000, respectively.

E-Commerce Issues

RCCL operates Web sites with customer booking capabilities for both Royal Caribbean and Celebrity Cruises. The two Web sites allow customers to experience what a RCCL cruise would be like, including a virtual tour of the various ships. RCCL has streamlined the documentation process by providing passengers electronic documents from the Web sites, and also offers guests the ability to complete their embarkation forms online prior to the embarkation date. In addition, it provides online access to shore excursion booking via its Web sites. A Web browser-based booking tool, *CruiseManager*, has also been launched to make it easier for travel agents to book cruises on RCCL ships.

RCCL is using the latest information technology software to manage its operations. These software packages enable the company to optimize decisions about pricing, inventory, and marketing actions. One such package, FormScape, manages financial transaction documents. Using FormScape, RCCL has automated internal and external business information processing, allowing for rapid delivery of key business transaction information which in the past required numerous vendor/supplier verification calls and printed document handling and mailing. For a separate application, RCCL selected Informatica's data integration platform to consolidate information from numerous shipboard and land-based customer managements and human resource and supply chain systems. It also integrates data from Web- and phone-based reservations systems, multiple customer-management applications, and key operational systems into one data warehouse for analysis and making operational decisions. RCCL was the first company in the cruise industry to develop an automated booking system, *CruiseMatch® 2000*. To make travel agent booking easier, *CruiseMatch®*, gives travel agents direct access to RCCL's computer reservation system.

External Issues

Economic Issues

Demand for leisure activities is influenced by general economic conditions. Although the U.S economy officially came out of a recession in the fourth quarter of 2001 and has been growing since then at an average rate of about 2 percent per year, and the U.S. stock market has recently posted gains of about 20 percent in 2003, U.S unemployment continues to hold at a level of about 6 percent. Failure of the economy to make a full recovery thus far puts pricing pressure on the cruise industry and results in lower operating margins and profits.

U.S. inflation rates in 2003 remained low. The 12-month running CPI ended August 2003 was at a 2.27 percent level. This should have had a positive effect on controlling operating costs within the industry. Fuel costs, however, were substantially higher in 2002 and 2003 rising some 60 percent, which had a negative effect on operating costs since fuel costs are typically about 5 percent of total expenses. The prime rate in September 2003 fell to 4 percent, a historically low level, which had a positive effect on debt financing costs, a significant expense for RCCL.

Internationally, European economies, which represent 30 percent of world GDP, are a mixed bag. Europe in general has experienced three years of slow growth with some recent signs of improvement. One bright spot is Great Britain where the GDP increased by 0.6 percent in the third quarter of 2003. France, on the other hand, experienced declining GDP as well as declining job growth in 2003.

Royal Caribbean's agreement with the Finnish shipyards for the construction of future new ships hinges in part on a better euro–dollar exchange rate. The euro has risen 25.2 percent in the past year versus the U.S. dollar. In 2002, the euro was at 94.48 cents; in August 2003 it was at 1.18 dollars.

In the Asian market, China, Japan, and South Korea recently agreed to increase cooperation in a range of fields, including security, technology, and energy, a sign that a free-trade zone between North East Asia's three largest economies may be on the horizon. North East Asia, including Hong Kong and Taiwan, account for 20 percent of world GDP and include some of the fastest-growing economies in the world. On a similar note, a free-trade agreement, dubbed ASEAN, was signed in October 2003, between ten South East Asian countries, aimed at creating a European-style economy in the region by 2020.

Suppliers' Issues

The majority of RCCL's supplier purchases are for travel agency commissions, food and related items, port facility utilization, airfare, advertising, fuel, hotel supplies, and products related to guest accommodations. Most of these supplies are readily available from multiple sources at competitive prices. No one supplier provided goods or services in excess of 10 percent of RCCL's 2002 expenditures.

The majority of RCCL bookings occur through more than 30,000 independent travel agencies worldwide. For this reason, independent travel agencies are a critical distribution channel for RCCL. It has one of the largest sales forces in the industry which has the primary function of assisting travel agencies in marketing RCCL cruises. This sales force is critical since independent travel agencies have direct influence over customer choices and typically also represent RCCL's competitors. In addition to independent travel agencies, RCCL operates two internal, direct reservation call centers as well as online booking through the RCCL and Celebrity Web sites.

Another key supplier is the shipyards that fabricate cruise ships. These shipyards are relied upon to deliver ships, as part of RCCL's expansion program, on a timely basis and in excellent working order. Delays in ship construction or poor quality have in the past resulted in delays or cancellation of cruises, or have required unplanned ship repairs which impact customer satisfaction. For example, RCCL has experienced mechanical problems with the pod propulsion units on the new Millennium-class ships. These mechanical problems resulted in cruise cancellations and more than $10 million in lost profits in 2003.

Natural Environment Issues

Some environmental groups have lobbied for more stringent regulation of cruise ships, and some groups have generated negative publicity about the cruise industry and its environmental impact. Stricter environmental and health and safety regulations, brought about by this publicity, could affect RCCL operations thereby increasing the cost of compliance and adversely affecting the cruise industry.

According to an ocean advocacy group, Oceana, RCCL's claim that it adheres to "strict" environmental policies is absurd. Only three ships out of RCCL's fleet have advanced state-of-the-art sewage treatment systems. These ships were upgraded primarily for visits to Alaska, because the laws in that state require ships to meet stricter water quality standards. While RCCL touts its policy of treating its sewage, it fails to point out that it has made no commitment to treat sewage to a safe standard. According to the National Association of Attorneys General, 75 percent of the so-called "treated sewage" tested by the state of Alaska exceeded standards for dangerous fecal coliform bacteria, and 86 percent exceeded standards for suspended solids in sewage. As a result, Oceana will launch an intensive public campaign to create the political, consumer, and economic pressure to encourage RCCL to cease this practice. (**www.Oceana.org.**)

Oceana's campaign will focus on stopping RCCL from continuing to profit from dumping its sewage. It will educate consumers about Royal Caribbean's disregard for the pristine ocean waters and sea life that are highlighted in its advertising and encourage cruise passengers to spend their vacation dollars elsewhere. Consumer research shows that passengers are shocked to discover that the company is dumping fecal matter directly into the sea.

For RCCL's part, the company has taken several actions to boost its environmental reputation. First, it has instituted a senior level Safety and Environment position within its management structure. Second, in cooperation with the EPA the company has participated in studies of waste water discharge from its ships. The results of the study showed that waste discharge dilution rates for moving ships was much higher than predicted and thus has no impact on marine life. Third, an annual award program was created to encourage long-standing commitment to environmental innovation and improvement within the company. Competition for the award assists the company in progressively advancing its environmental performance in ways that go above and beyond regulatory compliance. Finally, RCCL is providing financial support to various organizations involved with ocean conservation.

Capacity Issues

Passenger cruise travel in the first two quarters of 2003 increased by 9 percent over 2002 levels, according to Maritime Administration data. The top 10 cruise lines carried 2 million passengers on 932 North American cruises in the second quarter of 2003. However, passenger growth has come at the price of lower margins due to pricing pressure brought on by increasing industry capacity.

Cruising capacity has grown in recent years at a rate of about 8 percent per year and is expected to continue to increase at this rate in the future as both RCCL and Carnival Cruise Lines, the two largest cruise operators, are expected to continue to introduce new ships. In order to utilize new capacity in the future, the cruise vacation industry will need to capture an ever-increasing percentage of the overall vacation market. Since 1970, cruising has been one of the fastest-growing sectors of the vacation market. As shown in Exhibit 5, the number of North American guests has grown to an estimated 7.6 million in 2002 from 0.5 million in 1970, a compound annual growth rate of approximately 9 percent.

According to Cruise Lines International Association, the North American market was served by an estimated 117 ships with approximately 163,187 berths at the end of 2002. The increase in capacity over the last five years is net of approximately

EXHIBIT 5
North American Cruise Market Guests and Average Number of Berths

YEAR	PASSENGERS	NUMBER OF BERTHS
1998	5,428,000	118,747
1999	5,894,000	130,152
2000	6,886,000	144,499
2001	6,906,000	151,690
2002	7,640,000	163,187

Source: RCCL *Form 20-F*, 2002, p. 7

36 ships with approximately 27,500 berths that have either been retired or moved out of the North American market. For the total industry in North America, there are a number of cruise ships on order with an estimated 54,900 berths which will be placed in service between 2003 and 2006.

Competitors

As shown in Exhibit 6, RCCL's principal competitor is Carnival Corporation. RCCL and Carnival compete on the basis of cruise pricing and on the types of ships and services they offer cruise passengers. Due to Carnival's larger market share, 52 percent versus RCCL's 33 percent, and Carnival's wide portfolio of cruise brands, it has stronger financial flexibility and greater access to capital markets than RCCL. Carnival also has better access to the travel agency distribution network and to berthing facilities in various ports throughout the world.

Carnival Corporation is a global cruise vacation and leisure travel company that offers various cruise brands serving the contemporary cruise sector through Carnival Cruise Lines and Costa Cruises, the premium cruise sector through Holland America Line, the premium/luxury cruise sectors through Cunard Line,

EXHIBIT 6
North American Cruise Line Market Share for 2nd Quarter 2003

CRUISE LINE	PASSENGERS	PERCENT OF TOTAL PASSENGERS
Carnival Cruise Line	723,000	36.2
Princess Cruises	156,000	7.8
Holland America Line	141,000	7.0
Cunard Cruise Line	13,000	0.6
Costa Cruise Lines	8,000	0.4
Royal Caribbean International	510,000	25.5
Celebrity Cruises	153,000	7.6
Star/Norwegian Cruise Line	186,000	9.3
Disney Cruise Line	101,000	5.1
Crystal Cruises	7,000	0.3
Total	1,998,000	100.0

Source: Maritime Administration Web site, **www.marad.dot.gov/marad_statistics**.

and the luxury cruise sector through Seabourn Cruise Line and Windstar Cruises. In April 2003, the company combined with P&O Princess Cruises. The combined passenger capacity has grown to over 75,000 berths, and 41 ships. In addition to its cruise business, the company operates Holland America Tours and offers services in the state of Alaska and the Canadian Yukon. Holland America Tours also markets sightseeing packages, both separately and as part of its cruise/tour packages.

A distant third with respect to size is Star Cruises; Norwegian Cruise Lines was acquired by Hong Kong's Star Cruises in 2000 after a takeover battle waged by Star Cruises and Carnival. Carnival eventually dropped its bid, and Star purchased the company. NCL operates eight cruise ships. As the third-largest cruise operator, Star Cruises offers cruises to more than 200 destinations worldwide on its fleet of 20 ships (which operate under the Star Cruises, Norwegian Cruise Line, and Orient Lines names). Ships range from the *SuperStar Virgo* (2,000-passenger capacity) to the *MegaStar Taurus*, designed for private charters.

Conclusion

Demand for cruises and other vacation products has been and is expected to continue to be affected by the public's attitude toward the safety of travel. In addition, demand for cruises is also dependent on the underlying economic strength of the countries in which cruise companies operate. Economic changes that reduce disposable income in the countries in which cruise lines operate will reduce demand for vacations, including cruise vacations, which will force cruise companies to discount prices, reducing the profitability. Other variables which affect profitablity are those that impact operating costs such as interest rates, fuel prices, and insurance rates, as shown in Exhibits 7 and 8 which are also subject to change due to economic conditions and the geopolitical climate.

Considering these risks, cruise line companies continue to expand their fleets and available berths at a rate of about 8 percent per year. It must also be considered that cruise berths are perishable assets that disappear once the cruise ship leaves port. If a berth is not filled, any potential to generate revenue from it in the future is lost. Despite what appears to be a steady increase in demand for cruise vacations, cruise operators will suffer financially if there is too much supply in the market either through overexpansion, or a drop in demand due to economic conditions, safety concerns, or bad publicity over flu outbreaks or environmental mismanagement.

In response to these external factors, RCCL is pursuing several strategies. The company plans to slow its pace of capital expansion, reducing its fleet expansion from around 17 percent per year in recent years to about 5 percent per year over the next three years, beginning in 2004. RCCL plans to operate a greater number of bases of operation within the United States to target vacationers who want to avoid air travel. Plans are to continue to increase the percentage of European travelers through European itineraries and bases of operation, and through its strategic alliance with First Choice Holidays PLC and the formation of its Island Cruises brand. It also plans to utilize aggressive media advertising to target customers who are "Explorers" and build name recognition for its Royal Caribbean and Celebrity brands. RCCL says it will offer the best cruising experience available to its customers on the basis of innovation in quality of ships, quality of service, variety of itineraries, and price. RCCL will continue to control costs and optimize revenue per berth through the integration of the latest yield management systems, software packages, and the Internet.

EXHIBIT 7

Royal Caribbean CR (RCL)—Income Statement

IN MILLIONS OF U.S. DOLLARS (EXCEPT FOR PER SHARE ITEMS)	12 MONTHS ENDING 12/31/03	12 MONTHS ENDING 12/31/02	12 MONTHS ENDING 12/31/01
Revenue	$3,784.20	3,434.30	3,145.30
Other Revenue	—	—	—
Total Revenue	**3,784.20**	**3,434.30**	**3,145.30**
Cost of Revenue	2,381.00	2,113.20	1,934.40
Gross Profit	**1,403.20**	**1,321.10**	**1,210.90**
Selling/General/Administrative Expenses	514.3	431.1	454.1
Research & Development	—	—	—
Depreciation/Amortization	362.7	339.1	301.2
Interest Expense (Income), Net Operating	—	—	—
Unusual Expense (Income)	—	—	—
Other Operating Expenses	—	—	—
Total Operating Expense	**3,258.10**	**2,883.40**	**2,689.60**
Operating Income	**526.2**	**551.0**	**455.6**
Interest Expense, Net Non-Operating			
Interest/Investment Income, Non-Operating	4.5	12.4	24.5
Interest Income (Expense), Net Non-Operating			
Gain (Loss) on Sale of Assets	—	—	—
Other, Net	18.4	54.7	27.5
Income Before Tax	**280.7**	**351.3**	**254.5**
Income Tax	0	0	0
Income After Tax	**280.7**	**351.3**	**254.5**
Minority Interest	—	—	—
Equity in Affiliates	—	—	—
Net Income Before Extra. Items	**280.7**	**351.3**	**254.5**
Accounting Change	—	—	—
Discontinued Operations	—	—	—
Extraordinary Items	—	—	—
Net Income	$ **280.7**	**351.3**	**254.5**
Preferred Dividends	—	—	0
Income Available to Common Excl. Extra. Items	**280.7**	**351.3**	**254.5**
Income Available to Common Incl. Extra. Items	**280.7**	**351.3**	**254.5**
Basic/Primary Weighted Average Shares	194.1	192.5	192.2
Basic/Primary EPS Excl. Extra. Items	**1.446**	**1.825**	**1.324**
Basic/Primary EPS Incl. Extra. Items	**1.446**	**1.825**	**1.324**
Dilution Adjustment	0	0	0
Diluted Weighted Average Shares	197.3	195.7	193.5
Diluted EPS Excl. Extra. Items	**1.422**	**1.795**	**1.315**
Diluted EPS Incl. Extra. Items	**1.422**	**1.795**	**1.315**
Dividends per Share—Common Stock	—	0.52	0.52
Gross Dividends—Common Stock	—	100.1	100
Stock Based Compensation	—	20.5	37

Source: www.investor.stockpoint.com.

EXHIBIT 8

Royal Caribbean CR (RCL)—Balance Sheet

IN MILLIONS OF U.S. DOLLARS (EXCEPT FOR PER SHARE ITEMS)	AS OF 12/31/03	AS OF 12/31/02	AS OF 12/31/01
Cash & Equivalents	$ 330.1	242.6	727.2
Short Term Investments	—	—	—
Cash and Short Term Investments	330.1	242.6	727.2
Trade Accounts Receivable, Net	89.5	79.5	72.2
Other Receivables	—	—	—
Total Receivables, Net	89.5	79.5	72.2
Total Inventory	53.3	37.3	33.5
Prepaid Expenses	101.7	88.3	53.2
Other Current Assets	—	—	—
Total Current Assets	**574.6**	**447.7**	**886.1**
Property/Plant/Equipment—Gross	—	—	—
Accumulated Depreciation	—		
Property/Plant/Equipment, Net	9,943.50	9,276.50	8,605.40
Goodwill, Net	278.6	278.6	278.6
Intangibles, Net	—	—	—
Long Term Investments	—	—	—
Other Long Term Assets	526.1	535.7	598.7
Total Assets	**$11,322.70**	**10,538.50**	**10,368.80**
Accounts Payable	187.8	171.2	144.1
Accrued Expenses	271.9	308.3	283.9
Notes Payable/Short Term Debt	—	—	—
Current Port. LT Debt/Capital Leases	360.0	122.5	238.6
Other Current Liabilities	729.6	568.0	446.1
Total Current Liabilities	**1,549.30**	**1,169.90**	**1,112.60**
Long Term Debt	5,475.80	5,322.30	5,407.50
Capital Lease Obligations	—	—	—
Total Long Term Debt	**5,475.80**	**5,322.30**	**5,407.50**
Total Debt	**5,835.80**	**5,444.80**	**5,646.10**
Deferred Income Tax	—	—	—
Minority Interest	—	—	—
Other Liabilities	34.7	11.6	92
Total Liabilities	**7,059.80**	**6,503.80**	**6,612.20**
Redeemable Preferred Stock	—	—	—
Preferred Stock—Non Redeemable, Net	—	—	—
Common Stock	2.0	1.9	1.9
Additional Paid-In Capital	2,100.60	2,053.60	2,045.90
Retained Earnings (Accum. Deficit)	2,162.20	1,982.60	1,731.40
Treasury Stock—Common			
Other Equity	5.8	3.7	
Total Equity	**4,262.90**	**4,034.70**	**3,756.60**
Total Liability & Shareholders' Equity	**$11,322.70**	**10,538.50**	**10,368.80**
Shares Outs.—Common Stock	195.6	192.5	191.8
Total Common Shares Outstanding	**195.6**	**192.5**	**191.8**
Total Preferred Stock Shares Outs.	—	—	—
Employees (actual figures)	—	27,300.00	24,000.00
Number of Common Shareholders (actual figures)	—	—	—

Source: www.investor.stockpoint.com.

References

Investor's Business Daily. October 7, 2003, p. B16.

Royal Caribbean Cruises LTD. *Annual Report*, 2002.

Royal Caribbean Cruises LTD. *Form 20-F*, March 24, 2003.

The Economist. September 13–19, 2003, pp. 11, 41–42.

U.S.News and World Report. September 29, 2003, pp. 28–32, 36.

www.royalcaribbean.com

www.celebrity.com

www.rclinvestor.com

www.islandcruises.com

www.marad.dot.gov/marad_statistics.

www.cruising.org.

www.investor.stockpoint.com.

www.oceana.org.

www.fool.com.

www.cnn.com.

www.whitehouse.gov/fsbr/esbr.html.

www.iccl.com.

www.cruisemates.com.

www.carnival.com.

www.hollandamerica.com.

14 The Quarry, Inc., Indoor Climbing Center—2004

Harold L. Koch
Utah Valley State College

www.TheQuarry.net

It is a beautiful, sunny day in Provo, Utah, and Jeff Pedersen is driving in to open up for business at The Quarry, Inc. (801-418-0266). A little sore from the previous day's climbing clinic out in Rock Canyon, Jeff is thinking about the news interview he just heard on the local radio station with a rock climber in Utah's Canyonlands National Park, Aron Ralston. Ralston, while climbing alone last spring, had been trapped by an 800-pound boulder for several days and, to survive, self-amputated his lower right arm with a dull pocketknife. While bringing national attention to rock climbing, the event could, in the long term, result in a negative impact for the sport. "We'll soon see," Jeff thinks.

Today will most likely not be a full day of activity in The Quarry climbing gym, as people tend to stay outside in good weather. Jeff remembers, however, as he turns off I-15 onto University Parkway, the class of 25 Boy Scouts from Troop 55 that will be in the building for an evening of indoor rock climbing to earn their Climbing Merit Badge.

"We have to work harder and apply more formal business knowledge to survive as a small business," Jeff muses. The Quarry cannot absorb another year of financial losses and hope to grow in this rather delicate environment; in 2003–2004 a concerted focus on planning and strategy is a must and no longer an option, especially when the SBA and local banks are becoming more cautious in the face of the national economic stagnation. With all these thoughts running around in his head, Jeff turns into the parking lot in front of the tall building that houses "the wall." This is Jeff's life and passion.

Source: The Quarry Records.

Industry Information

Overview

The person looking for fitness coupled with social interaction and outdoor adventure has many options: hiking, camping, kayaking, rock climbing, mountain biking, snowboarding, in-line skating, helicopter skiing, and white water rafting, among others. And, of course, some of the same needs could be met by joining indoor fitness clubs like Golds Gym (**www.GoldsGym.com**), which has 650 facilities from California to Russia and 24 Hour Fitness, which operates 300 franchise clubs serving 2.7 million members globally (**www.24hourfitness.com/html/company/**). These well-known centers offer aerobics, swimming, tennis, tanning facilities, and weightlifting. A survey conducted by the Outdoor Industry Association in 2003 reports that more than two-thirds of Americans participate in at least one outdoor activity each year and cumulatively spend $13.6 billion annually on outdoor/athletic merchandise, including gear, apparel, and footwear.

The Emergence of the Indoor Climbing Gym

The indoor climbing gym was born in the mid–1980s as an adjunct to mountain and rock climbing. Originally conceived as a place for experts to climb on rainy days and for the novice to learn the basics, it has become more than that today: it can also be a fun date, instead of a movie, for the university student; a source of self-esteem for the young single mother, or physical conditioning for the individualistic teenager; or a tool for teaching the principles of teamwork for the modern corporation looking to create a cooperative management culture. These needs and interests, coupled with a booming economy in the 1990s, engendered approximately 350 indoor walls (gyms) in the United States and many more abroad in Australia, Canada, England, and Brazil (**www.climbingcourses.co.uk/**; **www. aquaterra-ventures.com/wa/climbing_western_australia.html**).

The gyms construct their walls in such a way that there can be a variety of climbing experiences (from overhangs to slabs to vertical), adjusted to create very easy "routes" for beginners to very difficult, vertical terrain for experts. The designers of climbing gym facilities, such as Vertical World of Seattle, Washington (**www.verticalworld.com/walls.htm**), conceive and construct a free-standing "real rock" look. Concrete shell climbing walls, ideal for retail stores and outdoor bouldering walls in public parks, are common.

The "Industry" of the Climbing Gym

The climbing gym is difficult to place in any one "industry" as some owners see it in the Physical Fitness Services (SIC7991), which focus on aerobic exercise, fitness, and recreational sports centers; others believe they belong in the Clubs-Memberships Sports and Recreation family (SIC7997) because they sell memberships similar to golf and tennis clubs; some identify with the Amusement and Recreational Services industry (SIC7999), home for the ski resorts and recreational goods rentals. Finally, many of the artificial wall owners/managers attend the Sporting Goods Manufacturers Association (SGMA) trade shows, which merchandise the clothing, equipment, and hardware necessary for all outdoor sports.

In addition to the standard industry classifications mentioned above, the *Encyclopedia of Emerging Industries* (2000) describes a new industry which includes rock climbing: "Extreme Sports." It is noted that rock climbing and artificial wall climbing are the most popular of such sports and experienced an annual growth rate of 50 percent in the mid-1990s.

In-line skating is by far the most common, with nearly 28 million people slipping on a pair of skates at least once in 1999. Eight other sports associated with the extreme moniker, including skateboarding, snowboarding, wakeboarding, mountain biking, and rock climbing, claimed more than a million U. S. participants each during 1999.

Finally, there is a voluntary Climbing Gym Association (CGA) with which an owner can affiliate; the CGA is soon to begin publishing a journal (**www. adventuresafety.org/services/risk_mgt_sub/wall.htm**).

Ownership and Gym Nature

Climbing gyms are 90 percent individually owned, with the remaining 10 percent owned in multiples (2–5 climbing gyms per owner). They can be categorized by the space dedicated to their walls and gross sales: small climbing gyms have approximately 5,000 square feet with gross revenues of around $120,000 per year; the medium-sized gyms boast around 7,500 square feet and generate about $250,000 yearly; the larger ones have between 12,000 and 20,000 square feet and garner from $500,000 to $1 million in sales per year.

Jeff and his partners constructed 9,000 square feet of wall at $23.00 per square foot. Like most other climbing gyms it was conceived as an extension of his extreme passion for rock climbing. Since then, approximately 6 percent of the original 350 gyms that started this way have closed. The key to financial viability is to be good at marketing and financial management; the indoor climbing gym can no longer be an exotic toy for big kids.

The Basic Climber Profile

The sport of rock climbing has attracted a wide range of people since the mid-1980s; with 60 percent of the climbers being male and 40 percent female; sport climbing is most popular among the 25- to 34-year-old age group, followed by the 18- to 24-year-old category. The hard-core climber like Jeff represents a very small percentage of total revenues; the sport is becoming more and more oriented toward satisfying social needs.

The Sporting Goods Manufacturers Association (SGMA) places the number of enthusiasts for climbing at 2.1 million; however, 95 percent of them participate infrequently (less than 15 times a year), a real challenge for an indoor facility like The Quarry. The state of Utah ranks number two in the nation behind Wyoming in the climbing of artificial walls, with 89,518 Utahans participating.

External Issues in 2003

Since 9/11/01 and the continuing military operations in Iraq, spending and travel for outdoor adventures like rock climbing has stagnated along with the rest of the U. S. economy. Given that most large cities throughout the United States have at least one climbing gym, the short-term need to travel to unique places like Utah can be postponed. As income growth continues to slow, consumers are cutting back, especially on the luxuries of life such as cable TV and vacations. Many people are skeptical of air travel, which has negatively impacted sports in Utah, specifically skiing, by about 15 percent during the 2002–2003 seasons; the expected boom from the high profile 2001–2002 International Winter Olympics never materialized. Higher fuel costs discourage new-car purchases even though household spending grew 3 percent in 2003. Both business travel and international travel suffered declines, leaving tourism employment and traveler spending constant in 2002 and 2003.

Company Profile

History

Jeff and two close friends founded The Quarry, Inc., in Provo, Utah, in late 2000. Pedersen is a very well-known rock climber who has competed nationally and has been featured in articles published in trade magazines such as *Rock & Ice* (**www.rockandice.com/**). A graduate of Brigham Young University, Jeff came to Utah to study geology and fell in love with the topography and nature-loving lifestyle. He founded and managed a retail climbing equipment store called Mountainworks from 1993 until 2001, at which time he sold his equity to a friend who now runs the 1,000-square-foot shop located on the first floor of The Quarry, to dedicate himself to the new entrepreneurial endeavor. The store carries all of the ropes, harnesses, clothing, boots, and hardware necessary to climb at any skill level and complements Jeff's climbing target market and business perfectly.

The Balance Sheets (Exhibit 3) show that the capital needed for start-up was raised through a $380,000 loan from the SBA, $485,000 from a local bank, and $300,000 financed by the builder. The significant capital needed for start-up (the basic climbing surface alone cost $186,000) was also partially capitalized through a special offering of 400,000 shares of Common Stock (no par value) at $1.00 per share. As can be seen in the Statement of Operations (Exhibit 1), the small company that vowed to become "the largest and finest indoor climbing facility in the Intermountain West" is hoping to break even in the third year of operation. However, Jeff had to accept a large debt base from the SBA and local lenders, which is constantly a headache when it comes time to pay the bills. Cash flow management is sometimes more difficult than rock climbing.

Location

The Quarry is located in one of Provo's busiest shopping centers in a town that is home to BYU with 30,000 students. Just a mile toward highway I-15 down University Parkway in Orem is Utah Valley State College with 24,000 more students. Orem and Provo are located in a county of 360,000 inhabitants where 36 percent of the residents

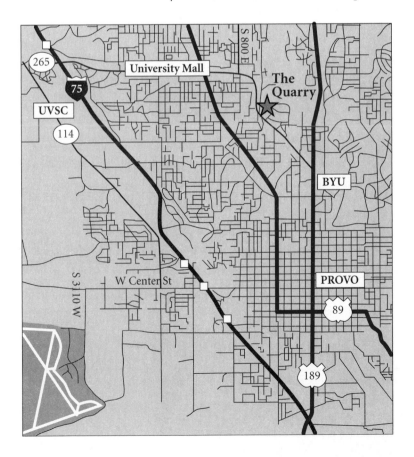

EXHIBIT 1

Consolidated Statement of Operations

	YEAR ENDED DECEMBER 31,		
	2001	2002	2003 (8 MONTHS)
Revenue			
Automated Payment System Plans (EFT)	$121,654	$185,025	$113,505
Family Memberships (18.2%)			
College Students (60%)			
Noncollege Individual Clients (21.8%)			
Day Sales (walk-ins)[1]	295,041	260,338	152,578
16–17 years old (3.5%)			
18–34 years old (96.5%)			
University Classes	440	13,200	20,878
Corporate Group Memberships	—	—	7,031
Other Sales (Equipment-Shoe Rental, Vending)	11,264	39,672	15,174
Less: Returns and Discounts	(1,248)	(4,450)	(3,161)
Total Net Revenue	**$427,151**	**$493,785**	**$302,135**
Expenses			
Operating Expenses			
Automobiles	$10,685	$15,294	—
Utilities	21,035	21,349	14,168
Repairs	1,335	986	135
Depreciation	68,223	59,021	38,333
Part-Time Climbing Instructor Fees	988	21,256[2]	3,822
Custodial	17,612	4,586	1,678
Gym Supplies (Cleaning, Ropes, Hardware)	22,676	43,137	6,624
Payroll, Taxes & FICA[3]	224,804	231,360	63,061
Part-Time (40%)			
Salaried (60%)			
Total Operating Expenses	**$367,358**	**$396,989**	**$127,791**
Marketing Expenses			
Advertising	$11,708	$8,489	$4,439
Design, Photography, Prizes	2,069	6,889	—
Signs, Printing, Direct-Mail Pieces	—	5,288	1,701
Total Marketing Expenses	**$13,777**	**$20,666**	**$6,140**
Administrative Expenses			
Interest Expense (SBA and Bank)	$114,506	$122,447	$83,965
Bank Service Charges	4,558	13,918	6,728
Insurance (Life, Property, Medical)	23,572	30,120	17,472
Travel and Entertainment	3,475	—	144
Contributions, Dues, and Licenses	3,410	195	401
Education and Equipment	14,423	11,668	—
Land Improvement	—	11,988	—
Consulting & Professional Services (route setting)	—	46,227	48,004
Miscellaneous	6,845	3,826	8,837
Total Administrative Expenses	**$170,789**	**$236,563**	**$165,551**
Net Income (Loss)	**($124,773)**	**($160,433)**	**$2,653**

[1]These sales represent the "recreation"-oriented individual who perceives artificial rock climbing in the same category as a movie, bowling, a date alternative on Saturday evening, or video parlor games. They come infrequently, thus they are not motivated to purchase the EFT Membership Plan.
[2]This figure is larger than either of the two other years as it reflects an instructor who worked nearly full-time who is no longer with The Quarry.
[3]In 2001 there were four full-time employees and by 2003 they were reduced to two: Jeff Pederson and Matt Nielson.

Source: The Quarry, Inc., Company Records (consolidated/reconciled by the case author).

are between the ages of 18 and 39 and the forecasted growth is 6 percent annually over the next five years. Utah offers an excellent combination of outdoor, western beauty and a lifestyle that is attractive for raising families and retirement. University enrollments in Utah have been growing at about 8 percent annually, faster than most other states in the United States.

Mission Statement

One of Jeff's original partners, Josh Miller, was studying for his MBA at Brigham Young and, along with Nate Maughan, the three wrote the mission statement that would drive the marketing and operations of The Quarry. They sincerely believed in what they wrote.

> Climbing inherently promotes a healthy lifestyle of friendship and fulfillment, responsibility, ethics and achievement.
>
> Our Purpose is to provide the highest quality experience for all climbers from novice to expert. We strive to maintain a clean, friendly and inspiring environment that is constantly new and challenging. We do not chase competitors; we run with our customers. The highest standard for improvement is ourselves.
>
> Our Goal is to be aggressively innovative, financially profitable, socially responsible, and to promote the sport we love. We anticipate The Quarry being known by individuals around the world as the reason they become climbers for life.

Company Organization and Personnel

The original founders and management team were three entrepreneurs who under-stood that their market went far beyond the hard-core, adventure-seeking rock climber like Jeff Pedersen or Aron Ralston. Each person brought something special to The Quarry. Jeff, a graduate of BYU in geology, today serves as the CEO and has been living and climbing in Utah for over 18 years. He is widely acknowledged as one of the most prolific sport climbers in the United States and, along with Bill Boyle and Boone Speed, he created most of the sport climbing in American Fork Canyon—a limestone area that was key in the progression of climbing development in the United States. As a result of his high profile and local expertise, visitors to the state of Utah frequently stop by The Quarry asking for advice about local climbing. In 2004, Jeff still handles day-to-day management of The Quarry and is responsible for customer relations and employees. He is considered to be the Senior Climbing Instructor.

Josh Miller, also a graduate from BYU with a degree in linguistics, was a sea-soned entrepreneur, having served as the Vice President of Atomic Giant, an Internet company that in 2000 had a net worth of $1 million. A seasoned climber, he had com-peted in several regional competitions and in 1994 was the winner of the men's advanced division at the annual Rock Rodeo national competition held in El Paso, Texas. Josh, in tandem with Nate Maughan, was responsible for the business opera-tions of the gym up until May of 2003, when he finished his MBA and decided to enter the financial industry, thus divesting and leaving Jeff and Nate to carry The Quarry forward.

Nathan (Nate) Maughan received his degree in computer science in 1996 from BYU and recently completed a master's degree in international studies. He speaks four languages and is active in the fitness industry, participating in marathons, triathlons, and 10K races. No longer a full-time manager but a member of the board of directors, he pro-vides consulting on the computer system and financial accounting for The Quarry.

EXHIBIT 2
The Quarry Organizational Chart—2003

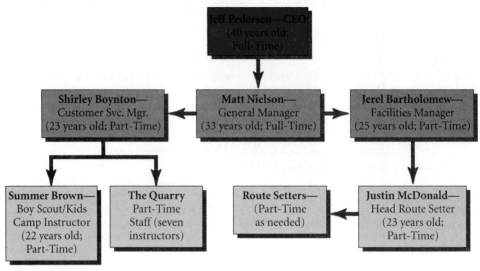

Source: Jeff Pedersen, CEO.

In early 2004, The Quarry has two full-time people; Jeff is the only one with a degree. (Matt Nielson was the head sales manager of Office Max for three years before coming to The Quarry). In addition, Jeff receives advice from an unpaid financial advisor and continues a close relationship with the builder of the wall of The Quarry, El Dorado Walls, which has constructed many successful gyms in Colorado, Pennsylvania, Alaska, West Virginia, and New Zealand. Several part-time climbing instructors (all college students) are needed, as the organizational chart Exhibit 2 reveals.

Facilities
Situated in the busiest commercial district of Provo, equidistant from Brigham Young University and Utah Valley State College, the facility of The Quarry greatly enhances its attractiveness. The exterior of the building has eye-catching signage and dramatic lighting visible from the busy thoroughfare; its spacious interior and quality surfaces are kept in immaculate shape and repair. The retail shop The Mountaineer can be seen below and to the right of the climbing walls.

Approximately 45,000 vehicles drive by the building daily and it is 50 feet west of Movies 8, the busiest theater in Provo. Close by in the same shopping center are an Olive Garden restaurant, a ShopKo discount store, and various other retail stores that generate traffic. The pictures below show a close-up of the climbing walls, which are the primary offering of The Quarry.

Target Audiences and Services of The Quarry
The Quarry offers a "product" for a variety of the consumer segment profiles mentioned earlier and reflected in the financial statements. In the most general of terms, the service offered by The Quarry is the climbing experience on the artificial wall, whether individually or in a group (family, corporate, Boy Scout, university, etc.). The client is fitted with a harness, climbing shoes, and ropes and, with the assistance of a climbing instructor (or friend/partner), then chooses a "route" from different difficulty levels for the climb to the top of the 45-foot wall. S/he then either repeats the

View from the North. Note the Finger Cracks on the left.

experience, requests a new "route," or takes a turn holding the safety rope so that her/his partner can climb.

The largest group of people who climb artificial walls are the "walk-ins" between 18 and 34 years of age, who equate the artificial climbing experience to a movie, bowling, the video arcade, or a date, mostly a social activity with a touch of adventure and physical challenge. Because they are in the category of 95 percent "infrequent users" they do not choose to affiliate with a membership. The walk-ins are heavy users of the Saturday Night Date Night ($5 per person from 9–12 P.M.) climbing social, when The Quarry features kaleidoscopic black lights and popular music that adds excitement to the climbing experience (the "Cosmic Climb," as the Web site of The Quarry calls it).

The second-largest income generator is the monthly Electronic Fund Transfer (EFT) membership. This plan is promoted and priced in a way that is similar to exercise centers like Gold's Gym and 24 Hour Fitness centers, which offer a $13 per-month single membership. The Quarry client is billed automatically via an electronic funds transfer assignment and is allowed unlimited climbing time. There are several plans from which a client can choose, all with a $39 one-time enrollment fee up front: 24 months at $19 per month ($456); 12 months for $29 per month ($348); 6 months for $39 per month ($234); 1 month for $69 ($69).

In addition, Jeff has created a series of seven "packages" all priced at $99 each to smooth out the uneven utilization of instructors and facilities. These packages complement the monthly EFT membership regulars, walk-in climbers (Jeff recently lowered the daily walk-in price from $13 to $9 to cope with the aggressive campaigns of the physical fitness clubs in the area), and scheduled groups such as Boys Scouts, corporate team-building sessions, family groups, and university classes. The following example of the seven packages, described in a threefold handout and on its Web site, typifies The Quarry's special offerings.

New Segments of Climbers

The corporate membership segment in the first eight months of 2003 has already produced $7,000 in revenues, and Jeff is sitting within 45 minutes of headquarters and regional offices of very important companies such as Novell, Inc.; Black Diamond Equipment, LTD.; Iomega Inc.; Nu Skin Enterprises; Huntsman Chemical Corporation;

EXHIBIT 3
Consolidated Balance Sheet

| | YEAR ENDED DECEMBER 31, | | |
	2001	2002	2003 (8 MONTHS)
Assets			
Current Assets:			
Cash and cash equivalents	$16,023	$6,865	$4,319
Receivables, less doubtful account allowance	—	—	1,523
Total Current Assets	16,023	6,865	5,842
Fixed Assets:			
Property and Equipment at Cost			
Climbing Wall	$ 242,540	$ 242,540	$ 242,540
Climbing Holds	28,000	28,000	28,000
Land	238,000	238,000	238,000
Building	725,452	725,452	725,452
Other	10,000	10,000	10,000
Equipment & Furniture	6,168	6,168	6,168
Less Accumulated Depreciation	68,223	127,254	165,587
Total Property and Equipment, net	1,181,937	1,122,906	1,084,573
Total Assets	**$1,197,960**	**$1,129,771**	**$1,090,415**
Liabilities and Stockholders' Equity			
Current Liabilities:			
Accounts Payable	$16,958	$ 48,855	$ 25,898
Credit Card Payable	6,549	10,266	9,730
Notes Payable	9,750	87,400	102,997
Taxes Payable (Income and Sales)	27,326	23,874	3,283
Other	3,079	4,100	3,665
Total Current Liabilities	$63,662	$174,495	$145,573
Long-Term Liabilities			
SBA Loan	$ 381,966	$ 371,601	$ 364,699
Bank Loan	484,155	474,000	468,215
Supplier Note	303,950	305,881	305,481
	1,170,071	1,151,482	1,138,395
Stockholders' Equity			
Capital stock common, par value $1.00, authorized 400,000	$ 89,000	$ 89,000	$ 89,000
Retained Earnings	(124,773)	(285,206)	(282,553)
Total Stockholder's Equity	(35,773)	(196,206)	(193,553)
Total Liabilities and Stockholders' Equity	**$1,197,960**	**$1,129,771**	**$1,090,415**

Source: The Quarry, Inc., Company Records (consolidated/reconciled by the case author).

and Franklin Covey, Inc., to name a few. To date there has been no concerted effort to sell "Team Building" packages but Jeff has been thinking about the possibility.

Finally, The Quarry has teamed up with Utah Valley State College and offers PE credit courses with climbing as the physical emphasis, drawing an average group of 23 students. As can be seen on the financials, in only eight months during 2003 the revenues for this activity have exceeded the entire year of 2002.

ing and financial management. The three men resigned from their positions at RBC Centura and began filing the necessary paperwork to found a community-based financial institution.

During the transition of resigning from RBC Centura and founding the new bank, Saunders worked tirelessly at designing and developing his master plan for success. This master plan dealt less with making the most profit at any cost and more with building solid personal relationships with every customer that entered that bank. Saunders knew that this would not be an easy task, and in order to be successful in achieving this master plan, he would have to develop a set of goals, morals, and values for himself and his employees to live by. These goals, morals, and values would not only apply during business hours, but would apply 24 hours a day, 7 days a week, 365 days a year. After reading countless books on motivation and management while at the same time drawing on his own personal experience and knowledge, Saunders and his team developed what is today known as the Reliance Focus. The Reliance Focus is a pledge made to customers that guarantees each person excellent customer service and a flawless banking experience by hiring competent, well-qualified employees to provide them with the best products available to meet their financial needs. The founders of the bank believed that the Reliance Focus, along with the set of values developed for the bank, would set the institution apart from the run-of-the-mill banking experience.

On August 16, 1999, First Reliance Bank was opened for business in a small mobile unit on Palmetto Street. The mobile unit was a temporary location for the bank until the main office was completed in June of 2000. During this phase, First Reliance Bank set out to raise capital by way of a stock offering. In many cases, raising sufficient capital for a start-up financial institution takes many months and sometimes over a year. In the case of First Reliance Bank, the necessary capital of $7.2 million was raised in just 60 days by over 950 stockholders. This act alone served as a strong indicator that First Reliance Bank was not only needed but was definitely wanted in the community. This achievement made First Reliance Bank the most successful de novo bank ever started in Florence County. Exhibits 1 and 2 illustrate the growth of First Reliance Bank by way of income statement and balance sheet.

Once the stock offering was completed and the main office building was up and running, First Reliance Bank was on its way to achieving its vision of becoming recognized as the largest and most profitable bank in South Carolina. In April of 2001, First Reliance Bank opened the doors to its first branch office on Second Loop Road. While the main office is located in the western part of Florence, the Second Loop Road office was opened to better serve customers who lived in the southern part of Florence. The maps in Exhibit 3 illustrate the locations of the main office and the Second Loop branch in Florence.

The values and focus set forth by the founders have taken First Reliance Bank from nothing more than a dream back in 1998 to the fourth-largest bank in Florence as of September 2003. The aggressive growth strategy coupled with the deep desire to build strong customer relationships has helped propel First Reliance Bank past many other fledgling community banks as well as many deep-rooted financial institutions in the Florence area. Given the success of First Reliance Bank with its main office on Palmetto Street and its only branch office on Second Loop Road, expansion of this business model and philosophy seems inevitable.

Once all the dust settled, a pretax net income of $1.3 million was reported for the year 2002. This figure illustrated a growth of over 40 percent from the previous year's pretax earnings of $928,652. In April 2003, First Reliance Bank witnessed

EXHIBIT 1
Balance Sheet

FIRST RELIANCE BANCSHARES, INC.
Consolidated Balance Sheets

	DECEMBER 31	
	2002	2001
Assets		
Cash and cash equivalents:		
Cash and due from banks	→ $ 3,789,927	$ 1,987,594
Federal funds sold	2,856,000	1,057,000
Total cash and cash equivalents	6,645,927	3,044,594
Investment securities:		
Securities available-for-sale	→ 23,448,775	14,305,686
Nonmarketable equity securities	250,000	142,400
Total investment securities	23,698,775	14,448,086
Loans receivable	→ 81,558,827	64,875,191
Less allowance for loan losses	(1,137,337)	(1,045,014)
Loans, net	80,421,490	63,830,177
Premises, furniture and equipment, net	3,993,363	3,675,541
Accrued interest receivable	698,590	687,611
Other real estate owed	120,872	86,988
Other assets	497,574	421,537
Total assets	→ **$116,076,591**	**$86,194,534**
Liabilities		
Deposits:		
Noninterest-bearing transaction accounts	$ 16,470,767	$12,175,551
Interest-bearing transaction accounts	16,489,757	9,251,381
Savings	15,492,740	14,237,621
Time deposits $100,000 and over	21,525,185	14,874,927
Other time deposits	30,344,632	25,147,164
Total deposits	→ 100,323,081	75,686,644
Securities sold under agreements to repurchase	1,881,750	1,927,164
Advances from Federal Home Loan Bank	4,500,000	—
Accrued interest payable	376,961	472,848
Other liabilities	350,621	449,871
Total liabilities	→ **107,432,413**	**78,536,527**
Commitments and contingencies (Notes 6, 7, and 15)		
Shareholders' Equity		
Common stock, $0.01 par value, 5,000,000 shares authorized; 1,448,830 and 724,115 shares issued and outstanding at December 31, 2002 and 2001, respectively	14,488	11,488
Capital Surplus	→ 7,091,562	7,167,775
Retained earnings	→ 1,309,803	415,500
Accumulated other comprehensive income	→ 228,325	63,244
Total shareholders' equity	8,644,178	7,658,007
Total liabilities and shareholders' equity	→ **$116,076,591**	**$86,194,534**

The Balance Sheet data represents the financial period ending 12/31/2002.

EXHIBIT 2
Income Statement

FIRST RELIANCE BANCSHARES, INC.
Consolidated Statements of Income

	FOR THE YEARS ENDED DECEMBER 31		
	2002	**2001**	**2000**
Interest income			
Loans, including fees	$5,939,949	$5,236,089	$3,697,084
Investment securities:			
Taxable	662,951	766,410	422,465
Tax exempt	232,807	93,623	1,155
Federal funds sold	84,277	149,072	280,343
Other interest income	11,759	6,332	19,146
Total	6,931,743	6,251,526	4,420,193
Interest expense			
Time deposits $100,000 and over	706,350	784,115	496,167
Other deposits	1,504,468	2,018,091	1,497,317
Other interest expense	126,154	84,100	61,322
Total	2,336,972	2,886,306	2,054,806
Net interest income	4,594,771	3,365,220	2,365,387
Provision for loan losses	348,533	347,000	628,312
Net interest income after provision for loan losses	4,246,238	3,018,220	1,737,075
Noninterest income			
Service charges on deposit accounts	590,168	504,582	327,697
Residential mortgage origination fees	829,808	716,203	424,654
Securities and insurance brokerage commissions	101,963	82,279	—
Credit life insurance commissions	31,588	51,320	74,638
Other service charges, commissions, and fees	82,121	28,828	14,981
Gain of sales of securities available-for-sale	79,785	7,413	—
Other	18,084	12,937	12,800
Total	1,733,517	1,403,562	854,770
Noninterest expenses			
Salaries and benefits	2,641,032	1,876,552	1,151,218
Occupancy	173,565	167,849	96,000
Furniture and equipment	221,658	244,136	70,462
Other operating	1,643,238	1,204,593	811,747
Total	4,679,493	3,493,130	2,129,427
Income before income taxes	1,300,262	928,652	462,418
Income tax expense	405,959	312,098	169,400
Net income	$ 894,303	$ 616,554	$ 293,018
Earnings per share			
Basic	$0.62	$0.43	$0.20
Diluted	$0.59	$0.42	$0.20

The Income Statement data represents the financial period ending 12/31/2002.

EXHIBIT 3

Maps of the Main Office and Second Loop Locations

**The Main Office of First Reliance Bank can be
located on the map provided below:**

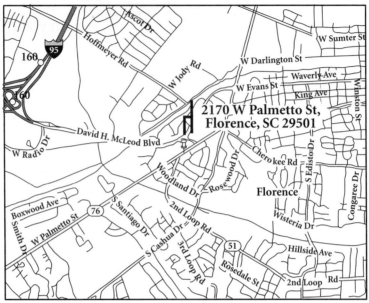

**The Second Loop Branch of First Reliance Bank can be
located on the map provided below:**

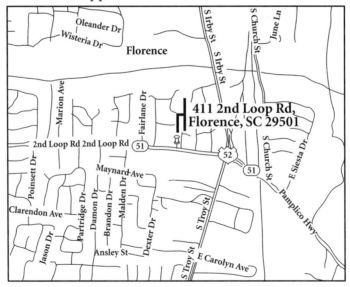

continued growth as it unveiled its new state-of-the-art Operations Center containing the latest high-tech equipment for processing and tracking account transactions in the most efficient manner. The Operations Center was built with intentions of servicing the ever-increasing loan portfolio and deposit operations of First Reliance Bank. It also freed up much-needed space on the second floor of the main office. Vacant space left by the operations staff will make room for expansion and

<u>EXHIBIT 4</u>
Executive Team Organizational Structure

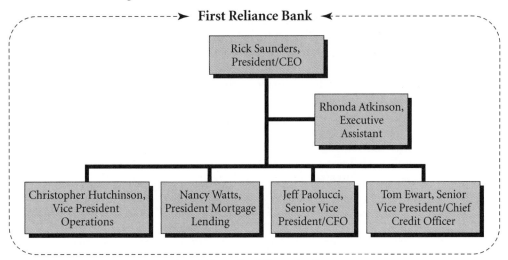

First Reliance Bank Executive Team

The Organizational Structure comes directly from the First Reliance Bank intranet as of October 2003.

hiring of more employees in the main branch. Additional employees hired at the main branch will better serve First Reliance Customers on front-end transactions.

The month of April set yet another financial milestone in the brief history of First Reliance Bank as the second stock offering was completed and provided a capital injection of $8 million. This additional capital opened the door for service to larger corporate/commercial customers as well as the opportunity for future branches in other markets. The additional capital injection coupled with the aggressive style of the Business Banking Department helped First Reliance Bank to reach $150 million in total assets in June 2003. This was truly a milestone for a bank that had not even celebrated its fourth birthday. Each of these goals was undoubtedly achieved by adhering to the Reliance Focus, as well as the hard work and dedication from the staff of over 65 employees.

The executive structure of First Reliance Bank can be viewed in Exhibit 4. The Executive Team makes nearly all of the long-term decisions that ultimately trickle down to each division of the bank. The profit center structure of First Reliance Bank is divided into four major areas of financial services along with the day-to-day deposit transactions. These four divisions are Business Banking, Consumer Banking, Mortgage Banking, and Investment Services. Each division is briefly discussed above.

Personal Banking
The personal banking division of First Reliance Bank provides customers with day-to-day financial needs such as checking and savings account products, certificates of deposit that are handled by branch managers and personal bankers. Personal Banking also encompasses consumer loans for personal purchases such as cars and boats. Consumer lenders and sales development leaders located at the main office or the second Loop branch handle each loan. Each loan that is granted is determined by the financial strength of the borrower and the discretion of the consumer lender. In the year 2002, consumer loans decreased 12 percent to $9,944,293 from 2001's $11,310,260.

Business Banking

The Business Banking division of First Reliance Bank provides the business owners of the Florence community with various commercial loans and lines of credit. These loans can be in amounts as small as $100,000 and as large as $2.4 million in-house, but with an unlimited cap through loan participations. Loans may involve the purchase of real estate, the purchase of equipment, or the refinancing of existing purchases. Lines of credit may be used for construction projects or for the financing of day-to-day operations. Each loan made by the Business Banking Department is thoroughly analyzed during an underwriting phase and submitted to the business banker. The loan is then subject to the approval of the business banker as well as the chief credit officer. Loans involving larger amounts that exceed the CEO or chief credit officer's authority (currently $500,000 as of 9/2003) must be approved at various committee levels listed below:

- $0 to $200,000—   Approval by Business Banker
- $200,001 to $500,000—   Approval by President or Chief Credit Officer
- $500,001 to $1,500,000—   Approval by Management Loan Committee
- $1,500,001 and over—   Approval by Director's Loan Committee

Since the inherent risk is much greater in business and commercial loans the approval process is much more thorough. It involves intense discussion of each loan and the review of the financial analysis submitted by the underwriter at each committee level. The commercial loan portfolio enjoyed 12 percent growth in the year 2002. These loans increased to $15,627,587 from $13,977,706 in 2001.

Mortgage Banking

The Mortgage Banking Department at First Reliance Bank provides the origination of residential mortgages in the Florence area. Once the loans are originated and closed by the Mortgage Department, they are brokered off to large mortgage buyers seeking long-term sound investments that are well secured. The Mortgage Department is mainly driven by fee income that is created when mortgages are originated. Due to the low interest rate environment, the Mortgage Department enjoyed explosive profits in the year 2002 and again in 2003. Fees collected from mortgage originations increased 16 percent to $829,808.00 in 2002.

Investment Services

The Investment Services division provides a wide array of financial services to the clients it serves. These include the establishment and maintenance of 401k's, stock purchases, retirement planning, and the funding of college educations.

Exhibit 5 illustrates the concentration of loans for each banking product, while Exhibit 6 represents the year-over-year comparisons for each loan product that is offered at First Reliance Bank.

Internal Forces

It is the top priority of First Reliance Bank to hire and retain competent employees. This is of great importance due to the fact that there is a constant stream of new internal challenges facing First Reliance Bank as it grows larger and larger. The major internal factors are marketing, IT, and management. Several of the internal factors faced by First Reliance Bank are described below.

Given the fierce competition in banking in Florence, proper marketing tools must be used in order to effectively increase market share. Given that First Reliance Bank is only four years old and is up against well-established, larger financial institu-

EXHIBIT 5

Loan Portfolio Concentration (as of 12/31/2002)

COMPOSITION OF THE LOAN PORTFOLIO (IN MILLIONS)				
	2002		2001	
	AMOUNT	PERCENT OF TOTAL	AMOUNT	PERCENT OF TOTAL
Commercial and Industrial	$15,628	19.16%	$13,978	21.55%
Real Estate	55,425	67.96%	39,406	60.76%
Consumer	9,944	12.19%	11,310	17.43%
Other	561	0.69%	181	0.28%
Total	$81,558	100%`	$64,875	100%

EXHIBIT 6

Year-over-Year Performance for Each Product Type

MAJOR CLASSIFICATIONS OF LOANS RECEIVABLE		
TYPE OF LOAN	12/31/2002	12/31/2001
Residential 1–4 Family	$17,113,018	$11,720,240
Commercial	20,632,111	15,029,012
Construction	9,799,410	6,748,992
Second Mortgages	4,491,109	4,266,248
Equity Lines of Credit	3,389,463	1,641,940
Commercial and Industrial	15,627,587	13,977,706
Consumer	9,944,293	11,310,260
Other	561,836	180,793
Total	$81,558,827	$64,875,191

tions, one major challenge is to boost name recognition. First Reliance Bank has achieved this by the use of billboards, newspaper advertisements, print ads in local magazines, and the sponsorship of various community events. It is also a goal of First Reliance Bank to raise awareness of the bank by donating many promotional items and time to charity fundraisers in the Florence community.

While name recognition is of great importance, it is also important to point out the products and services First Reliance Bank offers. One major advantage for the bank is the fact that many of its customers have long-standing relationships with its employees. This marketing concept cannot be bought or taught; it is achieved by hiring friendly, knowledgeable associates that are willing to assist the public no matter where they are. The concept is paramount in the business banking field because a strong customer rapport will lead to referrals and future financing opportunities.

The First Reliance staff achieves this not only during banking hours but also outside the bank in the form of community service and fundraisers. In the year 2002, First Reliance Bank employees donated over 2,030 hours of community services to

124 various civic and charity groups. Each event that is attended by First Reliance employees helps to serve as excellent PR for the bank and its values.

In the Spring of 2003, First Reliance Bank opened the doors of the new Operations Center, located adjacent to the main office. This Operations Center was designed with future growth in mind, which is centered on the values of the bank and the technology needed to support those values. The First Reliance Bank Operations Center is equipped with the most high-tech and advanced equipment. There is a strong belief that the ultimate vision of becoming recognized as the largest, most profitable bank in South Carolina depends heavily on the technology supporting the bank.

External Forces

Like many other businesses in a capitalistic economy, First Reliance Bank is faced with an endless string of competitors. The products it offers in terms of checking/savings accounts and loans are quite similar to those of its institutional competitors. As of September 2002, there were 12 banks and 3 savings institutions operating 35 offices within the Florence city limits; and there were 6 credit unions and 6 finance companies that also compete for many of the customers in Florence. First Reliance Bank is currently ranked fourth in terms of size and market share in the Florence market. Its three largest competitors are Wachovia, BB&T, and First Federal ranked first to third, respectively. All of these banks are well established and have been in existence in the Florence community for many years. Another advantage these competitors have is the fact that each bank has branches located throughout the state and the Southeast, thus creating economies of scale which lead to more competitive pricing. The competitive pricing due to the size of the bigger banks presents a negative for First Reliance Bank, especially on large commercial loans. Note in Exhibit 7 that the Florence County market share is commanded by the three major competitors of First Reliance Bank.

EXHIBIT 7
Depository Market Share for Florence County

FLORENCE, SOUTH CAROLINA, DEPOSIT MARKET SHARE (AS OF 5/2/2003)			
	NUMBER OF FLORENCE OFFICES	DEPOSITS (IN MILLIONS)	PERCENT OF MARKET SHARE
Wachovia Bank	8	$ 315,458.00	22.43%
Branch Bank and Trust (BB&T)	3	252,809.00	17.98%
People's Federal	5	180,466.00	12.83%
Citizens Bank	4	88,602.00	6.30%
First Reliance Bank	2	86,407.00	6.14%
Bank of America	3	84,772.00	6.03%
First Citizens Bank	4	81,555.00	5.80%
Carolina First Bank	3	49,332.00	3.51%
RBC Centura	4	48,359.00	3.44%
Florence National Bank	1	43,549.00	3.10%
Others	13	175,047.00	12.44%
Total	50	$1,406,356.00	100%

- *First Federal*—First Federal was previously known as People's Federal in the Florence area. It has over $180 million on deposit with 12.83 percent of the market share in the Florence area. First Federal, then known as People's Federal, witnessed a decrease of 3 percent in total assets from just the year before.

- *BB&T*—BB&T has over $252 million on deposit with 17.98 percent of the market share in the Florence area. It increased total assets by 6 percent from just one year before. BB&T is a multistate mega-bank with operations in South Carolina, North Carolina, Virginia, Maryland, and Georgia, among others.

- *Wachovia*—Wachovia Corporation has over $315 million on deposit and 22.43 percent of the Florence market share. It strengthened its market share by merging with First Union in 2002. In terms of total assets, the merger of these two banks helped Wachovia gain a large lead for market share in Florence.

Source: Market share data per FDIC Web site as of 6/30/2003.

First Reliance Bank does face competition from other banks in the area. Even though it is larger than several of the "community" banks in Florence, there is still a fierce battle for the best pricing and customer service. Other community banks in the area include Florence National Bank, SC Bank and Trust, and Anderson Brothers. First Reliance Bank is the only bank in Florence County that is owned by the stockholders in the county which it serves. All other "community" banks in the Florence area are owned by parent banks with stockholders in other markets.

The banking industry as a whole has been affected by the recent downturn in the economy beginning in 2001. This downturn has resulted in the lowering of the prime rate to its current level of 4.0 percent. The current status of the prime rate has resulted in more competition and a constant battle to win over the best customers. The low rate environment has also been quite lucrative for the Mortgage Banking Department in terms of residential refinances as well as the Business Banking Department in terms of construction loans and commercial refinances. This low rate environment is not expected to last and careful measures must be taken to secure customer loyalty and proper pricing in regard to future rate hikes.

The target market for First Reliance Bank includes Florence County and the communities surrounding Florence County. According to the Florence Chamber of Commerce Web site, Florence County has a population of over 125,000 with a median age of 36 years. The population has grown nearly 10 percent since 1990 and over 13 percent since 1980. Florence County is expected to grow another 10 percent to 137,000 by the year 2010. The median income for the region is over $33,000 with a cost of living that is 5 percent lower than the national average. The largest sector of employment in Florence County is the service industry, which employs over 40 percent of the county's workforce. Each of these factors was considered in founding the bank, along with looking ahead to the possibilities for future success.

The technological makeup of the United States is changing rapidly. Sizable portions of bank customers are quickly becoming technologically savvy and expect to be able to obtain information on demand. In the United States alone there are over 126 million active Internet users as of October 2003 (**cyberatlas.internet.com**). With that in mind, the use of the most advanced technology is paramount when competing against other financial institutions where the use of the Internet is involved.

Financial Condition

The financial condition of First Reliance Bank yielded the following analysis for the year ending 12/31/2002:

Income Statement

Income Statement analysis illustrated the strong growth in the following areas for First Reliance Bank:

- Overall net income grew 45 percent in 2002 to over $894k.
- Earnings per share grew 44 percent to $.62 a share. This takes into account the 1-for-1 stock dividend given to its shareholders and the 2-for-1 stock split dividend given to the shareholders.
- Other notable points are the strong growth in the origination fees from residential refinances and the growth in salary/benefits which increased due to bank growth.

Balance Sheet

Balance Sheet analysis for First Reliance Bank produced the following financial highlights for the year ending 2002:

- Total cash and equivalents listed for 2002 increased 118 percent to over $6.6 million from just over $3 million in the year 2001.
- Total assets for First Reliance Bank grew to over $116 million in 2002, which was an increase of 35 percent from just over $86 million in 2001.
- The offsetting total liabilities were calculated to be just over $100 million, which is a $25 million increase from the year before. The increase in total liabilities is solely due to the growth and expansion of First Reliance Bank.

Future Outlook for First Reliance Bank

With the vision in mind to be recognized as the "largest, most profitable bank in South Carolina," the outlook for First Reliance Bank seems very bright. The challenge will be to fend off its competitors and continue to gain market share from its top three competitors. Future and continued endeavors for First Reliance Bank may include the following:

- Expand to other potentially high profit markets in the state of South Carolina, perhaps Charleston, Columbia, Greenville, Spartanburg, and Myrtle Beach. Each of these markets presents opportunity for growth and expansion.
- Hire and retain a competent, hard-working staff that believes strongly in the values and goals of First Reliance Bank.
- Ongoing development of products and services that attract and maintain customers.
- Continuous improvement of associates on staff through intense education and training courses.
- Maintain profitability and maximize shareholder wealth while offering customers competitively priced financial services and products.

References

cyberatlas.internet.com.
First Reliance Bank *Annual Report*.
First Reliance Bank Annual Shareholder's Presentation.
First Reliance Bank Stock Offering Prospectus.
www.fcedp.com.
www.FDIC.gov.
www.firstreliance.com.
www.investor.stockpoint.com.
www.mappoint.msn.com.

16 Bridal Gallery—2003

Carol Cumber and Bianca Ornclas
South Dakota State University
Paul Reed
Sam Houston State University

Recently graduated from Sam Houston State University, Huntsville, Texas, and newly engaged to her college sweetheart, a 22-year-old woman walked into the store with a smile and thoughts of an exciting future. A three-tiered, elaborately decorated wedding cake stood as greeting at the door of the small bridal boutique. Her attention was quickly drawn to the center of the shop where the "dress of the week" was highlighted. The elegant yet simple ivory satin column gown was beautifully displayed on a mannequin, complete with veil, shoes, jewels, and other accessories. She pictured herself floating down the aisle in that selection, feeling and looking like a princess. Beyond that, she saw the large section of the gallery that was filled with a selection of stylish, high-quality bridal gowns.

Watching the customer enter the store was Vickie Cangelose. As owner and operator of the Bridal Gallery; (936–295–8895) a specialty store with a full range of bridal products and services, Cangelose prided herself on giving personalized attention to every customer. As she came out from behind the counter to warmly greet the new customer, she thought, "Let's see what I can do to help her have a 'storybook' wedding."

Background and History

In the early 1990s, Vickie Cangelose started in the bridal gown business by buying used wedding gowns at garage sales and offering them for sale in her mother's antique store. She quickly realized that this was her calling and in 1995 decided to open up her own bridal store with some money she had inherited. The building she occupied was only 11 feet by 60 feet, so as her business began to grow there was a need for a larger store. A few years later she decided to move her bridal business to a new location. The Bridal Gallery, which specialized in a full range of bridal products and services, was relocated to a shopping center in the south end of Huntsville, Texas, near Sam Houston State University. The location was not entirely visible from the road.

Since Vickie's mother had operated her own wedding cake business out of her home for twenty years, they decided to equally share the rental of the new bridal store, where the visibility would be increased, and her mother's cake-making and works of art of her mother's cake artistry could be displayed. They agreed that Vickie would be the hands-on owner of the store and would be responsible for the day-to-day upkeep of the Bridal Gallery while her mother would remain the silent partner. It was at this location that the business began to take off. The 1,800 square-foot store provided a large array of dresses to appeal to young women.

Bridal Gallery's Products and Services

The Bridal Gallery is in the business of pampering its clients by providing free one-on-one consultation, and offering a full range of bridal products and services, from bridal and bridesmaids gowns to garters, shoes, and jewels. Tuxedo rentals are also available. In one of her flyers, Cangelose stated that her store is a place "Where expert advice saves you time and money." Her philosophy is that every client should be given personalized attention and high-quality, reasonably priced products to make her dreams an affordable reality.

The service begins with a personalized consultation with the client, during which Cangelose tries to define the most appropriate style of dress. The bride is then led around the store so she can find that special gown. Although the Bridal Gallery is only 1,800 square feet, including three large changing rooms, there are 100–150 styles and sizes of bridal gowns in the store at a given time. Over 75 bridesmaids' dresses in every color of the rainbow also are stocked.

In addition, the Bridal Gallery provides additional bridal services such as tuxedo rentals, dyeable shoes, lingerie, and even candelabras. The Bridal Gallery maintains several business relationships with outside companies to offer the bride the option of not having to run all over town to find that perfect caterer, wedding cake, flower shop, limousine service, or reception hall. It recently expanded the product line to include an offering of 125 styles and sizes of prom dresses. Cangelose is cautiously optimistic that the new line will be a good revenue generator. She believes she can develop a competitive advantage in this new market by offering a service where she registers the prom gown so that no two identical Bridal Gallery prom dresses would be worn at the same high school's prom.

The inventory maintained at the Bridal Gallery is from outside vendors at wholesale costs. Cangelose maintains a personal relationship with her sales representatives to ensure that the inventory of bridal and bridesmaid dresses meets her high quality standards. She also buys her merchandise from bridal shows and catalogues.

Vickie Cangelose attributes part of her competitive advantage to incentives she offers Bridal Gallery customers. The incentives include two free steamings (for the portrait session and day of the wedding, a ($150 value), wedding gown travel bag ($25 value), free spot cleaning, and free consultative advice that includes everything from fashion to proper etiquette and wording on wedding invitations.

Bridal Gallery's Culture and Organizational Structure

The Bridal Gallery fosters an environment that encourages a pampered experience for every bride. This service is provided either directly by Cangelose or her one employee, who is a part-time bridal consultant who shares Cangelose's service philosophy. She works on straight commission. The target market is women between the ages of 17 and 24. The hours of operation are Monday thru Friday 10:00 A.M. to 6:00 P.M. and Saturday 10:00 A.M. to 3:00 P.M., with after-hour appointments available upon request.

Since the bridal business operates in a cyclical industry that reflects the latest fashions and trends, Cangelose and her bridal consultant often go to bridal shows and sales training seminars to stay up-to-date with their target market. In addition, they both shop local as well as other major cities' bridal stores to be aware of their competitors in an attempt to remain a leader in providing high-quality products at affordable prices.

The city of Huntsville, Texas, is located approximately 70 miles north of Houston. This growing community of 35,078 includes over 13,000 Sam Houston State University students. Recent studies indicate that marriage is a major life goal for the majority of today's college women, who want to meet a spouse while at college.

The Bridal Gallery is popular among young women. It offers that special experience that many young women dream about. Cangelose loves giving advice and helping to make wishes come true. Her motto is "Home of the Pampered Bride! Where expert advice saves you time and money." Cangelose sees Sam Houston State University students as her core customers.

Bridal Gallery Promotion

The billboard in front of the gallery is a bit dated and in need of renovation, but Cangelose believes that fully 75 to 80 percent of her customers are based on word-of-mouth recommendations. She advertises primarily through the yellow pages and the local newspaper. Radio and TV ads are seen as ineffective due to the Bridal Gallery's narrow target market. Interestingly, given the belief that their target customer is the Sam Houston State University student, advertising in the college paper has not been effective. The Bridal Gallery belongs to a bridal association and participates in the yearly bridal show, where it showcases its products and services. A serendipitous benefit for promotion of the business is location, and although Bridal Gallery is not very visible from the road, it is located across the street from an organization frequented by college students—Planned Parenthood.

Bridal Gallery's Competition

Although there are traditional department stores that offer bridal products, Cangelose believes that the two other local bridal stores in the Huntsville area are her primary competitors. They are:

Doran's

Doran's is owned and operated by Ruth Erwin. It has been around for over twenty years as an upscale specialty store that caters to women over the age of 30. The store provides top-name-brand dresses at a premium price. It is less than two miles away from the Bridal Gallery, and it's not uncommon for Doran's clients to check out the Bridal Gallery because of its reputation for exceptional service and affordable prices.

Jessica's Fashion

Jessica's Fashion is located approximately three miles from the Bridal Gallery. It has been in business for over five years. Jessica's Fashions offers wedding dresses, prom dresses, and quincernera dresses at affordable costs. Although the selection is quite large, the dresses are of lower quality. Cangelose does not feel the prices for her dresses need to be lowered to compete with Jessica's Fashion because she believes that young women (or their parents) are willing to pay for quality.

Although Cangelose entered the prom dress market in 2003, she does not feel she faces strong competition in this market, as there is just one other specialty shop for prom gowns in Huntsville.

Bridal Gallery's Finances

The Bridal Gallery sees a lot of ups and downs in this cyclical business that emphasizes the "June bride." Cangelose has not had a steady paycheck during the entire life of the business. Throughout the eight-year history of the business, half of the years have resulted in negative net income. She is not discouraged, however, for she believes that it is not realistic for a small business to expect big profits in the early years. Interestingly, her "best" and "worst" years occurred only one year apart.

Year 2001 saw the best financial performance the business has ever seen. This might have been somewhat deceptive, however, because a change in bookkeeping systems was responsible for factoring in the rent in the "other income" column in 2001, but not in 2002.

In 2002, although revenues were up, expenses increased which resulted in a decline in net income of over $44,000 from the end of 2001 to the end of 2002. She rationalized that 2002 was a down year due to factors such as the aftermath of the horror of September 11, 2001, a depressed economy, and the fact that she had significantly increased inventory costs because of the purchase of the new line of prom gowns. Although cost of goods sold increased by almost 50 percent, she attributed some of this to expenses such as acquiring a business loan and an increase in taxes. The Bridal Gallery's financial summary can be found in Exhibits 1 and 2.

EXHIBIT 1
Bridal Gallery's Balance Sheet

	DECEMBER 31, 2001	DECEMBER 31, 2002
Current Assets		
Cash and cash equivalents	$24,670.00	$18,084.00
Accounts Receivable	(15,306.00)	(16,000.00)
Inventory	43,333.00	77,194.00
Other Current Assets	1,449.00	965.00
Total Assets	**$54,146.00**	**$80,243.00**
Current Liabilities		
Accounts Payable	$ 4,618.00	$ 5,097.00
Payroll Liabilities	271.00	192.00
Taxes Payable	$ 2,486.00	$10,842.00
Shareholders' Equity		
Opening Bal. Equity	$ 1,964.00	$26,234.00
Personal Draw	(2,146.00)	(4,092.00)
Retained Earnings	7,876.00	46,953.00
Net Income	39,077.00	(4,983.00)
Total Equity	**$54,146.00**	**$80,243.00**

EXHIBIT 2
Bridal Gallery's Income Statement

FOR THE YEAR ENDED	DECEMBER 31, 2001	DECEMBER 31, 2002
Revenues	$89,148.00	$100,278.00
Cost of Goods Sold	28,917.00	43,442.00
General Expenses	44,254.00	62,101.00
Other Income	23,100.00	282.00
Net Income	$39,077.00	$ (4,983.00)

First-quarter earnings for the new prom dress product line offered in spring 2003 showed a promising net profit of $16,543. Cangelose was thrilled to calculate that 90 percent of the inventory of 125 prom gowns was sold.

Local Area
Huntsville, Texas, is located along Interstate 45, approximately 70 miles north of Houston and 170 miles south of Dallas/Fort Worth. When Interstate 45 was constructed in the 1960s, the highway was located about a mile west of Huntsville. During the ensuing 40 years, the geometric center of the town has gravitated toward the interstate. This movement of the town toward the interstate should continue since the city of Huntsville has recently constructed a wastewater treatment facility and a north–south arterial road on the west side on Interstate 45. This additional infrastructure should stimulate development on the west side of town.

Huntsville, the county seat of Walker County (with a 2000 population of 61,758), in many respects is a typical east Texas county seat, which serves as the

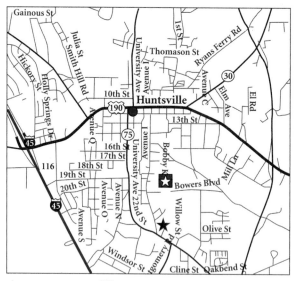

★ Bridal Gallery   ◼★ Sam Houston State University

trade center for the county and the surrounding rural population. Huntsville is also home to Sam Houston State University (SHSU) and is the headquarters for the Texas Department of Criminal Justice (TDCJ). Additional employment is supported by the city, county, school district, Huntsville Memorial Hospital; and by the typical small service, retail, and light industry-type firms present in the community. The 2000 census placed the population of Huntsville at 35,078. In addition to the local citizens, the population totals include 8,904 inmates housed in the prisons, and over 13,000 university students. Many of the university students come from the Houston area and find the availability of recreational and social activities limited in Huntsville.

17 Champions Hydro-Lawn, Inc.—2003

Joseph Kavanaugh, Marilyn Butler, and Misty Poissoit
Sam Houston State University
Leslie Toombs
University of Texas at Tyler

www.championshydrolawn.com

It was the first meeting of the New Year for the Houston Northwest Business Men's Association. Its monthly breakfast meetings provided small business owners an opportunity to network, sharing ideas, recent accomplishments, and concerns. Lou Triche, owner of Champions Hydro-Lawn (281–445–2614), sat at the table with Gerry, a longtime friend and confidant. Gerry, a casualty of downsizing in the oil industry, was currently working as a consultant. He listened as Lou described the difficult year just completed.

Lou, sole proprietor of a turf establishment business for eighteen years, had just experienced a year-end loss, only the second in the company's history, and this one during a period of local economic growth. The previous year-end loss occurred during a nationwide recession and resulted from an unprofitable contract and the theft of internal documentation by a disgruntled employee, which had required a complete reconstruction of records. "This time, it was different," Lou told Gerry, "I bid a large mowing and maintenance contract that was beyond the organization's capability, a major tactical error." He continued telling Gerry how the experience cost Champions Hydro-Lawn the profit for the year and placed it in an unwanted debt position. With the difficulty in the collection of accounts receivable, increasing interest rates, fuel costs at an all-time high, and a downturn in the market, his company was no longer in a desired position of strength for transition or change. Had the past year been an expensive lesson, or had it been a valuable, timely experience? "You know, Gerry, the turf establishment business has really changed. They used to call us the squirt and go guys. Now, we are an important part of the erosion control industry striving to protect and preserve the environment and," Lou paused, "make a buck." As he and Gerry continued to discuss the details, a plan began to emerge.

Erosion Control Industry, Harris County, Texas

The uncontrolled movement of soil by water and wind is an enormous ecological problem, which created the erosion control industry. Sediment, the result of erosion, is responsible for more than two-thirds of pollutants that flow into U.S. waterways. Approximately $13 billion is spent annually in the United States to alleviate erosion and sedimentation.

Flood control projects balance the use of the land with its capacity to store and transport flood waters. Harris County consisted of more than 17,000 square miles (twice the size of Rhode Island), 22 major watersheds, and 3,000 miles of networked waterways. Plentiful rainfall and a growing population had created a need to maxi-mize the use of public lands. The Harris County Flood Control District (HCFCD), one of the nation's largest, designed flood control improvements, carried out capi-tal improvement projects, maintained drainage facilities, approved subdivision drainage plans and, in cooperation with the Office of Emergency Management, provided flood watch and flood alert programs. Funded by Harris County, the HCFCD also received financial and research support from the state of Texas and the federal government. A broad range of professions had evolved in the erosion con-trol industry with the following major objectives: the prevention of soil erosion, the establishment of vegetation, and the trapping of sediment before it entered the waterways. HCFCD was the major source of turf establishment contracts in Harris County.

In the late 1980s, strategic changes occurred at the Harris County Flood Control District (HCFCD). Over budget and missing the mark with flood control, management changes redirected the goals of the organization, and shifted the emphasis from short-term maintenance to long-term ecological concerns. Large maintenance contracts, the bulk of its work, were privatized, thereby creating a new market and a need for the turf establishment business. The Harris County Flood Control District had further defined itself in the past five years from an organization that grew and mowed grass and other vegetation to one that designed areas that would encourage succession, the establishment of progressive growth from grass to shrubs to trees. According to Dr. Sherri Dunlap, manager for the Harris County Flood Control District (HCFCD), "Erosion control had an enormous impact on vir-tually every aspect of what the HCFCD did: maintenance and repair frequency, the need to de-silt channels to reestablish flow lines, water quality protection, riparian habitat, and aesthetics."

The Turf Establishment Industry in Harris County, Texas

Turf establishment was an initial step and a vital link in the ecological chain of water management. Southeast Texas, replete with bayous, streams, tributaries, and rivers, all headed for the Gulf of Mexico, presented major ecological concerns: flood con-trol, erosion, safe drinking water, ship channel commerce, wetland preservation, migratory water fowl habitat, and environmentally sensitive coastal estuaries and salt water marshes. With an ever-increasing population, the flow of water and the quality of water was a major ecological concern to individuals, builders, and devel-opers, as well as local, state, and federal governments. The turf establishment busi-ness as a science had also matured from the distribution of grass seeds to the growth of vegetation to control erosion and improve water quality. One of the methods that was used to accomplish this was the evaluation of soil to determine specifications to maximize seed germination, minimize the use of fertilizer, and increase plant heartiness.

Three primary methods of turf establishment were used in the Greater Houston area: broadcast seeding, hydro mulch seeding, and laying of sod. A dry application method was seed planted with a broadcast seeder or a cultipactor. The seed was planted one-quarter-inch deep and rolled with a cultipactor after seeding to promote the absorption of water. Using specialized trucks, hydro seeding with mulch sprayed an application of a homogeneous aqueous mixture of seed, water, fertilizer, dye, wood fiber mulch, and tackifier (a soil binder), to the prepared area to control erosion and encourage revegetation. Sod, used in places where seed growth was difficult, was tightly placed by panels in rows and secured with metal staples, twelve inches long, into a prepared seedbed. A costly alternative, sod was an effective application for steep slopes and sheer embankments. Hydro mulch seed spraying and broadcast seeding were the methods most frequently utilized in Harris County, Texas.

The History of Champions Hydro Lawn

Lou Triche, a sole proprietor, owns Champions Hydro-Lawn, a leading turf establishment company providing erosion control in the Greater Houston area. His customer base consists of engineering firms, landscape architects, commercial construction contractors, commercial landscapers, county flood control districts, the state of Texas, and federal flood control agencies. Champions Hydro-Lawn bids on and fulfills contracts that assist in the mitigation and control of erosion by the establishment of grass on areas disturbed by construction, and provides erosion control and mowing services, almost exclusively within Harris County, Texas. The turf establishment business is very seasonal, with the peak period being from March to November. Champions Hydro-Lawn employs approximately thirty people year-round and forty seasonal laborers primarily from Mexico and Central America.

The company is located in an unrestricted area of Northwest Harris County on approximately two acres of land in a mixed residential and commercial area central to its labor pool. The office is a converted three-bedroom house with three attached, large metal multiuse warehouse buildings used for repair and maintenance of equipment and storage of hydro mulch supplies. Located on the back of the property are three diesel storage tanks and a variety of trucks, flatbeds, and other lawn maintenance equipment.

Champions Hydro-Lawn owns the largest inventory of hydro mulch equipment in the local industry. An in-house mechanic maintains the equipment in excellent condition, ready to respond. Hydro mulch products, ordered in volume directly from the manufacturer, are stored on the property.

Current Organizational Challenges for Champions Hydro-Lawn

The profitability of Champions Hydro-Lawn results from successful bids of erosion control contracts. Total revenue increased 28.6 percent in 2001 and just over 12 percent in 2002. The company, in spite of good revenue increases, incurred a net loss in 2002 of $392,000, resulting from its bid on a large mowing contract too large for the company to successfully complete with current resources. In order to complete that mowing contract, six Kubota tractors were purchased and additional equipment rented, increasing capital investment by 40 percent from 2001 to 2002. This placed Champions Hydro-Lawn in an unwanted debt position, contributing to an unprofitable year.

The office manager is responsible for scheduling, accounting and payroll, human resource concerns, inventory management, and the coordination of internal and external operations. The inside sales person serves as backup support for the office manager, but very limited redundancy exists in the system. The office manager, responsible for coordinating the "throughput" of the organization, could be a single point of failure. There is no cross-training among office personnel. In some cases, individuals are quite protective of their "territories."

Accounts receivable are a major concern for Champions Hydro-Lawn. Most bids are contracted and subcontracted, which extends collection time and causes problematic cash flow issues.

Inventory control is another major concern for Champions Hydro-Lawn. There are few safeguards to prevent theft of costly equipment or hydro mulch products. A purchase order system was put in place in January 2003 to control purchases, but there is no system for tracking the inventory of hydro mulch products.

Most of the hourly and temporary laborers live in the United States on a temporary visa and use English as a second language. The barriers created by language and cultural differences represent another significant challenge for the company.

The Competition in the Hydro Mulch Industry in Harris County, Texas

In Harris County, Texas, there are three major companies that compete in this segment of the industry: Champions Hydro-Lawn, A-1 Hydro Mulch, and C-Mark. The owners of both A-1 and C-Mark are former employees of Champions Hydro-Lawn, who learned the hydro mulch business while there. The hydro mulch industry in the Greater Houston area is fiercely competitive. All are seasonal businesses that use contract laborers primarily from Mexico and Central America, function with a minimal, full-time staff, and are owned by a sole proprietor. In Harris County, Champions Hydro-Lawn is number one in the industry. The firm is able to bid multiple contracts, large and small, because it has the labor pool, the equipment, and the product to complete the job. Additionally, Lou Triche has an excellent reputation in the hydro mulch industry, a superior performance bond rating, and offers a one-year warranty on all hydro mulch contracts.

External Environment

The Greater Houston area has recently experienced one of the longest sustained periods of economic growth in the past twenty-five years. As a result, there is an enormous amount of construction in the area, which disturbs soils and impacts the 3,000 miles of networked waterways in the flood control district. The district is responsible for the balanced use of the land in consideration of the land's ability to store and move flood waters. Ten years ago, HCFCD had a major shift in focus from maintenance to the establishment of ecological systems. The shift resulted in the privatization of flood control projects to private contractors, and the turf establishment business boomed in response.

The turf establishment business is based on science. When a project is bid, agronomists are consulted to test the soil and determine the best seed for the area. Fertilizers are examined to determine minimal use and optimum value, as fertilizer can be detrimental to the ecology. Industry organizations have set national standards, and local standards have been established through research associated with the HCFCD. Equipment design has been reengineered to establish and maintain growth in an efficient manner that creates the least amount of disruption to the soil and vegetation.

Computer technology has streamlined organizations and created new channels of distribution. The turf establishment industry utilizes technology extensively for customer service, education, and the marketing of products through a Web site presence.

Harris County, Texas, located near the southern border of the United States, has a growing Hispanic/Latino population. The 2000 census statistics for Texas indicated a 39 percent increase in the ethnic group during the past ten years. Language and culture create barriers among different ethnic groups but the Houston area is culturally diverse with educational and community services established to integrate and support the cultural diversity.

The current administration has established a dispensation plan for immigrants from Mexico and Central America that allows laborers to get green cards and begin the naturalization process to become U.S. citizens.

Environmental legislation pending in the state of Texas could significantly affect the lawn maintenance business by restricting and controlling emissions from gasoline and diesel-powered, heavy-use equipment. This is a serious potential concern to the entire industry and places erosion control, striving to protect the water supply, and emissions control, striving to improve air quality, at cross purposes.

The current trend in erosion control is to utilize the land in a manner that would allow for proper drainage and flood control. Once proper drainage is established, maintenance becomes the focus. Harris County, Texas, has an estimated $4 billion in flood control infrastructure. Maintenance includes the removal of silt beds deposited by passing storm water, repairs to channel banks, and mowing weeds and tall grass that impede the flow of water. Additionally, the district seeks to identify and cultivate vegetation that would reduce erosion along the waterways and improve the water supply.

Internal Environment

Champions Hydro-Lawn has approximately thirty full-time, year-round employees, twelve are staff and the balance hourly workers. During the peak period from March to November, experienced, seasonal laborers are also contracted to complete jobs. Including Lou Triche, there are twelve staff positions, listed as follows: production superintendent, engineering manager, outside sales manager, two field superintendents, account representative, office manager, inside sales, shop manager, senior mechanic, and a receptionist/accounts receivable clerk. (See Exhibit 1.)

Champions Hydro-Lawn does not have a vision or mission statement. Staff meetings are held weekly to discuss new and prospective business and report on

EXHIBIT 1
Current Organizational Chart for Champions Hydro-Lawn, Inc.

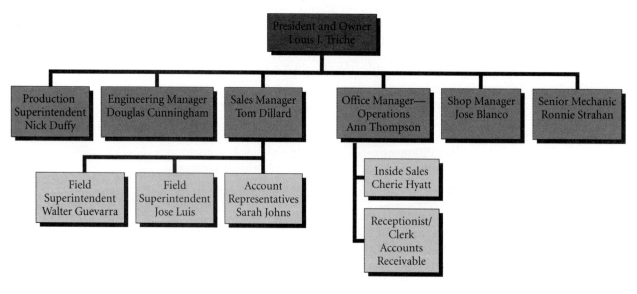

active contracts. Organizational meetings are held monthly for communication and encouragement. With the work at Champions Hydro-Lawn being seasonal, it is very important to keep the laborers informed regarding availability of work and also to incorporate them as integral team members.

There is a real sense of family among the employees of Champions Hydro-Lawn. Laborers are encouraged to participate in a company-sponsored savings plan at a local credit union. Because of the seasonal nature of the work, it is important that the laborers save to carry them through the off-season, and there is always the risk that quality employees would leave to take year-round jobs. Bilingual education and Graduate Equivalency Degree (GED) classes are offered to laborers and their families at Casa Juan Diego, a ministry for migrant workers. Financial support for the $75 filing fee as well as encouragement is given to those seeking permanent residency. A bonus is awarded to any laborer who completes the required training and receives a Texas Commercial Driver's License that enables the laborer to drive the company's commercial equipment. Company parties are given two to three times a year and the staff, laborers, family members, and friends of the company are invited, further promoting a sense of family among the employees of Champions Hydro-Lawn. Out of a sense of charity, the owner routinely extends loans to employees.

Champions Hydro-Lawn purchases hydro mulch products (seed, fertilizer, hay, and tactifier) in bulk directly from the manufacturer. It is the only company in the local industry able to purchase hydro mulch product in this manner. The location of three diesel tanks on the property allows the circumvention of the $.50 per-gallon fuel tax when trucks and mowing equipment are transported to the site on flatbed trailers, and also gives additional pricing leverage when contracts are bid.

The largest inventory of hydro mulch equipment and product combined with a one-year warranty of satisfaction gives Champions Hydro-Lawn an excellent reputation and an advantage in the industry. The company leads the industry in pricing, and with its A+ Performance Bond rating, extensive equipment inventory, products supply, unconditional warranty, and outstanding customer service, Champions Hydro-Lawn is the number-one hydro mulch company in the Greater Houston area, according to Dr. Sherri Dunlap of the HCFCD.

Internal operations are critical to the success of Champions Hydro-Lawn. Schedules are set and posted daily by the office manager who arrives at approximately 4:00 A.M. to assess work completed the prior day, reset the day's schedule, assign work teams to ongoing projects, and allocate equipment and product inventory. Laborers arrive ready for work between 6:00 and 7:00 A.M. to check the job board for the postings by the office manager. All work teams travel with two-way radios and cell phones for communication and trouble shooting from the field.

The office manager is the primary point of contact and is responsible for human resource concerns, maintenance of the company's books, tracking accounts receivable and accounts payable, preparing the weekly payroll, and keeping up with the inventory. The company receptionist assists with accounts receivable collections. The inside sales person is responsible for contract fulfillment and assists the office manager. Cash flow is always a major concern for the organization. The office manager maintains inventory, which is critical to operations. All records are kept by hand and on a small computer networking system. Accounting records are outsourced for balancing on a monthly basis.

Seed is the most important component of the hydro mulch mix and the most costly. Seed prices are secured through the commodities market, purchased in bulk, and stored in the warehouse on the property.

Repeat and referral customers are sources for contracts obtained. New business is generated from leads received through the Dodge Room, a county source for the posting of recent construction permits. Customer service, Lou's outstanding salesmanship, and referrals have been the company's marketing strategy. Champions Hydro-Lawn does not have a Web site presence.

Champions Hydro-Lawn has a small computer network that is used by three of the office staff for operations, inventory, accounting, and contracts. Lou does not use a computer. A facsimile (FAX) machine is a major source of communication and bidding on contracts.

Ecological techniques, including the specification of seeds, fertilizer, and mulch, are a science that requires continuing education for current trends and new technology. Lou and the engineering manager attend industry seminars to acquire the latest information on seeds and the application to specific areas. The HCFCD, with its emphasis on ecological systems, establishes the specifications and standards in the county and conducts extensive research which offers cutting-edge technology for the industry. When a contract is bid, soil samples are submitted to an agronomist for evaluation and satisfaction of the specifications of the contract.

Financial Analysis

Champions Hydro-Lawn had about $3.9 million in net revenue in 2002. The cost structure of contracts is based on 61 percent labor and 31 percent materials. Contracts are bid on a per diem basis and have to be completed on time to be profitable.

According to Lou, cash flow is the greatest financial concern due to delays in collecting receivables. It cost between $800 and $900 every time a hydro mulch truck rolls off the lot. The average collection period is thought to be over sixty days. Invoices are sent biweekly with contracts specifying thirty-day terms for nongovernment jobs and forty-five days for government jobs. Over-due bill notices are sent when accounts are forty-five days in arrears and, if there is no response, contract liens are filed when accounts are sixty days past due. Bad debt write-off was approximately $94,000 for 2001 and $53,000 for 2002. Problems with cash flow routinely result in nonsufficient-funds charges from the bank.

Lou is responsible for all capital equipment purchases. He seeks to maintain minimum debt due to the uncertainties of cash flow, the weather, and economic conditions. He also wants to be in a position to respond quickly to business opportunities.

The office manager maintains the day-to-day finances of the organization. The Quick Books accounting software package is used to track accounts receivable, accounts payable, and the weekly payroll. A purchase order system is utilized and receipts are required for reimbursement. Monthly, a certified public accountant balances the company books. On an annual basis, an accounting firm completes a review of the books and files all necessary tax information.

The Plan

As Gerry continued to listen, Lou shared his plans for the company. "My goal for Champions Hydro-Lawn, at the turn of the century, was to grow the company from $4 million in revenue to $10 million in revenue over the next ten years. I have worked hard to position the business for acquisition or merger but now we are entering a much different market and I am not getting any younger. The retirement plans I discussed with my financial planner a year ago must now be

EXHIBIT 2
Champions Hydro-Lawn, Inc.—Income Statement

	FOR THE PERIOD ENDED DECEMBER 31		
	2002	2001	2000
Revenues			
Sales	$3,928,551	3,516,768	2,777,308
Services	8,700	10,500	—
Total Revenues	3,937,251	3,527,268	2,777,308
Less: Cash Discounts	(15,407)	(10,986)	(43,005)
Net Revenues	3,921,844	3,516,282	2,734,303
Cost of Sales	(749,451)	(943,296)	(814,003)
Gross Profit	3,172,393	2,572,986	1,920,300
Expenses			
Payroll Expenses	2,162,911	1,371,322	1,124,113
Bad Debts/Write Offs	52,911	93,512	—
Depreciation Expense	220,652	119,202	85,183
Insurance	116,791	117,388	121,934
Gasoline/Diesel	161,047	109,125	112,515
Repairs and Maintenance	238,704	161,957	230,794
Miscellaneous	37,342	105,696	30,971
Telephone	41,321	29,665	24,867
Shop and Office Expenses	128,119	63,525	49,981
Professional Fees and Development	32,099	28,311	17,876
Utilities	11,810	18,067	15,086
Advertising	8,531	15,809	13,901
Crew Expenses	27,977	16,702	—
Travel & Entertainment	38,770	30,558	7,568
Donations	11,411	16,528	5,842
Property Taxes	16,924	18,409	6,864
Contract Labor	6,251	16,342	10,143
Printing, Reproduction, and Data Services	9,173	13,089	15,748
Employee Medical	11,760	10,991	4,980
Employee Incentives/Gifts	22,266	6,954	5,401
Safety & Other Equipment	3,865	3,579	9,222
Equipment Rental	82,364	—	5,940
Franchise and Other Taxes	3,591	4,567	1,813
Postage & Delivery	2,444	1,256	4,241
Auto Expenses	38,896	20,211	39,965
Bank Service Charges	12,365	2,524	4,623
Total Expenses	3,500,296	2,395,291	1,949,571
Net Ordinary Profit	(327,903)	177,695	(29,271)
Other Income and Expenses			
Interest Expenses	(116,784)	(38,269)	(50,453)
Interest Income	226	8,885	1,027
Other Expenses	(17,452)	—	—
Other Income	68,948	11,934	—
Net Other Expenses	(65,061)	(17,450)	(49,426)
Net Profit Before Taxes	(392,964)	160,245	(78,697)
Provision for Income Taxes	—	(41,750)	(23,009)
Net Profit After Taxes	**$ (392,964)**	**118,495**	**(101,706)**

EXHIBIT 3

Champions Hydro-Lawn, Inc.—Balance Sheet

	DECEMBER 31,		
	2002	2001	2000
ASSETS			
Current Assets			
Cash in Bank—Republic National Bank	$ (21,615)	(2,126)	21,846
Notes Receivable	25,000	800	800
Accounts Receivable—Trade	503,956	662,584	360,733
Less: Allowance for Bad Debts	(11,056)	—	—
Net Accounts Receivable	492,900	662,584	360,733
Employee and Officer Advances	56,032	43,791	193,466
Officers' Life Insurance	42,070	—	—
Insurance Claims Receivable and			
Prepaid Insurance	13,130	—	16,322
Inventory	96,896	181,309	146,232
Total Current Assets	**704,413**	**886,358**	**739,399**
Fixed Assets			
Land	25,000	25,000	25,000
Property, Plant & Equipment	2,069,375	1,507,511	1,147,565
Subtotal—Cost	2,094,375	1,532,511	1,172,565
Less: Accumulated Depreciation	(1,373,733)	(1,158,455)	(1,039,253)
Net Fixed Assets	720,642	374,055	133,312
Other Assets			
Deferred Interest	—	24,509	—
Prepaid Federal Income Taxes	20,167	19,079	—
Deposits	10,340	10,091	10,091
Total Other Assets	30,507	53,679	10,091
TOTAL ASSETS	**$1,455,562**	**1,314,092**	**882,802**
LIABILITIES & EQUITY			
LIABILITIES			
Current Liabilities			
Notes Payable—Republic National Bank	$ —	110,837	181,997
Sales Tax Payable	1,104	2,165	—
Federal Income Tax Payable	—	41,851	20,101
Accounts Payable	103,578	196,483	104,870
Other Current Liabilities	1,132,725	—	—
Total Current Liabilities	1,237,406	351,336	306,968
Long-Term Liabilities			
Notes Payable—Republic National Bank	—	268,426	—
TOTAL LIABILITIES	**1,237,406**	**619,763**	**306,968**
EQUITY			
Capital			
Common Stock	2,000	2,000	2,000
Additional Paid-In Capital	89,524	71,567	71,567
Total Capital	91,524	73,567	73,567
Retained Earnings			
Beginning Balance	519,596	502,267	502,267
Current Net Profit	(392,964)	118,495	
Ending Balance	126,632	620,762	502,267
TOTAL EQUITY	**218,156**	**694,329**	**575,834**
TOTAL LIABILITIES & EQUITY	**$1,455,562**	**1,314,092**	**882,802**

reassessed." Further, Lou told Gerry, "In order to fund my retirement, I need to sell or merge the company. I still believe I need to reach $10 million in revenues and make a consistent profit for the sale or merger to generate enough cash to fund a retirement account of at least $2 million. What changes can I make to still reach this revenue goal by 2012?" Gerry responded, "Let's talk, my friend, about a plan for Champions Hydro-Lawn that will assist in obtaining your goals and securing your future."

18

The Audubon Nature Institute—2003©*

Caroline M. Fisher
Loyola University New Orleans

www.auduboninstitute.org

"Louisiana's wetlands are vanishing at the alarming rate of more than 35 square miles each year. Of the total U.S. wetlands loss reported annually, 80 percent occurs in Louisiana. Such staggering loss threatens not only the survival of countless animals that flourish in the wetlands, but our way of life as well. Louisiana, and the nation, depend on wetlands for food, jobs, and protection from hurricanes and floods," said Ron Forman, president and CEO of the Audubon Nature Institute, in its *2002 Annual Report*. The Audubon Nature Institute (504-581-4629) is committed to increasing public awareness of the coastal erosion problem and communicating effective ways to address the problem as part of its mission to "preserve native Louisiana habitats."

Background

Formed in 1988, the Audubon Nature Institute is a not-for-profit "family of museums and parks dedicated to nature and unified with a purpose of celebrating life through nature." Its purpose of "celebrating the wonders of nature" guides its mission to:

1. Provide a guest experience of outstanding quality.
2. Exhibit the diversity of wildlife.
3. Preserve native Louisiana habitats.
4. Educate our diverse audience about the natural world.
5. Enhance the care and survival of wildlife through research and conservation.
6. Provide opportunities for recreation in natural settings.
7. Operate a financially self-sufficient collection of facilities.
8. Weave quality entertainment through the guest experiences.

Ron Forman says the essence of the institute's purpose is to "teach children, especially inner-city children, to love nature and to value living things." Another goal of the institute is to contribute to the economic development of the New Orleans area by encouraging tourism, especially family tourism, and creating jobs. The institute's mission statements are provided in Exhibit 1.

In 2003, the Audubon Nature Institute was in charge of the (1) Audubon Park, (2) Audubon Zoological Garden, (3) Audubon Center for Research of Endangered Species, (4) Audubon Louisiana Nature Center, (5) Audubon Wilderness Park,

---

* This case was prepared by Caroline M. Fisher as a basis for class discussion. It is not intended to illustrate either effective or ineffective handling of an administrative situation.
© 2003 Caroline M. Fisher.

EXHIBIT 1
Audubon's Mission Statements

AUDUBON PARK/AUDUBON ZOO

Mission Statement. The mission of the Audubon Park/Audubon Zoo is to connect people with nature by providing superior recreational, educational, zoological, and botanical experiences.

ACRES/AUDUBON FREEPORT-MCMORAN SPECIES SURVIVAL CENTER

Mission Statement. The mission of the Audubon Center for Research of Endangered Species/Audubon Freeport-McMoRan Species Survival Center is to safeguard wildlife for future generations through innovative scientific programs that accelerate reproduction and preserve the earth's genetic heritage.

AUDUBON LOUISIANA NATURE CENTER/AUDUBON WILDERNESS PARK

Mission Statement. The mission of the Audubon Louisiana Nature Center/Audubon Wilderness Park is to lead and inspire a diverse audience to a better understanding and deeper appreciation of the natural world.

AQUARIUM OF THE AMERICAS/AUDUBON ENTERGY IMAX® THEATER/WOLDENBERG RIVERFRONT PARK

Mission Statement. The mission of the Aquarium of the Americas/Audubon Entergy IMAX® Theater/Woldenberg Riverfront Park is to inspire our audience to respect, to inspire our audience to respect the natural environment.

AUDUBON CENTRAL ORGANIZATION

Mission Statement. The mission of the Audubon Central Organization is to provide Audubon facilities with an outstanding array of shared support services that facilitates doing business while achieving the mission of the overall organization.

---

(6) Audubon Aquarium of the Americas, (7) Entergy IMAX® Theatre, (8) Freeport-McMoRan Audubon Species Survival Center, and (9) Woldenberg Riverfront Park.

The Audubon Zoo

The main outward purpose of the Audubon Park Zoo is entertainment. Many of the promotional efforts of the zoo are aimed at creating an image of the zoo as an entertaining place to go. Obviously, such a campaign is necessary to attract visitors to the zoo. Behind the scenes, the zoo also preserves and breeds many animal species, conducts research, and educates the public.

The *2000 Annual Report* stated that

> Ensuring the survival of endangered species becomes possible only when people learn about these animals and embrace efforts to save them. That's our goal every time visitors walk into our facilities. The more they come, the more they learn—and the more they want to help.

In 2003, the zoo's Louisiana Swamp played an important role as a learning lab that closely resembles its wild counterpart. Louisiana habitats were a recurring theme in many learning adventures from the after-school WIKD science program to such special events as Swamp Fest.

The Aquarium of the Americas

The Aquarium of the Americas consists of the 14-acre Woldenberg Park and the 110,000 square-foot Aquarium that includes six permanent exhibits: the Caribbean Reef, the Amazon Rainforest, the Mississippi River, the Gulf of Mexico, and Living in Water. The aquarium has added educational shows, a summer program for students in grades seven to ten called Aquakids, and Discovery Cove where children can see and touch aquatic species. The aquarium is headquarters for the Louisiana Marine Mammal and Sea Turtle Rescue program which is committed to the care and treatment of injured, ill, or out-of-habitat marine mammals and sea turtles. For example, the aquarium provides injured turtles with rescue and rehabilitation. In 2002, the network returned five endangered Kemp's ridley turtles and a green sea turtle to their native Gulf of Mexico home. A large-scale wetlands exhibit and a major traveling exhibit are planned for 2004 to attract attention to wetlands loss across the nation.

Like the zoo, the aquarium is constantly changing. The year 2000 saw the opening of a highly popular exhibit titled "Seahorses," praised by *Southern Living* as an Official Southern Travel Treasure. Summer 2001 saw the introduction of Frogs!, an exciting collection in the Changing Exhibit Gallery, featuring over two dozen species from around the globe. A new exhibit on the Flower Garden Banks National Marine Sanctuary, an undersea preserve that mirrors a Caribbean habitat with colorful coral reefs and tropical sea life, debuted in 2003.

The Freeport-McMoRan Audubon Species Survival Center

The Freeport-McMoRan Audubon Species Survival Center (FMASSC) provides endangered animals a refuge where they can breed and eventually boost their numbers. Located on a 1,200-acre site, the center houses such animals as the Mississippi sandhill crane and the Baird's tapir. The Survival Center's 130-acre wetlands area is a busy breeding site for resident birds and a critical stopover habitat for migrating birds that breed farther north. In 2002, 126 birds were banded by the Audubon MAPS banding station at the Survival Center. Another milestone was reached in 2002 when a male sandhill crane (a species that continues to battle the threat of extinction) that was hatched and reared at the Survival Center fathered a chick in the wild.

The Audubon Louisiana Nature and Science Center

The stated purpose of the Louisiana Nature and Science Center, an 86-acre site, is to provide ecological and environmental science programs to the entire community. Newspapers across the state have spotlighted the nature center's innovative Louisiana YES! Program. This annual Youth Environmental Summit (YES) brings together students, teachers, politicians, businessmen, and other professionals to brainstorm solutions to the state's environmental problems. The students then embark on projects in their home areas.

A new exhibit at the nature center completed in 2002 focused attention on the plight of the Louisiana black bear. An interactive display tracked the species' decline and the conservation efforts to save it. The nature center started its Learning, Excitement, Adventure, and Discovery (LEAD) project in 2002. This project impacts first through fifth-grade students in ten New Orleans public schools. Its format incorporates in-school outreach programs, mentoring by Audubon experts, and classroom "discovery boxes."

The Entergy IMAX Theatre

The Entergy IMAX® Theatre, the largest of its kind in the Gulf South, includes 354 seats and a nearly a 6-story-high screen. Movies shown at the IMAX Theatre are changed regularly. In fall 2003, the theatre presented *Haunted Castle 3D, The Nutcracker 3D, Lewis & Clark: The Great Journey West, Into the Deep 3D, Mysteries of Egypt, Matrix Reloaded,* and *Matrix Revolution.* A planned IMAX feature on Louisiana's wetlands will tell the story of coastal erosion and its impacts around the world.

The Audubon Center for Research of Endangered Species

The Audubon Center for Research of Endangered Species (ACRES) studies advanced breeding techniques, animal behavior, and nutrition. The Center has a 36,000 square-foot building that includes labs for reproduction, molecular genetics, cryogenics, and veterinary care, and has made an international splash with several of its research projects. First, in an unprecedented embryo transfer, a common house-cat gave birth to Jazz, an African wildcat, in 1999. ACRES director Dr. Betsy Dresser commented on the significance of this birth, "By using non-endangered species as surrogates, we can increase the number of births of endangered and rare animals." Second, the first two test-tube caracals (African wildcats) were born via *in vitro* fertilization using frozen sperm in 2000. The use of frozen sperm, embryos, and other genetic material of vanishing animals promises to help the scientific community preserve endangered species.

Dr. Dresser, Audubon's research head, who was responsible for the embryo transfer, earned the prestigious Chevron Conservation Award in 2000. She was praised as "an internationally recognized pioneer." A local weekly newspaper, *Gambit,* named Dr. Dresser the New Orleanian of the Year for 2000. The Research Center has been hailed in such national publications as the *Washington Post, U.S. News and World Report, Popular Science,* and *Scientific American.*

In 2002, the center banded nearly 1,500 brown pelicans, an endangered species, on the Chandeleur Islands to help scientists track their movements. It also created sand fences to help protect the disappearing coastal wetlands and barrier islands.

A new scientist was added to the Center's staff in 2002: Dr. Carol A. Brenner. Her extensive experience in molecular reproduction will be another important tool in the center's use of technology to breed wildlife in danger of disappearing from habitats around the world.

Parks

The Audubon Nature Institute owns and operates three free public parks, the Audubon Park next to the Zoo in uptown New Orleans, the Audubon Wilderness Park on the Westbank, and Woldenberg Park on the riverfront in downtown New Orleans. The Audubon Wilderness Park features an orientation center, hiking trails, and wetland facts. This park is dedicated to preserving the natural environment of Louisiana and providing opportunities for family recreation in a natural setting. Groups like the Boy Scouts use this park for group camping outings; reservations are handled by the Audubon Nature Center. The long-term goal for the Wilderness Park is for it to serve as a major urban park. Woldenberg Park complements the Aquarium and provides an extensive area from which the public can view the river and its traffic.

Audubon Park includes many very-old oak trees, a jogging path, picnic areas, riding stables, and the Audubon Golf Course. Extensive renovation of the golf course, a resurfaced jogging track, and other improvements designed to maximize opportunity for outdoor recreation at the Audubon Park were begun in 2001. After some controversial feedback, the plans for the clubhouse and parking lot for the golf course were scaled back in size. Work on the golf course was completed in 2002 and it was opened as a model for balancing development with habitat, wildlife, and resource conservation in the midst of a metropolitan area.

The Audubon Nature Institute

The Audubon Nature Institute has a 24-member governing board. Yearly elections are held for six members of the board who serve four-year terms. The board oversees the policies of the Audubon Nature Institute and sets guidelines for memberships, concessions, fundraising, and marketing. However, actual policy making and operations are controlled by the Audubon Commission which sets Zoo hours, admission prices, and so on.

Through its volunteer programs, the Audubon Nature Institute staffs many of the Audubon programs. The vast majority of the volunteers work at the Zoo or the aquarium. Volunteers from members of the Audubon Nature Institute help with education, membership, public relations, graphics, clerical work, research, or even exhibit and animal care. In 2002, 889 volunteers provided over 95,000 hours of service, valued at $1,575,170.

Membership in the Audubon Nature Institute is open to anyone who joins the Zoo, Aquarium, the Nature Center, or any combination of the three. Annual fees for an individual are $45 for one facility, $65 for two, and $85 for all three. Participation in hands-on, behind-the-scenes, members-only events at the Zoo, Aquarium, and Nature Center are benefits of membership in addition to unlimited free admission and free parking at some facilities. Members also receive discounts on tickets to the Entergy IMAX Theatre, discounts on selected merchandise in Institute gift shops, and a free subscription to *Audubon Up Close,* a quarterly publication for members only.

Marketing

The Audubon Nature Institute publishes a quarterly newsletter for members called *Audubon Up Close.* This publication received a Silver Award for design excellence from the American Institute of Graphic Arts in 2000, its first year of publication. The colorful eight-page newsletter is crammed full of pictures and articles about recent achievements and upcoming events at all the facilities.

The American Association of Zoological Parks and Aquariums reported that most zoos find the majority of their visitors live in close proximity to the park. Thus, in order to sustain attendance over the years, zoos must attract the same visitors repeatedly. A large number of the Zoo's promotional programs and special events are aimed at just that.

The Audubon Nature Institute conducts a multitude of very successful promotional programs. The effect is to have continual parties and celebrations going on, attracting a variety of people to the Zoo and other facilities (and raising additional revenue). Key among these annual events are the Zoo-to-Do; the Swamp Fest, a Cajun music festival held over two weekends in October; and the Boo at the Zoo Halloween. In addition to these annual promotions, the Audubon Nature Institute schedules special family weekends throughout the year.

EXHIBIT 2

Admission Fees

FACILITY	ADULTS	CHILDREN	SENIORS
Aquarium	$13.50	$ 6.50	$10.00
IMAX	7.75	5.00	6.75
IMAX & Aquarium	17.25	10.50	14.00
Nature Center	4.75	2.50	3.75
Zoo	9.00	4.75	5.75

Source: The Audubon Institute.

Many educational activities are conducted all year long. These include (1) a Junior Zoo Keeper program for seventh and eighth graders, (2) a Student-Intern program that enables college students to receive zookeeper training, (3) a "Swamp School" for third graders, (4) the "Wild Science" after-school program for fifth graders, and (5) "AquaKids" at the Audubon Aquarium.

In 2003, the Audubon Nature Institute charged admission fees for all its facilities, as indicated in Exhibit 2. However, admission is free for members and for children on school field trips. Nearly 300,000 students visited the nine facilities on such trips during 2000.

Finances and Fund Raising

The Zoo generates operating funds from attendance and creative special events and programs. A history of adequate operating funds allows the Zoo to guarantee capital donors that their gifts will be used to build and maintain top-notch exhibits. A comparison of the 2000, 2001, and 2002 combined statements of income and expenses for the Audubon Nature Institute is provided in Exhibit 3. Exhibit 4 shows the breakdown of income and expenses by facility; Exhibit 5 shows the balance sheet for December 31, 2002.

The Audubon Nature Institute raises funds through five major types of activities: membership, concessions, the annual fund, Adopt an Animal, Zoo-to-Do, and capital fund drives. Zoo managers from around the country come to the Audubon Park Zoo for tips on fundraising, especially to learn about the Zoo-to-Do.

Zoo Parents' pay a fee to "Adopt an Animal," the fee varying with the animal chosen. Zoo Parents' names are listed on a large sign inside the Zoo. They also have their own celebration, Zoo Parents' Day, held at the Zoo yearly.

Zoo-To-Do is a black-tie fundraiser held annually with live music, food and drink, and original, high-class souvenirs such as posters or ceramic necklaces. Admission tickets, limited to 3,000 annually, are priced starting at $150 per person. The Zoo-To-Do is a popular sellout every year. In 2000, the Zoo-To-Do and the Zoo-To-Do for Kids brought in more than $1 million. The Zoo-To-Do continues to sell out annually and remains a major fundraiser as well as a great public relations event for the Zoo.

The Audubon Zoo Development Fund was established in 1973. Corporate/industrial support of the Zoo is strong; many corporations have underwritten construction of Zoo displays and facilities. A sponsorship is considered to be for the life

EXHIBIT 3

Statement of Institute Operating Income and Expenses ($000)

	2002	2001	2000
OPERATING INCOME			
Admissions	$12,541	12,867	12,997
Concessions, Catering, & Gift Shops	8,716	8,923	6,251
Membership Support	2,571	2,546	2,413
Marketing Events & PR	327	183	211
Recreational & Educational Programs	878	876	1,040
Other	753	487	601
TOTAL OPERATING INCOME	$25,786	25,882	23,423
NONOPERATING ITEMS*			
Debt Service Funded by Operations	(807)	(852)	(895)
Dedicated Tax Millage	3,556	3,170	2,999
Interest/Endowment Income	684	630	804
Fundraising Transfer to Operations	2,735	2,536	2,086
TOTAL INCOME	$31,954	31,367	28,417
OPERATING EXPENSES*			
Operations, Maintenance, & Utilities	6,820	7,014	6,792
Curatorial and Research	5,888	5,198	4,888
Food Service, Catering, & Gift Shops	5,736	5,585	3,856
Membership	932	926	856
Recreational & Educational	1,344	1,270	1,200
Marketing & Promotions	2,114	1,980	1,925
Visitor Services & Volunteers	1,521	1,455	1,392
Administration, Personnel, & MIS	4,570	4,981	3,920
Fringe Benefits	2,187	2,022	2,265
TOTAL EXPENSES	31,141	30,433	27,094
REVENUES—EXPENSES	813	934	1,413
CAPITAL EXPENDITURES	$ 9,860	9,637	11,989

*Excludes capital revenues and expenditures and depreciation associated with buildings and fixed exhibitry.
Source: Audubon Institute *Annual Reports.*

of the exhibit. The development department operates on a 12 percent overhead rate, which means 88 cents of every dollar raised goes toward the projects.

The Audubon Annual Fund, used to pay for day-to-day operations at all Audubon facilities, raises over $200,000 annually. The Institute also is awarded state, federal, and private grants from time to time to perform research and special projects.

The Institute has additional revenue-generating potential by operating the Jerome S. Glazer Audubon Tea Room at the Audubon Zoo. The Tea Room provides 10,000 square feet of space available to rent for elegant occasions such as weddings, corporate gatherings, and other special events.

The Institute organizes and conducts several expeditions yearly. In 2000, it offered three different safaris to Kenya, to Zimbabwe/Zambia/South Africa, and to Botswana. In 2001, it offered an African safari to Tanzania, an expedition to Australia,

EXHIBIT 4
2001 Financial Summary for Audubon Nature Institute

	AUDUBON ZOO AUDUBON PARK	AQUARIUM IMAX® WOLDENBERG RIVERFRONT PARK	RESEARCH CENTER/ SPECIES SURVIVAL CENTER	NATURE CENTER	2001 TOTALS
OPERATING REVENUES AND SUPPORT*					
Admissions	$ 3,133,258	$ 9,629,329	—	$104,538	$12,867,125
Concessions, Catering & Gift Shop	5,057,020	3,817,425	—	48,127	8,922,572
Membership Support	1,399,339	1,042,964	—	103,406	2,545,709
Marketing, Events & PR	137,990	44,912	—	—	182,902
Recreational & Educational Activities	634,056	34,111	—	208,292	876,459
Other	193,768	276,956	13,923	2,322	486,969
NON-OPERATING ITEMS*					
Debt Service Funded by Operations	—	(851,959)	—	—	(851,959)
Dedicated Tax Millage	360,178	2,810,043	—	—	3,170,221
Interest/Endowment Income	38,667	237,484	300,000	54,258	630,409
Operating Transfers	2,696,229	(2,696,971)	(10,269)	11,011	0
Fundraising Transfer to Operations	687,248	40,417	1,592,646	215,899	2,536,210
TOTAL REVENUES	$14,337,753	$14,384,711	$1,896,300	$747,853	$31,366,617
OPERATING EXPENSES*					
Curatorial & Research Activities	2,304,152	1,710,402	1,183,316	—	5,197,870
Operations, Maintenance & Utilities	2,236,215	4,001,763	732,522	43,947	7,014,447
Food Service, Catering & Gift Shops	3,441,821	2,111,976	6,336	25,143	5,585,276
Membership Services	504,236	384,940	—	36,926	926,102
Recreational & Educational	816,376	191,030	—	262,988	1,270,394
Marketing & Promotions	653,692	1,326,177	—	—	1,979,869
Visitor Services & Volunteers	598,715	742,086	—	114,505	1,455,306
Administration, Personnel, MIS	2,379,188	2,333,257	10,047	258,556	4,981,048
Fringe Benefits	1,197,939	726,667	70,621	27,255	2,022,482
TOTAL OPERATING EXPENSES	$14,132,334	$13,528,298	$2,002,842	$769,320	$30,432,794
EXCESS (DEFICIT) OF REVENUES OVER EXPENDITURES	$205,419	$856,413	($106,542)	($21,467)	$933,823
CAPITAL EXPENDITURES	$7,286,453	$2,167,979	$126,986	$55,441	$9,636,859

FACILITY	VOLUNTEERS	HOURS WORKED	FACILITY	VOLUNTEERS	HOURS WORKED
Audubon Zoo	571	45,504	Nature Center	156	14,900
Aquarium	285	35,262	Research Center	11	4,400

*Excludes capital revenues and expenditures and depreciation associated with buildings and fixed exhibitry.
Source: Audubon Institute *Annual Reports.*

and an ecotour to Ecuador and the Galapagos Islands. For 2002, a 12-day birding and wildlife adventure in Costa Rica was conducted. This expedition took participants from lush rainforests to an active volcano.

Management
The Audubon Nature Institute's organizational chart is shown in Exhibit 6. The Institute has relatively few layers of management between Ron Forman and the frontline staff. In 2002, Forman was elected president of the local chamber of commerce.

EXHIBIT 5
2002 Financial Summary for Audubon Nature Institute

	AUDUBON ZOO AUDUBON PARK	AQUARIUM IMAX® WOLDENBERG RIVERFRONT PARK	RESEARCH CENTER/ SPECIES SURVIVAL CENTER	NATURE CENTER	2002 TOTALS
OPERATING REVENUES AND SUPPORT*					
Admissions	$2,963,013	$9,492,803	—	$85,175	$12,540,991
Concessions, Catering & Gift Shop	5,227,294	3,441,372	—	47,635	8,716,301
Membership Support	1,421,259	1,033,575	—	116,045	2,570,879
Marketing, Events & PR	218,576	108,199	—	—	326,775
Recreational & Educational Activities	689,403	15,553	—	173,539	878,495
Other	233,036	473,765	44,446	2,053	753,300
NON-OPERATING ITEMS*					
Debt Service Funded by Operations	—	(807,307)	—	—	(807,307)
Dedicated Tax Millage	383,407	3,172,504	—	—	3,555,911
Interest/Endowment Income	92,188	239,720	300,000	52,500	684,408
Operating Transfers	2,155,754	(2,131,496)	(73,272)	49,014	0
Fundraising Transfer to Operations	654,943	70,883	1,788,587	220,247	2,734,660
TOTAL REVENUES	**$14,038,873**	**$15,109,571**	**$2,059,761**	**$746,208**	**$31,954,413**
OPERATING EXPENSES*					
Curatorial & Research Activities	2,561,212	1,861,871	1,464,846	—	5,887,929
Operations, Maintenance & Utilities	2,244,500	3,882,186	657,590	35,488	6,819,764
Food Service, Catering & Gift Shops	3,760,072	1,946,059	4,866	24,517	5,735,514
Membership Services	544,631	348,575	—	39,052	932,258
Recreational & Educational	818,638	257,653	—	267,788	1,344,079
Marketing & Promotions	662,839	1,481,576	—	—	2,144,415
Visitor Services & Volunteers	668,387	736,631	—	115,613	1,520,631
Administration, Personnel, MIS	2,270,867	2,019,921	13,470	265,682	4,569,940
Fringe Benefits	1,196,662	882,311	72,152	35,712	2,186,837
TOTAL OPERATING EXPENSES	**$14,727,808**	**$13,416,783**	**$2,212,924**	**$783,852**	**$31,141,367**
EXCESS (DEFICIT) OF REVENUES OVER EXPENDITURES	**($688,935)**	**$1,692,788**	**($153,163)**	**($37,644)**	**$813,046**
CAPITAL EXPENDITURES	**$8,379,412**	**$1,100,585**	**$174,962**	**$204,555**	**$9,859,514**

FACILITY	VOLUNTEERS	HOURS WORKED	FACILITY	VOLUNTEERS	HOURS WORKED
Audubon Zoo	512	44,600	Nature Center	112	12,310
Aquarium	253	32,844	Research Center	12	5,480

*Excludes capital revenues and expenditures and depreciation associated with buildings and fixed exhibitry.

*Source: Audubon Institute Annual Reports.

E-Commerce

The Audubon Nature Institute has its own Web site, is listed on important informational Web sites, and has used eBay to raise funds for its work. The Institute uses its Web site to provide outgoing information, to provide a means for incoming information through e-mail addresses for key Institute staff, and to sell admission tickets online.

The Institute is listed on a number of Web sites that promote recreational activities in the New Orleans area to tourists and locals. Among these are neworleans.net, neworleans.com, gambit-no.com, louisianatravel.com, and nawlins.com. In addition,

EXHIBIT 6

Audubon Institute Organizational Chart

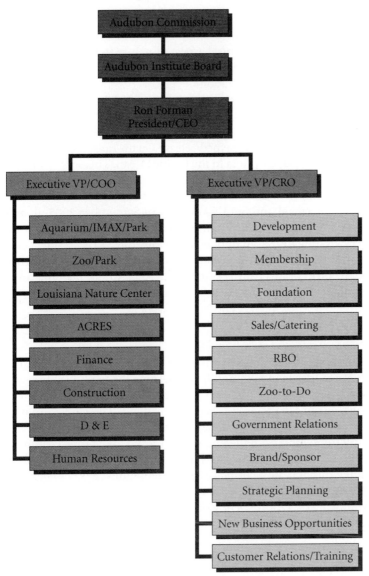

Source: The Audubon Institute.

using paintings created by the orangutans at the Audubon Zoo, the Audubon chapter of the American Association of Zookeepers sold orangutan-created paintings on eBay, raising money to support a wide range of conservation organizations, from the World Wildlife Fund to the Dian Fossey Gorilla Fund.

The Natural Environment

The Audubon Nature Institute is "dedicated to nature and unified with a purpose of celebrating life through nature." Its purpose of "celebrating the wonders of nature" guides its mission. Five of the eight parts of its mission (see the list earlier in this case) are directly related to nature. Its strategic plan reflects its purpose and mission.

An indicator of the Institute's dedication to nature is the change made in its name in 2000. Prior to that year, it was called Audubon Institute. The word "nature" was added to its name to emphasize the central aspect of nature to the organization. The name was paired with a new look designed to strengthen its unity of purpose—nature—and the broad scope of the organization.

Many of the efforts of the Institute to preserve and celebrate nature were described earlier. Even the Zoo, contrary to the public image of most zoos, is involved in efforts to return endangered species to the wild and not just preserve a few specimens in captivity. In 2000, the Zoo staff helped release Guam rails, including four chicks born at the Zoo, on the island of Rota in the Pacific Ocean. This species of bird was wiped out on the island of Guam by the brown tree snake, a species accidentally introduced to Guam. The Zoo also saw the birth of three baby jaguars in 2001—an endangered species from Central and South America. In September 2003, it witnessed the birth of a baby southern white rhino, Satchmo, who weighed in at 80 pounds. "This is a very exciting time at Audubon Nature Institute," says president and CEO Ron Forman. "Captive breeding is an important, proactive way of ensuring species survival, and the birth of this baby is a wonderful result of our ongoing commitment to wildlife conservation."

The Future

The Audubon Insectarium

This living science museum is scheduled to open in the U.S. Custom House on Canal Street in downtown New Orleans in fall 2004. It will become the tenth facility operated by the Audubon Nature Institute. Exhibits will include "Termites: The Second Battle of New Orleans," "Louisiana Swamp," "Field Camp," and "Life Underground," in which guests are shrunk to bug size as inhabitants of the first two inches of top soil. The very popular Butterfly exhibit from the Zoo will be moved to the Insectarium. In this exhibit, butterflies hatch from cocoons and fly freely around the many flowers and the visitors walking through. Ron Forman sees this museum as a way to help the economic development of the city of New Orleans and bring local people back to Canal Street in downtown New Orleans. The Zoo's Bugmobile is heralding the coming opening of the Insectarium as it travels to schools and community centers to provide outreach education.

The Jeri and Bob Nims Community Center

In October 2003, the Institute's new community center opened and is used to deliver exciting new programs celebrating the wonders of nature to visitors of all ages. Located at the entrance to the Zoo, the Center will include a community room available for use by nonprofit groups, an early childhood classroom, real scientific equipment and computers to encourage children and their teachers to investigate science, and an outdoor classroom.

Other Opportunities

Ron Forman holds the future of the Audubon Nature Institute in a tremendously optimistic light, considering the forces opposing them. The Institute faces a rather weak New Orleans economic situation; it operates in a city where many attractions compete for the leisure dollar of natives and tourists. It has to vie with the

French Quarter, Dixieland Jazz, the Superdome, casinos, and the greatest attraction of all, Mardi Gras.

Plans to continue to "preserve native Louisiana habitats" and promote wetlands conservation include a comprehensive range of learning tools, such as a large-scale, permanent wetlands exhibit at the Aquarium and a major traveling exhibit designed to attract attention to wetlands, in addition to the planned IMAX feature mentioned earlier.

19 Central United Methodist Church—2004

Robert T. Barrett
Francis Marion University

www.centralmethodist.net

Look in any newspaper and the headlines indicate that the economy remains weak, poverty and jobless rates are soaring, and wars and terrorism threaten. As the needy become more needy, demands on nonprofit organizations continue to rise. Budgets for these nonprofit organizations are increased in attempts to meet these ever-increasing demands. Needs of low-income families, the uninsured, and others are pronounced in economic downturns, [since many of the primary support individuals find themselves out of work.] In addition to the spiritual support of their own congregations as they struggle with difficult times, what role should churches play in supporting financial needs of the poor, particularly in bad times? What impact will decisions of this nature have on operating budgets? Indeed, how should a local church set priorities to balance its financial support between the local church needs and outreach commitments beyond the church walls?

Should a local church make decisions based on majority rule? Should certain groups of members carry more weight (e.g., individuals who have been members for 50 years and up)? What does "for the good of the whole" mean in a church of 2,000-plus members? Should strategic planning be initialized? Are visionaries welcome as churches strive to minister to their congregations and beyond?

Central United Methodist Church (843-662-3218) is located in the heart of downtown Florence, South Carolina. Central's annual operating budget, which covers internal operating expenses as well as local outreach and conference benevolence giving, has grown from $0.9 million in the late 1990s to over $1.3 million in 2003. Indications from proposals of the church committees are that the budget will be even larger in 2004. The church is also looking to move to the second phase of a building campaign that could add between $1 million and $5 million to the $1.6 million current debt of the church.

The church has moved to a new administrative structure that will require some creative and cooperative work to help this new programming body succeed. This new structure changed the programming operations of the church from the previous structure that had been in place for over 20 years.

Mission Statements

The United Methodist Church

The mission of the church is to make disciples of Jesus Christ. Local churches provide the most significant arena through which disciple making occurs. The statement that follows was taken from the Disciplines of the United Methodist Church.

Central United Methodist Church exists to serve and glorify God as revealed in Jesus Christ by making disciples through worship, fellowship, education and service to the Church and the community.

Central United Methodist Church—Past and Present

Central United Methodist Church was established in the late 1800s and moved to its present site at the corner of Irby and Cheves Streets in 1913. Through a variety of land and property acquisitions since 1913, Central's main campus has grown to include approximately 200 feet of frontage on Irby Street and 300 feet of frontage on Cheves Street. With its downtown location, a limited number of acquisition possibilities remain available to Central. In the mid-1900s, it had the opportunity to purchase a house that was adjacent to church property for a cost of $30,000. The church turned down this opportunity, and the owner sold the property to a group that developed a hotel and cafeteria on the property. After the hotel failed, the church was able to buy the property in 1980 for $100,000. In 1984, Central purchased a building adjacent to the property that serves as both the primary facility for the youth ministry and the location of other Sunday school classes. Central continues to actively seek property for building and parking purposes.

Church Property

In addition to the main church campus in the downtown Florence location at Cheves and Irby Streets, Central United Methodist Church owns a large tract of land just outside of Florence, named Camp Sexton (after the donor), and a Boy Scout hut a few miles from the main church property. Most church programs are held at the downtown location. A summer camp for children is held for several weeks at Camp Sexton. Camp Sexton hosts special programs during the year and Sunday afternoon swim sessions for church members during the summer. The church sponsors Boy Scout troop meetings weekly in the Boy Scout hut.

The church sanctuary seats approximately 400 people. Attendance averages for the two Sunday morning services are shown for the past 14 years in Exhibit 1. The sanctuary overflows for performances of the Masterworks Choir, the Christmas Eve services, Easter and Mother's Day Sunday services, and large funerals and weddings.

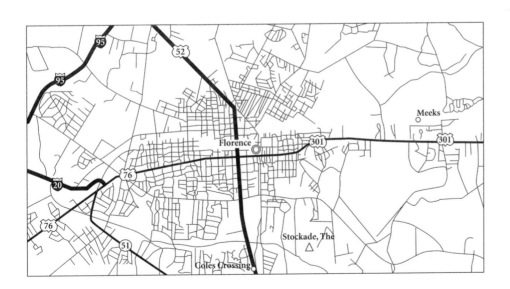

EXHIBIT 1

Central United Methodist Church Membership and Attendance Levels

YEAR	CHURCH MEMBERSHIP	AVERAGE WORSHIP ATTENDANCE	SUNDAY SCHOOL MEMBERSHIP	AVERAGE ATTENDANCE
2002	2,008	693	1,136	362
2001	1,976	637	1,992	330
2000	1,944	609	1,913	334
1999	1,901	604	1,872	333
1998	1,899	617	1,757	443
1997	1,874	593	1,399	325
1996	1,863	589	1,572	322
1995	1,866	590	1,416	380
1994	1,855	551	1,376	331
1993	1,826	535	1,206	323
1992	1,801	522	1,111	308
1991	1,797	523	1,088	338
1990	1,795	540	1,091	336
1989	1,800	534	1,048	342

Source: Central United Methodist Church.

In 2001, Central completed Phase I of an ambitious building project designed to expand programming capabilities of the church. With the completion of the building project, church capacity increased by almost one-third. The Davis Christian Life Center, named for the former minister who pushed the church to begin the building project, and his wife, is an excellent facility for larger informal programs. The tile-floored facility has a full-length basketball court that is flanked by a raised stage for music programs, the annual talent show, and other church fellowship programs. The very popular Wednesday Night Supper program, now scheduled in the Davis Life Center, has drawn over 300 members and averaged over 200 attendees, up a full 33 percent over previous years when the smaller fellowship hall had seating limitations. The new Davis Christian Life Center has truly made growth possible. The expansion also brought several new Sunday school classrooms for children and allowed space previously dedicated to the children's ministries to be allocated to other age-group programs. A beautiful and welcoming commons area became the new main entrance to the church with better access for the physically handicapped.

Membership Profile and Contributions

Exhibit 1 shows the membership levels for Central for 14 years. Approximately 23 percent of the members are younger than 10 years of age (note that young people on rolls prior to joining the church formally in seventh grade are only considered to be "Preparatory Members"), approximately 12 percent are in the 11- to 20-year age bracket, approximately 16 percent are in the 21- to 30-year age bracket, approximately 14 percent are in the 31- to 40-year age bracket, approximately 12 percent are in both the 41- to 50- and 51- to 60-year age brackets, and the remaining 11 percent are age 61 or older. Note that over 60 percent of the members are younger than 40, with 35 percent of this group being classified as children and youth. Another interesting breakdown of church membership shows that approximately 60 percent of the members are married, with a bulk of the remaining 40 percent being in the children and youth age brackets. This demonstrates commitment of the membership to strong family values,

EXHIBIT 2
Central United Methodist Church Contributions

YEAR	OPERATING BUDGET	BUILDING FUND	BUILDING FUND EXTRA
2002	$1,207,231.44	$337,607.46	—
2001	1,174,367.00	—	—
2000	997,187.00	—	—
1999	968,110.00	614,814.00	$104,133.72
1998	868,987.00	592,400.00	75,108.00
1997	820,610.00	145,231.33	6,464.75
1996	830,009.91	131,661.41	7,251.00
1989	499,069.64		

Source: Central United Methodist Church.

but it could also reflect weak emphasis on or consideration for adult singles. In a time of declining memberships in churches across the country, Central has been able to maintain membership and participation levels.

Exhibit 2 gives information on contributions to the operating budget, to the building fund, and to the category labeled "Building Fund Extra," which is for designated project gifts. Contributions have steadily increased in recent years. Church budgets in excess of $800,000 were overpledged (and collected) in the late 1990s. However, with more and more contributions going to the building fund to pay for the new building, the operating budget suffered. Pledges to the operating budget were down at the start-up of the capital campaign, and the church had to scramble to meet the operating budget obligations. In the early years of the twenty first century, Central members increased total pledges each year. In 2002, Central UMC earned the five-star award from the South Carolina Annual Conference of the United Methodist Church by receiving all of the pledges in full, along with meeting some other criteria.

Church Property and the Annual Budget
Exhibit 3 gives the value of property owned by Central and debt owed by Central over the last seven years. The value of church property has grown, while debt service

EXHIBIT 3
Central United Methodist Church Assets and Debt

YEAR	VALUE OF CHURCH CAMPUS PROPERTY	PARSONAGE & FURNITURE	OTHER ASSETS	DEBT
2002	$14,224,880	$439,290	$ 622,239	$1,776,000
2001	14,224,880	436,290	630,931	2,183,943
2000	12,365,340	495,000	1,138,347	970,000
1999	9,376,600	475,000	2,737,150	0
1998	9,298,340	457,900	2,143,500	0
1997	8,880,000	421,000	918,000	0
1996	8,223,700	432,700	476,997	103,100

Source: Central United Methodist Church.

EXHIBIT 4

Central United Methodist Annual Budget, 2003 and 2004

ACCOUNT	2003 ANNUAL BUDGET	2004 ANNUAL BUDGET
Staff-Parish Committee	$ 569,012	$ 623,643
Education and Spiritual Growth	55,183	59,133
Membership Care Ministry Team	6,600	5,600
Outreach Ministry Team	28,000	30,250
Worship Ministry Team	23,750	24,600
Evangelism Ministry Team	24,700	26,200
Fellowship, Recreation, and Leisure Ministry Team	20,100	23,650
Stewardship Ministry Team	5,000	2,000
Board of Trustees	307,338	352,870
Camp Sexton Program	5,200	5,200
Annual Conference Apportionments	255,792	157,850
Operations	79,100	99,400
Total Budget	$1,379,775	$1,410,396

Source: Central United Methodist Church.

has continued to decline over recent years. The annual budget for 2003 and 2004 are given in Exhibit 4.

Florence, South Carolina

Founded in 1850, Florence historically was and remains a railroad city. It is located in a region of South Carolina called the Pee Dee, named after a tribe of Indians who inhabited the area. The local chamber of commerce touts Florence as the trade, industrial, medical, transportation, cultural, financial, and educational center of the Pee Dee. Located where Interstate I-95 and I-20 intersect, Florence sees many travelers headed north to New York, south to Florida, east to Myrtle Beach, and west to the Appalachian Mountains.

The city of Florence has more than 33,500 residents, a total that is projected to double by the year 2010. Florence County has 127,000 residents, and it projects growth to 132,000 by 2010. Florence has churches of all denominations; within three miles of the downtown location of Central United Methodist Church are Baptist, Presbyterian, Lutheran, Episcopal, and other Methodist churches. In the city of Florence, there are five Methodist churches, and many other churches have chosen to locate in areas on the outskirts of town. Thus, as the population of Florence grows, there is increased "competition" for parishioners.

Church Organization
Church Staff

Central United Methodist Church is served by a staff of twenty-three. The senior pastor acts as the chief administrative officer of this staff. Other primary staff members include one associate pastor, a music director, a director of children's

EXHIBIT 5

Central United Methodist Church, Salaries for Key Personnel

ACCOUNT	2003 ANNUAL BUDGET	2004 ANNUAL BUDGET
Pastor	$87,000	$90,000
Associate Pastor	48,000	50,000
Director of Children's Ministry	39,000	20,500
Director of Youth Ministries	16,377	17,196
Director of Adult Ministries	22,726	23,271
Director of Young Adult Ministries	12,500	12,500
Business Manager	30,020	30,020
Administrative Secretary	20,400	21,828
Staff Secretary	17,279	17,279
Communications Director	25,000	25,600
Music Director/Organist	52,272	53,526
Building/Property Superintendent	19,000	22,800

Source: Central United Methodist Church.

ministries, a part-time director of adult ministries, a part-time director of young adult ministries, and a part-time director of youth ministries. Clerical and custodian assistants make up most of the remaining staff positions. The church has adopted a strategy of successfully using part-time staff. The benefits of using a part-time staff are apparent in efficiencies and quality of service. This strategy allows the church to hire a person who is skilled in a particular function for the limited amount of time needed for that job. Salaries of these key personnel are presented in Exhibit 5.

Central United Methodist Church has moved aggressively into Internet communication. The Web site (**www.centralmethodist.net**) is updated on a regular basis. The Web site has pages describing many of the church committees. The senior minister sends a weekly e-mail newsletter to church members, keeping them apprised of church programs and important church news as well as providing a weekly devotional thought. Church committees are informed of meeting schedules and agendas through e-mail. Church members contact staff members with concerns and news via the Web. The church also has recently initiated a newsletter entitled *Messenger* that is printed and mailed to members each month. The *Messenger* reports timely information regarding programs, new members, and other church initiatives.

Volunteer Structure

Like most churches, much of the Central United's work is carried out by volunteers. The committee structure that helps to govern and carry out church programs is headed by the newly formed Church Council. Under the current structure, all committees report on a bimonthly basis to the Church Council. The new church programming structure is described below.

In 2001, a steering committee guided the church through an evaluation of alternative volunteer administrative structures. In addition to proposing the Church

Council structure described below, this task force listed Core Values that drive the ministries of Central United Methodist Church.

- Central's primary purpose is to make disciples.
- All programs should be evaluated by this purpose: Will it aid in the making and nurturing of disciples?
- We believe we have a responsibility to our community and world.
- We will trust in the Spirit to lead us and not be afraid to move in new directions.
- We believe every person is gifted by God and needs to discover and use their gift(s).

Because of this, Central UMC will be a lay-driven church.

- All volunteers, chairs, and chair-elects will be trained and nurtured in their work.
- We are committed to excellence in all we do.
- We grant to every church member permission to dream, initiate, and organize other church members in programs that serve the above purpose.
- We will treat one another with respect and love and, if necessary, agree to disagree.

The result of this year-long process to analyze church structure was the consolidation of the Administrative Board and Council on Ministries committees into the Church Council. The primary argument in favor of this structure was to cut down on duplication of meetings and efforts of church members, thus helping to prevent burnout. The Church Council is made up of six primary planning committees/teams: Worship Ministry Team; Membership Care Ministry Team; Missions and Advocacy Ministry Team; Evangelism and Witness Ministry Team; Leisure, Recreation, and Fellowship Ministry Team; and Education and Spiritual Growth Ministry Team. In addition, there are seven standing support committees that are appointed or elected each year: Board of Trustees, Staff-Parish Relations Committee, Committee on Finance, Endowment Fund Committee, Committee on Nominations, Stewardship Committee, and Long Range Planning Committee. Other ad hoc committees are added when needed.

Major Challenges
There are a number of major challenges ahead for Central United Methodist Church. The church must develop a plan to prioritize the wants, desires, and needs of the various groups within and outside of the church. If the church is to move on to the second phase of the facility expansion plan developed in the 1990s (Phase II), there is a need to consider fresh strategies for fundraising. The church is also working to become comfortable with the new administrative structure for volunteers that will help spread the burden/opportunity for service across the congregation.

New building initiatives
In its Long Range Plan, Central United Methodist Church indicated a need to increase space to carry out programs for the ever-growing membership. The renovated facility came online in 2001. Over half of the expected costs were collected prior to beginning the construction. The congregation made pledges to cover the remainder of the $5.0 million addition.

EXHIBIT 6

Organizational Chart Central United Methodist Church

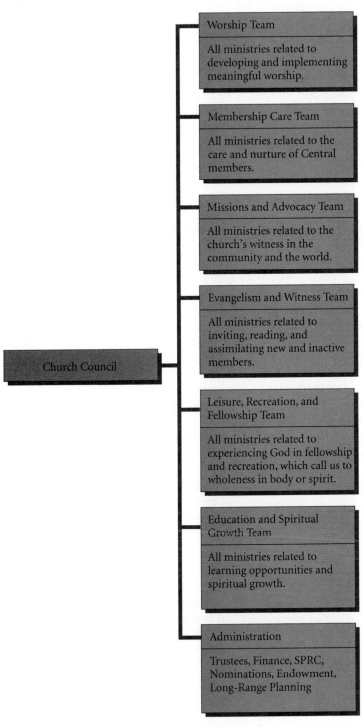

In 2003, the Building Committee was charged with the task of developing a plan to accomplish all or part of Phase II of the building project set forth by the Long Range Planning Committee of the mid-1990s. The Building Committee also needed to estimate current costs for the proposal. The Building Committee report was made to the congregation in the fall of 2003. The major categories under consideration were:

1. Major improvements to the Scout Hut.
2. An administrative office complex to be built in existing space.
3. Completion of the second floor of the children's building, which included the new media center.
4. Construction of a port cochere (space to drive under to let people out of the car in inclement weather).
5. New elevator and additional access to sanctuary building.
6. Major renovation/addition to the sanctuary.

Suggestions 1 through 5 would likely cost between $1 million and $2.5 million. The modification to the sanctuary would increase seating capacity from about 600 to about 800 and would cost an additional $2 million. As was anticipated, there were major objections expressed (most by longtime members) to the renovation of the sanctuary. The primary objections to the other facility changes were associated with the costs of the renovations. With approximately $1.6 million left on the loan from Phase I of the building project, many are concerned that adding to this financial burden will overly tax resources of church members. Also, in previous capital campaigns, pledges to the Capital Campaign have offset pledges (and contributions) to the annual Operating Budget of the church.

For a number of years, Central has used the Pass-It-On process for the annual Stewardship Campaign. In this process, over 100 Neighborhood Packets are set up with between 5 and 10 families who live in close proximity to each other. Neighborhood Team Leaders start the process by picking up their packets at the kick-off breakfast, prayerfully considering the financial commitment they will make to the church, filling out their pledge card, and passing the packet on to the next family on the list. When all families have had an opportunity to make their pledges, the packets are returned to the church. An independent firm records and monitors the pledges, notifying families throughout the year of how they are doing in satisfying their pledges.

Conclusion

Many churches take in a lot of money and spend a lot of money. The strategic planning process is being used more and more by churches to effectively obtain contributions and allocate funds according to the best wishes of the members.

Develop a three-year strategic plan for Central United Methodist Church that is consistent with the church's mission. Also, answer the following questions about conducting the strategic planning process in a church:

1. To what extent should the congregation be involved and how? Should a vote by members be taken on major issues?
2. How should a church decide among spending monies locally or globally to win disciples to Jesus Christ?

3. Are there competing interests within churches? If so, how should the budgeting process be structured to allocate funds to different groups?

4. If the church decides to limit the budget for the new building initiatives to $1 million, how should the membership determine the projects to pursue at this time? Make some suggestions regarding capital campaign fundraising.

5. What are the pros and cons of using the "Pass-It-On" process of fundraising?

20 The United States Postal Service—2004

Lori L. Lyerly
Francis Marion University

www.usps.com

> In a world that's gone virtual, it seems that everyone is searching for the authentic. They're looking for roots. Tradition. Values. Real Experience. They want something they can hold. Something they can touch. Something that's still here tomorrow—and the day after. Mail—the real kind—has it all. Always has. Always will. Authentic? That's mail. It's an original. It's as creative as you are, and it's created just for you. It can be a simple envelope or a colorful package. But there's no mistaking the sight or the feel of it. Mail. It's real. There's nothing like it in the world. And it's yours!
>
> *Source:* Adapted from USPS *Annual Report* 2002, p. 3.

The United States Postal Service (USPS) is an independent federal agency that makes deliveries to more than 140 million addresses every day and is the only service provider to deliver to every address in the nation. The USPS is the world's leading provider of mail and delivery services, offering some of the most affordable postage rates in the world, while building annual revenues of over $67 billion. The USPS delivers some 203 billion letters, advertisements, periodicals, and packages a year—and serves 7 million customers each day at its 38,000 retail locations nationwide. It handles nearly 43 percent of the world's mail volume.

Mission and Vision

The Postal Reorganization Act of 1970 defines the mission of the Postal Service and charges:

> The Postal Service is to bind the nation together through the correspondence of the people, to provide access in all communities, and to offer prompt, reliable postal services at uniform prices.

History

Correspondence between colonists, colonies, and England depended primarily on friends, merchants, and the Native Americans. In 1639 the first official notice of a postal service appeared in the colonies. It was the responsibility of local authorities to operate postal routes. A Continental Congress was organized in Philadelphia in May 1775 to establish an independent government. One of its first questions was how to deliver the mail. Benjamin Franklin led the Committee of Investigation to establish a postal system. On July 26, 1775, over 225 years ago, the Continental Congress appointed Franklin as Postmaster General. Following the adoption of the

Constitution in May 1789, the Act of September 22, 1789, temporarily established a post office and created the Office of the Postmaster General. At that time there were 75 post offices and about 2,000 miles of post roads, although as late as 1780 the postal staff consisted only of a Postmaster General, a Secretary/Comptroller, three surveyors, one Inspector of Dead Letters, and 26 post riders.

The Post Office Department was not specifically established as an executive department by Congress until June 8, 1872 (17 Stat. 284–4). As mail delivery evolved from foot to horseback, stagecoach, steamboat, railroad, automobile, and airplane, with intermediate and overlapping use of balloons, helicopters, and pneumatic tubes, mail contracts ensured the income necessary to build the great highways, rail lines, and airways that eventually spanned the continent. By the turn of the ninteenth century, the Post Office Department had purchased a number of stagecoaches for operation on the nation's better post roads—a post road being any road on which the mail traveled—and continued to encourage new designs to improve passenger comfort and carry mail more safely.

By the mid-1960s however, the Post Office Department was in deep trouble. Years of financial neglect and fragmented control had finally impaired its ability to function in terms of facilities, equipment, wages, and management efficiency, as well as in terms of the highly subsidized rates that existed on all classes of mail — rates that for many years bore little relation to costs. In May 1969, four months after he became a member of President Richard Nixon's cabinet, Postmaster General Winton M. Blount proposed a basic reorganization of the Post Office Department. The president asked Congress to pass the Postal Service Act of 1969, calling for removal of the Postmaster General from the cabinet and creation of a self-supporting postal corporation wholly owned by the federal government. The Post Office Department was transformed into the United States Postal Service, an independent establishment of the executive branch of the government of the United States. The Postal Reorganization Act of 1970 stated:

> The United States Postal Service shall be operated as a basic and fundamental service provided by the government of the United States, authorized by the Constitution, created by an Act of Congress, and supported by the people. The Postal Service shall have as its basic function the obligation to provide postal services to bind the nation together through the personal, educational, literary, and business correspondence of the people. It shall provide prompt, reliable, and efficient services to patrons in all areas and shall render postal services to all communities.

Source: Adapted from USPS *Annual Report*, 2002 p. 3.

The Postal Reorganization Act required that the government agency be self-supporting. This was achieved in 1982 and the postal services have been free from taxpayer support since then. This achievement was one of the first and most important results sought by the Postal Reorganization Act. Financial self-sufficiency is a major goal in strategic planning for the postal service. In the early 1990s, the Postal Service's management reviewed the mission and developed a Statement of Purpose:

> To provide every household and business across the United States with the ability to communicate and conduct business with each other and the world through prompt, reliable, secure and economical services for the collection, transmission, and delivery of messages and merchandise.

The Postal Service receives no taxpayer dollars for routine operations, but derives its operating revenues solely from the sale of postage, products, and services.

2002

September 11, 2001, is a date no American will soon forget. It sent our country into a state of terror and recession. The attacks affected nearly every industry, every city, and every business in the United States including the USPS. Mail volume declined by 4.6 billion by the end of 2001. The threat of anthrax greatly affected the mail system and the network of the USPS. In 2002 the USPS invested over $978 million in new or improved buildings and equipment, and operating revenue grew 1.0 percent to $66.5 billion, on a volume decline of 2.2 percent. This marked the second consecutive year of mail volume decline and the greatest rate of volume decline since 1946.

The Postal Service suffered the largest decline in history for year-end 2002. The economic recession followed into 2003. Historically, mail volume has tracked the economy, usually with some delay. Decline in the advertising market damaged volumes immensely. Exhibit 1 illustrates mail volume by type historically and for the future. Standard Mail volume fell by 2.6 percent in 2002 as a result of the weakness of the advertising market and declined most sharply early in the year in the wake of September 11 and the anthrax attacks. Priority Mail volume dropped most sharply early in the year. This was due to the disruption in air delivery. Priority Mail growth was further hindered by the 35 percent price increases in 2001. Priority Mail service is part of the highly competitive expedited package market. FedEx began to cover the entire nation and UPS became far more aggressive which in turn affected growth and volumes of Priority Mail. Total volume of Package Services declined 2.3 percent, although Parcel Post volume grew 5.1 percent from 2001 to 2002. Some of the growth is due to the shift from Priority Mail.

2003

The shape of the U.S. economy has impacted all industries and agencies including the USPS. The year-to-date net income at third quarter ending May 16, 2003 was $1.9 billion compared to a plan of $1.5 billion. With a volume of 47 billion pieces of mail, revenues at third-quarter-end were $16.0 billion. Operating revenue grew 5.2 percent due to the impact of rate increases but was $490 million and 785 million pieces below plan. Revenue and volume of First-Class Mail, Priority Mail, and Express Mail, the highest-margin products, had the largest shortfalls. The volume performance was less unfavorable for Standard Mail. These results reflect the impact of electronic diversion, competition, and an economy growing less rapidly than had been forecasted.

Third-quarter 2003 showed First-Class Mail revenue of $8.7 billion was $352 million, or 3.9 percent. Priority Mail volume fell 14.0 percent and revenues were 2.7 percent below the same quarter last year. Express Mail volume and revenue also fell: volume dropped 12.3 percent and revenue dropped 4.3 percent from the same quarter last year. These product lines continue to be negatively affected by businesses moving packages to ground delivery services, the sluggish economy, and intense competition in the air and ground package delivery markets. Standard Mail volume increased by 638 million pieces, and was 3.1 percent over the same quarter last year. This is the fourth consecutive quarter of growth for Standard Mail. Standard Mail revenue increased 10.0 percent compared to the same quarter last year, but was $56 million, or 1.4 percent, below plan. Standard Mail volume actually grew by 638 million pieces in the third quarter, or 3.1 percent over the same period last year. This was the only source of significant volume

EXHIBIT 1
Operating Statistics

(IN MILLIONS OF UNITS INDICATED) CLASS OF MAIL	2003	2002	2001
First-Class Mail			
Pieces, number	**99,058.7**	102,378.6	103,655.6
Weight, pounds	**4,236.3**	4,283.6	4,362.8
Revenue	**$37,048.3**	$36,483.2	$35,876.0
Priority Mail			
Pieces, number	**859.6**	998.2	1,117.8
Weight, pounds	**1,622.9**	1,875.1	2,149.7
Revenue	**$4,494.3**	$4,722.5	$4,916.4
Express Mail			
Pieces, number	**55.8**	61.3	69.4
Weight, pounds	**53.2**	59.1	72.1
Revenue	**$888.1**	$910.5	$995.7
Mail grams			
Pieces, number	**2.8**	2.8	3.3
Revenue	**$1.2**	$1.4	$1.4
Periodicals			
Pieces, number	**9,319.9**	9,689.8	10,077.4
Weight, pounds	**3,995.0**	4,006.1	4,408.3
Revenue	**$2,234.8**	$2,164.9	$2,205.2
Standard Mail			
Pieces, number	**90,358.5**	87,230.6	89,938.4
Weight, pounds	**10,797.3**	10,315.5	10,822.2
Revenue	**$17,203.1**	$15,816.8	$15,704.9
Package Services			
Pieces, number	**1,128.5**	1,075.1	1,093.0
Weight, pounds	**3,793.8**	3,690.6	3,801.7
Revenue	**$2,215.7**	$2,080.1	$1,993.9
International Economy Mail			
Pieces, number	**29.9**	38.6	60.4
Weight, pounds	**60.5**	65.3	80.3
Revenue	**$145.9**	$150.4	$177.7
International Airmail			
Pieces, number	**909.2**	865.2	1,022.1
Weight, pounds	**183.0**	151.8	171.6
Revenue	**$1,469.4**	$1,429.4	$1,554.0
U.S. Postal Service			
Pieces, number	**391.4**	424.9	380.6
Weight, pounds	**80.1**	87.5	82.3
Free Mail for the Blind and Handicapped			
Pieces, number	**70.4**	56.8	44.6
Weight, pounds	**29.8**	28.1	24.9
Totals			
Pieces, number	**202,184.7**	202,821.9	207,462.6
Weight, pounds	**24,851.9**	24,562.7	25,975.9
Revenue	**$65,700.7**	$63,761.1	$63,425.2

Source: www.usps.com/history/anrpt03/html/statistics1.htm

growth. But this growth was insufficient to offset the volume declines in First-Class Mail, Priority Mail, Express Mail, and Periodicals.

Internal Factors

Business Structure

The Board of Governors of the U.S. Postal Service is similar to a Board of Directors. The board of nine Governors are appointed by the president and approved by the Senate. The Governors are chosen to represent the public interest and no more than five can come from the same political party. The nine Governors select the Postmaster General who becomes a member of the board. The Postmaster General serves for an indefinite term as well as the Deputy Postmaster, who is also selected by the board. The Postmaster General and the Deputy Postmaster General participate with the Governors on all matters except for voting on rate or classification adjustments, adjustments to the budget of the Postal Rate Commission, or election of the Chairman of the Board. They work together on approval of rate and class changes. The organizational chart is shown in Exhibit 2.

Technology

The Postal Service, like virtually every other large enterprise today, is adapting to the changes created by the development of the Internet. The effects of this are already being realized, as reflected in the decrease in revenues. Introduction of new technology is diversifying the mailing industry. Businesses want to reduce handling of documents and are therefore looking for more cost-effective, customized approaches to this. Detailed studies of consumer decision making in the future suggest that consumers will change how they search for information, entertain them-

EXHIBIT 2
Organizational Chart

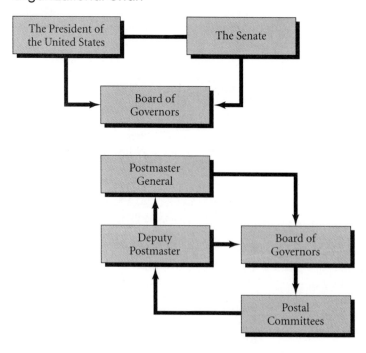

selves, shop, and conduct transactions. Consumers want convenience. This represents a major challenge for the Postal Service in the future. The USPS Product Development teams created several new First-Class Mail application enhancements in 2002, including the Micro Payment® service, Friend-To-Friend Mail™ service, and Repositionable Notes.

In Managed Service Points (MSP) carriers scan delivery points at selected locations on their routes to ensure that the Postal Service is providing consistent time-of-day delivery. This is a use of technology to ensure customer satisfaction with on-time delivery. Another method of improving technology that is now used by the USPS is a new automated sorter that brings the processing efficiency of letter mail to flat-size mail—oversized envelopes, magazines, and catalogs. By sorting three times faster than the last generation of flat-sorting equipment, costs are better controlled. One final technological improvement is the CONFIRM® service. Customers can track their mail as it moves through the system. The information it provides helps customers plan and manage inventory and other resources better than ever. Click-N-Ship® also allows customers to print postage and mailing labels from home or office computers.

Marketing Technology and Channel Management
During 2002, Marketing Technology and Channel Management continued its commitment to leverage advances in technology. The USPS wanted to significantly improve the customer experience for business mailers. The USPS Marketing Technology and Channel Management targeted the following two areas: dramatically improve acceptance, streamline and improve the overall payment and account management. The Postal Service continues to explore new and better ways to extend and enhance its traditional products by leveraging today's quickly evolving technology. For the past two years, Online Payment Services have been available through the USPS. NetPost Mailing Online saves customers time, effort, and money. These printing and mailing services allow customers to send their mailings from their office or home. NetPost will print, fold, insert, and apply the postage and if mail is ordered by 2:00 P.M. EST, it will be printed and mailed the next day.

The Postal Service completed operational deployment of CONFIRM. This provides the customer with valuable information concerning a flat or letter. Reports are available to subscribers on the Internet. Postal operations also have been improved using information technology. The deployment of the Delivery Operations Information System (DOIS) was completed in September 2002, which allows supervisors access to information that will better enable effective management.

Legislation
In April 2003, the Postal Service delivered its Transformation Plan to Congress. It defines the short- and long-term strategies that will enable the Postal Service to successfully carry out its long-standing mission of providing affordable, universal service. Also in August 2003, *Public Law 107–210* was signed by the president and allows the Customs Service to open outbound international mail weighing more than 16 ounces.

The Postal Reorganization Act, as specified by Congress, was to ensure that residents of both urban and rural communities have access to an effective Postal Service. The Postal Service has established a nationwide network of facilities, centralized delivery units, and rural and highway contract delivery routes. A change in community postal needs or the loss of suitable facilities may lead to the closing of a Post Office but customers who may lose a postal service are still provided benefits.

For Employees

The Postal Service has nine collective bargaining agreements with seven unions covering approximately 726,000 employees. Postal Service unions cover a full range of topics involving wages, benefits, and conditions of employment. The Postal Service wants to ensure leadership continuity and build talent from within the organization. The objectives are: to develop people for corporate needs, to identify individuals who can move into executive positions, and to foster diversity among leadership ranks. Individuals are identified as potential successors based on their leadership skills, functional and management expertise, and performance results. After completing the eighth full year of succession planning, less than 1 percent of executive vacancies were filled by outside hires. The Management Intern Program and Professional Specialist Intern Program were implemented in 2002. These exist to attract and develop outstanding internal and external candidates who possess graduate degrees. In 2002, the Postal Service continued to emphasize the importance of the Merit Performance Evaluation process. This process evaluates and rewards the performance of professional and managerial personnel based on yearly objectives. The USPS also provides its employees with excellent insurance, retirement, and leave programs.

External Factors

The Postal Service has significant competition in every major category of service by world-class competitors. Major competitors to the USPS, include FedEx, UPS, and e-mail.

FedEx

Mission Statement

FedEx Corporation will produce superior financial returns for its shareowners by providing high value-added logistics, transportation and related information services through focused operating companies. Customer service requirements will be met in the highest quality manner appropriate to each market segment served. FedEx Corporation will strive to develop mutually rewarding relationships with its employees, partners and suppliers. Safety will be the first consideration in all operations. Corporate activities will be conducted to the highest ethical and professional standards.

Source: Adapted from the FedEx Web site: www.fedex.com.

FedEx Ground began in 1985 as RPS (Roadway Package System), a division of Roadway Services, which became Caliber System Inc., in 1996. RPS revolutionized the small-package ground-shipping market. It was the first in the ground business to use bar coding and automated sorting. In 1993, RPS exceeded $1 billion in annual revenue after being in business for only nine years. This represented the fastest growth of any ground transportation company. RPS had 100 percent coverage in North America in 1996; it was officially named FedEx Ground in January 2000. Later that year, the company launched FedEx Home Delivery. This is a business-to-consumer service designed to help catalog and online retailers meet the needs of the residential market with standard features such as evening and Saturday deliveries. In September 2002, FedEx Home Delivery completed its expansion and is now available nationwide, serving virtually every U.S. address. Today, FedEx Ground is the only small-package ground carrier operating a network of automated facilities, and ships 2.1 million packages every business day.

FedEx is a global provider of transportation, e-commerce, and supply chain management services, offering integrated business solutions through a network of independently operating subsidiaries. Fiscal year ending 5/31/03 showed revenues rose 9 percent. The growth is a result of the volume growth in the ground and international express shipments. FedEx Ground provides 100 percent coverage to every business address in Canada and Puerto Rico. Among its many competitive service options, FedEx Ground offers C.O.D. service for both domestic and international destinations.

United Parcel Service

Founded in 1907 as a messenger company in the United States, UPS has grown into a $30 billion corporation. UPS is a global company with one of the most recognized and admired brands in the world. It is the world's largest package delivery company and services more than 200 countries. UPS offers to manage inventory, to do order fulfillment, to manage logistics services, and to provide customer service. One positive thing for UPS is that for the fourth year in a row, it ranks among the best of the nation's major companies in minority employment. *Fortune* magazine's July 7, 2003, issue ranks UPS eleventh on its "Best Companies for Minorities" list. Notably, UPS remains the highest ranked transportation/delivery service provider for the fourth consecutive year.

E-mail

The Internet is another competitor for the USPS. The Internet offers customers the ability to receive statements or bills, to receive payments, and to provide information about products and services. Electronic commerce, known as e-commerce, allows people to exchange goods and services immediately worldwide. Any time of the day or night, you can go online and buy almost anything you want. E-commerce companies offer products and services that substitute for traditional postal services. E-mail has indeed become one of the most common means of communication for people across the country and throughout the world. It saves people time, money, and useless effort. The well-known phrase "you've got mail" has become a significant part of the English language. People have become extremely reliant upon the instantaneous delivery and short response time provided by e-mail and the Internet, and this has made it a significant competitor of the USPS.

Global Issues

International mail revenues declined 8.8 percent to $1.580 billion during 2002. Associated volume and weight also declined by 16.5 percent and 13.8 percent, respectively. The Postal Service continues a multiyear process of improving the reliability and features of its expedited and package service offerings. Global Express Guaranteed™ was established in 2000 and provides a guaranteed, day-certain package delivery option for customers. International Business has taken steps to transform its existing Global Express Mail™ and Global Air Parcel services into a consistent and reliable menu of companion options that are predicated on days to delivery and geographic service area. Foreign postal administrations that have entered the U. S. market are contesting the package delivery market and have been open about their interest in serving U. S. customers in more fundamental ways. These foreign posts include the Germans, the Dutch, the British, and the Canadians. All are free to enter the U. S. market and even to offer services that would be regulated if offered by the Postal Service. These competitors mainly affect the Priority Mail sector of the USPS.

EXHIBIT 3
Statement of Operations

(DOLLARS IN MILLIONS)	YEAR ENDED SEPTEMBER 30		
	2003	2002	2001
Operating revenue	$68,529	66,463	65,834
Operating expenses:			
Compensation and benefits	50,428	51,557	51,351
Transportation	4,989	5,132	5,056
Other	8,485	8,545	9,233
Total operating expenses	63,902	65,234	65,640
Income from operations	4,627	1,229	194
Interest and investment income	58	46	35
Interest expense on deferred retirement liabilities	(116)	(1,601)	(1,603)
Interest expense on borrowings	(334)	(340)	(306)
Debt repurchase expense	(360)	—	—
Emergency preparedness appropriations	177	179	—
Emergency preparedness expense	(184)	(189)	—
Net income (loss)	$ 3,868	(676)	(1,680)

Source: www.usps.com/history/anrpt03/html/sofops.htm

Natural Environment

The Postal Service safety and health program was faced with a serious challenge as a result of the mailing of letters containing anthrax. Even though the attacks occurred at the end of 2001, effects of the attacks continued into 2002. The five deaths that occurred as a result of the anthrax attacks included two Postal Service employees. Bioterrorism attacks closed two major processing and distribution centers in the eastern United States, and contaminated 21 other postal facilities. The Postal Service also had to deal with more than 17,000 hoaxes that disrupted operations across the country. A nationwide safety and health alert system is operated through the National Postal Operations Center (NPOC). Over 17,000 Postal Service employees who might have been exposed to anthrax were given precautionary medication by NPOC.

Future Outlook

The outlook for the USPS is somewhat gloomy. A weak economy, advertising decreases, e-mail, FedEx, and UPS all hurt the USPS, which is having to downsize. Some analysts argue that the USPS should convert to a centralized mailbox delivery system rather than home delivery to all. This change would save millions. Other analysts suggest that the USPS should cease to continue with cooperative agreements with FedEx and UPS. It has been said that these companies gain more from the USPS than they give, so therefore the deals are not in the best interest of the USPS.

EXHIBIT 4
Balance Sheet

(DOLLARS IN MILLIONS)	SEPTEMBER 30	
	2003	2002
Assets		
Current Assets		
Cash and cash equivalents	**$2,266**	$1,156
Receivables:		
Foreign countries	**744**	592
U.S. government	**359**	125
Consignment	**50**	55
Other	**144**	137
Receivables before allowances	**1,297**	909
Less allowances	**106**	112
Total receivables, net	**1,191**	797
Supplies, advances and prepayments	**366**	327
Total Current Assets	**3,823**	2,280
Other Assets, Principally Revenue Forgone		
Appropriations Receivable	**365**	368
Property and Equipment at Cost		
Buildings	**19,759**	19,513
Equipment	**17,166**	16,421
Land	**2,809**	2,776
Leasehold improvements	**1,060**	1,098
	40,794	39,808
Less allowances for depreciation and amortization	**18,717**	16,895
	20,077	22,913
Construction in progress	**977**	1,223
Total Property and Equipment, Net	**23,054**	24,136
Deferred Retirements Costs—	**—**	32,231
Total Assets	**$27,242**	$59,015

Source: www.usps.com/history/anrpt03/html/balancesheet1.htm

References
FedEx *Annual Report*, 2002.
Fortune, July 7, 2003.
The United States Postal Service *Annual Report*, 2002.
The USPS Comprehensive Statement, 2002.
The USPS Five-Year Plan.
The USPS News and Events (found at **www.usps.com**).
The USPS Transformation Plan.
www.fedex.com
www.ups.com
www.usatoday.com
www.usps.com
www.wsj.online.com

21   American Red Cross—2004

Stefanie Schaller
Francis Marion University

www.redcross.org

When it comes to a disaster, the American Red Cross (ARC) is the master in providing relief to victims, blood to hospital patients, health and safety training to the public, and emergency social services to U.S. military families. The ARC is a member of the International Red Cross and Red Crescent Movement, a nonprofit and non-government organization. As a voluntary organization, the ARC depends on the generosity of people for both time and money to provide disaster relief. All disaster relief given by the ARC is given free of charge as a gift from the American people. Led by 1.2 million volunteers and 30,000 employees, the ARC annually mobilizes relief to families affected by more than 67,000 disasters, trains almost 12 million people in lifesaving skills, and exchanges more than a million emergency messages for U.S. military service personnel and their families.

Total ARC operating revenues and gains for fiscal year 2003 decreased 26 percent to $3.03 billion.

History

Clara Barton founded the ARC in Washington, D.C., on May 21, 1881. Barton was the head of the ARC for 23 years when the organization conducted its first domestic and overseas disaster relief efforts.

The ARC obtained its first congressional charter in 1900 and a second in 1905, the year after Barton retired. The 1905 charter, which is still in effect today, promotes the purposes of the organization that include giving relief to and serving as a medium of communication between members of the American armed forces and their families and providing national and international disaster relief and mitigation.

With the outbreak of the First World War, ARC gained phenomenal growth as the number of local chapters increased from 107 in 1914 to 3,864 in 1918 and membership rose from 17,000 to more than 20 million adult and 11 million Junior Red Cross members. In 1951, President Truman established a federal blood program for national defense purposes and named the ARC the official blood-collecting agency for the country for the duration of the Korean conflict. This first nationwide civilian blood program now supplies nearly 50 percent of the blood and blood products in this country.

In 1991, the transformation of the Red Cross Blood Services was launched. It overhauled the way the organization collects, processes, and distributes blood to ensure that the ARC provides the safest possible blood supply. The ARC expanded its position in biomedical research and started doing business in the new field of human tissue banking and distribution.

Over the years, ARC enlarged its service, always with the aim of preventing and relieving suffering. Fields such as civil defense, CPR/AED training, HIV/AIDS education, and the provision of emotional care and support to disaster victims and their survivors were included into the service of the ARC. Moreover it helped the federal government form the Federal Emergency Management Agency (FEMA) and serves as its principal supplier of mass care in federally declared disasters. The ARC works closely with the International Committee of the Red Cross on matters of international conflict and social, political, and military crisis. As a member of the International Federation of Red Cross and Red Crescent Societies, which ARC helped found in 1919, the organization assists in more than 175 other national societies, helping victims of disasters throughout the world.

ARC is the nation's premier emergency-response organization. This is evidenced by the fact that ARC workers and volunteers were the first to arrive on the scene the morning of September 11, 2001. More than 55,000 volunteers from all 50 states were involved in helping victims of the terrorist attacks. A year after the attacks, ARC contributed an average of $115,000 to each family of the deceased and seriously injured, through the Liberty Disaster Relief Fund. This fund consists of more than $1 billion.

External Assessment Information
Charitable Nonprofit Organizations
With more than 1.4 million charities, including religious congregations, in the United States, and donations from about 70 percent of the households in any given year, charitable nonprofit organizations play a major role in the nonprofit sector of the United States. Based on Giving USA 2003 findings, total charitable giving reached an estimated $240.92 billion for 2002, compared to $238.46 billion in 2001. The estimate for charitable giving in 2002 is 2.3 percent of the gross domestic product. This is just slightly lower than the 2.4 percent of GDP in 2001, compared to 2.3 percent in 2000 and somewhat higher than the 2.2 percent of GDP in 1999. Exhibit 1 shows that charitable giving can be broken down into four sections: giving by individuals, giving through bequests, giving by foundations, and giving by corporation. Giving by corporation increased the most from 2001 to 2002, whereas giving by individuals represents the major source of all giving sources with 76.3 percent. Note in Exhibit 2 that religious institutions, with 35 percent of total contribution, received the most help from volunteers. Health and human services organizations just received 7.8 and 7.7 percent, respectively.

EXHIBIT 1
Breakdown and Changes in Giving by Source from 2001 to 2002

SOURCE	2002 $BILLION	2001 $BILLION	CHANGE IN %	% OF SOURCE OF ALL GIVING SOURCES IN 2002
Individuals	$183.73	182.47	0.7	76.3
Bequests	18.10	17.74	2.0	7.5
Foundations	26.90	27.22	−1.2	11.2
Corporations	12.19	11.03	10.5	5.0
Total	$240.92	238.46		100.0

Source: AAFRC Trust for Philanthropy/Giving, USA, 2003.

EXHIBIT 2

2002 Contributions by Type of Recipient Organization

RECIPIENT ORGANIZATION	$BILLION IN 2002	% OF THE TOTAL CONTRIBUTION
Religious Institutions	84.28	35.0
Educational Institutions	31.64	13.2
Unallocated Giving	30.45	12.6
Foundations	22.00	9.2
Health Organizations	18.87	7.8
Human Services Organizations	18.65	7.7
Arts, Culture, and Humanities Charities	12.22	5.1
Public-society Benefit Organizations	11.60	4.8
Environmental/Animal Charities	6.59	2.7
International Affairs	4.62	1.9
Total	**240.92**	**100.0**

Source: AAFRC Trust for Philanthropy/Giving USA, 2003.

Americans are not alone in volunteering. The international nonprofit sector is increasing in organized voluntary activity and the creation of private, nonprofit, or nongovernmental organizations. Around the world, one person in four donates time to nonprofit organizations. The recent rise in volunteer activity around Europe can be explained by a growing public dissatisfaction with, and lack of trust in, government and other established democratic channels. Based on Judith Nichols' article "Giving and Volunteering in 5 Countries," Exhibit 3 informs that Spain was the leading country in volunteering with 71 percent, followed by Britain 65 percent, Canada 62 percent, the United States 55 percent, and France with 27 percent in 1997.

Competitors

ARC's main competitors in the nonprofit sector are the Salvation Army, the United Way, the American Cancer Society, and Amnesty International.

The Salvation Army is an international evangelical organization with 40,000 employees and approximately 1.5 million volunteers in the United States. The organization has four main territories in the United States, with headquarters in Des

EXHIBIT 3

Giving and Volunteering in 5 Different Countries in 1997

	BRITAIN	CANADA	FRANCE	SPAIN	U.S.
Percentage of population donating to charity	65%	62%	27%	71%	55%
Average donation ($US per month) (Adjusted for cost of living and rounded to nearest dollar)	$14	$43	$8	$15	$38
Percentage of population volunteering for charity	15%	25%	10%	11%	20%
Average time volunteered (in hours per month)	1.8	5.2	1.6	1.6	2.2

Source: Charities Aid Foundation as presented by Judith Nichols at the Second NSFRE Fund Raising Congress, Toronto, November 1997.

Plaines, Illinois; West Nyack, New York; Atlanta, Georgia; and Long Beach, California. The corps community centers represent the basic service unit of the Salvation Army. They provide a variety of local programs, like religious services, evangelistic campaigns, family counseling, day care centers, youth activities, and general programs.

The United Way is an international nonprofit organization that operates in 42 countries and is dedicated to strengthening communities and improving lives around the world. The United Way in the United States is called the United Way of America. It is a national organization whose purpose is to improve life in every community across America. The United Way movement includes approximately 1,400 community-based United Way organizations, each being independent and governed by local volunteers. In 2001–2002, United Way of America generated an estimated $5 billion, which represents an increase of 6.8 percent from $4.7 billion in 2000.

The American Cancer Society is a national community-based voluntary health organization working to eliminate cancer by preventing it, and saving lives through extensive research, education, advocacy, and service. It is one of the oldest and largest voluntary health organizations in the United States, with approximately 2 million volunteers. The American Cancer Society, Inc., has a National Society, with includes chartered divisions in the United States and over 3,400 local units.

Amnesty International is an international organization whose main focus is on internationally recognized human rights in an effort to prevent and stop grave abuse of the rights of physical and mental integrity and promote freedom from discrimination. It cooperates with other nongovernmental organizations like the United Nations and regional intergovernmental organizations. Amnesty International has more than 1.5 million members and regular donors in more than 150 countries, including the United States. Its nerve center is the International Secretariat in London, with more than 410 staff members and over 120 volunteers from over 50 countries.

The ARC's tracking poll, conducted in February 2001, reflects that the ARC outperforms the Salvation Army, the United Way, and the American Cancer Society in the following dimensions: brand awareness, recall, favorability, and trust of the organization. Exhibit 4 represents a broad overview of the results of the 2001 tracking poll, including the Salvation Army and the American Cancer Society.

EXHIBIT 4
Broad Overview of the American Red Cross 2001 Tracking Poll

ISSUES	AMERICAN RED CROSS	SALVATION ARMY	AMERICAN CANCER SOCIETY
Name charitable organization that help people nationwide & in community	47%	29%	NA
Name nonprofit organization that help save lives	45%	>13%	>13%
Recall life-saving organization, hearing or seeing info about during the past three months	37%	NA	19%
Having a very favorable perception of nonprofit organization	78%	NA	69%
Trust of the organization	85%	78%	NA
Donate in the next twelve months	36%	NA	NA
Contacted by a nonprofit organization within the past twelve months	27%	31%	41%

Source: American Red Cross Mid-Carolina Chapter—General Information.

In the blood supply industry, ARC as a nonprofit organization has to compete with HemaCare Corporation. HemaCare Corporation, the only for-profit company, was founded in 1978. The company and its subsidiary, Coral Blood Services, customizes blood management programs for healthcare facilities and supplies blood products and services to over 160 hospitals in southern California and on the East Coast. It operates in California, Connecticut, Maine, Massachusetts, New Hampshire, New Jersey, New York, North Carolina, Pennsylvania, Rhode Island, and Tennessee. It is accredited by the Food and Drug Administration (FDA), and is approved by the American Association of Blood Banks (AABB).

Demographic, Cultural, and Social Trends

Several demographic factors influence the amount of income that individuals donate to charity organizations and the time volunteered for an organization. The most important are age, marital status, and church participation. Primarily, older individuals who have been married and who attend church regularly tend to donate a larger percentage of their income to charitable organizations than do young, single, non-church-attending individuals. According to the article "Philanthropy in the American Economy," people aged 65 and over are approximately 25 percent more likely to make a charitable donation than younger individuals, and give $500–$600 more per year on average. A survey by the Independent Sector found that 84 percent of those attending religious services weekly in 1998 made household contributions, with an average for all households in the survey of 70.1 percent. But church attendance has been declining since the 1980s. In 1981, 60 percent of Americans attended church, which decreased in 1998 to 55 percent and in 2001 to 42 percent, according to the article "Church Attendance Drops." The level of personal income influences the type of organization to which an individual donates. Upper-income individuals are more likely to give to the arts and humanities, environmental organizations, and educational institutions. Lower-income individuals tend to give to religious congregations and human service groups. The baby boom generation is predicted to inherit $10 trillion in the next 30 years, which is the largest transfer of wealth ever, and which may help to increase the growth of giving over the next decades. Some of this wealth will go to charitable organizations, but a greater number of people need to be encouraged to consider using the bequest as a method to ensure that their money goes to the causes they support. Volunteering is a big part of philanthropy in the United States. As the Independent Service survey suggests, volunteering has increased over the years. However, the United Way of America conducted an involvement survey in September 2002 and found that 97 percent of Americans believe it is important to volunteer, but only 34 percent of those volunteered in 2001; 43 percent of seniors aged 75 and over reported volunteering in 1998, which is an increase of 8 percentage points since 1995. Seniors aged 75 and over represent 5.9 percent of the total national population. However, individuals between the ages of 35 and 44 represent the highest percentage of volunteering for a charitable organization, and account for 16 percent of the population. African-American and Hispanic families are less likely to give and give less than white families, because they have on average lower income and wealth. Preliminary results from the Independent Sector survey show that 75 percent of whites reported making contributions in 1998 compared to 52 percent of African Americans and 63 percent of Hispanics, but both African-Americans and Hispanic giving has increased over the years.

According to the ARC, one in every 200 Americans serves as an ARC volunteer. The fastest-growing segment of the volunteering population is young people, who currently represent 35 percent of the organization. Youth between the ages of 10 and 19 represent 15.5 percent of the total population.

During the summer, less blood donations are given: This is a big challenge for blood centers. During the school year, donations from high school and college students account for approximately 15 percent of ARC blood collections. In the summer, it becomes more difficult to collect from these groups, although the need remains.

Economic Conditions

The latest U. S. economic outlook for 2003 and 2004 reports that the economy faces moderate growth and inflation and is still heavily dependent on global economic recovery. The economic recession and the war with Iraq are indices for a pessimistic outlook in the United States.

The level of charitable giving as a percentage of income and economic output has remained relatively constant for decades. But donations do tend to track economic conditions, meaning that an improvement in the economy tends to leverage a more rapid increase in giving. Surveys do indicate that people's tendency to give is quite sensitive to their view of the economy. For example, a fast economic growth and high consumer confidence results in a rise in both the volume of donations by individuals and corporations and the percentage of income donated. The Independent Sector survey found that only 55 percent of the households that worry a lot about money make contributions, while 71 percent make contributions when they are not worried about their finances.

E-Commerce Issues

More and more nonprofit organizations make use of the Internet either to present information or to receive donations. Before the terrorist attacks on September 11, 2001, less than 6 percent of Americans made a charitable contribution online. The Independent Sector survey found that 81 percent of those who gave to September 11 relief efforts had never made an online donation before. According to Arts Law Memo, it is easier and more effective to donate online for 51 percent of Americans. Online givers are generally females, ages 18 to 34. Moreover, Arts Law Memo informs, about a third of adult Americans would be very likely to use the Internet to get information about charities. They are most interested in how a charity spends its money.

Political Trends

President George W. Bush's tax plan calls for reductions in marginal tax rates, elimination of the estate tax (the death tax), and reinstatement of the "above-the-line" tax deduction for charitable donations by households who do not itemize their tax returns and thus do not qualify for that deduction today. The concern is that under the Bush plan, tax rates would be decreased, thereby lowering the tax savings and hence the incentive to donate.

However, a recent survey of wealthy individuals, reported in *The Chronicle of Philanthropy*, suggests that reducing or eliminating the estate tax would have little impact on contributions. According to *The Chronicle of Philanthropy*, "[e]liminating the federal estate tax would not cause most people, including the wealthiest Americans, to change their charitable-giving habits."

Legal Events

In December 2000, HemaCare Corporation filed a lawsuit against the ARC, saying that the ARC illegally tries to keep blood supply competitors out of certain markets and tries to eliminate existing competition. HemaCare claims that the ARC distributes blood products below cost and will not provide any blood to hospitals, which arrange blood supply from another organization. The ARC has to be aware of its competitors and legal actions they might undertake.

Internal Assessment Information

Vision and Mission

ARC Vision and Mission Statements can be found on its Web site, **www.redcross.org**. The Vision is: "Together, we can save a life." The Mission Statement reads: "The American Red Cross, a humanitarian organization led by volunteers and guided by its Congressional Charter and the Fundamental Principles of the International Red Cross Movement, will provide relief to victims of disasters and help people prevent, prepare for, and respond to emergencies."

In addition to the Mission Statement, the ARC is guided by its long-standing congressional charter and its values. Those seven values—humanitarianism, stewardship, helping others, respect, voluntary spirit, continuous learning, and integrity—not only operate in national campaigns and at the highest levels of administration but also play an important role in guiding the actions of local initiatives.

Management and Structure

Although closely associated with the federal government in promoting its objectives, the ARC is an independent, volunteer-led organization, financially supported by voluntary public contributions and cost-reimbursement charges.

The organization is led by a 50-member volunteer Board of Governors, which meets twice a year in Washington, D. C., and once at a national convention. The president of the United States, who is the honorary chairman of the ARC, appoints eight governors, including the chairman of the board. The chairman, David McLaughlin, nominates and the board elects the president of the ARC, currently Marsha Johnson Evans, who is responsible for carrying into effect the policies and programs of the board. The Board of Governors defines policy and appoints governance to local chapter boards of directors, consistent with corporate policy and external regulatory bodies. This decentralized responsibility for service delivery connected with centralized policy and management allows the ARC to contribute immediate, effective, and efficient support. Exhibit 5 shows the organizational chart of the ARC.

The ARC consists of nearly 1,000 chapters, 36 blood services, and 18 national headquarters departments. The chapters are the local units of the ARC and are located in communities all over the United States. They are responsible for all local Red Cross activities within jurisdiction and are subject to the policies and regulations of the corporation. The 36 blood services are the main business of the biomedical service sector, which is operationally separated from the chapters. Its primary purpose is to collect, process, and distribute blood and blood products to over 3,000 hospitals and medical centers. The national headquarters offers oversight to the chapters and biomedical services. Furthermore, they provide corporate service in the field of insurance, legal, human resources, communication and marketing, finance, audit, information technology, and fundraising. Exhibit 6 shows that Ohio has the most chapters with 46, followed by Pennsylvania with 41, and California with 39. In Ohio and Pennsylvania the most biomedical services, 3 respectively, can be found.

Marketing

The ARC has an incredibly strong focus on marketing. In order to maintain its strong position, Marsha J. Evans, ARC president and CEO, announced the appointment of Dennis L. Dunlap, CEO of the American Marketing Association, as a Volunteer Advisor for Marketing Strategy for the ARC, effective September 1, 2003. Together they want to foster and drive donations, create new growth, and generate new prospects for the ARC. One promotion strategy, which the ARC launched, is the ARC Entertainment Outreach Program. The ARC works closely with the entertainment

EXHIBIT 5

American Red Cross Organizational Chart

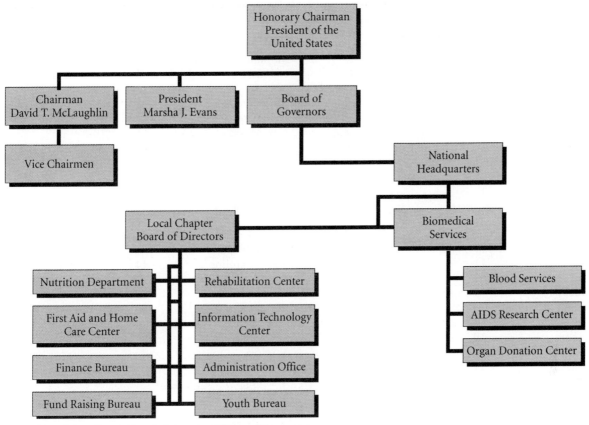

Source: Adapted from the *American Red Cross Annual Report 2002.*

industry in order to encourage the American public to donate their time, blood, and money as a way to help continue the ARC's humanitarian efforts. The Entertainment Outreach Program operates exclusively out of the national headquarters in Washington, D.C. The current outreach to the entertainment community consists of two areas:

The National Celebrity Cabinet

Developed in 2002 to help ARC to highlight important initiatives and response efforts, this is an award-winning combination of well-respected actors, television personalities, musical artists, sports figures, and a clothing designer, who are "on-call" to help the ARC by donating their time, skills, passion, and energy for a one-year term to assist the organization when it's needed most. Heidi Klum, Al Roker, Ruben Blades, and Nicole Miller are just a few of the celebrities in the 2003 National Celebrity Cabinet.

The Entertainment Production Assistance

The ARC offers production companies posters, signage, and background materials, which are often used as set dressing and props. Approvals for use of protected ARC emblems and symbols and approvals of requests to shoot in and around ARC properties can be gained here.

EXHIBIT 6

Breakdown of ARC's Chapters and Biomedical Services

STATE	CHAPTERS	BIOMEDICAL SERVICES	STATE	CHAPTERS	BIOMEDICAL SERVICES
Alaska	2		Montana	1	1
Alabama	9	2	Nebraska	8	1
Arizona	2		Nevada	3	
Arkansas	7	1	New Hampshire	8	
California	39	2	New Jersey	21	
Colorado	5		New Mexico	5	
Connecticut	16	1	New York	24	1
Delaware	1		North Carolina	28	1
Florida	22		North Dakota	2	
Georgia	16	1	Ohio	46	3
Hawaii	1		Oklahoma	7	1
Idaho	1		Oregon	11	1
Illinois	19		Pennsylvania	41	3
Indiana	19	1	Rhode Island	1	
Iowa	11		South Carolina	14	
Kansas	9	1	South Dakota	2	
Kentucky	9	1	Tennessee	12	1
Louisiana	6		Texas	23	
Maine	5	1	Utah	4	1
Maryland	10	1	Vermont	3	
Massachusetts	12		Virginia	25	2
Michigan	21	2	Washington	19	
Minnesota	17	1	Washington, D.C.	1	
Mississippi	4		West Virginia	7	
Missouri	10		Wisconsin	18	1

Source: Adapted from www.redcross.org/where/chapts.html.

The ARC uses the Internet as a marketing tool to communicate with the American public. The organization operates with Advertising.com's e-mail market-ing programs. Advertising.com helps the ARC to raise needed funds for multiple organizational priorities and to establish one-to-one, continuous relationships with its donors and prospects. An average of 300,000 personalized text and HTML e-mails are transferred monthly to ARC's e-mail database.

All these marketing strategies contribute to the enormous brand awareness, recall, favorability, and trust the organization has achieved.

Financial Data

All financial information is contained in Exhibits 7, 8, and 9. Special Project Funds, which are invested for the benefit of all ARC operating units, and the net assets and operations of Boardman Indemnity Ltd., a 100 percent owned captive insurance sub-sidiary, are included in the consolidated financial statements.

Information Technology (IT)

Although the ARC does not have a huge IT budget, it will undertake some major changes in the future to improve the organization's IT redundancy. The organization has already built more capacity in its backup sites in order to get scalability. On

EXHIBIT 7

Consolidated Statement of Financial Position

JUNE 30, 2003
(WITH SUMMARIZED INFORMATION AS OF JUNE 30, 2002)
(IN THOUSANDS)

ASSETS	UNRESTRICTED	TEMPORARILY RESTRICTED	PERMANENTLY RESTRICTED	TOTALS 2003	TOTALS 2002
Current assets:					
Cash and cash equivalents	$ 184,108	262,042	742	446,892	609,973
Investments	265,809	12,825	10,726	289,360	310,706
Receivables, net of allowance for doubtful accounts of $17,022 in 2003 and $19,604 in 2002:					
Trade	223,977	15,241	—	239,218	319,801
Contributions, current portion	15,697	97,370	162	113,229	126,570
Other	—	—	23,448	23,448	15,825
Inventories, net of allowance for obsolescence of $6,925 in 2003 and $7,750 in 2002	167,940	2,981	—	170,921	203,654
Other assets	11,022	4,177	203	15,402	15,892
Total current assets	868,553	394,636	35,281	1,298,470	1,602,421
Investments	599,994	79,751	346,715	1,026,460	1,029,545
Contributions receivable	3,151	23,644	637	27,432	34,826
Pension intangible asset	15,632	—	—	15,632	
Land, buildings, and other property, net	930,110	—	—	930,110	823,541
Other assets	11,153	2,880	21,052	35,085	35,293
Total assets	2,428,593	500,911	403,685	3,333,189	3,525,626
Liabilities and Net Assets					
Current liabilities:					
Accounts payable and accrued expenses	344,857	26,936	—	371,793	296,662
Current portion of debt and capital leases	75,505	—	—	75,505	39,894
Postretirement benefits	12,828	—	—	12,828	18,924
Other current liabilities	30,997	2,589	44	33,630	23,556
Total current liabilities	464,187	29,525	44	493,756	379,036
Debt and capital leases	344,912	—	—	344,912	357,453
Pension and postretirement benefits	237,741	—	—	237,741	120,042
Other liabilities	88,816	1,113	35	89,964	93,823
Total liabilities	1,135,656	30,638	79	1,166,373	950,354
Net assets	1,292,937	470,273	403,606	2,166,816	2,575,272
Commitments and contingencies					
Total liabilities and net assets	**$2,428,593**	**500,911**	**403,685**	**3,333,189**	**3,525,626**

Source: Adapted from *American Red Cross Annual Report 2003.*

September 11, 2001, cellular and landline telephone communication infrastructure was destroyed. The ARC is working on alternative ways, such as satellite-based communication, to stay in touch with disaster workers. The more traditional strategy is to have multiple avenues, multiple pathways that people can use to get connected.

Furthermore, the ARC uses GetActive Software to fulfill critical blood donation needs. The new online service provides blood donors with an easy-to-use registration

EXHIBIT 8

Consolidated Statement of Activities

YEAR ENDED JUNE 30, 2003
(WITH SUMMARIZED INFORMATION FOR THE YEAR ENDED JUNE 30, 2002)
(IN THOUSANDS)

	TOTALS	
	2003	2002
Operating revenues and gains:		
Public Support:		
United Way and other federated	$ 176,493	188,068
Disaster relief	57,575	133,376
Liberty disaster relief—Sept 11 response	12,121	989,060
Legacies and bequests	93,781	95,885
Services and materials	61,071	118,256
Grants	75,191	88,411
Other contributions	216,185	250,909
Products and services:		
Biomedical	2,016,768	1,924,077
Program materials	148,692	137,488
Contracts	59,970	58,171
Investment income	69,485	82,463
Other revenues	46,443	51,097
Net assets released from restrictions	—	—
Total operating revenues and gains	3,033,775	4,117,261
Operating expenses:		
Program services:		
Armed Forces Emergency Services	67,743	61,513
Disaster services	367,435	308,156
Liberty disaster relief—Sept 11 response	209,117	617,960
Biomedical services	2,033,915	1,872,967
Health and safety services	221,619	213,614
Community services	153,180	152,902
International services	17,618	32,736
Total program services	3,070,627	3,259,848
Supporting services:		
Fund raising	122,946	136,901
Management and general	176,080	174,182
Total supporting services	299,026	311,083
Total operating expenses	3,369,653	3,570,931
Change in net assets from operations	(335,878)	546,330
Nonoperating gains (losses)	(18,475)	(135,195)
Additional minimum pension liability	(54,103)	—
Change in net assets	(408,456)	411,135
Net assets, beginning of year	2,575,272	2,164,137
Net assets, end of year	$2,166,816	2,575,272

Source: Adapted from *American Red Cross Annual Report 2003.*

EXHIBIT 9
Statement of Functional Expenses

YEAR ENDED JUNE 30, 2003
(WITH SUMMARIZED INFORMATION FOR THE YEAR ENDED JUNE 30, 2002)
(IN THOUSANDS)

PROGRAM SERVICES

	ARMED FORCES EMERGENCY SERVICES	DISASTER SERVICES	LIBERTY DISASTER RELIEF - SEPT 11 RESPONSE	BIOMEDICAL SERVICES	HEALTH AND SAFETY SERVICES	COMMUNITY SERVICES	INTERNATIONAL SERVICES	TOTAL PROGRAM SERVICES
Salaries and wages	$36,754	84,873	7,971	798,330	102,571	65,728	7,127	1,103,354
Employee benefits	8,621	19,859	1,417	193,728	23,270	15,433	1,709	264,037
Subtotal	45,375	104,732	9,388	992,058	125,841	81,161	8,836	1,367,391
Travel and maintenance	1,549	29,078	1,200	36,329	4,681	3,917	759	77,513
Equipment maintenance and rental	1,182	14,226	647	58,332	4,385	5,837	236	84,845
Supplies and materials	4,191	21,407	583	443,959	46,955	20,401	505	538,001
Contractual services	9,270	51,679	8,715	430,242	29,198	22,370	2,491	553,965
Financial and material assistance	3,993	136,319	188,584	24,649	2,744	13,809	4,414	374,512
Depreciation and amortization	2,183	9,994	—	48,346	7,815	5,685	377	74,400
Total expenses	$67,743	367,435	209,117	2,033,915	221,619	153,180	17,618	3,070,627

SUPPORTING SERVICES

	FUND RAISING	MANAGEMENT AND GENERAL	TOTAL SUPPORTING SERVICES	TOTAL EXPENSES 2003	TOTAL EXPENSES 2002
Salaries and wages	$ 46,154	84,612	130,766	1,234,120	1,165,085
Employee benefits	10,541	20,484	31,025	295,062	249,808
Subtotal	56,695	105,096	161,791	1,529,182	1,414,893
Travel and maintenance	3,338	5,582	8,920	86,433	111,447
Equipment maintenance and rental	1,470	4,833	6,303	91,148	104,619
Supplies and materials	20,837	6,770	27,607	565,608	564,702
Contractual services	36,970	39,419	76,389	630,354	628,127
Financial and material assistance	1,233	2,689	3,922	378,434	660,252
Depreciation and amortization	2,403	11,691	14,094	88,494	86,891
Total expenses	$122,946	176,080	299,026	3,369,653	3,570,931

Source: Adapted from American Red Cross Annual Report 2003.

site: alerts blood donors to critical blood needs in their area; reminds potential donors when they are eligible to donate; and helps them locate a donation center, schedule an appointment, and "Tell-a-Friend" to make an appointment to donate blood.

The ARC uses a centralized Citrix MetaFrame Presentation system that makes application access transparent and thus enables the relief workers to spend less time on paperwork and more time with the victims. This centralized application administration helps the ARC save time and money that would be spent on traveling to remote offices for support.

Future Outlook

Most of the balance of the Liberty Disaster Relief Fund, approximately $133 million, will be spent over the next three to five years to help families with long-term needs including healthcare, mental health, and family support services. The Liberty Fund will be kept as a separate, segregated account and all of the funds will be spent to help families most directly affected by the tragedies. The organization estimates that it will offer mental health services for 16,000 people over the next five years based on its September 11 Recovery Program.

The ARC will improve the IT system, increasing security and implementing new applications that support people behind the scenes. Furthermore, the ARC will implement a ten-year, multidimensional plan in order to improve the facilities and the procedures of the biomedical services division. President and CEO Marsha Johnson Evans says that "gaining and maintaining the confidence of key constituents-blood donors, recipients of blood and blood products and the Food and Drug Administration—is our top priority."

Despite the healthy state of volunteering in the United States, other concerns remain. The following list presents some concerns the ARC might consider:

- The ARC needs to continue to encourage the young, the retired, the unemployed, and those from minority backgrounds to volunteer.
- Over the next few decades, the ARC could see an increase in the number of older people who want to volunteer. It should find new ways to recruit volunteers who are nearing retirement in the 55–64 age group.
- How can the ARC recruit the baby boomers, who will inherit $10 trillion in the next 30 years?
- How can the ARC deal with the increased migration of Americans to disaster-prone regions of the country?
- The Internet is an important medium to educate the public about the work of nonprofits, and how to give and volunteer. However, personal motivations to give and volunteer are complex and diverse; therefore people may be concerned about their privacy when sharing personal or financial information online.
- From a charitable organization's point of view it can be unreliable and expensive to raise money from the general public. Increasing competition for funds raises strategic issues about competing or cooperating with other organizations, emphasizing uniqueness, or collaborating to secure more income for common causes.
- The increasing spread of HIV is a major concern for blood supply.

References

"AAFRC Trust for Philanthropy/Giving USA 2003." www.givingusa.org.
"AAFRC Trust Press Releases." www.aafrc.org/press_releases/trustreleases/charityholds.html.
"American Red Cross." www.advertising.com/Casestudies/html.
"American Red Cross *Annual Report 2002*." www.redcross.org/pubs/#report.

"American Red Cross Case Study." www.diversityroundtable.net/08.htm.

"American Red Cross Mid-Carolina Chapter—General Information." www.donrey.koz.com.

"Arts Law Memo. Online *Annual Reports*." www.vlaa.org.

"California Lawsuit Charges American Red Cross with Unfair Business Practices." www.ama-assn.org/amnews/pick_01/prsd0219.htm.

Chang, C. F., A. A. Okunade, and Ned Kumar. "Motives Behind Charitable Bequests." *Journal of Nonprofit & Public Sector Marketing*, 6(4) (1999): 69–85.

"Charitable Giving Increases in 2002, 'Giving USA' Reports." www.the-dma.org.

"Church Attendance Drops." www.umich.edu/news/Releases/2000/Jan00/r011100.html.

Dee, J. R., and A. B. Henkin. "Communication and Donor Relations: A Social Skills Perspective." *Nonprofit Management and Leadership* (1997): 107–119(1–8).

"Economic Conditions and Charitable Behavior." www.independentsector.org/GandV/s_econ.htm.

"Giving and Volunteering in Five Countries." www.charityvillage.com/cv/research/rsta19.html.

"Key Findings." www.independentsector.org/GandV/s_keyf.htm.

Schervish, Paul G. "Philanthropy Can Thrive without an Estate Tax." *The Chronicle of Philanthropy,* January 11, 2002.

"Philanthropy in the American Economy. A Report by the Council of Economic Advisers." www.oslerbooks.com/damon/pdf/philanthropy.pdf.

"Q&A: Thomas Schwaninger, CIO of the American Red Cross." www.computerworld.com/industrytopics/healthcare/story/0,10801,64887,00.html.

Schneider, J. C. "Philanthropic Styles in the United States: Toward a Theory of Regional Differences." *Nonprofit and Voluntary Sector Quarterly* 25(2) (1996): 190–210.

"The Relationship Between Religious Involvement and Charitable Behavior." www.independentsector.org/GandV/s_rela2.htm.

"United Way of American Research, September 2002. Involvement Survey." national.unitedway.org/surveys/survey0902/files/TelephoneSurveyReport.pdf.

"Why the Bush Tax Cuts Are No Threat to Philanthropy." www.heritage.org/Research/Taxes/BG1417.cfm.

www.amnesty.org.

www.cancer.org.

www.donorsforum.org/resource/restrends.html.

www.salvationarmyusa.org.

www.unitedway.org.

22 The Classic Car Club of America—2004

Matthew C. Sonfield
Hofstra University

www.classiccarclub.org

A line of automobiles is passing through your city or town. Most of the cars have large chrome headlamps, a big vertical radiator grill, sweeping fenders, running boards, and outside spare wheels and tires at the sides of the engine or behind the trunk. What's going on? It may be some members of the Classic Car Club of America (847-390-0443) driving on a club tour or traveling to a club auto show.

In 1952 a small group of devotees of old cars established the Classic Car Club of America, Inc. (CCCA). These enthusiasts were especially interested in the luxury cars of the late 1920s and 1930s. A listing of certain high-priced, high-quality, and limited production cars were designated as "Classic Cars," and the period from 1925 to 1942 was chosen as the limits of the "Classic Era." It was felt that cars built prior to 1925 had not yet reached technical maturity, and that after World War II the quality of most so-called luxury cars had succumbed to the economic pressures of mass production. Some pictures of Classic Cars are provided in Exhibit 1.

Over the years the list of CCCA recognized Classic Cars was modified and expanded, and the time period was extended both backward and forward, to include certain car models from as early as 1918 and as late as 1948, which were basically the same as the 1925–1942 models. All cars included on the list were of considerably higher price and quality than the mass-production cars of this era, and most had original prices in the $2,000 to $5,000 range. (This was a considerable amount of money at that time. For example, in 1930 a Ford Model A [*not* a Classic Car] sold new for about $450.) Some of the most luxurious Classic Cars, such as the American Duesenberg, the English Rolls-Royce, the French Hispano-Suiza, and the Italian Isotta-Fraschini, were even more expensive than most Classic Cars and sold new in the $10,000 to $20,000 range! Exhibit 2 lists those cars recognized as Classic Cars by the CCCA in 2004.

The Mission Statement of the CCCA, as stated in its legal bylaws is:

> The purposes for which the club is founded are: for the development, publication and interchange of technical, historical and other information for and among members and other persons who own or are interested in fine or unusual foreign or domestic motor cars built between and including the years 1925 and 1948, but including cars built before 1925 that are virtually identical to 1925 Classics, and distinguished for their respective fine design, high engineering standards and superior workmanship, and to promote social intercourse and fellowship among its members; and to maintain

EXHIBIT 1
Some Examples of Classic Cars
1926 Duesenberg (below); 1934 Rolls Royce (top right); 1941 Packard (right).

Source: The Classic Car Club of America, Inc.

references upon and encourage the maintenance, restoration and preservation of all such Classic cars.

The Collector Car Hobby

The "collector car" hobby in the United States is a broad and wide-reaching activity involving a large number of Americans. Basically, a "collector car" is any automobile owned for purposes other than normal transportation. The most widely read collector car hobby magazine, *Hemmings Motor News*, had an average circulation of about 250,000 in 2003. Another magazine, *Car Collector*, estimates that nearly 1 million Americans are engaged in the old-car hobby.

"Collector car" is a loose term, ranging from turn-of-the-century "horseless carriages" to currently built but limited-production cars, such as the Ferrari and other Italian super-sports cars. Naturally, owners of collector cars enjoy the company of other persons with similar interests, and thus a wide variety of car clubs exist, to suit almost any particular segment of this vast hobby. Some of these clubs have a broad focus and attract people with many different makes of cars of many different ages, while other clubs have a narrow focus on only one make of car or only a narrow time period. The largest of these clubs is the Antique Automobile Club of America, which caters to owners of virtually all cars 25 years old or older, and it has a membership of more than 60,000 (**www.aaca.org**). Examples of narrow-focused car clubs are the Pierce-Arrow Society (**www.pierce-arrow.org**) and the Stutz Club (**www.stutzclub.org**), each with only a few hundred members. The CCCA falls somewhere between these two extremes.

EXHIBIT 2
CCCA-Recognized Classic Cars

A.C.	Excelsior*	M.G.*
Adler*	Farman*	Minerva*
Alfa Romeo	Fiat*	N.A.G.*
Alvis*	FN*	Nash*
Amilcar*	Franklin*	Packard*
Armstrong-Siddeley*	Georges Irat*	Peerless
Aston Martin*	Graham*	Pierce-Arrow
Auburn*	Graham-Paige*	Railton*
Austro-Daimler	Hispano-Suiza*	Raymond Mays*
Ballot*	Horch	Renault*
Bentley*	Hotchkiss*	Reo*
Benz*	Hudson*	Revere
Blackhawk	Humber*	Roamer*
B.M.W.*	Invicta	Rochet Schneider*
Brewster*	Isotta-Fraschini	Rohr*
Brough Superior*	Itala	Rolls-Royce
Bucciali*	Jaguar*	Ruxton
Bugatti	Jensen*	Squire
Buick*	Jordan*	S.S. and S.S. Jaguar*
Cadillac*	Julian*	Stearns-Knight
Chenard-Walcker*	Kissell*	Stevens-Duryea
Chrysler*	Lagonda*	Steyr*
Cord	Lanchester*	Studebaker*
Cunningham	Lancia*	Stutz
Dagmar*	La Salle*	Sunbeam*
Daimler*	Lincoln*	Talbot*
Darracq*	Lincoln Continental	Talbot-Lago*
Delage*	Locomobile*	Tatra*
Delahaye*	McFarlan	Triumph*
Delaunay Belleville*	Marmon*	Vauxhall*
Doble	Maserati*	Voisin
Dorris	Maybach	Wills St. Claire
Duesenberg	Mercedes	Willys-Knight*
Du Pont	Mercedes-Benz*	
Elcar*	Mercer	

*Indicates that only certain models of this make are considered Classic. Some other 1925–1948 custom-bodied cars not listed above may be approved as Classic upon individual application.
Source: The Classic Car Club of America, Inc.

CCCA Organization and Activities
When the CCCA's 2002 fiscal year ended on December 31, 2002, the club had 5,918 members, as indicated below:

Active (regular membership—2004 dues @$45/year)	4,425
Associate (for spouses, no publications—$7/year)	1,204
Life (after ten years, one-time fee of $800)	217
Life Associate (spouse of Life—$80)	69
Honorary (famous car designers, etc.)	3
TOTAL	5,918

EXHIBIT 3

Selected CCCA Membership Data (At End of Fiscal Year)

	2003	2002	2001	2000
Active Members	4,351	4,400	4,425	4,198
Associate Members	1,264	1,220	1,204	1,113
Life Members	211	208	217	215
Life Associate Members	64	65	69	69
Honorary Members	3	3	3	3
Total	5,893	5,896	5,918	5,598

Source: The Classic Car Club of America, Inc.

Most of these members own more than one Classic Car and many own other non-Classic collector cars as well. Most also belong to other car clubs besides the CCCA. (Exhibit 3 gives a comparison of membership figures for recent years.)

CCCA members receive a variety of benefits from their membership. A magazine, *The Classic Car*, is published four times a year. It is high in quality and highly respected by automotive historians, and it features 48 pages or more of articles and photos of Classic Cars. A CCCA *Bulletin* is also published eight times a year, and contains club and hobby news, technical columns, and members' and commercial ads for Classic Cars, parts, and related items. A further publication is the club's *Handbook and Directory*, published annually. It contains a current listing of club members and the Classic Cars they own, so that club members can locate other members with similar cars or who live nearby. Commercial car-related advertisements are solicited for this *Handbook and Directory*, and its cost is fully paid for by these advertisements. Advertisements also cover some of the costs of the magazine and bulletin. Most other car clubs also publish magazines, newsletters, and directories, with quality and frequency depending on the club's size and budget. Also, there are a number of old-car magazines published commercially rather than by car clubs. Most CCCA members subscribe to some of these commercial publications as well.

The CCCA also sponsors three types of national events each year. The Annual Meeting in January includes business meetings and a car judging meet, and is held in a different location in the United States each year. In the spring and summer a series of "Grand Classic" judging meets are held (some simultaneously) in 10 to 12 locations around the country, with a total of 400 to 600 Classic Cars being exhibited and judged. At CCCA judging meets, cars are evaluated by a point system which takes into account the quality and authenticity of restoration and the general condition of the car, both mechanically and cosmetically. CCCA judging meets are not usually publicized to the general public, and access to view the cars is generally restricted to club members and their guests only. Most CCCA members also bring their Classic Cars to meets sponsored by other clubs or organizations. For example, a CCCA member who owns a Rolls-Royce might belong to the Rolls-Royce Owners Club (**www.rroc.org**) and attend some of that club's events, or he or she might take that Rolls-Royce to a judging meet sponsored by a local charity. As an example, the best-known charity-run car show takes place each August at Pebble Beach, California (**www.pebblebeachconcours.net**) and attracts highly restored collectable automobiles from across the United States and Canada, and even from other countries.

Each year the club sponsors several "Classic CARavans" in various parts of the United States and Canada. The "CARavan" is a tour in which members in as many as 100 Classic Cars join together in a week-long planned itinerary. Every few years, a cross-country "CARavan" of several weeks' duration is run. Other car clubs also run similar tours. The Annual Meeting, Grand Classics, and CARavans are designed to be financially self-supporting, with attending members paying fees that cover all the costs of the events.

The CCCA has members who have volunteered to be technical advisors, to assist other members. Furthermore, the club makes available for sale to members certain club-related products, such as hats, ties, shirts, and umbrellas with a Classic Car design. In still another member-oriented venture, the CCCA in 1990 and 2001 commissioned the club's publications editor to write two 750-page hardcover books about Classic Cars and the era in which they were built (*The Classic Car* and *The Classic Era*). Each of these books included over 1,500 photographs of members' Classic Cars. They were published by the club and sold to members and through book stores to the general public, and have brought additional revenue and publicity to the CCCA.

The CCCA also maintains a World Wide Web site (**www.classiccarclub.org**). This attractive Web site provides a wide range of information about the club and about Classic Cars. At this site, one can join the club, buy the club's books, see many Classic Cars, and find much more. As of late 2003, the site had received more than 275,000 "hits."

The club is managed by a 15-member Board of Directors, with a president, vice president, treasurer, secretary, and so on. All are club member volunteers (from all over the United States) who have shown a willingness and ability to help run the CCCA, and have been elected by the total membership to three-year terms of office. These officers and directors are not reimbursed for their expenses, which include attending eight board meetings each year, most of which are held at club headquarters which are located in a club-owned office condominium in Des Plaines, Illinois (a site chosen because of its central location within the United States, and its close proximity to Chicago's main airport). Another member volunteers as "Executive Administrator" and oversees the club's employees and its daily operations. The only paid employees of the club are a full-time office secretary, a part-time clerical worker, and the publications editor, who is a freelance automotive writer/editor doing other work besides that for the CCCA. An organization chart of the CCCA is shown in Exhibit 4.

In addition to belonging to the national CCCA, the majority of members also pay dues and belong to a local CCCA. As of 2004 there are 27 regions throughout the United States. Each region sponsors a variety of local activities for members and their Classic Cars, and also publishes its own magazine or newsletter. Many of the regions also derive revenues from the sale of Classic Car replacement parts, service items, or clothing, offered to all members of the national club.

A Classic Car Club of America Museum has also been established by the club. It is legally separate from the CCCA and its regions. It has its own building on the grounds of a larger old-car museum in Hickory Corners, Michigan (**www.gilmorecarmuseum.org**), and displays a variety of Classic Cars and related items that have been donated to it. The CCCA Museum, unlike the CCCA itself, is eligible to receive tax-deductible gifts of money and property (such as cars). Although the CCCA has granted the museum the right to use the "CCCA" name, the museum has a separate Board of Trustees and is run totally apart from the club. Because of this legal separation, the club's directors do not have the authority to make strategic decisions for the museum, nor can the museum's performance and finances directly benefit the club.

EXHIBIT 4
2004 CCCA Organizational Chart

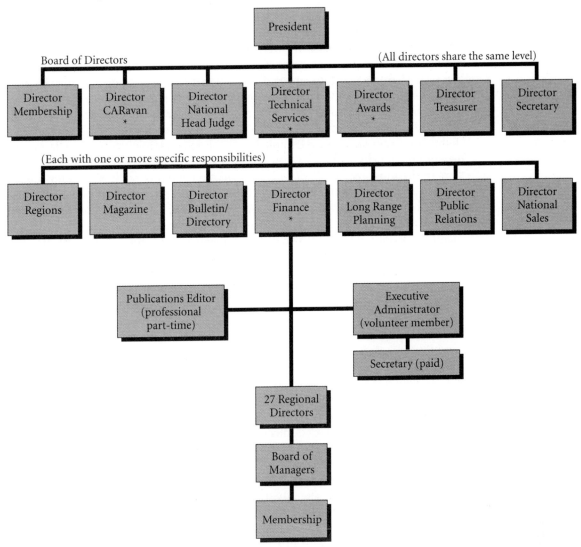

*This director chairs a committee for this functional responsibility, composed of other directors and members.
Source: The Classic Car Club of America, Inc.

Current Concerns

While the officers and directors of the CCCA believe the club to be strong, both financially and in its value to its members, a variety of concerns about the future exist. One concern involves the use of the word "Classic" as it refers to collector cars. While the CCCA uses this term to denote the specific listing of 1920 through 1948 luxury cars the club has designated as "Classic Cars," many other collector car hobbyists use the term more loosely, to refer to any collector car which they see as special. Thus one can find the word "Classic" used to describe 1928 Fords and 1955 Chevrolets. While the CCCA cannot legally protect and limit the hobby's use of the word "Classic," the club has legally registered the term "Full Classic" to refer to CCCA-designated Classic Cars. In its publications and publicity, the CCCA now refers to its members' cars as "Full

Classics" and it is hoped that this trade mark registration and usage will help to protect and clarify the term "Classic" as used by the club.

Another concern is the continuing effect of rising costs upon the club's ability to maintain its current level of services and benefits to the membership. In particular, the cost of its publications and its headquarters office administration have risen considerably over the years. The Board of Directors has responded by raising annual dues several times (from $10 in the 1960s to an increase in 2001 to $45 per year), but it recognizes that certain cost increases are unavoidable, and that raising dues too high may result in a loss of members. (CCCA financial statements are provided in Exhibits 5 and 6).

One way to overcome this problem is to increase the number of members and thus create greater revenues for the club. (The number of members has risen only slightly in recent years—see Exhibit 3.) The directors know that many Classic Car owners do not belong to the CCCA. While CCCA members listed about 7,500 Classic Cars in the most recent *Handbook and Directory*, no one really knows how many Classic Car owners are *not* in the club. Club efforts in recent years to increase membership have been targeted at people who own Classic Cars but are not members of the CCCA. Letters have been sent to past members who failed to renew their CCCA membership (about 5% to 10% each year), region officers have contacted local non-CCCA members known to own Classic Cars, mailings have been made to Classic Car–owning persons found in the directories of other old-car clubs, articles about CCCA activities as well as a few paid advertisements have been placed in various old-car hobby magazines, and membership ads have been placed in single-marque car clubs (such as the Packard club) in return for allowing those clubs to place their membership ads in the CCCA's publications.

Furthermore, while some CCCA members do not own Classic Cars, most do, for much of the pleasure of belonging to the club derives from participating in the various activities with a Classic Car. Thus, while Classic enthusiasts who do not own a Classic Car might also be an appropriate target for CCCA new membership recruitment efforts, the primary focus has been on persons currently owning a Classic Car.

Currently, very few CCCA members live outside the United States. About 2 percent of the membership lives in Canada, and less than 2 percent lives outside of North America (mainly in Western Europe). While countries beyond the United States might be good targets for membership recruitment efforts, the club's directors have never been able to determine whether this is the case, and no formal attempts at international recruitment have ever been made.

The club's membership recruitment efforts have only been moderately successful. While new members have offset the annual 5 to 10 percent attrition rate, total membership has risen only slightly in recent years. Yet, unless the listing of recognized Classic Cars is expanded, the number of Classic Cars in existence is fixed, and with it, by and large, is the number of Classic Car owners.

There is ongoing discussion among CCCA members with regard to expanding the current listing of club-recognized "Classic Cars." There are two directions for such an expansion. One way is to add further makes and/or models within the 1925–1948 year limits. Another way is to add cars built before or after the currently accepted time frame.

Several times in recent years, the Board of Directors has voted to add additional models of existing Classic makes to the CCCA's listing (for example, by adding a Packard model line slightly lower in original price to already-listed Packard model lines of the same year). Also, a few lesser-known makes of this time period have been added (such as the American Elcar and the French Georges Irat), but only a handful of these cars still exist. These additions have drawn a mixed reaction from the membership. Some members feel that such additions dilute the meaning of "Classic Car" while most other members seem to support the directors' decisions, or have no strong opinion.

EXHIBIT 5
CCCA Statements of Receipts and Disbursements (Cash Flow Basis)

	2003	2002	2001
RECEIPTS			
Active Membership Dues (dues received for current FY)	$ 17,243	$ 21,289	$ 18,462
Prepaid Active Dues (dues received for next FY)	179,160	179,648	177,603
Associate Membership Dues	1,001	1,099	1,008
Prepaid Associate Dues	7,881	7,853	7,425
Life Memberships	6,400	0	3,600
Life Associate Memberships	270	0	180
Publication Sales	1,153	2,103	1,558
Awards Income (member registration fees for meets, etc.)	12,980	13,195	12,977
CARavan Income	32,373	30,900	27,640
National Sales Items	12,149	18,249	9,045
Insurance Income (from regions)	8,060	7,700	4,225
Book Income	23,923	24,190	67,716
Advertising Income-Bulletin	24,216	26,521	25,228
Advertising Income-Magazine	2,000	1,500	2,000
Advertising Income-Directory	17,525	30,125	15,750
Interest Income	3,960	4,179	7,005
Miscellaneous Income	2,327	2,855	6,182
TOTAL RECEIPTS	352,621	371,405	387,604
DISBURSEMENTS			
Membership Expense (recruitment)	3,470	4,872	6,543
Annual Meeting Expense	10,162	13,482	10,792
Awards Expense (meets, etc.)	24,048	10,478	22,933
CARavan Expense	21,268	15,917	21,474
National Sales Items	4,703	9,929	12,261
Book Expense	1,763	1,871	40,599
Bulletin Editor Fee	11,702	11,671	10,221
Bulletin Printing	49,091	62,488	43,587
Magazine Editor Fee	10,000	10,449	10,000
Magazine Printing	77,671	83,709	78,163
Directory Printing	15,725	14,791	16,325
General Administration (supplies, postage, telephone, etc.)	22,150	31,095	19,252
Office (wages, condo expenses)	59,722	45,921	58,021
Insurance	14,198	13,842	8,936
Professional Services	4,460	16,308	6,424
Miscellaneous Expenses	4,933	5,649	7,253
TOTAL EXPENSES	335,067	352,472	372,784
EXCESS RECEIPTS OVER DISBURSEMENTS (DEFICIT)	$ 17,553	$ 18,934	$ 14,820

Note: Certain unusual one-time receipts and disbursements omitted.
Source: The Classic Car Club of America, Inc.

EXHIBIT 6
CCCA Balance Sheets

	2003	2002	2001	2000
ASSETS				
Bank Balance	$ 33,859	$ 20,267	$ 20,500	$ 35,815
Investments (at cost) (money market funds, govt. notes, etc.) (includes life membership fund)	393,501	398,384	389,959	291,215
Office Condominium	153,527	158,926	166,636	148,071
TOTAL ASSETS	580,887	577,577	577,095	475,101
LIABILITIES	0	0	0	0
OWNERS' EQUITY	**$580,887**	**$577,577**	**$577,095**	**$475,071**

Source: The Classic Car Club of America, Inc.

In 2002, after conducting a vote of the entire membership, the CCCA Board of Directors voted to expand the listing of recognized Classic Cars to all earlier models that were virtually identical to already-accepted 1925 models. The CCCA's Board of Directors has no plans to extend the current listing of "Classic Cars" any further. While further changes, especially to years after 1948, might add new (and perhaps younger) members and more dues revenues, the club's mission and focus might be diluted by any further expansion. Would a broader focus and listing of accepted "Classics" reduce the attraction of the club to its existing members, who have many other old-car clubs to choose from?

While some less exotic and unrestored Classic Car models can be found for under $15,000, most sell for $20,000 to $75,000, and the most desirable Classic Cars (convertible models with custom bodies, 12- and 16-cylinder engines, etc.) can sell for $100,000 and more. (A very small number of especially exotic and desirable Classic Cars have sold in the $250,000 to $1,000,000 range, and a 1929 Bugatti Royale reportedly sold in 1987 for over $9.8 million!) Furthermore, judging meets have become very serious events, with awards and high scores adding significantly to a Classic Car's sales value. Thus, many highly desirable and/or top scoring Classic Cars are now hardly driven at all, and are transported in enclosed trailers to and from judging meets. While most Classic Car owners still enjoy driving their cars, and the CCCA CARavans continue to be highly popular among club members, some members yearn for the "old days" when there was less emphasis on judging and on a car's value, and when CCCA members could drive and park their Classic Cars anywhere.

Future Direction
Together for their regular Board of Directors' meetings, the 15 officers and directors of the CCCA ask themselves the following questions:

1. What are the various criteria we should consider when making strategic decisions for the club? How do we balance financial objectives and nonfinancial objectives? Which are primary and which are secondary?
2. Does the CCCA have "competition" as most businesses do? Who or what constitutes this competition?
3. How important are, and how should we deal with, rising costs to the club?

4. If we are forced to choose between raising dues or lowering the services provided to the members, which takes priority?

5. Should the club be offering more services to its members, even if this requires an increase in dues? If so, which services should be expanded?

6. Is any further expansion of the listing of recognized Classic Cars desirable?

7. What are the pros and cons of adding post–1948 luxury cars to the current CCCA listing of "Classic Cars"?

8. How important is it to increase the number of members in the club? What are some alternative ways to increase membership?

9. How serious is the aging membership of the club? Should the CCCA try to attract younger people to the club and, if so, how? What are some specific strategies to accomplish this?

10. Are there other possible sources of revenue to the club? What might some be?

11. How important is protecting the term "Classic Car"? What else can the CCCA do to further such protection?

12. Are there other long-range issues or concerns that the club has not yet addressed?

23 Utah Valley State College—2004

Lowell M. Glenn, David W. Johnson, and Bradley A. Winn
Utah Valley State College

www.uvsc.edu

Dr. William A. Sederburg, the new president of Utah Valley State College (801–863–INFO) (UVSC), swung around in his chair and looked out at the campus from his window in the corner of the administration building. He'd just told the local Chamber of Commerce that he hadn't come here to "fix things; UVSC is already a healthy school." But the challenge of maintaining the dynamic growth that had characterized the institution over the last decade would require the very best that he, his staff, the faculty, and the community of students could muster to sustain the momentum.

His predecessor, President Romesburg, had been widely recognized for successfully transforming the community college in to a four-year institution, and had his sights set on creating a university. His battles in the higher education system of the state and with the legislature had been legend during this growth period, but progress had come at a price. The good times of economic prosperity during much of this growth were now being replaced by a period of economic retrenchment. State resources were decreasing and the higher education system had recently announced a moratorium on expanding programs. Public announcements as to where limited funding for higher education would be directed in the future were not favorable to UVSC.

Over the last decade, UVSC had grown from a student body size of under 10,000 to one approaching 25,000. While student tuition/fees had increased more than 45 percent over the last two years, students still flooded the campus. New faculty members were hired at an unprecedented pace and new academic deans were demanding, and getting, more doctorally qualified faculty. Faculty were more often being hired through national, rather than local, searches and many came with an interest in the university model. Faculty teaching loads were being reduced, closer to the levels of four-year institutions, and faculty members were increasingly expected to produce scholarly works. As schools within the college began seeking professional accreditation, it appeared that UVSC was on a track aimed at adding graduate programs and attaining university status.

It was clear that if these institutional expectations were to occur amidst the challenges of reduced resource levels and opposition among varied sectors of the higher education system within the state of Utah, UVSC would have to produce a major planning effort to justify its aspirations. This case describes the strategic planning process that occurred at UVSC between early 2000 and the issuance of a final report in April 2002.

UVSC had its inception in 1941, as the shadow of war loomed on the horizon. During the 2002–2003 academic year, Dr. Lucille Stoddard returned from retirement (she had previously served as the Vice President of Academic Affairs) to again

EXHIBIT 1

Top Levels of UVSC's Governance Hierarchy

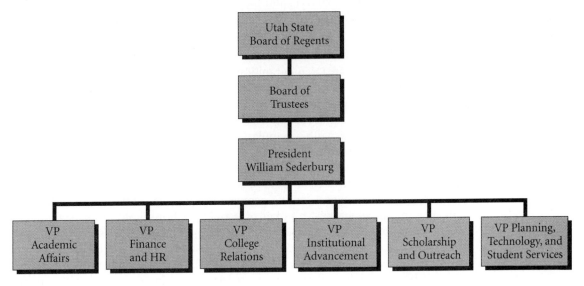

serve as Interim President of UVSC. Her efforts were primarily aimed at keeping the college operational. Most strategic issues were put on hold until the arrival of President Sederburg in June of 2003.

Organizational Structure

Dr. Stoddard provided President Sederburg with a detailed organization chart showing his new domain. Exhibit 1 shows the top levels of UVSC's governance hierarchy.

The UVSC Board of Trustees consists of citizens, many from the local community, who are appointed by the governor to provide local direction and oversight to UVSC administration. The Vice President of Academic Affairs, sometimes referred to as the Provost, is responsible for most academic programs at UVSC. The deans of the academic schools report to the Provost. These schools include Business; Computer Science and Engineering Technology; Education; General Academics; Humanities, Arts, and Social Sciences; Science and Health; Trades, Technology and Industry; and the Wasatch Campus. Also reporting to the Provost are Athletics, the Faculty Senate president, and the Center for Teaching Excellence.

To forward his interest in creating a strategic plan that would lead UVSC toward university status, President Romesburg had established the position of Vice President for Planning, Technology, and Student Services with responsibility for the Offices of Planning, Institutional Research, Information Technology, Web Services, Admissions and Registration, and Academic and Career Advising.

The existing organization is essentially the creation of President Romesburg. His entrepreneurial style often rewarded individuals with positions of power based upon accomplishment and personality. This has resulted in some questionable placements of function which in turn have raised conflicts and issues. Since President Romesburg's departure, the academic deans have asserted their influence and have strengthened their base of power within UVSC. One of their biggest concerns has been the method of allocation of budget funds. The budgeting process begins with the allocation of funds by the state legislature. UVSC has not fared well in this allocation, obtaining the least funding and facilities per student of all higher educational institutions in the entire state.

Culture of the Region

Utah is an interesting area demographically. More than three-fourths of Utah's 2.3 million residents live in a four-county area 80 miles long sheltered by the western face of the Wasatch Mountains. This so-called Wasatch Front runs between Ogden to the north and Provo/Orem to the south. Utah County is the fastest growing of those four Wasatch Front counties with a population of nearly 400,000 as of 2003 and over 17 percent of the state's people.

A report to the state's governor shows an estimated 325,000 people between the ages of 18 and 24 living in Utah. Utah ranks first among all states in the nation when comparing the percentage of young people under 17 to the total population of the state. It also has the highest number of people per household of any state in the nation. In one analysis of cumulative school-age population increases between 2000 and 2030, Utah County is projected to have an absolute increase of 69,130, almost as large as Salt Lake County, despite having less than half of the population of its northern neighbor. This will result in an estimated 81 percent increase in school-age population for Utah County contrasted to only a 45 percent increase for the same period in Salt Lake County.

Utah is the headquarters for the Church of Jesus Christ of Latter-day Saints (Mormons). About 70 percent of the population of the entire state is Mormon, but in Utah County nearly 90 percent of the people adhere to the religious beliefs of the church. Mormons are, for the most part, politically conservative. Utah has voted Republican since the first Eisenhower administration in the 1950s. They have larger than average families; in 2000 the average Utah family had 3.57 persons compared to the national average of 3.14 persons per family. Mormon parents emphasize the importance of education. Utah ranked fourth highest among all states in 2000 with the proportion of persons over 25 with at least a high school diploma (87.7%). In the preceding decade there was a 17 percent increase in the proportion of people over 25 with at least a bachelor's degree. By the year 2000, 26.1 percent of Utahans over 25 held a bachelor's degree or higher.

Located within ten miles of UVSC, Brigham Young University (BYU) is a Mormon-sponsored institution that has grown rapidly in size and reputation over the last several decades. When the Mormon Church had a membership of 1 or 2 million, and most of its members lived in the western United States, BYU was a magnet that drew many young people to its doors for higher education. But now the church has some 11 million members scattered around the world and there is a limit to the number of people who can attend BYU. This has resulted in frustration for the young people who wanted to follow their parents to BYU.

Selection and admission processes at BYU have been continually revised upward to include only the most qualified in terms of high school achievement and standard testing scores. In addition, BYU administrators have often given preference to out-of-area/state applicants, further limiting the opportunities of college-age students in the Utah County area. The Mormon Church recognized the number of its youth in the Utah County area that began to feel excluded from access to BYU. One alternative was for these young people to go up to Rexburg, Idaho, where the church converted a two-year junior college to a four-year satellite of the Provo campus. But another, closer-to-home, alternative was the development of an LDS Institute of Religion on the UVSC campus where Mormon youth could access religious courses just like they do at BYU. These centers for religious study have been set up at a number of institutions of higher learning around the world, but the UVSC Institute is by far the largest and best attended. These factors, coupled with the rapid growth of the Utah County area as outlined above, have resulted in a tremendous pent-up demand for collegiate education in the community. The obvious alternative became UVSC.

In mid–2002 a private group was formed in response to the governor's concern about how education could be better supported through the economic downturn. It called itself the Employer's Education Coalition (EEC) and looked at all levels of educational issues in the state. The University of Utah and Utah State University were encouraged to return to the objective of identifying a few areas where they could excel and to allocate their resources into those activities. UVSC was identified as the low-cost institution, teaching students for an average cost of $4,500 per person (contrasted to $10,000 per student at Utah). The position of the Employer's Education Coalition was that UVSC should just keep doing it cheaply and stop pushing for resources to expand to a satellite in Heber City, as it was doing at the time. The EEC also stated that UVSC should stop its attempt to become a university and "stay in its box." Two-year schools were encouraged to "become the best and most cost-effective" two-year programs possible.[1]

UVSC in the Utah Higher Education Environment

Utah Valley State College is one of ten institutions in the higher education system of the state of Utah. Exhibit 2 illustrates the relative status of UVSC contrasted to the other institutions of higher education for the budget year 2002–2003. UVSC ranks fifth among the group in terms of total budget for the period despite the fact that it is the second largest in terms of enrollment. Over the last ten years, growth has averaged more than 10 percent annually at UVSC. The 16,258 FTE student enrollment of 2002–2003 was 118 percent higher than the 7,473 FTE reported in the 1992–1993 academic year. Unfortunately, during that same period total expenditures per FTE only expanded just over 20 percent, tax funding per FTE grew only 18 percent, and tuition levels per FTE expanded by over 30 percent. UVSC had the lowest expenditure per student among any of the ten institutions in the state.

UVSC's efforts to upgrade the level of resources to make it more competitive with other institutions that offer baccalaureate degrees presents an interesting problem for the other schools in the state. UVSC is often compared with a similar institution in Ogden, Utah: Weber State University. Observers of resources allocated to UVSC over the last ten years become concerned when they compare funding levels for these two institutions. As Exhibit 3 illustrates, between 1995 and projected fiscal 2004, Weber State's budgets grew from $63.6 million to $91.3 million. Over that same period UVSC, which had only just begun issuing four-year degrees in 1995, expanded its budgets from $37.1 million to $84.9 million—nearly 129 percent higher than the decade earlier.

The Board of Regents prepared some comparisons of Utah higher education institutions with a series of "comparables" in other parts of the country. UVSC was significantly below its group of comparable colleges with only 70 percent of the expenditure levels of the comparable group. Another measure of an ability to meet student needs is the square feet per student of physical facilities available in the varied institutions of the Utah higher education system. Despite being the second-largest institution in the state system, UVSC ranks fifth among all schools in the number of square feet available to provide instruction and support. By way of

EXHIBIT 2

Revenues and Expenditures

			REVENUES			EXPENDITURES			
Institution	Total Rev/Exp	State Tax Funds	Tuition & Fees	Federal/Other	Sal & Benefits	Nonpersonal Services	Enrollment FTE*	Cost Per Student
2002–03 Budget								
University of Utah	$303,916,100	$205,408,300	$ 89,570,200	$ 8,937,600	$260,737,349	$ 43,178,751	22,336	$13,607
Utah State Univ.	176,910,500	123,838,900	48,167,000	4,904,600	147,958,200	28,952,000	14,964	11,822
Weber State Univ.	84,611,600	55,227,400	29,384,200		72,240,140	12,371,460	13,049	6,484
Salt Lake Community	80,817,200	53,672,900	27,144,300		66,957,200	13,860,000	14,209	5,688
Utah Valley State	76,640,500	39,872,500	36,768,000		66,046,695	10,593,805	16,258	4,714
Southern Utah Univ.	36,707,836	26,055,900	10,651,936		30,242,436	6,465,400	4,961	7,399
Dixie State College	22,777,300	16,138,400	6,638,900		17,187,803	5,589,497	4,256	5,352
Snow College	19,274,700	15,190,500	4,084,200		12,326,204	6,948,496	2,755	6,996
College Eastern Utah	14,722,200	12,121,600	2,600,600		11,493,728	3,228,472	1,683	8,748
Total Utah Higher Ed.	$816,377,936	$547,526,400	$255,009,336	$13,842,200	$685,189,755	$131,187,881		
Reported	$836,156,136	$566,347,400	$255,275,136	$14,533,600	$689,845,711	$146,310,425		
Difference	$19,778,200	$18,821,000	$265,800	$691,400	$4,655,956	$15,122,544		

*Education & General

Source: Utah System of Higher Education: Data Book 2003–2004.

EXHIBIT 3
Utah System of Higher Education

	STATE TAX FUNDS APPROPRIATED	% OF TOTAL	TUITION AND FEES	% OF TOTAL	OTHER REVENUE	% OF TOTAL	TOTAL REVENUES
Weber State University							
FY 1995	$42,099,200	66.2%	$16,963,733	29.6%	$4,492,147	7.1%	$63,555,080
FT 2000	50,418,900	72.4%	21,653,859	31.1%	−2,448,104	−3.5%	69,626,665
FY 2004 Request	60,397,600	66.2%	30,867,600	33.8%	0	0.0%	91,265,200
Utah Valley State College							
FY 1995	19,782,700	53.3%	14,340,975	38.6%	3,005,945	8.1%	37,129,620
FT 2000	32,941,800	58.8%	21,875,400	39.0%	1,246,628	2.2%	56,063,828
FY 2004 Request	46,520,600	54.8%	38,332,400	45.2%	0	0.0%	84,853,000

Source: Utah System of Higher Education: Data Book 2003–2004.

comparison, Utah State University had 14,964 FTE students in 2003 compared to UVSC's 16,258. But with over 4 million square feet of facility, USU had more than 2.6 times the square feet of facility space compared to UVSC's 1.5 million square feet of facility (Exhibit 4).

The problem is that the growth of the past decade is only a harbinger of what is to come over the next decade. Projections at the turn of the millennium suggested there would be a 19.2 percent population growth in Utah by the year 2010. But again the region served by UVSC is expected to grow even faster. Counties within this region, including Utah and Summit Counties, are projected to grow by more than 23 percent in each case. Another county within UVSC's service region, Wasatch County, is projected to grow an unprecedented 28.6 percent.

A 2002 Utah State Board of Regents projection estimates that UVSC would have 27,560 students by 2007 and 32,340 by 2012. But UVSC's Office of Institutional Research estimates there will be over 29,000 students by 2005 and nearly 38,000 by

EXHIBIT 4
Total Space by Institution—Utah System of Higher Education

INSTITUTION	CLASSROOM	LAB AND RESEARCH	OFFICE	RESIDENTIAL	OTHER	TOTAL	FTE STUDENT ENROLLMENT
University of Utah	264,422	1,475,469	1,699,592	1,510,843	5,704,403	10,654,729	22,336
Utah State University	155,412	677,804	618,454	850,810	1,746,078	4,048,558	14,964
Weber State University	147,954	245,536	282,137	179,943	1,489,693	2,345,263	13,046
Southern Utah University	62,094	144,258	132,134	84,359	785,851	1,208,696	4,961
Snow College	43,711	71,760	58,335	95,190	381,796	650,792	2,755
Dixie State College	49,948	130,897	89,169	49,611	356,070	675,695	4,256
College of Eastern Utah	33,367	76,682	49,320	82,725	306,641	548,735	1,683
Utah Valley State College	96,932	285,192	211,183	5,705	928,379	1,527,391	16,258
Salt Lake Community College	160,316	373,247	195,004	0	903,325	1,631,892	14,209

Source: Utah System of Higher Education: Data Book 2003–2004.

2010, if current trends continue. The early 2003 decision by the State Board of Regents to impose a moratorium on new programs was in part designed to limit this increase in UVSC growth. It may all be problematic, however, as students continue to flock to the campus despite higher tuition costs and all the other restraints that policy makers have tried to impose on these growth patterns.

A more detailed outline of UVSC revenues and expenditures is provided in Exhibit 5. A number of observers believe that as long as the economic recession continues in Utah it will be necessary to find alternative means for funding UVSC's expansion. One possibility is to increase student tuition. In 2003, the Utah State Legislature authorized a variety of tuition increases for each of the state colleges and universities ranging from 6 percent to as high as 23 percent. UVSC raised tuition levels 12.5 percent to 14.5 percent within this time frame. In their push to structure UVSC more like a university, officials have sought to expand tuition to bring it more in line with Weber State University and have raised tuition some 45 percent over the period between 2001 and 2003.

Summary of UVSC Strategic Plan

President Sederburg was a strong proponent of strategic management while he was president of Ferris State University, the institution from which he came to UVSC. As he looked over the UVSC Strategic Plan document, he read the following mission statement.

> Utah Valley State College is a community of learners where every individual is welcomed, encouraged, and supported. We strive for excellence in liberal arts and sciences, the professions, and applied technology education. UVSC offers a full spectrum of educational opportunities including college preparation and certificates, associate and baccalaureate degrees and advanced professional education. Our programs prepare students for career success, personal enrichment and lifelong learning and enhance their ability to contribute to society.
>
> Utah Valley State College values its students, faculty, staff and community and affirms the value of learning and scholarship, excellence and innovation, ethics and integrity, academic freedom, diversity and international understanding.

From studies of UVSC made prior to his interviews, President Sederburg recalled that this mission statement was not the same one he had read on the college Web site.

> Utah Valley State College is a state college comprised of two interdependent divisions. The lower division embraces and preserves the philosophy and mission of a comprehensive community college, while the upper division consists of programs leading to baccalaureate degrees in areas of high community demand and interest. Utah Valley State College is dedicated to providing a broad range of quality academic, vocational, technical, cultural, and social opportunities designed to encourage students in attaining their goals and realizing their talents and potential, personally and professionally. The College is committed to meeting student and community lower division and upper division needs for occupational training; providing developmental, general, and transfer education; meeting the needs for continuing education for personal enrichment and career enhancement; and providing diverse social, cultural, and international opportunities, and student support services.

EXHIBIT 5

Operating Expenditures and Revenues by Object—Utah Valley State College

	2000–01 ACTUAL	2001–02 ACTUAL	2002–03 BUDGET
A. EXPENDITURES AND TRANSFERS OUT			
1. Regular Faculty	$12,695,639	$15,575,181	$18,754,813
2. Adjunct/Wage Rated Faculty	5,673,730	6,754,805	7,092,589
3. Teaching Assistants	0	0	0
4. Executives	2,074,887	2,307,161	2,250,063
5. Staff	14,593,213	17,094,704	17,826,324
6. Wage Payroll	2,377,028	2,890,980	2,822,697
7. Total Salaries and Wages	37,414,497	44,622,831	48,746,486
8. Employee Benefits	13,032,216	15,321,972	17,300,209
9. Total Personal Services	50,446,713	59,944,803	66,046,695
10. Travel	671,376	723,016	592,164
11. Current Expense	6,385,030	7,169,217	7,866,881
12. Fuel and Power	1,349,555	1,655,765	1,520,141
13. Equipment	874,516	1,673,701	614,619
14. Total Non-Personal Services	9,280,477	11,221,699	10,593,805
15. Total Expenditures	59,727,190	71,166,502	76,640,500
16. Transfers to Other Funds	190,000	592,281	0
17. **Total Expenditures + Transfers**	**$59,917,190**	**$71,758,783**	**$76,640,500**
B. REVENUES AND TRANSFERS IN			
18. Tuition and Fees	$25,688,592	$30,577,806	$36,275,000
19. Sales and Services of Educational Activities	16,334	14,624	18,000
20. Other Sources	206,924	480,819	475,000
21. Total General Dedicated Credits	25,911,850	31,073,249	36,768,000
22. Federal Appropriations	0	0	0
23. Trust Funds	0	0	0
24. Mineral Lease Funds	0	0	0
25. Total Other Revenues	0	0	0
26. Uniform School Fund	0	0	0
27. Income Tax	5,034,600	9,755,900	4,300
28. State General Fund	31,516,300	31,464,000	39,868,200
29. Total State Tax Funds	36,500,900	41,219,900	38,872,500
30. Total Revenues	62,462,750	72,293,149	76,640,500
31. Balance Carried Forward	1,539,868	4,314,273	0
32. Transfers From Other Funds	228,845	636,181	0
33. **Total Available**	**$64,231,463**	**$77,243,603**	**$76,640,500**
C. FUND & CARRY FORWARD BALANCE			
34. Fund Balance	$4,314,273	$5,484,820	$0
35. Less Commitments & Other Deductions	2,547,625	0	0
36. **Net Carryforward Balance**	**$1,766,648**	**$5,484,820**	**$0**

Note: Budget amounts for FY 2003 are based on reductions through the July 2002 Special Session (HB 5009).
Source: UVSC Internal Report.

Upon inquiry, he found that the mission statement from the strategic plan had been approved by the Board of Trustees but had been put on hold by the Board of Regents. In analyzing the two statements, the phrase "advanced professional education" caught his eye. UVSC wants to be a university, he thought. His review of the remaining portions of the strategic plan found the following Strategic Priorities and Goals.

Strategic Priority I: Attract, Retain, and Promote Excellent Faculty, Staff, and Students

> GOAL 1: Attract, Retain, and Promote Excellent Faculty
>
> GOAL 2: Attract, Retain, and Promote Excellent Staff
>
> GOAL 3: Attract Students Who Will Gain from and Contribute to UVSC

Strategic Priority II: Create a Vibrant Teaching and Learning Environment

> GOAL 1: Offer High Quality Programs
>
> GOAL 2: Pursue Excellence in Teaching and Scholarship
>
> GOAL 3: Utilize Nontraditional Delivery Methods for Special Populations
>
> GOAL 4: Develop Learning Resources Required for a Baccalaureate-Granting Institution

Strategic Priority III: Create a Supportive Student and Campus Environment

> GOAL 1: Provide Student Support Services which Facilitate and Promote Student Success
>
> GOAL 2: Enrich the Extracurricular Life of Students
>
> GOAL 3: Expand Athletics to Prepare for NCAA Competition

Strategic Priority IV: Create a Collaborative and Effective Work Environment

> GOAL 1: Improve Internal Communications
>
> GOAL 2: Improve External Communications
>
> GOAL 3: Foster Higher Levels of Service

Strategic Priority V: Develop a Quality Infrastructure

> GOAL 1: Expand Funding Sources
>
> GOAL 2: Acquire Land and Facilities to Meet Current and Future Demand for Access
>
> GOAL 3: Use Technology to Improve Learning and Administrative Processes

Each goal had an additional three to five objectives to round out the strategic plan. No priorities were included for any of the plan elements. To the new president, the plan seemed like a laundry list of things needing to be done at UVSC. He wondered how the plan had been developed and what steps had been taken toward its implementation.

Strategic Planning Process

In 1999, Dr. Bradley A. Winn was brought on board as the Vice President for Planning and Student Services. Dr. Winn had previously worked at the University of Michigan where he had completed a comprehensive strategic plan for the university. In the year 2000, President Romesburg had stated, "The time has come for UVSC to reassess where we are and where we are heading. We need a full comprehensive examination of our future as the college serving the mountainland region of Utah."

A bottom-up, comprehensive strategic planning process was proposed by Dr. Winn, who had convinced President Romesburg to lead the effort supported by Dr. Winn and his staff along with a Strategic Planning Council comprised of administrative, faculty, staff, and student leadership of the institution. Four key questions were asked.

1. What are the two or three major issues and concerns facing UVSC now and in the short term? (These may be college-wide issues, or departmental.)
2. What are the two or three biggest problems the college faces in meeting the needs and expectations of the community? (Whether or not the expectations are realistic is really not the issue.)
3. What are we doing that we should do differently or better?
4. What are we missing? What two or three things should we be doing that we are not? (These can be new degrees or majors or they can be services or functions.)

Everyone was asked to provide input, including faculty, staff, students, and community members. Over 250 pages of feedback were received. From this, the Planning Council identified nine major themes, including: technology, mission and core values, quality of instruction, space, communication, service quality, funding sources, athletics, and enrollment management/growth. Campus Conversation Groups were then organized around these nine themes and charged with providing recommendations to the UVSC Strategic Planning Council on the issues and action steps pertaining to their group. The deliberations returned from the Campus Conversation Groups were then combined by the Planning Council into a single institutional strategic plan.

This plan contained a new vision/mission/values statement and five strategic priorities supported by a series of goals and 70 specific objectives. Each of the 70 objectives from the plan was assigned to one of the vice presidents for implementation. Action plans with performance indicators and expected delivery dates were then developed by each vice president for their assigned objectives. These efforts were then summarized into a Redline/BlueLine/Greenline version of the strategic plan for internal use only. The redline indicated the next action step for an objective, the blueline indicated the responsible vice president, and the greenline the target date. Vice presidents devoted a meeting a week to furthering the college's strategic priorities.

As the college transitioned from designing the strategic plan to implementing it, several significant accomplishments occurred, including:

- A new School of General Academics was established to support open-enrollment students needing remedial help.
- New faculty hiring was focused primarily at the Ph.D. level.

- Adjunct faculty salaries were increased.
- Faculty research and scholarship increased.
- The number of online/distance education classes increased dramatically.
- A PR video extolling the virtues of UVSC was completed.
- Efforts at attracting external funding increased. The previous dean of the School of Business who had been successful at attracting funds to the Business School was named the new Vice President of Institutional Advancement.
- A Career Employment Office was established and rapidly expanded to support students in career placement and part-time employment.
- An ambitious five-year roll-out of a new ERP system (BANNER) for the college was instituted.
- The athletic director became a catalyst for upgrading the athletic programs to NCAA Division I level beginning with basketball (UVSC does not have a football program).
- Construction of a new liberal arts building was begun and an elementary school campus and land adjacent to campus was purchased.

Then in 2002, President Romesburg announced that he was taking another position in Nevada, and Dr. Winn accepted the Provost position at Snow College. With these two key architects and drivers of the strategic plan gone, implementation efforts slowed and many of the issues were put on hold pending the arrival of the new president. Several of the Vice Presidents continued work on their own portions of the plan. In academics, several of the deans also began work at developing their own strategic plans that would be required for future accreditation reviews.

Conclusion

As he sat in his new office overlooking the campus, President Sederburg realized the great progress that UVSC had made over the past years and thought about its even greater future potential. His first attention should undoubtedly be directed at organizing his executive team. Beyond that, he realized that there were numerous issues still to be resolved. Some of these could be solved organizationally; however, many would require his best efforts at strategic management. He had been given several lists of issues from various constituents. The list from the Faculty Senate included the following as their top-ten items:

1. Faculty Salaries
2. Lowest funding per student in the state
3. Overall UVSC budget system
4. Faculty workload
5. Adjunct pay and working conditions
6. "Top heavy" administration
7. Fewest square feet of facilities per student in the state
8. Not enough money placed on actual education
9. Underfunded and understaffed UVSC Police Department
10. Merit raise system that does not reward outstanding performance

Hard decisions remained. Priorities needed to be determined in light of declining state revenues. Could UVSC continue to do more with less? Internal programs needed reviewing. The budget allocation process needed revision. The balance between centralization and decentralization needs examination. Information technology would need to be better utilized to support faculty and students as well as the administration. Improving UVSC's image and reputation locally and in Salt Lake must surely be a priority. Again President Sederburg looked out his office window at his beautiful campus surrounded by the towering Wasatch Mountains, home of the 2002 Winter Olympics. A vision of UVSC reaching new heights sparked his imagination.

Note

1. "A State at Risk." Executive Summary of the Exployers' Educational Coalition, June 2002, p. 28.

24   Harley-Davidson, Inc.—2004

Richard A. Cox
Francis Marion University

HDI

www.harley-davidson.com

There is something about the power of this brand and this company that intrigues us all. Whether you are a rider or an investor—or whether you are just interested—you have to admit that the way this company connects with its customers truly sets Harley-Davidson apart. Harley-Davidson has customers who are very passionate about their products. The name Harley-Davidson and its logo no doubt represent symbols of American individualism and even a bit of American rebelliousness. Everyone has seen at least one person with the famous Harley Bar & Shield logo tattooed on his or her arm. What is it about this company that would cause someone to want to be associated with it in such a permanent way? Is it the people and events that draw riders to Harley-Davidson? The company sponsors rides and rallies everywhere from Daytona to Houston—or even in international cities like Saint-Tropez, Sungwoo, and Lillehammer. From Mexico to Mount Fuji or from Austria to Australia, riders today can experience Harley at events in more than 100 countries. For some riders, however, the thrill may just be the back roads and riding alone on a lazy Saturday afternoon. Others could have been lured by the distinctive sound of a Harley-Davidson. Even the Harley Web site roars. No other motorcycle has the same sound as the company's legendary V-twin. The famous uneven rumble or "potato, potato, potato" sound has survived for generations and is as distinctive as the customers who ride the bikes. Whatever the reason, this type of loyalty has helped Harley-Davidson to survive against fierce international competition and to maintain a strong financial performance.

History

In 1903, what was to become a legendary motorcycle company was formed in the Davidson family's backyard. The Davidson brothers, William D., Walter, Arthur, and William S. Harley, made their first motorcycle there. In 1909, Harley-Davidson introduced its first V-twin engine. This engine is still the company standard to this day.

During World War I, Harley-Davidson supplied the military with some 20,000 motorcycles. During this time there were major advancements in the design of motorcycles, and Harley was the leader. However, a decade after the war ended, the Great Depression devastated the motorcycle industry. Only Harley-Davidson and Indian (Hendee Manufacturing) survived through the 1930s.

In 1941, World War II called, and Harley-Davidson answered with more than 90,000 motorcycles. After the war, demand for motorcycles exploded, and Harley-Davidson added additional facilities in Milwaukee in 1947. That same year, the company began selling what was to become the classic black leather motorcycle jacket. After Indian closed in 1953, Harley-Davidson was the sole American motorcycle manufacturer for the next 46 years. Harley ended family ownership in 1965 with a public offering. Only four years later, the company merged with the American Machine and Foundry Company (AMF), a longtime producer of leisure products.

By the early 1970s, the United States was importing huge numbers of lower-priced Japanese motorcycles. Japanese firms were able to capture a large portion of Harley's market share. Because it had expanded production so quickly, Harley was also having quality problems. In 1981, thirteen of Harley's senior executives purchased the business from AMF. The company then convinced President Ronald Reagan, by relying on a recommendation from the International Trade Commission (ITC), to impose additional tariffs on imported heavyweight Japanese motorcycles that were 700cc or larger for five years, starting in 1983. Then in 1986, Harley-Davidson, Inc., became publicly held for the first time since 1969. That same year, Harley regained its place at the top of the U.S. super-heavyweight market, beating out Honda. The next year, the company asked the ITC to remove the tariffs one year early. This move made both business and American history, and President Reagan praised the company as an "American success story." Harley's U.S. market share continued to grow, and the company was listed on the New York Stock Exchange in 1987. It had not only survived a difficult time, but some would say that it became an American icon.

Harley celebrated its 100th year anniversary in 2003 by conducting Harley gatherings and trips worldwide.

Mission and Vision Statements

Harley's mission statement says, "We fulfill dreams through the experiences of motorcycling, by providing to motorcyclists and to the general public an expanding line of motorcycles, branded products and services in selected market segments."

Harley's vision statement is as follows: Harley-Davidson is an action-oriented, international company, a leader in its commitment to continuously improve [its] mutually beneficial relationships with stakeholders (customers, suppliers, employees, shareholders, government, and society). Harley-Davidson believes the key to success is to balance stakeholders' interests through the empowerment of all employees to focus on value-added activities.

Harley Divisions

Harley-Davidson is divided into two segments: (1) motorcycles and related products and (2) financial services. The motorcycles and related products segment designs, manufactures, and sells motorcycles, motorcycle parts, accessories, and general merchandise. The financial services segment consists of Harley's wholly owned subsidiary, Harley-Davidson Financial Services, Inc. (HDFS). HDFS provides financial service programs to Harley and Buell dealers and consumers in the United States and Canada.

The average purchaser of a U.S. Harley-Davidson motorcycle is a married male in his mid-forties, with a household income of approximately $78,600. Over two-thirds of the sales of Harley-Davidson motorcycles are to buyers with at least one year of education beyond high school, and 30 percent have college degrees. Only about 9 percent of Harley's U.S. retail motorcycle sales are to women. Repeat business is strong as about 42 percent of motorcycle purchasers have owned a Harley previously.

Harley's heavyweight class of motorcycles is divided into four segments: standard, performance, touring, and custom. The standard segment emphasizes simplicity and cost, and the performance segment emphasizes handling and acceleration.

The touring segment focuses on comfort for long-distance travel; Harley-Davidson pioneered this segment of the heavyweight market. Harley's custom segment gives owners the opportunity to customize their bikes.

Harley-Davidson makes twenty-eight models of touring and custom heavyweight motorcycles, with retail prices ranging from $5,975 to $27,995. The prices of Harley's custom bikes on the high end can be as much as 50 percent more than its competitors' custom motorcycles. Harley's custom segment makes up the highest number of its bikes sold and demands a higher price because of its features, styling, and high resale value.

Harley has one custom model that is priced competitively with comparable motorcycles available in the market—the 883cc Sportster. This model serves as sort of an introduction bike for new Harley-Davidson customers. The company's surveys of retail purchasers indicate that over 75 percent of the purchasers of its Sportster model have previously owned competitive-brand motorcycles, are new to the sport of motorcycling, or have been out of the sport for five or more years. The company also has research indicating that more than 92 percent of its motorcycle customers intend to repurchase. Harley is hoping that the purchasers of the lower-priced Sportster models will be tempted to purchase a higher-priced custom model the next time around.

The Buell motorcycle line serves the standard and performance segments of the market. Buell sells four heavyweight performance models, with retail prices ranging from $8,795 to $13,700. The company also introduced the Buell Blast in 2000 for the standard market, with a price tag of about $4,595. The Blast is smaller and lighter than the other motorcycles offered by Buell. The bike also has a single-cylinder engine as opposed to the trademark V-engine configuration. The company's studies indicate that almost half of Buell Blast purchasers have never owned a motorcycle before, and over 50 percent are women. Harley-Davidson bought a minority interest in Buell, a sport bike company, in 1992 and purchased full interest in 1998. Production of the new Buell Firebolt XB9R began in 2001.

Harley-Davidson Financial Services (HDFS) finances about 35 percent of retail purchases of a new or used Harley. HDFS also offers wholesale financing, with services including floorplan and open account financing of motorcycles and accessories. In addition, the company often makes real estate loans, computer loans, and showroom remodeling loans to many dealers. In the United States and Canada, where these services are offered, they were used by about 97 percent of all dealers.

Marketing and Distribution

Harley-Davidson has approximately 630 independently owned full-service dealerships in the United States. The marketing efforts are divided between dealer promotions, customer events, magazine and direct-mail advertising, and public relations. Harley also sponsors racing activities and special promotional events, and it participates in all major motorcycle consumer shows and rallies. The Harley Owners Group (HOG), which was founded in 1983, currently has approximately 750,000 members worldwide and is the industry's largest company-sponsored motorcycle enthusiast organization (**www.hog.com**). The Buell Riders' Adventure Group (BRAG) was also formed in recent years and has grown to approximately 10,000 members. Both HOG and BRAG sponsor events, including national rallies and rides, across the United States and around the world for motorcycle enthusiasts. Harley faces competitive forces from the likes of Honda,

Suzuki, Kawasaki, and Yamaha in maintaining its dominant 48 percent overall market share in the U.S. heavyweight motorcycle market.

Harley-Davidson is one of the most admired and recognized companies in the world today. Recently, the company has attempted to create an increased awareness of the Harley-Davidson brand name among the nonriding public and to provide a wide range of products for enthusiasts by licensing the Harley-Davidson name. The company has licensed the production and sale of T-shirts, jewelry, small leather goods, toys, and other products. The company also licenses the Harley-Davidson name to two cafes, one located in New York City and one in Las Vegas.

Harley has created an Academy of Motorcycling for those interested in learning to ride a motorcycle. The Academy, which is called "Rider's Edge," introduced more than 1,000 aspiring motorcyclists to the sport in 2000. Those riders learned aboard the new single-cylinder Buell Blast. The participating dealers are creating new customers today that could lead to lifelong relationships. Almost half of all Harley's U.S. dealers have opened new retail stores or completed major renovations to their existing facilities in the past three years.

Harley has an online catalog featuring its genuine motor accessories and motor clothes. In addition to browsing and making a wish list, customers can actually purchase these products at the Web site. The orders are then distributed to local dealers who can ship the products directly or hold the items for pickup.

International Sales

In Europe, Harley considers the unique tastes of many individual countries that together represent a market about the size of the U.S. market. Also, the European Union's motorcycle noise standards are lower than those of the U.S. Environmental Protection Agency (EPA). This causes research and development costs related to motorcycle noise emissions to be higher for motorcycles produced for the European market. The European heavyweight motorcycle market is made up of 74 percent of the standard and performance segments. Harley has only recently started to compete in the performance market with the addition of its Buell motorcycles. Harley has about 7 percent market share in Europe. The company has had difficulty growing its market share in European markets. In the European region, there are about 350 Harley-Davidson dealerships.

Harley has about 22 percent of the motorcycle market share in Asia. It is now easier to obtain a heavyweight motorcycle driver's license in Japan. There are currently about 213 Harley-Davidson outlets serving eight country markets in the Asia/Pacific region.

Harley has an assembly facility in Manaus, Brazil, the first such operation outside the United States. The facility imports U.S.-made components for final assembly in Brazil. This increases the availability of Harley's motorcycles in Brazil, and reduces duties and taxes, making them more affordable to a larger group of Brazilian customers. In the past, only the wealthy in Brazil could afford a Harley because of the steep import tariffs. The facility currently assembles fewer than 1,000 motorcycles per year.

Competition

The U.S. and international heavyweight (651+cc) motorcycle market is highly competitive. Some of Harley's major competitors have larger financial and marketing resources and are more diversified. For example, only about half of the sales of Yamaha Motor Company are motorcycles. Competition in the heavyweight motorcycle market is based on price, quality, reliability, styling, and customer preference.

Harley-Davidson does not emphasize price in its heavyweight bikes partly because the resale prices for used Harley-Davidson motorcycles are generally higher priced than that of its competitors.

Since 1986, Harley has led the industry in domestic sales of heavyweight motorcycles. Harley's share of the U.S. heavyweight (651+cc) market is about 48 percent compared to its next largest competitor in the domestic market, Honda, which has about 18 percent market share.

A recent new potential domestic threat for Harley-Davidson is Polaris, an American snowmobile/ATV manufacturer, that produces "Victory" motorcycles. Polaris motorcycles are all priced below the Harley (see **www.polarisindustries.com**), and it has more than 300 dealers in the United States, Canada, United Kingdom, and Australia, with plans for future expansion. Motorcycles currently represent less than 5 percent of overall sales at Polaris. The president of Polaris, Tom Tiller, stated in a February 2001 press release, "We are in the motorcycle business for the long-term and remain confident in Victory's ability to contribute to profitable growth for Polaris" (**www.americanmotor.com/news**).

Suzuki Motor Corporation and Kawasaki Heavy Industries, Ltd., have formed a strategic alliance in the areas of product development, design, engineering, and manufacturing of motorcycles (see **www.suzukicycles.com**). The alliance strengthened both companies' global motorcycle businesses. The market share of Suzuki and Kawasaki rivals that of Honda, Harley's number-one competitor in the United States.

Strategic Plan for Sustainable Growth

Harley has moved assembly operation of its "Dyna Glide" family of motorcycles to its facility in Kansas City, Missouri, from York, Pennsylvania. Harley has also just built a new $145 million, 350,000 square-foot assembly plant in York on the site of its existing manufacturing facility. The president of the company feels that this new facility, coupled with the movement of production between the plants, will provide strong and flexible manufacturing capabilities. Harley also continues its focus on research and development with its 218,000 square-foot Product Development Center (PDC), which is currently in the process of being expanded with 165,000 additional square feet of space.

Harley plans to continue to increase its motorcycle production to be able to sustain its annual double-digit growth rate for units shipped. Harley produced and sold 263,653 Harley-Davidson motorcycles in 2002, up 12.4 percent from the 244,386 shipped in 2001. As recently as 1999, the company had envisioned reaching an annual production target of 200,000, but not until the year 2003. Harley may have underestimated the growth in the demand for its bikes, the growth in the worldwide heavyweight market, and its ability to increase production.

The Buell division sold 10,943 motorcycles in 2002, up from the 9,925 units shipped in 2001. This was due to the growth in sales of the new Buell Blast.

The Future

Domestically, Harley has the kind of name recognition and brand loyalty that is the envy of the industry. Could it ever develop a similar customer relationship abroad? Recognizing that part of the Harley image was built on tradition, how can Harley stay true to the things (and people) that helped to make it what it is and still grow as it has in the past few years?

Prepare a three-year strategic plan for Harley-Davidson. Address the specific issues of international growth opportunities in European countries as well as

EXHIBIT 1

Harley-Davidson, Inc. (HDI)—Income Statement

IN MILLIONS OF U.S. DOLLARS (EXCEPT FOR PER SHARE ITEMS)	12 MONTHS ENDING 12/31/03	12 MONTHS ENDING 12/31/02	12 MONTHS ENDING 12/31/01
Revenue	$4,624.30	4,091.00	3,406.80
Other Revenue	279.5	211.5	181.5
Total Revenue	**3,903.70**	**4,302.50**	**3,588.30**
Cost of Revenue	3,070.30	2,780.40	2,374.10
Gross Profit	**1,554.00**	**1,310.60**	**1,032.70**
Selling/General/Administrative Expenses	684.2	639.4	551.7
Research & Development	—	—	—
Depreciation/Amortization	—	—	—
Interest Expense (Income), Net Operating	—	—	—
Unusual Expense (Income)	—	—	—
Other Operating Expenses	—	—	—
Total Operating Expense	**3,754.50**	**3,419.80**	**2,925.80**
Operating Income	**1,149.30**	**882.7**	**662.5**
Interest Expense, Net Non-Operating	—	—	—
Interest/Investment Income, Non-Operating	—	—	—
Interest Income (Expense), Net Non-Operating	23.1	16.5	17.5
Gain (Loss) on Sale of Assets	—		0
Other, Net			
Income Before Tax	**1,166.00**	**885.8**	**673.5**
Income Tax	405.1	305.6	235.7
Income After Tax	**760.9**	**580.2**	**437.7**
Minority Interest	—	—	—
Equity In Affiliates	—	—	—
Net Income Before Extra. Items	**760.9**	**580.2**	**437.7**
Accounting Change	—	—	—
Discontinued Operations	—	—	—
Extraordinary Items	—	—	—
Net Income	**$760.9**	**580.2**	**437.7**
Preferred Dividends	—	—	—
Income Available to Common Excl. Extra. Items	**760.9**	**580.2**	**437.7**
Income Available to Common Incl. Extra. Items	**760.9**	**580.2**	**437.7**
Basic/Primary Weighted Average Shares	302.3	302.3	302.5
Basic/Primary EPS Excl. Extra. Items	**2.517**	**1.919**	**1.447**
Basic/Primary EPS Incl. Extra. Items	**2.517**	**1.919**	**1.447**
Dilution Adjustment	0	0	0
Diluted Weighted Average Shares	304.5	305.2	306.2
Diluted EPS Excl. Extra. Items	**2.499**	**1.901**	**1.429**
Diluted EPS Incl. Extra. Items	**2.499**	**1.901**	**1.429**
Dividends per Share—Common Stock	—	0.14	0.12
Gross Dividends—Common Stock	—	41.5	35.4
Stock Based Compensation	—	12.2	11.8

Source: www.investor.stockpoint.com.

EXHIBIT 2
Harley-Davidson, Inc. (HDI)—Balance Sheet

INDUSTRY: RECREATIONAL PRODUCTS
SECTOR: CONSUMER CYCLICAL

IN MILLIONS OF U.S. DOLLARS (EXCEPT FOR PER SHARE ITEMS)	AS OF 12/31/03	AS OF 12/31/02	AS OF 12/31/01
Cash & Equivalents	$ 812.4	280.9	439.4
Short Term Investments	510.2	514.8	196.0
Cash and Short Term Investments	1,322.70	795.7	635.4
Trade Accounts Receivable, Net	112.4	108.7	118.8
Other Receivables	1,002.00	855.8	656.4
Total Receivables, Net	1,114.40	964.5	775.3
Total Inventory	207.7	218.2	181.1
Prepaid Expenses	84.3	46.8	34.4
Other Current Assets	—	41.4	39.0
Total Current Assets	**2,729.10**	**2,066.60**	**1,665.30**
Property/Plant/Equipment—Gross	—	—	—
Accumulated Depreciation	—		
Property/Plant/Equipment, Net	—	1,032.60	891.8
Goodwill, Net	—	49.9	49.7
Intangibles, Net	—	—	—
Long Term Investments	—	—	—
Other Long Term Assets	2,194.00	712.1	511.7
Total Assets	**$4,923.10**	**3,861.20**	**3,118.50**
Accounts Payable	631.5	227.0	194.7
Accrued Expenses	—	380.5	304.4
Notes Payable/Short Term Debt	—	—	—
Current Port. LT Debt/Capital Leases	324.3	382.6	217.1
Other Current Liabilities	—	—	—
Total Current Liabilities	**955.8**	**990.1**	**716.1**
Long Term Debt	670	380	380
Capital Lease Obligations	—	—	—
Total Long Term Debt	**670**	**380**	**380**
Total Debt	994.3	762.6	597.1
Deferred Income Tax	—	29.5	17.8
Minority Interest	—	—	—
Other Liabilities	339.6	228.8	248.3
Total Liabilities	**$1,965.40**	**1,628.30**	**1,362.20**
Redeemable Preferred Stock	—	—	—
Preferred Stock—Non Redeemable, Net	—	—	—
Common Stock	—	3.3	3.2
Additional Earnings (Accum. Deficit)	—	386.3	359.2
Treasury Stock—Common	—		
Other Equity	2,957.70	2,372.10	1,833.20
Total Equity	**2,957.70**	**2,232.90**	**1,756.30**
Total Liability & Shareholders' Equity	**$4,923.10**	**3,861.20**	**3,118.50**
Shares Outs.—Common Stock	302.2	302.7	302.8
Total Common Shares Outstanding	**302.2**	**302.7**	**302.8**
Total Preferred Stock Shares Outs.	**—**	**—**	**—**
Employees (actual figures)	—	9,100.00	8,650.00
Number of Common Shareholders (actual figures)	—	85,475.00	76,935.00

Source: www.investor.stockpoint.com.

domestic competitive threats from Honda and the new alliance of Suzuki and Kawasaki. Examine the strengths of the Harley-Davidson brand along with the continuing weakness of ongoing capacity constraints. Imagine you are chairman and CEO Jeffery L. Bleustein and have the task of leading this company as it prepares to meet the growing demand for its motorcycles in the coming years. What specific actions would you take? Should your recommendations be financed with debt or equity? Develop projected financial statements to assess the impact of your changes.

25 Winnebago Industries—2004

Eugene M. Bland
Texas A&M—Corpus Christi
John G. Marcis
Coastal Carolina University

WGO

www.winnebagoind.com

Saving money is nice, but it is not the real reason that people travel in a motor home. Motor homing is just plain fun. Motor homers are an adventurous lot—they like to go, see, and do. Florida residents have replaced Californians as the most active motor home campers. New Yorkers are third on the "most on the go" list. Recreational vehicle (RV) owners say that they not only save money when camping but can avoid the bother of having to stop for restaurants and bathrooms.

Motor home traveling is purported to be much less expensive than traveling by car or plane and staying in a motel. Motor homers stop when there is something to see and do. They often spend summers where it is cool and winters where it is warm. In fact, industry advertisements tout the RV lifestyle with the slogan "Wherever you go, you're always at home."

Winnebago Industries is a leading manufacturer of motor homes. The company builds quality products with state-of-the-art, computer-aided design and manufacturing systems on automotive-style assembly lines. Although Winnebago competes with Fleetwood and Coachman, the name "Winnebago" is considered synonymous with the term "motor home."

Company revenues for the fiscal year ended August 30, 2003, increased to a record $842.2 million (52 weeks) from $825.3 million in 2002 (53 weeks). Motor home shipments (Class A and C) during the 52-week fiscal 2003 were 10,726 units, a decrease of 328 units from the 53-week fiscal 2002 shipment of 11,054. For the first eight calendar months of 2003, the firm's market share of Class A and Class C motor homes market decreased from 21.0 percent to 19.2 percent for the same period as 2002.

Winnebago was founded in 1958 and has always been headquartered in Forest City, Iowa (641–582–3535). The company's common stock is listed on the New York, Chicago, and Pacific Stock Exchanges and traded under the symbol WGO. Options for the Winnebago's common stock are traded on the Chicago Board Options Exchange. Winnebago's homepage can be accessed at **www.winnebagoind.com** and corporate press releases are available at **www.prnewswire.com**.

Winnebago Industries is financially stable: the firm owns its land, buildings, and equipment, and has no long-term debt; it has an enviable cash and marketable securities balance of $99,381,000 fiscal year-end August 2003. This provides the company with the opportunity for future long-term growth. In 1998, the Board of Directors approved a general plan to repurchase outstanding shares of the firm's stock. The repurchase initiatives in 1998 and 1999 resulted in 13.1 percent of the outstanding shares of Winnebago's stock being repurchased by the firm. In 2003, the board authorized the eighth repurchase initiative of an additional $20 million worth of stock. In fiscal 2003, the company repurchased nearly 676,200 shares. Further, the board authorized the doubling of the cash dividend for fiscal 2004. Winnebago Industries will now pay a $.10 per-share quarterly dividend, instead of a semiannual dividend. The company is devoted to focusing resources on building RVs, increasing its share of the RV market, and enhancing profitability.

In April 2003, the company announced the sale of its dealer financing receivables in the Winnebago Acceptance Corporation (WAC) to GE Commercial Distribution Finance Corporation for nearly $34 million. Bruce Hertzke, chairman, CEO, and president, said, "We welcome GE Commercial Distribution Finance Corporation's continued commitment to the RV industry. The sale of the WAC receivables will allow Winnebago Industries to focus on what we do best, the production of high quality motor homes."

Early Motor Homing

The first motor home was built in 1915 to take people from the Atlantic Coast to San Francisco. It had wooden wheels and hard rubber tires. It was promoted as having all the comforts of an ocean cruiser. By the 1920s, the house car had become a fixture in the United States and a symbol of freedom. All kinds of house cars could be seen traveling across America's dirt roads. They ranged from what looked like large moving cigars to two-story houses with porches, on wheels. But these house cars featured poor weight distribution, poor insulation, and poor economy. From the 1930s to the 1950s they gave way in popularity to the trailer.

In the mid-1950s motor homes were called motorized trailers. They were overweight, underpowered, and poorly insulated, but they were still a vast improvement over the house cars of the 1920s. In the 1960s motor homing became much more popular, largely as a result of the innovations of Winnebago. From Forest City, Iowa, where the company was founded in 1958, Winnebago set the pace for new development of motor homes. The Winnebago name became a household word. Buyers of motor homes were asked, "When will your Winnebago be delivered?"

Corporate Profile

Corporate Mission Statement

Winnebago's motto is "Quality is a Journey—Not a Destination." From the beginning, the company recognized the critical roles played by employees, customers, and dealers in the total quality process. Winnebago Industries' commitment to quality is illustrated by its Mission Statement, Statement of Values, and its Statement of Guiding Principles (provided in Exhibit 1).

Production Facilities

Winnebago has major production facilities in Forest City, Iowa. Currently, over 20 buildings at this location comprise over 2 million square feet (approximately 60 acres under roof) and contain the company's manufacturing, maintenance, and service operations. There are also satellite-manufacturing facilities at Hampton and Lorimor, Iowa. These two facilities add another 700,000 square feet of manufacturing space. All corporate facilities in Forest City are located on approximately 784 acres of land owned by Winnebago. In March 2003, the newest production facility in Charles City, Iowa, began operation. This $12.5 million, 204,000 square-foot facility increases

EXHIBIT 1

Winnebago Industries, Inc. Mission Statement

MISSION STATEMENT

Winnebago Industries, Inc. is a leading manufacturer of recreation vehicles (RVs) and related products and services. Our mission is to continually improve our products and services to meet or exceed the expectations of our customers. We emphasize employee teamwork and involvement in identifying and implementing programs to save time and lower production costs while maintaining the highest quality values. These strategies allow us to prosper as a business with a high degree of integrity and to provide a reasonable return for our shareholders, the ultimate owners of our business.

VALUES

How we accomplish our mission is as important as the mission itself. Fundamental to the success of the Company are these basic values we describe as the four P's:

People—Our employees are the source of our vast strength. They provide our corporate intelligence and determine our reputation and vitality. Involvement and teamwork are our core human values.

Products—Our products are the end result of our team's efforts, and they should be the best in meeting or exceeding our customers' expectations worldwide. As our products are viewed, so are we viewed.

Plant—The Company believes its plant is the most technologically advanced in the RV industry. We continue to review facility improvements that will increase the utilization of our plant capacity and enable us to build the best quality product for the investment.

Profitability—Profitability is the ultimate measure of how efficiently we provide our customers with the best products for their needs. Profitability is required to survive and grow. As our respect and position within the marketplace grows, so will our profit.

GUIDING PRINCIPLES

Quality comes first—To achieve customer satisfaction, [we must make] the quality of our products and services . . . be our number one priority.

Customers are central to our existence—Our work must be done with our customers in mind, providing products and services that meet or exceed the expectations of our customers. We must not only satisfy our customers, we must also surprise and delight them.

Continuous improvement is essential to our success—We must strive for excellence in everything we do: in our products, in their safety and value, as well as in our services, our human relations, our competitiveness, and our profitability.

Employee involvement is our way of life—We are a team. We must treat each other with trust and respect.

Dealers and suppliers are our partners—The Company must maintain mutually beneficial relationships with dealers, suppliers, and our other business associates.

Integrity is never compromised—The Company must pursue conduct in a manner that is socially responsible and that commands respect for its integrity and for its positive contributions to society. Our doors are open to all men and women alike without discrimination and without regard to ethnic origin or personal beliefs.

Source: Winnebago Industries, 1999 *Annuual Report*, p. 21.

the manufacturing capacity of the firm by nearly 30 percent. By October 2003, this facility was producing over 50 Class C motor homes per week. The goal is to increase production of Class C motor homes in Charles City and allow the Forest City plant to specialize in the production of Class A motor homes.

Winnebago has three 900-foot assembly lines for final assembly of motor homes. Statistical process control is practiced at Winnebago and has enhanced the quality of its van products. As a motor home moves down the assembly line, quality control is carefully monitored. Units are taken randomly from the line for a thorough examination. The performance of every RV is tested before it is delivered to a dealer's lot. The company makes sure that all of its motor home components meet or exceed federal and durability standards. Some of the tests routinely performed include lamination strength, appliance performance, chip resistance, vibration, drop, salt spray, and crash tests.

Research and Development

Winnebago uses computer technology to design its motor homes. The company has a state-of-the-art, computer-aided design/computer-aided manufacturing (CAD/CAM) system. This system aids in producing low-cost sheet metal parts, new paint lines for steel and aluminum parts, and modifications of assembly equipment.

One of Winnebago's product-testing facilities at Forest City houses some of the most sophisticated technology being used in the RV industry (such as high- and low-temperature chambers for subjecting parts to extreme temperatures and high stress).

Product Line

In 2004, Winnebago Industries expanded its offerings to 78 different floor plans. One-third of these models are either new or redesigned for the 2004 model year. Winnebago manufactures two principle kinds of recreational vehicles as indicated in Exhibit 2: Class A Motor Homes and Class C Motor Homes (Mini). Class A motor homes are constructed on a chassis that already has the engine and drive components. They range in length from 23 to 37 feet and can sell for over $250,000. Class A motor homes include the Winnebago Adventurer, Brave, Chieftain, and Journey; and Itasca Suncruiser, Sunrise, Sunflyer, and Horizon; and Ultimate Advantage and Freedom as indicated in Exhibit 3. Although the Winnebago Adventurer and Itasca Suncruiser are popular, the Winnebago Brave and Itasca Sunrise models are the company's top-selling vehicles. Motor home shipments (Class A and C) during the 52-week fiscal 2003 were 10,726 units, a decrease of 328 units from the 53-week fiscal 2002 shipment

EXHIBIT 2
Motor Home Product Classification

CLASS A MOTOR HOMES
These are conventional motor homes constructed directly on medium-duty truck chassis which include the engine and drive train components. The living area of the driver's compartment is designed and produced by Winnebago Industries. Class A motor homes from Winnebago Industries include Winnebago Brave, Adventurer, Chieftain, and Journey; Itasca Sunrise, Suncruiser, Sunflyer, and Horizon; and Ultimate Advantage and Freedom.

CLASS B VAN CAMPERS
These are panel-type trucks to which sleeping, kitchen, and toilet facilities are added. These models also have a top extension to provide more headroom. Winnebago Industries converts the EuroVan Camper, which is distributed by Volkswagen of America and Volkswagen of Canada.

CLASS C MOTOR HOMES (MINI)
These are minimotor homes built on a van-type chassis onto which Winnebago Industries constructs a living area with access to the driver's compartment. Class C motor homes from Winnebago industries include Winnebago Minnie and Minnie Winnie; Itasca Spirit and Sundancer; and Rialta.

Source: Winnebago Industries, 2001 *Annual Report*, p. 16.

EXHIBIT 3

Winnebago Industries, Inc., Unit Sales of Recreation Vehicles

YEAR ENDED	AUGUST 30, 2003	AUGUST 31, 2002	AUGUST 25, 2001	AUGUST 26, 2000	AUGUST 28, 1999
Class A	6,705	6,725	5,666	6,819	6,054
Class C	4,021	4,329	3,410	3,697	4,222
Total	10,726	11,054	9,076	10,516	10,276

Source: 2002 *Annual Report* and 2003 *Fourth Quarter Report.*

of 11,054. Market share decreased from 21 percent in 2002 to 19.2 percent in 2003. However, the 2003 market share is higher than the 18.8 percent share reported in 2001 and the 17 percent share of the year 2000 Class A and C motor home market. As of August 30, 2003, back orders for Class A and Class C motor homes was 2,632 units (compared to the abnormally high 3,248 in August of 2002).

Class C motor homes are constructed on a van chassis; the driver's compartment is accessible to the living area. These motor homes are compact and easy to drive. They range from 21 to 29 feet in length and have 5 popular floor plans. Typical options of a Class C vehicle include 6 feet of headroom, shower, stove, sink, refrigerator, and 2 double beds. Winnebago's Minnie and Minnie Winnie are among the most popular Class C motor homes in the country. The company's Itasca Sundancer and Itasca Spirit also are popular.

Marketing

Consumer research reveals that demographics for motor home buyers are undergoing change. Traditionally, buyers have been "woofies" (representing "well-off older folks" and defined as people over 50 years of age with discretionary income available) with time to enjoy leisure travel and outdoor recreation. According to research, an individual in the United States is turning 50 every 7.5 seconds, contributing an additional 350,000 people per *month* to that prime target market. Available demographic information indicates that this trend will continue for the next 30 years. Additionally, a 2001 University of Michigan "RV Consumer Demographic Study" found that the age of interested consumers has been expanding to include younger buyers as well.

The peak selling season for RVs has historically been spring and summer. Class A and Class C motor homes are marketed under the Winnebago and Itasca brand names and are sold through a network of approximately 250 unique dealers in 2003 in the United States and, to a limited extent, in Canada and other foreign countries. At Winnebago, the trend is toward a smaller number of dealers who have larger market areas. These fewer, but larger dealers are expected to offer more services to customers and should be better able to provide customer support after the sale.

Winnebago Industries believes it has the most comprehensive service program in the RV industry. With the purchase of any new Class A or Class C motor home (except the Rialta, which has a 24-month/24,000-mile warranty), Winnebago offers a comprehensive 12-month/15,000-mile warranty, a 3-year/36,000-mile warranty on sidewalls and slideout room assemblies, and a 10-year fiberglass roof warranty. Winnebago also instituted a "toll-free hotline" where experienced service advisors respond to inquiries from prospective customers and expedite and resolve warranty issues. Every owner of a new Winnebago motor home receives free roadside assistance for 12 months.

Recent Years

Winnebago celebrated its 45th anniversary in 2003 with a record year for revenues. Revenues reached $845.21 million for the fiscal year (compared with $ 825.3 million for the 2002 fiscal year). Income from continuing operations for the year was down 7.8 percent from the previous fiscal year to $49.9 million from $52.9 million. By the end of fiscal year 2003, with interest rates rebounding from 45-year lows, Winnebago had a sales order backlog of over 2,600 units, down from the abnormally high 3,248 unit backlog a year earlier.

Winnebago's fortunes were mixed in 2003. The year started with sales at a record pace. However, uncertainty about the war with Iraq, declining consumer confidence in the economy, rebounds from record low interest rates, and increases in gas prices caused sales to decline at the end of the fiscal year. Production for the 52-week 2003 period was down 328 units (3 percent) from the 53-week 2002 period. Higher unit manufacturing costs resulting from lower volume, start up costs associated with the Charles City facility, and higher discounts hurt profits. In an attempt to sell the existing inventory, manufacturers and dealers started to offer sales incentives, which put pressure on operating margins. By the end of the fourth quarter of fiscal 2003, and the start of the 2004 model year, however, wholesale and retail sales appeared to have normalized.

Winnebago's External Environment

Winnebago's motor homes can attract a low-frills buyer desiring the most stripped-down RV, the person with expensive tastes desiring the ultimate in RV luxury, and everyone in between. RVs can be purchased or rented. Many families unable to buy a mobile home rent one to take on vacation. As the baby boomers age and approach retirement, many of them will consider selling their primary residence, purchasing and moving into a motor home, and traveling to any point they desire in North America.

The motel and hotel industries have been experiencing an oversupply of available rooms, which has resulted in low rates for rooms. Compared to the cost of owning/renting and operating an RV, the costs of staying in a motor home versus a motel are about the same if not a bit lower in favor of the motel. Motor home sales historically increase whenever travel, tourism, and vacationing gain in popularity. The converse is also true.

There are about 122,000 camp sites in U.S. state parks, including 4,500 maintained by the U.S. Forest Service and 100 in the National Parks System. In addition, there are more than 15,000 private campgrounds and over 1,620 county parks. Winnebagos can access nearly all of these sites. However, the economic uncertainly introduced since the terrorist attacks of September 11, 2001, and the continued "War on Terror" have served to cloud the fiscal picture of leisure-related activities like RVing.

In August 2001, Winnebago Industries and its retirement plans were served with a lawsuit alleging 23 separate causes of action including breach of fiduciary duty, unjust enrichment, violation of ERISA vesting provisions, and violations of ERISA funding requirements. The case is set for trial in June of 2004, but so far, the case has not been certified as a class-action suit. The company has accrued legal fees, but since the risk of an adverse verdict or the amount of any potential exposure are not known, no other expenses have accrued.

In 2003, interest rates reached their lowest levels in 40 years. This low interest rate environment reduces the cost of financing the purchase of an RV and likely will increase firm and industry sales. However, Winnebago Industries has no long-term debt. While this financial structure all but eliminates the company's default risk, it also means that the firm is foregoing the benefit that the tax deductibility of interest payments provide. The lack of long-term debt, and resultant reliance on equity financing, raises the company's weighted average cost of capital. Many other industrial firms have used this low interest rate period to refinance existing debt and even to issue new debt.

Major Competitors

Company (Stock Symbol)	Headquarters Location
Coachman Industries, Inc. (COA)	Elkhart, IN
Fleetwood Enterprises, Inc. (FLE)	Riverside, CA
Monaco Coach Corp. (MNC)	Junction City, OR
Thor Industries, Inc. (THO)	Jackson, OH

Major changes occurred among the larger firms in the RV industry in 2002 and 2003. Coachman Industries, a producer of both RVs and modular housing, in 2003 announced that it would establish a finance division that would provide exclusive financing services to its RV dealers and that there was strong dealer response to COA's new RV product line. Fleetwood Enterprises produces motor homes and travel trailers, as well as manufactured housing. Throughout the 1990s, Fleetwood was the largest firm in the RV industry in terms of sales. Historically, Monaco Coach Corporation specialized in the production of premium RVs, producing bus-sized, diesel-fueled RVs ranging in price from $100,000 to $1.1 million. However, in 2000–2001, Monaco started to diversify into the smaller Class C motor home market. As a result, Monaco had a substantial rate of growth for the period 1993 to 2002. Thor Industries emerged in 2002–2003 as a major firm in the RV industry. In 2002, Thor acquired Keystone RV Company and in July 2003, Thor completed the acquisition of Damon Corporation, a privately held manufacturer of motor homes with annual sales of approximately $200 million, for $46 million in cash. With these recent acquisitions, it is possible that Thor will consolidate some production facilities and emerge as a very lean, competitive firm in the RV industry. Thor, like Winnebago, has issued no long-term debt.

Industry Outlook

Calendar years 2002 and 2003 were lackluster ones for the RV industry. During the first six months of 2002, the national economy suffered from faltering consumer confidence in the aftermath of the terrorist attacks of September 11, 2001, and from a weak national economy. In the first half of 2003, uncertainty regarding the conflict in Iraq led to declining consumer confidence, and higher fuel prices depressed RV sales. Moreover, like auto manufacturers, RV manufacturers started to offer sales incentives to reduce the existing inventory and this reduced operating profit margins. The RV industry saw a modest expansion in unit sales in the last six months of 2003 as gasoline prices fell and interest rates reached multi-decade lows.

Regarding the long-term prospects for the RV industry, the size of the 55-to-64 age group is expected to increase by approximately 45 percent over the next decade (as compared with an overall population growth rate of about 8 percent) and this portends increased sales growth of RVs into the next decade. Industry sales should also be positively influenced by the factors that increase the wealth and incomes of this group. Continued low financing rates, low fuel prices, tax cuts on capital gains and dividends, healthcare reform, and the growth of the national economy and the

EXHIBIT 4
Winnebago Industries Inc. (WGO)

ANNUAL INCOME STATEMENT IN MILLIONS OF U.S. DOLLARS (EXCEPT FOR PER SHARE ITEMS)	52 WEEKS ENDING 8/30/03	53 WEEKS ENDING 8/31/02	52 WEEKS ENDING 8/25/01
Revenue	$845.2	825.3	671.7
Other Revenue	—	—	—
Total Revenue	**845.2**	**825.3**	**671.7**
Cost of Revenue	731.8	708.9	588.6
Gross Profit	**113.4**	**116.4**	**83.1**
Selling/General/Administrative Expenses	36.1	38.3	31.8
Research & Development	—	—	—
Depreciation/Amortization	—	—	—
Interest Expense (Income), Net Operating	—	—	—
Unusual Expense (Income)	—	—	—
Other Operating Expenses	—	—	—
Total Operating Expense	**767.9**	**747.2**	**620.3**
Operating Income	**77.3**	**78.1**	**51.4**
Interest Expense, Net Non-Operating	—	—	—
Interest/Investment Income, Non-Operating	—	—	—
Interest Income (Expense), Net Non-Operating	1.4	3.3	4.4
Gain (Loss) on Sale of Assets	—	—	—
Other, Net	—	—	—
Income Before Tax	**78.7**	**81.3**	**55.8**
Income Tax	30.0	28.4	14.3
Income After Tax	**48.7**	**52.9**	**41.5**
Minority Interest	—	—	—
Equity In Affiliates	—	—	—
Net Income Before Extra. Items	**48.7**	**52.9**	**41.5**
Accounting Change	—	—	—
Discontinued Operations	1.2	1.8	2.3
Extraordinary Item	—	—	—
Net Income	**$49.9**	**54.7**	**42.7**
Preferred Dividends	—	—	—
Income Available to Common Excl. Extra. Items	**48.7**	**52.9**	**41.5**
Income Available to Common Incl. Extra. Items	**49.9**	**54.7**	**42.7**
Basic/Primary Weighted Average Shares	18.5	19.9	20.7
Basic/Primary EPS Excl. Extra. Items	**2.636**	**2.651**	**2.001**
Basic/Primary EPS Incl. Extra. Items	**2.698**	**2.741**	**2.06**
Dilution Adjustment	—	—	0
Diluted Weighted Average Shares	18.8	20.4	21
Diluted EPS Excl. Extra. Items	**2.59**	**2.595**	**1.972**
Diluted EPS Incl. Extra. Items	**2.651**	**2.682**	**2.03**
Dividends per Share—Common Stock	0.2	0.2	0.2
Gross Dividends—Common Stock	3.7	4.0	4.1
Stock Based Compensation	2	1.8	1.7

EXHIBIT 5

Winnebago Industries Inc. (WGO)

ANNUAL BALANCE SHEET IN MILLIONS OF U.S. DOLLARS (EXCEPT FOR PER SHARE ITEMS)	AS OF 8/30/03	AS OF 8/31/02	AS OF 8/25/01
Cash & Equivalents	$ 99.4	42.2	102.3
Short Term Investments	—	—	—
Cash and Short Term Investments	99.4	42.2	102.3
Trade Accounts Receivable, Net	30.9	28.4	61.8
Other Receivables	—	—	—
Total Receivables, Net	30.9	28.4	61.8
Total Inventory	114.3	113.7	79.8
Prepaid Expenses	4.8	4.3	3.6
Other Current Assets	7.9	4.5	6.7
Total Current Assets	**257.3**	**233.6**	**254.3**
Property/Plant/Equipment—Gross	—	—	—
Accumulated Depreciation			
Property/Plant/Equipment, Net	63.3	48.9	46.5
Goodwill, Net	—	—	—
Intangibles, Net	—	—	—
Long Term Investments	22.8	23.5	22.2
Other Long Term Assets	34.1	31.1	28.9
Total Assets	**$377.5**	**337.1**	**351.9**
Accounts Payable	52.2	44.2	40.7
Accrued Expenses	40.2	41.8	34.4
Notes Payable/Short Term Debt	—	—	—
Current Port. LT Debt/Capital Leases	—	—	—
Other Current Liabilities	0	2.6	4.9
Total Current Liabilities	**92.4**	**88.6**	**80.0**
Long Term Debt	—	—	—
Capital Lease Obligations	—	—	—
Total Long Term Debt	—	—	—
Total Debt	—	—	—
Deferred Income Tax	—	—	—
Minority Interest	—	—	—
Other Liabilities	74.4	68.7	64.5
Total Liabilities	**$166.8**	**157.3**	**144.5**
Redeemable Preferred Stock	—	—	—
Preferred Stock—Non Redeemable, Net	—	—	—
Common Stock	12.9	12.9	12.9
Additional Paid-In Capital	26.0	25.7	22.3
Retained Earnings (Accum. Deficit)	331.0	284.9	234.1
Treasury Stock—Common			
Other Equity	—	—	—
Total Equity	**210.6**	**179.8**	**207.5**
Total Liability & Shareholders' Equity	**$377.5**	**337.1**	**351.9**
Shares Outs.—Common Stock	18.2	18.7	20.8
Total Common Shares Outstanding	**18.2**	**18.7**	**20.8**
Total Preferred Stock Shares Outs.	—	—	—
Employees (actual figures)	3,750.00	3,685.00	3,325.00
Number of Common Shareholders (actual figures)	4,565.00	4,922.00	5,513.00

return on the stock market positively impact the wealth and disposable incomes of this group, and will influence the strength of this industry.

Conclusion

Let's say you just took a management job with Winnebago and your first assignment is to prepare a three-year strategic plan for the company. Devise a plan based on what you know about Winnebago Industries. Actually, this request is quite common as part of the management development program in many large firms. Winnebago currently does no business outside the U.S. Do you think they should?

26 Avon Products, Inc.—2004

James W. Camerius
Northern Michigan University

AVP

www.avon.com

On Tuesday May 20, 2003, Andrea Jung, Chairman of the Board and Chief Executive Officer of Avon Products, Inc., arrived at her New York office early to reflect on the company's progress under her leadership during the past three years. Andrea Jung assumed the position of president and CEO of Avon Products in 1999 at the age of 41, becoming the first woman to lead Avon and one of the few *Fortune* 500 women CEOs. On September 6, 2001, she also assumed the additional post of chairman of the Board of Directors.

Avon enjoys a global reputation stemming largely from its formidable world-wide network of independent sales agents. But the effectiveness of the sales force has waned in recent years as the company grapples with how best to sell cosmetics, jewelry, and apparel to an increasingly sophisticated customer, and how to compete against other mass merchandisers. Balance sheet and income statement data for Avon are shown in Exhibits 1 and 2. For 2003, Avon's revenues increased 10 percent to $6.88 billion while net income increased 24 percent to $664.8. As of February 2004, Avon had 45,000 employees.

Avon Products

Avon is the world's largest direct-selling organization and merchandiser of beauty and beauty-related products. From corporate offices in New York City, Avon markets product lines to women in 143 countries through 3.9 million independent sales representatives who sell primarily on a door-to-door or direct-selling basis. Avon's product line includes skin care items, makeup, fragrances for men and women, and toiletries for bath, hair care, personal care, hand and body care, and sun care. It also includes an extensive line of fashion jewelry, apparel, gifts, and collectibles. Recognizable brand names such as Anew, Skin-So-Soft, Avon Color, Advance Techniques Hair Care, and Avon Wellness are featured. There are approximately 600 items in the product line. Globally, the company's product line is marketed primarily at moderate price points. The marketing strategy emphasizes department store quality at discount store prices. Global marketing efforts resulted in a number of highly successful global "power" brands in the areas of cosmetics, skin care, and fragrance (i.e., products such as Anew, Avon Color, Avon Solutions, Skin-So-Soft, Avon Naturals, and the new global product called mark™).

Avon is also the world's largest manufacturer and distributor of fashion jewelry, and it markets an extensive line of gifts and collectibles. The product line also includes watches, shoes, purses, CDs, videos, toys, and a wide array of other products from around the world. The major categories and subcategories of products are

EXHIBIT 1

Consolidated Balance Sheets

AVON PRODUCTS, INC.
(IN MILLIONS, EXCEPT SHARE DATA)

DECEMBER 31	2002	2001
Assets		
Current assets		
Cash, including cash equivalents of $413.8 and $45.1	$ 606.8	$ 508.5
Accounts receivable (less allowance for doubtful accounts of $49.5 and $45.1)	555.4	519.5
Inventories	614.7	612.5
Prepaid expenses and other	271.3	244.6
Total current assets	2,048.2	1,885.1
Property, plant and equipment, at cost		
Land	51.5	49.4
Buildings and improvements	694.4	664.0
Equipment	802.5	836.0
	1,548.4	1,549.4
Less accumulated depreciation	779.3	777.7
	769.1	771.7
Other assets	510.2	524.2
Total assets	$3,327.5	$3,181.0
Liabilities and Shareholders' (Deficit) Equity		
Current liabilities		
Debt maturing within one year	$605.2	$88.8
Accounts payable	379.9	404.1
Accrued compensation	175.7	145.2
Other accrued liabilities	336.6	338.2
Sales and taxes other than income	125.1	108.8
Income taxes	353.0	371.9
Total current liabilities	1,975.5	1,457.0
Long-term debt	767.0	1,236.3
Employee benefit plans	560.4	436.6
Deferred income taxes	35.4	23.0
Other liabilities (including minority interest of $37.0 and $29.0)	116.9	103.2
Commitments and Contingencies		
Shareholders' (deficit) equity		
Common stock, par value $.25—authorized: 800,000,000 shares; issued 358,382,162 and 356,312,680 shares	89.6	89.1
Additional paid-in capital	1,019.5	983.0
Retained earnings	1,735.3	1,389.4
Accumulated other comprehensive loss	(791.4)	(489.5)
Treasury stock, at cost—123,124,530 and 119,631,574 shares	(2,180.7)	(2,002.1)
Total shareholders' (deficit) equity	(127.7)	(75.1)
Total liabilities and shareholders' (deficit) equity	$3,327.5	$3,181.0

Source: Avon's 2002 *Annual Report*, p. 45.

EXHIBIT 2

Consolidated Statements of Income

AVON PRODUCTS, INC.—2002
(IN MILLIONS, EXCEPT PER-SHARE DATA)

YEARS ENDED DECEMBER 31	2002	2001	2000
Net sales	$6,170.6	$5,957.8	$5,681.7
Other revenue	57.7	42.5	40.9
Total revenue	6,228.3	6,000.3	5,722.6
Costs, expenses and other:			
Cost of sales*	2,344.4	2,268.4	2,171.3
Marketing, distribution and administrative expenses	2,979.6	2,889.5	2,761.4
Contract settlement gain, net of related expenses	—	(25.9)	—
Special charges, net	34.3	94.9	—
Operating profit	870.0	773.4	789.9
Interest expense	52.0	71.1	84.7
Interest income	(15.2)	(14.1)	(8.5)
Other expense, net	(2.4)	27.0	21.5
Total other expenses	34.4	83.7	97.7
Income from continuing operations before taxes, minority interest and cumulative effect of accounting changes	835.6	689.7	692.2
Income taxes	292.3	240.3	202.2
Income before minority interest and cumulative effect of accounting changes	543.3	449.4	490.0
Minority interest	(8.7)	(4.5)	(4.2)
Income from continuing operations before cumulative effect of accounting changes	534.6	444.9	485.8
Cumulative effect of accounting changes, net of tax	—	(0.3)	(6.7)
Net income	$ 534.6	$ 444.6	$ 479.1
Basic earnings per share:			
Continuing operations	$ 2.26	$ 1.88	$ 2.04
Cumulative effect of accounting changes	—	—	(.03)
	$ 2.26	$ 1.88	$ 2.01
Diluted earnings per share:			
Continuing operations	$ 2.22	$ 1.85	$ 2.02
Cumulative effect of accounting changes	—	—	(.03)
	$ 2.22	$ 1.85	$ 1.99
Weighted-average shares outstanding			
Basic	236.06	236.83	237.67
Diluted	245.47	246.05	242.95

*2002 and 2001 included amounts of $2.0 and $2.5, respectively, for inventory write-downs related to the special charges.

Source: Avon's 2002 *Annual Report*, p. 44.

shown in Exhibit 3. Consolidated net sales by classes of principal products for the years ended December 31, 2002, 2001, and 2000 are shown in Exhibit 4.

History

In the late 1800s, David McConnell, a door-to-door book salesman, had an idea he believed would encourage women to buy his books. Following a common trade practice of the period, he gave prospective customers a gift of perfume to arouse their interest. Before long, he discovered that the perfume was more popular than the books. He

EXHIBIT 3
Avon Product Line

SKIN CARE PRODUCTS

Anew: Age management skin care
Avon Skin Care: Specific skin care concerns
Basics: Affordable, easy to use skin care
Clearskin: Acne-fighting products
Moisture Therapy: Dry-skin care products

MAKEUP

Avon Color: Basic global cosmetics brand
Beyond Color: Anti-aging line
Hydra Finish: Sheer and natural cosmetics
Perfect Wear: Transfer-proof, long-wearing products
Color Trend: Global, trendy, chic colors at low prices

HAIR CARE

Advance Techniques: Alternative hair-care products
Herbal Care: Natural global botanical products

FRAGRANCES

(includes one new product introduction each year)

BATH

Skin-So-Soft: Bath oil, bug repellent, and sunscreen
Naturals: Moisturizing cleansers
Aromatherapy: Candles, creams, lotions, bath products
Footworks: Foot care line
Avon Bubble Bath: In assorted fragrances
Milk Made: Vitamin enriched items for bath and body

JEWELRY & MORE

JEWELRY (fashion, classic, and seasonal)
APPAREL (watches, shoes, and purses)
GIFT LINE (collectibles, toys, and unique gifts)

Source: Company record.

formed a new firm, which he called the California Perfume Company. "I started in a space scarcely larger than an ordinary kitchen pantry," McConnell noted in 1900. "My ambition was to manufacture a line of goods superior to any other and take those goods through canvassing agents directly from the laboratory to the consumer." McConnell based his business upon several factors: (1) products sold directly to the consumer, (2) an image of the company that captured the beauty and excitement of the state of California, and (3) a national network of sales agents he had organized during his years as a bookseller.

In the early 1950s, the sales representatives' territories were reduced in size, a strategy that led to a quadrupling of the sales force and increased sales sixfold over the next twelve years. Avon advertisements appeared on television for the first time

EXHIBIT 4
Avon's Segment Financial Data

YEARS ENDED DECEMBER 31	2002 OPERATING		2001 OPERATING		2000 OPERATING	
	NET SALES	PROFIT (LOSS)	NET SALES	PROFIT (LOSS)	NET SALES	PROFIT (LOSS)
North America						
U.S.	$2,151.2	$ 424.7	$2,024.2	$ 373.4	$1,901.7	$ 343.5
U.S. Retail*	8.8	(25.9)	12.3	(25.9)	8.5	(4.5)
Other†	252.2	32.2	242.4	33.1	244.3	29.2
Total	2,412.2	431.0	2,278.9	380.6	2,154.5	368.2
International						
Latin America‡	1,700.1	378.8	1,898.5	427.5	1,839.9	415.5
Europe	1,228.6	212.4	1,008.5	167.0	884.2	129.5
Pacific	829.7	133.9	773.7	112.6	803.1	117.8
Total	3,758.4	725.1	3,680.7	707.1	3,527.2	662.8
Total from operations	6,170.6	1,156.1	5,959.6	1,087.7	5,681.7	1,031.0
Global expenses	—	(249.8)	(1.8)	(242.8)	—	(241.1)
Contact settlement gain, net of related expenses	—	—	—	25.9	—	—
Special charges, net§	—	(36.3)	—	(97.4)	—	—
Total	$6,170.6	$ 870.0	$5,957.8	$ 773.4	$5,681.7	$ 789.9

*Includes U.S. Retail and Avon Center.

†Includes Canada and Puerto Rico.

‡Avon's operations in Mexico reported net sales for 2002, 2001, and 2000 of $661.8, $619.7 and $554.8, respectively. Avon's operations in Mexico reported operating profit for 2002, 2001, and 2000 of $163.9, $154.8, and $136.0, respectively.

§ The 2002 and 2001 special charges of $36.3 and $97.4, respectively, were included in the Consolidated Statements of Income as special charges ($34.3 in 2002 and $94.9 in 2001) and as inventory write-downs in cost of sales ($2.0 in 2002 and $2.5 in 2001).

Source: Avon's 2002 *Annual Report,* p. 63.

during this period. The famous slogan "Ding Dong, Avon Calling" was first used in 1954. In 1960, total sales were $168.2 million, international sales were $11.3 million, and the company consisted of 6,800 employees and 125,000 sales representatives. Sales continued to grow dramatically throughout the 1960s. By 1969, total sales had grown to $676.7 million, international sales were $193.2 million, and the firm had 20,800 employees and over 400,000 sales representatives. Manufacturing plants, distribution centers, and sales branches were opened throughout the world as part of an expansion program.

In 2000, Avon increased its research and development budget 46 percent to get the newly developed "blockbuster" products to market faster. Normally, Avon spends at least three years developing new products, but Janice Teal, head of R&D, recalls Jung saying to her, "You've got two years. I need a breakthrough, and that's the goal." Avon's strategy also includes making the direct-selling system more relevant to the contemporary woman. This strategy meant providing more meaningful career opportunities as well as harnessing technology to make Avon more user-friendly for the sales representatives. "If Avon stops adding numbers of active representatives, the fuel and the lifeblood of the business slows down," Jung suggested. A new motivation and recruiting program was implemented as part of the strategic plan.

Competition

Competition in the direct-selling industry consists of a few large, well-established firms and many small organizations that sell about every product imaginable, including toys, cookware, animal food, collectibles, plant care products, clothing, computer software, and financial services. In addition to Avon, the dominant companies include Mary Kay (cosmetics), Amway (home maintenance products), Shaklee Corporation (vitamins and health foods), Encyclopedia Britannica (reference books and learning systems), Tupperware (plastic dishes and food containers), Electrolux (vacuum cleaners), and Fuller (brushes and household products). Avon is substantially larger in terms of sales representatives, sales volume, and resources than Mary Kay Cosmetics, Inc., its nearest competitor in direct sales.

Headquartered in Dallas, Texas, Mary Kay's product line includes more than 200 products in eight categories: facial skin care, color cosmetics, nail care, body care, sun protection, fragrances, men's skin care, and dietary supplements. Mary Kay is a privately held company whose wholesale sales for 2002 were approximately $1.6 billion. Since opening its first international venture in Australia in 1971, Mary Kay, Inc., has expanded and is now sold in 34 markets worldwide. Mary Kay Ash served as Chairman Emeritus of Mary Kay, Inc., from 1987 until her death on November 22, 2001. In mid-2001, her son and cofounder, Richard Rogers, became CEO of the company.

Several other firms, such as Procter & Gamble Co., Unilever NV, Revlon, Inc., Estée Lauder, and France's L'Oréal, sell cosmetics and personal care products primarily through department stores and mass merchandisers, and they are considered important competitors in the marketplace. Revlon, whose image varies by product line, built a multibillion dollar business by buying out old established lines like Max Factor, Charles of the Ritz, Germain Monteil, Diane Von Furstenberg, and Almay. Some international firms, such as Shiseido, Japan's largest cosmetics maker, are experimenting with beauty service centers in the United States and other countries. The centers offer free lessons in massage techniques and information on how to apply makeup. Shiseido found that many customers who visited such centers soon made a purchase in the department stores where Shiseido products were sold.

International Expansion

For the three years ended 2002, 2001, and 2000, Avon derived approximately 60 percent of both its consolidated net sales and consolidated pretax income from the operations of its international subsidiaries (see Exhibit 4). Total international sales in 2002 were $3.76 billion, compared to Avon North America sales of $2.41 billion. Total international operating profit in 2002 was $725.1 million, compared to Avon North America profit of $431.0 million. The international operations of the company are divided into four geographic regions: (1) North America, which includes Canada, Puerto Rico, and the United States; (2) Latin America, which includes Brazil, Mexico, Argentina, and Venezuela; (3) Pacific region, which includes the Philippines, Thailand, Japan, New Zealand, Australia, and China; and (4) the European region, which comprises the United Kingdom, central and eastern Europe, and Russia.

Avon management feels that it is time to reevaluate and map out the long-term future of the firm's beauty businesses on a global level. Senior management realizes that the traditional Avon system of door-to-door house calls worked wonderfully in developing nations. The company has direct investments in 53 markets and through distributorships, specially appointed representatives, and licensees in 143 countries, including a significant presence in Egypt, Greece, and Saudi Arabia.

Enormous growth opportunities exist in countries with huge populations such as China, Indonesia, and India. Avon's management also sees potential in Poland,

Czech Republic, Slovakia, and Hungary. In the Pacific Rim area, countries like Vietnam, Cambodia, and Laos are targeted as market opportunities. The second area of potential growth is to continue to emphasize direct selling in the emerging and developing markets of Latin America, the Pacific Rim, and other areas. In those markets, the retail infrastructure is undeveloped, especially in the interiors of those countries. The Avon representative provides consumers with an opportunity to buy a wide range of quality products at acceptable prices. In some developing markets, where access to quality goods has been particularly prized, Avon's direct-selling method opened up unprecedented prospects for women. In China, for example, women are so eager for Avon products that a projected six-month inventory of lotion sold out in only two weeks.

Growth in the markets of central and eastern Europe are considered primary targets by Avon's management in the new millennium. Avon Russia rebounded in 2000, reversing a downturn in 1999–2001. In 2002, higher sales resulted from an improved local economy, coupled with an increase in the average order resulting from a 2001 change in the commission structure.

The number of people buying from Avon in markets like the United States had been dwindling by 2 to 3 percent per year for about 12 years. "We applied all the tried-and-true stimuli to our direct-selling system: changes in recruiting, incentives, commissions, brochures, and more," suggested Preston when he was CEO. "We had some success. But we didn't stop the decline of customer purchasing activity." Management felt growth would come if it were to update the direct-selling channel.

Global Marketing

Satisfying the subtleties and intricacies of customer demand around the world means that a firm's business varies from country to country and market to market. In the United States, for example, Avon tested Avon Select, an early direct-marketing program, to enable customers to buy Avon products in various settings. Customers could order products via any one of four methods: (1) through an Avon representative, (2) by mail though special select catalogs, (3) by the 1-800-FOR-AVON telephone number, or (4) by fax.

The traditional door-to-door method, with the Avon lady as the homemakers' friend and beauty consultant, made the company the world's largest cosmetics firm and the number-one direct seller. The approach was viewed as expensive (the salesperson got a 20 to 50 percent commission), and there were the problems associated with hiring, training, managing, and motivating the sales force. Avon recently strengthened its traditional direct-selling channel through a program called Sales Leadership, a business model designed to attract and retain sales representatives through initiatives focused on business and beauty training. Each representative who signs up for the leadership program gets a percentage of the sales of every representative she recruits and every representative that the recruit herself recruits—and so on down through three "generations" of Avon representatives.

Avon has reached an agreement with the JC Penney Co. to set up shops called beComing within 90 retail stores operated by the firm. The shops are to be built around an assisted open-selling concept, which allows customers to browse racks that feature the beComing brand. Each shop has six areas featuring color cosmetics, skin care, fragrance, aromatherapy, mother-and-baby beauty products, and nutritional products for active lifestyles. beComing is designed specifically with one thought in mind: to avoid cannibalizing core Avon lines and the business done by traditional Avon sales representatives. It is priced and designed to target shoppers in mass department and specialty stores. The line is priced between mass-marketed lines such as L'Oréal Paris and 10 percent to 15 percent below the entry-level department store brands. Following a strategic review of options in early 2003 to reposition the beComing beauty brand in the United

States, Avon announced that it was ending the alliance with JC Penney and would now offer this product line through its traditional direct selling of sales representatives.

Avon also is continuing to test a direct-mail catalog, which would allow customers to bypass the Avon representative and place orders themselves. The success of a mail-order catalog will depend greatly upon Avon's ability to manage its mailing and customer lists, to control inventory carefully, to offer quality merchandise, and to project a distinctive customer-benefiting image. In a limited test of a catalog, Avon reached a more upscale customer who placed an average order of $40, more than double that of orders placed through the regular Avon sales brochure.

Growth Strategies

Upgrading the Avon global image is considered by management to be extremely important. One important element of the image upgrade was the announcement of a global advertising strategy. By consolidating worldwide advertising, Avon management believes it can expand its global presence and communicate a more unified brand image throughout its international markets (to view a recent organizational chart, see Exhibit 5). In 2000, management increased advertising expenditures by 50 percent to more than $90 million, and created Let's Talk, the company's first-ever global advertising campaign. Let's Talk television and print advertisements featured young sports professionals who serve as role models.

A new global product line of women's health and well-being products called Avon Wellness was part of this image program. It was aimed at expanding the definition of beauty to encompass inner health as well as outward appearance, and it featured vitamins and nutritional supplements as well as various exercise, fitness, and stress relief items. The image campaign also featured the theme, "The Company for Women." This line and other corporate strategies reflect the Avon corporate vision "to be the company that best understands and satisfies the product, service and self-fulfillment needs of women globally." The broad-based vision of the firm includes not only beauty, but health, fitness, self-empowerment, and financial independence. Such programs as the Avon Breast Cancer Crusade, the Avon Foundation, Avon's Worldwide Fund for Women's Health, and Avon Women of Enterprise are examples the application of this corporate mission.

Avon has changed its direct sales approach by connecting its U.S. representatives to a marketing tool called youravon.com. It empowered them with the technology of the World Wide Web. As e-representatives, they have a global reach and the technological advantage of the Internet, which enables them to direct sales and establish customer relationships. The company also opened kiosks, called Avon Centers, in about 40 high-traffic shopping malls. The centers are designed to display an upscale beauty image, showcase the company's beauty brands, and encourage customer trials of products. The centers were modeled after similar initiatives in Malaysia, the Philippines, Taiwan, Spain, Chile, Venezuela, and Mexico. They are small but attractive, 400- to 600-square-foot environments that add significantly to the company's retail presence in locations where retail and direct selling have a history of being able to coexist.

In 2003, Avon announced that it was introducing an entirely new beauty business called mark™, "celebrating young women and the mark they are making in the world." The mark™ line consists of nearly "300 innovative, first-to-market and exclusive products in fun, modern packaging." A "magalog" (combination of magazine plus catalog) called *meetmark* is delivered to an initial target audience of 10 million young (16–24 years old) women every four to six weeks, and features the mark™ products, up-to-the-minute trends, and inspiring lifestyle stories. To maintain the social spirit of the new brand, mark™ representatives and customers are able to connect with each other 24 hours a day at **www.meetmark.com** or by telephone at 1-800-meetmark. Avon has also retained the Creative Artists Agency (CAA) to provide entertainment-based marketing strategies for

EXHIBIT 5
Avon Products, Inc. Senior Management Organization Chart 2002

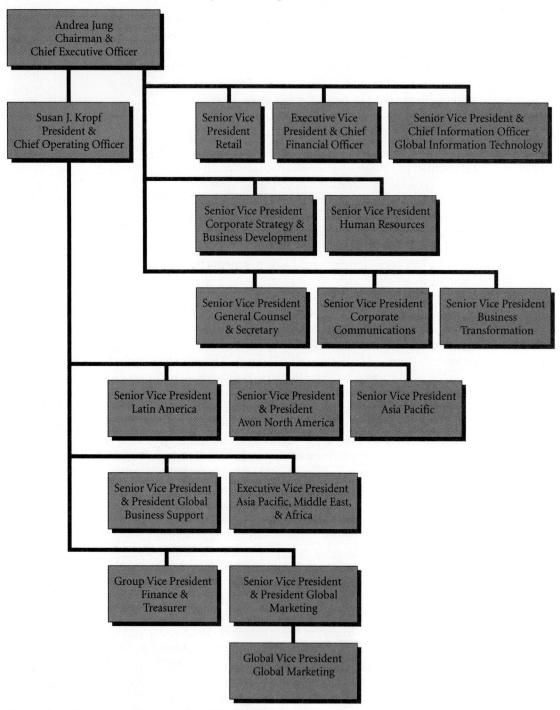

Source: Adapted from Avon Products, Inc., *Annual Report,* 2002.

EXHIBIT 6

Total Sales by Product Line—Avon Products, Inc.—2002

DECEMBER 31	2002	2001	2000
Sales			
Beauty*	$3,895.4	$3,716.5	$3,529.8
Beauty Plus†	1,144.5	1,157.7	1,148.7
Beyond Beauty‡	932.7	927.9	956.4
Health and Wellness§	198.0	155.7	46.8
Total net sales	$6,170.6	$5,957.8	$5,681.7

*Beauty includes cosmetics, fragrances, and toiletries.

†Beauty Plus includes fashion jewelry, watches and apparel and accessories.

‡Beyond Beauty includes home products, gift and decorative and candles.

§ Health and Wellness includes vitamins, aromatherapy products, exercise equipment, stress relief and weight management products.

Source: Avon's 2002 *Annual Report*, p. 64.

the launch of the new product line. CAA has marketing expertise and extensive relationships in the entertainment industry to create brand-building opportunities for mark™ in film, television, and music, and well as to create marketing alliances with entertainment properties, personalities, and industry decision makers.

Conclusion

Avon is part of a fiercely competitive industry. CEO Jung needs to put in place a solid strategy for the 2004—2006 time period, including clear recommendations and support of pro forma financial statements. Let's say she asks you, as an outside management consultant, to perform this work for Avon. Do the best job that you can to explain what your strategy would be.

EXHIBIT 7

Total Assets—Avon Products, Inc.—2002

DECEMBER 31	2002	2001	2000
North America			
U.S.	$ 627.0	$ 637.0	$ 639.3
U.S. Retail	29.8	28.6	12.0
Other	128.2	109.3	114.7
Total	785.0	774.9	766.0
International			
Latin America North*	541.0	603.3	594.4
Europe	667.3	508.3	443.2
Pacific	426.5	393.6	400.1
Total	1,634.8	1,505.2	1,437.7
Corporate and other	909.7	900.9	607.6
Total assets	$3,327.5	$3,181.0	$2,811.3

*Avon's operations in Mexico reported total assets at December 31, 2002, 2001, and 2000 of $205.7, $211.0, and $189.9, respectively.

Source: Avon's 2002 *Annual Report,* p. 64.

27 Revlon, Inc.—2004

M. Jill Austin
Middle Tennessee State University

REV

www.revlon.com

The vision of Revlon is to "provide glamour, excitement and innovation to consumers through high-quality products at affordable prices." Early in 2003, Jack Stahl, Revlon president and CEO, reflected on the prior year.

> We clearly exited the year a much different company than the one that entered it. We have a sound plan and we are making progress against it. We are beginning to grow and we have attracted resources needed to execute our plan. We are making the investments necessary to position Revlon for long-term, profitable growth.

The company's objectives for the new Revlon include: creating the most preferred consumer brands available, developing effective partnerships with retailers, and becoming a company of choice for employees. Net sales for 2002 decreased by $158.2 million (12.4 percent) to $1,119.4 billion (compared to $1,277.6 billion in 2001) and net losses in 2002 were $286.5 million while the company had a loss of $153.7 million in 2001. For the nine months ended September 30, 2003, revenues rose 3 percent to $930 million but net losses rose 32 percent to $141 million.

Revlon products are sold in more than 100 countries around the world with sales outside the United States and Canada accounting for approximately 32 percent of total sales in 2002. Product categories for the company include skin care, cosmetics, personal care, fragrance, and professional products. Some of the company's most recognized brand names include Revlon, Ultima II, ColorStay, Almay, Charlie, Flex, Mitchum, and Jean Naté.Successful products developed recently by the company include Revlon Skinlights, Revlon High Dimension Haircolor, Almay Kinetin Skincare Advanced Anti-Aging products, and Moisturous Lipcolor. Exhibit 1 shows the company products in each business category.

It is the long-term mission of Revlon to emerge as the dominant cosmetics and personal care firm through the twenty-first century by appealing to young/trendy women, health-conscious women (skin care), and older women with its variety of brands.

History

Revlon, Inc., was formed in 1932 by brothers Charles and Joseph Revson and Charles Lachmann with a $300 investment. Charles Lachmann was a nail polish supplier who is most notably remembered for his contribution of the "l" in the Revlon name. Charles Revson was the primary force behind the success of Revlon until his death in

EXHIBIT 1

Revlon, Inc., Products and Business Categories

BRAND	COSMETICS	SKIN CARE	FRAGRANCES	PERSONAL CARE PRODUCTS
Revlon	Revlon ColorStay ColorStay Overtime Stay Natural Always On Revlon Age Defying Super Lustrous New Complexion Skinlights High Dimension Illuminance Lipglide Moisturous	Eterna 27 Vitamin C Absolutes Revlon Absolutes	Charlie Ciara	High Dimension Colorsilk Frost & Glow Flex Outrageous Aquamarine Mitchum Hi & Dri Jean Naté Revlon Beauty Tools
Almay	Almay Time-Off Amazing Lasting One Coat Skin Stays Clean Organic Fluoride Plus Lip Vitality Clear Complexion Skin Smoothing Foundation Pure Tints	Almay Kinetin Almay Milk Plus		Almay
Other Brands	Ultima II Jeanne Gatineau Cutex	Ultima II Jeanne Gatineau		Bozzano Juvena

Source: Revlon, Inc. 2002 *Form 10-K*, p. 5.

1968. In the early years, Revson developed a near monopoly on beauty parlor sales by selling his nail polish door-to-door at salons. He expanded into the lipstick market with the slogan "Matching Lips and Fingertips." Some of the landmark advertising campaigns directed by Revson included "Fatal Apple" and "Fire and Ice." Revson was a hard taskmaster, expecting the same whole-life devotion of his workers that he gave to Revlon. He would hold meetings until two in the morning, call employees at home to discuss business, curse employees, and pretend to fall asleep during some presentations.

The company started with only one product—nail enamel. Revlon nail enamel was manufactured with pigments instead of the dyes typically used in this type of manufacturing. This approach allowed Revlon to market a large number of color options to consumers relatively quickly. It took the three company founders just six years to transform their small nail enamel company into a multimillion-dollar organization. This successful collaboration launched one of the most recognizable brands and companies in the world.

Originally, Revlon offered its nail enamels through a limited distribution system in which professional salons carried the products. However, as the 1930s progressed, the products were distributed widely in select drug stores and department stores. As the world entered World War II, Revlon contributed to the war effort by providing first aid kits and dye markers for the U. S. Navy. After the war, Revlon expanded its product lines with the introduction of manicure and pedicure instruments (a natural compliment to the nail enamel products). Revlon management recognized global demand potential, and began offering company products in a number of new markets. Stock was first offered in the company in 1955. The 1960s were associated with the "American Look" campaign designed to introduce the All-American girl to the world cosmetics market via well-known U. S. models. Further identifying with the changing role of women in the market and society, the Charlie fragrance line was introduced in the early 1970s. Sales for this extremely popular line surpassed $1 billion by 1977.

After the death of Charles Revson, Michel Bergerac took control of the company. He built up the pharmaceutical side of the business. By 1985 two-thirds of Revlon's sales were healthcare products such as TUMS and Oxy acne medications and the company was losing ground in cosmetics. Millionaire Ronald Perelman made five offers to purchase Revlon and eventually took over the company for $1.8 billion in a leveraged buyout. Perelman returned the company to its roots and sold off the healthcare products. He refocused the company to become an internationally known manufacturer and seller of cosmetics and fragrances. Perelman took the company private in 1987 by buying the stock of all public shareholders. A subsidiary of MacAndrews & Forbes stills holds 83 percent of the outstanding shares of Revlon and Perelman is chairman and Chief Executive Officer of MacAndrews & Forbes Holdings, Inc. The company was taken public in 1996 and is traded on the New York Stock Exchange (NYSE).

In September 1996, Revlon was given approval to manufacture, distribute, and market Revlon products in China and the first manufactured goods rolled off the production line in December 1996. The company acquired Bionature S.A., a South American manufacturer of hair and personal care products in 1997. The completion of acquisitions in South America increased distribution and manufacturing capabilities in these markets.

In an effort to reduce expenses, the company's worldwide professional products line was sold for $315 million in March 2000 and two months later, the Argentinian brand Plusbelle was sold for $46 million. In November 2000, the company closed three manufacturing plants and reduced its workforce by 1,115 employees (14 percent of the workforce) in an effort to improve efficiency. Additional cost reductions were made in 2001 when warehouse and manufacturing space were reduced by 55 percent. The company closed its in-house advertising division the same year. The Colorama brand of cosmetics was sold in 2001 for $50 million to L'Oréal. Managers reviewed the strengths and weaknesses of Revlon in 2002, in an attempt to evaluate the company's businesses so improvements could be planned.

Present Conditions

The company has continued to struggle in recent years and has debt of almost $2 billion. Despite these struggles, Revlon continues to launch or reintroduce new product lines. The 33-year-old Ultima II brand was reintroduced in 2001 and Charlie perfume was reintroduced in 2002. Revlon and Pacific World Corporation agreed in October 2002 to jointly manufacture a line of nail and nail care products. Moisturous Lipcolor (24 shades of hydrating lipstick) was sold beginning in 2002 and the Moonlit Mauve color collection and Almay Bright Eyes products were introduced in fall 2003.

In February 2003, the company received cash in the amount of $150 million from MacAndrews & Forbes Holdings, Inc., so the company could implement some of its growth and stabilization plans. This $100 million loan and a $40–$65 million line of credit will be used primarily for product development. MacAndrews & Forbes Holdings, Inc., is indirectly owned by Ronald Perelman through REV Holdings. Perelman controls 93 percent of the voting power of Revlon. Even with its financial difficulties, Revlon is the number-one brand in the U.S. mass market for color cosmetics.

Demographic and Social Trends

The cosmetics and personal care industry is impacted by two major changes in the demographic composition of the United States: the aging population and the change in proportions of racial and ethnic populations. Aging baby boomers make up a significant proportion of the adult U.S. population. The 75 million Americans born between 1946 and 1964 are a significant market for the cosmetics/personal care industry. The aging of the population has been coupled with a mini–baby boom. Many baby boomers have high levels of disposable income and are brand-loyal consumers. In addition, it appears that baby boomers' consumption patterns and rates have not necessarily changed as they have aged. The number of people in the mature market (55 and older) also continues to increase in number. Many of these consumers are wealthier and more willing to spend than ever before. Also, women in the mature age group remain active in the workforce for longer periods of time than in the past. Another market segment of interest to cosmetics companies is the U. S. teen market (ages 12–19) since females in this age group will number almost 20 million by 2010.

The ethnic/racial makeup of the American population is shifting. While African Americans represent the largest minority segment, the Hispanic American segment is the fastest-growing segment and is projected to be the largest minority segment in the United States by the year 2010, with approximately 40.5 million individuals. The result is that the non-Hispanic white share of the U.S. population is expected to decline to 68 percent by the year 2010. The Asian American population is also growing rapidly. International sales of cosmetics/skin care products are also impacted by ethnic/racial issues. There are significant opportunities for companies in Asian countries (60 percent of world's population). The youthful, increasingly affluent Latin American countries also represent a growth opportunity. Since the majority of personal care products are currently sold in the United States, Japan, Canada, and European countries (less than 20 percent of world's population), the potential for sales of personal care products around the world is excellent.

Other social and demographic issues that may impact the industry include consumers' concerns about product safety and the use of animal testing by cosmetics companies. Increasingly, cosmetics/personal care is not an industry for women only; men purchase personal care products such as skin creams and hair care products/dyes and many men are trying cosmetics in an effort to improve their appearance. The market for hair coloring has expanded with teenagers and adults wanting more vibrant coloring options.

Competition

Competition is intense in the cosmetics/skin care industry. In the past, the retail cosmetics industry was dominated by sales of cosmetics in specialty stores and department stores with beauty consultants providing service. Today large numbers of women prefer purchasing these items at drug stores, supermarkets, mass volume retailers such as Kmart and Wal-Mart, door-to-door sellers such as Avon, and on the Internet. Revlon's major competitors include: Procter & Gamble; Avon Products; Estée Lauder Companies, Inc.; L'Oréal; and Unilever. The cosmetics and skin care industry was a $200 billion business worldwide in 2003.

Other competitors include small companies such as Urban Decay; specialty stores such as Bath & Body Works, Body Shop, and H20; and retailers selling their own brands such as Benneton, Banana Republic, and Victoria's Secret. Competition for the African-American market is also increasing with brands such as Fashion Fair and cosmetics lines launched by Iman and Patti LaBelle. A discussion of major competitors of Revlon, Inc., follows.

Procter and Gamble

Procter & Gamble (P&G) is a multinational company offering products in a wide range of categories including personal care, cosmetics, fragrances, hair care, and skin care. Some of the P&G products not in the cosmetics/skin care industry include diapers, baking mixes, bleach, dish care products, juice, laundry products, oral care products, and peanut butter. The company operates in more than 70 countries.

Revlon faces competition from P&G in a number of product categories. P&G offers hair care products through its Pantene, Vidal Sassoon, and Pert brands. P&G skin care lines include Oil of Olay, Noxzema, and Clairol. Fragrance lines sold by P&G include Giorgio, Hugo Boss, Old Spice, and Helmut Lang. The P&G cosmetics line includes Cover Girl and Max Factor. In 2003, beauty care products contributed $12.2 billion to revenue and $2 billion to profit for P&G. Currently, Faith Hill and Queen Latifeh promote Cover Girl products. Selected financial information for Procter & Gamble is shown in Exhibit 2.

L'Oréal

L'Oréal is the world's largest cosmetics firm. L'Oréal acquired Maybelline, one of its leading competitors, in 1996 for $758 million. This move was an attempt to strengthen its position in the U. S. market. L'Oréal had previously held only a 7.5 percent share of the market, but the acquisition of Maybelline made it the number-two cosmetics firm in the United States. L'Oréal competes with Revlon in the area of cosmetics (L'Oréal, Maybelline, Biotherm, and Helena Rubenstein), hair care (L'Oréal and Redken), and fragrances (Giorgio Armani and Ralph Lauren perfumes). In 1998, L'Oréal acquired Soft Sheen, an ethnic hair care business, and introduced a quick-dry nail polish call Jet-Set. Some of the advertising spokespersons for the company are Beyonce Knowles and Natalie Imbruglia. Ben Affleck signed a $1.5 million contract in 2003 to promote L'Oréal men's products. Financial information for L'Oréal is shown in Exhibit 3.

EXHIBIT 2
Financial Information for Procter & Gamble

($ IN MILLIONS)	2002	2003
Net Sales	$40,238	43,377
Operating Income	6,678	7,853
Net Earnings	4,352	5,186
Long-Term Debt	11,201	11,475
Shareholders' Equity	$13,706	16,186

Source: www.pg.com.

EXHIBIT 3
Financial Information for L'Oréal

(EUROS IN MILLIONS)	2001	2002
Sales	$13,740	14,288
Net Profits (before capital gains and losses)	1,033	1,236
Fixed Assets	8,140	8,130
Current Assets	6,724	6,843
Loans and Debt	2,939	2,646
Shareholders' Equity	$ 7,210	7,434

Source: www.loreal-finance.com.

Unilever

Unilever is an Anglo-Dutch firm that until recently has been noted as a manufacturer of soap/detergent products and food products. The company also manufactures personal care products. Some of the Unilever brands include: mass skin care (Dove, Pond's, Vaseline); hair care (Dove, Sunsilk, Suave, Organics, Salon Selectives); and prestige fragrance lines (Calvin Klein, Karl Lagerfeld, and Chloe). Some of the top prestige fragrances include Obsession, Eternity, and Escape.

The company is a world leader in prestige fragrances and leads the hair care market in Africa, the Middle East, Latin America, and Asia/Pacific. Its skin care products lead the market in North America, Africa, Latin America, Asia/Pacific, and the Middle East. Financial results for Unilever are shown in Exhibit 4.

Avon Products, Inc.

Avon is the number-one direct seller of cosmetics and beauty products in the world. Its direct sales force numbers 3 million people in 143 countries. Some brand names for Avon products include Avon Color, Avon Skin Care Solutions, Anew, Skin-So-Soft, and Advance Techniques. In 2001, Avon began selling vitamins and nutritional supplements. It also sells jewelry, gift items, lingerie, and a skin care line for older women. Venus and Serena Williams were hired in February 2001 to promote Avon products in the "Dream big . . . let's talk Avon" advertising campaign. A new brand for women ages 16–24 called "mark" was launched in the United States in fall 2003 and the global launch is scheduled for spring 2004.

The company's products can be purchased through its Internet site, **www.avon.com**, but 98 percent of Avon revenue is generated by sales representatives. In an attempt to address the sales representatives' concerns that Internet sales would take away their sales, Avon is allowing sales representatives to have their own Web sites. Avon also now sells its products at Avon Centers in some JC Penney stores. Avon posted sales of nearly $6 billion dollars in 2002. Selected financial information is provided in Exhibit 5.

Estée Lauder

The Estée Lauder Companies, Inc., manufactures and markets cosmetics, fragrances, skin care products, and hair care products. Some of the company's cosmetics/skin care brands include Estée Lauder and Clinique. Fragrances are sold under the brands Beautiful, Intuition, and Youth Dew. In addition, Estée Lauder holds the worldwide license for fragrances and cosmetics with the brand names Tommy Hilfiger and Donna Karan

EXHIBIT 4

Financial Information for Unilever

(EUROS IN MILLIONS)	2001	2002
Profit on Ordinary Activities before Taxation	$ 3,624	3,979
Net Income	1,838	2,129
Total Assets	52,766	44,598
Total Assets Less Current Liabilities	29,554	23,996
Creditors Due within One Year	23,212	20,602
Long-Term Debt	$29,554	23,996

Source: **www.unilever.com.**

EXHIBIT 5

Financial Information for Avon Products, Inc.

($ IN MILLIONS)	2001	2002
Net Sales	$5,957.8	6,170.6
Operating Profit	773.4	870.0
Net Income	444.6	534.6
Total Assets	3,181.0	3,327.5
Long-Term Debt	$1,236.3	767.0

Source: www.avon.com.

(DKNY). Estée Lauder acquired two new companies in 1998: jane (a color cosmetics line targeted toward young women) and Aveda (a prestige brand of products for hair care). The company also has an investment in MAC (Make-Up Art Cosmetics, Limited). Other Estée Lauder brands include Bobbi Brown Essentials, Aramis, Prescriptives, Stila Cosmetics, kate spade, and Darphin. Some of the advertising spokespersons for the company are models Liya Kebede and Carolyn Murphy and actress Elizabeth Hurley. Selected financial information for Estée Lauder is shown in Exhibit 6.

Internal Factors for Revlon

Organization/Management

In 1990, then Chairman Levin led the company in recruiting a strong team of experienced managers who would work to achieve leadership in the cosmetics/skin care industry. It was at about this same time that Revlon developed its vision to "provide glamour, excitement, and innovation to consumers through high-quality products at affordable prices." The company set up the Revlon Learning Center and developed training programs to communicate its strategic principles to employees. Training provided a means for ensuring that the company's teamwork approach remained effective. In 1994, Revlon established the "Charlie Awards" to recognize employees whose accomplishments significantly impacted Revlon. A number of these awards are given to deserving employees each year.

At the core of the Revlon organization is the belief in individual values and the integrity of the firm and its actions. Revlon and its employees are active in supporting women's health programs and other community efforts. In the last decade Revlon

EXHIBIT 6

Financial Information for Estée Lauder
Companies, Inc.

($ IN MILLIONS)	2001	2002
Net Sales	$4,667.7	4,743.7
Gross Profit	3,441.3	3,470.3
Net Income	305.2	191.9
Total Assets	3,218.8	3,416.5
Long-Term Debt	$ 410.9	403.9

Source: www.esteelauder.com.

spent more than $25 million on services and research that help women. One of the events that Revlon sponsors is the Revlon Run/Walk in Los Angeles and New York, which raised $5 million in 2002. The company established a partnership with the National Council of Negro Women in 1998 to help support wellness programs for African-American women.

Revlon began restructuring the company by downsizing by 720 employees in 1998. Additional downsizing occurred in 1999 and 2000. Several executive positions were eliminated to save resources and three manufacturing plants were closed in 2000. In addition to downsizing, the company merged its cosmetics and beauty care sales forces in an effort to build brands rather than product categories. The restructuring program continued from 2000 through 2002 and included a termination of an additional 2,500 employees, sale of a manufacturing facility in Arizona, and consolidation of manufacturing operations into the North Carolina manufacturing facility.

CEO Jack Stahl, a former Coca-Cola executive, was hired for the top Revlon job in February 2002. In an attempt to learn the business quickly, Stahl worked with 250 laborers to install new Revlon displays in New York drugstores, went with marketing researchers to interview consumers in their homes, began creating a more decentralized structure, and asked lots of questions of everyone. Some of the major management positions are shown in Exhibit 7.

EXHIBIT 7
Organization Chart for Revlon, Inc.

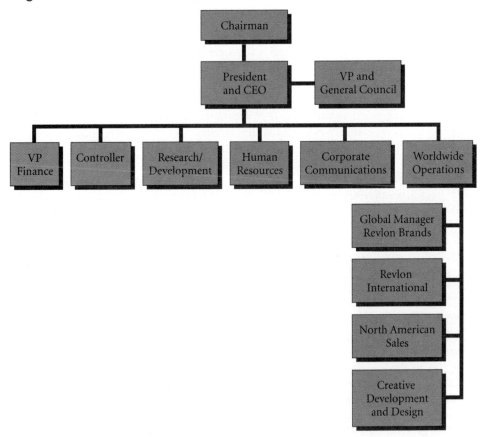

Source: Revlon, Inc., 2002, *Form 10-K.*

Marketing

The primary customers for Revlon products are large mass merchandisers and chain drug stores. Some of the major retail customers are Walgreen's, Wal-Mart, Target, Kmart, CVS, Eckerd, and Rite Aid. Revlon provides point-of-sale displays and samples for these stores. Wal-Mart sales were 22.5 percent of total Revlon sales in 2002. Revlon's products are also sold through its Web sites **www.revlon.com** and **www.almay.com**.

Advertising continues to be one of the primary areas of promotion spending by Revlon. The company made a strategic decision in 2001 to hire outside advertising agencies to handle promotional efforts for Revlon. Its managers hired the two firms Kirshenbaum, Bond & Partners and Deutsch to develop marketing ideas for the company's products. Longtime Revlon spokesperson Cindy Crawford, one of the most recognizable faces in the cosmetics world, promoted Revlon products for 18 years. However, in 2001 the company decided to discontinue Crawford's contract and hire four relatively unknown models to promote its brands. In summer 2001, Revlon teamed with Absolut Vodka and W Hotels to promote its Absolutely Fabulous products. These parties for models and celebrities were held in Los Angeles, New York, Chicago, and Atlanta and were used to promote Absolutely Fabulous on Revlon's Web site. In 2002, Revlon was included in a thirteen-week storyline for the soap "All My Children" and a marketing campaign coordinated with the James Bond movie "Die Another Day," staring Revlon spokesperson Halle Berry. Hiring Berry represents the company's return to using famous women as spokespersons. Her contract expired in 2003. Revlon spent approximately $281.2 million on advertising in 2002.

New product development continues to be a primary objective of Revlon even in bad financial times. It spent $23 million on research and development efforts for new products in 2002 and employed 160 people in this effort. In addition to development efforts, Revlon has plans to revitalize some of its long-established products. The chief marketing officer Debra Leipman-Yale left the company in fall 2003 after disappointing sales results from her promotion efforts. She had only been in her marketing position for eighteen months. The final promotion developed by Leipman-Yale was a televised concert called "Revlon Rocks the Holiday," which was developed to support the holiday 2003 Red Rocks line.

Manufacturing/Distribution

Globalization of the company's manufacturing and distribution efforts has enabled the consolidation of production facilities. This consolidation and coordination between markets has provided increased operating efficiency and better use of capital assets. The number of production facilities has been reduced and centralized to cover core regions. Currently, the company has U.S. production facilities in Oxford, North Carolina, and Irvington, New Jersey. Production facilities are also located in Mexico, Venezuela, Argentina, South Africa, China, and France. Several of the company's plants have ISO-9000 certification signifying their commitment to quality manufacturing standards. Planning for long-term growth includes a focus on and utilization of top-notch production facilities and distribution systems.

The Revlon Phoenix Site Distribution Center handles components and raw materials as well as finished stocks of cosmetics and personal care products. The distribution center maintains a 99 percent rating in both inventory accuracy and order accuracy. An automated-materials-handling system was installed at the distribution center in 1980 and several improvements have been made in the system since that time. In 1984 the company moved to a "paperless" receiving process and bar coding was first used in 1988. Software enhancements were made in 1994 to increase capacity of operations. The company's emphasis on continuous improvement means that Revlon managers look for ways to provide greater efficiency in company operations on an ongoing basis.

Financial Conditions

Significant financial issues impact the company's operations. Long-term debt at the end of 2002 was nearly $2 billion. For this reason, the company continues its restructuring program that was started in 1998. Costs associated with these restructurings include employee severance, personnel benefits, and factory/warehouse/office costs.

Note in Exhibit 8 (statement of operations) that sales decreased during 2000–2002 and that the company had net losses in 2002 of $286.5 million. According to balance sheet information in Exhibit 9, current assets and total assets decreased while current liabilities and total liabilities increased from 2001 to 2002.

EXHIBIT 8

Revlon, Inc., Consolidated Statement of Operations

	YEAR ENDED DECEMBER 31,		
($ IN MILLIONS EXCEPT PER SHARE DATA)	2002	2001	2000
Net sales	$ 1,119.4	$ 1,277.6	$ 1,409.4
Cost of sales	503.7	544.2	574.3
Gross profit	615.7	733.4	835.1
Selling, general and administrative expenses	717.0	679.2	765.1
Restructuring costs and other, net	13.6	38.1	54.1
Operating (loss) income	(114.9)	16.1	15.9
Other expenses (income):			
Interest expense	159.0	140.5	144.5
Interest income	(3.5)	(3.9)	(2.1)
Amortization of debt issuance costs	7.7	6.2	5.6
Foreign currency losses, net	1.4	2.2	1.6
Loss (gain) on sale of product line, brands and facilities, net	1.0	14.4	(10.8)
Loss on early extinguishment of debt	—	3.6	—
Miscellaneous, net	1.2	2.7	(1.8)
Other expenses, net	166.8	165.7	137.0
Loss before income taxes	(281.7)	(149.6)	(121.1)
Provision for income taxes	4.8	4.1	8.6
Net loss	$ (286.5)	$ (153.7)	$ (129.7)
Basic and diluted loss per common share:			
Net loss per common share	$ (5.49)	$ (2.94)	$ (2.49)
Weighted average number of common shares outstanding:			
Basic and diluted	$52,199,468	$52,199,349	$52,166,980

Source: Revlon, Inc. 2002 *Form 10-K*, p. F-4.

EXHIBIT 9

Revlon, Inc., Consolidated Balance Sheet

($ IN MILLIONS EXCEPT PER SHARE DATA)	DECEMBER 31, 2002	DECEMBER 31, 2001
ASSETS		
Current assets:		
Cash and cash equivalents	$ 85.8	$ 103.3
Marketable securities	—	2.2
Trade receivables, less allowances of $24.0 and		
$15.4, respectively	212.3	203.9
Inventories	128.1	157.9
Prepaid expenses and other	39.6	45.6
Total current assets	465.8	512.9
Property, plant and equipment, net	133.4	142.8
Other assets	154.4	156.0
Goodwill, net	185.9	185.9
Total assets	$ 939.5	$ 997.6
LIABILITIES AND STOCKHOLDERS' DEFICIENCY		
Current liabilities:		
Short-term borrowings–third parties	$ 25.0	$ 17.5
Accounts payable	92.9	87.0
Accrued expenses and other	392.3	281.3
Total current liabilities	510.2	385.8
Long-term debt–third parties	1,726.0	1,619.5
Long-term debt–affiliates	24.1	24.1
Other long-term liabilities	320.0	250.9
Stockholders' deficiency:		
Preferred stock, par value $.01 per share; 20,000,000		
shares authorized, 546 shares of Series A Preferred Stock		
issued and outstanding	54.6	54.6
Preferred stock, par value $.01 per share; 20,000,000		
shares authorized, 4,333 shares of Series B Convertible		
Preferred Stock issued and outstanding	—	—
Class B Common Stock, par value $.01 per share; 200,000,000		
shares authorized, 31,250,000 issued and outstanding	0.3	0.3
Class A Common Stock, par value $.01 per share; 350,000,000		
shares authorized, 20,516,135 issued and outstanding, respectively	0.2	0.2
Capital deficiency	(201.3)	(201.3)
Accumulated deficit since June 24, 1992	(1,361.9)	(1,075.4)
Accumulated other comprehensive loss	(132.7)	(61.1)
Total stockholders' deficiency	(1,640.8)	(1,282.7)
Total liabilities and stockholders' deficiency	$ 939.5	$ 997.6

Source: Revlon, Inc., 2002 *Form 10-K*, p. F-3.

Future Outlook

Critics suggest that Revlon will deplete its financial resources by mid-2004 and may have to file for Chapter 11 bankruptcy unless the company receives additional loans. The company has $700 million in debt that must be paid off by 2005. As Revlon deals with its debt problems and tries to continue its strategy of innovation, product development, and globalization, several issues must be considered:

1. Should Revlon concentrate its efforts on international markets?
2. Should Revlon diversify its operations or develop joint ventures with other cosmetics companies?
3. What role does innovation play in the strategic planning of Revlon? Which specific types of innovation might Revlon use?
4. What is the role "branding" should play in future growth strategies of Revlon?
5. How will competitive reactions impact Revlon's future plans?
6. What is the impact of social trends and economic trends on companies in the cosmetics/skin care industry?
7. What plans should Revlon develop to pay off long-term debt?

References

Atlas, Riva. "Revlon Running Near Empty." http://www.NYTimes.com (August 28, 2003).

Bayot, Jennifer. "Private Sector: A Shaker, Not a Stirrer, At Revlon." *New York Times* (December 1, 2002): 2.

Byrnes, Nanette. "Avon—The New Calling." *BusinessWeek* (September 18, 2000): 136.

Davis, Riccardo. "Revlon to Shut Plant, Ax 900 Jobs in Valley." *Arizona Republic* (November 2, 2000): A1.

Fairclough, Gordon. "Revlon Takes Down 'for Sale' Sign, As Shares Sink 34%." *Wall Street Journal* (October 4, 1999): B6.

Grossman, Andrea. "Teens, Males Boost Color Sales." *Drug Store News* (November 23, 1998): 53.

Kelpacki, Laura. "Ultima Plans a Makeover." *WWD* (December 15, 2000): 10.

Mack, Ann. "Casting Call." *Adweek Southwest* (April 9, 2001): 16.

Neff, Jeff. "CMO Out as Ad Costs Rise." *Advertising Age* (October 13, 2003): 3.

Revlon. 2000, 2002 *Annual Report*.

Spears, John. "Revlon to Shed 120 Jobs in Shift to U.S." *The Toronto Star* (October 25, 2000).

www.avon.com.
www.loreal.com.
www.pg.com.
www.revlon.com.
www.unilever.com.

28 Pilgrim's Pride Corporation— 2004

James L. Harbin
Texas A & M University—Texarkana

CHX

www.pilgrimspride.com

Headquartered in Pittsburg, Texas, Pilgrim's Pride Corporation (903-855-1000) is engaged in the production, processing, and marketing of fresh chicken and further processed and prepared chicken products. It is the second-largest poultry producer in both the United States and Mexico. Its prepared foods are sold throughout the United States; and its fresh chickens are sold regionally in the central, southwestern, and western United States and northern and central Mexico. Additionally, the company exports approximately 12 percent of its product line to overseas markets such as Russia and eastern Europe.

Among the many companies that Pilgrim's serves are Wal-Mart, KFC, PepsiCo., Kraft, Nestlé, Wendy's, Grandy's, Burger King, Church's, Chili's, and Long John Silver. At year-end 2003, Pilgrim's employed nearly 24,800 people and processed more than 44 million pounds of chicken a week in the United States and 11 million pounds a week in Mexico. Pilgrim's had approximately $2.5 billion in 2002 sales. Sales exceeded $2.6 billion in 2003.

Pilgrim's remarkable growth has taken place in a commodity industry in which, every year for the past 50 years, economists have been predicting doom and gloom. Citing industry sales as an indicator, experts have also deduced that the chicken industry has finally matured. The big question facing Pilgrim's today is whether it can continue to grow in an industry undergoing increased consolidation through additional marketing techniques, further cost curtailment, increased integration (gaining control over supplies and distribution), improved genetics, and growing techniques.

Bo Pilgrim's Background and Philosophy

Lonnie "Bo" Pilgrim's story is a classic one of deprivation and determination and then success. Born in northwest Texas in 1928, he was the fourth of seven children. His father died when Bo was nine, and he left home at twelve to live with his grandmother.

His entrepreneurial spirit had early roots. One of his first goals in life, he says, was "to be able to buy a soda when I wanted it. My father would, on occasion, give me money for a cold drink, but only after I had finished some work he wanted done for it." He learned at an early age that he could buy his own soft drinks. He bought sodas from his father's general merchandise store and sold them at a profit to the local factory workers. He later peddled newspapers, raised chickens and hogs, hauled gravel, picked peas and cotton, and sacked groceries—all before he turned eighteen.

He likens business to "a game, even a war." Commenting on how he spends his time, he says, "I spend one-third of my working days dealing with the government, one-third with lawyers, and the remaining one-third of my time is spent constructively."

On entrepreneurship, Pilgrim said, "It is more than just shooting from the hip. A company has four resources—people, dollars, time, and facilities. Our company's objective is to gain optimum use of these four through planning, building pride, and rewarding your employees."

When asked about his secret of success, Bo responded, "Take your abilities, season them with experience on the job, and combine that with drive and motivation, and you will be successful. The way to make a difference in your life is to make that mind-boggling decision not to be average."

Most Texans know Bo as the chicken king who dresses up as a Pilgrim to hawk his chicken in television commercials. "It's a mind-boggling thing. I'd put it right up there with marriage and my first bicycle," he told viewers in 1984, when introducing whole boneless chicken. He also promoted Pilgrim's leaner chicken with the tagline, "Nobody likes a fat chicken." Bo Pilgrim was one of the first American corporate executives to appear in company advertising.

Visitors to corporate headquarters get parking spaces marked with a picture of a chicken and the words "Pullet in here." The first-floor lobby walls are festooned with more than 300 samples of memorabilia of Pilgrim and his company—wooden thank-you plaques, framed newspaper clippings, and photographs of him with prominent politicians. In the second-floor executive office suite, representations of chickens are everywhere—there are ceramic chickens, oil paintings of chickens, photographs of chickens, and stuffed chickens.

History

Because commodity chicken down cycles had almost bankrupted Pilgrim's twice over the years, the company has increasingly emphasized value-added and branded products, including its chill-pack and further processed and prepared food lines. In the late 1980s, Pilgrim's began a major strategic shift to the prepared foods segment of the chicken industry. Such products generate higher prices per pound, exhibit lower price volatility, and result in higher and more consistent profit margins than non-value-added products, such as whole ice-pack chicken. Prepared foods currently account for approximately 50 percent of Pilgrim's total U. S. sales. Sales of further-processed chicken for Pilgrim's have more than doubled from 1998 through 2002, while frozen raw chicken sales have increased by slightly more than 50 percent.

In order to crack the food service business with processed and prepared chicken, Pilgrim's had to price its products below Tyson Foods, Inc. (its chief competitor), at a loss. The company also had to spend approximately $6 million to $8 million a year on advertising, promotion, and supermarket-slotting allowances to entice this business.

Pilgrim's Pride lost about $50 million over three years trying to enter the prepared chicken market. In fiscal 1988, the company lost a net $8 million on $506 million in sales. "I never envisioned how difficult it would be," Bo said, "It was like getting on the wrong ski lift, you might wish you hadn't done it, but there was no other way to get back down." Disgruntled investors dumped the stock, which had just had an initial public offering in January 1987. The value of Bo Pilgrim's stake shrank by 76 percent to $61 million.

Pilgrim's finally turned the corner with a strategic retreat from the supermarkets and a major advance into the food service market. In food service, Pilgrim's positioned itself as an alternative to Tyson, aiming at those customers who are leery of being too dependent on one supplier. "A lot of buyers gave us information to help us duplicate the products they were buying from Tyson," Pilgrim says. With over forty of the country's largest restaurant chains as customers, the company now has been able to raise its prices to be in line with Tyson.

Mission

A large group of Pilgrim's employees representing all areas of the company recently met to brainstorm the company's direction, vision, and mission. Many in the group were afraid that rather than developing a mission, they might end up with a mission statement. The difference, according to Monty Henderson, then president and CEO, was "that a mission statement becomes very wordy and usually winds up as a long paragraph or two that no one—not even the authors—can remember and usually winds up in a file somewhere. A mission, by contrast, is known by everyone, practiced daily by everyone, and becomes a way of life."

After much discussion about the business, the customers, and the competition, the group came to a consensus that Pilgrim's vision is "to achieve and maintain leadership in each product and service that we provide." To achieve this goal, the group felt that its mission was summed up as follows: "Our job is outstanding customer satisfaction . . . every day." Because of the increased emphasis on the international market, Pilgrim's later amended its vision: "To be a world class chicken company—better than the best."

Bo Pilgrim's personal vision for the company stretches beyond the continental United States. "The mission behind Pilgrim's is to help save rural America in the United States and the people of Mexico by providing jobs in the production of chickens. They must be versatile, economical, and wholesome chickens to feed the rest of the world. We'll use the best affordable technology and science to improve our systems. That's broader than just making money out of chickens."

Competition

Pilgrim's competes with other integrated chicken companies and to a lesser extent with local and regional poultry companies that are not fully integrated. The primary competitive factors in the chicken industry include price, product line, and customer service. Although its products are competitively priced and generally supported with in-store promotions and discount programs, the company believes that product quality, brand awareness, and customer service are the primary methods through which it competes. Pilgrim's believes that it has only one competitor (Tyson) with a more complete line of value-added products.

Tyson, the number-one poultry processor, generates 23 percent of the U.S. poultry production. Gold Kist has 9 percent, and Perdue Farms has 7 percent. With the 2003 acquisition of ConAgra, Pilgrim's will have approximately 16 percent.

Acquisitions have fueled Tyson's growth over the years. Since 1985 it has acquired over 20 different companies. In 1988, the *Wall Street Journal* reported that Tyson would acquire Pilgrim's for approximately $162 million, but the deal fell through. Tyson, in the early 1990s, attempted to sustain its growth by transferring its poultry-processing expertise to beef, pork, and seafood. By 1999, Tyson was ready to acknowledge that this strategy was a failure and was making preparations to return to just chicken. In 2001 however, under the new leadership of Don Tyson's son John, the company acquired IBP Inc., the world's largest producer of fresh beef and pork, in an approximate $3 billion-plus deal. IBP had $16.9 billion in 2000 sales. Tyson, with the IBP acquisition, has about 28 percent of the U. S. beef market, 23 percent of the chicken market, and 18 percent of the pork market. Tyson now has a goal of becoming a one-stop shop for protein. The belief is that its customers will be drawn to the ease of buying from one single supplier.

"Our marketing strategy for success is simple—segment, concentrate, dominate. We identify a promising market segment, concentrate our resources in it, and ultimately gain for Tyson Foods a dominate share of that segment," stated a recent Tyson annual report. "Our customers include all of the nation's top 50 food service distributors, 88 of the top 100 restaurant chains, 100 of the top retail supermarket chains, and every major wholesale club."

Mexico

Pilgrim's plants are geographically located to serve over 85 percent of the Mexican market. Its business strategy for Mexico calls for using its U. S. management expertise to solidify its position as the most efficient operator in Mexico and, at the same time, to develop a strong consumer and trade franchise for the Pilgrim's Pride brand. With the Mexican market maturing at an accelerated rate and customers increasingly selecting value-added products, it appears that Pilgrim's entry is particularly timely. Pilgrim's sales in Mexico rose to $343 million in 2002, an increase of 50 percent from its 1996 sales of $228 million.

The Broiler Industry

Before the 1950s, farmers were reluctant to undertake chicken farming because investments in buildings, equipment, feed, chicks, and other inputs could easily be lost due to disease or natural calamities. Chicken feed suppliers recognized that they could increase their own sales by extending credit to farmers, enabling them to remain in business while they paid off their debts. This risk-sharing arrangement spurred chicken production and eventually evolved into the kind of grower-contracting arrangements that are now common to all poultry production. Meanwhile, the feed suppliers edged further into slaughter and processing operations, which are the integrated chicken firms of today.

Through contracting arrangements, integrated chicken firms accept much of the risk of chicken growing in exchange for greater control over both the quality and quantity of the birds. Usually, the firm provides company-owned chicks and feed, while the contract farmer provides the housing and labor and then returns the fully grown chickens to the firm for processing. The firm, typically, pays a pre-established fee per pound for live broilers plus a bonus or penalty for performance relative to other chicken farmers.

Industry leaders recognized early on that if they owned the chicken throughout the production cycle—from farm to grocery case—they could reduce manufacturing costs, streamline production, improve quality, and, therefore, increase profit margins. Efficiency in chicken production has increased from 1935 when it took 112 days and 4.4 pounds of feed to grow a 2.85-pound chicken, to today's figures of 47 days and 1.95 pounds of feed to grow a 5.0-pound chicken.

Vertical integration in the poultry industry was listed as one of the top-ten events having the greatest impact on the meat industry during the twentieth century. Other top-ten events pertinent to the poultry industry were the passage of the Federal Meat Inspection Act (1906), the development of refrigerated rail cars and trucks and the national interstate highway system, the growth of fast-food chains, and the passage of both the Humane Slaughter Act (1958) and the Poultry Products Inspection Act (1957).

Profitability

Industry profitability is primarily a function of the consumption of chicken and competing meats and the costs of feed grains. Historically, the broiler industry operated on a fairly predictable cycle of about three years: a year of good profits, followed by a year of expanded output and declining profits, followed by a year of losses and production cuts.

The chicken companies have spent much of their energy trying to escape the commodity cycle through marketing and further processing. Frank Perdue, with his classic commercials, was the first to demonstrate that a company could charge a premium price for a brand name bird. Today, the biggest producers all play the brand-loyalty game. This leaves the chicken producers in an odd situation: they are commodity concerns trying to behave like consumer-products companies. As Prudential-Bache's John McMillin foretold in the 1980s, "The 1990s chicken industry will be better capitalized, more competitive—and less profitable." That prediction came true.

Industry profitability can be significantly influenced by feed costs, which are influenced by a number of factors unrelated to the broiler industry, including legislation that provides discretion to the federal government to set price and income supports for grain. Historically, feed costs have averaged approximately 50 percent of total production costs of non-value-added products and have fluctuated substantially with the price of corn, milo, and soybean meal. By comparison, feed costs typically average approximately 25 percent of total production costs of further processed and prepared chicken products such as nuggets, fillets, and deli products; as a result, increased emphasis on sales of such products by chicken producers reduces the sensitivity of earnings to feed cost movements.

Although feed costs may vary dramatically, the production costs of chicken are not as severely affected by changing feed ingredient prices as are the production costs of beef and pork. Chickens require approximately two pounds of dry feed to produce one pound of meat, compared to cattle and hogs, which require approximately seven and three pounds, respectively, of feed.

Problems

The poultry industry is one beset with multiple common problems. These range from labor recruitment/retention, working conditions, growers who are dissatisfied with their income and contracts, pollution and waste generated throughout the various stages of operations, meat that arrives at the market place contaminated with salmonella or listeriosis, and various animal rights groups attempting to impose their views on the meat industry, just to name a few. Taken individually or collectively, these problems result in bad public relations and negative impacts on the bottom line for an industry whose margins are already razor thin.

The industry struggles to find enough cheap, unskilled labor to staff its processing plants. Turnover is extremely high and often runs to 100 percent annually. Pilgrim's seems to do better than the industry as a whole; according to past CEO David Van Hoose, "our employee turnover rate in prepared foods division amounts to 18 percent annually against an industry average of 60 percent." Industry leader Tyson's alleged use of illegal immigrants did little to help positive public relations. Solutions are automation and higher wages. Labor makes up only about 10 percent of the total cost of production, meaning that raising wages would result in only minor cost increases to the consumer. But in an industry where two cents a pound can make a difference, no company seems willing to make the first move.

Conditions on the production line can be tough. Injury statistics from the Occupational Safety and Health Administration for 2000 reveal that one out of every seven poultry workers was injured on the job, more than double the average for all private industries. Poultry workers are also 14 times more likely to suffer debilitating injuries from repetitive trauma.

The industry's biggest worry may be microscopic in physical size. The growing and processing of chickens encourages the growth of bacteria such as salmonella and listeriosis. About 6 million Americans are made ill by such bacteria every year, and about 1,300 die. Scientists at the Centers for Disease Control say chickens may be the cause of up to half of those cases. Partly to hold down the price of poultry, the industry has put little effort into producing cleaner chickens, relying instead on consumers to cook the meat thoroughly. In October of 2002, Pilgrim's recalled 27 million pounds of chicken and turkey meat processed at its recently acquired WLR Foods facilities that might have been contaminated with listeria monocytogenes. It was the largest meat recall in USDA history. Pilgrim's currently face lawsuits from several deaths and illnesses alleged to have came from that product.

Consolidation has resulted in a highly centralized and vertically integrated industry in which the four top players control 55 percent of American production. As a result, the country has been carved up into regional buying monopolies, and each region's dominant processor can dictate terms to the growers. The vast majority of growers receive only short-term contracts from the processors, with no formal assurances of long-term business relationships. Farmers are at a distinct disadvantage when negotiating contract terms since they are financially unable to risk falling into disfavor with the processors.

A report from the Texas Commissioner of Agriculture concluded that although "the grower makes a substantial capital investment and takes most of the risk, he or she is not sharing in the success of the industry." In some cases, growers have received as little as $579 in annual income per 20,000-bird-capacity chicken house.

The processors defend their practices by pointing out that growers are guaranteed a price for adult chickens, typically about 3.5 cents to 4 cents a pound. Thus, the processors contend, growers are sheltered from much of the risk of the volatile chicken market. Bill Roenigk, spokesperson for the National Broiler Council, a processor trade group, says studies have shown that chicken farmers' average return on investment is 5 percent, which is higher than the return in many other agriculture operations.

Animal rights groups, such as People for the Ethical Treatment of Animals (PETA) have had little success in the past in imposing their views on the industry. In the fall of 2003, however, PETA did gain some notable reforms from restaurant chains KFC, McDonald's, and Burger King. Ken Klippen, a vice president of United Egg Producers, a trade group based in Georgia said, "customers used to tell us what they wanted to eat. Now they tell us how they want it produced."

Changing Demand and Supply

Before 1970, most poultry bought by consumers was whole chickens and turkeys, and the export business was almost nonexistent. It would have been difficult to find a restaurant or fast-food outlet selling chicken sandwiches or nuggets. Deboned chicken breasts did not exist. Today, exports account for almost one-sixth of U.S. poultry production, and consumers are confronted with an endless variety of chicken products.

Few Americans, before the 1950s, ate much chicken. Per capita poultry consumption was approximately 9 pounds in the early 1950s. In 2002, per capita consumption in the United States was approximately 78 pounds. Pounds per capita of chicken consumption surpassed beef consumption in the early 1990s. The gap has increased almost every year since, with Americans now eating slightly less than 70 pounds of beef per capita. The USDA estimates that chicken consumption will increase at a 3 percent compounded annual growth rate into the future. Consumption of chicken in Mexico has accelerated from less than 30 pounds in 1989 to almost 50 pounds per capita in 2002.

The major factors influencing this growth are consumer awareness of the health and nutritional characteristics of chicken, the price advantage of chicken relative to red meat, and the convenience of further processed and prepared chicken products. This growth has been enhanced by new product forms and packaging that increase convenience and product versatility. A larger, more affluent, mobile population has created a demand for more convenient foods. People are willing to trade dollars for time, and the industry has cashed in by providing value-added products.

Chicken firms have further segmented the market by observing that Americans are willing to pay much higher prices for white meat breasts than for dark meat thighs and drumsticks. They have also learned—and benefited—from the fact that overseas countries provide a market for low-value parts (chicken feet, tails, wingtips, gizzards) at a higher price than Americans are willing to pay. "Upgrading dark meat sales options is the biggest opportunity for our industry and this company over the next ten years," says O. B. Goolsby, appointed as Pilgrim's president in November of 2003, "we are currently deboning a huge percentage of our white-meat production, leaving us somewhat dependent on what is happening in the dark-meat commodity export markets around the world."

The poultry sector isn't solely chicken; it also includes turkey, duck, goose, and quail. But the poultry industry in America is chicken-driven. Chicken nuggets account for about 10 percent of total U. S. broiler output and showed chicken companies what could happen if they went beyond selling what are called, in the trade, "feathers-off, guts-out birds."

Chicken, priced pound-per-pound, is one-third the cost of beef and one-half the cost of pork. Non-value-added chickens are selling for less than they did in 1923, when Mrs. Wilmer Steele of Ocean View, Delaware, sold what chicken historians say was the nation's first flock of commercial broilers for 62 cents a pound. Why is chicken cheaper than the competition? The answer has to do with the fact that a chicken is highly efficient at converting feed to flesh. As noted, to produce a pound of meat, a chicken consumes less than two pounds of feed, compared with six or seven pounds for a cow and three for a pig.

Also, a chicken doesn't live long. The shorter a creature's life cycle, the quicker its generations can be manipulated genetically. Chicken breeders have steadily developed birds that grow bigger on less feed in less time. Breeders may be approaching the limits of practicality on this score; modern chickens have "put on so much weight that they have some real problems mating," said Walter Becker, professor emeritus of genetics and cell biology at Washington State University.

Furthermore, chickens don't graze. Raising cattle requires an investment in land; raising chickens doesn't. Chickens used to need to run around in the sun; otherwise, they would develop a vitamin D deficiency and rickets. But in the 1920s, poultry producers solved the vitamin D problem by adding cod-liver oil to chicken feed. Since then, they have been able to raise thousands of chickens in confinement, allowing about 0.7 square foot per bird.

The Future

During the next few years, per capita consumption of chicken could more than double throughout the world. In the domestic market, fewer and fewer meals consumed at home are made from scratch. In 1999, Americans spent approximately $970 million a day eating out. With 70 percent of mothers working outside of the home and 40 percent of consumers not knowing what they will eat as late as four o'clock in the afternoon, meal planning and preparation take a back seat to convenience and eating out.

Pilgrim's made two major acquisitions in 2000 and 2003. It acquired WLR Foods, Inc., for approximately $300 million in September of 2000. This allowed it to expand into the mid-Atlantic region. At that time, WLR Foods was the fifth-largest chicken company and the fourth-largest turkey company in the United States. One analyst described the WLR deal as pricey (Pilgrim's paid about twice per share what WLR stock was trading at when the deal was announced). Another described WLR as a company "going nowhere fast" that will benefit from being absorbed by a bigger and more competitive player. He went on to say, "that the last thing this industry needs is more capacity, so you have to congratulate (Pilgrim's) management for choosing this route to grow, which doesn't add to the industry's overcapacity problems."

In 2003, Pilgrim's acquired the chicken division of ConAgra Foods, Inc., for approximately $590 million. ConAgra was the fourth-largest producer with an 8 percent share of the market and sales of over $2 billion in 2002. Some analysts describe the deal as a dice roll for both ConAgra and Pilgrim's because of the cyclical nature and the traditional excess capacity of the industry. Both acquisitions created synergistic opportunities and expanded Pilgrim's domestic and international presence. They also contribute to Bo's goal of "doubling in size every five to ten years through internal growth and acquisitions." He further emphasizes that "we won't get far from chicken." From 1992 to 2003, Pilgrim's has been able to more than double its growth rate (9.7%) as compared to the industry growth rate (4.5%). Sustaining this rate of growth, while facing integration difficulties along with a more leveraged situation, presents a formidable future challenge. Management continues to be pressured to improve margins and stock performance (see Exhibits 1, 2, and 3 for details).

EXHIBIT 1
Pilgrim's Pride Corporation and Subsidiaries September 29, 2001 (in thousands)

	FISCAL YEAR ENDED		
	SEPTEMBER 29, 2001 (52 WEEKS)	SEPTEMBER 30, 2000 (52 WEEKS)	OCTOBER 2, 1999 (53 WEEKS)
Net Sales to Customers			
Chicken and Other Products			
United States	$1,652,199	$1,192,077	$1,102,903
Mexico	323,678	307,362	254,500
Sub-total	1,975,877	1,499,439	1,357,403
Turkey	238,835	—	—
Total	$2,214,712	$1,499,439	$1,357,403
Operating Income			
Chicken and Other Products			
United States	$78,096	$45,928	$ 88,177
Mexico	12,157	34,560	21,327
Sub-total	90,253	80,488	109,504
Turkey	4,289	—	—
Total	$94,542	$80,488	$109,504
Depreciation and Amortization[b]			
Chicken and Other Products			
United States	$38,155	$24,444	$23,185
Mexico	11,962	11,583	11,351
Sub-total	50,117	36,027	34,536
Turkey	5,273	—	—
Total	$55,390	$36,027	$34,536
Total Assets			
Chicken and Other Products			
United States	$ 764,073	$496,173	
Mexico	247,681	209,247	
Sub-total	1,011,754	705,420	
Turkey	203,941	—	
Total	$1,215,695	$705,420	
Capital Expenditures[a]			
Chicken and Other Products			
United States	$ 80,173	$69,712	
Mexico	29,425	22,417	
Sub-total	109,598	92,129	
Turkey	3,034	—	
Total	$112,632	$92,129	

(a) Excludes business acquisition cost of $239,539, incurred in connection with the acquisition of WLR Foods on January 27, 2001.

(b) Includes amortization of capitalized financing costs of approximately $0.9 million, $1.2 million, and $1.1 million in fiscal years 2001, 2000, and 1999, respectively.

Source: Pilgrim's Pride, 2001 *Annual Report,* p. 65.

EXHIBIT 2

Pilgrim's Pride Corporation (PPC)

ANNUAL INCOME STATEMENT IN MILLIONS OF U.S. DOLLARS (EXCEPT FOR PER SHARE ITEMS)	52 WEEKS ENDING 9/27/03	52 WEEKS ENDING 9/28/02	52 WEEKS ENDING 9/29/01
Revenue	$2,619.30	2,533.70	2,214.70
Other Revenue	—	—	—
Total Revenue	**2,619.30**	**2,533.70**	**2,214.70**
Cost of Revenue	2,465.30	2,369.30	2,000.80
Gross Profit	**154**	**164.4**	**214**
Selling/General/Administrative Expenses	136.9	135.3	119.4
Research & Development	—	—	—
Depreciation/Amortization	—	—	—
Interest Expense (Income), Net Operating	—	—	—
Unusual Expense (Income)	−46.5	−0.8	—
Other Operating Expenses	—	—	—
Total Operating Expenses	**2,555.70**	**2,503.80**	**2,120.20**
Operating Income	**63.6**	**29.9**	**94.5**
Interest Expense, Net Non-Operating	—	—	—
Interest/Investment Income, Non-Operating	—	—	—
Interest Income (Expense), Net Non-Operating	−38	−32	−30.8
Gain (Loss) on Sale of Assets	—	—	—
Other, Net	37.6	4	−0.5
Income Before Tax	**63.2**	**1.9**	**63.3**
Income Tax	7.2	−12.4	21.3
Income After Tax	**56**	**14.3**	**42**
Minority Interest	—	—	—
Equity In Affiliates	—	—	—
Net Income Before Extra. Items	**56**	**14.3**	**42**
Accounting Change	—	—	—
Discontinued Operations	—	—	—
Extraordinary Items	0	0	−0.9
Net Income	**56**	**14.3**	**41.1**
Preferred Dividends	—	—	—
Income Available to Common Excl. Extra. Items	**56**	**14.3**	**42**
Income Available to Common Incl. Extra. Items	**56**	**14.3**	**41.1**
Basic/Primary Weighted Average Shares	41.1	41.1	41.1
Basic/Primary EPS Excl. Extra. Items	**1.363**	**0.349**	**1.022**
Basic/Primary EPS Incl. Extra. Items	**1.363**	**0.349**	**1.001**
Dilution Adjustment	0	0	0
Diluted Weighted Average Shares	41.1	41.1	41.1
Diluted EPS Excl. Extra. Items	**1.363**	**0.349**	**1.022**
Diluted EPS Incl. Extra. Items	**1.363**	**0.349**	**1.001**
Dividends per Share—Common Stock	—	—	—
Gross Dividends—Common Stock	2.5	2.5	2.5
Stock Based Compensation	—	—	—

Source: www.investor.stockpoint.com.

EXHIBIT 3

Pilgrim's Pride Corporation (PPC)

ANNUAL BALANCE SHEET IN MILLIONS OF U.S. DOLLARS (EXCEPT FOR PER SHARE ITEMS)	AS OF 9/27/03	AS OF 9/28/02	AS OF 9/29/01
Cash & Equivalents	$ 16.6	14.9	20.9
Short Term Investments	—	—	—
Cash and Short Term Investments	16.6	14.9	20.9
Trade Accounts Receivable, Net	127	85.3	95
Other Receivables	—	—	—
Total Receivables, Net	127	85.3	95
Total Inventory	340.9	326.8	314.4
Prepaid Expenses	—	—	—
Other Current Assets	6.2	16.9	12.9
Total Current Assets	$ 490.7	443.9	443.3
Property/Plant/Equipment—Gross	—	—	—
Accumulated Depreciation	−465	−401.3	−338.6
Property/Plant/Equipment, Net	735.5	762	752.4
Goodwill, Net	—	—	—
Intangibles, Net	—	—	—
Long Term Investments	—	—	—
Other Long Term Assets	31.3	21.9	20.1
Total Assets	$ 1,257.50	1,227.90	1,215.70
Accounts Payable	159.2	163.9	151.3
Accrued Expenses	107.5	84.6	78.7
Notes Payable/Short Term Debt	—	—	—
Current Port. LT Debt/Capital Leases	2.7	3.5	5.1
Other Current Liabilities	10.2	12.9	4.9
Total Current Liabilties	279.6	264.9	239.9
Long Term Debt	416	450.2	467.2
Capital Lease Obligations	—	—	—
Total Long Term Debt	416	450.2	467.2
Total Debt	418.6	453.6	472.3
Deferred Income Tax	114	116.9	126.7
Minority Interest	1.2	1.6	0.9
Other Liabilities	—	—	—
Total Liabilities	$ 810.8	833.6	834.8
Redeemable Preferred Stock	—	—	—
Preferred Stock—Non Redeemable, Net	—	—	—
Common Stock	0.4	0.4	0.4
Additional Paid-In Capital	79.6	79.6	79.6
Retained Earnings (Accum. Deficit)	368.2	314.6	302.8
Treasury Stock—Common	−1.6	−1.6	−1.6
Other Equity	0	1.2	−0.3
Total Equity	446.7	394.3	380.9
Total Liabilities & Shareholders' Equity	$ 1,257.50	1,227.90	1,215.70
Shares Outs.—Common Stock	—	—	—
Total Common Shares Outstanding	41.1	41.1	41.1
Total Preferred Stock Shares Outs.	—	—	—
Employees (actual figures)	24,800.00	24,800.00	24,500.00
Number of Common Shareholders (actual figures)	33,074.00	39,698.00	45,725.00

Source: www.investor.stockpoint.com.

29 Anheuser-Busch Companies, Inc.—2004

Michelle Ghoens
Francis Marion University

BUD

www.anheuserbusch.com

Anheuser-Busch Companies, Inc., continued to achieve record operation performance in 2003 despite declining stock market numbers, corporate scandals, increased governmental regulations, and international instability. Some of the company's foremost competitors reported declining numbers, yet Anheuser-Busch's stock prices were up, sales were up, and earnings per share were up.

Anheuser-Busch, originally founded in St. Louis in 1852 and named Bavarian Brewery, has been the beer industry leader for nearly five decades. Barrel sales have increased from a mere 8,000 in 1865 produced in a single brewery to 127.9 million in 2003 produced in 12 breweries. In 1919, the company incorporated and, as Anheuser-Busch, Inc., has undisputedly become the world's leading brewer. It has also been the industry's leader in using technological innovations to ensure quality products. During the 1870s, the company was the first to use the process of pasteurization and employed a fleet of 40 artificially refrigerated train cars for distribution to the West Coast and Texas. It also began construction of railside icehouses to support refrigerated rail cars for beer distribution.

National Prohibition took effect in 1920, and Anheuser-Busch, Inc., introduced products such as ginger ale, root beer, and, more importantly for its profitability margins, ice cream. In 1933, Prohibition was repealed, and beer production resumed again, though Anheuser-Busch remained profitable in its default. The year 1957 was a trademark year because Anheuser-Busch became the beer industry leader and has remained as such since that year. More broadly, today the company has charged into and made substantial headway in the entertainment and packaging industries.

Internal Operations

Anheuser-Busch operations consist of the following business divisions: domestic beer, international beer, packaging, entertainment, and other.

Domestic and International Beer

Beer is Anheuser-Busch's foremost product. It is produced and distributed by its subsidiary, Anheuser-Busch, Inc. (ABI), which sells approximately 2.5 times the volume of its closest domestic competitor. Approximately 30 beers and three nonalcoholic malt beverages are produced by ABI, including but not limited to the following notable brand names: Budweiser, Bud Light, Michelob, Busch, Natural Light, and O'Doul's. In addition to these, new products include Michelob ULTRA, a low-carbohydrate beer, and Bacardi Silver. Most of the aforementioned products are sold in both packaged and draft forms, and most are sold on a nationwide basis.

ABI has 12 strategically located domestic breweries to maintain an effective nationwide distribution system. In addition, the multiple breweries are maintained in order to preserve and provide the highest-quality product to consumers nationwide. ABI maintains its competitive advantage, which has and continues to be based on quality and freshness by the following ongoing efforts: initiating modernization programs, using controlled environment warehouses, and utilizing rigorous monitoring policies.

International strategies concentrate on the growth potential of newly developing markets. Anheuser-Busch attempts to establish equity partnerships with other leading brewers in order to establish a reputable foundation abroad for the Budweiser brand and, of course, sizable sales volume. In 2002, global sales reached approximately 8 million barrels. These numbers are partially due to Anheuser-Busch's ownership of breweries in Mexico, Chile, and China, which are discussed in the Global Issues section.

Packaging

Anheuser-Busch is among the largest U.S. manufacturers of aluminum beverage containers and is the world's largest recycler of aluminum beverage containers. The firm's packaging operations are handled through the following subsidiaries: Metal Container Corporation (MCC), Anheuser-Busch Recycling Center (ABRC), Precision Printing and Packaging, Inc. (PPPI), Eagle Packaging, Inc. (EPI), and Longhorn Glass Corporation (LGC).

First, Metal Container Corporation (MCC) manufactures cans and beverage can lids for sale to ABI, U.S. soft drink customers, and Grupo Modelo. Anheuser-Busch Recycling Center (ABRC) recycles aluminum cans at its plant in Hayward, California. It helps reduce container costs and is the world's largest recycler of aluminum beverage containers. Precision Printing and Packaging, Inc. (PPPI), produces more than 25 billion metalized and paper labels at its plant in Clarksville, Tennessee, for Anheuser-Busch and other customers. This particular company provides approximately 80 percent of Anheuser-Busch's labels. Eagle Packaging, Inc. (EPI), supplies all of Anheuser-Busch's liner material. Longhorn Glass Corporation (LGC), located in Jacinto City, Texas, produces more than 60 percent of the glass bottles for the nearby Houston Brewery.

Theme Parks

Anheuser-Busch has one of the largest adventure theme park operators in the United States, Busch Entertainment Corporation (BEC), which owns and directs nine theme parks. BEC offers families the experience of fun and educational marine-life parks, theme parks, splash rides, natural animal habitats, and so on. BEC operates Busch Gardens in three cities, SeaWorld in three cities, as well as Adventure Island, Water Country USA, Sesame Place, and Discovery Cove. In fact, Busch Entertainment has been cited for its emphasis on quality of wildlife conservation, entertainment quality, and customer/guest service.

Real Estate

Through its subsidiary, Busch Properties, Inc. (BPI), Anheuser-Busch has become engaged in real estate development. BPI owns and operates The Kingsmill Resort and Conference Center in Williamsburg, Virginia, which offers world-class recreational amenities and accommodations. It is located near Busch Gardens and Water Country USA. Anheuser-Busch also owns and operates Busch Creative Services Corporation, which is a marketing communications business, and Manufacturers Railway Co., a transportation service business.

Rivals

Consumption in the alcoholic beverage industry, which includes beer, wine, and liquor, is not growing. A slow decline in consumption for an entire generation is attributed to an increase in regulatory restrictions (i.e., raising of minimum drinking age and increasing federal excise taxes on alcoholic beverages) and a general trend toward moderation in alcohol consumption. This trend may be attributed to a national inclination toward health consciousness as well as social concern. The number of consumers reaching legal drinking age has grown in recent years. The number of 21- to 24-year-olds has increased for the first time in 20 years. The increase in this particular age group is expected to contribute an additional 1 percent gain in annual beer volume for the next few years. This projection is based on analyses that contend beer is the alcoholic beverage of choice for this age group.

Anheuser-Busch's closest competitors are Miller Brewing Company and Coors Brewing Company. These two industry players are briefly discussed below.

Miller Brewing Company

Miller Brewing Company, headquartered in Milwaukee, Wisconsin, has grown to become the second-largest brewery in the United States. With the establishment of Miller Brewing International, Miller has become the seventh-largest brewer in the world, with sales in more than 80 countries. Principal foreign markets are located in both North and South America, as well as Europe and Asia. In Mexico, Ireland, South Korea, and Norway, Miller brands are the leading imports.

Miller was the first national brewer to begin recycling aluminum and has become even more environmentally conscious. Miller has gone so far as to capture excess carbon dioxide from fermentation and sold it for use in refrigeration and freezing operations, and has reduced the weight of bottles in order to save glass.

Miller offers over 50 brands of beer including the very popular Miller Lite. South Africa Breweries has merged with Miller Brewing Company to form SABMiller Brewing Company.

Adolph Coors Company

Adolph Coors Company is ranked among the 500 largest publicly traded corporations in the United States. Its principal subsidiary is Coors Brewing Company, the nation's third-largest brewer. The company also owns Coors Brewers Limited, the second-largest brewer in the United Kingdom. Among Coors Company's products is Coors Light, the fourth-largest selling beer in the nation. Coors products are available throughout the United States and in more than 30 international markets in North America, Latin America, the Caribbean, Europe, and Asia. In addition, Coors owns and is a partner in operating the nation's largest aluminum can manufacturing plant, and is a partner in a glass bottles manufacturing plant.

Global Issues

U.S. brewers are trying hard to establish a global presence in developing markets of Asia, eastern Europe, and Latin America. This is being accomplished through exports and purchases of equity interests in local brewers. U.S. brewers are engaging in joint ventures with local brewers and distributors to establish their strongholds abroad.

Foreign companies are also taking advantage of potentially lucrative global markets. These markets are considered to be those newly developing nations as well as those nations that have not traditionally been considered beer-drinking societies, in Latin America, Asia, and eastern Europe. The beer market is much like other consumer markets in that the products have a tendency to be somewhat provincial according to local preferences. For instance, Germans and Austrians tend to prefer heavier lagers, while Americans favor lighter pilsners. Furthermore, distribution networks are complicated due to trade barriers among countries.

Anheuser-Busch continues to be the most aggressive brewer regarding global market expansion. Since 1993, it has established business arrangements in China, Japan, Brazil, India, Italy, France, Switzerland, and Spain. Anheuser-Busch has also established a joint venture with Kirin Brewing Company of Japan, and has done the same with Chile's Compania Cervecerias Unidas S.A. and Argentina's Buenos Aires Embotelladora S.A. (BAESA). It has purchased equity interests in Redhook Ale Brewery, Inc., and Widmer Brothers Brewing Company, and in addition, has raised its ownership interest in Mexico's largest brewer, Grupo Modelo S. A., to 50.2 percent. This market expansion is made possible by numerous changes within the various nations, including market reforms and rising prosperity in much of Latin America as well as a shift in customer preferences among traditional wine-drinking nations toward beer. Chileans and Argentinians increasingly prefer American beers, among other products, instead of local wines.

Marketing

Anheuser-Busch focuses its advertising efforts on younger drinkers. Hardly anyone is unfamiliar with the "Bud frogs" or the "whassup?" commercials. These marketing campaigns have helped it gain market share among the aforementioned target market. The company uses the annual Super Bowl and other notable sports venues as well as music icons such as Tim McGraw to effectively market products.

Anheuser-Busch maintains a good public image by continually publicizing safe drinking practices through television, radio, and journal advertising. It is also done in those places where products are offered. For instance, Anheuser-Busch uses gift card promotions at bars, restaurants, grocery stores, and so on, in conjunction with American Express to promote its "Sober Driver" slogan.

Future Outlook

According to 2003 sales, the future of Anheuser-Busch looks keen. Record sales and earnings continued throughout the year. Sales to wholesalers continued to rise in 2003, as did sales from wholesalers to resalers. Anheuser-Busch plans to expand further into newly developing markets such as Latin America and China, where great interest in its products has been manifested.

The beer industry continues to be the main focus at Anheuser-Busch Companies, Inc., though theme parks play a major role as well in future planning. Anheuser-Busch executives have planned less on building new theme parks and more on selling the less profitable ones or expanding those that have proven to retain adventurers and attract new ones.

EXHIBIT 1

Vision and Mission Statements

VISION
"Through all of our products, services and relationships, we will add to life's enjoyment."
MISSION
Anheuser-Busch's mission is to ensure the following three goals are met: • Be the world's beer company • Enrich and entertain a global audience • Deliver superior returns to our shareholders

Source: www.anheuserbusch.com.

EXHIBIT 2

Net Income of Anheuser-Busch and Nearest Competitors

(IN MILLIONS)	2003	2002	2001	2000
Anheuser-Busch Companies	$664	1933.8	1,704.5	1,551.6
Miller	$ 64	189		
Coors	$161.7	123.0	109.6	92.3

Note: 2003 income recordings for Miller are through March 31, yet 2003 income recordings for Anheuser-Busch are through September 30.

Note: Income statements prior to acquisition by SABMiller no longer provided.

EXHIBIT 3

Organizational Structure Strategy Committee—Anheuser-Busch Companies, Inc.

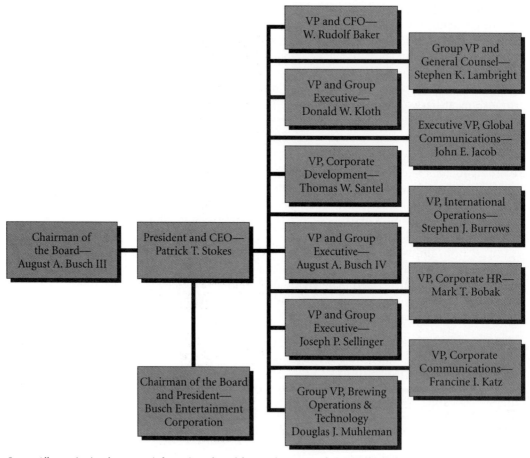

Source: All organizational structure information adapted from Anheuser-Busch Companies, Inc. 2002 *Annual Report*.

EXHIBIT 4

Anheuser Busch (BUD)

ANNUAL INCOME STATEMENT IN MILLIONS OF U.S. DOLLARS (EXCEPT FOR PER SHARE ITEMS)	12 MONTHS ENDING 12/31/03	12 MONTHS ENDING 12/31/02	12 MONTHS ENDING 12/31/01
			Reclass. 12/31/02
Revenue	$14,146.70	13,566.40	12,911.50
Other Revenue	—	—	—
Total Revenue	**14,146.70**	**13,566.40**	**12,911.50**
Cost of Revenue	8,449.10	8,131.30	7,950.40
Gross Profit	**5,697.60**	**5,435.10**	**4,961.10**
Selling/General/Administrative Expenses	2,498.30	2,455.40	2,255.90
Research & Development	—	—	—
Depreciation/Amortization	—	—	—
Interest Expense (Income), Net Operating	—	—	—
Unusual Expense (Income)	—	—	—
Other Operating Expenses	—	0	−17.8
Total Operating Expense	**10,947.40**	**10,586.70**	**10,188.50**
Operating Income	**3,199.30**	**2,979.70**	**2,723.00**
Interest Expense, Net Non-Operating	−377.1	−351	−334.3
Interest/Investment Income, Non-Operating	1.7	1.3	1.1
Interest Income (Expense), Net Non-Operating	−375.4	−349.7	−333.2
Gain (Loss) on Sale of Assets	—	—	—
Other, Net	0.4	−6.4	−12.2
Income Before Tax	**2,824.30**	**2,623.60**	**2,377.60**
Income Tax	1,093.30	1,041.50	927.5
Income After Tax	**1,731.00**	**1,582.10**	**1,450.10**
Minority Interest	—	—	—
Equity In Affiliates	344.9	351.7	254.4
Net Income Before Extra. Items	**2,075.90**	**1,933.80**	**1,704.50**
Accounting Change	—	—	—
Discontinued Operations	—	—	—
Extraordinary Item	—	—	—
Net Income	**$ 2,075.90**	**1,933.80**	**1,704.50**
Preferred Dividends	—	—	—
Income Available to Common Excl. Extra. Items	**2,075.90**	**1,933.80**	**1,704.50**
Income Available to Common Incl. Extra. Items	**2,075.90**	**1,933.80**	**1,704.50**
Basic/Primary Weighted Average Shares	826.2	866	890.1
Basic/Primary EPS Excl. Extra. Items	**2.513**	**2.233**	**1.915**
Basic/Primary EPS Incl. Extra. Items	**2.513**	**2.233**	**1.915**
Dilution Adjustment	0	0	0
Diluted Weighted Average Shares	837	878.9	901.6
Diluted EPS Excl. Extra. Items	**2.48**	**2.2**	**1.891**
Diluted EPS Incl. Extra. Items	**2.48**	**2.2**	**1.891**
Dividends per Share—Common Stock	—	0.75	0.69
Gross Dividends—Common Stock	—	649.5	614.1
Stock Based Compensation	—	93.1	68.6

Source: www.investor.stockpoint.com.

EXHIBIT 5
Anheuser Busch (BUD)

ANNUAL BALANCE SHEET IN MILLIONS OF U.S. DOLLARS (EXCEPT FOR PER SHARE ITEMS)	AS OF 12/31/03	AS OF 12/31/02	AS OF 12/31/01
			Reclass. 12/31/02
Cash & Equivalents	$ 191.1	188.9	162.6
Short Term Investments	—	—	—
Cash and Short Term Investments	191.1	188.9	162.6
Trade Accounts Receivable, Net	669.4	630.4	620.9
Other Receivables	—	—	—
Total Receivables, Net	669.4	630.4	620.9
Total Inventory	587.5	563.6	591.8
Prepaid Expenses	—	—	—
Other Current Assets	182.3	121.8	175.1
Total Current Assets	**$ 1,630.30**	**1,504.70**	**1,550.40**
Property/Plant/Equipment—Gross	—	—	—
Accumulated Depreciation	—	−7,604.00	−7,088.30
Property/Plant/Equipment, Net	8,498.90	8,363.90	8,390.00
Goodwill, Net	—	—	—
Intangibles, Net	486.6	437.7	—
Long Term Investments	3,052.00	2,827.90	2,855.00
Other Long Term Assets	1,021.70	985.3	1,149.50
Total Assets	**$14,689.50**	**14,119.50**	**13,944.90**
Accounts Payable	1,093.70	986.6	945
Accrued Expenses	452	468.5	416.9
Notes Payable/Short Term Debt	—	—	—
Current Port. LT Debt/Capital Leases	—	—	—
Other Current Liabilities	311.5	332.6	374.6
Total Current Liabilities	**$ 1,857.20**	**1,787.70**	**1,736.50**
Long Term Debt	7,285.40	6,603.20	5,983.90
Capital Lease Obligations	—	—	—
Total Long Term Debt	**7,285.40**	**6,603.20**	**5,983.90**
Total Debt	**7,285.40**	**6,603.20**	**5,983.90**
Deferred Income Tax	1,462.10	1,345.10	1,367.20
Minority Interest	—	—	—
Other Liabilities	1,373.10	1,331.20	795.8
Total Liabilities	**$11,977.80**	**11,067.20**	**9,883.40**
Redeemable Preferred Stock	—	—	—
Preferred Stock—Non Redeemable, Net	—	—	—
Common Stock	1,457.90	1,453.40	1,445.20
Additional Paid-In Capital	1,194.00	1,024.50	810.2
Retained Earnings (Accum. Deficit)	13,935.40	12,544.00	11,258.20
Treasury Stock—Common	−12,939.00	−11,008.60	−8,981.60
Other Equity	−890.3	−870.7	−338.3
Total Equity	**2,711.70**	**3,052.30**	**4,061.50**
Total Liabilities & Shareholders' Equity	**$14,689.50**	**14,119.50**	**13,944.90**
Shares Outs.—Common Stock	813.3	846.6	879.1
Total Common Shares Outstanding	**813.3**	**846.6**	**879.1**
Total Preferred Stock Shares Outs.	**—**	**—**	**—**
Employees (actual figures)	—	23,176.00	23,432.00
Number of Common Shareholders (actual figures)	—	57,259.00	57,347.00

Source: www.investor.stockpoint.com.

References

Anheuser-Busch Companies 2001 *Annual Report*.

Anheuser-Busch Companies 2003 *Annual Report*.

Serwer, Andy. "Beers to Ya! In a Skunky Market, Budweiser and Coors Just Keep Chugging Along." *Fortune* (September 2, 2002).

"Still the King of Beers: Anheuser-Busch Executes Another strong Year with New Products and Effective Marketing." *Beverage Industry*, 94 (January 2003): 22.

www.anheuserbusch.com.

www.coors.com.

www.millerbrewing.com.

30   Boeing—2004

Carolyn R. Stokes
Francis Marion University

BA

www.boeing.com

The Boeing Company (312–544–2000), headquartered in Chicago, Illinois, is the largest aerospace firm in world, as measured by total sales; and has been the world's leading manufacturer of commercial aircraft for the last 20 years with an average of over 60 percent of the market, a global leader in military aircraft, and the largest contractor for NASA. Boeing is one of the largest U.S. companies with over $50 billion in sales in 2002, as indicated in Exhibit 1.

Boeing has two main business units: Commercial Aircraft and Integrated Defense Systems, and Boeing Capital Corporation with new frontiers in Connexion by Boeing[SM] and Air Traffic Management. Jetliners currently in production include the families of the Boeing 717, 737, 747, 757, 767, and 777 models. It also manufactures helicopters, military aircraft, electronic systems, and missiles; provides communication services for aerospace-related activities; and is a major contractor in the Space Station.

The aerospace industry remains greatly impacted by the terrorist attacks of September 11, 2001. For the first time in U.S. history, all air traffic was grounded. With high security, airports gradually reopened with fewer flights and fewer passengers. Airlines, the major customer of Boeing's commercial jets, canceled some orders and placed fewer orders for aircraft. The U.S. President and Congress declared war on terrorism. In the war of "Enduring Freedom," the United States and its Allies continue their effort to fight terrorism by maintaining a military presence in Iraq and Afghanistan as they work to reestablish order. In this ongoing effort to ensure freedom, the military is depreciating its aircraft and consuming its arsenal of weapons. U.S. intelligence is using state-of-the-art technological equipment such as the unmanned aircraft and satellites that Boeing produces.

Led by chairman and CEO Harry Stonechipher, Boeing had revenue of $50.5 billion with deliveries of 281 commercial jet aircraft and 87 military aircraft and missile deliveries in 2003 as compared with $54.1 billion with deliveries of 381 commercial jet aircraft and 108 military aircraft and missile deliveries in 2002. In the Defense and Space segments Boeing recorded an operating profit of $0.77 billion on sales of $27.4 billion in 2003. This revenue includes $15.0 billion from military aircraft and missiles, and $12.4 billion from space and communications. Boeing faces decreasing demand for commercial aircraft, increasing demand for aerospace communication systems, and steady demand for defense and space contracts due to replacement needs for aircraft and missiles used in the war with Iraq.

Industry experts are still predicting world air traffic to double by 2020. With improved cost management, well-designed aircraft and equipment, and continued

EXHIBIT 1

Boeing Company (BA)

ANNUAL INCOME STATEMENT IN MILLIONS OF U.S. DOLLARS (EXCEPT FOR PER SHARE ITEMS)	12 MONTHS ENDING 12/31/03	12 MONTHS ENDING 12/31/02	12 MONTHS ENDING 12/31/01
		Reclass. 12/31/03	
Revenue	$50,485.00	54,061.00	58,198.00
Other Revenue	—	—	—
Total Revenue	**50,485.00**	**54,061.00**	**58,198.00**
Cost of Revenue	44,330.00	45,988.00	48,778.00
Gross Profit	**6,155.00**	**8,073.00**	**9,420.00**
Selling/General/Administrative Expenses	3,224.00	2,981.00	2,767.00
Research & Development	1,651.00	1,639.00	1,936.00
Depreciation/Amortization	—	—	—
Interest Expense (Income), Net Operating	—	—	—
Unusual Expense (Income)	892	−2	935
Other Operating Expenses	−7	−44	−21
Total Operating Expense	**50,062.00**	**50,611.00**	**54,302.00**
Operating Income	**423**	**3,450.00**	**3,896.00**
Interest Expense, Net Non-Operating	−358	−320	−650
Interest/Investment Income, Non-Operating	—	—	—
Interest Income (Expense), Net Non-Operating	−358	−320	−650
Gain (Loss) on Sale of Assets	—	—	—
Other, Net	444	50	318
Income Before Tax	**509**	**3,180.00**	**3,564.00**
Income Tax	−189	861	738
Income After Tax	**698**	**2,319.00**	**2,826.00**
Minority Interest	—	—	—
Equity In Affiliates	—	—	—
Net Income Before Extra. Items	**698**	**2,319.00**	**2,826.00**
Accounting Change	0	−1,827.00	1
Discontinued Operations	—	—	—
Extraordinary Items	—	—	—
Net Income	**$ 698**	**492**	**2,827.00**
Preferred Dividends	—	—	—
Income Available to Common Excl. Extra. Items	**698**	**2,319.00**	**2,826.00**
Income Available to Common Incl. Extra. Items	**698**	**492**	**2,827.00**
Basic/Primary Weighted Average Shares	802.3	799	816.2
Basic/Primary EPS Excl. Extra. Items	**0.87**	**2.902**	**3.462**
Basic/Primary EPS Incl. Extra. Items	**0.87**	**0.616**	**3.464**
Dilution Adjustment	0	0	0
Diluted Weighted Average Shares	808.9	808.4	829.3
Diluted EPS Excl. Extra. Items	**0.863**	**2.869**	**3.408**
Diluted EPS Incl. Extra. Items	**0.863**	**0.609**	**3.409**
Dividends per Share—Common Stock	0.68	0.68	0.68
Gross Dividends—Common Stock	—	570	577
Stock Based Compensation	—	—	—

Source: www.investor.stockpoint.com.

research to develop customer products, Boeing should remain a major competitor in the aerospace industry. Boeing's three fundamental goals are to: run healthy core businesses, leverage strengths into new markets, and open new frontiers. The company needs a clear strategic plan for the future.

Commercial Aircraft

Boeing has reduced the number of labor hours required to produce a Boeing 737 from 30,000 to under 10,000, to better compete. Since 2000, Boeing has streamlined its aircraft production operations, which resulted in a four-day reduction in the production of the 737. To match capacity with output to remain profitable, Boeing vacated and disposed of more than 4.5 million square feet of facilities and reduced the supplier base by 16 percent. Reducing the production time results in product cost reduction and better customer response time. Boeing has also streamlined the production of the 717 and 757 and plans to extend these innovations to the 747, 767, and 777 assembly operations.

Boeing's backlog of orders dropped from $89.8 billion in 2000 to $75.9 billion in 2001, and down to $63.9 in 2003. Backlogs have averaged about $78 billion over the past five years. Boeing worked to solve any possible delays in production by rapidly ramping-up the production process. The increased production rate helped to keep the backlog of orders under $70.0 billion. For two decades Boeing has averaged over a 60 percent share of the world market for commercial jets. In 2002 the number of undelivered jetcraft units under firm order was 1,083 as compared with 1,598 in 2000. As of December 2002, Boeing's expected number of commercial jet transport deliveries for 2002 was approximately 381, down 22 percent from the 489 aircraft delivered in 2000.

By the middle of November 2003 Boeing had received only 178 gross orders. Even with the decline in orders from Asian markets, approximately 33 percent of Boeing's 2002 airline sales were from non-U.S. carriers, down from 34 percent in 2000, and 47 percent in 1998. The backlogs, possible increases in military orders for aircraft, and possible returns to normal passenger demand may push production levels upward in the near future.

Considering the increased demand for passenger nonstop travel between cities, Boeing decided not to continue development of the Sonic Cruiser, but instead is developing the new Boeing 7E7 that will seat 200–250 passengers and fly 7,000 to 8,000 nautical miles, which uses technologies developed for the Sonic Cruiser. The 7E7 exceptional performance will come from improvements in engine technology, aerodynamics, materials, and systems; the jetcraft will set new standards for environmental responsibility and comfort. According to J. Lynn Lunsford, in "Boeing's New Baby" in the November 18, 2003, *Wall Street Journal,* the new 7E7 will not only be 20 percent more efficient, but it will have a rotunda entry with high ceiling, large windows, and mood lighting that will lead to 7E7 passenger appeal. These features added to the broadband Internet service of Connexion by Boeing[SM] being installed on Boeing planes should motivate passengers to request this aircraft. Boeing is developing the aircraft as a possible replacement for the Boeing 757s and 767s and a possible competitor with the Airbus 300s and 330s. About 3,000 orders possibly could come from the 7E7; the company plans to have the 7E7 ready for delivery by 2008.

Boeing commercial airjet segment currently produces the 717, 737, 747, 757, 767, and 777 families. Its commercial airjet development has focused on the new extended range derivatives of the 747 and 777 families, and the development of the new Boeing 7E7. Boeing is pleased with the response to the Boeing 777 family first put into service in 1995. The 777 was developed to meet the need for more efficient, comfortable, and high-capacity jets. The 777-200 and 777-300 series with recently launched extended range derivatives can seat from 305 to 550 passengers and have ranges from 5,925 to 8,865 miles. A Boeing survey produced results showing that three out of four passengers preferred the Boeing 777. Boeing had received a total of 619 orders and had delivered 424 aircraft by the end of 2002.

The smallest member of the Boeing jetliner family is the 737, the best-selling aircraft of all time with 4,379 deliveries by the end of 2002. The 737 family, developed for short- to medium-range, is designed for greater range, speed, and compliance with recent noise and emission standards. The 600, 700, 800, and 900 members of the 737 family have outsold all aircraft in their market. The 737 family includes two Boeing Business Jets, derivatives of the 737-700 and -800 members; Boeing had received 5,177 orders and had delivered a total of 4,379 by the end of 2002.

The Boeing 757 and 767 are medium-capacity, fuel-efficient twinjets that meet FAA requirements for extended-range operations. The 757 can carry 200 passengers as far as 3,900 nautical miles. In 1999, Boeing introduced the 757-300 which has 20 percent additional seating and 10 percent lower per-seat operating costs than the 757-200. The 757-300 can carry 280 passengers up to 3,995 miles. Boeing had received 1,049 orders and had delivered a total of 1,022 by the end of 2000.

The 767 is larger, carrying about 260 passengers in mixed class, with a range on some versions in excess of 6,000 nautical miles. The 767-200 can carry 181–224 passengers a range of 7,618 miles, and the 767-300, which comes in an extended range version, can carry 20 percent more passengers. This 767-400ER can carry 304–375 passengers up to a range of 6,501 miles. In 2000 Boeing committed to the production of a longer-range version of the 767-400ER; it had received 931 orders and had delivered a total of 892 by the end of 2002.

The flagship of the Boeing airplane family, the 747-400, can carry 568 passengers more than 8,000 nautical miles, and offers airline customers the lowest seat-mile costs of any twin-aisle commercial jetcraft in the world. The new extended range version offers a range of 8,850 miles. The 747-400 has both an all-cargo and a Combi model for passengers and freight. The Boeing 747 freight aircraft is in great demand at the Tokyo International Airport, which handles more than 1.5 million tons of freight, more than any other airport in the world. The 747-400F gives Boeing's airline customers the capability of carrying 20 tons more payload on the routes they can fly compared to 747-200 freighters, or carrying the same payload 800 nautical miles farther. Boeing had received orders for 1,371 and delivered a total of 1,319 by the end of 2002.

Deliveries with leased aircraft in parenthesis, as reported by the company, were as follows:

	2003	2002	2001	2000
717	12(11)	20	49(10)	32
737 Classic	0	—	—	2
737 NG	173	223(2)	299(5)	279
747	19(1)	27(1)	31(1)	25
757	14	29	45	45
767	24(5)	35(1)	40	44
777	39	47	61	55
MD-90	0	—	2	4
MD-11	0	—	—	3

The company reported the following key financial information for the Commercial Aircraft segment for the most recent three years (numbers are all in millions of dollars):

	2003	2002	2001	2000
Revenues	$22,408	$28,387	$35,056	$31,171
Operating Income	707	2,017	2,632	2,736
Assets	—	9,726	10,851	10,367
Liabilities	—	6,051	8,211	8,539
Research and Development cost	676	768	858	574
Contractual back-log of rders	63,900	68,159	75,850	89,780

These operating profits translate into operating margins of 7.1 percent in 2002, and 6.7 percent in 2001. For the nine months ended September 30, 2003, revenues were $40,308 million, compared to $37,287 million for the same period in 2002. The increase was made even with strong competition from Airbus.

Competition in Commercial Aircraft

Boeing's most formidable competitor in the commercial aircraft industry is Airbus, formed in 1970 as a loose federation of four European countries. By 2000, the company had become the European Aeronautic Defense and Space Co. (EADS), formed from aerospace groups in Germany, France, and Spain. In 2001, president and CEO Noel Forgeard changed the ownership structure, and Airbus is now 80 percent owned by EDS, a publicly traded company, and 20 percent owned by British Aerospace. Alex Taylor III, in his November 2003 *Fortune* article "Lord of the Air," wrote that Airbus is expected to deliver 300 aircraft versus 280 Boeing deliveries and has a backlog of 1,500 aircraft that is 400 more than Boeing. The 7.0 percent operating return for Airbus in 2002 is almost the same as the 7.1 percent return for Boeing. Boeing and Airbus have greatly differing forecasts for the size of commercial plane that airlines will be most inclined to purchase to meet their passenger needs. Airbus is forecasting a future demand for a large number of super jumbo commercial airplanes that will seat up to 555 passengers, and Boeing is forecasting a future demand for a large number of midsized commercial aircraft seating 200–250 passengers to satisfy passenger demand for nonstop travel between cities. To meet the future demand in its forecast, Airbus is developing the A380, a large, double-decker aircraft that will seat 555 passengers and have a cost per passenger mile of only 2.5 cents, according to Taylor. Airbus already has over 100 A380 aircraft orders that should be sufficient to break even at the full price, and expects to deliver the first aircraft in 2005. The first purchasers possibly are getting discounts of up to 30 or 40 percent, so Airbus may need many additional orders to break even.

Airbus is depending on future passengers wanting the large aircraft. Boeing is banking on the forecast that there will be only a small market for large aircraft and a large market for a 200–250 passenger aircraft like the Boeing 7E7. One argument for the super-sized A380 is that many airlines have difficulty getting slots at airports due to scarce space. According to Andy Pasztor, in the October 2, 2003, *Wall Street Journal* article "Airports Brace for Delays (Again)," the problem of gridlock at airports is returning. Chicago O'Hare, Dallas/Fort Worth International, Miami International, Denver International, and Cincinnati/Northern Kentucky air terminals are planning multimillion-dollar, long-term expansions. Boeing's Air Traffic Management (ATM) program could reduce gridlock earlier and also help during the major expansion operations. The ATM system Boeing has under development would make more efficient use of airports, thereby allowing more aircraft to land and depart. The size aircraft demanded in the near future will have significant impact on Boeing's commercial airplane production. With planning, quality, service, cost/management, and competitive pricing, Boeing's airliners now provide over 12,000 of the world fleet.

Customer Service

Boeing is meeting the needs of the customer, and the customer's customer. In the highly competitive market for commercial aircraft, its reputation for customer service is an effective marketing tool. Boeing provides regional world centers for proactive, value-added maintenance, parts and training, and provides ready access to parts and training programs using the WEB and ED-ROM technologies. Customers can access parts information on the Web site MyBoeingFleet.com. Information availability of parts, maintenance, engineering, and operational data are provided for customers. Boeing is also focusing on serving the customer by serving the customer's customer. Connexion by Boeing^{SM} and ATM are beginning to play key roles in enhancing the services that Boeing offers.

Boeing Frontiers

Connexion by Boeing^{SM}

Connexion by Boeing^{SM} is a dynamic breakthrough in consumer and commercial airline service that is beginning to provide air travelers an unparalleled array of high-speed data communication services via a space-based network. The venture's strategic focus is on broadband, high-speed real-time Web service to commercial, business, and military customers. Boeing, leading the airborne broadband communications frontier, has excelled at blending creative innovation with large-scale integration. Its competency in satellite systems, commercial aircraft construction, and high-speed critical data transfer methodology gives it a competitive advantage that no narrow-band provider can match. On May 7, 2002, Connexion by Boeing^{SM} received the first FAA certification for an onboard broadband information system. On January 15, 2003, Lufthansa passengers became the first to experience in flight Internet connectivity. Scandinavian Airlines, All Nippon Airways, Singapore Airlines, Japan Airlines, and others have signed for the Connection broadband Internet access. The service can also play a role in enhancement of aerospace security. Connexion by Boeing^{SM} is an example of a new frontier developed by using the company's core strengths.

Air Traffic Management

Boeing is developing an Air Traffic Management (ATM) system to replace the current ground-based program. The proposed ATM would integrate today's separate control, communications, navigation, surveillance, and weather services into a single, seamless Common Information Network (CIN). The new ATM will rely primarily on Global Positioning Satellites (GPS). The system should be relatively inexpensive and easy to install on older airlines, both Boeing and Airbus. Boeing's new planes come equipped with the technology that allows them to fly from place to place without ground control. According to a May 17, 2001, *Wall Street Journal* article by J. Lynn Lunsford, United Parcel Service (UPS) Airlines and Federal Express have already been using an early satellite version to improve operations at large hubs.

On October 20, 2003, Boeing announced that the International Organization for Standardization (ISO) has awarded the ATM the ISO 9001:2000 Certification. The ISO certified the ATM as meeting or exceeding its requirements for quality management systems. The ATM could be implemented in the near future. The objectives of the ATM are to make flying safer and more secure, increase capacity, dramatically reduce congestion and delays, and keep aviation affordable and accessible for commercial, military, business, and general aviation operators.

As global air travel and air freight business increase, the current ground-based system becomes more overloaded. The proposed new Boeing ATM program may be the answer. However, the new program will require cooperation of all stakeholders in the airline industry to be successful.

Integrated Defense Systems

Military Aircraft and Missiles

Nuclear proliferation in North Korea, Operation "Enduring Freedom," and the continued war against terrorism highlight the need for defense systems. Boeing is a major player in the field of military aircraft and missiles, its biggest customer being the U.S. Department of Defense. Boeing also sells to foreign governments under licenses granted by the U.S. government to its Allies.

This segment of the company produces tactical fighters, trainers, helicopters, military transports, tankers, strike missiles, and special purpose planes. It also provides aerospace support products and services. The biggest programs in this industry segment are the C-17 Globemaster transport program and the F/A-18E/F Super Hornet fighter program. The segment also includes the AH-64 Apache, JADM, F-22 Raptor, F-15 Eagle, V-22 Osprey, and CH-47 Chinook programs.

Deliveries with leased aircraft in parenthesis, as reported by the company, were as follows:

	2003	2002	2001	2000
C-17 Globemaster	16	16	14(4)	13
F/A-18E/F Super Hornet	44	40	36	26
T-45TS Goshawk	12	14	15	16
F-15 Eagle	4	3	—	5
CH-47 Chinook	0	7	11	7
737 C-40A Clipper	1	3	4	—
AH-64 Apache	0	15	7	8

The company reported the following key financial information for the Military Aircraft and Missiles segment for the most recent three years (numbers are all in millions of dollars):

	2003	2002	2001	2000
Revenues	$14,984	$13,990	$12,451	$11,924
Operating Income	1,894	1,645	1,346	1,245
Assets	—	2,232	2,162	2,950
Liabilities	—	1,499	1,297	1,104
Research and Development cost	419	345	258	257
Contractual back-log of orders	25,300	21,073	17,630	17,113

These operating profits translate into operating margins of 11.8 percent in 2002, 10.8 percent in 2001, and 10.4 percent in 2000. Revenues were $14.0 billion in 2002, up from $12.5 billion in 2001 and $11.9 billion in 2000. For the nine months ending September 30, 2003, revenues were $11,214 million, compared to $10,244 million for the same period in 2002, an increase of over 9 percent.

Boeing is using its "customer knowledge, technical strength, and large-scale systems integration capabilities to shape the market." The company spent $345 million on research in 2002, up from $258 million in 2001. The focus of the increase in research spending was on the development of the 767 Tanker programs for the U.S. military and international customers. The Boeing 767 Tanker serves transport needs and provides a reliable aerial refueling system. Italy is the first customer for the 767 Tanker scheduled for delivery in 2005.

Boeing research dollars are also spent on innovative products such as unmanned, reusable aircraft to fly bombing missions. These craft combine some of the best features of missiles with those of manned aircraft: (1) the aircraft loses no people if shot down; and (2) the aircraft delivers its payload and returns the delivery system for reuse, unlike missiles, which destroy the delivery system with the payload.

The U.S. commitment to the war against terrorism and maintaining a military presence in Iraq and Afghanistan seem to indicate that the government will be procuring additional military hardware and services in the years to come. Boeing's Military Aircraft and Missile segment is poised to benefit from additional purchases of equipment and services.

Space and Communications

The Space and Communications segment, which is the newest and smallest of Boeing's segments, seems to be the fastest growing. The five major areas of operations in this segment are integrated battlespace, missile defense, human space flight and exploration, launch and satellite, and homeland security. Boeing's president set a goal of making Boeing "number one in space." Boeing has Delta programs that are rocket boosters used by NASA and some private satellite-launch groups to put satellites in orbit and to launch other space-related activities. In November 2002, Boeing successfully launched the Delta IV rocket powered by the newest rocket engine since the 1980s.

Deliveries of products in this segment are as follows:

	2003	2002	2001	2000
Delta II	4	3	12	10
Delta III	2	1	—	—
BSS Satellites	3	6	7	5
Network Satellites	1	—	—	—

The company reported the following key financial information for the Space and Communications for the most recent three years (numbers are all in millions of dollars):

	2003	2002	2001	2000
Revenues	$12,376	$10,964	$10,364	$8,039
Operating Income	(1,128)	364	619	(243)
Assets	—	10,521	10,299	9,629
Liabilities	—	3,406	3,123	2,903
Research and Development cost	427	397	526	526
Contractual back-log of orders	15,600	14,941	13,111	13,707

These operating profits translate into margins of 3.2 percent in 2002 and 5.9 percent in 2001, and a loss of 3 percent in 2000. Revenues were $11.0 billion in 2002, up slightly from $10.4 billion in 2001. For the nine months ending September 30, 2003, revenues were $8,901 million, compared to $7,701 million for a similar period in the previous year, an increase of over 15 percent.

Competition in Integrated Defense Systems

Lockheed Martin, the major competitor for Boeing Integrated Defense Systems, produces military aircraft, rocket launchers, and other space equipment. In 2002, 57 percent of Lockheed Martin's sales were from the U.S. Department of Defense, 20 percent from NASA and other government agencies, and 17 percent from international customers. In 2002, Boeing IDS operating income of $2.009 billion exceeded that of Lockheed Martin operating income of 1.158 by only $851 million. Earlier, Lockheed Martin had suffered a $1.046 billion operating loss in 2001 and a $.519 billion loss in 2000. In 2002, Lockheed Martin with sales of $26.562 billion managed to top Boeing IDS sales of $24.957 by $1.605 billion.

The prospects for this segment are quite varied. For its governmental customers Boeing offers airborne mission systems, space systems, satellite systems, and security services, and for commercial customers, the company offers satellite manufacturing, hybrid network systems, security systems, and telecommunications. The launch services sector is dependent on NASA and the commercial satellite launch market. This is a highly competitive area. The information and communication services sector is positioned to experience rapid growth. In 2002, Boeing Homeland Security and Service unit was selected to implement some U.S. Department of Homeland Security Operation Safe Commerce pilot programs. The human space flight sector expects relatively flat growth over the next ten years. Boeing's activities will include completing existing contracts for the International Space Station and operations and maintenance on the Space Shuttle program.

Capital Financing

Budget crunches are motivating commercial and military customers to be interested in Boeing Capital Company (BCC) for financing arrangements. The BCC acts as a captive finance subsidiary and provides market-based leases and loans mainly for airlines. BCC has about 22 percent of its work in the commercial equipment leasing and financing arrangement markets. Customer and consumer finance segment revenues are made up primarily of interest from financing receivables and lease income from equipment leased to others under operating leases. A major expense of the segment is depreciation on the equipment leased. No interest expense on debt incurred by the company is included in the calculation of segment income. (The interest and debt expense for the company is reported as a single amount on the income statement. It is not allocated to the segments.)

The revenues from the segment were $994 million, $815 million, and $545 million for the years 2002, 2001, and 2000, respectively. Comparable operating incomes were $482 million, $562 million, and $397 million, respectively. The segment employed assets of $11.840 billion, $9.252 billion, and $5.391 billion; and had liabilities of $345 million, $316 million, and $198 million in 2002, 2001, and 2000. The book value of Boeing Capital Company went up over 28 percent from 2001 to 2002 and up 72 percent from 2000 to 2001.

This segment is likely to continue to grow as long as airline companies and others need additional airplanes. Because of the high cost of purchasing a commercial aircraft, many of Boeing's customers will opt for either financing the purchase or leasing the aircraft from the company due to tight budget constraints. This should provide a steady source of revenue for Boeing Capital. As long as interest rates are low, the segment can make a good profit.

Conclusion

The war, "Enduring Freedom," has reduced our nation's supply of aircraft, missiles, and other aerospace products, thereby requiring repletion of these products by Boeing and other manufacturers. The airline passenger business is expected to double over the next 20 years with the air cargo business expected to double over the same period. The space and communications market is looking forward to significant increases in the commercial market. Boeing has greatly reduced the labor cost of commercial aircraft. However, it still has to compete with Airbus, a major commercial jetliners manufacturer; Lockheed Martin, a major defense contractor; and with others in the aerospace market. Boeing also has to continue to work on coordinating activities and reducing costs of its many operations.

With expertise in each of the areas, Boeing should be able to compete with technological innovations and costs, and to open more frontiers. The aerospace business environment remains uncertain but Boeing, with its extraordinary resources and magnificent record in aerospace, with an excellent strategic plan should continue to be the world leader in aerospace.

Prepare a strategic plan for CEO Philip M. Condit. Keep in mind that according to the 2002 *Annual Report,* Boeing's plan for the future is to move from being market driven to market shaping. Boeing will work to understand and appreciate where the customer and customer's customer want to go and blaze a trail or pave a way for them.

EXHIBIT 2
Boeing Company (BA)

ANNUAL BALANCE SHEET IN MILLIONS OF U.S. DOLLARS (EXCEPT FOR PER SHARE ITEMS)	AS OF 12/31/03	AS OF 12/31/02	AS OF 12/31/01
		Reclass. 12/31/03	
Cash & Equivalents	$ 4,633.00	2,333.00	633
Short Term Investments	—	—	—
Cash and Short Term Investments	4,633.00	2,333.00	633
Trade Accounts Receivable, Net	4,474.00	5,007.00	5,156.00
Other Receivables	201	—	—
Total Receivables, Net	4,675.00	5,007.00	5,156.00
Total Inventory	5,338.00	6,184.00	7,559.00
Prepaid Expenses	—	—	—
Other Current Assets	2,570.00	3,331.00	3,497.00
Total Current Assets	**17,216.00**	**16,855.00**	**16,845.00**
Property/Plant/Equipment—Gross	—	—	—
Accumulated Depreciation	—	—	—
Property/Plant/Equipment, Net	8,432.00	8,765.00	8,459.00
Goodwill, Net	1,913.00	2,760.00	5,127.00
Intangibles, Net	1,035.00	1,128.00	1,320.00
Long Term Investments	—	—	—
Other Long Term Assets	24,397.00	22,834.00	17,227.00
Total Assets	**52,993.00**	**52,342.00**	**48,978.00**
Accounts Payable	13,563.00	13,739.00	14,237.00
Accrued Expenses	—	—	—
Notes Payable/Short Term Debt	—	—	—
Current Port. LT Debt/Capital Leases	1,144.00	1,814.00	1,399.00
Other Current Liabilities	3,719.00	4,257.00	4,930.00
Total Current Liabilities	**18,426.00**	**19,810.00**	**20,566.00**

(continued)

EXHIBIT 2
Continued

ANNUAL BALANCE SHEET IN MILLIONS OF U.S. DOLLARS (EXCEPT FOR PER SHARE ITEMS)	AS OF 12/31/03	AS OF 12/31/02	AS OF 12/31/01
Long Term Debt	13,299.00	12,589.00	10,866.00
Capital Lease Obligations	—	—	—
Total Long Term Debt	**13,299.00**	**12,589.00**	**10,866.00**
Total Debt	**14,443.00**	**14,403.00**	**12,265.00**
Deferred Income Tax	—	0	177
Minority Interest	—	—	—
Other Liabilities	13,149.00	12,247.00	6,544.00
Total Liabilities	**44,874.00**	**44,646.00**	**38,153.00**
Redeemable Preferred Stock	—	—	—
Preferred Stock—Non Redeemable, Net	—	—	—
Common Stock	5,059.00	5,059.00	5,059.00
Additional Paid-In Capital	2,880.00	2,141.00	1,975.00
Retained Earnings (Accum. Deficit)	14,387.00	14,262.00	14,340.00
Treasury Stock—Common	−8,322.00	−8,397.00	−8,509.00
Other Equity	−4,145.00	−4,045.00	−488
Total Equity	**8,119.00**	**7,696.00**	**10,825.00**
Total Liabilities & Shareholders' Equity	**$52,993.00**	**52,342.00**	**48,978.00**
Shares Outs.—Common Stock	800.3	799.7	797.9
Total Common Shares Outstanding	**800.3**	**799.7**	**797.9**
Total Preferred Stock Shares Outs.	**—**	**—**	**—**
Employees (actual figures)	157,000.00	166,000.00	186,900.00
Number of Common Shareholders (actual figures)	—	138,000.00	—

Source: www.investor.stockpoint.com.

EXHIBIT 3
The Boeing Company and Subsidiaries Sales by Geographic Area (in millions)

	YEAR ENDED DECEMBER 31,		
	2002	2001	2000
Asia, other than China	$ 7,614	$ 7,112	$ 5,568
China	1,442	1,504	1,026
Europe	5,871	8,434	9,038
Oceania	1,813	895	887
Africa	525	573	542
Non-U.S. Western Hemisphere	669	875	559
United States	36,135	38,805	33,701
Total Sales	$54,069	$58,198	$51,321

EXHIBIT 4
Boeing's Organizational Chart

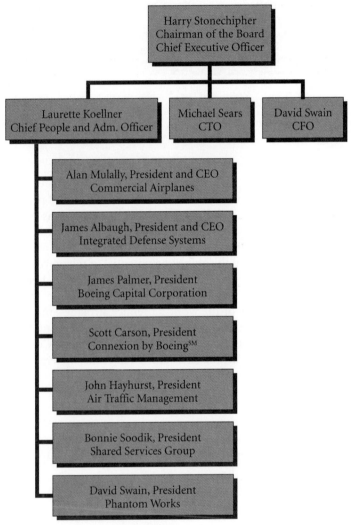

Source: Adapted from 2003 *Annual Report.*

31 Lockheed Martin Corporation—2004

Jim Meshaw
Francis Marion University

LMT

www.lockheedmartin.com/
The effects of war: death; loss of loved ones; mass destruction of public and private property; burning oil fields; the threat of biological and chemical weapons being used; unknowns about the economy; declining consumer confidence; increased focus on the war and less attention to education and other needed public programs; increased scrutiny by other nations around the globe; the potential of taking years to recover from the devastation—amidst these negative events, some companies benefit when war or the threat of war occurs. One such company is Lockheed Martin, which develops, produces, and distributes many of the world's premier airplanes, missiles, and defense systems. Some of the company's products include the famous F-16 fighter, F/A-22, C-5, and C-130 aircraft; support for the F-117 Stealth, Aegis Combat System, Patriot Advanced Capability missile, the Atlas and Titan rocket systems, and various homeland security systems.

History

The Lockheed Martin Corporation was formed in 1995, when the Lockheed Aircraft Company acquired Martin Marietta. Although these were two separate companies, they had similar histories.

Lockheed

After his first venture into the aircraft business failed, Allan Loughead formed the Lockheed Aircraft Company in 1926 in Hollywood, California. Two years after the company's inception, its Vega model was used to make the first transcontinental flight in the United States. Amelia Earhart utilized a later model of the Vega in her transatlantic flight from the United States to Ireland in 1932, the first flight of this type performed by a woman.

During the 1930s and 1940s, Lockheed placed much emphasis on developing aircraft that were to be used by the U.S. military. In 1944, the first American jet fighter was flown, the Lockheed XP-80 Shooting Star. The company reached several milestones during the 1950s: the C-130 Hercules was first produced in 1954; this plane is still in production and holds the record as being the military airlifter that has been in use for the longest period of time. Also, the Polaris ballistic missile was developed in 1956, with the help of the U.S. Navy.

Other notable projects advanced by Lockheed are the Deep Quest underwater research vehicle, the Trident missile program, the development of heat-resistant tiles for the Space Shuttle, and assistance in developing the Stealth fighters.

Martin

The Glenn L. Martin Company, founded in 1912, merged with the Wright Company in 1916 and then, in 1917, backed out of this merger and was reestablished. In 1918 the company built the MB-2, the first twin-engine bomber, and in 1935 the first transpacific fight was completed, utilizing the M-130.

Like Lockheed, Martin placed much emphasis on the development of military aircraft. In 1945, its B-29 bombers dropped the atomic bombs on Hiroshima and Nagasaki. During the 1950s, the ballistic missile programs were ramped up at Martin, with the development of the Pershing Missile program and the Titan I ICBM. Other notable projects for Martin and Martin Marietta were the docking adapter for Skylab, the Titan II, III, and IV missiles and the Magellan spacecraft.

Lockheed and Martin Marietta merged in 1995 and became one of the largest defense and technology companies in the world. Following this event, in 1998, Lockheed Martin attempted to merge with Northrop Grumman. This proposed merger, which would have made the company the largest in the world at the time, did not receive governmental support because of antitrust regulations, and was not successful.

Internal Assessment

Lockheed Martin, headquartered in Bethesda, Maryland, today operates 939 facilities in 457 cities; the company also conducts business from 56 foreign nations. Lockheed Martin currently employs approximately 125,000 workers, including 50,000 scientists and engineers and 20,000 software and systems engineers. The company utilizes many process improvement techniques, including Six Sigma and lean manufacturing, to reduce its costs and improve the quality of its products. Lockheed Martin expects that the savings generated by these programs during the last five years will exceed $2.6 billion.

Lockheed Martin is primarily involved in researching, designing, developing, manufacturing, integrating, and operating advanced technology systems, products, and services. Effectively accomplishing these tasks will enable the company to achieve its vision—"To be the world's best advanced technology systems integrator."

As shown in Exhibit 1, Lockheed Martin generated $31.8 billion in sales in 2003, approximately 80 percent of which were derived from the U.S. government, with an additional 14 percent of its sales coming from foreign governments. Net income more than doubled in 2003 to over $1 billion. Commercial customers generated the remaining 6 percent of its revenue, created mainly by sales of satellites, launch services, and information technology services. Lockheed Martin is separated into four business segments—systems integration, space systems, aeronautics, and technology services, which are briefly described below.

As 80 percent of Lockheed Martin's volume is generated by sales to the U.S. government, the company is heavily involved in political action committees. From 1990 to 2000 the company contributed in excess of $10.6 million to various candidates and committees, including $4.2 million in 1999. These expenditures were followed by lobbying contributions of $9.8 million in 2000. The majority of this funding is directed toward influential leaders who have the ability to make decisions that may positively affect Lockheed Martin.

EXHIBIT 1

Net Sales by Customer

(IN MILLIONS)	2002	2001	2000
U.S. Government			
Systems Integration	$ 7,741	$ 6,952	$ 6,855
Space Systems	6,276	5,956	5,932
Aeronautics	4,483	3,437	2,784
Technology Services	2,735	2,269	2,120
	$21,235	$18,614	$17,691
Foreign Governments			
Systems Integration	$1,583	$1,790	$2,231
Space Systems	60	94	79
Aeronautics	1,971	1,899	2,061
Technology Services	76	104	117
	$3,690	$3,887	$4,488
Commercial			
Systems Integration	$ 279	$ 272	$ 561
Space Systems	1,048	786	1,328
Aeronautics	17	19	40
Technology Services	293	390	413
	$1,637	$1,467	$2,342

Source: Lockheed Martin 2002 *Annual Report*, p. 78.

Business Segments

Systems Integration

This business unit designs and produces various systems for air, land, and sea applications. The preeminent components of this business unit are Naval Electronics and Surveillance Systems; Missiles and Fire Control Systems; Command, Control, Communications, Computers and Intelligence Systems; and Systems Integration, which is comprised of various business solutions. Some of the primary products for this segment are missile defense systems, precision-guided weapons, vessel and submarine combat systems, fingerprint identification systems, and simulation and training systems. This diverse business segment, which contains over 1,000 programs, generates approximately 36 percent of Lockheed's sales.

Note in Exhibit 2 that after having a poor year in 2001, where net sales declined 7 percent and operating profit declined 8 percent in comparison to 2000, Systems Integration net sales grew 7 percent in 2002, driven primarily by growth in three specific areas:

- $285 million increase in Missile and Fire Control due mainly to increased volume in missile programs.
- $275 million increase in Command, Control, Communications, Computers and Intelligence, primarily due to increased information superiority programs.
- $145 million increase in Naval Electronics and Surveillance due to higher volumes in radar systems and surface systems.

EXHIBIT 2

Selected Financial Data by Business Segment

(IN MILLIONS)	2002	2001	2000
Net Sales			
Systems Integration	$ 9,603	$ 9,014	$ 9,647
Space Systems	7,384	6,836	7,339
Aeronautics	6,471	5,355	4,885
Technology Services	3,104	2,763	2,649
	$26,562	$23,968	$24,520
Operating Profit			
Systems Integration	$ 952	$ 906	$ 981
Space Systems	443	360	345
Aeronautics	448	329	280
Technology Services	177	114	106
	$1,158	$833	$1,105

Source: Lockheed Martin 2002 *Annual Report,* p. 39.

These increased sales helped this segment to realize a 5 percent increase in operating profit over the previous year.

Space Systems

The Space Systems segment designs, develops, engineers, and produces satellites, ground systems, launches, and strategic missiles. This business segment, which generated approximately 28 percent of Lockheed Martin's sales in 2002, has developed various satellites for both commercial and governmental use; the Titan and Atlas launch vehicles; and strategic missiles, including the Trident, Polaris, and Poseidon programs. Lockheed Martin believes that future government contracts in this area will include global positioning, space-based radar planetary exploration, and ground reconnaissance programs, and the company intends to compete in each of these.

Net sales for Space Systems rebounded from a weak 2001, where net sales decreased 7 percent in comparison to 2000, and grew by 8 percent in 2002, mainly due to increased volume in government space. Operating profit, which had increased 4 percent from 2000 to 2001, grew 23 percent from 2001 to 2002, led by the Commercial Space business.

Aeronautics

The Aeronautics unit, which generated 24 percent of Lockheed Martin's 2002 sales, designs and develops military fighters, airlift aircraft, and technologies that are associated with each. Some of the more famous of these aircraft are the F/A-22, the F-16, the F-35, and the C-130J. Historically, much of the design and development of these aircraft has been influenced by the U.S. Department of Defense and the U.S. Armed Forces, but as the international portion of Lockheed Martin's business grows in this area, other countries may play a larger role than previously.

Net sales for this segment increased by 21 percent from 2001 to 2002, primarily due to the F-35, F/A-22, F-16, and C-5 programs, which collectively generated approximately $1.6 billion more revenue in 2002. These increases contributed to the

36 percent increase in operating profit from 2001 to 2002. From 2000 to 2001, net sales and operating profit grew by 10 percent and 18 percent, respectively.

Technology Services

The smallest business unit, generating 12 percent of company sales in 2002, is the Technology Services unit. This segment provides services to both governmental and commercial groups, with offerings consisting of, but not limited to, program management, systems development, simulation engineering, network services, applications development, and consulting.

Technology Services net sales and operating profit grew by 12 percent and 55 percent, respectively, from 2001 to 2002. The two primary contributors to these were more effective performance in commercial information technology and increased volume in the government information technology. From 2000 to 2001, net sales increased 4 percent, while operating profit increased 8 percent.

Technology

Lockheed Martin must continue to engineer and manufacture new products in order to keep up with developing needs. As most, if not all, of these products are highly technologically advanced, there are huge costs associated with the research and development that is necessary for the company's products. It is interesting to note that after increasing research and development (R&D) expenditures in 2001 from $863 million to $875 million, the company reduced R&D spending to $830 million in 2002. Additionally, Lockheed Martin did not undertake production of any new products or lines of business in 2002, other than increasing the development of launch vehicles.

Natural Environment

Lockheed Martin has incurred liabilities in the past and is currently involved in several additional lawsuits. Under investigation is the former facility in Redlands, California, where the California Regional Water Quality Control Board has issued several orders against Lockheed Martin, with regard to the perchlorate concentration in the water. Lockheed Martin currently holds $185 million on its balance sheet to cover this liability. In a separate case, Lockheed Martin has also been involved with potential groundwater and soil contamination in Burbank and Glendale, California. It is expected that these occurrences may cost the company an additional $60 million. Possible soil and groundwater contamination may also have occurred in Great Neck, New York, due to Lockheed Martin's operations; it is expected that Lockheed Martin will incur an additional $70 million in costs to resolve these issues.

External Factors

Competitors

Lockheed Martin's primary competitors are Boeing, General Dynamics, Northrop Grumman, Raytheon, and United Technologies Corporation. These same companies are also sometimes partners with Lockheed Martin, as exemplified by the current United Space Alliance, a 50–50 partnership with Boeing. This relationship is responsible for the U.S. Air Force space-related operations and the ground processing of the Space Shuttle fleet. There are varying degrees to which these companies have the U.S. government as a customer, ranging from Raytheon's 73 percent of 2002 sales to United Technologies Corporation's 16 percent of 2002 sales.

Boeing is comprised of four primary business segments: Commercial Airplanes, Military Aircraft and Missile Systems, Space and Communications, and Boeing Capital Corporation. Boeing's 2002 sales were $54.1 billion, generated by serving customers in 145 countries around the globe. Currently, Boeing employs approximately 160,000 people, in 38 states and in 70 countries. Boeing is one of the dominant forces in the commercial jet aircraft segment, manufacturing the 737, 747, 767, and 777 class jets, in addition to the MD-80 and MD-90 models. Boeing is currently under contract for the Space Shuttle Flight Operations and Space Shuttle Main Engine also. Some of Lockheed Martin's principal competitors from Boeing, in the defense sector, are the Osprey aircraft, the Comanche helicopter, and the Harpoon class missiles.

General Dynamics is comprised of four main business units: Information Systems and Technology, Combat Systems, Marine Systems, and Aerospace; sales in 2002 were $13.8 billion, 64 percent of which were generated by the U.S. government. In addition to providing systems integration capabilities, General Dynamics manufactures military battle tanks, rockets, warheads, nuclear submarines, combat ships, and Gulfstream jets. General Dynamics is currently partnering with Lockheed Martin on the F-35 project, as the gun systems integrator.

Northrop Grumman is a global defense company that focuses on systems integration, defense electronics, advanced aircraft, space technology, and shipbuilding. Sales in 2002 were $17.2 billion, with revenues rather evenly distributed across the business units. Northrop Grumman currently employs approximately 120,000 people, across all 50 states and in 25 countries. Some of the products in competition with those of Lockheed Martin are the AWACS early warning radar, Longbow Hellfire missile, Longbow Apache helicopter, and B-2 Spirit stealth bomber. Northrop Grumman also designs and constructs nuclear-powered aircraft carriers and submarines.

Raytheon is comprised of five strategic business units—electronic systems, command, control, communication and information systems, technical services, commercial electronics, and aircraft. Collectively, the business units generated 2002 sales of $16.7 billion, being led by the electronics systems unit, with sales of $8.9 billion. Raytheon operates on a global scale and employs approximately 76,000. The company manufactures a variety of missiles, air traffic management systems, radar systems, aircraft components, and business jets, including the Hawker and Beechcraft. Raytheon is a strong competitor of Lockheed Martin in the missile arena, with its Patriot, Tomahawk, and Stinger programs.

United Technologies Corporation, a global company with 2002 sales of $28.2 billion, is comprised of four diverse segments: Otis—elevator and escalator manufacturing, installation, and service; Carrier—heating and air conditioning systems; Pratt & Whitney—aircraft engines; and Flight Systems—aviation components and military helicopters. The Flight Systems segment is the only segment directly in competition with Lockheed Martin, producing the Black Hawk and new RAH-66 Comanche helicopters.

Raw Materials

Aluminum and titanium, which are required for the production of Lockheed Martin's products, are not unusually scarce, and there is little concern that these will become unavailable. However, carbon fiber, nicalon fiber, and aluminum lithium are currently provided by a sole supplier and an interruption of supply would probably lead to delays in production.

Government

As the majority of Lockheed Martin's business volume is conducted with the government, it is heavily regulated. Within this environment, fines may be levied or contracts may be terminated for either lack of performance by Lockheed Martin or at the convenience of the government. While Lockheed Martin utilizes various types of contracts, in most instances, should a contract be terminated, the company would receive compensation for any completed work.

Labor Market

The current labor market is a strong concern to all companies in the aerospace and defense industry. On the rise are average earnings and weekly hours worked, while the supply of skilled labor, mechanics in particular, is not sufficient.

There is also a shortage of manufacturers in the machine tool field, a vital component of the aerospace and defense industry. There are currently only four or five machine tool companies in the world that are able to produce the advanced machinery that is required in the production of aircraft frames and engines. This scarcity of resources has been experienced firsthand by Lockheed Martin from the summer of 2002 until the present. After being awarded the Joint Strike Fighter (JSF) contract in 2002, Lockheed Martin placed a significant order, $12.3 million, with Ingersoll Milling Machine Company, one of the few companies capable of fulfilling this request. In April of 2003, after Lockheed Martin had received no portion of this order, it was discovered that Ingersoll had shut down and filed for bankruptcy. Lockheed Martin was forced to find another supplier in order to continue with the JSF program.

Another factor in this area is a recent political development whereby any new weapon for the United States must be manufactured by American machine tools. With the insufficient supply of labor that exists in this area, alternatives need to be developed. If American companies do not develop plans to turn this sector around, there could be dire consequences for the defense industry.

Declining Satellite Market

Much concern exists in the Space Systems unit, with regard to the commercial segment. There is currently an overcapacity of approximately 35–50 percent in satellite manufacturing. This overcapacity of production, combined with declining consumer demand, and low margins, approximately 5 percent, has caused underutilization of the resources and has led to company bankruptcies over the last several years; these bankruptcies include Globalstar, Iridium, and Orbcomm.

Industry Outlook

While the mid- to late 1990s saw much growth in the aerospace and defense industry, analysts predict that over the next several years, the growth in the industry will be slow to moderate, between 3 and 5 percent. The Bush administration has requested substantial increases in defense spending for 2004. These conditions, coupled with increasing focus on budget deficits, healthcare costs, education, and Social Security, leads many to believe that high growth in the industry will not be experienced in future years.

Current News

Space Exploration

In August 2003, Lockheed Martin, accompanied by Jet Propulsion Laboratory and the University of Arizona, was awarded development of NASA's Mars Scout program.

This $325 million program will be used to engineer and develop a spacecraft to be sent to Mars in order to conduct analysis of several planetary factors. The vehicle is scheduled to be launched in 2007 and land on Mars in May 2008.

Upcoming Projects

The U.S. Department of Homeland Security is developing a program whose purpose is to monitor the entry, status, and departure of foreign nationals in the United States. The U.S. Visitor and Immigrant Status Indicator Technology (to be known as US VISIT) system will be the vehicle to monitor and measure these activities. Lockheed Martin has announced that it will bid on the project, whose expected cost to the U.S. government is $1.5 billion.

Lockheed Martin has also been awarded a five-year, $140 million contract with the Federal Bureau of Investigation, in which Lockheed Martin will support the development of the security architecture for the FBI's computers and networks. This program will be designed to increase the quantity of safeguards within the FBI's systems.

Legal Issues

Lockheed Martin is suing one of its leading competitors in the launch vehicle segment, Boeing, alleging that Boeing used proprietary pricing information from Lockheed Martin during the bids for the Evolved Expendable Launch Vehicle in 1998, which Boeing ultimately won. Speculatively, the penalties that may be levied against Boeing are at least $500 million in damages and potentially $1.5 billion in punitive damages. Additionally, Lockheed Martin may seek further damages from Boeing in order to recapture three times its lost profits on the venture.

Resulting from another legal matter, Lockheed Martin will be forced to reimburse the U.S. government $37.9 million, stemming from allegations that the company overbilled the Air Force for navigation pods and infrared targeting. Although Lockheed Martin denies any wrongdoing in this matter, a spokesperson for the company stated that the fines would be paid in order to eliminate further distractions regarding this matter.

Conclusion

For the last two years, Lockheed Martin has focused on reducing its backlog, improving its credit rating, yielding greater financial flexibility, and increasing its cash flow. In the years to come, the company envisions streamlining and bolstering its position within the commercial satellite industry, generating more value from the Space Systems programs and increasing its attention to F/A-22 and Space-Based Infrared System programs. The company foresees greater cash generation, margin expansion, and the continued recruiting and hiring of the best available talent.

Over the last several years, Lockheed Martin has reaped the benefits from a renewed American focus on defense and anti-terrorism. This focus has led to the support of new Stealth fighter programs, strong interest in domestic safety programs, and various military programs. However, there may be a lessening of support of these types of programs as politicians are forced to examine and solve domestic problems, such as education, healthcare, and deficit issues, just to name a few.

EXHIBIT 3
Lockheed Martin Corp (LMT)

ANNUAL INCOME STATEMENT IN MILLIONS OF U.S. DOLLARS (EXCEPT FOR PER SHARE ITEMS)	12 MONTHS ENDING 12/31/03	12 MONTHS ENDING 12/31/02
Revenue	$31,824.00	26,578.00
Other Revenue	—	—
Total Revenue	**31,824.00**	**26,578.00**
Cost of Revenue	29,805.00	24,629.00
Gross Profit	**2,019.00**	**1,949.00**
Selling/General/Administrative Expenses	—	—
Research & Development	—	—
Depreciation/Amortization	—	—
Interest Expense (Income), Net Operating	—	—
Unusual Expense (Income)	—	—
Other Operating Expenses	—	—
Total Operating Expense	**29,805.00**	**24,629.00**
Operating Income	**2,019.00**	**1,949.00**
Interest Expense, Net Non-Operating	—	−581
Interest/Investment Income, Non-Operating	—	—
Interest Income (Expense), Net Non-Operating	—	−581
Gain (Loss) on Sale of Assets	—	—
Other, Net	−487	−791
Income Before Tax	**1,532.00**	**577**
Income Tax	479	44
Income After Tax	**1,053.00**	**533**
Minority Interest	—	—
Equity In Affiliates	—	—
Net Income Before Extra. Items	**1,053.00**	**533**
Accounting Change	—	—
Discontinued Operations	0	−33
Extraordinary Items	—	—
Net Income	**$ 1,053.00**	**500**
Preferred Dividends	—	—
Income Available to Common Excl. Extra. Items	**1,053.00**	**533**
Income Available to Common Incl. Extra. Items	**1,053.00**	**500**
Basic/Primary Weighted Average Shares	446.5	445.1
Basic/Primary EPS Excl. Extra. Items	**2.358**	**1.197**
Basic/Primary EPS Incl. Extra. Items	**2.358**	**1.123**
Dilution Adjustment	0	0
Diluted Weighted Average Shares	450	452
Diluted EPS Excl. Extra. Items	**2.34**	**1.179**
Diluted EPS Incl. Extra. Items	**2.34**	**1.106**
Dividends per Share—Common Stock	0.48	0.44
Gross Dividends—Common Stock	261	199
Stock Based Compensation	—	67

Source: www.investor.stockpoint.com.

EXHIBIT 4

Lockheed Martin Corp (LMT)

IN MILLIONS OF U.S. DOLLARS (EXCEPT FOR PER SHARE ITEMS)	AS OF 12/31/03	AS OF 12/31/02
Cash & Equivalents	$ 1,010.00	2,738.00
Short Term Investments	240	0
Cash and Short Term Investments	1,250.00	2,738.00
Trade Accounts Receivable, Net	4,039.00	3,655.00
Other Receivables	—	—
Total Receivables, Net	4,039.00	3,655.00
Total Inventory	2,348.00	2,250.00
Prepaid Expenses	—	—
Other Current Assets	1,764.00	1,983.00
Total Current Assets	**9,401.00**	**10,626.00**
Property/Plant/Equipment—Gross	—	—
Accumulated Depreciation	—	−5,058.00
Property/Plant/Equipment, Net	3,489.00	3,258.00
Goodwill, Net	7,879.00	7,380.00
Intangibles, Net	807	814
Long Term Investments	1,060.00	1,009.00
Other Long Term Assets	2,708.00	2,671.00
Total Assets	**$25,344.00**	**25,758.00**
Accounts Payable	1,434.00	1,102.00
Accrued Expenses	—	—
Notes Payable/Short Term Debt	—	—
Current Port. LT Debt/Capital Leases	136	1,365.00
Other Current Liabilities	7,591.00	7,354.00
Total Current Liabilities	**9,161.00**	**9,821.00**
Long Term Debt	6,072.00	6,217.00
Capital Lease Obligations	—	—
Total Long Term Debt	**6,072.00**	**6,217.00**
Total Debt	**6,208.00**	**7,582.00**
Deferred Income Tax	—	0
Minority Interest	—	—
Other Liabilities	3,355.00	3,855.00
Total Liabilities	**$18,588.00**	**19,893.00**
Redeemable Preferred Stock	—	—
Preferred Stock—Non Redeemable, Net	—	—
Common Stock	—	455
Additional Paid-In Capital	—	2,796.00
Retained Earnings (Accum. Deficit)	—	4,262.00
Treasury Stock—Common	—	—
Other Equity	6,756.00	−1,598.00
Total Equity	**6,756.00**	**5,865.00**
Total Liabilities & Shareholders' Equity	**$25,344.00**	**25,758.00**
Shares Outs.—Common Stock	445.2	455
Total Common Shares Outstanding	**445.2**	**455**
Total Preferred Stock Shares Outs.	**—**	**—**
Employees (actual figures)	—	125,000.00
Number of Common Shareholders (actual figures)	—	45,425.00

Source: www.investor.stockpoint.com.

EXHIBIT 5
Lockheed Martin Organizational Chart

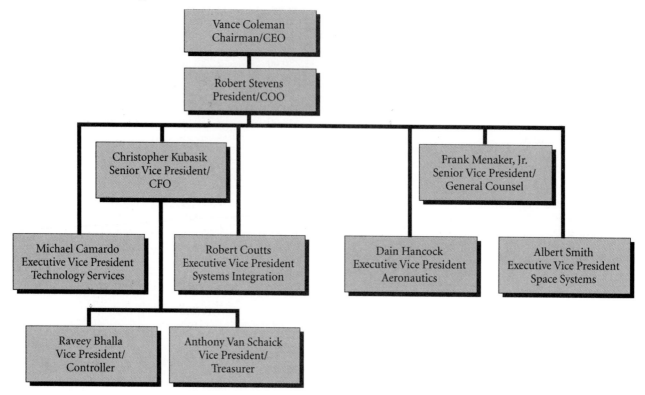

References

Aviation Week & Space Technology (August 4, 2003): 32.
Aviation Week & Space Technology (August 11, 2003): 35.
Aviation Week & Space Technology (August 18, 2003): 18.
Aviation Week & Space Technology (July 28, 2003): 48–50.
Lockheed Martin 2002 *Annual Report*.
Lockheed Martin 2003 *Form 10-K*.
S & P Industry Survey, Aerospace and Defense.
Boeing Company 2003 *Form 10-K*.
General Dynamics 2003 *Form 10-K*.
Northrop Grumman Corporation 2003 *Form 10-K*.
Raytheon Company 2003 *Form 10-K*.
United Technologies Corporation 2003 *Form 10-K*.
www.economy.com/store/download_sample_getfile.asp?f=ind_Aerospace.pdf&id=54
www.graduatingengineer.com/industryfocus/defense.html
investor.stockpoint.com/leftnav/NewsDisp.asp?News_Count=10&TimeStamp=10/4/
2003+3:04:20+PM&Symbol=LMT&slider=5&Headline5=Lockheed+settles+
with+U.S.+for+overcharging+Air+Force&Vendor5=2&FileName5=20030828/
COM0002.xml&StoryID5=8025423
www.reachingcriticalwill.org/dd/lm.html p.2

Other Web sites to Visit
www.aia-aerospace.org/stats/stats.cfm.
www.boeing.com.
www.generaldynamics.com.
www.northgrum.com.
www.raytheon.com.
www.utc.com.

32   Apple Computer, Inc.—2004

K. Suzanne Harrington
Francis Marion University

www.apple.com

Apple's (AAPL) motto is "Think Differently," a concept that Macintosh does very well by creating innovative products that continue to define the world of computer design. Other computer manufacturers have attempted to replicate the iconoclastic appeal of the Apple design, but none have succeeded in the manner of Apple. When Steve Jobs assumed the post of CEO in 1998, he re-revolutionized the entire Apple platform, rescinding previous attempts to license the operating system. Jobs identified four basic platforms based on the demographics of computer buyers, from the most basic "I know nothing" people to the experts able to code their own software. Under his command, Apple introduced the outstanding iMac, iBook, PowerBook, and G series computers, all designed to fit the needs of such diverse buyers. And in 2003, Apple continued to forge ahead in design as the introduction of iTunes, iMovie, iPhoto, and iPod inspired replication by its rivals. Millions of Personal Computer (PC) owners had gone to **www.apple.com** and downloaded iTunes, purchasing songs for 99 cents. Apple seems to be yet again in the forefront of a revolution of technology, integrating music, images, and animation.

Mission

Apple ignited the personal computer revolution in the 1970s with the Apple II and reinvented the personal computer in the 1980s with the Macintosh. Apple is committed to bringing the best personal computing experience to students, educators, creative professionals and consumers around the world through its innovative hardware, software and Internet offerings.

History

Founded in 1976 in a garage in Santa Clara, California, Apple is the brainchild of Steve Wozniak and Jobs, two college dropouts who sought to provide a user-friendly computer to a new and distinct market of small computer users. Between 1978 and 1980, sales increased from $7.8 million to $117 million and in 1980 the company went public. In 1983, Steve Wozinak left Apple, and Jobs hired John Sculley away from Pepsi to be the company's president. After experiencing several product failures, Apple unveiled the Macintosh computer in 1984 to overwhelming success, setting the stage for Apple's rise and its recognition as a household name.

By 1985, relations between Sculley and Jobs became contentious, and Jobs was ousted in a boardroom coup. Additionally, Sculley, now overseeing Apple, ignored Microsoft founder Bill Gates's appeal for Apple to license its products to them and make the Microsoft platform an industry standard, which prompted the emergence and subsequent dominance of PC/ Wintel computers.

Apple entered the desktop publishing market in 1986 with its Mac Plus and LaserWriter printers, and in 1987 formed the software firm known as Claris. Apple further established itself as a prominent player in the corporate world, particularly in the publishing market, and courted the education sector by offering huge discounts. However, by the late 1980s, competition from Microsoft's Windows operating system and the abject failure of Apple's Newton handheld computer plunged the earnings of Apple, forcing a reduction in its workforce, including the resignation of John Sculley. And in a rather unwise move, Apple began ventures into licensing its own operating system, a little too late.

In 1997, CEO Gilbert Amelio, successor to Sculley, purchased the company NeXT software from former founder Steve Jobs in an attempt to upgrade and overhaul the Apple operating system. Regardless of these myriad changes within Apple, sales in the corporate and education sector continued to fall, and Apple was forced again to trim its workforce by 30 percent, canceling projects and trimming research costs.

Apple's fortunes turned upward in 1998 when CEO Gilbert Amelio was ousted, and Jobs triumphantly returned as interim CEO, "iCEO" as he referred to himself. Jobs took immediate control of Apple by forging a surprising relationship with Microsoft, which included releasing a Mac version of Microsoft's popular office software.[2] In order to protect Apple's declining market share, Jobs rescinded the licensing of Apple's OS from chief imitator Power Computing, subsequently putting the firm out of business. Apple also implemented other cost-saving measures, including the death of the Newton handheld device and the production of printers; but in an effort to improve software applications, Claris software was integrated into Apple's main platform. Additionally, Jobs streamlined Apple's product line with introduction of Apple's iMac and iBook lines for the general consumer; the G series and PowerBooks for the more advanced user; a new UNIX-based operating system ingeniously titled X; and an online build-to-order system to mimic the success of competitors like Gateway and Dell.

2000–2003 Condition

January 2000 introduced Apple's new Internet strategy: a suite of Mac-only Internet-based applications called "iTools" and an exclusive partnership with Earthlink. Moreover, Apple ventured into the bricks and mortar end of the business by opening a number of retail stores that sold not only Apple computers, but various third-party "digital lifestyle" products such as MP3 players, digital still and video cameras, and PDAs (Personal Digital Assistant). The successful iPod is a small, hard-drive-based MP3 player, which represents Apple's first hardware addition to its "digital hub" strategy. At a price of $299, the iPod faces a similar challenge to the woeful, yet cleverly designed, G4 Cube: favoring style and form-factor over price. Nevertheless, and contrary to the dismal sales of the Cube, the iPod has fast become the MP3 player to have because of its versatility.

In July 2002, the free iTools service was rolled into a new fee subscription-based "dotMac" service. Apple released iLife, a bundled software package that included iTunes, iPhoto, iMovie, and iDVD, for $50 (all but iDVD could be freely downloaded from Apple's site), in a play to further push the digital-hub concept into the consumer space. Apple continued to show profits through the first two quarters of 2002.

Current Products

In January 2003, Apple introduced two new PowerBook models: (1) the 17-inch PowerBook G4 weighing as little as 6.8 pounds and (2) the 12-inch PowerBook G4, which features a 12-inch, active-matrix display weighing approximately 4.6 pounds. Apple continued to innovate its Macintosh line of professional desktop systems with faster processors, FireWire 800, and internal support for 54Mbps AirPort Extreme and Bluetooth wireless networking, and at a reduced cost. Additionally, Apple introduced the 20-inch Apple Cinema Display and introduced significant price reductions on its 23-inch Cinema HD Display and its 17-inch Apple Studio Display. The company continued to upgrade its software products and existing software systems.

One of Apple's newest products, Final Cut Express, enables small business users, educators, students, and advanced hobbyists to perform professional-quality digital video editing. Final Cut Express is a powerful video editing tool that uses hundreds of special effects and offers easy delivery of output to DVD, the Internet, or tape. The Cohen brothers, directors of such films as "Raising Arizona" and "Fargo," used Apple's Final Cut Pro on their latest film.

Keynote, Apple's new presentation software, provides users with the ability to create high-quality presentations. Keynote includes such items as professionally designed themes, advanced typography, professional-quality image resizing, and animated charts and tables that can be created quickly with cinematic-quality transitions.

Internal Factors

Marketing

Apple has truly taken the road less traveled in marketing it various products. Unlike Dell, Microsoft, and Gateway, who tend to target the common denominator in consumers, Apple has chosen to selectively target its audience, focusing on the less-mainstream computer users. While Apple does seek to increase its share of the computer consumers, it does so in a most offbeat manner. It creates offbeat marketing strategies of its products such as computer HAL 2000 from the movie *2001: A Space Odyssey,* such actors as Jeff Goldblum, and the very funny commercials of former PC users who have converted to the Mac OS. Apple's marketing strategy is not a broad spectrum one: no talking cows or colorful butterflies or dumb-spoken college boys.

Business Structure

Note from Apple's organizational chart in Exhibit 1 that the company manages its business primarily on a geographic basis, with offices in the Americas, Europe, Japan, and Asia Pacific. Apple operates 51 retail stores with the majority located in California; its assembly of products is conducted in Sacramento, California; Cork, Ireland; and by external vendors in Fullerton, California; Taiwan, Korea, the People's Republic of China, and the Czech Republic. Jobs is the guiding force for Apple. While his tactics do not make sense even to some of those who work closely with him, his ability to design and envision new products has reinvigorated the Apple family of products. Exhibit 2 shows locations of Apple's stores. Apple products can be purchased online at its 24-hour sales department or by calling 1-800-MY-APPLE.

EXHIBIT 1
Organizational Structure

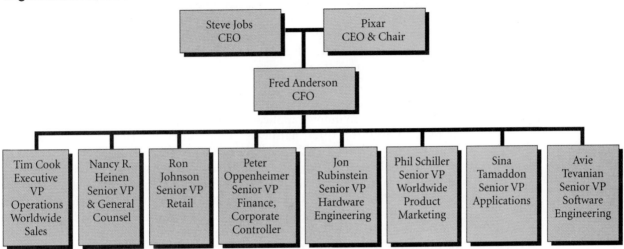

Source: Adapted from Apple Computer's *Notice of Annual Meeting of Shareholders,* March 24, 2003.

EXHIBIT 2
Store Locations

Arizona—4 locations	**Missouri**—1 location
California—24 locations	**Nevada**—1 location
Colorado—4 locations	**New Hampshire**—1 location
Connecticut—2 locations	**New Jersey**—5 locations
Florida—10 locations	**New York**—14 locations
Georgia—2 locations	**North Carolina**—1 location
Hawaii—1 location	**Ohio**—4 locations
Illinois—5 locations	**Pennsylvania**—1 location
Indiana—1 location	**Tennessee**—2 locations
Maryland—1 location	**Texas**—6 locations
Massachusetts—5 locations	**Virginia**—6 locations
Michigan—3 locations	**Washington**—5 locations
Minnesota—3 locations	**Wisconsin**—1 location

Source: Adapted from **www.apple.com/buy/**.

Jobs, and his partner Pixar, who co-founded the Academy Award–winning animation studios in 1986, are co-CEOs of Apple Computer. Pixar Studios created five of the most successful and beloved animated films of all time: the Academy Award–winning *Toy Story* (1995); *A Bug's Life* (1998); Golden Globe–winner *Toy Story 2* (1999); *Monsters, Inc.* (2001); and *Finding Nemo* (2003). Pixar's five films have earned more than $2 billion in worldwide box office receipts to date.

Competition

The largest competitor to the Apple Computer's platform is none other than Microsoft and its Windows application, designed to mimic the Apple operating system. Apple's top-three hardware competitors are Dell, Hewlett-Packard/Compaq, and IBM. With the computer market continuing to be characterized by rapid technological advances in both hardware and software development, all computer manufacturers face steep competition for a shrinking market share of consumers. This has created a most advantageous opportunity for the savvy computer purchaser. With a surplus of cheaper and cheaper PCs readily available, Apple faces a showdown with its competitors, particularly in terms of pricing. As of yet, Apple still has not created a computer that can undersell its competition. However, on a positive front, Apple buyers tend to be loyal to the brand, nearly fanatical, in fact. Additionally, Apple has an excellent track record in regard to customer service.

Dell

Mission Statement

> Dell's mission is to be the most successful computer company in the world at delivering the best customer experience in markets they serve.

Founded in 1984 by Michael Dell, Dell Computers has streamlined its own offerings: the Dimension series for desktop PCs; the Inspiron series for laptop computers; the Axim series for PDA devices; and it has complemented all of the above with its own line of printers. In 2003, the company's profits rose 19 percent to $2.1 billion with shipments increasing in the first quarter by 25 percent, faster than any of its competitors. For the time being, Dell products are purchased only online at **www.Dell4me.com** or by phone at 1-800-915-3344.

Dell's name has been limited to a number of product categories such as printers, network switches outside of its core computer hardware, projectors, and USB storage devices. However, due to increased growth in the digital market and the slowing computer business, Dell is diversifying its product line into consumer electronics. The company, which also sells several consumer-electronics products via its software and peripheral business and online store, has begun to branch out into other areas by launching its own music download store, digital music jukebox, and wireless personal digital assistant, even going so far as to market flat-panel televisions. Apple, via its iTunes, iPhoto, and iMovies, has shown that music, movies, and photos are a natural extension for the computer user. Dell's most damaging effect on Apple Computers is its ability to drive down costs through its direct-sales approach. Its computers are manufactured once an order has been received, thus reducing overheard and ensuring that products do not sit on a shelf, collecting dust. Additionally, its lack of a bricks-and-mortar locations provides a financial cutting edge as well.

Hewlett-Packard
Mission Statement

> Providing innovative, reliable products and services is a key element in
> satisfying customer needs, but there are other important elements as well.
> HP offers many different products and services to a broad set of
> customers.

Bill Hewlett and Dave Packard, both of whom attended Stanford University, founded Hewlett-Packard (HP) in 1939. In 2002, HP acquired Compaq Computer Corp., which was the largest computer technological merger in history and one that created a horrific schism between the CEO of HP and the descendents of both Hewlett and Packard. Today, HP is a leading global provider of products, technologies, solutions, and services to consumers and businesses; its offerings span IT infrastructure, personal computing and access devices, global services, and imaging and printing. In an attempt to expand its market share, HP, in September 2003, announced the Smart Office initiative for the small and medium-sized business (SMB) market, one of the fastest-growing and most important segments of the global economy. The Smart Office initiative is innovative in design as it offers more than 100 different products, solutions, and services.

Computers manufactured by HP lost $56 million in the third quarter of 2003, compared with a $21 million profit in the second quarter. Even its printers, for which the company is known worldwide, lost ground. Operating margins fell to 14.1 percent from 16.6 percent during that time, while sales in the printer division totaled $5.2 billion, up from $4.7 billion in 2002. But on a positive front, HP's laptop computer business sales are strong with a growth of 27 percent in the third quarter of 2003. Like Dell, HP poses a serious threat to Apple's growth. HP can capitalize on the longevity of its name and offer a desktop computer at a far less cost than Apple.

International Business Machines (IBM)
Mission Statement

> Strives to lead the world in the creation, development and manufacture of
> the industry's most advanced information technologies, including
> computer systems, software, networking systems, storage devices and
> microelectronics.

On September 30, 2003, IBM reported net earnings of $1.79 billion, a rise of 37 percent over 2002. Revenue rose about 9 percent to $21.52 billion from $19.82 billion in 2002. Additionally, IBM expects to add 10,000 new jobs around the world in 2004; its services division is a bright spot in the computer world where revenue jumped 17 percent to $10.4 billion in one year.

IBM, also known as Big Blue, plans to sign more than $15 billion in service contracts in the third quarter of 2003, most of which will be long-term deals. The second-biggest slice of IBM's business, the hardware division, saw a 1 percent drop in revenue to $6.7 billion compared to 2002, but the worst blight on IBM's results remained in its semiconductor operations, which had to cut jobs and pay at several factories. The earnings report showed continued trouble in the technology group: a pretax loss of $96 million and a 30 percent drop in revenue to $882 million. For 2003,

IBM's earnings came to $4.9 billion on revenues of $63.2 billion. Those figures are an improvement on the first three quarters of 2002, where IBM earned $2.6 billion on revenues of $57.5 billion.

For Apple Computers, IBM is a thorn in its side because it is also able to capitalize on the history of its name and its longevity in the computer business; and, like other Apple competitors, IBM offers a far more affordable PC than Apple.

Natural Environment

Today's computers are made of plastic, which is nothing more than a composite of oil. This method of production has created millions of "throw away" computers which are dumped into our already limited landfill space. Exhibit 3 details statistics regarding computer disposal. As early as 1992, the Environmental Protection Agency (EPA) banned the landfill dumping of CRTs. The following year, the EPA began targeting companies that dispose large quantities of CRTs through landfills. In an attempt to follow the EPA stance, many state and local agencies are now monitoring the disposal of CRTs and other computer equipment.

On the international side, the European Union Parliament is working to finalize the Waste Electrical and Electronic Equipment Directive, which makes manufacturers of electrical goods, including personal computers, financially responsible for the collection, recycling, and safe disposal of past and future products. This will serve as a point of interest and a source of future expense to Apple once the directive is in place.

EXHIBIT 3
Landfill Statistics

- 3.2 million tons is the amount of PC equipment currently in landfills.
- 150 million is the minimum number of personal computers that will have been burned in United States landfills by 2005, according to a study by Carnegie Mellon University.
- 20.6 million is the minimum number of PCs that have fallen into disuse since 1998, according to the National Safety Council.
- 11 percent is the percentage of those that have been recycled.
- Computers can contain up to 6.3 percent lead.
- CRTs (computer monitors) contain lead to shield users from radiation and this lead could pose an environmental hazard when used CRTs are incinerated.
- The Environmental Protection Agency says lead can make up as much as 25 percent of the weight of monitors weighing anywhere from 15 to 90 pounds.
- 80 percent of all American trash and waste is landfilled.
- Two-thirds of our landfills were closed down in the last decade.
- Plastics and computer-related scrap fill our landfills while contaminating our ground and water daily.
- Only 10 percent of our nation's plastics are actually being recycled.

Source: www.interconrecycling.com/landfill.htm.

Technological Environment

The worldwide PC market grew more quickly than expected in the third quarter of 2003. All geographic regions showed double-digit, year-on-year growth, with the exception of Latin America. The PC market as a whole grew 15.7 percent compared with the same period in 2002. Figures showed a growth rate of about 14.1 percent worldwide. PC shipments in the United States increased 16.1 percent from 2002 to 2003. In a battle that's now becoming familiar, Dell held on to the PC market share crown during the third quarter of 2003, but Hewlett-Packard substantially cut the lead. Dell saw shipments grow by 27.9 percent worldwide, while HP saw sales grow 28 percent. Dell's worldwide market share was 15.3 percent, compared with 15.1 percent for HP. IBM was a distant third with a worldwide market share of 5.3 percent.

Exhibit 4 shows computer firms' U.S. market share. Apple's share increased 1 percent from 2002 to 2003 for a grand total of 3 percent. Dell's market also increased from 25 percent in 2002 to 27.4 in 2003. Hewlett-Packard went from 18 percent in 2002 to 19.4 percent, while IBM moved from 4.3 percent in 2002 to 4.6 percent in 2003.

E-Commerce Issues

Apple maintains an up-to-date e-store that allows customers to browse and find the latest products available each day. Apple recognizes the need to have previous customers revisit the site to make future purchases and is capitalizing on this through iTunes, music that can be purchased only at Apple's Web site and downloaded to its iPod (a music playing device). Dell, in an attempt to replicate Apple's success, has entered this realm with its Jukebox software where customers can download music for a fee or listen to Internet radio at no charge.

There are three key trends leading IT professionals to take a second look at Apple. The first is the Unix workstation; the second is the rise of the laptop's popularity; the third, and most potent, is the growing frustration with the Microsoft monoculture and its all-too-common worm attacks that gum up corporate networks and leave all Windows-based computers vulnerable to future attacks. Virus threats are becoming an increasing burden to all companies who have computers. Few IT departments have considered eliminating their Windows systems altogether; however, they are starting to think they need to have a few Macs around as

EXHIBIT 4

Market Share for U.S. Computer Firms

	MARKET IN UNITED STATES FOR 2002 (%)	MARKET IN UNITED STATES FOR 2003 (%)
Apple	2	3
Dell	25	27.4
HP	18	19.4
IBM	4.3	4.6

Source: Adapted from **www.macnn.com/news/21595**.

well, to effectively manage their networks. Apple is the only hardware alternative to Window-Intel (Wintel) PCs.

In the corporate realm, CEOs and CFOs tend to gravitate toward Unix workstations, especially the use of laptops, because it provides employees with greater work flexibility. Apple has been at the forefront of this trend for some time. In fact, Steve Jobs declared 2003 as the year of the laptop. Apple continues to develop designs that appeal to the consumer and ones that reflect a more competitive price. While Dell and HP were the undisputed leaders of laptop sales for 2003, Apple may very well begin to make inroads with laptop consumers.

Future Outlook

Refinement of speech recognition programs will soon make the operation of a computer even easier. Virtual reality, the technology of interacting with a computer using all of the human senses, will also contribute to better human and computer interfaces. Apple's history of innovation and its motto of "thinking differently" will be the key advantages for keeping it in the forefront with its current users, and in enticing new customers. Originality has been a hallmark for Apple from the very beginning, and it is that sense of style that enables it to prosper in this ever-growing and changing market.

Apple's recent successes and expansion has led CEO Steve Jobs to predict that Apple's market share will double from 5 percent to 10 percent in the near future (Apple's market share of the home computer market might seem small at 5 percent, but this percentage is still larger than the combined market share of Mercedes and BMW in the United States). Moreover, Apple is currently the most profitable computer company in the industry despite the dampened economy and its small size relative to the industry giants. Its continuing success hinges on its ability to expand market share.

Some questions pondered by Apple are: How can we best capitalize on the needs of the business world for a safer, virus-free, worm-free system? Should we enter the consumer electronics business like Dell and Gateway? Should we remain a lone wolf in operating systems or adopt a cross-platform format compatible with Wintel? How much emphasis should we place on developing the next generation of voice recognition computers?

EXHIBIT 5

Apple Computer Inc. (AAPL)

ANNUAL INCOME STATEMENT IN MILLIONS OF U.S. DOLLARS (EXCEPT FOR PER SHARE ITEMS)	12 MONTHS ENDING 9/27/03	12 MONTHS ENDING 9/28/02	12 MONTHS ENDING 9/29/01
Revenue	$6,207.00	5,742.00	5,363.00
Other Revenue	—	—	—
Total Revenue	**6,207.00**	**5,742.00**	**5,363.00**
Cost of Revenue	4,499.00	4,139.00	4,128.00
Gross Profit	**1,708.00**	**1,603.00**	**1,235.00**
Selling/General/Administrative Expenses	1,212.00	1,109.00	1,138.00
Research & Development	471	446	430
Depreciation/Amortization	—	—	—
Interest Expense (Income), Net Operating	—	—	—
Unusual Expense (Income)	26	31	11
Other Operating Expenses	—	—	—
Total Operating Expense	**6,208.00**	**5,725.00**	**5,707.00**
Operating Income	**−1**	**17**	**−344**
Interest Expense, Net Non-Operating	−8	−11	−16
Interest/Investment Income, Non-Operating	69	118	218
Interest Income (Expense), Net Non-Operating	61	107	202
Gain (Loss) on Sale of Assets	10	−42	88
Other, Net	22	5	2
Income Before Tax	**92**	**87**	**−52**
Income Tax	24	22	−15
Income After Tax	**68**	**65**	**237**
Minority Interest	—	—	—
Equity In Affiliates	—	—	—
Net Income Before Extra. Items	**68**	**65**	**−37**
Accounting Change	1	0	12
Discontinued Operations	—	—	—
Extraordinary Items	—	—	—
Net Income	$ **69**	**65**	**−25**
Preferred Dividends	—	—	—
Income Available to Common Excl. Extra. Items	**68**	**65**	**−37**
Income Available to Common Incl. Extra. Items	**69**	**65**	**−25**
Basic/Primary Weighted Average Shares	360.6	355	345.6
Basic/Primary EPS Excl. Extra. Items	**0.189**	**0.183**	**−0.107**
Basic/Primary EPS Incl. Extra. Items	**0.191**	**0.183**	**−0.072**
Dilution Adjustment	0	0	0
Diluted Weighted Average Shares	363.5	361.8	345.6
Diluted EPS Excl. Extra. Items	**0.187**	**0.18**	**−0.107**
Diluted EPS Incl. Extra. Items	**0.19**	**0.18**	**−0.072**
Dividends per Share—Common Stock	0	0	0
Gross Dividends—Common Stock	0	0	0
Stock Based Compensation	166	229	371

Source: www.investor.stockpoint.com.

EXHIBIT 6
Apple Computer Inc. (APPL)

ANNUAL BALANCE SHEET IN MILLIONS OF U.S. DOLLARS (EXCEPT FOR PER SHARE ITEMS)	AS OF 9/27/03	AS OF 9/28/02	AS OF 9/29/01
Cash & Equivalents	$3,396.00	2,252.00	2,310.00
Short Term Investments	1,170.00	2,085.00	2,026.00
Cash and Short Term Investments	4,566.00	4,337.00	4,336.00
Trade Accounts Receivable, Net	766	565	466
Other Receivables	—	—	—
Total Receivables, Net	766	565	466
Total Inventory	56	45	11
Prepaid Expenses	—	—	—
Other Current Assets	499	441	330
Total Current Assets	**5,887.00**	**5,388.00**	**5,143.00**
Property/Plant/Equipment—Gross	—	—	—
Accumulated Depreciation	−505	−436	−396
Property/Plant/Equipment, Net	669	621	564
Goodwill, Net	85	—	—
Intangibles, Net	24	119	76
Long Term Investments	—	39	128
Other Long Term Assets	150	131	110
Total Assets	**$6,815.00**	**6,298.00**	**6,021.00**
Accounts Payable	1,154.00	911	801
Accrued Expenses	899	747	717
Notes Payable/Short Term Debt	—	—	—
Current Port. LT Debt/Capital Leases	304	—	—
Other Current Liabilities	—	—	—
Total Current Liabilities	**2,357.00**	**1,658.00**	**1,518.00**
Long Term Debt	0	316	317
Capital Lease Obligations	—	—	—
Total Long Term Debt	**0**	**316**	**317**
Total Debt	**304**	**316**	**317**
Deferred Income Tax	235	229	266
Minority Interest	—	—	—
Other Liabilities	—	—	—
Total Liabilities	**$2,592.00**	**2,203.00**	**2,101.00**
Redeemable Preferred Stock	—	—	—
Preferred Stock—Non Redeemable, Net	—	—	0
Common Stock	1,926.00	1,826.00	1,693.00
Additional Paid-In Capital	—	—	—
Retained Earnings (Accum. Deficit)	2,394.00	2,325.00	2,260.00
Treasury Stock—Common	—	—	—
Other Equity	−97	−56	−33
Total Equity	**4,223.00**	**4,095.00**	**3,920.00**
Total Liabilities & Shareholders' Equity	**6,815.00**	**6,298.00**	**6,021.00**
Shares Outs.—Common Stock	366.7	359	350.9
Total Common Shares Outstanding	**366.7**	**359**	**350.9**
Total Preferred Stock Shares Outs.	**0**	**0**	**0**
Employees (actual figures)	10,912.00	10,211.00	9,603.00
Number of Common Shareholders (actual figures)	29,015.00	28,310.00	26,992.00

Source: www.investor.stockpoint.com.

References

BBC News. "Apple Could Double Market Share."
news.bbc.co.uk/hi/english/business/newsid_2005000/2005495.stm, May 23, 2002 ESM
    210, week 3 notes, Magali Delmas.
Rogers, Paul. "Valley Industrial Pollution Plunges; Tougher Laws Credited with Statewide Drop."
    Mercury News (May 24, 2002).
www.apple.com.
www.businessweek.com.
www.census.gov/.
www.ecommercetimes.com/perl/story/31726.html.
www.forbes.com.
www.hp.com.
www.ibm.com/us/.
www.theapplemuseum.com/.

33 Gateway, Inc.—2004

Xiwu (Ben) Zhang
Francis Marion University

GTW

www.gateway.com

"I'm confident that the direction we're going is the absolute right direction," said Theodore Waitt, CEO of Gateway, during an interview with Reuters in the spring of 2003. Gateway did make some major advances in its industry by introducing an industry-leading customer service and support program, wireless personal computer connectivity, and a strategic relationship with IBM Global Services to provide on-site and field support for Gateway's systems and networking division. With these efforts, one would think Gateway is a profitable company. However, the numbers tell a different story. In October 2003, Gateway posted its eleventh loss in 12 quarters, as revenue fell due to cutthroat pricing in the personal computer (PC) industry. Gateway's third-quarter revenue declined to $883 million from $1.1 billion a year earlier, as net losses increased to $139 million from $73 million. Gateway is in trouble. However, CEO Theodore Waitt says:

> We're pleased with the progress we're making in transforming from a traditional PC company to a branded integrator. We have a lot of work to do, but every step in our transformation is being taken from a position of increased strength and momentum. We expect to keep delivering on our milestones and goals through the balance of the year and beyond.

History

In 1985, Theodore Waitt started Gateway in an Iowa farmhouse with a $10,000 loan from his grandmother, a rented computer, and a three-page business plan. He turned Gateway into a one of America's best-known brands with innovations that helped shape the technology industry. In less than ten years, Gateway transformed itself into a multinational *Fortune* 500 corporation with annual sales of nearly $3.6 billion.

Gateway has been a pioneer for numerous PC industry trends and practices. It was the first PC company to offer systems with standard color monitors and a standard three-year warranty, and the first to advertise on television. It was one of the nation's early "bricks and clicks" retailers, and it was among the first direct retailers to sell its own branded consumer electronics. In 2002, Gateway's products and services received more than 90 awards and accolades and the company's retail stores outperformed competitors in a "mystery shopper" comparison. In 2003, Gateway was named the second most admired American company in the computer industry by *Fortune* magazine.[1]

Gateway's strategy today is to profitably grow its PC business, diversify into digital technology products, and optimize its cost structure. As one of the leading suppliers of PCs to the U.S. consumer market, Gateway currently holds an estimated

6 percent market share. It sells its products online, by telephone, and in Gateway Country retail stores. Due to poor financial performance, Gateway closed 80 of its retail stores in 2002 as sales revenue decreased to $4.1 billion from its revenue of $9.2 billion in 2001. Gateway's gross profit in 2002 declined to $0.6 billion, a decrease of approximately 32 percent from 2001. Revenues fell to $3.4 billion in 2003 and net income fell to negative $514 million.

Internal Factors

Gateway's vision and mission statements are provided below:

> Vision Statement:
> To improve the quality of life through technology.

> Mission Statement:
> To be the leading integrator of personalized technology solutions. To profitably grow our business faster than the competition by better understanding and serving the desires of our customer and aggressively marketing the highest value directly to our chosen markets.

Gateway sells products and technology solutions directly to customers primarily through three complementary distribution channels—telephone sales, Web sales, and its nationwide network of Gateway retail stores. During 2002, its business sales and marketing activities focused on its core market segments: small and medium businesses, including education and government. Gateway has developed the Gateway eMarketplace to facilitate both online purchases and sales of a wide range of technology and products that help businesses run. It initially focused on desktop PCs, mobile PCs, and servers, but is rapidly expanding its offerings to include a wide range of branded technology products and services, such as plasma-screen displays, DLP projectors, tablet PCs, and systems and networking solutions.

Gateway operates three manufacturing facilities in the United States, located in North Sioux City and Sioux Falls, South Dakota, and Hampton, Virginia. Gateway is determined to save the environment and conducts safety and usability tests to ensure that its products not only meet customer performance requirements but also meet or surpass safety standards. Gateway has designed its manufacturing process to provide a simplified line of products with standardized configurations as well as products that are "built to order" or custom-configured to meet customer specifications. Production teams are used to assemble desktop PCs and servers with each member trained to do several tasks.

Business Structure

As indicated in Gateway's organization chart, seen in Exhibit 1, the company is structured based on geographic segments: North America; Europe, Middle East, Africa (EMEA); and Asia Pacific (A-P). The North America segment is further divided into the Consumer and Business segments. The Business segment manages the business, education, and government markets while the Consumer Segment deals with individual customers. The Gateway Business division accounts for nearly 48 percent of gross profits and nearly half of the company's $7.5 billion in revenues in 2002. Gateway has been growing the business-to-business segment for several years, but the majority of revenues have traditionally come from small businesses. In the Business segment, Gateway invests throughout the year in new products, services, and support, and continues to enhance its range of mobile products for businesses.

The Consumer segment has had a significant positive effect on gross margin, which grew from 12 percent in January to 16 percent in March 2003. Gateway plans

EXHIBIT 1
Gateway's Organizational Structure

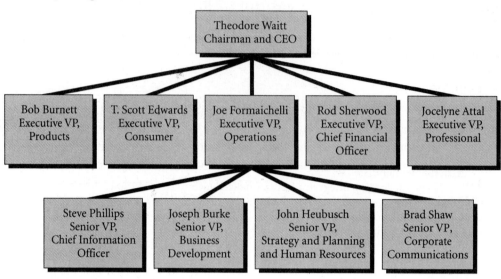

Source: www.gateway.com/about/news_info/executive_bios.shtml.

to further diversify its mix of products and services beyond its core PC business and into higher-margin areas that now include a 42-inch plasma TV, digital displays, audio products, and video gear.

Gateway's income statement by segment is provided in Exhibit 2. Note that only the Business section in North America had a positive operating income in 2002. In the third quarter of 2003, the improved seasonal demand helped Gateway increase revenue by 14 percent. Total Consumer revenue was $427 million, including sales of 224,000 PCs. In the Professional segment, total revenue was $456 million, with 334,000 PC units sold. On a year-over-year basis, Professional revenue decreased 6 percent and PC unit sales decreased 2 percent. Gateway's gross margin in this quarter was 10.0 percent compared with 17.2 percent in the previous quarter and 15.0 percent in the third quarter of 2002.

Gateway's goal is to generate more profit from consumer electronics rather than PC sales and to regain its status in the market by 2005. As part of the strategy, it introduced 50 new products in 2003, ranging from handheld computers to four-way servers. Gateway's income statements and balance sheets are provided in Exhibit 3 and Exhibit 4.

External Factors

Many computer makers have greater financial, marketing, manufacturing, and technological resources than Gateway and consolidation in the PC industry has resulted in even larger and stronger competitors. Gateway expects that average sales prices for PCs will continue to decline. Gateway sold 558,000 PCs in the third quarter of 2003. However, only the under-$800 PCs experienced increasing unit sales.

In 2002, PC shipments globally edged up, after falling 4 percent in 2001, according to International Data Corporation (IDC). However, growth was just 1.4 percent, and the outlook for 2003 is not much better. Currently, IDC projects unit growth of 6.9 percent, down from its earlier prediction of 8.3 percent growth

EXHIBIT 2

Gateway's Income Statement by Segment

(IN THOUSANDS)	2002	2001	2000
North America			
Net Sales			
Consumer	$2,356,573	2,955,747	5,056,530
Business	1,814,752	2,430,815	2,832,936
	4,171,325	5,386,562	7,889,466
Operating income			
Consumer	(222,295)	15,303	61,811
Business	161,076	219,773	382,512
	(61,219)	235,076	1,000,623
Income tax expense	(178,028)	(292,643)	164,149
Depreciation and amortization	159,458	185,739	169,602
Segment assets	2,478,951	2,930,953	3,695,002
Long-lived assets	554,035	740,143	1,742,015
Europe, Middle East, Africa			
Net sales	NA	229,026	5,863,621
Operating loss	NA	(53,493)	(55,126)
Income tax expense	NA	8,034	(2,689)
Depreciation and amortization	NA	8,118	10,974
Segment assets	21,239	34,944	243,917
Long-lived assets	NA	NA	60,489
Asian Pacific			
Net sales	NA	322,308	776,256
Operating loss	NA	(37,548)	4,799
Income tax expense	NA	10,377	(7,870)
Depreciation and amortization	NA	6,119	8,508
Segment assets	9,217	20,960	241,726
Long-lived assets	NA	NA	40,564
Operating income			
Segment operating income	(61,219)	144,035	950,296
Nonsegment operating expenses			
Restructuring and other special charges			
Cost of goods sold	(15,604)	(216,327)	(51,369)
Selling, general and administrative expenses	(83,403)	(759,170)	(43,368)
Other non-segment operating expenses	(351,376)	(352,468)	(350,304)
Total operating income	(511,242)	(1,183,930)	505,255

Source: www.gateway.com/about/investors/docs/02_annual_report.pdf.

for 2003. Standard & Poor's forecasts a 5 percent increase in PC shipments for 2003. The lackluster U.S. economy hurts PC demand.

U.S. gross domestic product (GDP) grew by a modest 2.4 percent (in real terms) in 2002, according to Standard & Poor's economists. Based on data from IDC for the first quarter of 2003, worldwide PC shipments rose 2.1 percent, year-to-year, as consumer spending remained weak and commercial PC demand failed to recover materially. Although commercial demand is expected to also remain weak in 2003, the consumer market continues to outperform. IDC projects the consumer market to

EXHIBIT 3

Gateway Inc. (GTW)

ANNUAL INCOME STATEMENT IN MILLIONS OF U.S. DOLLARS (EXCEPT FOR PER SHARE ITEMS)	12 MONTHS ENDING 12/31/03	12 MONTHS ENDING 12/31/02	12 MONTHS ENDING 12/31/01
			Restated 12/31/02
Revenue	$3,402.40	4,171.30	5,937.90
Other Revenue	—	—	—
Total Revenue	**3,402.40**	**4,171.30**	**5,937.90**
Cost of Revenue	2,938.80	3,605.10	5,099.70
Gross Profit	**463.6**	**566.2**	**838.2**
Selling/General/Administrative Expenses	974.1	994.4	2,022.10
Research & Development	—	—	—
Depreciation/Amortization	—	—	—
Interest Expense (Income), Net Operating	—	—	—
Unusual Expense (Income)	—	83	—
Other Operating Expenses	—	—	—
Total Operating Expense	**3,912.90**	**4,682.60**	**7,121.80**
Operating Income	**−510.6**	**−511.2**	**−1,183.90**
Interest Expense, Net Non-Operating	—	—	—
Interest/Investment Income, Non-Operating	—	—	—
Interest Income (Expense), Net Non-Operating	—	—	—
Gain (Loss) on Sale of Assets	—	—	—
Other, Net	19.3	35.5	−101.9
Income Before Tax	**−491.2**	**−475.7**	**−1,285.80**
Income Tax	23.6	−178	−274.2
Income After Tax	**−514.8**	**−297.7**	**−1,011.60**
Minority Interest	—	—	—
Equity In Affiliates	—	—	—
Net Income Before Extra. Items	**−514.8**	**−297.7**	**−1,011.60**
Accounting Change	—	0	−23.9
Discontinued Operations	—	—	—
Extraordinary Items	—	0	4.3
Net Income	**$−514.8**	**−297.7**	**−1,031.10**
Preferred Dividends	−11.1	−11.3	—
Income Available to Common Excl. Extra. Items	**−526**	**−309**	**−1,011.60**
Income Available to Common Incl. Extra. Items	**−526**	**−309**	**−1,031.10**
Basic/Primary Weighted Average Shares	324.2	324	323.3
Basic/Primary EPS Excl. Extra. Items	**−1.622**	**−0.954**	**−3.129**
Basic/Primary EPS Incl. Extra. Items	**−1.622**	**−0.954**	**−3.189**
Dilution Adjustment	0	0	0
Diluted Weighted Average Shares	324.2	324	323.3
Diluted EPS Excl. Extra. Items	**−1.622**	**−0.954**	**−3.129**
Diluted EPS Incl. Extra. Items	**−1.622**	**−0.954**	**−3.189**
Dividends per Share—Common Stock	0	0	0
Gross Dividends—Common Stock	0	0	0
Stock Based Compensation	—	35.3	72.5

Source: www.investor.stockpoint.com.

EXHIBIT 4
Gateway Inc. (GTW)

ANNUAL BALANCE SHEET IN MILLIONS OF U.S. DOLLARS (EXCEPT FOR PER SHARE ITEMS)	AS OF 12/31/03	AS OF 12/31/02	AS OF 12/31/01
			Restated 12/31/02
Cash & Equivalents	$ 409.2	465.6	731
Short Term Investments	679.8	601.1	435.1
Cash and Short Term Investments	1,089.00	1,066.70	1,166.10
Trade Accounts Receivable, Net	210.2	197.8	220
Other Receivables	—	—	—
Total Receivables, Net	210.2	197.8	220
Total Inventory	114.1	88.8	120.3
Prepaid Expenses	—	—	—
Other Current Assets	250.2	602.1	616.6
Total Current Assets	**1,663.50**	**1,955.40**	**2,122.90**
Property/Plant/Equipment—Gross	—	—	—
Accumulated Depreciation	—	−552.5	−440
Property/Plant/Equipment, Net	330.9	481	608.4
Goodwill, Net	—	—	—
Intangibles, Net	14	23.3	36.3
Long Term Investments	—	—	—
Other Long Term Assets	20.1	49.7	219.2
Total Assets	**2,028.40**	**2,509.40**	**2,986.90**
Accounts Payable	416	278.6	341.1
Accrued Expenses	325.9	421.4	604.3
Notes Payable/Short Term Debt	—	—	—
Current Port. LT Debt/Capital Leases	—	—	—
Other Current Liabilities	257.1	240.3	200.6
Total Current Liabilities	$ 999	940.3	1,146.00
Long Term Debt	—	—	—
Capital Lease Obligations	—	—	—
Total Long Term Debt	—	—	—
Total Debt	—	—	—
Deferred Income Tax	—	—	—
Minority Interest	—	—	—
Other Liabilities	109.7	127.1	82.6
Total Liabilities	**1,108.70**	**1,067.50**	**1,228.70**
Redeemable Preferred Stock	197.7	195.4	193.1
Preferred Stock—Non Redeemable, Net	—	200	200
Common Stock	—	3.2	3.2
Additional Paid-In Capital	—	732.8	731.6
Retained Earnings (Accum. Deficit)	—	307.4	616.4
Treasury Stock—Common	—	—	0
Other Equity	722	3.1	13.8
Total Equity	**919.7**	**1,441.90**	**1,758.20**
Total Liability & Shareholders' Equity	**$2,028.40**	**2,509.40**	**2,986.90**
Shares Outs.—Common Stock	324.4	324.1	324
Total Common Shares Outstanding	**324.4**	**324.1**	**324**
Total Preferred Stock Shares Outs.	**0.1**	**0.1**	**0.1**
Employees (actual figures)	—	11,500.00	14,000.00
Number of Common Shareholders (actual figures)	—	4,927.00	4,681.00

Source: www.investor.stockpoint.com.

advance by 11.3 percent in 2003. Among the top-five PC makers, Dell, Hewlett-Packard (HP), International Business Machines (IBM), Fujitsu Siemens, and Toshiba, only HP experienced a year-to-year unit decline in the first quarter of 2003.

International markets present a promising opportunity for computer manufacturers in the coming years. Areas like the Asia-Pacific region and Latin America witnessed stronger growth than the worldwide average. In 2002, Asia-Pacific PC sales outpaced all other major regions with 10 percent growth. PC sales in Europe grew by 1.8 percent and the United States saw 3.2 percent unit growth.

Competition

The PC industry is characterized by aggressive pricing, short product life cycles, and price sensitivity by customers who expect excellent service. Gateway competes primarily on the basis of customer intimacy, value, technology, product offerings, operation efficiency, quality, and reliability. It also focuses on maintaining good customer service, support, and supplier relationships to enable products to be brought quickly to market. Dell, Apple, HP, and IBM are fierce PC competitors. Dell and HP continue to battle for the most market, as indicated in Exhibit 5.

Dell designs, develops, manufactures, markets, services, and supports a range of computer systems, including enterprise systems (servers, storage and networking products, and workstations), notebook computer systems, desktop computer systems, and software and peripherals. Generally managed on a geographic basis, Dell is located in the Americas, Europe, and Asia Pacific-Japan. Dell's second quarter 2003 revenue was $9.8 billion, up 16 percent from the same period in 2002. During this quarter, Dell's performance continued to outpace the industry. Dell increased its worldwide share by 2.6 points to 18 percent and strengthened its position as the world's number-one supplier of personal computing systems. Dell's low-cost structure and efficient, direct-to-customer model has enabled the firm to consistently achieve market share growth while maximizing profitability.

HP is a global provider of products, technologies, solutions, and services to consumers and businesses. As of October 31, 2002, HP had five business segments: the Imaging and Printing Group (IPG), the Personal Systems Group (PSG), the Enterprise Systems Group (ESG), the HPS Group, HP Services (HPS), and HP Financial Services (HPFS) Group. HP provides a broad range of value-added financial service offerings that

EXHIBIT 5
Top Ten Computer Hardware Manufacturing Companies (revenues in thousands)

RANK	COMPANY NAME	2002 SALES	2001 SALES
1	International Business Machines	$81,186,000	$85,866,000
2	Hewlett-Packard	56,588,000	45,226,000
3	Dell Computer	35,404,000	31,168,000
4	Sun Microsystems	12,496,000	18,250,000
5	Apple Computer	5,742,000	5,363,000
6	NCR	5,585,000	5,917,000
7	Gateway	4,171,300	6,080,000
8	Diebold	1,940,200	1,760,300
9	Silicon Graphics	1,341,400	1,854,500
10	Palm	1,030,800	1,559,312

Source: www.plunkettresearch.com/technology/infotech_statistics_1.htm.

enable customers worldwide to acquire complete IT solutions, including hardware, software, and services. Hewlett-Packard has undergone extensive restructuring under the leadership of CEO Carly Fiorina, who spearheaded the largest deal in tech-sector history: the acquisition of Compaq Computer in a stock transaction valued at approximately $19 billion. HP reported third quarter of 2003 revenue of $17.35 billion compared to $16.54 billion in the prior year period. Revenues increased 5 percent year-over-year.

Apple Computer historically had urged customers to "Think Differently" but now wants them to "Think Digital." Apple Computer's desktop and laptop computers feature a very user-friendly operating system. Apple designs, manufactures, and markets PCs and related personal-computing solutions for sale primarily to education, creative, consumer, and business customers. Its net sales during the third quarter of 2003 increased 8 percent or $116 million from the same period in 2002, and increased 4 percent or $193 million for the first nine months of fiscal 2003 compared to the same period in 2002. Apple, however, is experiencing "ongoing weakness" in its U.S. education business.

E-Commerce

In February 1999, Gateway became the first PC manufacturer to bundle its own Internet service with sales of its personal computers. Through Gateway.com, Gateway customers are able to purchase an entire computing solution from one Web site offering personalized PCs plus thousands of peripherals, software, and related products. Personalization of Gateway.com is based on a strategy of collecting customer information from various sources. Gateway.com collects customer attributes information from its site using cookies and requires visitors to assign themselves to different divisions (home office, corporate, education, small business, and government). Additional information is also collected through various advertising and affiliate programs with other Web sites.

Gateway.com personalizes a visitor's experience to the site without the visitor noticing. Gateway is most interested in where visitors come from, their navigational paths in Gateway.com, and their drop-off point during the purchasing process. At Gateway.com, free services, such as e-mail newsletters, Gateway Guide publication, and store location finder are offered to site visitors in exchange for personal information. Customers provide their geographic location when they input their zip code into the store location finder; they provide their e-mail addresses when they request e-mail services. By offering the Gateway Guide publication, Gateway.com collects visitors' full address, phone number, and e-mail address. In addition to the static services offered, Gateway.com offers visitors dynamic services such as online chat with technical support and sales associates. It also acquires customers through promotion of its products at university sites such as Ohio University and University of South Carolina. Gateway.com also has strategic alliances with technology-oriented sites such as Znet.com, where it has a preferred vendor spot on Znet.com's homepage. It also has a preferred spot on other Gateway-owned sites such as Gateway.net and Spotshop.com. By offering these services, Gateway is able to focus on the benefits that customers seek.

Dell.com is the most well-known e-commerce Web site. Customers in the United States are segmented on the Dell.com into home and home office, medium and large organizations, Internet providers, healthcare business, federal government, state and local government, and education. Each customer segment has a different mix of products and services available. Customers can select and price different configurations and select various add-ons such as software, peripherals, and digital cameras.

Dell sells products in 13 languages around the world with its homepage. In Japan, for example, 80 percent of Dell's sales are driven by the Web and 40 percent of sales are actually online. Dell and Gateway are not the only two PC manufacturers that sell products online. IBM and Apple also have increasing revenue from sales through their Web sites.

Natural Enviroment

More than 12 million get thrown away every year in the United States alone. Are we talking about cars? Telephones? No, computers! By 2004, as many as 315 million computers will be obsolete. Many old computers end up gathering dust in homes and many more are simply thrown out with the trash. The Silicon Valley Toxics Coalition reported in 2002 that as much as 80 percent of electronic waste collected for recycling in the United States was shipped to Asia, mainly China, India, and Pakistan. A growing number of computer makers, including HP, Dell, and IBM, take back old computer equipment for disposal with little or no cost to consumers.

Japan, home of electronics manufacturers Fujitsu and Canon, passed a law in 2001 requiring computer manufacturers to recycle certain parts. Japan also requires disclosure of chemicals used in production plants. While many people are throwing away good computers, others cannot even afford one. Hundreds of organizations are working to resolve this problem by collecting, repairing, and upgrading old computers. Some high schools and colleges also teach computer repair skills, as well. "Old" computers often go to schools, charities, and needy individuals, or may be put to good use in Third World countries. Donating a used computer can turn one person's trash into someone else's treasure—and cut down on waste!

Gateway, as one of the leading PC manufacturers in the world, has been assessed and certified as meeting requirements of the International Organization for Standardization (ISO) 9002 since 1995. ISO9002 provides a foundation for continuous improvement through consistent procedures, regular internal audits, and corrective action plans and improves internal manufacturing processes to ensure consistent quality within an entire manufacturing facility. Gateway designs products with a focus on reducing energy consumption and extending the product life span so that they meet or exceed all applicable federal standards and environmental regulations. Gateway's computer assembly process leaves almost no component waste materials, and all raw packaging material is either recycled or returned to the supplier for reuse. The company's "Asset Recovery Services" program helps eliminate the hassle of equipment disposal, and helps it comply with complex local, state, and Environmental Protection Agency (EPA) disposal standards. Gateway also recycles and employs reusable materials wherever practical.

Conclusion

Both Dell and Gateway are diversifying into television and other consumer electronics. Gateway is heavily advertising its new line of plasma televisions. However, do you believe diversification is a good strategy for Gateway. Rather than diversification, should Gateway be building more Gateway retail stores and expanding again globally? Re-entry into China's market may be a better strategy for Gateway since the PC market there is expected to grow in that country about 17 percent in 2003. Gateway was the most famous PC brand in China in 2000 and is still popular. China is the biggest PC market in the world and that economy has the highest growth rate in the world at 8 percent each year. The Chinese government encourages investment in China and offers a series of favorable policies to foreign investors.

Another strategy that Gateway might pursue would be extensive research and development to support a product development strategy aimed at voice recognition computers, and simply more advanced PCs. Gateway is known for innovation and "firsts" and could capitalize on this reputation by leading the industry in new, improved laptop, notebook, and desktop PCs, but this strategy would require substantial technological expenditures.

After conducting a thorough analysis of Gateway, develop a three-year strategic plan for the firm. A clear plan for the future is needed. Profit margins have decreased severely in the PC industry due to intense competition, so there is not much room for error in Gateway's strategy formulation and implementation efforts. Gateway's very survival may be at stake with the strategic plan developed today.

Note

1. www.ud.com/company/news/press/05122003.htm.

References

Apple's Web site: www.apple.com.

Baughier, Barry, Bijay Kusle, Kelton Lemons, Sharrzan Clay, and Sokunthea Sok. "Recovering Gateway" (June 26, 2003). boisdarc.tamu-commerce.edu/~bkusle/mkt/Gateway_mkt_plan.pdf.

Dell's Web site: www.dell.com.

"Gateway Posts Wider Second-Quarter Loss." *Reuters* (July 24, 2003). www.forbes.com/newswire/2003/07/24/rtr1037190.html.

"Gateway Reports 2003 Second Quarter Results." *PRNewswire* (July 25, 2003). www.eetimes.com/pressreleases/prnewswire/89693.

Gateway's Web site: www.gateway.com.

HP's Web site: www.hp.com.

Martell, Duncan. "Gateway to Invest More in Its Stores to Spur Growth" (June 2, 2003). in.tech.yahoo.com/030601/137/24t3a.html.

San Jose. "Computer Makers Slammed for E-Waste" (January 10, 2003). www.cbsnews.com/stories/2003/01/10/tech/main535959.shtml.

Standard & Poor's Industry Surveys: Computer Hardware (June 5, 2003).

"2002–2003 Annual General report on China Computer Market." www.dri.co.jp/auto/report/ccid/ccid00103.htm.

Wall, Mark. "Henry Fund Research, Gateway Inc." (November 25, 2002). www.biz.uiowa.edu/hebry/gtw.pdf.

Weiss, Todd R. "Gateway Posts Net Loss, Lower Revenue for Q1 2003" (April 18, 2003). www.computerworld.com/hardwaretopics/hardware/desktops/story/0,10801,80467,00.htm.

34 Stryker Corporation—2004

Henry H. Beam
Western Michigan University

SYK

www.strykercorp.com

Stryker Corporation is a leading maker of specialty surgical and medical products based in Kalamazoo, Michigan. Although not yet a household name, Stryker is one of America's most consistently profitable growth companies. In 2003, Stryker posted record sales of $3.6 billion and net income of $453 million. After John Brown became chairman in 1977, Stryker achieved 20 percent or more annual earnings per share growth every year until 1998, a remarkable record. In 1998, Stryker acquired Howmedica, the orthopedic division of Pfizer. The acquisition nearly doubled Stryker's size, but restructuring charges associated with the acquisition interrupted the streak of 20 percent per year earnings per share growth for two years. By 2000, the company was once again attaining its "Gold Standard" of 20 percent or better annual earnings growth. Stryker's success has gained the attention of Wall Street, where its stock is increasingly on the recommended list of the leading brokerage firms.

All this growth comes from making products that people hope they never have to use—but are glad to have available when they need them. Stryker develops, manufactures, and markets a wide variety of surgical products and specialty hospital beds that are sold primarily to physicians and hospitals throughout the world; it also provides outpatient physical therapy services in the United States. Stryker's mission statement, taken from its 2002 *Annual Report,* is "to serve patients, surgeons and health-care systems around the world with best-in-class surgical and medical products."

In the 1950s and 1960s, Stryker's reputation was enhanced by good publicity about some of its unique products. Roy Campanella, the Brooklyn Dodger baseball star who had been paralyzed from injuries incurred in an automobile accident in 1958, was cared for on Stryker equipment. *Life* magazine did a story about the Tennessee American Legion buying a Circ-O-Lectric Hospital Bed for Sergeant Alvin York, the World War I Medal of Honor winner who had become an invalid by the early 1960s. When Senator Edward Kennedy suffered a back injury in a plane crash in 1964, he was cared for on Stryker equipment. More recently, former First Lady Barbara Bush had Osteonics hip replacements. Such favorable publicity has enhanced the image of the company in the public's eye.

History

The Stryker Corporation takes its name from its founder, Dr. Homer Stryker, a remarkable and multitalented man who believed hard work and inventiveness could overcome any challenge. After serving briefly in World War I, Stryker earned his medical degree from the University of Michigan in 1925, chose orthopedics as his specialty, and located his medical practice in his home town of Kalamazoo, Michigan. Throughout his life, he liked to fiddle with gadgets. During the early years of his medical practice, Stryker invented a mobile hospital bed and a cast-cutting saw. The mobile bed had a frame that pivoted from side to side so physicians could position injured patients for treatment while keeping them immobile. He won a contract to supply the U.S. Army with his beds during World War II and was soon running a small business as well as his medical practice. The contract was terminated when the war ended in 1945, but the business continued with other products such as the cast-cutting saw, which was used to remove casts from patients' arms and legs. The rapid acceptance of the cast cutter by physicians and hospital beds by the army convinced Dr. Stryker that he had more than a part-time business on his hands. In 1946, he started the Orthopedic Frame Company with himself as the sole shareholder. While Dr. Stryker continued with his medical practice, his business was growing rapidly. His son Lee joined him in the business in 1955 after earning a bachelor's degree in business from Syracuse University. Lee's business sense balanced his father's desire to use the company as an outlet for his inventive talents.

In 1964, the company changed its name to Stryker Corporation. With new products coming regularly, sales reached $4.7 million in 1966. Although Stryker's medical equipment business would make him wealthy, he gave away hundreds of ideas and techniques free of charge to other physicians. After Dr. Stryker retired from the company in 1969, it continued to grow under the guidance of Lee Stryker until his tragic death in an airplane crash in Wyoming in July 1976. Later that year, John Brown accepted an offer to become president of Stryker.

Brown graduated from Auburn University in 1957 with a degree in chemical engineering. He had held management positions with Ormet, Thiokol, and Bristol-Myers Squibb before assuming the top position at Stryker. Brown took charge of a firm with sales of $23 million and net income of $1.5 million. He quickly decentralized the company, creating the autonomous divisional structure it has today. When he realized that salespeople were quitting because the compensation system had been changed from commission to salaries and bonuses, he restored commissions as their dominant form of compensation. He also established the ambitious goal of 20 percent annual growth in earnings per share, a goal which everyone at Stryker takes very seriously.

Acquisitions have played an important part in Stryker's growth. In December 1998, it acquired Howmedica, the orthopedic unit of Pfizer, for $1.65 billion in cash. Howmedica made a wide variety of innovative products for the orthopedic market, including craniofacial trauma products through Leibinger, a German company it had purchased in 1996. At the time of the acquisition, Howmedica had sales of $850 million. Stryker's strong cash flow has allowed it to pay down virtually all of the debt it incurred to buy Howmedica in just six years.

Stryker continued to make niche acquisitions, such as Colorado Biomedical, which makes the Colorado Micro Needle used in precision electro-surgery, and Image Guided Technologies, which made three-dimensional optical measurement devices used in image-guided surgery. In 2002, Stryker acquired the spinal implant business of Surgical Dynamics from Tyco International for $135 million. This completed its portfolio of spinal products in the United States, where the demand is the greatest.

Although located mainly in Kalamazoo, Michigan, Stryker also leases facilities in other U.S. cities as well as in France, Germany, Ireland, Switzerland, Canada, and Puerto Rico. The Stryker family trust owns about a third of the shares of the company. Stryker's financial statements are shown in Exhibits 1 and 2.

EXHIBIT 1

Stryker Corporation (SYK)

ANNUAL INCOME STATEMENT IN MILLIONS OF U.S. DOLLARS (EXCEPT FOR PER SHARE ITEMS)	12 MONTHS ENDING 12/31/03	12 MONTHS ENDING 12/31/02	12 MONTHS ENDING 12/31/01
Revenue	$3,625.30	$3,011.60	$2,602.30
Other Revenue	—	—	—
Total Revenue	**3,625.30**	**3,011.60**	**2,602.30**
Cost of Revenue	1,312.40	1,111.20	963.8
Gross Profit	**2,312.90**	**1,900.40**	**1,638.50**
Selling/General/Administrative Expenses	1,416.00	1,165.40	985.4
Research & Development	180.2	141.4	142.1
Depreciation/Amortization	—	—	—
Interest Expense (Income), Net Operating	—	—	—
Unusual Expense (Income)	0	17.2	0.6
Other Operating Expenses	—	—	—
Total Operating Expense	**2,908.60**	**2,435.20**	**2,091.90**
Operating Income	**716.7**	**576.4**	**510.4**
Interest Expense, Net Non-Operating	−22.6	−40.3	−67.9
Interest/Investment Income, Non-Operating	—	—	—
Interest Income (Expense), Net Non-Operating	−22.6	−40.3	−67.9
Gain (Loss) on Sale of Assets	—	—	—
Other, Net	−41.6	−29.4	−36.8
Income Before Tax	**652.5**	**506.7**	**405.7**
Income Tax	199	161.1	133.9
Income After Tax	**453.5**	**345.6**	**271.8**
Minority Interest	—	—	—
Equity In Affiliates	—	—	—
Net Income Before Extra. Items	**453.5**	**345.6**	**271.8**
Accounting Change	—	—	—
Discontinued Operations	—	—	—
Extraordinary Items	—	0	−4.8
Net Income	**$ 453.5**	**345.6**	**267**
Preferred Dividends	—	—	—
Income Available to Common Excl. Extra. Items	**453.5**	**345.6**	**271.8**
Income Available to Common Incl. Extra. Items	**453.5**	**345.6**	**267**
Basic/Primary Weighted Average Shares	198.9	197.5	196.3
Basic/Primary EPS Excl. Extra. Items	**2.28**	**1.75**	**1.385**
Basic/Primary EPS Incl. Extra. Items	**2.28**	**1.75**	**1.36**
Dilution Adjustment	—	—	—
Diluted Weighted Average Shares	203.4	203.8	203
Diluted EPS Excl. Extra. Items	**2.23**	**1.696**	**1.339**
Diluted EPS Incl. Extra. Items	**2.23**	**1.696**	**1.315**
Dividends per Share—Common Stock	0	0.12	0.1
Gross Dividends—Common Stock	0	23.7	19.7
Stock Based Compensation	—	17.1	11.8

Source: www.investor.stockpoint.com.

EXHIBIT 2
Stryker Corporation (SYK)

ANNUAL BALANCE SHEET IN MILLIONS OF U.S. DOLLARS (EXCEPT FOR PER SHARE ITEMS)	AS OF 12/31/03	AS OF 12/31/02	AS OF 12/31/01
Cash & Equivalents	$ 65.9	$ 37.8	$ 50.1
Short Term Investments	—	—	—
Cash and Short Term Investments	65.9	37.8	50.1
Trade Accounts Receivable, Net	498.6	406.7	332.1
Other Receivables	—	—	—
Total Receivables, Net	498.6	406.7	332.1
Total Inventory	467.9	426.5	399.8
Prepaid Expenses	—	52.8	39.6
Other Current Assets	365.2	227.5	171.5
Total Current Assets	**1,397.60**	**1,151.30**	**993.1**
Property/Plant/Equipment—Gross	—	—	—
Accumulated Depreciation	—	−405.5	−312.9
Property/Plant/Equipment, Net	604.7	519.2	444
Goodwill, Net	965.5	460	434.3
Intangibles, Net	—	475.1	368
Long Term Investments	—	—	—
Other Long Term Assets	191.3	209.9	184.2
Total Assets	**3,159.10**	**2,815.50**	**2,423.60**
Accounts Payable	—	106	108.5
Accrued Expenses	—	432.1	334.8
Notes Payable/Short Term Debt	—	—	—
Current Port. LT Debt/Capital Leases	—	10.7	1.7
Other Current Liabilities	850.5	158.7	88.4
Total Current Liabilities	**850.5**	**707.5**	**533.4**
Long Term Debt	18.8	491	720.9
Capital Lease Obligations	—	—	—
Total Long Term Debt	**18.8**	**491**	**720.9**
Total Debt	**18.8**	**501.7**	**722.6**
Deferred Income Tax	—	—	—
Minority Interest	—	—	—
Other Liabilities	135	118.8	113.1
Total Liabilities	**$1,004.30**	**1,317.30**	**1,367.40**
Redeemable Preferred Stock	—	—	—
Preferred Stock—Non Redeemable, Net	—	—	—
Common Stock	—	19.8	19.7
Additional Paid-In Capital	—	120.7	83.2
Retained Earnings (Accum. Deficit)	—	1,442.60	1,120.70
Treasury Stock—Common	—	—	—
Other Equity	2,154.80	−84.9	−167.4
Total Equity	**2,154.80**	**1,498.20**	**1,056.20**
Total Liabilities & Shareholders' Equity	**$3,159.10**	**2,815.50**	**2,423.60**
Shares Outs.—Common Stock	199.5	198.1	196.7
Total Common Shares Outstanding	**199.5**	**198.1**	**196.7**
Total Preferred Stock Shares Outs.	—	—	—
Employees (actual figures)	—	14,045.00	12,839.00
Number of Common Shareholders (actual figures)	—	3,132.00	2,988.00

Source: www.investor.stockpoint.com.

External Environment

Stryker's future will be influenced by three important trends in its external environment, (1) fewer hospitals, (2) an aging population, and (3) competitors.

The number of hospitals in the United States has been declining for over 20 years. With about a third of all hospitals in the United States considered to be excess capacity, industry consolidation is likely to continue. As purchasing decisions in the 1980s and 1990s shifted away from individual physicians to buying alliances, producers of medical products were increasingly forced to demonstrate the cost-effectiveness of their products. About two-thirds of all medical device purchases in the United States are now made by managed-care buyers such as Health Maintenance Organizations (HMOs) and national buying groups. Additionally, over half of all surgeries performed at community hospitals are now done on an outpatient basis. This is due to restricted reimbursement policies for inpatient care and the development of less invasive surgical procedures that do not require overnight stays in hospitals. For example, removal of the gallbladder now requires a single day in the hospital, followed by a week of convalescence. In contrast, traditional gallbladder surgery entailed about a week in the hospital and a month's convalescence.

In terms of the aging population, the baby-boom generation—the large number of people born in the United States (and worldwide) between 1947 and 1961—is aging. A baby boomer turns 50 every seven seconds. Worldwide, there are over 600 million people aged 60 and that number is projected to rise to 1.2 billion by 2025. As the population ages, it will be in greater need of the reconstructive products and rehabilitative services that Stryker offers.

Regarding competitors, Stryker's primary rival is Zimmer Holdings, of Warsaw, Indiana, which had sales of $1.4 billion and net income of $258 million in 2002. Zimmer was spun off from Bristol-Myers Squibb in 2001 and competes directly with Stryker in many of its product lines in the United States and abroad. Zimmer designs and markets orthopedic products such as reconstructive implants and fracture management devices. Products include the NexGen knee implant series and the Versys system for hips. International sales are about 40 percent of Zimmer's total sales, with Japan accounting for about half of that market. In 2003, Zimmer acquired Centerpulse, a Swiss firm that makes reconstructive joint, spine, and dental implants. The acquisition increased Zimmer's annual sales to $2 billion and made it the leader in both the United States and Europe in the hip replacement market.

Stryker's Organization

Stryker is organized into five major product divisions: Howmedica; MedSurg Equipment; Physiotherapy; Biotech, Spine, and Trauma; and International. Each Stryker product unit competes against medical equipment subsidiaries of large firms (e.g., DePuy of Johnson & Johnson, Hill-Rom of Hillenbrand Industries) as well as independent firms such as Biomet, Medtronic Midas Rex, U.S. Surgical, and Zimmer.

Howmedica Osteonics

The Howmedica Osteonics division produces a variety of hip, knee, and shoulder implants. It is a combination of the former Stryker Osteonics division and the Howmedica acquisition. This is Stryker's largest unit, accounting for over half of sales. Every year, about half a million people in the United States and a comparable number abroad, many of them elderly, undergo joint replacement surgery to regain some of their previous mobility. Most hip and knee replacements result from osteoarthritis (a condition in which joints become painful and mobility is reduced) and rheumatoid arthritis (a disease that destroys cartilage at the joint's surface). Orthopedic research has led to development of a broad array of prosthetic devices. Recent innovations include porous hip and knee replacements, which allow bone to grow directly into the metal implant.

Stryker MedSurg

The MedSurg (medical and surgical) division has four major segments: Stryker Instruments, Stryker Endoscopy, Stryker Medical, and Stryker Leibinger.

Stryker Instruments produces a wide range of high-quality operating room equipment that is utilized primarily in orthopedic procedures, such as bone saws and drills. It is a market leader for battery-powered, heavy-duty surgical instruments. Its Stryker 940 cast removal system is the newest version of Dr. Stryker's original cast cutter.

Stryker Endoscopy makes a broad range of medical video imaging equipment and instruments for arthroscopy and general surgery. In an endoscopic (less invasive) surgical procedure, the surgeon removes or repairs damaged tissue through several small punctures rather than through an open incision. Patients experience reduced trauma and pain, less time in the hospital, and a quicker return to health. Imaging technology plays a crucial role in endoscopic procedures. Stryker is a leader in medical video imaging systems. Its miniaturized color video camera was the first to offer surgeons a broadcast-quality image. This division also makes digital cameras to assist with endoscopic procedures. Stryker Endoscopy recently signed a distribution agreement with Regeneration Technologies to supply human allograft tissue in the U.S. for sports medicine surgeries such as reconstruction and repair of the knee, hip, shoulder, wrist, elbow, foot, or ankle.

Stryker Medical produces specialty stretchers and hospital beds which facilitate the transportation, transfer, and treatment of patients. It designed a line of innovative stretchers as a result of a close analysis of hospital needs, focusing on reducing the number of patient transfers (from bed to stretcher to operating table and back again) that must be performed in a hospital. It also produces accessories such as bedside stands and overbed tables.

Stryker Leibinger is a leading maker of surgical instruments and products primarily used for head, neck, and hand surgery. Its headquarters are in Germany.

The Physiotherapy Associates division operates nearly 400 outpatient rehabilitation centers in over 25 states. Following an orthopedic or neurological injury, the centers provide physical, occupational, and speech therapy to help speed a patient's return to work or full activity. Each center averages $400,000 in revenue per year. In the outpatient physical therapy market, Stryker's principal competitors are independent practices and hospital-based services. Competition is also provided by national rehabilitation companies such as HealthSouth, NovaCare, and Rehability.

Stryker Biotech, Spine, and Trauma

Stryker Biotech, Spine, and Trauma provides both implants and instruments to assist in the repair of the human spine. Trauma products are used primarily in repairing fractures resulting from sudden injury. An estimated 10,000 spinal injuries occur each year in the United States, nearly half of which are related to automobile and motorcycle accidents. About one-third of all spine procedures are fusions, in which surgeons seek to stop painful motion in the back by fusing unstable vertebrae. One of Stryker's promising new biotechnology products is its OP-1 bone growth protein, designed to help with difficult-to-heal fractures and spinal fusions.

International

In the early 1990s, Stryker sought to improve the distribution of its products internationally by investing in Matsumoto, the largest Japanese distributor of orthopedic, general surgery, and emergency care products. In addition to Stryker products, Matsumoto also distributed devices from other leading American and European medical device makers. Shortly after Stryker took a majority ownership position in Matsumoto in 1995, several medical instrument companies stopped distributing through Matsumoto because they felt uncomfortable with Stryker's majority stake.

As a result, sales of non-Stryker products fell over 50 percent from 1995 to 1996. In 1999, Stryker purchased the remaining shares of Matsumoto stock, bringing its direct ownership to 100 percent. Matsumoto is now called Stryker Japan. Stryker Europe and Stryker Pacific (all except Japan) comprise Stryker's other international operations. Overall, international sales account for about a third of Stryker's sales.

Manufacturing

Stryker's manufacturing processes consist primarily of precision machining, metal fabrication, assembly operations, and the investment (precision) casting of cobalt chrome and finishing of cobalt chrome and titanium. The principal raw materials used by the company are stainless steel, aluminum, cobalt chrome, and titanium alloys. In all, purchases from outside sources are about half of the company's total cost of sales.

Two Stryker manufacturing facilities have won awards. In 1998, *Industry Week* named Howmedica Osteonics, located in Allendale, New Jersey, as one of the top-ten manufacturing plants in the United States. Then in 2000, the Stryker Instruments manufacturing facility in Kalamazoo, Michigan, was similarly honored by *Industry Week*. All of the plant's workforce participates in self-directed work teams. More than 99 percent of all finished products meet quality requirements at initial inspection, and 98 percent of all deliveries are made on time.

Research and Development

Many of the company's products and product improvements have been developed internally. The company maintains close working relationships with physicians and medical personnel in hospitals and universities, who assist in product research and development. Research and development is under the direct control of the operating divisions, where it can be focused on specific markets. Stryker seeks to obtain patent protection on its products whenever possible. It currently holds over 1,500 patents worldwide on products it has developed. The company spent $180.2, $141.4, and $142.1 million, respectively, in 2003, 2002, and 2001 on research, development, and engineering.

Stryker's Corporate Culture

Since John Brown became CEO, Stryker has developed a distinctive, no-nonsense corporate culture that is sometimes described as "a lot like being in the Marine Corps," although senior executives try to downplay that image. Sayings representing Stryker's core beliefs are prominently written on walls in lobbies and cafeterias. One of the most common, "First be best, then be first," refers to the competitive corporate philosophy established by Dr. Stryker that Stryker should first make the best products and then seek market leadership for those products. Another slogan that appears on Stryker promotional literature is, "Good for the customer. Good for us. Otherwise, no deal."

Although there are no time clocks visible in Stryker facilities, employees wear scanning ID cards that keep track of when they arrive for work and when they leave. Lunch time is restricted to 30 minutes, just enough time to eat in the company cafeteria. Given the pressure of the 20 percent annual increase in earnings goal, the workweek for white-collar workers is typically between 50 and 60 hours. It is common for executives to work evenings or on weekends. In return for their hard work ethic, employees are encouraged to share in the company's prosperity through a generous stock purchase plan. Employees can contribute up to 14 percent of their earnings to purchase Stryker stock. The company will match the first 8 percent contributed by the employees.

Most of the company's products are marketed in the United States directly to more than 7,500 hospitals and to doctors and other healthcare facilities by its 2,000-person salesforce. The company maintains dedicated sales forces for each of its principal product lines to provide focus and a high level of expertise to each medical speciality served. The domestic salesforce is compensated in large part by commissions. Stryker has been referred to as a "salesperson's paradise," where the best performers can earn $200,000 or more a year. Hourly workers can earn pay increases or bonuses for meeting quality objectives.

A manager at Stryker Instruments made the following connection between Stryker's culture and its success: "There is nothing particularly special about what we do from a manufacturing standpoint, in comparison to our competitors. The difference is in our culture. We aren't the only smart guys out there, but we do have the most highly defined, tangibly strong culture. And that is what, above all, we need to protect."

The Future

Stryker has prospered for more than 25 years under the direction of John Brown. Despite its past success, the company may find it increasingly difficult to make its target of 20 percent annual earnings growth. First, most of Stryker's major markets have shown annual growth rates of 5 percent or less over the last few years. This means Stryker's divisions need to grow more rapidly than the market segments in which they compete in order to meet the 20 percent per year earnings growth goal. Second, mergers and acquisitions within the healthcare sector will probably continue at a rapid pace. This could lead to the emergence of larger and more powerful buying groups, such as Novation, that could put increased pressure on the suppliers of medical equipment, such as Stryker, to reduce the cost of their products. Third, employees may tire of the high-pressure Stryker culture and look for less stressful jobs with other companies.

Stryker does have some opportunities available to it to help make its growth goals. One opportunity is to use its strong financial position to continue making selected acquisitions in new markets, as it did when it entered the trauma business in 1996 with its acquisition of Osteo Holdings. It can also increase its share of existing markets, as it did with its 2002 acquisition of Surgical Dynamics. A second opportunity for growth is to add centers to its Physical Therapy Services division. A third opportunity would be to place increased emphasis on Stryker Biotech, its corporate research and development laboratory, to come up with new products.

In 2003, Stephen MacMillan, 38, was appointed president of Stryker, providing an indication of who would eventually succeed John Brown, who is 68 years old. Brown retained the titles of chairman and CEO. Prior to joining Stryker, MacMillan was Vice President, Global Specialty Operations for Pharmacia Corporation until it was acquired by Pfizer in 2002. Prior to Pharmacia, MacMillan held management and marketing positions at Johnson & Johnson and Procter & Gamble. MacMillan is a graduate of Davidson College and the Harvard Business School Advanced Management Program.

John Brown was highly successful in taking Stryker from a small company with sales of $23 million in 1977 to a company listed on the New York Stock Exchange with sales of $3.6 billion in 2003. His heir-apparent, Steve MacMillan, will face a very different set of challenges now that Stryker is a *Fortune* 500 company. In addition to dealing with the competitive threat posed by Zimmer, he will have to consider whether it is time to change any of the goals and polices that were so instrumental in Stryker's past success, such as:

- Insisting that earnings per share increases 20 percent a year, every year.
- Commission as the dominant form of compensation system for the salesforce.
- Its quasi-military corporate culture and fast-paced work ethic.

35   Biomet, Inc.—2004

Satish P. Deshpande
Western Michigan University

BMET

www.biomet.com

Consolidation is occurring in the orthopedic industry. Large firms are acquiring smaller companies to fill gaps in their product lines or increase market share. Indiana-based Zimmer and Britain's Smith & Nephew recently got into a bidding war over Switzerland's Centerpulse. Switzerland's Synthes-Stratec also made a bid for privately held Mathys Medical. This sector is attractive to investors looking for a safe haven to invest their money in an industry that is relatively impervious to a slowing economy. The global market for orthopedic devices is around $16 billion and growing at an annual rate of 12 percent.

Biomet, Inc., operates in the musculoskeletal products business segment of the healthcare sector. The company is a specialty manufacturer, designer, and marketer of orthopedic products, including reconstructive and fixation devices, electrical bone growth stimulators, bone substitutes, orthopedic support devices, operating room supplies, general surgical instruments, dental reconstructive implants, and arthroscopy products.

Biomet has its corporate headquarters in Warsaw, Indiana, and operates in over 30 countries. The company and its subsidiaries distribute products primarily aimed at musculoskeletal medical specialists who work in the fields of both surgical and nonsurgical therapy in over 100 countries, and it employs over 5,000 people worldwide.

Biomet reported record sales for its fiscal year ending May 31, 2003, as sales increased 17 percent to $1.39 billion. Net income increased 20 percent to $286.7 million. Revenues reflect the continued market penetration of the reconstructive, fixation, spinal, and other product lines of the company. The fourth quarter of fiscal 2003 was Biomet's one-hundredth consecutive quarter of record year-over-year sales and earnings, excluding litigation charges in the fourth quarter of fiscal 1999 and third quarter of fiscal 2001.

Orthopedic implant manufacturers have faced increasing pressure to contain their costs as hospitals seek various ways to limit expensive inventories. Burdensome regulations, expensive product liability, and managed care have led many manufacturers to develop and manufacture their products abroad. On the other hand, the Food and Drug Administration (FDA) has come under increasing public and political pressure to speed up approvals of drugs and medical devices. In Senate hearings, the FDA has been attacked for failing to provide timely access to new medical technology. Congressional leaders in the past have called for privatization of the governmental agency. In response, the federal government has announced a number of steps to ease restrictions. These are positive signals for Biomet.

History

Biomet, Inc., was incorporated in 1977 in Indiana by Dane A. Miller, Niles L. Noblitt, Jerry Ferguson, and Ray Harroff. Today, Miller is president and CEO of Biomet, Ferguson is vice chairman of the board, and Noblitt is board chairman. Miller, as well as several other key managers, worked at the Zimmer Division of Bristol-Myers before forming their own company. The company initially sold orthopedic support products through ten distributors. Biomet entered the reconstructive device market in the early 1980s when it introduced a titanium alloy-based hip system. Biomet further enhanced its reputation with a number of technological advances in hip replacement systems as well as in total knee replacement. Biomet was founded on the premise that major orthopedic companies, which were primarily divisions of large pharmaceutical companies, had neglected a service orientation approach to orthopedic surgeons' needs. Through a dedication to high levels of service and a variety of innovative products, Biomet has rapidly penetrated the growing market for orthopedic products.

In 1992, Biomet purchased Walter Lorenz Surgical Instruments, Inc. (Lorenz Surgical), for $19 million. Lorenz Surgical, based in Jacksonville, Florida, was a leading marketer of oral-maxillofacial products used by oral surgeons. Its product offerings include orthognathic instruments (used for jaw alignment), craniofacial instruments (used to treat severe skull deformities), rigid fixation systems, TMJ instruments, exodontial instruments, and a transmandibular implant system. These products were principally used to correct deformities, to assist in the repair of trauma fractures, and for cosmetic applications.

In 1994, Biomet purchased Kirschner Medical Corporation of Maryland for $38.9 million ($13.3 million over the fair value). Kirschner (as does Biomet) produced joint replacements for hips, knees, and shoulders, along with fracture fixation products. Kirschner was a market leader in shoulder implants; it also produced braces, supports, splints, and cast materials. It had four manufacturing plants in the United States and one in Spain. During fiscal year 1996, Kirschner's orthopedic operations were consolidated into Biomet, eliminating duplicative administrative and overhead expenses. During the same period, Biomet Europe was established to coordinate manufacturing, development, and sales activities in Europe. In early 1998, Biomet entered into a joint venture agreement with Merck KgaA, a pharmaceutical and chemical company located in Darmstadt, Germany. Under this agreement, the two companies joined their European orthopedic and biomaterials business operations to form Biomet Merck.

Biomet formed an alliance with Selective Genetics, Inc., during the fourth quarter of fiscal year 1999 to develop gene therapy products for the musculoskeletal market. In late 1999, Biomet acquired Implant Innovation Inc. ("3i"), a worldwide leader in the dental reconstructive implant market, in a stock-for-stock exchange in which 7.8 million shares were issued for all outstanding shares. Subsequently, in late 2000, Biomet, through its subsidiary EBI, acquired Biolectron, Inc., for $90 million in cash. Biolectron's products are aimed at the spinal fusion, fracture healing, and arthroscopy markets. During fiscal year 2002 and 2001, Biomet acquired a number of foreign distributors and/or businesses. In early 2002, it entered into a partnership with Z-KAT, Inc., to co-develop and distribute image-guided software and intelligent instrumentation for musculoskeletal applications. During the fourth quarter of 2002 the company determined that its nearly $6 million investment in preferred stock of Selective Genetics was permanently impaired and took a charge of $5.5 million.

Today, 63 percent of Biomet's business is in reconstructive devices, and almost 70 percent of the company's business is domestic. It employs over 2,000 sales representatives worldwide. The major subsidiaries (**www.biomet.com/corporate/subsidiaries.cfm/**) of Biomet are:

- Arthrotek, which is the company's sports medicine division. Arthrotek offers a complete line of arthroscopy products, including resorbable arthroscopic fixation products. It is based in Warsaw, Indiana, with manufacturing sites in Ontario and Redding, California.
- Electro-Biology, Inc. (EBI), which is the market leader in the electrical stimulation and external fixation market segments. EBI also offers products in the spinal and orthopedic support market segments. It is based in Parsippany, New Jersey, and operates plants in Guaynabo, Puerto Rico; Parsippany and Allendale, New Jersey; and Marlow, Oklahoma.
- Lorenz Surgical, which is a pioneer in the craniomaxillofacial market segment, is based in Jacksonville, Florida. The Lorenz product line includes the industry's first resorbable craniomaxillofacial fixation system.
- Implant Innovations, Inc., which is a major presence in the dental reconstructive implant market. It is located in Palm Beach Gardens, Florida.
- BioMer C. V., which is a 50–50 joint venture between Biomet, Inc., and Merck KGaA, a German chemical and pharmaceutical company. The partnership significantly expands Biomet's presence in the European marketplace while providing the company with worldwide access to key biomaterials technologies.

External Issues

As shown in Exhibit 1, the 2003 musculoskeletal products market in the United States is estimated to be nearly $9.53 billion. Reconstructive devices make up nearly 40 percent of the orthopedic market. Exhibit 2 provides detailed information on the reconstructive market in the United States. This $3.81 billion market segment includes total hip, knee, and shoulder replacements and is expected to grow between 13 and 15 percent annually. The hip market is estimated to be $1.63 billion and is growing 10 to 12 percent annually. The $2.04 billion knee market is estimated to be growing at an

EXHIBIT 1

2003 Sales of Musculoskeletal Products in the United States

MARKET SEGMENT	SALES (IN MILLIONS)
1. Orthopedic Reconstructive Devices	$3,810
2. Spinal Products	2,180
3. Fixation	1,170
4. Arthroscopy	770
5. Softgoods and Bracing	525
6. Dental Reconstructive Implants	390
7. O.R. Supplies	300
8. Powered Surgical Equipment	205
9. Bone Cement and Accessories	180
	$9.53 billion

Source: Biomet *Annual Report,* 2003, p. 4.

EXHIBIT 2

2003 Sales of Orthopedic Reconstructive in the United States

MARKET SEGMENT	SALES (IN MILLIONS)
1. Knees	$2,035
2. Hips	1,625
3. Shoulders	100
4. Others	50
	$3.81 billion

Source: Biomet *Annual Report*, 2003, p. 4.

annual rate of 12 to 14 percent. The shoulder market is estimated around $100 million, with an 8 percent annual growth rate.

Biomet's major competitors include DePuy, Inc., a subsidiary of Johnson & Johnson; Stryker Howmedica Osteonics, a subsidiary of Stryker Corp.; Zimmer, Inc., a subsidiary of Zimmer Holdings, Inc.; Smith & Nephew plc and Centerpulse Orthopedics, a division of Centerpulse AG. Johnson & Johnson/DePuy and Stryker/Howmedica are the leaders in the reconstructive field, followed by Zimmer. Biomet is the fourth-largest participant in the market. According to Exhibit 3, unlike other companies, Biomet is well diversified in different segments of the market. Growth in the reconstructive market has been attributed to better products and techniques that improve surgical outcomes, cost-effective techniques, and demographics. Recent products last longer and require less surgical time in the operating room, thereby lowering costs.

People today are living longer, which accounts for the expanded patient pool. Life expectancies have increased by approximately 5 percent over the past two decades. Male life expectancy has increased to 71 years, while female life expectancy has increased to 78 years. Of the estimated 37 million Americans who suffer from arthritis, approximately 14 million of them (38 percent) are between the ages of 45 and 64. A more active

EXHIBIT 3

Biomet's Position in Different Segments of the Musculoskeletal Market

MARKET SEGMENT	BMET	SYK	ZMH	SNN
1. Reconstructive Total Joints	✓	✓	✓	
2. Spinal Products	✓	✓		
3. Fixation	✓	✓		✓
4. Dental Implants	✓			
5. Procedure-Specific Arthroscopy	✓	✓		✓
6. Ortho-Biologics	✗	✗		
7. Bone Growth Stimulation	✓			✓

✓ Top 4 Market Position in United States

✗ In Development with Products on the Market

Source: Biomet *Annual Report*, 2003, p. 4.

lifestyle, according to Biomet officials, has led to joint replacement at younger ages. Likewise, the pool of people 75 and over is increasing. Clearly, demographics are favorable for Biomet.

The general population growth rate from 1989 to 2010 is projected to be only 14 percent. But the 55–74 year age sector is expected to grow 40 percent between 1997 and 2010, an increase of 16 million people. The over–75 population is expected to grow by 16 percent to 18 million people over the same period. The over–65 population segment accounts for more than two-thirds of total healthcare expenditures. Competition in the implant market is based primarily on service and product design, while competition in the sale of generic internal fixation devices tends to be based more on price. Purchasing decisions for hospitals are being made increasingly through buying groups that are able to negotiate price discounts from the manufacturers.

Two additional factors squeezing profits are (1) the higher utilization of lower-priced implants for the elderly, who require less functionality and longevity of implants; and (2) the fact that surgeons are becoming more cooperative with hospital administrators and are narrowing their choices of products, thereby allowing hospitals to deal with fewer manufacturers.

Biomet's Products

Biomet's products are divided into four groups: Reconstructive Products, Fixation Products, Spinal Products, and Other Products. Exhibit 4 gives sales by product group for three fiscal years ended May 31: 2003, 2002, and 2001.

Reconstructive Products

Biomet's net sales of reconstructive devices worldwide increased around 20 percent during fiscal year 2003 to more than $867 million. These devices replace joints that have deteriorated either from diseases such as arthritis or through injury. Reconstructive joint surgery involves modification of the area surrounding the affected joint and insertion of one or more manufactured joint components. Biomet's primary reconstructive products concern the hip, knee, shoulder, and dental implants, although the company can produce peripheral joints for the wrist, elbow, finger, or large toe. A hip prosthesis consists of a femoral head, neck, and stem manufactured in a variety of head sizes, neck lengths, stem lengths, and con-

EXHIBIT 4

Biomet's Sales of Reconstructive Devices

	YEARS ENDED MAY 31,					
	2003		2002		2001	
(dollar amounts in thousands)	Net Sales	% Sales	Net Sales	% Sales	Net Sales	% Sales
Reconstructive products	$ 867,602	63%	721,004	61%	614,308	60%
Fixation devices	237,117	17%	215,544	18%	202,152	19%
Spinal products	143,607	10%	125,119	11%	91,103	9%
Other products	141,974	10%	130,235	10%	123,100	12%
Total	$1,390,300	100%	1,191,902	100%	1,030,663	100%

Source: Biomet 2003 Annual Report.

figurations. Hip sales increased by 19 percent in the United States and 23 percent worldwide in the third quarter of 2003. The M^2a Taper Metal-on-Metal Articulation System, specially designed for young active patients, continues to experience increased market acceptance in the United States. Ten new hip products were introduced during fiscal year 2003 and the company has a number of hip products, including the Freedom Constrained Liner, scheduled to the released in fiscal year 2004.

The minimally invasive Repicci II Unicondylar Knee and the Ascent Total Knee System drive Biomet's market-leading knee performance in the United States. In addition, the AGC Total Knee System was introduced in 1983 and has shown excellent long-term clinical results. The product features left and right femoral components, matching tibial components, and appropriately sized patella components for resurfacing. Biomet's various major knee systems, with their variety of options, are one of the most versatile and comprehensive available in the orthopedic market. Knee sales increased by 15 percent in the United States and 20 percent worldwide in 2003. Biomet also has a Patient-Matched-Implant (PMI) services group, which designs, manufactures, and delivers one-of-a-kind reconstructive and trauma devices for orthopedic surgeons. The company acquired a patent in 1990 that allows a physician to create, prior to surgery (through the use of CT or MRI data), electronic 3-D models that are then translated into a PMI design for manufacture. Nine new knee products were introduced during fiscal year 2003.

Three new shoulder and extremity products were introduced during fiscal year 2003, including the Comprehensive Shoulder System Fracture Stem. Extremity products increased 11 percent in the United States and 15 percent worldwide during third quarter of fiscal year 2003. The Osseotite Dental Reconstructive Implant System helped U. S. dental reconstructive implant sales increase 20 percent in third quarter fiscal year 2003. Biomet entered the bone cements and accessories market five years ago and currently holds the second position in the $180 million U. S. market. The company's Cell Factor Technologies subsidiary's Gravitational Platelet Separation System is a cost-effective way of collecting large concentrations of platelets from a small volume of blood. Clinical evaluations began during second quarter fiscal year 2004 on a procedure-specific software developed in conjunction with Z-KAT, Inc.

Fixation Products

Every year, around 10 million fractures occur in the United States. The 2003 fixation market was estimated to be $1.17 billion and it is growing at an estimated 9 percent per year. It includes products used to stabilize broken bones and to promote healing. Biomet's net sales in this market increased by around 10 percent to $237 million. EBI is a market leader in both the $165 million external fixation market segment and the $160 million electrical stimulation market.

External fixation is typically used to immobilize fractured bones when traditional casting is not an option. The company introduced a number of extensions to its DynaFix Rail System, a well-known modular system for treating factures. During fiscal year 2002, the company introduced the lightweight Vision Pin-to-Bar System which allows x-ray visualization of the fracture site.

The EBI Model Bone Healing System continues to be a market leader in the domestic electrical simulation market. This product is used on fractured bones that do not heal using normal methods. A coil connected to a battery-operated treatment unit is placed on the fracture. The system produces a pulsating electromagnetic field

(PEMF) which affects the cells. Since the system is noninvasive, it poses no surgical risks and has no known side effects. The company introduced a compact version of the system during fiscal year 1998 and a lighter, more patient-friendly model in 2000. The acquisition of Biolectron, Inc., helped EBI broaden and improve its already strong product line. Biomet's Lorenz Surgical subsidiary is ranked third in the $185 million craniomaxillofacial fixation market. The LactoSorb Craniomaxillofacial Fixation System consists of a copolymer comparable in strength to existing titanium systems, but it is completely resorbed within nine to twelve months. This system is especially beneficial for pediatric surgical procedures, since it eliminates the need for a second surgery to remove plates and screws. During fiscal 2003, Lorenz Surgical introduced three new products into the market.

Spinal Products

The U. S. spinal implant market is about $2.18 billion (see Exhibit 1). Growing by at least 20 percent annually, this is the fastest-growing segment of the musculoskeletal products market. Back injuries cost society nearly $16 billion every year. Over 2 million spinal procedures were performed worldwide in 2003. Nearly half of the more than 300,000 vertebral fusion procedures performed in the United States every year utilize some type of instrumentation. Spinal sales increased 11 percent during third quarter fiscal year 2003. Currently, EBI is the fourth-largest participant in the market. The Biolectron acquisition provided EBI with the SpinalPak noninvasive simulation system, which offers surgeons a patient-friendly device for noninvasive stimulation. EBI has a broad spectrum of spinal products in development including an artificial disk replacement.

Other Products

Biomet's "other product" sales during fiscal 2003 were approximately $142 million. This was a 9 percent increase in the United States over the previous fiscal year, and was in great part due to Arthrotek's arthroscopy products, EBI's line of soft goods and bracing products, and various operating room supplies from Biomet Merck.

Operations

Research and Development

Biomet has spent nearly $150 million on research and development from 2001 to 2003. A number of biomaterials projects are in progress to address issues like designing better implants for various applications and bone substitute materials and cements. The company is placing more emphasis on finding ways to help the body heal itself naturally. Biomet's innovative new technology development efforts primarily take place in Warsaw, Indiana, and Darmstadt, Germany. On the other hand, evolutionary developments including product line extensions are driven by the individual subsidiaries. Biomet's research and development efforts have produced nearly 340 new products and services during the last four years.

International Operations

Biomet has operations in over 30 countries and distributes its products to over 100 countries; its business segments are managed primarily on a geographic basis. These segments are comprised of the United States, Europe, and the category labeled "Others" (Canada, South America, Mexico, Japan, and the Pacific Rim). Biomet eval-

EXHIBIT 5
Biomet's Sales by Geographic Area

(IN THOUSANDS)	2003	2002	2001
Net Sales			
United States	$ 966,638	$ 856,375	$ 722,381
Europe	332,053	260,420	237,444
Rest of World	91,609	75,107	70,838
	$1,390,300	$1,191,902	$1,030,663
Operating Income			
United States	$388,841	$326,906	$251,927
Europe	41,924	39,152	34,772
Other	1,540	4,636	3,988
	$432,305	$370,694	$290,687
Long-Lived Assets			
United States	$238,249	$226,406	$213,339
Europe	141,950	121,253	109,758
Other	13,742	10,061	8,532
	$393,941	$357,720	$331,629

Source: Biomet Inc., and Subsidiaries Notes to Consolidated Financial Statements, 2003 *Annual Report*.

uates performance based on the operating income of each geographic unit. Exhibit 5 shows the performance of each segment. The Net sales to customers in Europe increased by 28 percent to $332 million and those in the "Others" category increased by 22 percent to $91 million over the previous year. Biomet's consolidated financial information is given in Exhibits 7 and 8.

Biomet Merck provides Biomet with the exclusive rights to Merck KGaA's current and future biomaterials-based products. Currently, with a local presence in all the major markets, it is the fourth largest orthopedic company in Europe. This is partly due to the successful integration of Biomet's and Merck KGaA's operations. The company started selling its products directly in Japan during fiscal 2002. The $1 billion market in Japan offers significant opportunities for Biomet.

Management Philosophy

Biomet prides itself on having "the responsiveness and innovation of a small company, with the resources and market presence of a large company." In the absence of a formal vision statement, the phrase "The most responsive company in orthopedics" could be seen as an informal vision statement. On its Web site (**www.biomet.com/investors/faq.cfm**), Biomet explicitly states that it has no written mission statement. But the following statement, based on information in its 2002 *Annual Report*, may act as a mission statement:

> The Biomet team is committed to the compassionate care of patients throughout the world. We do this by connecting, building, and nurturing long-term relationships with our customers and patients that allows us to deliver technologically advanced quality products with unsurpassed

service. We are also committed to ensure that our team members have the best technology, educational tools, resources, and work environment in the industry. We believe that by connecting people, ideas, technology, products, and service, we provide a network that is critical to our patients and customers; and ultimately to the future success of the company.

Team Biomet

According to CEO Dane Miller, who ranks sixth in *Forbes* magazine's (May 12, 2003) "Best Bosses for the Buck" list, the major reasons for the success of Biomet are: "(1) We remain close to the market and listen to the needs of our customers, (2) We function as a team to get the job done, and (3) Our team has creative and innovative members in place to succeed." The team concept was started at Biomet in 1977 and is today an integral part of the firm's philosophy. One characteristic of the concept is that Biomet has decentralized decision making so that decisions can be made at the appropriate levels. Teams are composed of employees from several functional areas (e.g., design, manufacturing, quality, and production planning). Physically, employees are located by functional areas within the facility where routine decisions are handled. Only those decisions related to large commitments of capital expenditures or changes in strategic policies require presidential or vice presidential signatures.

Communications between subsidiaries and departments is frequent and open. Members of management interact with the workers on a daily basis. In addition, there are many corporate events that foster camaraderie. When Dane Miller and his colleagues started the company, his goal was to "create an organization that could grow unencumbered by the bureaucratic structures and conservatism that [we believed] stifle initiative and creativity at many large firms." Although Miller and his colleagues keep an open door for employees, they are constantly on the shop floor talking to employees in their work setting. The team concept is stressed in company brochures and meetings. There is a Biomet Team Appreciation Day and company picnics, Christmas parties, and other special events. The quarterly in-house publication Bio Briefs serves as an effective communication tool to keep employees informed of corporate and product information, as well as to recognize special events such as promotions, birthdays, births, anniversaries, and so on.

Biomet's team concept offers every employee financial incentives including cash bonuses, company shares, and stock options. The team concept also extends to the medical profession. When patients face unusual circumstances, Biomet officials are often called upon to design specialty products. Biomet enjoys a healthy reputation in the medical profession for its "team effort." This concept, first announced in 1989, is reinforced in daily operations. In the absence of a formal organization chart, Exhibit 6 provides an organizational chart based on titles of the officers of Biomet, Inc., which are reported in the company's Web page.

Conclusion

Prices of orthopedic devices in the United States are expected to grow at a modest 2 percent rate in the future. Biomet will have to continue its strategy of finding a niche such as spinal implants and stimulators. With $418 million in cash and investments, the company is well positioned to continue making selective acquisitions. But Biomet could itself become a target of a pharmaceutical company such as Novartis,

EXHIBIT 6
Organizational Chart, Biomet, Inc.

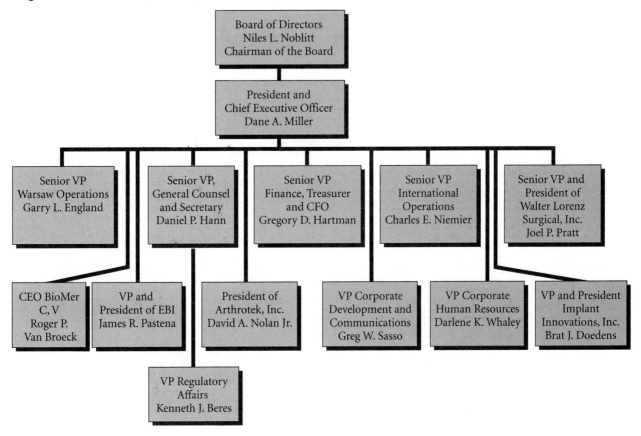

Source: Adapted from information in Biomet's 2003 *Annual Report* and www.biomet.com.

EXHIBIT 7
Consolidated Financial Information

ANNUAL INCOME STATEMENT (IN THOUSANDS)	PERIOD ENDING MAY 31,	
	2003	2002
Net sales	$1,390,300	$1,191,902
Cost of sales	407,295	332,727
Gross profit	983,005	859,175
Selling, general and administrative expenses	501,191	437,731
Research and development expense	55,309	50,750
Other charges/(credits)	(5,800)	—
Operating income	432,305	370,694
Other income, net	19,438	5,421
Income before income taxes and minority interest	451,743	376,115
Provision for income taxes	156,961	127,665
Income before minority interest	294,782	248,450
Minority interest	8,081	8,710
Net income	$ 286,701	239,740

Source: Biomet's 2003 *Annual Report* and www.biomet.com.

EXHIBIT 8

Biomet, Inc., and Subsidiaries Consolidated Balance Sheets

	AT MAY 31,	
(IN THOUSANDS, EXCEPT PER-SHARE DATA)	2003	2002
Assets		
Current assets:		
Cash and cash equivalents	$ 225,650	$ 154,297
Investments	37,337	30,973
Accounts and notes receivable, less allowance for doubtful receivables (2003—$18,742 and 2002—$13,175)	418,095	365,148
Inventories	356,270	335,348
Deferred income taxes	54,262	49,523
Prepaid expenses and other	20,141	17,655
Total current assets	1,111,755	952,944
Property, plant and equipment:		
Land and improvements	22,285	17,854
Buildings and improvements	127,030	102,957
Machinery and equipment	319,650	268,643
	468,965	389,454
Less, Accumulated depreciation	215,519	170,393
Property, plant and equipment, net		
Investments	155,607	201,247
Goodwill, net of accumulated amortization (2003—$44,011 and 2002—$42,972)	126,706	125,157
Other intangible assets, net of accumulated amortization (2003—$29,704 and 2002—$25,163)	10,874	8,532
Other assets	13,781	14,782
Total assets	$1,672,169	$1,521,723
Liabilities & Shareholders' Equity		
Current liabilities:		
Short-term borrowings	$ 114,120	$ 90,467
Accounts payable	42,106	36,318
Accrued income taxes	12,453	17,483
Accrued wages and commissions	43,715	35,106
Accrued insurance	11,568	14,383
Accrued litigation	—	5,864
Other accrued expenses	42,692	38,078
Total current liabilities	266,654	237,699
Deferred federal income taxes	7,031	3,332
Other liabilities	462	406
Total liabilities	274,147	241,437
Minority interest	111,888	103,807
Commitments and contingencies		
Shareholders' equity:		
Preferred shares, $100 par value: Authorized 5 shares; none issued	—	—
Common shares, without par value: Authorized 500,000 shares; issued and outstanding 2003—257,489 shares and 2002—263,651 shares	141,931	124,417
Additional paid-in capital	54,081	48,868
Retained earnings	1,100,462	1,054,020
Accumulated other comprehensive loss	(10,340)	(50,826)
Total shareholders' equity	1,286,134	1,176,479
Total liabilities and shareholders' equity	$1,672,169	$1,521,723

Source: Biomet's 2003 *Annual Report.*

or American Home Products that wants to get into the musculoskeletal products market. The company has a Shareholders' Rights Plan expiring in 2009 that protects it against any hostile takeover. In the international arena, a strong dollar could hurt U.S. exports. Biomet should develop further initiatives to make an impact in the Japanese market.

Develop a three-year strategic plan for Biomet.

36 Nike—2004

M. Jill Austin
Middle Tennessee State University

Nike

www.nike.com

The year 2003 was a year of "firsts" for Nike. The company had the highest revenue in its history and also earned more revenue outside the United States for the first time. However, the company continues to deal with controversies on a number of fronts such as manufacturing ethics, lawsuits, and criticism of the high endorsement fees paid to athletes. CEO Phil Knight seems resigned that his view of Nike and the public's view may not always mesh.

> One thing hasn't changed. I still can't capture the essence of this company. The world will never view Nike as I do. Where others see controversy, I see impact. Where they see record sales, I see next year's goal. Where the world sees endorsement contracts, I see validation by the greatest athletes of our time. When the world is in doubt about Nike is when I am most certain of our ability to compete and win.

The company's vision and mission are shown in Exhibit 1.

Net income in 2003 for Nike ($740 million) increased by 11 percent over 2002. For the fiscal year 2003, revenues at Nike increased by 8 percent over 2002 to $10.7 billion. Nike sells athletic shoes, accessories, sports equipment, and clothing for men, women, and children. The Nike name and logo have such high consumer awareness

EXHIBIT 1
Nike Vision and Mission

Vision—"To bring inspiration and innovation to every athlete* in the world."

Mission—Nike is the "largest seller of athletic footwear and athletic apparel in the world. Performance and reliability of shoes, apparel, and equipment, new product development, price, product identity through marketing and promotion, and customer support and service are important aspects of competition in the athletic footwear, apparel, and equipment industry . . . We believe we are competitive in all of these areas." The company aims to "lead in corporate citizenship through proactive programs that reflect caring for the world family of Nike, our teammates, our consumers, and those who provide services to Nike."

*Nike co-founder Bill Bowerman defined an athlete by saying, "If you have a body, you're an athlete."
Source: nikebiz.com and Nike Form 10-K, 2001, 2003.

that the company no longer includes the Nike name on its products; the "swoosh" logo is all that is needed. The company's products are sold to approximately 18,000 retail accounts in the United States including department stores, footwear stores, and sporting goods stores. Nike also sells its products through independent distributors, licensees, and subsidiaries in 200 countries around the world. Approximately 30,000 international retail outlets sell Nike products. Nike operates a total of 24 distribution centers in several different international markets: Asia, Canada, Latin America, Europe, and Australia, and operates 161 retail stores in the United States including 75 factory outlets, 4 Nike Stores, 65 Cole Haan stores, 4 employee-only stores, and 13 NikeTown stores.

Over 50 percent of total revenue in 2003 came from international sales. Countries that have the largest Nike business include: United Kingdom, Japan, France, Italy, Spain, Germany, and Canada. Revenues increased in the Europe and Asia Pacific geographic regions in 2003, while the U.S. and Americas footwear segments and the Americas apparel regions had decreases in sales from the previous year. Domestic and international revenues for Nike are shown in Exhibit 2.

EXHIBIT 2
Domestic and International Revenues for Nike

($ IN MILLIONS)	FISCAL 2003	FISCAL 2002	FY03 vs. FY02 % CHG	FISCAL 2001	FY02 vs. FY01 % CHG
U.S. Region					
Footwear	$ 3,019.5	$3,135.5	(4)%	$3,167.4	(1)%
Apparel	1,351.0	1,255.7	8%	1,207.9	4%
Equipment	287.9	278.4	3%	273.6	2%
Total U.S.	4,658.4	4,669.6	—	4,648.9	—
Europe, Middle East, and Africa (EMEA) Region					
Footwear	1,896.0	1,543.8	23%	1,415.7	9%
Apparel	1,133.1	977.9	16%	961.0	2%
Equipment	212.6	174.8	22%	176.3	(1)%
Total EMEA	3,241.7	2,696.5	20%	2,553.0	6%
Asia Pacific Region					
Footwear	732.4	640.2	14%	617.5	4%
Apparel	499.3	403.3	24%	356.1	13%
Equipment	127.1	98.7	29%	91.5	8%
Total Asia Pacific	1,358.8	1,142.2	19%	1,065.1	7%
Americas Region					
Footwear	337.3	359.1	(6)%	355.2	1%
Apparel	148.1	167.1	(11)%	152.1	10%
Equipment	41.6	41.9	(1)%	31.8	32%
Total Americas	527.0	568.1	(7)%	539.1	5%
	9,785.9	9,076.4	8%	8,806.1	3%
Other	911.1	816.6	12%	682.7	20%
Total Revenues	$10,697.0	$9,893.0	8%	$9,488.8	4%

Source: Nike 2003 *Form 10-K*, p. 3.

History

Philip Knight, a dedicated long-distance runner, developed a plan to make low-cost running shoes in Japan and to sell them in the United States as part of his work toward an MBA degree at Stanford University. After graduation, Knight teamed up with Bill Bowerman, his former track coach at the University of Oregon, to make his plan a reality by starting Blue Ribbon Sports in 1964. Blue Ribbon Sports shoes gained a cult following among serious runners because Knight distributed the shoes, called Tigers, at track meets. In 1971, Blue Ribbon Sports received a trademark on its "Swoosh" logo and the Nike brand name was also introduced. Blue Ribbon Sports officially changed its name to Nike in 1978. During the late 1970s and early 1980s, Nike researchers used their technological expertise to develop several types of athletic shoes that revolutionized the industry. The company became more and more successful each year with profits increasing steadily during this time.

In 1988, Nike purchased New Hampshire–based Cole Haan for $64 million. The subsidiary currently has several brand names including CH, Gseries by Cole Haan, Bragano, and Cole Haan. Nike's casual footwear business grew 16 percent the following year. Nike also acquired the Cole-Haan Accessories Company in 1990, a distributor of premium quality belts, braces, and small leather goods. That same year, Nike opened its first retail store, called NikeTown, in Portland, Oregon; it purchased a cap-making company called Sports Specialties (now called Nike Team Sports, Inc.) in 1993, and in 1994, the Outdoor division added a new shoe called "Air Mada" and the Nike sport sandal became the top seller in the market. In 1995, Nike acquired Canstar Sports, Inc. (the world's largest hockey equipment maker), for $409 million. Canstar, now called Bauer Nike Hockey, Inc., manufactures in-line roller skates, ice skates and blades, protective gear, hockey sticks, and hockey jerseys. The Michael Jordan collection of basketball clothing was launched in 1998. Clothing designed for young men who want the "urban look" was added to the Michael Jordan collection and sports stars Randy Moss and Derek Jeter were hired to promote the Jordan brand in 1999. A new line called ACG (All Conditions Gear) that sells gear for snowboarding, skateboarding, surfing, and mountain biking was launched in 1999.

Present Conditions

The company has made several changes in recent years in its attempts to gain market share and offer a broader range of sports shoes and apparel products. Two Nike Goddess stores, geared toward the sale of women's clothing and footwear, were opened in Los Angeles in 2001. Nike purchased Impact Golf Technologies in 2002 so the company could manufacture golf clubs. It began selling three brands of apparel in spring 2002 to provide different brands to different types of customers: Nike Performance (for athletes), Nike Active ("gym to street" wear), and Nike Fusion (stylish clothing made of high performance fabrics). In September 2003, Nike acquired Converse for $305 million to increase its offerings in the currently popular retro and classic shoe market. The company's Hurley brand, acquired in 2002, sells youth-oriented shoes and apparel for surfing, skateboarding, and snowboarding.

Foot Locker announced in 2002 that it would purchase only about half as many Nike products in the future, because of a company decision that Foot Locker would sell more lower-priced shoes and not as many high-priced Nike shoes. This is a significant issue since 10.9 percent of Nike revenue came from Foot Locker in fiscal 2002

($800 million in wholesale cost). Foot Locker canceled millions of dollars in Nike orders in protest of high wholesale prices, and Nike retaliated by stopping shipments of its most popular shoes to Foot Locker stores. This disagreement will be a significant cost to Nike in the short run.

Competition

The athletic shoe industry has changed tremendously since "sneakers" were invented. In 1873, the "sneaker" was developed from India rubber and canvas material. Dunlop became the dominant seller of sneakers in 1938. Keds and PF Fliers dominated the children's market in the 1960s. Adult standard brands such as Adidas and Converse were well accepted by sports enthusiasts for years. When Nike entered the market in the late 1960s, the industry changed forever. In addition to new competition, lifestyles began to change and companies began to contract manufacturing rather than invest in plant and equipment to manufacture their own products.

The major competitors in the athletic shoe industry are Nike and Reebok, who hold 39 percent and 11 percent market share respectively. Some of the other two dozen competitors in the industry include Adidas-Salomon AG, New Balance, K-Swiss, Fila, Asics, and Keds. Designer brands such as Tommy Hilfiger and Nautica have entered the athletic shoe market by providing shoes for fashion-minded young people. Fashion shoe brands, such as Vans and Skechers, which appeal to teenagers and young adults, are taking some market share from the major competitors. Vans, a California company specializing in skateboarding shoes, earned $15.5 million in 2001, but lost $2.6 million in 2002. Skechers had almost $1 billion in sales in 2002 and a net income of $47 million. The most intense competition continues to be among the industry leaders: Nike, Reebok, and Adidas.

Reebok International, Ltd.

Reebok designs and develops athletic shoes and clothing for sale worldwide. The company sells athletic shoes in different color combinations for aerobics, cycling, volleyball, tennis, fitness, running, basketball, soccer, walking, and children's footwear, and recently diversified its offerings to include more types of casual shoes, sports clothing, other types of athletic shoes, and sports-related equipment. There are currently 204 Reebok factory direct stores in the United States. The company's four product divisions include: Reebok, Greg Norman Collection, Rockport, and Ralph Lauren footwear.

In the early 1980s, Reebok sold aerobic shoes primarily to women, but by the mid-1980s large numbers of men were buying Reebok shoes. The company's shoes are designed to make a fashion statement and are marketed to build on this image. Reebok took the lead in revenues from Nike in 1987, but Nike regained its lead over Reebok in 1990. Despite Reebok's marketing efforts, the company continued to lose ground to Nike in the 1990s.

Reebok developed a series of marketing campaigns around sports stars in an effort to increase its market share. Some of the sports personalities who signed marketing contracts with Reebok include Julie Foudy, Venus Williams, Allen Iverson, Peyton Manning, Byron Leftwich, Ray Lewis, Andy Roddick, Greg Norman, and Roger Clemens. In August 2001, Reebok signed a ten-year contract with the National Basketball Association to provide all court apparel beginning with the 2004–2005 season. Reebok has 300 National Football League endorsers; 50 to 75 are high-profile football stars. Reebok

EXHIBIT 3

Selected Financial Information for Reebok

($IN MILLIONS EXCEPT PER SHARE AMOUNT)	2001	2002
Gross Revenue	$2992.9	3127.9
Net Income	102.7	131.5
Long-term Debt	351.2	353.3
Net Worth	719.9	884.6
Net Profit Margin(%)	3.4	4.2
Earnings Per Share	$ 1.66	2.04

Source: Value Line.

introduced the Rbx brand in 2002, and launched a retro footwear line inspired by Jay Zee in 2003 and a shoe called the G-Unit Collection that is promoted by 50 Cent. Current NFL and NBA teams that are supplied apparel exclusively by Reebok have been paid a total of $450 million by Reebok. Selected financial information for Reebok is shown in Exhibit 3.

International Competition

Competition is increasing in Europe. Adidas-Salomon AG, a German company, is the number-one seller of athletic shoes in Europe and number two worldwide. Analysts believe that doing well in the European market is crucial to the continued success of companies in the athletic shoe industry. Nike sales in Europe, Asia, Canada, and Latin America increased to almost $4.4 billion in 2002 and to $5.127 billion in 2003. Both Nike and Reebok hope to continue increasing their presence in the international retail market.

Adidas, the top European-owned competitor, will be fighting to maintain its 15 percent worldwide share of the competitive market for athletic shoes. Founded in 1948, Adidas outfitted such sports stars as Al Oerter (1956 Olympics) and Kareem Abdul-Jabbar (NBA). Family disputes in this family-owned company threatened its success after it gained a 70 percent market share in the United States. One brother became so angry he founded the rival company Puma. During this time, the U.S. market share dropped from 70 percent to 2 percent. The company was sold in 1989 for $320 million. The new owner became involved in other issues and neglected the company. By the time the current CEO took over in 1993, Adidas was losing about $100 million per year. When asked what he knew about the athletic shoe industry, then CEO Robert Louis-Dreyfus replied, "All I did was borrow what Nike and Reebok were doing. It was there for everybody to see." By 1996, the company's successes were evident: it equipped 3,000 Olympic athletes and these athletes won a total of 220 medals; U.S. market share doubled in 1998 to 12 percent and the following year the company added in-line skates to its product mix.

Adidas-Salomon AG brands include: Adidas (footwear, balls, bags, and apparel), Salomon (ski equipment and apparel, hiking boots, and in-line skates), Cliché (skateboarding), ArcTreyx (outdoor clothing and equipment), Taylor Made (golf equipment), Mavic (cycle components), and Bonfire (winter sports clothing). Some of the sports stars who currently have endorsement contracts with Adidas include NBA players Tracy McGrady and Tim Duncan. Adidas bought a high-altitude climbing and clothing company called ArcTeryx in 2002. Adidas sales and

EXHIBIT 4
Selected Financial Information for Adidas

(EUROS IN MILLIONS EXCEPT PER-SHARE AMOUNT)	2001	2002
Net Sales	$6,112	6,523
Net Income	208	229
Net Total Borrowings	1,679	1,498
Total Assets	4,183	4,261
Net Profit Margin (%)	3.4	3.5
Earnings Per Share	$ 4.60	5.04

Source: www.adidas-salomon.com.

net income in U.S. dollars were $6.8 billion and $240 million respectively. Selected financial information for Adidas is shown in Exhibit 4.

Economic Conditions

Total U.S. sales of athletic shoes increased in 2002 to $15.69 billion, representing a 2.5 percent increase over 2000. Beginning in fall 2000, consumer confidence began to decline and slow general economic growth continued through 2003. After the terrorist attacks on September 11, 2001, the U.S. economy continued to falter and there was a sharp drop in demand for athletic shoes. Athletic shoe manufacturers have also experienced economic crises in some international markets. For example, in fall 2002 there was a two-week lockout of dockworkers that delayed some shipments of Far East manufactured goods to retailers. In addition, the impact of foreign currency fluctuations and interest rate changes has the potential to create financial problems for athletic shoe manufacturers. The transition toward the euro has also created some economic pressures in the European Union countries that recently converted their currency to the euro. Ten new countries are scheduled to join the EU in May 2004, making the EU market that has common currency and trade rules much larger for competitors.

Most athletic shoe companies contract with manufacturing companies in the Far East to produce their shoes. Some of the countries that manufacture shoes for Nike, Reebok, and other companies include South Korea, Taiwan, China, Thailand, Malaysia, and Indonesia. The athletic shoe companies develop design specifications and new technology for the shoes in the United States and then send these to the factory to be produced. The primary advantage of foreign contract manufacturing is that no capital investment is required and the athletic shoe companies can operate with very little long-term debt. There are also several disadvantages to contract manufacturing. Some countries, such as Korea, that have produced large numbers of athletic shoes in the past are developing the expertise and contacts to begin producing more sophisticated electronics products and do not have available capacity to continue producing athletic shoes. Some additional disadvantages of overseas production include labor unrest, political unrest, delays caused by shipping, and unreliability of quota systems (embargoes).

Social Factors

Beginning in the late 1970s, athletic shoe buyers became brand-conscious and the major competitors relied on their well-known brand names to sell their products. In recent years, consumers have changed their view of athletic footwear/clothing as fashion accessories. Athletic shoe companies began having some difficulty selling their products to the youth market in 1997 due to the youth demand shift to hiking boots and casual leather shoes. Most recently, the fashion for athletic shoes is a classic look or "retro" style athletic shoe.

The ages of potential consumers present some unique challenges for athletic shoe/apparel companies. Generation Y children (born between 1979 and 1994) rival the size of the baby-boom generation; they are 60 million strong and will be a significant market in the future. Generation Y consumers prefer fashion-oriented sportswear rather than athletic brand clothing. The Generation Y population responds differently to advertising than other generations; this group is not swayed by glossy national advertising campaigns. They respond to truth in advertising and are more cynical and practical than other generations. Typically, Generation Y members prefer to use the Internet as a source for product information; they are an important target market for athletic shoe companies. Members of the large baby boomer generation are interested in staying fit and healthy and became obsessed with exercise in the late 1980s. Currently, exercise is not as popular a pastime for baby boomers as it was in the early 1990s, but demand for clothing/footwear for leisure activities continues to increase for this group.

Changes in lifestyles of girls/women will likely impact the industry. Since the mid-1990s women have purchased more athletic shoes than men have. In addition, more girls are involved in sports today than ever before. There are currently more than 13 million women and girls who play basketball and approximately 7 million who play soccer.

Legal/Regulatory Issues

The global marketplace has many legal restrictions that athletic shoe manufacturers must consider. Both the North American Free Trade Agreement (NAFTA) and the General Agreement on Tariffs and Trade (GATT) provide better access to world trade. Companies operating in Mexico and Canada will benefit from reduced import/export duties outlined in the NAFTA agreement. GATT provides commitments for access to international markets and tariff reductions on many products. The European Union (EU) increased the power of European countries to control imports, and has also provided a single, coordinated market rather than many different markets in Europe. In 1995, at the request of European footwear manufacturers, the EU imposed anti-dumping duties on athletic footwear imported to the EU from China and Indonesia. In 1995, the United States restored diplomatic relations with Vietnam, a potential high-volume producer of athletic shoes. President Clinton awarded most favored nation status (MFN) to China and Congress supported the president's decision in 1999. Since China is a major source of footwear production, it is critical for athletic shoe companies that MFN status for China continues. In May 2003, President Bush renewed Normal Trade Relations for Vietnam, providing additional manufacturing opportunities for athletic shoe companies. These legal changes, along with country-specific laws, will provide for many opportunities and some threats for international business operations.

Nike Internal Factors

Five primary internal factors for Nike include superior research and development efforts for the company's products, marketing/distribution expertise, social responsibility, management style/culture, and financial returns.

Nike Research and Development

Nike is able to stay on the cutting edge in technology because research and development in the athletic shoe industry is largely design innovation and does not require a large investment in equipment. In 1980, the company formed the Nike Sport Research Laboratory (NSRL), which uses video cameras and traction testing devices and researches several types of concerns including: children's foot morphology, "turf toe," and apparel aerodynamics. In addition, NSRL evaluates ideas that have been developed by the Advanced Product Engineering (APE) group. APE is involved in long-term product development. Shoes are created for five years in the future. This group developed cross-training shoes, the Nike Footbridge stability device, inflatable fit systems, and the Nike 180 air cushioning system. The company also uses its knowledge of technology to improve sports clothing. In June 2000, Nike introduced the Swift Suit, a full-length body suit designed to help runners keep muscles warm and reduce "drag." One of the newest footwear developments is a spring-loaded shoe called Nike Shox that was introduced after sixteen years of research and development.

In addition to their laboratory work, Nike designers visit athletes to learn more about shoe technology. In 1996, Nike staff worked with the Philadelphia 76ers to test a variety of shoes and Nike's 1999 Air Seismic cross-trainer was the result. In 1997, Nike designers visited Mia Hamm to learn her expectations of women's soccer shoes and the company designed a lightweight shoe with a fiber cushion and foam. Nike continues to rely on superior technological developments to differentiate its products from competitors. Exhibit 5 indicates the major recent Nike technological developments.

Marketing

Since Nike does not actually produce shoes, the main focus of the company is creating and marketing its products. Nike sells its products online through **www.nike.com** and Phil Knight meets with the Internet team daily. The online store sells a variety of products including shoes, equipment, and apparel. Nike positions its products as high-performance shoes designed with high-technology features. The general target market for Nike athletic shoes is males and females between the ages of 18 and 34. Nike's current strategy is to target women more aggressively. The company created Nike Goddess stores and began marketing more toward women who have an "active lifestyle." In 2002, Nike introduced a women's yoga shoe in an attempt to appeal to health-conscious women who do not see themselves as athletes. Currently, 20 percent of Nike's sales are to women while the industry average is 50 percent.

EXHIBIT 5
Recent Nike Technological Developments

DATE	DEVELOPMENT	PURPOSE
1997	Air Flightposite shoe	Dual-pigmented material with metallic hues that can be molded into a shoe
2000	Air Presto	Fashion shoes made almost entirely of stretch mesh
2002	Shox VCII	Spring sole foot bed that runs the length of the shoe
2003	Shox NZ, Shox TL	Spring sole cushioning system that helps return energy to the runner

Nike advertises its products in a variety of ways and targets its ads to specific groups or types of people. Advertising expenditures were $1.0279 billion in 2002 and $1.168 billion in 2003. The company continues to spend advertising dollars on TV ads during professional and college sports events, prime time programs, and late night programs. Prime time ads are intended to reach a broad range of adults and late night TV advertising is geared toward younger adults. Print is also very important in advertising Nike products. Print media such as *Sports Illustrated*, *People*, *Runner's World*, *Glamour*, *Self*, *Tennis*, *Money*, *Bicycling*, and *Weight Watchers* are also very important in advertising Nike products. The company had significant sponsorships for the 2003 Tour de France bicycling team with Lance Armstrong, who won the event for a record fifth time. Currently, Nike sponsors the Turkish, Mexican, and Korean national soccer teams and the company sponsored the International Inline Skating Association Marathon Tour in 2003.

Some of the celebrity spokespersons for Nike include Michael Jordan, Andre Agassi, Mia Hamm, Marion Jones, Brandi Chastain, Vince Carter, David Duval, Kobe Bryant, and Tiger Woods. Tiger Woods signed a reported $90 million deal in 1999 to promote Nike golf wear. In September 2000, Woods signed a five-year extension on his endorsement contract worth an estimated $100 million. In 2003, 18-year-old professional basketball star LeBron James signed a $90 million contract. Exhibit 6 shows some of Nike's advertising campaigns.

EXHIBIT 6
Nike Advertisements

THEME	VISUAL IMAGE
"Hangtime"	Air Jordan basketball shoe promotion featuring Michael Jordan and Spike Lee.
"Revolution"	Beatles song "Revolution" played and images of sports stars were shown.
"Bo Knows"	Illustrates the range of Nike shoes (20 different sport categories).
"Just Do It"	Shows people from many walks of life exercising in Nike shoes.
"Multiple Bo's"	Bo Jackson meets Sonny Bono and fourteen other Bo Jacksons who represent different sports.
"Rock and Roll Tennis"	Andre Agassi shows his tennis skills in rock video format.
"I am not a role model"	Charles Barkley says sports stars are not role models, but parents should be role models.
"Aerospace Jordan"	Cartoon characters Bugs Bunny, Looney Tunes bay guy Marvin Martin, and Michael Jordan travel to Mars. (Super Bowl XXVII)
"Air Swoopes"	An ad with Sheryl Swoopes introducing the Air Swoopes basketball shoe and announcing Nike sponsorship of the women's U.S. Olympic basketball team
"Broad-Minded"	An advertisement with Tiger Woods. The statement made is "We're not just canvas and leather shoes. We're big—and broad-minded."
"Date"	The U.S. Women's Soccer Team says "we will take on the world as a team" and everyone on the team goes on a date with one person
"Two Fillings"	The U.S. Women's Soccer Team all want fillings when Brandi Chastain said she had two fillings. Each woman stands and says, "I will have two fillings."
"Chicks Dig the Long Ball"	Pitchers Tom Glavine and Greg Maddox try to get Heather Locklear's attention from Mark McGwire.

International marketing efforts continue. Nike has operations in 200 countries on 6 continents. Nike is already number one in the overall footwear market in Spain, France, Belgium, Holland, Luxembourg, Finland, Italy, and the United Kingdom. Some of the new markets that are now being pursued include Chile, Peru, Bolivia, India, Mexico, South Africa, and several eastern European countries. Wieden and Kennedy, the advertising agency responsible for most of Nike's ads, has offices in London, Tokyo, and Amsterdam so that advertising can be developed by local people to fit with local cultures.

Distribution

Nike opened a 630,000 square-foot apparel distribution center in Memphis in 1992 that is called Nike Next Day. Footwear is distributed from centers in Greenland, New Hampshire; Wilsonville, Oregon; and Memphis, Tennessee. Nike apparel is shipped from the Memphis distribution center. Cole Haan and Bauer products are distributed from Greenland, New Hampshire, and Hurley products are shipped from Costa Mesa, California. The company operates a "Futures" ordering program that allows retailers to order up to six months in advance and be guaranteed to receive their order within a certain time period and at a certain price. However, Futures retailers can receive apparel orders the next day if they place their orders by 7:00 P.M. the day before. Nike's automatic replenishment system provides automatic shipments to high-volume merchandisers in an effort to ensure constant supply for retailers. In 2003, 91 percent of U.S. footwear and 67 percent of U.S. apparel shipments were ordered under the futures program.

Knight worries that the brand will lose its image as a technically superior sports shoe if international marketing is not monitored carefully. Nike has purchased the distribution operations of many of its worldwide distributors in an attempt to control marketing of Nike products. Some of these "Nike-owned" countries include: Singapore, Taiwan, Hong Kong, New Zealand, Korea, Japan, and Malaysia. The Severe Acute Respiratory Syndrome (SARS) outbreak in China in 2002/2003 made it hard for Nike to coordinate its production and distribution efforts and to ensure quality, since travel was restricted to some areas where production and distribution centers were located.

Social Responsibility

Nike has been criticized in the past few years for employment practices at its international manufacturing sites. Some consumers are concerned about the exploitive practices of managers in some Asian countries. For example, in 2001, Indonesian factory managers making Nike products were charged with sexual harassment, physical and verbal abuse, restrictions in health services, and forced overtime. In addition, some of these managers were charged with requiring employees who misbehave or are late for work to run laps or clean toilets. Nike promised to investigate and improve inappropriate conditions whenever they exist.

The company first set up a labor practices department in 1996 and in 1998 the position of Vice President of Social Responsibility was created. In 1998, Nike joined the Fair Labor Association (FLA), a sweatshop-monitoring organization founded by a presidential taskforce made up of apparel manufacturers and human rights organizations. The company also belongs to the Global Alliance for Workforce and Communities (GAWC), a business group whose objective is to improve factory employees' work lives. Nike's leadership on labor initiatives in factories producing its products is shown in Exhibit 7.

EXHIBIT 7
Nike Recent Labor Initiatives

- 1998—Nike joined the Fair Labor Association (FLA), a sweatshop-monitoring organization founded by a presidential taskforce made up of apparel manufacturers and human rights organizations. Companies involved include Nike, Reebok, Liz Claiborne, and Phillips Van Heusen. Many of the apparel manufacturers and some retailers joined an effort through the American Apparel Manufacturing Association that has less stringent requirements than FLA. The group, United Students Against Sweatshops (students from 100 universities), created a more rigorous plan for monitoring sweatshops than required by the FLA. The student group demanded that companies disclose the locations of their foreign factories so that independent investigations of labor practices could occur.
- 1999—Nike joined the Global Alliance for Workers and Communities, a labor-monitoring project.
- 2001—Nike began revealing the results of monitoring on its Web site on a quarterly basis.
- 2003—Nike conducted more than 1,000 SHAPE Audits (Safety, Attitude, People, and Environment). This process included evaluation of more than 100 factors by Nike staff. When warranted, some factors will receive further scrutiny. Plans call for two yearly inspections at apparel plants and four inspections per year at footwear plants.

Sources: "Nike Puts Its Code of Conduct in the Pocket of Workers." *PR Newswire* (September 17, 1997); "Sweatshop Reform: How to Solve the Standoff." *BusinessWeek* (May 3, 1999); **www.nikebiz.com.**

In addition to its membership in the FLA and GAWC, Nike has developed a process for ensuring that its factories comply with the company's code of conduct. The Nike Code of Conduct can be seen in Exhibit 8.

Nike has developed several programs that show its concern about social responsibility issues and the company provides contributions to several charitable and nonprofit organizations. Some of the organizations Nike supports include: World Wildlife Fund, Boys and Girls Clubs of America, National Head Start Association, Special Olympics, YWCA of the USA, and the junior golf program. Nike's target is to give 3 percent of pretax profits to charitable causes; in 2003, it gave $30.7 million in cash and in-kind gifts to charities.

EXHIBIT 8
Nike Code of Conduct

Nike looks for contractors who share our commitment to best practices and continuous improvement in:
- Management practices that respect the rights of all employees, including the right to free association and collective bargaining.
- Minimizing our impact on the environment.
- Providing a safe and healthy workplace.
- Promoting the health and well-being of all employees.

Source: **www.nikebiz.com.**

EXHIBIT 9
Nike Environmental Initiatives

- Reuse-A-Shoe Program—Grind Material from shoes (rubber, foam, and fabric) is used to make other products. The granulated rubber is used to make football, soccer, and baseball fields and weight room flooring. Foam is used for synthetic basketball courts, playground surfacing, and tennis courts. Fabric is used for padding under hardwood basketball floors.
- Sustainability Philosophy—The company management evaluates the environmental impact of day-to-day operations. The goal is for sustainability to become a part of daily business decision making.
- Climate Impact—The Nike Virtual Logistics team evaluates the environmental impact of the company's distribution activities and attempts to change operations that have a negative impact.
- Air to Earth—Nike's educational program for elementary and middle school students provides opportunities for students to study recycling and conservation.

Source: www.nikebiz.com.

N.E.A.T. (Nike Environmental Action Team) was formed in 1993. The purpose of this group is to pursue environmental initiatives in regard to recycling old athletic shoes and reusing them in new products. Nike recovers 2 million pairs of shoes each year in its "Reuse-A-Shoe" program for recycling. Exhibit 9 provides examples of Nike's attempts to reduce its impact on the environment through the Reuse-A-Shoe program and other initiatives.

In addition to bad public relations due to manufacturing ethics, the company had to defend itself against a false advertising lawsuit in 2002. Marc Kasky sued Nike for false advertising after accusing Phil Knight of lying when Knight responded to questions about Nike sweatshops in a letter to the editor printed in the *New York Times*. The California Supreme Court ruled this speech as commercial speech that is regulated by the Federal Trade Commission and subject to deceptive advertising regulations. In June 2003, The U.S. Supreme Court dismissed the case, but suggested that the speech by Knight was not purely commercial speech. The case was sent back to the California Supreme Court to be reviewed.

Management Style/Culture

Phil Knight has created a strong culture at Nike based on company loyalty and locker room camaraderie. Most corporate employees are health-conscious young people and Knight trusts these employees to "Just Do It." His philosophy is "Play by the rules, but be ferocious. . . . It's all right to be Goliath, but always act like David." The 74-acre corporate campus of Nike provides a sense of the culture: it has wooded areas, running trails, a lake, and a fitness center. Knight believes that people should find a "sense of peace at work."

During 1998 and 1999, Nike restructured the company to take advantage of cost savings and to improve operating efficiency. Employees were terminated from all areas of Nike including international and domestic workers. Phil Knight called a meeting of all company headquarters employees in 1998 and apologized for not paying more attention during the company's boom years and for not being prepared for the years of hard times that followed. Mark Parker and Charlie Denson took over day-to-day operations as co-presidents of Nike in 2002. Parker had Nike experience in

EXHIBIT 10
Nike Organization Chart

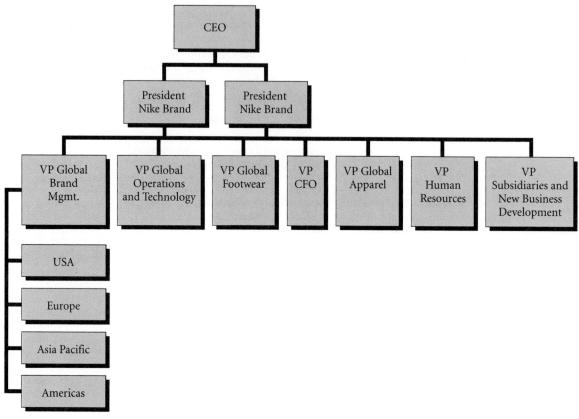

Source: Nike *Form 10-K*, 2003.

product research and development and Denson had previously worked in a variety of sales management positions with the company. In 2003, Knight admitted that Nike "got to be a $9 billion company with a $5 billion management." Major divisions of the company are shown in Exhibit 10.

Finance/Accounting
During its years of rapid growth, Nike managers encouraged free spending to develop and market company products. After cost-cutting layoffs and a search for efficiency that started in 1998, vice presidents began to spend more time making employees aware of the necessity of financial accountability. Each geographic region manager was given a profit-and-loss statement in 1998, and now compensation is partly tied to performance. Note in the income statement in Exhibit 11 that revenues for 2003 increased by 8 percent over 2002 while net income increased by 11 percent. The balance sheet (Exhibit 12) provides information on assets and liabilities for the last two years.

Future Outlook
Even with limited U.S. growth and intense global competition in the athletic shoe/apparel markets, Nike managers expect that the company will perform well in the future. It plans to double its current sales level of women's products ($1.5 bil-

EXHIBIT 11
Consolidated Statements of Income

(IN MILLIONS, EXCEPT PER-SHARE DATA)	YEAR ENDED MAY 31,		
	2003	2002	2001
Revenues	$10,697.0	$9,893.0	$9,488.8
Cost of sales	6,313.6	6,004.7	5,784.9
Gross Margin	4,383.4	3,888.3	3,703.9
Selling and administrative	3,137.6	2,820.4	2,689.7
Interest expense	42.9	47.6	58.7
Other income/expense, net	79.9	3.0	34.1
Income before income taxes and cumulative effect accounting change	1,123.0	1,017.3	921.4
Income taxes	382.9	349.0	331.7
Income before cumulative effect of accounting change	740.1	668.3	589.7
Cumulative effect of accounting change, net of income taxes of ($-, $3.0 and $-)	266.1	5.0	—
Net income	$ 474.0	$ 663.3	$ 589.7
Basic earnings per common share—before accounting change	$ 2.80	$ 2.50	$ 2.18
Cumulative effect of accounting change	1.01	0.02	—
	$ 1.79	$ 2.48	$ 2.18
Diluted earnings per common share—before accounting change	$ 2.77	$ 2.46	$ 2.16
Cumulative effect of accounting change	1.00	0.02	—
	$ 1.77	$ 2.44	$ 2.16

Source: Nike 2003 *Form 10-K*, p. 36.

lion) by 2005. More Nike Goddess stores are planned in 2004 and beyond. By 2007, Nike expects global soccer revenues to reach $1 billion. The company believes that Hurley products and Converse's retro styles will allow Nike to appeal to younger people.

Consider the following questions regarding Nike's future:

1. Is Nike trying to supply products for too many sports? Should Nike narrow its product line in athletic shoes?
2. What types of acquisitions would you suggest to Philip Knight for Nike?
3. Should Nike begin producing some of its own products?
4. Is Nike taking the correct approach in marketing its shoes internationally?
5. What changes in product and advertising should the company pursue to appeal to the aging baby boomers? To Generation Y?
6. How can Nike maintain a competitive advantage over Reebok?
7. Is Nike responding correctly to concerns about the treatment of employees in international manufacturing facilities?
8. How much emphasis should Nike place on increasing international sales?
9. Has Nike chosen the appropriate targets for new marketing efforts? Can the company be successful in gaining market share among women?

EXHIBIT 12
Consolidated Balance Sheet

	MAY 31,	
(IN MILLIONS EXCEPT PER-SHARE AMOUNT)	2003	2002
ASSETS		
Current Assets:		
Cash and equivalents	$ 634.0	$ 575.5
Accounts receivable, less allowance for doubtful accounts of $87.9 and $80.4	2,101.1	1,804.1
Inventories	1,514.9	1,373.8
Deferred income taxes	163.7	140.8
Prepaid expenses and other current assets	266.2	260.5
Total current assets	4,679.9	4,154.7
Property, plant and equipment, net	1,620.8	1,614.5
Identifiable intangible assets, net	118.2	206.0
Goodwill	65.6	232.7
Deferred income taxes and other assets	229.4	232.1
Total assets	$6,713.9	$6,440.0
LIABILITIES AND SHAREHOLDERS' EQUITY		
Current Liabilities:		
Current portion of long-term debt	$ 205.7	$ 55.3
Notes payable	75.4	425.2
Accounts payable	572.7	504.4
Accrued liabilities	1,054.2	765.3
Income taxes payable	107.2	83.0
Total current liabilities	2,015.2	1,833.2
Long-term debt	551.6	624.9
Deferred income taxes and other liabilities	156.1	141.6
Commitments and contingencies	—	—
Redeemable Preferred Stock	0.3	0.3
Shareholders' Equity:		
Common Stock at stated value:		
Class A convertible—97.8 and 98.1 shares outstanding	0.2	0.2
Class B—165.8 and 168.0 shares outstanding	2.6	2.6
Capital in excess of stated value	589.0	538.7
Unearned stock compensation	(0.6)	(5.1)
Accumulated other comprehensive loss	(239.7)	(192.4)
Retained earnings	3,639.2	3,495.0
Total shareholders' equity	3,990.7	3,839.0
Total liabilities and shareholders' equity	$6,713.9	$6,440.0

Source: Nike 2003 *Form 10-K*, p. 37.

References

Bernstein, Aaron. "Sweatshop Reform: How to Solve the Standoff." *BusinessWeek* (May 3, 1999): 186.

Chandrasekaran, Rajiv. "Indonesian Workers in Nike Plants List Abuses." *Washington Post* (February 23, 2001): E1.

Garrahan, Matthew. "How to Keep Doing It All Over the World: Branding." *Financial Times (London)* (August 5, 2003): 10.

Grant, Lorrie. "Reebok Goes Toe to Toe with Nike." *USA Today* (September 4, 2001): B1.

Holmes, Stanley. "Free Speech or False Advertising." *BusinessWeek* (April 28, 2003).

Holmes, Stanley, and Christine Tierney. "How Nike Got Its Game Back." *BusinessWeek* (November 4, 2002).

Kapner, Suzanne. "Sneaker Cease-Fire—Nike, Footlocker Near End to Painful Dispute." *New York Post* (July 24, 2003): 33.

Lee, Louise. "Can Nike Still Do It?" *BusinessWeek* (February 21, 2000): 121.

Neubrone, Ellen, and Kathleen Kerwin. "Generation Y." *BusinessWeek* (February 15, 1999): 80.

Nike *Annual Reports*, 2001, 2003.

Nike *Press Release*: "Statement on Today's Protocol Decision by the U.S. Supreme Court in First Amendment Case" (June 27, 2003).

Parloff, Roger. "Can We Talk?" *Fortune* (September 2, 2002): 102.

"Team Mia." *AdWeek* (June 21, 1999): 42.

Wallace, Charles. "Adidas Back in the Game." *Fortune* (August 18, 1997): 176.

Wang, Edward. "Nike Trying New Strategies for Women; Company Seeks Merger of Athletics and Fashion." *New York Times* (June 19, 2001): C1.

Warner, Fara. "Nike's Women's Movement." *Fast Company* (August 2002): 70.

37 Reebok International, Ltd. (RBK)—2004

Todd Butler
Francis Marion University

RBK

www.reebok.com

Can an athlete's performance be traced to what he or she is wearing? Nike, Reebok, and all other manufacturers of shoes and apparel claim to give their customers a competitive edge. How is this possible? Is this fact or just a great marketing ploy to get you to buy the latest shoe on the market because the endorser of the product is having great success? A good question to ask the endorsers of the different brands is, "What products did you wear before you became famous or would you switch to another product for more money?"

Reebok International is a worldwide designer, marketer, and distributor of sports, fitness, and casual footwear and apparel. Reebok sells under the Reebok, Rockport, Ralph Lauren and Polo, and Greg Norman Brands. It is headquartered in Canton, Massachusetts, and currently employees around 7,400 full- and part-time employees globally; its sales were $3.1 billion in 2002. Sales increased to $3.4 billion in 2003.

A vision statement could not be found for Reebok; its mission statement, Exhibit 1, is a detailed description of what Reebok hopes to accomplish as a business.

History

J. W. Foster and Sons, known as Reebok today, was founded in 1890 on the basis that athletes wanted to run faster. The United Kingdom–based company made some of the first running shoes with spikes on the bottom. During the early years, J. W. Foster and Sons made shoes by hand for the best-known athletes. Later, Reebok earned recognition and started to make shoes for the best athletes around the world. One highlight of J. W. Foster was the making of shoes for the 1924 Summer Games. This was later celebrated in the film "Chariots of Fire."

In 1958, two of J. W. Foster's grandsons introduced a companion company known as Reebok. Reebok is named for an African gazelle. In 1979, an entrepreneur named Paul Fireman noticed Reebok's shoes at an international trade show and negotiated a licensing agreement with Reebok to market the shoes in the United States. At $60 a pair, Reebok was the most expensive running shoe on the market.

By 1981, Reebok's sales topped $1.5 million and it was setting the stage for the future. In 1982, it introduced the first women's athletic shoe called the Freestyle™. By the late 1980s, Reebok was selling shoes in over 170 countries and had gone public with stock options to raise capital. The company continued to grow and introduced the Pump® technology which continues on today.

During the 1990s, Reebok began to shift its image by making many different types of sports shoes that ranged from basketball shoes to soccer shoes, and began

EXHIBIT 1
Reebok's Mission Statement

Reebok is a global sports and fitness company with a heritage dating back to 1895. We are a leader in the design and development of authentic products and services, and we influence the athletic lifestyle trends of the world. Reebok is a true partner with its customers and is relentlessly committed to their success. Built on a foundation of trust, listening and innovation, we are our customers' most valued resource for quality products and information and the leading authority in sports and fitness.

Our purpose is to ignite a passion for winning, to do the extraordinary, and to capture the customer's heart and mind. Reebok has a fun, energetic culture driven by the value we place on people, our greatest asset. We embrace diversity in its fullest sense. We act with integrity and operate through confident, empowered teams. With courageous leadership, we stay focused on what is most important to our customers. We have a deep-felt commitment to operate in a socially responsible way and we stand for human rights throughout the world.

We are committed to excellence and innovation in everything we do. We demonstrate our excellence by setting exceptional performance standards, which we then achieve through focused perseverance and vigorous execution. Innovation and magical ideas drive our company to create powerful breakthrough products and inspirational marketing and advertising.

Our passion for winning creates our possibilities. We harness the boundless creative energy of every individual to make the differences that count—to captivate the consumer and create an exceptional global brand and organization.

> We make a difference:
> To our customers
> To our employees
> To our shareholders
> To our athletes
> And to the world in which we live

Source: www.Reebok.com

advertising the shoes with professional athletes. It signed Venus Williams in 1995 and Allen Iverson in 1996 to endorse its shoes and athletic wear.

Reebok has entered long-term contracts with the rights to market and sell apparel for the National Basketball Association (NBA), National Football League (NFL), Women's National Basketball Association (WNBA), and the Indy Racing League (IRL). In 2002, Reebok introduced RBK, which targets another sector of the market, or the street-inspired footwear and apparel industry. In 2003, Venus Williams surpassed tennis supermodel Anna Kournikova as the top paid female endorser, thanks to a five-year $40-million deal with Reebok.

Research and Brands

Reebok is committed to bring its customers innovative technology in both its footwear and apparel products, and spent $44.8 million on R&D in 2002 compared to approximately $41.7 million in 2001 and approximately $49.8 million in 2000. The company has placed a strong emphasis on footwear technologies, which consist of cushioning, stability, and lightweight features in its products. Most of Reebok's R&D is performed at its headquarters where employees work in a state-of-the-art product development facility to design and develop technologically advanced athletic and fitness footwear. Reebok also has development centers in China, Taiwan, and Indonesia.

Reebok has four principal brands: Reebok®, Rockport®, Ralph Lauren® and Polo®, and Greg Norman®. Under these brands, the company markets sports and fitness products, including footwear, apparel, and accessories. Each of the brands is described below, with a list of direct competitors for each brand.

The Reebok® Brand

Reebok's RBK product collection features street-inspired footwear apparel and accessories. This collection appeals to younger and more fashionably oriented customers. Athletes who seek performance from their footwear use the performance product collection. The Reebok line includes footwear for basketball, running, walking, fitness, football, soccer, tennis, and other sports. The classic category includes both longtime Reebok footwear and redesigns of the company's past models. All designs include new technologies, fabrics, and materials. Some of Reebok's competitors include Nike, Adidas, New Balance, Puma, Converse, Fila, Skechers, FUBU, Mecca, and ENYCE.

The Rockport® Brand

Reebok designs and markets comfortable footwear for men, women, and children under the Rockport brand. Rockport has product lines in casual, dress, and performance shoes. There are four collections of men's footwear, which are the Rockport Reserve, Rockport, Rocs by Rockport, and XCS. Some of Rockport's competitors include Timberland, Clarks, Ecco, Mephisto, Bostonian, Merrel, and Easy Spirit.

The Ralph Lauren® and Polo® Brands

The Ralph Lauren Collection includes the traditional classic as well as Polo Sport. The Polo Jeans Co. line targets males ages 16–25. The Ralph Lauren and Polo Brand children's line targets boys and girls ages 5–12. All Ralph Lauren footwear products are sold in top-tier retailers and Polo-owned retail stores. Polo Jeans Co. and Polo Sport lines are sold in major department stores as well as in Polo specialty stores. Some of Ralph Lauren and Polo's competitors include Cole Haan, Timberland, Tommy Hilfiger, Prada, Gucci, Puma, Adidas, and Diesel.

The Greg Norman® Brand

The Greg Norman Collection consists of a wide range of men's apparel and accessories marketed under the Greg Norman name and logo. Originally, the Norman collection featured only golf apparel, but now it consists of leather jackets and sweaters as well. These products are sold in upper-end department stores, men's specialty stores, pro shops, golf specialty stores, and Greg Norman shops. Some of Greg Norman's competitors include Ashworth, Cutter & Buck, and Tommy Bahama.

Present Conditions

There is intense global competition in the sports and fitness footwear business as well as the apparel business; Reebok is facing competition from both established companies and new entrants into the market daily. It currently ranks third in the market share of athletic footwear and apparel in the world and is continuing to experience growth. A list of each category in which Reebok competes globally is given below:

- Design
- Product performance
- Quality
- Price
- Brand image
- Marketing and promotion
- Customer service
- Delivery times

Reebok International sells its products through subsidiaries and independent retailers in 170 countries. In the United States, the company operates more than 200 Reebok, Rockport, and Greg Norman stores, primarily in factory outlet malls.

External Conditions

Historically, retail stores often carried inventories well in advance of the seasonal increases in demands; they now keep inventories low to reduce their holding cost, which places more pressure on suppliers like Reebok to provide quick exceptional service. Reebok has shortened its design and production time and transports products quickly to stores once orders are placed.

Prices are falling in this industry due to influx of imports, retail promotions, and market share gained by discounters. Rapid price deflation has forced the industry to seek new ways to boost profits, so it has adopted offshore outsourcing extensively.

Consumer confidence is volatile due to factors such as the increase in unemployment, the war with Iraq, and depressed stock prices. People are acting cautiously when spending money and consider many options before purchasing any consumer goods. According to the Standard & Poor's Industry Survey, total U.S. apparel sales fell 1.8 percent in 2002 to $163 billion from 2001's level of $166 billion. Total footwear sales declined 5 percent from $42.58 billion in 2001 to $40.56 billion in 2002. Although total footwear sales declined, athletic footwear sales rose 2.5 percent to $15.69 million in 2002 from $15.31 million in 2001.

Global Issues

U.S. manufacturers of apparel and footwear have moved much of their operations from the United States to Asia, Mexico, the Caribbean, Central America, and sub-Saharan Africa. Companies are struggling to find ways to compete or to gain competitive advantage. One competitive advantage for Reebok is that it pays a lower wage for employees in the international countries compared to the U.S. wage rates of domestic facilities. Reebok pledges to do what is right for the people in all countries in which it operates.

Reebok has adopted a Human Rights Standard, as follows:

> Reebok's devotion to human rights worldwide is a hallmark of our corporate culture. As a corporation in an ever more global economy, we will not be indifferent to the standards of our business partners around the world. We believe that incorporation of internationally recognized human rights standards into our business practice improves worker morale and results in a

higher quality working environment and higher quality products. In developing this policy, we have sought to use standards that are fair, that are appropriate to diverse cultures and that encourage workers to take pride in their work.

Dita Indah Sari, an Indonesian women's labor rights activist, criticizes the Reebok Human Rights Award. Dita is the main labor rights campaigner and unionist within the left-wing People's Democratic Party (PDP) in Indonesia. She also founded the National Front for Indonesian Workers' Struggle. Dita started her campaign of rallies aimed at getting her fellow low-income workers a better deal. She is now also successfully building a union of workers in plants across Java. Reebok factories in Indonesia pay only the absolute minimum government wage that is equivalent to less than $2 a day, and Nike has been questioned about employing children in their factories.

E-Commerce

In 2002, the Internet accounted for less than 5 percent of apparel sales but it has great potential as a distribution channel because consumers may shop anytime. The Internet also has disadvantages like not being able to touch, feel, or try on apparel or shoes.

Reebok's products are sold through many different stores on the Internet. In addition, it has its own online store at **www.reebok.com**, where customers can purchase apparel and footwear along with many different types of accessories at the suggested retail price.

Marketing Strategy

Reebok has sought to raise its brand image and customer brand loyalty by entering into agreements with professional athletes and sports teams. The company believes this is a good way to increase awareness as well as the image of its brand by using the best athletes to endorse its products. Reebok's strategy is to build up the "vector" logo so that it symbolizes Reebok like the golden arches for McDonald's and the swoosh for rival Nike. On August 23, 2003, Reebok began marketing the vector logo in a $50 million global, 18-month ad campaign saying, "Wear the Vector. Outperform."

Reebok has license agreements with the National Football League (NFL), National Basketball Association (NBA), and the Women's National Basketball Association (WNBA). Under the NFL agreement, Reebok is the exclusive supplier of uniforms, apparel, and coaches' wear for all 32 NFL teams in the league. Under the NBA license agreement, Reebok is the exclusive supplier of uniforms, shooting shirts, warm-ups, and practice wear beginning in 2002–2003. By season 2004–2005, Reebok will be the exclusive supplier for all 29 NBA teams. It has been the exclusive supplier for the WNBA since 2001.

In May 2003, Reebok launched an ad campaign that featured three-year-old Mark Mayes. In the clip, Mark made 18 basketball shots in a row, at an age when most kids could not even pick up a ball. Reebok is focusing on young adults by communicating the message to start early and keep training to succeed. One of the largest age groups in 2003, according to the U.S. Department of Commerce, is the 5- to 14-year old population. Harris Interactive, a market research firm in New York, recently found that teenage girls spend 75 percent of their earnings on clothing and related accessories compared to 52 percent for teenage boys. The research firm also noted that teens often quickly change preferences, so it is risky to target them.

Reebok is partnering with Limited Too to reach teenage girls. The partnership allows Limited Too's stores to sell Reebok footwear to the trend-conscious girls between the ages of 7 and 14. The partnership, launched in March 2003, is now in 510 Limited Too stores nationwide and in catalogs mailed to over 4 million girls several times per year.

Reebok is taking advantage of the wide use of broadband to air commercials that feature Reebok's office linebacker Terry Tate. Broadband is currently in 18 percent of U.S. homes and is a way for Reebok to reduce reliance on television commercials to advertise its products. Reebok has created **www.terrytate.reebok.com**, which allows down-loaders to check out Terry's latest commercials, send links and video to friends via e-mail, and to download screensavers and wallpapers to their personal computers. Currently, more than 7 million consumers have gone to the Reebok site to download the first three of the four planned Web films of Terry Tate. In one of Terry's popular commercials, he tackles a streaker in Reebok's parody of a Nike ad. The trend of downloading commercials from the Internet is growing and catching the eye of other major companies, but Reebok is one of the early pioneers of the strategy.

In mid-2003, Reebok teamed with today's most popular rapper, known as 50 cent. He has been shot and stabbed numerous times, according to his lyrics and news reports. Reebok is using the rapper to promote the street-designed footwear and hopes to attract interest in its street line of shoes and apparel.

Management Structure

Reebok could best be described as a firm that has grown by acquiring competitors. The company operates as individual business units, as illustrated in the Organizational Chart, Exhibit 2.

EXHIBIT 2
Organizational Chart of Reebok's Top Management

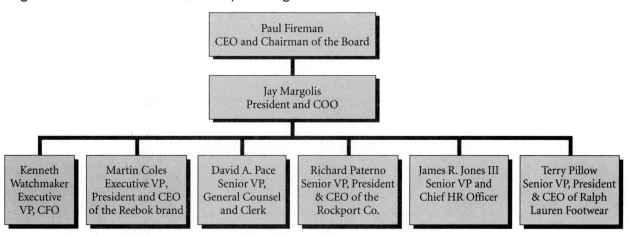

Source: Organizational chart constructed from data in Reebok's 2003 *Annual Report.*

Competitors

Although there are many competitors in the footwear and apparel industry, the top three to Reebok are Nike, Adidas, and Fila. Nike and Adidias are larger than Reebok. Nike, Adidas, and Fila's sales for 2002 were $10.6 billion, $6.8 billion, and $955 million, respectively, as seen in Exhibit 3. The current order of market share has not changed in 2003. Nike's 2002 sales for apparel and footwear were $3,132 million and $5,985 million, respectively.

Nike has challenged the NFL's agreement with Reebok. Nike is sending all its endorsed athletes (approximately 80 percent of all NFL players) letters stating that they may loose their endorsements if they support the competitor's product by wearing Reebok caps on the NFL sidelines. Nike dropped its on-field apparel rights before last season and Reebok quickly picked them up. NFL and Nike may have to go to court to determine the issue. The NFL's position is that "Players have the right to wear a team-identified cap supplied by Reebok on the field." The NFL sidelines provide marketers like Reebok with hours of in-game exposure to the always hard-to-reach male audience. The NFL considers its ownership of the sidelines one of the most profitable pieces of marketing directly controlled by the league.

Tiger Woods, who has a five-year $125 million endorsement contract with Nike, switched back to the Nike club after laying down his Titleist model. Tiger quit using the Nike club after having control problems off the tee, and has not used the Nike driver since July 2003. Michael Jordan announced that Jordan, a division of Nike, has signed basketball stars Gary Payton and Jason Kidd to represent the Jordan brand of footwear and apparel. The Jordan brand has a casual, sport, and style line of apparel, footwear, and accessories.

Adidas competes in the apparel, footwear, and accessories market but focuses most of its energy on athletic shoes for tennis, running, and basketball. Bankruptcy recently haunted Adidas but it is making a comeback by shifting its operations to Asia and increasing its marketing budget. Adidas supports sports activities worldwide, and is the sponsor for the Euro 2004 Tournament and the Athens Olympics. Athletes from 45 nations will wear Adidas products at these events.

Fila is a subsidiary of Sport Brands International (SBI). Fila products are sold in 50 countries worldwide at more than 771 outlet stores and retail stores. Some of Fila's paid endorsers for its products are Jennifer Capriati, Grant Hill, and Barry Bonds. Fila has also supported major tennis events. Fila and Sports Authority together supported the 2002 and 2003 Tennis U.S. Open. Fila markets a 2003 U.S. Open Collection of tennis apparel and footwear.

EXHIBIT 3
Competitor Analysis

	NIKE	ADIDAS	REEBOK	FILA
Fiscal Year-End	May	December	December	December
2002 Sales (mill.)	$10,697	$6,837.2	$3,127.9	$955.2
1-Year Sales Growth	8.1%	26.3%	4.5%	13.4%
2002 Net Income	$1,006.2	$239.6	$126.4	($85)
1-Year Net Income Growth	51.7%	29.7%	23.1%	(16.3%)
2002 Employees	23,300	14,716	7,400	2,301
1-Year Employee Growth	2.6%	5.6%	2.4%	(11.9%)

Source: Hoover's Online. Nike's data reflect time period May 2002–May 2003.

Industry Outlook

As indicated in Exhibit 4, the overall share of total personal consumption expenditures on apparel and footwear is on the decline in the United States. This could be due to many factors that are hard to identify since it has steadily declined for the last 30 years. This is evidence that the apparel and footwear industry is not as important to consumers as it was in 1973.

Reebok's products are manufactured or assembled in the United States and many other countries including China, Indonesia, Thailand, Hong Kong, Taiwan, and South Korea. Reebok is very vulnerable to changing economic conditions in these countries, which could be influenced by inflation, devaluation, recessions, change in currency trading, import tariffs, and political instability.

In 2002, the Standard & Poor's Industry Survey revealed that stores made 31 percent of apparel sales in 2002 and 2001. Specialty stores had 25 percent of sales in 2002 up from 24 percent in 2001. Department store sales decreased to 19 percent in 2002 from 20 percent in 2001. National chains sold 16 percent in 2002 and 15 percent in 2001. The remaining 9 percent was sold through mail order, the Internet, factory outlets, and other outlets.

According to Standard & Poor's Industry Survey, 25 percent of all shoes sold in 2002 were sold through discount stores, 19 percent were sold in self-service stores, and 11 percent through high-end shoe stores. The remaining shoes were sold through catalogs, mail order, sporting goods stores, and off-price outlets.

Conclusions

Reebok is gaining market share in the footwear and apparel industry. Its current strategies seem to be working since it has increased sales over the last 3 years in an industry that has seen a decline in spending over the last 30 years. The company's financial statements are provided in Exhibits 5 and 6. Reebok must be careful not to

EXHIBIT 4

Apparel and Footwear as a Share of Total Personal Consumption Expenditures

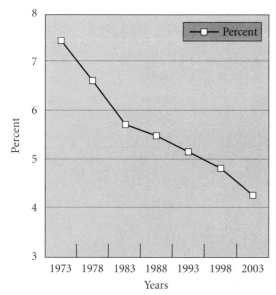

Source: U.S. Department of Commerce.

EXHIBIT 5

Reebok International, Ltd. (RBK)

ANNUAL INCOME STATEMENT IN MILLIONS OF U.S. DOLLARS (EXCEPT FOR PER SHARE ITEMS)	12 MONTHS ENDING 12/31/03	12 MONTHS ENDING 12/31/02	12 MONTHS ENDING 12/31/01
Revenue	$3,485.30	3,127.90	2,992.90
Other Revenue	—	—	—
Total Revenue	**3,485.30**	**3,127.90**	**2,992.90**
Cost of Revenue	2,147.10	1,957.80	1,894.50
Gross Profit	**1,338.20**	**1,170.00**	**1,098.40**
Selling/General/Administrative Expenses	1,085.80	954.6	913.9
Research & Development	—	—	—
Depreciation/Amortization	—	—	—
Interest Expense (Income), Net Operating	17.4	23.8	31
Unusual Expense (Income)	—	−0.4	−0.5
Other Operating Expenses	0.8	5.9	11.5
Total Operating Expense	**3,251.10**	**2,932.50**	**2,837.10**
Operating Income	**234.2**	**195.4**	**155.8**
Interest Expense, Net Non-Operating	—	—	—
Interest/Investment Income, Non-Operating	—	—	—
Interest Income (Expense), Net Non-Operating	—	—	—
Gain (Loss) on Sale of Assets	—	—	—
Other, Net	—	—	—
Income Before Tax	**234.2**	**195.4**	**155.8**
Income Tax	72.1	60.6	48.3
Income After Tax	**162.1**	**134.8**	**107.5**
Minority Interest	−4.8	−3.3	−4.8
Equity In Affiliates	—	—	—
Net Income Before Extra. Items	**157.3**	**131.5**	**102.7**
Accounting Change	0	−5.1	—
Discontinued Operations	—	—	—
Extraordinary Items	—	—	—
Net Income	$ **157.3**	**126.5**	**102.7**
Preferred Dividends	—	—	—
Income Available to Common Excl. Extra. Items	**157.3**	**131.5**	**102.7**
Income Available to Common Incl. Extra. Items	**157.3**	**126.5**	**102.7**
Basic/Primary Weighted Average Shares	59.3	59.5	58.6
Basic/Primary EPS Excl. Extra. Items	**2.652**	**2.211**	**1.754**
Basic/Primary EPS Incl. Extra. Items	**2.652**	**2.126**	**1.754**
Dilution Adjustment	7.5	7.3	6.1
Diluted Weighted Average Shares	67.8	68	65.5
Diluted EPS Excl. Extra. Items	**2.432**	**2.042**	**1.662**
Diluted EPS Incl. Extra. Items	**2.432**	**1.967**	**1.662**
Dividends per Share—Common Stock	—	0	0
Gross Dividends—Common Stock	—	0	0
Stock Based Compensation	—	7	6.1

Source: www.investor.stockpoint.com.

EXHIBIT 6
Reebok International, Ltd. (RBK)

ANNUAL BALANCE SHEET IN MILLIONS OF U.S. DOLLARS (EXCEPT FOR PER SHARE ITEMS)	AS OF 12/31/03	AS OF 12/31/02	AS OF 12/31/01
Cash & Equivalents	$ 693.6	642.4	413.3
Short Term Investments	—	—	—
Cash and Short Term Investments	693.6	642.4	413.3
Trade Accounts Receivable, Net	532.3	421.8	383.4
Other Receivables	—	—	—
Total Receivables, Net	532.3	421.8	383.4
Total Inventory	352.7	399.7	362.9
Prepaid Expenses	—	32.1	30.8
Other Current Assets	148.2	117.6	104.3
Total Current Assets	**1,726.80**	**1,613.60**	**1,294.70**
Property/Plant/Equipment—Gross	—	—	—
Accumulated Depreciation	—	−244.3	−215.5
Property/Plant/Equipment, Net	149.8	134.8	134
Goodwill, Net	—	23.4	31.3
Intangibles, Net	67	43.8	45.4
Long Term Investments	—	—	—
Other Long Term Assets	46.1	45.2	37.8
Total Assets	**$1,989.70**	**1,860.80**	**1,543.20**
Accounts Payable	—	166.1	127.3
Accrued Expenses	—	350	262.5
Notes Payable/Short Term Debt	8.1	19	19
Current Port. LT Debt/Capital Leases	0.2	0.1	0.1
Other Current Liabilities	—	44.7	40.5
Total Current Liabilities	**565.9**	**579.9**	**449.4**
Long Term Debt	353.2	353.3	351.2
Capital Lease Obligations	—	—	—
Total Long Term Debt	**353.2**	**353.3**	**351.2**
Total Debt	**361.5**	**372.4**	**370.3**
Deferred Income Tax	—	—	—
Minority Interest	36.9	43	22.6
Other Liabilities	—	—	—
Total Liabilities	**$ 956**	**976.2**	**823.2**
Redeemable Preferred Stock	—	—	—
Preferred Stock—Non Redeemable, Net	—	—	—
Common Stock	—	1	1
Additional Paid-In Capital	—	—	—
Retained Earnings (Accum. Deficit)	—	1,602.50	1,453.30
Treasury Stock—Common	—	−660.4	−660.4
Other Equity	1,033.70	−58.5	−74
Total Equity	**1,033.70**	**884.6**	**719.9**
Total Liabilities & Shareholders' Equity	**$1,989.70**	**1,860.80**	**1,543.20**
Shares Outs.—Common Stock	59.3	60.2	59
Total Common Shares Outstanding	**59.3**	**60.2**	**59**
Total Preferred Stock Shares Outstanding	—	—	—
Employees (actual figures)	—	7,400.00	6,700.00
Number of Common Shareholders (actual figures)	—	6,106.00	6,082.00

Source: www.investor.stockpoint.com.

EXHIBIT 7
Reebok's Comparative Sales Analysis

REPORTED DOLLARS (IN MILLIONS EXCEPT PER SHARE DATA)	SIX MONTHS ENDED JUNE 30,		
	2003	2002	CHANGE 2003/2002
Reebok:			
U.S.A.—Footwear	$ 528.8	496.3	6.5%
U.S.A.—Apparel	198.2	157.1	26.2%
	727.0	653.4	11.3%
International—Footwear	335.7	308.7	8.7%
International—Apparel	276.1	234.6	17.7%
	61.8	543.3	12.6%
Reebok Worldwide—Footwear	864.5	805.0	7.4%
Reebok Worldwide—Apparel	474.3	391.7	21.1%
	1,338.8	1,196.7	11.9%
Rockport	177.6	182.7	−2.8%
Other Brands	84.5	74.0	14.2%
	$1,600.9	1,453.4	10.1%
Total Company:			
Footwear	1,094.7	1,034.0	5.9%
Apparel	506.2	419.4	20.7%
	$1,600.9	1,453.4	10.1%

Source: Reebok *Quarterly Report,* June 2003.

get comfortable or quit monitoring the environment because of its past success. Success today does not mean success in the future. Reebok should constantly look for new strategies to fit the market conditions at the time. For example, a company with a competitive position in a market that has slow growth might pursue a diversification strategy. Reebok needs to continually use strategic planning so it will be successful in the competitive industry of apparel and footwear sales.

References

Devaney, Polly. "Reebok Shoots from the Hip-hop in Sneaker Wars: Trailing Behind Nike in the Footwear Market, Reebok Has Decided to Sign up Rap Stars and Bad Boys, Rather Than Squeaky-Clean Role Models." *Marketing Week* 26, 31 (2003): 21(1).

Elkin, Tobi. "Making the Most of Broadband; Reebok, Visa, Others Use Fast Medium to Go Beyond TV As Redux." *Advertising Age* 74, 36 (2003): 86.

Elliott, Stuart. "The Reebok Campaign Joins the California Campaign." *New York Times* (August 12, 2003): C8.

Lefton, Terry. "Nike, Reebok Play NFL Head Games." *The Business Journal of Portland* (September 16, 2002). **portland.bizjournals.com/portland/stories/2002/09/16/daily4.html**.

Reebok *Annual Report*, 2003.

Thomaselli, Rich. "Reebok's Strategy: Play Up Vector Logo; Authenticity, Heritage Focus of $50 Million Global Ad Push." *Advertising Age* 74, 34 (2003): 6.

Wagle, Yogeesh. Standard Poor's Industry Survey: Apparel and Footwear (July 3, 2003).

www.freeedgar.com.

www.forbes.com.

www.hooversonline.com.
www.investor.stockpoint.com.
www.reebok.com.
www.strategyclub.com.
www.theindonesianinstitute.org.
www.usatoday.com.
www.valueline.com.
www.yahoo.com.
www.yahoo.multexinvestor.com.

38 Callaway Golf Company—2004

Mark Bube
Francis Marion University, and
Forest David
Campbell University

Ely

www.callawaygolf.com

Callaway Golf Company (CGC) won the bidding war on September 4, 2003 for Top-Flite Golf, with a $174 million offer that ended a struggle with rival Adidas-Salomon, owner of Taylor Made Golf. Top-Flite is a leading manufacturer of golf balls and has a high reputation among professionals and recreational players. Privately held Top-Flite was formerly Spalding Sports Worldwide. The name was changed in April 2003, after the company sold the Spalding brand and its line of inflatable balls to Russell Corp., the Atlanta-based athletic wear maker. Top-Flite, the nation's second-largest golf ball maker behind industry leader Titleist, had $250 million in year 2002 golf ball sales. The company's $530 million in debt and the highly competitive market forced it into bankruptcy. Under the deal, Callaway assumes Top-Flite's debt.

In 1982, Ely Callaway founded Callaway Hickory Stick USA, Inc., which later became Callaway Golf. CGC's products are designed and built on an eight-building campus in Carlsbad, California, where the majority of its 2,300 employees work. Callaway makes premium-priced golf clubs that are popular with both amateurs and professionals; it makes fairway woods, irons, wedges, Odyssey White Hot and Dual Force putters, and high-tech golf balls including the HX, CTU 30, and CB1. Callaway's drivers include the ERC II, Hawk Eye VFT, and Steelhead. Callaway also licenses its name for apparel, shoes, and other golf accessories.

In its early years, Callaway revolutionized the industry with golf clubs that were "very forgiving" and therefore very welcome to the average golfer. New technologies and production methods turned the smallest golf club manufacturer into the world's largest maker of premium golf clubs and a dominant force in the industry. During the years of growth, Callaway acquired well-known brands like Oddyssey, a manufacturer of putters; STRATA, a manufacturer of golf balls; and Ben Hogan, a competitor in golf clubs.

Vision and Mission

CGC does not have a written vision statement, but it does have a mission statement, given on its Web site, as follows:

> Callaway Golf Company is driven to be a world class organization that designs, develop, makes and delivers demonstrably superior and pleasing different golf products that incorporate breakthrough technologies, backs those products with noticeably superior customer service, and generates a return to the shareholders in excess of the cost of capital. We share every

golfer's passion for the game, and commit our talents and our technology to increasing the satisfaction and enjoyment all golfers derive from pursuing that passion.

Current Operations

In the beginning of 2003, CGC's stock price fell below $10 a share from $15 a year earlier. High costs related to Callaway's pro endorsement expenses, declining interest in golf, and intense competitiveness in the industry have hindered the company's profitability. CGC experienced an operating loss of $25.6 million in the golf ball business in 2002 due to the expansion of its production line, the reduction of prices to remain competitive, and the necessity to defend its market share.

There has been low acceptance of Callaway's new product introduction of the C4 driver, which was supposed to capture a large portion of the market; nonetheless, CGC's financial position remains strong since the company has no long-term debt and high liquidity. CGC recently signed a licensing contract with TRG Accessories to sell CGC travel gear and gift items, and signed a licensing contract with the watch manufacturing company Fossil to design a Callaway Golf Timepiece collection.

Product Sales

Note in Exhibit 1 that CGC's sales of woods in 2002 decreased 21 percent, sales of irons declined 17 percent, and sales of putters decreased 65 percent compared to 2001. Overall, Callaway's 2002 sales declined 3 percent to $792.1 million but then increased to $814 million in 2003. These are not good numbers. Internationally, note in Exhibit 2 that Callaway's sales declined in all regions of the world in 2002 except Europe. Sales were down 21 percent in Japan and 1 percent in the United States. Golf Datatech reports that the number of golf rounds played in the United States declined 2.9 percent in 2002, as compared to 2001. The product life cycle with higher-priced titanium metal woods has shortened. This hurts Callaway's sales.

Business Ethics

CGC adopted a corporate Code of Conduct and Ethics Policy in 1997 applicable to all employees and directors, including senior financial officers. CGC previously permitted loans to employees, including executive officers, in restricted amounts (up to $150,000) and for limited purposes (purchase of a primary residence). There are currently no outstanding loans to executive officers under this program, and only two loans outstanding to nonexecutive officers.

EXHIBIT 1
CGC Sales Information by Product Category

(IN MILLIONS)	2002	FOR THE YEARS ENDED DEC. 31, GROWTH/(DECLINE)		2001			2000
		DOLLARS	PERCENT		DOLLARS	PERCENT	
Woods	$310.00	($82.90)	−21%	$392.90	($10.00)	−2%	$403.00
Irons	243.5	−5.4	−2%	248.9	−51	−17%	299.9
Putters	11.5	44	65%	67.5	12.3	22%	55.2
Golf balls	66	11.1	20%	54.9	20.9	62%	34
Accessories	61.1	9.1	18%	52	6.5	14%	45.5
Total	792.1	−24.1	−3%	816.2		−3%	837.6

2002 compared to ⟶ to 2001, compared to ⟶ to 2000

Source: Callaway Golf Company *Form K-10,* 2002.

EXHIBIT 2
Callaway's International Sales

(IN MILLIONS)	2002	DOLLARS	PERCENT	2001	DOLLARS	PERCENT	2000
			FOR THE YEARS ENDED DEC. 31, GROWTH/(DECLINE)				
USA	$438.70	−$5.40	−1%	$444.10	−$7.10	−2%	$451.20
Europe	136.9	18.5	16%	118.4	7.1	−6%	125.5
Japan	102.6	−28.1	−21%	130.7	8.7	7%	122
Rest Of Asia	58	−5.9	−9%	63.9	−18.5	−22%	82.4
Other countries	55.9	−3.2	−5%	59.1	2.6	5%	56.5
Total	792.1	−24.1	−3%	816.2		−3%	837.6

2002 compared to ⟶ to 2001, compared to ⟶ to 2000

Source: Callaway Golf Company *Form K-10*, 2002.

CEO/CFO certification procedures pursuant to Section 302 of Sarbanes-Oxley, established in November 2002, have been implemented at CGC. The company also has an insider trading policy that is written, distributed to all employees, and accompanied by training. Officers and key employees are subject to "gatekeeper" review and approval by the CGC's legal department.

Business Operations

CGC and its subsidiaries design, manufacture, and sell high-quality golf clubs and golf balls for both the average and professional player. Golf clubs include drivers, fairway woods, irons, wedges, and putters. The company also sells golf accessories like golf bags, golf gloves, headwear, travel covers and bags, towels, and umbrellas. CGC has subsidiaries all over the world; those wholly owned by CGC include: Callaway Sales Company, Callaway Golf Europe Ltd., Callaway Golf K.K., Callaway Golf Korea Ltd., Callaway Golf Canada Ltd., and Callaway Golf South Pacific PTY Ltd. CGC distributes directly to the retailers, or to the wholly owned subsidiaries and third-party distributors. The company also licenses its trademarks and service marks to third parties in exchange for royalty fees.

CGC owns the trademark Ben Hogan, under which it sells very exclusive and expensive golf clubs; in the putter market, CGC owns the trademark Odyssey. Experiencing losses with its own golf ball company, CGC bought Top-Flite to reform that aspect of the business.

CGC and its subsidiaries currently employ 2,300 full-time employees, 625 in sales and marketing, about 150 in the research and development and product engineering, and approximately 1,200 in production. The remaining full-time employees are in the administrative and support staff. CGC's organizational structure is a divisional design based on geographic regions of the world, as illustrated in Exhibit 3. Note that there is an America division and also an International division that is further broken down into continents and countries.

The golf business is highly seasonal. In the busy summer season, CGC employees are required to work many hours of overtime, whereas in the winter, production capacity is only about 68 percent. These special conditions require a special employment contract based on a working-hours-account, which allows employees to use overtime work-hours, gathered during high production, to make up the unused work time in the off season.

EXHIBIT 3
Organizational Chart

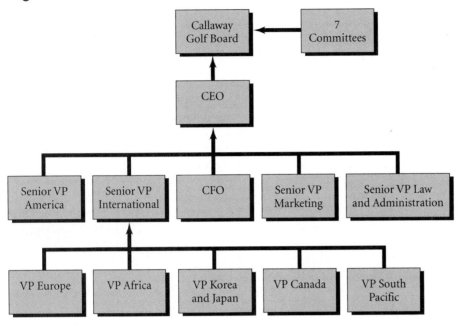

Source: www.nasbic.org/success/stories/callaway.cfm.

Marketing

Rapid introduction of new golf clubs or golf balls could result in close-outs of existing inventories at both wholesale and retail levels. Close-outs result in reduced margins on the sale of older products, as well as reduced sales of new products. Callaway's marketing is limited and focused on promotion through professional players on the PGA Tour, like Carlos Franco, Charles Howell III, and Arnold Palmer; and players on the LPGA-Tour like Annika Sorenstam, as well as TV commercials during coverage of big golf events like the Masters in Augusta and the U.S. Open. Callaway also uses point-of-purchase displays for its products in golf shops and retail stores worldwide.

External Factors

During the ordinary course of its manufacturing process, CGC creates toxic waste through the use of special materials and production processes. The waste is transported off-site on a regular basis by registered waste haulers. As a standard procedure, a comprehensive audit of the treatment, storage, and disposal facilities with which the company contracts for the disposal of hazardous waste are performed annually by CGC.

The ongoing conflict in Iraq has decreased the level of demand for the company's products, which are recreational in nature, and therefore discretionary purchases for consumers. Any decrease in consumer confidence, or adverse economic conditions, or political unrest diverts interest from playing golf and hurts Callaway's business.

Golf is not a growth industry. There are 26 million recreational players in the United States, but on average 3 million customers enter and 3 million customers exit the industry annually. The net effect is zero growth. It takes a lot of time to play golf.

People today have so many other ways to spend their time. A positive trend for CGC, however, is that the world's population is aging and many older individuals both play golf and have discretionary income to purchase golf equipment. Golf courses are overbuilt in the United States; the number of rounds played was down 6 percent in the United States in 2003 from 2002. More and more companies are chasing the same customers, which means that a gain in market share for one is a loss for another.

Competitors

More and more well-known athletic goods manufacturers such as Nike, Wilson, and Adidas, just to mention a few, are diversifying and expanding into the market. These companies have very good reputations, which helps them enter the golf equipment and accessories market. Several companies that produce high-quality tennis racquets, such as Prince, Fila, Head, and Wilson, are becoming a big threat to Callaway Golf. Wilson already does substantial golf business.

Worldwide, golf equipment is a $4 billion business ($2 billion in the United States). Industry leaders spend millions on endorsement contracts for the game's best players to entice recreational players. For example, Nike pays Tiger Woods to use and endorse its products and Titleist pays Phil Mickelson. A popular but expensive way to gain market share is using PGA Tour players to promote your product. "The PGA Tour is the one bright spot in the whole industry," says Drapeau. "The TV ratings are up; the attendance is up. A large part of that is due to Tiger Woods." Woods is so popular that Nike signed him to an endorsement contract and then over time built an entire golf division around him. Woods once played Titleist equipment, but in the last two years he has gradually shifted to Nike. Each time he changed, he said he would not have changed unless Nike made the best product for him to play.

Nike's shares in the market are modest: 7 percent for golf balls, 2 percent for woods, and 5 percent for irons. On the other hand, Callaway had 20 percent of the woods and 14 percent of the irons in 2002. Titleist had approximately 50 percent of the ball market and $1 billion in worldwide sales in 2002.

"With respect to metal woods and irons, CGC's major domestic competitors are Taylor Made, Titleist, Cobra, Cleveland and Ping." For putters, the major domestic competitors are Ping and Titleist. In the golf ball business, CGC faces competition from Titleist, Nike, Spalding, Sumitomo Rubber Industry, Bridgestone (Precept), and MaxFli (bought by TaylorMade). Titleist has an estimated market share in excess of 50 percent and is therefore leading in the golf ball industry.

TaylorMade-Adidas Golf (TAG), one of the largest golf club manufacturers in the world, is a subsidiary of Adidas-Salomon A.G. TAG announced record first quarter 2003 revenue of EUR 176 million, a 14 percent increase over the previous first quarter record established a year ago. The first quarter results marked the twelfth consecutive quarter in which quarterly revenues exceeded those in the prior year. TAG's international revenues increased 20 percent during the quarter, while U.S. revenues gained 9 percent. Revenue growth was led by Asia, whose revenues rose 26 percent due to significant gains in Korea as well as continued growth in Japan. In Europe, revenues increased 19 percent, driven by gains in metal woods, golf balls, and golf apparel.

Titleist is another of CGC's major competitors. Titleist manufactures all kinds of golf clubs, as well as balls, equipment, and accessories. Titleist brand names are FootJoy, Cobra, and Pinnacle. The company is very strong in the golf shoe market and is the leading producer in golf balls, with a market share of 50 percent. Titleist is also one of the leading manufacturers of woods.

Nike went into the golf business with Tiger Woods. Nike's market share in golf balls is 7 percent, 2 percent in woods, and 5 percent in irons. The market share in these categories is still low, but the company is steadily growing in the golf industry, increasing with Tiger Wood's success.

Global Issues

The global golf market is uniform in the sense that firms do not have to develop different products for different markets. But different economic and competitive situations in global markets make it sometimes difficult to place products in the right way with the right price, and at the same time generate profit. Rules vary for different professional tours, like the PGA Tour, the European Tour, the Canadian Tour, and the Asian-Pacific Tour. It is difficult to introduce and market a new product which conflicts with rules for the professional players. An innovation is difficult to market if professional players are not allowed to play with the new equipment. Recreational players will never see new equipment developed for their game.

A negative factor CGC has to face is the mass amount of imitation of its products, especially in the Asian-Pacific area. It is very difficult for the company to track the imitations, which results in high administration costs, and loss of revenues. Interruptions in air carrier or shipping services, anti-American sentiments, and social, economic, and political instability all negatively affect the performance of CGC.

Conclusion

For golfers, the current business climate means bargains. The National Golf Foundation, an industry group, reports that the number of golfers has held steady at about 26 million in recent years. Americans are not playing as much golf this year as they did last year. Many public and private golf clubs are experiencing weak demand and have been lowering prices in order to attract customers. Golf equipment is selling but at lower prices. Compared with 2002, prices are down 8.5 percent for woods, 5.3 percent for irons, and 3.4 percent for balls. The discounting has taken its toll. A few golf companies have declared bankruptcy, including San Diego–based Carbite Inc., a wedge and putter maker. Some equipment manufacturers, including Plano-based Adams Golf Inc., are struggling as well, and CGC itself laid off 100 employees at the end of 2002.

The ongoing war on terrorism and basic rift between America and Europe hurts Callaway. Golf products are discretionary rather than essential items. Other factors that also harm the golf business include high unemployment, increased consumer debt levels, and declining consumer confidence and spending.

Prepare a clear three-year strategic plan for Callaway Golf Company.

References

Adam, Richard. "Golf At a Downside." *Dallas Morning News* (February 21, 2003).

Brigham, E., and F. Houston. *Fundamentals of Financial Management.* Forth Worth, TX: Harcourt Brace Company, 1999.

Callaway *Annual Report,* 2002.

Callaway Golf Company *Form 10-K,* 2002.

Golf Datatech.

Golf Magazine. April 2003.

San Diego Union Tribune.

www.callaway.com.

www.comdirekt.de

www.investor.stockpoint.com

www.yahoo.com/finance

EXHIBIT 4

Callaway Golf Company (ELY)

ANNUAL INCOME STATEMENT IN MILLIONS OF U.S. DOLLARS (EXCEPT FOR PER SHARE ITEMS)	12 MONTHS ENDING 12/31/03	12 MONTHS ENDING 12/31/02	12 MONTHS ENDING 12/31/01
		RECLASS. 12/31/03	
Revenue	$ 814	793.2	816.2
Other Revenue	—	—	—
Total Revenue	**814**	**793.2**	**816.2**
Cost of Revenue	445.4	393.1	411.6
Gross Profit	**368.6**	**400.2**	**404.6**
Selling/General/Administrative Expenses	273.2	256.9	259.4
Research & Development	29.5	32.2	32.7
Depreciation/Amortization	—	—	—
Interest Expense (Income), Net Operating	—	—	—
Unusual Expense (Income)	—	—	—
Other Operating Expenses	—	—	—
Total Operating Expense	**748.2**	**682.2**	**703.6**
Operating Income	**65.9**	**111.1**	**112.5**
Interest Expense, Net Non-Operating	—	—	−1.6
Interest/Investment Income, Non-Operating	—	—	—
Interest Income (Expense), Net Non-Operating	—	—	−1.6
Gain (Loss) on Sale of Assets	—	—	—
Other, Net	2	0.6	−12.8
Income Before Tax	**67.9**	**111.7**	**98.2**
Income Tax	22.4	42.2	39.8
Income After Tax	**45.5**	**69.4**	**58.4**
Minority Interest	—	—	—
Equity In Affiliates	—	—	—
Net Income Before Extra. Items	**45.5**	**69.4**	**58.4**
Accounting Change	—	—	0
Discontinued Operations	—	—	—
Extraordinary Items	—	—	—
Net Income	**45.5**	**69.4**	**58.4**
Preferred Dividends	—	—	—
Income Available to Common Excl. Extra. Items	**45.5**	**69.4**	**58.4**
Income Available to Common Incl. Extra. Items	**45.5**	**69.4**	**58.4**
Basic/Primary Weighted Average Shares	66	66.5	69.8
Basic/Primary EPS Excl. Extra. Items	**0.689**	**1.044**	**0.836**
Basic/Primary EPS Incl. Extra. Items	**0.689**	**1.044**	**0.836**
⸍ution Adjustment	0	0	—
⸍ted Weighted Average Shares	66.5	67.3	71.3
⸍d EPS Excl. Extra. Items	**0.685**	**1.032**	**0.819**
⸍ EPS Incl. Extra. Items	**0.685**	**1.032**	**0.819**
⸍ per Share—Common Stock	0.28	0.28	0.28
⸍ends—Common Stock	—	21.5	21.7
⸍ompensation	—	11	14.6

EXHIBIT 5
Callaway Golf Company (ELY)

ANNUAL BALANCE SHEET IN MILLIONS OF U.S. DOLLARS (EXCEPT FOR PER SHARE ITEMS)	AS OF 12/31/03	AS OF 12/31/02	AS OF 12/31/01
		Reclass. 12/31/03	
Cash & Equivalents	$ 47.3	108.5	84.3
Short Term Investments	—	0	6.4
Cash and Short Term Investments	47.3	108.5	90.7
Trade Accounts Receivable, Net	100.7	63.9	48.7
Other Receivables	—	—	—
Total Receivables, Net	100.7	63.9	48.7
Total Inventory	185.4	151.8	167.8
Prepaid Expenses	—	—	—
Other Current Assets	50.1	44.9	47.6
Total Current Assets	**383.5**	**369**	**354.7**
Property/Plant/Equipment—Gross	—	—	—
Accumulated Depreciation	—	−158.9	−133
Property/Plant/Equipment, Net	164.8	167.3	133.3
Goodwill, Net	—	18.2	16.8
Intangibles, Net	169.9	103.1	104.5
Long Term Investments	—	—	—
Other Long Term Assets	30.5	22.2	38.3
Total Assets	**$748.6**	**679.8**	**647.6**
Accounts Payable	—	—	—
Accrued Expenses	38.2	36.6	60.2
Notes Payable/Short Term Debt	—	—	—
Current Port. LT Debt/Capital Leases	0.2	3.2	2.4
Other Current Liabilities	12	7.6	1.1
Total Current Liabilities	**130.2**	**109.2**	**101.9**
Long Term Debt	—	—	3.2
Capital Lease Obligations	—	—	—
Total Long Term Debt	**—**	**—**	**3.2**
Total Debt	**0.2**	**3.2**	**5.5**
Deferred Income Tax	—	—	—
Minority Interest	—	—	—
Other Liabilities	29	27.3	28.2
Total Liabilities	**$159.2**	**136.5**	**133.3**
Redeemable Preferred Stock	—	—	—
Preferred Stock—Non Redeemable, Net	—	—	—
Common Stock	—	0.8	0.8
Additional Paid-In Capital	—	371.5	419.5
Retained Earnings (Accum. Deficit)	—	439.5	388.6
Treasury Stock—Common	—	−130.3	−83.9
Other Equity	589.4	−3.9	−4.6
Total Equity	**589.4**	**543.4**	**514.3**
Total Liabilities & Shareholders' Equity	**$748.6**	**679.8**	**647.6**
Shares Outs.—Common Stock	66.7	65.7	67
Total Common Shares Outstanding	**66.7**	**65.7**	**67**
Total Preferred Stock Shares Outs.	**—**	**—**	**—**
Employees (actual figures)	—	2,300.00	2,500.00
Number of Common Shareholders (actual figures)	—	9,000.00	9,000.00

Source: www.investor.stockpoint.com.

39   UST Inc.—2004

Marilyn M. Helms
Dalton State College (GA)

UST

www.ustinc.com or www.ussmokelesstobacco.com

Even though UST suffered a huge litigation loss in a 2002 antitrust appeal with rival Conwood, and paid the $1.05 billion fine and accrued interest against the firm's 2002 earnings, Vincent A. Gierer Jr., UST chairman, president, and CEO, is optimistic about the growth of the company and of the smokeless tobacco segment in general. The company's superior cash flow even allowed a strong and growing dividend and the company is investing $450 million in share repurchases over the next three years to add even more shareholder value. Yet Gierer pondered whether the continued deployment of troops and reservists overseas could have a negative impact on the company's retail activity shares and volume. UST recently was the subject of controversy for mailing free samples of smokeless tobacco to Marines stationed in Iraq; military people appear to be significantly higher users of smokeless tobacco than the rest of the adult population. The wine segment of the business also faced competition caused by an oversupply of grapes, cheaper imports, and a reduction in wholesale inventories.

Scope and Products

UST is a holding company with a market capitalization of more than $6 billion, revenue of more than $1.7 billion, and net earnings exceeding $490 million. In 2003, net sales increases were due largely to higher selling prices, and partially offset by lower unit volume for moist smokeless tobacco products and higher-premium case sales for wine products. Higher smokeless tobacco segment sales represented about 70 percent of 2003's consolidated net sales.

UST Inc., has a company history dating to 1822 and the name U.S. Tobacco Company dates back to 1922. Copenhagen, UST's flagship brand, which was introduced in 1822, represents one of America's oldest trademarks and remains the best-selling moist smokeless tobacco in the world. Based in Greenwich, Connecticut, UST is a holding company for four wholly owned subsidiaries: (1) United States Tobacco Company; (2) International Wine & Spirits Ltd.; (3) UST Enterprises Inc., and (4) UST International Inc., employing approximately 4,800 employees combined. UST, through its subsidiary, U.S. Smokeless Tobacco Company (USSTC), is a leading producer and marketer of moist smokeless tobacco products including Copenhagen, Copenhagen Long Cut, Skoal, Skoal Long Cut, Skoal Bandits, Red Seal, and Rooster. Internationally, UST markets its products primarily to Canada and sales have been both profitable and stable for a number of years.

Other consumer products marketed by the company include premium wines sold nationally through the Chateau Ste. Michelle, Columbia Crest, Conn Creek, and Villa Mt. Eden wineries as well as sparkling wine produced under the Domaine Ste. Michelle label. Wine sales increased 7.8 percent to $203.5 million and represented

12.1 percent of consolidated net sales for 2002. Case volume for premium wine rose 7.5 percent and was the main driver for the sales increase in the wine segment in 2002. Premium case volume increased 7.5 percent and was the main driver for the net sales increase. The company's two leading brands, Chateau Ste. Michelle and Columbia Crest, had increased case volume of 14.4 percent and 1.8 percent, respectively, and together comprised 78.5 percent of the company's total case volume. The company is making premium wines available in mainstream restaurants like The Olive Garden and Red Lobster and through supermarkets and warehouse clubs.

Cigars that are marketed by UST subsidiaries include Don Tomás, Don Tomás Dominican Selection, Helix, Astral, and Astral Talanga Valley Selection premium cigars. This segment had a net sales increase of 4.9 percent to $32.2 million and was 1.9 percent of consolidated net sales in 2002, attributable to higher cigar volume but offset by lower levels of sales internationally. All other operations reported an operating loss of $3.7 million.

USSTC

UST's subsidiary USSTC is the world's leading producer and marketer of the only growing segment of the tobacco industry, moist smokeless tobacco. The company's leading brands, Copenhagen and Skoal, each represent more than $1 billion at retail. The company sells more than 1.7 million cans per day, or approximately 650 million cans annually. In 2001, the company changed its name from United States Tobacco Company to U.S. Smokeless Tobacco Company (USSTC), to more accurately reflect its unique position in the tobacco industry.

Vision and Social Responsibility

The company's vision is as follows: "Our smoke-free products will be recognized by adults as the preferred way to experience tobacco satisfaction." This vision represents the company's distinctly different position in the tobacco industry. To accompany that vision, USSTC adopted the following four key strategies: (1) Breaking Down Barriers—expanding the marketplace beyond the current 5 million adult moist smokeless tobacco consumers. This means reaching out to the 40 to 50 million adult cigarette smokers, many of whom are looking for alternative forms of tobacco satisfaction. This strategy involves product improvements, creation of new brands, advertising, and product sampling with the ultimate objective of building awareness of the smokeless tobacco category, increasing social acceptability of its products, and improving the ease of use; (2) Improving the Value Equation—offering value enhancements through quality and price initiatives, including product improvements and line extensions, as well as increased advertising support and promotional strategies. UST will continually provide greater value and higher quality to ensure consumers have a wide array of smokeless tobacco product choices; (3) Effective Resource Allocation—a reallocation of spending and cost-savings will be used to boost premium can sales by targeting spending for increased product support, enhanced product promotions, and increased advertising, resulting in an expansion of spending for print media and in-store merchandising programs; and (4) Next-Generation Products—focusing on innovation by developing new products and bringing them to the marketplace.

The company demonstrates social responsibility in a number of ways, including its 175-year relationship with the American farmer. UST purchases only 100 percent American-grown tobacco. The company also works to reduce youth access to smokeless tobacco products and has taken an active stance on its own and in cooperation with retailers to discourage sales of its products to minors. Among the many initiatives taken by the company, USSTC is the only smokeless tobacco manufacturer to sign the

Smokeless Tobacco Master Settlement Agreement (STMSA). Under the STMSA, the company voluntarily adopted an array of advertising and promotional restrictions and agreed to pay $100 million toward programs to reduce youth access to tobacco products and combat youth substance abuse.

Internal Factors

Marketing

Internally, the company has new products in development and 50 percent of capital expenditures in 2002 were directed at new products, up from 33 percent in the prior year and the trend in spending on R&D is expected to continue. UST also is a promotional sponsor for a number of motorsports activities and events that are aligned with the customers' lifestyles, where it hands out samples and offers free product coupons. In accordance with the Smokeless Tobacco Master Settlement Agreement's sponsorship restrictions, the company sponsors the two-car Skoal Racing[SM] funny car team that competes on the National Hot Rod Association (NHRA) circuit. The cars, owned by racing legend Don "The Snake" Prudhomme, are driven by two of the sport's leading stars, Ron Capps and Tommy Johnson Jr. At dozens of events each year, associated with EA Sports Supercross Series, the company has a major presence with two mobile marketing units—the Skoal Racing[SM] Tour and the U.S. Smokeless Tobacco Company Motorsports Experience[SM] Tour. These interactive exhibits, which are set up as adult-only facilities, feature memorabilia, artifacts, and a variety of simulated competitions.

The company has become actively involved in sponsoring rodeo and bull-riding competitions throughout the year, with a major presence at events conducted by both the Professional Rodeo Cowboys Association (PRCA) and Professional Bull Riders, Inc., (PBR). It supports the National Intercollegiate Rodeo Association (NIRA) by providing scholarships to adult student-athletes. A mobile marketing unit, part of the U.S. Smokeless Tobacco Company Western Legends[SM] Tour, is also present with an interactive exhibit highlighting the Western lifestyle. USSTC signed the recently retired Ty Murphy, "King of the Cowboys," to be a spokesperson for the company and to make national appearances.

Current Litigation

Snuff is a finely ground or shredded form of tobacco, most commonly sold in small tin cans or pouches. Users put a pinch between their lower lip or cheek and gum. Snuff contains nicotine and a variety of cancer-causing chemicals that are absorbed into the blood. Because snuff is held in the mouth for minutes at a time, some argue more of the chemicals enter the body than they would from cigarette smoking.

Since the early 1950s, there have been some 50 claims against smokeless tobacco companies, which is far fewer than the 1,000 individual claims and class-action lawsuits faced by cigarette manufacturers. UST has other claims pending in West Virginia, Illinois, Florida, Kentucky, and Mississippi. In these cases, the company is charged with manipulating nicotine levels in smokeless products, or its products are alleged to cause injuries.

West Virginia has legislation pending to impose the state's first smokeless tobacco tax. The bill (SB116) would impose a 7 percent excise (or sin) tax on smokeless tobacco products. This follows similar legislation passed in California to tax smokeless tobacco products. Even more disturbing to the industry is a June 2003 report by the Surgeon General Richard H. Carmona, who told a congressional committee he would support a total ban on all tobacco products, insisting they have no benefit to society.

The Campaign for Tobacco-Free Kids (**www.tobaccofreekids.org**) president, Matthew Myers, testified in June 2003 before the U.S. House Energy and Commerce Committee's subcommittee on Commerce, Trade and Consumer Protection on whether smokeless tobacco use can cure smoking. His answer was "no" and he pointed to other organizations that have reported serious disease risks of smokeless tobacco products. These groups include the Surgeon General, the National Cancer Institute, the American Cancer Society, the American Dental Association, and the Scientific Advisory Committee to the World Health Organization.

There is ongoing concern over health hazards associated with spit tobacco. The various forms of spit tobacco have been found to cause mouth cancer, a disease responsible for more than 8,000 deaths annually. Aside from oral cancer, spit tobacco also leads to bad breath, teeth stains, cancer of the mouth and throat, leukoplakia, potential cardiovascular problems, and peptic ulcers. The American Dental Association also agrees smokeless tobacco is not a safe alternative to cigarettes (**www.ada.org/prof/resources/positions/statements/smokeless.asp**).

In May 2003, anti-tobacco forces asked the Cal Poly (California) rodeo to cut all ties to chewing tobacco including the local scholarships provided by the U.S. Smokeless Tobacco Company. The rodeo has previously banned tobacco advertising. A new, coconut-based product, Kikit, has been targeted to help smokeless tobacco users kick their addiction and was developed by former smokeless tobacco user Steve Rousch. UST's new product Revel has also been criticized as discouraging smokers from quitting altogether, and critics point out that smokeless tobacco is not a safe substitute for smoking cigarettes. Yet UST hopes to attract smokers in states, including California, Delaware, New York, Florida, and Massachusetts, that have bans on smoking in restaurants and other public places.

While smokeless tobacco users remain loyal to their brands and to the product category, several substitutes are entering the market to compete with nicotine-based products (rather than gum or sugared candy). Ariva is a new product offering nicotine in a snuff-based product marketed to smokers to urge them to quit. Like UST's Revel, it provides a jolt of nicotine when smokers can't smoke—on airplanes, in movie theaters, or in smoke-free offices. Star Scientific, Inc., of Chester, Virginia, makes Ariva (**www.starscientific.com/frame_pages/release_frame.htm**). Other substitutes include nicotine gum, nicotine patches, nasal sprays, or nicotine inhalers to deliver nicotine as well as tobacco-free alternatives.

External Factors

The Smokeless Tobacco Industry

Today, the U.S. tobacco industry is a $53 billion industry, with cigarettes accounting for nearly 94 percent of the total. The remaining 6 percent of usage is for cigars, moist smokeless tobacco, chewing tobacco, and snuff (Standard & Poor's Industry Surveys). The smokeless tobacco industry (NAICS 312229) is divided into two major areas—chewing tobacco and snuff—with each area comprising different products. The chewing tobacco area consists of loose-leaf, moist, firm plug, and twist/roll products. The snuff group consists of dry and moist, depending on the amount of moisture added to the tobacco during manufacturing. At present, moist smokeless tobacco accounts for only 3 percent of the entire tobacco category at the retail level. Consumption patterns have shifted from loose-leaf to moist snuff. Consumers of moist smokeless tobacco products are brand loyal to extreme and demand product freshness. Research shows consumers looking for their brand will go elsewhere if they don't find it, rather than purchase another brand. Out-of-stock sales can hurt sales performance, but carrying excess inventory can result in stale products. Retailers work with suppliers to develop selections to maintain stock and to preserve product freshness.

The aggregate tobacco industry is classed with oligopolistic industries. Implications for all firms are high capital costs, hazardous antitrust and legal action, severe price-cutting, and monopolistic accusations if firms join in a concerted action. The increased scale needed to compete in the industry has erected very high barriers to entry.

The smokeless tobacco industry is highly concentrated near the tobacco-producing region of the United States. The five states that have the greatest number of workers in the industry are Kentucky, Tennessee, Georgia, North Carolina, and Illinois. Georgia and Illinois have replaced Virginia and Pennsylvania as leading employers of smokeless tobacco workers. Over one-half of the employment in the industry is concentrated in Kentucky. The reasons for this geographic concentration are obvious, the first being a desire to locate factories close to raw materials. Another reason is that the industry is concentrated in the South, which has traditionally been considered the prime market for the smokeless industry.

Product/Market Shifts

UST Inc., seems to be benefiting from higher cigarette prices. As a maker of moist smokeless tobacco products, UST isn't necessarily luring new consumers who don't want to pay more for cigarettes, but the company is actually winning over its own customers who don't want to pay more for cigarettes. About one-fourth of UST's customers also smoke cigarettes, so instead of using both, many tobacco users are moving away from higher-priced cigarettes and buying more snuff. While growth in moist snuff volume has increased, the Tobacco Merchants Association indicates that the chewing tobacco industry has been plummeting since 1988.

Changes in the smokeless tobacco market are consumer driven and all of the smokeless market is striving to meet the changing trend. One of the growing trends in smokeless tobacco, besides the cut (fine cut or long cut) is the move toward added flavors. Mint or ice seems to be the favorite among the younger consumers. Other smokeless products that are appearing are tobacco-free and nicotine-free chews and herbal snuffs. Since their introduction in mid-1995, the Skoal Flavor Packs have been marketed to "smokers who can't smoke." Skoal Bandits, a moist snuff, packaged in portion packs similar to small tea bags, along with other smokeless products, are aiding profits. In contrast to the increase in moist snuff, chewing tobacco, a longer-cut tobacco sold in foil packages, has been continually losing ground.

Most competitors in the smokeless category have added a discount brand. Coupled with this bargain trend, they are linking their products to sporting events as a promotional strategy. Another factor that helps to boost the trend toward increasing sales of moist snuff is its availability within the market. This product can be purchased in locations such as supermarkets, smoke shops, mass merchandisers, and discount and convenience stores. The products can even be purchased online at retailers like **www.freshsnuff.com/orderonline.htm**. Additionally, as the number of places where people can smoke are further restricted, moist snuff sales should grow because it is easy to use anywhere. Driving the trend further is aggressive advertising, which is directed at the moist snuff segment of the market. Smokeless tobacco usage in 2002 edged up 10.5 percent to 116.5 million pound versus 2001, according to the *Maxwell Report*.

UST introduced three new premium products in 2002, Skoal Long Cut Berry Blend, Copenhagen Pouches, and Skoal Wintergreen pouches. These three products contributed approximately 13.6 million cans. In addition, Skoal Winter Blend was introduced as the first seasonal product. UST's newest product, Revel, comes in packs designed for the nation's some 46 million adult smokers interested in an alternative to cigarettes, and is priced competitively with a pack of premium cigarettes.

Retail Distribution of Moist Snuff

Manufacturers typically sell moist snuff to independent wholesalers who then resell to retailers. While over 300,000 retail stores in the U.S. sell moist snuff, sales volume is concentrated in large chains including mass merchandisers and convenience stores. There are no agreements between retailer and moist snuff manufacturers requiring retailers to exclusively sell the products of only one manufacturer.

In offering new products, each manufacturer must justify the retailers' allocation of space to them. Manufacturers provide free display racks to retail stores and work to design very visible displays. Some retailers use separate racks provided by each moist snuff manufacturer for its own products, but Wal-Mart uses a single, customized cabinet for the display of moist snuff products in order to provide greater uniformity, aid inventory management, and maximize shelf space efficiency. Due to restrictions on self-service and theft problems, products are no longer displayed on open shelves, but increasingly are restricted to locked cabinets and secured behind-the-counter areas.

Manufacturers offer retailers' incentive programs and rebates for providing sales data, participating in promotional programs, or for giving a manufacturer the best placement of racks and displays. Manufacturers have sales personnel in the field who visit retail stores each day to routinely check racks, check that stock is current, and introduce new products and promotions.

Competitors

The *Federal Trade Commission Report* to Congress for the years 2000 and 2001 (issued in 2003) indicates that of the five major domestic manufacturers of smokeless tobacco (Conwood Company, National Tobacco Company, Swedish Match North America, Inc., Swisher International, Inc., and United States Smokeless Tobacco Company), USSTC led the industry market share for smokeless tobacco in terms of pounds sold. For the major domestic manufacturers of the moist snuff segment of the smokeless tobacco industry, U.S. Tobacco continued to lead the industry in 2001 with a 74 percent market share, followed by Conwood at 13 percent and Swedish Match at 8 percent in terms of pounds sold.

Conwood

Conwood makes Kodiak, Kodiak Straight, Grizzly, Long Cut Cougar, Hawken Wintergreen, and Kodiak Ice smokeless tobacco. Conwood's major brands of chewing tobacco are Levi Garrett and H.B. Scot's. Based in Memphis, Tennessee, Conwood is controlled through a complicated ownership scheme by Chicago's powerhouse Pritzker family, who took the firm private in a $400 million buyout in 1985.

Swisher International Group, Inc.

This company produces mass-market large cigars, premium cigars, and little cigars. It also makes smokeless tobacco products. Its moist and dry snuff offerings include the Silver Creek, Kayak, Redwood, and Navy brands; loose-leaf chewing tobacco sells under the Mail Pouch, Lancaster, and Chattanooga Chew names. The firm has been privately held since 1999. Headquartered in Jacksonville, Florida, Swisher International, Inc., produces large cigars, such as Swisher Sweets, King Edward, Blackstone, and Optimo for the mass market. It also produces Bering, La Primadora, and Siglo 21 in the premium cigar category.

Swedish Match

Formerly Pinkerton Tobacco Co. (Nasdaq: SWMAY), Swedish Match is owned by Volvo and produces cigars, smokeless tobacco, and pipe tobacco as well as smoking accessories such as matches and lighters. Swedish Match's products are made in 15 countries and sold in 140 countries. The firm was founded in 1915 and is organized in five product/geographic divisions—North Europe, Continental Europe, North America, Overseas, and Matches. The head office is located in Stockholm. Its goal is to strengthen its position as a leading global player in the area of niche tobacco products, particularly in the European and North American markets, and to continue developing its position in certain selected markets in other parts of the world.

More than one in ten Swedish adults is a user and Swedish Match has a market share above 90 percent in that country. However, in the United States, the company believes it has the largest potential since the U.S. market is growing by 3 percent a year while Swedish Match's sales grew 19 percent in volume in 2002, mainly through its popular Timber Wolf brand in the low-priced snuff segment. Swedish Match's largest moist snuff brand is Timber Wolf, which is one of the leaders in the value-priced segment. During the past few years, the value-priced segment has recorded a two-digit annual growth rate. New flavor variants are Timber Wolf Long-Cut Mint and Timber Wolf Long-Cut Natural. The Swedish-produced Catch and General brands were launched in New York and Washington, D.C. The main target group is the many Swedes residing in these cities. Swedish Match's North American range also includes Renegades portion-packed snuff. Its popular chewing tobacco brands are Red Man, Granger Select, JD's Blend, Red Man Golden Blend, Red Man Select, and Southern Pride.

Advertising and Demographics

UST, like other smokeless tobacco manufacturers, is changing its marketing strategies. As reported in the August 2003 document *Federal Trade Commission Smokeless Tobacco Report for the Years 2000 and 2001,* advertising and promotion expenditures for smokeless tobacco products reached $236.7 million in 2001. Sales too have continued to increase every year since 1985 reaching $2.13 billion for the smokeless tobacco industry in 2001. The five major manufacturers spend $236.68 million on advertising during 2001 and this was the highest amount recorded for marketing expenditures.

Interestingly, the advertising mix is changing for the industry. Promotional allowances and retail value-added offers (such as "buy one, get one free" or "buy three, get a free hat,") received the greatest share of the advertising expenditures. Spending on advertising in magazines, newspapers, and point-of-sale advertising, public entertainment, and spending to distribute free product samples decreased. Spending on outdoor billboard advertising remained flax. The industry reported no expenditures for audio visual advertising or for-transit advertising. Spending for promotional allowances increased as did direct mail, coupons, Internet advertising, and endorsements. Moist snuff generates more revenue than any other type of smokeless tobacco and also receives the greatest advertising and promotional support.

Some 7.6 million people in the U.S. age 12 and older use smokeless tobacco. Among youth, 15 percent of male high school students use smokeless products along with 6 percent of male middle school students. A study by the Department of Health and Human Services found that 19 percent of high school males use smokeless tobacco. Usage by the under-19 age group is highest in the South and the Midwest and in particular, in the states of Tennessee and Montana. Of student-athletes who use smokeless tobacco products, 57 percent play baseball and 40 percent play football. Many consumers use both snuff and chewing tobacco.

According to the National Tobacco Incidence Study 2000, the typical adult moist smokeless tobacco consumers are white males between the ages of 18 and 34. The average age of the consumer is increasing and a diminishing labor market working in agriculture and other outdoor sectors is also declining. Consumption of tobacco and snuff is traditionally associated with outdoor work and leisure activities like hunting and fishing. Consumers tend to be employed full-time, earning $25,000 to $40,000 per year. The number of adults consuming continues to increase while consumption of cigarettes, cigars, and loose-leaf are on the decline. The top-third of the adult consumers are responsible for 63 percent of the smokeless tobacco segment purchases, buying an average of 7.5 cans per week. Multipacks represent 69 percent and single cans represent 31 percent.

Smokeless tobacco producers are now expanding their customer base into other consumer segments, including active outdoor people, sports enthusiasts, business executives, and professional people. New, younger consumers, many of whom have never used any form of tobacco before, are being attracted to smokeless tobacco products, especially the moist snuff. These younger consumers like the moist snuff because it is

EXHIBIT 1

UST Inc. (UST)

ANNUAL INCOME STATEMENT IN MILLIONS OF U.S. DOLLARS (EXCEPT FOR PER SHARE ITEMS)	12 MONTHS ENDING 12/31/03	12 MONTHS ENDING 12/31/02	12 MONTHS ENDING 12/31/01
			Reclass. 12/31/02
Revenue	$1,742.60	1,682.90	1,626.00
Other Revenue	—	—	—
Total Revenue	**1,742.60**	**1,682.90**	**1,626.00**
Cost of Revenue	392.7	365.1	349.6
Gross Profit	**1,349.90**	**1,317.80**	**1,276.40**
Selling/General/Administrative Expenses	475.8	455.5	443.4
Research & Development	—	—	—
Depreciation/Amortization	—	—	—
Interest Expense (Income), Net Operating	—	—	—
Unusual Expense (Income)	0	1,260.50	0
Other Operating Expenses	—	—	—
Total Operating Expense	**868.6**	**2,081.10**	**793.0**
Operating Income	**874.1**	**−398.2**	**833.0**
Interest Expense, Net Non-Operating	—	−69.1	−66.2
Interest/Investment Income, Non-Operating	—	23.0	32.5
Interest Income (Expense), Net Non-Operating	−76.9	−46.1	−33.8
Gain (Loss) on Sale of Assets	—	—	—
Other, Net	—	—	—
Income Before Tax	**797.2**	**−444.4**	**799.3**
Income Tax	304.5	−172.9	307.7
Income After Tax	**492.7**	**−271.5**	**491.6**
Minority Interest	—	—	—
Equity In Affiliates	—	—	—
Net Income Before Extra. Items	**492.7**	**−271.5**	**491.6**
Accounting Change	—	—	—
Discontinued Operations	—	—	—
Extraordinary Items	—	—	—
Net Income	$ **492.7**	**−271.5**	**491.6**
Preferred Dividends	—	—	—
Income Available to Common Excl. Extra. Items	**492.7**	**−271.5**	**491.6**
Income Available to Common Incl. Extra. Items	**492.7**	**−271.5**	**491.6**
Basic/Primary Weighted Average Shares	166.6	168.8	164.3
Basic/Primary EPS Excl. Extra. Items	**2.958**	**−1.608**	**2.993**
Basic/Primary EPS Incl. Extra. Items	**2.958**	**−1.608**	**2.993**
Dilution Adjustment	—	0	—
Diluted Weighted Average Shares	167.7	168.8	165.7
Diluted EPS Excl. Extra. Items	**2.938**	**−1.608**	**2.967**
Diluted EPS Incl. Extra. Items	**2.938**	**−1.608**	**2.967**
Dividends per Share—Common Stock	2.0	1.92	1.84
Gross Dividends—Common Stock	—	324.2	303.3
Stock Based Compensation	—	4.4	4.9

EXHIBIT 2
UST Inc. (UST)

ANNUAL BALANCE SHEET IN MILLIONS OF U.S. DOLLARS (EXCEPT FOR PER SHARE ITEMS)	AS OF 12/31/03	AS OF 12/31/02	AS OF 12/31/01
			Reclass. 12/31/02
Cash & Equivalents	$ 438.0	382.0	272.0
Short Term Investments	—	—	—
Cash and Short Term Investments	438.0	382.0	272.0
Trade Accounts Receivable, Net	—	77.6	85.4
Other Receivables	—	—	0
Total Receivables, Net	—	77.6	85.4
Total Inventory	573.3	535.7	493.8
Prepaid Expenses	—	24.3	23.9
Other Current Assets	122.7	1,271.60	16.9
Total Current Assets	**1,134.10**	**2,291.30**	**892.0**
Property/Plant/Equipment—Gross	—	—	—
Accumulated Depreciation	—	−346.2	−320.6
Property/Plant/Equipment, Net	377.9	389.9	369.6
Goodwill, Net	—	—	—
Intangibles, Net	—	—	—
Long Term Investments	—	—	—
Other Long Term Assets	101.4	84.1	750.2
Total Assets	**1,613.40**	**2,765.30**	**2,011.70**
Accounts Payable	—	—	—
Accrued Expenses	0	1,260.50	0
Notes Payable/Short Term Debt	—	0	3.3
Current Port. LT Debt/Capital Leases	—	—	—
Other Current Liabilities	238.6	18.3	47.6
Total Current Liabilities	**238.6**	**1,462.40**	**222.5**
Long Term Debt	1,140.00	1,140.00	862.6
Capital Lease Obligations	—	—	—
Total Long Term Debt	**1,140.00**	**1,140.00**	**862.6**
Total Debt	**1,140.00**	**1,140.00**	**865.9**
Deferred Income Tax	—	0	183.5
Minority Interest	—	—	—
Other Liabilities	176.2	209.8	162.1
Total Liabilities	**1,554.70**	**2,812.30**	**1,430.60**
Redeemable Preferred Stock	—	—	—
Preferred Stock—Non Redeemable, Net	—	—	—
Common Stock	103.8	102.7	101.7
Additional Paid-In Capital	752.5	696.9	635.4
Retained Earnings (Accum. Deficit)	480.0	320.3	916.0
Treasury Stock—Common	−1,254.10	−1,104.00	−1,053.80
Other Equity	−23.5	−62.9	−18.3
Total Equity	**58.7**	**−47.0**	**581.1**
Total Liability & Shareholders' Equity	**1,613.40**	**2,765.30**	**2,011.70**
Shares Outs.—Common Stock	165.7	168.0	167.6
Total Common Shares Outstanding	**165.7**	**168.0**	**167.6**
Total Preferred Stock Shares Outs.	**—**	**—**	**—**
Employees (actual figures)	—	4,911.00	4,691.00
Number of Common Shareholders (actual figures)	—	7,550.00	7,800.00

Source: www.investor.stockpoint.com.

more socially acceptable than chewing tobacco and snuff can be used indoors as well as outdoors, since one does not have to "spit." Internationally, most find the practice of "dipping" and "spitting" to be "gross" and not a social custom taken up by many people.

Future
Given the state of the company and the industry, Mr. Gierer pondered the following issues as he brainstormed future strategies:

- Will health claims and litigation against smokeless tobacco users increase?
- Can smokeless alternative snuff products garner a larger market share? How can the firm attract new users and capture current and former cigarette smokers?
- Should UST continue to base its reputation on premium brands or create lower-priced brands? Will lower-priced brands steal business away from Skoal and Copenhagen?
- How will the industry's growth be affected by excise or "sin" taxes, smoking use restrictions, and the growing health concerns of smoking and/or smokeless tobacco?
- Is diversification beyond wine, cigars, and smokeless tobacco a key to survival? What products could be added and why?
- Should the company launch new brands and packaging improvements? Can snuff be made more socially acceptably? Should it develop more nonspit products like Revel? How can the industry attract women and white-collar professionals as potential new customers?
- Should it try to acquire an international competitor to exceed its current 2–3 percent growth per year?
- Will the changes in marketing expenditures result in higher sales? Is the advertising mix appropriate given current legislation and consumer groups?

For Additional Information
U.S. Tobacco Co., Greenwich, CT, 1–800–421–3276, or **www.ustshareholder.com**, or **www.ustinc.com**, or 1–800–777–1UST.

Wine Subsidiaries
Chateau Ste. Michelle, **www.ste-michelle.com**.
Columbia Crest, **www.columbia-crest.com**.
Stimson Lane, **www.stimson-lane.com**.

Competitors
Conwood Co. LP., Memphis, TN, 1–800–238–5990, **www.cwdlp.com/webpages/default.htm**.
Swedish Match Richmond, VA, 1–812–426–7796, **www.swedishmatch.be**.
Swisher International Inc., Jacksonville, FL, 1–800–843–3731, **swisher.com**.

Industry Data
Bureau of Alcohol, Tobacco, and Firearms (ATF), **www.atf.treas.gov**, 202–720–2791.
Food and Drug Administration, **www.fda.com**.
Tobacco International, New York, 1–212–391–2060, **www.tobaccointernational.com**.
Tobacco Merchants Association of the U.S., Princeton, NJ, 1–609–275–4900, **www.tma.org/tma/default.htm**.
Tobacco Reporter, **www.tobaccoreporter.com**.
Tobacco Situation and Outlook Report, Washington, DC, 1–800–999–6779, **www.eldis.org/static/DOC1248.htm**.
U.S. Department of Agriculture, **www.usda.com**.
A list of tobacco industry addresses is also available at **www.tobacco.org/Resources/tob_indy.html**.

40 R.J. Reynolds Tobacco Company—2004

Cleat Weaver
Francis Marion University

rjr

www.rjrt.com

In an effort to increase profit, Reynolds Holdings, the parent company of R.J. Reynolds Tobacco Company (RJR), plans to delete 2,600 jobs, or 40 percent of its workforce, by 2005. RJR Packaging, with approximately 1,000 employees, has also been put up for sale. Job cancellations, along with other decreases, are expected to save $1 billion over the next five years. In February 2003, RJR ended its sponsorship of Winston Cup Racing. Additionally, RJR is downsizing its brand focus from four brands to two, with Camel and Salem slated to receive a majority of its marketing efforts and promotional spending, while Winston and Doral are expected to receive much less attention. Lawsuits against cigarette manufacturers are rampant. Amid all this turmoil, it is uncertain whether RJR can continue to remain competitive alone and is considering a merger with Brown & Williamson Tobacco Company.

Camel was RJR's first highly recognized cigarette and the company's only brand to experience increased market share in the past few years. As indicated in Exhibit 1, Camel is a higher-priced, premium cigarette yielding higher profits. On the other hand, analysts are somewhat confused about the choice to make Salem RJR's second priority behind Camel, since Salem has taken a path of long-run decline. However, new packaging and a new slogan, "Stir the Senses," were introduced to Salem's advertising campaign. While Salem was once the favored menthol brand in the United States, comprising 4.2 percent of the 1994 cigarette market, Salem controlled only 2.5 percent of the market share in mid-2003.

EXHIBIT 1
RJR's Top Four Brands

NATIONAL RANKING BY SHARE	RJR BRAND	2002 RETAIL MARKET SHARE	BRAND'S CIGARETTE CATEGORY
#3	Camel	6.1%	Premium
#4	Doral	5.9%	Savings
#6	Winston	4.7%	Premium
#9	Salem	2.4%	Premium

Source: IRI/Capstone.

EXHIBIT 2

2002 Retail Market Share by Manufacturer

Phillip Morris	49.4%
R.J. Reynolds Tobacco	22.9%
BAT/Brown & Williamson	10.0%
Lorillard	8.2%
Liggett & Myers	2.3%
Other	7.2%

Source: www.rjrt.com.

Operations

As indicated in Exhibit 2, RJR is the second-largest tobacco company in the United States, behind Phillip Morris, and manufactures about one of every four cigarettes sold in the United States. Santa Fe Natural Tobacco Company, Inc., a subsidiary of RJR, manufactures Natural American Spirit cigarettes and other tobacco products, and markets them both nationally and internationally.

Headquartered in Winston-Salem, North Carolina, RJR's largest plant is located in Tobaccoville, North Carolina, a 2 million square-foot facility. The Whitaker Park plant in Winston-Salem was built in 1961 and is about 1 million square feet. RJR has important research and development facilities in Winston-Salem and also operates a packaging division called RJR Packaging. In the 1950s, the packaging business, which had traditionally supplied material for the company's cigarette manufacturing operations, began expanding and now produces flexible packaging materials for a number of external customers, including food and pharmaceutical companies.

RJR considers its production facilities to be among the most technologically advanced in the world, with the capacity to produce approximately 150 billion cigarettes annually. However, RJR's profit margin has declined approximately 74 percent in the past four years. Whereas the profit per 1,000 cigarettes was $21.93 in 1999, current profit levels have decreased to $5.79. In contrast, however, chief competitor Phillip Morris continues to make a profit of approximately $21.05 per 1,000 cigarettes. As shown in Exhibit 3, RJR incurred a loss of $3.4 billion in 2003 compared to loss of $44 million in 2002. However, RJR repurchased $500 million of outstanding stock in 2002 and increased its dividend payment 8.6 percent.

History

R.J. Reynolds Tobacco Company was founded in 1875 in Winston, North Carolina, when 25-year-old Richard Joshua Reynolds started a chewing-tobacco manufacturing operation. The town of Winston subsequently merged with a nearby community called Salem, thus giving rise to the name Winston-Salem. Despite having only a few hundred residents and no paved roads, the town of Winston hdeld great potential as a center for business since it was a production center for flue-cured tobacco leaf and since it was in close proximity to a newly built railroad line. Mr. Reynolds was a man of great vision. Having anticipated the future popularity of smoking tobacco, pipe tobaccos were introduced, followed by cigarette blends.

EXHIBIT 3

R.J. Reynolds Tobacco Company (RJR)

ANNUAL INCOME STATEMENT IN MILLIONS OF U.S. DOLLARS (EXCEPT FOR PER SHARE ITEMS)	12 MONTHS ENDING 12/31/03	12 MONTHS ENDING 12/31/02	12 MONTHS ENDING 12/31/01
			Reclass. 12/31/02
Revenue	$ 5,267.00	6,211.00	6,269.00
Other Revenue	—	—	—
Total Revenue	**5,267.00**	**6,211.00**	**6,269.00**
Cost of Revenue	3,218.00	3,732.00	3,560.00
Gross Profit	**2,049.00**	**2,479.00**	**2,709.00**
Selling/General/Administrative Expenses	1,327.00	1,463.00	1,429.00
Research & Development	—	—	—
Depreciation/Amortization	—	0	362
Interest Expense (Income), Net Operating	—	—	—
Unusual Expense (Income)	4,563.00	237	0
Other Operating Expenses	—	—	—
Total Operating Expense	**9,108.00**	**5,432.00**	**5,351.00**
Operating Income	**−3,841.00**	**779**	**918**
Interest Expense, Net Non-Operating	−111	−147	−150
Interest/Investment Income, Non-Operating	29	62	137
Interest Income (Expense), Net Non-Operating	−82	−85	−13
Gain (Loss) on Sale of Assets	—	—	—
Other, Net	5	−11	−13
Income Before Tax	**−3,918.00**	**683**	**892**
Income Tax	−229	265	448
Income After Tax	**−3,689.00**	**418**	**444**
Minority Interest	—	—	—
Equity In Affiliates	—	—	—
Net Income Before Extra. Items	**−3,689.00**	**418**	**444**
Accounting Change	0	−502	0
Discontinued Operations	122	40	−9
Extraordinary Item	121	0	0
Net Income	**$−3,446.00**	**−44**	**435**
Preferred Dividends	—	—	—
Income Available to Common Excl. Extra. Items	**−3,689.00**	**418**	**444**
Income Available to Common Incl. Extra. Items	**−3,446.00**	**−44**	**435**
Basic/Primary Weighted Average Shares	83.7	88.7	97
Basic/Primary EPS Excl. Extra. Items	**−44.076**	**4.711**	**4.575**
Basic/Primary EPS Incl. Extra. Items	**−41.172**	**−0.496**	**4.483**
Dilution Adjustment	0	0	0
Diluted Weighted Average Shares	83.7	90.2	99
Diluted EPS Excl. Extra. Items	**−44.076**	**4.635**	**4.485**
Diluted EPS Incl. Extra. Items	**−41.172**	**−0.488**	**4.395**
Dividends per Share—Common Stock	3.8	3.725	3.3
Gross Dividends—Common Stock	—	332	324
Stock Based Compensation	—	8	−1

Source: www.investor.stockpoint.com.

An employee stock plan was developed in 1912 for employees to have as much control as possible and to ensure their financial stability in the coming years. In 1913, Camel cigarettes were produced from several different types of tobacco and later became known as "the American blend." Supported by strong advertising, Camel became the first nationally known cigarette brand in the United States.

In addition to developing cigarettes, Reynolds established nearly every packaging standard in the industry, including the 20-cigarette pack established in 1913, and the one-piece, 10-pack carton started in 1915. Reynolds also became the first company to use a moisture-proof, sealed cellophane outer wrap packaging to preserve freshness (in 1931). Winston, the first filter cigarette, was introduced in 1954 followed by Salem, the first filter-tipped menthol cigarette, in 1956 and Doral in 1969. Reynolds Tobacco became the leading U.S. cigarette manufacturer in 1958, a standing it held until 1983. Reynolds' Tobaccoville Manufacturing Center was opened in 1986. By the 1960s, Reynolds Tobacco began diversifying into food and other nontobacco businesses, and so in 1970 it established a new parent company called R.J. Reynolds Industries, Inc. Nabisco was acquired in 1985 and the parent company was renamed RJR Nabisco, Inc. A merger agreement ensued between RJR Nabisco and Kohlberg Kravis Roberts & Co.(KKR) for the acquisition of RJR by KKR. Completed in 1989 and valued at $25 billion, the acquisition was labeled the largest corporate transaction in history at that time. The company stock returned to the stock market in 1991 after being privately held for some time. Then in 1995, KKR divested its remaining holdings in RJR Nabisco.

In 1999, R.J. Reynolds Tobacco Holdings, Inc., became an independent publicly traded company again with RJR as its wholly owned subsidiary. In 2000, R.J. Reynolds Tobacco Holdings, Inc., received $1.5 million in cash when it acquired its former parent company, Nabisco Group Holdings (NGH). In 2002, the company acquired Santa Fe Natural Tobacco Company for $340 million.

Mission

R.J. Reynolds Tobacco Company (RJRT) is the second-largest cigarette manufacturer in the United States, with four of the nation's 10 best-selling cigarette brands: Camel, Winston, Salem and Doral. RJRT's mission is to strengthen the equity and performance of our key brands and thereby deliver strong financial results to our parent company. RJRT's strategy is to stabilize, then grow, its key brands—focusing on enhancing the brand equity while maintaining a competitive price. The cornerstone of building brand equity is offering adult smokers brands with meaningful points of difference in product, packaging and programs.

We will continually strive to meet the preferences of adult smokers better than our competitors by developing, manufacturing and marketing distinctive, high quality tobacco products, and by developing technologies that have the potential to reduce the health risks associated with smoking.

We conduct our business in a responsible and ethical manner, recognizing the risks associated with the use of cigarettes, and committed to being a constructive participant in various public policy issues involving cigarettes.

Source: RJRT Web site.

External Factors

Cigarette shipments, as displayed in Exhibit 4, have seen a steady decline in the United States since 1987 and cigarette prices of the larger producers increased $.52 per pack between 1999 and 2001. Numerous laws and regulations are placed on the tobacco industry in regard to sales, advertising, and taxes. There is a threat that Congress may further increase federal excise taxes and regulation of the cigarette industry. Cigarette sales are almost certain to be negatively affected in the coming years by these factors.

From 1998 to 2002, American cigarette prices increased by $1.45 a pack, leading to declines in cigarette consumption. The industry is restricted in its marketing abilities due to the 1998 Master Settlement Agreement that limits advertising in areas such as billboards and sporting events. In contrast to the major cigarette producers in the United States, deep-discount brands are not affected as significantly. Groups against smoking have tried to limit cigarette sales and advertising as well as development of new tobacco products. Higher taxes and selling prices have heightened competition and have led to deep discounting as a means for major producers to remain competitive.

The industry in which RJR operates is extremely competitive with a few large participants. Data collected by Information Resources Inc./Capstone indicate that Phillip Morris Incorporated had market shares of 50.45 percent, 50.37 percent, and 49.58 percent in 2001, 2000, and 1999, respectively, while RJR had market shares of 23.42 percent, 23.58 percent, and 23.92 percent in the same years, with smaller manufacturers controlling the remaining market shares. Phillip Morris controlled 49.4 percent of the U.S. market share in 2002, while RJR held only 22.9 percent. Competition remains fierce in today's market as producers all compete for a portion of an industry whose overall size has steadily declined.

Factors affecting competition include manufacturers' brands, positioning, consumer loyalty, retail display, promotion, and price. The emergence of deep-discount brands has occurred, selling prices have risen, and cigarette taxes have increased.

Global Issues

RJR formed a joint venture with Gallaher Group Plc in 2002 to produce and sell a limited variety of American-blend cigarette brands that will be marketed in France, Spain, Italy, and the Canary Islands. The company, known as R.J. Reynolds-Gallaher International Sarl, is based in Switzerland. RJR has a large global presence, with subsidiaries in 57 countries including Finland, Vietnam, Poland, and Tanzania. RJR now controls nearly 4 percent of the international cigarette market and has witnessed a 75 percent global sales increase since 1990.

Global sales now account for 41 percent of total tobacco sales for RJR. RJR purchased a majority share of the Tanzanian Cigarette Company in 1995 for $55 million. This was the largest single investment in the country since it achieved independence in 1961. The Dar Es Salaam plant was quickly renovated and will soon produce 4 billion cigarettes per year, making it one of the largest producers in Africa. RJR's facilities also operate in Turkey where they account for half of the country's exports.

Health Considerations

In the 1990s, RJR began experimenting with a large variety of nicotinic compounds that may have had therapeutic benefits. Targacept, Inc., a company that arose out of R.J. Reynolds, develops and tests products that interact with nicotinic receptors in the

EXHIBIT 4

R.J. Reynolds Tobacco Company (RJR)

ANNUAL BALANCE SHEET IN MILLIONS OF U.S. DOLLARS (EXCEPT FOR PER SHARE ITEMS)	AS OF 12/31/03	AS OF 12/31/02	AS OF 12/31/01
			Reclass. 12/31/02
Cash & Equivalents	$1,523.00	1,584.00	2,020.00
Short Term Investments	107	595	207
Cash and Short Term Investments	1,630.00	2,179.00	2,227.00
Trade Accounts Receivable, Net	—	96	106
Other Receivables	—	—	—
Total Receivables, Net	—	96	106
Total Inventory	—	762	730
Prepaid Expenses	—	—	—
Other Current Assets	1,701.00	955	865
Total Current Assets	**3,331.00**	**3,992.00**	**3,928.00**
Property/Plant/Equipment—Gross	—	—	—
Accumulated Depreciation	—	−1,221.00	−1,330.00
Property/Plant/Equipment, Net	—	940	1,050.00
Goodwill, Net	3,292.00	7,090.00	6,875.00
Intangibles, Net	1,759.00	2,085.00	2,773.00
Long Term Investments	—	—	—
Other Long Term Assets	1,295.00	544	496
Total Assets	**$9,677.00**	**14,651.00**	**15,122.00**
Accounts Payable	—	60	74
Accrued Expenses	2,809.00	2,618.00	2,675.00
Notes Payable/Short Term Debt	—	—	—
Current Port. LT Debt/Capital Leases	56	741	43
Other Current Liabilities	—	8	0
Total Current Liabilities	**2,865.00**	**3,427.00**	**2,792.00**
Long Term Debt	1,671.00	1,755.00	1,631.00
Capital Lease Obligations	—	—	—
Total Long Term Debt	**1,671.00**	**1,755.00**	**1,631.00**
Total Debt	**1,727.00**	**2,496.00**	**1,674.00**
Deferred Income Tax	806	1,236.00	1,798.00
Minority Interest	—	—	—
Other Liabilities	1,278.00	1,517.00	875
Total Liabilities	**$6,620.00**	**7,935.00**	**7,096.00**
Redeemable Preferred Stock	—	—	—
Preferred Stock—Non Redeemable, Net	—	—	—
Common Stock	—	1	1
Additional Paid-In Capital	—	7,401.00	7,371.00
Retained Earnings (Accum. Deficit)	—	1,217.00	1,593.00
Treasury Stock—Common	—	−1,286.00	−776
Other Equity	3,057.00	−617	−163
Total Equity	**3,057.00**	**6,716.00**	**8,026.00**
Total Liabilities & Shareholders' Equity	**$9,677.00**	**14,651.00**	**15,122.00**
Shares Outs.—Common Stock	83.7	86	94.2
Total Common Shares Outstanding	**83.7**	**86**	**94.2**
Total Preferred Stock Shares Outstanding	—	—	—
Employees (actual figures)	—	8,200.00	8,200.00
Number of Common Shareholders (actual figures)	—	27,000.00	38,000.00

Source: www.investor.stockpoint.com.

EXHIBIT 5
Organizational Structure

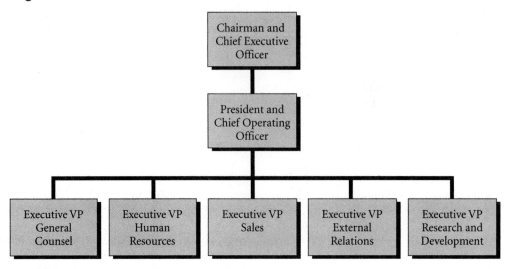

human nervous system and which may be able to treat various conditions such as Alzheimer's disease, Parkinson's disease, depression, obesity, and anxiety, among others. Scientists at RJR have made great strides in the study of tobacco and its medicinal effects and are leaders in testing methods to identify harmful effects of cigarette smoke. These efforts have assisted R.J. Reynolds Tobacco in developing cigarettes that have reduced traditional risks attributable to smoking.

In the 1970s and 1980s, RJR focused much effort on developing cigarettes with lower levels of tar and nicotine and was successful in reducing yields of these substances by nearly 70 percent. Also, in the 1980s, RJR developed Premier, a cigarette that heats, rather than burns tobacco, which greatly decreases secondhand smoke and other harmful substances associated with smoking. RJR recently initiated a new cigarette brand called Eclipse, which also heats rather than burns tobacco. RJR does not advocate Eclipse as providing reduced risks of heart disease or complicated pregnancy. It is speculated that, in comparison with tobacco-burning cigarettes, Eclipse may pose less of a threat of cancer, bronchitis, and emphysema.

Conclusion
With a 15 percent decline in revenues in 2003 and billion dollar losses, R.J. Reynolds is in severe trouble. Prepare a three-year strategic plan for the company.